CARIBBEANA 1900-1965

Editorial Research Assistant:
CAROL FEIST DICKERT

Consultant on Netherlands Caribbean:
ANNEMARIE DE WAAL MALEFIJT

Caribbeana 1900-1965

A TOPICAL BIBLIOGRAPHY

By Lambros Comitas

PUBLISHED FOR

Research Institute for the Study of Man

UNIVERSITY OF WASHINGTON PRESS
Seattle and London

The production of this bibliography was financed in part
by a grant (GN-401) from the Office of Science Information Service,
National Science Foundation.

To Vera Rubin

PREFACE

Recent years have witnessed fundamental rearrangements in the social and political ordering of West Indian societies despite the tenacity of a colonial heritage. In the British Caribbean, for example, the independence of Jamaica, Trinidad and Tobago, Guyana, and Barbados has inaugurated an era of unprecedented autonomy. After centuries of bondage to the metropole, and after an abortive federation of British West Indian territories, these four new nations and the other self-governing islands have now shouldered the arduous task of directing their own national destinies. Following a different political formula, Surinam and the Netherlands Antilles have associated in equal partnership with the Kingdom of the Netherlands, while French Guiana and the islands in the French Caribbean have become integral parts of the Republic of France.

It is obvious that the level and form of political development varies in the Caribbean. Nevertheless, for the first time throughout much of the region, the tangled path to the future is being cleared by West Indians for West Indians. In a region which has long had to look to Europe and the United States for example and for approval, the conscious efforts to reorient the population to West Indian values and to instill a West Indian content and outlook in the school curriculum are significant steps to the development of national identity. For the serious work ahead, West Indians involved in national development will want to have a thorough knowledge of the Caribbean past together with an objective understanding of the present. Foreign scholars are also increasingly looking to scientific materials on the area. Unlike many other regions of the developing world, much has been written about the West Indies — a good deal of it scattered and forgotten — that needs only to be brought methodically to the surface. CARIBBEANA 1900-1965 has gathered together references to most of the scholarly writings on the non-Hispanic Caribbean. It is offered as a bibliographic guide to all those engaged in scholarly and technical pursuits in this complex region.

CARIBBEANA 1900-1965 is a one-volume bibliography of material that has been published in the twentieth century. Originally, it was intended to help stimulate and to aid research in social science and related disciplines in the West Indies. During the long period of bibliographic research, it became obvious that the collection had outgrown the original intent and that it could be of value to a much larger readership. In part, this is due to the nature of social science inquiry, especially the broad bibliographic requirements of the holistically-oriented anthropologists. Since many social scientists seek systematic data from a wide variety of fields, it became important that this broad range of potential interests be reflected in the collection. As a consequence, while the volume, in my opinion, is still particularly suited to the social scientist, CARIBBEANA 1900-1965 should prove eminently useful to scholars in other disciplines, to administrators, to planners, to government extension workers, to teachers, and to students.

vii

Geographically, the bibliography focuses on the non-Hispanic territories of the Caribbean region. These include the mainland and insular possessions or former possessions of Great Britain, France, The Netherlands, and the United States of America. As delimited, the area covered by this bibliographic study subsumes Surinam, French Guiana, and British Guiana (now Guyana) in South America, British Honduras in Central America and all the islands of the Antilles with the exception of Haiti and the Spanish-speaking territories. Also excluded are the Bahama Islands, since publications on this group are very limited. I have excluded Haiti and the Spanish-speaking islands from this volume since a number of bibliographies already exist for these territories. Actually, to have dealt systematically with the printed matter on Puerto Rico, Cuba, the Dominican Republic, and Haiti would have meant an extraordinary expansion of the bibliography and a concomitant increase in the years of research and preparation. The geographic areas finally selected, in my opinion, form a meaningful unit. Despite cultural and ecological differences, they have in common many historical, structural, and economic characteristics. More importantly, to the best of my knowledge, no previous attempt has been made to provide comparative coverage for this increasingly significant part of the world.

The primary organization of the bibliography is topical rather than geographical. A volume organized along geographical lines would be difficult to utilize with any efficiency given the large number of territories and the wide differential in the number of publications about each. The basic objective of facilitating research would seriously suffer. Subject classifications were developed out of the material itself. No classificatory scheme from either library science or social science was used in whole or in part. By allowing the data to generate the subject categories, the main currents or themes in Caribbean research become easily identified. The resulting organization reflects a more accurate picture of the actual state of West Indian studies. From the number of subject chapters, it is obvious that this approach favors specificity rather than generality. In my judgment, this should be an aid rather than a hindrance to the reader. Although this procedure has resulted in chapters of uneven length — some quite long and some rather short, it has the tangential benefit of indicating the relative strengths and weaknesses of research on specific topics.

CARIBBEANA 1900-1965 contains over seven thousand complete references to authored books, monographs, reports, articles, and miscellaneous publications. Doctoral dissertations and master's theses are also included. Although technically they are not printed matter, these manuscripts are available through the author's university, and can usually be purchased in microfilm or other forms of reproduction. Since they are generally unknown outside the particular discipline for which they are written, their inclusion here should be helpful to the reader. Publications such as government reports have not been listed in the bibliography if they had no printed indication as to authorship or could not be located for purposes of review and analysis. In other words, no unauthored or unseen publications have been included in this volume. Also regrettably excluded are a small number of materials published in 1965 but unavailable for review before the manuscript was prepared for printing in 1966.

No attempt was made to assess critically the publications which were reviewed. The philosophy followed in this regard was neatly stated by H. Ian Hogbin in his Introduction to C.R.H. Taylor's *A Pacific Bibliography*, "Some of the minor publications, it may be thought, would have been decently left in oblivion. But Mr. Taylor believes, in my opinion rightly, that we should not prejudge. Subsequent generations may well discover significant material in the most unlikely places." With this I am in full accord.

Four years have gone into the preparation of this volume. To say that many were involved in all its phases is to cite the obvious. Nevertheless, without the support of scores of institutions and individuals, the bibliography would not have been completed. I am indebted to all those specialists on the Caribbean who, on request, forwarded their reprints for review. Since well over a hundred kindly responded, I can only acknowledge them here collectively. Many of the articles and reports sent would have been troublesome to find. After having been processed for the bibliography, all reprints were permanently deposited in the Caribbean library of the Research Institute for the Study of Man.

I am also indebted to the great libraries of New York City. The Caribbean literature scattered throughout their stacks staggers the imagination. To the staffs of these libraries, who so willingly cooperated in our work, I extend my sincere appreciation. I must mention particularly the librarians at the American Museum of Natural History; the Medical Library, College of Physicians and Surgeons at Columbia University; and Helen Vogel, Lynn Mullins, and Tom Dailey at the American Geographical Society, who went far beyond professional courtesy to facilitate us in every way in the completion of our work.

Several libraries in the West Indies also contributed heavily to this effort. In particular, I wish to thank Marjorie Lumsden, Chief Librarian of the Central Library of Trinidad and Tobago in Port of Spain. Miss Lumsden made scarce publications available to us on loan; over the years, she forwarded the valuable West Indian reference lists compiled by her staff, and she gave much of her time when on leave in New York City to review, comment, and advise on many matters pertaining to the bibliography. I am also grateful to Judith E. Richards of the West India Reference Library in Jamaica, to Stella E. Merriman of the Public Library in Georgetown, Guyana, and to Mrs. M. Prescod of the Public Library in Castries, St. Lucia, for their able assistance. Mr. Neville Connell, Director of The Barbados Museum and Historical Society, generously offered the facilities of the Society's library during my stay in the island in 1964. Valerie Bloomfield, Librarian of the Institute of Commonwealth Studies, University of London, kindly made available West Indian materials for our use.

Inter-library loans from the West Indies were expedited through the courtesy of the Trinidad and Tobago and the Jamaican governments. I wish to acknowledge the good offices of His Excellency Sir Ellis Clarke, C.M.G., Ambassador for Trinidad and Tobago to the United States of America; Mr. Charles Archibald, Deputy Permanent Representative of Trinidad and Tobago to the United Nations; His Excellency Mr. E.R. Richardson, C.M.G., Ambassador, Permanent Representative of Jamaica to the United Nations and Valerie C. Nelson, Registrar/Librarian of the Permanent Mission of Jamaica to the United Nations. I am most appreciative of their gracious cooperation.

A special word of thanks must be given to my colleague, Dr. David Lowenthal of the American Geographical Society, who made his West Indian collection available and who generously assisted in locating and checking references, both in New York City and in London. Thanks are extended also to my colleague, Professor Jerome Handler of Southern Illinois University, who carefully verified publications for the bibliography while he was conducting research in Barbados.

The arduous and time consuming task of producing the finished plates for this work was accomplished by the typesetting skill of Charlotte Singer and Mildred Hagler. Acknowledgment is made to Marion Brown, Linda Elfenbein, Ariane Brunel, Maynard Briggs Witherell and Sushila Raghavan who contributed to various aspects of the production.

Professor Annemarie de Waal Malefijt of Hunter College accepted the responsibility of reviewing all references written in the Dutch language. Her expertese and thoroughness is gratefully acknowledged.

Throughout the life of the project, I have been ably seconded by Carol Feist Dickert, Research Assistant on the staff of the Research Institute for the Study of Man. She has been integrally involved with every phase of the operation from the research stage through all the intricate aspects of the production. Her skill and cooperation were invaluable ingredients in the successful completion of the volume.

What I owe to the Research Institute for the Study of Man goes beyond expressions of gratitude. An anthropological foundation long interested in the advancement of Caribbean studies, the Research Institute initiated, sponsored, and nurtured this bibliography. It has generously covered most of the research and production costs and it has provided the office space for all phases of the work. A staff member was permanently assigned to work with the project and its excellent collection of West Indian publications was made available at all times. In addition, continuous support was provided by regular staff members of the Institute. I am beholden particularly to the Librarian, Jane Lowenthal, to Andrea Talbutt and to Dena Hirsch. It is my hope that this bibliography will at least partially justify the extraordinary support and wholehearted cooperation I received.

New York City
June, 1967

Lambros Comitas

TABLE OF CONTENTS

NOTES ON STYLE AND USE

CARIBBEANA 1900-1965 is organized with the specific intent of facilitating scholarly research on the West Indies and culturally related areas. The book is divided thematically into ten major sections: Introduction to the Caribbean; The Past; The People; Elements of Culture; Health, Education and Welfare; Political Issues; The Environment and Human Geography; Socioeconomic Activities and Institutions; Soils, Crops and Livestock; and Economic and Social Prospects. Each section is further sub-divided into topically related chapters. The total of sixty-seven chapters, therefore, represents that many discrete topics.

The reference style in CARIBBEANA 1900-1965 is a modified version of that utilized by the *American Anthropologist,* the journal of the American Anthropological Association, as well as by a growing number of other professional publications.

All publications selected for inclusion as references in this bibliography have been examined, catalogued as to subject matter, and assigned to one of the sixty-seven substantive chapters for primary affiliation. Those publications which deal meaningfully with more than one topic are cross-listed appropriately in one or more of the other pertinent chapters as well. This procedure assures as complete a listing as possible for each chapter-topic. Since many references listed in CARIBBEANA 1900-1965 deal with more than one topic, there is considerable cross-listing. Consequently, for reasons of brevity and economy, two varieties of the reference style have been employed — a complete form and an abbreviated form.

The Complete Reference

A complete reference appears only once for any publication. This full form is found in the chapter of primary affiliation, that is, the chapter most closely related to the major theme of the publication. In addition to standard bibliographic data, the complete reference includes a coded notation as to the geographical area or areas covered by the publication; where applicable, a translation into English of the non-English title of the publication; also where applicable, a notation of other chapters in which the reference is cross-listed; and for most references, a coded notation as to the library in the New York City area where the publication can be found. The additional information offers a capsule annotation for the interested reader. The following example serves to illustrate the organization of and the data included in a complete reference:

HERSKOVITS, MELVILLE JEAN

19.019   GC   1938 Les noirs du Nouveau Monde: sujet de recherches africanistes [The
                          New World Negroes: a subject for Africanist research]. *J Soc Afr*
                          8(1): 65-82.   [11,67]   [*AMN*]

NAME OF AUTHOR(S) An author's name is listed exactly as it appears in his publications.
In instances, however, where the author's publications themselves vary as to the spelling or
usage of his name, the bibliography employs the most complete form or that which is known
to be the author's preference. In the example given, the author is Melville Jean Herskovits.

REFERENCE NUMBER Each publication listed has only one reference number. In a complete reference, this number is in bold print. The first two digits indicate the chapter to
which the reference is primarily assigned. In the example given, the number **19.019** indicates by its first two digits that the complete reference is located in Chapter 19, Cultural
Continuities and Acculturation. The last three digits indicate the position of the reference
within its primary chapter. This position is based on an alphabetical listing of authors'
surnames. The reference number is the key to locating complete references in CARIBBEANA
1900-1965.

GEOGRAPHICAL CODE Each reference includes a geographical notation, in bold print,
which is located to the immediate right of the reference number. This notation indicates
the most specific geographical region or regions considered by an author in his publication.
Up to three geographical areas can be listed for each entry. If more than three areas are
discussed, *or* if those areas together encompass a common geographical grouping, the next
larger geographical unit is employed. If, for example, the publication deals with British
Guiana, French Guiana and Surinam, the geographical code for Guianas-General is employed.
In the example given, the notation GC stands for General Caribbean, the area which the
author delimits in this particular article. When scanning a page of references, the geographical notations form a clearly identifiable column which allows the reader to locate rapidly
references for specific areas. The geographical divisions used in CARIBBEANA 1900-1965,
and the code to its geographical units appear on pages xlix and l.

YEAR OF PUBLICATION This information is in a column to the right of the geographical
notation, so that the reader can find, at a glance, references for specific time periods. In
the example given, 1938 is the year of publication.

TITLE OF REFERENCE The title of an article, as in the example given above, appears in
lower case letters. Titles of books, monographs and other separate publications are in small
capital letters, as in the following illustration: REBEL DESTINY: AMONG THE BUSH NEGROES OF
DUTCH GUIANA. For both articles and separate publications written in other than the English
language, the original title of publication is followed, in brackets, by an English translation.

PUBLICATION INFORMATION   In the case of an article, the following information is provided: a modified abbreviation, in italics, of the name of the journal. (Periodical Abbreviations appear in the section immediately following this one); its volume and issue numbers; and its pagination.   For books, monographs and other separate publications, the following information is provided: the place of publication; the publisher; the number of pages.

SECONDARY TOPICS   In addition to a primary topic, many of the publications listed provide systematic data about other subjects as well.   These are dealt with in other chapters of the bibliography.   In such cases, the appropriate chapter numbers of the bibliography are given in bold print, within brackets, immediately following the pagination.   This notation also indicates that the reference is included in abbreviated form in the chapters enumerated. In the example given, the reference includes the bracketed numbers [11,67] specifying that the publication contains material pertinent to Chapter 11 (Population Segments: Negroes) and to Chapter 67 (Theory and Methodology).   These notations, where they appear, enable the reader to make a general assessment of the scope of the work.

LIBRARY CODE   The majority of complete references carry a notation of a library in the New York City area where the publication is located.   The library notation is set in capital italic letters, within brackets, and it is placed at the extreme right-hand corner of the last line of the reference.   In the example given, the notation [AMN] indicates that the publication is accessible at the library of the American Museum of Natural History.   The code to New York City libraries can be found at the end of the Periodical Abbreviations section.

The Abbreviated Reference

Whenever a publication is cross-listed, the complete reference is given only in the chapter of primary affiliation.   For listing in other chapters to which the publication has relevance, the abbreviated reference form is utilized. This truncated form is illustrated below:

HERSKOVITS, MELVILLE JEAN
19.019   **GC**   1938   Les noirs du Nouveau Monde: sujet de recherches africanistes [The New World Negroes: a subject for Africanist research].

Only the name of the author(s), the reference number, the geographical code, the year of publication and the title of publication (as well as translation, wherever necessary) are retained in the abbreviated form.   While the reference number remains the same as in the complete reference, it is set in italics to distinguish it easily from the complete references in a given chapter.   The placement of abbreviated references in a chapter is based solely on the alphabetical order of the authors' surnames and does not depend on reference numbers. If complete information for an abbreviated reference is required, the primary chapter of that reference should be consulted.

Indexes

For the readers' convenience, two indexes can be found following Chapter 67. The AUTHOR INDEX lists all authors alphabetically, followed by the reference number(s) of their work(s). No distinction is made in the index between first and second authors. The GEOGRAPHICAL INDEX has grouped together by reference numbers all entries on a given geographical area. The reader is advised to progress from the most specific region of interest to the more general geographical groupings. For example, to locate publications on St. Lucia, one should first consult the section on St. Lucia and then proceed to the sections on the Windward Islands and on the British Caribbean. As a guide to these geographical divisions, refer to the listing entitled GEOGRAPHICAL DIVISIONS FOR CARIBBEANA 1900-1965, on page xlix.

Chapter Headings and Contents

A serious effort has been made to provide chapter titles which are both succinct and informative. In some cases, however, the title alone is insufficient to give the reader a sense of both the scope and limitations of the chapter. In order to limit ambiguities and to clarify the conceptualization of the more complex chapters, a number of short chapter annotations are provided below:

CHAP. 2 - GENERAL WORKS   Scholarly writings of a broad or comprehensive nature; studies of regions or communities without a specific or narrowly delimited subject or problem focus; general handbooks on a scholarly level.
See also [3] Travel and Description; [43] Human Geography.

CHAP. 3 - TRAVEL AND DESCRIPTION   Travel journals; guide books; handbooks.

CHAP. 5 - GENERAL HISTORY   All general historical writings except those publications dealing with slavery or emancipation. Primary references to publications in other chapters which have historical pertinence are included in this chapter in abbreviated form as secondary references.
See also [4] Archeology and Ethnohistory; [6] Slavery and Emancipation.

CHAP. 6 - SLAVERY AND EMANCIPATION
See also [45] Plantation Systems.

CHAP. 7 - DEMOGRAPHY AND POPULATION TRENDS
See also [43] Human Geography.

CHAP. 8 - SOCIAL ORGANIZATION   Social structure; social stratification; organization of age groups.
See also [9] Kinship Organization; [10] Population Segments: Overview; [20] Values and Norms; [22] Music, Art and Recreation; [23] Religion, Cults and Magic; [24] Folklore; [31] Personality and Mental Health; [43] Human Geography.

CHAP. 10 - POPULATION SEGMENTS: OVERVIEW   Writings which deal comparatively with a number of ethnic or racial groups in a given area; writings on pluralism.
See also [8] Social Organization; [16] Race Relations; [19] Cultural Continuities and Acculturation; [21] Cultural and National Identity.

CHAP. 11 - POPULATION SEGMENTS: NEGROES   Writings which focus on the Negro in the Caribbean. Given the racial composition of the region, a high proportion of all publications in this bibliography deal directly or indirectly with the Negro population. However, many of these references do not specifically identify the racial group under discussion; they have consequently not been listed as secondary cross-references in this chapter.
See also [10] Population Segments: Overview; [16] Race Relations; [19] Cultural Continuities and Acculturation.

CHAP. 13 - POPULATION SEGMENTS: AMERINDIANS   Writings on mainland tribal groups in the Guianas; on contemporary Caribs in the Antilles; on Black Caribs.
See also [4] Archeology and Ethnohistory; [10] Population Segments: Overview.

CHAP. 14 - POPULATION SEGMENTS: BUSH NEGROES
See also [6] Slavery and Emancipation; [10] Population Segments: Overview; [19] Cultural Continuities and Acculturation.

CHAP. 15 - POPULATION SEGMENTS: OTHERS   Chinese; Indonesians; Javanese; Jews.

CHAP. 18 - WEST INDIANS ABROAD   Writings that deal with various facets of the life of West Indians residing outside of the Caribbean area. This growing body of literature should be of considerable research value to Caribbeanists. When appropriate, secondary cross-references have been listed in other pertinent chapters.

CHAP. 25 - CREOLE LANGUAGES   French Creole; English Creole; Bush Negro dialects; Papiamento; language and society.

CHAP. 28 - HEALTH AND PUBLIC HEALTH   Clinical studies; epidemiological studies; water supply; sanitation; insect control.
See also [33] Social Welfare.

CHAP. 32 - EDUCATION   Secondary cross-references in this chapter include childrens' textbooks on all subject matter.

CHAP. 33 - SOCIAL WELFARE
See also [28] Health and Public Health; [30] Nutrition; [32] Education; [35] Housing and Architecture; [36] Urban Issues; [44] General Economic Studies; [50]   Labor, Labor Relations and Trade Unions.

CHAP. 40 - GEOLOGY AND LAND FORMS
See also [54] Mining and Economic Geology.

CHAP. 41 - PLANT AND ANIMAL LIFE
See also [64] Sylviculture and Lumbering.

CHAP. 43 - HUMAN GEOGRAPHY   This chapter brings together references to publications which deal with a region in broad geographical terms, often with an ecological orientation. Typically, such publications include sections on physical geography, natural resources, local history, demographic factors, and economics.   Many also offer sections on social structure and prospects for development.
See also [2] General Works; [7] Demography and Population Trends; [44] General Economic Studies.

CHAP. 44 - GENERAL ECONOMIC STUDIES   Comprehensive writings on Caribbean economics; national account studies; topics such as household budget analyses which are not treated in other economics-oriented chapters.

CHAP. 52 - TRANSPORTATION AND COMMUNICATION   Transport; radio; journalism.
See also [51] External Trade and Internal Marketing.

CHAP. 57 - SOILS AND SOIL SURVEYS
See also [43] Human Geography; [46] Land Use and Agricultural Economics.

CHAP. 58 - THE SUGAR COMPLEX   All references to publications principally concerned with sugar are grouped in this chapter. References include those that stress the agricultural dimensions, the labor factors, the historical perspectives, and the social and cultural implications.
See also [44] General Economic Studies; [45] Plantation Systems; [46] Land Use and Agricultural Economics.

CHAP. 66 - DEVELOPMENT AND CHANGE   Comprehensive plans for the development of a region; progress reports about such programs.   References to publications dealing with development in a specific or a narrowly delimited field, such as housing, appear as primary references in appropriate subject chapters and as secondary cross-references in this chapter.

CHAP. 67 - THEORY AND METHODOLOGY   The bulk of references are for publications in the social sciences, particularly anthropology and sociology.

PERIODICAL ABBREVIATIONS

A

Acad Sci Colon C R Séanc . . *Academie des Sciences Coloniales, Comptes Rendus des Séances.* Paris.

Adult Educ . . . . *Adult Education.* London.

Afr Mus . . . . *African Music.* Transvaal, S. Africa.

Afr Women . . . . *African Women.* London.

Afroamerica . . . . *Afroamerica.* Mexico, D. F.

Agenda . . . . *Agenda.* London.

Agric Am . . . . *Agriculture in the Americas.* Washington, D. C.

Agric Hist . . . . *Agricultural History.* Baltimore; Chicago.

Agric J Br Gui . . . . *Agricultural Journal of British Guiana.* Georgetown.

Agric Prat Pays Chauds . . . . *L'Agriculture Pratique des Pays Chauds.* Paris.

Agron Colon . . . . *L'Agronomie Coloniale.* Paris.

Agron Trop . . . . *L'Agronomie Tropicale.* Paris.

Am Anthrop . . . . *American Anthropologist.* Various places.

Am Antiq . . . . *American Antiquity.* Menasha, Wis.; Salt Lake City.

Am Cath Sociol Rev . . . . *American Catholic Sociological Review.* Various places.

Am Cons B . . . . *American Consular Bulletin.* Washington, D. C.

Am Fed . . . . *The American Federationist.* Washington, D. C.

Am Heb . . . . *American Hebrew.* New York.

Am Hist Rev . . . . *American Historical Review.* Lancaster, Pa.; New York.

Am J Econ Sociol . . . . *American Journal of Economics and Sociology.* Lancaster, Pa.

Am J Hum Gntcs . . . . *American Journal of Human Genetics*. Baltimore.

Am J Hyg . . . . *The American Journal of Hygiene*. Baltimore.

Am J Int Law . . . . *American Journal of International Law*. Concord, N. H.; Washington, D. C.

Am J Med . . . . *The American Journal of Medicine*. New York.

Am J Nurs . . . . *The American Journal of Nursing*. New York.

Am J Orth-psych . . . . *American Journal of Orthopsychiatry*. Menasha, Wis.

Am J Phys Anthrop . . . . *American Journal of Physical Anthropology*. Philadelphia.

Am J Psychol. . . . . *American Journal of Psychology*. Austin, Tex.; Ithaca, N. Y.

Am J Publ Heal . . . . *American Journal of Public Health*. New York.

Am J Sci . . . . *American Journal of Science*. New Haven.

Am J Sociol . . . . *American Journal of Sociology*. Chicago.

Am J Trop Med . . . . *American Journal of Tropical Medicine*. Baltimore.

Am J Trop Med Hyg . . . . . . *American Journal of Tropical Medicine and Hygiene*. Baltimore.

Am Jew Archs . . . . *American Jewish Archives*. Cincinnati.

Am Jew Hist Q . . . . *American Jewish Historical Quarterly*. New York.

Am Mercury . . . . *The American Mercury*. New York.

Am Mus J . . . . *American Museum Journal*. New York.

Am Neptune . . . . *The American Neptune*. Salem, Mass.

Am Perspect . . . . *American Perspective*. Washington, D. C.

Am Scand Rev . . . . *American Scandinavian Review*. New York.

Am Sociol Rev . . . . *American Sociological Review*. Menasha, Wis.; New York.

Am Speech. . . . . *American Speech*. Baltimore; New York.

America . . . . *America*. New York.

Américas. . . . . *Américas*. Washington, D. C.

Americas. . . . . *The Americas*. Washington, D. C.

An Univ Chile . . . . *Anales de la Universidad de Chile*. Santiago de Chile.

Ann Am Acad Polit
    Social Sci . . . . *Annals of the American Academy of Political and Social Sciences*. Philadelphia.

Ann Ass Am Geogr . . . . *Annals of the Association of American Geographers*. Lancaster, Pa.; Washington, D. C.

Ann Geogr. . . . . *Annales de Géographie*. Paris.

Ann Hyg Med Colon . . . . . . *Annales d'Hygiène et Médecine Coloniale*. Paris.

Ann Min . . . . *Annales des Mines.* Paris.

Ann N Y Acad Sci . . . . *Annals of the New York Academy of Sciences.* New York.

Ann Soc Lin Lyon . . . . *Annales de la Société Linéenne de Lyon.* Lyons.

Ann Trop Med Paras . . . . . *Annals of Tropical Medicine and Parasitology.* Liverpool.

Annls Inst Past . . . . *Annales de l'Institut Pasteur.* Paris.

Annls Med Pharm Colon . . . . *Annales de Médecine et de Pharmacie Coloniales.* Paris.

Annuar Fr Dr Int . . . . *Annuaire Francais de Droit International.* Paris.

Anthrop Ling . . . . *Anthropological Linguistics.* Bloomington, Ind.

Anthrop Q . . . . *Anthropological Quarterly.* Washington, D.C.

Anthropologica . . . . *Anthropologica.* Various places.

Anthropologie . . . . *Anthropologie.* Paris.

Anthropos . . . . *Anthropos.* Various places.

Antioch Rev . . . . *The Antioch Review.* Yellow Springs, Ohio.

Antiques . . . . *Antiques.* New York.

Anuar Estud Am . . . . *Anuario de Estudios Americanos.* Seville.

Architecture . . . . *Architecture.* New York.

Archs Inst Past Guy . . . . . . *Archives de l'Institut Pasteur de la Guyane et du Territoire de l'Inini.* Cayenne, F.G.

Archs Inst Past Guy Ter l'In. *Archives de l'Institut Pasteur de la Guyane Francaise et du Territoire de l'Inini.* Cayenne, F.G.

Archs Inst Past Mart . . . . . . *Archives de l'Institut Pasteur de la Martinique.* Fort-de-France, Mart.

Archs Path . . . . *Archives of Pathology.* Chicago.

Arena . . . . *Arena.* Boston.

Army Navy Life . . . . *Army and Navy Life.* New York.

Art J . . . . *The Art Journal.* London.

Arts . . . . *The Arts.* New York.

Asia Afr Rev . . . . *Asia and Africa Review.* London.

Asiat Rev . . . . *Asiatic Review.* London.

Atlan Mon . . . . *Atlantic Monthly.* Boston.

Atlanten . . . . *Atlanten.* Copenhagen.

Auk . . . . *The Auk.* Lancaster, Pa.

B

B Acad Med . . . . *Bulletin de l'Academie de Médecine.* Paris.

B Ag Econ Colon Auto
  Ter Afr . . . . *Bulletin de l'Agence Economique des Colonies Autonomes et des Territoires Africains sous Mandat.* Melun, France.

B Ag Gen Colon . . . . *Bulletin de l'Agence Générale des Colonies.* Melun, France; Paris.

B Am Ass Petrol Geol . . . . . *Bulletin of the American Association of Petroleum Geologists.* Tulsa, Okla.

B Am Geogr Soc . . . . *Bulletin of the American Geographical Society.* New York.

B Am Pal . . . . *Bulletins of American Paleontology.* Ithaca, N.Y.

B Ass Av Sci . . . . *Bulletin de l'Association Francaise pour l'Avancement des Sciences.* Paris.

B Ass Geogr Fr . . . . *Bulletin de l'Association de Géographes Francais.* Paris.

B Br Mus. . . . . *Bulletin of the British Museum.* London.

B Bur Am Ethnol . . . . *Bulletin of the Bureau of American Ethnology.* Washington, D.C.

B Colon Comp . . . . *Bulletin de Colonisation Comparée.* Brussels.

B Colon Inst Amst . . . . . . *Bulletin of the Colonial Institute of Amsterdam.* Amsterdam.

B Friends Hist Ass . . . . . . *Bulletin of the Friends' Historical Association.* Haverford, Pa.

B Geogr Soc Phila . . . . . . *Bulletin of the Geographical Society of Philadelphia.* Philadelphia.

B Geol Soc Am. . . . . *Bulletin of the Geological Society of America.* New York.

B Imp Inst. . . . . *Bulletin of the Imperial Institute.* London.

B Inst Fr Afr Noire . . . . . . *Bulletin de l'Institut Francais d'Afrique Noire.* Dakar.

B Inst Jam Sci . . . . *Bulletin of the Institute of Jamaica, Science Series.* Kingston.

B Mem Soc Anthrop . . . . . . *Bulletins et Memoires de la Société d'Anthropologie.* Paris.

B Mus Hist Nat . . . . *Bulletin du Muséum d'Histoire Naturelle.* Paris.

B Off Int Hyg Publ . . . . . . *Bulletin de l'Office International d'Hygiène Publique.* Paris.

B Pan Am Un. . . . . *Bulletin of the Pan American Union.* Washington, D.C.

B Pedag . . . . *Bulletin Pédagogique.* Pointe-à-Pitre, Guad.

B Perm Int Ass Nav Congr . . *Bulletin of the Permanent International Association of Navigation Congresses.* Brussels.

B Soc Anthrop . . . . *Bulletin de la Société d'Anthropologie.* Paris.

B Soc Fr Hist Nat Ant . . . . . *Bulletin de la Société Francaise d'Histoire Naturelle des Antilles*. Fort-de-France, Mart.

B Soc Geogr . . . . *Bulletin de la Société de Géographie de Lille*. Lille.

B Soc Geogr Comml Paris . . . *Bulletin de la Société de Géographie Commerciale de Paris*. Paris.

B Soc Geogr Etud
   Colon Mars . . . . *Bulletin de la Société de Géographie et d'Etudes Coloniales de Marseille*. Marseilles.

B Soc Geogr Mars . . . . *Bulletin de la Société de Géographie de Marseille*. Marseilles.

B Soc Geogr Paris . . . . *Bulletin de la Société de Géographie de Paris*. Paris.

B Soc Geogr Toul . . . . *Bulletin de la Société de Géographie de Toulouse*. Toulouse.

B Soc Geol Fr, Notes Mem . . *Bulletin de la Société Géologique de France, Notes et Mémoires*. Paris.

B Soc Oceanogr Fr . . . . . . *Bulletin de la Société d'Océanographie de France*. Paris.

B Soc Path Exot . . . . *Bulletin de la Société de Pathologie Exotique*. Paris.

B Soc Path Exot Fil . . . . . *Bulletin de la Société de Pathologie Exotique et de ses Filiales*. Paris.

Bett Crops Pl Fd . . . . *Better Crops with Plant Food*. Washington, D.C.

Bib Transl . . . . *Bible Translator*. London.

Bijd Dierkunde . . . . *Bijdragen tot de Dierkunde*. Leiden, The Netherlands.

Bijd Volk . . . . *Bijdragen tot de Taal, Land- en Volkenkunde*. The Hague.

Bijd Volk Ned-Indie. . . . . . *Bijdragen tot de Taal- Land- en Volkenkunde van Nederlandsch-Indië*. The Hague.

Bim . . . . *Bim*. Bridgetown.

Biotypologie . . . . *Biotypologie*. Paris.

Bklyn Mus Q . . . . *Brooklyn Museum Quarterly*. Brooklyn, N.Y.

Blwd Mag . . . . *Blackwood's Magazine*. Edinburgh.

Bois For Trop . . . . *Bois et Forêts des Tropiques*. Paris.

Boll Soc Geogr It . . . . *Bolletino de la Società Geografica Italiana*. Rome.

Boln Indig . . . . *Boletín Indigenista*. Mexico, D.F.

Boln Inst Caro Cuerva . . . . . *Boletín del Instituto Caro y Cuerva*. Bogotá.

Boln Latam Mus Inst
   Inter-Amer Music . . . . . . *Boletín Latinoamericano de Música*. Montevideo.

Boricua . . . . *Boricua*. San Juan.

Boston Coll Press,
    Anthrop Ser . . . . *Boston College Press Anthropological Series.* Chestnut Hill,
                    Mass.

Br Car Suppl . . . . *British Caribbean Supplement of New Commonwealth.* London.

Br Gui Med Annual . . . . *British Guiana Medical Annual.* Georgetown.

Br J Educ Stud . . . . *British Journal of Education Studies.* London.

Br J Psych . . . . *British Journal of Psychiatry.* London.

Br J Sociol . . . . *British Journal of Sociology.* London.

C

C R Mens Séanc Acad
    Sci Colon . . . . *Comptes Rendus Mensuels des Séances de l'Académie des
                    Sciences Coloniales.* Paris.

Cah Cent Etud Reg
    (Ant-Guy) . . . . *Les Cahiers du Centre d'Etudes Régionales (Antilles-Guyane).*
                    Fort-de-France, Mart.

Cah O-M . . . . *Les Cahiers d'Outre-Mer.* Bordeaux.

Cah Sociol Econ . . . . *Cahiers de Sociologie Economique.* Le Havre.

Calif Geogr . . . . *The California Geographer.* Los Angeles.

Can Forum . . . . *The Canadian Forum.* Toronto.

Can Geogr . . . . *The Canadian Geographer.* Ottawa.

Can Geogr J . . . . *Canadian Geographical Journal.* Ottawa.

Can Hist Rev . . . . *The Canadian Historical Review.* Toronto.

Can Inst Int Aff . . . . *Canadian Institute of International Affairs.* Toronto.

Can J Econ Polit Sci . . . . . . *The Canadian Journal of Economics and Political Science.*
                    Toronto.

Can J Zool . . . . *Canadian Journal of Zoology.* Ottawa.

Can Mag . . . . *Canadian Magazine.* Toronto.

Can Mag Polit Sci Art Lit . . *The Canadian Magazine of Politics, Science, Art and Litera-
                    ture.* Toronto.

Can-W I Mag . . . . : . . *Canada-West Indies Magazine.* Huntington, Quebec.

Car Commn Mon Inf B . . . . . *Caribbean Commission Monthly Information Bulletin.* Port of
                    Spain.

Car Econ Rev . . . . *Caribbean Economic Review.* Port of Spain.

Car For . . . . *The Caribbean Forester.* Rio Piedras, P. R.

Car Hist Rev . . . . *Caribbean Historical Review.* Port of Spain.

Car Med J . . . . *Caribbean Medical Journal.* Port of Spain.

Car Q . . . . *Caribbean Quarterly.* Port of Spain.

Car Stud . . . . *Caribbean Studies.* Rio Piedras, P. R.

Caribbean . . . . *The Caribbean.* Port of Spain.

Cent Mag . . . . *Century Magazine.* New York.

Ch Hist . . . . *Church History.* New York.

Cha J . . . . *Chambers' Journal (or Chambers's Journal).* London.

Chem Indus . . . . *Chemistry and Industry.* London.

Children . . . . *Children.* Washington, D. C.

China Wkly Rev . . . . *The China Weekly Review.* Shanghai.

Chr Cent . . . . *The Christian Century.* Chicago.

Chr Sci Monit Mag . . . . . . *Christian Science Monitor Magazine.* Boston.

Chron Med . . . . *Chronique Médicale.* Paris.

Chron Min Colon . . . . *La Chronique des Mines Coloniales.* Paris.

Chron Social Fr . . . . *Chronique Sociale de France.* Lyons.

Chron W I Comm . . . . *Chronicle of the West India Committee.* London.

Civilisations . . . . *Civilisations.* Brussels.

Colon Geol Miner Rsrc . . . . *Colonial Geology and Mineral Resources.* London.

Colon Mar . . . . *Colonies et Marine.* Paris.

Commerce Reports . . . . *Commerce Reports.* Washington, D. C.

Commonw Dev . . . . *Commonwealth Development.* London.

Commonw J . . . . *Commonwealth Journal.* London.

Commonweal . . . . *Commonweal.* New York.

Community Dev B . . . . *Community Development Bulletins.* London.

Comp Stud Soc Hist . . . . . . *Comparative Studies in Society and History.* The Hague.

Concours Méd . . . . *Le Concours Médical.* Paris.

Connoisseur . . . . *Connoisseur.* London.

Cons Com Exter . . . . *Le Conseiller du Commerce Extérieur.* Paris.

Contemp Rev . . . . *Contemporary Review.* London.

Context . . . . *Context.* Chicago.

Contrib Mus Am Indn . . . . . . *Contributions from the Museum of the American Indian.* New York.

Copeia . . . . *Copeia.* Ann Arbor, Mich.

Cornhill Mag . . . . *The Cornhill Magazine.* London.

Corona . . . . *Corona.* London.

Craft Hor . . . . *Craft Horizons.* New York.

Crisis . . . . *Crisis.* New York.

Crown Colon . . . . *Crown Colonist.* London.

Ctry Life . . . . *Country Life.* London.

Cuadernos . . . . *Cuadernos.* Paris.

Curr Hist . . . . *Current History.* New York; Philadelphia.

D

Dalh Rev . . . . *Dalhousie Review.* Halifax, Nova Scotia.

Dance Notat Rec . . . . *Dance Notation Record.* New York.

Dep St B . . . . *Department of State Bulletin.* Washington, D. C.

Dial Notes . . . . *Dialect Notes.* New Haven.

Dock Harb Auth . . . . *The Dock and Harbour Authority.* London.

Docum Med Geogr Trop . . . . *Documenta de Medicina Geographica et Tropica.* Amsterdam.

Docum Ned Indo
    Morbis Trop . . . . *Documenta Neerlandica et Indonesica de Morbis Tropicis.* Amsterdam.

Dt Rdsch . . . . *Deutsche Rundschau.* Gelsenkirchen, Germany.

E

East Anthrop . . . . *The Eastern Anthropologist.* Lucknow, India.

Ecl Geol Helv . . . . *Eclogae Geologicae Helvetiae.* Basel.

Ecol Monogr . . . . *Ecological Monographs.* Durham.

Ecology . . . . *Ecology*. Durham, N. C.

Econ Dev Cult Chg . . . . . . *Economic Development and Cultural Change*. Chicago.

Econ Geogr . . . . *Economic Geography*. Worcester, Mass.

Econ J . . . . *The Economic Journal*. London.

Ed Res Rep. . . . . *Editorial Research Reports*. Washington, D. C.

Edin Rev . . . . *Edinburgh Review*. London.

Edn Hebd J Déb . . . . *Edition Hebdomadaire du Journal de Débats*. Paris.

Education . . . . *Education*. Boston.

Emp Dig . . . . *Empire Digest*. Toronto.

Emp For J . . . . *The Empire Forestry Journal*. London.

Emp For Rev . . . . *The Empire Forestry Review*. London.

Emp J Expl Agric . . . . *The Empire Journal of Experimental Agriculture*. Oxford.

Emp Prod Exp . . . . *Empire Production and Export*. London.

Emp Rev . . . . *Empire Review (title varies)*. London.

Empl Secur Rev . . . . *Employment Security Review*. Washington, D. C.

Encounter . . . . *Encounter*. London.

Ency Mens O-M . . . . *Encyclopedie Mensuelle d'Outre-Mer*. Paris.

Engl Hist Rev . . . . *English Historical Review*. London.

Engl Lang Tch . . . . *English Language Teaching*. London.

Engng Min J . . . . *Engineering and Mining Journal*. New York.

Enterprise . . . . *Enterprise*. Various places.

Erde . . . . *Die Erde*. Berlin.

Erdkunde . . . . *Erdkunde*. Bonn.

Esprit . . . . *Esprit*. Paris.

Esso Ant . . . . *Esso in the Antilles*. [Port of Spain?]

Ethnology . . . . *Ethnology*. Pittsburgh, Pa.

Ethnomusicology . . . . *Ethnomusicology*. Middletown, Conn.

Etud O-M . . . . *Etudes d'Outre-Mer*. Marseilles.

Etudes . . . . *Etudes*. Paris.

Eug Q . . . . *Eugenics Quarterly*. New York.

Explor J . . . . *Explorers Journal.* New York.

Explor Rev . . . . *Exploration Review.* London.

Ext Rev Fr . . . . *(Extrait de) La Revue Francaise.* Paris.

Extra-Mural Reptr . . . . *Extra-Mural Reporter.* Mona, Jamaica.

F

Facts Fig . . . . *Facts and Figures.* Washington, D. C.

Far East Rev . . . . *The Far Eastern Review.* Shanghai.

Farmer . . . .*The Farmer; Journal of the Jamaica Agricultural Society.* Kingston.

Fellowship . . . . *Fellowship.* Nyack, N. Y.

Fert Ster . . . . *Fertility and Sterility.* New York.

Fla Hist Q . . . . *The Florida Historical Quarterly.* St. Augustine.

Fld Col Mus . . . . *Field Columbian Museum Publications.* Chicago.

Fld Mus Nat Hist . . . . *Field Museum of Natural History, Publications.* Chicago.

Focus . . . . *Focus.* New York.

Fol Civ . . . . *Folia Civitatis.* Amsterdam.

Folk . . . . *Folk.* Copenhagen.

Folk-Lore . . . . *Folk-Lore.* London.

Folkeskolen . . . . *Folkeskolen.* Copenhagen.

For Aff . . . . *Foreign Affairs.* New York.

For Agric . . . . *Foreign Agriculture.* Washington, D. C.

For Com Wkly . . . . *Foreign Commerce Weekly.* Washington, D. C.

For Policy Rep . . . . *Foreign Policy Reports.* New York.

Foren Dansk Samv
    Dansk Atlha . . . . *Foreningen Dansk Samvirke de Dansk Atlanterhavsøer.* Copenhagen.

Fortnightly . . . . *The Fortnightly.* London.

Fortune . . . . *Fortune.* Chicago.

Forum . . . . *Forum.* New York.

Fra Natnmus Arbsm . . . . *Fra Nationalmuseets Arbejdsmark.* Copenhagen.

Free Lab Wld . . . . *Free Labour World*. Brussels.

Freedomways . . . . *Freedomways*. New York.

G

Geneesk Tijdschr Ned-Indie . . *Geneeskundig Tijdschrift voor Nederlandsch-Indië*. Batavia, (Djakarta).

Geogr Tidsskrift . . . . *Geografisk Tidsskrift*. Copenhagen.

Geogr J . . . . *Geographical Journal*. London.

Geogr Mag . . . . *Geographical Magazine*. London.

Geogr Rdsch . . . . *Geographische Rundschau*. Braunschweig; Frankfort.

Geogr Rev . . . . *Geographical Review*. New York.

Geogr Tchr . . . . *The Geographical Teacher*. Aberystwyth, Wales.

Geogr Tijdschr . . . . *Geografisch Tijdschrift*. The Hague.

Géographie . . . . *La Géographie*. Paris.

Geography . . . . *Geography*, Manchester, Eng.

Geol Mag . . . . *Geological Magazine*. London.

Geol Mijnb . . . . *Geologie en Mijnbouw*. The Hague.

Geol Soc Am . . . . *The Geological Society of America Bulletin*. New York.

Globe . . . . *The Globe*. Geneva; Manchester.

Globus . . . . *Globus*. Braunschweig.

Gunton's Mag . . . . *Gunton's Magazine*. New York.

H

Harper's Mag . . . . *Harper's Magazine*. New York.

Harper's Mon Mag . . . . *Harper's Monthly Magazine*. New York.

Harv Educ Rev . . . . *Harvard Educational Review*. Cambridge.

Hdwd Rec . . . . *Hardwood Record*. Chicago.

Hibbert J . . . . *The Hibbert Journal*. London.

Hispan Am Hist Rev . . . . . . *Hispanic American Historical Review*. Durham, N. C.

Hispania . . . . *Hispania*. Menasha, Wis.

Hist J . . . . *The Historical Journal.* Cambridge, Eng.

Hist Mag Prot Epsc Ch . . . . *Historical Magazine of the Protestant Episcopal Church.* New Brunswick, N. J.

Hist Tchr Mag . . . . *History Teacher's Magazine.* Philadelphia.

Hist Today . . . . *History Today.* London.

History . . . . *History.* London.

Holiday . . . . *Holiday.* Philadelphia.

Home Geogr Mon . . . . *Home Geographic Monthly.* Worcester, Mass.

L'Homme . . . . *L'Homme. Revue Francaise d'Anthropologie.* Paris.

Hommes Mondes . . . . *Hommes et Mondes.* Paris.

Hum Org . . . . *Human Organization.* New York.

Hum Rel . . . . *Human Relations.* London.

I

Iberoamer Archiv . . . . *Ibero-Amerikanisches Archiv.* Berlin.

Illus Lond News . . . . *Illustrated London News.* London.

Imp Asiat Q Rev . . . . *The Imperial and Asiatic Quarterly Review.* London.

Imp Inst B . . . . *Imperial Institute Bulletin.* London.

In Context . . . . *In Context.* New Haven.

Independent . . . . *The Independent.* Boston; New York.

India Q . . . . *India Quarterly.* New Delhi.

India Rubb Wld . . . . *India Rubber World.* New York.

Indisch Genoot . . . . *Indisch Genootschap.* The Hague.

Indn Notes . . . . *Indian Notes.* New York.

Indn Notes Monogr . . . . *Indian Notes and Monographs.* New York.

Indo-Asian Cult . . . . *Indo-Asian Culture.* New Delhi.

Indonesië . . . . *Indonesië.* The Hague.

Indus Lab Rel Rev . . . . *Industrial and Labor Relations Review.* Ithaca, N.Y.

Inf B Scient Res Coun . . . . . *Information; Bulletin of the Scientific Research Council.* Kingston.

Inf Geogr . . . . *L'Information Géographique.* Paris.

Inst Past Guy Ter l'In . . . . . *Institut Pasteur de la Guyane et du Territoire de l'Inini, Publications.* Cayenne, F. G.

Int Aff . . . . *The International Affairs.* London.

Int Archiv Ethnogr . . . . *Internationales Archiv für Ethnographie.* Leiden, The Netherlands.

Int Archs Ethnogr . . . . *International Archives of Ethnography.* Leiden, The Netherlands.

Int Com . . . . *International Commerce.* Washington, D. C.

Int Comp Law Q . . . . *The International and Comparative Law Quarterly.* London.

Int Free Trade Un . . . . . . *International Free Trade Union News.* New York.

Int J . . . . *International Journal.* Toronto.

Int J Am Ling . . . . *International Journal of American Linguistics.* Various places.

Int J Comp Sociol . . . . *International Journal of Comparative Sociology.* Dharwar, India.

Int J Social Psych. . . . . *International Journal of Social Psychiatry.* London.

Int Lab Rev . . . . *International Labour Review.* Geneva; London.

Int Ment Heal Res Newsl . . . *International Mental Health Research Newsletter.* New York.

Int Org . . . . *International Organization.* Boston.

Int Ref Serv . . . . *International Reference Service.* Washington, D. C.

Int Rev Educ . . . . *International Review of Education.* The Hague.

Int Rev Miss . . . . *International Review of Missions.* London.

Int Spectator . . . . *Internationale Spectator.* The Hague.

Int Sug J . . . . *International Sugar Journal.* London.

Inter-Amer Econ Aff . . . . . . *Inter-American Economic Affairs.* Washington, D. C.

Inter-Amer Q . . . . *Inter-American Quarterly.* Washington, D. C.

Inter-Ocean . . . . *Inter-Ocean.* Batavia, (Djakarta).

Ir Eccles Rec . . . . *Irish Ecclesiastical Record.* Dublin.

J

J Ab Social Psychol . . . . . . *Journal of Abnormal and Social Psychology.* New York.

J Agric Econ . . . . *Journal of Agricultural Economics.* Reading, Eng.

J Agric Soc Trin Tob . . . . . . *Journal of the Agricultural Society of Trinidad and Tobago.* Port of Spain.

J Am Folk . . . . *Journal of American Folklore.* Various places.

J Arn Arb . . . . *Journal of the Arnold Arboretum.* Cambridge, Mass.

J Barb Mus Hist Soc . . . . . . *Journal of the Barbados Museum and Historical Society.* Bridgetown.

J Bd Agric Br Gui . . . . *The Journal of the Board of Agriculture of British Guiana.* Georgetown.

J Comp Leg Int Law . . . . . . *Journal of Comparative Legislation and International Law.* London.

J Ecol . . . . *Journal of Ecology.* Various places.

J Econ . . . . *Journal des Economistes.* Paris.

J Econ Hist . . . . *Journal of Economic History.* New York.

J Educ Sociol . . . . *Journal of Educational Sociology.* New York.

J For . . . . *Journal of Forestry.* Washington, D.C.

J Geogr . . . . *Journal of Geography.* Chicago; Menasha, Wis.

J Geol . . . . *Journal of Geology.* Chicago.

J Geophys Res . . . . *Journal of Geophysical Research.* Washington, D.C.

J Hered . . . . *Journal of Heredity.* Washington, D.C.

J Indn Psychoan Inst . . . . . . *Samiska (Journal of the Indian Psychoanalytic Institute).* Calcutta.

J Int Folk Mus Coun . . . . . . *Journal of the International Folk Music Council.* Cambridge, Eng.; Leiden, The Netherlands.

J Inter-Amer Stud . . . . *Journal of Inter-American Studies.* Gainesville, Fla.

J Med Educ . . . . *Journal of Medical Education.* Evanston, Ill.

J Mod Hist . . . . *The Journal of Modern History.* Chicago.

J N Y Bot Gdn . . . . *Journal of the New York Botanical Garden,* New York.

J Negro Educ . . . . *Journal of Negro Education.* Washington, D.C.

J Negro Hist . . . . *Journal of Negro History.* Lancaster, Pa.; Washington, D.C.

J Polit . . . . *Journal of Politics.* Gainesville, Fla.

J Polit Econ . . . . *Journal of Political Economy.* Chicago.

J Proj Tech . . . . *Journal of Projective Techniques.* Glendale, Calif.

J Psychol . . . . *Journal of Psychology.* Provincetown, Mass.

J Roy Anthrop Inst
   Gt Br Ire . . . . *Journal of the Royal Anthropological Institute of Great Britain
    and Ireland.* London.

J Roy Commonw Soc . . . . . . *Journal of the Royal Commonwealth Society.* London.

J Roy Inst Br Archit . . . . . . *Journal of the Royal Institute of British Architects.* London.

J Roy Soc Arts . . . . *Journal of the Royal Society of Arts.* London.

J Roy United Serv Instn . . . . *Journal of the Royal United Service Institutions.* London.

J Soc Afr . . . . *Journal de la Sociéte' des Africanistes.* Paris.

J Soc Am . . . . *Journal de la Société des Américanistes.* Paris.

J Soc Am Paris . . . . *Journal de la Société des Américanistes de Paris.* Paris.

J Soc Comp Leg . . . . *Journal of the Society of Comparative Legislation.* London.

J Social Psychol . . . . *Journal of Social Psychology.* Provincetown, Mass.

J Social Sci . . . . *Journal of the Social Sciences.* New York.

J Soil Sci . . . . *The Journal of Soil Science.* Oxford.

J Trop Ped . . . . *Journal of Tropical Pediatrics.* Calcutta.

J Wash Acad Sci . . . . *Journal of the Washington Academy of Sciences.* Baltimore;
    Washington, D.C.

Jam Hist Rev . . . . *Jamaican Historical Review.* Kingston.

Janus . . . . *Janus.* Leiden, The Netherlands.

Jb Städt Mus Volk Lpz . . . . *Jahrbuch des Städtischen Museums für Völkerkunde zu Leip-
    zig.* Leipzig.

Jew Fron . . . . *Jewish Frontier.* New York.

Jew Q Rev . . . . *The Jewish Quarterly Review.* London.

Jubilee . . . . *Jubilee.* New York.

K

Kenyon Rev . . . . *The Kenyon Review.* Gambier, Ohio.

Kirk Saml . . . . *Kirkehistoriske Samlinger.* Copenhagen.

Knick Wkly . . . . *Knickerbocker Weekly*, New York.

Kon Veren Indische Inst . . . *Koninklijke Vereeniging Indische Instituut.* Amsterdam.

Kon Veren Kol Inst G . . . . . *Koninklijke Vereeniging Koloniaal Instituut Gids in het Volk-enkundig Museum.* Amsterdam.

L

Language . . . . *Language.* Baltimore; Menasha, Wis.

Life Lett . . . . *Life and Letters.* London.

Lingua . . . . *Lingua.* Amsterdam.

Listener . . . . *The Listener.* London.

Listener BBC Telev Rev . . . *Listener and B. B. C. Television Review.* London.

Liv Age . . . . *Living Age.* Boston; New York.

M

Man . . . . *Man.* London.

Mar Mirror . . . . *Mariner's Mirror.* Cambridge, Eng.

March India . . . . *March of India.* Delhi.

Marr Fam Liv . . . . *Marriage and Family Living.* Chicago; Minneapolis.

Mass Educ B . . . . *Mass Education Bulletin.* London.

Med Newsmag . . . . *MD Medical Newsmagazine.* New York.

Meded Kon Akad Wetensch
  Afd Lettk . . . . *Mededeelingen der Koninklijke Akademie van Wetenschappen Afdeeling Letterkunde.* Amsterdam.

Meded Kon Veren
  Indisch Inst . . . . *Mededeeling Koninklijke Vereeniging Indisch Instituut.* Amsterdam.

Meded Rijksmus Volk . . . . . *Mededeelingen van het Rijksmuseum voor Volkenkunde.* Leiden, The Netherlands.

Mem Mus Comp Zool
  Harv Coll . . . . *Memoirs of the Museum of Comparative Zoology at Harvard College.* Cambridge.

Menorah J . . . . *The Menorah Journal.* Concord, N. H.

Mens Mij . . . . *Mens en Maatschappij.* Groningen.

Mens Mij Twee Tijdschr . . . *Mens en Maatschappÿ Tweedmaandelijks Tÿdschrift.* Groningen.

Mentor . . . . *Mentor.* New York; Springfield, Ohio.

Mercure Fr . . . . *Mercure de France.* Paris.

Metron (Int Rev Statist) . . . . *Metron (International Review of Statistics).* Ferrara, Italy.

Mezhdunarodnaia Zhizn . . . . *Mezhdunarodnaia Zhizn.* Moscow.

Midwest Folk. . . . . *Midwest Folklore.* Bloomington, Ind.

Mines Mag . . . . *Mines Magazine.* Denver.

Min Mag . . . . *Mining Magazine.* London.

Min Metall . . . . *Mining and Metallurgy.* New York.

Min Qua Engng . . . . *Mine and Quarry Engineering.* London.

Miss Rev Wld . . . . *Missionary Review of the World.* New York.

Missi Valley Hist Rev . . . . . *The Mississippi Valley Historical Review.* Lincoln, Neb.

Mod Philol . . . . *Modern Philology.* Chicago.

Mon Rev . . . . *Monthly Review.* New York.

Mon Weath Rev . . . . *Monthly Weather Review.* Washington, D. C.

Monde Colon Illus . . . . *Le Monde Colonial Illustré.* Paris.

Month . . . . *The Month. (London Catholic Truth Society).* London.

Morav Miss . . . . *Moravian Missions.* London.

Mosq News . . . . *Mosquito News.* Selma, Calif.

Mot Boating . . . . *Motor Boating.* New York.

Mus Q . . . . *The Musical Quarterly.* New York.

N

N W I G . . . . *Nieuwe West-Indische Gids.* The Hague, Amsterdam.

Names . . . . *Names.* Berkeley; Los Angeles.

Nat Hist . . . . *Natural History.* New York.

Nation . . . . *The Nation.* New York.

Natn Coun Outlook . . . . *National Council Outlook.* New York.

Natn Geogr Mag . . . . *The National Geographic Magazine.* New York; Washington, D. C.

Natn Guardian . . . . *National Guardian.* New York.

Natn Munic Rev . . . . *National Municipal Review.* Worcester, Mass.

Natn Petrol News . . . . *National Petroleum News.* Cleveland.

Natn Rev . . . . *The National Review.* London.

Nature . . . . *La Nature.* Paris.

Ned Jurbl . . . . *Nederlands Juristenblad.* Zwolle, The Netherlands.

Negro Hist B . . . . *The Negro History Bulletin.* Washington, D.C.

Neophilologus . . . . *Neophilologus.* Groningen.

Neth J Agric Sci . . . . *Netherlands Journal of Agricultural Science.* Wageningen.

New Cent Rev . . . . *New Century Review.* London.

New Commonw . . . . *New Commonwealth.* London.

New Commonw,
    Br Car Suppl. . . . . *New Commonwealth, British Caribbean Supplement.* London.

New Republ. . . . . *New Republic.* New York.

New Soc . . . . *New Society.* London.

New Stsm . . . . *New Statesman.* London.

New Stsm Natn. . . . . *New Statesman and Nation.* London.

New Wld Antiq . . . . *New World Antiquity.* London.

New Wld Q . . . . *New World Quarterly.* Georgetown; Mona, Jamaica.

New Wld Rev . . . . *New World Review.* New York.

N Y Acad Sci Trans Ann . . . *New York Academy of Sciences: Transactions, Annals.* New York.

New Yorker . . . . *The New Yorker.* New York.

Nieuwe W I G . . . . *Nieuwe West-Indische Gids.* Amsterdam; The Hague.

Nineteenth Cent After . . . . . *The Nineteenth Century and After.* New York.

Nord Tidsskr Straf . . . . *Nordisk Tidsskrift for Strafferet.* Copenhagen.

Norsk Geogr Tidsskr . . . . . . *Norsk Geografisk Tidsskrift.* Oslo.

Nth Am Rev. . . . . *North American Review.* New York.

Nth Caro Hist Rev . . . . *North Carolina Historical Review.* Raleigh.

Nueva Revta Filol Hispan . . *Nueva Revista de Filología Hispánica.* Mexico, D.F.

O

Oost West . . . . *Oost en West.* The Hague.

Opbouw . . . . *Opbouw*. Utrecht, The Netherlands.

Opportunity . . . . *Opportunity*. New York.

Oversea Educ . . . . *Oversea Education*. London.

P

Pacif Hist Rev . . . . *The Pacific Historical Review*. Berkeley.

Pacif Sociol Rev . . . . *Pacific Sociological Review*. Eugene, Or.

Pan Am Mag . . . . *Pan American Magazine*. Washington, D. C.

Parl Aff J Hans Soc . . . . . . *Parliamentary Affairs, Journal of the Hansard Society*. London.

Partijn Zhizn . . . . *Partinaia Zhizn*. Moscow.

Peab Mus Pap . . . . *Peabody Museum Papers*. Cambridge, Mass.

Pêche Marit . . . . *La Pêche Maritime*. Paris.

Pelican . . . . *Pelican*. Mona, Jamaica.

Penant . . . . *Penant*. Paris.

Pepperpot . . . . *Pepperpot*. Kingston.

Pet Geogr Mitt . . . . *Petermanns Geographische Mitteilungen*. Gotha, Germany; Leipzig.

Pet Mitt . . . . *Petermanns Mitteilungen*. Gotha, Germany.

Phil Trans Roy Soc Lond . . . *The Philosophical Transactions of the Royal Society of London*. London.

Philol Q . . . . *Philological Quarterly*. Iowa City.

Phylon . . . . *Phylon*. Atlanta, Ga.

Plaisir Fr . . . . *Plaisir de France*. Paris.

Pol J . . . . *Police Journal*. London.

Polit Q . . . . *The Political Quarterly*. London.

Polit Sci Q . . . . *Political Science Quarterly*. New York.

Polit Stud . . . . *Political Studies*. Oxford.

Pop Sci Mon . . . . *Popular Science Monthly*. New York.

Popul I . . . . *Population Index*. Princeton, N. J.; Washington, D. C.

Popul Rev . . . . *Population Review*. Madras.

Popul Stud . . . . *Population Studies*. London.

Population . . . . *Population*. Paris.

Prefabrication. . . . . *Prefabrication*. London.

Présence Afr . . . . *Présence Africaine*. Dakar; Paris.

Presse Med . . . . *La Presse Médicale*. Paris.

Problemy Mira Sots . . . . *Problemy Mira i Sotsializma*. Prague.

Proc Acad Nat Sci Phil . . . . *Proceedings of the Academy of Natural Sciences of Philadelphia*. Philadelphia.

Proc Agric Soc Trin Tob . . . *Proceedings of the Agricultural Society of Trinidad and Tobago*. Port of Spain.

Proc Am Antiq Soc . . . . *Proceedings of the American Antiquarian Society*. Worcester, Mass.

Proc Am Phil Soc . . . . *Proceedings of the American Philosophical Society*. Philadelphia, Pa.

Proc Geol Ass . . . . *Proceedings of the Geologists' Association*. Colchester, Eng.

Proc Ind Acad Sci . . . . *Proceedings of the Indiana Academy of Sciences*. Indianapolis.

Proc Natn Acad Sci . . . . . . *Proceedings of the National Academy of Sciences*. Washington, D. C.

Proc Zool Soc Lond . . . . . . *Proceedings of the Zoological Society of London*. London.

Psychiatry . . . . *Psychiatry*. Baltimore; Washington, D. C.

Psychol Monogr . . . . *Psychological Monographs*. Evanston, Ill.; Lancaster, Pa.

Publ Law . . . . *Public Law*. London.

Publs Am Econ Ass . . . . . . *Publications of the American Economic Association*. New York.

Publs Am Folk Soc . . . . *Publications of the American Folklore Society*. Philadelphia.

Pubs Mod Lang Ass Am . . . . *Publications of the Modern Language Association of America*. New York.

Punch . . . . *Punch*. London.

Q

Q J Geol Soc . . . . *Quarterly Journal of the Geological Society*. London.

Q Rev . . . . *The Quarterly Review*. London.

Quest Diplom Colon . . . . . . *Questions Diplomatiques et Coloniales*. Paris.

R

Race . . . . *Race.* London.

Reporter . . . . *The Reporter.* New York.

Rev Bl Polit Lit . . . . *Revue Bleue Politique et Littéraire.* Paris.

Rev Deux Mondes . . . . *Revue des Deux Mondes.* Paris.

Rev Econ Fr . . . . *Revue Economique Francaise.* Paris.

Rev Etud Coop . . . . *Revue des Etudes Coopératives.* Paris.

Rev Fr . . . . *La Revue Francaise.* Paris.

Rev Fr Etr Colon . . . . *Revue Francaise de l'Etranger et des Colonies.* Paris.

Rev Fr Hist O-M . . . . *Revue Francaise d'Histoire d'Outre Mer.* Paris.

Rev Gen Sci . . . . *Revue Générale des Sciences.* Paris.

Rev Guad . . . . *Revue Guadeloupéenne.* Basse-Terre, Guad.

Rev Hist . . . . *Revue Historique.* Paris.

Rev Hist Colon . . . . *Revue d'Histoire des Colonies.* Paris.

Rev Hist Colon Fr . . . . *Revue de l'Histoire des Colonies Francaises.* Paris.

Rev Hist Econ Social . . . . . *Revue d'Histoire Economique et Sociale.* Paris.

Rev Jur Polit Un Fr . . . . . . *Revue Juridique et Politique de l'Union Francaise.* Paris.

Rev Ling Rom . . . . *Revue de Linguistique Romane.* Paris.

Rev Med Fr . . . . *Revue Medicale Francaise.* Paris.

Rev Polit Parl . . . . *Revue Politique et Parlementaire.* Paris.

Rev Soc Hist Geogr Haiti . . . *Revue de la Société d'Histoire et de Geographie d'Haiti.* Port-au-Prince, Haiti.

Rev Social . . . . *Revue Socialiste.* Paris.

Rev Univ . . . . *Revue Universitaire.* Paris.

Rev Univers Min Metall Trav
   Publ Sci Arts
     Appl Indus . . . . *Revue Universelle des Mines, de la Metallurgie des Travaux Publics, des Sciences et des Arts appliqués à l'Industries.* Liége, Belgium.

Revta Brasil Mala Do Trop . . *Revista brasileira de Malariologia e Doencas Tropicais.* Rio de Janeiro.

Revta Brasil Polit Int . . . . . *Revista Brasileira de Política Internacional.* Rio de Janeiro.

Revta Cienc Social . . . . . . Revista de Ciencias Sociales. Rio Piedras, P. R.

Revta Geogr Am . . . . Revista Geográfica Americana. Buenos Aires.

Revta Hist Am . . . . Revista de Historia de América. Mexico, D. F.

Revta Indias . . . . La Revista de Indias. Madrid.

Revta Inst Etnol. . . . . Revista del Instituto de Etnología. Tucumán, Argentina.

Revta Mex Geogr . . . . Revista Mexicana de Geografía. Mexico, D. F.

Revta Mus Paul . . . . Revista do Museu Paulista. Sao Paulo.

Revta Policl Cara . . . . Revista de la Policlínica Caracas. Caracas.

Revta Soc Brasil Geogr . . . . Revista da Sociedade Brasileira de Geografia. Rio de Janeiro.

Revta Soc Geogr Rio Jan . . . Revista da Sociedade de Geografia do Rio de Janeiro. Rio
de Janeiro.

S

S Am . . . . South American. New York.

S Atlan Q . . . . South Atlantic Quarterly. Durham, N. C.

Sch Soc . . . . School and Society. New York.

Schakels . . . . Schakels, Suriname. The Hague.

Science . . . . Science. New York.

Scient Am . . . . The Scientific American. New York.

Scient Am Suppl . . . . Scientific American Supplement. New York.

Scient Mon . . . . Scientific Monthly. New York.

Scott Geogr Mag . . . . The Scottish Geographical Magazine. Edinburgh.

Scott Hist Rev . . . . The Scottish Historical Review. Edinburgh; Glasgow.

Shell Mag . . . . Shell Magazine. [Port of Spain?]

Shell Trin . . . . Shell Trinidad. [Port of Spain].

Smithson Misc Colln . . . . . . Smithsonian Miscellaneous Collections. Washington, D.C.

So Econ J . . . . The Southern Economic Journal. Chapel Hill, N. C.

So Work . . . . Southern Workman. Hampton, Va.

Social Econ Stud . . . . Social and Economic Studies. Mona, Jamaica.

Social Forces . . . . Social Forces. Chapel Hill, N. C.

Social Sci . . . . Social Scientist. Mona, Jamaica.

Sociol Gids . . . . *Sociologische Gids*. Meppel, The Netherlands.

Sociol Rev . . . . *Sociological Review*. Keele, Eng.; London.

Sociol Social Res . . . . *Sociology and Social Research*. Los Angeles.

Sociologia . . . . *Sociologia*. Sao Paulo.

Soil Sci . . . . *Soil Science*. Baltimore.

Sov Ethnogr . . . . *Sovetskaia Etnografiia*. Moscow.

Sp Miss . . . . *Spirit of Missions*. New York.

Spectator . . . . *Spectator*. London.

Spotlight . . . . *Spotlight*. Kingston.

Statist . . . . *The Statist*. London.

Stud Left . . . . *Studies on the Left*. Madison, Wis.

Stud Philol . . . . *Studies in Philology*. Chapel Hill, N.C.

Studio . . . . *The Studio*. London.

Stuttgarter Geogr Stud . . . . . *Stuttgarter Geographische Studien*. Stuttgart.

Sug Azucar . . . . *Sugar y Azúcar*. New York.

Sug B . . . . *Sugar Bulletin*. New Orleans.

Suppl Social Econ Stud . . . . *Supplement to Social and Economic Studies*. Mona, Jamaica.

Sur Landb . . . . *De Surinaamse Landbouw*. Paramaribo.

Surv Graphic . . . . *Survey Graphic*. East Stroudsberg, Pa.

Sw J Anthrop . . . . *Southwestern Journal of Anthropology*. Albuquerque, N.M.

T

Taal Tong . . . . *Taal en Tongval*. Antwerp.

Taxes . . . . *Taxes*. Chicago.

Tchr Coll Rec . . . . *Teachers College Record*. New York.

Temps Mod . . . . *Les Temps Modernes*. Paris.

Tex J Sci . . . . *Texas Journal of Science*. Austin, Texas.

Tex Q . . . . *The Texas Quarterly*. Austin, Texas.

Th Arts . . . . *Theatre Arts.* New York.

Tijdschr Econ Geogr . . . . . . *Tijdschrift voor Economische Geographie.* The Hague.

Tijdschr Econ Social Geogr . *Tijdschrift voor Economische en Sociale Geographie.* Rotterdam.

Tijdschr Ned Aar Genoot . . . *Tijdschrift van het (Koninklijk) Nederlandsch Aardrijkskundig Genootschap.* Amsterdam; Leiden, The Netherlands.

Tijdschr Ned Taalen Lettk . . *Tijdschrift voor Nederlandsche Taalen Letterkunde.* Leiden, The Netherlands.

Tilskueren . . . . *Tilskueren.* Copenhagen.

Timehri . . . . *Timehri.* Georgetown.

Times Br Colon Rev . . . . . . *The Times British Colonies Review.* London.

Tomorrow . . . . *Tomorrow.* New York.

Torch . . . . *Torch.* Kingston.

Town Ctry Plann . . . . *Town and Country Planning.* London.

Town Plann Rev . . . . *The Town Planning Review.* Liverpool.

Trans Am Inst Min
 Metall Engn . . . . *Transactions of the American Institute of Mining and Metallurgical Engineers.* New York.

Trans Am Res Free Acc
 Masons . . . . *Transactions of the American Lodge of Research Free and Accepted Masons.* New York.

Trans Ill St Acad Sci . . . . . *Transactions of the Illinois State Academy of Science.* Carbondale, Ill.

Trans N Y Acad Sci . . . . . . *Transactions of the New York Academy of Sciences.* New York.

Trans Roy Soc Trop
 Med Hyg . . . . *Transactions of the (Royal) Society of Tropical Medicine and Hygiene.* London.

Travel . . . . *Travel.* New York.

Tribus . . . . *Tribus.* Stuttgart.

Trop Agric . . . . *Tropical Agriculture.* London.

Trop Geogr Med . . . . *Tropical and Geographical Medicine.* Amsterdam.

Trop Sci . . . . *Tropical Science.* London.

Trop Wd . . . . *Tropical Woods.* New Haven.

Tropiques . . . . *Tropiques*. Paris.

Tubercle . . . . *Tubercle*. London.

Twen Cent . . . . *The Twentieth Century*. London.

U

U N Wld . . . . *United Nations World*. Bristol, Conn.

U S Natn Herb . . . . *United States National Herbarium, Contributions*. Washington, D.C.

U S Navl Inst Proc . . . . *United States Naval Institute, Proceedings*. Annapolis.

U S Navl Med B . . . . *U. S. Naval Medical Bulletin*. Washington, D.C.

United Emp . . . . *United Empire*. London.

Univ Calif Press
  Publs Hist . . . . *University of California Press, Publications in History*. Berkeley; Los Angeles.

Univ Fla Contrib Fla St
  Mus Social Sci . . . . *University of Florida, Contributions of the Florida State Museum, Social Sciences*. Gainesville.

Univ Mus B . . . . *University Museum, Bulletin*. Philadelphia.

L'Universo . . . . *L'Universo*. Florence.

V

Vc Miss . . . . *Voice of Missions*. New York.

Venture . . . . *Venture*. London.

Vie It Am Lat . . . . *Le Vie d'Italia e dell'America Latina*. Milan.

Vie It Mondo . . . . *Le Vie d'Italia e del mondo*. Milan.

Vie Mondo . . . . *Le Vie del Mondo*. Milan.

Vopr Ekon . . . . *Voprosy Ekomomiki*. Moscow.

Vox Guy . . . . *Vox Guyanae*. Paramaribo.

Vse Pro Dviz . . . . *Vsemirnoe Profsoiuznoe Dvizhenie*. Moscow.

W

W I B . . . . *West Indian Bulletin*. Bridgetown.

W I Comm Circ . . . . *West India Committee Circular*. London.

W I Econ. . . . . *The West Indian Economist*. Kingston.

W I G . . . . *West-Indische Gids*. Amsterdam; The Hague.

W I Med J . . . . *The West Indian Medical Journal*. Kingston.

W I Rev . . . . *West Indian Review*. Kingston.

Weather . . . . *Weather*. London.

Welf Reptr. . . . . *Welfare Reporter*. Kingston.

West Polit Q . . . . *The Western Political Quarterly*. Salt Lake City.

Wester Mh . . . . *Westermanns Monatshefte*. Braunschweig, Ger.

Wld Aff. . . . . *World Affairs*. London.

Wld Aff Q . . . . *World Affairs Quarterly*. Los Angeles.

Wld Crops . . . . *World Crops*. London.

Wld Ment Heal . . . . *World Mental Health*. London.

Wld Polit . . . . *World Politics*. Princeton, N. J.

Wld Today. . . . . *World To-day*. London.

Wld Trade Un Mov. . . . . . . *World Trade Union Movement*. London.

Wld Trav. . . . . *World Traveler*. New York.

Wld Work. . . . . *World's Work*. London; New York.

Wm Mary Q . . . . *The William and Mary Quarterly*. Williamsburg.

Word . . . . *Word*. New York.

Y

Yb Ass Pacif Cst Geogr . . . *The Yearbook of the Association of Pacific Coast Geographers*. Cheney, Wash.

Ymer . . . . *Ymer*. Stockholm.

Z

Z Dt Geol Ges A Abh . . . . . *Zeitschrift der Deutschen Geologischen Gesellschaft A. Abhandlungen*. Stuttgart.

Z Franz Spr . . . . *Zeitschrift für französische Sprache und Literatur*. Jena & Leipzig.

Z Ges Erdk Berl . . . . *Zeitschrift der Gesellschaft für Erdkunde zu Berlin.* Berlin.

Z Kryst Miner . . . . *Zeitschrift für Krystallographie und Mineralogie.* Leipzig.

Z Polit . . . . *Zeitschrift für Politik.* Various places.

Z Rassk . . . . *Zeitschrift für Rassenkunde.* Stuttgart.

Zaire . . . . *Zaire.* Brussels.

Zoologica . . . . *Zoologica.* New York.

CODE TO NEW YORK CITY LIBRARIES

Most references in this bibliography have the library source identified by code. All references with such identification can be located in New York City. References without library notations are from a number of private collections or libraries in the United States, Canada and the West Indies. Such references were lent to the Research Institute for the Study of Man for review and inclusion in the bibliography, or were examined at the source.

ACM   *NEW YORK ACADEMY OF MEDICINE*
        (2 East 103rd Street)

AGS   *AMERICAN GEOGRAPHICAL SOCIETY*
        (Broadway & 156th Street)

AMN   *AMERICAN MUSEUM OF NATURAL HISTORY*
        (Central Park West & 79th Street)

COL   *COLUMBIA UNIVERSITY*
        (Broadway & 116th Street)

NYP   *NEW YORK PUBLIC LIBRARY*
        (Fifth Avenue & 42nd Street)

RIS   *RESEARCH INSTITUTE FOR THE STUDY OF MAN*
        (162 East 78th Street)

SCH   *SCHOMBURG COLLECTION OF THE NEW YORK PUBLIC LIBRARY*
        (103 West 135th Street)

TCL   *TEACHERS COLLEGE LIBRARY*
        (525 West 120th Street)

UNL   *UNITED NATIONS LIBRARY*
        (United Nations Plaza)

UTS   *UNION THEOLOGICAL SEMINARY*
        (Broadway & 120th Street)

GEOGRAPHICAL DIVISIONS FOR

CARIBBEANA 1900-1965

I. General Caribbean

II. British Caribbean

    Barbados

    British Guiana (Guyana)

    British Honduras

    British Virgin Islands
      Tortola

    Jamaica
      Caicos Islands
      Cayman Islands
      Turks Islands

    Trinidad & Tobago
      Tobago

    Leeward Islands
      Anguilla
      Antigua
      Montserrat
      Nevis
      Saint Kitts (Saint Christopher)

Windward Islands
    Dominica
    Grenada
    Grenadines
      Bequia
      Carriacou
    St. Lucia
    St. Vincent

III. French Caribbean
    French Guiana
    French Antilles
      Guadeloupe
      Desirade
      Les Saintes
      Marie Galante
      Saint Barthelemy
      Saint Martin
      Martinique

IV. Netherlands Caribbean
    Netherlands Antilles
      Netherlands Leeward Islands
        Aruba
        Bonaire
        Curacao
      Netherlands Windward Islands
        Saba
        Saint Eustatius
        Saint Maarten
    Surinam

V. United States Virgin Islands
    Saint Croix
    Saint John
    Saint Thomas

VI. Composite Units
    Guianas—General
      (British, French & Dutch)
    Saint Martin/St. Maarten
    Saint Kitts/Nevis/Anguilla
    Turks & Caicos Islands
    Virgin Islands—General
      (British & United States)

CODE TO GEOGRAPHICAL UNITS

AG	Anguilla		MG	Marie Galante
AR	Aruba		MS	Montserrat
AT	Antigua		MT	Martinique
BB	Barbados			
BC	British Caribbean		NA	Netherlands Antilles
BG	British Guiana		NC	Netherlands Caribbean
BH	British Honduras		NL	Netherlands Leeward Islands
BN	Bonaire		NV	Nevis
BQ	Bequia		NW	Netherlands Windward Islands
BV	British Virgin Islands			
CC	Caicos Islands		SA	Saba
CM	Cayman Islands		SB	Saint Barthelemy
CR	Carriacou		SC	Saint Croix
CU	Curacao		SE	Saint Eustatius
			SJ	Saint John
DM	Dominica		SK	Saint Kitts
DS	Desirade		SL	Saint Lucia
			SM	Saint Martin/St. Maarten
FA	French Antilles		SR	Surinam
FC	French Caribbean		ST	Saint Thomas
FG	French Guiana		SV	Saint Vincent
GC	General Caribbean			
GD	Guadeloupe		TB	Tobago
GG	Guianas—General		TC	Turks and Caicos Islands
GN	Grenadines		TR	Trinidad and Tobago
GR	Grenada		TT	Tortola
JM	Jamaica		UV	United States Virgin Islands
KNA	St. Kitts—Nevis—Anguilla		VI	Virgin Islands—General
LS	Les Saintes			
LW	Leeward Islands		WW	Windward Islands

1

CARIBBEANA 1900-1965

INTRODUCTION
TO THE
CARIBBEAN

Chapter 1

BIBLIOGRAPHICAL REFERENCES

ABONNENC, E.; HURAULT, J.; SABAN, R., et al.

1.001   FG   1957 Bibliographie de la Guyane Francaise [Bibliography of French Guiana]. Vol. 1. Paris, Editions Larose, 278p. [RIS]

ALCALA, V. O.

28.005   GC   1959 Instructional material for healthy living.

ANIKINA, E. B., et al., comps

1.002   GC   1964 Trinidad i Tobago. Iamaika. Kolonial'nye territorii [Trinidad and Tobago. Jamaica. Colonial territories]. In their Latinskaia America v sovetskoi pechati: bibliografiia . . . 1946-1962 gg. [Redkollegiia: E. B. Ananova . . . et al.] [Latin America in the Soviet Press]. Moscow, Akademiia Nauk SSSR, Institut Latinskoi Ameriki, p.92, 104, 107-112. [RIS]

BELL, HERBERT C.; PARKER, DAVID W., et al.

1.003   GC   1926 Guide to British West Indian archive materials, in London and in the islands, for the history of the United States. Washington, Carnegie Institution of Washington, 435p. (Publication no. 372.) [5] [COL]

BLACK, CLINTON VANE de BROSSE

1.004   BG   1955 Report on the archives of British Guiana. Georgetown, Printed for the Govt. of British Guiana by the "Daily Chronicle", 23p. [37]

CANTON, BERTHE E.

1.005   FC   1954 The French Caribbean Departments: sources of information: 1946-1955. In Current Caribbean bibliography. Port of Spain, Caribbean Commission, v. 4, p. 1-36. [RIS]

CHAPMAN, T. & HERRERA, E.

1.006   TR   1961 List of completed research work carried out at the Imperial College of Tropical Agriculture on crop husbandry. J Agric Soc Trin Tob. 61(4), Dec.: 489-503; 1962 62(1), Mar.: 72-91. [46] [AMN]

5

COOLHAAS, W. PH.

1.007   NC   1960 A CRITICAL SURVEY OF STUDIES ON DUTCH COLONIAL HISTORY. The
                       Hague: Koninklijk Instituut voor Taal-, Land- en Volkenkunde,
                       154p. (Bibliographical series, 4.)   [5]   [*RIS*]

CRUICKSHANK, J. GRAHAM

1.008   BB   1935 A bibliography of Barbados. *J Barb Mus Hist Soc* 2(3),May: 155-165;
                       2(4), Aug.: 220-225.   [*AMN*]

CUNDALL, FRANK

1.009   JM   [1908?] BIBLIOGRAPHIA JAMAICENSIS. Kingston, Institute of Jamaica, 83,38p.
1.010   GC   1909 BIBLIOGRAPHY OF THE WEST INDIES (EXCLUDING JAMAICA). Kingston,
                       Institute of Jamaica, 179p.   [*COL*]

DAMPIERRE, JACQUES de

1.011   FA   1904 ESSAI SUR LES SOURCES DE L'HISTOIRE DES ANTILLES FRANCAISES
                       (1492-1664) [STUDY OF THE HISTORICAL SOURCES ON THE FRENCH
                       ANTILLES (1492-1664)]. Paris, A. Picard, 238p. (Mémoires et docu-
                       ments de la Société de l'école des chartes, Vol. 6.) [5]   [*COL*]

DEBIEN, GABRIEL

1.012   FA   1961 Les travaux d'histoire sur les Antilles Francaises; chronique
                       bibliographique (1959 et 1960) [Historical works on the French
                       Antilles; bibliographical chronicle (1959 and 1960)]. *Rev Fr Hist
                       O-M* 48(170): 267-308. [5]   [*COL*]
1.013   FA   1963 Chronique de l'histoire d'outre-mer, les Antilles Francaises (1961
                       et 1962) [Historical chronicle of the overseas territories, the French
                       Antilles (1961 and 1962)]. *Rev Fr Hist O-M* 50(179):227-267.   [5]
                                                                                        [*COL*]

EASTON, DAVID K.

1.014   TB   1950 Preliminary survey of the archives of Tobago. *Car Hist Rev* 1,
                       Dec.: 133-135.
1.015   GC   1955 The Caribbean Commission Library. *Caribbean* 8(8), Mar.: 166-168.
                                                                                        [*COL*]

FELHOEN KRAAL, JOHANNA L. G.

1.016   GC   1953 Territoires de la Commission des Caraïbes 1953 [Territories of the
                       Caribbean Commission, 1953]. *Civilisations* 3(4):615-617.   [*NYP*]
1.017   NC   1955 Antillas Neerlandesas y Suriname [The Netherlands Antilles and
                       Surinam]. *Anuar Estud Am* 12:695-734. [2]   [*NYP*]
1.018   NC   1956/ Libraries and archives for research in West Indian history. *W I G*
                  57   37:71-92. [5]   [*COL*]
1.019   NC   1956 Netherlands Antilles and Surinam: developments 1946-1956, as
                       reflected in publications on these countries. *In* CURRENT CARIBBEAN
                       BIBLIOGRAPHY. Port of Spain, Caribbean Commission, v.6, p.1-49.
                                                                                        [*RIS*]

GAZIN GOSSEL, JACQUES

1.020   FA   1926 ELÉMENTS DE BIBLIOGRAPHIE GÉNÉRALE MÉTHODIQUE ET HISTORIQUE DE
                       LA MARTINIQUE (ANTILLES FRANCAISES) [FOUNDATIONS FOR A GENERAL,

SYSTEMATIC AND HISTORICAL BIBLIOGRAPHY OF MARTINIQUE (FRENCH ANTILLES)]. Fort-de-France, Impr. Antillaise, 348p.   [*COL*]

GRIFFIN, A. P. C.

1.021   UV   1901 A LIST OF BOOKS ON THE DANISH WEST INDIES. Washington, U. S. Govt. Print. Off., 18p.

GROPP, ARTHUR E.

1.022   BC/   1941 GUIDE TO LIBRARIES AND ARCHIVES IN CENTRAL AMERICA AND THE WEST
           FA/   INDIES, PANAMA, BERMUDA, AND BRITISH GUIANA SUPPLEMENTED WITH
           UV   INFORMATION ON PRIVATE LIBRARIES, BOOKBINDING, BOOKSELLING, AND
                    PRINTING. New Orleans, Middle American Research Institute, Tulane University of Louisiana, 721p.

HARDY, F.

1.023   BC   1936 Studies in West Indian soils. *Trop Agric* 13(10), Oct.: 268-273. [57]
                                                                                      [*AGS*]

HOFF, B. J.

1.024   NC   1956 Lijst van geschriften van Professor C. H. de Goeje [List of the writings of Professor C. H. de Goeje]. *W I G* 36:91-94.   [*RIS*]

HOLDSWORTH, H.

1.025   JM   1953 The Library of the University College. *W I Med J* 2(1), Mar.: 81-84. [32]   [*COL*]

KEMP, JAMES F.

40.101   BV   1926 Introduction and review of the literature on the geology of the Virgin Islands.

KUYP, EDWIN van der

1.026   SR   1962 Literatuuroverzicht betreffende de voeding en de voedingsgewoonten van de Boslandcreool in Suriname [Bibliography about nutrition and food habits of the Bush Negroes in Surinam]. *N W I G* 41(3), May: 205-271.   [14, 28, 30]   [*COL*]

LACROIX, ALFRED

2.123   FC   1932 NOTICE HISTORIQUE SUR LES MEMBRES ET CORRESPONDANTS DE L'ACADÉMIE DES SCIENCES AYANT TRAVAILLÉ DANS LES COLONIES FRANCAISES DE LA GUYANE ET DES ANTILLES DE LA FIN DU XVIIᵉ SIÈCLE AU DÉBUT DU XIXᵉ [HISTORICAL ACCOUNT OF THE MEMBERS AND CORRESPONDENTS OF THE ACADEMY OF SCIENCES WHO WORKED IN THE FRENCH COLONIES OF GUIANA AND THE ANTILLES FROM THE END OF THE 17TH TO THE BEGINNING OF THE 19TH CENTURY].

LINCOLN, WALDO

1.027   GC   1926 LIST OF NEWSPAPERS OF THE WEST INDIES AND BERMUDA. Worcester, Mass., American Antiquarian Society.

MEILINK-ROELOFSZ, M. A. P.

1.028   NA   1955 A survey of archives in the Netherlands pertaining to the history of the Netherlands Antilles. *W I G* 35:1-38.   [*COL*]

MORAIS, ALLAN I.

1.029   GC   1953 Useful sources of Caribbean statistics. *Car Commn Mon Inf B* 7(1), Aug.: 7-9, 24.   [*AGS*]

1.030   GC   1954 SELECT BIBLIOGRAPHY OF TRADE PUBLICATIONS WITH SPECIAL REFERENCE TO CARIBBEAN TRADE STATISTICS. Compiled in the Statistical Unit, Research Branch, Central Secretariat, Caribbean Commission. [Introd. signed: Allan Morais. Statistician...]. Port of Spain, Caribbean Commission, 54p. [51]   [*RIS*]

OUDSCHANS DENTZ, FRED

1.031   GC   1936/ Musea in West Indië [Museums in the West Indies]. *W I G* 18:139-152. 37 [2]   [*COL*]

1.032   SR   1938 Surinaamsche journalistiek [Surinam journalism]. *W I G* 20:33-44, 65-76, 289-290. [52]   [*COL*]

RAGATZ, LOWELL JOSEPH

1.033   BC   1923 A CHECK LIST OF HOUSE OF COMMONS SESSIONAL PAPERS RELATING TO THE BRITISH WEST INDIES AND TO THE WEST INDIAN SLAVE TRADE AND SLAVERY, 1763-1834. London, Bryan Edwards Press, 42p. [5, 6]   [*COL*]

1.034   BC   1931 A CHECK-LIST OF HOUSE OF LORDS SESSIONAL PAPERS RELATING TO THE BRITISH WEST INDIES AND TO THE WEST INDIAN SLAVE TRADE AND SLAVERY, 1763-1834. London, Bryan Edwards Press, 13p. [6, 37] [*NYP*]

1.035   BC   1932 A GUIDE FOR THE STUDY OF BRITISH CARIBBEAN HISTORY, 1763-1834, INCLUDING THE ABOLITION AND EMANCIPATION MOVEMENTS. Washington, U.S. Govt. Print. Off., 725p. [5]   [*RIS*]

1.036   FA   1949 EARLY FRENCH WEST INDIAN RECORDS IN THE ARCHIVES NATIONALES. [n.p.] ("Reprinted from vol. 1, no. 3, of the Inter-American Bibliographical Review [Fall, 1941]", p.151-190). [5]   [*RIS*]

REID, CHARLES FREDERICK

1.037   UV   1941 BIBLIOGRAPHY OF THE VIRGIN ISLANDS OF THE UNITED STATES. New York, H. W. Wilson, 225p.   [*TCL*]

ROSE, F. G. & CHOW, J. E.

28.450   BG   1923 A resume of the scientific work published by medical men in British Guiana from 1769 to the present day.

ROTH, VINCENT

1.038   BG   1948 BIBLIOGRAPHY OF BRITISH GUIANA, COMPILED UNDER THE AEGIS OF THE BRITISH GUIANA BIBLIOGRAPHY COMMITTEE BY ITS CHAIRMAN. [Georgetown?] Microfilm copy of the typewritten manuscript. Made in 1951 for the Library of Congress. Negative. Collation of the original: 1 v. (unpaged).   [*RIS*]

RUBIN, JOAN

1.039   GC   1963 A bibliography of Caribbean Creole languages. *Car Stud* 2(4), Jan.: 51-61. [25]   [*RIS*]

RUTTEN, L. M. R.

1.040   GC   1938 BIBLIOGRAPHY OF WEST INDIAN GEOLOGY. Utrecht, 103p. (Geographische en geologische mededeelingen, Physiographisch-geologische reeks, no. 16). [40]   [*AGS*]

SAVAGE, ERNEST A.

1.041   BC/   1934 THE LIBRARIES OF BERMUDA, THE BAHAMAS, THE BRITISH WEST INDIES,
        UV   BRITISH GUIANA, BRITISH HONDURAS, PUERTO RICO, AND AMERICAN
                      VIRGIN ISLANDS: REPORT TO THE CARNEGIE CORPORATION OF NEW YORK.
                      London, Library Association, 104p. [COL]

SHILSTONE, E. M.

40.165   BB   1938 A descriptive list of maps of Barbados.

STEENHUIS, J. F.

1.042   GG/   1951 DE GEOLOGISCHE LITERATUUR OVER OF VAN BELANG VOOR NEDERLANDS
        NA   GUYANA (SURINAME) EN DE NEDERLANDSE WESTINDISCHE EILANDEN
                      [THE GEOLOGICAL LITERATURE ABOUT OR OF IMPORTANCE TO DUTCH
                      GUIANA (SURINAM) AND THE DUTCH WEST INDIAN ISLANDS]. The Hague,
                      Boek-en Kunstdrukkerij Mouton, 108p. (Vervolgen 2-6, 1934-1950 en
                      addenda voor de jaren voor 1934, nos. 651-1574.) [40] [AGS]

VALKHOFF, MARIUS

25.104   GC   1960 Contributions to the study of Creole. I. Contributions to the study
                      of Creole. III. Some notes on Creole French.

WAGENAAR HUMMELINCK, P.

1.043   CU   1946 Literatuur betreffende het natuurwetenschappelijk onderzoek in
                      Curacao gedurende de oorlogsjaren [Literature about natural sci-
                      ence research in Curacao during the war]. *W I G* 27:363-375.
                      [40, 41] [COL]

1.044   SR   1946 Literatuur betreffende het natuurwetenschappelijk onderzoek in
                      Suriname gedurende de oorlogsjaren [Literature about natural
                      science research in Surinam during the war]. *W I G* 27:300-310.
                      [40, 41] [COL]

WILES, D. A.

1.045   BB   1949 The history of the Barbados Public Library. *Car Commn Mon Inf B*
                      3(2), Sept.: 61-62. [5] [COL]

WILLIAMS, ERIC EUSTACE

1.046   GC   1952 A West Indian book collection. *Car Commn Mon Inf B* 6(3), Oct.:
                      59-62, 72. [COL]

1.047   GC   1954 A bibliography of Caribbean history: a preliminary essay. Part 1:
                      1492-1898. *Car Hist Rev* 3-4, Dec.: 208-250. [5] [RIS]

WILLIAMS, JAMES

1.048   BG   1917 Indian languages. *Timehri* 3d ser., 4(21), June: 83-86. [26] [AMN]

1.049   GG   1924 The Arawak Indians and their language. *In* PROCEEDINGS OF THE
                      TWENTY-FIRST INTERNATIONAL CONGRESS OF AMERICANISTS [1st
                      Sess.]. The Hague, Aug. 12-16, 1924. The Hague, p.355-370. [13, 26]
                      [AGS]

WILSON, P. N. & HERRERA, E.

1.050   TR   1961 List of completed research work carried out at the Imperial College
                      of Tropical Agriculture on animal and grassland husbandry. *J Agric*
                      Soc Trin Tob 61(1), Mar.: 63-86. [65] [AMN]

WINTER, JOHANNA MARIA van

1.051   NC   1953 Lijst van bronnen betreffende de afschaffing van de slavernij in
                    Nederlands West-Indië [List of sources on the abolition of slavery
                    in the Dutch West Indies]. *W I G* 34:91-102.   [6]   [*COL*]

WORK, MONROE N.

1.052   GC   1928 A BIBLIOGRAPHY OF THE NEGRO IN AFRICA AND AMERICA. New York,
                    H. W. Wilson, 698p. [11]   [*COL*]

ZIMMERMAN, IRENE

1.053   GC   1961 A GUIDE TO CURRENT LATIN AMERICAN PERIODICALS: HUMANITIES AND
                    SOCIAL SCIENCES. Gainesville, Kallman, 355p.   [*RIS*]

Chapter 2

GENERAL WORKS

ABRAHAMS, PETER

2.001   JM   1957   JAMAICA: AN ISLAND MOSAIC. London, H. M. S. O., 284p. (The Corona library.)   [*RIS*]

ADEMOLLO, UMBERTO

2.002   FA   1940   Le colonie francesi delle Antille, Guadalupa e Martinica [The French colonies in the Antilles, Guadaloupe and Martinique]. *Vie Mondo* 8(9), Sept.: 863-874.   [*AGS*]

2.003   FG   1942   Una metà agognata del super-imperialismo statunitense: la Guiana Francese [A coveted goal of American super-imperialism: French Guiana]. *Vie Mondo* 10(3), Mar.: 251-258.   [*AGS*]

ALEXANDER, WILLIAM H.

2.004   SK   1901   St. Christopher, West Indies. *B Am Geogr Soc* 33(1):42-46.   [*AGS*]

ANDERSON, A. H.

2.005   BH   1948   BRIEF SKETCH OF BRITISH HONDURAS. Rev. ed. Belize, Govt. Printer, 86p.   [*NYP*]

ANDERSON, ROBERT M., ed.

2.006   SV   1938   HANDBOOK OF ST. VINCENT. 5th ed. Kingstown, St. Vincent, Office of the Vincentian, 453p.   [*UTS*]

ARNOLD, PERCY

2.007   BC   1955   Political and economic advance. *New Commonw, Br Car Suppl* 30(9), Oct. 31: iv-vi.   [*AGS*]

ASPINALL, Sir ALGERNON E.

2.008   BC   1912   THE BRITISH WEST INDIES: THEIR HISTORY, RESOURCES, AND PROGRESS. London, Sir Isaac Pitman, 434p.   [*NYP*]

2.009   BC   1926   THE HANDBOOK OF THE BRITISH WEST INDIES, BRITISH GUIANA AND BRITISH HONDURAS, 1926-27. London, West India Committee, 212p.   [*AGS*]

BAILEY, LEE

2.010   BC   1948   Whose future in the Caribbean? *Life Lett* 57(128), Apr.: 13-19.   [*COL*]

11

BALDWIN, RICHARD
2.011   BG   1946 THE RUPUNUNI RECORD. Georgetown, British Guiana Bureau of Pub-
                   licity & Information, 57p.   [*RIS*]

BALEN, CHRISTIAN van
2.012   CU   1944 La isla de Curacao y demás Antillas holandesas [The island of
                   Curacao and the other Dutch Antilles]. *Revta Geogr Am* 21(128),
                   May: 269-278.   [*AGS*]

BALEN, W. J. van
2.013   CU   1939 The territory of Curacao. *B Colon Inst Amst* (Published in colla-
                   boration with the Netherlands Pacific Institute) 2(2), Feb.: 115-121.
                                                                                     [*AGS*]

BARBOUR, WILLIAM R.
2.014   UV   1931 Possibilities of the Virgin Islands. *Pan Am Mag* 44(5), May: 354-362.
                                                                                     [*COL*]

BAUDE, THEODORE
2.015   MT   1931 Martinique. *In* GUADELOUPE, GUYANE, MARTINIQUE, SAINT-PIERRE ET
                   MIQUELON. Paris, Société d'éditions géographiques, maritimes et
                   coloniales, 29p. (Exposition Coloniale internationale de Paris.)[*NYP*]

BECKWITH, MARTHA WARREN
11.004   JM   1929 BLACK ROADWAYS: A STUDY OF JAMAICAN FOLK LIFE.

BESSON, MAURICE; LEBLOND, MARIUS-ARY;
ROULLIER, JEAN & HEILLY, G. d'
2.016   FC   1936 Les colonies francaises d'Amérique, à l'occasion du tricentenaire
                   des Antilles [The French colonies in the Americas, on the occasion
                   of the tercentenary of the Antilles]. *In* ENCYCLOPÉDIE COLONIALE
                   ET MARITIME. Paris, fasc. 1, May, p.2-37.   [*NYP*]

BICKERTON, DEREK
12.003   TR   1962 THE MURDERS OF BOYSIE SINGH.

BLANKENSTEIJN, M. van
2.017   SR   1923 SURINAME, Rotterdam, 339p.   [*AGS*]

BOLT, ANNE
2.018   BH   1958 British Honduras. *Geogr Mag* 31(1), May: 27-31.   [*AGS*]
2.019   BC   1961 A diversity of islands: The West Indian Federation. *Geogr Mag*
                   34(5), Sept.: 271-283.   [38]   [*AGS*]

BONNET, P.
2.020   GD   1955 La vie antillaise (Guadeloupe) [Life in the Antilles (Guadeloupe)].
                   Etud O-M 38, Feb.: 83-88.   [*NYP*]

BOOY, THEODOOR de & FARIS, JOHN T.
2.021   UV   1918 THE VIRGIN ISLANDS: OUR NEW POSSESSIONS AND THE BRITISH ISLANDS.
                   Philadelphia, Lippincott, 292p.   [*AGS*]

BRONS, J. C.

2.022   SR   1952 HET RIJKSDEEL SURINAME [SURINAM, A TERRITORY OF THE NETHER-LANDS]. Haarlem, De Erven F. Bohn, 214p. (Volksuniversiteits bibliotheek, 2nd ser., no. 44.)   [AGS]

BROWN, JOHN, ed.

2.023   LW   1961 LEEWARDS: WRITINGS, PAST AND PRESENT, ABOUT THE LEEWARD ISLANDS. [Bridgetown?] Barbados, Dept. of Extra-Mural Studies, Leeward Islands, University College of the West Indies, 74p.   [RIS]

BRUNINGS, LOUIS

2.024   SR   1951 Surinam. *Americas* 3(10), Oct.: 13-16, 41.   [AGS]

BRYCE, WYATT E., ed.

2.025   JM   1946 REFERENCE BOOK OF JAMAICA. Kingston, Wyatt Bryce, 404p.   [COL]

BUISKOOL, J. A. E.

2.026   SR   1946 SURINAME NU EN STRAKS [SURINAM NOW AND THEN]. Amsterdam, W. L. Salm, 247p.   [NYP]

BURDON, Sir JOHN ALDER

2.027   BH   1928 BRIEF SKETCH OF BRITISH HONDURAS: PAST, PRESENT AND FUTURE. 2d rev. ed. London, West India Committee, 53p.   [AGS]

2.028   BH   1931 ARCHIVES OF BRITISH HONDURAS. London, Sifton Praed (on behalf of West India Committee), 3v. [5]   [COL]

BURNHAM, Viscount

2.029   BC   1923 The West Indies. *J Roy Soc Arts* 72(3708), Dec. 14:60-71.

CAIGER, STEPHEN L.

2.030   BH   1951 BRITISH HONDURAS: PAST AND PRESENT. London, George Allen & Unwin, 240p.   [RIS]

CAPRA, GIUSEPPE

2.031   JM   1938 Nelle Grandi Antille, "Giamaica" [In the Greater Antilles, "Jamaica"]. *Vie Mondo* 6(8), Aug.: 793-805.   [AGS]

CARGILL, MORRIS

2.032   JM   1956 Jamaica and Britain. *Hist Today* 6(10), Oct.: 655-663.   [COL]

CARLEY, MARY MANNING

2.033   JM   1963 JAMAICA: THE OLD AND THE NEW. London, George Allen and Unwin, 212p.   [RIS]

CECIL, C. H.

2.034   BG   1931 British Guiana— "Terra incognita." *Can-WI Mag* 20(6), May: 195-198.   [NYP]

CELARIE, HENRIETTE

2.035   GD   1930 Karukéra, l'île d'émeraude [Karukera, the emerald isle]. *Rev Deux Mondes* 56, Mar. 15:378-403.   [COL]

CHEMIN DUPONTES, P.

2.036   GC   1909 LES PETITES ANTILLES: ÉTUDE SUR LEUR ÉVOLUTION ÉCONOMIQUE [THE LESSER ANTILLES: A STUDY OF THEIR ECONOMIC DEVELOPMENT]. Paris, 362p. (Librairie orientale & americaine.)   [AGS]

CHISHOLM, HESTER DOROTHY

37.063   LW/   1938 A COLONIAL EVALUATION OF THE BRITISH LEEWARD ISLANDS AND THE UV   VIRGIN ISLANDS OF THE UNITED STATES.

CLARKE, C. BELFIELD

2.037   BC   1951 The West Indies re-visited. *United Emp* new ser., 42(1), Jan.-Feb.: 12-19.   [AGS]

CLELAND, HERDMAN F.

2.038   CU   1909 Curacao, a losing colonial venture. *B Am Geogr Soc* 41(3): 129-138.   [AGS]

COAGE, JEFFERSON S.

2.039   UV   1924 The Virgin Islands. U.S.A. *Crisis* 28(6), Oct.: 276-277.   [COL]

COLL, C. van

2.040   SR   1903 Gegevens over land en volk van Suriname [Data about the country and people of Suriname]. *Bijd Volk Ned-Indie* 55:451-650. [10]
2.041   SR   1905 Toegift tot de "Gegevens over land en volk van Suriname" [Addition to the "Data about the country and people of Suriname"]. *Bijd Volk Ned-Indie* 58:465-480. [13]

COLLIER, H.C.

2.042   BG   1938 British Guiana—a possible refuge haven. *Can-W I Mag* 27(12), Dec.: 29-38. [17]   [NYP]
2.043   BG   1941 British Guiana—past, present—and future? *Can-W I Mag* 30(5), May: 7-10; 30(6), June: 8-9, 29-31.   [NYP]
2.044   BB   1944 Barbados in brief. *Can-W I Mag* 33-34(11), Nov.: 19-23.   [NYP]
2.045   LW   1945 The Leeward Islands. *Can-W I Mag* 35(7), Aug.-Sept.: 9, 11-15.   [NYP]
2.046   WW   1945 The Windward Islands. *Can-W I Mag* 35(7), Aug.-Sept.: 43, 45-57.   [NYP]
2.047   JM   1946 About Jamaica. *Can-W I Mag* 36(3), May: 55-57, 59, 61, 63, 65. [NYP]
2.048   JM   1946 Climate, population, resources and industry. *Can-W I Mag* 36(3), May: 9-11, 13.   [NYP]

COLLINS, DOREEN

2.049   TC   1961 The Turks and Caicos Islands—some impressions of an English visitor. *Car Q* 8(3), Dec.: 163-167.   [RIS]

CRACKNELL, EVERILL M.W.

2.050   BB   1934 THE BARBADIAN DIARY OF GEN. ROBERT HAYNES 1787-1836. Hampshire, Azania Press, 70p. [5]

CROWLEY, DANIEL JOHN

2.051   SL   1956 Report from St. Lucia. *Jubilee* Dec.: 2.   [*RIS*]

CURTIN, PHILIP D.

2.052   JM   1955 TWO JAMAICAS: THE ROLE OF IDEAS IN A TROPICAL COLONY, 1830-1865. Cambridge, Mass., Harvard University Press, 270p. [5, 8, 10] [*RIS*]

DANGOISE, ARTHUR & POTTEREAU, L.

2.053   FG   [n.d.] NOTES, ESSAIS ET ÉTUDES SUR LA GUYANE FRANCAISE ET LE DEVELOPPEMENT DE SES RESSOURCES VARIÉES ET SPÉCIALEMENT DE RICHESSES AURIFERES, FILONIENNES ET ALLUVIONNAIRES [NOTES, DISCUSSIONS, AND STUDIES ON FRENCH GUIANA AND THE DEVELOPMENT OF ITS VARIED RESOURCES, PARTICULARLY ITS GOLD, LODE-METAL AND ALLUVIAL RESOURCES]. Paris, Impr. Roberge, 225p. [54]   [*SCH*]

DAVIES, SAMUEL HENRY

2.054   DM   1921 Cinderella of the Antilles—Dominica's plight and the remedy. *W I Comm Circ* 36(587), Mar. 31:120-122.   [*NYP*]

DAVSON, Sir EDWARD R.

2.055   BC   1915 The West Indies: their common interest and imperial aim. *Timehri* 3d ser., 3(20B), May: 333-344.

DELPEY, GENEVIEVE

2.056   FA   1939 Influence des phénomènes actuels aux Antilles Francaises [The influence of current events on the French Antilles]. *Geographie* 71(1), Jan.: 13-19.   [*AGS*]

DELPH, C. N. & ROTH, VINCENT, eds.

2.057   BG   1948 WHO IS WHO IN BRITISH GUIANA 1945-1948. 4th ed. Georgetown, Daily Chronicle, 851p.   [*NYP*]

DENIS, SERGE, ed.

2.058   FA   1935 NOS ANTILLES [OUR ANTILLES]. Orléans, Luzeray, 378p.   [*AGS*]

DESSARRE, EVE

2.059   JM/   1965 CAUCHEMAR ANTILLAIS [ANTILLES NIGHTMARE]. Paris, Francois
        TR/   Maspero, 160p. [37]   [*RIS*]
        FA

DIGBY, ERNEST S.

2.060   TB   1934 When history was made in Tobago. *Can-W I Mag* 23(4), Mar.: 121-123. [5]   [*NYP*]

DOMINGO, W. A.

2.061   BC   1926 The West Indies. *Opportunity*, 4(47), Nov.: 339-342.

DONALD, ALAN H.

2.062   CM   1961 A view of the Cayman Islands. *Corona* 13(1), Jan.: 9-12.   [*AGS*]

DORAN, EDWIN BEAL, Jr.

2.063   CM   1956 Cayman Islands—a sketch. *Caribbean* 10(2), Sept.: 31-32,42.   [*RIS*]

DOW, HENRY, comp.

2.064   TR   1952 THE TRINIDAD AND TOBAGO YEAR BOOK FOR THE YEAR OF OUR LORD
                  1952. [Port of Spain?] Yuille's Printerie, 584p.   [*RIS*]

2.065   TR   1964 TRINIDAD & TOBAGO YEAR BOOK 1964-65. Port of Spain, Yuille's
                  Printerie, 474p.   [*RIS*]

2.066   TR   1965 TRINIDAD AND TOBAGO YEAR BOOK FOR THE YEARS OF OUR LORD 1965-6,
                  JULY-JUNE. Port of Spain, Yuille's Printery, 492p.   [*RIS*]

DUGUE, JOSEPH

2.067   FG   1932 Réhabilitation de la Guyane [The rehabilitation of Guiana]. *Rev
                  Econ Fr* 54(6), Nov.-Dec.: 362-366.   [*NYP*]

DUMORET, RANDAL

2.068   BC   1953 The British West Indies. *Can-W I Mag* 43(7), July: 5-7,9-13.   [*NYP*]

DUNBAR, ELIZABETH U.

2.069   CU   1934 What oil did to Curacao. *J Geogr* 33(9), Dec.: 340-345. [54] [*AGS*]

DUNCAN, EBENEZER

2.070   BC   1946 FOOTPRINTS OF WORTHY WESTINDIANS. [Bridgetown?] Barbados,
                  Advocate Co., 28p.   [*RIS*]

ECCARD, FREDERIC

2.071   FC   1936 Le tricentenaire des Antilles Francaises [The tercentenary of the
                  French Antilles]. *Rev Deux Mondes* 31, Feb. 15:800-817.   [*COL*]

EGERTON, Sir WALTER

2.072   BG   1918 British Guiana and the problem of its development. *J Roy Soc Arts*
                  66(3419), May 31:453-458; 66(3420), June 7:459-471. [66]   [*AGS*]

EMERSON, GUY

2.073   UV   1917 The Virgin Islands of the United States. *S Am* 5(8), June: 5-8.

EMERUWA, LINDA

2.074   BC   1962 THE WEST INDIES. London, Longmans, 74p. (Commonwealth countries
                  series.)

EVANS, WALDO

2.075   UV   1928 THE VIRGIN ISLANDS OF THE UNITED STATES: A GENERAL REPORT BY
                  THE GOVERNOR. Washington, U.S. Govt. Print. Off., 101p.   [*NYP*]

FAUQUET, G.

2.076   MT   1912 Note sur la population de la Martinique (eléments ethniques et
                  catégories sociales) [Memorandum on the population of Martinique
                  (ethnic elements and social classes)]. *B Mem Soc Anthrop* 6th ser.,
                  3:154-161. [10]   [*AMN*]

FELHOEN KRAAL, JOHANNA L. G.

2.077   NC   1949 The Netherlands, West Indies. *Man* 49(117), Aug.: 85-87.   [*COL*]
1.017   NC   1955 Antillas Neerlandesas y Suriname [The Netherlands Antilles and
                  Surinam].

FORBES, ROSITA

2.078   GC   1950 ISLANDS IN THE SUN. 3d ed. London, Evans, 167p.   [*SCH*]

FOYLE, MONTAGUE L.

2.079 SB 1926 St. Bartholomew—a little known French possession. *Can-W I Mag* 15(11), Sept.: 252-253. [*NYP*]

FRAZIER, E. FRANKLIN & WILLIAMS, ERIC, eds.

2.080 GC 1944 THE ECONOMIC FUTURE OF THE CARIBBEAN. Washington, D.C., Howard University Press, 94p. [44] [*COL*]

GAAY FORTMAN, B. de

2.081 CU 1927/ Curacao en onderhorige eilanden [Curacao and subordinate islands]. 28 *W I G* 9:1-16, 49-66, 97-110, 241-264, 363-378, 417-432, 497-518, 561-574;
1928/ 10:1-10. [5, 44]
29 [*COL*]

GAILLARD, ROBERT

5.065 FA 1953 EN PARCOURANT LES ISLES DES ANTILLES [THROUGH THE ANTILLES].

GAMMANS, L.D.

2.082 BC 1944 The West Indies in war-time. *United Emp* 35(5), Sept.-Oct.: 147-152. [*AGS*]

GARRIGOU-LAGRANGE, ANDRE

2.083 FA 1960 Connaissance des Antilles Francaises [The study of the French Antilles]. *Cah Sociol Econ* 3, Nov.: 263-270. [*AGS*]

GITTENS-KNIGHT, E., comp.

2.084 GR 1946 THE GRENADA HANDBOOK AND DIRECTORY 1946. Bridgetown, Advocate Co., 392p.

GOLDSTEIN, GERALD

2.085 TR 1961 BASIC DATA ON THE ECONOMY OF TRINIDAD AND TOBAGO. Washington, U.S. Govt. Print. Off., 12p. (World Trade Information Service, Economic reports, pt. 1, no. 61-29.) [*AGS*]

GOSLINGS, B.M.

10.015 SR [n.d.] De Indianen en Boschnegers van Suriname [The Indians and Bush Negroes of Surinam].

GREENIDGE, C.W.W.

2.086 BC 1949 The present outlook in the British West Indies. *Car Commn Mon Inf B* 2(12), July: 361-363. [66] [*COL*]

GRIER, Sir SELWYN

2.087 BC 1942 Some West Indian problems. *United Emp* new ser., 33(2), Mar.-Apr.: 33-35.

GRIEVE, S.

2.088 DM 1906 NOTES UPON THE ISLAND OF DOMINICA (BRITISH WEST INDIES). London, Adam and Charles Black, 126p. [17] [*COL*]

GRITZNER, CHARLES F.

2.089   FG   1963 French Guiana: developmental trends in post-prison era. *J Geogr* 62(4), Apr.: 161-168.   [*AGS*]

GUERIN, DANIEL

10.016   GC   1956 LES ANTILLES DÉCOLONISÉES [THE INDEPENDENT ANTILLES].
2.090   GC   1961 THE WEST INDIES AND THEIR FUTURE. London, Dennis Dobson, 191p.
                                                                        [*RIS*]

HARLOW, VINCENT TODD & MADDEN, FREDERICK

2.091   BC   1953 BRITISH COLONIAL DEVELOPMENTS 1774-1834: SELECT DOCUMENTS. Oxford, Clarendon Press, 619p. [5]   [*COL*]

HARMAN, CARTER & the editors of LIFE

2.092   GC   1963 THE WEST INDIES. New York, Time Inc., 158p.   [*AGS*]

HARMAN, JEANNE PERKINS

2.093   UV   1958 The $25,000,000 was well spent. *Caribbean* 11(7), Feb.: 150-152.
                                                                        [*COL*]

HARRIS, Sir C. ALEXANDER & VILLIERS, J. A. J. de, comps.

2.094   BG   1911 STORM VAN'S GRAVESANDE: THE RISE OF BRITISH GUIANA..London, Hakluyt Society, 2v. (703p.) (2d ser., nos. 27-28.) [5]   [*COL*]

HARTOG, JOHAN

5.079   AR   1953 ARUBA ZOALS HET WAS, ZOALS HET WERD, VAN DE TIJD DER INDIANEN TOT OP HEDEN [ARUBA AS IT WAS, AND AS IT BECAME, FROM THE TIME OF THE INDIANS TO THE PRESENT].
5.080   AR   1961 ARUBA, PAST AND PRESENT.
2.095   CU   1961 CURACAO: VAN KOLONIE TOT AUTONOMIE [CURACAO: FROM COLONY TO AUTONOMY]. [Oranjestad?] Aruba, de Wit, 2v. (1156p.)

HEIM, ROGER

2.096   FG   1953 Paradoxes sur la Guyane [Guianese paradoxes]. *C R Mens Seanc Acad Sci Colon* 13, Sept.-Oct.: 421-435.   [*RIS*]

HENRIQUES, FERNANDO

2.097   JM   1960 JAMAICA: LAND OF WOOD & WATER. 2d ed. London, MacGibbon & Kee, 215p.   [*COL*]

HIRSCHFELD, MARY

2.098   SA   1955 Saba. *Americas* 7(10), Oct.: 21-25.   [*AGS*]

HISS, PHILIP HANSON

2.099   CU/   1943 Dutch West Indies: Curacao and Surinam. *In* LANDHEER
         SR   BARTHOLOMEW, ed. THE NETHERLANDS. Berkeley and Los Angeles, University of California Press, p.392-408.   [*AGS*]

HOLDRIDGE, DESMOND

2.100   BG   1939 An investigation of the prospect for white settlement in British Guiana. *Geogr Rev* 29(4), Oct.: 622-642. [66]   [*AGS*]

HOOG, J. de
2.101 SR 1958 SURINAME, EEN LAND IN OPKOMST [SURINAM, A COUNTRY ON THE RISE]. Delft, Ethnografisch Museum, 36p. (Serie Monografieën, v.1.) [13, 14]

HOOVER, DONALD D.
2.102 UV 1926 The Virgin Islands under American rule. *For Aff* 4(3), Apr.: 503-506. [*AGS*]

HOUSTON, HILL
2.103 SR 1941 Surinam. *For Com Wkly* 5(6), Nov. 8:4-5, 36-37. [*AGS*]

HOYER, W. M.
2.104 AR 1945 A BRIEF HISTORICAL DESCRIPTION OF THE ISLAND OF ARUBA IN ENGLISH AND PAPIAMENTO. [Willemstad?] Curacao, Boekhandel Bethencourt, 26p. [25] [*AGS*]

HOYOS, F. A.
2.105 BB 1960 BARBADOS: OUR ISLAND HOME. London, Macmillan, 184p.

HUGHES, COLIN A.
2.106 BH 1953 Progress in British Honduras. *Venture* 5(2), Apr.: 8. [*COL*]

HUGHES, RICHARD
2.107 JM 1939 Jamaica today. *Geogr Mag* 10(2), Dec.: 105-114. [*AGS*]

HURAULT, JEAN
2.108 FG 1952 La Guyane, Département francais et terre inconnue [Guiana, French *Département* and unknown land]. *In* EXPLORATIONS OUTRE-MER A TRAVERS L'UNION FRANCAISE. Paris, La Documentation francaise, p. 199-219. [*AGS*]
13.039 FG 1963 Les Indiens de Guyane Francaise: problèmes pratiques d'administration et de contacts de civilisation [The Indians of French Guiana: practical problems of administration and culture contact].

HUTSON, Sir JOHN
2.109 BB 1948 MEMORIES OF LONG LIFE. [Bridgetown?] Barbados, Cole's Printery, 51p.

IM THURN, EVERARD F.
2.110 BG 1913 The hinterland of British Guiana. *W I Comm Circ* Dec. 16:579-581; Dec. 30:604-608. [*NYP*]
2.111 BG 1934 THOUGHTS, TALKS AND TRAMPS. London, Oxford University Press, 285p. [*COL*]

INNISS, LEWIS OSBORN
2.112 TR 1910 TRINIDAD AND TRINIDADIANS: A COLLECTION OF PAPERS, HISTORICAL, SOCIAL AND DESCRIPTIVE, ABOUT TRINIDAD AND ITS PEOPLE. Port of Spain, Mirror Print. Works, 165p. [*SCH*]

JAMES, PRESTON E.
2.113 TR 1926 L'isola di Trinidad [The island of Trinidad]. *Vie It Am Lat* 32(11), Nov.: 1231-1236. [*AGS*]

JARVIS, JOSE ANTONIO

2.114   VI   1944 THE VIRGIN ISLANDS AND THEIR PEOPLE. Philadelphia, Dorrance,
                     178p.   [COL]

JENGER, ALBERT

2.115   FA   1962 Les Antilles Francaises doivent, elles aussi, évoluer [The French
                     Antilles, too, must develop]. *Rev Guad* 46, Jan.-Mar.: 15-18.   [RIS]

JENNINGS, JOHN E., Jr.

2.116   UV   1938 OUR AMERICAN TROPICS. New York, Thomas Y. Crowell, 265p. [AGS]

JONES, JOSEPH M.

2.117   GC   1944 Caribbean laboratory. *Fortune* 29(2), Feb.: 124-127, 256, 258, 260,
                     262, 264, 266, 269-270, 272.   [AGS]

KINGSBURY, ROBERT C.

2.118   VI   1961 The Virgin Islands. *Focus* 11(7), Mar.: 1-6.   [RIS]

KRUIJER, GERARDUS JOHANNES

2.119   GC   1956 Caribische sociologie [Caribbean sociology]. *Sociol Gids* 3(8),
                     Oct.: 157-160.   [RIS]
8.036   JM   1956 SOCIOLOGICAL REPORT ON THE CHRISTIANA AREA.
2.120   GG   1960 SURINAME EN ZIJN BUURLANDEN: LICHTPLEKKEN IN HET OERWOUD VAN
                     GUYANA, 3d ed. [SURINAM AND ITS NEIGHBORS: CLEARINGS IN THE
                     PRIMEVAL FOREST]. Meppel, Holland, J. A. Boom, 285p.   [RIS]

**KRUIJER, GERARDUS JOHANNES, VEENENBOS, J. S. & WESTERMANN,
J. H., comps.**

2.121   NW   1953 BOVENWINDENRAPPORT [REPORT ON THE WINDWARD ISLANDS]. Amsterdam,
                     Voorlichtingsinstituut voor het Welvaartsplan Nederlandse Antillen,
                     [393]p.

LABROUSSE, PAUL

2.122   FA   [1935?] DEUX VIEILLES TERRES FRANCAISES, (GUADELOUPE AND MARTINIQUE)
                     [TWO OLD FRENCH LANDS, GUADELOUPE ET MARTINIQUE]. Colombes,
                     Impr. Leroux, 191p.   [COL]

LACROIX, ALFRED

2.123   FC   1932 NOTICE HISTORIQUE SUR LES MEMBRES ET CORRESPONDANTS DE L'ACA-
                     DÉMIE DES SCIENCES AYANT TRAVAILLÉ DANS LES COLONIES FRANCAISES
                     DE LA GUYANE ET DES ANTILLES DE LA FIN DU XVIIe SIÈCLE AU DÉBUT
                     DU XIXe [HISTORICAL ACCOUNT OF THE MEMBERS AND CORRESPONDENTS
                     OF THE ACADEMY OF SCIENCES WHO WORKED IN THE FRENCH COLONIES
                     OF GUIANA AND THE ANTILLES FROM THE END OF THE 17th TO THE BE-
                     GINNING OF THE 19th CENTURY]. Paris, Gauthier-Villars, 99p.   [1]
                                                                                       [AMN]

LAMONT, Sir NORMAN

2.124   BC   1912 PROBLEMS OF THE ANTILLES. London, Simpkin, Marshall, Hamilton,
                     Kent & Co., 178p.   [NYP]
2.125   TR   1933 PROBLEMS OF TRINIDAD: BEING A COLLECTION OF SPEECHES AND WRIT-
                     INGS ON SUBJECTS CONNECTED WITH THE COLONY. Trinidad, Yuille's
                     Printerie, 304p.   [SCH]

LASSERRE, GUY

43.096   GD   1961 La Guadeloupe: étude géographique [Guadeloupe: a geographic study].

La VARRE, WILLIAM J., Jr.

2.126   BG   1919 A real El Dorado: British Guiana possesses natural resources of vital importance which now lie dormant. *Nat Hist* 19(6), Dec.: 715-22.   [*AGS*]

LEBLOND, MARIUS-ARY

2.127   FA   1937 Belles et fières Antilles [The beautiful and proud Antilles]. Paris, Jean Crès, 252p.   [*SCH*]

LEE, KENDRICK

2.128   GC   1943 Problems of the Caribbean area. *Ed Res Rep* 1(22), June 14:379-395.   [*COL*]

LEECHMAN, ALLEYNE, ed.

2.129   BG   1913 The British Guiana handbook 1913. Georgetown, Argosy, 283p.   [*COL*]

LEEUW, HENDRIK de

2.130   SR   1942 Surinam, America's friendly comrade. *Knick Wkly* 2(7), Apr. 13: 25-31.   [*COL*]

LEGRAY, JACQUES,

2.131   GC   1952 Quelques éléments de l'avenir antillais [Some aspects of the future of the Antilles]. *Rev Polit Parl* 207(618), May: 158-168; 207(619), June: 289-297.   [*COL*]

2.132   BG   1953 En Guyane Britannique [In British Guiana]. *Rev Deux Mondes* Nov. 15: 313-324.   [*NYP*]

LEIRIS, MICHEL

2.133   FA   1955 Contacts de civilisations en Martinique et en Guadeloupe [Culture contact in Martinique and Guadeloupe]. Paris, UNESCO, 192p.   [*RIS*]

LE PAGE, ADRIEN

2.134   GD   1931 Guadeloupe. *In* Guadeloupe, Guyane, Martinique, Saint-Pierre et Miquelon. Paris, Société d'Editions Géographiques, Maritimes et Coloniales, 72p. (Exposition coloniale internationale de Paris.) [*NYP*]

LEROI-GOURHAN, ANDRE; POIRIER, JEAN; HAUDRICOURT, ANDRE-GEORGES & CONDOMINAS, GEORGES

2.135   FA   1953 Les Antilles. *In* Ethnologie de l'Union Francaise (territoires exterieurs) vol. 2: Asie, Océanie, Amérique. Paris, Presses universitaires de France, p.833-860. (Pays d'outre-mer. 6th ser.: Peuples et civilisations d'outre-mer, 2.)   [*COL*]

2.136   FG   1953 La Guyane. *In* Ethnologie de l'Union Francaise (territoires exterieurs) vol. 2: Asie, Océanie, Amérique. Paris, Presses universitaires de France, p.861-890. (Pays d'outre-mer. 6th ser.: Peuples et civilisations d'outre-mer, 2.)   [*COL*]

LEVO, JOHN E.
2.137   BV   1921 The British Virgin Islands—where perpetual summer reigns. *W I Comm Circ* 36(595), July 21:300-301.   [*NYP*]

LISSER, H. G. de
2.138   JM   1913 TWENTIETH CENTURY JAMAICA. Kingston, Jamaica Times, 208p. [*NYP*]

LOKKE, CARL L.
2.139   FC   1958 Society in the French Caribbean. *In* WILGUS, A. CURTIS, ed. THE CARIBBEAN: BRITISH, DUTCH, FRENCH, UNITED STATES [PAPERS DE-LIVERED AT THE EIGHTH CONFERENCE ON THE CARIBBEAN HELD AT THE UNIVERSITY OF FLORIDA, DEC. 5-7, 1957]. Gainesville, University of Florida Press, p.125-136. (Publications of the School of Inter-American Studies, ser. 1, v. 8.)   [*RIS*]

LONG, E. JOHN
2.140   JM   1961 JAMAICA. Garden City, N.Y., Nelson Doubleday with the cooperation of American Geographical Society, 64p. (Around the world program.)
                                                                          [*AGS*]

LOVETT, ROBERT MORSS
2.141   UV   1937 The Virgins: problem children. *New Republ* 90(1161), Mar. 3: 105-107.   [*COL*]

LOWENTHAL, DAVID
2.142   FG   1960 French Guiana: myths and realities. *Trans N Y Acad Sci* 22(7), May: 528-540. [7, 37, 44]   [*RIS*]

LUKE, Sir HARRY
2.143   BH   1948 New lease of life for British Honduras. *Crown Colon* 18(196), Mar.: 125-127.   [*AGS*]
2.144   BC   1949 The West Indies since the Moyne Report. *Geogr Mag* 22(5), Sept.: 165-176.
2.145   GC   1950 CARIBBEAN CIRCUIT. London, Nicholson & Watson, 262p.   [*NYP*]

LYNCH, LOUIS
2.146   BB   1964 THE BARBADOS BOOK. London, Andre Deutsch, 254p.   [*RIS*]

MacDERMOT, T. H.
2.147   BC   1919 Our West Indian colonies. *United Emp* 10(11), Nov.: 506-511. [*AGS*]

MacMILLAN, ALLISTER, ed.
2.148   GC   [1911] THE WEST INDIES. London, Collingridge, 424p.   [*NYP*]

MACMILLAN, MONA
2.149   JM   1957 THE LAND OF LOOK BEHIND: A STUDY OF JAMAICA. London, Faber and Faber, 224p.   [*RIS*]

MACMILLAN, W. M.
2.150   BC   1936 WARNING FROM THE WEST INDIES: A TRACT FOR AFRICA AND THE EMPIRE. London, Faber and Faber, 213p.   [*COL*]

MEEK, GEORGE

2.151   JM   1962 Island in the sun: a profile of Jamaica. *Americas* 14(12), Dec.:
                22-31.   [*RIS*]

MELVILLE, EDWINA

2.152   BG   1956 THIS IS THE RUPUNUNI. [Georgetown?] B.G., Govt. Information
                Services, 56p. [32]   [*RIS*]

MENDES, ALEX L.

2.153   TR   1933 Patos— a Caribbean outpost. *Can-W I Mag* 22(11), Oct.: 345-347.
                                                                                   [*NYP*]

MENKMAN, W.R.

2.154   NC   1932/ Amerikaansch Nederland op het Congres "Nederland Overzee"
                33 [The American Netherlands at the Congress, "The Netherlands
                Overseas"]. *W I G* 14:193-205.   [*COL*]

25.076 CU   1936/ Curacao, zijn naam en zijn taal [Curacao, its name and its language].
                37

MERRILL, GORDON CLARK

2.155   BC   1958 The British West Indies—the newest Federation of the Common-
                wealth. *Can Geogr J* 56(2), Feb.: 60-69. [38]   [*AGS*]

MIELCHE, HAKON

2.156   UV   1943 DREI KLEINE INSELN [THREE SMALL ISLANDS]. Munich, Zinnen-
                Verlag, 283p.   [*NYP*]

MINTZ, SIDNEY W., comp.

2.157   GC   1960 PAPERS IN CARIBBEAN ANTHROPOLOGY. New Haven, Dept. of
                Anthropology, Yale University, 26, 24, 11, 33, 26, 37, 11, 58p. (Yale
                University publications in anthropology, no. 57-64.)   [*RIS*]

MITCHELL, Sir HAROLD

2.158   GC   1962 The West Indies: a kaleidoscope of territories. *Wld Today* 18(11),
                Nov.: 487-494.   [*COL*]

MITTELHOLZER, EDGAR

2.159   BG   1963 A SWARTHY BOY. London, Putnam, 157p. [8,16]   [*RIS*]

MORAIS, ALLAN I.

2.160   GC   1952 Statistical organisation in the Caribbean. *Car Commn Mon Inf B*
                6(4), Nov.: 84-86. [67]   [*AGS*]
2.161   GR   1955 This is Grenada. *Caribbean* 9(5), Dec.: 101-105. [42]   [*COL*]

MOYNE, BRYAN WALTER GUINNESS, baron

2.162   GC   1940 The West Indies in 1939, by Lord Moyne. *Geogr J* 96(2), Aug.:
                85-92.   [*AGS*]

MUHLENFELD, AUGUST

2.163   NC   1944 The Dutch West Indies in peace and war. *Int Aff* 20(1), Jan.: 81-93.
                                                                                   [*AGS*]

MUNTSCH, ALBERT

2.164   BH   1961 Xaibe—a Mayan enclave in northern British Honduras. *Anthrop Q*
                34(2), Apr.: 121-126.   [*RIS*]

MURPHY, JOSEPH

2.165   BH   1931 A day of dread. *W I Comm Circ* 46(862), Oct. 15:407-409.   [*NYP*]

NAIPAUL, V. S.

2.166   GC   1963 THE MIDDLE PASSAGE: THE CARIBBEAN REVISITED. London, Macmillan,
                       232p. [3]   [*RIS*]

NEWMAN, A. J.

2.167   JM   [1946?] JAMAICA: THE ISLAND AND ITS PEOPLE. 5th ed. of the Times geography
                       and history of Jamaica. [Kingston, Printed by Jamaica Times Press].
                       141p. [32]   [*SCH*]

NEY, ROBERT MORSE

37.280   BH/   1938 THE COLONIAL VALUE OF BRITISH HONDURAS, BRITISH GUIANA, AND
           BG/   JAMAICA.
           JM

OLIVIER, SYDNEY, 1st Baron RAMSDEN

2.168   JM   1936 JAMAICA, THE BLESSED ISLAND, by Lord Olivier. London, Faber and
                       Faber, 466p.   [*COL*]

O'NEAL, J. R.

2.169   BV   1958 Fascinating isles with colourful names. *Caribbean* 12(4), Nov.:
                       80-82.   [*COL*]

OTTLEY, CARLTON ROBERT

2.170   TB   [n.d.] THE COMPLETE HISTORY OF THE ISLAND OF TOBAGO IN THE WEST INDIES.
                       Port of Spain, Guardian Commercial Printery, 148p. [5]   [*AGS*]
2.171   TR   1957 Trinidad—capital of the West Indies. *Caribbean* 10(10), May: 245,
                       248-250.   [*COL*]

OUDSCHANS DENTZ, FRED

1.031   GC   1936/ Musea in West Indië [Museums in West India].
                  37

OUDSCHANS DENTZ, FRED & MENKMAN, W. R.

2.172   CU/   1928 ONZE WEST [OUR WEST]. The Hague, T. C. B. Ten Hage.
           SR

PANHUYS, L. C. van

2.173   SR   1905 Naschrift op "Gegevens over land en volk van Suriname" [Postscript
                       to "Data about the country and people of Surinam"]. *Bijd Volk
                       Ned-Indie* 58:481-482. [10]
2.174   SR   1906 Uber die letzte niederländische expedition nach Surinam [Notes on
                       the last Dutch expedition to Surinam]. *In* INTERNATIONALER AMERIKAN-
                       ISTEN-KONGRESS, 14th SESSION, STUTTGART 1904 [PROCEEDINGS].
                       Berlin, W. Kohlhammer, pt. 2, 427-433.   [*AGS*]
2.175   SR   1924/ Americanism in Holland. *W I G* 6:217-222.   [*COL*]
                  25
2.176   SR   1931/ Surinaamsche onderwerpen op het Amerikanisten-Congres te Hamburg
                  32   [Surinam topics from the Congress of Americanists at Hamburg].
                       W I G 13:203-216, 310-316.   [*COL*]

PASSERA, GINO de'

2.177   BG   1925 La Guiana Britannica [British Guiana]. *Vie It Am Lat* 31(4), Apr.:
                       407-414.   [*AGS*]

PATTERSON, BRUCE

2.178   BC   1954 Britain's Caribbean colonies: tragic, doomed lands? *Int J* 9(1),
               Winter: 34-40.   [66]   [*AGS*]

PEARSE, ANDREW C.

2.179   GC   1955 Caribbean folk culture. *Caribbean* 9(3), Oct.: 62-65.   [8]   [*COL*]

PELAGE AL.

2.180   GD   [n.d.] LA GUADELOUPE VUE PAR AL. PELAGE: GRAVURES ET DESSINS HUMOR-
               ISTIQUES [GUADELOUPE AS SEEN BY AL. PELAGE: HUMOROUS PRINTS
               AND DRAWINGS]. Basse Terre, Impr. officielle, 22p.   [22, 25]   [*RIS*]

PESCETTO, U.

2.181   ST   1906 S. Thomas (Antille Danesi) [Saint Thomas (Danish Antilles)].
               Boll Soc Geogr It 4th ser., 7(2):1099-1108.   [*NYP*]

PETIONI, C. AUGUSTIN

2.182   GC   1944 West Indians and the post war world. *In* FRAZIER, E. F. & WILLIAMS,
               E., eds. THE ECONOMIC FUTURE OF THE CARIBBEAN. Washington, D.C.,
               Howard University Press, p.33-36.

PHILEMON, CESAIRE

2.183   MT   1931 GALERIES MARTINIQUAISE: POPULATION, MOEURS, ACTIVITÉS DIVERSES ET
               PAYSAGES DE LA MARTINIQUE. [MARTINIQUE IMAGES. PEOPLE, CUSTOMS,
               VARIED ACTIVITIES AND LANDSCAPES OF MARTINIQUE]. Paris, Exposi-
               tion coloniale internationale, 430p.   [*NYP*]

POUQUET, JEAN

2.184   FA   1952 LES ANTILLES FRANCAISES [THE FRENCH ANTILLES]. Paris, Presses
               universitaires de France, 128p.   [*AGS*]

PREIJ, L. C.

2.185   SR   Jaarcijfers van Suriname, by L. C. Prey [Statistics of Surinam].
               1939 *WIG* 21:48-55, 116-122, 146-147, 179-183, 127-129, 292-295, 319-321,
                    389-393;
               1940 22:122-125, 186-190, 250-254, 314-319, 377-383;
               1941 23:60-62, 294-301.   [*COL*]

PRICE, A. GRENFELL

2.186   SA   1934 White settlement in Saba Island, Dutch West-Indies. *Geogr Rev*
               24(1), Jan.: 42-60.   [*AGS*]

PROUDFOOT, MARY

2.187   VI   1954 BRITAIN AND THE UNITED STATES IN THE CARIBBEAN: A COMPARATIVE
               STUDY IN METHODS OF DEVELOPMENT. London, Faber and Faber, 434p.
                                                                           [*RIS*]

QUARRY, JOHN

2.188   GC   1956 THE WEST INDIES. London, Adam and Charles Black, 84p. (The
               Lands and Peoples series.)

RENNER, GEORGE T.

2.189   BH   1925 British Honduras. *J Geogr* 24(3), Mar.: 111-117.   [*AGS*]

REVERT, EUGENE

2.190   GC   1954 LES ANTILLES [THE ANTILLES]. Paris, Librairie Armand Colin, 220p. [RIS]

2.191   FC   1955 LA FRANCE D'AMERIQUE: MARTINIQUE, GUADELOUPE, GUYANE, SAINT-PIERRE ET MIQUELON [THE FRENCH LANDS IN THE AMERICAS: MARTINIQUE, GUADELOUPE, GUYANE, SAINT-PIERRE AND MIQUELON]. Paris, Editions maritimes et coloniales, 255p. [RIS]

2.192   GC   1958 ENTRE LES DEUX AMÉRIQUES: LE MONDE CARAÏBE [BETWEEN THE TWO AMERICAS: THE CARIBBEAN WORLD]. Paris, Editions francaises, 252p. [NYP]

RICE, HARMON EDMOND

2.193   BB   1954 The Barbados' consistent climate provides one of the most alluring appeals. *Can W I Mag* 44(8), Aug.: 13, 15, 17, 19-21; 44(9), Sept.: 13, 15-16. [NYP]

RICHARDS, ALFRED, comp.

2.194   TR   1927 DISCOVERY DAY CELEBRATION, 1927: SOUVENIR. Port of Spain, Franklin's Electric Printery, 128p. [SCH]

RICHARDSON, W. A.

2.195   BC   [1958?] THE WEST INDIES 1958. Port of Spain, Trin., Federal Information Services, 36p. [AGS]

RICOUX, EMILE

2.196   FA   1937 Les Antilles Francaises [The French Antilles]. *B Soc Geogr Etud Colon Mars* 57:67-81. [AGS]

2.197   FG   1938 Une visite à la Guyane Francaise: richesses naturelles et possibilités économiques [A visit to French Guiana: natural resources and economic possibilities]. *B Soc Geogr Mars* 58:78-89. [AGS]

ROBERT, GERARD

33.040   GD   1935 LES TRAVAUX PUBLICS DE LA GUADELOUPE [PUBLIC WORKS IN GUADELOUPE].

ROBERTS, WALTER ADOLPHE, ed.

2.198   JM   1960 THE GLEANER GEOGRAPHY AND HISTORY OF JAMAICA. (REV.). Kingston, United Printers, 80p. [43] [RIS]

ROBINSON, JESSE S.

2.199   GC   1941 An economist looks at the West Indies. *Education* 61(5), Jan.: 278-281. [TCL]

RODWAY, JAMES

2.200   GG   1912 GUIANA: BRITISH, DUTCH AND FRENCH. London, T. Fisher Unwin, 318p. [COL]

RODWAY, JAMES & STARK, JAMES H.

2.201   BG   [n.d.] STARK'S GUIDE-BOOK AND HISTORY OF BRITISH GUIANA. Boston, James H. Stark, 120p. [AMN]

RODWELL, Sir CECIL

2.202   BG   1927 The problems of British Guiana. *United Emp* new ser., 18(12), Dec.: 680-684. [AGS]

ROSE-ROSETTE, FELIX

2.203   MT   1953 LA MARTINIQUE. Paris, A. & P. Jarach, 113p.   [RIS]

ROTH, VINCENT

2.204   BG   1951 The British Guiana Museum; its origin, history and vicissitudes.
                Timehri 4th ser., 1(30), Nov.: 21-29;
                1952 4th ser., 1(31), Nov.: 29-42.

RUBIN, VERA, ed.

2.205   GC   1960 CARIBBEAN STUDIES: A SYMPOSIUM. 2d ed. Seattle, University of
                Washington Press, 124p.   [RIS]

SANDERSON, IVAN T.

2.206   TR   1951 A GUIDE TO TRINIDAD. New York, Frederick Farnam Associates, 32p.
                                                                                 [AGS]

2.207   SR   1963 SURINAM. 2d ed. Garden City, Nelson Doubleday, with the coopera-
                tion of the American Geographical Society, 64p. (Around the world
                program.)   [AGS]

SANJURJO, MARIA ANTONINA

37.358   FC   1938 AN APPROACH TO THE COLONIAL EVALUATION OF THE FRENCH WEST INDIES
                AND FRENCH GUIANA.

SATINEAU, MAURICE

2.208   GD   1928 HISTOIRE DE LA GUADELOUPE SOUS L'ANCIENT RÉGIME, 1635-1789
                [HISTORY OF GUADELOUPE UNDER THE OLD REGIME, 1635-1789]. Paris,
                Payot, 400p. [5]   [NYP]

SCHAAD, J. D. G.

2.209   SR   1954 Naar de Bovenlandse Indianen in Suriname; medische expeditie
                [Medical expedition to the upland Indians in Surinam]. *Oost West*
                47(8), Aug. 28: 7-8. [13]   [RIS]

SCHRIEKE, B. J. O. & RUTGERS, A. A. L., eds.

2.210   SR   1947 ONS KONINKRIJK IN AMERIKA: WEST-INDIË [OUR KINGDOM IN THE
                AMERICAS: THE WEST INDIES]. The Hague, W. van Hoeve, 381p.
                                                                                 [AGS]

SHARP, G. F., ed.

2.211   BB   1934 THE BARBADOS YEAR BOOK 1933-34. [Bridgetown?] Barbados, Advo-
                cate Press, 268p.

2.212   BB   1935 THE BARBADOS YEAR BOOK 1935. [Bridgetown?] Barbados, Advocate
                Press, 332p.

SHARP, G. F. & GALE, C. A. L., eds.

2.213   BB   1937 BARBADOS YEAR BOOK AND WHO'S WHO 1937. [Bridgetown?] Barbados,
                Advocate Press, 244p.

SHAW, EARL BENNETT

2.214   ST   1934 St. Thomas; the keystone of the Antilles. *J Geogr* 33(4), Apr.: 131-
                139.   [AGS]

2.215   UV   1935 The poorhouse of the United States. *Scient Mon* 41, Aug.: 131-140.
                                                                                 [AGS]

SHAZAMAN, SABZALI

2.216   TR   1947 Workers in Trinidad. *Can Forum* 27(316), May: 36-37.   [NYP]

SHEPPARD T.

2.217   BB   1936 Report on the Barbados Museum. *J Barb Mus Hist Soc* 3(4), Aug.:
               197-204.   [*AMN*]

SHERLOCK, PHILIP M.

2.218   GC   1963 CARIBBEAN CITIZEN. 3d ed. London: Longmans, 120p. [21, 66]   [*RIS*]

SHILSTONE, E. M.

2.219   BB   1940 Barbados in the year 1840. *J Barb Mus Hist Soc* 8(1), Nov.: 3-12.
               [5]   [*AMN*]

SIMEY, THOMAS S.

33.048 BC   1946 WELFARE AND PLANNING IN THE WEST INDIES.

SIMMONDS, W. AUSTIN

2.220   TR   1963 Trinidad and Tobago; one nation, two islands, many peoples.
               Americas 15(3), Mar.: 8-13.   [*AGS*]

SMITH, LLOYD SIDNEY, ed.

2.221   JM/   1941 PUBLIC LIFE AND SPORT: JAMAICA—GRENADA—TRINIDAD. Port of Spain,
         GR/   Trinidad Pub. Co., 368p.   [*SCH*]
         TR
2.222   BC   1957 THE BRITISH CARIBBEAN—WHO, WHAT, WHY, 1955-56. Glasgow, Bell
               and Bain, 868p.   [*RIS*]
2.223   BC   1965 THE CARIBBEAN—WHO, WHAT, WHY 1965. Amsterdam, Drukkerij
               Holland, 844p.   [*RIS*]

SMITH, M. G. & KRUIJER, G. J.

67.025 JM   1957 A SOCIOLOGICAL MANUAL FOR EXTENSION WORKERS IN THE CARIBBEAN.

SMITH, RAYMOND THOMAS

2.224   BG   1962 BRITISH GUIANA. London, Oxford University Press, 218p.   [*RIS*]

SOLA, RALPH A.

2.225   UV   1951 Life on the Virgin Islands. *U N Wld* 5(2), Feb.: 64-65.   [*COL*]

SPENCER-SMITH, D. C.

2.226   JM   1938 Reflections on Jamaica. *Cornhill Mag* Nov.: 678-687.

STAAL, G. J.

2.227   SR   1923/ Vijf en twintig jaren 1898-1923 [Twenty-five years 1898-1923].
               24 *W I G* 5:225-258.   [*COL*]
2.228   SR   1924 Something about Dutch Guiana (Surinam). *In* PROCEEDINGS OF THE
               TWENTY-FIRST INTERNATIONAL CONGRESS OF AMERICANISTS [1st
               session]. The Hague, Aug. 12-16, 1924. The Hague, p.377-380. [*AGS*]
2.229   SR   1926 La Guiana Olandese (Surinam) [Dutch Guiana (Surinam)]. *Vie It Am
               Lat* 32(10), Oct.: 1125-1130.

STANNARD, HAROLD

2.230   BG   1945 The British West Indies. *In* FABIAN COLONIAL ESSAYS. London, George
               Allen & Unwin, p.202-214.   [*NYP*]

STARKEY, OTIS P.

2.231   BC   1960 How we live in the West Indies. *J Geogr* 59(3), Mar.: 123-127. [*AGS*]

STEELE, WESLEY

16.031   JM   1954 ENGULFED BY THE COLOR TIDE; STUDIES FROM JAMAICA: CONSEQUENCES OF THE SLAVE TRADE AND BRITISH COLONIALISM.

STORY, CHRISTOPHER

2.232   BG   1962 British Guiana: unremitting struggle. *Contemp Rev* 202, Sept.: 125-129.   [*COL*]

SWAN, MICHAEL

2.233   BG   1957 BRITISH GUIANA: THE LAND OF SIX PEOPLES. London, H.M.S.O., 235p. (The Corona library.)   [*RIS*]

SWAYNE, Sir ERIC J. E.

2.234   BH   1917 British Honduras. *Geogr J* 50(3), Sept.: 161-179.   [*AGS*]

TAYLOR, CHARLES EDWIN

2.235   UV   1902 St. Thomas, St. Croix, and St. John. *Independent* 54(2790), May 22: 1223-1230.

THOMPSON, E. W.

2.236   BC   1942 DON'T FORGET THE WEST INDIES. London, Edinburgh House Press, 24p. (World issues no. 12.)   [*NYP*]

THOMPSON, W. L.

2.237   UV   1929 The Virgin Islands of the United States. *U S Navl Inst Proc* 55(314), Apr.: 289-295.   [*AGS*]

THOMSON, JAY EARLE

2.238   UV   1928 OUR ATLANTIC POSSESSIONS. New York, Charles Scribner, 219p. [*NYP*]

THORP, WILLIAM

16.033   JM   1904 How Jamaica solves the Negro problem.

TODMAN, McW.

2.239   VI   1955 The Virgin Islands. *Corona* 7(3), Mar.: 89-93.   [*AGS*]

VANDENBOSCH, AMRY

2.240   NC   1941 The Dutch colonies in the Western World. *J Polit* 3(3), Aug.: 308-317.   [*COL*]

VAUGHAN, HERBERT M.

2.241   BG   1927 British Guiana. *Edin Rev* 246(502), Oct.: 273-286.   [*COL*]

VIGNON, ROBERT

2.242   FG   1954 La Guyane Francaise au sein de la Communauté Francaise (situation politique, juridique et économique) [French Guiana at the heart of the French community]. *Cons Com Exter* 32(20-21), Aug.-Sept.: 12-23. [37]

VOCHEL, LUCIEN
2.243   BG   [n.d.] L'Arrondissement de L'Inini. La Guyane francaise. *Rev Fr* 60:11-13.

WADDELL, DAVID A. G.
2.244   BH   1961 BRITISH HONDURAS: A HISTORICAL AND CONTEMPORARY SURVEY. London,
                 New York, Oxford University Press, 151p.   [*RIS*]

WALKER, HENRY W.
2.245   BG   1931 British Guiana: its possibilities and opportunities. *Emp Rev* 54(369),
                 Oct.: 270-276.   [*NYP*]

WALLE, J. van de
2.246   SR   1958 Het oude en het nieuwe Suriname [The old and the new Surinam]. *In*
                 WALLE, J. van de & WIT, H. de, eds. SURINAME IN STROOMLIJNEN.
                 Amsterdam, Wereld Bibliotheek, p. 7-19.

WALLE, J. van de & WIT, H. de, eds.
2.247   SR   1958 SURINAME IN STROOMLIJNEN [SURINAM IN STREAMLINES]. Amsterdam,
                 Wereld Bibliotheek, 133p.

WARNER, ARTHUR
2.248   UV   1924 Our neglected crown colony. *Forum* 72(2), Aug.: 175-182.   [*COL*]

WATKINS, FREDERICK HENRY, comp.
2.249   LW   1924 HANDBOOK OF THE LEEWARD ISLANDS. London, West India Committee,
                 308p.   [*AGS*]

WAUGH, ALEC
2.250   GC   1958 THE SUGAR ISLANDS. London, Cassell, 319p.

WEATHERLY, U. G.
67.027   GC   1923 The West Indies as a sociological laboratory.

WESTERMANN, J. H.
46.235   NA   1947 Natuurbescherming op de Nederlandsche Antillen, haar etische,
                 aesthetische, wetenschappelijke en economische perspectieven
                 [The protection of nature on the Dutch Antilles, its ethical, esthet-
                 ical, scientific and economic perspectives].

WHITBECK, R. H.
2.251   GC   1933 The Lesser Antilles—past and present. *Ann Ass Am Geogr* 23(1),
                 Mar.: 21-26.   [*AGS*]

WHITSON, AGNES M. & HORSFALL, LUCY F.
2.252   BC   1948 BRITAIN AND THE WEST INDIES. London, Longmans, Green, 87p. [*AGS*]

WILDE, A. NEIJTZELL de
2.253   NC   1938 The Netherlands as a colonial power. *Asiat Rev* 34(120), Oct.:
                 702-718.   [*NYP*]

WILGUS, A. CURTIS, ed.
2.254   GC   1951 THE CARIBBEAN AT MID-CENTURY [PAPERS DELIVERED AT THE FIRST
                 ANNUAL CONFERENCE ON THE CARIBBEAN HELD AT THE UNIVERSITY OF

FLORIDA, DEC. 7-9, 1950]. Gainesville, University of Florida Press, 284p. (Publications of the School of Inter-American Studies, ser. 1, v. 1.)   [RIS]

WILGUS, A. CURTIS, ed.

2.255   GC   1952 THE CARIBBEAN: PEOPLES, PROBLEMS AND PROSPECTS [PAPERS DELIV-
                ERED AT THE SECOND ANNUAL CONFERENCE ON THE CARIBBEAN, HELD AT
                THE UNIVERSITY OF FLORIDA, DEC. 1951]. Gainesville, University of
                Florida Press, 240p. (Publications of the School of Inter-American
                Studies, ser. 1, v. 2.)   [RIS]

2.256   GC   1953 THE CARIBBEAN: CONTEMPORARY TRENDS [PAPERS DELIVERED AT THE
                THIRD ANNUAL CONFERENCE ON THE CARIBBEAN HELD AT THE UNI-
                VERSITY OF FLORIDA, DEC. 18-20, 1952]. Gainesville, University of
                Florida Press, 292p. (Publications of the School of Inter-American
                Studies, ser. 1, v. 3.)   [RIS]

2.257   GC   1955 THE CARIBBEAN: ITS CULTURE [PAPERS DELIVERED AT THE FIFTH CON-
                FERENCE ON THE CARIBBEAN HELD AT THE UNIVERSITY OF FLORIDA,
                DEC. 2-4, 1954]. Gainesville, University of Florida, 277p. (Pub-
                lications of the School of Inter-American Studies, ser. 1, v. 5.)
                                                                                     [RIS]

2.258   GC   1957 THE CARIBBEAN: CONTEMPORARY INTERNATIONAL RELATIONS [PAPERS
                DELIVERED AT THE SEVENTH CONFERENCE ON THE CARIBBEAN HELD AT
                THE UNIVERSITY OF FLORIDA, DEC. 6-8, 1956]. Gainesville, Uni-
                versity of Florida Press, 330p. (Publications of the School of Inter-
                American Studies, ser. 1, v. 7.) [38]   [RIS]

2.259   GC   1958 THE CARIBBEAN: BRITISH, DUTCH, FRENCH, UNITED STATES [PAPERS
                DELIVERED AT THE EIGHTH CONFERENCE ON THE CARIBBEAN HELD AT THE
                UNIVERSITY OF FLORIDA, DEC. 5-7, 1957]. Gainesville, University of
                Florida Press, 331p. (Publications of the School of Inter-American
                Studies, ser. 1, v. 8.)   [RIS]

2.260   GC   1959 THE CARIBBEAN: NATURAL RESOURCES [PAPERS DELIVERED AT THE NINTH
                CONFERENCE ON THE CARIBBEAN HELD AT THE UNIVERSITY OF FLORIDA,
                DEC. 4-6, 1958]. Gainesville, University of Florida Press, 315p.
                (Publications of the School of Inter-American Studies, ser. 1, v. 9.)
                                                                                     [RIS]

WILLIAMS, ERIC EUSTACE

2.261   BC   1940 The Negro in the British West Indies. In WESLEY, CHARLES, H.,
                ed. THE NEGRO IN THE AMERICAS. Washington, D. C., Graduate School,
                Division of the Social Sciences, Howard University, p. 7-19. [11]
                                                                                     [RIS]
11.027   GC   1942 The Negro in the Caribbean.   [COL]
2.262   BG   1945 The historical background of British Guiana's problems. J Negro
                Hist 30(4), Oct.: 357-381. [5, 58]   [COL]
2.263   TR   1962 HISTORY OF THE PEOPLE OF TRINIDAD AND TOBAGO. Port of Spain,
                PNM Pub. Co., 294p.   [RIS]
66.165   TR   1960 PERSPECTIVES FOR THE WEST INDIES.
2.264   TR   1964 Trinidad and Tobago: international perspectives. Freedomways
                4(3), Summer: 331-340. [37]   [RIS]
2.265   BC   1952 DOCUMENTS ON BRITISH WEST INDIAN HISTORY, 1807-1833. Port of
                Spain, Trinidad Pub. Co., 406p. [5]   [RIS]

WILLIAMS, ERLE R.

2.266   SC   1953 St. Croix—past and present. *Negro Hist B* 16(8), May: 171-175, 180.
                                                                              [*COL*]

WILLIAMS, JOSEPH J.

2.267   JM   1925 WHISPERINGS OF THE CARIBBEAN: REFLECTIONS OF A MISSIONARY.
                 New York, Benziger Brothers, 252p.   [*AGS*]

WYK, EUGENE C. van

2.268   NA   1942 The Netherlands West Indies. *Knick Wkly* 2(7), Apr. 13: 14-21.
                                                                              [*COL*]

ZABRISKIE, LUTHER K.

2.269   UV   1918 VIRGIN ISLANDS OF THE UNITED STATES OF AMERICA. New York, G. P.
                 Putnam, 339p.   [*NYP*]

Chapter 3

TRAVEL AND DESCRIPTION

ABONNENC, E.

3.001   FG   1950 GUIDE DE LA GUYANE CÔTIÈRE [GUIDE TO COASTAL GUIANA]. Paris, Impr. de l'Institut Géographique Nationale, 90p.   [*NYP*]

ADAMS, HARRIET CHALMERS

3.002   SR   1907 Picturesque Paramaribo; the city which was exchanged for New York. *Natn Geogr Mag* 18(6), June: 365-373.   [*AGS*]

AIKEN, JAMES

3.003   SR   1912 Notes on a trip to Surinam, *Timehri* 3d ser., 2(19A), July: 143-153.   [*AMN*]

ALFORD, CYRIL E. R.

3.004   TB   [1949?] THE ISLAND OF TOBAGO. London, Longmans (Dorchester), 158p. [*RIS*]

ALLMON, CHARLES

3.005   BB   1952 Barbados, outrider of the Antilles, *Natn Geogr Mag* 101(3), Mar.: 363-392.   [*AGS*]

3.006   TR   1953 Happy-go-lucky Trinidad and Tobago. *Natn Geogr Mag* 103(1), Jan.: 35-75.   [*AGS*]

ALLMON, GWEN DRAYTON

3.007   MT   1959 Martinique, a tropical bit of France. *Natn Geogr Mag* 115(2), Feb.: 255-283.   [*AGS*]

ANDERSON, ROBERT M.

3.008   SV   1938 THE ST. VINCENT HANDBOOK. Kingstown, St. Vincent, Office of the "Vincentian," 453p.   [5]

ANDERSON, ROBERT M., ed.

3.009   SV   1937 NOTES AND REFLECTIONS ON ST. VINCENT. 2d ed. Kingstown, St. Vincent, Office of the "Vincentian," 58p.   [*NYP*]

ARBUTHNOT, JOAN

3.010   BG   1936 MORE PROFIT THAN GOLD. New York, Scribner, 287p.   [*NYP*]

ASPINALL, Sir ALGERNON E.

3.011   GC   1920 The West Indies revisited. *W I Comm Circ* 35(566-580), June 10-
             Dec. 23: 167-168, 183-185, 202-203, 215-216, 231-232, 248-249,
             263-264, 279-280, 293-294, 310-311, 327-328, 342-343, 361-362,
             379-380, 396-397;
             1921 36(581-606), Jan. 6-Dec. 22: 11-12, 30-31, 48-49, 67-68, 88-90,
             108-109, 131-133, 150-151, 172-173, 196-199, 217-219, 239-240,
             260-261, 286-288, 307-308, 327-328, 347-348, 364-365, 394-395,
             415-416, 434-435, 457-458, 479-480, 499-501, 524-526, 544-545;
             1922 37(607-622), Jan. 5-Aug. 3: 16, 37-38, 60-62, 79-80, 102-103, 124-
             126, 148-150, 171-173, 193-194, 219-221, 246-247, 268-269, 295-
             297, 316-318, 341-342, 362-364.   [*NYP*]
3.012   GC   1928 A WAYFARER IN THE WEST INDIES. London, Methuen, 244p.   [*NYP*]
3.013   GC   1960 THE POCKET GUIDE TO THE WEST INDIES... 10th ed., rev. London,
             Methuen, 474p.   [*RIS*]

ATTENBOROUGH, DAVID

3.014   BG   1956 Expedition to British Guiana. *Timehri* 4th ser., 1(35), Oct.: 32-36.
41.020 BG   1956 ZOO QUEST TO GUIANA.

BAKHUIS, L. A.

3.015   SR   1902 Verslag der Coppename-Expeditie [Report of the Coppename Ex-
             pedition]. *Tijdschr Ned Aar Genoot* 19:695-852.

BALDWIN, RICHARD

3.016   BG   1950 The forgotten river. *Timehri* 4th ser., 1(29), Aug.: 36-39.
3.017   BG   1951 The cattle trail. *Timehri* 4th ser., 1(30), Nov.: 37-40.
52.005 BG   1956 The river boathand of Guiana: a disappearing character.

BARBANSON, W. L. de

3.018   SB   1934/ St. Barthélémy. *W I G* 16:177-191.   [*COL*]
             35
5.010   SB   1935/ St. Barthélémy in den Zweedschen tijd [St. Barthelemy during the
             36 Swedish epoch].

BAYLEY, GEORGE D.

3.019   BG   1909 HANDBOOK OF BRITISH GUIANA, 1909. Georgetown, Argosy Co., 607p.

BECCARI, NELLO

3.020   BG   1933 Naturalisti italiani nella Guiana Britannica [Italian naturalists in
             British Guiana]. *Vie It Mondo* 1(2), Feb.: 191-208.   [*AGS*]

BEEBE, MARY BLAIR & BEEBE, WILLIAM

41.039 BG   1910 OUR SEARCH FOR A WILDERNESS.

BEEBE, WILLIAM

3.021   BG   1918 JUNGLE PEACE. New York, Holt, 297p. [41]   [*AGS*]

BELL, ARCHIE

3.022   GC   1926 THE SPELL OF THE CARIBBEAN ISLANDS. Boston, L.C. Page, 361p.

BELL, HENRY HESKETH

3.023   DM   [1946?] GLIMPSES OF A GOVERNOR'S LIFE. London, Sampson Low, Marston, 212p. [37]   [*NYP*]

BELLAMY, ROBIN

3.024   LW/   1964 Poverty in paradise. *Geogr Mag* 36(11), Mar.: 653-663.   [*AGS*]
     WW

BERKEL, ADRIAAN van

3.025   BG/   1941 ADRIAAN VAN BERKEL'S TRAVELS IN SOUTH AMERICA BETWEEN THE
     SR   BERBICE AND ESSEQUIBO RIVERS AND IN SURINAM 1670-1689. Ed. by Walter Edmund Roth. Georgetown, Daily Chronicle, 145p.   [5]

BLACK, CLINTON VANE de BROSSE

3.026   JM   1960 SPANISH TOWN, THE OLD CAPITAL. Spanish Town, Jamaica, Parish Council of St. Catherine, 63p. [5]   [*NYP*]

BODKIN, G. E.

3.027   BG   1918 A fishing trip on the upper waters of the Mazaruni River. *Timehri* 3d ser., 5(22), Aug.: 64-73. [56]   [*AMN*]

BONNE, C.

28.044   SR   1923/Hygienische ervaring te Moengo [Hygienic experience in Moengo]. 24

BONSAL, STEPHEN

3.028   GC   1912 THE AMERICAN MEDITERRANEAN. New York, Moffat, Yard, 488p. [*RIS*]

BORDEAUX, ALBERT

3.029   FG   1906 LA GUYANE INCONNUE: VOYAGE À L'INTÉRIEUR DE LA GUYANE FRAN-CAISE [UNKNOWN GUIANA: JOURNEY TO THE INTERIOR OF FRENCH GUIANA]. Paris, Plon-Nourrit, 286p.   [*AGS*]

BOSCH, I. G. J. van den

3.030   SR   1930/ Indruk van Suriname [Impressions of Surinam]. *W I G* 12:339-349. 31   [*COL*]

BOURGOIS, JEAN-JACQUES

3.031   FA   1958 MARTINIQUE ET GUADELOUPE: TERRES FRANCAISES DES ANTILLES [MAR-TINIQUE AND GUADELOUPE: FRENCH LANDS IN THE ANTILLES]. Paris, Horizons de France, 154p.   [*AGS*]

BOWEN, CALVIN, comp.

3.032   JM   1958 GUIDE TO JAMAICA. Kingston, Jamaica Tourist Board, 221p.   [*NYP*]

BRACEWELL, SMITH

3.033   BG   1948 The discovery of Kaieteur Fall by Charles Barrington Brown. *Timehri* 4th ser., 1(28), Dec.: 10-14.

BRAUW, W. de

5.020   SA   1934/ Het eiland Saba en zijn bewoners [The Island of Saba and its 35 inhabitants].

BRIERLEY, J. N.
3.034   TR   1912 TRINIDAD: THEN AND NOW. Port of Spain, Franklin's Electric Printery,
                   348p.   *[SCH]*

BRINNIN, JOHN MALCOLM
3.035   GC   1961 Caribbean island-hopping. *Atlan Mon* 207(4), Apr.: 96-99.   *[COL]*
3.036   BB   1962 Barbados. *Atlan Mon* 209(2), Feb.: 104-107.   *[COL]*

BROOKE, M. E.
3.037   ST   1929 Casual glimpses of St. Thomas, the island of Blackbeard and bay
                   rum. *B Geogr Soc Phila* 27, Jan.: 43-53.   *[AGS]*

BROWN, G. M. L.
3.038   CU   1905 A month in Curacao. *Can Mag Polit Sci Art Lit* 24(3), Jan.: 203-209.
                                                                                        [COL]

BROWN, WENZELL
3.039   GC   1947 ANGRY MEN—LAUGHING MEN: THE CARIBBEAN CALDRON. New York,
                   Greenberg, 369p.   *[NYP]*

BURDON, KATHARINE JANET
3.040   KNA   1920 A HANDBOOK OF ST. KITTS—NEVIS ... London, West India Committee,
                   247p.   *[NYP]*

BUTLER, G. PAUL & ERICA
3.041   GC   1960 CARIBBEAN AND CENTRAL AMERICA, AND THE BAHAMAS AND BERMUDA.
                   Princeton, N. J., D. Van Nostrand, 438p.   *[NYP]*

CADBURY, HENRY J.
3.042   BB   1942 An account of Barbados 200 years ago. *J Barb Mus Hist Soc* 9(2),
                   Feb.: 81-83. [5]   *[RIS]*
3.043   BB   1943 A Quaker account of Barbados in 1718. *J Barb Mus Hist Soc* 10(3),
                   May: 118-124. [5, 23]   *[AMN]*

CAINE, W. RALPH HALL
3.044   JM   1908 THE CRUISE OF THE PORT KINGSTON. London, Collier, 351p. [5, 23, 44]
                                                                                        [COL]

CAPPELLE, H. van
3.045   SR   1903 DE BINNENLANDEN VAN HET DISTRICT NICKERIE [THE INTERIOR OF THE
                   NICKERIE DISTRICT]. Baarn, [Netherlands], Hollandia, 240p.   *[NYP]*
3.046   SR   1905 AU TRAVERS DES FORÊTS VIERGES DE LA GUYANE HOLLANDAISE [THROUGH
                   THE VIRGIN FORESTS OF DUTCH GUIANA]. Baarn, [Netherlands],
                   Hollandia, 198p.   *[NYP]*

CARR, DAVID & THORPE, JOHN
3.047   BH   1961 FROM THE CAM TO THE CAYS: THE STORY OF THE CAMBRIDGE EXPEDI-
                   TION TO BRITISH HONDURAS 1959-60. London, Putnam, 190p.

CARREL, FRANK
3.048   BG   1938 Life at its best—in South America. *Can-W l Mag* 27(5), May: 23-26.
                                                                                        [NYP]

CASE, HENRY W.

3.049   BB/   1910 ON SEA AND LAND, ON CREEK AND RIVER. London, Morgan and Scott,
         BG   159p. [23]   [*UTS*]

CAVE, HUGH B.

3.050   JM   1962 FOUR PATHS TO PARADISE: A BOOK ABOUT JAMAICA. London, Alvin
                   Redman, 308p.

CECIL, C. H.

3.051   BC   1931 Parts and pleasant places. *Can-W I Mag* 20(5), Apr.: 164-168. [*NYP*]

CELARIE, HENRIETTE

3.052   FC   1930 LE PARADIS SUR TERRE: MARTINIQUE-GUADELOUPE-GUYANE [PARADISE
                   ON EARTH: MARTINIQUE-GUADELOUPE-GUIANA]. Paris, Librairie
                   Hachette, 223p.   [*COL*]
3.053   FG   1930 Le visage de la Guyane [The face of Guiana]. *Rev Deux Mondes* 56,
                   Apr. 15:817-842; 57, May 15:381-401.   [*COL*]

CHANDOS, DANE

3.054   GC   1955 ISLES TO WINDWARD. London, Michael Joseph, 238p.

CHAPMAN, ESTHER, ed.

3.055   JM   1961 PLEASURE ISLAND: THE BOOK OF JAMAICA. 5th ed. Kingston, Arawak
                   Press, 324p.   [*RIS*]

CHOT, ROBERT

3.056   FG   1949 En Guyane rouge [In red (Amerindian) Guiana]. *Rev Fr* 18, Apr.:
                   40-43. [13]   [*NYP*]

CINQUABRE, P.

3.057   GC   1948 Escales caraïbes [Caribbean ports of call]. *Tropiques* new ser.,
                   46(302), Aug.-Sept.: 3-14.   [*NYP*]

CLARK, SYDNEY

3.058   GC   1960 ALL THE BEST IN THE CARIBBEAN INCLUDING THE BAHAMAS AND BERMUDA.
                   New York, Dodd, Mead, 470p.

CLEGG, JOHN G.

3.059   WW   1963 Warm wind over the water. *Chron W I Comm* 78(1384), May: 262-263.
                                                      [*NYP*]

CLEMENTI, Sir CECIL

3.060   BG   1917 A journey to Mount Roraima across the Savannah Highlands of
                   British Guiana. *Timehri* 3d ser., 4(21), June: 1-26.   [*AMN*]

COCHRAN, HAMILTON

3.061   UV   1937 THESE ARE THE VIRGIN ISLANDS. New York, Prentice-Hall, 236p.
                                                      [*NYP*]

COLLIER, H. C.

3.062   BG   1936 Dutch courage. *Can-W I Mag* 25(5), Apr.: 21-23.   [*NYP*]
3.063   SK   1938 Golden gateways of the stars. *Can-W I Mag* 27(7), July: 23-26.
                                                      [*NYP*]

3.064 DM 1939 "Poetry of earth." *Can-W I Mag* 28(12), Christmas: 21-25. [*NYP*]

3.065 TB 1940 Escape to paradise. *Can-W I Mag* 29(3), Mar.: 19-22. [*NYP*]

CONNELL, NEVILLE

3.066 BB 1957 Father Labat's visit to Barbados in 1700. *J Barb Mus Hist Soc* 24(4), Aug.: 160-174. [5, 23] [*AMN*]

COOK, E. M.

3.067 JM 1924 JAMAICA, THE LODESTONE OF THE CARIBBEAN. Bristol, J.W. Arrowsmith, 187p. [*AGS*]

CORMACK, J.

3.068 CU 1930 A glimpse of modern Curacao. *Cha J* 7th ser., 20(1042), Nov.: 809-812. [*NYP*]

COULTHARD, G. R.

3.069 JM 1964 The enchanted garden. *Car Q* 10(1), Mar.: 25-30. [*RIS*]

CRABOT, CHRISTIAN & DELAPLACE, JEAN

3.070 MT 1960 GUIDE DE LA MARTINIQUE [GUIDE TO MARTINIQUE]. Paris, Société d'édition géographique et touristique, 145p. [*NYP*]

CRAMPTON, Professor

3.071 BG 1912 Latest journey to Roraima. *Timehri* 3d ser., 2(19A), July: 13-19. [*AMN*]

CRITCHELL, LAURENCE SANFORD

3.072 TR 1937 Crossroads of the Caribbean. *Natn Geogr Mag* 83(3), Sept.: 319-344. [*AGS*]

CRONE, KENNEDY

3.073 JM 1932 Jamaica, island jewel of the Caribbean Sea. *Can Geogr J* 4(4), Apr.: 243-264. [*AGS*]

CURTIS, JOHN GOULD

3.074 JM 1932 Jamaica, land of springs. *Home Geogr Mon* 1(11), May: 30-35. [*AGS*]

DAVIS, HASSOLDT

3.075 FG 1949 On the flowing highway in Guiana forests. *Travel* 92(6), June: 4-9, 31. [14] [*AGS*]

3.076 FG 1952 THE JUNGLE AND THE DAMNED. New York, Duell, Sloan and Pearce, 306p. [13, 14, 37] [*NYP*]

DAVIS, WILLIAM MORRIS

41.073 LW/ 1926 THE LESSER ANTILLES.
    WW

DEAN, CORINNE
3.077   BG   1945 Belize: a story of practical amalgamation. *J Negro Hist* 30(4), Oct.:
                    432-436.   [*COL*]

DECKERS, L. N.
3.078   GC   1939 Een studiereis naar de West [A study trip to the West]. *W I G* 21:65-
                    71, 97-107, 129-139, 193-205, 257-274.   [*COL*]

DES VOEUX, Sir G. WILLIAM
3.079   BG/   1903 MY COLONIAL SERVICE IN BRITISH GUIANA, ST. LUCIA, TRINIDAD, FIJI,
         SL/   AUSTRALIA, NEWFOUNDLAND, AND HONG KONG WITH INTERLUDES. Vol. 1.
         TR   London, John Murray, 408p.   [*COL*]
3.080   BG   1948 EXPERIENCE OF A DEMERARA MAGISTRATE, 1863-1869. Georgetown,
                    B.G., Daily Chronicle, 148p. (originally published in 1903.)   [*RIS*]

DIJK, M. van
5.046   SE   1929/ Nog eens: verzuimd Sint Eustatius [Once again: neglected St.
               30 Eustatius].

DOFLEIN, FRANZ
3.081   GC   1900 VON DEN ANTILLEN ZUM FERNEN WESTEN [FROM THE ANTILLES TO THE
                    FAR-OFF WEST]. Jena, Gustav Fischer, 180p.   [*NYP*]

DORAN, EDWIN BEAL, Jr.
52.024 CC   1957 Caicos cruise.

DOUGLAS-JONES, MARGUERITE
3.082   BG   1934 The road. *Timehri* 4th ser., no. 25, Dec.: 4-7.   [*RIS*]

DYKE, JOHN C. van
3.083   GC   1932 IN THE WEST INDIES: SKETCHES AND STUDIES IN TROPIC SEAS AND
                    ISLANDS. New York, Scribner, 211p.   [*COL*]

EADIE, HAZEL BALLANCE
3.084   TT   1931 LAGOONED IN THE VIRGIN ISLANDS. London, George Routledge, 443p.
                                                                                  [*NYP*]

EARLY, ELEANOR
3.085   CU/   1939 LANDS OF DELIGHT: A CRUISE BOOK TO NORTHERN SOUTH AMERICA AND
         TT   THE CARIBBEAN. Boston, Houghton, 214p.   [*AGS*]

ECKERT, BERTHA M.
3.086   JM   1928 Jamaica, isle of beauty. *So Work* 57(2), Feb.: 65-71.

EDSON, WESLEY
3.087   GC   1964 RETIRING TO THE CARIBBEAN. Garden City, Doubleday, 324p.   [*SCH*]

EGAN, JAMES
3.088   SM   1964 St. Maarten: a Caribbean find. *Atlan Mon* 213(1), Jan.: 106,108-109.
                                                                                  [*NYP*]

EGGLESTON, GEORGE T.
3.089   VI   1959 VIRGIN ISLANDS. Princeton, N.J., Van Nostrand, 208p.   [*AGS*]
3.090   SL   1963 ORCHIDS ON THE CALABASH TREE. London, Frederick Muller, 255p.[*NYP*]

EILERTS de HAAN, J. G., et al.

40.059   SR   1910 Verslag van de expeditie near de Suriname-Rivier [Account of the
                      expedition to the Surinam River].

ELIAS, EDUARD

3.091   CU   1954 Curacao revisited. *Car Commn Mon Inf B* 7(1), Jan.: 150-151,164.
                                                                                [*COL*]

ELLAM, PATRICK

3.092   GC   1957 THE SPORTSMAN'S GUIDE TO THE CARIBBEAN. New York, A.S. Barnes,
                      130p. [22]

ELLIOTT, STUART E.

3.093   DM   1951 The mouth of hell. *Nat Hist* 60(10), Dec.: 440-445,476.   [*AGS*]

ENGELS, C. J. H.

24.026   CU   1954 De culturele plaats van de Antillen in het Koninkrijk [The cultural
                      position of the Antilles in the Kingdom].

EUWENS, P. A.

3.094   CU   1925/ Klein-Curacao. *W I G* 7:401-410.   [*COL*]
                26
3.095   BN   1933/ De "Brandaris", de hoogste bergtop van het eiland Bonaire [The
                34   "Brandaris", the highest mountain top of the island Bonaire].
                      W I G 15:257-272, 289-298.   [*COL*]

EBANS, Mrs. L. CONWAY

3.096   BG   1929 El Dorado. *W I Comm Circ* 44(793), Feb. 21: 67-68; 44(794), Mar.
                      7:92-93.   [*NYP*]

FAIRCHILD, DAVID

3.097   GC   1934 Hunting useful plants in the Caribbean. *Natn Geogr Mag* 66(6),
                      Dec.: 705-737. [41]   [*AGS*]

FARABEE, WILLIAM CURTIS

3.098   BG   1917 A pioneer in Amazonia: the narrative of a journey from Manaos to
                      Georgetown. *B Geogr Soc Phila* 15, Jan.-Oct.: 57-103. [13] [*AGS*]

FENGER, FREDERIC ABILDGAARD

3.099   GC   1917 ALONE IN THE CARIBBEAN. New York, George H. Doran, 353p. [*NYP*]

FERMOR, PATRICK LEIGH

3.100   GC   1950 THE TRAVELLER'S TREE. London, John Murray, 403p.   [*RIS*]

FFRENCH, C. O'B.

3.101   TR   1943 Trinidad, the crossroads of the world. *Can Geogr J* 26(4), Apr.:
                      188-201.   [*AGS*]

FIUMI, LIONELLO

3.102   FA   1937 IMMAGINI DELLE ANTILLE [IMAGES OF THE ANTILLES]. Rome, Augustea,
                      156p.   [*NYP*]

FLU, P. C.

3.103   SR   1922/ Sanitaire verhoudingen in Suriname [Sanitary situations in Surinam]. 23 *W I G* 4:577-596. [28]   [*COL*]

FOLLETT, HELEN

3.104   GC   1943 ISLANDS ON GUARD. New York, Charles Scribner, 170p.   [*NYP*]

FOLLIARD, EDWARD T.

3.105   MT   1941 Martinique, Caribbean question mark. *Natn Geogr Mag* 79(1), Jan.: 47-55.   [*AGS*]

FOSTER, HARRY L.

3.106   GC   1928 THE CARIBBEAN CRUISE. New York, Dodd, Mead, 350p.   [*NYP*]
3.107   GC   1929 COMBING THE CARIBBEES. London, John Lane, 302p.   [*NYP*]

FOYLE, MONTAGUE L.

3.108   SA   1919 Saba—where the Dutch rule the Americans. *Cha J* 7th ser., 10(472), Dec. 13: 22-25.   [*NYP*]

FRANCE, HENRY de

3.109   FC   1941 UN SOURCIER AUX COLONIES [A DOWSER IN THE COLONIES]. Paris, Maison de la radiesthésie, 56p.   [*AMN*]

FRANCE-HARRAR, ANNIE

3.110   GC   1928 Mulattenwelt in Westindien [World of mulattos in the West Indies]. *Wester Mh* 144(862), June: 370-372. [11]   [*COL*]

FRANCK, HARRY A.

3.111   GC   1920 ROAMING THROUGH THE WEST INDIES. New York, Century Co., 486p.   [*COL*]

FRANSSEN HERDERSCHEE, A.

40.065   SR   1905 Verslag van de Gonini-Expeditie [Account of the Gonini Expedition].

FREETH, ZAHRA

3.112   BG   1960 RUN SOFTLY DEMERARA. London, George Allen & Unwin, 220p. [*RIS*]

FREITAS, C. P. de

3.113   BG   1944 On the frontier of British Guiana and Brazil. *Timehri* 4th ser., 1(26), Nov.: 122-145.   [*AMN*]

FREITAS, Q. B. de

3.114   BG   1948 Early experiences of a government medical officer in British Guiana. *Timehri* 4th ser., 1(28), Dec.: 24-27. [28]   [*AMN*]

FROIDEVAUX, HENRI

3.115   FG   1901 Les "lettres édifiantes" et la description de la mission de Kourou [The "edifying letters" and a description of the Kourou mission]. *J Soc Am Paris* 3:177-186. [5, 23]   [*AGS*]

FULLER, GEORGE S. B.

3.116   BC   1928 A winter cruise in the Caribbean. *Can-W I Mag* 17(5), Mar.: 108-109, 112.   [*NYP*]

FURLONG, CHARLES WELLINGTON

3.117   SR   1914 Through the heart of the Surinam jungle. *Harper's Mag* 128(765),
                     Feb.: 327-339. [14]   [*COL*]

3.118   SR   1915 The red men of the Guianan forests. *Harper's Mag* 131(784), Sept.:
                     527-537. [13]   [*COL*]

GAAY FORTMAN, B. de

3.119   NW   1920/ St. Martin, St. Eustatius en Saba. *W I G* 2:213-220.   [*COL*]
               21

3.120   SR   1948 Een vijfdaags bezoek aan Suriname in 1825 [A five-day visit to
                     Surinam in 1825]. *W I G* 29:13-19. [5]   [*COL*]

GANN, THOMAS W. F.

3.121   BH   1925 Mystery cities: explorations and adventure in Lubaantun. New
                     York, Scribner, 152p.   [*AGS*]

GEAY, F.

3.122   FG   1901 Compte-rendu de deux missions scientifiques dans l'Amérique
                     équatoriale [Account of two scientific expeditions to equatorial
                     America]. *B Mus Hist Nat* 7:148-158.   [*AMN*]

GETROUW, C. F. G.

3.123   SR   1946 Coronie. *W I G* 27:65-68.   [*COL*]

GIRAUD, J.

40.068   SR   1906 Au travers des forêts vierges de la Guyane Hollandaise [Through
                     the virgin forests of Dutch Guiana].

GOEJE, C. H. de

40.070   SR   1908 Verslag der Toemak Hoemak expeditie [Account of the Tumuc-
                     Humac expeditions].

5.066   GC   1936/ Op den oceaan voor en na Columbus [On the ocean before and after
               37   Columbus].

GONGGRIJP, J. W.

3.124   SR   1922/ Over het Orinoco-gebied [About the Orinoco region]. *W I G* 4:1-24.
               23   [*COL*]

GONGGRIJP, J. W. & STAHEL, G.

3.125   SR   1923/ Verslag van een reis naar den Hendriktop (Boven Saramacca) [Re-
               24   port on a trip to the Hendrik mountain (Upper Saramacca)]. *W I G*
                     5:1-20, 77-94, 129-150.   [*COL*]

GRANT, HERBERT T.

3.126   BH   1927 The Cockscombs revisited. *Geogr J* 70(6), Dec.: 564-572.   [*AGS*]

3.127   BH   1929 A second Cockscombs expedition in 1928. *Geogr J* 73(2), Feb.:
                     138-144. [40]   [*AGS*]

GUPPY, NICHOLAS

3.128   BG   1958 Wai-Wai: through the forest north of the Amazon. London, John
                     Murray, 375p.   [*AGS*]

GUTHRIE, W. E.
3.129   GC   1911 A CARIBBEAN CORRESPONDENCE. Bloomington, Ill., 84p.   *[NYP]*

HAMMOND, F. H.
3.130   TB   1910 A TOUR AROUND TOBAGO BY LAND AND SEA. [Port of Spain?] Trinidad,
        Franklin's Electric Printery, 70p.   *[SCH]*

HANNAU, HANS W.
3.131   GC   [1963?] ISLANDS OF THE CARIBBEAN. Munich, Wilhelm Andermann, 111p. *[SCH]*

HARLOW, VINCENT TODD, ed.
3.132   BC   1924 COLONISING EXPEDITIONS TO THE WEST INDIES AND GUIANA, 1623-
        1667. London, Hakluyt Society, 262p. (2d ser., no.56). [5] *[COL]*

HARMAN, CARTER
3.133   GC   1963 THE WEST INDIES. New York, Time Inc., 159p. (Life world library.)
        [SCH]

HARMAN, JEANNE PERKINS
3.134   BV   1961 THE VIRGINS: MAGIC ISLANDS. New York, Appleton-Century-Crofts,
        269p.   *[RIS]*

HARRINGTON, RICHARD
3.135   NL   1952 ABC Islands of the Netherlands West Indies. *Can Geogr J* 44(2),
        Feb.: 58-69.   *[AGS]*
3.136   SR   1952 Surinam, partner of the Netherlands. *Can Geogr J* 45(2), Aug.:
        42-53.   *[AGS]*

HARRIS, Sir C. ALEXANDER, ed.
3.137   GG   1928 A RELATION OF A VOYAGE TO GUIANA BY ROBERT HARCOURT 1613.
        London, Hakluyt Society, 188p. [5]

HEILPRIN, ANGELO
3.138   BG   1906 Impressions of a naturalist in British Guiana. *B Am Geogr Soc*
        38(9): 539-553. [41]   *[AGS]*
3.139   BG   1907 An impression of the Guiana wilderness. *Natn Geogr Mag* 18(6),
        June: 373-381.   *[AGS]*

HENDERSON, GILROY
3.140   BG   1952 Stone circles and tiger's lairs. *Timehri* 4th ser., 1(31), Nov.: 62-66.

HENDERSON, JOHN
3.141   JM   1905 THE WEST INDIES. Painted by A.S. Forrest. Described by John
        Henderson. London, Adam and Charles Black, 272p.   *[NYP]*

HENFREY, COLIN
13.035   BG   1964 THE GENTLE PEOPLE: A JOURNEY AMONG THE INDIAN TRIBES OF GUIANA.

HENLE, FRITZ & KNAPP, P. E.
3.142   GC   1957 THE CARIBBEAN: A JOURNEY WITH PICTURES. New York, Studio Publ.,
        207p.   *[AGS]*

HEPBURN, ANDREW
3.143   GC   1962 COMPLETE GUIDE TO THE CARIBBEAN AND BAHAMAS. Rev. ed. New York, Doubleday, 164p.

HERBERT, CHARLES W.
3.144   SA   1940 Saba, crater treasure of the Indies. *Natn Geogr Mag* 78(5), Nov.: 597-628.   [*AGS*]

HEYWARD, Du BOSE & RECK, DAISY
3.145   UV   1940 The American Virgins: after dark days, these adopted daughters of the United States are finding a new place in the Caribbean sun. *Natn Geogr Mag* 78(3), Sept.: 273-308.   [*AGS*]

HICKERTON, J. P.
3.146   BC   1958 CARIBBEAN KALLALLOO. London, Carey Kingsgate Press, 99p.

HILL, O. MARY
3.147   SV   1959 St. Vincent in the Windwards. *Can Geogr J* 59(5), Nov.: 162-167.   [*AGS*]

HINGSTON, R. W. G.
3.148   BG   1930 The Oxford University Expedition to British Guiana. *Geogr J* 76(1), July: 1-24. [41]   [*AGS*]
3.149   BG   1932 A new world to explore: in the tree-roof of the British Guiana forest flourishes hitherto-unknown life. *Natn Geogr Mag* 62(5), Nov.: 617-642. [41]   [*AGS*]

HOLDRIDGE, DESMOND
3.150   BG   1931 The people of the green mansions. *Bklyn Mus Q* 18(1), Jan.: 21-28.   [*AMN*]
3.151   GC   1937 ESCAPE TO THE TROPICS. New York, Harcourt, 272p.   [*NYP*]

HOPPE, E. O.
3.152   BH   1949 British Honduras. *Can Geogr J* 39(1), July: 18-32.   [*AGS*]

HOWES, PAUL GRISWOLD
3.153   DM   1929 The mountains of Dominica. *Nat Hist* 29(6), Nov.-Dec.: 595-610.   [*AGS*]

HUGHES, MARJORIE
3.154   JM   1962 THE FAIREST ISLAND. London, Victor Gollancz, 160p.   [*RIS*]

HURAULT, JEAN
3.155   FG   1948 NOTE SUR LA CONDUITE D'UNE MISSION DE RECONNAISSANCE DANS L'INTÉRIEUR DE LA GUYANE [ACCOUNT OF THE LEADING OF A RECONNAISSANCE EXPEDITION INTO THE INTERIOR OF GUIANA]. Paris, Impr. de l'Institut géographique national, 71p. [13,14]   [*NYP*]

IJZERMAN, J. W.
3.156   SR   1911 Twee reizen van Paramaribo [Two trips from Paramaribo]. *Tijdschr Ned Aar Genoot* 28:648-661.

JACKSON, T. B., ed.

3.157   TR   1904 THE BOOK OF TRINIDAD. Port of Spain, Muir, Marshall, 154p.

JADFARD, RENE

3.158   FG   1946 NUITS DE CACHIRI: RÉCIT GUYANAIS [CACHIRI NIGHTS: A GUIANA TALE]. Paris, Fasquelle, 155p.   [*SCH*]

JENMAN, G. S.

3.159   BG   1907 To KAIETEUR. Georgetown, Argosy Co., 39p.

JOHNSTON, JAS.

3.160   JM   1903 JAMAICA: THE NEW RIVIERA. London, Cassell, 95p.   [*COL*]

JORDAN, W. F.

3.161   FC   1922 CRUSADING IN THE WEST INDIES. New York, Revell, 202p. [23] [*NYP*]

JUNKER, L.

3.162   SR   1933/Herinneringen aan het corwoud uit mijn dagboek van 1921. [Memories 34 of the jungle from my diary of 1921]. *W I G* 15:177-190; 209-226. [*COL*]

3.163   SR   1941/Herinneringen aan het corwoud [Memories of the jungle]. *W I G* 23: 45 234-252, 302-316, 330-339, 353-364 (1941); 24:143-158 (1942); 26: 111-127, 129-146 (1944/45).   [*COL*]

KAHN, MORTON CHARLES

3.164   SR   1936 Where black man meets red. *Nat Hist* 37(5), May: 383-399. [13, 14, 28] [*AGS*]

KESLER, C. K.

5.108   TB   1928/ Tobago, een vergeten Nederlandsche kolonie [Tobago, a forgotten 29 Dutch colony].

5.112   TR   1941 Trinidad het grootste en schoonste der Kleine Antillen [Trinidad, the largest and most beautiful island of the Lesser Antilles].

5.113   BB   1942 Barbados.

KINGSBURY, ROBERT C. & PATRICIA

3.165   VI   1958 THE VIRGIN ISLANDS. Garden City, Nelson Doubleday, 64p. (Around the world program.)   [*RIS*]

KINGSLEY, CHARLES

3.166   BC   1900 AT LAST: A CHRISTMAS IN THE WEST INDIES. London, MacMillan, 465p. (First published 1871.)   [*RIS*]

KIRKE, HENRY

3.167   BG   1948 TWENTY-FIVE YEARS IN BRITISH GUIANA, 1872-1897. Georgetown, Daily Chronicle, 255p.   [*RIS*]

KLASS, SHEILA SOLOMON

12.014   TR   1964 Everyone in this house makes babies.

KNAPPERT, L.
5.120   SE   1929/ Verzuimd Sint Eustatius [Neglected St. Eustatius].
                      30

KRUIJER, GERARDUS JOHANNES
43.089   JM   1956 Met bulldozers en sociologie de bergen in [Trip into the mountains
                      with bulldozers and sociology].

La GORCE, JOHN OLIVER
3.168   JM   1927 Jamaica, the isle of many rivers. *Natn Geogr Mag* 51(1), Jan.: 1-55.
                                                                                        [*AGS*]

LANG, HERBERT
3.169   BG   1924 Into the interior of British Guiana. *Nat Hist* 24(4), July-Aug.:
                      467-478.   [*AGS*]

LANGEMEYER, F. S.
3.170   NW   1934/ Het klimaat en de natuurverschijnselen op onze Bovenwindsche
                      35   Eilanden [The climate and the natural phenomena on our Windward
                      Islands]. *W I G* 16:81-90. [42]   [*COL*]
5.121   SM   1940 Ver van 's werelds strijdgewoel: St. Maarten 1918-1920 [Far from
                      the troubles of the world: St. Maarten 1918-1920].

LANGLEY, ANNE RAINEY
3.171   BC   1941 British West Indian interlude. *Natn Geogr Mag* 79(1), Jan.: 1-46.
                                                                                        [*AGS*]

LANKS, HERBERT C.
3.172   JM/   1947 Through the West Indies by highway. *Can Geogr J* 34(5), May:
             TR   216-239.   [*AGS*]
3.173   JM/   1948 HIGHWAY ACROSS THE WEST INDIES. New York, Appleton-Century-
             TR   Crofts, 197p.   [*AGS*]

LARSEN, HENRY & PELLATON, MAY
3.174   FG   1958 BEHIND THE LIANAS; EXPLORATION IN FRENCH GUIANA. Edinburgh,
                      Oliver and Boyd, 211p.   [*AGS*]

LASSERRE, JEAN
3.175   FG   1934 LA PÈGRE DES TROPIQUES [RABBLE OF THE TROPICS]. Paris, Emile
                      Paul, 250p.   [*SCH*]

La VARRE, WILLIAM J., Jr.
3.176   BG   1919 UP THE MAZARUNI FOR DIAMONDS. Boston, Marshall Jones, 139p.
                                                                                        [*NYP*]
3.177   BG   1923 Discovering diamonds in British Guiana. *Wld Work* 41(243), Feb.:
                      274-282.   [*NYP*]

LAWS, GEOFFREY
3.178   BH   1928 The survey of the Lubaantun district in British Honduras. *Geogr J*
                      71(3), Mar.: 224-239. [4]   [*AGS*]

Le BOUCHER, LEON
3.179   GD   1931 LA GUADELOUPE PITTORESQUE: LES VOLCANS—LES RIVIÈRES DU SUD—

LES ETANGS [PICTURESQUE GUADELOUPE—THE VOLCANOES—THE SOUTHERN RIVERS—THE PONDS]. Paris, Société d'éditions géographiques, maritimes et coloniales, 256p. [40] [AGS]

LEEUW, HENDRIK de
3.180   CU/   1935 CROSSROADS OF THE CARIBBEAN SEA. New York, Messner, 331p. [RIS]
      SR

LEITCH, ADELAIDE
3.181   SB   1956 St. Barthélémy: stranger in the West Indies. *Can Geogr J* 52(1), Jan.: 30-35. [AGS]

LETHEM, Sir GORDON J.
3.182   BG   1950 Salute to adventurers. *Timehri* 4th ser., 1(26), Nov.: 35-41. [5]

Le TOUMELIN, JACQUES-YVES
3.183   FA/   1959 KURUN IN THE CARIBBEAN. London, Rupert Hart-Davis, 173p.
      WW

LICKERT, Rev.
13.047   BG   1912 Moruca.

LOGAN, HANCE
51.088   GC   1925 Hance Logan, M.P., gives Parliament account of his mission to West Indies.

LORD, W.T.
3.184   BG   1944 Exploring in British Guiana. *Timehri* 4th ser., 1(26), Nov.: 35-41. [AMN]

LYNCH, LOUIS
3.185   BB   1959 WEST INDIAN EDEN: THE BOOK OF BARBADOS. Glasgow, Robert Maclehose, 312p. [RIS]

McTURK, MICHAEL
3.186   BG   1911 My journey from Kalacoon to the Orinoco. *Timehri* 3d ser., 1(18B), July: 89-97. [AMN]

MAKIN, WILLIAM J.
3.187   JM   1939 CARIBBEAN NIGHTS. London, Robert Hale, 287p. [23] [SCH]

MANEN, W. H. R. van
3.188   SR   1909 Die Erforschung von Surinam während des letzten Jahrzehnts [The research of Surinam during the past decade]. *Globus* 95(7), Feb. 25: 104-110; 95(8), Mar. 4: 117-122. [COL]

MANNINGTON, GEORGE
3.189   GC   1925 THE WEST INDIES WITH BRITISH GUIANA AND BRITISH HONDURAS. London, Leonard Parsons, 304p. [NYP]

MANKOWITZ, WOLF
3.190   BB   1964 Flying fish and sugar cane; or, The joys of wintering in Barbados. *Holiday* 25(2), Feb.: 72-78, 91. [NYP]

MANOLIS, N.
3.191   GC   1933 THE TRAVELER'S GUIDE TO THE WEST INDIES AND GUIANAS. New York,
                           Cosmos Print. Co., 86p.   [*NYP*]

MARDEN, LUIS
37.249   BC   1942 Americans in the Caribbean.

MARVEL, EVALYN
3.192   UV   1961 GUIDE TO PUERTO RICO AND THE VIRGIN ISLANDS. New York, Crown,
                           254p.   [*NYP*]

MARVEL, TOM
3.193   GC   1937 CIRCLING THE CARIBBEAN. New York, Harcourt, Brace and Company,
                           302p.   [*NYP*]

MAUFRAIS, RAYMOND
3.194   FG   1952 ADVENTURES EN GUYANE: CARNETS [ADVENTURES IN GUIANA:(TRAVEL)
                           NOTES]. Paris, René Julliard, 255p.   [*NYP*]

MAZIERES, FRANCIS
3.195   FG   1955 EXPEDITION TUMAC-HUMAC. Garden City, N.Y., Doubleday, 249p.
                                                                                           [*AGS*]

MAZIERES, FRANCIS & DARBOIS, DOMINIQUE
3.196   FG   1952 Mission Guyane Tumuc-Humac: le carnet de route de Francis
                           Mazières [The Tumuc-Humac Guiana expedition: Francis Mazières'
                           notes]. *Plaisir Fr* 174(19), Oct.: 6-26. [13]   [*NYP*]

MEETEREN, N. van
5.133   BN   1949 Bonaire in het begin der negentiende eeuw [Bonaire in the early
                           part of the 19th century].

MELVILLE, EDWINA
3.197   BG   1957 Wapishana village. *Blwd Mag* 281(1696), Feb.: 155-168.   [*COL*]

MENKMAN, W.R.
5.137   CU   1934/ Drie reizen naar Curacao in den zeiltijd [Three trips to Curacao in
                      35   the era of sailing ships].
3.198   SR   1938 Moderne ontdekkingsreizen in het Surinaamsche binnenland [Modern
                           voyages of discovery in the interior of Surinam]. *W I G* 20:342-345.
                                                                                           [*COL*]
5.141   TT   1938 Tortola.
3.199   TB   1939 Tobago. *W I G* 21:218-236, 305-314, 369-381;
                      1940 22:33-46, 97-110, 129-133. [5]   [*COL*]
3.200   GC   1941 Aanteekeningen op Hamelberg's werken [Notes on Hamelberg's
                           writings]. *W I G* 23:1-22, 33-50, 65-77, 97-111, 161-176, 203-224,
                           321-329;
                      1946 27:157-158. [5]   [*COL*]
5.144   SR   1946 Uit de geschiedenis der opening van het Surinaamsche binnenland
                           [From the history of the opening of the interior of Surinam].
5.146   NC   1948 Onze West 1898-1948 [Our West 1898-1948].

METZGEN, MONRAD SIGRID & CAIN, HENRY EDNEY CONRAD, comps.

3.201   BH   1925 THE HANDBOOK OF BRITISH HONDURAS. London, West India Committee, 461p.   [*NYP*]

MIDAS, ANDRE

3.202   MT   1959 Une île amoureuse du vent [An island in love with the wind]. *Caribbean* 13(6), June: 106-109.   [*COL*]

MIELCHE, HAKON

3.203   GC   1962 CALYPSO ISLANDS. London, Herbert Jenkins, 157p.

MITCHELL, CARLETON

3.204   GC   1948 Carib cruises the West Indies. *Natn Geogr Mag* 93(1), Jan.: 1-56.
3.205   GC   1948 ISLANDS TO WINDWARD: CRUISING THE CARIBBEES. New York, D. van Nostrand, 287p.   [*AGS*]

MITCHELL, JOHN O'H.

3.206   BC   1922 The swizzle archipelago. *Can-W I Mag* 10(7), May: 184-186.   [*NYP*]

MITTELHOLZER, EDGAR

3.207   BC   1958 WITH A CARIB EYE. London, Secker & Warburg, 192p.   [*SCH*]

MOORE, W. ROBERT

3.208   CU/   1943 Curacao and Aruba on guard. *Natn Geogr Mag* 83(2), Feb.: 169-192.
         AR   [*AGS*]
3.209   JM   1954 Jamaica—hub of the Caribbean. *Natn Geogr Mag* 105(3), Mar.: 333-352.   [*AGS*]

MORAND, PAUL

3.210   GC   1929 HIVER CARAÏBE: DOCUMENTAIRE [CARIBBEAN WINTER: A DOCUMENTARY ACCOUNT]. Paris, Flammarion, 259p.   [*NYP*]

MORRIS, CLAUD

3.211   CM   1940 Lazy days in the sun. *Can-W I Mag* 29(8), Aug.: 25-27, 29.   [*NYP*]

MORTENSEN, THEODOR

3.212   UV   1908 Fra de dansk-vestindiske øer [From the Danish-West Indian Islands]. *Geogr Tidsskrift* 19:73-94.

MULVILLE, DAN

3.213   CU   1962 Curacao. *Geogr Mag* 34(11), Mar.: 658-670.   [*AGS*]
3.214   MT   1963 Martinique. *Geogr Mag* 36(1), May: 38-48.   [*AGS*]

MUNIER, CATHERINE

3.215   FG   1936 Impressions guyanaises [Impressions of Guiana]. *Rev Bl Polit Lit* 74(1), Jan.: 16-18.   [*NYP*]

MURRAY, REGINALD M.

3.216   JM   1928 Across the John Crow Mountains of Jamaica. *Geogr J* 71(3), Mar.: 272-274.   [*AGS*]
3.217   JM   1937 The John Crow Mountains. *W I Comm Circ* 52(1017), Sept. 23:371-373.   [*NYP*]

MURRAY, STEWART
3.218   UV   1951 THE COMPLETE HANDBOOK OF THE VIRGIN ISLANDS. New York, Duell, Sloan and Pearce, 178p.   [AGS]

NAIPAUL, V. S.
2.166   GC   1963 THE MIDDLE PASSAGE: THE CARIBBEAN REVISITED.

NARDAL, Mlle.; DEVEZ, G. & ROUSSIER, PAUL
3.219   FC   1931 MARTINIQUE, GUADELOUPE, GUYANE, ST. PIERRE-MIQUELON. Paris, Société d'éditions géographiques, maritimes et coloniales, 74, 66, 53, 34p.   [AGS]

NEITA, CLIFTON, ed.
3.220   JM   [1957?] WHO'S WHO, JAMAICA, BRITISH WEST INDIES, 1957. Kingston, Who's Who (Jamaica) Ltd., 520p.   [COL]

NORMAND, GILLES
3.221   FG   1924 AU PAYS DE L'OR: RÉCIT D'UN VOYAGE CHEZ LES INDIENS INCONNUS DE LA GUYANE FRANCAISE [IN THE LAND OF GOLD: ACCOUNT OF A JOURNEY TO THE UNKNOWN INDIANS OF FRENCH GUIANA]. Paris, Perrin, 341p. [13]   [NYP]

NORWOOD, VICTOR G. C.
3.222   BG   1956 MAN ALONE! ADVENTURES IN THE JUNGLES OF BRITISH GUIANA AND BRAZIL. London, T. V. Boardman, 234p.   [NYP]

NUGENT, MARIA
3.223   JM   1934 LADY NUGENT'S JOURNAL: JAMAICA ONE HUNDRED YEARS AGO. Ed. by Frank Cundall. London, Published for the Institute of Jamaica by the West India Committee, 404p. [5]   [COL]

NUTTING, C. C.
41.173   BB/   1919 BARBADOS-ANTIGUA EXPEDITION.
         AT

OAKLEY, AMY
3.224   GC   1951 BEHOLD THE WEST-INDIES. New York, Longmans, Green, 540p. [AGS]

OBER, FREDERICK ALBION
3.225   GC   1900 THE STORIED WEST INDIES. New York, D. Appleton, 291p.   [NYP]
3.226   GC   1904 OUR WEST INDIAN NEIGHBORS. New York, James Pott, 433p.   [COL]
3.227   GC   1914 A GUIDE TO THE WEST INDIES, BERMUDA AND PANAMA. New York, Dodd, Mead, 533p.   [COL]

OLIPHANT, J. N. & STEVENSON, DUNCAN
3.228   BH   1929 An expedition to the Cockscomb Mountains, British Honduras, in March 1928. Geogr J 73(2), Feb.: 123-137. [43]   [AGS]

OLLEY, PHILIP P.
3.229   JM   1952 GUIDE TO JAMAICA, 3d ed. Kingston, Tourist Trade Development Board, 330p.

ORR, FAY

3.230 GC 1941 FREIGHTER HOLIDAY. New York, Hastings House, 197p. [*NYP*]

OSWALD, A.

3.231 BG 1955 IT HAPPENED IN BRITISH GUIANA: STORIES BY AN OVERSEER ON A SUGAR ESTATE. Ilfracombe-Devon, Arthur H. Stockwell, 255.

OUDSCHANS DENTZ, FRED

54.051 SR 1920/ De bauxientnijverheid en de stichting van een nieuwe stad in
21 Suriname [The bauxite industry and the founding of a new city in Surinam].

23.114 SR 1948 Wat er overbleef van het kerkhof en de synagoge van de Joden-Savanne in Suriname[What is left of the cemetery and the synagogue of the Jewish-Savannah in Surinam].

OULIE, MARTHE

3.232 FA 1935 LES ANTILLES, FILLES DE FRANCE [THE ANTILLES, DAUGHTERS OF FRANCE]. Paris, Fasquelle, 308p. [*NYP*]

PACK, S. W. C.

3.233 BB 1964 WINDWARD OF THE CARIBBEAN. London, Alvin Redman, 226p. [*NYP*]

PALMER, KATHERINE V. W.

3.234 JM 1940 Some natural history descriptions of Jamaica. *Scient Mon* 51(4), Oct.: 321-328. [*AGS*]

PANHUYS, L. C. van

3.235 SR 1944/Naar het Lichtschip [To the Lightship]. *W I G* 26:19-23. [*COL*]
45

PARMER, CHARLES B.

3.236 GC 1937 WEST INDIA ODYSSEY: THE COMPLETE GUIDE TO THE ISLANDS OF THE CARIBBEAN. New York, Dodge, 285p.

PASSERA, GINO de'

3.237 BG 1925 La Cascata di Kaieuteur [The Kaieteur Waterfall]. *Vie It Am Lat* 31(5), May: 557-562. [*AGS*]

PERRET, JACQUES

3.238 FG 1932 La rivière et la forêt guyanaises [The rivers and forests of Guiana]. *Monde Colon Illus* 10(110), Oct.: 184-185. [*NYP*]

PERRET, JACQUES & GOREAUD, JEAN

3.239 FG 1932 Mission Monteux-Richard en Guyane Francaise [The Monteux-Richard expedition to French Guiana]. *B Ag Gen Colon* 25(279): 895-969. [*AGS*]

PFEIFFER, E. W.

3.240 BG 1940 Happy hunting ground. *Can-W I Mag* 29(5), May: 19-21; 29(7), July: 20-25. [*NYP*]

PHILLIPS, HENRY ALBERT

3.241 GC 1937 WHITE ELEPHANTS IN THE CARIBBEAN: A MAGIC JOURNEY THROUGH

ALL THE WEST INDIES. 2d ed. New York, Robert M. McBride, 301p.   [*NYP*]

PHILLIPS, ROSALIND
3.242   BG   1956 Journey to Kaieteur. *Caribbean* 9(7), Feb.: 153-156.   [*COL*]

PILKINGTON, FREDERICK
23.124   JM   1950 DAYBREAK IN JAMAICA.

POLL, WILLEM van de
3.243   NA   1951 THE NETHERLANDS WEST INDIES: THE ISLANDS AND THEIR PEOPLE. The Hague, W. van Hoeve, 64p.
3.244   SR   1951 SURINAM: THE COUNTRY AND ITS PEOPLE. The Hague, W. van Hoeve, 40p.   [*COL*]

POPE-HENNESSY, JAMES
3.245   BC   1943 WEST INDIAN SUMMER: A RETROSPECT. London, B.T. Batsford, 117p. [5]   [*AGS*]
3.246   WW/   1954 THE BATHS OF ABSOLOM: A FOOTNOTE TO FROUDE. London, Allan
         MT/   Wingate, 64p.   [*RIS*]
         TR

POST, CHARLES JOHNSON
3.247   CU   1909 A little paradise in the Dutch West Indies (Curacao). *Cent Mag* 79(2), Dec.: 176-184.   [*NYP*]

POWELL, E. ALEXANDER
3.248   GC   1936 AERIAL ODYSSEY. New York, Macmillan, 292p.   [*NYP*]

PRAKKEN, A. B. J.
3.249   NW   1919 De Bovenwindsche Eilanden der kolonie Curacao [The Windward Islands of the colony of Curacao]. *W I G* 2:402-417. [50]   [*COL*]

PULLEN-BURRY
3.250   JM   1905 ETHIOPIA IN EXILE: JAMAICA REVISITED. London, T. Fisher Unwin, 288p. [11]   [*NYP*]

QUESTEL, ANDRE
3.251   GC   1919 SOUVENIRS DE VOYAGE AUX ANTILLES ET GUYANES [RECOLLECTIONS OF A TRIP TO THE ANTILLES AND GUIANAS]. Paris, Impr. Pradier, 156p. [5]   [*SCH*]

RALPH, LESTER
3.252   SA   1914 Saba: an unknown island. *Can Mag* 43(1), May: 85-91.   [*NYP*]

RAMBERT, G.
3.253   GD   1955 Guadeloupe 1952: impressions de voyage [Guadeloupe 1952: Impressions of the voyage]. *Etud O-M* 38, Feb.: 71-76.   [*NYP*]

RAMPERSAD, FELIX ALBAN
3.254   TR   1963 TRINIDAD, GEM OF THE CARIBBEAN. Port of Spain: Quick-Service Printing Co., 128p.   [*RIS*]

REDGRAVE, WILLIAM J.

3.255   GC   1959 ISLANDS IN THE WIND. 3d ed. Greenlawn, N.Y., Harian Publications, 227p.   [*SCH*]

REED, HENRY A.

3.256   ST   1906 A trip to St.Thomas Island, Danish West Indies. *Army Navy Life* 9(6), Dec.: 561-566.   [*NYP*]

REID, GEO. RODHOUSE

3.257   SR   1934 A week in Suriname. *Timehri* 4th ser., no. 25, Dec.: 48-52.   [*RIS*]

RICHARDSON, GWEN

3.258   BG   1925 ON THE DIAMOND TRAIL IN BRITISH GUIANA. London, Methuen, 243p.   [*NYP*]

ROBERTS, WALTER ADOLPHE

3.259   GC   1948 LANDS OF THE INNER SEA, THE WEST INDIES AND BERMUDA. New York, Coward-McCann, 301p.   [*AGS*]

5.186   JM   1955 JAMAICA, THE PORTRAIT OF AN ISLAND.

ROTH, VINCENT

3.260   BG   1949 PATHFINDING ON THE MAZARUNI: THE JOURNAL OF SIX EXPEDITIONS ... 1922, 1923 AND 1924. Georgetown, B.G. Daily Chronicle, 270p.   [*RIS*]

3.261   BG   1952 Legislative council in north-west: a personal account of the Legislative Council's tour of the north west district, 27-31 March, 1952. *Timehri* 4th ser., 1(31), Nov.: 67-100.

ROTHERY, AGNES

3.262   MT   1930 Martinique. *Forum* 84(6), Dec., suppl.: xxxv-xxxvii.   [*COL*]

ROUX, HENRY D.

3.263   FG   1935 L'hinterland guyanais [The Guianese hinterland]. *Geographie* 64(4), Oct.: 205-227.   [*AGS*]

RUTTEN, L.M.R.

3.264   NA   1940 Het parelsnoer der Antillen en de gordel van smaragd [The pearl necklace of the Antilles and the girdle of emeralds]. *Tijdschr Ned Aar Genoot* 2d ser., 57(3), May: 362-396.   [*AGS*]

RUTTER, OWEN

3.265   GC   1933 IF CRAB NO WALK: A TRAVELLER IN THE WEST INDIES. London, Hutchinson, 288p.   [*NYP*]

ST. CLAIR, JAMES

3.266   JM   1929 A voyage to Jamaica in the forties. *W I Comm Circ* 44(805), Aug. 8: 307-308; 44(806), Aug. 22: 327-328; 44(807), Sept. 5: 437-438; 44(808), Sept. 19: 367-368: 44(809), Oct. 3: 388; 44(810), Oct. 17: 406-407; 44(811), Oct. 31: 426-427; 44(812), Nov. 14: 447-448; 44(813), Nov. 28: 467; 44(814). Dec. 12: 44(815), Dec. 26: 517. [5]   [*NYP*]

SANDERSON, IVAN T.
3.267   SR   1939 A journey in Dutch Guiana. *Geogr J* 93(6), June: 468-490.   [*AGS*]

SAVAGE, RAYMOND
3.268   BB   1936 BARBADOS, BRITISH WEST INDIES. London, Arthur Barker, 105p. [*NYP*]
3.269   BB   1937 BARBADOS, THE ENCHANTING ISLE. Philadelphia, J.B. Lippincott,
                      119p.   [*AGS*]

SAVARIA, EDMOND
3.270   FG   1933 SINNAMARY; OU, UNE PROMENADE EN GUYANE [SINNAMARY; OR, A
                      GUIANA TRIP]. Paris, André Tournon, 273p.   [*SCH*]

SCHELTEMA de HEERE, G. A. N.
3.271   SR/   1943 Bezoek van een Haarlemmer aan Suriname en Curacao in 1861-1862
          CU   [Visit of a person from Haarlem to Surinam and Curacao in 1861 and
                      1862]. *W I G* 25:321-343.   [*COL*]
3.272   SR   1947 De reis Nederland-Paramaribo in 1861 en sedert 1884 [The Nether-
                      land-Paramaribo journey in 1861 and after 1884]. *W I G* 28:74-87.
                      [52]   [*COL*]

SCHOMBURGK, RICHARD
3.273   BG   1953 RICHARD SCHOMBURGK'S TRAVELS IN BRITISH GUIANA 1840-1844. Ed.
                      by Walter E. Roth. Vol. 1. Georgetown, Daily Chronicle, 419p.   [5]

SCOFIELD, JOHN
3.274   UV   1956 Virgin Islands: tropical playland, U.S.A. *Natn Geogr Mag* 109(2),
                      Feb.: 201-232.   [*AGS*]

SEATON, GEORGE W.
3.275   GC   1938 LET'S GO TO THE WEST INDIES. New York, Prentice-Hall, 331p. [*NYP*]

SHARP, ROLAND HALL
3.276   SR   1942 In strategic Surinam. *Chr Sci Monit Mag* 34(104), Mar. 28: 4-14.
                                                                                       [*NYP*]

SHERLOCK, PHILIP M.
3.277   JM   1962 JAMAICA WAY. London, Longmans, Green, 104p.   [*RIS*]

SHIPLEY, Sir ARTHUR E.
3.278   BC   1924 ISLANDS WEST INDIAN-AEGEAN. London, Martin Hopkinson, 139p.[*AGS*]

SIMPICH, FREDERICK
3.279   GC   1931 Skypaths through Latin America. *Natn Geogr Mag* 59(1), Jan.: 27-29.
                                                                                       [*AGS*]

SINCKLER, E. GOULBURN
3.280   BB   1914 THE BARBADOS HANDBOOK. 3d ed. London, Duckworth and Co., 233p.
                                                                                       [*COL*]

SLOTHOUWER, L.
3.281   NW   1929/ De Nederlandsche Bovenwindsche Eilanden [The Dutch Windward
          30   Islands]. *W I G* 11:97-112. [5,66]   [*COL*]

SMITH, BRADLEY

3.282   GC   1956 Escape to the West Indies: a guidebook to the islands of the Caribbean. New York, Knopf, 415p. [*RIS*]

SMITH, GLANVILLE

3.283   GC   1937 Many a green isle. New York, Harper, 284p. [*NYP*]

SMITH, H. CARINGTON

3.284   BG   1938 On the frontier of British Guiana and Brazil. *Geogr J* 92(1), July: 40-54. [39] [*AGS*]

SMITH, NICOL

3.285   SR   1941 Bush master: into the jungles of Dutch Guiana. Indianapolis, Bobbs-Merrill, 315p. [*NYP*]

3.286   MT/   1942 Black Martinique—red Guiana. Indianapolis, Bobbs-Merrill, 312p.
      FG   [*AGS*]

3.287   FG   1943 Color glows in the Guianas, French and Dutch. *Natn Geogr Mag*
      SR   83(4), Apr.: 459-480. [*AGS*]

SNELLEMAN, J. F.

3.288   SR   1926/ Walter E. Roth. *W I G* 8:315-335. [*COL*]
          27

STAAL, G. J.

3.289   SR   1921/ Door de modder naar Coronie [Through the mud toward Coronie].
          22 *W I G* 3:466-469. [*COL*]

14.028   SR   1922/ Boschneger-herinneringen [Bush Negro reminiscences].
          23

STAHEL, GEROLD, et al.

3.290   SR   1926 De expeditie naar het Wilhelmina-Gebergte (Surinam) in 1926 [The expedition to the Wilhelmina mountains in 1926]. *Tijdschr Ned Aar Genoot* ser. 2, 43:545-596. [40, 41, 42]

STARR, IDA M. H.

3.291   ST/   1903 Gardens of the Caribbees: sketches of a cruise to the West
      MT/   Indies and the Spanish Main. Boston, L. C. Page, 2v. [*COL*]
      TR

STEDMAN, JOHN GABRIEL

3.292   SR   1962 The journal of John Gabriel Stedman 1744-1797 ... Ed. by Stanbury Thompson, London, Mitre Press, 437p. [*COL*]

STEDMAN, LOUISE

3.293   JM   1956 "Highlands" of Jamaica—from sea to Blue Mountain Peak. *Can-W I Mag* 46(9), Sept.: 5-7. [*NYP*]

STEELE, WILBUR DANIEL

3.294   SC   1918 The beleaguered island. *Harper's Mon Mag* 136(816), May: 817-829. [*NYP*]

STEWART, R. P.

3.295   BG   1912 To paradise: notes from an explorer's diary. *Timehri* 3d ser., 2(19B), Dec.: 365-372. [*AMN*]

STEWART, WILLIAM FORRES
3.296   TR   1953 Lucky strike island. *Can-W I Mag* 43(13), Jan.: 7-9,11.   [*NYP*]

STOCKUM, A. J. van
3.297   SR   1905 Een ontdekkingstocht in de binnenlanden van Suriname [An explora-
                tory expedition in the interior of Surinam]. Amsterdam, G.P. Tierie,
                324p.   [*NYP*]

STOKES, ANSON PHELPS
3.298   GC   1902 CRUISING IN THE WEST INDIES, ETC. New York, Dodd, Mead, 126p.
                                                                                     [*NYP*]
3.299   GC   1903 CRUISING IN THE CARIBBEAN WITH A CAMERA. New York, Dodd, Mead,
                21p.   [*NYP*]

STUART, STARR
3.300   BG   1942 British Guiana: "a journey into the interior." *Natn Rev* 118(710),
                Apr.: 369-376.   [*NYP*]

SWAN, MICHAEL
3.301   BG   1955 A letter from the bush. *Timehri* 4th ser., 1(34), Sept.: 42-47.
3.302   BG   1958 THE MARCHES OF EL DORADO: BRITISH GUIANA, BRAZIL, VENEZUELA.
                Boston, Beacon Press, 304p.

TAYLOR, JAN C.
3.303   BG   1960 British Guiana. *Explor Rev* Feb.: 29-33.   [*AGS*]

TEGANI, ULDERICO
3.304   CU   1929 Willemstad di Curacao [Willemstad of Curacao]. *Vie It Am Lat* 35(11),
                Nov.: 1147-1153.   [36]   [*AGS*]

THARP, GRAHAME
3.305   BV   1958 "You're welcome!" a visit to the British Virgin Islands. *Geogr Mag*
                31(3), July: 149-158.   [*AGS*]

THIONVILLE, CAMILLE
3.306   GD   1931 LA GUADELOUPE TOURISTIQUE [THE TOURIST'S GUADELOUPE]. Paris,
                Impr. Vve. Léger, 317p.   [*SCH*]

THOMPSON, R. W.
3.307   JM/   1946 BLACK CARIBBEAN. London, Macdonald, 286p.   [*RIS*]
         BH

TREVES, Sir FREDERICK
3.308   GC   1908 THE CRADLE OF THE DEEP: AN ACCOUNT OF A VOYAGE TO THE WEST
                INDIES. London, Smith, Elder, 378p.   [*NYP*]

TUZET, Y.
3.309   JM   1937 Images de la Jamäique [Jamaican images]. *Rev Deux Mondes* 41,
                Oct. 15: 850-879.   [*COL*]

VANDERCOOK, JOHN WOMACK
3.310   SR   1926 Jungle survival. *Harper's Mag* 152, Jan.: 235-241. [14]   [*COL*]

3.311   SR   1927 Surinam—South America's melting pot. *Wld Trav* 19(2), Feb.: 38-39,
                       56-57, 64, 66.   [*NYP*]
3.312   GC   1938 CARIBBEE CRUISE: A BOOK OF THE WEST INDIES. New York, Reynal
                       and Hitchcock, 349p.   [*AGS*]

VERRILL, ALPHEUS HYATT
3.313   GC   1915 ISLES OF SPICE AND PALM. New York, D. Appleton, 303p.   [*RIS*]
3.314   GC   1917 THE BOOK OF THE WEST INDIES. New York, E. P. Dutton, 485p. [*NYP*]
3.315   GC   1923 IN THE WAKE OF THE BUCCANEERS. London, Leonard Parsons, 374p.
                       [5]   [*AGS*]
3.316   BG/   1929 THIRTY YEARS IN THE JUNGLE. London, John Lane, 281p.   [*NYP*]
         DM

VINCENT, HARRY
59.053   TR   1910 THE SEA FISH OF TRINIDAD.

VINCKE, GASTON
3.317   FG   1935 AVEC LES INDIENS DE LA GUYANE [WITH THE INDIANS OF GUIANA]. Ed.
                       par la Comité du tricentaire des Antilles et de la Guyane. Paris,
                       28p. [22]   [*SCH*]

VOORHOEVE, JAN
3.318   SR   1960/ De handschriften van Mr. Adriaan Francois Lammens [The manu-
                 61   scripts of Mr. Adriaan Francois Lammens]. *N W I G* 40:27-49. [*COL*]

WAGENAAR HUMMELINCK, P.
3.319   GC   1955/ Caribische beelden [Caribbean images]. *W I G* 36:125-132.   [*COL*]
                 56

WALKER, H. De R.
3.320   BC   1902 THE WEST INDIES AND THE EMPIRE: STUDY AND TRAVEL IN THE WINTER
                       OF 1900-1901. New York, Dutton, 253p.   [11, 12, 37, 46]   [*NYP*]

WALLE, J. van de
3.321   NA   1954 DE NEDERLANDSE ANTILLEN: LAND, VOLK, CULTUUR. THE NETHERLANDS
                       ANTILLES: COUNTRY, PEOPLE, CULTURE [Text in Dutch and English].
                       Baarn, [Holland], Het Wereldvenster, 204p.   [*NYP*]

WARD, EDWARD
3.322   JM   1933 A trip to Jamaica: with a true character of the people and island.
                       In FIVE TRAVEL SCRIPTS COMMONLY ATTRIBUTED TO EDWARD WARD.
                       New York, Columbia University Press for the Facsimile Text
                       Society, [no. 1] (16p.)   [5]   [*COL*]

WARDLAW, C. W.
3.323   GC   1935 GREEN HAVOC: IN THE LANDS OF THE CARIBBEAN, Edinburgh, William
                       Blackwood, 318p.   [*NYP*]

WATSON, R. M.
3.324   BG   1962 Sifting the forest floor. *Geogr Mag* 34(9), Jan.: 541-550.   [*AGS*]

WAUGH, ALEC
3.325   MT   1938 La Martinique. *Geogr Mag* 8(2), Dec.: 121-132.   [*AGS*]

| 3.326 | GC | 1953 THE SUNLIT CARIBBEAN. London, Evans, 160p. |
| 3.327 | GC | 1958 LOVE AND THE CARIBBEAN: TALES, CHARACTERS AND SCENES OF THE WEST INDIES. New York, Farrar, Straus and Cudahy, 310p. |

WAUGH, EVELYN

3.328   BG   1934 NINETY-TWO DAYS: THE ACCOUNT OF A TROPICAL JOURNEY THROUGH BRITISH GUIANA AND PART OF BRAZIL. New York. Farrar and Rinehart, 238p.   [*NYP*]

WEEL, M. A. van

3.329   CU   1933/ Reisindrukken van Curacao [Travel impressions of Curacao]. *W I G* 34 15:145-157.   [*COL*]

WENT, F. A. F. C.

3.330   SR   1919 Natuur-wetenschappelijk onderzoek van de binnenlanden van Suriname [Natural-scientific research on the interior of Surinam]. *W I G* 1(1): 429-437.   [*COL*]

WHITE, WALTER GRAINGE

3.331   BG   [n.d.] AT HOME WITH THE MACUCHI. Ipswich, W. E. Harrison, 75p.   [13, 23]
                                                                                               [*NYP*]

WIJNAENDTS-FRANCKEN, C. J.

3.332   BG/   1915 DOOR WEST-INDIE: ANTILLEN, PANAMA, VENEZUELA, BRITSCH GUYANA,
         SR   SURINAME [TRAVELS IN WEST INDIA: THE ANTILLES, PANAMA, VENEZUELA, BRITISH GUIANA, SURINAM]. Haarlem, H.D. Tjeenk Willink, 238p.   [*AGS*]

WILDE, C. NOEL

3.333   BH   1933 British Honduras. *Can Geogr J* 7(6), Dec.: 275-285.   [*AGS*]

WILLIAMS, JAN

3.334   BQ   1949 Bequia—sleepy haven. *Can-W I Mag* 39(4), Apr.: 24-25.   [*NYP*]

THE PAST

Chapter 4

ARCHEOLOGY AND ETHNOHISTORY

ABONNENC, E.

4.001   FG   1952   Inventaire et distribution des sites archéologiques en Guyane Francaise [Listing and distribution of archaeological sites in French Guiana]. *J Soc Am Paris* new ser. 41:43-62.   [*AGS*]

AHLBRINCK, W.

4.002   SR   1960/   Een bezoek aan het museum in Costa Rica: oudheidkundige verwant-
              61   schap tussen Midden-Amerika en Suriname [A visit to the museum of Costa Rica: archeological relationships between Meso-America and Surinam]. *N W I G* 40:50-64.   [*COL*]

ANDERSON, A. H.

4.003   BH   [1952?] Glimpses of a lost civilization. *Car Q* 2(2):24-29.   [13]   [*RIS*]

4.004   BH   1954   The ancient Maya Indians. *Car Commn Mon Inf B* 8(1), Aug.: 2-4,9.   [*COL*]

4.005   BH   1958   Recent discoveries at Caracol Site, British Honduras. *In* PROCEEDINGS OF THE 32nd INTERNATIONAL CONGRESS OF AMERICANISTS, COPENHAGEN. Copenhagen, Munksgaard, p. 494-499.   [*AGS*]

4.006   BH   1962   Cave sites in British Honduras. *In* AKTEN DES 34. INTERNATIONALEN AMERIKANISTENKONGRESSES, Wien 1960. Vienna, Ferdinand Berger, p.326-331.   [*AGS*]

BALDWIN, RICHARD

4.007   BG   1946   Lost El Dorado. *Can-W I Mag* 36(5), July: 19-21; 36(6), Aug., 19-24; 36(7), Sept.: 13-14, 22-23.   [*NYP*]

BARTON, G. T.

4.008   BB   1953   THE PREHISTORY OF BARBADOS. [Bridgetown?] Barbados, Advocate Co., 88p. [13]

BELL, HENRY HESKETH

13.006   DM   1937   The Caribs of Dominica.

BOOY, THEODOOR de

4.009   CC   1912   Lucayan remains on the Caicos Islands. *Am Anthrop* new ser., 14(1), Jan.-Mar.: 81-105.   [*COL*]

| 4.010 | JM | 1913 | Certain kitchen-middens in Jamaica. *Am Anthrop* new ser., 15(3), July-Sept.: 425-434.   [*COL*] |

24.009   JM   1915   Certain West-Indian superstitions pertaining to celts.

4.011   UV   1917   Archeological investigations in the Virgin Islands: to solve the riddle of the origin of their aborigines. *Scient Am Suppl* 84(2180), Oct.: 232-234.   [*NYP*]

4.012   UV   1917   Archeological notes on the Danish West Indies: the petroglyphs of the island of St. John and of Congo Cay. *Scient Am Suppl* 84(2189), Dec. 15: 376-377.   [*NYP*]

4.013   BC   1917   Certain Archaeological investigations in Trinidad, British West Indies. *Am Anthrop* new ser., 19(4), Oct.-Dec.: 471-486.   [*COL*]

BOUGE, L. J.

4.014   GC   1948   Objets lithiques et pétroglyphes des Antilles: à l'origine–à l'arrivée de C. Colomb–aprés la conquête [Stone artifacts and petroglyphs of the Antilles: in early times–at the time of Columbus's arrival–post-conquest]. *In* ACTES DU 28. CONGRÈS INTERNATIONAL DES AMÉRICANISTES, Paris, 1947. Paris, Musée de l'homme, p.587-598.
                                                                             [*AMN*]

BRANCH, C. W.

4.015   SK/   1907   Aboriginal antiquities of St. Kitts and Nevis. *Am Anthrop* new
        NV   ser., 9(2), Apr.-June: 315-333.   [*COL*]

BULLBROOK, JOHN ALBERT

4.016   TR   1927   The aborigines of Trinidad. *In* RICHARDS, ALFRED, comp. DISCOVERY DAY CELEBRATION, 1927: SOUVENIR. Port of Spain, Franklin's Electric Printery. p.66-72.   [*SCH*]

4.017   GC   1941   THE ABORIGINAL REMAINS OF TRINIDAD AND THE WEST INDIES. [Port of Spain?] Trinidad, A.L. Rhodes, Govt. Printer, 14p.   [*NYP*]

4.018   GC   1949   The aboriginal remains of Trinidad and the West Indies. *Car Q* 1(1), Apr.-June: 16-21; 1(2) [n.d.]: 10-15.   [*RIS*]

4.019   TR   1953   ON THE EXCAVATION OF A SHELL MOUND AT PALO SECO, TRINIDAD, B.W.I. New Haven, Yale University Press, 114p. (Yale University publications in anthropology, no. 50.)   [27, 67]   [*RIS*]

4.020   TR   1956   The aborigines of Trinidad. *Shell Trin* 4(9), Christmas: 4-7.   [*RIS*]

4.021   TR   1957   The Carib-Arawak controversy. *Shell Trin* 4(10), Mar.: 7-9.   [5]
                                                                             [*RIS*]

BULLEN, RIPLEY P.

4.022   ST/   1962   Ceramic periods of St. Thomas and St. John Islands, Virgin Islands.
        SJ   *In* WILLIAM L. BRYANT FOUNDATION. AMERICAN STUDIES. REPORT NOS. 3-4. [Maitland, Fla., Central Florida Museum], Report no. 4 (74p.)

4.023   GC   1962   The Preceramic Krum Bay Site, Virgin Islands, and its relationship to the peopling of the Caribbean. *In* AKTEN DES 34. INTERNATIONALEN AMERIKANISTENKONGRESSES, Wien 1960. Vienna, Ferdinand Berger p.398-403.   [*AGS*]

4.024   GR   1964   Archeological research at Grenada, West Indies. *In* YEAR BOOK OF THE AMERICAN PHILOSOPHICAL SOCIETY, 1963. Philadelphia, George H. Buchanan, p.511-514.   [*NYP*]

4.025   GR   1964   THE ARCHAEOLOGY OF GRENADA, WEST INDIES. Gainesville, University of Florida, 67p. (Contributions of the Florida State Museum, Social sciences, no. 11.)   [*AGS*]

BULLEN, RIPLEY P. & SLEIGHT, FREDERICK W.

4.026 UV 1963 THE KRUM BAY SITE: A PRECERAMIC SITE ON ST. THOMAS, UNITED STATES VIRGIN ISLANDS. Orlando, Fla., William L. Bryant Foundation, 46p. (American studies report no. 5.) [*AGS*]

BUTT, AUDREY J.

13.010 BG 1958 Secondary urn burial among the Akawaio of British Guiana.

23.012 BG 1961/Symbolism and ritual among the Akawaio of British Guiana.
62

CARTER, J. E. L.

4.027 BG 1943 An account of some recent excavations at Seba, British Guiana. *Am Antiq* 9(1), July: 89-99. [*AGS*]

COE, WILLIAM R. & COE, MICHAEL D.

4.028 BH 1956 Excavations at Nohoch Ek, British Honduras. *Am Antiq* 21(4), Apr.: 370-382. [*COL*]

CONZEMIUS, EDUARD

13.011 BH 1928 Ethnographical notes on the Black Carib (Garif).

COOKSEY, C.

4.029 BB 1912 The first Barbadians. *Timehri* 3d ser., 2(19A), July: 142-144. [*AMN*]

COTTER, C. S.

4.030 JM 1946 The aborigines of Jamaica. *Jam Hist Rev* 1(2), Dec.: 137-141. [*COL*]

4.031 JM 1948 The discovery of the Spanish carvings at Seville. *Jam Hist Rev* 1(3), Dec.: 227-233. [*COL*]

DELAWARDE, JEAN-BAPTISTE

4.032 MT 1937 PRÉHISTOIRE MARTINIQUAISE: LES GISEMENTS DU PRÊCHEUR ET DU MARIGOT [THE PREHISTORY OF MARTINIQUE: THE SITES OF PRÊCHEUR AND MARIGOT]. Fort-de-France, Impr. officielle, 30p. [*AGS*]

De WOLF, MARIAN

4.033 JM 1953 Excavations in Jamaica. *Am Antiq* 18(3), Jan.: 230-238. [*RIS*]

Du RY, C. J.

4.034 NL 1960 Notes on the pottery of Aruba, Curacao and Bonaire. *N W I G* 40: 81-102. [67] [*RIS*]

EVANS, CLIFFORD & MEGGERS, BETTY J.

4.035 BG 1960 ARCHEOLOGICAL INVESTIGATIONS IN BRITISH GUIANA. Washington, U.S. Govt. Print. Off., 418p. (Bureau of American Ethnology, Bulletin 177.) [*RIS*]

FARABEE, WILLIAM CURTIS

4.036 BG 1916 Some South American petroglyphs. *In* ANTHROPOLOGICAL ESSAYS. PRESENTED TO WILLIAM HENRY HOLMES IN HONOR OF HIS SEVENTIETH BIRTHDAY, DEC. 1, 1916, BY HIS FRIENDS AND COLABORERS [sic]. Washington, [James William Bryan Press?], p.88-95. [*AGS*]

FERIZ, H.

4.037   SR   1962/Een merkwaardige stenen kraal uit Suriname [A curious stone bead
                 63 from Surinam]. *N W I G* 42:255-258.   [*COL*]

FEWKES, JESSE WALTER

4.038   GC   1907 ABORIGINES OF PORTO RICO AND NEIGHBORING ISLANDS. Washington,
                 U.S. Govt. Print. Off., 220p.   [*SCH*]

4.039   TR   1914 Prehistoric objects from a shell-heap at Erin Bay, Trinidad. *Am
                 Anthrop* new ser., 16(2), Apr.-June: 200-220.   [*COL*]

4.040   GC   1914 Relations of aboriginal culture and environment in the Lesser
                 Antilles. *B Am Geogr Soc* 46(9), Sept. 662-678. [13]   [*COL*]

4.041   GC   1915 ENGRAVED CELTS FROM THE ANTILLES. New York, Heye Foundation,
                 12p. (Contributions from the Museum of the American Indian, v.2,
                 no. 2.)   [*COL*]

4.042   JM   1922 A prehistoric island culture area of America. *In* BUREAU OF AMERICAN
                 ETHNOLOGY. 34th ANNUAL REPORT TO THE SECRETARY OF THE SMITH-
                 SONIAN INSTITUTION. Washington, U.S. Govt. Print. Off., p.35-281.
                                                                                  [*AGS*]

FROIDEVAUX, HENRI

4.043   GD   1920 La station des Trois-Rivières (Guadeloupe) et ses pétroglyphes
                 [The archaelogical site of Trois-Rivière (Guadeloupe) and its
                 petroglyphs]. *J Soc Am* 12:127-140.   [*AGS*]

GAAY FORTMAN, B. de

4.044   BN   1942 Geschiedkundige sprokkelingen: de Indianen op Bonaire [Historical
                 gleanings: The Indians on Bonaire]. *W I G* 24:251-256. [13] [*COL*]

GANN, THOMAS W. F.

4.045   BH   1918 THE MAYA INDIANS OF SOUTHERN YUCATAN AND NORTHERN BRITISH
                 HONDURAS. Washington, U.S. Govt. Print. Off., 146p. (Bureau of
                 American Ethnology, Smithsonian Institution, Bulletin 64.) [13] [*COL*]

4.046   BH   1930 Recently discovered Maya city in the southwest of British Honduras.
                 In PROCEEDINGS OF THE TWENTY-THIRD INTERNATIONAL CONGRESS OF
                 AMERICANISTS, N.Y., 1928. New York, p.188-192.   [*AGS*]

GANN, THOMAS W. T. & MARY

4.047   BH   1939 Archeological investigations in the Corozal district of British
                 Honduras. *In* SMITHSONIAN INSTITUTION, BUREAU OF AMERICAN ETH-
                 NOLOGY. BULLETIN 123. Washington, U.S. Govt. Print. Off., p.1-66.
                 (Anthropological papers no.7.)   [*AMN*]

GEIJSKES, D. C.

4.048   NW   1961/Het Eerste Internationale Congres voor de Studie van de Prae-
                 62 Columbiaanse Culturen in de Kleine Antillen [The First Inter-
                 national Congress for the Study of Pre-Columbian Cultures in the
                 Lesser Antilles]. *N W I G* 41:272-284.   [*COL*]

GOEJE, C. H. de

13.032   SR   1931/Oudheden uit Suriname: op zoek naar de Amazonen [Antiquities
                 32 from Surinam: in search of the Amazons].

4.049   SR   1943 Neolithische Indianen in Suriname [Neolithic Indians in Surinam].
              Tijdschr Ned Aar Genoot 60:334-374.   [*AGS*]

GOGGIN, JOHN M. & ROUSE, IRVING
4.050   GC   1948 A West Indian ax from Florida. *Am Antiq* 13(4, pt. 1), Apr.: 323-325.
                                                                                [*COL*]

GONGGRIJP, J. W.
4.051   SR   1920/ Sporen van voorhistorischen bewoners van Suriname [Traces of
              21   prehistoric inhabitants of Surinam]. *W I G* 2:1-16. [5]   [*COL*]

GOWER, CHARLOTTE D.
4.052   GC   1927 THE NORTHERN AND SOUTHERN AFFILIATIONS OF ANTILLES CULTURE.
              Menasha, Wis., American Anthropological Association, 60p. (Memoir
              no. 35.) [13]   [*COL*]

GOYHENECHE, E. & NICOLAS, MAURICE
5.071   FA   1956 DES ÎLES ET DES HOMMES [THE ISLANDS AND THE PEOPLE].

GRIFFIN, JOHN W.
4.053   GC   1943 The Antillean problem in Florida archaeology. *Fla Hist Q* 22(2),
              Oct.: 86-91.   [*RIS*]

GRUNING, E. L.
4.054   BH   1930 Report on the British Museum expedition to British Honduras, 1930.
              J Roy Anthrop Inst Gt Br Ire 60, July-Dec.: 477-483.   [*AGS*]

HARCOURT, RAOUL d'
4.055   MT   1952 Collections archéologiques martiniquaises du Musée de l'homme
              [The archaeological collections from Martinique of the Musée de
              l'homme]. *J Soc Am* new ser., 41:239-294.   [*RIS*]

HARRIS, W. R.
4.056   GC   1904 The Caribs of Guiana and the West Indies. *In* ANNUAL ARCHAEOLOGICAL
              REPORT OF THE ONTARIO PROVINCIAL MUSEUM, 1903, BEING PART OF
              APPENDIX TO THE REPORT OF THE MINISTER OF EDUCATION, ONTARIO,
              1904. Ontario, p.139-145.   [*AMN*]

HATT, GUDMUND
4.057   UV   1922 Den dansk-hollandske arkaeologiske ekspedition Vestindien [The
              Danish-Dutch archeological expedition to the West Indies]. *Geogr
              Tidsskrift* 26:236-237.
4.058   UV   1924 Archaeology of the Virgin Islands. *In* PROCEEDINGS OF THE TWENTY-
              FIRST INTERNATIONAL CONGRESS OF AMERICANISTS, [1st sess.] The
              Hague, Aug. 12-16, 1924. The Hague, pt. 1, p.29-42.   [*AGS*]

HEEKEREN, H. R. van
4.059   NL   1960 Studies on the archaeology of the Netherlands Antilles. II: A survey
              of the non-ceramic artifacts of Aruba, Curacao and Bonaire. *NWIG*
              40:103-120. [67]   [*RIS*]
4.060   NL   1963/ Studies on the archeology of the Netherlands Antilles. III: Pre-
              64   historical research on the islands of Curacao, Aruba and Bonaire in
              1960. *N W I G* 43:1-24.   [*RIS*]

HESHUYSEN, F. van

4.061   SR   1925/ Uit het Suriname Archief in Londen: mémoire sur les Indiens à
             26 Suriname, 22 sept. 1800 [From the Surinam Archives in London:
memorandum about the Indians in Surinam, Sept. 22, 1800]. *W I G*
7:346-349. [13] *[COL]*

HOSTOS, ADOLFO de

4.062   GC   1924 Antillean fertility idols and primitive ideas of plant fertilization
elsewhere. *In* PROCEEDINGS OF THE TWENTY-FIRST INTERNATIONAL
CONGRESS OF AMERICANISTS, first part, held at The Hague. AUG.
12-16, 1924. The Hague, p.247-252. *[AGS]*

4.063   GC   1924 Notes on West Indian hydrography in its relation to prehistoric
migrations. *In* ANNAES DO XX CONGRESSO INTERNACIONAL DE AMERICAN-
ISTAS, Rio de Janeiro, 1922. Rio de Janeiro, Impr. Nacional, pt. 1,
p.239-250. [17, 40] *[AGS]*

4.064   GC   1941 ANTHROPOLOGICAL PAPERS, BASED PRINCIPALLY ON STUDIES OF THE
PREHISTORIC ARCHAEOLOGY AND ETHNOLOGY OF THE GREATER ANTILLES.
San Juan, P. R., Govt. of Puerto Rico, Office of the Historian, 211p.
[RIS]

HOWARD, ROBERT R.

4.065   JM   1950 THE ARCHAEOLOGY OF JAMAICA AND ITS POSITION IN RELATION TO
CIRCUM-CARIBBEAN CULTURE. Ph. D. dissertation, Yale University,
498p.

4.066   JM   1956 The archaeology of Jamaica: a preliminary survey. *Am Antiq* 22(1),
July: 45-59. *[RIS]*

4.067   JM   1962 Aboriginal archaeology in Jamaica. *Inf B Scient Res Coun* 2(4),
Mar.: 61-65. *[RIS]*

HUCKERBY, THOMAS

4.068   SV   1914 Petroglyphs of Saint Vincent, British West Indies. *Am Anthrop* new
ser., 16(2), Apr.-June: 238-244. *[COL]*

4.069   GR/   1921 Petroglyphs of Grenada and recently discovered petroglyph in St.
       SV   Vincent. *Indn Notes Monogr* 1(3), Jan.: 143-164. [13] *[COL]*

HURAULT, JEAN; FRENAY, P. & RAOUX, Y.

4.070   FG   1963 Pétroglyphes et assemblages de pierres dans le sud-est de la
Guyane Francaise [Petroglyphs and stone assemblages in south-
eastern French Guiana]. *J Soc Am* new ser., 52:157-166. *[AMN]*

JESSE, C.

4.071   SL   1952 Rock-cut basins on Saint Lucia. *Am Antiq* 18(2), Oct.: 166-168. *[COL]*
4.072   BQ   [1953?] A note on Bequia. *Car Q* 3(1): 55-56. *[RIS]*
4.073   SL   1960 The Amerindians in Iouanalao. *J Barb Mus Hist Soc* 27(2), Feb.:
49-65. *[AMN]*

JOSSELIN de JONG, J. P. B. de

4.074   NL   1919/ De betekenis van het archeologisch onderzoek op Aruba, Curacao
          20 en Bonaire [The significance of archeological research on Aruba,
Curacao and Bonaire]. *W I G* 1(2): 317-334. *[COL]*

JOSSELIN de JONG, J. P. B. de

4.075   CU   1924 A natural prototype of certain three-pointed stones. *In* PROCEEDINGS
OF THE TWENTY-FIRST INTERNATIONAL CONGRESS OF AMERICANISTS,
The Hague, Aug. 1924. Leiden, E. J. Brill, p.43-45.   [*NYP*]

4.076   SA/   1947 Archeological material from Saba and St. Eustatius, Lesser Antilles.
        SE   *Meded Rijksmus Volk* No. 1 (54p.)   [*NYP*]

JOYCE, THOMAS A.

4.077   GC   1916 CENTRAL AMERICAN AND WEST INDIAN ARCHAEOLOGY. London, Philip
Lee Warnes, 270p. [13]   [*COL*]

4.078   BH   1926 Report on the investigations at Lubaantun, British Honduras, in
1926. *J Roy Anthrop Inst Gt Br Ire* 56:207-230.   [*AGS*]

4.079   BH   1929 British Museum Expedition to British Honduras. *Nature* 124(3138),
Dec. 21:964-965.   [*AGS*]

4.080   BH   1929 Report on the British Museum Expedition to British Honduras,
1929. *J Roy Anthrop Inst Gt Br Ire* 59:439-459.   [*AGS*]

JOYCE, THOMAS A.; CLARK, J. COOPER & THOMPSON, J. E.

4.081   BH   1927 Report on the British Museum Expedition to British Honduras,
1927. *J Roy Anthrop Inst Gt Br Ire* 57, July-Dec.: 295-323.   [*AGS*]

JOYCE, THOMAS A.; GANN, T.; GRUNING, E. L. & LONG, R. C. E.

4.082   BH   1928 Report on the British Museum Expedition to British Honduras,
1928 *J Roy Anthrop Inst Gt Br Ire* 58, July-Dec.: 323-350.   [*AGS*]

KRIEGER, HERBERT W.

4.083   UV   1938 Archeology of the Virgin Islands. *In* EXPLORATIONS AND FIELD WORK
OF THE SMITHSONIAN INSTITUTION IN 1937. Washington, D. C.; Smithsonian Institution, p.95-102.   [*AMN*]

LATHRAP, DONALD W.

4.084   BG   1964 An alternative seriation of the Mabaruma phase, northwestern
British Guiana. *Am Antiq* 29(3), Jan.: 353-359.   [*AGS*]

La TRY ELLIS, W. CH. de

6.040   NL   1960/ Historische aantekeningen omtrent de Nederlandse Antillen [His-
              61 torical notes about the Dutch Antilles].

LAWS, GEOFFREY

3.178   BH   1928 The survey of the Lubaantun district in British Honduras.

LEE, JAMES W.

4.085   JM   1962 Arawak stone artifacts. *Inf B Scient Res Coun* 2(4), Mar.: 70-72.
    [*RIS*]

LINK, MARION CLAYTON

4.086   JM   1960 Exploring the drowned city of Port Royal. *Natn Geogr Mag* 117(2),
Feb.: 151-183.   [*AGS*]

LONGLEY, G. C.

4.087   JM   1914 Kitchen middens of Jamaica. *Am Mus J* 14(8), Dec.: 295-303. [*NYP*]

LOVEN, SVEN

4.088   JM   1932 Stone dart points from the district of Old Harbour (Jamaica) and
                       qualified flint artifacts from the Antilles. *Revta Inst Etnol* 2:133-
                       138.   [*AMN*]

4.089   GC   1935 ORIGINS OF THE TAINAN CULTURE, WEST INDIES. Göteborg, Elanders
                       boktr. aktiebolag, 696p.   [*AGS*]

LUMIERE, CORNEL

4.090   JM   1956 Secrets of a sunken city. *Can-W 1 Mag* 46(1), Jan.: 7-10.   [*NYP*]

MACKIE, EUAN W.

4.091   BH   1961 New light on the end of classic Maya culture at Benque Viejo,
                       British Honduras. *Am Antiq* 27(2), Oct.: 216-224.   [*COL*]

McKUSICK, MARSHALL BASSFORD

4.092   GC   1960 Aboriginal canoes in the West Indies. *In* Mintz, SIDNEY W., comp.
                       PAPERS IN CARIBBEAN ANTHROPOLOGY. New Haven, Dept. of Anthro-
                       pology, Yale University, no. 63 (58p.) (Yale University publications
                       in anthropology, no. 57-64.) [13, 49]   [*RIS*]

4.093   GC   1960 THE DISTRIBUTION OF CERAMIC STYLES IN THE LESSER ANTILLES, WEST
                       INDIES. Ph.D. dissertation, Yale University, 220p.

MASON, GREGORY

4.094   BH   1928 Pottery and other artifacts from caves in British Honduras and
                       Guatemala. *Indn Notes Monogr* no. 47 (45p.)   [*COL*]

MEGGERS, BETTY J. & EVANS, CLIFFORD

4.095   BG   1955 Preliminary results of archaelogical investigations in British Guiana.
                       Timehri 4th ser., 1(34), Sept.: 5-26.

MEIGHAN, C. W. & BENNYHOFF, J. A.

4.096   BH   1951 A shell snake effigy from British Honduras. *Am Antiq* 16(4), Apr.:
                       352-353.   [*COL*]

METRAUX, A.

4.097   FG   1927 MIGRATIONS HISTORIQUES DES TUPI-GUARANI [HISTORICAL MIGRATIONS
                       OF THE TUPI-GUARANI]. Paris, Librairie orientale et américaine, 45p.
                                                                                         [*COL*]

MIDAS, ANDRE

4.098   FA   1960 Caribs and Frenchmen: the struggle for the islands. *Caribbean*
                       14(1), Jan.: 2-4, 10, 19.   [*COL*]

MILLER, GERRIT S.

4.099   JM   1932 Collecting in the caves and kitchen middens of Jamiaca. *In* EXPLO-
                       RATIONS AND FIELD WORK OF THE SMITHSONIAN INSTITUTION IN 1931.
                       Washington, D. C., Smithsonian Institution, 65-72. [41]   [*AMN*]

MORLEY, SYLVANUS G.

4.100   BH   1956 THE ANCIENT MAYA, 3d ed. Stanford University, Calif., Stanford
                       University Press, 494p. [5, 13]   [*RIS*]

OSGOOD, CORNELIUS

4.101   GC   1942 Prehistoric contact between South America and the West Indies. *Proc Natn Acad Sci* 28(1), Jan.: 1-4. [13]   [*RIS*]

4.102   BG   1946 BRITISH GUIANA ARCHEOLOGY TO 1945. New Haven, Yale University Press, 65p. (Publications in anthropology no. 36.)   [*COL*]

OWER, LESLIE H.

4.103   BH   1926 The colony of British Honduras. *W I Comm Circ* 41(716), Mar. 11:87. [40]   [*NYP*]

PEBERDY, P. STORER

4.104   BG   1948 Discovery of Amerindian rock-paintings in British Guiana. *Timehri* 4th ser., 1(28), Dec.: 54-58. [22]

PETER, IMELDA

4.105   DM   1934 The Caribs of Dominica—then and now. *Can-W I Mag* 23(8), July: 247-248, 250. [13]   [*NYP*]

PETITJEAN-ROGET, JACQUES

4.106   DM/   1963 The Caribs as seen through the dictionary of the Reverend Father
         GD   Breton. *In* [PROCEEDINGS OF THE] FIRST INTERNATIONAL CONVENTION FOR THE STUDY OF PRE-COLUMBIAN CULTURE IN THE LESSER ANTILLES. Fort-de-France, Société d'histoire de la Martinique, p.43-68. [26]

PICHARDO MOYA, FELIPE

4.107   GC   1956 LOS ABORÍGINES DE LAS ANTILLAS [THE ABORIGINES OF THE ANTILLES]. Mexico, Fondo de Cultura Económica, 140p.   [*AGS*]

PINCHON, ROBERT

4.108   MT   1952 Introduction à l'archéologie martiniquaise [Introduction to the archaeology of Martinique]. *J Soc Am* new ser., 41:305-352.   [*RIS*]

4.109   MT   1963 The archaeological problem in Martinique: a general view. *In* [PROCEEDINGS OF THE] FIRST INTERNATIONAL CONVENTION FOR THE STUDY OF PRE-COLUMBIAN CULTURE IN THE ANTILLES. Fort-de-France, Société d'histoire de la Martinique, p.75-80.

REICHLEN, HENRI & BARRET, PAULE

4.110   MT   1940 Contribution à l'archéologie de la Martinique: le gisement de l'anse Belleville [Contribution to the archaeology of Martinique: the site of Belleville Cove]. *J Soc Am* new ser., 32:227-274. [41]   [*AGS*]

4.111   MT   1941 Contribution à l'archéologie de la Martinique: le gisement de Paquemar [Contribution to the archaeology of Martinique: the Paquemar site]. *J Soc Am* new ser., 33:91-117.   [*AGS*]

4.112   FG   1943/ Contribution à l'archéologie de la Guyane Francaise [Contributions
         46   to the archaeology of French Guiana], par Henri et Paule Reichlen. *J Soc Am* new ser., 35:1-24.   [*AGS*]

RICKETSON, OLIVER, Jr.

27.035   BH   1931 Excavations at Baking Pot, British Honduras.

RIVET, P.

54.064   GC   1923 L'orfèvrerie précolombienne des Antilles, des Guyanes et du Vénézuela, dans ses rapports avec l'orfèvrerie et la métallurgie

des autres régions américaines [Precolombian metal-working in the
Antilles, Guianas, and Venezuela in relation to metal-working and
metallurgy in other parts of the Americas].

ROACH, C. N. C.
4.113   BB   1936 Old Barbados. *J Barb Mus Hist Soc* 3(3), May: 137-148; 3(4), Aug.:
                     211-222; 4(1), Nov.: 12-21;
                1937 4(2), Feb.: 53-67; 4(3), May: 109-122; 4(4), Aug.: 167-179; 5(1),
                     Nov.: 3-10;
                1938 5(2), Feb.: 85-100; 5(3), May: 130-143; 6(1), Nov.: 26-40;
                1939 6(2), Feb.: 74-85; 6(3), May: 139-151; 6(4), Aug.: 191-197.   [*AMN*]

ROBERTSON, WINDOM J.
4.114   GR   1958 The Caribs of Grenada. *C-W I Mag* 48(12), Dec.: 27-28.   [*NYP*]

RODWAY, JAMES
4.115   FG   1912 Guiana: the wild and wonderful. *Timehri* 3d ser., 2(19B), Dec.:
                     235-242.   [*AMN*]
4.116   FG   1919 "Timehri" or pictured rocks. *Timehri* 3d ser., 6(23), Sept.: 1-11.
                                                                                  [*AMN*]

ROTH, VINCENT
4.117   FG   1944 A stone-age bead factory on the Mahaica River. *Timehri* 4th ser.,
                     1(26), Nov.: 42-48.   [*AMN*]

ROUSE, IRVING
4.118   GC   1940 Some evidence concerning the origins of West Indian pottery-making.
                     Am Anthrop new ser., 42(1), Jan.-Mar.: 49-80.   [*AGS*]
4.119   TR   1947 Prehistory of Trinidad in relation to adjacent areas. *Man* 47(103),
                     July: 93-98.   [*COL*]
4.120   GC   1948 The West Indies; an introduction: the Arawak; the Carib. *In*
                     STEWARD, JULIAN H., ed. HANDBOOK OF SOUTH AMERICAN INDIANS,
                     VOL. 4: THE CIRCUM-CARIBBEAN TRIBES. Washington, U.S. Govt.
                     Print. Off., p.495-496, 507-546, 547-565. (Smithsonian Institution,
                     Bureau of American Ethnology, Bulletin 143.) [13]   [*RIS*]
4.121   GC   1949 The Southeast and the West Indies. *In* GRIFFIN, JOHN W., ed.
                     THE FLORIDA INDIAN AND HIS NEIGHBORS. Winter Park, Inter-American
                     Center, Rollins College, p.117-137.   [*COL*]
4.122   BC   1951 Areas and periods of culture in the Greater Antilles. *Sw J Anthrop*
                     7(3), Autumn: 248-265.   [*AGS*]
4.123   GC   1951 Prehistoric Caribbean culture contact as seen from Venezuela.
                     Trans N Y Acad Sci ser. 2, 13(8), June: 342-347.   [*COL*]
4.124   GC   1953 The Circum-Caribbean theory: an archaeological test. *Am Anthrop*
                     55(2, pt. 1), Apr.-June: 188-200.   [*RIS*]
4.125   GG   1953 GUIANAS: INDIGENOUS PERIOD. México, Instituto Panamericano de
                     Geografia e Historia, 100p. [13] (Program of the history of America.)
4.126   TR   1953 INDIAN SITES IN TRINIDAD: APPENDIX TO "ON THE EXCAVATION OF A
                     SHELL MOUND AT PALO SECO, TRINIDAD, B.W.I." by J.A. Bullbrook.
                     New Haven, Yale University Press, p.94.111. (Yale University
                     publications in anthropology, no. 50.)   [*COL*]
4.127   GC   1956 Settlement patterns in the Caribbean Area. *In* WILLEY, GORDON R.,
                     ed. PREHISTORIC SETTLEMENT PATTERNS IN THE NEW WORLD, New
                     York, Wenner-Gren Foundation for Anthropological Research, p.165-

172. (Viking Fund publications in anthropology, no. 23.) [COL]

4.128 GC 1958 Archeological similarities between the Southeast and the West Indies. In FAIRBANKS, CHARLES H., ed. FLORIDA ANTHROPOLOGY. Tallahassee, p.3-14. (Florida Anthropological Society, Publications, no. 4; Florida State University, Dept. of Anthropology, Notes in anthropology, v. 2.) [AMN]

4.129 GC 1960 The entry of man into the West Indies. In MINTZ, SIDNEY W., comp. PAPERS IN CARIBBEAN ANTHROPOLOGY. New Haven, Dept. of Anthropology, Yale University, no. 61 (58p.) (Yale University publications in anthropology, no. 57-64.) [RIS]

4.130 GC 1961 Archaeology in lowland South America and the Caribbean, 1935-60. Am Antiq 27(1), July: 56-62. [COL]

4.131 GC 1962 The intermediate area, Amazonia, and the Caribbean area. In BRAIDWOOD, R.J. & WILLEY, G.R., eds. COURSES TOWARDS URBAN LIFE [based on a symposium held at the European head-quarters of the Wenner-Gren Foundation for Anthropological Research at Burg Wartenstein, Austria, July 3-11, 1960]. New York, Aldine Pub. Co., p.34-59· (Viking Fund publications in anthropology no. 32.) [COL]

4.132 GC 1964 Prehistory of the West Indies. Science 144(3618), May 1: 499-513. [RIS]

ROUSE, IRVING; CRUXENT, J.M. & GOGGIN, J.M.

4.133 GC 1958 Absolute chronology in the Caribbean area. In PROCEEDINGS OF THE THIRTY-SECOND INTERNATIONAL CONGRESS OF AMERICANISTS, Copenhagen. Copenhagen, Munksgaard, p.508-515. [AGS]

SATTERTHWAITE, LINTEN, Jr.

4.134 BH 1951 Reconnaissance in British Honduras. Univ Mus B 16(1), May: 21-37. [RIS]

4.135 BH 1954 A modified interpretation of the "giant glyph" altars at Caracol, British Honduras. New Wld Antiq 1(1):1-3. [22] [RIS]

4.136 BH 1954 Sculptured monuments from Caracol, British Honduras. Univ Mus B 18(1-2), June: 3-45. [22] [RIS]

SHAW, EARL BENNETT

8.052 SC 1934 The villages of St. Croix.

SHERLOCK, PHILIP M.

4.137 JM 1939 THE ABORIGINES OF JAMAICA. Kingston, Institute of Jamaica, 20p. [AMN]

SINCKLER, E. GOULBURN

4.138 BB 1918 The Indians of Barbados. Timehri 3d ser., 5(22), Aug.: 48-55. [AMN]

SKINNER, ALANSON

4.139 SC 1925 Archeological specimens from St. Croix, Virgin Islands. Indn Notes 2(2), Apr.: 109-115.

SLEIGHT, FREDERICK W.

4.140 UV 1962 Archaeological reconnaissance of the island of St. John, United States Virgin Islands. In WILLIAM L. BRYANT FOUNDATION. AMERICAN

STUDIES. REPORT NOS. 3-4. [Maitland, Fla., Central Florida Museum], Report no. 3 (49p.)

STAHEL, GEROLD

4.141   SR   1921/ Een Indiaansche rotstekening aan de Kabelebo-rivier (Courantijn) 22 [An Indian petroglyph near the Kabelebo river (Courantyne)]. *W I G* 3:100-102.   [COL]

TAYLOR, DOUGLAS C.

4.142   GC   1946 Kinship and social structure of the Island Carib. *Sw J Anthrop* 2(2), Summer: 180-212. [13]   [AMN]

4.143   GC   1949 The interpretation of some documentary evidence on Carib culture. 5(4), Winter: 379-392.   [COL]

9.054   GC   1953 A note on marriage and kinship among the Island Carib.

TAYLOR, DOUGLAS C. & ROUSE, IRVING

4.144   GC   1955 Linguistic and archeological time depth in the West Indies. *Int J Am Ling* 21(2), Apr.: 105-115. [26, 67]   [COL]

THOMPSON, J. ERIC S.

4.145   BH   1931 ARCHAEOLOGICAL INVESTIGATIONS IN THE SOUTHERN CAYO DISTRICT, BRITISH HONDURAS. Chicago, Field Museum of Natural History, p.217-362. (Publication no. 301; Anthropological series, v. 17, no. 3.)   [COL]

4.146   BH   1939 EXCAVATIONS AT SAN JOSE, BRITISH HONDURAS, Washington, D.C., Carnegie Institution of Washington, 292p. (Publication no. 506.)   [AGS]

4.147   BH   1942 LATE CERAMIC HORIZONS AT BENQUE VIEJO, BRITISH HONDURAS. Washington, D.C., Carnegie Institution of Washington, p.1-35. (Publication no. 528; Contributions to American anthropology and history no. 35.)   [AGS]

THORPE, JOHN E.

4.148   BH   1961 Expedition to British Honduras. *Corona* 13(12), Dec.: 449-452.   [AGS]

TYNDALE-BISCOE, J. S.

4.149   JM   1962 The Jamaican Arawak—his origin, history, and culture. *J Am Hist Rev* 3(3), Mar.: 1-9.   [COL]

VERIN, PIERRE MICHEL

4.150   SL   1961 Les Caraïbes à Sainte Lucie depuis les contacts coloniaux [The Caribs in St. Lucia since the time of contact]. *N W I G* 41(2), Dec.: 66-82. [5, 13]   [RIS]

VERRILL, ALPHEUS HYATT

4.151   BG   1918 Prehistoric mounds and relics of the north west district of British Guiana. *Timehri* 3d ser., 5(22), Aug.: 11-20. [27]   [AMN]

4.152   BG   1918 A remarkable mound discovered in British Guiana. *Timehri* 3d ser., 5(22), Aug.: 21-25.   [AMN]

WAGENAAR HUMMELINCK, P.

4.153   NL   Rotstekeningen van Curacao, Aruba en Bonaire [Linear rock designs
              1953 of Curacao, Aruba and Bonaire. *W I G* 34:173-206;
              1957 37:5-41;
              1961 41:83-126. [67]   [*RIS*]

WILLCOX, HORACE

4.154   BH   1954 Removal and restoration of the monuments of Caracol. *Univ Mus B*
                    18(1-2), June: 47-72. [67]   [*RIS*]

WILLEY, GORDON R. & BULLARD, WILLIAM R., Jr.

4.155   BH   1956 Melhodo site, a house mound group in British Honduras. *Am Antiq*
                    22(1), July: 29-44.   [*COL*]

YDE, JENS

4.156   UV   1947 En vaerdifuld gave fra Vestindien [A valuable gift from the West
                    Indies]. *Fra Natnmus Arbsm* p.29-37.   [*RIS*]

ZERRIES, OTTO

4.157   BG   1961 Eine seltene Keule aus Guayana in Besitz des Linden-Museums
                    Stuttgart [A rare club from British Guiana in the possession of the
                    Linden Museum in Stuttgart]. *Tribus* 10, Sept.: 145-151.   [*AMN*]
4.158   BG   1962 Eine seltene Keule der Woyawai (Guayana) in Museo Pigorini zu
                    Rom [A rare Waiwai club (British Guiana) in the Pigorini Museum
                    in Rome]. *Tribus* 11, Nov.: 139-141.   [*AGS*]

Chapter 5

GENERAL HISTORY

ABONNENC, E.
7.002   FG   1948/ Aspects demographiques de la Guyane Francaise [Demographic as-
49   pects of French Guiana].

ACWORTH, A. W.
35.001   BC   1949 Treasure in the Caribbean: a first study of Georgian buildings
in the British West Indies.

ADHIN, J. H.
5.001   SR   1961/ De immigratie van Hindostanen en de afstand van de Goudkust [The
62   immigration of the Hindustanis and the cession of the Gold Coast].
N W I G 41:4-13.   [12, 17]   [*COL*]

AIKEN, JAMES
45.002   BG   1917 A voice from the past.

ALLAND, ALEXANDER
15.001   ST   1940 The Jews of the Virgin Islands; a history of the islands and candid
biographies of outstanding Jews born there.

ALVARADO, RAFAEL
39.001   BH   1958 La cuestión de Belice [The Belize question].

AMELUNXEN, C. P.
22.002   CU   1934/ De verdediging van Curacao bezongen [The defense of Curacao is
35   sung (praised)].

ANDERSON, ROBERT M.
3.008   SV   1938 The St. Vincent handbook.

ANDRADE, JACOB A. P. M.
15.002   JM   1941 A record of the Jews in Jamaica from the English conquest to
the present time.

APPLETON, S. E.
5.002   TR   1938 Old Tobago—some notes based on a perusal of the church registers.

W I Comm Circ 53(1044), Oct. 6: 397-398; 53(1045), Oct. 20: 421-422.
[23]   [*NYP*]

ARCINIEGAS, GERMAN

5.003   GC   1946 CARIBBEAN; SEA OF THE NEW WORLD. New York, Knopf, 464p. [*COL*]

ARMYTAGE, FRANCES

51.003   BC   1953 THE FREE PORT SYSTEM IN THE BRITISH WEST INDIES; A STUDY IN
                        COMMERCIAL POLICY, 1766-1822.

ARROYO, MANUEL

39.002   BH   1947/ A questão de Belice, Honduras Britânicas [The question of Belize,
                        48 British Honduras].

ASBECK, W. D. H. van

23.003   SR   1919 De Evangelische of Moravische Broeder-Gemeente in Suriname [The
                        Evangelical or Moravian Brethren in Surinam].

ASHCROFT, M. T.

28.015   BG   1962 The morbidity and mortality of enteric fever in British Guiana.

ASPINALL, Sir ALGERNON E.

5.004   BC   1912 WEST INDIAN TALES OF OLD. London, Duckworth, 259p. [24] [*NYP*]
38.009   BC   1919 West Indian Federation: its historical aspect.
5.005   BB   1942 "Rachel Pringle of Barbadoes." *J Barb Mus Hist Soc* 9(3), May:
                        112-119.   [*AMN*]
52.003   BC   1945 Some roads and their burdens.

ASTURIAS, FRANCISCO

39.003   BH   1941 BELICE.

AUGIER, F. R. & GORDON, SHIRLEY

5.006   GC   1962 SOURCES OF WEST INDIAN HISTORY. London, Longmans, 308p.   [*RIS*]

AUGIER, F.R.; HALL, D. G.; GORDON, S. C. & RECKORD, M.

5.007   GC   1960 THE MAKING OF THE WEST INDIES. London, Longmans, 310p.   [*RIS*]

AZEVDEO COSTA, J. A. de

39.004   FG   1945 Litígio entre o Brasil e a Franca—a questão do Território de Amapá
                        [Litigation between Brazil and France— the question of the Territory
                        of Amapá].

BAGUET, HENRI

43.005   FA   1905 DU RÉGIME DES TERRES ET LA CONDITION DES PERSONNES AUX ANTILLES
                        FRANCAISES AVANT 1789 [LAND ADMINISTRATION AND THE CONDITION OF
                        PEOPLE IN THE FRENCH ANTILLES PRIOR TO 1789].

BAKER, MARCUS

39.005   BG   1900 Anglo-Venezuelan boundary dispute.

BALEN, W. J. van

13.004   SR   1930/ Inca's in Surinam?
                   31

BALLOU, H. A.

41.023   BB   1937 Notes on the insects mentioned in Schomburgk's history.

BANBUCK, C. A.

5.008   MT   1935 HISTOIRE POLITIQUE, ÉCONOMIQUE ET SOCIALE DE LA MARTINIQUE SOUS
L'ANCIEN RÉGIME (1635-1789) [POLITICAL, ECONOMIC, AND SOCIAL HIS-
TORY OF MARTINIQUE UNDER THE OLD REGIME (1635-1789)]. PARIS,
Librairie des Sciences Politiques et Sociales, 335p.   [NYP]

BANGOU, HENRI

6.002   GD   1962 LA GUADELOUPE 1492-1848; OU, L'HISTOIRE DE LA COLONISATION DE
L'ÎLE LIÉE À L'ESCLAVAGE NOIR DE SES DÉBUTS À SA DISPARITION
[GUADELOUPE 1492-1848; OR, THE HISTORY OF THE COLONIZATION OF
THE ISLAND RELATED TO NEGRO SLAVERY FROM ITS BEGINNINGS TO ITS
DISAPPEARANCE].

5.009   GD   1963 LA GUADELOUPE 1848-1939; OU, LES ASPECTS DE LA COLONISATION
APRÈS L'ABOLITION DE L'ESCLAVAGE [GUADELOUPE 1848-1939; OR
ASPECTS OF COLONIZATION AFTER THE ABOLITION OF SLAVERY]. [Auril-
lac, France?] Editions du Centre, 311p.   [RIS]

BARBANSON, W. L. de

5.010   SB   1935/ St. Barthélémy in den Zweedschen tijd [St. Barthelemy during the
36   Swedish epoch], door P. de Barbanson.
[COL]

7.005   SB   1958 Grafschriften op Saint Barthélémy [Gravestone inscriptions on St.
Barthelemy].

BARBOUR, VIOLET

5.011   GC   1911 Privateers and pirates of the West Indies. Am Hist Rev 16(3), Apr.:
529-566.   [COL]

BAYLEY, HERBERT

52.006   BB   1940 The twopenny Barbados stamp of 1859.
52.007   BB   1941 The postmarks of the Barbados post offices 1852-1941.
52.008   BB   1944 Postmarks and cancelling marks used in Barbados 1841-1944.
52.009   BB   1952 The centenary of the Barbados Post Office: 1852-1952.

BEACHEY, RAYMOND W.

58.007   BC   1951 The period of prosperity in the British West Indian sugar industry
and the continental bounty system, 1865-1884.
58.008   BC   1954 Sugar technology in the British West Indies in the late nineteenth
century.
58.009   BC   1957 The British West Indies sugar industry in the late 19th century.

BELL, HERBERT C.

51.005   BC   1916 British commercial policy in the West Indies, 1783-1793.
51.006   BC   1917 The West India trade before the American Revolution.

BELL, HERBERT C.; PARKER, DAVID W., et al.

1.003   GC   1926 GUIDE TO BRITISH WEST INDIAN ARCHIVE MATERIALS, IN LONDON AND
IN THE ISLANDS, FOR THE HISTORY OF THE UNITED STATES.

BENJAMINS, H. D.

5.012   SR   1920/ Nog eens Aphra Behn [Aphra Behn once again]. *W I G* 2:517-538.
                   21   [*COL*]
7.008   BG/   1923 Bevolkingscijfers van Britsch Guyana en Suriname [Population
           SR   figures on British Guiana and Surinam].
51.008   SR   1924/ Iets over den ouden handel met de Indianen in Guiana. [Some facts
                   25   about the old trade with the Indians in Guiana].
29.006   SR   1929/ Treef en lepra in Suriname [Treyf and leprosy in Surinam].
                   30

BENNETT, J. HARRY, Jr.

32.018   BB   1950 Sir John Gay Alleyne and the Museum School, Codrington College,
                         1775-1797.
23.006   BB   1951 The S. P. G. and Barbadian politics, 1710-1720.
45.003   JM   1964 Cary Helyar, merchant and planter of seventeenth-century Jamaica.

BERGHE, PIERRE L. van den

16.004   GC   1963 Racialism and assimilation in Africa and the Americas.

BERKEL, ADRIAAN van

3.025   BG/   1941 ADRIAAN VAN BERKEL'S TRAVELS IN SOUTH AMERICA BETWEEN THE
           SR   BERBICE AND ESSEQUIBO RIVERS AND IN SURINAM 1670-1689.

BERNISSANT, P.

43.014   FA   1916 ETUDE SUR LE RÉGIME AGRICOLE DES ANTILLES FRANCAISES [STUDY
                         OF AGRICULTURAL CONDITIONS IN THE FRENCH ANTILLES].

BETHENCOURT, CARDOZO de

15.003   GC   1925 Notes on the Spanish and Portuguese Jews in the United States,
                         Guiana, and the Dutch and British West Indies during the seven-
                         teenth and eighteen centuries.

BEUKERING, J. A. van

46.012   SR   1952 Types of farming.

BEYERMAN, J. J.

5.013   BG   1934/ De Nederlandsche kolonie Berbice in 1771 [The Dutch colony
                   35   Berbice in 1771]. *W I G* 15:313-317.   [*COL*]

BIANCHI, WILLIAM J.

39.017   BH   1959 BELIZE: THE CONTROVERSY BETWEEN GUATEMALA AND GREAT BRITAIN
                         OVER THE TERRITORY OF BRITISH HONDURAS IN CENTRAL AMERICA.

BIJLSMA, R.

54.007   SR   1919/ Het mijnwerk der Societeit van Suriname op den Van den Bempden-
                   20   berg 1729-1743 [The mining operations of the Society of Surinam on
                         the Van den Bempden Mountain 1729-1743].
51.010   SR   1919/ Suriname's handelsbeweeging 1683-1712 [Surinam's commercial
                   20   development from 1683 to 1712].
40.013   SR   1920/ Alexander de Lavaux en zijne generale kaart van Suriname 1737
                   21   [Alexander de Lavaux and his general map of Surinam in 1737].

40.014   SR   1920/ De karteering van Suriname ten tijde van Gouverneur van Aerssen
              21   van Sommelsdijck [Surveying of Surinam at the time of Governor
                   van Aerssen van Sommelsdijck].

47.004   SR   1920/ De Surinaamsche grondbrieven ten tijde van Gouverneur van Aerssen
              21   van Sommelsdijck [The land certificates of Surinam during the time
                   of Governor van Aerssen van Sommelsdijck].

45.004   SR   1921/ Gouverneur Temmings plantage Berg en Daal bij den Parnassusberg
              22   in Suriname [Governor Temmings plantation "Berg en Daal" near
                   the Parnassus Mountain in Surinam].

43.015   SR   1921/ Surinaamsche plantage-inventarissen van het tijdperk 1713-1742
              22   [Surinam plantation inventories of the years 1713-1742].

45.005   SR   1922/ Aanwijzingen voor plantage-ondernemingen in Surinam in 1735
              23   [Directives for plantations in Surinam in the year 1735].

58.010   SR   1922/ Over bodemgesteldheid en suikerplantage-exploitatie in Suriname,
                   1765 [On soil conditions and sugar-plantation exploitation in
                   Surinam, 1765].

5.014   SR   1923/ De brieven van Gouverneur van Aerssen van Sommelsdijck aan de
              26   Directeuren der Societeit van Suriname uit het jaar 1648 [The
                   letters written by Governor van Aerssen van Sommelsdijck to the
                   Director of the Society of Surinam in the year 1648]. *W I G* 5:424-
                   437, (1923/24); 6:41-48, 593-602, (1924/25); 7:176-188, (1925/26).
                   [37]   [*COL*]

              BINDLEY, T. HERBERT
32.020   BB   1910 The evolution of a colonial college.

              BISWAMITRE, C. R.
5.015   SR   1938 Suriname gedurende de regeering van Koningin Wilhelmina [Surinam
                   during the rule of Queen Wilhelmina]. *W I G* 20:353-363. [7]   [*COL*]

              BITTER, B. A.
63.003   NA   1950 Geschiedenis van de bijenteelt op de Nederlandse Antillen [History
                   of apiculture on the Dutch Antilles].

              BLACK, CLINTON VANE de BROSSE
5.016   JM   1952 TALES OF OLD JAMAICA. Kingston, Pioneer Press, 121p. [24]   [*NYP*]
3.026   JM   1960 SPANISH TOWN, THE OLD CAPITAL.
5.017   JM   1961 HISTORY OF JAMAICA. 2d rev. ed. London, Collins Clear-type Press,
                   256p.   [*COL*]

              BLAIR
32.023   BG   1901 The system of education in British Guiana.

              BLANCHARD, RAE
45.006   BB   1942 Richard Steele's West Indian plantation.

              BLANCHE, LENIS
52.011   GD   1935 CONTRIBUTION À L'HISTOIRE DE LA PRESSE À LA GUADELOUPE [CONTRI-
                   BUTION TO THE HISTORY OF JOURNALISM IN GUADELOUPE].

5.018 GD 1938 HISTOIRE DE LA GUADELOUPE [HISTORY OF GUADELOUPE]. Paris, M.
          Lavergne imprimeur, 191p.   [*AGS*]

BLANT, ROBERT le
37.029 DS 1947 Les mauvais sujets à la Désirade, 1763-1767 [Undesirable indi-
          viduals in Desirade, 1763-1767].

BLOOMFIELD, L. M.
39.018 BH 1953 THE BRITISH HONDURAS-GUATEMALA DISPUTE.

BOUCAUD, J. E. A.
28.050 BC 1962 The practice of medicine in the British West Indies 1814-1953.

BOURNE, RUTH
5.019 GC 1939 QUEEN ANNE'S NAVY IN THE WEST INDIES. New Haven, Yale University
          Press, 34p.   [*NYP*]

BOUTRUCHE, ROBERT
51.016 FA 1935 Bordeaux et le commerce des Antilles Francaises au XVIIIe siècle
          [Bordeaux and the French Antillean trade in the 18th century].

BOYCE, Sir RUBERT W.
28.052 BC 1910 HEALTH PROGRESS AND ADMINISTRATION IN THE WEST INDIES.

BRAITHWAITE, LLOYD E.
38.024 BC 1957 Progress toward federation, 1938-1956.

BRAUW, W. de
5.020 SA 1934/ Het eiland Saba en zijn bewoners [The Island of Saba and its
          35 inhabitants]. *W I G* 16:304-317. [3, 7]   [*COL*]

BROU, ALEXANDRE
23.007 BC/ 1935 CENT ANS DE MISSIONS 1815-1934: LES JÉSUITES MISSIONNAIRES AU
     FG   XIXe ET AU XXe SIÈCLES [ONE HUNDRED YEARS OF MISSION WORK 1815-
          1934: THE JESUIT MISSIONARIES IN THE 19th AND 20th CENTURIES].

BROWN, AUDREY
5.021 SK 1962 La Chateau de la Montagne, Saint Christopher. *Chron W I Comm*
          77(1370), Mar.: 125-128. [35]   [*NYP*]

BROWN, E. ETHELRED
50.013 JM 1919 Labor conditions in Jamaica prior to 1917.

BROWN, JOHN
5.022 GC 1962 Du Plessis. *Chron-W I Comm* 77(1378), Nov.: 569-571. [*NYP*]
5.023 SL 1962 Sir John Moore: a study in integrity and humanity. *Chron-W I Comm*
          77(1368), Jan.: 25-27; 77(1369), Feb.: 71-73.   [*NYP*]
5.024 SL 1965 St. Lucia in the time of Henry Breen. *Chron-W I Comm* 80(1404),
          Jan.: 28-30.   [*NYP*]

BROWNE, C. A.
46.023 GC 1927 Some historical relations of agriculture in the West Indies to that
          of the United States.

BRUNOT, FERDINAND
25.010   FA   1935 Le francais hors d'Europe [French outside of Europe].

BRYCE, WYATT E., et al.
36.004   JM   1952 Historic Port Royal.

BULLBROOK, JOHN ALBERT
4.021   TR   1957 The Carib-Arawak controversy.

BURDON, Sir JOHN ALDER
2.028   BH   1931 Archives of British Honduras.

BURN, W. L.
5.025   BC   1951 The British West Indies. London, Hutchinson, 196p.   [*COL*]

BURNS, Sir ALAN CUTHBERT
5.026   BC   1954 History of the British West Indies. London, George Allen & Unwin, 821p.   [*RIS*]

BURR, GEORGE LINCOLN
39.019   BG   1900 The Guiana boundary: a postscript to the work of the American Commission.

BURT, ARTHUR E.
37.049   JM   1962 The first instalment of representative government in Jamaica, 1884.

BUTT, AUDREY J.
23.011   BG   1959/ The birth of a religion (the origins of 'Hallelujah' the semi-Christian
              60   religion of the Carib-speaking peoples of the borderlands of British Guiana, Venezuela and Brazil.)

CABON, A.
23.013   FG   1950 La clergé de la Guyane sous la Révolution [The Guiana clergy during the Revolution].

CADBURY, HENRY J.
23.014   BB   1940 Quakers, Jews and freedom of teaching in Barbados, 1686.
23.015   BB   1941 Barbados Quakers—1683 to 1761: Preliminary list.
3.042   BB   1942 An account of Barbados 200 years ago.
23.016   BB   1942 186 Barbados Quakeresses in 1677.
3.043   BB   1943 A Quaker account of Barbados in 1718.
23.017   BB   1946/ Witnesses of a Quaker marriage in 1689.
              47
23.018   BB   1948/ Further lists of early clergy.
              49
23.019   BB   1948 Clergymen licensed to Barbados, 1694-1811.
23.020   BB   1953 Glimpses of Barbados Quakerism 1676-9.

CAINE, W. RALPH HALL
3.044   JM   1908 The cruise of the Port Kingston.

CALDERON QUIJANO, JOSE ANTONIO
39.020   BH   1944 Belíce 1663(?)-1821: historia de los establecimientos británicos

DEL RÍO VALIS HASTA LA INDEPENDENCIA DE HISPANOAMÉRICA [BELIZE 1663(?)-1821: HISTORY OF THE BRITISH SETTLEMENTS OF THE VALIS RIVER UNTIL THE INDEPENDENCE OF SPANISH AMERICA].

CAMERON, NORMAN E.

32.039   BG   1961 Chronology of educational development in British Guiana from 1808 to 1957.

CAMERON, THOMAS W. M.

5.027   GC   1934 The early history of the Caribee islands (1493-1530). *Scott Geogr Mag* 50(1), Jan.: 1-18; 50(2), Mar.: 92-100.   [*COL*]

CAMPBELL, PERSIA CRAWFORD

15.006   BC   1923 Foreign competition for Chinese labour, 1845-74.

CANALES SALAZAR, FELIX

39.021   BH   1946 DERECHOS TERRITORIALES DE LA REPÚBLICA DE HONDURAS SOBRE HONDURAS BRITÁNICA O BELICE, ISLAS DEL CISNE Y COSTAS DE LOS INDIS MOSQUITOS [TERRITORIAL RIGHTS OF THE REPUBLIC OF HONDURAS OVER BRITISH HONDURAS OR BELIZE, SWAN ISLANDS AND THE MOSQUITO INDIAN COAST].

CANDACE, GRATIEN

51.019   FA   1935 Les Antilles dans la prospérité des ports francais depuis trois siècles [The Antilles' share in the prosperity of French ports over the last three centuries].

CAPLE, S. CANYNGE

22.016   BC   1957 ENGLAND V. THE WEST INDIES 1895-1957.

CAPPER, T.

32.041   JM   1901 The system of education in Jamaica.

CARMICHAEL, GERTRUDE

5.028   TR   1961 HISTORY OF THE WEST INDIAN ISLANDS OF TRINIDAD AND TOBAGO, 1498-1900. London, Alvin Redman, 463p.   [*RIS*]

CARTER, E. H.; DIGBY, G. W. & MURRAY, R. N.

5.029   GC   1959 HISTORY OF THE WEST INDIAN PEOPLES. BOOK III: FROM EARLIEST TIMES TO THE 17th CENTURY. London, Thomas Nelson, 178p.   [32]
                                                                            [*RIS*]

CASTA-LUMIO, LUCIEN

50.017   FC   1906 ETUDE HISTORIQUE SUR LES ORIGINES DE L'IMMIGRATION RÉGLEMENTÉE DANS NOS ANCIENNES COLONIES DE LA RÉUNION, LA GUADELOUPE, LA MARTINIQUE, ET LA GUYANE [HISTORICAL STUDY ON THE ORIGINS OF REGULATED IMMIGRATION INTO OUR FORMER COLONIES OF REUNION, GUADELOUPE, MARTINIQUE, AND GUIANA].

CAZANOVE, Dr.

28.086   FC   1935 Les épidémies de fièvre jaune aux Antilles et à la Guyane Francaise [Yellow fever epidemics in the Antilles and in French Guiana].

CECIL, C. H.
18.009   JM   1935 The maroons in Canada.

CHANDLER, ALFRED D.
17.005   BB   1946 The expansion of Barbados.

CHAPIN, HOWARD M.
52.018   BB   1934 Barbados signal books of 1814.

CHARPENTIER, GENEVIEVE
51.023   FA   1937 LES RELATIONS ÉCONOMIQUES ENTRE BORDEAUX ET LES ANTILLES
                AU SIÈCLE [ECONOMIC RELATIONS BETWEEN BORDEAUX AND THE ANTILLES
                IN THE 18th CENTURY].

CHEESMAN, E. E.
41.061   GC   1939 The history of introduction of some well known West Indian staples.

CHILSTONE, E. M.
37.062   BB   1939 Tercentenary of.the Barbados House of Assembly—growth of repre-
                sentative government.

CHRISTELOW, ALLAN
51.024   JM   1942 Contraband trade between Jamaica and the Spanish Main, and the
                Free Port Act of 1766.

CLEGHORN, ROBERT
23.022   BH   1939 A SHORT HISTORY OF BAPTIST MISSIONARY WORK IN BRITISH HONDURAS
                1802-1939.

CLEMENTI, Sir CECIL
5.030   BG   1922 Colonisation in British Guiana. *United Emp* new ser., 13(7), July:
                443-453. [17]   [*AGS*]
37.065   BG   1937 A CONSTITUTIONAL HISTORY OF BRITISH GUIANA.

COLLIER, H. C.
5.031   JM   1937 Old Port Royal lives again. *Can-W I Mag* 26(3), Mar.: 21-22.   [*NYP*]
5.032   AG   1937 "There was a day." *Can-W I Mag* 26(9), Sept.: 28-30.   [*NYP*]
5.033   JM   1938 Fragments of stone. *Can-W I Mag* 27(11), Nov.: 4-6.   [*NYP*]
11.007   JM   1939 The maroons of Jamaica.
5.034   BC   1941 Station for honour. *Can-W I Mag* 30(9), Sept.: 21-24.   [*NYP*]

COMITAS, LAMBROS
10.009   BC   1960 Metropolitan influences in the Caribbean: the West Indies.

COMVALIUS, TH. A. C.
22.032   SR   1938 Twee historische liederen in Suriname [Two historical songs in
                Surinam].

CONNELL, NEVILLE
23.026   BB   1953 St. George's Parish Church, Barbados.
3.066   BB   1957 Father Labat's visit to Barbados in 1700.
35.008   BB   1959 18th century furniture and its background in Barbados.

5.035   BB   1960 A SHORT HISTORY OF BARBADOS. Bridgetown, Barbados Museum and
                      Historical Society, 15p.

          COOLHAAS, W. PH.
1.007   NC   1960 A CRITICAL SURVEY OF STUDIES ON DUTCH COLONIAL HISTORY.

          COOPER, JOHN IRWIN
32.049   BC   1949 The West Indies, Bermuda, and the American mainland colleges.

          COTTER, C. S.
37.071   JM   1959 Ocho Rios in Jamaican history.

          COZIER, EDWARD L.
38.030   BC   1957 Foreshadows of federation.

          CRABB, J. A., ed.
23.027   JM   1951 CHRIST FOR JAMAICA.

          CRACKNELL, EVERILL M. W.
2.050   BB   1934 THE BARBADIAN DIARY OF GEN. ROBERT HAYNES 1787-1836.

          CRIST, RAYMOND E.
43.030   SK/   1949 Static and emerging cultural landscapes in St. Kitts and Nevis,
          NV   British West Indies.
43.032   AT   1954 Changing cultural landscapes in Antigua, B. W. I.

          CROUSE, NELLIS M.
5.036   FA   1940 FRENCH PIONEERS IN THE WEST INDIES, 1624-1664. New York,
                      Columbia University Press, 294p.   [*RIS*]

          CROWLEY, DANIEL JOHN
22.041   TR   1956 The traditional masques of Carnival.
66.031   SL   [1959?] CONSERVATISM AND CHANGE IN SAINT LUCIA: ACTAS DEL XXXIII CON-
                      GRESO INTERNACIONAL DE AMERICANISTAS, SAN JOSE, COSTA RICA,
                      JULY 20-27, 1958.

          CRUICKSHANK, J. GRAHAM
36.005   BG   1918 "King William's people."
8.014   BG   1921 The beginnings of our villages.
45.007   BG   1930 The wreckage of an industry.

          CUMPER, GEORGE E.
58.027   JM   1954 Labour demand and supply in Jamaican sugar industry, 1830-1950.
7.011   JM   1956 Population movements in Jamaica, 1830-1950.
50.021   BB   1959 Employment in Barbados.

          CUMPSTON, I. M.
50.026   BC   1953 INDIANS OVERSEAS IN BRITISH TERRITORIES, 1834-1854.

          CUNDALL, FRANK
5.037   JM   1900 STUDIES IN JAMAICA HISTORY. London, Sampson Low, Marston and Co.
                      for the Institute of Jamaica, 78p.   [*NYP*]
37.079   BC   1906 POLITICAL AND SOCIAL DISTURBANCES IN THE WEST INDIES: A BRIEF
                      ACCOUNT AND BIBLIOGRAPHY.
5.038   GC   1910 The colonization of the Caribbean. *United Emp* new ser., 1(9),
                      Sept.: 620-635.   [*AGS*]

5.039   JM   1913 Outlines of the history of Port Royal. *W I Comm Circ* 28(391), Sept.
                        23: 441-443; 28(392), Oct. 7: 466-468; 28(393), Oct. 21: 488-489;
                        28(394), Nov. 4: 514-516; 28(395), Nov. 18:537-538.   [*NYP*]
32.052   JM   1914 THE MICO COLLEGE JAMAICA.
5.040   JM   1915 HISTORIC JAMAICA. London, West India Committee for the Institute
                        of Jamaica, 424p.   [*COL*]
37.080   JM   1919/ Jamaica governors [Some items have title: Governors of Jamaica].
                        23
17.007   SR/   1919 The migration from Surinam to Jamaica.
           JM
5.041   BC   1920 Historical sidelights. II: The West India Committee in 1946. *W I*
                        Comm Circ 35(562), Apr. 15:108-109.   [*NYP*]
37.081   BC   1920 Royal visits to the West Indies.
22.048   JM   1924 Pine's painting of Rodney and his officers.
52.021   JM   1926 Early printing in Jamaica.
45.008   JM   1927 An historic Jamaica estate.
23.030   JM   1930 Three fingered Jack.
23.031   JM   1931 A BRIEF HISTORY OF THE PARISH CHURCH OF ST. ANDREW, JAMAICA.
5.042   JM   1931 The Palisadoes. *W I Comm Circ* 46(862), Oct. 15: 411-412; 46(863),
                        Oct. 29: 431-432; 46(864), Nov. 12: 451-452.   [*NYP*]
5.043   BC   1936 Early British efforts for the development of the West Indies. *W I*
                        Comm Circ 51(991), Sept. 24: 405-406, 51(992), Oct. 8: 425-426;
                        51(993), Oct. 22: 444; 51(994), Nov. 5: 464; 51(995), Nov. 19:484.
                                                                                         [*NYP*]
37.082   JM   1936 THE GOVERNORS OF JAMAICA IN THE SEVENTEENTH CENTURY.
37.083   JM   1937 THE GOVERNORS OF JAMAICA IN THE FIRST HALF OF THE EIGHTEENTH
                        CENTURY.

CUNDALL, FRANK; DAVIS, N. DARNELL & FRIEDENBERG, ALBERT M.
15.009   JM/   1915 Documents relating to the history of the Jews in Jamaica and
           BB   Barbados in the time of William III.

CUNDALL, FRANK & PIETERSZ, JOSEPH L.
5.044   JM   1919 JAMAICA UNDER THE SPANIARDS. Kingston, Institute of Jamaica, 115p.
                                                                                         [*COL*]

CURRY, HERBERT FRANKLIN, Jr.
37.084   BH   1956 British Honduras: from public meeting to crown colony.
38.033   BC   1958 THE MOVEMENT TOWARD FEDERATION OF THE BRITISH WEST INDIAN
                        COLONIES, 1624-1945.

CURTIN, PHILIP D.
51.043   BC   1954 The British sugar duties and West Indian prosperity.
2.052   JM   1955 TWO JAMAICAS: THE ROLE OF IDEAS IN A TROPICAL COLONY, 1830-1865.

DAM, C. F. A. van
5.045   CU   1961/ Curaçao in de eerste jaren na 1634 [Curacao during the first few
                        62 years after 1634]. *N W I G* 41:168-170.   [*COL*]

DAMPIERRE, JACQUES de

1.011   FA   1904 ESSAI SUR LES SOURCES DE L'HISTOIRE DES ANTILLES FRANCAISES
                     (1492-1664) [STUDY OF THE HISTORICAL SOURCES ON THE FRENCH
                     ANTILLES (1492-1664)].

DAUTHEUIL

28.120 FG   1936 Comment on devenait médecin au XVIIᵉ siècle "en l'isle de
                     Cayenne" [How one became a physician in the 17th century on
                     "Cayenne Island"].

DAVIS, N. DARNELL

15.010 BB   1909 Notes on the history of the Jews in Barbados.
28.121 NV   1911 Nevis as West Indian health resort.

DEBIEN, GABRIEL

50.033 FC   1942 LE PEUPLEMENT DES ANTILLES FRANCAISES AU XVIIᵉ SIÈCLE: LES
                     ENGAGÉS PARTIS DE LA ROCHELLE (1683-1715) [THE SETTLEMENT
                     OF THE FRENCH ANTILLES IN THE 17th CENTURY: THE BONDED SERVANTS
                     FROM LA ROCHELLE (1683-1715)].
50.034 FA   1951 Les engagés pour les Antilles (1634-1715) [Bonded servants signed
                     up for the Antilles (1634-1715)].
1.012   FA   1961 Les travaux d'histoire sur les Antilles Francaises; chronique
                     bibliographique (1959 et 1960) [Historical works on the French
                     Antilles; bibliographical chronicle].
1.013   FA   1963 Chronique de l'histoire d'outre-mer, les Antilles Francaises (1961
                     et 1962) [Historical chronicle of the overseas territories, the French
                     Antilles (1961 and 1962)].
30.009 FC   1964 La nourriture des esclaves sur les plantations des Antilles Fran-
                     caises aux XVIIᵉ et XVIIIᵉ siècles [The diet of slaves on the plan-
                     tations of the French Antilles in the 17th and 18th centuries].

De CAMP, DAVID

25.019 JM   1961 Social and geographical factors in Jamaican dialects.

DECLAREUIL, JEAN

37.094 FG   1927 LES SYSTÈMES DE TRANSPORTATION ET DE MAIN-D'OEUVRE PÉNALE AUX
                     COLONIES DAN LE DROIT FRANCAIS [THE COLONIAL PENAL TRANSPORTA-
                     TION AND FORCED LABOR SYSTEMS IN FRENCH LAW].

DEERR, NOEL

58.031 BC   1946 Sugar in the West Indies.

DELANY, FRANCIS X.

23.034 JM   1930 A HISTORY OF THE CATHOLIC CHURCH IN JAMAICA B.W.I. 1494 TO 1929.

DELAWARDE, JEAN-BAPTISTE

43.037 MT   1935 LES DÉFRICHEURS ET LES PETITS COLONS DE LA MARTINIQUE AUX
                     XVIIᵉ SIÈCLE [SETTLERS AND SMALL LAND HOLDERS IN MARTINIQUE IN
                     THE 17th CENTURY].

DesBRIERE, JUANITA

46.053 AR   1938 Aruba, Cinderella of the Caribbean.

DEVAS, RAYMUND P.

23.035   GR   1927/ The Catholic Church in Grenada, B.W.I. (1650-1927) by R.C. Devas.
              28

23.036   GR   1932 CONCEPTION ISLAND; OR, THE TROUBLED STORY OF THE CATHOLIC CHURCH IN GRENADA.

DIGBY, ERNEST S.

2.060   TB   1934 When history was made in Tobago.

DIJK, M. van

5.046   SE   1929/ Nog eens: verzuimd Sint Eustatius [Once again: neglected St.
             30 Eustatius]. *W I G* 11:412-421. [3, 66]   [*COL*]

DONOHOE, WILLIAM ARLINGTON

5.047   BH   1947 A HISTORY OF BRITISH HONDURAS. New York, Colorite Offset Print. Co., 118p.   [*COL*]

DUCHESNE-FOURNET, JEAN

43.045   GG   1905 LA MAIN-D'OEUVRE DANS LES GUYANES [MANPOWER IN THE GUIANAS].

DUNCAN, EBENEZER

5.048   SV   1963 A BRIEF HISTORY OF ST. VINCENT WITH STUDIES IN CITIZENSHIP. 3d rev. ed. Kingstown, St. Vincent Reliance Printery, 113p.   [37]
                                                   [*RIS*]

EDMUNDSON, GEORGE

17.009   BG/   1901 The Dutch in western Guiana.
         TB

39.025   BG   1923 The relations of Great Britain with Guiana.

EINAAR, J. F. E.

37.103   SR   1934 BIJDRAGE TOT DE KENNIS VAN HET ENGELSCH TUSSCHENBESTUUR VAN SURINAME, 1804-1816 [CONTRIBUTION TO KNOWLEDGE ABOUT THE ENGLISH INTERREGNUM IN SURINAM, 1804-1816].

EISNER, GISELA

44.056   JM   1961 JAMAICA, 1830-1930: A STUDY IN ECONOMIC GROWTH.

ELDER, J. D.

22.055   TR   1964 Color, music and conflict: a study of aggression in Trinidad with reference to the role of traditional music.

ELLIS, J. B.

23.041   BH/   1913 THE DIOCESE OF JAMAICA: A SHORT ACCOUNT OF ITS HISTORY, GROWTH,
         JM   AND ORGANIZATION.

EMMANUEL, ISAAC S.

15.011   GC   1955 New light on early American Jewry.

23.042   CU   1957 PRECIOUS STONES OF THE JEWS OF CURACAO; CURACAON JEWRY 1656-1957.

ERICKSON, EDGAR L.

50.044   BC   1934 The introduction of East Indian coolies into the British West Indies.

ESCALONA RAMOS, ALBERTO

39.026   **BH**   1941 Belice pertenece a México o a Guatemala? [Does Belize belong to Mexico or to Guatemala?]

ESPINET, CHARLES S. & PITTS, HARRY

22.059   **TR**   1944 LAND OF THE CALYPSO: THE ORIGIN AND DEVELOPMENT OF TRINIDAD'S FOLK SONG.

ETTINGER, J. van

53.012   **CU**   1926/ Een vergeten hoofdstuk uit de geschiedenis van het Curacaosche 27 circulatie-bankwezen [A forgotten chapter from the history of circulation banking on Curacao].

53.013   **SR**   1927/ Pogingen tot oprichting van eene circulatie-bank in Suriname 1849- 28 1864 [Attempts to establish a circulation bank in Surinam].

53.014   **CU**   1928/ Munt- en bankwezen in Curacao (1880-1905) [Money and banking in 29 Curacao (1880-1905)].

53.015   **CU**   1930/ Bankwezen in Curacao 1906-1928 [Banking institutions in Curacao, 31 1906-1928].

EUWENS, P. A.

5.049   **CU**   1919/ Curacao's eeuwfeest, 1816-1916 [Curacao's centennial, 1816-1916]. 20 *W I G* 1(2): 241-263.   [COL]

5.050   **CU**   1924/ De eerste dagen van het Engelsche bewind op Curacao in 1807 [The 25 first days of English rule on Curacao in 1807]. *W I G* 6:575-58].   [COL]

40.060   **CU**   1928/ De oudste kaarten van het eiland Curacao [The oldest maps of the 29 island Curacao].

15.012   **CU**   1930/ De eerste Jood op Curacao [The first Jew on Curacao]. 31

EVANS, LUTHER HARRIS

5.051   **UV**   1945 THE VIRGIN ISLANDS: FROM NAVAL BASE TO NEW DEAL. [Ann Arbor?] Michigan, Ann Arbor Press, 365p. [37]   [COL]

FABIUS, G. J.

47.011   **NA/**   1914 Het leenstelsel van de West-Indische Compagnie [The feudal system
             BG   of the West-Indian Company].

FARLEY, RAWLE

8.024   **BG**   1953 The rise of village settlements of British Guiana.
8.025   **BG**   1954 Rise of a peasantry in British Guiana.
44.058   **BG**   1955 The economic circumstances of the British annexation of British Guiana (1795-1815).
16.010   **BG**   1955 The substance and the shadow—a study of the relations between white planters and free coloured in a slave society in British Guiana.
37.110   **BG**   1955 The unification of British Guiana.
32.062   **BC**   1958 UNIVERSITIES AND THE EDUCATION OF WORKING PEOPLE.

FARRAR, P. A.

23.044   **BB**   1935 Christ Church.
15.013   **BB**   1942 The Jews in Barbados.

FAUCHILLE, PAUL

39.027   **BG**   1905 LE CONFLIT DE LIMITES ENTRE LE BRÉSIL ET LA GRANDE-BRETAGNE ET LA SENTENCE ARBITRALE DU ROI D'ITALIE [THE BOUNDARY DISPUTE

BETWEEN BRAZIL AND GREAT BRITAIN AND THE ARBITRATION RULING OF THE KING OF ITALY].

FAWKES, M. A.
28.150   TR   1957 A short history of yaws in Trinidad.

FELHOEN KRAAL, JOHANNA L. G.
1.018   NC   1956/ Libraries and archives for research in West Indian history.
               57

FERTIG, NORMAN ROSS
38.040   BC   1958 THE CLOSER UNION MOVEMENT IN THE BRITISH WEST INDIES.

FINDLAY, G. G. & HOLDSWORTH, W. W.
23.045   BC   1921 THE HISTORY OF THE WESLEYAN METHODIST MISSIONARY SOCIETY, v. 2.

FISHER, RUTH ANNA
15.015   JM   1943 Note on Jamaica.

FLETCHER, W. E. L.
52.027   BB   1961 The Barbados Railway.

FLOCH, HERVE ALEXANDRE
28.166   FG   1952/ La fièvre jaune en Guyane Francaise [Yellow fever in French
               53 Guiana].

FLORES, GIOVANNI
15.016   BH   1958 Gli italiani de Manatee [The Italians of Manatee].

FORT, Rev.
23.047   DM/   1903 La Dominique et Sainte Lucie [Dominica and St. Lucia].
          SV

FOSSUM, PAUL R.
39.028   BG   1928 The Anglo-Venezuelan boundary controversy.

FRANKLIN, C. B.
23.048   TR   1934 A CENTURY AND A QUARTER OF HANOVER METHODIST CHURCH HISTORY
               1809-1934.

FREEMAN, WILLIAM G.
58.045   BC   1930 The historic Bourbon cane.

FROIDEVAUX, HENRI
32.068   FC   1900 L'OEUVRE SCOLAIRE DE LA FRANCE DANS NOS COLONIES [THE FRENCH
               EDUCATIONAL TASK IN THE COLONIES].
3.115   FG   1901 Les "lettres édifiantes" et la description de la mission de Kourou
               [The "edifying letters" and a description of the Kourou mission].

FURNESS, ALAN
5.052   JM   1962 The Jamaican coffee boom and John Mackeson. *Jam Hist Rev* 3(3),
               Mar.: 10-21. [45, 63]   [COL]

GAAY FORTMAN, B. de

44.061	CU	1919 Curacao tegen het einde der West-Indische Compagnie [Curacao's position during the final years of the West Indian Company].
5.053	SE	1920/ Eene bladzijde uit de geschiedenis van St. Eustatius [A page from 21 the history of St. Eustatius]. *W I G* 2:558-572. *[COL]*
5.054	CU	1921/ Een gevecht voor de haven van Curacao [A fight over the harbor of 22 Curacao]. *W I G* 3:385-392. *[COL]*
5.055	CU	1924/ Een belangrijk dagboek [An important diary]. *W I G* 6:240-270. 25 *[COL]*
5.056	CU	1924/ Een bladzijde uit de geschiedenis van Curacao [A page from the 25 history of Curacao]. *W I G* 6:169-178. [37] *[COL]*
53.019	CU	1925/ Munt- en geldmoeilijkheden op Curacao voor 1 honderd jaar [Coin 26 and money difficulties in Curacao 100 years ago].
5.057	CU	1926/ Een wonderlijke onderneming tegen Porto-Rico [A strange under- 27 taking against Puerto Rico]. *W I G* 8:389-398. *[COL]*
2.081	CU	1927/ Curacao en onderhorige eilanden [Curacao and subordinate islands]. 29
5.058	SR	1928/ In Suriname vóór honderd jaar [In Surinam a hundred years ago]. 29 *W I G* 10:483-495. [6, 37] *[COL]*
53.020	CU	1928/ Munt- en geldmoeilijkheden op Curacao vóór honderd jaar [Coin 29 and money difficulties in Curacao a hundred years ago].
44.076	NA	1929/ De West-Indische Maatschappij [The West Indian Company]. 30
37.127	CU	1934/ Staatkundige geschiedenis van Curacao [Political history of 35 Curacao].
5.059	CU	1935/ Curacao in 1782. *W I G* 17:349-364. *[COL]* 36
44.081	CU	1935/ Staatkundige geschiedenis van Curacao: de Curacaosche begrooting 36 voor 1935 [Political history of Curacao: the budget of Curacao for the year 1935].
5.060	CU	1936/ Pamfletten over Curacao [Documents about Curacao]. *W I G* 18: 37 353-372. *[COL]*
44.082	CU	1936/ Staatkundige geschiedenis van Curacao: de Curacaosche begrooting 37 voor 1936 [Political history of Curacao: the budget of Curacao for the year 1936].
47.017	CU	1936/ Twee verzoekschriften aan den koning over den landbouwpolitiek 37 van Gouverneur van Raders in Curacao [Two petitions to the king about the agricultural policy of Governor van Raders in Curacao].
44.083	CU	1937 Staatkundige geschiedenis van Curacao: de Curacaosche begrooting voor 1937 [Political history of Curacao: the budget of Curacao for the year 1937].
5.061	CU	1938 Curacao onder de regeering van Koningin Wilhelmina 1898-1938 [Curacao under the government of Queen Wilhelmina 1898-1938]. *W I G* 20:262-269. [66] *[COL]*
44.085	CU	1938 Staatkundige geschiedenis van Curacao: de Curacaosche begrooting voor 1938 [Political history of Curacao: the budget of Curacao for the year 1938].
44.086	CU	1939 Staatkundige geschiedenis van Curacao: de Curacaosche begrooting van 1939 [Political history of Curacao: the budget of Curacao for the year 1939].
44.087	CU	1940 Staatkundige geschiedenis van Curacao: de Curacaosche begrooting voor 1940 [Political history of Curacao: the budget of Curacao for the year 1940].

5.062 NL 1942/ Curacao en onderhoorige eilanden Bonaire en Aruba van 1804-
     43 1866: het bestuur van den Gouverneur J. P. Changuion [Curacao
       and the subordinate islands Bonaire and Aruba from 1804-1866: the
       rule of the Governor J. P. Changuion]. *W I G* 24:361-382; 25:1-28.
                          [COL]

23.051 BG 1942 De geschiedenis der Luthersche geméente in Berbice [The history
       of the Lutheran congregation in Berbice].

37.130 CU 1943 Aanvulling van de Encyclopaedie van Nederlandsch West-Indië:
       De gouverneurs van Curacao [Addition to the Encyclopedia of the
       Netherlands West Indies: The governors of Curacao].

5.063 CU 1944/ De kolonie Curacao onder Engelsch bestuur van 1807 tot 1816 [The
     45 colony Curacao under English rule from 1807 to 1816]. *W I G* 26:
       229-246.   *[COL]*

37.132 CU 1947 Schets van de politieke geschiedenis der Nederlandsche Antillen
       in de twintigste eeuw (Curacao) [Sketch of the political history
       of the Netherlands Antilles in the twentieth century (Curacao)].

3.120 SR 1948 Een vijfdaags bezoek aan Suriname in 1825 [A five-day visit to
       Surinam in 1825].

5.064 CU 1960/ Over Curacao in 1829 [About Curacao in 1829]. *N W I G* 40:226-227.
     61   *[COL]*

GAILLARD, ROBERT
5.065 FA 1953 En parcourant les îsles des Antilles [Through the Antilles].
       Monte Carlo, Les Beaux Livres, 314p. [2]   *[NYP]*

GIBBONS, WILLIAM J.
7.024 GC 1961 Trends in Latin American population.

GLASS, RUTH
21.007 JM 1962 Ashes of discontent.

GOCKING, C. V.
37.141 JM 1960 Early constitutional history of Jamaica (with special reference to
       the period 1838-1866).

GODFREY, J. E.
37.142 BG 1912 Village administration and local government in British Guiana.

GOEJE, C. H. de
13.031 SR 1930/ Een oud bericht over Arowakken en Karaïben [An old report about
     31 Arawaks and Caribs].

13.032 SR 1931/ Oudheden uit Suriname: op zoek naar de Amazonen [Antiquities from
     32 Surinam: in search of Amazons].

40.071 GC 1936/ De namen der Antillen [The names of the Antilles].
     37

5.066 GC 1936/ Op den oceaan voor en na Columbus [On the ocean before and after
     37 Columbus]. *W I G* 18:65-81. [3, 52]

GOERKE, HEINZ
28.233 JM 1956 The life and scientific works of Dr. John Quier, practitioner of
       physic and surgery, Jamaica: 1738-1822:

GOMES, G. A.
28.238   BG   1934 Some medical worthies of the past in the colony: notes and reminiscences.

GONGGRIJP, J. W.
4.051   SR   1920/ Sporen van voorhistorischen bewoners van Suriname [Traces of 21 prehistoric inhabitants of Surinam].

GOODWIN, R. S. D.
5.067   AT   1928 Fort James, Antigua. *W I Comm Circ* 43(773), May 17:183-184. [*NYP*]

GOODWIN, WILLIAM B.
5.068   JM   1946 SPANISH AND ENGLISH RUINS IN JAMAICA. Boston, Meador, 239p. [*COL*]

GORDON, SHIRLEY C.
32.070   TR   1962 The Keenan report, 1869.
32.071   BC   1963 A CENTURY OF WEST INDIAN EDUCATION.
32.072   BB   1963 Documents which have guided educational policy in the West Indies: the Mitchinson report, Barbados 1875.
32.073   JM   1963 Documents which have guided educational policy in the West Indies —no. 5: report upon the condition of the juvenile population of Jamaica, 1879.
32.074   TR   1963 Documents which have guided educational policy in the West Indies —no. 3: Patrick Joseph Keenan's report 1869.
32.076   JM   1964 Documents which have guided educational policy in the West Indies: the Lumb report, Jamaica, 1898.

GORDON, WILLIAM E.
44.093   JM   1957 Imperial policy decisions in the economic history of Jamaica, 1664-1934.

GOSLINGA, C. CH.
23.058   GC   1956 Kerk, Kroon en Cariben [Church, crown and Caribs].

GOULD, CLARENCE P.
51.059   FA   1939 Trade between the Windward Islands and the continental colonies of the French Empire, 1683-1763.

GOVEIA, ELSA V.
5.069   BC   1956 A STUDY OF THE HISTORIOGRAPHY OF THE BRITISH WEST INDIES TO THE END OF THE NINETEENTH CENTURY. Mexico, Instituto Panamericano de Geografía e Historia, 177p.   [*RIS*]
66.056   BC   1965 Small societies in transition: past history and present planning in the West Indies.

GOYENECHE, EUGENE
5.070   MT   1956 Historical monuments of Martinique. *Caribbean* 10(5), Dec.: 123-125. [35]   [*COL*]

GOYHENECHE, E. & NICOLAS, MAURICE
5.071   FA   1956 DES ÎLES ET DES HOMMES [THE ISLANDS AND THE PEOPLE]. Fort-de-France, Editions des Horizons caraibes, 174p. [13, 27]   [*RIS*]

GRAHAM, J. W.
32.080   JM   1938 A century of education in Jamaica.

GRAHAM, GERALD S.
51.060   BC   1941 The origin of free ports in British North America.

GREAVES, IDA C.
53.022   BC   1952/Money and currency in Barbados.
                  53

GREENIDGE, C. W. W.
38.048   BB   1956 Barbados and the Pope Hennessy riots.
5.072   FC   1958 The French West Indies. *J Bar Mus Hist Soc*. 26(1), Nov.: 3-9.
                  [*AMN*]

GROOT, SILVIA W. de
14.004   SR   1963 VAN ISOLATIE NAAR INTEGRATIE: DE SURINAAMSE MARRONS EN HUN
                  AFSTAMMELINGEN, OFFICIELE DOCUMENTEN BETREFFENDE DE DJOEKA'S
                  (1845-1863) [FROM ISOLATION TO INTEGRATION: THE SURINAM MAROONS
                  AND THEIR DESCENDANTS, OFFICIAL DOCUMENTS CONCERNING THE DJUKA
                  TRIBE (1845-1863)].

GUASCO, ALEXANDRE
23.059   FG   1903 La Guyane francaise [French Guiana].

GUERRA Y SANCHEZ, RAMIRO
58.050   BB   1927 AZÚCAR Y POBLACIÓN EN LAS ANTILLAS [SUGAR AND POPULATION IN THE
                  WEST INDIES].

GUIRAL, PAUL
17.012   FA   1911 L'IMMIGRATION RÉGLEMENTÉE AUX ANTILLES FRANCAISES ET À LA
                  RÉUNION [REGULATED IMMIGRATION INTO THE FRENCH ANTILLES AND
                  REUNION].

GULCHER, C. F.
59.014   SR   1943 Een Surinaamsch koffieplanter uit de 18de eeuw (S.L. Neale)
                  [A Surinam coffee planter from the 18th century (S.L. Neale)].

HALL, DOUGLAS GORDON
45.011   BC   1954 The social and economic background to sugar in slave days (with
                  special reference to Jamaica).
44.096   JM   1959 FREE JAMAICA, 1838-1865: AN ECONOMIC HISTORY.
58.051   BC   1961 Incalculability as a feature of sugar production during the eighteenth
                  century.

HALLEMA, A.
51.062   NC   1933/Friesland en de voormalige compagnieën voor den handel op Oost
                  34 en West [Friesland and the former companies that traded with the
                  East and West].
37.153   CU   1934/Eenige gegevens over oude gevangenissen, aard der gevangenisstraf,
                  35 etc. op Curacao gedurende de 17de en 18de eeuw [Some data about
                  old prisons, nature of imprisonment, etc. on Curacao during the 17th
                  and 18th centuries].

37.154   SR/   1934/ Het jaar 1872 in de geschiedenis van het gevangeniswezen in de
           CU   35 West [The year 1872 in the history of the prison-system in the West].

HAMELBERG, J. H. J.
5.073   NL   1901 DE NEDERLANDERS OP DE WEST-INDISCHE EILANDEN [THE DUTCH ON
                      THE WEST INDIAN ISLANDS]. Amsterdam, J. H. de Bussy, 243p. [*COL*]

HAMILTON, BRUCE
37.157   BB   1944 The Barbados Executive Committee: an experiment in government.
38.049   BB   1950/ Barbados and British West Indian Confederation, 1871-1885.
                  51
38.050   BB   1956 BARBADOS AND THE CONFEDERATION QUESTION 1871-1885.

HARING, CLARENCE HENRY
5.074   GC   1910 THE BUCANEERS IN THE WEST INDIES IN THE XVII CENTURY. New York,
                      E. P. Dutton, 298p. (B. A. thesis, Oxford University, May 1909.)
                                                                          [*COL*]

HARLOW, VINCENT TODD
3.132   BC   1924 COLONISING EXPEDITIONS TO THE WEST INDIES AND GUIANA, 1623-1667.
5.075   BB   1926 A HISTORY OF BARBADOS 1625-1685. Oxford, Clarendon Press, 347p.
                                                                          [*COL*]

HARLOW, VINCENT TODD & MADDEN, FREDERICK
2.091   BC   1953 BRITISH COLONIAL DEVELOPMENTS 1774-1834: SELECT DOCUMENTS.

HARPER, BESSIE
5.076   AT   1945 Historic Antigua. *Can-W I Mag* Aug.-Sept.: 17-21.   [*NYP*]
5.077   AT   1950 Antigua "historically speaking." *Can-W I Mag* 40(10), Oct.: 19, 21.
                                                                          [*NYP*]

HARRIS, Sir C. ALEXANDER, ed.
3.137   GG   1928 A RELATION OF A VOYAGE TO GUIANA BY ROBERT HARCOURT 1613.

HARRIS, Sir C. ALEXANDER & VILLIERS, J. A. J. de, comp.
2.094   BG   1911 STORM VAN'S GRAVESANDE: THE RISE OF BRITISH GUIANA.

HARRIS, COLERIDGE
37.160   WW   1960 The constitutional history of the Windwards.

HARRIS, Sir JOHN
32.090   BC   1936 The vicissitudes of a legacy.

HARRISON, Sir JOHN B.
42.014   BG   1926 The climate of British Guiana.

HART, FRANCIS RUSSELL
5.078   GC   1922 ADMIRALS OF THE CARIBBEAN. Boston, Houghton, 203p.   [*COL*]

HART, RICHARD
50.062   JM   1952 THE ORIGIN AND DEVELOPMENT OF THE PEOPLE OF JAMAICA.

HARTLEY, HAZEL MORSE
46.088   BB   1949 Of the produce of the plantations.

HARTOG, JOHAN

23.062   AR   1952 Aruba's oudste kerk 1750-1816-1952 [Aruba's oldest church 1750-1816-1952].

5.079   AR   1953 ARUBA ZOALS HET WAS, ZOALS HET WERD, VAN DE TIJD DER INDIANEN TOT OP HEDEN [ARUBA AS IT WAS AND AS IT BECAME, FROM THE TIME OF THE INDIANS TO THE PRESENT]. [Oranjestad?] Aruba, de Wit, 451p. [2]   [*AGS*]

5.080   AR   1961 ARUBA, PAST AND PRESENT. Oranjestad, Aruba, D. J. de Wit, 451p. [2]   [*NYP*]

HASKELL, H. N.

32.091   BB   1941/Some notes on the foundation and history of Harrison College. 52

HAYNES, EDMUND C.; HAYNES, A. PERCY & HAYNES, EDMUND S. P., eds.

5.081   BB   1910 NOTES BY GENERAL ROBERT HAYNES OF NEW CASTLE AND CLIFTON HALL PLANTATIONS, BARBADOS AND OTHER DOCUMENTS OF FAMILY INTEREST. London, Argus Print. Co., 32p.

HEARNE, JOHN

19.016   JM   1963 European heritage and Asian influence in Jamaica.

HEIDLER, J. B.

5.082   JM   1929 The Jamaica insurrection and English men of letters. *Philol Q* 7(2), Apr.: 214-218. [37]   [*COL*]

HENDRICK, S. PURCELL

23.063   JM   1911 A SKETCH OF THE HISTORY OF THE CATHEDRAL CHURCH OF ST. JAGO DE LA VEGA, SPANISH TOWN IN THE PARISH OF ST. CATHERINE, JAMAICA.

HENGEL, J. W. A. van

53.023   CU   1938 De Curacaosche realen en stuivers van 1821 en 1822 [The Curacao realen and stivers of 1821 and 1822].

HENRY, ARTHUR

5.083   FG   1950 LA GUYANE FRANCAISE: SON HISTOIRE 1604-1946 [FRENCH GUIANA: ITS HISTORY 1604-1946]. Cayenne, Impr. Paul Laporte, 336p. [*RIS*]

HERMANS, HANS G.

37.173   NC   1958 Constitutional development of the Netherlands Antilles and Surinam.

HERMES, JOAO SEVERIANO da FONSECA

39.029   BH   1939 Questão de limites entre Guatemala e Honduras Ingleza [Boundary controversy between Guatemala and British Honduras].

HEYLIGERS, J. C. TH. G. J.

5.084   SK   1933/Brimstone Hill, "The Gibraltar of the West Indies." *W I G* 15:191-200. 34   [*COL*]

HIGHAM, C. S. S.

5.085   LW   1921 THE DEVELOPMENT OF THE LEEWARD ISLANDS UNDER THE RESTORATION,

1660-1688: A STUDY OF THE FOUNDATIONS OF THE OLD COLONIAL SYSTEM. Cambridge, Cambridge University Press, 266p.   [COL]

37.176 LW/ 1926 The General Assembly of the Leeward Islands.
        GR

37.177 BC   1926 Sir Henry Taylor and the establishment of crown colony government in the West Indies.

HILDEBRAND, INGEGERD

5.086   SB   1951 DEN SVENSKA COLONIN S:T BARTHÉLEMY OCH VÄSTINDISKA KOMPANIET FRAM TILL 1796 [THE SWEDISH COLONY ST. BARTHELEMY AND THE WEST INDIAN COMPANY UP TO 1796]. Växjö, [Sweden?] Smålandspostens boktr., 350p. (Ph. D. dissertation.)   [NYP]

HILFMAN, P.A.

15.019 SR   1909 Notes on the history of the Jews in Surinam.

HILL, Mrs. A. St.

7.032   BB   1937/ A census of the island of Barbados, West Indies.
             42

HILL, LUKE M.

36.008 BG   1911 Nomenclature of Georgetown: its streets and districts.
36.009 BG   1915 The municipality of Georgetown.

HINCKLEY, THEODORE C.

51.067 JM   1963 The decline of Caribbean smuggling.

HIRST, GEORGE S.S.

5.087   CM   [n.d.] NOTES ON THE HISTORY OF THE CAYMAN ISLANDS. Kingston, P.A. Benjamin Manufacturing Co., published privately.

HISS, PHILIP HANSON

5.088   NA   1943 NETHERLANDS AMERICA: THE DUTCH TERRITORIES IN THE WEST. London, Robert Hale, 225p. [44]   [RIS]

HOETINK, HARRY

8.031   CU   1958 HET PATROON VAN DE OUDE CARACAOSE SAMENLEVING [THE PATTERN OF THE OLD CURACAO SOCIETY].
10.019 CU   1960 Curacao como sociedad segmentada [Curacao as a segmented society].
16.017 CU/ 1961 Diferencias en relaciones raciales entre Curazao y Surinam [Differences in racial relations between Curacao and Surinam].
        SR

HOLLIS, Sir CLAUD

5.089   TR   1941 A BRIEF HISTORY OF TRINIDAD UNDER THE SPANISH CROWN. [Port of Spain?] Trinidad, A.L. Rhodes, Govt. Printer, 108p.   [NYP]

HOTTEN, JOHN C., ed.

17.013 BB   1931 THE ORIGINAL LISTS OF PERSONS OF QUALITY, EMIGRANTS, RELIGIOUS EXILES, POLITICAL REBELS, SERVING MEN ... WHO WENT FROM GREAT BRITAIN TO THE AMERICAN PLANTATIONS 1600-1700.

HOWARD, RICHARD A.

41.140 MS   1961 Why Montserrat?

HOY, DON R.

46.093   GD   1961 AGRICULTURAL LAND USE OF GUADELOUPE.

HOYER, W. M.

53.024   CU   1936/ De Curacaosche muntspeciën [The coins of Curacao].
                  37
40.091   AR   1938 De naam "Aruba" [The name "Aruba"].
40.092   CU   1938 De naam "Curacao" [The name "Curacao"].

HOYOS, F. A.

5.090   BB   [n.d.] PRINCESS MARGARET AND THE MEMORIES OF OUR PAST. [Bridgetown?]
                  Barbados, Advocate Co., 19p.   [RIS]
32.101   BB   1945 TWO HUNDRED YEARS: A HISTORY OF THE LODGE SCHOOL.
5.091   BB   1953 OUR COMMON HERITAGE. [Bridgetown?] Barbados, Advocate Press,
                  147p. [32]   [RIS]

HUBBARD, LUCIUS L.

5.092   GC   1931 Did Columbus discover the islands Antigua and St. Martin? *Geogr
                  Rev* 21(4), Oct.: 584-597.   [AGS]

HUGHES, COLIN A.

38.056   BC   1958 Experiments towards closer union in the British West Indies.

HUGHES, H. B. L.

23.072   JM   1945 The impact on Jamaica of the Evangelical Revival.
5.093   CM   1946 Notes on the Cayman Islands. *Jam Hist Rev* 1(2), Dec.: 154-158.
                                                                            [COL]

HULLU, J. de

5.094   CU   1913 Curacao in 1817. *Bijd Volk Ned-Indie* 67:563-609.
5.095   SE   1913 St. Eustatius in 1819, door A. de Veer, medegedeeld door J. de
                  Hullu [St. Eustatius in 1819, by A. de Veer, communicated by J. de
                  Hullu]. *Bijd Volk Ned-Indie* 68:429-444.
5.096   SE   1919/ Het leven op Sint Eustatius omstreeks 1792 [Life on St. Eustatius
                  20 around 1792]. *W I G* 1(2): 144-150.   [COL]
5.097   NW   1919 St. Eustatius, St. Martin en Saba op 't laatst van de 18de eeuw
                  [St. Eustatius, St. Martin and Saba at the end of the 18th century].
                  W I G 1(1): 385-393.   [COL]
51.069   SE   1921/ De handel van St. Eustatius in 1786 [The commerce of St. Eustatius
                  22 in 1786].
5.098   BN   1922/ Bonaire in 1816. *W I G* 4:504-512.   [COL]
                  23
37.189   NC   1922/ Memorie van den Amerikaanschen Raad over de Hollandsche bezit-
                  23 tingen in West-Indie in Juli 1806 [Memorandum of the American
                  Council about the Dutch possessions in the West Indies in July 1806].
5.099   AR   1923/ Aruba in 1816. *W I G* 5:371-382.   [COL]
                  24

HUMPHREYS, ROBERT ARTHUR

37.190   BH   1948 The Anglo-Guatemalan dispute.
37.191   BH   1961 THE DIPLOMATIC HISTORY OF BRITISH HONDURAS, 1638-1901.

HURAULT, JEAN
19.021   FG   1960 Histoire des noirs réfugiés boni de la Guyane Francaise [History of the black Boni refugees of French Guiana].

HURTADO AGUILAR, LUIS A.
39.030   BH   [1958?] BELICE ES DE GUATEMALA: TRATADOS, SITUACIÓN JURÍDICA, ACTUACIONES, OPINIONES [BELIZE BELONGS TO GUATEMALA: TREATIES, JURIDICAL SITUATION, PROCEEDINGS, RULINGS].

HURWITZ, SAMUEL J. & EDITH
15.020   JM   1965 The New World sets an example for the old: the Jews of Jamaica and political rights 1661-1831.

HUTCHINSON, J. B. & STEPHENS, S. G.
61.017   TB   1944 Note on the "French" or "small-seeded" cotton grown in the West Indies in the 18th century.

HUTTON, J. E.
23.073   GC   [1922?] A HISTORY OF MORAVIAN MISSIONS.

JACOBS, H. P.
5.100   GC   1956 History galore. *Caribbean* 9(9), Apr.: 194-200.   [*COL*]

JACQUEMIN, CH.
5.101   FC   1936 AUX ÎLES CARAÏBES, ANTILLES FRANCAISES [IN THE CARIBBEAN ISLANDS OF THE FRENCH ANTILLES]. Paris, Impr. Marcel Etaix, 225p.   [*COL*]

JAMESON, JOHN FRANKLIN
51.072   SE   1903 St. Eustatius in the American Revolution.

JARVIS, JOSE ANTONIO
5.102   UV   1938 BRIEF HISTORY OF THE VIRGIN ISLANDS. St. Thomas Art Shop, 258p.
[*NYP*]

JENKINS, CHARLES FRANCIS
23.074   TT   1923 Tortola, the chief of the British Virgin Islands.

JESSE, C.
23.075   FA   1960 Religion among the early slaves in the French Antilles.
5.103   SL   1962 OUTLINES OF ST. LUCIA'S HISTORY. 2d ed. [Bridgetown?] St. Lucia Archaeological & Historical Society, 61p.   [*RIS*]
5.104   GC   1963 The Spanish cédula of December 23, 1511, on the subject of the Caribs. *Car Q* 9(3), Sept.: 22-32. [13]   [*RIS*]

JONKERS, A.
66.075   NC   1953 Hoofdtrekken van de ontwikkeling van Suriname en de Nederlandse Antillen [Main features of the development of Surinam and the Dutch Antilles].

JORDAN, WINTHROP D.
16.021   BC   1962 American chiaroscuro: the status and definition of mulattoes in the British Colonies.

JOSA, F. P. LUIGI

23.076   BC   1910 ENGLISH CHURCH HISTORY OF THE WEST INDIAN PROVINCE.

JOSA, GUY

58.061   MT   1931 LES INDUSTRIES DU SUCRE ET DU RHUM A LA MARTINIQUE (1639-1931) [THE SUGAR AND RUM INDUSTRIES IN MARTINIQUE (1639-1931)].

JUDAH, GEORGE FORTUNATUS

15.022   JM   1909 The Jews' tribute in Jamaica.

JUNKER, L.

14.012   SR   1932/ Het einde van een dynastie—de dood van Jankosoe [The end of a
              33 dynasty—the death of Jankosoe].

KALFF, S.

5.105   SR   1924/ Westindische gedenkpenningen [West Indian commemorative medals].
             25 *W I G* 6:223-237.   [*COL*]

5.106   NA   1926/ Iets over Peter Stuyvesant [Some facts about Peter Stuyvesant].
             27 *W I G* 8:517-530.   [*COL*]

5.107   SE   1926/ Uit de geschiedenis van St. Eustatius [From the history of St.
             27 Eustatius]. *W I G* 8:405-420.   [*COL*]

37.210   NC   1927/ Vreemdelinger in het Westindische leger [Foreigners in the West-
             28 Indian army].

15.023   SR   1928 Javanese emigrants in Suriname.

37.211   CU   1931/ Curacaosche troebelen [Troubles of Curacao].
             32

KASTEEL, ANNEMARIE C. T.

37.212   NA   1956 DE STAATKUNDIGE ONTWIKKELING DER NEDERLANDSE ANTILLEN [THE POLITICAL EVOLUTION OF THE NETHERLANDS ANTILLES].

KAYSERLING, M.

15.024   JM   1900 The Jews in Jamaica and Daniel Israel Lopez Laguna.

KEITH, ALICE B.

51.077   BC   1948 Relaxations in the British restrictions on the American trade with the British West Indies, 1783-1802.

KELSICK, CECIL A.

37.214   LW   1960 Constitutional history of the Leewards.

KERVEGANT, D.

59.026   MT   1932 Le caféier à la Martinique [Coffee growing in Martinique].

KESLER, C. K.

23.079   SR   1923/ Nils Otto Tank (1800-1864).
             24

51.078   SR   1926/ Amsterdamsche bankiers en de West in de 18de eeuw [Amsterdam
             27 bankers and the West in the 18th century].

52.044   CU   1926/ De interoceanische verbinding voor 100 jaar [The inter-ocean con-
             27 nection 100 years ago].

25.056   NA   1926/ De naam Antillen [The name "Antilles"].
             27

| 5.108 | TB | 1928/ Tobago, een vergeten Nederlandsche Kolonie [Tobago, a forgotten 29 Dutch colony]. *W I G* 10:527-534. [3] [COL] |

5.108   TB   1928/ Tobago, een vergeten Nederlandsche Kolonie [Tobago, a forgotten
                 29 Dutch colony]. *W I G* 10:527-534. [3]   [COL]
28.307   BG   1929/ Een Duitsch medicus in Essequebo in de laatste jaren der 18e
                 30 eeuw [A German medical doctor in Essequibo during the last years
                 of the 18th century].
5.109   SM   1932/ Heeft Columbus St. Maarten ontdekt? [Did Columbus discover St.
                 33 Maarten?] *W I G* 14:76-78.   [COL]
16.022   SR   1932/ Na 100 jaar: branden in Paramaribo [After 100 years: fires in
                 33 Paramaribo].
23.080   NC/   1933/ Graaf von Zinzendorf in Holland [Count von Zinzendorf in Holland].
          ST   34
15.025   SR   1938 Javenen in Suriname reeds in het jaar 1714? [Were the Javanese
                 already in Surinam in the year 1714?]
23.081   SR   1939 Een Moravische Zuster uit de 18e eeuw: Anna Maria Kersten geb.
                 Tonn 1723-1807 [A Moravian Sister from the 18th century: Anna
                 Maria Kersten neé Tonn, 1723-1807].
5.110   MT   1941 Martinique: de geboorteplaats van een keizerin [Martinique: The
                 birthplace of an empress]. *W I G* 23:112-126.   [COL]
5.111   MT   1941 De ontdekking en de naam van het eiland Martinique [The discovery
                 and the name of the island Martinique]. *W I G* 23:340-345.   [COL]
5.112   TR   1941 Trinidad, het grootste en schoonste der Kleine Antillen [Trinidad,
                 the largest and most beautiful island of the Lesser Antilles]. *W I G*
                 23:257-268. [3]   [COL]
5.113   BB   1942 Barbados. *W I G* 24:201-213. [3]   [COL]
23.082   BG   1942 Moeilijkheden met betrekking tot eedsaflegging en het dragen van
                 wapenen in Berbice in de 18de eeuw [Problems about oath-taking
                 and carrying of weapons in Berbice in the 18th century].
5.114   GC   1944/ Hoe Spanje zijn bezittingen in de Caraïbische Zee verkreeg,
                 45 organiseerde en—verloor [How Spain obtained, organized, and—lost
                 its possessions in the Caribbean Sea]. *W I G* 26:39-60, 65-83. [COL]

KING, GEORGE H.

5.115   SK   1933 Sir Timothy's guns. *W I Comm Circ* 48(895), Jan. 19: 25-26.   [NYP]
5.116   SK   1940 The story of Brimstone Hill. *Can-W I Mag* 29(11), Nov.:19-21. [NYP]
5.117   SK   1954 BRIMSTONE HILL, THE GIBRALTAR OF THE WEST INDIES. 5th ed. Basse-
                 terre, St. Kitts, St. Kitts Printery, 11p.

KINGSBURY, ROBERT C.

43.082   CR   1960 Carriacou: an old world in the new.

KLERK, CORNELIS JOHANNES MARIA de

50.073   SR   1942 De Britisch-Indiërs in Suriname [The British Indians in Surinam].

KLEYNTJENS, J.

5.118   TB   1949 De Koerlandse kolonisatiepogingen op Tobago [The Courlande
                 attempts to colonize Tobago]. *W I G* 30:193-216.   [COL]

KLINGBERG, FRANK J.

32.112   BC   1939 The Lady Mico Charity Schools in the British West Indies, 1835-
                 1842.

KNAPLUND, PAUL

38.064   BC   1957 Introduction to Federation of the West Indies.

KNAPPERT, L.

23.087   CU   1925/ Koning Willem I en de Protestantsche gemeente op Curacao [King
26   William the First and the Protestant community on Curacao].

23.089   SM   1928/ Een heksenproces op Sint Maarten [A witch trial on St. Maarten].
29

5.119   NW   1929/ Geschiedenis van de Nederlandsche Bovenwindsche eilanden in de
33   18de eeuw [History of the Dutch Windward Islands in the 18th
century]. *W I G* 11:353-386, 421-436, 513-541, 559-574 (1929/30);
12:31-42, 73-84, 161-178, 279-290, 325-338, 423-440, 471-484,
573-590 (1930/31); 13:177-202, 249-268, 545-568 (1931/32); 14:
25-41 (1932/33).   *[COL]*

5.120   SE   1929/ Verzuimd Sint Eustatius [Neglected St. Eustatius]. *W I G* 11:
30   159-174. [3]   *[COL]*

23.090   CU   1939   Wigboldt Rasvelt en zijne gemeente op Curacao, 1730-1757 [Wig-
boldt Rasvelt and his congregation on Curacao].

KNOX, GRAHAM

37.217   JM   1963   British colonial policy and the problems of establishing a free
society in Jamaica, 1838-1865.

KOCH, L.

23.091   UV   1905   Den danske mission i Vestindien [The Danish mission in the West
Indies].

KUNZ, JOSEF L.

39.032   BH   1946   Guatemala vs. Great Britain: in re Belice.

LALUNG, HENRY de

13.046   GC   1948   LES CARAÏBES, UN PEUPLE ÉTRANGE AUJOURD'HUI DISPARU [THE CARIBS,
AN EXOTIC AND NOW EXTINCT PEOPLE].

LANGEMEYER, F. S.

52.051   SM   1937   Eene reis naar Sint Maarten in oorlogstijd [A voyage to St. Maarten
in time of war].

5.121   SM   1940   Ver van's werelds strijdgewoel: St. Maarten 1918-1920 [Far from
the troubles of the world: St. Maarten 1918-1920]. *W I G* 22:193-219.
[3]   *[COL]*

LANJOUW, J. & UITTIEN, H.

41.156   SR   1935/ Surinaamsche geneeskruiden in den tijd van Linnaeus [Surinam's
36   medicinal herbs during the age of Linnaeus].

LARA, ORUNO

5.122   GD   [1922?] LA GUADELOUPE—PHYSIQUE, ÉCONOMIQUE, AGRICOLE, COMMERCIALE,
FINANCIÈRE, POLITIQUE ET SOCIALE [PHYSICAL, ECONOMIC, AGRICUL-
TURAL, COMMERCIAL, FINANCIAL, POLITICAL AND SOCIAL ASPECTS OF
GUADELOUPE]. Paris, Nouvelle librairie universelle, 340p.   *[SCH]*

LARET, W. F. H.

51.082   SR   1949   Honderd jaren vrijhandel in Suriname [A hundred years of free trade
in Surinam].

LASHLEY, L. A. G. O.

37.223   SR   1954/ Het Koninkrijk is dood, leve het Koninkrijk [The Kingdom is dead,
55   long live the Kingdom].

LATOUR, M. D.

7.041   CU   1936/Familienamen op Curacao [Family names on Curacao].
               37

28.324   CU   1955/Het Sint Elisabeths Gasthuis op Curacao 1855-1955 [The St.
               56 Elisabeths Hospital on Curacao, 1855-1955].

LAURENCE, K. O.

5.123   TR   1963 The settlement of free Negroes in Trinidad before emancipation.
               Car Q 9(1-2): 26-52. [11[[*RIS*]

LAURENCE, STEPHEN M.

28.326   TR   1941 The evolution of the Trinidad midwife.

LEAKE, H. MARTIN

47.024   BC   1932 Studies in tropical land tenure. (2) The West Indies.

LEGER, MARCEL

28.330   FG   1917 La lèpre à la Guyane Francaise et ses réglementations successives
               [Leprosy in French Guiana and successive regulations about it].

LeMAIRE, G. W.

54.034   AR   1936 Aruba, Netherlands West Indies—the history and industrial
               development].

LEMERY, HENRY

5.124   MT   1936 LA RÉVOLUTION FRANCAISE À LA MARTINIQUE [THE FRENCH REVOLUTION
               IN MARTINIQUE]. Paris, Larose, 338p.   [*AGS*]

LE PAGE, R. B. & De CAMP, DAVID

25.067   JM   1960 JAMAICAN CREOLE: AN HISTORICAL INTRODUCTION TO JAMAICAN CREOLE,
               BY R. B. LE PAGE, AND FOUR JAMAICAN CREOLE TEXTS, WITH INTRO-
               DUCTION, PHONEMIC TRANSCRIPTIONS AND GLOSSES BY DAVID DE CAMP.

LESCENE, G. T.

28.336   JM   1955 Brief historical retrospect of the medical profession in Jamaica.

LETHEM, Sir GORDON J.

3.182   BG   1950 Salute to adventurers.

LEVY, BABETTE M.

23.095   BC   1960 The West Indies and Bahamas: Puritanism in conflict with tropical
               island life.

LEVY, CLAUDE

38.066   BC   1950 PROBLEMS IN BRITISH WEST INDIAN FEDERATION.

LEWIS, C. BERNARD

5.125   JM   1948 The history of the Pedro and Morant Cays. *Jam Hist Rev* 1(3), Dec.:
               302-309.   [*COL*]

LEWIS, GORDON K.

37.225   GC   1961 The Caribbean: colonization and culture.

LICHTVELD, U. M. & VOORHOEVE, J.
51.085   SR   1958 SURINAME: SPIEGEL DER VADERLANDSE KOOPLIEDEN [SURINAM: MIRROR OF THE DUTCH MERCHANTS].

LIER, RUDOLF A.J. van
8.040   NC   1955 Social and political conditions in Surinam and the Netherlands Antilles: Introduction.

LIER, WILLEM F. van
14.021   SR   1921/ Bij de Aucaners [Among the Aucanians].
            22

LIVINGSTON, Sir NOEL B.
23.097   JM   1946 Records of the Kingston vestry.

LLOYD-STILL, R.M.
31.050   BC   1955 The mental hospital.

LONG, ANTON V.
66.095   JM   1956 JAMAICA AND THE NEW ORDER 1827-1847.

LOW, F.O.
15.028   BG   1919 Hopetown Chinese settlement.

LOWE, ROBSON
5.126   BB/   1951 THE CODRINGTON CORRESPONDENCE 1743-1851. London, Robson Lowe,
      AT   112p.

LOWENTHAL, DAVID
5.127   FG   1952 Colonial experiments in French Guiana, 1760-1800. *Hispan Am Hist Rev* 32(1), Feb.: 22-43.   [*RIS*]
38.073   BC   1957 Two federations.

LUCAS, Sir CHARLES PRESTWOOD
43.103   BC   1905 HISTORICAL GEOGRAPHY OF THE BRITISH COLONIES. VOL. II: THE WEST INDIES.
5.128   GC   1913 The A B C of West Indian history. *Hist Tchr Mag* 4(7), Sept.: 183-187.   [*TCL*]

LUTHIN, REINHARD H.
5.129   SB   1934 St. Bartholomew: Sweden's colonial and diplomatic adventure in the Caribbean. *Hisp Am Hist Rev* 14(3), Aug.: 307-324.   [*NYP*]

LYNDEN, J.W. van
23.098   SR   1939 De Evangelische Broedergemeente in Suriname [The United Brethern in Surinam].

McCONNEY, E.J., comp.
17,016   BB   1963 Prisoners of the '45 rising.

MacDERMOT, T.H.
37.238   JM   1922 Jamaica, past and present.
37.239   JM   1922 The political constitution of Jamaica.

McDERMOTT, T. W. L.

38.080   BC   1933 Federation of the West Indies: Is it desirable?

MacINNES, C. M.

37.241   BC   1955 Constitutional development of the British West Indies.

MACKENZIE, V. St. CLAIR, ed.

37.242   BG   1923 Laws of British Guiana (1803-1921) Rev. ed.

MACMILLAN, W. M.

37.247   BC   1960 The road to self rule: a study in colonial evolution.

McMURTRIE, DOUGLAS C.

52.053   DM   1932 The first printing in Dominica.
52.054   BB   1933 Early printing in Barbados.
52.055   JM   1942 The first printing in Jamaica.

McNEILL, GEORGE

23.099   JM   1911 The story of our missions: the West Indies.

McTURK, MICHAEL

5.130   BG   1912 Some old graves in the Colony. *Timehri* 3d ser., 2(19B), Dec.:
                       357-363. [23]   [*AMN*]

MANDEVILLE, R. G. F.

58.068   BB   1963 A brief note on the history of sugar in Barbados.

MARCUS, JACOB RADER

15.031   GC   1953 The West India and South America expedition of the American
                       Jewish Archives.

MARCOS LOPEZ, FRANCISCO

39.034   BH   [n.d.] Quiebra y reintegración del derecho de gentes: Gibraltar,
                       Belice, Las Malvinas [The breaking and restoration of inter-
                       national law: Gibraltar, Belize, Las Malvinas].

MARSHALL, GLORIA ALBERTHA

53.028   BC   1959 Benefit societies in the British West Indies: the formative
                       years.

MARTIN, K.

40.114   NL   1920/ Vroegere rijzingen van den bodem in Nederlandsch West-Indië
                 21   [Ground elevations in the Dutch West Indies which occurred in
                       the past].
5.131   SR   1926/ De waardeering van Voltz als pionier voor Suriname [Appreciation
                 27   of Voltz as a pioneer of Surinam]. *W I G* 8:533-538.   [*COL*]

MARTINEAU, ALFRED

37.255   FA   1935 Il y a cent ans: les droits civils et politiques, le Conseil colonial
                       [One hundred years ago: civil and political rights, the colonial
                       Council].

MASEFIELD, G. B.

46.138 BC 1950 A short history of agriculture in the British colonies.

MATHIESON, WILLIAM LAW

5.132 BC 1936 The sugar colonies and Governor Eyre, 1849-1866. London, Longmans, Green, 243p. [6]   [*RIS*]

MATTHEWS, Dom BASIL

9.026 TR 1953 Crisis of the West Indian family.

MAY, ARTHUR J.

35.031 BC 1933 The architecture of the West Indies.

MAY, FRED

23.102 BG 1918 The Lutherans of Berbice.

MAY, LOUIS-PHILIPPE

43.106 MT 1930 Histoire économique de la Martinique (1635-1763) [Economic history of Martinique (1635-1763)].

MEETEREN, N. van

5.133 BN 1949 Bonaire in het begin der negentiende eeuw [Bonaire in the early part of the 19th century]. *W I G* 30:82-86, 97-104, 217-236. [3]   [*COL*]

MEIKLE, LOUIS S.

38.084 BC 1912 Confederation of British West Indies versus annexation to the United States of America.

MEILINK-ROELOFSZ, M.A.P.

5.134 BG 1961/ Archivalia betreffende de voormalige Nederlandse koloniën Esse-
     62 quebo, Demerary en Berbice in het Public Record Office te London [Items concerning the former Dutch colonies Essequibo, Demerara and Berbice in the Public Record Office in London]. *N W I G* 41: 127-140.   [*COL*]

MENDOZA, JOSE LUIS

39.035 BH 1942 Inglaterra y sus pactos sobre Belice [Great Britain and its treaties on Belize].

MENKMAN, W. R.

66.098 SE 1932/ Sint Eustatius' gouden tijd [The golden age of St. Eustatius].
     33

5.135 SE 1933/ Statiaansche toestanden in de XVIIIe eeuw [Statian conditions in
     34 the 18th century]. *W I G* 15:23-44, 105-123.   [*COL*]

5.136 SE 1933/ Het voorspel der verovering van St. Eustatius in 1781 [The prelude
     34 to the conquest of St. Eustatius in 1781]. *W I G* 15:321-337, 353-370.   [*COL*]

5.137 CU 1934/ Drie reizen naar Curacao in den zeiltijd [Three trips to Curacao in
     35 the era of sailing ships]. *W I G* 16:282-293. [3]   [*COL*]

44.153 NA 1934 De economische beteekenis der Nederlandsche Antillen, voorheen en thans [The economic importance of the Dutch Antilles, in the past and present].

5.138   NA   1935/ Sprokkelingen op het terrein der geschiedenis van de Nederlandsche
                36   Antillen [Gleanings from the history of the Dutch Antilles]. *W I G*
                     17:65-115.   [*COL*]
5.139   SR   1935/ Suriname onder Engelsch bewind [Surinam under English rule]. *W I G*
                36   17:322-334.   [37]   [*COL*]
25.076 CU   1936/ Curacao, zijn naam en zijn taal [Curacao, its name and its language].
                37
5.140   NA   1936/ De Nederlanders in de Caraïbische wateren: een nabetrachting [The
                37   Dutch in the Caribbean seas: in retrospect]. *W I G* 18:213-219.
                     [37, 52]   [*COL*]
24.049 GC   1937 Nog eens het eiland der reuzen [Once again the island of the giants].
5.141   TT   1938 Tortola. *W I G* 20:178-192.   [3]   [*COL*]
3.199   TB   1939/ Tobago.
                40
3.200   GC   1941/ Aanteekeningen op Hamelberg's werken [Notes on Hamelberg's
                46   writings].
5.142   NW   1943 Zuid Amerikaansche piraterie en onze Bovenwindsche Eilanden voor
                     vijf kwart eeuw [South American piracy and our Windward Islands
                     over a period of 125 years]. *W I G* 25:65-80, 97, 116, 129-154. [*COL*]
5.143   SR   1944/ Suriname in Willoughby's tijd [Surinam in the time of Willoughby].
                45   *W I G* 26:1-18.   [6]   [*COL*]
5.144   SR   1946 Uit de geschiedenis der opening van het Surinaamsche binnenland
                     [From the history of the opening of the interior of Surinam]. *W I G*
                     27:182-192, 289-299, 321-343.   [3, 14]   [*COL*]
5.145   CU   1948 Het eerste Nederlandsche bestuur van Curacao [The first Dutch
                     rule of Curacao]. *W I G* 29:328-338.   [*COL*]
5.146   NC   1948 Onze West 1898-1948. [Our West 1898-1948]. *W I G* 29:193-209.
                     [3, 7]   [*COL*]
5.147   SR   1949 De Surinaamse geschiedenis sociologisch behandeld [The history
                     of Surinam from a sociological viewpoint]. *W I G* 30:330-341. [*COL*]
23.104 SM/   1958 St. Maarten en St. Barthélemy, 1911-1951.
         SB

MERRILL, GORDON CLARK
19.031 BC   1961 The survival of the past in the West Indies.
15.032 GC   1964 The role of Sephardic Jews in the British Caribbean area during
                     the seventeenth century.

MEYER, J.
7.047   SR   1954 PIONEERS OF PAUROMA, CONTRIBUTION TO THE EARLIEST HISTORY OF
                     THE JEWISH COLONIZATION OF AMERICA.

MINTZ, SIDNEY W.
8.041   JM   1958 Historical sociology of the Jamaican church-founded free village
                     system.
58.070 JM   1959 Labor and sugar in Puerto Rico and in Jamaica, 1800-1850.
8.044   GC   1961 The question of Caribbean peasantries: a comment.
51.101 JM   1964 Currency problems in eighteenth-century Jamaica and Gresham's law.

MINTZ, SIDNEY W. & HALL, DOUGLAS
51.102 JM   1960 The origins of the Jamaican internal marketing system.

MITCHELL RONALD
11.019 JM   1950 The Maroons of Accompong.

MOLENGRAAFF, G. J. H.

28.375   CU   1930/ Korte uiteenzetting van de destijds door den mijnbouwkundigen
             31   dienst opgestelde plannen tot waterverzorging van de haven van
                 Willemstad en van die stad zelve op het eiland Curacao [Short
                 explanation of the former plans of the mining department for
                 the water supply of the port of Willemstad and of that city
                 itself on the island Curacao].

MOORE, RICHARD B.

37.273   GC   1964   Caribbean unity and freedom.

MORALES PADRON, FRANCISCO

5.148   JM   1952   Jamaica española [Spanish Jamaica]. Seville, Escuela de Estudios
                 Hispano-americanos de Sevilla, 497p.   [*NYP*]

MORLEY, SYLVANUS G.

4.100   BH   1956   The ancient Maya. 3d ed.

MORSINK, F.

14.022   SR   1934/ Nogmaals: de dood van Jankosoe. En: nog niet het einde van een
             35   dynastie [Once again: the death of Jankosoe. And: not yet the end
                 of a dynasty].

MOTHON, R. P.

23.109   TR   1903   La Trinidad.

MULDER, G. C. A.

44.159   SR   1960/ Suriname's economische stilstand in de vorige eeuw [Surinam's
             61   economic stagnation during the previous century].

MULLER, KARL

23.110   GC   1931   Westindien. Suriname [West Indies. Surinam].

MURRAY, C. GIDEON

38.088   BC   1912   A united West Indies.

MURRAY, D. J.

37.277   BC   1965   The West Indies and the development of colonial government.

MURRAY, R. N.

5.149   JM   1960   The road back—Jamaica after 1866. *Car Q* 6(2-3), May: 134-141.
                 [37]   [*RIS*]

NARDIN, J.C.

5.150   GR   1962   Les archives anciennes de la Grenade [Early records of Grenada].
                 Rev Fr Hist O-M 49:117-140.   [*COL*]

NATH, DWARKA

12.022   BG   1950   A history of the Indians in British Guiana.

NEHAUL, B. B. G.

28.392   BG   1955   History of the British Guiana Branch of the British Medical
                 Association.

28.395   BG   1956   Some public health legislation of British Guiana in the nineteenth
                 century.

NETTLEFORD, REX

19.033   JM   1963 The African connexion—the significance for Jamaica.

NEWMAN, PETER KENNETH

51.109   BC   1960 Canada's role in West Indian trade before 1912.

NEWTON, ARTHUR PERCIVAL

5.151   GC   1933 The European nations in the West Indies 1493-1688. London, A. &
                     C. Black, 356p.   [*RIS*]

NICOLE, CHRISTOPHER

22.102   BC   1957 West Indian cricket.

NOUSSANNE, HENRI de

23.112   FA/   1936 La France missionnaire aux Antilles: Guadeloupe, Martinique,
            TR   Trinidad [French missionaries in the West Indies: Guadeloupe,
                          Martinique, Trinidad].

NUGENT, MARIA

3.223   JM   1934 Lady Nugent's journal: Jamaica one hundred years ago.

OLIVER, VERE LANGFORD

23.113   BB   1915 The monumental inscriptions in the churches and churchyards
                        of the island of Barbados, British West Indies.

OLSCHKI, LEONARDO

40.134   GC   1943 The Columbian nomenclature of the Lesser Antilles.

O'NEIL, MAUD E.

35.032   BB   1949 Of the buildings in progress with which to house the College.

OPPENHEIM, SAMUEL

15.033   GG/   1907 An early Jewish colony in Western Guiana 1658-1666: and its rela-
            TB   tion to the Jews in Surinam, Cayenne and Tobago.
15.034   BG   1908 An early Jewish colony in Western Guiana: supplemental data.

ORIOL, T.

5.152   GD   1935 Les hommes célèbres de la Guadeloupe [Famous men of
                     Guadeloupe]. Basse-Terre, Impr. Catholique, 352p.   [*NYP*]

ORR, G. M.

5.153   GC   1927 The origin of the West India Regiment. *J Roy United Serv Instn*
                     72(485), Feb.: 129-136.   [*NYP*]

OTTLEY, CARLTON ROBERT

2.170   TB   [n.d.] The complete history of the island of Tobago in the West Indies.
5.154   TR   1955 An account of life in Spanish Trinidad. [Port of Spain?] Trinidad,
                     College Press, 135p.   [*RIS*]
5.155   TR   1962 The story of Port of Spain, capital of Trinidad, West Indies,
                     from the earliest times to the present day. [Port of Spain?]
                     Trinidad, Published by the author, 136p. [36]   [*RIS*]
37.294   TR   1964 A historical account of the Trinidad and Tobago police force
                        from the earliest times.

OUDSCHANS, DENTZ FRED

5.156	SR	1919	Surinam as a Dutch possession. *Timehri* 3d ser., 6(23), Sept.: 173-182. [*AMN*]

5.157 GG 1923/ Wapens en mottos [Coats of arms and mottoes]. *W I G* 5:421-423.
24 [*COL*]

5.158 SR 1927/ Hoe men in Suriname in de loop der eeuwen den tijd heeft aange-
28 geven [How the time was registered in Surinam during the course
of the centuries]. *W I G* 9:433-448. [*COL*]

37.296 SR 1928/ Nogmaals het wapen van Suriname [Surinam's coat of arms once
29 again].

28.406 SR 1930/ Dr. Constantin Hering en Christiaan Johannes Hering.
31

62.020 SR 1930/ Iets uit de geschiedenis van de rijstcultuur in Suriname [Some facts
31 from the history of rice culture in Surinam].

5.159 SM 1931/ Hoe het eiland Sint Maarten werd verdeeld [How the island St.
32 Maarten was divided]. *W I G* 13:163-164. [*COL*]

5.160 SM 1933/ De inbezitneming van het Fransche gedeelte van Sint Maarten door
34 de Nederlanders [The occupation of the French part of St. Maarten
by the Dutch]. *W I G* 15:280-281. [*COL*]

44.181 SR 1941 Een blik op den toestand van Suriname bij den overgang van het
Engelsche bestuur op dat der Bataafsche Republiek in 1802 [The
conditions in Surinam at the time of the change from English rule to
that of the Batavian Republic].

7.052 SR 1941 De geschiedenis van den burgelijken stand en van eenige famili-
enamen in Suriname [The history of the Civil Registration and of
some family names in Surinam].

5.161 SR 1941 Hoe Suriname anderhalve eeuw geleden tegen den buitenlandschen
vijand maatregelen nam [How Surinam took measures against the
foreign enemy one-and-a-half centuries ago]. *W I G* 23:186-191.
[*COL*]

51.111 SR 1942 De eerste handelsbetrekkingen van Suriname met de Amerikaansche
Republiek [The first trade relations of Surinam with the American
Republic].

32.148 CU 1942 De geschiedenis van het Collegium Neerlandicum, de eerste en
eenige middelbare onderwijsinrichting op Curacao, 1866-1871 [The
history of the Collegium Neerlandicum, the first and only advanced
education institute on Curacao, 1866-1871].

37.299 SR 1943 Aanvulling van de Encyclopaedie van Nederlandsch West-Indië:
De Gouverneurs van Suriname [Addition to the Encyclopedia of the
Dutch West Indies: The Governors of Surinam].

5.162 BG/ 1943 De kolonisatie van Guyana [The colonization of Guiana]. *W I G*
SR 25:248-287. [7] [*COL*]

22.104 SR 1943 De loopbaan van Krayenhoff van Wickera in Suriname [The career
of Krayenhoff van Wickera in Surinam].

37.300 SR 1948 De afzetting van het Groot-Opperhoofd der Saramaccaners Koffy in
1835 en de politieke contracten met de Boschnegers in Suriname
[The dismissal of Koffy, the headman of the Saramaccans, in 1835,
and the political contracts with the Bush Negroes in Surinam].

5.163 SR 1949 GESCHIEDKUNDIGE TIJDTAFEL VAN SURINAME [HISTORICAL-CHRONO-
LOGICAL TABLE OF SURINAM]. Amsterdam, J.H. de Bussy, 146p. [*RIS*]

23.115 SR 1949 De Hervormde Kerk in Suriname in haar begintijd [The Dutch Reformed Church in Surinam in her early years].

33.035   SR   1954 Een welvaartsplan voor Suriname in 1770 voorgesteld door Gouvern-
                          eur Jan Nepveu [A welfare plan for Surinam proposed by Governor
                          Jan Nepveu in 1770].
32.149   SR   1955/ Grepen uit de geschiedenis van het onderwijs in Suriname in de
                      56   17e en 18e eeuw [Aspects of the history of school education in
                           Surinam in the 17th and 18th centuries].

PADILLA, ELENA
45.018   GC   1959 Colonization and development of plantations.

PAGET, HUGH
8.046   JM   1945 The free village system in Jamaica.
36.013   JM   1946 The founding of Mandeville.

PANDAY, R. M. N.
46.163   SR   1959 AGRICULTURE IN SURINAM, 1650-1950: AN INQUIRY INTO THE CAUSES
                          OF ITS DECLINE.

PANHUYS, L. C. van
37.301   SR   1924/ De Gouverneur-Generaal Willem Benjamin van Panhuys [Governor-
                      25   General Willem Benjamin van Panhuys].
37.302   SR   1926/ De Nederlandsche Regeering tegenover de kolonie Suriname in
                      27   1816. [The Dutch Government versus the colony of Surinam in 1816].
37.303   SR   1934/ Mr. Lammers over het bestuur van Suriname in 1816 [Mr. Lammers
                      35   on the government of Surinam in 1816].
60.064   SR   1936/ De overbrenging van de banaan en de bacove uit Afrika naar
                      37   tropisch Amerika in het begin van de 16de eeuw [The importation
                           of the banana and the bacove from Africa into tropical America in
                           the beginning of the 16th century].

PANHUYS, L. C. van; HERSKOVITS, M. J. & MORDINI, A.
5.164   FG   1934 Un manuscrit de 1690 sur la Guyane Francaise [A 1690 manuscript
                          on French Guiana]. *In* Verhandlungen des XXIV Internationalen
                          Amerikanisten-Kongresses, Hamburg, 1930. Hamburg, Friederichsew,
                          de Gruyter, p.26-31.   [*AGS*]

PARES, RICHARD
5.165   GC   1936 WAR AND TRADE IN THE WEST INDIES 1739-1763. Oxford, Clarendon
                          Press, 631p. [37, 51]   [*NYP*]
37.304   GC   1937 Prisoners of war in the West-Indies in the eighteenth century.
5.166   BB   1938/ Barbados history from the records of the prize court. *J Barb Mus*
                      40   *Hist Soc* 5(4), Aug.: 186-189; 6(1), Nov.: 10-20 (1938); 6(2), Feb.:
                           59-66; 6(3), May: 117-128 (1939); 7(3), May: 136-138 (1940). [*AMN*]
45.019   NV   1950 A WEST INDIA FORTUNE.
51.113   GC   1956 YANKEES AND CREOLES: THE TRADE BETWEEN NORTH AMERICA AND THE
                          WEST INDIES BEFORE THE AMERICAN REVOLUTION.
45.020   GC   1960 MERCHANTS AND PLANTERS.

PARKER, C. SANDBACH
66.110   BG   1913 The development of British Guiana.

PARKER, FRANKLIN D.
37.305   FC   1958 Political development in the French Caribbean.

PARRY, JOHN HORACE
37.306   BC   1954 The Patent Offices in the British West Indies.

51.116   JM   1955   Eliphalet Fitch: a Yankee trader in Jamaica during the war of Independence.

44.166   JM   1962   Salt fish and ackee: an historical sketch of the introduction of food crops into Jamaica.

PARRY, JOHN HORACE & SHERLOCK, P. M.

5.167   GC   1956   A SHORT HISTORY OF THE WEST INDIES. London, Macmillan, 316p.
[RIS]

PAYNE, ERNEST A.

23.118   JM   1946   FREEDOM IN JAMAICA; SOME CHAPTERS IN THE STORY OF THE BAPTIST MISSIONARY SOCIETY. 2d ed.

PEARSE, ANDREW C.

22.115   TR   1956   Carnival in nineteenth century Trinidad.

PENDELTON, LEILA AMOS

5.168   UV   1917   Our new possessions—the Danish West Indies. *J Negro Hist* 2(3), July: 267-288.   [SCH]

PENSON, LILLIAN M.

5.169   BC   1920   Historical sidelights. *W I Comm Circ*; 1. *Early years of the West India Committee*, 35(559), Mar. 4:66; 35(560), Mar. 18:77; 3. *The Bristol West India club*, 35(564), May 13: 134-135.   [NYP]

37.311   BC   1924   COLONIAL AGENTS OF THE BRITISH WEST INDIES: A STUDY IN COLONIAL ADMINISTRATION, MAINLY IN THE EIGHTEENTH CENTURY.

37.312   BG   1926   The making of a crown colony: British Guiana, 1803-33.

PERCIVAL, D. A.

49.058   GC   1953   Industrialization: historical background, existing industries and industrial potential of the Caribbean area.

PETERS, FRED E.

35.035   MS   1931   SAINT ANTHONY'S CHURCH, MONTSERRAT, WEST INDIES.

PETITJEAN-ROGET, JACQUES

23.122   MT   1956   Les protestants à la Martinique sous l'ancien régime [The Protestants in Martinique under the old regime].

PHILLIPS, ULRICH B.

45.022   JM   1914   A Jamaica Slave Plantation.

45.023   AT   1926   An Antigua plantation, 1769-1818.

PIETERSZ, J. L. & JACOBS, H. P., eds.

5.170   JM   1952   Two Spanish documents of 1656. *Jam Hist Rev* 2(2), Oct.: 11-35.

PITMAN, FRANK WESLEY

58.076   BC   1917   THE DEVELOPMENT OF THE BRITISH WEST INDIES 1700-1763.

45.024   BC   1927   The West Indian absentee planter as a British Colonial type.

45.025   BC   1931   The settlement and financing of British West India plantations in the eighteenth century.

PLATT, RAYE R.
37.316   GC   1926 A note on political sovereignty and administration in the Caribbean.

PLENEL, ALAIN
37.317   FA   1963 Libération nationale et assimilation à la Martinique et à la
                          Guadeloupe [National liberation and (political) assimilation in
                          Martinique and Guadeloupe].

POPE-HENNESSY, JAMES
3.245   BC   1943 WEST INDIAN SUMMER; A RETROSPECT.
37.319   BC   1964 The Federation Riots, Barbados 1875-1876.

POTTER, THOMAS I.
46.170   TR   1932 The Agricultural Society and its affiliated branches.
46.171   TR   1932 River Estate: a brief history of the property.
5.171   TR   1933 The tragedy of San Francisco; a dark episode in Trinidad's history.
                          W I Comm Circ 48(915), Oct.: 439-440.   [*NYP*]

POYER, JOHN
37.322   BB   1954 History of the administration of the Rt. Hon. Lord Seaforth, etc.

PRICE, EDWARD T.
10.036   BB   1957 The Redlegs of Barbados.

PRIDMORE, F.
53.030   BB   1962 Notes on colonial coins: the Barbados issues of 1788 and 1792.
                          Are they coins or private tokens?
53.031   BB   1964 Notes on colonial coins: cut money of Barbados.

PROTAIN, Mrs. G.
5.172   GR   1962 Grenada's historical background. *Chron W I Comm* 77(1378), Nov.:
                          572-573.   [*NYP*]

PYTTERSEN, T.J.
46.178   SR   1929/ De mogelijke opleving van Suriname [The possible revival of
                    30   Surinam].

QUELLE, OTTO
10.037   GG   1951 Die Bevölkerungsentwicklung von Europäisch-Guayana: eine anthro-
                          pogeographische Untersuchung [The population growth of European
                          Guiana: an anthropo-geographical study].

QUESTEL, ANDRE
3.251   GC   1919 SOUVENIRS DE VOYAGE AUX ANTILLES ET GUYANES [RECOLLECTIONS OF
                          A TRIP TO THE ANTILLES AND GUIANAS].

QUINTUS BOSZ, A. J. A.
47.028   SR   1954 DRIE EEUWEN GRONDPOLITIEK IN SURINAME: EEN HISTORISCHE STUDIE
                          VAN DE ACHTERGROND EN DE ONTWIKKELING VAN DE SURINAAMSE RECHTEN
                          OP DE GROND [THREE CENTURIES OF LAND POLICY IN SURINAM: AN
                          HISTORICAL STUDY OF THE BACKGROUND AND DEVELOPMENT OF LAND
                          RIGHTS IN SURINAM].

37.326   SR   1960/ Misvattingen omtrent de staatkundige ontwikkeling van Suriname
            61 [Misunderstandings about the political development of Surinam].

RAGATZ, LOWELL JOSEPH
1.033   BC   1923 A CHECK LIST OF HOUSE OF COMMONS SESSIONAL PAPERS RELATING
               TO THE BRITISH WEST INDIES AND TO THE WEST INDIAN SLAVE TRADE
               AND SLAVERY, 1763-1834.
5.173   BC   1923 A GUIDE TO THE OFFICIAL CORRESPONDENCE OF THE GOVERNORS OF
               THE BRITISH WEST INDIA COLONIES WITH THE SECRETARY OF STATE,
               1763-1833. London, Bryan Edwards Press, 79p.   [*COL*]
45.026   BC   1925 THE OLD PLANTATION SYSTEM IN THE BRITISH CARIBBEAN.
51.117   BC   1927 STATISTICS FOR THE STUDY OF BRITISH CARIBBEAN ECONOMIC HISTORY,
               1763-1833.
45.027   BC   [1928?] ABSENTEE LANDLORDISM IN THE BRITISH CARIBBEAN 1750-1833.
45.028   GC   1928 FALL OF THE PLANTER CLASS IN THE BRITISH CARIBBEAN, 1763-1833.
45.029   BC   1931 ABSENTEE LANDLORDISM IN THE BRITISH CARIBBEAN, 1750-1833.
1.035   BC   1932 A GUIDE FOR THE STUDY OF BRITISH CARIBBEAN HISTORY, 1763-1834,
               INCLUDING THE ABOLITION AND EMANCIPATION MOVEMENTS.
5.174   BC   1935 Les Antilles dans l'histoire coloniale anglaise de l'Amerique du
               Nord [The Antilles in the British colonial history of North America].
               Rev Hist Colon 2:69-88.
5.175   BC   1935 THE WEST INDIAN APPROACH TO THE STUDY OF AMERICAN COLONIAL
               HISTORY. London, Arthur Thomas, 20p.   [*COL*]
1.036   FA   1949 EARLY FRENCH WEST INDIAN RECORDS IN THE ARCHIVES NATIONALES.

RAGHAVAN, SUSHILA
8.048   TT   1963 SOCIAL STRATIFICATION IN TORTOLA, BRITISH VIRGIN ISLANDS.

RAMESHWAR, S.M., et al.
12.026   TR   1945 INDIAN CENTENARY REVIEW: ONE HUNDRED YEARS OF PROGRESS, 1845-
               1945, TRINIDAD, B.W.I.

RAMPHAL, S.S.
38.100   BC   1959 The West Indies—constitutional background to federation.
38.101   BC   1960 Federalism in the West Indies.

RAYMOND, URSULA
5.176   GC   1959 Pere Labat. *Shell Trin* 5(9), Christmas: 24-27.

RAYNER, Sir THOMAS CROSSLEY, ed.
37.329   BG   1905 LAWS OF BRITISH GUIANA. New and rev. ed.

REECE, J.E. & CLARK-HUNT, C.G., eds.
23.126   BB   1925 BARBADOS DIOCESAN HISTORY.

RENNARD, J.
5.177   FA   1935 BAAS, BLÉNAC, OU LES ANTILLES FRANCAISES AU XVIIᵉ SIÈCLE [BAAS,
               BLÉNAC, OR THE FRENCH ANTILLES IN THE 17th CENTURY]. Fort de
               France, M. Alexander, 245p.   [*NYP*]
23.127   FA   1935 Organisation des paroisses [The parish organization].
5.178   MT   1938 TRINITÉ. Annemasse [France] Impr. Granchamp, 131p.   [*RIS*]

23.128   MT   1951 LA MARTINIQUE HISTORIQUE DES PAROISSES: DES ORIGINES À LA SÉPARATION [PARISH HISTORY OF MARTINIQUE, FROM CONTACT TO SEPARATION].

RENS, L. L. E.
15.035   SR   1954 Analysis of annals relating to early Jewish settlement in Surinam.

REYNE, A.
59.037   SR   1924/ Geschiedenis der Cacaocultuur in Surinam [History of the cultiva-
              25 tion of cocoa in Surinam].

ROBERTS, GEORGE WOODROW
17.023   BC   1954 Immigration of Africans into the British Caribbean.
38.106   BC   1957 Some demographic considerations of West Indian federation.

ROBERTS, WALTER ADOLPHE
5.179   JM   1936 Sir Henry Morgan as Statesman. *Can-W I Mag* 25(10), Sept.: 23-25.
                                                                          [*NYP*]
5.180   GC   1940 THE CARIBBEAN: THE STORY OF OUR SEA OF DESTINY.New York, Bobbs-
              Merrill, 361.   [*COL*]
5.181   FA   1942 THE FRENCH IN THE WEST INDIES. Indianapolis, Bobbs-Merrill
              Company, 335p.   [*COL*]
5.182   JM   1949 Henry Morgan—sinner turned saint. *Can-W I Mag* 39(3), Mar.: 27-29.
                                                                          [*NYP*]
5.183   JM   1952 Simon Bolivar in Jamaica. *Jam Hist Rev* 2(2), Oct.: 1-10.
5.184   JM   1952 SIR HENRY MORGAN, BUCCANEER AND GOVERNOR. Rev. ed. Kingston,
              Pioneer Press, 165p. [37, 44]
5.185   JM   1952 SIX GREAT JAMAICANS. Kingston, Pioneer Press, 117p.
36.015   JM   1955 THE CAPITALS OF JAMAICA.
5.186   JM   1955 JAMAICA: THE PORTRAIT OF AN ISLAND. New York, Coward-McCann,
              247p. [3]   [*RIS*]
35.037   JM   1962 Old King's House, Spanish Town.

ROBERTSON, E. ARNOT
5.187   JM   1959 THE SPANISH TOWN PAPERS. London, Cresset Press, 199p.   [*COL*]

RODNEY, WALTER
67.020   BC   1963/ The role of the historian in a developing West Indies.
              64

RODWAY, JAMES
45.030   BG   1911 Names of our plantations.
39.036   BG   1911 Our boundary war scare.
5.188   BG   1917 War in Demerara 1781-2. *Timehri* 3d ser., 4(21), June: 154-159. [*AMN*]
67.021   BG   1918 The "good old times" in Guiana.
50.098   BG   1919 Labour and colonization.

ROMANETTE, IRMINE
32.168   MT   1925 L'enseignement secondaire des jeunes filles à la Martinique
              [Secondary education for girls in Martinique].

ROOS, J. S.
15.036   SR   1905 Additional notes on the history of the Jews in Surinam.

ROSE, F. G. & CHOW, J. E.

28.450 BG 1923 A resume of the scientific work published by medical men in British Guiana from 1769 to the present day.

ROSS, WILLIAM GILLIES

5.189 AT 1960 THE HISTORICAL GEOGRAPHY OF ANTIGUA. M.A. thesis, McGill University, 191p. [43]

ROTH, VINCENT

5.190 BG 1953 Reminiscences of the old Demerara. *Timehri* 4th ser., 1(32), Nov.: 28-31.

58.083 BG 1953 Some sugar biography.

5.191 BG 1955 Great fires of Georgetown. *Timehri* 4th ser., 1(34), Sept.: 62-67.

ROUSSIER, PAUL

32.169 MT 1930 Une maison d'education pour les jeunes personnes à la Martinique au temps où l'impératrice Joséphine était enfant [An educational institution for young ladies in Martinique at the time when Empress Josephine was a child].

22.128 MT 1935 Fêtes d'autrefois à la Martinique [Festivals of the past in Martinique].

RUHOMON, PETER

12.028 BG 1946 CENTENARY HISTORY OF THE EAST INDIANS IN BRITISH GUIANA, 1838-1938.

RUTGERS, A. A. L.

5.192 SR 1938 Suriname onder de regering van Koningin Wilhelmina 1898-1938 [Surinam under the Government of Queen Wilhelmina 1898-1938]. *W I G* 20:257-261. [66]   [COL]

RUTTEN, L. M. R.

40.149 NL 1931/ De geologische geschiedenis der drie Nederlandsche Beneden-
       32 windsche Eilanden [The geological history of the three Dutch Leeward Islands].

SABLE, VICTOR

37.353 FC 1955 LA TRANSFORMATION DES ISLES D'AMÉRIQUE EN DÉPARTEMENTS FRANCAIS [THE CONVERSION OF THE AMERICAN ISLANDS INTO FRENCH *Départements*].

ST. CLAIR, JAMES

3.266 JM 1929 A voyage to Jamaica in the forties.

SAINT-OMER, ROMAINE

5.193 FG 1945 BLANC, QU'EST-CE QUE LA GUYANE [WHITE MAN, WHAT IS GUIANA?] Paris, Lib.-Imp. réunies, 30p.   [SCH]

SAMSON, PH. A.

52.078 SR 1950 De Surinaamse pers gedurende het Engelse tussenbestuur [The Surinam press during the English interregnum].

22.129 SR 1954 Aantekeningen over kunst en vermaak in Suriname voor 1900 [Notes on art and entertainment in Surinam prior to 1900].

SAMUEL, WILFRED S.
15.037   BB   1928 A REVIEW OF THE JEWISH COLONISTS IN BARBADOS IN THE YEAR 1680.

SANTISO GALVEZ, GUSTAVO
39.037   BH   1941 EL CASO DE BELICE A LA LUZ DE LA HISTORIA Y EL DERECHO INTER-
                        NACIONAL [THE BELIZE QUESTION IN THE LIGHT OF HISTORY AND INTER-
                        NATIONAL LAW].

SATINEAU, MAURICE
2.208   GD   1928 HISTOIRE DE LA GUADELOUPE SOUS L'ANCIEN RÉGIME, 1635-1789
                        [HISTORY OF GUADELOUPE UNDER THE OLD REGIME, 1635-1789].
5.194   FC   1948 SCHOELCHER, HÉROS DE L'ABOLITION DE L'ESCLAVAGE DANS LES POS-
                        SESSIONS FRANCAISES [SCHOELCHER, HERO OF THE ABOLITION OF
                        SLAVERY IN THE FRENCH POSSESSIONS]. Paris, Mellotée, 156p. [*NYP*]

SAUL, SAMUEL BERRICK
44.207   BC   1957 The economic significance of "constructive imperialism."

SCHELVEN, A.A. van
5.195   SR   1922/ Suriname in de 18e eeuw [Surinam in the 18th century]. *W I G*
                  23   4:65-90.   [*COL*]

SCHOENRICH, OTTO
39.038   BG   1949 The Venezuela-British Guiana boundary dispute.

SCHOMBURGK, RICHARD
3.273   BG   1953 RICHARD SCHOMBURGK'S TRAVELS IN BRITISH GUIANA 1840-1844.

SCHULLER, RUDOLF
5.196   GG   1916 The Ordaz and Dortal Expeditions in search of El-Dorado, as
                        described on sixteenth century maps. *Smithson Misc Colln* 66(4)
                        (15p.) [40]   [*AGS*]

SCHULZE, ADOLF
23.136   GC   1931/ 200 Jahre Brüdermission [200 years of the Brothers' missions].
                  32

SCHUTZ, JOHN A.
23.139   BB   1946 Christopher Codrington's will: launching the S.P.G. into the
                        Barbadian sugar business.

SCHUTZ, JOHN A. & O'NEIL, MAUD E., eds.
23.140   BB   1946 Arthur Holt, Anglican clergyman, reports on Barbados, 1725-1733.

SCROGGS, WILLIAM
37.363   JM   1962 Jamaicans are English.

SEHEULT, R.
28.479   TR   1940 A brief historical survey of the surgeons-general of Trinidad.
28.480   TR   1940 A short historical survey of three notable medical men of the past
                        century.
28.481   GC   1944 A brief sketch of the history of yellow fever in the West Indies.
28.483   TR   1946 A review of the evolution of health services in Trinidad—1814-1934.

SEMMEL, BERNARD

5.197   JM   1962   THE GOVERNOR EYRE CONTROVERSY. London, MacGibbon and Kee, 188p.   [*NYP*]

16.029   JM   1962   The issue of "race" in the British reaction to the Morant Bay Uprising of 1865.

SERTIMA, J. van

53.033   BG   1913   The British Guiana Bank.

36.017   BG   1915   The municipality of New Amsterdam.

SHEPHARD, C.Y.

58.088   BC   1929   The sugar industry of the British West Indies and British Guiana with special reference to Trinidad.

59.040   TR   1932/ The cacao industry of Trinidad; some economic aspects.
                    37

51.123   GC   1939   British West Indian economic history in imperial perspective.

46.200   LW/   1947   Peasant agriculture in the Leeward and Windward Islands. Part I:
           WW   The development of peasant agriculture.

SHEPHEARD, WALWYN P. B.

38.111   BC   1900   The West Indies and confederation.

SHERLOCK, PHILIP M.

8.053   GC   1955   THE DEVELOPMENT OF THE MIDDLE CLASS IN THE CARIBBEAN.

5.198   GC   1960   WEST INDIAN STORY. London, Longmans, Green, 134p.

37.368   JM/   1962   Nouvelles nations dans les Antilles [New nations in the Caribbean].
           TR

SHILSTONE, E. M.

37.370   BB   1934   The evolution of the general assembly of Barbados.

37.371   BB   1935   The thirteen Baronets.

23.143   BB   1936   Parish churches in Barbados.

40.165   BB   1938   A descriptive list of maps of Barbados.

5.199   BB   1939   Captain Henry Hawley and the House of Assembly at Barbados. *J Barb Mus Hist Soc* 6(4), Aug.: 175-185.   [*AMN*]

2.219   BB   1940   Barbados in the year 1840.

5.200   BB   1944   Historic Barbados. *Can-W I Mag* 33-34(11), Nov.: 7-9, 73-74.   [*NYP*]

5.201   BB   1953   The Washingtons and their doctors in Barbados. *J Barb Mus Hist Soc* 20(2), Feb.: 71-80.   [*AMN*]

23.144   BB   1958   MONUMENTAL INSCRIPTIONS IN THE BURIAL GROUND OF THE JEWISH SYNAGOGUE AT BRIDGETOWN, BARBADOS.

52.085   BB   1958   Some notes on early printing presses and newspapers in Barbados.

SHORROCKS, FRANCIS

23.145   BB   1958   History of the Catholic Church in Barbados during the 19th century.

SIRES, RONALD VERNON

5.202   JM   1936   JAMAICA IN DECLINE, 1834-1856. Ph.D. dissertation, University of Wisconsin, 257p. [6, 37]

37.377   JM   1940   Constitutional change in Jamaica, 1834-60.

50.115   JM   1940   Negro labor in Jamaica in the years following emancipation.

50.116   JM   1940   Sir Henry Barkly and the labor problem in Jamaica 1853-1856.

37.378   JM   1953   Governmental crisis in Jamaica, 1860-1866.

37.380   JM   1954 The Jamaica Constitution of 1884.
37.381   JM   1955 The experience of Jamaica with a modified crown colony government.
37.382   BC   1957 Government in the British West Indies: an historical outline.

SLOAN, JENNIE A.
39.039   BG   1938 Anglo-American relations and the Venezuelan boundary dispute.

SLOMAN, E.
35.041   BG   1912 St. George's Cathedral.

SLOTHOUWER, L.
3.281   NW   1929/ De Nederlandsche Bovenwindsche Eilanden [The Dutch Windward
            30   Islands].

SLUITER, ENGEL
39.040   SR   1933 Dutch Guiana: a problem in boundaries.

SMELSER, MARSHALL
5.203   FA   1955 THE CAMPAIGN FOR THE SUGAR ISLANDS, 1759: A STUDY OF AMPHIBIOUS
                   WARFARE. Chapel Hill, N.C., University of North Carolina Press,
                   212p.   [*NYP*]

SMITH, Rev. G.W.
23.156   GC   [1939?] CONQUESTS OF CHRIST IN THE WEST INDIES: A SHORT HISTORY OF EVAN-
                   GELICAL MISSIONS.

SMITH, M.G.
8.056   BC   1953 Some aspects of social structure in the British Caribbean about
                   1820.

SPURDLE, FREDERICK G.
37.389   BB/   [n.d.] Early West Indian government, showing the progress of government
            JM/   in Barbados, Jamaica and the Leeward Islands, 1660-1783.
            LW

STAAL, G.J.
10.051   SR   1927/ Stroomingen in Suriname [Currents in Surinam].
            28

STAEHELIN, F.
23.160   SR/   [1912?] DIE MISSION DER BRÜDERGEMEINE IN SURINAME UND BERBICE IM ACHT-
            BG   ZEHNTEN JAHRHUNDERT [THE MORAVIAN BRETHREN MISSION IN SURINAM
                   AND BERBICE IN THE 18TH CENTURY].

STEMBRIDGE, E.C.
32.193   JM   1939 Romance of a charity—intended marriage "dot" that benefited
                   thousands.
32.194   BB   1939 Soldier-poet who founded a college.

STEPHENS, S.G.
61.030   BC   1944 Cotton growing in the West Indies during the 18th and 19th centuries.

STEVENS, PETER
35.042   BB   1959 Planning and preservation.

STEVENSON, G. C.
61.031   BG   1949 Some historical notes on the cultivation of cotton in British Guiana.
58.098   BB   1959 Sugar cane varieties in Barbados: an historical review.

STEWART, ALICE R.
38.119   BC   1950 Canadian-West Indian union, 1884-1885.
38.120   BC   1951 Documents on Canadian-West Indian relations, 1883-1885.

STRONG, L. A. G.
58.099   BC   1954 THE STORY OF SUGAR.

SUMMIT, ALPHONS
15.039   SR   1940 The Jews of Surinam.

SWABEY, CHRISTOPHER
64.109   BG   1950 Note on the development of forest policy in British Guiana.
64.110   BG   1951 Note on the development of forest policy in British Guiana.

SYPHER, W.
21.025   BC   1939 The West Indian as a character in the 18th century.

TANSILL, C. C.
37.396   UV   1932 THE PURCHASE OF THE DANISH WEST INDIES.

TAYLOR, RONALD V.
45.034   BB   1957 Two Barbados estate plans.

TAYLOR, S. A. G.
37.397   JM   1949 Military operations in Jamaica 1655-1660: an appreciation.
5.204   JM   1954 PAGES FROM OUR PAST. Kingston, Pioneer Press, 183p.   [*NYP*]
5.205   JM   1962 When the French invaded Jamaica. *Chron W I Comm* 77(1731),
                        Apr.: 179-180.   [*NYP*]
5.206   JM   1963 The "Pass" at Craigellachie. *Chron W I Comm* 78(1386), July:
                        373-375.   [*NYP*]
5.207   JM   1965 The settlers from Nevis. *Chron W I Comm* 80(1405), Feb.: 77-79.
                                                                                [*NYP*]

THAMAR, MAURICE
37.398   FG   1935 LES PEINES COLONIALES ET L'EXPÉRIENCE GUYANAISE [COLONIAL PENAL
                        SENTENCES AND THE GUIANA EXPERIMENT].

THOMPSON, ROBERT WALLACE
46.219   JM   1959 Vázquez de Espinosa and Jamaica.

THORNE, A. A.
32.199   BG   1911/ Education in British Guiana.
                  12

THORNTON, A. P.

51.137   TR   1954 Some statistics of West Indian produce, shipping and revenue, 1660-1685.

5.208   JM/   1956 West India policy under the Restoration. Oxford, Clarendon
          BB   Press, 280p.   [*RIS*]

THORNTON, H. P.

5.209   JM   1952 The Modyfords and Morgan. *Jam Hist Rev* 2(Publ. no. 2), Oct.: 36-60.

TOOKE, CHARLES W.

44.236   UV   1900 The Danish colonial fiscal system in the West Indies.

TORO, ELIAS

39.041   BG   1905 Por las selvas de Guayana: delimitación de Venezuela con
                       Guayana Británica [Through the forests of Guiana: the boundary
                       between Venezuela and British Guiana].

TUCKER, LEONARD, comp.

23.164   JM   1914 "Glorious liberty": the story of a hundred years' work of the
                       Jamaica Baptist Mission.

TURNER, H. E.

65.075   BG   1938 A short history of the Rupununi savannahs with special reference
                       to the livestock industry.

UGARTE, MANUEL

39.042   BH   1940 Guatemala's claims in British Honduras.

UTTLEY, K. H.

28.528   AT   1958 The mortality from erysipelas over the last hundred years in Antigua,
                       the West Indies.

28.529   AT   1959 The epidemiology of tetanus in the Negro race over the last hundred
                       years in Antigua, the West Indies.

28.530   AT   1959 The mortality and epidemiology of filariasis over the last hundred
                       years in Antigua, British West Indies.

28.531   AT   1960 The epidemiology and mortality of whooping cough in the Negro
                       over the last hundred years in Antigua, British West Indies.

28.532   AT   1960 The mortality and epidemiology of diphtheria since 1857 in the
                       Negro population of Antigua, British West Indies.

28.533   AT   1960 The mortality and epidemiology of typhoid fever in the coloured
                       inhabitants of Antigua, West Indies, over the last hundred years.

28.534   AT   1960 The mortality of yellow fever in Antigua, West Indies, since 1857.

28.535   AT   1960 Smallpox mortality in the Negro population of Antigua, West Indies;
                       a historical note.

28.536   AT   1961 Epidemiology and mortality of malaria in Antigua, B. W. I., 1857-1956.

28.537   AT   1961 The epidemiology of puerperal fever and maternal mortality in An-
                       tigua, West Indies, over the last hundred years, including a com-
                       parison with recent trends in neighbouring territories.

VALLEE, LIONEL

9.057   ST   1964 The Negro family in St. Thomas: a study in role differentiation.

VANDERCOOK, JOHN WOMACK

15.040   SR   1928 Jungle Jews.

VERIN, PIERRE MICHEL

4.150   SL   1961 Les Caraïbes à Sainte Lucie depuis les contacts coloniaux [The
                     Caribs in St. Lucia since the time of contact].

40.199   SL   1961 Toponymie de l'île de Sainte-Lucie [Toponymy of the island of
                     St. Lucia].

VERRILL, ALPHEUS HYATT

3.315   GC   1923 IN THE WAKE OF THE BUCCANEERS.

VERTEUIL, ERIC de

28.540   TR   1941 Trinidad malaria in prospect and retrospect.

VIGNOLS, LEON

50.124   FC   1928 Les Antilles Francaises sous l'Ancien Régime: Aspects écono-
                     miques et sociaux: L'institution des engagés (1626-1774) [The
                     French Antilles under the old regime: economic and social aspects:
                     The institution of bonded servants (1626-1774)].

5.210   FC   1928 Les Antilles Francaises sous l'Ancien Régime: Aspects écono-
                     miques et sociaux: Un produit social de guerre; filibuste et boucane
                     (XVIe-XVIIIe siècles) [The French Antilles under the old regime:
                     Economic and social aspects: A social by-product of war; Fili-
                     busters and buccaneers (16th–18th centuries)]. *Rev Hist Econ
                     Social* 16(2): 137-181.

VILLIERS, J. A. J. de

5.211   BG   1911 The foundation and development of British Guiana. *Geogr J* 38(1),
                     July: 8-26.   [*AGS*]

39.044   BG   1912 The boundaries of British Guiana.

VOLLENHOVEN, C. van

5.212   SR   1916 Politieke contracten met de Boschnegers in Suriname [Political
                     contracts with the Bush Negroes of Surinam]. *Bijd Volk Ned-Indië*
                     71:371-411. [14, 37]

VOULLAIRE, W. R.

23.168   SR   1926 SURINAM: LE PAYS, LES HABITANTS ET LAS MISSION MORAVE [SURINAM:
                     THE LAND, THE INHABITANTS, AND THE MORAVIAN MISSION].

VRYMAN, L. C.

5.213   FG   1936/ Iets over de Nederlandsche volksplanting in "Cayanen" gedurende
              37   de zeventiende eeuw [Some facts about the Dutch settlement in
                    "Cayanen" during the 17th century]. *W I G* 18:13-24. [7]   [*COL*]

WADDELL, DAVID A. G.

37.407   BH   1957 British Honduras and Anglo-American relations.
37.408   BH   1959 British Honduras and Anglo-American relations: a correction.
37.409   BH   1959 Great Britain and the Bay Islands 1821-61.

WAGENAAR HUMMELINCK, P.

45.035   SR   1947 Het dagelijksch leven op de Surinaamsche koffieplantage "Kokswoud" in 1828 [Daily life on the coffee plantation "Koswoud"
in 1828].

WARD, EDWARD

3.322   JM   1933 A trip to Jamaica with a true character of the people and island.

WATERMAN, I. D.

28.552   TR   1958 A century of service.

WATERMAN, THOMAS T.

35.044   BB   1946 Some early buildings of Barbados.

WATTS, ARTHUR P.

5.214   BC   1924 UNE HISTOIRE DES COLONIES ANGLAISES AUX ANTILLES (DE 1649 À
1660) [A HISTORY OF THE BRITISH COLONIES IN THE ANTILLES (FROM
1649 TO 1660)]. Paris, Presses universitaires de France, 516p.
[*NYP*]

5.215   NV/   1925 NEVIS AND ST. CHRISTOPHER'S 1782-1784 (UNPUBLISHED DOCUMENTS).
SK   Paris, Presses universitaires de France, 159p.   [*NYP*]

WATTS, DAVID

41.260   BB   1963 PLANT INTRODUCTION AND LANDSCAPE CHANGE IN BARBADOS 1625-1830.

WATTS, Sir FRANCIS

46.229   BC   1920 Tropical departments of agriculture, with special reference to the
West Indies.
20:019   BC   1926 History as affecting outlook in the West Indies.
46.232   BC   1927 West Indian notes.

WAUGH, ALEC

5.216   GC   1964 A FAMILY OF ISLANDS: A HISTORY OF THE WEST INDIES FROM 1492 TO
1898, WITH AN EPILOGUE SKETCHING EVENTS FROM THE SPANISH-
AMERICAN WAR TO THE 1960'S. Garden City, Doubleday, 348p.   [*RIS*]

WEBBER, A. R. F.

5.217   BG   1931 A CENTENARY HISTORY AND HANDBOOK OF BRITISH GUIANA. Georgetown, Argosy Co., 363p.   [*NYP*]

WEISS, H.

23.169   SR   1919 Het zendingswerk der Herrnhutters in de Oerwouden van de Boven-
Suriname [Missionary work of the Moravian Brethren in the jungles
of the Upper-Surinam River].

23.170   SR   1920/ De zending der Hernhutters onder de Indianen in Berbice en Sur-
21 iname, 1738-1816 (The mission of the Moravians among the Indians
in Berbice and Surinam, 1738-1816].

WELLS, HENRY

37.417   UV   1955 Outline of the constitutional development of the United States
Virgin Islands.

WESLEY, CHARLES H.

32.212   BC   1932/ Rise of Negro education in the British Empire.
33

11.026   BC   1934   The emancipation of the free colored population in the British Empire.

WESTERGAARD, WALDEMAR
45.037   SC   1938   A St. Croix map of 1766: with a note on its significance in West Indian plantation economy.
5.218   UV   1957   THE DANISH WEST INDIES: UNDER COMPANY RULE (1671-1754) WITH SUPPLEMENTARY CHAPTER; 1755-1917. New York, Macmillan, 359p.
[*NYP*]

WESTRA, P.
37.420   SR   1919   De Koloniale Staten van Suriname [The Colonial Council of Surinam].

WHITE, RALPH J.
23.171   BG   1919   The Berbice Lutheran Church.

WHITSON, AGNES M.
37.423   JM   1929   THE CONSTITUTIONAL DEVELOPMENT OF JAMAICA, 1660 TO 1729.

WIJK, H. L. A. van
25.119   CU   1958   Orígenes y evolución del papiamentu [Origins and development of Papiamento].

WILES, D. A.
1.045   BB   1949   The history of the Barbados Public Library.

WILLIAMS, ERIC EUSTACE
58.128   BC   1943   Laissez faire, sugar and slavery.
58.129   BG   1944   The historical background of British Guiana's problems.
2.262   BG   1945   The historical background of British Guiana's problems.
2.265   BC   1952   DOCUMENTS ON BRITISH WEST INDIAN HISTORY, 1807-1833.
1.047   GC   1954   A bibliography of Caribbean history: a preliminary essay. Part I: 1492-1898.
16.035   GC   1955   THE HISTORICAL BACKGROUND OF RACE RELATIONS IN THE CARIBBEAN.
38.127   BC   1963   THE FUTURE OF THE WEST INDIES AND GUYANA. ADDRESS DELIVERED AT QUEENS COLLEGE, GEORGETOWN, GUYANA, UNDER THE AUSPICES OF THE EXTRA-MURAL DEPARTMENT, UNIVERSITY OF THE WEST INDIES, 13TH MARCH 1963.
5.219   BC   1964   BRITISH HISTORIANS AND THE WEST INDIES. Port of Spain, P.N.M. Pub. Co., 187p. [67]   [*RIS*]

WILLIAMS, ERIC EUSTACE, ed.
38.128   BC   1954   The historical background of the British West Indian Federation: select documents.
5.220   GC   1963   DOCUMENTS OF WEST INDIAN HISTORY, VOL. I: 1492-1655, FROM THE SPANISH DISCOVERY TO THE BRITISH CONQUEST OF JAMAICA. Port of Spain, Printed by P.N.M. Pub. Co., 310p.   [*RIS*]

WILLIAMS, J. F.
58.132   BG   1951   Development of the cane sugar industry in British Guiana.

WILLIAMS, JAMES
47.033   BG   1936   The aborigines of British Guiana and their land.

WILLIAMS, JOSEPH J.

23.172   JM   1932 VOODOOS AND OBEAHS, PHASES OF WEST INDIA WITCHCRAFT.
10.052   JM/   1932 WHENCE THE "BLACK IRISH" OF JAMAICA?
           BB
11.028   JM   1938 The Maroons of Jamaica.

WILLIAMSON, JAMES A.

5.221   BG/   1923 ENGLISH COLONIES IN GUIANA AND ON THE AMAZON, 1604-1668. Oxford,
           SR   Clarendon Press, 191p.   [COL]
5.222   SK/   1926 THE CARIBBEE ISLANDS UNDER THE PROPRIETARY PATENTS. New York,
           BB   Oxford University Press, 234p.   [AGS]

WINZERLING, E. O.

5.223   BH   1946 THE BEGINNING OF BRITISH HONDURAS 1506-1765. New York, North
                         River Press, 90p.   [AGS]

WISEMAN, H. V.

5.224   BC   1950 A SHORT HISTORY OF THE BRITISH WEST INDIES. London, University
                         of London Press, 159p.   [COL]

WOLSTENHOLME, G. L.

41.268   BG   1953 Jenman and the Georgetown Botanic Gardens.

WOODING, H. O. B.

37.432   TR   1960 The constitutional history of Trinidad and Tobago.

WOOLF, S. H.

5.225   BB   1949 Rum and roguery—Barbados, 1710. *Life Lett* 62(143), July: 25-33.
                                                                                [COL]

WRIGHT, RICHARDSON

22.148   JM   1937 REVELS IN JAMAICA, 1682-1838.
8.066   JM   1938/Freemasonry on the island of Jamaica.
                     39

WRONG, HUME

37.433   BC   1923 GOVERNMENT OF THE WEST INDIES.

WROTH, LAWRENCE C.

5.226   FG   1925 Some early French Guiana tracts: an addition to the early biblio-
                         graphy of El Dorado. *Proc Am Antiq Soc* new ser., 35, Apr.: 28-45.

YOUNG, ALLAN

36.021   BG   1957 SOME MILESTONES IN VILLAGE HISTORY.
37.435   BG   1958 THE APPROACHES TO LOCAL SELF-GOVERNMENT IN BRITISH GUIANA.

YOUNG, J. G.

36.022   JM   1946 Who planned Kingston?
52.095   JM   1959 Old road laws of Jamaica.

ZANS, V. A.

40.227   JM   1958 Geology and mining in Jamaica: a brief historical review.

ZWARTS, JAC

15.045   SR   1927/Een episode uit de Joodsche kolonie van Guyana, 1660 [An episode
                     28 from the Jewish colony of Guiana, 1660].

Chapter 6

SLAVERY AND EMANCIPATION

ABBENHUIS, M. F.

6.001   CU/   1953 De requesten van Pater Stöppel en Perfect Wennekers in 1817 en
        SR   1819 [The petitions of Father Stöppel and Perfect Wennekers in
                      1817 and 1819]. *W I G* 34:38-50. [23]   [*COL*]

BANGOU, HENRI

6.002   GD   1962 LA GUADELOUPE 1492-1848; OU L'HISTOIRE DE LA COLONISATION DE
                    L'ÎLE LIÉE À L'ESCLAVAGE NOIR DE SES DÉBUTS À SA DISPARITION
                    [GUADELOUPE 1492-1848; OR, THE HISTORY OF THE COLONIZATION OF
                    THE ISLAND RELATED TO NEGRO SLAVERY FROM ITS BEGINNINGS TO ITS
                    DISAPPEARANCE]. [Aurillac, France?]. Editions du Centre, 350p. [5]
                                            [*RIS*]

BAUDE, PIERRE

6.003   MT   1948 L'AFFRANCHISSEMENT DES ESCLAVES AUX ANTILLES FRANCAISES,
                    PRINCIPALEMENT À LA MARTINIQUE, DU DÉBUT DE LA COLONISATION À
                    1848 [THE EMANCIPATION OF SLAVES IN THE FRENCH ANTILLES, PAR-
                    TICULARLY IN MARTINIQUE, FROM THE ONSET OF COLONIZATION TO 1848].
                    Fort de France, Impr. du gouvernement, 174p.   [*NYP*]

BEHN, APHRA

6.004   SR   1919/ De geschiedenis van den koninklijken slaaf [The history of the
             20   royal slave]. *W I G* 1(1):477-495; 1(2):52-70, 339-360, 435-461. [16]
                                              [*COL*]

BENJAMINS, H. D.

7.008   BG/   1923 Bevolkingscijfers van Britsch Guyana en Suriname [Population
        SR   figures on British Guiana and Surinam].

BENNETT, J. HARRY, Jr.

6.005   BB   1949 Of the Negroes thereon. *In* KLINGBERG, FRANK J., ed. CODRINGTON
                    CHRONICLE: AN EXPERIMENT IN ANGLICAN ALTRUISM ON A BARBADOS
                    PLANTATION, 1710-1834. Berkeley and Los Angeles, University of
                    California Press, p.85-103. (Publications in history no. 37.)
6.006   BB   1951/ The problems of slave labor: supply at the Codrington plantations.
             52   pts. I-II. *J Negro Hist* 36(4), Oct.: 406-441; 37(2), Apr.: 115-141.
                                              [*RIS*]

6.007   BB   1958 BONDSMEN AND BISHOPS: SLAVERY AND APPRENTICESHIP ON THE COD-
               RINGTON PLANTATIONS OF BARBADOS, 1710-1838. Berkeley and Los
               Angeles, University of California Press, 176p. (Publications in
               history no. 62.)   [*RIS*]

               BURN, W. L.
6.008   BC   1937 EMANCIPATION AND APPRENTICESHIP IN THE BRITISH WEST INDIES.
               London, Jonathan Cape, 196p. [50]   [*RIS*]

               CAMERON, N. E.
11.005   GC   1929/ THE EVOLUTION OF THE NEGRO.
               34

               COUSINS, WINIFRED M.
9.004   BC   1935 Slave family life in the British colonies 1800-1834.

               CRUICKSHANK, J. GRAHAM
11.008   BG   1919 African immigrants after freedom.
8.015   BG   1933 "Good time" in slavery days.

               CUNDALL, FRANK
6.009   JM   1920 Richard Hill. *J Negro Hist* 5(1), Jan.: 37-44.   [*COL*]

               DAVIS, DAVID B.
6.010   BC   1960/ James Cropper and the British anti-slavery movement, 1821-1823.
               61 *J Negro Hist* 45(4), Oct. 1960: 241-258; 46(3), July 1961: 154-173.
                                                                                  [*COL*]

               DEBIEN, GABRIEL
6.011   MT   1960 Destinées d'esclaves à la Martinique [Lives of Martinique slaves].
               B Inst Fr Afr Noire 22(1-2), Jan.-Apr.: 1-91.   [*AMN*]
30.009   FC   1964 La nourriture des esclaves sur les plantations des Antilles Fran-
               caises aux XVIIe et XVIIIe siècles [The diet of slaves on the
               plantations of the French Antilles in the 17th and 18th centuries].

               DEBIEN, GABRIEL & FELHOEN KRAAL, JOHANNA L. G.
6.012   SR   1955/ Esclaves et plantations de Surinam vus par Malouet, 1777. [Slaves
               66 and plantations of Surinam as seen by Malouet, 1777]. *W I G* 36:53-
               60.   [*COL*]

               DRIMMELEN, C. van
11.009   SR   1925/ De Neger en zijn cultuur geschiedenis [The Negro and his cultural
               26 history].

               ERICKSON, ARVEL B.
6.013   JM   1959 Empire or anarchy: the Jamaican rebellion of 1865. *J Negro Hist*
               44(2), Apr.: 99-122. [11]   [*COL*]

               FINDLAY, G. G. & HOLDSWORTH, W. W.
23.045   BC   1921 THE HISTORY OF THE WESLEYAN METHODIST MISSIONARY SOCIETY, V. 2.

               FISHER, RUTH ANNA
6.014   BB   1942 Manuscript materials bearing on the Negro in British archives. *J
               Negro Hist* 27(1), Jan.: 83-93.   [*AMN*]

GAAY FORTMAN, B. de

5.058   SR   1928/ In Suriname voor honderd jaar [In Surinam a hundred years ago].
              29

6.015   SR   1930/ Suriname op den drempel van de afschaffing der slavernij [Surinam
              31   on the threshold of the abolition of slavery]. *W I G* 12:401-422. [37]
                                                                                 [*COL*]

GASTON-MARTIN

6.016   FA   1948   HISTOIRE DE L'ESCLAVAGE DANS LES COLONIES FRANCAISES [HISTORY
                    OF SLAVERY IN THE FRENCH COLONIES]. Paris Presses universitaires
                    de France, 318p.   [*RIS*]

GETROUW, C. F. G.

6.017   SR   1953   De stemming van de bevolking voor, tijdens, en na de emancipatie
                    van de slaven in Suriname [The mood of the population before,
                    during, and after the emancipation of the slaves in Surinam]. *W I G*
                    34:3-12.   [*COL*]

GOSLINGA, C. CH.

6.018   GG   1956/ Juan de Ampués, vredelievende Indianenjager [Juan de Ampués,
              57   peaceloving Indian slave hunter]. *W I G* 37:169-187.   [*COL*]

6.019   NL   1956   EMANCIPATIE EN EMANCIPATOR [EMANCIPATION AND EMANCIPATOR].
                    Assen, Van Gorcum, 187p.   [*RIS*]

GOVEIA, ELSA V.

6.020   GC   1960   The West Indian slave laws of the eighteenth century. *Revta Cienc*
                    Social 4(1), Mar.:75-105.   [*AGS*]

GROL, G. J. van

46.079   ' SE   1920/ Econmische arbeid op St. Eustatitus van gouvernementswege 1903-
              21   1918 [Government supported economic work on St. Eustatius 1903-
                    1918].

HALL, DOUGLAS GORDON

6.021   JM   1953   The apprenticeship period in Jamaica, 1834-38. *Car Q* pp.3(3),
                    Dec.: 142-166.   [*RIS*]

6.022   BC   1962   Slaves and slavery in the British West Indies. *In* SINGHAM, A. &
                    BRAITHWAITE, L. E., eds. Special number [of *Social Econ Stud*]
                    on the Conference on Political Sociology in the British Caribbean,
                    Social Econ Stud 11(4), Dec.: 305-318. [45]   [*RIS*]

HALL, GWENDOLYN MIDLO

6.023   GC   1964   Negro slaves in the Americas. *Freedomways* 4(3), Summer: 319-330.
                                                                               [*RIS*]

HALLEMA, A.

6.024   NC   1939   Koloniale vraagstukken ten opzichte van onze West anderhalve
                    eeuw geleden [Colonial problems in connection with our West one-
                    and-a-half centuries ago]. *WIG* 21:78-86, 108-115. [44,51] [*COL*]

HARRIS, Sir JOHN

6.025   BC   1933   A CENTURY OF EMANCIPATION. London, J.H. Dent, 287p.   [*COL*]

HART, RICHARD

6.026   JM   1950 Cudjoe and the first Maroon war in Jamaica. *Car Hist Rev* 1, Dec.:
                       46-79.   [*COL*]

HARTOG, JOHAN

6.027   SE   1948 Oud nummer van de "St. Eustatius Gazette" [Old issue of the
                       "St. Eustatius Gazette"]. *W I G* 29:161-174.   [*COL*]

HELLMER-WULLEN, HILDA von

6.028   GC   1939 Der Sklavenhandel—die historische Grundlage der Negerfrage in
                       Amerika: statistische Aufzeichnungen von 1492-1807 [The slave
                       trade—the historical basis of the Negro issue in America: statistical
                       records from 1492-1807]. *Z Rassk* 9(2):97-103.   [*AGS*]

HESSELBERG, ENGELBRET

6.029   SC   1926 Account of the Negro rebellion on St. Croix, Danish West Indies,
                       1759 (WALDEMAR C. WESTERGAARD, ed.) *J Negro Hist* 11,
                       Jan.: 50-61.   [*AMN*]

HIGHAM, C. S. S.

6.030   BB   1925 / The Negro policy of Christopher Codrington. *J Negro Hist* 10(2),
                       Apr.: 150-153.   [*SCH*]

HOUDAILLE, J.; MASSIO, R.; & DEBIEN, G.

6.031   FA   1963 Les origines des esclaves des Antilles [The origins of the slaves
                       of the Antilles]. *B Inst Fr Afr Noire* ser. B, 25(3-4): 215-265. [*COL*]

JESSE, C.

23.075   FA   1960 Religion among the early slaves in the French Antilles.

JONES, SAMUEL B.

11.013   BC   1911 The British West Indian Negro.

JOUBERT, E.

6.032   FA   1948 Conséquences géographiques de l'émancipation des noirs aux
                       Antilles (1848) [Geographic consequences of the emancipation of
                       the blacks in the Antilles (1848)]. *Cah O-M* 1(2), Apr.-June: 105-118.
                                                                                      [*AGS*]

KATZ, WALLACE

6.033   BC/   1958/ Slavery and caste: plantation society in the British and French
          FA   59   Caribbean in the eighteenth century. Kings Crown Essays, Columbia
                       College *J Social Sci* 6(1), Winter: 13-44.   [*RIS*]

KENNEDY, MELVIN D.

6.034   MT   1960 The Bissette affair and the French colonial question. *J Negro Hist*
                       45(1), Jan.: 1-10.   [*COL*]

KESLER, C. K.

11.014   SR   1926/ Naar aanleiding van "De Neger en zijne cultuurgeschiedenis" [With
                 27   reference to "The Negro and his cultural history"].
28.307   BG   1929/ Een Duitsch medicus in Essequebo in de laatste jaren der 18e eeuw
                 30   [A German medical doctor in Essequibo during the last years of the
                       18th century].

6.035   SR   1940 Slavenopstanden in de West [Slave rebellions in the West]. *W I G*
             22:157-170, 189-302.   [*COL*]
6.036   NC   1940 Uit de eerste dagen van den West-Indischen slavenhandel [About
             the first days of the West Indian slave trade]. *W I G* 22:175-185.
             [13]   [*COL*]

KIELSTRA, J. C.
44.125 SR   1925 Wirtschaftliche und soziale Probleme in Niederländisch-Westindien
             [Economic and social problems in the Dutch West Indies].

KLINGBERG, FRANK J.
6.037   BB   1938 British humanitarianism at Codrington. *J Negro Hist* 23(4), Oct.:
             451-486. [8, 32]   [*AMN*]
6.038   JM   1942 As to the state of Jamaica in 1707. *J Negro Hist* 27(3), July: 288-
             294. [23]   [*AMN*]

KLINGBERG, FRANK J., ed.
45.012 BB   1949 CODRINGTON CHRONICLE: AN EXPERIMENT IN ANGLICAN ALTRUISM ON A '
             BARBADOS PLANTATION, 1710-1834.

KNAPLUND, PAUL
6.039   BC   1950 Sir James Stephen: the friend of the Negroes. *J Negro Hist* 35(4),
             Oct.: 368-407.   [*COL*]

LACASCADE, PIERRE
50.079 FA   1907 ESCLAVAGE ET IMMIGRATION. LA QUESTION DE LA MAIN-D'OEUVRE AUX
             ANTILLES: LE DÉCRET DU 13 FÉVRIER 1852 ET LA CONVENTION ANGLAISE
             DU 1ᵉʳ JUILLET 1861 [SLAVERY AND IMMIGRATION. THE QUESTION OF
             MANPOWER IN THE ANTILLES: THE DECREE OF 13 FEBRUARY 1852 AND
             THE BRITISH CONVENTION OF JULY 1861].

LATOUR, M. D.
11.015 CU   1940 Boessaalsche Negers [Recently arrived ("greenhorn") Negroes].

La TRY ELLIS, W. CH. de
6.040   NL   1960/ Historische aantekeningen omtrent de Nederlandse Antillen [Histor-
             61   ical notes about the Dutch Antilles]. *N W I G* 40:201-220. [4] [*COL*]

LEVY, CLAUDE
6.041   BB   1959 Barbados: the last years of slavery 1823-1833. *J Negro Hist* 44(4),
             Oct.: 308-345.   [*COL*]

LEWIS, GORDON K.
37.225 GC   1961 The Caribbean: colonization and culture.

LIER, RUDOLF A. J. van
6.042   SR   1954 Negro slavery in Surinam. *Car Hist Rev* 3-4, Dec.: 108-148.   [*RIS*]

LINDE, J. M. van der
6.043   SR   1953 De emancipatie der Negerslaven in Suriname en de zendingsarbeid
             der Moravische Broeders [The emancipation of the Negro slaves in
             Surinam and the missionary work of the Moravian Brethren]. *W I G*
             34:23-37. [23]   [*COL*]

LOPEZ, AMY K.
50.085 JM   1948 Land and labour to 1900.

McPHERSON, JAMES M.

6.044 GC 1964 Was West Indian emancipation a success? The abolitionist argument during the American Civil War. *Car Stud* 4(2), July: 28-34.   *[RIS]*

MARCHAND-THEBAULT, MARIE-LOUISE

6.045 FG 1960 L'esclavage en Guyane Francaise sous l'ancien régime [Slavery in French Guiana under the old regime]. *Rev Fr Hist O-M* 47(166): 5-75.   *[RIS]*

MATHIESON, WILLIAM LAW

6.046 BC 1926 BRITISH SLAVERY AND ITS ABOLITION. London, Longmans, Green, 318p.   *[RIS]*

6.047 BC 1932 BRITISH SLAVE EMANCIPATION, 1838-49. London, Longmans, Green, 243p. [47, 50]   *[NYP]*

5.132 BC 1936 THE SUGAR COLONIES AND GOVERNOR EYRE, 1849-1866.

MENKMAN, W. R.

6.048 BG/ 1932/ Essequibosche correspondentie [Correspondence from Essequebo].
     SR   33 *W I G* 14:59-68.   *[COL]*

6.049 CU 1935/ Slavenhandel en rechtsbedeeling op Curacao op het einde der 17e
        36 eeuw [Slave trade and administration of justice on Curacao at the end of the 17th century]. *W I G* 17:11-26. [37]   *[COL]*

6.050 CU 1944/ Nederlandsche en vreemde slavenvaart [Dutch and foreign slave
        45 trade]. *W I G* 26:97-110.   *[COL]*

5.143 SR 1944/ Suriname in Willoughby's tijd [Surinam in the time of Willoughby].
        45

6.051 NC 1953 Slavernij—slavenhandel—emancipatie [Slavery, slave trade and emancipation]. *W I G* 34:103-112.   *[COL]*

MIDAS, ANDRE

6.052 FA 1950 Victor Schoelcher and emancipation in the French West Indies. *Car Hist Rev* 1, Dec.: 110-124.   *[COL]*

NIDDRIE, DAVID L.

6.053 TR 1963 Kaye Dowland's book: a record of mid-19th century Tobago. *Car Q* 9(4), Dec.: 44-51.   *[RIS]*

OUDSCHANS DENTZ, FRED

6.054 SR 1928/ Het einde van de legende Dahlberg-Baron [The end of the legend
        29 Dahlberg-Baron]. *W I G* 10:165-167.   *[COL]*

45.017 SR 1944/ De herkomst en de beteekenis van Surinaamsche plantagenamen
        45 [The origin and meaning of the names of the plantations in Surinam].

PADILLA, ELENA

45.018 GC 1959 Colonization and development of plantations.

PAYNE, ERNEST A.

23.118 JM 1946 FREEDOM IN JAMAICA; SOME CHAPTERS IN THE STORY OF THE BAPTIST MISSIONARY SOCIETY. 2d ed.

PETERS, FRED E.

6.055 BC 1934 THE ABOLITION OF SLAVERY. Bridgetown, Advocate Press, 16p.

PITMAN, FRANK WESLEY
6.056   BC   1926   Slavery on the British West India plantations in the eighteenth century. *J Negro Hist* 11(4), Oct.: 584-668. [23, 45]   [*AMN*]

RAGATZ, LOWELL JOSEPH
1.033   BC   1923   A CHECK LIST OF HOUSE OF COMMONS SESSIONAL PAPERS RELATING TO THE BRITISH WEST INDIES AND TO THE WEST INDIAN SLAVE TRADE AND SLAVERY, 1763-1834.
1.034   BC   1931   A CHECK-LIST OF HOUSE OF LORDS SESSIONAL PAPERS RELATING TO THE BRITISH WEST INDIES AND THE WEST INDIAN SLAVE TRADE AND SLAVERY, 1763-1834.

KENNARD, J.
6.057   FC   1948   1848-1948: centennaire de la liberté [1848-1948 centenary of freedom]. *Rev Hist Colon* 35(1): 27-69.   [*NYP*]

ROBERTS, GEORGE WOODROW
7.063   BC   1952   A life table for a West Indian slave population.
17.023   BC   1954   Immigration of Africans into the British Caribbean.

RODNEY, WALTER & AUGUSTUS, EARL
6.058   GC   1964   The Negro slave. *Car Q* 10(2), June: 40-47. [45]   [*RIS*]

ROMONDT, PH. F. W.
6.059   NW   1941   Pieter Hassell. *W I G* 23:78-88. [37]   [*COL*]

RUIZ, R. E.
11.024   GC   [1965?]   A historical perspective on Caribbean Negro life.

SAMSON, PH. A.
6.060   SR   1953   De status van Piekie-Njan [The status of Piekie-Njan]. *W I G* 34: 51-55.   [*COL*]

SCHOELCHER, VICTOR
6.061   GD   1935   LETTRES INÉDITES À VICTOR SCHOELCHER (1848-1851) [UNPUBLISHED LETTERS TO VICTOR SCHOELCHER (1848-1851)]. Basse-Terre, Impr. catholique, 176p. [23]   [*RIS*]
6.062   FA   1948   ESCLAVAGE ET COLONISATION [SLAVERY AND COLONIZATION]. Paris, Presses universitaires de France, 218p. (Colonies et empires, 2d ser.: Les classiques de la colonisation, 11.)   [*COL*]

SCHUYLER, ROBERT LIVINGSTON
37.361   BC   1925   The constitutional claims of the British West Indies; the controversy over the slave registry bill of 1815.

SHERIDAN, RICHARD B.
6.063   BC   1961   The West India sugar crisis and British slave emancipation, 1830-1833. *J Econ Hist* 21(4), Dec.: 539-551. [58]   [*COL*]

SIRES, RONALD VERNON
5.202   JM   1936   JAMAICA IN DECLINE, 1834-1856.
6.064   JM   1942   The Jamaica slave insurrection loan, 1832-1863. *J Negro Hist* 27(3), July: 295-319.   [*AMN*]

SMITH, M.G.

6.065   JM   1954 Slavery and emancipation in two societies. *Social Econ Stud* 3(3-4), Dec.: 239-290.   [*NYP*]

SMITH, ROBERT WORTHINGTON

6.066   JM   1945 The legal status of Jamaican slaves before the anti-slavery movement. *J Negro Hist* 30(3), July: 239-290. [37]   [*COL*]

23.159   BC   1950 Slavery and Christianity in the British West Indies.

SPINGARN, LAWRENCE P.

6.067   UV   1957 Slavery in the Danish West Indies. *Am Scand Rev* 45(1), Mar.: 35-43.

STAAL, G. J.

6.068   SR   1928/ Nettelbecks plannen [The plans of Nettelbeck]. *W I G* 10:283-286.
            29 [66]   [*COL*]

6.069   SR   1928/ Uit den slaventijd [About the era of slavery]. *W I G* 10:168-173.
            29 [45]   [*COL*]

TANNENBAUM, FRANK

6.070   GC   1947 SLAVE AND CITIZEN; THE NEGRO IN THE AMERICAS. New York, Alfred A. Knopf, 128p. [8, 23]   [*RIS*]

VOORHOEVE, JAN

6.071   SR   1962/ De nalatenschap van A. H. A. Mamin, 1804-1837, en de plantage
            63 Vrouwenvlijt [The estate left by A. H. A. Mamin, 1804-1837, and the plantation "Vrouwenvlijt"]. *N W I G* 42:259-268.   [*COL*]

6.072   SR   1962/ W. E. H. Winkels: blankof'cier met palet en papier (W. E. H. Winkels:
            63 white official with palette and paper]. *N W I G* 42:269-288. [*COL*]

WAGENAAR HUMMELINCK, P.

45.035   SR   1947 Het dagelijksch leven op de Surinaamsche koffieplantage "Kokswoud" in 1828 [Daily life on the coffee plantation "Kokswoud" in 1828].

WESLEY, CHARLES H.

6.073   BC   1932 The neglected period of emancipation in Great Britain, 1807-1823. *J Negro Hist* 17(2), Apr.: 156-179.   [*AMN*]

6.074   BC   1932 The Negro in the West Indies: slavery and freedom. *J Negro Hist* 17(1), Jan.: 51-66.   [*AMN*]

6.075   BC   1938 The abolition of Negro apprenticeship in the British Empire. *J Negro Hist* 23(2), Apr.: 155-199.   [*AMN*]

WILLIAMS, ERIC EUSTACE

6.076   BC   1938 THE ECONOMIC ASPECT OF THE ABOLITION OF THE BRITISH WEST INDIAN SLAVE TRADE AND SLAVERY. Ph. D. dissertation, Oxford University, 408p. [58]   [*COL*]

6.077   BC   1940 The golden age of the slave system in Britain. *J Negro Hist* 25(1), Jan.: 60-106.   [*AMN*]

6.078   BC   1942 The British West Indian slave trade after its abolition in 1807. *J Negro Hist* 27(2), Apr.: 175-191.   [*AMN*]

58.128   BC   1943 Laissez-faire, sugar and slavery.

6.079   BC   1944 CAPITALISM AND SLAVERY. Chapel Hill, University of North Carolina Press, 285p. [44]   [*RIS*]

6.080   BC   1954 The British West Indies at Westminster. Part I: 1789-1823. [Port of Spain?] Trinidad, Govt. Print. Off., 136p. [37]   [*RIS*]

WINTER, JOHANNA MARIA van

1.051   NC   1953 Lijst van bronnen betreffende de afschaffing van de slavernij in Nederlands West-Indië [List of sources on the abolition of slavery in the Dutch West Indies].

6.081   SR/   1953 De openbare mening in Nederland over de afschaffing der slavernÿ
        CU   [The public opinion in the Netherlands about the abolition of slavery]. *W I G* 34:61-90.   [*COL*]

WYNDHAM, H.A.

6.082   BC/   1937 The West Indies. *In his* The Atlantic and emancipation. London,
        FA   Oxford University Press, p.79-125.

ZOOK, GEORGE F.

6.083   BB/   1919 The royal adventures and the plantations. *J Negro Hist* 4(2), Apr.:
        JM   206-231.   [*SCH*]

THE PEOPLE

Chapter 7

DEMOGRAPHY AND POPULATION TRENDS

ABBOTT, GEORGE C.
7.001   BC   1963 Estimates of the growth of the population of the West Indies to 1975 (two projections). *Social Econ Stud* 12(3), Sept.: 236-245.
[*RIS*]

ABONNENC, E.
7.002   FG   1948/ Aspects demographiques de la Guyane Francaise [Demographic
           49 aspects of French Guiana]. I. Historique [Historical]. II. Demographic actuelle [Present day demography]. III. Avenir de la population [Future of the population]. *Inst Past Guy Ter L'In* 180, Oct. (24p.); 182, Dec. (20p.) (1948); 184, Jan. (12p.) (1949). [5,10,28] [*ACM*]

ABONNENC E. & ISSARTE, A.
7.003   FG   1952 Démographie de la Guyane Francaise; structure de la population d'après le recessement de 1946 [Demography of French Guiana; Population structure according to the 1946 census]. *B Soc Path Exot* 45(2), Mar.-Apr.: 261-273. [10] [*ACM*]

ASHCROFT, M. T.
28.015   BG   1962 The morbidity and mortality of enteric fever in British Guiana.

AUGELLI, JOHN P. & TAYLOR, HARRY W.
7.004   TR   1960 Race and population patterns in Trinidad. *Ann Ass Am Geogr* 50(2), June: 123-138. [10, 44] [*RIS*]

BARBANSON, W. L. de
7.005   SB   1958 Grafschriften op Saint Barthélémy [Gravestone inscriptions on St. Barthelemy]. *WIG* 38:97-105. [5, 23] [*COL*]

BAYLEY, GEORGE D.
20.002   BG   1911 Census comicalities.
7.006   BG   1912 REPORT ON THE RESULTS OF THE CENSUS OF THE POPULATION, 1911. Georgetown, Argosy Co., 70p. [*AGS*]

BENJAMIN, ELSIE
7.007   JM   1944 Jamaica takes a census. *Surv Graphic* 33(12), Dec.: 488-490, 512. [67] [*COL*]

BENJAMINS, H.D.

7.008   BG/   1923 Bevolkingscijfers van Britsch Guyana en Suriname [Population
        SR   figures on British Guiana and Surinam]. *W I G* 6:197-215.   [5,6]
                                                                        [*COL*]

BISWAMITRE, C. R.

5.015   SR   1938 Suriname gedurende de regeering van Koningin Wilhelmina [Surinam
                   during the rule of Queen Wilhelmina].

BRAITHWAITE, LLOYD E.

17.003   JM   [1961?] Population, migration and urbanization.

BRAUW, W. de

5.020   SA   1934/ Het eiland Saba en zijn bewoners [The island of Saba and its
                   35 inhabitants].

CLARAC

28.094   FG   1902 La Guyane Francaise; notes de géographie médicale, d'ethnographie
                   et de pathologie [French Guiana: medical geography, ethnography,
                   and pathology].

COINTET, ANDRE

7.009   FA   1954 Le surpeuplement des Antilles Francaises en particulier de la
                   Guadeloupe [Overpopulation in the French Antilles, particularly in
                   Guadeloupe]. *Rev Étud Coop* 26(96), Apr.-June: 111-124..   [10]
                                                                  [*NYP*]

COUSINS, WINIFRED M.

7.010   BC   1935 The sex-ratio among Negroes as illustrated by certain British
                   colonies. *Sociol Rev* 27(4), Oct.: 423-440.   [10]   [*COL*]

CRUICKSHANK, J. GRAHAM

11.008   BG   1919 African immigrants after freedom.

CUMPER, GEORGE E.

7.011   JM   1956 Population movements in Jamaica, 1830-1950. *Social Econ Stud* 5(3),
                   Sept.: 261-280.   [5, 47]   [*RIS*]
50.021   BB   1959 Employment in Barbados.
44.046   BB   1962 The differentiation of economic groups in the West Indies.
7.012   JM   1963 Preliminary analysis of population growth and social characteristics
                   in Jamaica, 1943-60. *Social Econ Stud* 12(4), Dec.: 393-431.   [*RIS*]

CUMPSTON, I. M.

50.026   BC   1953 INDIANS OVERSEAS IN BRITISH TERRITORIES, 1834-1854.

DALE, EDMUND H.

7.013   BC   1963 The demographic problem of the British West Indies. *Scott Geogr
                   Mag* 79(1), Apr.: 23-31.   [17]   [*AGS*]

DELOBEZ, A.

44.049   MT   1963 La population et l'économie de la Martinique en 1960 [The popula-
                   tion and economy of Martinique in 1960].

DEY, MUKUL K.

7.014   TR   1962 The Indian population in Trinidad and Tobago. *Int J Comp Sociol*
                   3(2), Dec.: 245-253.   [12]   [*COL*]

DORAN, EDWIN BEAL, Jr.

27.018   CM   1952 Inbreeding in an isolated island community.

DUNCAN, W. J.

7.015   BG   1916 The public health statistics of the colony. *Br Gui Med Annual 1915*
                     21:173-179   [10,28]   [*ACM*]
7.016   BG   1919 The public health and medical statistics of the colony. *Br Gui Med
                     Annual 1919* 22:115-131.   [10, 28]   [*ACM*]

EDGE, P. GRANVILLE

7.017   BC   1944 Infant mortality in British West Indies. *Trans Roy Soc Trop Med
                     Hyg* 38(2), Nov.: 117-132.   [10, 28]   [*COL*]

ENGLISH, E. W. F., et al.

7.018   BG   1907 Report of the Mortality Commission. *Br Gui Med Annual 1906* 15:1-
                     42.   [10, 28, 30]   [*ACM*]

ERICKSEN, E. GORDON

7.019   BC   1962 THE WEST INDIES POPULATION PROBLEM: DIMENSIONS FOR ACTION.
                     Lawrence, University of Kansas, 194p. (University of Kansas
                     publications, Social science studies.) [9, 36, 66]   [*RIS*]

FLOCH, HERVE ALEXANDRE

7.020   GD   1935 Cinq années de démographie au Moule (Guadeloupe) [Five years of
                     demography in Moule (Guadeloupe)]. *Annls Med Pharm Colon* 34(2),
                     Apr.-June: 325-346.   [*ACM*]
28.173   FG   1956 Influence de la lutte antipaludique sur la natalité, la mortinatalité
                     et la mortalité infantile en Guyane Francaise [Influence of the fight
                     against malaria on birth rate, stillbirth rate, and infantile mortality
                     in French Guiana].
7.021   FG   1956 Influence du paludisme sur la natalité, mortinatalité et mortalité
                     infantile [The influence of malaria on the birthrate, stillbirth rate,
                     and infantile mortality]. *Revta Brasil Mala Do Trop* 8(4), Oct.: 541-
                     544. [28]   [*COL*]
28.174   FG   1956 Natalité, mortinatalité, mortalité infantile et paludisme [Birth rate,
                     stillbirth rate, infantile mortality, and malaria].

GAAY FORTMAN, B. de

7.022   NL   1936/ Bevolkingscijfers van Curacao [Population figures of Curacao].
                37   *W I G* 18:51-60.   [*COL*]
23.049   CU   1941 Lutherschen op Curacao [Lutherans on Curacao].
23.050   BG/   1941 Lutherschen op St. Eustatius en in Essequebo [Lutherans on St.
         SE   Eustatius and in Essequibo].
7.023   NA   1959 Toelating, verblijf, vestiging, en uitzetting in de Nederlandse
                     Antillen [Admission, residence, settlement and expulsion in the
                     Netherlands Antilles]. *W I G* 39:1-27. [37]   [*COL*]

GANGULEE, N.

12.007   BC   1947 INDIANS IN THE EMPIRE OVERSEAS: A SURVEY.

GIBBONS, WILLIAM J.

7.024   GC   1961 Trends in Latin American population.

GOEJE, C. H. de

7.025   BG/   1933/ Sterven de Indianen uit [Are the Indians dying off]? *W I G* 16:232-233.
         SR   34 [13]   [*COL*]
7.026   GC   1938 De bevolking van Amerika [The population of America]. *W I G* 20:
                     129-136. [13]   [*COL*]

GREENE, MARC T.
7.027   BC   1954 Problems of the West Indies. *Contemp Rev* 186, Dec.: 349-353.
                                                                                    [*COL*]

HAREWOOD, JACK
50.060   JM/   1960 Overpopulation and underemployment in the West Indies.
          TR
7.028   TR   1963 Population growth of Trinidad and Tobago in the twentieth century.
                       Social Econ Stud 12(1), Mar.: 1-26.   [*RIS*]

HAUGER, JEAN
7.029   FG   1957 La population de la Guyane Francaise [The population of French
                       Guiana]. *Ann Geogr* 66(358), Nov.-Dec.: 509-518. [10]   [*AGS*]

HAWLEY, AMOS H.
7.030   AR   1960 THE POPULATION OF ARUBA, A REPORT BASED ON THE CENSUS OF 1960.
                       [Oranjestad?] Aruba, Office of Vital Statistics and Census, 35p.
                                                                                    [*RIS*]

HESSLING, H. A.
7.031   AR   1933/ Beeld van Aruba in cijfers [Statistical picture of Aruba]. *W I G*
                 34   15:385-389. [44]   [*COL*]

HEWICK, J. E.
10.018   BG   1911 Our people.

HILL, Mrs. A. St.
7.032   BB   1937/ A census of the island of Barbados, West Indies. *J Barb Mus Hist*
                 42   *Soc* 4(2), Feb.: 72-82; 4(3), May: 141-144; 4(4), Aug.: 196-200; 5(1),
                       Nov.: 39-42 (1937); 5(2), Feb.: 109-112; 5(4), Aug.: 194-203; 6(1),
                       Nov.: 41-44 (1938); 6(2), Feb.: 87-90; 6(3), May: 152-159; 6(4), Aug.:
                       218-225; 7(1), Nov.: 50-53 (1939); 7(2), Feb.: 87-98; 7(4), Aug.:
                       194-198; 8(1), Nov.: 36-41 (1940); 8(3), May: 138-143 (1941); 9(3),
                       May: 144-151 (1942). [5]   [*AMN*]

HUGGINS, H. D.
7.033   BC   1955 Population and migration. *New Commonw, Br Car Suppl* 30(9), Oct.
                       31: xv-xvi. [17]   [*AGS*]

HUGGINS, H. D., ed.
44.110   BC   1958 [PROCEEDINGS OF THE] STUDY CONFERENCE ON ECONOMIC DEVELOPMENT
                       IN UNDERDEVELOPED COUNTRIES [held at the University College of
                       the West Indies, Aug. 5-15, 1957].

HUGGINS, H. D. & CUMPER, G. E.
44.111   JM/   1958 Economic development in a context of low population pressure.
          BG
HURAULT, JEAN
7.034   FG   1959 Etude démographique comparée des indiens oayana et des noirs
                       réfugiés boni du haut-Maroni (Guyane Francaise) [Comparative
                       demographic study of the Oyan Indians, and the black Boni refugees
                       from upper Maroni (French Guiana)]. *Population* 14(3), July-Sept.:
                       509-534. [13]   [*RIS*]

KALFF, S.
7.035   SR   1929/ Franschen in Suriname [French people in Surinam]. *W I G* 11:316-
                 30   334. [45]   [*COL*]

KESLER, C. K.

15.025   SR   1938 Javanen in Suriname reeds in het jaar 1714 [Were the Javanese already in Surinam in the year 1714]?

KLERK, CORNELIS JOHANNES MARIA de

50.073   SR   1942 De Britisch-Indiërs in Suriname [The British Indians in Surinam].

KONDAPI, C.

12.016   BC   1951 INDIANS OVERSEAS, 1838-1949.

KRUIJER, GERARDUS JOHANNES

36.010   SR   1951 Urbanisme in Suriname [Urbanism in Surinam].

50.078   NW   1953 Enquête onder de arbeiders- an boerenbevolking van de Bovenwindse Eilanden, 1951 [Survey of the labor and farming population of the Windward Islands, 1951].

7.036   SR   1954 De onderscheiding naar landaard in de demografische statistiek van Surinam [Distinguishing ethnic origin in the demographic statistics of Surinam]. *Mens Mij Twee Tijdschr* p.152-158. [10] *[RIS]*

7.037   NW   1955 Demografie van de Bovenwindse Eilanden [Demography of the Windward Islands]. *WIG* 36(1): 81-84. *[RIS]*

KUCZYNSKI, R. R.

7.038   BC   1953 DEMOGRAPHIC SURVEY OF THE BRITISH COLONIAL EMPIRE, VOL. III: WEST INDIAN AND AMERICAN TERRITORIES. London, Oxford University Press, 497p. *[RIS]*

KUYP, EDWIN van der; WALVIS, W. Chr. & LIER, R. A. J. van

7.039   SR   1959 Report on the demographic problems of Surinam. *Vox Guy* 3(3), Mar.: 97-162.

LAMPE, P. H. J.

28.321   SR   1927 Suriname, sociaal-hygienische beschouwingen [Surinam, social-hygienic observations].

LASSERRE, GUY

7.040   GD   1959 Présentation de cartes des densités de la population en Guadeloupe [Density maps of the Guadeloupe population]. *B Ass Geogr Fr* 280-281, Jan.-Feb.: 33-48. *[AGS]*

LATOUR, M. D.

7.041   CU   1936/Familienamen op Curacao [Family names on Curacao]. *W I G* 18: 37 195-199. [5] *[COL]*

LENS, TH.

17.015   SR   1927/ Emigratie naar Suriname [Emigration to Surinam].
                28

LEWIS, W. ARTHUR

49.050   BC   1956 The industrialization of the British West Indies.

LOWENTHAL, DAVID

43.098   JM   1958 Population and production in Jamaica.

2.142   FG   1960 French Guiana: myths and realities.

43.101   GG   1960 Population contrasts in the Guianas.

McARTHUR, J. SIDNEY

10.028   BG   1912 Our people; a rejoinder to the paper of Mr. J. E. Hewick.

MARTIAL & BEAUDIMENT
7.042   FC   1938 Essai de démographie des colonies francaises [Demographic study of the French colonies]. *B Off Int Hyg Publ* 30(2): suppl. (154p.)
[*COL*]

MENKMAN, W. R.
7.043   SR   1927/Dokteren over de West [Attempt to improve the West]. *W I G* 9:78-88.
              28 [17, 66]   [*COL*]

17.018   SR   1927/Nog een emigratie van Nederlanders naar Suriname [Another emigra-
              28 tion of Dutch people to Surinam].

46.142   SR   1937 Welke kansen biedt Suriname voor landbouwkolonisatie door blanken [What possibilities can Surinam offer for agricultural colonization by whites]?

5.146   NC   1948 Onze West 1898-1948. [Our West 1898-1948].

7.044   SR   1949 Een buitengewoon Surinaams verslag [A special report on Surinam]. *W I G* 30:116-126. [28]   [*COL*]

7.045   SR   1949 Het Surinaamse verslag [The Surinam report]. *W I G* 30:9-14. [44]
[*COL*]

MEYER, H.
7.046   SR   1961/Suriname en het Wereldbevolkingsvraagstuk [Surinam and the prob-
              62 lem of world population]. *N W I G* 41:38-45. [34]   [*COL*]

MEYER, J.
7.047   SR   1954 Pioneers of Pauroma, contribution to the earliest history of the Jewish colonization of America. Paramaribo, 52p. [5, 23]

MINETT, E. P.
7.048   BG   1923 Brief review of the public health statistics of the colony. *Br Gui Med Annual 1923* 23:137-147. [28]   [*ACM*]

7.049   BG   1923 Infantile mortality. *Br Gui Med Annual 1923* 23:148-150.   [*ACM*]

NAIDOO, M. B.
12.020   TR   1960 The East Indian in Trinidad—a study of an immigrant community.

NATH, DWARKA
12.022   BG   1950 A history of the Indians in British Guiana.

NEWLING, BRUCE E.
36.012   JM   1962 The growth and spatial structure of Kingston, Jamaica.

NIDDRIE, DAVID L.
43.112   TB   1961 Land use and population in Tobago: an environmental study.

NORRIS, OLIVER
7.050   DM   1964 Situation et perspectives de la démographie dominicaine [Statistics and vistas of Dominica demography]. *Cah Cent Etud Reg Ant-Guy* 5, Nov. (71p.) [8]   [*RIS*]

OLIVIERA, A. T.
7.051   SR   1923/De natuurlijke aanwas der bevolking van Suriname [The natural
              24 population increase of Surinam]. *W I G* 5:561-600.   [*COL*]

OUDSCHANS DENTZ, FRED
7.052   SR   1941 De geschiedenis van den burgelijken stand en van eenige famili-
enamen in Suriname [The history of the Civil Registration and of some family names in Surinam]. *W I G* 23:51-59. [5]   [*COL*]

7.053 SR 1941 Een Hugenoten-afstammeling in Surinam [A descendent from the Huguenots in Surinam]. *W I G* 23:89-91. [*COL*]

5.162 BG/ 1943 De kolonisatie van Guyana [The colonization of Guiana].
   SR

45.017 SR 1944/ De herkomst en de beteekenis van Surinaamsche plantagenamen 45 [The origins and meanings of the names of the plantations in Surinam].

7.054 SR 1944/ Volkstellingen in Suriname [Census in Surinam]. *W I G* 26:191-192. 45 [*COL*]

7.055 SR 1947 De bevolking van Suriname [The population of Surinam]. *W I G* 28: 9-10. [*COL*]

23.114 SR 1948 Wat er overbleef van het kerkhof en de synagoge van de Joden-Savanne in Suriname [What is left of the cemetery and the Synagogue of the Jewish-Savannah in Surinam].

PECK, H. AUSTIN
44.183 JM 1958 Economic planning in Jamaica: a critique.

PIVETEAU, ALBERT
7.056 GD 1951 Some observations on the population of Guadeloupe. *Car Commn Mon Inf B* 5(3), Oct.: 73-74. [*AGS*]

PROUDFOOT, MALCOLM J.
17.021 GC 1950 POPULATION MOVEMENTS IN THE CARIBBEAN.

PROUDFOOT, MARY
7.057 BC 1956 Population problems. *Statist* Sept.: 13.

PYTTERSEN, T.J.
46.176 SR 1927/ Europeesche kolonies in Suriname [European colonies in Surinam]. 28

QUELLE, OTTO
10.037 GG 1951 Die Bevölkerungsentwicklung von Europäisch-Guayana: eine anthropogeographische Untersuchung [The population growth of European Guiana: an anthropo-geographical study].

REVERT, EUGENE
7.058 MT 1938 Note sur la population de la Martinique [Note on the population of Martinique]. *In* ACTES DU CONGRÈS INTERNATIONAL DE LA POPULATION, 1937. Paris, Hermann, V.6, p.27-41. [*AGS*]

ROBERTS, GEORGE WOODROW
7.059 BC [n.d.] POPULATION TRENDS IN THE BRITISH CARIBBEAN. Port of Spain, Guardian Commercial Printery, 24p. [*RIS*]

7.060 BG 1948 Some observations on the population of British Guiana. *Popul Stud* 2(2), Sept.: 185-218. [10] [*COL*]

7.061 JM 1950 A note on mortality in Jamaica. *Popul Stud* 4(1), June: 64-85. [*COL*]

7.062 BC 1951 Population trends in the British Caribbean colonies, 1946-61. *Car Econ Rev* 3(1-2), Oct.: 179-200. [*RIS*]

7.063 BC 1952 A life table for a West Indian slave population. *Popul Stud* 5(3), Mar.: 238-243. [6] [*COL*]

7.064 BC 1956 Recent demographic trends in Cuba, Haiti and the British Caribbean. *In* POPULATION BULLETIN OF THE UNITED NATIONS, NO. 5, New York, United Nations, p.42-50. [*UNL*]

7.065   JM   1957   THE POPULATION OF JAMAICA. Cambridge [Eng.], Published for the
                          Conservation Foundation at the University Press, 356p.   [*RIS*]
38.106   BC   1957   Some demographic considerations of West Indian federation.
7.066   GC   1958   The Caribbean islands. *Ann Am Acad Polit Social Sci* 306, Mar.:
                          127-136.   [*RIS*]
7.067   BC   1958   Note on population and growth. *In* HUGGINS, H. D., ed. [PROCEED-
                          ING OF THE] STUDY CONFERENCE ON ECONOMIC DEVELOPMENT IN UNDER-
                          DEVELOPED COUNTRIES (held at the University College of the West
                          Indies, Aug. 5-15, 1957). *Social Econ Stud* 7(3), Sept.: 24-41.   [66]
                                                                                          [*RIS*]
7.068   BC   1960   Movements in population and the labour force. *In* CUMPER, G. E.,
                          ed. THE ECONOMY OF THE WEST INDIES. Kingston, Institute of Social
                          and Economic Research, University College of the West Indies,
                          p.24-47.   [17, 50]   [*RIS*]
7.069   JM   [1961?]   Population growth in Jamaica. *In* CUMPER, G. E., ed. REPORT OF
                          THE CONFERENCE ON SOCIAL DEVELOPMENT IN JAMAICA. Kingston,
                          Standing Committee on Social Services, p.23-26.   [*RIS*]
7.070   BC   1962   Prospects for population growth in the West Indies. *In* SINGHAM, A.
                          & BRAITHWAITE, L.E., eds. SPECIAL NUMBER [of *Social Econ Stud*]
                          ON THE CONFERENCE ON POLITICAL SOCIOLOGY IN THE BRITISH CARIB-
                          BEAN, Dec. 1961. *Social Econ Stud* 11(4), Dec.: 333-350. [66]   [*RIS*]
7.071   GC   1963   The demographic position of the Caribbean. *In* U.S. HOUSE OF REPRE-
                          SENTATIVES. COMMITTEE ON THE JUDICIARY. STUDY OF POPULATION
                          AND IMMIGRATION PROBLEMS: WESTERN HEMISPHERE (II). Washington,
                          U.S. Govt. Print. Off., p.81-124. (Special series no.6.) [66] [*RIS*]
7.072   BC   1963   Improving vital registration in the West Indies. *In* [PROCEEDINGS OF
                          THE] INTERNATIONAL POPULATION CONFERENCE, New York, 1961.
                          London, John Wright, v. 2, p.420-426.
7.073   JM   1963   Provisional assessment of growth of the Kingston-St. Andrew area
                          1960-70. *Social Econ Stud* 12(4), Dec.: 432-441.   [*RIS*]

          SAMSON, PH. A.
7.074   SR   1939   Uit het verleden van Suriname [From Surinam's past]. *WIG* 21:12-13.
                          [23]   [*COL*]

          SENIOR, CLARENCE
66.134   BC   1958   Demography and economic development. *In* HUGGINS, H.D., ed.
                          [PROCEEDINGS OF THE] STUDY CONFERENCE ON ECONOMIC DEVELOPMENT
                          IN UNDERDEVELOPED COUNTRIES (held at the University College of the
                          West Indies, Aug. 5-15, 1957). *Social Econ Stud* 7(3), Sept.: 9-23.

          SHAW, EARL BENNETT
7.075   VI   1935   Population adjustments in our Virgin Islands. *Econ Geogr* 11(3),
                          July: 267-279.   [8, 36]   [*AGS*]

          SIMPSON, GEORGE EATON
10.041   GC   1962   The peoples and cultures of the Caribbean area.

          SIRES, RONALD VERNON
50.116   JM   1940   Sir Henry Barkly and the labor problem in Jamaica 1853-1856.

SMITH, RAYMOND THOMAS

12.031   BG   1959 Some social characteristics of Indian immigrants to British Guiana.

SNEATH, P. A. T.

7.076   BG   1941 A study of crude birth/death ratio (vital index) in British Guiana. *Trans Roy Soc Trop Med Hyg* 35(2), Sept.: 105-117. [10, 28] [*COL*]

STANDARD, KENNETH L.

7.077   BB   1961 An analysis of child mortality in Barbados, West Indies. *W I Med J* 10(4), Dec.: 250-263. [*COL*]

STERN, PETER M.

7.078   GC   1958 Population factors. *In* WILGUS, A. CURTIS, ed. THE CARIBBEAN: BRITISH, DUTCH, FRENCH, UNITED STATES [papers delivered at the Eighth Conference on the Caribbean held at the University of Florida Dec. 5-7, 1957]. Gainesville, University of Florida Press, p.233-246. (Publications of the School of Inter-American Studies, ser. 1.) [66] [*RIS*]

STOLNITZ, GEORGE J.

28.506   GC   1958 The revolution in death control in nonindustrial countries.

SUNDARAM, LANKA

12.035   BC   1933 INDIANS OVERSEAS: A STUDY IN ECONOMIC SOCIOLOGY.

TAEUBER, IRENE

7.079   BG   1952 British Guiana: some demographic aspects of economic development. *Popul I* 18(1), Jan.: 3-19. [*AGS*]

TAYLOR, DOUGLAS C.

26.028   DM   1955/ Names on Dominica.
            56

26.049   SV   1958 Names on Saint Vincent.

TJON SIE FAT, HOWARD CYRIL

28.519   NW   1954 ONDERZOEK NAAR DE SOCIAAL-HYGIËNISCHE TOESTAND OP DE BOVINWINDSE EILANDEN DER NEDERLANSE ANTILLEN [INVESTIGATION OF SOCIAL-HYGIENIC CONDITIONS ON THE WINDWARD ISLANDS OF THE NETHERLANDS ANTILLES].

VERKADE-CARTIER van DISSEL, E. F.

7.080   SR   1937 DE MOGELIJKHEID VAN LANDBOUW-KOLONISATIE VOOR BLANKEN IN SURINAME AMSTERDAM [THE POSSIBILITY OF AGRICULTURAL SETTLEMENT FOR WHITES IN SURINAM]. H. J. Paris, 326p. [17, 46]

VERMEULEN, L. P.

7.081   NA   [196-] De bevolkingsstructuur der Nederlandse Antillen [Population patterns in the Netherlands Antilles]. *Tijdschr Ned Aar Genoot* 79(1): 34-58. [8, 10] [*RIS*]

7.082   NA   [1963?] De volkstelling 1960 in de Nederlandse Antillen [The 1960 census in the Dutch Antilles]. *Tijdschr Ned Aar Genoot* 80:186-192. [*RIS*]

VRYMAN, L. C.

5.213   FG   1936/ Iets over de Nederlandsche volksplanting in "Cayanen" gedurende
                   37 de zeventiende eeuw [Some facts about the Dutch settlement in
                   "Cayanen" during the 17th century].

WALLBRIDGE, J. S.

7.083   BG   1907 Remarks on the Mortality Commission Report. *Br Gui Med Ann 1906*
                   15:43-50. [10, 28]   [*ACM*]

WESTERMANN, J. H.

7.084   GC   1958 Demografische Conferentie van de Caraibische Commissie, Trinidad,
                   1957 [Demographic Conference of the Caribbean Commission,
                   Trinidad, 1957]. *W I G* 38:129-143.   [*COL*]

WILLIAMS, GERTRUDE

44.251   BC   1953 THE ECONOMICS OF EVERYDAY LIFE IN THE WEST INDIES.

WILLIAMS, JOSEPH J.

10.052   JM/   1932 WHENCE THE "BLACK IRISH" OF JAMAICA?
           BB

WISE, K. S.

7.085   BG   1912/ The public health, statistics, and medical institutions of the
                   13 Colony. *Br Gui Med Annual 1910, 1911, 1912* 17:lxxxvii-xcvi (1912);
                   18:xxiv-xxxi; 19: v-xiv (1913). [10, 28]   [*ACM*]

WISHART, W. de W.

7.086   BG   1902 The influence of rainfall on death-rate in the tropics. *Br Gui Med
                   Annual* [12?]: 76-78. [28, 42]   [*ACM*]

7.087   BG   1943 The Georgetown vital index as related to rainfall. *Br Gui Med
                   Annual 1943* 26:169-171. [28, 42]   [*ACM*]

WOLFF, J. W.

7.088   SR   1924 Some statistics about Suriname (Dutch Guiana). *Metron* 4(2), Dec.:
                   371-377.   [*AGS*]

WYTHENSHAWE, Lord SIMON of

7.089   BB   1954 POPULATION AND RESOURCES OF BARBADOS. Bloomcroft, Didsbury,
                   privately printed, 27p. [34]

ZANTEN, J. H. van

7.090   SR   1929 Demografie van de in Suriname levende volken [Demography of
                   peoples living in Surinam]. *Mens Mij* 5:201-219.

Chapter 8

SOCIAL ORGANIZATION

ADAMS, INES & MASUOKA, J.
8.001   TR   1961 Emerging elites and culture change. *Social Econ Stud* 10(1), Mar.: 86-92. [12, 66]   [*RIS*]

ALLEYNE, MERVIN C.
25.001   SL   1961 Language and society in St. Lucia.

ARONSON, ROBERT L.
50.006   JM   1961 Labour commitment among Jamaican bauxite workers; a case study.

ASSENDERP, ANDRE L. van
10.002   SR   1958 Some aspects of society in the Netherlands Antilles and Surinam.

BACK, E. H.
30.002   JM   1956 A nutritional survey of small farmers in Jamaica in 1955.
30.003   JM   1961 The dietary of small farmers in Jamaica.

BANKS, E. P.
13.005   DM   1956 A Carib Village in Dominica.

BECKETT, J. EDGAR
11.003   BG   1917 The black peasant proprietor.

BELL, WENDELL
38.012   JM   1960 Attitudes of Jamaican elites toward the West Indies Federation.
37.021   JM   1960 Images of the United States and the Soviet Union held by Jamaican elite groups.
37.022   JM   1962 Equality and attitudes of elites in Jamaica.
37.023   JM   1964 JAMAICAN LEADERS: POLITICAL ATTITUDES IN A NEW NATION.

BENOIST, JEAN
56.005   MT   1959 Individualisme et traditions techniques chez les pecheurs martiniquais [Individualism and technical tradition among Martinique fishermen].

BIJLSMA, R.
43.015   SR   1921/ Surinaamsche plantage-inventarissen van het tijdperk 1713-1742
                  22 [Surinam plantation inventories of the years 1713-1742].

BISWAMITRE, C. R.
12.004   SR   1937 Miskenning [Misjudgment].

BLAKE, JUDITH; STYCOS, J. MAYONE & DAVIS, KINGSLEY
34.006   JM   1961 FAMILY STRUCTURE IN JAMAICA: THE SOCIAL CONTEXT OF REPRODUCTION.

BONE, LOUIS W.
32.027   GG   1962 SECONDARY EDUCATION IN THE GUIANAS.

BRAITHWAITE, LLOYD E.
8.002   TR   1953 Social stratification in Trinidad. *Social Econ Stud* 2(2-3), Oct.:
                  5-175. [10, 19]   [*RIS*]
10.006   TR   1954 Cultural integration in Trinidad.
38.023   BC   1957 'Federal' associations and institutions in the West Indies.
34.007   BC   1957 Sociology and demographic research in the British Caribbean.
32.029   BC   1958 The development of higher education in the British West Indies.
8.003   BC   1960 Social stratification and cultural pluralism. *In* RUBIN, VERA, ed.
                  SOCIAL AND CULTURAL PLURALISM IN THE CARIBBEAN. New York, New
                  York Academy of Sciences, p.816-836. (Annals of the New York
                  Academy of Sciences, v.83, art.5.) [10]   [*RIS*]

BROOM, LEONARD
8.004   JM   1954 The social differentiation of Jamaica. *Am Sociol Rev* 19(2), Apr.:
                  115-125. [10]

BUCHLER, IRA R.
8.005   CM   1962 Caymanian folk racial categories. *Man* 62(287-290), Dec.: 185-186.
                  [16]   [*RIS*]

CALLENDER, CHARLES VICTOR
53.005   JM   1965 The development of the capital market institutions of Jamaica.

CHATEAU, E. D.
8.006   SR   1955 Groepsvorming onder de straatjeugd van Paramaribo [Group-forming
                  among streetcorner youth of Paramaribo]. *Vox Guy* 1(6): ᴠ179-184.
                  [9]

CLARKE, EDITH
9.003   JM   1957 MY MOTHER WHO FATHERED ME: A STUDY OF THE FAMILY IN 3 SELECTED
                  COMMUNITIES IN JAMAICA.

COHEN, YEHUDI A.
8.007   JM   1953 A STUDY OF INTERPERSONAL RELATIONS IN A JAMAICAN COMMUNITY.
                  Ph. D. dissertation, Yale University, 485p. [31]
8.008   JM   1954 The social organization of a selected community in Jamaica.
                  Social Econ Stud 2(4), Mar.: 104-133.   [*AGS*]
31.019   JM   1955 Character formation and social structure in a Jamaican community.
31.020   JM   1955 A contribution to the study of adolescence: adolescent conflict in
                  a Jamaican community.

8.009   JM   1955 Four categories of interpersonal relationships in the family and community in a Jamaican village. *Anthrop Q* 3(4), Oct.: 121-147. [9, 20, 44]   [*RIS*]

31.021   JM   1956 Structure and function: family organization and socialization in a Jamaican community.

COLERIDGE, P. E.

8.010   SR   1958 Vrouwenleven in Paramaribo [Women's life in Paramaribo]. *In* WALLE, J. van de & WIT, H. de, eds. SURINAME IN STROOMLIJNEN. Amsterdam, Wereld Bibliotheek, p.86-93. [20, 36]

COLLINS, SYDNEY

8.011   JM   1956 Social mobility in Jamaica, with reference to rural communities and the teaching profession. *In* TRANSACTIONS OF THE THIRD WORLD CONGRESS OF SOCIOLOGY, Amsterdam, Aug. 1956. London, International Sociological Association, v.3, p.267-276. [32]   [*COL*]

8.012   JM   1960 The school teacher in his role as leader in West Indian and African societies. *Civilizations* 10(3): 315-325. [32]   [*RIS*]

COMITAS, LAMBROS

56.017   JM   1962 FISHERMEN AND COOPERATION IN RURAL JAMAICA.

50.020   JM   1964 Occupational multiplicity in rural Jamaica.

CROPPER, J. B.

8.013   BG   1912 Our villages and country parts. *Timehri* 3d ser., 2(19B), Dec.: 235-258.   [*AMN*]

CROWLEY, DANIEL JOHN

24.020   SL   1958 La Rose and La Marguerite Societies in St. Lucia.

CRUICKSHANK, J. GRAHAM

8.014   BG   1921 The beginnings of our villages. *Timehri* 3d ser., 7(24), Aug.: 65-76. [5, 11]   [*AMN*]

8.015   BG   1933 "Good time" in slavery days. *W I Comm Circ* 48(919), Dec. 21: 507-508. [6,19]   [*NYP*]

CUMPER, GEORGE E.

8.016   JM   [n.d.] THE SOCIAL STRUCTURE OF JAMAICA. Kingston, Extra-Mural Dept., University College of the West Indies, 90p.   [*NYP*]

8.017   BC   [n.d.] SOCIAL STRUCTURE OF THE BRITISH CARIBBEAN (EXCLUDING JAMAICA). Kingston, Extra-Mural Dept., University College of the West Indies, 3 pts.   [*RIS*]

46.044   JM   1958 The Jamaican family: village and estate.

44.044   BB   1961 Household and occupation in Barbados.

50.024   JM/   1961/ Labour and development in the West Indies.
        BB   62

8.018   JM   [1961?] Notes on social structure in Jamaica. *In* CUMPER, GEORGE E., ed. REPORT OF THE CONFERENCE ON SOCIAL DEVELOPMENT IN JAMAICA. Kingston, Standing Committee on Social Services, p.3-11. [66] [*RIS*]

44.046   BB   1961/ The differentiation of economic groups in the West Indies.
              62

CUNDALL, FRANK

37.079   BC   1906 POLITICAL AND SOCIAL DISTURBANCES IN THE WEST INDIES: A BRIEF
                       ACCOUNT AND BIBLIOGRAPHY.

CURTIN, PHILIP D.

2.052   JM   1955 TWO JAMAICAS: THE ROLE OF IDEAS IN A TROPICAL COLONY, 1830-
                       1865.

DAVENPORT, WILLIAM HUNT

8.019   JM   1956 A COMPARATIVE STUDY OF TWO JAMAICAN FISHING COMMUNITIES.
                       Ph. D. dissertation, Yale University, 463p. [44, 66]
9.005   JM   1961 The family system of Jamaica.
8.020   BC   1961 Working papers on Caribbean social organization: Introduction.
                       Social Econ Stud 10(4), Dec.: 380-385.   [*RIS*]

DAVIDSON, H. K. & MINKES, A. L.

66.035   JM   1954 Social factors in the economic problems of Jamaica.

De CAMP, DAVID

25.019   JM   1961 Social and geographical factors in Jamaican dialects.

DESPRES, LEO A.

67.003   BG   1964 The implications of nationalist politics in British Guiana for the
                       development of cultural theory.

DORAN, EDWIN BEAL Jr.

51.048   CC   1958 The Caicos Conch Trade.

DUKE, JAMES TAYLOR

20.004   JM   1963 EQUALITARIANISM AMONG EMERGENT ELITES IN A NEW NATION.

ELLIS, ROBERT ARTHUR

8.021   JM   1955 SOCIAL STRATIFICATION IN A JAMAICAN MARKET TOWN. Ph. D. disserta-
                       tion, Yale University, 295p. [67]
8.022   JM   1956 Social status and social distance. *Sociol Social Res* 40(4), Mar.-
                       Apr.: 240-246.   [*RIS*]
8.023   JM   1957 Colour and class in a Jamaican market town. *Sociol Social Res*
                       41:354-360. [16]   [*RIS*]

FARLEY, RAWLE

8.024   BG   1953 The rise of village settlements of British Guiana. *Car Q* 3(2),
                       Sept.: 101-109. [5, 11]   [*RIS*]
8.025   BG   1954 Rise of a peasantry in British Guiana. *Social Econ Stud* 2(4), Mar.:
                       87-103. [5, 11]   [*AGS*]
16.010   BG   1955 The substance and the shadow—a study of the relations between
                       white planters and free coloured in a slave society in British
                       Guiana.
49.022   BC   1958 NATIONALISM AND INDUSTRIAL DEVELOPMENT IN THE BRITISH CARIBBEAN.
32.062   BC   1958 UNIVERSITIES AND THE EDUCATION OF WORKING PEOPLE.

FREILICH, MORRIS

10.013   TR   1960 CULTURAL DIVERSITY AMONG TRINIDADIAN PEASANTS.

GILLIN, JOHN P.

8.026   BG   1934 Crime and punishment among the Barama River Carib of British Guiana. *Am Anthrop* new ser., 36(3), July-Sept.: 331-344.   [13]
                 [*COL*]

8.027   BG   1935 Social life of the Baram River Caribs of British Guiana. *Scient Mon* 40(3), Mar.: 227-236. [13]   [*AGS*]

GLASS, RUTH

21.007   JM   1962 Ashes of discontent.

GODFREY, J. E.

37.142   BG   1912 Village administration and local government in British Guiana.

GREENFIELD, SIDNEY M.

9.009   BB   1959 FAMILY ORGANIZATION IN BARBADOS.
47.018   BB   1960 Land tenure and transmission in rural Barbados.

HADLEY, C. V. D.

31.032   BC   1949 Personality patterns, social class, and aggression in the British West Indies.

HANDELMAN, DON

18.024   GC   1964 VOLUNTARY ASSOCIATIONS AMONG WEST INDIANS IN MONTREAL.

HARNARINE, HAROLD

44.097   BC   1963/ Business enterprise and Asiatic groups in the West Indies.
              64

HELWIG, G. V.

10.017   JM   1958 Society in the British West Indies.

HENRIQUES, FERNANDO

9.016   JM   1953 FAMILY AND COLOUR IN JAMAICA.

HENRY, FRANCES

8.028   TR   1965 Social stratification in an Afro-American cult. *Anthrop Q* 38(2), Apr.: 72-78. [23]   [*RIS*]

HERSKOVITS, MELVILLE JEAN

8.029   SR   1930 The social organization of the Bush Negroes of Suriname. *In* PROCEEDINGS OF THE TWENTY-THIRD INTERNATIONAL CONGRESS OF AMERICANISTS, New York, 1928. New York, p.713-727. [14]   [*AGS*]

HERSKOVITS, MELVILLE JEAN & FRANCES S.

11.012   TR   1947 TRINIDAD VILLAGE.

HICKERSON, HAROLD

8.030   BG   1954 SOCIAL AND ECONOMIC ORGANIZATION IN A GUIANA VILLAGE. Ph.D. dissertation, Indiana University, 449p. [11, 12]

HOCKEY, SIDNEY W.

21.010   BC   1958 An emerging culture in the British West Indies.

HOETINK, HARRY

8.031   CU   1958 HET PATROON VAN DE OUDE CURACAOSE SAMENLEVING [THE PATTERN OF
THE OLD CURACAO SOCIETY]. Assen, Holland, 189p. [5]   [*RIS*]

9.017   GC   1961 Gezingsvormen in het Caribisch gebied [Family types in the Caribbean area].

HOROWITZ, MICHAEL M.

8.032   MT   1959 MORNE-PAYSAN: PEASANT COMMUNITY IN MARTINIQUE; AN APPROACH TO
A TYPOLOGY OF RURAL COMMUNITY FORMS IN THE CARIBBEAN. PH. D.
dissertation, Columbia University, 203p.   [*COL*]

67.013   GC   1960 A typology of rural community forms in the Caribbean.

HUGGINS, H. D.

62.016   BG   1941 An economic survey of rice farming in West Demerara.

HUSSEIN, AHMED & TAYLOR, CARL C.

66.068   JM/   1953 Report of the Mission on Rural Community Organization and De-
TR   velopment in the Caribbean area and Mexico.

JAMES, ERIC GEORGE

37.208   JM   1956 ADMINISTRATIVE INSTITUTIONS AND SOCIAL CHANGE IN JAMAICA, BRITISH
WEST INDIES—A STUDY IN CULTURAL ADAPTATION.

JAMES, S. A.

32.106   SL   1962 Adult education and community development.

JAYAWARDENA, CHANDRA

8.033   BG   1963 CONFLICT AND SOLIDARITY IN A GUIANESE PLANTATION. London, Ath-
lone Press, 159p. (London School of Economics, monographs on
social anthropology no. 25.) [12, 20, 27, 50]   [*RIS*]

JEPHCOTT, PEARL

33.017   BG   1956 REPORT ON THE NEEDS OF THE YOUTH OF THE MORE POPULATED COASTAL
AREAS OF BRITISH GUIANA: WITH PARTICULAR REFERENCE TO THE RE-
CREATION AND INFORMAL EDUCATION OF THOSE AGED 13-19.

KLASS, MORTON

12.013   TR   1961 EAST INDIANS IN TRINIDAD: A STUDY OF CULTURAL PERSISTENCE.

KLERK, CORNELIS JOHANNES MARIA de

50.074   SR   1953 DE IMMIGRATIE DER HINDOESTANEN IN SURINAME [THE IMMIGRATION
OF HINDUS TO SURINAM].

KLINGBERG, FRANK J.

6.037   BB   1938 British humanitarianism at Codrington.

KNOPP, SYLVIA

8.034   TR   1959 SHANTY TOWN: THE STUDY OF A NEWLY FORMED OUTCASTE GROUP IN
TRINIDAD. M. A. thesis, Columbia University, 74p.   [*RIS*]

KNOX, GRAHAM

37.217   JM   1963 British colonial policy and the problems of establishing a free
society in Jamaica, 1838-1865.

KOVATS, EDITH

9.022   MT   1964 MARIAGE ET COHÉSION SOCIALE CHEZ LES BLANCS CRÉOLES DE LA

MARTINIQUE [MARRIAGE AND SOCIAL COHESION AMONG THE WHITE CREOLES OF MARTINIQUE].

KRUIJER, GERARDUS JOHANNES

32.113   JM   1952 De 4-H Clubs van Jamaica.

8.035   NW   1953 De Bovenwindse Eilanden sociografisch [The Windward Islands 'sociographically']. *In* KRUIJER, G.J.; VEENENBOS, J.S. & WESTERMANN, J.H., comps. BOVENWINDENRAPPORT. Amsterdam, Voorlichtingsinstituut voor het Welvaartsplan Nederlandse Antillen, 24p. [10]

8.036   JM   1956 SOCIOLOGICAL REPORT ON THE CHRISTIANA AREA. [Kingston?] Jamaica, Christiana Area Land Authority, 108p. [2, 66]

8.037   JM   1957 The impact of poverty and undernourishment on man and society in rural Jamaica. *Mens Mij Twee Tijdschr* p.284-290. [30, 31, 46] [*RIS*]

LIER, RUDOLF A. J. van

8.038   GC   1950 THE DEVELOPMENT AND NATURE OF SOCIETY IN THE WEST INDIES. Amsterdam, Koninklijke Vereeniging Indische Instituut, 19p. (Mededeling no. 92, Afdeling Culturele en physische anthropologie no. 37.) [10]   [*AGS*]

8.039   GC   1951 The problem of the political and social elite in the West Indies and the Guyana's. *In* RECORD OF THE XXVIth MEETING [OF THE] INTERNATIONAL INSTITUTE OF DIFFERING CIVILIZATIONS (INSTITUT INTERNATIONAL DES CIVILISATIONS DIFFERENTES "INCIDI") held in Paris on the 12th, 13th, 14th and 15th March 1951. Brussels, p.340-351. [10, 37]   [*RIS*]

8.040   NC   1955 Social and political conditions in Suriname and the Netherlands Antilles: Introduction. *In* DEVELOPMENTS TOWARDS SELF-GOVERNMENT IN THE CARIBBEAN: A SYMPOSIUM HELD UNDER THE AUSPICES OF THE NETHERLANDS UNIVERSITIES FOUNDATION FOR INTERNATIONAL COOPERATION AT THE HAGUE, SEPT. 1954. The Hague, W. van Hoeve, p.125-133. [5, 10, 37]   [*RIS*]

LONG, ANTON V.

66.095   JM   1956 JAMAICA AND THE NEW ORDER 1827-1847.

LONGABAUGH, RICHARD HAROLD

18.044   BB   1962 THE DESCRIPTION OF MOTHER-CHILD INTERACTION.

LOSONCZI, E.

30.035   BH   1958 Social anthropology in health education with particular reference to nutrition.

LOW, F. O.

15.028   BG   1919 Hopetown Chinese settlement.

LOWENTHAL, DAVID

10.027   GC   1960 The range and variation of Caribbean societies.

MALEFIJT, ANNEMARIE de WAAL

15.029   SR   1963 THE JAVANESE OF SURINAM: SEGMENT OF A PLURAL SOCIETY.

15.030   SR   1963 Het sociaal-economisch vermogen van de Javanen in Suriname [The socio-economic potential of the Javanese in Surinam].

MALLIET, A. M. WENDELL
11.017   BC   1926 Some prominent West Indians.

MANLEY, DOUGLAS R.
32.130   JM   1963 Mental ability in Jamaica (an examination of the performance of children in the Jamaican common entrance examination, 1959).

MARSHALL, GLORIA ALBERTHA
53.028   BC   1959 Benefit societies in the British West Indies: the formative years.

MAU, JAMES A.; HILL, RICHARD J. & BELL, WENDELL
20.012   JM   1961 Scale analyses of status perception and status attitude in Jamaica and the United States.

MINTZ, SIDNEY W.
51.099   JM   1956 The role of the middleman in the internal distribution system of a Caribbean peasant economy.
8.041   JM   1958 Historical sociology of the Jamaican church-founded free village system. *W I G* 38(1-2):46-70. [5]   [*RIS*]
51.100   JM   1959 Internal market systems as mechanisms of social articulation.
45.016   GC   1959 The plantation as a socio-cultural type.
8.042   GC   1961 A final note [to special issue of *Social Econ Stud* on Caribbean social organization]. *Social Econ Stud* 10(4), Dec.: 528-535.
8.043   JM   [1961?] The house and the yard among three Caribbean peasantries. *In* Actes du VIe Congrès international des sciences anthropologiques, et ethnologiques, Paris 1960. [Paris?] v. 2, p. 1. p.591-596. [*RIS*]
8.044   GC   1961 The question of Caribbean peasantries: a comment. *Car Stud* 1(3), Oct.: 31-34. [5]   [*RIS*]

MINTZ, SIDNEY W. & DAVENPORT, WILLIAM, eds.
8.045   GC   1961 Caribbean social organization. *Social Econ Stud* 10(4), Dec.: 380-535.

MINTZ, SIDNEY W. & HALL, DOUGLAS
51.102   JM   1960 The origins of the Jamaican internal marketing system.

MITTELHOLZER, EDGAR
2.159   BG   1963 A swarthy boy.

MOSKOS, CHARLES CONSTANTINE, Jr.
37.274   BC   1963 The sociology of political independence: a study of influence, social structure and ideology in the British West Indies.

MOSKOS, CHARLES CONSTANTINE, Jr. & BELL, WENDELL
37.275   BC   1964 Attitudes towards democracy among leaders in four emergent nations.
21.017   BC   1964 West Indian nationalism.

NIEHOFF, ARTHUR
12.023   TR   1959 The survival of Hindu institutions in an alien environment.

NORRIS, KATRIN
21.019   JM   1962 Jamaica: the search for an identity.

NORRIS, OLIVER

7.050   DM   1964 Situation et perspectives de la démographie dominicaine [Status and vistas of Dominica demography].

OBERG, KALERVO & HINDORI, GEORGE

46.154   SR   1963 GROOT HENAR POLDER: POLDER SETTLEMENT STUDY NO. II.

PADILLA, ELENA

10.033   GC   1960 Peasants, plantations, and pluralism.

PAGET, HUGH

8.046   JM   1945 The free village system in Jamaica. *Jam Hist Rev* 1(1), June 31-48.
        [5]   *[NYP]*

PASS, Mrs. E. A. de

8.047   TR   1929 The West Indies Boy Scouts. *W I Comm Circ* 44(807), Sept. 5: 343-344. [22, 32]   *[NYP]*

PATTERSON, H. ORLANDO

32.153   JM   1962 The social structure of a university hall of residence.

PEARSE, ANDREW C.

2.179   GC   1955 Caribbean folk culture.

POWRIE, BARBARA E.

20.013   TR   1956 The changing attitude of the coloured middle class towards Carnival.

RAGHAVAN, SUSHILA

8.048   TT   1963 SOCIAL STRATIFICATION IN TORTOLA, BRITISH VIRGIN ISLANDS, M. A. thesis, Brandeis University, 59p. [5]   *[RIS]*

RENSELAAR, H. C. van

11.023   SR   1963 Het sociaal-economisch vermogen van de Creolen in Suriname [The socio-economic potential of the Creoles in Surinam].

RIVIERE, P. G.

13.061   SR   1965 THE SOCIAL ORGANISATION OF THE TRIO INDIANS OF SURINAM.

RODMAN, HYMAN

8.049   GC   1959 On understanding lower-class behaviour. *Social Econ Stud* 8(4), Dec.: 441-450. [9, 67]   *[RIS]*
9.034   TR   1961 Marital relationships in a Trinidad village.

ROSE, W. V.

56.047   BB   1955 Memorandum on the Barbados fishing industry for consideration by the Marketing Committee.

ROSS, STELLA V. B.

8.050   BG   1962 Women in the Guianese society. *Afr Women* 5(1), Dec.: 21-22.
        [NYP]

RUBIN, VERA

20.015   TR   1961 Family aspirations and attitudes of Trinidad youth.
20.016   BC   1962 Culture, politics and race relations.
31.064   TR   1963 The adolescent; his expectations and his society.

SCHWARTZ, BARTON M.

8.051   TR   1963 THE DISSOLUTION OF CASTE IN TRINIDAD. Ph.D. thesis, University
                         of California at Los Angeles, 196p. [12,19]   [*RIS*]
23.141   TR   1964 Ritual aspects of caste in Trinidad.

SEAGA, EDWARD P. G.

32.176   JM   1955 Parent-teacher relationships in a Jamaican village.

SEGGAR, W. H.

66.133   BG   1959 Community development amongst Amerindians.

SHAW, EARL BENNETT

8.052   SC   1934 The villages of St. Croix. *B Geogr Soc Phila* 32, Jan.-Oct.: 10-24.
                         [11, 35]   [*AGS*]
7.075   VI   1935 Population adjustments in our Virgin Islands.

SHERLOCK, PHILIP M.

8.053   GC   1955 THE DEVELOPMENT OF THE MIDDLE CLASS IN THE CARIBBEAN. London,
                         7p. (Working paper for the 29th Study Session of the International
                         Institute of Differing Civilizations, Sept. 13-16.) [5,10]   [*RIS*]

SIMONS, R. D.

36.018   SR   1958 Stad en platteland [The city and the rural areas].

SIMPSON, GEORGE EATON

36.019   JM   1954 Begging in Kingston and Montego Bay.
29.024   TR   1962 Folk medicine in Trinidad.
8.054   GC   1962 Social stratification in the Caribbean. *Phylon* 1st quarter: 29-46.
                         [10, 66]   [*RIS*]

SKINNER, ELLIOTT P.

10.043   BG   1955 ETHNIC INTERACTION IN A BRITISH GUIANA RURAL COMMUNITY: A STUDY
                         OF SECONDARY ACCULTURATION AND GROUP DYNAMICS.
8.055   BG   1960 Group dynamics and social stratification in British Guiana. *In*
                         RUBIN, VERA, ed. SOCIAL AND CULTURAL PLURALISM IN THE
                         CARIBBEAN. New York, New York Academy of Sciences, p.904-916.
                         (Annals of the New York Academy of Sciences, v. 83, art. 5.)
                         [10,16]   [*RIS*]

SMITH, M. G.

8.056   BC   1953 Some aspects of social structure in the British Caribbean about
                         1820. *Social Econ Stud* 1(4), Aug.: 55-80. [5]   [*RIS*]
67.024   GC   [1955?] A FRAMEWORK FOR CARIBBEAN STUDIES.
8.057   JM   1956 Community organization in rural Jamaica. *Social Econ Stud* 5(3),
                         Sept.: 295-312.   [*RIS*]
50.117   JM   1956 A REPORT ON LABOUR SUPPLY IN RURAL JAMAICA.
20.018   JM   1960 Education and occupational choice in rural Jamaica.
10.046   JM   1961 The plural framework of Jamaican society.
9.039   CR   1962 KINSHIP AND COMMUNITY IN CARRIACOU.
9.040   CR   1962 WEST INDIAN FAMILY STRUCTURE.
8.058   JM   1963 Aimless, wandering adolescent groups. *In* CARTER, SAMUEL E.,
                         ed. THE ADOLESCENT IN THE CHANGING CARIBBEAN: PROCEEDINGS OF THE
                         THIRD CARIBBEAN CONFERENCE FOR MENTAL HEALTH, Apr. 4-11, 1961,
                         UCWI, Jamaica. Kingston, The Herald, p.78-79. [67]   [*RIS*]

10.048	BC	1965	THE PLURAL SOCIETY IN THE BRITISH WEST INDIES.
8.059	GR	1965	STRATIFICATION IN GRENADA. Berkeley and Los Angeles, University of California Press, 271p.
8.060	GR	1965	Structure and crisis in Grenada, 1950-1954. *In his* THE PLURAL SOCIETY IN THE BRITISH WEST INDIES. Berkeley and Los Angeles, University of California Press, p.262-303. [37, 44, 66] [*RIS*]

SMITH, M. G. & KRUIJER, G. J.

67.025	JM	1957	A SOCIOLOGICAL MANUAL FOR EXTENSION WORKERS IN THE CARIBBEAN.

SMITH, RAYMOND THOMAS

9.041	BG	1953	Aspects of family organization in a coastal Negro community in British Guiana.
9.042	BG	1953	Aspects of family organization in a coastal Negro community in British Guiana: a preliminary report.
47.030	BG	1955	Land tenure in three Negro villages in British Guiana.
9.043	BG	1956	THE NEGRO FAMILY IN BRITISH GUIANA: FAMILY STRUCTURE AND SOCIAL STATUS IN THE VILLAGES.
12.031	BG	1959	Some social characteristics of Indian immigrants to British Guiana.
9.045	GC	1963	Culture and social structure in the Caribbean: some recent work on family and kinship studies.
8.061	BG	1964	Ethnic difference and peasant economy in British Guiana. *In* FIRTH, RAYMOND & YAMEY, B. S., eds. CAPITAL, SAVING AND CREDIT IN PEASANT SOCIETIES. London, George Allen and Unwin, p.305-329. [10, 20, 44] [*RIS*]

SPECKMANN, JOHAN DIRK

8.062	SR	1962	Hindostaanse bevolkingsgroep in Suriname [Hindustani population group in Surinam]. *Oost West* 55, Jan.: 22-25. [12]
12.033	SR	1963	De positie van de Hindostaanse bevolkingsgroep in de sociale en ekonomische struktuur van Suriname [The position of the Hindustani population group in the social and economic structure of Surinam].

SPENCE, ELEANOR JEAN

51.130	BB	1964	MARKETING ACTIVITIES AND HOUSEHOLD ACTIVITIES OF COUNTRY HAWKERS IN BARBADOS.

STYCOS, J. MAYONE & BACK, KURT

34.019	JM	1958	Contraception and Catholicism in Jamaica.

TANNENBAUM, FRANK

6.070	GC	1947	SLAVE AND CITIZEN; THE NEGRO IN THE AMERICAS.

TAYLOR, COUNCILL SAMUEL

8.063	JM	1955	COLOR AND CLASS: A COMPARATIVE STUDY OF JAMAICAN STATUS GROUPS. Ph. D. dissertation, Yale University, 363p. [10, 16]

VALLEE, LIONEL

9.057	ST	1964	THE NEGRO FAMILY IN ST. THOMAS: A STUDY IN ROLE DIFFERENTIATION.

VERIN, PIERRE-MICHEL

43.147	SL	1963	LA POINTE CARAÏBE (SAINTE-LUCIE).

VERMEULEN, L. P.
7.081   NA   [196-] De bevolkingsstructuur der Nederlandse Antillen [Population patterns in the Netherlands Antilles].

WAGLEY, CHARLES
8.064   GC   1959 Recent studies of Caribbean local societies. *In* WILGUS, A. CURTIS, ed. THE CARIBBEAN: NATURAL RESOURCES [papers delivered at the Ninth Conference on the Caribbean held at the University of Florida, Dec. 4-6, 1958]. Gainesville; Univ. of Florida Press, 1959, p.193-204. (Publications of the School of Inter-American Studies, ser. 1, v.9.)   [*RIS*]

WAGLEY, CHARLES & HARRIS, MARVIN
8.065   MT   1958 MINORITIES IN THE NEW WORLD: SIX CASE STUDIES. New York, Columbia University Press, 320p. [16]   [*RIS*]

WEEVER, P. M. de
46.233   BG   1921 Our future peasantry.

WELLS, A. F. & D.
53.042   BC   1953 FRIENDLY SOCIETIES IN THE WEST INDIES.

WENGEN, G. D. van
15.041   SR   1963 Tajoeb, een prestige-feest bij de Javanen in Suriname [Tajub, a prestige festival among the Javanese of Surinam].

WRIGHT, RICHARDSON
8.066   JM   1938/ Freemasonry on the island of Jamaica. *Trans Am Res Fr Acc Masons* 39 3(1), Oct./Oct.: 126-155. [5]   [*NYP*]

YOUNG, ALLAN
37.435   BG   1958 THE APPROACHES TO LOCAL SELF-GOVERNMENT IN BRITISH GUIANA.

Chapter 9

KINSHIP ORGANIZATION

ADHIN, J. H.
9.001   SR   1960/Over de "joint family" der Hindostanen [On the joint family of
             61 the Hindustani]. *N W I G* 40:17-27. [12]   *[COL]*

BEAUBRUN, MICHAEL H.
31.005   TR   1963 The role of father in Trinidad adolescence.
31.007   GC   [1965?] Keynote address.

BENOIST, JEAN
27.007   FA   1964 Quelques facteurs sociaux de la différenciation raciale aux Antilles
             Francaises [Some social aspects of racial differentiation in the
             French Antilles].

BENOIT, GUY
31.009   GD   1963 Attitudes and problems of adolescents in Guadeloupe.
31.010   GD   [1965?] Essai sur la structure familiale vecue en Guadeloupe [Essay on
             family structure in Guadeloupe].

BLAKE, JUDITH
34.004   JM·   1955 FAMILY INSTABILITY AND REPRODUCTIVE BEHAVIOR IN JAMAICA: CURRENT
             RESEARCH IN HUMAN FERTILITY.
34.005   JM   1958 A reply to Mr. [Lloyd E.] Braithwaite [*Social Econ Stud* 6(4), Dec.
             1957: 523-571].

BLAKE, JUDITH; STYCOS, J. MAYONE & DAVIS, KINGSLEY
34.006   JM   1961 FAMILY STRUCTURE IN JAMAICA: THE SOCIAL CONTEXT OF REPRODUCTION.

BLUMBERG, B.; McGIFF, J. & GUICHERIT, I.
28.039   SR   1953 A survey of intestinal parasites in the schoolchildren of Moengo,
             Surinam, 1950.

BRAITHWAITE, LLOYD E.
34.007   BC   1957 Sociology and demographic research in the British Caribbean.
31.013   GC   1961 Social and economic changes in the Caribbean.

BRAITHWAITE, LLOYD E. & ROBERTS, G. W.

9.0ᴜ2   TR   1963 Mating patterns and prospects in Trinidad. *In* [PROCEEDINGS OF THE] INTERNATIONAL POPULATION CONFERENCE, New York, 1961. London, John Wright, v. 2, p.173-181. [11, 12]

CHATEAU, E. D.

8.006   SR   1955 Groepsvorming onder de straatjeugd van Paramaribo [Group-forming among streetcorner youth of Paramaribo].

COUSINS, WINIFRED M.

9.004   BC   1935 Slave family life in the British colonies 1800-1834. *Sociol Rev* 27(1), Jan.: 35-55. [6]   [*COL*]

CLARKE, EDITH

47.010   JM   1953 Land tenure and the family in four communities in Jamaica.
9.003   JM   1957 MY MOTHER WHO FATHERED ME: A STUDY OF THE FAMILY IN 3 SELECTED COMMUNITIES IN JAMAICA. London, George Allen and Unwin, 215p. [8, 47]   [*RIS*]

CLOSE, KATHRYN

31.018   GC   1961 Youth in the Caribbean—reaching for maturity.

COHEN, YEHUDI A.

31.019   JM   1955 Character formation and social structure in a Jamaican community.
31.020   JM   1955 A contribution to the study of adolescence: adolescent conflict in a Jamaican community.
8.009   JM   1955 Four categories of interpersonal relationships in the family and community in a Jamaican village.
31.021   JM   1956 Structure and function: family organization and socialization in a Jamaican community.

CROWLEY, DANIEL JOHN

19.006   SL   1956 Naming customs in St. Lucia.

CUMPER, GEORGE E.

46.044   JM   1958 The Jamaican family: village and estate.
44.043   BB   1960 West Indian household budgets.
44.044   BB   1961 Household and occupation in Barbados.
50.024   JM/   1961/Labour and development in the West Indies.
           BB   62

DAVENPORT, WILLIAM HUNT

9.005   JM   1961 The family system of Jamaica. *Social Econ Stud* 10(4), Dec.: 420-454. [8]   [*RIS*]

DAVIDS, LEO

9.006   BG/   1964 The East Indian family overseas. *Social Econ Stud* 13(3), Sept.:
           TR   383-396. [12, 19]   [*RIS*]

DAVIDSON, H. K. & MINKES, A. L.

66.035   JM   1954 Social factors in the economic problems of Jamaica.

ERICKSEN, E. GORDON

7.019   BC   1962 THE WEST INDIES POPULATION PROBLEM: DIMENSIONS FOR ACTION.

FILL, J. HERBERT

31.025 UV 1963 The sexual dilemma of the Caribbean adolescent.

FOCK, NIELS

9.007 GG 1960 South American birth customs in theory and practice. *Folk* 2:51-69. [13, 19] [*COL*]

GOODE, WILLIAM J.

9.008 GC 1960 Illegitimacy in the Caribbean social structure. *Am Sociol Rev* 25(1), Feb.: 21-30. [*RIS*]

GOURDON J.

31.027 GD [1965?] Hygiène mentale et relations familiales [Mental health and family relations].

GREENFIELD, SIDNEY M.

9.009 BB 1959 FAMILY ORGANIZATION IN BARBADOS. Ph. D. dissertation, Columbia University, 212p. [8] [*COL*]
47.018 BB 1960 Land tenure and transmission in rural Barbados.
9.010 BB 1961 Socio-economic factors and family form: a Barbadian case study. *Social Econ Stud* 10(1), Mar.: 72-85. [44] [*RIS*]
9.011 GC 1962 Households, families and kinship systems in the West Indies. *Anthrop Q* 35(3), July: 121-132. [67] [*RIS*]

HAGLUND, ELSA

35.019 GC 1958 HOUSING AND HOME IMPROVEMENT IN THE CARIBBEAN.

HAJARY, H. N.

9.012 SR 1937 De verwacht wordende groote gebeurtenis onder de Britsch-Indiërs in Suriname [The expected big event among British Indians in Surinam]. *W I G* 19:1-4. [12, 66] [*COL*]

HENRIC, S.

9.013 GD [1965?] La famille guadeloupéenne [The Guadeloupe family]. *In* FAMILY RELATIONSHIPS: [PROCEEDINGS OF THE] FOURTH CARIBBEAN CONFERENCE FOR MENTAL HEALTH, Curacao, Apr. 16-23, 1963, Netherlands Antilles. [Willemstad? Boek- en Offset Drukkerij "De Curacaosche Courant"] p.151-154. [31] [*RIS*]

HENRIQUES, FERNANDO

9.014 JM 1949 West Indian family organization. *Am J Sociol* 55(1), July: 30-37. [11] [*COL*]
9.015 JM 1951 Kinship and death in Jamaica. *Phylon* 12(3):272-278. [19] [*COL*]
9.016 JM 1953 FAMILY AND COLOUR IN JAMAICA. London, Eyre and Spottiswood, 196P. [8, 11] [*RIS*]

HOETINK, HARRY

9.017 GC 1961 Gezinsvormen in het Caribisch gebied [Family types in the Caribbean area]. Mar.-Apr.: 81-93. [8] [*RIS*]
9.018 GC 1965 Contemporary research; the Caribbean family and its relation to the concept of mental health. *In* FAMILY RELATIONSHIPS: [PROCEEDINGS OF THE] FOURTH CARIBBEAN CONFERENCE FOR MENTAL HEALTH, Curacao, Apr. 16-23, 1963, Netherlands Antilles. [Willemstad? Boek-en Offset Drukkerij "De Curacaosche Courant"] p.36-45. [31] [*RIS*]

HOROWITZ, MICHAEL M. & SYLVIA H.
9.019   MT   1963 A note on marriage in Martinique. *Marr Fam Liv* 25(2), May: 160-161.
                                                                                    [*RIS*]

HOYT, ELIZABETH E.
50.066   JM   1960 Voluntary unemployment and unemployability in Jamaica with special reference to the standard of living.

HURAULT, JEAN
13.036   FG   1961 Les Indiens oayana de la Guyane Francaise [The Oayana Indians of French Guiana].
13.038   FG   1962 Les Indiens oyampi de la Guyane Francaise [The Oyampi Indians of French Guiana].

IBBERSON, DORA
34.008   JM   1956 A note on the relationship between illegitimacy and the birthrate.

JAYAWARDENA, CHANDRA
9.020   BG   1960 Marital stability in two Guianese sugar estate communities. *Social Econ Stud* 9(1), Mar.: 76-100. [12, 45]   [*RIS*]
9.021   BG   1962 Family organisation in plantations in British Guiana. *Int J Comp Sociol* 3(1), Sept.: 43-64. [12, 44, 45]   [*RIS*]

KLASS, SHEILA SOLOMON
12.014   TR   1964 EVERYONE IN THIS HOUSE MAKES BABIES.

KOVATS, EDITH
9.022   MT   1964 MARIAGE ET COHÉSION SOCIALE CHEZ LES BLANCS CRÉOLES DE LA MARTINIQUE [MARRIAGE AND SOCIAL COHESION AMONG THE WHITE CREOLES OF MARTINIQUE]. M. A. thesis, University of Montreal, 107p. [8]   [*RIS*]

KREISELMAN, MARIAM
9.023   MT   1958 THE CARIBBEAN FAMILY: A CASE STUDY IN MARTINIQUE. Ph. D. dissertation, Columbia University, 304p.

KRUIJER, GERARDUS JOHANNES
34.009   JM   1958 Family size and family planning; a pilot survey among Jamaican mothers.

LEWIS, E. P.
9.024   TR   1964 Adoption and foster homes. *In* REPORT OF CONFERENCE ON CHILD CARE IN TRINIDAD AND TOBAGO HELD BY TRINIDAD AND TOBAGO ASSOCIATION FOR MENTAL HEALTH, SUB-COMMITTEE ON CHILDREN AND YOUTH, COMMUNITY EDUCATION CENTRE, St. Ann's, Apr. 18th, 1964. [Port of Spain?] Government Printery, p.30-32. [37]   [*RIS*]

LOUILOT, LILIANE
9.025   FA   1961 La famille aux Antilles [The family in the Antilles]. *Chron Social Fr* 69(2), Mar. 31: 113-125.   [*NYP*]

MASON, JOYCE
32.134   SL   1962 Adult education and family life.

MATTHEWS, Dom BASIL

9.026   TR   1953 CRISIS OF THE WEST INDIAN FAMILY. Port of Spain, Extra-Mural Dept., University College of the West Indies, 117p. [5, 19]   [RIS]

MOSER, C. A.

44.158   JM   1957 THE MEASUREMENT OF LEVELS OF LIVING WITH SPECIAL REFERENCE TO JAMAICA.

MOSKOS, CHARLES CONSTANTINE, Jr.

37.274   BC   1963 THE SOCIOLOGY OF POLITICAL INDEPENDENCE: A STUDY OF INFLUENCE, SOCIAL STRUCTURE AND IDEOLOGY IN THE BRITISH WEST INDIES.

MURRA, JOHN V.

9.027   FA   1957 Studies in family organization in the French Caribbean. *Trans N Y Acad Sci* 2d ser., 19(4), Feb.: 372-378. [67]   [RIS]

NIEHOFF, ARTHUR

12.023   TR   1959 The survival of Hindu institutions in an alien environment.

OTTERBEIN, KEITH F.

9.028   JM/   1964 A comparison of the land tenure systems of the Bahamas, Jamaica,
          BB   and Barbados: the implications it has for the study of social systems shifting from bilateral to ambilineal descent. *Int Archs Ethnogr* 50(1): 31-42. [47]   [RIS]

9.029   GC   1965 Caribbean family organization: a comparative analysis. *Am Anthrop* 67(1), Feb.: 66-79.   [RIS]

PATCHETT, K. W.

9.030   BC   1959 Some aspects of marriage and divorce in the West Indies. *Int Comp Law Q* 8(4), Oct.: 632-677. [10,37]   [NYP]

PRINS, J.

9.031   SR   1963 Een Surinaams rechtsgeding over een Moslimse verstoting [A Surinam lawsuit about a Moslem divorce]. *N W I G* 42(2), Feb.: 201-207. [12, 37]   [RIS]

RAY, MICHAEL

9.032   BG   1935 Bamboo marriage. *Can-W I Mag* 24(5), Apr.: 21-22. [12]   [NYP]

ROBERTS, GEORGE WOODROW

34.013   BC   1953 Motherhood tables of the 1946 census.
34.014   BC   1955 Cultural factors in fertility in the British Caribbean.
34.015   GC   1955 Some aspects of mating and fertility in the West Indies.

ROBERTS, GEORGE WOODROW & BRAITHWAITE, LLOYD

34.016   TR   1960 Fertility differentials by family type in Trinidad.
34.017   TR   1961 A gross mating table for a West Indian population.
9.033   TR   1962 Mating among East Indian and non-Indian women in Trinidad. *Social Econ Stud* 11(3), Sept.: 203-240. [11, 12]   [RIS]

RODMAN, HYMAN

8.049   GC   1959 On understanding lower-class behaviour.
9.034   TR   1961 Marital relationships in a Trinidad village. *Marr Fam Liv* 23(2), May: 166-170. [8]   [RIS]

RUBIN, VERA

20.015   TR   1961 Family aspirations and attitudes of Trinidad youth.

31.064   TR   1963 The adolescent: his expectations and his society.

9.035   GC [1965?] The West Indian family retrospect and prospect. *In* FAMILY RELA-
TIONSHIPS: [PROCEEDINGS OF THE] FOURTH CARIBBEAN CONFERENCE
FOR MENTAL HEALTH, Curacao, Apr. 16-23, 1963, Netherlands An-
tilles [Willemstad? Boek- en Offset Drukkerij "De Curacaosche
Courant"] p.53-65. [20, 31]   [*COL*]

SAMPATH, MARTIN

28.457   TR   1953 The influence of socio-anthropological factors on the incidence of
syphilis in a heterogenous group of pregnant women in Trinidad.

SCHWARTZ, BARTON M.

9.036   TR   1965 Patterns of East Indian family organization in Trinidad. *Car Stud*
5(1), Apr.: 23-36. [12]   [*RIS*]

SIMPSON, GEORGE EATON

10.041   GC   1962 The peoples and cultures of the Caribbean area.

SMITH, M. G.

47.029   CR   1956 The transformation of land rights by transmission in Carriacou.

9.037   JM   1957 Family patterns in rural Jamaica. *Welf Reptr* 16(3), May-June:
24-25,28. [44]

9.038   CR   1961 Kinship and household in Carriacou. *Social Econ Stud* 10(4),
Dec.: 454-477.   [*RIS*]

9.039   CR   1962 KINSHIP AND COMMUNITY IN CARRIACOU. New Haven, Yale University
Press, 347p. [8]   [*RIS*]

9.040   CR   1962 WEST INDIAN FAMILY STRUCTURE. Seattle, University of Washington
Press, 311p. (A monograph from the Research Institute for the Study
of Man.) [8,36]   [*RIS*]

SMITH, RAYMOND THOMAS

9.041   BG   1953 Aspects of family organization in a coastal Negro community in
British Guiana. *Timehri* 4th ser., 1(32), Nov.: 49-70. [8, 11]

9.042   BG   1953 Aspects of family organization in a coastal Negro community in
British Guiana: a preliminary report. *Social Econ Stud* 1(1), Feb.:
1-24. [8, 11]   [*RIS*]

9.043   BG   1956 THE NEGRO FAMILY IN BRITISH GUIANA: FAMILY STRUCTURE AND SOCIAL
STATUS IN THE VILLAGES. London, Routledge and Kegan Paul, 282p.
[8, 11]   [*RIS*]

9.044   GC   1960 The family in the Caribbean. *In* RUBIN, VERA, ed. CARIBBEAN
STUDIES: A SYMPOSIUM. 2d ed. Seattle, University of Washington
Press, p.67-79.   [*RIS*]

9.045   GC   1963 Culture and social structure in the Caribbean: some recent work on
family and kinship studies. *Comp Stud Soc Hist* 6(1), Oct.: 24-46.
[8, 67]   [*RIS*]

SMITH, RAYMOND THOMAS & JAYAWARDENA, C.

9.046   BG   1958 Hindu marriage customs in British Guiana. *Social Econ Stud* 7(2),
June: 178-194. [12]   [*RIS*]

9.047   BG   1959 Marriage and the family amongst East Indians in British Guiana.
Social Econ Stud 8(4), Dec.: 321-376. [12]   [*RIS*]

SOLIEN, NANCIE L.

9.048 BH 1958 THE CONSANGUINEAL HOUSEHOLD AMONG THE BLACK CARIB OF CENTRAL AMERICA. Ph. D. dissertation, University of Michigan, 234p. [11, 13] [*NYP*]

9.049 BH 1959 The nonunilineal descent group in the Caribbean and Central America. *Am Anthrop* 61(4), Aug.: 578-583. [13] [*RIS*]

9.050 BH 1960 Changes in Black Carib kinship terminology. *Sw J Anthrop* 16(2), Summer: 144-159. [13, 26] [*RIS*]

9.051 GC 1960 Household and family in the Caribbean. *Social Econ Stud* 9(1), Mar.: 101-106. [*RIS*]

SPECKMANN, JOHAN DIRK

9.052 SR 1965 MARRIAGE AND KINSHIP AMONG THE INDIANS IN SURINAM. Assen [Netherlands?] VanGorcum, 302p. (Ph. D. dissertation, Rijksuniversiteit.) [12] [*RIS*]

SPENCE, ELEANOR JEAN

51.130 BB 1964 MARKETING ACTIVITIES AND HOUSEHOLD ACTIVITIES OF COUNTRY HAWKERS IN BARBADOS.

STRAW, K. H.

30.051 BB 1954 Household budgets and nutritional analysis of food consumption in Barbados.

STYCOS, J. MAYONE & BACK, KURT

34.019 JM 1958 Contraception and Catholicism in Jamaica.

STYCOS, J. MAYONE & BLAKE, JUDITH

9.053 JM 1954 The Jamaican Family Life Project: some objectives and methods. *Social Econ Stud* 3(3-4), Dec.: 342-349. [67] [*NYP*]

TANCOCK, CATHERINE BRIDGET

18.067 BB 1961 A STUDY OF HOUSEHOLD STRUCTURE AND CHILD TRAINING IN A LOWER CLASS BARBADIAN GROUP.

TAYLOR, DOUGLAS C.

9.054 GC 1953 A note on marriage and kinship among the Island Carib. *Man* 53 (art. 175), Aug.: 117-119. [4] [*COL*]

9.055 GC 1957 Marriage, affinity, and descent in two Arawakan tribes: a sociolinguistic note. *Int J Am Ling* 23(4), Oct.: 284-290. [13, 26] [*COL*]

26.038 GC 1957 A note on some Arawakan words for *man*, etc.

9.056 GC 1961 Some remarks on teknonymy in Arawakan. *Int J Am Ling* 27(1), Jan.: 76-80. [26] [*COL*]

TIETZE, CHRISTOPHER

34.020 BB 1957 THE FAMILY PLANNING SERVICE IN BARBADOS.

34.021 BB 1958 THE EFFECTIVENESS OF THE FAMILY PLANNING SERVICE IN BARBADOS.

TIETZE, CHRISTOPHER & ALLEYNE, CHARLES

34.022 BB 1959 A family planning service in the West Indies.

VALLEE, LIONEL

9.057   ST   1964 THE NEGRO FAMILY IN ST. THOMAS: A STUDY IN ROLE DIFFERENTIATION. Ph. D. dissertation, Cornell University, 244p. [5, 8, 11]

WATERMAN, JAMES A.

9.058   TR   1962 Illegitimacy in Trinidad and Tobago. *Car Med J* 24(1-4): 76-79. [*COL*]

WELSH, BRONTE

31.071   KNA [1965?] Paper on mental health and family relationship.

WILSON, GLADSTONE

9.059   JM   [1961?] New stresses in the family. *In* CUMPER, GEORGE, ed. REPORT OF THE CONFERENCE ON SOCIAL DEVELOPMENT IN JAMAICA. Kingston, Standing Committee on Social Services, p. 91-93. [*RIS*]

Chapter 10

POPULATION SEGMENTS: OVERVIEW

ABONNENC, E.

7.002   FG   1948/ Aspects demographiques de la Guyane Franciase [Demographic
49   aspects of French Guiana].

ABONNENC, E. & ISSARTE, A.

7.003   FG   1952 Démographie de la Guyane Francaise; structure de la population
d'après le recensement de 1946 [Demography of French Guiana
population structure according to the 1946 census].

ADHIN, J. H.

10.001   SR   1954/ De culturele invloed van de Aziatische bevolkingsgroep op Sur-
55   iname [The cultural influence of the Asiatic population group upon
Suriname]. *Vox Guy* 1(4-5), Nov.-Jan.: 29-34.

ARCHIBALD, CHARLES H.

38.006   BC   1961 Question-mark over the Caribbean.

ARNEAUD, JOHN D. & YOUNG, OSWALD

27.001   TR   1955 A preliminary survey of the distribution of A B O and Rh blood
groups in Trinidad, B. W. I.

ASHCROFT, M. T.

28.015   BG   1962 The morbidity and mortality of enteric fever in British Guiana.

ASSENDERP, ANDRE L. van

10.002   SR   1958 Some aspects of society in the Netherlands Antilles and Surinam.
In WILGUS, A. CURTIS, ed. THE CARIBBEAN: BRITISH, DUTCH,
FRENCH, UNITED STATES [papers delivered at the Eighth Conference on the Caribbean held at the University of Florida. Dec.
5-7, 1957]. Gainesville, University of Florida Press, p.86-94.
(Publications of the School of Inter-American Studies, ser 1, v. 8.)
[8]   [RIS]

AUGELLI, JOHN P. & TAYLOR, HARRY W.

7.004   TR   1960 Race and population patterns in Trinidad.

BAKHUIS, L. A.

10.003   SR   1903 De bevolking van Suriname [The population of Surinam]. *Tijdschr Ned Aar Genoot* 20(1):311-316.

BENOIST, JEAN

27.003   MT   [1958?] Données comparatives sur la croissance somatique des enfants de couleur et des enfants de race blanche nés et élevés à la Martinique [Comparative data on the somatic growth of colored children and white children born and bred in Martinique].

27.006   MT   1963 Les Martiniquais: anthropologie d'une population métissée [The people of Martinique: the anthropology of a hybrid population].

BETHENCOURT, CARDOZO de

15.003   GC   1925 Notes on the Spanish and Portuguese Jews in the United States, Guiana, and the Dutch and British West Indies during the seventeenth and eighteenth centuries.

BLUMBERG, B.; McGIFF, J. & GUICHERIT, I.

28.037   SR   1951 Filariasis in Moengo (Surinam) in 1950.

BOAS, J. H.

10.004   SR   1944 Jungle harmony. *Can-W I Mag* 33-34(4), Apr.: 23-27.   [*NYP*]

BOISSIERE, JEAN de

10.005   TR   1933 The street of all races. *Can-W I Mag* 23(1), Dec.: 20-21.   [*NYP*]

BRAITHWAITE, LLOYD E.

8.002   TR   1953 Social stratification in Trinidad.
10.006   TR   1954 Cultural integration in Trinidad. *Social Econ Stud* 3(1), June: 82-96.
                         [8, 19]   [*RIS*]
8.003   BC   1960 Social stratification and cultural pluralism.

BROOM, LEONARD

8.004   JM   1954 The social differentiation of Jamaica.
36.003   JM   1960 Urbanization and the plural society.

BURKHARDT, W.

23.008   SR   1927 Surinam.

BYAS, VINCENT W.

27.011   MT   1943 Ethnologic aspects of the Martinique Creole.

CAPPELLE, H. van

10.007   SR   1903 Bij de Indianen en Boschnegers van Suriname [Visit to the Indians and Bush Negroes of Surinam]. *Tijdschr Ned Aar Genoot* 20: 282-283.

24.012   SR   1926 Mythen en sagen uit West-Indië [Myths and legends from the West Indies.

CHARPENTIER, [GUY?] SUZY

10.008   FG   [n.d.] Peaux rouges et noires [Amerindians and Negroes]. *Rev Fr* 60: 5-10.

COIA, A. G.
28.101   BG   1933 Some racial statistics of uterine fibroids in British Guiana.

COINTET, ANDRE
7.009   FA   1954 Le surpeuplement des Antilles Francaises en particulier de la Guadeloupe [Overpopulation in the French Antilles, particularly in Guadeloupe].

COLL, C. van
2.040   SR   1903 Gegevens over land en volk van Suriname [Data about the country and people of Surinam].

COLLIER, W. A. & FUENTE, A. A. de la
28.103   SR   1953 The histoplasmine test in Surinam.

COLLIER, W. A. & La PARRA, D. A. de
27.014   SR   1952 Sickle-cell trait in Surinam Creoles.

COLLIER, W. A.; WOLFF, A. E. & ZAAL, A. E. G.
27.015   SR   1952 Contributions to the geographical pathology of Surinam. I: Blood groups of the Surinam population.

COMITAS, LAMBROS
10.009   BC   1960 Metropolitan influences in the Caribbean: the West Indies. *In* RUBIN, VERA, ed. SOCIAL AND CULTURAL PLURALISM IN THE CARIBBEAN. New York, New York Academy of Sciences, p.809-815. (Annals of the New York Academy of Sciences, vol. 83, art. 5.) [5]   [*RIS*]

COUSINS, WINIFRED M.
7.010   BC   1935 The sex-ratio among Negroes as illustrated by certain British colonies.

CROWLEY, DANIEL JOHN
53.007   JM/   1953 American credit institutions of Yoruba type.
          TR
10.010   TR   1957 Plural and differential acculturation in Trinidad. *Am Anthrop* 59(5), Oct.: 817-824. [19, 21]   [*RIS*]
10.011   GC   1960 Cultural assimilation in a multiracial society. *In* RUBIN, VERA, ed. SOCIAL AND CULTURAL PLURALISM IN THE CARIBBEAN. New York, New York Academy of Sciences, p.850-854. (Annals of the New York Academy of Sciences, v. 83, art. 5.) [19]   [*RIS*]

CRUICKSHANK, E. K., et al.
28.116   JM   1955 Sickle cell anaemia: symposium at the University College of the West Indies, May 26th, 1954.

CURTI, MARGARET WOOSTER
31.022   CM   1960 Intelligence tests of white and colored school children in Grand Cayman.

CURTIN, PHILIP D.
2.052   JM   1955 TWO JAMAICAS: THE ROLE OF IDEAS IN A TROPICAL COLONY, 1830-1865.

DAVENPORT, C. B. & STEGGERDA, MORRIS
27.017   JM/   1929 RACE CROSSING IN JAMAICA.
          CM

DESPRES, LEO A.
67.003   BG   1964 The implications of nationalist politics in British Guiana for the development of cultural theory.

DRIDZO, A. D.
10.012   JM   1962 Naselenie Iamaĭki [The population of Jamaica]. *Sov Ethnogr* 5:100-110.   [*COL*]

DROOGLEEVER, FORTUYN, A. B.
27.020   SR   1952 AGE, STATURE AND WEIGHT IN SURINAM CONSCRIPTS.

DUNCAN, W. J.
7.015   BG   1916 The public health statistics of the colony.
7.016   BG   1919 The public health and medical statistics of the colony.

EDGE, P. GRANVILLE
7.017   BC   1944 Infant mortality in British West Indies.

EDGHILL, H. B.
28.144   BG   1961 Filariasis at Port Mourant and its environs Corentyne coast, British Guiana.

ENGLISH, E. W. F., et al.
7.018   BG   1907 Report of the Mortality Commission.

EVANS, HARRY
50.045   BG   1962 Profsoiuzy Britanskoi Gviany na raspute [by] Garri Evans [The trade unions of British Guiana in disarray].

FAUQUET, G.
2.076   MT   1912 Note sur la population de la Martinique (eléments ethniques et catégories sociales) [Memorandum on the population of Martinique (ethnic elements and social classes)].

FERGUSON, J. E. A.
28.151   BG   1906 The climate of the Peter's Hall District and its effects on the inhabitants.

FERNANDES, H. P.
28.153   BG   1951 Streptomycin in the treatment of tuberculosis in British Guiana.

FIELD, F. E.
28.154   BG   1913 Observations on dysentery, with special reference to its treatment by hypodermic injections of emetine.
28.155   BG   1916 Report on the amelioration and control of ankylostomiasis in the Belle Vue (West Bank) District of British Guiana.

FLOCH, HERVE ALEXANDRE; DURIEUX C. & KOERBER, R.
28.178   FG   1953 Enquête épidémiologique sur la fièvre jaune en Guyane Francaise [Epidemiological survey of yellow fever in French Guiana].

FLOCH, HERVE ALEXANDRE & LAJUDIE, P. de
28.183   FG   1946 Sur la lèpre en Guyane Francaise [Regarding leprosy in French Guiana].

27.022   FG   1947 Répartition des groupes sanguins en Guyane Francaise [Distribution of blood groups in French Guiana].

FRANCIS, OLIVER M.
28.188   BG   1943 Social, economic and dietetic features of tuberculosis in British Guiana.
28.189   BG   1943 Tuberculin tests in British Guiana.
28.190   BG   1944 Tuberculosis in British Guiana.

FREILICH, MORRIS
10.013   TR   1960 CULTURAL DIVERSITY AMONG TRINIDADIAN PEASANTS. Ph.D. dissertation, Columbia University, 178p. [8, 12]   [*RIS*]
67.006   TR   1963 The natural experiment, ecology and culture.

FUNG-KEE-FUNG, C.O.
28.206   BG   1962 Observations on endometrioses in British Guiana and a suggested origin.

GIGLIOLI, GEORGE
28.221   BG   1956 Medical services on the sugar estates of British Guiana.

GILLIN, JOHN P.
10.014   GC   1951 Is there a modern Caribbean culture? *In* WILGUS, A. CURTIS, ed. THE CARIBBEAN AT MID-CENTURY [papers delivered at the First Annual Conference on the Caribbean held at the University of Florida, Dec. 7-9, 1950]. Gainesville, University of Florida Press, p.129-135. (Publications of the School of Inter-American Studies, ser. 1, v. 1.) [21, 67]   [*RIS*]

GOSLINGS, B.M.
10.015   SR   [n.d.] De Indianen en Boschnegers van Suriname [The Indians and Bush Negroes of Surinam]. *Kon Veren Kol Inst G* 13:127p. [2]   [*AGS*]

GREWAL, N.
28.257   BG   1959 Surgical treatment of peptic ulcer in British Guiana.

GUERIN, DANIEL
10.016   GC   1956 LES ANTILLES DÉCOLONISÉES [THE INDEPENDENT ANTILLES]. Paris, Présence africaine, 188p. [2]   [*RIS*]

HAAN, J.H. de & HENDRIKS, J.A.H.
46.082   SR   1954 Lelydorp project—a pilotscheme for land-development in Surinam.

HARNARINE, HAROLD
44.097   BC   1963/64 Business enterprise and Asiatic groups in the West Indies.

HAUGER, JEAN
7.029   FG   1957 La population de la Guyane Francaise [The population of French Guiana].

HELWIG, G.V.
10.017   JM   1958 Society in the British West Indies. *In* WILGUS, A. CURTIS, ed. THE

CARIBBEAN: BRITISH, DUTCH, FRENCH, UNITED STATES [papers delivered at the Eighth Conference on the Caribbean held at the University of Florida, Dec. 5-7, 1957]. Gainesville, University of Florida Press, p.27-38. (Publications of the School of Inter-American Studies, ser. 1, v. 8.) [8]   [*RIS*]

HENRY, M. U. & POON-KING, T.

28.276   TR   1961 Blood groups in diabetes (a preliminary survey in South Trinidad).

HEWICK, J. E.

10.018   BG   1911 Our people. *Timehri* 3d ser., 1(18C), Dec.: 231-238. [7]   [*AMN*]

HOETINK, HARRY

10.019   CU   1960 Curacao como sociedad segmentada [Curacao as a segmented society]. *Revta Cienc Social* 4(1), Mar.: 179-193. [5]   [*AGS*]
20.009   GC   1961 Colonial psychology and race.
10.020   NA   1962 DE GESPLETEN SAMENLEVING IN HET CARAIBISCHE GEBIED [THE DIVIDED SOCIETY IN THE CARIBBEAN AREA]. Assen,[Netherlands], van Gorcum, 314p. [16]

HOROWITZ, MICHAEL M.

10.021   FA   1960 Metropolitan influences in the Caribbean: the French Antilles. *In* RUBIN, VERA, ed. SOCIAL AND CULTURAL PLURALISM IN THE CARIBBEAN. New York, New York Academy of Sciences, p.802-808. (Annals of the New York Academy of Sciences, v. 83, art. 5.)   [*RIS*]

JONKERS, A. H.; DOWNS, W. G.; AITKEN, T. H. G. & SPENCE, L.

28.298   SR   1964 Arthropod-borne encephalitis viruses in northeastern South America. Part I: A serological survey of Northeastern Surinam.

KALFF, S.

10.022   CU   1926/ Joden op het eiland Curacao [Jews on the island of Curacao]. *W I G* 27 8:69-84. [23]   [*COL*]

KEUR, DOROTHY L.

10.023   NA   1960 Metropolitan Influences in the Caribbean: The Netherlands Antilles. *In* RUBIN, VERA, ed. SOCIAL AND CULTURAL PLURALISM IN THE CARIBBEAN. New York, New York Academy of Sciences, p.796-801. (Annals of the New York Academy of Sciences, v. 83, art. 5.)   [*RIS*]

KLASS, MORTON

10.024   TR   1960 East and West Indian: cultural complexity in Trinidad. *In* RUBIN, VERA, ed. SOCIAL AND CULTURAL PLURALISM IN THE CARIBBEAN. New York, New York Academy of Sciences, p.855-861. (Annals of the New York Academy of Sciences, v. 83, art. 5.) [12]   [*RIS*]

KRUIJER, GERARDUS JOHANNES

36.010   SR   1951 Urbanisme in Suriname [Urbanism in Surinam].
8.035   NW   1953 De Bovenwindse Eilanden sociografisch [The Windward Islands 'sociographically'].
7.036   SR   1954 De onderscheiding naar landaard in de demografische statistiek van Suriname [Distinguishing ethnic origin in the demographic statistics of Surinam].

10.025	NC	1956	Samenwerking Suriname en Nederlandse Antillen [Cooperation between Surinam and the Netherlands Antilles]. *Oost West* 49(2):3-5.
66.084	SR	1958	Sociale consequenties van het Tien-jarenplan [Social consequences of the Ten Year Plan].

KUYP, EDWIN van der

28.314	SR	1951	Yellow fever in Surinam.
28.316	SR	1961	Schistosomiasis in the Surinam district of Surinam.

LASHLEY, L. A. G. O.

37.223	SR	1954/ 55	Het Koninkrijk is dood, leve het Koninkrijk [The Kingdom is dead, long live the Kingdom].

LEE, C. U.

28.327	BG	1923	A preliminary report on the incidence of filarial infection amongst Chinese, East Indians, Portuguese, blacks and mixed races in Georgetown.

LELYVELD, TH. van

19.028	SR	1919/ 20	De kleeding der Surinaamsche bevolkingsgroepen [The way of dressing of the Surinam population groups].

LE PAGE, R. B.

25.064	BC	1955	The language problem of the British Caribbean.

LICHTVELD, LOU

32.125	NA	1954/ 55	The social and economic background of education in Surinam and the Netherlands Antilles.
35.030	SR	1960	Native arts in modern architecture.

LIER, RUDOLF A. J. van

10.026	SR	1949	SAMENLEVING IN EEN GRENSGEBIED: EEN SOCIAAL-HISTORISCHE STUDIE VAN DE MAATSCHAPPIJ IN SURINAME [SOCIETY IN A FRONTIER AREA: A SOCIO-HISTORICAL STUDY OF THE SOCIETY OF SURINAM]. The Hague, Nijhoff, 425p. [*COL*]
8.038	GC	1950	THE DEVELOPMENT AND NATURE OF SOCIETY IN THE WEST INDIES.
8.039	GC	1951	The problem of the political and social elite in the West Indies and the Guyana's.
8.040	NC	1955	Social and political conditions in Surinam and the Netherlands Antilles: Introduction.

LOSONCZI, E.

30.035	BH	1958	Social anthropology in health education with particular reference to nutrition.

LOWENTHAL, DAVID

38.074	BC	1958	The West Indies chooses a capital.
43.101	GG	1960	Population contrasts in the Guianas.
10.027	GC	1960	The range and variation of Caribbean societies. *In* RUBIN, VERA, ed. SOCIAL AND CULTURAL PLURALISM IN THE CARIBBEAN. New York, New York Academy of Sciences, p.786-795. (Annals of the New York Academy of Sciences, v. 83, art. 5.) [8, 16] [*RIS*]
20.011	BC	1961	Caribbean views of Caribbean land.

LUYKEN, R. & LUYKEN-KONING, F. W. M.

30.039	SR	1960/ 61	Studies on the physiology of nutrition in Surinam.

LUYKEN, R.; LUYKEN-KONING, F. W. M. & DAM-BAKKER, A. W. I. van
30.040   NW   1959 Nutrition survey on the Windward Islands (Netherlands Antilles).

McARTHUR, J. SIDNEY
10.028   BG   1912 Our people: a rejoinder to the paper of Mr. J. E. Hewick. *Timehri*
                        3d ser., 2(19A), July: 20-28. [7]   [*AMN*]

McCOWAN, ANTHONY
37.236   BG   1956 British Guiana.

MALEFIJT, ANNEMARIE de WAAL
23.100   SR   1964 Animism and Islam among the Javanese in Surinam.

MARRIOTT, F. C.
50.088   TR   1918 Labour exchanges.

MENKMAN, W. R.
11.018   SR   1927/ Lanti sa pai [The country will pay for it].
                  28

MINETT, E. P.
28.371   BG   1913 The treatment of leprosy by nastin and benzoyl chloride.

MONTESTRUC, ETIENNE; BERDONNEAU, ROBERT;
BENOIST, JEAN & COLLET, ANDRE
27.032   MT   1959 Hémoglobines anormales et groupes sanguins, A, B, O, chez les
                        Martiniquais [Abnormal hemoglobins and blood groups A, B, O,
                        among the people of Martinique].

MOSKOS, CHARLES CONSTANTINE, Jr. & BELL, WENDELL
10.029   BG/   1965 Cultural unity and diversity in new states. *Tchr Coll Rec* 66(8),
           TR   May: 679-694. [21, 37]   [*RIS*]

MURRAY, GIDEON
10.030   BC   1924 The native and coloured races of the British West Indies, British
                        Guiana, British Honduras, the Bahamas and Bermuda. *In* LAGDEN,
                        Sir GODFREY, ed. THE NATIVE RACES OF THE EMPIRE. New York,
                        Henry Holt, p.297-335.   [*SCH*]

NEHAUL, B. B. G.
23.387   BG   1943 Report on the physical development and health of a sample of school
                        children in the Island of Leguan, British Guiana, 1941.

NICHOLSON, C. C.
30.043   BG   1947 Nutritional survey of pupils of elementary schools, Mahaicony
                        District, February-March, 1947.
30.044   BG   1956 Assessment of the nutritional status of elementary school children
                        of British Guiana by periodic sampling surveys and evaluation of
                        the beneficial effects of supplementary feeding.

OBERG, KALERVO
10.031   SR   1955 INTERACTION AND DEVELOPMENT OF ETHNIC GROUPS IN SURINAM. Rio de
                        Janeiro: USOM. [66]
46.153   SR   1964 A STUDY OF FARM PRODUCTIVITY IN THE SANTO BOMA SETTLEMENT PRO-
                        JECT SURINAM.

OGILVIE, J. A.

10.032   JM   1946 Jamaica—a racial melting pot. *Can-W I Mag* 36(3), May: 29,31,33.
                                                                            [*NYP*]

OZZARD, A. T.

28.411   BG   1914 Enteric fever in the Public Hospital, Georgetown.

PADILLA, ELENA

10.033   GC   1960 Peasants, plantations, and pluralism. *In* RUBIN, VERA, ed. SOCIAL
                    AND CULTURAL PLURALISM IN THE CARIBBEAN. New York, New York
                    Academy of Sciences, p.837-842. (Annals of the New York Academy
                    of Sciences, v. 83, art. 5.) [8, 45, 67]   [*RIS*]

PANHUYS, L. C. van

2.173   SR   1905 Naschrift op "Gegevens over land en volk van Suriname" [Post-
                    script to "Data about the country and people of Surinam"].

22.107   SR   1912 Les chansons et la musique de la Guyane Néerlandaise [The songs
                    and music of Dutch Guiana].

28.413   SR   1913 Recent discoveries in Dutch Guiana.

10.034   SR   1919 Een adres over Boschnegers en Indianen [A talk about Bush-
                    Negroes and Indians]. *W I G* 1(1):71-72.   [*COL*]

PATCHETT, K. W.

9.030   BC   1959 Some aspects of marriage and divorce in the West Indies.

PENARD, F. P. & A. P.

23.120   SR   1913 Surinaamsch bijgeloof: iets over *winti* en andere natuurbegrippen
                    [Surinam superstition: about *winti* and other supernatural notions].

PILKINGTON, FREDERICK

10.035   JM   1948 Jamaica. *Contemp Rev* 173(990), June: 349-353.   [*COL*]

PINTO, HEATHER

31.060   TR   [1965?] Group therapy among alcoholics.

PRICE, EDWARD T.

10.036   BB   1957 The Redlegs of Barbados. *Yb Ass Pacif Cst Geogr* 10:35-39.   [5]

PROCTOR, JESSE HARRIS, Jr.

38.098   TR   1961 East Indians and the federation of the British West Indies.

QUELLE, OTTO

10.037   GG   1951 Die Bevölkerungsentwicklung von Europäisch-Guayana: eine anthro-
                    pogeographische Untersuchung [The population growth of European
                    Guiana: an anthropo-geographical study]. *Erde* 3:366-378.   [5, 7]
                                                                            [*AGS*]

RENSELAAR, H. C. van, & VOORHOEVE, J.

10.038   SR   1962 Rapport over een ethnologische studiereis naar Mata [Report about
                    an ethnological field trip to Mata]. *Bijd Volk* 118:328-361.

RICHARDSON, E. C.

37.333   TR   [n.d.] TRINIDAD: REVOLUTION OR EVOLUTION; A CRITICAL ANALYSIS.

ROBERTS, GEORGE WOODROW

| 7.060 | BG | 1948 Some observations on the population of British Guiana. |
| 34.013 | BC | 1953 Motherhood tables of the 1946 census. |

RODWAY, JAMES

| 13.062 | BG | 1902 Forest people of British Guiana. |
| 66.121 | BG | 1917 Tropical development. |

ROSE, F. G.

28.446   BG   1919 An investigation into the causes of still-birth and abortion in the city of Georgetown.

28.448   BG   1926 Leprosy statistics and legislation in British Guiana.

ROWLAND, E. D.

28.451   BG   1912 Remarks on sixty-four cases of enteric fever treated in the Public Hospital, Georgetown, from December, 1908, to June, 1910.

28.452   BG   1913 Enteric fever in the Public Hospital, Georgetown.

28.453   BG   1914 Pneumonia in British Guiana.

RUBIN, VERA

10.039   TR   1959 Approaches to the study of national characteristics in a multi-cultural society. *Int J Social Psych* 5(1), Summer: 20-26.   [31] [*RIS*]

RUBIN, VERA, ed.

10.040   GC   1960 SOCIAL AND CULTURAL PLURALISM IN THE CARIBBEAN. New York, New York Academy of Sciences, 761-916p. (Annals of the New York Academy of Sciences, v. 83, art. 5.)   [*RIS*]

SHERLOCK, PHILIP M.

8.053   GC   1955 THE DEVELOPMENT OF THE MIDDLE CLASS IN THE CARIBBEAN.

SIMPSON, GEORGE EATON

10.041   GC   1962 The peoples and cultures of the Caribbean area. *Phylon* 3d quarter: 240-257.   [7, 9, 19, 20, 67]   [*RIS*]

8.054   GC   1962 Social stratification in the Caribbean.

SINGH, H. P.

10.042   TR   1955 Trinidad: why the various elements that comprise the population of Trinidad live amicably together. *Can-W I Mag* 45(2), Feb.: 5, 7, 16. [*NYP*]

SKINNER, ELLIOTT, P.

10.043   BG   1955 ETHNIC INTERACTION IN A BRITISH GUIANA RURAL COMMUNITY: A STUDY OF SECONDARY ACCULTURATION AND GROUP DYNAMICS. Ph. D. dissertation, Columbia University, 288p. [8, 19]   [*RIS*]

8.055   BG   1960 Group dynamics and social stratification in British Guiana.

SMITH, M. G.

10.044   BC   1957 ETHNIC AND CULTURAL PLURALISM IN THE BRITISH CARIBBEAN. [Brussels, Imp. Puvrez]. 9p. (Working paper for the 30th Study Session of the International Institute of Differing Civilizations, Lisbon, 15th-18th Apr. 1957. Doc. 11.)   [*RIS*]

10.045   GC   1960 Social and cultural pluralism. *In* RUBIN, VERA, ed. SOCIAL AND CULTURAL PLURALISM IN THE CARIBBEAN. New York, New York

			Academy of Sciences p.763-785. (Annals of the New York Academy of Sciences, v. 83, art. 5.) [67] [*RIS*]

10.046 JM 1961 The plural framework of Jamaican society. *Br J Sociol* 12(3), Sept.: 249-262. [8] [*RIS*]

10.047 GC 1961 West Indian culture. *Car Q* 7(3), Dec.: 112-119. [21] [*RIS*]

37.385 BC 1962 Short-range prospects in the British Caribbean.

10.048 BC 1965 THE PLURAL SOCIETY IN THE BRITISH WEST INDIES. Berkeley & Los Angeles, University of California Press, 359p. [8] [*RIS*]

SMITH, RAYMOND THOMAS

21.023 BG 1958 British Guiana.

37.386 BG 1963 British Guiana's prospects.

8.061 BG 1964 Ethnic difference and peasant economy in British Guiana.

SNEATH, P. A. T.

7.076 BG 1941 A study of crude birth/death ratio (vital index) in British Guiana.

28.488 BG 1943 Contemporary facts on the incidence of tuberculosis in British Guiana.

SNELLEMAN, J. F.

10.049 SR 1927/ Indianen en Negers [Amerindians and Negroes]. *W I G* 9:230-238.
28 [*COL*]

19.038 SR 1928/ De West-Indische zaal in het Museum van het Koloniaal Instituut
29 [The West Indian room in the museum of the Colonial Institute].

SPECKMANN, JOHAN DIRK

10.050 SR 1963 The Indian group in the segmented society of Surinam. *Car Stud* 3(1), Apr.: 3-17. [12, 19] [*RIS*]

STAAL, G. J.

10.051 SR 1927/ Stroomingen in Suriname [Currents in Surinam]. *W I G* 9:337-362.
28 [5, 16, 66] [*COL*]

STAFFORD, J. L.; HILL, K. R. & ARNEAUD, J. D.

27.036 GC 1955 Rhesus factor distribution in the Caribbean: preliminary communication.

STEVEN, GEORGE H.

28.500 BG 1936 Post-mortem notes on the spleen in various races of British Guiana: a comparison with 1893.

TAYLOR, COUNCILL SAMUEL

8.063 JM 1955 COLOR AND CLASS: A COMPARATIVE STUDY OF JAMAICAN STATUS GROUPS.

TEIXEIRA, J.

28.513 BG 1904 The recent epidemic of small-pox.

28.514 BG 1906 Report on smallpox treated at the Isolation Hospital at the "Best."

THEZE, J.

28.515 FG 1916 Pathologie de la Guyane Francaise [Pathology of French Guiana].

THOMAS, J. H.

28.516 BC 1960 Respiratory tuberculosis in the Caribbean.

VERMUELEN, L. P.

7.081 NA [196-] De bevolkingsstructuur der Nederlandse Antillen [Population patterns in the Netherlands Antilles].

WALLBRIDGE, J. S.
7.083   BG   1907 Remarks on the Mortality Commission Report.

WATTLEY, GEORGE H.
28.572   TR   1959 Myocardial infarction in South Trinidad.

WIERSEMA, J. P. & BARROW, R. S.
28.588   SR   1961 Cancer, especially of the cervix uteri, in Surinam.

WILLIAMS, JOSEPH J.
10.052   JM/   1932 WHENCE THE "BLACK IRISH" OF JAMAICA? New York, Dial Press,
           BB   97p. [5, 7]   [*AGS*]

WILTERDINK, J. B.; METSELAAR, D.; KUYP, E. van der
           & VERLINDE, J. D.
28.593   SR   1964 Poliomyelitis in Surinam.

WISE, K. S.
28.596   BG   1909 *Filaria bancroftii.*
7.085   BG   1912/ The public health, statistics, and medical institutions of the Colony.
                   13
28.597   BG   1912 The nastin treatment of leprosy in British Guiana.
28.598   BG   1914 The pathological effects of *filaria bancroftii* with reference to
                         septic complications.

WOLFF, J. W.; COLLIER, W. A.; ROEVER-BONNET, H. de
           & HOEKSTRA, J.
28.606   SR   1958 Yellow fever immunity in rural population groups of Surinam (with a
                         note on other serological investigations).

WRIGHT, H. B. & TAYLOR, BELLE
28.607   TR   1958 The incidence of diabetes in a sample of the adult population in
                         south Trinidad.

WYLIE, A.
28.608   BG   1906 On cataract disease in British Guiana.

YOUNG, ALLAN
37.435   BG   1958 THE APPROACHES TO LOCAL SELF-GOVERNMENT IN BRITISH GUIANA.

ZAVALLONI, MARISA
20.021   TR   1960 YOUTH AND THE FUTURE: VALUES AND ASPIRATIONS OF HIGH SCHOOL
                         STUDENTS IN A MULTICULTURAL SOCIETY IN TRANSITION—TRINIDAD, W. I.

ZONNEVELD, J. I. S. & KRUIJER, GERARDUS JOHANNES
47.034   SR   1951 Nederzettings- en occupatie-vormen in Suriname [Settlements and
                         other forms of territorial occupation in Surinam].

Chapter 11

POPULATION SEGMENTS: NEGROES

ABBENHUIS, M. F.
11.001   SR   1938 Creolen? [Creoles?]. *W I G* 20:148-149.   *[COL]*

ABEL, THEODORA M.
31.001   MS   1960 Differential responses to projective testing in a Negro peasant community: Montserrat, B. W. I.

ABEL, THEODORA M. & METRAUX, RHODA
31.003   MS   1959 Sex differences in a Negro peasant community: Montserrat, B. W. I.

ACHILLE, LOUIS T.
16.001   FC   1940 Notes on the Negro in the French West Indies.

ANDERSON, IZETT & CUNDALL, FRANK, comps.
24.002   JM   1910 JAMAICA NEGRO PROVERBS AND SAYINGS, COLLECTED AND CLASSIFIED ACCORDING TO SUBJECTS.

ASBECK, W. D. H. van
32.014   SR   1921/Negers en onderwijs in de Vereenigde Staten van America [Negroes
          22 and education in the U. S. A.].

BEALS, CARLETON
11.002   GC   1931 The Black Belt of the Caribbean. *Am Mercury* 24(94), Oct.: 129-138.   *[COL]*

BECKETT, J. EDGAR
11.003   BG   1917 The black peasant proprietor. *Timehri* 3d ser., 4(21), June: 30-37.
          [8, 46, 66]   *[AMN]*

BECKWITH, MARTHA WARREN
11.004   JM   1929 BLACK ROADWAYS: A STUDY OF JAMAICAN FOLK LIFE. Chapel Hill, University of North Carolina Press, 243p. [2, 24]   *[AGS]*

BOWER, B. D.
28.051   JM   1958 Tay-Sach's disease in a West Indian of African origin.

BRAITHWAITE, LLOYD E. & ROBERTS, G. W.
9.002   TR   1963 Mating patterns and prospects in Trinidad.

179

CAMERON, N. E.

11.005   GC   1929/ THE EVOLUTION OF THE NEGRO. Georgetown, Argosy Co., 2v. [6, 19]
                   34   [NYP]

CAMERON, NORMAN E.

11.006   GC   1950 The background of the Afro-American. *Timehri* 4th ser., 1(29),
                   Aug.: 21-24. [19]

CAMPBELL, ALBERT A.

31.015   ST   1943 St. Thomas Negroes—a study of personality and culture.   [COL]

CARR, ANDREW T.

19.004   TR   1953 A Rada community in Trinidad.   [RIS]

CECIL, C. H.

18.009   JM   1935 The Maroons in Canada.

COLLIER, H. C.

11.007   JM   1939 The Maroons of Jamaica. *Can-W I Mag 28(7)*, Aug.:6-10. [5, 18]   [NYP]

COULTHARD, G. R.

20.003   FA   1961 The French West Indian background of negritude.
16.007   GC   1962 RACE AND COLOUR IN CARIBBEAN LITERATURE.

CROWLEY, DANIEL JOHN

24.021   GC   1962 Negro folklore: an Africanist's view.

CRUICKSHANK, J. GRAHAM

25.017   BB   1911 Negro English, with reference particularly to Barbados.
25.018   BG/   1916 "BLACK TALK": BEING NOTES ON NEGRO DIALECT IN BRITISH GUIANA,
            BB   WITH (INEVITABLY) A CHAPTER ON THE VERNACULAR OF BARBADOS.
19.007   BG   1917 Among the "Aku" (Yoruba) in Canal No. 1, West Bank, Demerara
                         River.
11.008   BG   1919 African immigrants after freedom. *Timehri* 3d ser., 6(23), Sept.:
                         74-85. [6, 7, 50]   [AMN]
8.014   BG   1921 The beginnings of our villages.
22.046   BG   1924 An African dance in the colony.

CUNDALL, FRANK

23.030   JM   1930 Three fingered Jack.

DILLARD, J. L.

25.023   GC   1964 The writings of Herskovits and the study of the language of the
                         Negro in the New World.

DRIMMELEN, C. van

11.009   SR   1925/ De Neger en zijn cultuur geschiedenis [The Negro and his cultural
            26   history]. *W I G* 7:385-400. [6, 19]   [COL]

DUNHAM, KATHERINE

11.010   JM   1946 JOURNEY TO ACCOMPONG. New York, Holt, 162p.   [COL]

EGAN, CECILIA M.

23.040   MT   1943 Martinique—the isle of those who return.

ERICKSON, ARVEL B.
6.013   JM   1959 Empire or anarchy: the Jamaican rebellion of 1865.

FARLEY, RAWLE
8.024   BG   1953 The rise of village settlements of British Guiana.
8.025   BG   1954 Rise of a peasantry in British Guiana.

FRANCE-HARRAR, ANNIE
3.110   GC   1928 Mulattenwelt in Westindien [World of mulattos in the West Indies].

FREITAS, Q. B. de
28.197   BG   1933 Notes on cardiac dilation.

GOEJE, C. H. de
24.028   SR   1947 Anansi, l'araignée rusée [Anansi, the wily spider].

GREEN, HELEN BAGENSTOSE
31.030   TR   1964 Socialization values in the Negro and East Indian subcultures of
                      Trinidad.
20.008   TR   1965 Values of Negro and East Indian school children in Trinidad.

GRINDER, ROBERT E.; SPOTTS, WENDY S.; & CURTI, MARGARET
WOOSTER
31.031   JM   1964 Relationships between Goodenough draw-a-man test performance
                      and skin color among preadolescent Jamaican children.

HARPER, W. F.
27.027   JM   1959 Cranial vault sutures in the Jamaican Negro.

HENRIQUES, FERNANDO
9.014   JM   1949 West Indian family organization.
9.016   JM   1953 Family and colour in Jamaica.

HERSKOVITS, MELVILLE JEAN
11.011   GC   1930 The Negro in the New World: the statement of a problem. *Am Anthrop*
                      new ser., 32(1), Jan.-Mar.: 145-155 [67]   [COL]
67.007   GC   1931 The New World Negro as an anthropological problem.
67.008   GC   1938 African ethnology and the New World Negro.
19.019   GC   1938 Les noirs du Nouveau Monde: sujet de recherches africanistes [The
                      New World Negroes: a subject for Africanist research].
22.073   GC   1941 El estudio de la música negra en el hemisferio occidental [The
                      study of Negro music in the Western Hemisphere].
22.074   GC   1941 Patterns of Negro music.
67.009   GC   1946 Problem, method and theory in Afroamerican studies.
67.011   GC   1951 The present status and needs of Afroamerican research.
31.034   GC   1952 Some psychological implications of Afroamerican studies.
67.012   GC   1960 The ahistorical approach to Afroamerican studies: a critique.

HERSKOVITS, MELVILLE JEAN & FRANCES S.
24.033   SR   1936 SURINAM FOLK-LORE (with transcriptions and Surinam songs and
                      musicological analysis by Dr. M. Kolinski).
11.012   TR   1947 TRINIDAD VILLAGE. New York, Alfred A. Knopf, 351p. [8, 19] [RIS]

HICKERSON, HAROLD
8.030   BG   1954 SOCIAL AND ECONOMIC ORGANIZATION IN A GUIANA VILLAGE.

HURAULT, JEAN
43.071   FG   1965 La vie matérielle des noirs réfugiés Boni et des Indiens Wayana
                du Haut-Maroni (Guyane Francaise): agriculture, économie et
                habitat [the material life of the Black Boni refugees and the
                Waiyana Indians of the upper Maroni (French Guiana): agricul-
                ture, economy and habitat].

JONES, SAMUEL B.
11.013   BC   1911 The British West Indian Negro. *So Work* 40(4), Apr.: 201-205; 40(6),
                June: 330-335; 40(10), Oct.: 580-589. [6]   [COL]

KESLER, C. K.
11.014   SR   1926/ Naar aanleiding van "De Neger en zijne cultuurgeschiedenis" [With
          27   reference to "The Negro and his cultural history"]. *W I G* 8:59-68.
                [6,16]   [COL]

KLINGBERG, FRANK J.
31.112   BC   1939 The Lady Mico Charity Schools in the British West Indies, 1835-1842.

KRUIJER, GERARDUS JOHANNES
31.044   SM/   1953 St. Martin and St. Eustatius Negroes as compared with those of St.
          SE/   Thomas; a study of personality and culture.
          ST

LATOUR, M. D.
11.015   CU   1940 Boessaalsche Negers [Recently arrived ("greenhorn") Negroes].
                W I G 22:161-165. [6]   [COL]

LAURENCE, K. O.
5.123   TR   1963 The settlement of free Negroes in Trinidad before emancipation.

LEACH, MacEDWARD
24.043   JM   1961 Jamaican duppy lore.

LEIRIS, MICHEL
19.027   FA   1950 Martinique, Guadeloupe, Haiti.

LISSER, H. G. de
11.016   BC   1900 The Negro as a factor in the future of the West Indies. *New Cent
                Rev* 7(37), Jan.: 1-6. [50]   [NYP]

MAINBERGER, GONSALV
21.015   MT   1963 Mythe et realité de l'homme noir; à la mémoir de Frantz Fanon
                [Myth and reality of the Negro; in memory of Frantz Fanon].

MALLIET, A. M. WENDELL
11.017   BC   1926 Some prominent West Indians. *Opportunity* 4(47), Nov.: 348-351.
                [8]   [COL]

MARSHALL, GLORIA ALBERTHA
53.028   BC   1959 Benefit societies in the British West Indies: the formative
                years.

MARTIN, KINGSLEY
23.101   JM   1961 The Jamaican volcano.

MENKMAN, W. R.
11.018   SR   1927/ Lanti sa pai [The country will pay for it]. *W I G* 9:289-296. [10,20]
              28   [COL]

MINTZ, SIDNEY W.
67.015   GC   1964 Melville J. Herskovits and Caribbean studies: a retrospective tribute.

MISCHEL, FRANCES
23.106   TR   1957 African "powers" in Trinidad: the Shango cult.
29.017   TR/   1959 Faith healing and medical practice in the southern Caribbean.
           GR

MITCHELL, RONALD
11.019   JM   1950 The Maroons of Accompong. *Geogr Mag 23(1)*, May 1-5. [5]   [AGS]

MOORE, JOSEPH GRAESSLE
23.107   JM   1953 RELIGION OF JAMAICAN NEGROES: A STUDY OF AFRO-JAMAICAN ACCUL-
                       TURATION.

MORPURGO, A. J.
11.020   SR   1934/ De Kótómisi [The Kotomisi]. *W I G* 16: 393:400. [16]   [COL]
              35

NETTLEFORD, REX
19.033   JM   1963 THE AFRICAN CONNEXION—THE SIGNIFICANCE FOR JAMAICA.

NEWMAN, PETER KENNETH
16.026   BG   1962 Racial tension in British Guiana.

NORTH, LIONEL
22.103   GC   1932 Songs of the Afro-Indian.

OLIVIER, SYDNEY, 1st Baron RAMSDEN
46.157   JM   1929 The improvement of Negro agriculture, by Lord Olivier.
11.021   JM   1929 Progress of a Negro peasantry, by Lord Olivier. *Edin Rev* 249(507),
                     Jan.: 105-116. [44,66]
16.027   JM   1935 A key to the colour question, by Lord Olivier.

OUDSCHANS DENTZ, FRED
25.083   SR   1937 De plaats van de Creool in de literatuur van Suriname [The place
                     of Creole in the literature of Surinam].

PANHUYS, L. C. van
24.053   NC   1932/ Folklore in Nederlandsch West-Indië [Folklore in the Netherlands
              33 West Indies].
24.054   NC   1933/ Aanvulling Folklore in Nederlandsch West-Indië [Addition to folk-
              34 lore in the Netherlands West-Indies].

PILKINGTON, FREDERICK
11.022   JM   1940 Rising race of coloured people. *Crown Colon* 10(108), Nov.:489. [NYP]

POWRIE, BARBARA E.
20.013   TR   1956 The changing attitude of the coloured middle class towards Carnival.

PULLEN-BURRY, B.
3.250   JM   1905 ETHIOPIA IN EXILE: JAMAICA REVISITED.

RENSELAAR, H. C. van
11.023   SR   1963 Het sociaal-economisch vermogen van de Creolen in Suriname [The
                       socio-economic potential of the Creoles in Surinam]. *Tijdschr Kon
                       Ned Aar Genoot* 80(4): 474-481. [8,44]   [COL]

ROBERTS, GEORGE WOODROW & BRAITHWAITE, LLOYD
34.016   TR   1960 Fertility differentials by family type in Trinidad.
34.017   TR   1961 A gross mating table for a West Indian population.
9.003   TR   1962 Mating among East Indian and non-Indian women in Trinidad.

ROMITI, CESARE
28.442   BG   1933 Three cases of pleuricystic adamantinomata of the jaw, observed
                       in Negroes.
28.445   BG   1957 Statistical report on the incidence of fibroids and malignant tumors
                       of the uterus in British Guiana.

RUBIN, VERA
20.015   TR   1961 Family aspirations and attitudes of Trinidad youth.
20.016   BC   1962 Culture, politics and race relations.

RUIZ, R. E.
11.024   GC   [1965] A historical perspective on Caribbean Negro life. *In* FAMILY RELA-
                       TIONSHIPS [PROCEEDINGS OF THE] FOURTH CARIBBEAN CONFERENCE FOR
                       MENTAL HEALTH, Curacao, Apr. 16-23, 1963, Netherlands Antilles.
                       [Willemstad? Boek- en Offset Drukkerij "De Curacaosche Courant"]
                       p.46-52. [6,19]   [RIS]
                       [

SAMPATH, MARTIN
28.457   TR   1953 The influence of socio-anthropological factors on the incidence of
                       syphilis in a heterogenous group of pregnant women in Trinidad.

SAR, A. van der & WINKEL, C. A.
28.464   CU   1959 Non-specific spondylitis in Negroid children in Curacao.

SCHUCHARDT, HUGO
25.092   SR   1914 Die Sprache der Saramakkaneger in Surinam [The language of the
                       Saramacca Negroes of Surinam].

SCHUTZ, JOHN A. & O'NEIL, MAUD E., eds.
23.140   BB   1946 Arthur Holt, Anglican clergyman, reports on Barbados, 1725-1733.

SHAW, EARL BENNETT
8.052   SC   1934 The villages of St. Croix.
50.110   ST   1935 St. Thomas carries its coal.

SIMPSON, GEORGE EATON
23.147   JM   1955 Culture change and reintegration found in the cults of West Kings-
                       ton, Jamaica.
23.148   JM   1955 Political cultism in West Kingston, Jamaica.
23.149   JM   1955 The Ras Tafari movement in Jamaica: a study of race and class
                       conflict.

23.152   JM   1962 The Ras Tafari movement in Jamaica in its millennial aspect.
23.153   TR   1962 The Shango cult in Nigeria and in Trinidad.
23.154   TR   1964 The acculturative process in Trinidadian Shango.
23.155   TR   1965 THE SHANGO CULT IN TRINIDAD.

SIRES, RONALD VERNON
50.115   JM   1940 Negro labor in Jamaica in the years following emancipation.

SMITH, M. G.
19.037   GC   1960 The African heritage in the Caribbean.
23.157   GR   1963 DARK PURITAN.

SMITH, M. G.; AUGIER, ROY & NETTLEFORD, REX
23.158   JM   1960 THE RAS TAFARI MOVEMENT IN KINGSTON, JAMAICA.

SMITH, RAYMOND THOMAS
9.041   BG   1953 Aspects of family organization in a coastal Negro community in British Guiana.
9.042   BG   1953 Aspects of family organization in a coastal Negro community in British Guiana: a preliminary report.
47.030   BG   1955 Land tenure in three Negro villages in British Guiana.
9.043   BG   1956 THE NEGRO FAMILY IN BRITISH GUIANA: FAMILY STRUCTURE AND SOCIAL STATUS IN THE VILLAGES.

SOLIEN, NANCIE L.
13.074   JM/   1959 West Indian characteristics of the Black Carib.
          BH/
          TR

SPENCE, ELEANOR JEAN
51.130   BB   1964 MARKETING ACTIVITIES AND HOUSEHOLD ACTIVITIES OF COUNTRY HAWKERS IN BARBADOS.

STEDMAN, LOUISE
11.025   JM   1936 The romance of Accompong in Jamaica. *Can W I Mag* 25(6), May, 23-26.   [*NYP*]

STEWART, T.D.
27.039   GC   1939 Negro skeletal remains from Indian sites in the West Indies.

SWELLENGREBEL, N. H.
28.509   SR   1940 The efficient parasite.

UTTLEY, K. H.
28.529   AT   1959 The epidemiology of tetanus in the Negro race over the last hundred years in Antigua, the West Indies.
28.531   AT   1960 The epidemiology and mortality of whooping cough in the Negro over the last hundred years in Antigua, British West Indies.
28.532   AT   1960 The mortality and epidemiology of diphtheria since 1857 in the Negro population of Antigua, British West Indies.
28.533   AT   1960 The mortality and epidemiology of typhoid fever in the coloured inhabitants of Antigua, West Indies, over the last hundred years.

28.535   AT   1960 Smallpox mortality in the Negro population of Antigua, West Indies; a historical note.

28.538   AT   1961 Tuberculosis mortality in the Negro population of Antigua, British West Indies, over the last hundred years.

VALLEE, LIONEL
9.057   ST   1964 THE NEGRO FAMILY IN ST. THOMAS: A STUDY IN ROLE DIFFERENTIATION.

WALKER, H. De R.
3.320   BC   1902 THE WEST INDIES AND THE EMPIRE: STUDY AND TRAVEL IN THE WINTER OF 1900-1901.

WASHBURN, B. E.
28.550   BG/   1960 AS I RECALL.
            TR

WATERMAN, JAMES A.
28.555   TR   1941 Haemophilia in the Afro-West Indian.

WATERMAN, RICHARD ALAN
22.145   TR   1943 AFRICAN PATTERNS IN TRINIDAD NEGRO MUSIC.

WEINSTEIN, B.
28.577   BG   1962 Diabetes: a regional survey in British Guiana (preliminary report).

WESLEY, CHARLES H.
32.212   BC   1932/ Rise of Negro Education in the British Empire.
                  33
11.026   BC   1934 The emancipation of the free colored population in the British Empire. *J Negro Hist* 19(2), Apr.: 137-170. [5]   [*COL*]

WILLIAMS, ERIC EUSTACE
2.261   BC   1940 The Negro in the British West Indies.
11.027   GC   1942 THE NEGRO IN THE CARIBBEAN. Washington, D.C., Associates in Negro Folk Education, 119p. (Bronze booklet no. 8.) [2]   [*COL*]

WILLIAMS, JOSEPH J.
11.028   JM   1938 The Maroons of Jamaica. *Boston Coll Press, Anthrop Ser* 3(no.4, serial no. 12), Dec.: 379-480. [5]   [*AMN*]

WORK, MONROE N.
1.052   GC   1928 A BIBLIOGRAPHY OF THE NEGRO IN AFRICA AND AMERICA.

ADAMS, HARRIET CHALMERS

12.001   TR/   1907 The East Indians in the New World. *Natn Geogr Mag* 18(7), July:
         BG   485-491.   [*AGS*]

ADAMS, INEZ & MASUOKA, J.

8.001   TR   1961 Emerging elites and culture change.

ADHIN, J. H.

9.001   SR   1960/ Over de "joint family" der Hindostanen [On the joint family of the
                   61 Hindustani].

5.001   SR   1961/ De immigratie van Hindostanen en de afstand van de Goudkust [The
                   62 immigration of the Hindustanis and the cession of the Gold Coast].

50.001   SR   1963 De economisch-historische betekenis van de Hindostaanse immi-
                     gratie voor Suriname [The economic-historical value of the Hindus-
                     tani immigration for Surinam].

AHSAN, SYED REZA

12.002   TR   1963 EAST INDIAN AGRICULTURAL SETTLEMENTS IN TRINIDAD; A STUDY IN
                     CULTURAL GEOGRAPHY. Ph.D. dissertation, University of Florida,
                     299p. [43]

ANDREWS, C. F.

50.005   BG/   1930 "India's emigration problem."
         TR

BECKWITH, MARTHA WARREN

23.005   JM   1924 THE HUSSAY FESTIVAL IN JAMAICA.

BERTRAM, G. C. L.

34.003   BG   1962 The Indians of British Guiana.

BICKERTON, DEREK

12.003   TR   1962 THE MURDERS OF BOYSIE SINGH. London, Arthur Barker, 230p. [2] [*RIS*]

BISWAMITRE, C. R.

12.004   SR   1937 Miskenning [Misjudgment]. *W I G* 19: 176-188. [8,20]   [*COL*]

BRAITHWAITE, LLOYD E. & ROBERTS, G. W.

9.002   TR   1963 Mating patterns and prospects in Trinidad.

CAMMAERTS, E.

50.014   BC   1914 L'importation des coolies dans les Indes occidentales [The importation of coolies into the West Indies].

CROWLEY, DANIEL JOHN

12.005   TR   1954 East Indian festivals in Trinidad life. *Car Commn Mon Inf B* 7(9), Apr.: 202-204,208. [19,22]   [*RIS*]

24.019   TR   1955 A Trinidad Hindi riddle tale.

CUMPSTON, I. M.

50.026   BC   1953 INDIANS OVERSEAS IN BRITISH TERRITORIES, 1834-1854.

12.006   BG/   1956 A survey of Indian immigration to British tropical colonies to 1960.
              TR   *Popul Stud* 10(2), Nov.: 158-165. [17]   [*COL*]

DAVIDS, LEO

9.006   BG/   1964 The East Indian family overseas.
           TR

DEANE, C. G.

30.008   TR   1938 Deficiency diseases in East Indians of the labouring class.

DEERR, NOEL

50.036   GC   1938 Indian labour in the sugar industry.

DEY, MUKUL K.

7.014   TR   1962 The Indian population in Trinidad and Tobago.

ERICKSON, EDGAR L.

50.044   BC   1934 The introduction of East Indian coolies into the British West Indies.

FREILICH, MORRIS

10.013   TR   1960 CULTURAL DIVERSITY AMONG TRINIDADIAN PEASANTS.

FREITAS, Q. B. de

28.197   BG   1933 Notes on cardiac dilation.

GANGULEE, N.

12.007   BC   1947 INDIANS IN THE EMPIRE OVERSEAS: A SURVEY. London, New India Pub. House, 263p. [7]   [*NYP*]

GIGLIOLI, GEORGE

32.028   BG   1958 An outline of the nutritional situation on the sugar estates of British Guiana in respect to the eradication of malaria: recent developments in the production of green vegetables and fruit by individual units.

GLASENAPP, HELMUTH von

12.008   BG/   1937 Die Inder in Trinidad und Guayana [The Indians in Trinidad and
              TR   Guiana]. *Z Rassk* 6(3), Nov.: 307-311.   [*AMN*]

GREEN, HELEN BAGENSTOSE

31.030   TR   1964 Socialization values in the Negro and East Indian subcultures of Trinidad.

20.008   TR   1965 Values of Negro and East Indian school children in Trinidad.

GREENWOOD, THOMAS

50.054   BC   1921 East Indian emigration: the Indian government's policy.

HABIB, GEORGE G.

28.262   TR   1964 Nutritional vitamin B_{12} deficiency among Hindus.

HAJARY, H. N.

9.012   SR   1937 De verwacht wordende groote gebeurtenis onder de Britsch-Indiërs in Suriname [The expected big event among British Indians in Surinam].

HALE, C. M.

12.009   BG   1911 An Indian colony. *Imp Asiat Q Rev* 3d ser., 31(62), Apr.: 345-350.
[17]   [*NYP*]

HICKERSON, HAROLD

8.030   BG   1954 SOCIAL AND ECONOMIC ORGANIZATION IN A GUIANA VILLAGE.

HILL, ARTHUR H.

50.063   BG   1919 Emigration from India.

HOROWITZ, MICHAEL M.

23.068   MT   1963 The worship of South Indian deities in Martinique.

HOROWITZ, MICHAEL M. & KLASS, MORTON

23.069   MT   1961 The Martiniquan East Indian cult of Maldevidan.

HOUTE, I. C. van

25.044   SR   1963 Het bilinguisme van de Hindostaanse kinderen in Suriname [Bilingualism of Hindustani children in Surinam].

IBBOTSON, PETER

12.010   TR   1962 Indians in Fiji, Trinidad and Mauritius. *Asia Afr Rev* 2(4), Apr.:
13-14.   [*NYP*]

JAYAWARDENA, CHANDRA

9.020   BG   1960 Marital stability in two Guianese sugar estate communities.
9.021   BG   1962 Family organisation in plantations in British Guiana.
8.033   BG   1963 CONFLICT AND SOLIDARITY IN A GUIANESE PLANTATION.

JOLLY, A. L.

46.100   TR   1948 Peasant farming in two districts of the Oropouche Lagoon, June 1944-5.

JOSA, F. P. LUIGI

12.011   BG   1912 The Hindus in the West Indies. *Timehri* 3d ser., 2(19B), Dec.:
305-308;
1913 3(20, pt. 1), May: 25-31.   [*AMN*]

JUGLALL, W. E.

32.108   SR   1963 Het onderwijs aan nakomelingen van Brits-Indische immigranten in Suriname [The education of descendants of British Indian immigrants in Surinam].

KARAMAT ALI, M. A.

66.077   SR   1963 De evolutie van de Hindostanse volksgroep in het kader van de Surinaamse samenleving [The evolution of the Hindustani group within the framework of Surinam society].

KARSTEN, RUDOLF

12.012   SR   1930 DE BRITISCH-INDIERS IN SURINAME, BENEVENS EEN HANDLEIDING VAN DE BEGINSELEN VAN HET HINDOSTAANS [THE BRITISH INDIANS IN SURINAM, AND A MANUAL OF THE PRINCIPLES OF THE HINDOSTANI LANGUAGE]. The Hague, M. Nijhoff. [25]

KLASS, MORTON

10.024   TR   1960 East and West Indian: cultural complexity in Trinidad.

12.013   TR   1961 EAST INDIANS IN TRINIDAD: A STUDY OF CULTURAL PERSISTENCE. New York, Columbia University Press, 265p.   [8, 19]   [*RIS*]

KLASS, SHEILA SOLOMON

12.014   TR   1964 EVERYONE IN THIS HOUSE MAKES BABIES. Garden City, N. Y., Doubleday, 174p.

KLERK, CORNELIS JOHANNES MARIA de

50.073   SR   1942 De Britisch-Indiërs in Suriname [The British Indians in Surinam].

23.084   SR   1951 CULTUS EN RITUEEL VAN HET ORTHODOXE HINDOËISME IN SURINAME [CULTS AND RITUAL OF ORTHODOX HINDUISM IN SURINAM].

50.074   SR   1953 DE IMMIGRATIE DER HINDOESTANEN IN SURINAME [THE IMMIGRATION OF HINDUS TO SURINAM].

50.075   SR   1963 DE KOMST EN VESTIGING VAN DE BRITS-INDIËRS IN SURINAME [THE ARRIVAL AND SETTLEMENT OF THE BRITISH INDIANS IN SURINAM].

23.085   SR   1963 OVER DE RELIGIE DER SURINAAMSE HINDOSTANEN [ON THE RELIGION OF THE HINDUSTANIS IN SURINAM].

KONDAPI, C.

12.015   TR   1948 Indians overseas: the position in Trinidad. *India Q* 4(3), July-Sept.: 265-273.   [*AGS*]

12.016   BC   1951 INDIANS OVERSEAS, 1838-1949. Bombay, Oxford University Press, 558p. [7]   [*COL*]

KRUIJER, GERARDUS JOHANNES

46.127   BG/   1950 Landbouw-cooperatie onder de Aziatische bevolkingsgroepen van
            SR   Suriname en Brits Guyana [Agrarian cooperation among the Asiatic population groups of Surinam and British Guiana].

LASSERRE, GUY

43.094   GD   1953 Les Indiens de la Guadeloupe [The Indians of Guadeloupe].

LONG, EDWARD E.

50.084   BG   1925 British Guiana and Indian immigration.

LUCKHOO, E. A.

12.017   BG   1912 East Indians in British Guiana. *Timehri* 3d ser., 2(19B), Dec.: 309-314.   [*AMN*]

LUCKHOO, J. A.

12.018   BG   1919 The East Indians in British Guiana: from their advent to this colony to the present time; a survey of the economic, educational and political aspects. *Timehri* 3d ser., 6(23), Sept.: 53-65.   [*AMN*]

LUTCHMAN, W. I., ed.

12.019   SR   1963 VAN BRITS-INDISCH EMIGRANT TOT BURGER VAN SURINAME [FROM BRIT-
                         ISH INDIAN EMIGRANT TO CITIZEN OF SURINAM]. The Hague, Drukkerij
                         Wieringa.

MASSON, GEORGE H.

28.352   TR   1910 Indentured labour and preventable diseases.
28.354   TR   1922 The treatment of ankylostomiasis on the high seas by the intensive
                         method of thymol administration.

NAIDOO, M. B.

12.020   TR   1960 The East Indian in Trinidad—a study of an immigrant community.
                         J Geogr 59(4), Apr.: 175-181. [7,19]   [*RIS*]

NAIR, K. SANKARAN-KUTTY

12.021   BG   1958 Indians in British Guiana. *Indo-Asian Cult* 6(4), Apr.: 417-421. [*COL*]

NATH, DWARKA

12.022   BG   1950 A HISTORY OF THE INDIANS IN BRITISH GUIANA. London, Thomas
                         Nelson, 251p. [5,7,46]   [*RIS*]

NEHAUL, B. B. G.

27.033   BG   1947 Physical measurements of East Indian boys in Leguan, British
                         Guiana.
28.393   BG   1955 Influence of Indian immigration.
28.396   BG   1958 Serum protein levels in a group of East Indians in a hospital.

NEWMAN, PETER KENNETH

16.026   BG   1962 Racial tension in British Guiana.

NIEHOFF, ARTHUR

12.023   TR   1959 The survival of Hindu institutions in an alien environment. *East
                         Anthrop* 12(3), Mar.-May: 171-187. [8,9,19,66]   [*RIS*]

NIEHOFF, ARTHUR & J.

12.024   TR   1960 EAST INDIANS IN THE WEST INDIES. Milwaukee, Wis., Milwaukee
                         Public Museum, 192p. (Publications in anthropology no. 6.)   [*RIS*]

PANDAY, R. M. N.

12.025   SR   1963 De sociaal-economische betekenis van de Hindustaanse bevolk-
                         ings-groep in Suriname [The socio-economic importance of the
                         Hindustani community in Surinam]. *In* LUTCHMAN, W. I., ed. VAN
                         BRITS-INDISCH EMIGRANT TOT BURGER VAN SURINAME. The Hague,
                         Drukkerij Wieringa, p.39-48. [66]

PHILLIPS, LESLIE H. C.

23.123   BG   1960 Kali-mai puja.

PRINS, J.

23.125   SR   1961/ De Islam in Suriname: een oriëntatie [Islam in Surinam: an
                   62   orientation].
9.031   SR   1963 Een Surinaams rechtsgeding over een Moslimse verstoting [A Suri-
                         nam lawsuit about a Moslem divorce].

PROCTOR, JESSE HARRIS, Jr.

38.098   TR   1961 East Indians and the federation of the British West Indies.

RAMESHWAR, S. M., et al.

12.026   TR   1945 INDIAN CENTENARY REVIEW: ONE HUNDRED YEARS OF PROGRESS, 1845-
1945, TRINIDAD, B.W.I. Port of Spain, Trinidad, Printed by Guardian
Commercial Printery for the Indian Centenary Review Committee,
208p. [5]   [RIS]

RAY, MICHAEL

9.032   BG   1935 Bamboo marriage.

ROBERTS, GEORGE WOODROW & BRAITHWAITE, LLOYD

34.016   TR   1960 Fertility differentials by family type in Trinidad.
9.033   TR   1962 Mating among East Indian and non-Indian women in Trinidad.

RODWAY, JAMES

50.098   BG   1919 Labour and colonization.

ROMITI, CESARE

28.445   BG   1957 Statistical report on the incidence of fibroids and malignant tumors
of the uterus in British Guiana.

RUBIN, VERA

20.015   TR   1961 Family aspirations and attitudes of Trinidad youth.
20.016   BC   1962 Culture, politics and race relations.

RUHOMAN, JOSEPH

12.027   BG   1921 The Creole East Indian. Timehri 3d ser., 7(24), Aug.: 102-106.
[66]   [AMN]

RUHOMON, PETER

12.028   BG   1946 CENTENARY HISTORY OF THE EAST INDIANS IN BRITISH GUIANA, 1838-
1938. Georgetown, Daily Chronicle, 298p. [5]   [RIS]

SAMPATH, HUGH

12.029   TR   1951 AN OUTLINE OF THE SOCIAL HISTORY OF THE INDIANS IN TRINIDAD. M.A.
thesis, Columbia University, 59p.   [COL]

SAMPATH, MARTIN

28.457   TR   1953 The influence of socio-anthropological factors on the incidence of
syphilis in a heterogenous group of pregnant women in Trinidad.

SCHWARTZ, BARTON M.

8.051   TR   1963 THE DISSOLUTION OF CASTE IN TRINIDAD.
23.141   TR   1964 Ritual aspects of caste in Trinidad.
37.362   TR   1965 Extra-legal activities of the village pandit in Trinidad.
9.036   TR   1965 Patterns of East Indian family organization in Trinidad.

SERTIMA, J. van

50.109   BG   1919 An aching industrial void.

SINGH, H. P.

12.030   TR   1961 Indians in Trinidad. March India 13(3), Mar.: 14-16.   [NYP]

SIRES, RONALD VERNON

50.116   JM   1940 Sir Henry Barkly and the labor problem in Jamaica 1853-1856.

SMITH, RAYMOND THOMAS

62.024   BG   1957   Economic aspects of rice production in an East Indian community in British Guiana.

12.031   BG   1959   Some social characteristics of Indian immigrants to British Guiana. *Popul Stud* 13(1), July: 34-39.   [7, 8, 23]   [*RIS*]

SMITH, RAYMOND THOMAS & JAYAWARDENA, C.

9.046   BG   1958   Hindu marriage customs in British Guiana.

9.047   BG   1959   Marriage and the family amongst East Indians in British Guiana.

SMITH, ROBERT JACK

12.032   TR   1963   MUSLIM EAST INDIANS IN TRINIDAD: RETENTION OF ETHNIC IDENTITY UNDER ACCULTURATIVE CONDITIONS. Ph.D. dissertation, University of Pennsylvania, 230p.   [19]

SPECKMANN, JOHAN DIRK

8.062   SR   1962   Hindostaanse bevolkingsgroep in Suriname [Hindustani population group in Surinam].

10.050   SR   1963   The Indian group in the segmented society of Surinam.

12.033   SR   1963   De positie van de Hindostaanse bevolkingsgroep in de sociale en ekonomische struktuur van Suriname [The position of the Hindustani population group in the social and economic structure of Surinam]. *Tijdschr Kon Ned Aar Genoot* 80(4): 459-466.   [8, 44]

12.034   SR   1963   Het proces van sociale verandering bij de Hindostaanse bevolkingsgroep in Suriname [The process of social change among the Hindustanis in Surinam]. *In* LUCHTMAN, W.I., ed. VAN BRITS-INDISCH EMIGRANT TOT BURGER VAN SURINAME. The Hague, Drukkerij Wieringa, p.51-58.   [16, 66]

9.052   SR   1965   MARRIAGE AND KINSHIP AMONG THE INDIANS IN SURINAM.

STEMBRIDGE, E. C.

50.120   BG   1914   Indian immigration in British Guiana.

SUNDARAM, LANKA

12.035   BC   1933   INDIANS OVERSEAS: A STUDY IN ECONOMIC SOCIOLOGY. Madras, G.A. Natesan, 177p.   [7]   [*NYP*]

SWAYNE, Sir ERIC J. E.

50.121   BH   1910   India and British Honduras.

THIJS, M. D.

12.036   SR   1963   Het onbekende beeld [The unknown picture]. *In* LUCHTMAN, W.I., ed. VAN BRITS-INDISCH EMIGRANT TOT BURGER VAN SURINAME. The Hague, Drukkerij Wieringa, p.99-101.

TYSON, J. D.

12.037   JM/   1939   REPORT ON THE CONDITION OF INDIANS IN JAMAICA, BRITISH GUIANA
         BG/   AND TRINIDAD. Simla, Govt. of India Press, 110p.   [*AGS*]
         TR

WALKER, H. De R.

3.320   BC   1902   THE WEST INDIES AND THE EMPIRE: STUDY AND TRAVEL IN THE WINTER OF 1900-1901.

WASHBURN, B. E.
28.550   BG/   1960 As I RECALL.
           TR

WEINSTEIN, B.
28.577   BG   1962 Diabetes: a regional survey in British Guiana (preliminary report).

Chapter 13

POPULATION SEGMENTS: AMERINDIANS

ABRAHAM, E. A. V.
29.001 BG 1912 Materia medica Guian. Britt.

AHLBRINCK, W.
13.001 GG 1924 Carib life and nature. *In* Proceedings of the Twenty-first International Congress of Americanists, The Hague, Aug. 12-16, 1924. Leiden, E.J. Brill, pt. 1, p.217-225. [*AGS*]

ANDERSON, A. H.
4.003 BH [1952?] Glimpses of a lost civilization.

ANTHON, MICHAEL
23.002 BG 1957 The Kanaima.

AUBERT DE LA RUE, EDGAR
13.002 FG 1950 Quelques observations sur les Oyampi de l'Oyapock (Guyane Francaise) [Some observations on the Oyampi of the Oyapock (French Guiana)]. *J Soc Am* new ser., 39: 85-96. [*AGS*]
13.003 FG 1951 La Guyane Francaise. pt. II: Les populations [French Guiana. pt. II: The peoples]. *Nature* 79(3199), Nov.: 332-339. [For pt. I see 40.004.] [*AGS*]

BALEN, W. J. van
13.004 SR 1930/ Inca's in Suriname? *W I G* 12: 353-359. [5] [*COL*]
          31

BANKS, E. P.
24.004 GC 1955 Island Carib folk tales.
13.005 DM 1956 A Carib village in Dominica. *Social Econ Stud* 5(1), Mar.: 74-86. [8] [*RIS*]

BANNISTER, A. A.
32.017 BG 1951 Amerindian education in British Guiana.

BARTON, G. T.
4.008 BB 1953 'The prehistory of Barbados.

BELL, HENRY HESKETH
13.006 DM 1937 The Caribs of Dominica. *J Barb Mus Hist Soc* 5(1), Nov.: 18-31. [*AMN*]

BENJAMINS, H. D.

51.008   SR   1924/ Iets over den ouden handel met de Indianen in Guiana [Some facts
                25 about the old trade with the Indians in Guiana].

BODKIN, G. E.

13.007   BG   1919 The gun-trap of the Guiana Indians. *Timehri* 3d ser., 6(23), Sept.:
                202-206.   [*AMN*]

BRETT, WILLIAM HENRY & LAMBERT, LEONARD, eds.

24.010   BG   1931 GUIANA LEGENDS.

BRINDLEY, MAUD D.

13.008   BG   1924 The canoes of British Guiana. *Mar Mirror* 10(2), Apr.: 124-132.
                [52]   [*COL*]

BUTT, AUDREY J.

23.009   BG   1953 The burning fountain whence it came; a study of the beliefs of the
                Akawaio.
23.010   BG   1954 The burning fountain from whence it came (a study of the system of
                the beliefs of the Carib-speaking Akawaio of British Guiana).
29.008   BG   1956 Ritual blowing: taling—a causation and cure of illness among the
                Akawaio.
13.009   BG   1957 The Mazaruni scorpion (a study of the symbolic significance of
                tattoo patterns among the Akawaio). *Timehri* 4th ser., 1(36), Oct.:
                40-54. [19]
13.010   BG   1958 Secondary urn burial among the Akawaio of British Guiana. *Timehri*
                4th ser., no. 37, Sept.: 74-88.   · [*AMN*]
23.011   BG   1959/ The birth of a religion (the origins of 'Hallelujah' the semi-Christian
                60 religion of the Carib-speaking peoples of the borderlands of British
                Guiana, Venezuela and Brazil).
23.012   BG   1961/ Symbolism and ritual among the Akawaio of British Guiana.
                62

CHARPENTIER, S. & G.

66.028   FG   1954 An Indianist experiment in French Guiana.

CHOT, ROBERT

3.056   FG   1949 En Guyane rouge [In red (Amerindian) Guiana].

COLL, C. van

2.041   SR   1905 Toegift tot de "Gegevens over land en volk van Suriname" [Addi-
                tion to the "Data about the country and people of Surinam"].

COLLIER, H. C.

24.015   BG   1938 The woman who stuck in the sky.
56.016   BG   1941 Fishing without fiction.
29.010   BG   1942 Copper skin's secret.
63.012   BG/   1942 East goes west in cassava.
          JM/
          SV
29.011   BG   1946 Jungle dope.

COLLIER, W. A.

27.012   SR   1955 The M-N blood-groups in the Arawaks of Matta, Surinam.

COLLIER, W. A.; FROS, J. & SCHIPPER, J. F. A.
27.013   SR   1952 Blood groups of some American Indian settlements.

CONZEMIUS, EDUARD
13.011   BH   1928 Ethnographical notes on the Black Carib (Garif). *Am Anthrop* new
                        ser., 30(2), Apr.-June: 183-205.   [*COL*]

COOKSEY, C.
13.012   BG   1912 Indians of the North Western District. *Timehri* 3d ser., 2(19B),
                        Dec.: 327-335.   [*AMN*]
24.016   BG   1921 Warao stories.

CREGAN, K. H.
13.013   BG   1931 Blowpipes, spears, bows and arrows, and clubs: weapons of the
                        aboriginals of Guiana. *Illus Lond News* 179, Aug. 15: 258-259, 272.
                        [19].

DARBOIS, DOMINIQUE
13.014   FG/   1955 The Oyana Indians of Guiana. *Geogr Mag* 28(1): 40-41.   [*AGS*]
           SR
13.015   FG   1956 YANAMALE, VILLAGE OF THE AMAZON. London, Collins, 63p.   [*AGS*]

DAVIS, HASSOLDT
3.076   FG   1952 THE JUNGLE AND THE DAMNED.

DELAWARDE, JEAN-BAPTISTE
13.016   DM   1938 Les derniers Caraïbes: leur vie dans une réserve de la Dominique
                        [The last Caribs: their way of life on a Dominica reservation].
                        J Soc Am new ser., 30: 167-204.   [*AGS*]

DEYROLLE, E.
13.017   FG   1916 Notes d'anthropologie guyanaise [Notes on Guianese anthropology].
                        B Mem Soc Anthrop 6th ser., 7: 153-164.   [*AMN*]

DOLPHIN, CELESTE
22.052   BG   1946 Arawak rhythm.
52.023   BG   1959 Good afternoon, schools.

DROOGLEEVER FORTUYN, A.B.
27.019   SR   1946 SOME DATA ON THE PHYSICAL ANTHROPOLOGY OF OAJANA INDIANS.

EVANS, CLIFFORD & MEGGERS, BETTY J.
13.018   BG   1955 Life among the Wai Wai Indians. *Natn Geogr Mag* 107(3), Mar.: 329-
                        346.   [*AGS*]

FARABEE, WILLIAM CURTIS
3.098   BG   1917 A pioneer in Amazonia: the narrative of a journey from Manaos to
                        Georgetown.
13.019   BG   1918 THE CENTRAL ARAWAKS. Philadelphia: University Museum, Universi-
                        ty of Pennsylvania, 288p. (Anthropological publications, v. 9.) [*COL*]
13.020   BG   1924 THE CENTRAL CARIBS. Philadelphia: University Museum, University
                        of Pennsylvania, 209p. (Anthropological publications, v. 10.) [*COL*]

FERMOR, PATRICK LEIGH
13.021   DM   1950 The Caribs of Dominica. *Geogr Mag* 23(6), Oct.: 256-264.   [*AGS*]

FEWKES, JESSE WALTER
4.040   GC   1914 Relations of aboriginal culture and environment in the Lesser Antilles.

FIRSCHEIN, I. LESTER
27.021   BH   1961 Population dynamics of the sickle-cell trait in the Black Caribs of British Honduras, Central America.

FOCK, NIELS
13.022   BG   1958 Cultural aspects and social functions of the "oho" institution among the Waiwai. *In* PROCEEDINGS OF THE 32D INTERNATIONAL CONGRESS OF AMERICANISTS, 1956. Copenhagen, Munksgaard, p. 136-140. [19][*AGS*]
9.007   GG   1960 South American birth customs in theory and practice.
23.046   BG   1963 WAIWAI: RELIGION AND SOCIETY OF AN AMAZONIAN TRIBE.

FROS, J.
28.205   SR   1956 Filariasis in South-American Indians in Surinam.

FURLONG, CHARLES WELLINGTON
3.118   SR   1915 The red men of the Guianan forests.

GAAY FORTMAN, B. de
4.044   BN   1942 Geschiedkundige sprokkelingen: de Indianen op Bonaire [Historical gleanings: The Indians on Bonaire].

GANN, THOMAS W. F.
4.045   BH   1918 THE MAYA INDIANS OF SOUTHERN YUCATAN AND NORTHERN BRITISH HONDURAS.

GIGLIOLI, G.
13.023   BG   [n.d.] THE AMERINDIANS OF THE GUIANA HIGHLANDS AND SAVANNAHS: A STORY IN PHOTOGRAPHS. Georgetown, Daily Chronicle.

GILLIN, JOHN P.
8.026   BG   1934 Crime and punishment among the Barama River Carib of British Guiana.
8.027   BG   1935 Social life of the Baram River Caribs of British Guiana.
13.024   BG   1936 The Barama River Caribs of British Guiana. *Peab Mus Pap* 14(2): 166p.   [*RIS*]
13.025   GG   1948 Tribes of the Guianas. *In* STEWARD, JULIAN H., ed. HANDBOOK OF SOUTH AMERICAN INDIANS. Washington, U.S. Govt Print. Off., v. 3, p.799-860. (Smithsonian Institution. Bureau of American Ethnology. Bulletin no. 143.)   [*RIS*]

GLASENAPP, HELMUTH von
13.026   GC   1933/ Die Inder in Guayana und Westindien [The Indians in Guiana and the
                34   West Indies]. *Ibero Amer Archiv* 7(3): 295-305.   [*AGS*]

GOEJE, C. H. de
13.027   SR   1906 Bijdrage tot de ethnographie der Surinaamsche Indianen [Contribution to the ethnography of the Surinam Indians]. *Int Archiv Ethnogr* 17, suppl.
26.003   GG   1909 ETUDES LINGUISTIQUES CARAIB [CARIB LINGUISTIC STUDIES]. [PART 1].

13.028	SR	1910	Beiträge zur Völkerkunde von Surinam [Contributions to the ethnology of Surinam]. *Int Archiv Ethnogr* 19: 1-34. [*AMN*]
13.029	GG	1924/25	Karaïben en Guiana [Caribs and Guyana]. *W I G* 6: 465-471. [26] [*COL*]
13.030	GG	1924	Guayana and Carib tribal names. *In* PROCEEDINGS OF THE TWENTY-FIRST INTERNATIONAL CONGRESS OF AMERICANISTS, FIRST PART, held at The Hague, Aug. 12-16, 1924. The Hague, p.212-215. [26] [*AGS*]
26.004	BG/SR	1928	THE ARAWAK LANGUAGE OF GUIANA.
23.052	SR	1929/30	A. Ph. Penard over inwijding en wereld-beschouwing der Karaïben [A. Ph. Penard on initiation and worldview of the Caribs].
13.031	SR	1930/31	Een oud bericht over Arowakken en Karaïben [An old report about Arawaks and Caribs]. *W I G* 12: 485-491. [5] [*COL*]
13.032	SR	1931/32	Oudheden uit Suriname: op zoek naar de Amazonen [Antiquities from Surinam: in search of the Amazons]. *W I G* 13: 449-482, 497-530. [5] [*COL*]
7.025	BG/SR	1933/34	Sterven de Indianen uit? [Are the Indians dying off?].
26.011	GC	1935	Fünf Sprachfamilien Südamerikas [Five South American linguistic families].
7.026	GC	1938	De bevolking van Amerika [The population of America].
13.033	SR	1941	De Oayana-Indianen [The Oayana Indians]. *Bijd Volk* 100: 71-125.
23.053	SR	1942	De inwijding tot medicijnman bij de Arawakken (Guyana) in tekst en mythe [The initiation of medicinemen among the Arawaks (Guiana) in word and myths].
20.007	GC	1943	Philosophy, initiation and myths of the Indians of Guiana and adjacent countries.
23.055	SR	1948	ZONDVLOED EN ZONDEVAL BIJ DE INDIANEN VAN WEST-INDIE [THE DELUGE AND THE FALL AMONG THE INDIANS OF THE WEST-INDIES].
22.067	GC	1950	Verwanten van de Curacaose wiri [Relatives of the Curacao wiri].
23.056	GC	1952	The physical world, the world of magic, and the moral world of Guiana Indians.
23.057	NA	1956/57	Enkele beschouwingen over de Indianen der Nederlandse Antillen en hun geestesleven [Some observations about the Indians in the Netherlands Antilles and their spiritual life].

GOSLINGA, C. CH.

23.058	GC	1956	Kerk, kroon en Cariben [Church, crown and Caribs].

GOUGH, W. F.

13.034	BG	1912	A few remarks about the Macusis. *Timehri* 3d ser., 2(19A): 139-141.

GOWER, CHARLOTTE D.

4.052	GC	1927	THE NORTHERN AND SOUTHERN AFFILIATIONS OF ANTILLEAN CULTURE.

GOYHENECHE, E. & NICOLAS, MAURICE

5.071	FA	1956	DES ÎLES ET DES HOMMES [THE ISLANDS AND THE PEOPLE].

HAWEIS, STEPHEN

19.015	DM	1947	The death of a basket.

HENFREY, COLIN

37.170	BG	1961	The Amerindians of British Guiana.

66.060   BG   1961 S.O.S. from Guiana.
13.035   BG   1964 THE GENTLE PEOPLE: A JOURNEY AMONG THE INDIAN TRIBES OF GUIANA.
                       London, Hutchinson, 286p.   [*BB*]

HESHUYSEN, F. van
4.061   SR   1925/ Uit het Suriname Archief in Londen: mémoire sur les Indiens à
                 26   Suriname, 22 sept. 1800 [From the Surinam Archives in London:
                       memorandum about the Indians in Surinam, Sept. 22, 1800].

HODGE, W. H.
46.091   DM   1942 Plants used by the Dominica Caribs.

HOLMER, NILS M.
19.020   GC   1960/ Indian place names in South America and the Antilles.
                 61

HOOG, J. de
2.101   SR   1958 SURINAME, EEN LAND IN OPKOMST [SURINAM, A COUNTRY ON THE RISE].

HUCKERBY, THOMAS
4.069   GR/   1921 Petroglyphs of Grenada and recently discovered petroglyph in St.
           SV   Vincent.

HURAULT, JEAN
3.155   FG   1948 NOTE SUR LA CONDUITE D'UNE MISSION DE RECONNAISSANCE DANS L'IN-
                       TERIEUR DE LA GUYANE [ACCOUNT OF THE LEADING OF A RECONNAISSANCE
                       EXPEDITION INTO THE INTERIOR OF GUIANA].
7.034   FG   1959 Etude démographique comparée des Indiens Oayana et des noirs
                       réfugiés Boni du haut-Maroni (Guyane Francaise) [Comparative
                       demographic study of the Oyana Indians and the black Boni refugees
                       from upper Maroni (French Guiana)].
13.036   FG   1961 Les Indiens Oayana de la Guyane Francaise [The Oyana Indians
                       of French Guiana]. *J Soc Am* new ser., 50: 135-183. [9]   [*RIS*]
13.037   FG   1962/ Les Indiens de Guyane et le milieu géographic [The Indians of Guiana
                 63   and the geographical environment]. *N W I G* 42:84-186. [43]   [*COL*]
13.038   FG   1962 Les Indiens oyampi de la Guyane Francaise [The Oyampi Indians of
                       French Guiana]. *J Soc Am* new ser., 51: 65-82. [9]   [*RIS*]
13.039   FG   1963 Les Indiens de Guyane Francaise: problèmes pratiques d'adminis-
                       tration et de contacts de civilisation [The Indians of French Guiana:
                       practical problems of administration and culture contact]. *N W I G*
                       42(2), Feb.: 81-186. [2,66]   [*RIS*]
13.040   FG   1963 Les Indiens du littoral de la Guyane Francaise: Galibi et Arawak
                       [The Indians of the littoral of French Guyana: Galibi and Arawak].
                       Cah O-M 16: 145-183.   [*RIS*]
43.071   FG   1965 LA VIE MATÉRIELLE DES NOIRS RÉFUGIÉS BONI ET DES INDIENS WAYANA
                       DU HAUT-MARONI (GUYANE FRANCAISE): AGRICULTURE, ÉCONOMIE ET
                       HABITAT [THE MATERIAL LIFE OF THE BLACK BONI REFUGEES AND
                       THE WAIYANA INDIANS OF THE UPPER MARONI (FRENCH GUIANA): AGRI-
                       CULTURE, ECONOMY AND HABITAT].

HURAULT, JEAN & FRENAY, P.
13.041   FG   1963 Les Indiens emerillon de la Guyane Francaise [The Emerillon Indi-
                       ans of French Guiana]. *J Soc Am* 52: 132-156.   [*AMN*]

HURAULT, JEAN & FRIBOURG-BLANC, ANDRE
43.072   FG   1949 MISSION ASTRO-GÉODESIQUE DE L'OYAPOC (GUYANE FRANCAISE) JUILLET

à novembre 1947 [Astro-geodetic expedition to the Oyapoc (French Guiana) July to November 1947].

IM THURN, EVERARD F.

22.080   BG   1901   Games of the red-men of Guiana.

JESSE, C.

13.042   SL   1960   The Amerindians in St. Lucia (Iouanalao). [Bridgetown?] Barbados, St. Lucia Archaeological and Historical Society, 17p.   [RIS]

5.104   GC   1963   The Spanish cédula of December 23, 1511, on the subject of the Caribs.

JONES, C. R.

28.295   BG   1954   The health of the Amerindian.

28.296   BG   1954   Tuberculosis amongst the Amerindians of British Guiana.

JOYCE, THOMAS A.

4.077   GC   1916   Central American and West Indian archaeology.

KAHN, MORTON CHARLES

3.164   SR   1936   Where black man meets red.

KATE, HERMAN F. C. ten

13.043   SR   1920/ De Indiaan in de letterkunde [The Indian in literature]. *W I G* 2:95-21   108.   [COL]

KENSWIL, F. W.

13.044   BG   1946   Children of the silence. [Georgetown, B.G.?] Interior Development Committee, 24p.   [NYP]

KESLER, C. K.

6.036   NC   1940   Uit de eerste dagen van den West-Indischen slavenhandel [about the first days of the West Indian slave trade].

KOCH-GRUNBERG, T.

13.045   BG   1918   Uber die Kultur der Indianer Guayanas [On the culture of the Guiana Indians]. *JB Städt Mus Volk Lpz 1915/17*, 7: 63-66   [AMN]

KUNIKE, HUGO

19.026   GG   1912   Der Fisch als Fruchtbarkeitssymbol bei den Waldindianern Sudamerikas [The fish as a fertility symbol among the South American forest Indians].

LALUNG, HENRY de

13.046   GC   1948   Les Caraïbes, un peuple étrange aujourd'hui disparu [The caribs, an exotic and now extinct people]. Paris, Editions Bourrelier, 94p. [5]   [RIS]

LEKIS, LISA

22.087   GC   1955   The dance as an expression of Caribbean folklore.

LICHTVELD, LOU

14.020   SR   1958   Van Bosnegers en Indianen [About Bush Negroes and Amerindians].

LICKERT, Rev.

13.047   BG   1912   Moruca. *Timehri* 3d ser., 2(19B), Dec.: 315-325.   [AMN]

LOMBARD, JEAN

13.048   FG   1928 Recherches sur les tribus indiennes qui occupaient le territoire de la Guyane Francaise vers 1730 (d'après des documents de l'époque) [Researches on the Indian tribes that occupied the territory of French Guiana ca. 1730 (after documents of the time)]. *J Soc Am* 20: 121-153.   *[AGS]*

LUKE, Sir HARRY

13.049   DM   1947 Remnants of a Caribbean conquering race: I: Last refuge of Island Caribs in Dominica: impressions of a visit to a remote reserve. *Crown Colon* 17(193), Dec.: 639-643.   *[AGS]*

LUTZ, FRANKE

22.091   BG   1912 String-figures from the upper Potaro.

McKUSICK, MARSHALL BASSFORD

4.092   GC   1960 Aboriginal canoes in the West Indies.

MAZIERES, FRANCIS & DARBOIS, DOMINIQUE

3.196   FG   1952 Mission Guyane Tumuc-Humac: le carnet de route de Francis Mazières [The Tumuc-Humac Guiana expedition: Francis Mazières' notes].

MELVILLE, EDWINA

13.050   BG   1961 "Rupununi kakup-ri" (Wapishiana for "Rupununi life") *Timehri* 4th ser. (no. 40), Oct.: 35-43.   *[AMN]*

METRAUX, A.

13.051   FG   1928 LA CIVILISATION MATÉRIELLE DES TRIBUS TUPI-GUARANI [THE MATERIAL CULTURE OF THE TUPI-GUARANI]. Paris, Librarie Orientaliste Paul Geuthner, 331p.   *[COL]*

23.105   FG   1928 LA RELIGION DES TUPINAMBA ET SES RAPPORTS AVEC CELLE DES AUTRES TRIBUS TUPI-GUARANI [THE RELIGION OF THE TUPINAMBA AND ITS RELATIONSHIP TO THAT OF THE OTHER TUPI-GUARANI TRIBES].

13.052   GG   1950 LES PEAUX-ROUGES DE L'AMÉRIQUE DU SUD [THE INDIANS OF SOUTH AMERICA]. Paris, Editions Bourrelier, 123p.   *[NYP]*

MORLEY, SYLVANUS G.

4.100   BH   1956 THE ANCIENT MAYA.

MYERS, IRIS

13.053   BG   1944 The Makushi of British Guiana—a study in culture contact. *Timehri* 4th ser., 1(26), Nov.: 66-77;
1946 4th ser., 1(27), July: 16-38. [19]   *[AGS]*

NEVEU-LEMAIRE, M.

13.054   DM   1921 Les Caraïbes des Antilles: leurs représentants actuels dans l'île de la Dominique [The Caribs of the West Indies: their present descendants on the island of Dominica]. *Geographie* 35(2), Feb.: 127-146.   *[AGS]*

NORDENSKIOLD, ERLAND

26.018   GG   1922 DEDUCTIONS SUGGESTED BY THE GEOGRAPHICAL DISTRIBUTION OF SOME POST-COLUMBIAN WORDS USED BY THE INDIANS OF S. AMERICA.

NORMAND, GILLES

3.221   FG   1924 AU PAYS DE L'OR: RÉCIT D'UN VOYAGE CHEZ LES INDIENS INCONNUS DE LA GUYANE FRANCAISE [IN THE LAND OF GOLD: ACCOUNT OF A JOURNEY TO THE UNKNOWN INDIANS OF FRENCH GUIANA].

NORWOOD, VICTOR G. C.

13.055   GG   1964 JUNGLE LIFE IN GUIANA. London, Robert Hale, 191p.   [*RIS*]

OSGOOD, CORNELIUS

4.101   GC   1942 Prehistoric contact between South America and the West Indies.

PANHUYS, L. C. van

27.034   FG   1905 Are there pygmies in French Guiana?

13.056   SR   1920/ De toekomst van de Indianen in Canada en in Suriname [The future 21 of the Indians in Canada and in Surinam]. *WIG* 2: 513-516.   [*COL*]

24.057   SR   1934/ Het kikvorschmotief in Suriname en elders [The frog motif in Suri- 35 nam and elsewhere].

29.020   SR   1935/ Opvattingen van Zuid-Amerikaansche Indianen nopens ziekten en 36 geneeswijzen [South American Indian ideas about illness and cures].

PENARD, A. P.

23.119   SR   1928 Het pujai-geheim der Surinaamsche Caraiben [The pujai-secret of the Caribs of Surinam].

PENARD, THOMAS E.

25.087   TR   1927/ Remarks on an old vocabulary from Trinidad. 28

PENARD, THOMAS E. & ARTHUR P.

22.116   SR   1925/ Four Arawak Indian songs. 26

PERRET, JACQUES

13.057   FG   1933 Nouvelles observations ethnographiques sur la Guyane Francaise [New ethnographic observations on French Guiana]. *B Ass Av Sci* 111, Apr.: 101-105.   [*RIS*]

13.058   FG   1933 Observations et documents sur les Indiens emerillon de la Guyane Francaise [Observations and documentation on the Emerillon Indians of French Guiana]. *J Soc Am* new ser., 25(1): 65-97.   [*AGS*]

PETER, IMELDA

4.105   DM   1934 The Caribs of Dominica—then and now.

PINCHON, R. P.

13.059   FG   1955 En remontant le Maroni chez les Indiens roucouyennes de Guyane Francaise [Up the Maroni among the Rukuien Indians of French Guiana]. *B Soc Fr Hist Nat Ant* 5(23p.)   [*RIS*]

PRICE-MARS, JEAN

13.060   GC   1941 L'archeólogie, l'ethnologie et la linguistique; état actuel de ces sciences appliquées à l'aire géographique du golfe du Mexique et du bassin des Caraïbes, études comparatives et possibilités de co-ordination scientifique [Archaeology, ethnology, and linguistics;

present position of these sciences as applied to the geographical area of the Gulf of Mexico and the Caribbean, comparative studies, and possibilities of scientific coordination]. *Rev Soc Hist Geogr Haiti* 12(41), Apr.: 1-12.   [*AGS*]

RIVIERE, P. G.

13.061   SR   1965 THE SOCIAL ORGANISATION OF THE TRIO INDIANS OF SURINAM. Ph.D. dissertation, Magdalen College, Oxford University, 383p. [8]   [*RIS*]

ROBINSON, ALBAN

22.124   BG   1918 Some figures in string from the Makushis on the Ireng and Takutu Rivers.

RODWAY, JAMES

13.062   BG   1902 Forest people of British Guiana. *B Am Geogr Soc* 34(3-4): 211-216; 283-294. [10]   [*AGS*]

13.063   BG   1917 Indian Charms. *In* BEEBE, W.; HARTLEY, G.I. & HOWES, P.G., eds. TROPICAL WILD LIFE IN BRITISH GUIANA, vol. 1. New York, New York Zoological Society, p.488-499. [19]   [*AGS*]

ROMITI, CESARE

28.441   BG   1933 Rare hernias in aboriginal Indians of British Guiana.

ROTH, HENRY D.

23.130   BG   1950 The Kanaima.

ROTH, VINCENT

37.350   BG   1952 Amerindians and the state: a brief history of the Guiana Amerindians vis-a-vis the government.

ROTH, WALTER EDMUND

13.064   BG   1910 Some technological notes from the Pomeroon district, British Guiana, Part II. *J Roy Anthrop Inst Gr Br Ire* 40:23-38.   [*AGS*]

13.065   BG   1911 Old time Indians: their manners and customs. *Timehri*, 3d ser., 1(18A), Jan.: 62-75.   [*AMN*]

30.048   BG   1912 On the native drinks of the Guianese Indian.

13.066   BG   1913 The narcotics and stimulants of the Guianese Indian. *Br Gui Med Annual* 18: 1-9. [29]   [*ACM*]

23.131   BG   1915 An inquiry into the animism and folklore of the Guiana Indians.

29.022   BG   1919 A few notes on the medical practises of the Guiana Indians.

13.067   BG   1921 Some examples of Indian mimicry, fraud and imposture. *Timehri* 3d ser., 7(24), Aug.: 29-40 [19]   [*AMN*]

13.068   BG   1924 An introductory study of the arts, crafts, and customs of the Guiana Indians. *In* THIRTY-EIGHTH ANNUAL REPORT OF THE BUREAU OF AMERICAN ETHNOLOGY, 1916-1917. Washington, U.S. Govt. Print. Off.,p.25-745.   [*AGS*]

13.069   BG   1929 ADDITIONAL STUDIES OF THE ARTS, CRAFTS, AND CUSTOMS OF THE GUIANA INDIANS, WITH SPECIAL REFERENCE TO THOSE OF SOUTHERN BRITISH GUIANA. Washington, U.S. Govt. Print. Off., 110p. (Smithsonian Institute, Bureau of American Ethnology, Bulletin no. 91.) [22, 49]   [*NYP*]

ROUSE, IRVING

4.120   GC   1948 The West Indies; an introduction: the Arawak; the Carib.

4.125   GG   1953 Guianas: indigenous period.

ROUX, HENRY D.

13.070   FG   1936 Les Néo-Amérindiens en Guyane Francaise [Neo-Amerindians in French Guiana]. *Rev Gen Sci* 47(8), Apr. 30: 225-226.   [*COL*]

SAUSSE, ANDRE

28.465   FG   1951 Pathologie comparée des populations primitives noires et indiennes de la Guyane Francaise [Comparative pathology of the primitive Negro and Indian populations of French Guiana].

13.071   FG   Populations primitives du Maroni (Guyane Francaise) [Primitive peoples of the Maroni (French Guiana)]. Paris, Institut Géographique National, 133p. [14,28]   [*RIS*]

SAVILLE, MARSHALL H.

13.072   BG   1921 Bladed warclubs from British Guiana. New York, Museum of the American Indian, Heye Foundation, 12p. (Indian notes and monographs, Miscellaneous series, no. 14.)   [*COL*]

SCHAAD, J. D. G.

2.209   SR   1954 Naar de Bovenlandse Indianen in Suriname; medische expeditie [Medical expedition to the upland Indians in Surinam].

28.470   SR   1960 Epidemiological observations in Bush Negroes and Amerindians in Surinam.

SEGGAR, W. H.

13.073   BG   1952 The Mazaruni Amerindian district. *Timehri* 4th ser., 1(31), Nov.: 43-51. [66]

66.132   BG   1954 Some aspects of development of a remote interior district.

37.365   BG   1959 Amerindian local authority elections: upper Mazaruni Amerindian district.

66.133   BG   1959 Community development amongst Amerindians.

SOLIEN, NANCIE L.

9.048   BH   1958 The consanguineal household among the Black Carib of Central America.

9.049   BH   1959 The nonunilineal descent group in the Caribbean and Central America.

13.074   JM/   1959 West Indian characteristics of the Black Carib. *Sw J Anthrop* 15(3), Autumn: 300-307. [11, 19]   [*RIS*]
        BH/
        TR

9.050   BH   1960 Changes in Black Carib kinship terminology.

STAEHELIN, F.

23.160   SR/   [1912?] Die Mission der Brüdergemeine in Suriname und Berbice im Achtzehnten Jahrhundert [The Moravian Brethren mission in Surinam and Berbice in the 18th century].
        BG

STEWARD, JULIAN H.

13.075   GC   1948 The Circum-Caribbean tribes: an introduction. *In* STEWARD, JULIAN H., ed. Handbook of South American Indians. Washington, U.S. Govt. Print. Off., v. 4, p. 1-41. (Smithsonian Institution, Bureau of American Ethnology. Bulletin no. 143.)   [*RIS*]

STEWARD, JULIAN H., ed

13.076   GC   1948 Handbook of South American Indians. Volume 4: The Circum-Caribbean tribes. Washington, U.S. Govt. Print. Off., 609p. (Smithsonian Institution, Bureau of American Ethnology. Bulletin 143.) [*RIS*]

STOKES-ROBERTS. A. E.

13.077   BG   1947 Among the shy tenants of Green Mansions: an account of a visit to
                      the Ackwoi Indians of British Guiana. *Can W-I Mag* 37(1), Mar.:
                      18-19, 21.   [*NYP*]

STURTEVANT, WILLIAM C.

13.078   GC   1960 The significance of ethnological similarities between southeastern
                      North America and the Antilles. *In* MINTZ, SIDNEY W., comp.
                      PAPERS IN CARIBBEAN ANTHROPOLOGY. New Haven, Dept. of Anthro-
                      pology, Yale University, no.64(58p.) (Yale University publications
                      in anthropology, nos. 57-64.)   [*RIS*]

TACOMA J.

27.040   AR   1959 Indian skeletal remains from Aruba.
27.041   AR   1964 Kunstmatige schedeldeformatie in Aruba [Artificial skull deforma-
                      tion in Aruba].

TAYLOR, DOUGLAS C.

13.079   DM   1935 The Island Caribs of Dominica. *Am Anthrop* new ser., 37(2, pt. 1)
                      Apr.-June: 265-272. [26]   [*COL*]
13.080   DM   1936 Additional notes on the Island Carib of Dominica, B.W.I. *Am Anthrop*
                      new ser., 38(3, pt. 1) July-Sept.: 462-468. [26]   [*COL*]
13.081   DM   1938 The Caribs of Dominica.   *In* Smithsonian Institution. Bureau of
                      American Ethnology.   Bulletin no. 119. Washington, U.S. Govt.
                      Print. Off., p.103-159. (Anthropological papers, no. 3.)
13.082   WW   1941 Columbus saw them first. *Nat Hist* 48(1), June: 40-49.   [*AGS*]
23.161   DM   1945 Carib folk beliefs and customs from Dominica, B.W.I.
4.142   GC   1946 Kinship and social structure of the Island Carib.
24.073   DM   1946 Notes on the star lore of the Caribbees.
13.083   DM/   1950 The meaning of dietary and occupational restrictions among the
          BH   Island Carib. Menasha, Wisconsin: *Am Anthrop* 52(3), July-Sept.:
                      343-349. [19]   [*RIS*]
13.084   BH   1951 THE BLACK CARIB OF BRITISH HONDURAS. New York, Wenner-Gren
                      Foundation for Anthropological Research, 176p. (Viking Fund pub-
                      lications in anthropology, no. 17.)   [*RIS*]
24.074   DM   1952 Tales and legends of the Dominica Caribs.
9.055   GC   1957 Marriage, affinity, and descent in two Arawakan tribes: a socio-
                      linguistic note.

TAYLOR, DOUGLAS, C. & MOORE, HARVEY C.

49.069   DM   1948 A note on Dominican basketry and its analogues.

THOMAS, LEON

13.085   DM   1953 La Dominique et les derniers Caraïbes insulaires [Dominica and the
                      last Island Caribs]. *Cah O-M* 6(21), Jan.-Mar.: 37-60.   [*RIS*]
13.086   BH   1955 Les Caraïbes noirs du Honduras Britannique [The Black Caribs of
                      British Honduras]. *Cah O-M* 8(30), Apr.-June: 196-202.   [*AGS*]
43.145   DM   1955 La Dominique, asile des derniers autochtones antillais [Dominica,
                      haven of the last Caribbean aborigines].

THOMPSON, J. ERIC S.

13.087   BH   1930 ETHNOLOGY OF THE MAYAS OF SOUTHERN AND CENTRAL BRITISH HONDURAS.
                      Chicago, Field Museum of Natural History, p.27-213. (Publication
                      274, Anthropological series v. 17, no. 2.)   [*COL*]

TWISTON-DAVIES, SUZANNE
13.088   TR   1963 Carib Indians: a vanishing race. *Contemp Rev* 204, Oct.: 203-204, 208.   [*COL*]

VERIN, PIERRE MICHEL
13.089   SL   1959 Sainte-Lucie et ses derniers Caraïbes [St. Lucia and its last Caribs]. *Cah O-M* 12:349-361.   [*RIS*]
4.150   SL   1961 Les Caraïbes à Sainte Lucie depuis les contacts coloniaux [The Caribs in St. Lucia since the time of colonial contact].

VERRILL, ALPHEUS HYATT
13.090   BG   1917 The tribal relationships of the Akawoias. *Timehri* 3d ser., 4(21), June: 107-116.   [*AMN*]

VINCKE, GASTON
3.317   FG   1935 Avec Les Indiens de la Guyane [With the Indians of Guiana].

WAGENAAR HUMMELINCK, P.
27.042   AR/   1959 Indiaanse skeletvondsten op Aruba en Curacao [Indian skeletal dis-
       CU   coveries in Aruba and Curacao].

WHITE, WALTER GRAINGE
3.331   BG   [n.d.] At home with the Macuchi.

WILLIAMS, JAMES
13.091   BG   1912 The Americans of the interior of British Guiana. *Timehri* 3d ser., 2(19A), July: 135-137.   [*AMN*]
19.041   BG   1922 The name "Guiana."
1.049   GG   1924 The Arawak Indians and their language.
13.092   BG   1928 The Warau Indians of Guiana and vocabulary of their language. *J Soc Am* new ser., 20: 193-252.
                    1929 new ser., 21: 201-261.   [*AGS*]
47.033   BG   1936 The aborigines of British Guiana and their land.

WOOD, B. R.
13.093   BG   1944 Curare. *Timehri* 4th ser., 1(26), Nov.: 117-120. [19,41]   [*AMN*]

YDE, JENS
46.243   BG   1957 The agricultural level of the Waiwai Indians.
13.094   BG   1959 Resist-dyed bark costumes of the Waiwai Indians. *Folk* 1: 59-66. [19]   [*COL*]
46.244   BG   1960 Agriculture and division of work among the Waiwai.
13.095   BG   1962 Britisch-Guiana und Nord-Pará [British Guiana and Northern Pará (Brazil)]. *In* Bulletin of the International Committee on Urgent Anthropological and Ethnological Research, no. 5. Vienna, pub. by the Committee's Secretariat, p.112-116. [67]   [*RIS*]

ZERRIES, OTTO
23.175   GC   1961 Die Religionen der Naturvölker Südamerikas und Westindiens [The religions of the primitive peoples of South America and the West Indies].

Chapter 14

POPULATION SEGMENTS: BUSH NEGROES

BENJAMINS, H. D.

14.001   SR   1929/ Een Amerikaansche professor over Surinaamsche Boschnegers [An
             30 American professor discusses Surinam Bushnegroes]. *W I G* 11:
                   483-487.   *[COL]*

29.006   SR   1929/ Treef en lepra in Suriname [Treyf and leprosy in Surinam].
             30

BLUMBERG, B.; McGIFF, J. & GUICHERIT, I.

28.038   SR   1952 Malaria survey among the Bush Negroes of Marowyne District, Suri-
                 nam, S.A. in 1950.

BONNE, C.

25.009   SR   1920/ Het Boschnegerschrift van Afaka [The Bush-Negro writing system
             21 of Afaka].

BRUIJNING, C. F. A.

28.072   SR/   1957 Man-biting sandflies (*Phlebotomus*) in the endemic leishmaniasis
           FG   area of Surinam.

BUTTS, DONALD C. A.

27.009   SR   1955 Blood groups of the Bush Negroes of Surinam.

CAPPELLE, H. van

24.011   SR   1916 Surinaamsche Negervertellingen [Folktales of the Surinam Negroes].

CHARPENTIER, S. & G.

66.028   FG   1954 An Indianist experiment in French Guiana.

COMVALIUS, TH. A. C.

22.031   SR   1935/ Het Surinaamsche Negerlied: de banja en de doe [The Surinam Negro
             36 song: the banja and the doe].

COVARRUBIAS, MIGUEL

14.002   SR   1946 Los Djukas: "Bush Negroes" de la Gayana Holandesa [The Djuka:
                 Bush Negroes of Dutch Guiana]. *Afro America* 2(3): 121-122. *[AMN]*

CROWLEY, DANIEL JOHN

22.039   BG   1956 Bush Negro combs: a structural analysis.

CRUICKSHANK, J. GRAHAM
19.008   BG   1929   Negro games.

DARK, PHILIP J. C.
22.050   SR   1951   Some notes on the carving of calabashes by the Bush Negroes of Surinam.
22.051   SR   1954   BUSH NEGRO ART: AN AFRICAN ART IN THE AMERICAS.

DAVIS, HASSOLDT
3.075   FG   1949   On the flowing highway in Guiana forests.
3.076   FG   1952   THE JUNGLE AND THE DAMNED.

DELAFOSSE, MAURICE
14.003   SR   1925   Survivances africaines chez les Nègres "Bosch" de la Guyane [African survivals among the Bush Negroes of Guiana]. *Anthropologie* 35(5-6): 475-494. [19]   [*COL*]

DONICIE, A. C.
23.038   SR   1948   Sterfhuis en begrafenis bij de Saramakkanen [House of the deceased and funeral among the Saramaccans].
19.011   SR   1953   Iets over de tall en de sprookjes van Suriname [On the language and the fairy-tales of Surinam].

ESSED, W. F. R.
28.147   SR   1930/ Eenige opmerkingen naar aanleiding van de artikelen over treef en
            31   lepra in dit tijdschrift verschenen [Some remarks in connection with the articles about treyf and leprosy that appeared in this magazine].

FURLONG, CHARLES WELLINGTON
3.117   SR   1914   Through the heart of the Surinam jungle.

GOEJE, C. H. de
23.054   SR   1947   Negers in Amerika [Negroes in the Americas].

GONGGRIJP, J. W.
25.032   SR   1960   The evolution of a Djuka-script in Surinam, by J. W. Gonggryp.

GONGGRIJP, J. W. & DUBELAAR, C.
25.033   SR   1960   Pater Morssink en Afaka [Pater Morssink and Afaka].
25.034   SR   1963   De geschriften van Afaka in zijn Djoeka-schrift [The papers of Afaka in Djuka script], [by] W. Gonggryp & C. Dubelaar.

GROOT, SILVIA W. de
14.004   SR   1963   VAN ISOLATIE NAAR INTEGRATIE: DE SURINAAMSE MARRONS EN HUN AF-STAMMELINGEN, OFFICIELE DOCUMENTEN BETREFFENDE DE DJOEKA'S (1845-1863) [FROM ISOLATION TO INTEGRATION: THE SURINAM MAROONS AND THEIR DESCENDANTS, OFFICIAL DOCUMENTS CONCERNING THE DJUKA TRIBE (1845-1863)]. The Hague, Martinus Nijhoff, 100p. (Verhandelingen van het Koninklijk Instituut voor Taal-, Land- en Volkenkunde, v. 41.) [5, 37]   [*RIS*]

HERSKOVITS, MELVILLE JEAN
19.017   SR   1928/ Preliminary report of an ethnological expedition to Suriname, 1928.
            29

14.005   SR   1929/ The second Northwestern University Expedition for the Study of the
                  30   Surinam Bush-Negroes, 1929. *W I G* 11: 393-402.   [*COL*]
19.018 SR   1929 Adjiboto, an African game of the Bush-Negroes of Dutch Guiana.
8.029   SR   1930 The social organisation of the Bush Negroes of Suriname.
67.007 GC   1931 The New World Negro as an anthropological problem.
67.008 GC   1938 African ethnology and the New World Negro.
67.009 GC   1946 Problem, method and theory in Afroamerican studies.
22.075 SR   1949 Afro-American art.
31.034 GC   1952 Some psychological implications of Afroamerican studies.

HERSKOVITS, MELVILLE JEAN & FRANCES S.
22.076 SR   1930 Bush-Negro art.
14.006   SR   1934 REBEL DESTINY: AMONG THE BUSH NEGROES OF DUTCH GUIANA. New
                        York, Whittlesey House, McGraw-Hill, 366p. [19, 20]   [*RIS*]
24.033 SR   1936 SURINAME FOLK-LORE (with transcriptions and Suriname songs and
                        musicological analysis by Dr. M. Kolinski.)

HOOG, J. de
2.101   SR   1958 SURINAME, EEN LAND IN OPKOMST [SURINAM, A COUNTRY ON THE RISE].

HURAULT, JEAN
3.155   FG   1948 NOTE SUR LA CONDUITE D'UNE MISSION DE RECONNAISSANCE DANS L'IN-
                        TÉRIEUR DE LA GUYANE [ACCOUNT OF THE LEADING OF A RECONNAISSANCE
                        EXPEDITION INTO THE INTERIOR OF GUIANA].
19.021 FG   1960 Histoire des noirs réfugiés Boni de la Guyane Francaise [History of
                        the black Boni refugees of French Guiana].
14.007   FG   1961 Canots africains en Guyane [African canoes in Guiana]. *Bois For*
                        Trop 78, July-Aug.: 45-55. [19,52]   [*RIS*]
14.008   FG   1961 LES NOIRS RÉFUGIÉS BONI DE LA GUYANE FRANCAISE [THE BLACK BONI
                        REFUGEES OF FRENCH GUIANA]. Ifan Dakar, Institut francais d'Afri-
                        que noire, 362p. Mémoires de l'Institut francais d'Afrique noire,
                        no. 63.)   [*RIS*]

JUNKER, L.
14.009   SR   1922/ Eenige mededeelingen over de Saramaccaansche Boschnegers [Some
                  23   information about the Saramaccan Bush Negroes]. *W I G* 4: 449-
                        480.   [*COL*]
14.010   SR   1923/ Over de afstamming der Boschnegers [About the ancestry of the
                  24   Bush Negroes]. *W I G* 5: 310-317.   [*COL*]
14.011   SR   1924/ Godsdienst, zeden en gebruiken der Boschnegers [Religion, man-
                  25   ners and customs of the Bush Negroes]. *WIG* 6:73-81. [19]   [*COL*]
23.077 SR   1925/ De godsdienst der Boschnegers [The religion of the Bush Negroes].
                  26
14.012   SR   1932/ Het einde van een dynastie—de dood van Jankosoe [The end of a
                  33   dynasty—the death of Jankosoe]. *WIG* 14:49-58. [5, 37]   [*COL*]
14.013   SR   1932/ Een Staat in den Staat [A State within the State]. *W I G* 14:267-284,
                  33   321-336. [37]   [*COL*]
14.014   SR   1940 Primitief communism [Primitive communism]. *WIG* 22:277-283 [*COL*]
37.209 SR   1947 De benoeming van een grootopperhoofd der Boschnegers [The ap-
                        pointment of a headman of the Bush Negroes].

KAHN, MORTON CHARLES
14.015   SR   1928 The Bush Negroes of Dutch Guiana. *Nat Hist* 28(3), May-June:
                        243-252. [19]   [*AGS*]

14.016	SR	1929	Notes on the Saramaccaner Bush Negroes of Dutch Guiana. *Am Anthrop* new ser., 31(3), July-Sept.: 468-490. [COL]
22.084	SR	1931	Art of the Dutch Guiana Bush Negro.
14.017	SR	1931	DJUKA, THE BUSH NEGROES OF DUTCH GUIANA. New York, Viking Press, 233p. [19] [RIS]
3.164	SR	1936	Where black man meets red.
19.023	SR	1939	Africa's lost tribes in South America.
19.024	SR	1954	Little Africa in America: the Bush Negroes.
19.025	SR	1959	The Djukas of Surinam.

KLUGE, H. C.

14.018   SR   1923   Curious loggers of the world, the Boschneger of Suriname: descendants of escaped slaves fill important place in South American logging. *Hdwd Rec* 55(10), Sept. 10:18-20, 22. [64]   [NYP]

KUYP, EDWIN van der

1.026   SR   1962   Literatuuroverzicht betreffende de voeding en de voedingsgewoonten van de Boslandcreool in Suriname [Bibliography about, nutrition and food habits of the Bush Negroes in Surinam].

LAMBERTERIE, R. de

14.019   FG   [1947]   Notes sur les Bonis de la Guyane Francaise [Notes on the Boni of French Guiana]. *J Soc Am Paris* new ser., 35:123-147.   [AGS]

LAMPE, P. H. J.

29.014   SR   1928/   "Het Surinaamsche treefgeloof", een volksgeloof betreffende het
                          29   ontstaan van de melaatschheid ["The treyf belief in Surinam", a superstition about the cause of leprosy].

LIACHOWITZ, CLAIRE, et al.

28.339   SR   1958   Abnormal hemoglobins in the Negroes of Surinam.

LICHTVELD, LOU

29.015   SR   1930/   Een Afrikaansch bejgeloof: snetji-koti [An African superstition:
                          31   "snakebite cure"].

29.016   SR   1932/   Een oude getuigenis over de genezing van slangenbeet en aardeten
                          33   [An old testimony about the cure of snakebite and the eating of earth].

14.020   SR   1958   Van Bosnegers in Indianen [About Bush Negroes and Amerindians]. *In* WALLE, J. van de & WIT, H. de, eds. SURINAME IN STROOMLIJNEN. Amsterdam, Wereld Bibliotheek, p.59-75. [13]

LIER, WILLEM F. van

14.021   SR   1921/   Bij de Aucaners [Among the Aucanians]. *W I G* 3:1-30;
                          22   598-612.
                  1922/   4:205-230. [5,19]
                          23

LIER, WILLEM F. van & GOEJE, C. H. de

23.096   SR   1940   Aanteekeningen over het geestelijk leven en de samenleving der Djoeka's in Suriname [Notes on the spiritual life and society of the Djukas in Surinam].

LINDBLOM, K. G.

22.089   SR   1926   EINIGE DETAILS IN DER ORNAMENTIK DER BUSCHNEGER SURINAMS [SOME DETAILS OF THE ORNAMENTS OF THE BUSH NEGROES OF SURINAM].

LUQUET, G. H.

22.090   SR   1933   Exposition d'ethnographie guyanaise au Trocadéro [Exhibit of Guianese ethnography at the Trocadéro].

MENKMAN, W. R.

5.144   SR   1946   Uit de geschiedenis der opening van het Surinaamsche binnenland [From the history of the opening of the interior of Surinam].

MORPURGO, A. J.

24.050   SR   1935/ Folklore in Suriname.
             36

MORSINK, F.

14.022   SR   1934/ Nogmaals: de dood van Jankosoe. En: nog niet het einde van een
             35   dynastie [Once again: the death of Jankosoe. And: not yet the end of a dynasty]. *W I G* 16:91-105. [5,23]   [*COL*]

OUDSCHANS DENTZ, FRED

14.023   SR   1935/ Het Boschnegerdeurslot (klavierslot), zijn oorsprong en toepassing
             36   [The door-lock of the Bush Negroes, its origin and uses]. *W I G* 17:
                228-230.   [*COL*]

37.300   SR   1948   De afzetting van het Groot-Opperhoofd der Saramaccaners Koffy in 1835 en de politieke contracten met de Boschnegers in Suriname [The dismissal of Koffy, the headman of the Saramaccans, in 1835, and the political contracts with the Bush Negroes in Surinam].

PANHUYS, L. C. van

14.024   SR   1904   About the ornamentation in use by savage tribes in Dutch Guiana. *Bijd Volk Ned-Indie* 56:618-621. [19]

22.106   SR   1905   About the ornamentation in use by savage tribes in Dutch Guiana and its meaning.

14.025   SR   1906   Näheres über die Ornamente der Naturvölker Surinams [Details on the ornaments of the primitive peoples of Surinam]. *In* INTERNATIONALER AMERIKANISTEN-KONGRESS, 14TH SESSION, Stuttgart, [Proceedings], Berlin, W. Kohlhammer, pt. 2, p.437-439. [19]   [*AGS*]

14.026   SR   1910   Mitteilungen über surinamsche Ethnographie und Kolonisationsgeschichte... [Notes on the ethnography and colonial history of Surinam]. *In* VERHANDLUNGEN DES XVI. INTERNATIONALEN AMERIKANSTEN-KONGRESSES, Wien, 1908. Vienna, A. Hartleben, pt. 2, p.521-540. [19]   [*AGS*]

22.108   SR   1913   Development of ornament amongst the Bush-Negroes in Suriname.

23.116   SR   1913   The heathen religion of the Bush Negroes in Dutch Guiana.

29.019   SR   1924   The trafe-superstition in Surinam.

22.109   SR   1930   Ornaments of the Bush Negroes in Dutch Guiana; a further contribution to research in Bush-Negro art.

22.110   SR   1931/ Boschnegerkunst [Bush Negro art].
             32

24.056   SR   1934/ Folklore in Suriname.
             35

14.027   SR   1934   Die Bedeutung einiger Ornamente der Buschneger von Niederländisch Guyana [The significance of some Bush Negroes' ornaments from Dutch Guiana]. *In* VERHANDLUNGEN DES XXIV INTERNATIONALEN AMERIKANSTEN-KONGRESSES, Hamburg, 1930. Hamburg, Friederichsen, de Gruyter, p.196-206. [19]   [*AGS*]

| 24.059 | SR | 1935/
36 | Surinaamsche folklore (liederenverzameling Van Vliet) [Folklore of Surinam (Song collection of Van Vliet)]. |
| 29.021 | SR | 1943 | "Sneki-koti," inenting tegen den bijt van vergiftige slangen ["Sneki-koti," immunization against the bite of poisonous snakes]. |

PENARD, F. P. & A. P.

| 24.065 | SR | 1926/
27 | Negro riddles from Surinam. |

PRINS, J.

| 37.323 | SR | 1952 | Vragen inzake Bosneger-volksrecht [Questions concerning public rights of the Bush Negroes]. |

RATELBAND, K.

| 25.089 | SR | 1944/
45 | Een Boschnegerschrift van West-Afrikaanschen oorsprong [A Bush Negro system of writing of West African origin]. |

SAUSSE, ANDRE

| 28.465 | FG | 1951 | Pathologie comparée des populations primitives noires et indiennes de la Guyane Francaise [Comparative pathology of the primitive Negro and Indian populations of French Guiana]. |
| 13.071 | FG | 1951 | POPULATIONS PRIMITIVES DU MARONI (GUYANE FRANCAISE) [PRIMITIVE PEOPLES OF THE MARONI (FRENCH GUIANA)]. |

SCHAAD, J. D. G.

| 28.470 | SR | 1960 | Epidemiological observations in Bush Negroes and Amerindians in Surinam. |

STAAL, G. J.

| 37.391 | SR | 1921/
22 | Het voorspel der installatie van den posthouder bij de Aucaners [The prelude to the installation of the representative among the Aucaner]. |
| 14.028 | SR | 1922/
23 | Boschneger-herinneringen [Bush Negro reminiscences]. *W I G* 4:42-47. [3]   [*COL*] |

STAEHELIN, F.

| 23.160 | SR/
BG | [1912?] | DIE MISSION DER BRÜDERGEMEINE IN SURINAME UND BERBICE IM ACHTZEHNTEN JAHRHUNDERT. [THE MORAVIAN BRETHREN MISSION IN SURINAM AND BERBICE IN THE 18TH CENTURY]. |

STAGE, H. H.

| 14.029 | SR | 1947 | DDT has a namesake in Dutch Guiana (an application of DDT to cognomination). *Mosq News* 7(2), June: 55-57.   [*COL*] |

VANDERCOOK, JOHN WOMACK

14.030	SR	1926	Eternal life in the jungle. *Harper's Mag* 152, Mar.: 510-516. [*COL*]
14.031	SR	1926	Jungle commonwealth and jungle marriage. *Harper's Mag* 152, May: 771-779. [*COL*]
3.310	SR	1926	Jungle survival.
14.032	SR	1926	We find an African tribe in the South American jungle. *Mentor* 14(3), Apr.: 19-22. [*COL*]
29.026	SR	1927	Magic is the jungle science: the black tribes of Guiana do not believe in death.

VOLLENHOVEN, C. van
5.212   SR   1916 Politieke contracten met de Boschnegers in Suriname [Political contracts with the Bush Negroes of Surinam].

VOULLAIRE, R.
23.167   SR   1907 A journey among the bush men of Surinam.

WAYS, P.; BRYANT, J. & GUICHERIT, I. D.
28.576   SR   1956 Histoplasmin sensitivity among the Bush Negroes of Surinam.

WONG, E.
14.033   SR   1938 Hoofdenverkiezing, stamverdeling en stamverspreiding der Boschnegers van Suriname in de 18e en 19e eeuw [Election of headmen,
organization and distribution of the Bush Negro tribes of Surinam in
the 18th and 19th centuries]. *Bijd Volk Ned-Indie* 97:295-362.

Chapter 15

POPULATION SEGMENTS: OTHERS

AHRENS, H.

50.002   SR   1922/ Kolonisatie op particulier land in Suriname met Javanen onder con-
          23 tract onder de thans geldende immigratie wetten [Colonization with
             Javanese contract laborers on privately owned land in Surinam under
             the current immigration laws].

ALLAND, ALEXANDER

15.001   ST   1940 The Jews of the Virgin Islands; a history of the islands and candid
              biographies of outstanding Jews born there. *AmHeb* 146(20), Mar.
              29:5,12-13,16; 146(21), Apr. 5:6-7; 146(24), Apr. 26:5,12-13; 147(1),
              May 17:5,12. [5,23]   [*NYP*]

ANDRADE, JACOB A. P. M.

15.002   JM   1941 A RECORD OF THE JEWS IN JAMAICA FROM THE ENGLISH CONQUEST TO
              THE PRESENT TIME. Kingston, Jamaica Times, 282p. [5,23]   [*NYP*]

BETHENCOURT, CARDOZO de

15.003   'GC   1925 Notes on the Spanish and Portuguese Jews in the United States,
              Guiana, and the Dutch and British West Indies during the seven-
              teenth and eighteenth centuries. *In* PUBLICATIONS OF THE AMERICAN
              JEWISH HISTORICAL SOCIETY. New York, The Society, no. 29, p.7-38.
              [5,23]   [*COL*]

BIJLSMA, R.

15.004   SR   1920/ De stichting van de Portugeesch-Joodsche gemeente en synagoge
          21 in Suriname [The founding of the Portuguese-Jewish community and
             synagogue in Surinam]. *W I G* 2:58-60. [23]   [*COL*]

BONNE, C.

28.044   SR   1923/ Hygienische ervaring te Moengo [Hygienic experience in Moengo].
          24

BOUBEE, JOSEPH

15.005   ST   1923 Aux îles Vierges: une paroisse francaise inconnue [In the Virgin
              Islands: an unknown French parish] *Etudes* 60(176), July-Sept.:
              79-92.   [*NYP*]

CADBURY, HENRY J.

23.014   BB   1940 Quakers, Jews and freedom of teaching in Barbados, 1686.

CAMPBELL, PERSIA CRAWFORD

15.006   BC   1923 Foreign competition for Chinese labour, 1845-74. *In her* CHINESE
COOLIE EMIGRATION TO COUNTRIES WITHIN THE BRITISH EMPIRE. Lon-
don, P.S. King, ch. 3, p.86-160. [5,50]   [*AGS*]

CLEMENTI, Sir CECIL

15.007   BG   1915 THE CHINESE IN BRITISH GUIANA. Georgetown, Argosy Press, 416p.
[17]   [*NYP*]

COUSINS, WINIFRED M.

15.008   GC   1927 The Chinese in the Caribbean. *Liv Age* 332(4297), Jan.: 16-21. [*COL*]

CUNDALL, FRANK; DAVIS, N. DARNELL & FRIEDENBERG, ALBERT M.

15.009   JM/   1915 Documents relating to the history of the Jews in Jamaica and Bar-
BB   bados in the time of William III. *In* PUBLICATIONS OF THE AMERICAN
JEWISH HISTORICAL SOCIETY. New York, The Society, no. 23, p.25-29.
[5,23]

DAVIS, N. DARNELL

15.010   BB   1909 Notes on the history of the Jews in Barbados. *In* PUBLICATIONS OF
THE AMERICAN JEWISH HISTORICAL SOCIETY. New York, The Society,
no. 18, p.129-148. [5,23]   [*NYP*]

EMMANUEL, ISAAC S.

15.011   GC   1955 New light on early American Jewry. *Am Jew Archs* 7(1), Jan.: 3-64.
[5,23]   [*NYP*]
23.042 CU   1957 PRECIOUS STONES OF THE JEWS OF CURACAO; CURACAON JEWRY 1656-
1957.

EUWENS, P. A.

15.012   CU   1930/ De eerste Jood op Curacao [The first Jew on Curacao]. *W I G* 12:
31 360-366. [5]   [*COL*]
23.043 CU   1934/ De Joodsche Synagoge op Curacao [The Jewish Synagogue on Cura-
35 cao].

FARRAR, P. A.

15.013   BB   1942 The Jews in Barbados. *J Barb Mus Hist Soc* 9(3), May: 130-133.
[5,23]   [*AMN*]

FELHOEN KRAAL, JOHANNA L. G.

15.014   GC   1952 Territoires de la Commission des Caraïbes, 1945-1952 [Territories
of the Caribbean Commission, 1945-1952]. *Civilisations* 2(4), Dec.:
617-622.   [*COL*]

FISHER, RUTH ANNA

15.015   JM   1943 Note on Jamaica. *J Negro Hist* 28(2), Apr.: 200-203. [5,23,37,44][*COL*]

FLORES, GIOVANNI

15.016   BH   1958 Gli italiani di Manatee [The Italians of Manatee]. *Universo* 38(5),
Sept.-Oct.: 795-800. [5,17]   [*AGS*]

FRIED, MORTON H.

15.017   BG   1956 Some observations on the Chinese in British Guiana. *Social Econ
Stud* 5(1), Mar.: 54-73.   [19]   [*RIS*]

HEEMSTRA, J.

15.018   SR   1952/ De Indonesiërs in Suriname [The Indonesians in Surinam]. *Indonesie*
                  53   6:429-438. [37]

HILFMAN, P. A.

15.019   SR   1909 Notes on the history of the Jews in Surinam. *In* PUBLICATIONS OF THE
                  AMERICAN JEWISH HISTORICAL SOCIETY.   New York, The Society, no.
                  18, p.179-207. [5,23]   [*NYP*]

HURWITZ, SAMUEL J. & EDITH

15.020   JM   1965 The New World sets an example for the old: the Jews of Jamaica
                  and political rights 1661-1831. *Am Jew Hist Q* 55(1), Sept.: 37-56.
                  [5,23,37]   [*RIS*]

ISMAEL, JOSEPH

15.021   SR   1950/ De positie van de Indonesiër in het nieuwe Suriname [The position
                  51   of the Indonesian in present-day Surinam]. *Indonesie* 4:177-193.

JUDAH, GEORGE FORTUNATUS

15.022   JM   1909 The Jews' tribute in Jamaica.   *In* PUBLICATIONS OF THE AMERICAN
                  JEWISH HISTORICAL SOCIETY.   New York, The Society, no. 18, p.149-
                  177. [5,23,37]   [*NYP*]

KALFF, S.

15.023   SR   1928 Javanese emigrants in Suriname.   *Inter-Ocean* 9(10), Oct.: 544-548.
                  [5,17]   [*NYP*]

KAYSERLING, M.

15.024   JM   1900 The Jews in Jamaica and Daniel Israel Lopez Laguna. *Jew Q Rev*
                  12(48), July: 708-717. [5]   [*COL*]

KESLER, C. K.

15.025   SR   1938 Javanen in Suriname reeds in het jaar 1714? [Were the Javanese al-
                  ready in Surinam in the year 1714?]. *WIG* 20:270-274. [5,7] [*COL*]

KROEF, J. M. van der

15.026   SR   1951 The Indonesian minority in Surinam. *Am Sociol Rev* 16:672-679.

LAMPE, P. H. J.

28.320   SR   1927/ Suriname, sociaal-hygienische beschouwingen [Surinam, social-
                  28   hygienic observations].

LIND, ANDREW W.

15.027   JM   1958 Adjustment patterns among the Jamaican Chinese. *Social Econ Stud*
                  7(2), June: 144-164. [16,17]   [*RIS*]

LOW, F. O.

15.028   BG   1919 Hopetown Chinese settlement. *Timehri* 3d ser., 6(23), Sept.: 66-67.
                  [5,8]   [*AMN*]

MALEFIJT, ANNEMARIE de WAAL

15.029   SR   1963 THE JAVANESE OF SURINAM: SEGMENT OF A PLURAL SOCIETY. Assen,
                  [Netherlands] VanGorcum, 206p. [8,19]   [*RIS*]

15.030   SR   1963 Het sociaal-economisch vermogen van de Javanen in Suriname [The socio-economic potential of the Javanese in Surinam]. *Tijdschr Kon Ned Aar Genoot* 80(4): 467-473. [8,44]

23.100   SR   1964 Animism and Islam among the Javanese in Surinam.

MARCUS, JACOB RADER
15.031   GC   1953 The West India and South America expedition of the American Jewish Archives. *Am Jew Archs* 5(1), Jan.: 5-21. [5,23]

MERRILL, GORDON CLARK
15.032   GC   1964 The role of Sephardic Jews in the British Caribbean area during the seventeenth century. *Car Stud* 4(3), Oct.: 32-49. [5,23]   [*RIS*]

OPPENHEIM, SAMUEL
15.033   GG/   1907 An early Jewish colony in Western Guiana 1658-1666: and its rela-
         TB   tion to the Jews in Surinam, Cayenne and Tobago. *In* PUBLICATIONS OF THE AMERICAN JEWISH HISTORICAL SOCIETY. New York, The Society, no. 16, p.95-186. [5,23]   [*COL*]
15.034   BG   1908 An early Jewish colony in Western Guiana: supplemental data. *In* PUBLICATIONS OF THE AMERICAN JEWISH HISTORICAL SOCIETY. New York, the Society, no. 17, p.53-70. [5,23]

OUDSCHANS DENTZ, FRED
23.114   SR   1948 Wat er overbleef van het kerkhof en de synagoge van de Joden-Savanne in Suriname [What is left of the cemetery and the synagogue of the Jewish-Savannah in Surinam]. *W I G* 29:210-224.

PRINS, J.
23.125   BB   1961/ De Islam in Suriname: een oriëntatie [Islam in Surinam: an orienta-
         62   tation]. *N W I G* 41(1): 14-37.

RENS, L. L. E.
15.035   SR   1954 Analysis of annals relating to early Jewish settlement in Surinam. *Vox Guy* 1(1), May: 19-38. [5]   [*RIS*]

ROOS, J. S.
15.036   SR   1905 Additional notes on the history of the Jews in Surinam. *In* PUBLICATIONS OF THE AMERICAN JEWISH HISTORICAL SOCIETY. New York, The Society, no. 13, p.127-136. [5,23]   [*NYP*]

SAMUEL, WILFRED S.
15.037   BB   1936 A REVIEW OF THE JEWISH COLONISTS IN BARBADOS IN THE YEAR 1680. London, printed by Purnell, for the Jewish Historical Society of England, 125p. [5,23]   [*NYP*]

SHAW, EARL BENNETT
15.038   ST   1934 The Chachas of St. Thomas. *Scient Mon* 38, Feb.: 136-145.   [*AGS*]

SHILSTONE, E. M.
23.144   BB   1958 MONUMENTAL INSCRIPTIONS IN THE BURIAL GROUND OF THE JEWISH SYNAGOGUE AT BRIDGETOWN, BARBADOS.

SIRES, RONALD VERNON
50.116   JM   1940 Sir Henry Barkly and the labor problem in Jamaica 1853-1856.

SNELLEMAN, J. F.

17.027   SR   1920/ Chineesche immigranten in Suriname [Chinese immigrants to Suri-
21   nam].

SUMMIT, ALPHONS

15.039   SR   1940 The Jews of Surinam. *Am Heb* 146(22), Apr. 12: 14, 44-45, 48. [5,
17, 23]   [*NYP*]

SWELLENGREBEL, N. H. & KUYP, E. van der

28.511   SR   1940 HEALTH OF WHITE SETTLERS IN SURINAM.

TERVOOREN, E. P. M.

66.149   SR   1954/ De financiering van het Tienjarenplan en de Nederlandse bijstand
55   [The financing of the Ten Year Plan of Development and the contribution of the Netherlands].

VANDERCOOK, JOHN WOMACK

15.040   SR   1928 Jungle Jews. *Menorah J* 14(3), Mar.: 238-246. [5]   [*COL*]

WAAL, L. de

46.224   SR   1927/ Java-methoden voor Suriname? [Javanese methods for Surinam?].
28

WENGEN, G. D. van

15.041   SR   1963 Tajoeb, een prestige-feest bij de Javanen in Suriname [Tajub, a
prestige festival among the Javanese of Surinam]. *Bijd Volk*, 119:
106-121. [8,44]

YOUNG, ARTHUR A.

54.085   TR   1928 A Chinese pioneer of Trinidad's oil wells.
15.042   TR   1929 The Chinese in the West Indies. *China Wkly Rev* 48(11), May 11:
466.   [*NYP*]
15.043   TR   1929 Progressive Chinese in Trinidad. *China Wkly Rev* 51(3), Dec. 21:
114   [*NYP*]
15.044   TR   1931 The fight to keep Chinese out reaches Trinidad. *China Wkly Rev*
56(9), May 2: 308.   [NYP]

ZWARTS, JAC

15.045   SR   1927/ Een episode uit de Joodsche kolonie van Guyana, 1660 [An episode
28   from the Jewish colony of Guiana, 1660]. *W I G* 9:519-530.   [5,45]
[*COL*]

Chapter 16

RACE RELATIONS

ACHILLE, LOUIS T.

16.001   FC   1940 Notes on the Negro in the French West Indies. *In* WESLEY, CHARLES
H., ed. THE NEGRO IN THE AMERICAS. Washington, D.C., Graduate
School, Division of the Social Sciences, Howard University, p.20-23.
[11]

BAKER, CECIL SHERMAN

16.002   GC   1930 Climatic influences in the Caribbean. *C-W I Mag* 19(5), Mar.: 107-
108. [42]   [*NYP*]

BECKLES, LYNNE

16.003   JM   1961 Race and colour in Jamaica. *W I Econ* 4(1-2), July-Aug.: 5-6 [66]
[*RIS*]

BEHN, APHRA

6.004   SR   1919/ De geschiedenis van den koninklijken slaaf [The history of the royal
20   slave].

BERGHE, PIERRE L. van den

16.004   GC   1963 Racialism and assimilation in Africa and the Americas. *Sw J Anthrop* 19(4), Winter: 424-432. [5,19]   [*RIS*]

BRAITHWAITE, LLOYD E.

31.014   GC   1963 The changing social scene.

BUCHLER, IRA R.

8.005   CM   1962 Caymanian folk racial categories.

BYLES, G. LOUIS

16.005   BC   1946 Way to real unity in the West Indies. *Crown Colon* 16(176), July:
473-474. [21]   [*AGS*]

CAHNMAN, WERNER J.

16.006   GC   1943 The Mediterranean and Caribbean regions—a comparison in race and
culture contacts. *Social Forces* 22(2), Dec.: 209-214.   [*RIS*]

COULTHARD, G. R.

16.007   GC   1962 RACE AND COLOUR IN CARIBBEAN LITERATURE. London, Oxford University Press, 152p. [11,21]   [*RIS*]

CUNDALL, FRANK

37.079   BC   1906 POLITICAL AND SOCIAL DISTURBANCES IN THE WEST INDIES: A BRIEF AC-
COUNT AND BIBLIOGRAPHY.

ELDER, J. D.

22.055   TR   1964 Color, music and conflict: a study of aggression in Trinidad with
reference to the role of traditional music.

ELLIS, ROBERT ARTHUR

8.023   JM   1957 Colour and class in a Jamaican market town.

FANON, FRANTZ

16.008   FA   1952 PEAU NOIRE, MASQUES BLANCS [BLACK SKIN, WHITE MASKS].   Paris,
Editions du Seuil, 222p. [18]   [*NYP*]

16.009   FA   1955 Antillais et Africains [West Indians and Africans]. *Esprit* 23(223),
Feb.: 261-269.   [*COL*]

FARLEY, RAWLE

16.010   BG   1955 The substance and the shadow—a study of the relations between
white planters and free coloured in a slave society in British Guiana. *Car Q* 4(2), Dec.: 132-151. [5,8,45,66]   [*RIS*]

FRAZIER, E. FRANKLIN

16.011   GC   1944 Race relations in the Caribbean. *In* FRAZIER, E. F. & WILLIAMS,
E., eds. THE ECONOMIC FUTURE OF THE CARIBBEAN. Washington, D.C.,
Howard University Press, p.27-31.

GRINDER, ROBERT E.

27.025   JM   1964 Negro-white differences in intellectual performance: a receding controversy.

GUMPERT, MARTIN

16.012   UV   1947 Land without conflict. *Nation*, 164(14), Apr. 5: 395-396.   [*COL*]

HALPERIN, ERNST

37.156   BG   1965 Racism and Communism in British Guiana.

HART, ANSELL

16.013   JM   1955 Jamaica checkerboard: a history of colour question in Jamaica.
Pepperpot 5: 10-13.

HENRIQUES, FERNANDO

16.014   JM   1944 The colour bar in the West Indies. *New Stsm Natn* 28(717), Nov. 18:
334-335.   [*NYP*]

16.015   JM   1951 Colour values in Jamaican society. *Br J Sociol* 2(2), June: 115-121.
[*COL*]

HERRICK, ROBERT

16.016   BC/   1924 The race problem in the Caribbean. *Nation* 18(3075), June 11: 675-
FA   676; 118(3076), June 18: 699-700.   [*COL*]

HOETINK, HARRY

16.017   CU/   1961 Diferencias en relaciones raciales entre Curazao y Surinam [Differ-
SR   ences in racial relations between Curacao and Surinam]. *Revta
Cienc Social* 5(4), Dec.: 499-514. [5]   [*RIS*]

10.020 NA 1962 DE GESPLETEN SAMENLEVING IN HET CARAIBISCHE GEBIED [THE DIVIDED SOCIETY IN THE CARIBBEAN AREA].

HUGHES, COLIN A.
16.018 BC 1954 Colour and caste in the Caribbean. *Venture* 6(1), Apr.: 7-8. [*COL*]

HUNTE, GEORGE HUTCHINSON
16.019 BC 1946 West Indian unity: measures and machinery. *Crown Colon* 16(171), Feb.: 88-89. [21,38] [*AGS*]

JACOBS, H. P.
16.020 JM 1961 Reality and race: a reply to 'Realism and race.' *W I Econ* 3(10), Apr.: 13-18. [50] [*BB*]

JORDAN, WINTHROP D.
16.021 BC 1962 American chiaroscuro: the status and definition of mulattoes in the British Colonies. *Wm Mary Q* 3d ser., 19(2), Apr.: 183-200. [5,20][*COL*]

KALFF, S.
37.210 NC 1927/ Vreemdelingen in het Westindische leger [Foreigners in the West-
28 Indian Army].

KERR, MADELINE
31.039 JM 1953 Some areas in transition: Jamaica.

KESLER, C. K.
11.014 SR 1926/ Naar aanleiding van "De Neger en zijne cultuurgeschiedenis" [With
27 reference to "The Negro and his cultural history"].
16.022 SR 1932/ Na 100 jaar: branden in Paramaribo [After 100 years: fires in Para-
33 maribo]. *W I G* 14: 164-174. [5] [*COL*]

KNOX, GRAHAM
37.217 JM 1963 British colonial policy and the problems of establishing a free society in Jamaica, 1838-1865.

LAGROSILLIERE, J.
37.221 MT 1903 LA QUESTION DE LA MARTINIQUE [THE QUESTION OF MARTINIQUE].

LEWIS, GORDON K.
37.225 GC 1961 The Caribbean: colonization and culture.

LIND, ANDREW W.
15.027 JM 1958 Adjustment patterns among the Jamaican Chinese.

LOWENTHAL, DAVID
10.027 GC 1960 The range and variation of Caribbean Societies.

MARSHALL, MARGARET
16.023 JM 1947 Notes on Jamaica. *Nation* 164(15), Apr. 12: 422-423; 164(17), Apr. 26: 476-478. [*COL*]

MARTIN, KINGSLEY
23.101 JM 1961 The Jamaican volcano.

MATHER, FRANK JEWETT
16.024   JM   1906 Object-lesson in the solution of race problems. *Arena* 36(203),Oct.:
              364-369.   [*COL*]

MITTELHOLZER, EDGAR
2.159   BG   1963 A SWARTHY BOY.

MORITZEN, JULIUS
16.025   JM   1901 Has Jamaica solved the color problem? *Gunton's Mag* 20, Jan.: 31-
              46.   [*COL*]

MORPURGO, A. J.
11.020   SR   1934/ De Kótómisi [The Kotomisi].
              35

NETTLEFORD, REX
21.018   JM   1965 National identity and attitudes to race in Jamaica.

NEWMAN, PETER KENNETH
16.026   BG   1962 Racial tension in British Guiana. *Race* 3(2), May: 31-45. [11,12,
              37,44]   [*RIS*]

NORRIS, KATRIN
21.019   JM   1962 JAMAICA: THE SEARCH FOR AN IDENTITY.

OLIVIER, SYDNEY, 1st Baron RAMSDEN
50.093   BC   1910 WHITE CAPITAL AND COLOURED LABOR, by Lord Olivier.
16.027   JM   1935 A key to the colour question, by Lord Olivier. *Contemp Rev* 148
              (840), Dec.: 665-673. [11,66]   [*AGS*]

PENISTON-BIRD, CYNTHIA
16.028   JM   1940 "Jamaica for the Jamaicans!" *Natn Rev* 114(687), May: 603-610. [*NYP*]

ROBERTS, WALTER ADOLPHE
37.339   BC   1941 Caribbean headaches.

RUBIN, VERA
20.016   BC   1962 Culture, politics and race relations.

SEMMEL, BERNARD
16.029   JM   1962 The issue of "race" in the British reaction to the Morant Bay Up-
              rising of 1865. *Car Stud* 2(3), Oct.: 3-15. [5,37]   [*RIS*]

SHERLOCK, PHILIP M.
37.369   JM/ 1963 Prospects in the Caribbean.
         TR

SIMPSON, GEORGE EATON
23.147   JM   1955 Culture change and reintegration found in the cults of West Kingston,
              Jamaica.
23.148   JM   1955 Political cultism in West Kingston, Jamaica.
23.149   JM   1955 The Ras Tafari movement in Jamaica: a study of race and class
              conflict.
50.114   GC   1962 Employment policy problems in a multiracial society.
23.152   JM   1962 The Ras Tafari movement in Jamaica in its millennial aspect.

SKINNER, ELLIOTT P.

8.055 BG 1960 Group dynamics and social stratification in British Guiana.

SMITH, M. G.; AUGIER, ROY & NETTLEFORD, REX

23.158 JM 1960 THE RAS TAFARI MOVEMENT IN KINGSTON, JAMAICA.

SPECKMANN, JOHAN DIRK

16.030 SR 1963 De houding van de Hindostaanse bevolkingroep in Suriname ten opzichte van de Creolen [The attitude of the Hindustani community in Surinam towards the Creoles]. *Bijd Volk* 119(1): 76-92. [*RIS*]

12.034 SR 1963 Het proces van sociale verandering bij de Hindostaanse bevolkingsgroep in Suriname [The process of social change among the Hindustanis in Surinam].

STAAL, G. J.

37.391 SR 1921/ Het voorspel der installatie van den posthouder bij de Aucaners [The 22 prelude to the installation of the representative among the Aucaner].

10.051 SR 1927/ Stroomingen in Suriname [Currents in Surinam]. 28

STEELE, WESLEY

16.031 JM 1954 ENGULFED BY THE COLOR TIDE; STUDIES FROM JAMAICA: CONSEQUENCES OF THE SLAVE TRADE AND BRITISH COLONIALISM. New Britain, Pa., The author, 24p. [2,34] [*AGS*]

TAYLOR, COUNCILL SAMUEL

8.063 JM 1955 COLOR AND CLASS: A COMPARATIVE STUDY OF JAMAICAN STATUS GROUPS.

THORNTON, A. P.

16.032 BC 1960 Aspects of West Indian Society. *Int J* 15(2), Spring: 113-121. [*AGS*]

THORP, WILLIAM

16.033 JM 1904 How Jamaica solves the Negro problem. *Wld Work* 8(2), June: 4908-4913. [2] [*NYP*]

WAGLEY, CHARLES & HARRIS, MARVIN

8.065 MT 1958 MINORITIES IN THE NEW WORLD: SIX CASE STUDIES.

WELLS, HENRY

37.418 UV 1955 Outline of the nature of United States Virgin Islands politics.

WILLIAMS, ERIC EUSTACE

37.427 GC 1942 Crossways of the Caribbean.
16.034 UV 1945 Race relations in Puerto Rico and the Virgin Islands. *For Aff* 23(2), Jan.: 308-317. [*AGS*]

16.035 GC 1955 THE HISTORICAL BACKGROUND OF RACE RELATIONS IN THE CARIBBEAN. [Port of Spain, Printed by the College Press for the publisher, Dr. Eric Williams], 35p. (Teachers Economic and Cultural Association, People's Education Movement, Public affairs pamphlet no. 3.) [5] [*RIS*]

16.036 GC 1960 Race relations in Caribbean society. *In* RUBIN, VERA, ed. CARIBBEAN STUDIES: A SYMPOSIUM. 2d ed. Seattle, University of Washington Press, p.54-66. [37] [*RIS*]

Chapter 17

MIGRATION

ACHARD, CH.
28.001   FG   1939 Mission en Guyane [Guiana expedition].

ADHIN, J. H.
5.001   SR   1961/ De immigratie van Hindostanen en de Afstand van de Goudkust [The
62   immigration of the Hindustanis and the cession of the Gold Coast].
50.001   SR   1963 De economisch-historische betekenis van de Hindostaanse immigratie voor Suriname [The economic-historical value of the Hindustani immigration for Surinam].

AHRENS, H.
50.002   SR   1922/ Kolonisatie op particulier land in Suriname met Javanen onder con-
23   tract onder de thans geldende immigratie wetten [Colonization with
Javanese contract laborers on privately owned land in Surinam under
the current immigration laws].

ANDREWS, C. F.
50.005   BG/   1930 "India's emigration problem."
TR

ARCHIBALD, CHARLES H.
17.001   BC   1961 How many immigrants? *New Commonw* 39(6), June: 374-376.[18][*AGS*]

BASCOM, F. C. S.
50.008   BG   1912 The labour question: the problem stated.

BEYLERS, H. de
17.002   FG   1951 Immigration en Guyane [Immigration into Guiana]. *Ency Mens O-M*
1(15), Nov.: 323-325. [46, 66]   [*NYP*]

BRAITHWAITE, LLOYD E.
17.003   JM   [1961?] Population, migration and urbanization. *In* CUMPER, GEORGE, ed.
REPORT OF THE CONFERENCE ON SOCIAL DEVELOPMENT IN JAMAICA.
Kingston, Standing Committee on Social Services, p.63-69. [7,34,36]
[*RIS*]

BRANDON, H. G.
44.022   SR   1924/ Het Suriname vraagstuk [The problem of Surinam].
25

CAMMAERTS, E.

50.014   BC   1914 L'importation des coolies dan les Indes occidentales [The importation of coolies into the West Indies].

CARASCO, F. J. & SCHOUTEN, S. A.

17.004   SR/   1947 Emigration to Surinam. *Car Commn Mon Inf B* 1(4), Nov.: 19-25.
          BC   [66]   [*COL*]

CASTA-LUMIO, LUCIEN

50.017   FC   1906 ETUDE HISTORIQUE SUR LES ORIGINES DE L'IMMIGRATION RÉGLEMENTÉE DANS NOS ANCIENNES COLONIES DE LA RÉUNION, LA GUADELOUPE, LA MARTINIQUE, ET LA GUYANE [HISTORICAL STUDY ON THE ORIGINS OF REGULATED IMMIGRATION INTO OUR FORMER COLONIES OF RÉUNION, GUADELOUPE, MARTINIQUE, AND GUIANA].

CHANDLER, ALFRED D.

17.005   BB   1946 The expansion of Barbados. *J Barb Mus Hist Soc* 13(3-4): 106-136.
                    [5]   [*AMN*]

CHEVALIER, LOUIS

17.006   GC   1949 Les mouvements de la population dans les dépendances caraïbes [Population movements in the Caribbean dependencies]. *Population* 4(2), Apr.-June: 356-361.   [*COL*]

CLEMENTI, Sir CECIL

15.007   BG   1915 THE CHINESE IN BRITISH GUIANA.
5.030   BG   1922 Colonisation in British Guiana.

COLLIER, H. C.

2.042   BG   1938 British Guiana—a possible refugee haven.

CUMPSTON, I. M.

12.006   BG/   1956 A survey of Indian immigration to British tropical colonies to 1960.
          TR

CUNDALL, FRANK

17.007   SR/   1919 The migration from Surinam to Jamaica. *Timehri* 3d ser., 6(23),
          JM   Sept.: 145-172. [5]   [*AMN*]

DALE, EDMUND H.

7.013   BC   1963 The demographic problem of the British West Indies.

DAMBAUGH, LUELLA N.

17.008   GC   1957 Recent Caribbean migration. *In* WILGUS, A. CURTIS, ed. THE CARIBBEAN: CONTEMPORARY INTERNATIONAL RELATIONS [papers delivered at the Seventh Conference on the Caribbean held at the University of Florida, Dec. 6-8, 1956]. Gainesville, University of Florida Press, p.196-232. (Publications of the School of Inter-American Studies, ser. 1, v. 7).
                                                                                    [*RIS*]

DEBIEN, GABRIEL

50.033   FC   1942 LE PEUPLEMENT DES ANTILLES FRANCAISES AU XVIIᵉ SIÈCLE: LES ENGAGÉS PARTIS DE LA ROCHELLE (1683-1715) [THE SETTLEMENT OF THE FRENCH ANTILLES IN THE 17TH CENTURY: THE BONDED SERVANTS FROM LA ROCHELLE (1683-1715)].

50.034   FA   1951 Les engagés pour les Antilles (1634-1715) [Bonded servants signed up for the Antilles (1634-1715)].

DEERR, NOEL
50.036   GC   1938 Indian labour in the sugar industry.

EDMUNDSON, GEORGE
17.009   BG/   1901 The Dutch in western Guiana. *Engl Hist Rev* 16(64), Oct.: 640-675.
          TB   [5]   [*COL*]

EEKHOUT, J. J. W.
66.041   SR   1926 Heeft Suriname een toekomst? [Does Surinam have a future?].

ERICKSON, EDGAR L.
50.044   BC   1934 The introduction of East Indian coolies into the British West Indies.

FLORES, GIOVANNI
15.016   BH   1958 Gli italiani di Manatee [The Italians of Manatee].

GAUNT, MARY
17.010   JM   1924 Garden settlement in the West Indies. *W I Comm Circ* 39(677), Sept. 11: 357-358.   [*NYP*]

GRANSAULL, EDWARD
17.011   TR   1916 Causes of emigration from the colony. *Proc Agri Soc Trin Tob* 16(8), Aug.: 289-294. [66]   [*AMN*]

GREENWOOD, THOMAS
50.054   BC   1921 East Indian emigration: the Indian government's policy.

GRIEVE, S.
2.088   DM   1906 Notes upon the island of Dominica (British West Indies).

GUIRAL, PAUL
17.012   FA   1911 L'immigration réglementée aux Antilles Francaises et à la Reunion [Regulated immigration into the French Antilles and Reunion]. Paris, Jouve, 154p. (Ph.D. dissertation) [5]   [*COL*]

HALE, C. M.
12.009   BG   1911 An Indian colony.

HILL, ARTHUR H.
50.063   BG   1919 Emigration from India.

HOSTOS, ADOLFO de
4.063   GC   1924 Notes on West Indian hydrography in its relation to prehistoric migrations.

HOTTEN, JOHN C., ed.
17.013   BB   1931 The original lists of persons of quality, emigrants, religious exiles, political rebels, serving men...who went from Great Britain to the American plantations 1600-1700. New York, G.A. Baker, 580p. [5]   [*COL*]

HUGGINS, H. D.
7.033   BC   1955 Population and migration.

JONES, CLAUDIA
18.031   BC   1964 The Caribbean community in Britain.

KALFF, S.
15.023   SR   1928 Javanese emigrants in Suriname.

KLERK, CORNELIS JOHANNES MARIA de
50.073   SR   1942 De Britisch-Indiërs in Suriname [The British Indians in Surinam].
50.074   SR   1953 DE IMMIGRATIE DER HINDOESTANEN IN SURINAME [THE IMMIGRATION OF HINDUS TO SURINAM].
50.075   SR   1963 DE KOMST EN VESTIGING VAN DE BRITS-INDIËRS IN SURINAME [THE AR-RIVAL AND SETTLEMENT OF THE BRITISH INDIANS IN SURINAM].

KRUIJER, GERARDUS JOHANNES
17.014   NW   1953 Enquête onder be Bovenwinders op Curacao en Aruba (Juli-Augustus 1951) [Investigation among Windward Islanders on Curacao and Aruba (July-August 1951)]. *In* KRUIJER, G. J.; VEENENBOS, J. S. & WESTERMANN, J. H., comps. BOVENWINDENRAPPORT. Amsterdam, Voorlichtingsinstituut voor het Welvaartsplan Nederlandse Antillen, 17p. [22]

LACASCADE, PIERRE
50.079   FA   1907 ESCLAVAGE ET IMMIGRATION. LA QUESTION DE LA MAIN-D'OEUVRE AUX ANTILLES: LE DÉCRÉT DU 13 FÉVRIER 1852 ET LA CONVENTION ANGLAISE DU 1ER JUILLET 1861 [SLAVERY AND IMMIGRATION. THE QUESTION OF MANPOWER IN THE ANTILLES. THE DECREE OF 13 FEBRUARY 1852 AND THE BRITISH CONVENTION OF 1 JULY 1861].

LENS, TH.
17.015   SR   1927/ Emigratie naar Suriname [Emigration to Surinam]. *W I G* 9:137-151.
                 28   [7,66]   [*COL*]

LIND, ANDREW W.
15.027   JM   1958 Adjustment patterns among the Jamaican Chinese.

LONG, EDWARD E.
50.084   BG   1925 British Guiana and Indian immigration.

LOWENTHAL, DAVID & COMITAS, LAMBROS
43.102   MS   1962 Emigration and depopulation: some neglected aspects of population geography.

McCONNEY, E. J., comp.
17.016   BB   1963 Prisoners of the '45 rising. *J Barb Mus Hist Soc* 31(2), May: 73-90. [5,37]   [*AMN*]

MASSON, GEORGE H.
28.354   TR   1922 The treatment of ankylostomiasis on the high seas by the intensive method of thymol administration.

MAUNDER, W. F.

17.017   JM   1955 The new Jamaican emigration. *Social Econ Stud* 4(1), Mar.: 38-63.
                                                                                    [*RIS*]

MENKMAN, W. R.

7.043   SR   1927/ Dokteren over de West [Attempt to improve the West].
              28
17.018   SR   1927/ Nog een emigratie van Nederlanders naar Suriname [Another emigra-
              28   tion of Dutch people to Surinam]. *W I G* 9: 213-229. [7,46]   [*COL*]
17.019   NC   1937 Landverhuizing naar de tropen of aansluiting bij Duitschland [Immi-
                   gration to the tropics or affiliation with Germany]. *W I G* 19: 171-
                   175.   [*COL*]

MINTZ, SIDNEY W.

17.020   SC   1955 Puerto Rican emigration: a threefold comparison. *Social Econ Stud*
                   4(4), Dec.: 311-325. [19]   [*RIS*]

NEHAUL, B. B. G.

28.393   BG   1955 Influence of Indian immigration.

PROUDFOOT, MALCOLM J.

17.021   GC   1950 POPULATION MOVEMENTS IN THE CARIBBEAN. Port of Spain, Caribbean
                   Commission, 187p. [66]   [*COL*]

REUBENS, EDWIN P.

17.022   BC   [n.d.] MIGRATION AND DEVELOPMENT IN THE WEST INDIES. Mona, Institute of
                   Social and Economic Research, University College of the West In-
                   dies, 84p. (Studies in federal economics no. 3.)   [*RIS*]

ROBERTS, GEORGE WOODROW

17.023   BC   1954 Immigration of Africans into the British Caribbean. *Popul Stud* 7(3),
                   Mar.: 235-262. [5,6,46]   [*COL*]
17.024   BB   1955 Emigration from the island of Barbados. *Social Econ Stud* 4(3), Sept.:
                   245-288.   [*RIS*]
7.068   BC   1960 Movements in population and the labour force.

ROBERTS, GEORGE WOODROW & MILLS, D. O.

17.025   JM   1958 Study of external migration affecting Jamaica: 1953-55. *Social Econ
                   Stud* 7(2), June: suppl. (126p.)   [*RIS*]

ROMER, R.

28.440   SR   1919/ Sanitaire beschouwing in verband met immigraties van werkkrachten
              20   in Suriname [Essay on sanitation in connection with the immigration
                   of labor forces into Surinam].

ROSEN, JOSEPH A.

66.124   BG   1939 Problem of large scale settlement of refugees from middle European
                   countries in British Guiana.

SENIOR, CLARENCE

17.026   SC   1947 THE PUERTO RICAN MIGRANT IN ST. CROIX. Rio Piedras, P.R., Social
                   Science Research Center, University of Puerto Rico, 42p. [19] [*RIS*]

SNELLEMAN, J. F.
17.027   SR   1920/ Chineesche immigranten in Suriname [Chinese immigrants to Suri-
          21   nam]. *W I G* 2: 225-248. [15]   [*COL*]

STEMBRIDGE, E. C.
50.120   BG   1914 Indian immigration in British Guiana.

SUMMIT, ALPHONS
15.039   SR   1940 The Jews of Surinam.

SWAYNE, Sir ERIC, J. E.
50.121   BH   1910 India and British Honduras.

SWELLENGREBEL, N. H.
17.028   SR   1940 Over de vraag of een proefneming tot vestiging van politieke uit-
                gewekenen in Suriname hygienisch te verantwoorden is [On the
                question whether an attempt to settle political refugees in Surinam
                is advisable from a hygienic viewpoint]. *W I G* 22: 65-82. [27,28]
                                                                                          [*COL*]

VERKADE-CARTIER van DISSEL, E. F.
7.080   SR   1937 DE MOGELIJKHEID VAN LANDBOUW-KOLONISATIE VOOR BLANKEN IN SURI-
                NAME [THE POSSIBILITY OF AGRICULTURAL SETTLEMENT FOR WHITES IN
                SURINAM].

VIGNOLS, LEON
50.124   FC   1928 Les Antilles Francaises sous l'Ancien Régime: Aspects économi-
                ques et sociaux: L'institution des engagés (1626-1774) [The French
                Antilles under the old regime: Economic and social aspects: The
                institution of bonded servants (1626-1774)].

VINK, G. J.
17.029   SR   1941 Over de mogelijkheid van kolonisatie van blanken in Suriname [On
                the possibility of colonization of whites in Surinam]. *Tijdschr Ned
                Aar Genoot* 2d ser., 58(5): 675-692. [42]   [*AGS*]

Chapter 18

WEST INDIANS ABROAD

ARCHIBALD, CHARLES H.
17.001   BC   1961 How many immigrants?

BANTON, MICHAEL
18.001   BC   1953 The changing position of the Negro in Britain. *Phylon* 14(1), 1st quarter: 74-83.   [*COL*]
18.002   BC   1953 The economic and social position of Negro immigrants in Britain. *Sociol Rev* new ser., 1(2), Dec.: 43-62.   [*COL*]
18.003   BC   1953 Recent migration from West Africa and the West Indies to the United Kingdom. *Popul Stud* 7(1), July: 2-13.   [*COL*]
18.004   BC   1955 THE COLOURED QUARTER: NEGRO IMMIGRANTS IN AN ENGLISH CITY. London, Jonathan Cape, 253p.   [*SCH*]
18.005   BC   1960 WHITE AND COLOURED: THE BEHAVIOUR OF BRITISH PEOPLE TOWARDS COLOURED IMMIGRANTS. New Brunswick, N.J., Rutgers University Press, 223p.   [*RIS*]

BAYLISS, F. J. & COATES, J. B.
18.006   BC   1965 West Indians at work in Nottingham. *Race* 7(2), Oct.: 156-166.   [50]
   [*RIS*]

BENTZ, DOROTHY
25.008   BB   1938 American English as spoken by the Barbadians.

CALLEY, MALCOLM J. C.
18.007   BC   1962 Pentecostal sects among West Indian migrants. *Race* 3(2), May: 55-64. [23]   [*COL*]

CAREY, A. T.
18.008   GC   1956 COLONIAL STUDENTS: A STUDY OF THE SOCIAL ADAPTATION OF COLONIAL STUDENTS IN LONDON. London, Secker and Warburg, 267p.   [*RIS*]

CECIL, C. H.
18.009   JM   1935 The Maroons in Canada. *Can-W I Mag* 24(10), Sept.: 23-25. [5,11]
   [*NYP*]

COLLIER, H. C.
11.007   JM   1939 The Maroons of Jamaica.
18.010   BB   1941 Barbados answers the call. *Can-W I Mag* 30(10), Oct.: 17,24. [*NYP*]

COLLINS, SYDNEY

18.011   BC   1952 Social processes integrating coloured people in Britain, by Sidney Collins. *Br J Sociol* 3(1), Mar.: 20-29.   [*COL*]

18.012   BC   1957 Coloured minorities in Britain: studies in British race relations based on African, West Indian, and Asiatic immigrants. London, Lutterworth Press, 258p.   [*NYP*]

CUMPER, GEORGE E.

18.013   BB   1957 Working class emigration from Barbados to the United Kingdom, 1955. *Social Econ Stud* 6(1), Mar.: 76-83.   [*RIS*]

DAVISON, R. B.

18.014   BC   1962 West Indian Migrants: the social and economic facts of migrations from the British West Indies. Issued under the auspices of the Institute of Race Relations. London, Oxford University Press, 89p.   [*RIS*]

18.015   JM   1964 Commonwealth immigrants. Issued under the auspices of the Institute of Race Relations. London, Oxford University Press, 87p.   [*RIS*]

DRAKE, St. CLAIR

18.016   BC   1955 The colour problem in Britain. *Sociol Rev* 3(2), Dec.: 197-217. [*COL*]

EGGINTON, JOYCE

18.017   BC   1957 They seek a living. London, Hutchinson, 192p.

EMBRA, SHIRLEY

18.018   BC   1959 Caribbean students club. *Can-W I Mag* 49(2), Feb.: 15-16. [32]   [*NYP*]

FANON, FRANTZ

16.008   FA   1952 Peau noire, masques blancs [Black skin, white masks].

FIGUEROA, JOHN JOSEPH

18.019   BC   1957 Exiles from the Caribbean. *Commonweal* 65(16), Jan. 18: 402-404.   [*COL*]

18.020   BC   1958 British West Indian immigration to Great Britain. *Car Q* 5(2), Feb.: 116-120.   [*RIS*]

FLOCH, HERVE ALEXANDRE

28.175   FG   1956 Le traitement suppressif du paludisme chez les immigrants en Guyane Francaise [Medical control of malaria among the immigrants in French Guiana].

GLASS, RUTH

18.021   BC   1960 Newcomers: the West Indians in London. London, Allen and Unwin, 278p.   [*COL*]

GRIFFITH, J. A. G.

18.022   BC   1960 Legal aspects of immigration. *In* GRIFFITH, J.A.G., et al. Coloured immigrants in Britain. London, Oxford University Press, p.159-177. [37]   [*RIS*]

GRIFFITH, J. A. G., et al.

18.023   BC   1960 Coloured immigrants in Britain. Issued under the auspices of the Institute of Race Relations. London, Oxford University Press, 225p.   [*RIS*]

HANDELMAN, DON

18.024   GC   1964   VOLUNTARY ASSOCIATIONS AMONG WEST INDIANS IN MONTREAL. M.A. thesis, McGill University, 180p. [8]

HEIDE, H. ter

18.025   BC   1963   West Indian migration to Great Britain. *N W I G* 43(1), Sept.: 75-88.   [*RIS*]

HENDERSON, JUDITH

18.026   BC   1960   A sociological report. *In* GRIFFITH, J.A.G., et al. COLOURED IM-MIGRANTS IN BRITAIN. London, Oxford University Press, p.47-121.   [*RIS*]

HILL, CLIFFORD S.

18.027   BC   1958   BLACK AND WHITE IN HARMONY: THE DRAMA OF WEST INDIANS IN THE BIG CITY FROM A LONDON MINISTER'S NOTEBOOK. London, Hodder and Stoughton, 119p.   [*NYP*]

18.028   BC   1963   WEST INDIAN MIGRANTS AND THE LONDON CHURCHES. Issued under the auspices of the Institute of Race Relations. London, Oxford University Press, 89p. [23]   [*RIS*]

HUXLEY, ELSPETH

18.029   BC   1964   Settlers in Britain: blacks next door. *Punch* 246(6438), Jan. 29: 154-157.   [*NYP*]

HYNDMAN, ALBERT

18.030   BC   1960   The West Indian in London. *In* RUCK, S.K., ed. THE WEST INDIAN COMES TO ENGLAND. London, Routledge & Kegan Paul, p.65-154.   [*RIS*]

JONES, CLAUDIA

18.031   BC   1964   The Caribbean community in Britain. *Freedomways* 4(3), Summer: 341-357. [17]   [*RIS*]

KIEV, ARI

31.042   JM   1963   Beliefs and delusions of West Indian immigrants to London.

31.043   BC   1964   Psychiatric illness among West Indians in London.

18.032   BC   1964   Psychotherapeutic aspects of Pentecostal sects among West Indian immigrants to England. *Br J Sociol* 15(2), June: 129-138. [23, 31]   [*RIS*]

18.033   BC   1965   Psychiatric morbidity of West Indian immigrants in an urban group practice. *Br J Psych* 111(470), Jan.: 51-56. [31]   [*RIS*]

LEE, FRANK F.

18.034   BC   1959   Race conflict in Britain. *Fellowship* 25(13), July 1: 13-16.   [*COL*]

18.035   BC   1960   A comparative analysis of coloured grade school children: Negroes in the U.S. and West Indians in Britain. *J Educ Sociol* 34(3), Nov.: 127-136. [32]   [*RIS*]

18.036   BC   1960   Racial patterns in a British city: an institutional approach. *Phylon* 21(1), Spring: 40-50.   [*RIS*]

18.037   BC   1960   Social controls in British race relations. *Sociol Soc Res* 44(5), May-June: 326-334.   [*RIS*]

LEE, ROSEMARY

18.038   BC   1965 The education of immigrant children in England. *Race* 7(2), Oct.:
                      131-145. [32]   [*RIS*]

LEEFMANS, J.

18.039   SR   1958 Ambassadeurs zonder geloofsbrieven [Ambassadors without creden-
                      tials].*In* WALLE, J. van de & WIT, H. de, eds. SURINAME IN STROOM-
                      LIJNEN. Amsterdam, Wereld Bibliotheek, p.104-116.

LEEUWIN, R. S.

18.040   SR   1962 Microfilaraemia in Surinamese living in Amsterdam. *Trop Geogr Med*
                      14(4), Dec.: 355-360. [28]   [*COL*]

LEWIS, E. R.

18.041   BC   [n.d.] THE WHITES AND THE COLOUREDS. London, Susan Tully, 13p.   [*RIS*]

LITTLE, KENNETH L.

18.042   BC   1948 NEGROES IN BRITAIN; A STUDY OF RACIAL RELATIONS IN ENGLISH SO-
                      CIETY. London, Kegan Paul, Trench, Trubner & Co., 292p.   [*RIS*]
18.043   BC   1958 Integration without tears. *New Stsm* 56(1436), Sept. 20: 370.   [*COL*]

LONGABAUGH, RICHARD HAROLD

18.044   BB   1962 THE DESCRIPTION OF MOTHER-CHILD INTERACTION. Ph.D. dissertation,
                      Harvard University, 314p.   [8, 67]   [*RIS*]

MacINNES, COLIN

18.045   BC   1956 Short guide for Jumbles (to the life of their coloured brethren in Eng-
                      land). *Twen Cent* 159(949), Mar.: 247-254.   [*COL*]

MADDOX, H.

18.046   BC   1960 The assimilation of Negroes in a dockland area in Britain. *Sociol
                      Rev* 8(1), July: 5-15.   [*COL*]

MALCIOLN, JOSE V.

18.047   GC   1964 Panamá. *Freedomways* 4(3), Summer: 383-391.   [*RIS*]

MANLEY, DOUGLAS R.

18.048   BC   1955 The formal associations of a Negro community in Britain. *Social
                      Econ Stud* 4(3), Sept.: 231-244.   [*RIS*]
18.049   BC   1960 The West Indian background. *In* RUCK, S.K., ed. THE WEST INDIAN
                      COMES TO ENGLAND.   London, Routledge & Kegan Paul, p.3-50. [*RIS*]

MORRIS, MERVYN

18.050   BC   1962 A West Indian student in England (a personal reaction). *Car Q* 8(4),
                      Dec.: 17-29.   [*RIS*]

NORTHCOTT, CECIL

18.051   BC   1957 The colour problem in Britain. *Contemp Rev* 191, Feb.: 91-93.   [*COL*]

OTTLEY, ROI

18.052   GC   1943 NEW WORLD A'COMING. New York, Literary Classics, Inc., 364p.   [*COL*]

PATTERSON, SHEILA

18.053   BC   1960   A recent West Indian immigrant group in Britain. *Race* 1(2), May: 27-39.   [*COL*]

18.054   BC   1963   DARK STRANGERS: A SOCIOLOGICAL STUDY OF THE ABSORPTION OF A RECENT WEST INDIAN MIGRANT GROUP IN BRIXTON, SOUTH LONDON. London, Tavistick Publications, 470p. [19]   [*COL*]

PEACH, CERI

18.055   BC   1965   West Indian migration to Britain: the economic factors. *Race* 7(1), July: 31-46.   [*RIS*]

PILKINGTON, FREDERICK

18.056   JM   1951   Jamaicans in England. *Contemp Rev* 179, Mar.: 168-170.   [*COL*]

RAPHAEL, LENNOX

18.057   BC   1964   West Indians and Afro-Americans. *Freedomways* 4(3), Summer: 438-445.   [*RIS*]

REID, IRA deA.

18.058   GC   1940   Race, migration and citizenship: an essay on the interrelations of the West Indian Negro and the United States Negro. *In* WESLEY, CHARLES H., ed. THE NEGRO IN THE AMERICAS. Washington, D.C., Graduate School, Division of the Social Sciences, Howard University, p.55-71.

RICHMOND, ANTHONY H.

18.059   BC   1954   COLOUR PREJUDICE IN BRITAIN: A STUDY OF WEST INDIAN WORKERS IN LIVERPOOL, 1941-1951. London, Routledge and Kegan Paul, 184p.
                                                                                [*COL*]

18.060   BC   1956   Immigration as a social process: the case of coloured colonials in the U.K. *Social Econ Stud* 5(2), June: 185-201.   [*RIS*]

18.061   BC   1961   THE COLOUR PROBLEM. Rev. ed. [Baltimore], Penguin Books, 374p.
                                                                                [*RIS*]

RUCK, S. K., ed.

18.062   BC   1960   THE WEST INDIAN COMES TO ENGLAND: A REPORT PREPARED FOR THE TRUSTEES OF THE LONDON PAROCHIAL CHARITIES BY THE FAMILY WELFARE ASSOCIATION. London, Routledge & Kegan Paul, 187p.   [*RIS*]

SECRETAIN, ROGER

18.063   FA   1935   Les Antillais en France [French West Indians in France]. *In* DENIS, SERGE, ed. NOS ANTILLES. Orléans, Luzeray, p.278-286.   [*AGS*]

SENIOR, CLARENCE & MANLEY, DOUGLAS

18.064   JM   1955   A REPORT ON JAMAICAN MIGRATION TO GREAT BRITAIN. Kingston, Printed by the Govt. Printer, 67p.   [*RIS*]

18.065   JM   1956   THE WEST INDIAN IN BRITAIN. London, Fabian Colonial Bureau, 29p. (Fabian research series 179.)   [*RIS*]

SOUZA, IVO de

18.066   BC   1960   Arrival. *In* RUCK, S.K., ed. THE WEST INDIAN COMES TO ENGLAND. London, Routledge & Kegan Paul, p.51-64.   [*RIS*]

TANCOCK, CATHERINE BRIDGET
18.067   BB   1961 A STUDY OF HOUSEHOLD STRUCTURE AND CHILD TRAINING IN A LOWER
                      CLASS BARBADIAN GROUP. Ed.D. project, Harvard University, 167p.
                      [9,31]   [*RIS*]

WOOD, DONALD M.
18.068   BC   1960 A general survey. *In* GRIFFITH, J.A.G., et al. COLOURED IMMI-
                      GRANTS IN BRITAIN. London, Oxford University Press, p.3-43.   [*RIS*]
18.069   BC   1962 The migrants. *Statist* 176(4391), May 4: 315-316.   [*COL*]

WOOD, DONALD M.; HOOD, JESSIE; THOMPSON, K. ALDOUS & W. B.
18.070   BC   1960 The West Indian in the provinces. *In* RUCK, S.K., ed. THE WEST
                      INDIAN COMES TO ENGLAND. London, Routledge & Kegan Paul, p.155-
                      167.   [*RIS*]

ELEMENTS
OF
CULTURE

Chapter 19

CULTURAL CONTINUITIES AND ACCULTURATION

ADAM, LUCIEN
26.001   WW   1906 Le caraïbe du Honduras et le caraïbe des îles [The Carib [language] of Honduras and the Carib of the islands].

BASTIEN, REMY
19.001   GC   1964 Procesos de aculturacion en las Antillas [Processes of acculturation in the Antilles. *Revta Indias* 95-96, Jan.-June: 177-196. [*RIS*]

BECKWITH, MARTHA WARREN
23.005   JM   1924 THE HUSSAY FESTIVAL IN JAMAICA.

BECKWITH, MARTHA WARREN & ROBERTS, HELEN H.
23.005   JM   1923 CHRISTMAS MUMMINGS IN JAMAICA.

BENOIST, JEAN
56.005   MT   1959 Individualisme et traditions techniques chez les pêcheurs martiniquais [Individualism and technical traditions among Martinique fishermen].

BERGHE, PIERRE L. van den
16.004   GC   1963 Racialism and assimilation in Africa and the Americas.

BOWEN, CALVIN
22.013   JM   1954 Jamaica's John Canoe.

BRAITHWAITE, LLOYD E.
8.002   TR   1953 Social stratification in Trinidad.
10.006   TR   1954 Cultural integration in Trinidad.

BRUTON, J. G.
19.002   JM   1945 Influencias espagñoles sobre el inglés de Jamaica [Spanish influences on Jamaican English]. *Boln Inst Caro Cuerva* 1(2), May-Aug.: 375-376. [25]   [*NYP*]

BUNEL, FRANCOIS
19.003   GD   [1962?] RECUEIL DE SCÈNES VÉCUES À LA GUADELOUPE [TRUE EPISODES OF GUADELOUPE—A MISCELLANY]. Pointe-à-Pitre, Guad., Impr. Parisienne Anibal Lautric.   [25]   [*RIS*]

BUTT, AUDREY J.

13.009   BG   1957 The Mazaruni scorpion (a study of the symbolic significance of tattoo patterns among the Akawaio).

13.010   BG   1958 Secondary urn burial among the Akawaio of British Guiana.

BYAS, VINCENT W.

27.011   MT   1943 Ethnologic aspects of the Martinique Creole.

CAMERON, N. E.

11.005   GC   1929/ THE EVOLUTION OF THE NEGRO.
                  34

CAMERON, NORMAN E.

11.006   GC   1950 The background of the Afro-American.

CARR, ANDREW T.

19.004   TR   1953 A Rada community in Trinidad. *Car Q* 3(1): 36-54. [11,23]   [*RIS*]

22.018   TR   1956 Pierrot Grenade.

CASSIDY, FREDERIC G.

25.012   JM   1957 Iteration as a word-forming device in Jamaican folk speech.

25.015   JM   1961 Some footnotes on the "junjo" question.

CECIL, C. H.

22.020   BC   1937 I—you, and the Devil take the loser!

COLLIER, H. C.

22.024   BC   1935 "Warri," an African game transplanted to the West Indies.

22.026   TR   1939 Trinidad fantasia.

22.030   TR   1943 Carnival capers in calypso land.

COMITAS, LAMBROS

56.017   JM   1962 FISHERMEN AND COOPERATION IN RURAL JAMAICA.

COMVALIUS, TH. A. C.

22.034   SR   1946 Oud-Surinaamsche rhythmische dansen in dienst van de lichamelijke opvoeding [Old Surinamese rhythmic dances in the service of physical education].

CONNELL, NEVILLE

19.005   BC   1957 Punch drinking and its accessories. *J Barb Mus Hist Soc* 25(1), Nov.: 1-17. [30]   [*AMN*]

COULTHARD, G. R.

20.003   FA   1961 The French West Indian background of negritude.

CREGAN, K. H.

13.013   BG   1931 Blowpipes, spears, bows and arrows, and clubs: weapons of the aboriginals of Guiana.

CROWLEY, DANIEL JOHN

53.007   JM/   1953 American credit institutions of Yoruba type.
          TR

12.005   TR   1954 East Indian festivals in Trinidad life.

22.038	TR	1954	THE MEANINGS OF CARNIVAL.
23.028	SL	1955	Festivals of the calendar in St. Lucia.
22.040	TR	1956	The midnight robbers.
19.006	SL	1956	Naming customs in St. Lucia. *Social Econ Stud* 5(1), Mar.: 87-92: [9] [RIS]
22.041	TR	1956	The traditional masques of Carnival.
10.010	TR	1957	Plural and differential acculturation in Trinidad.
22.042	SL	1957	Song and dance in St. Lucia.
24.020	SL	1958	La Rose and La Marguerite Societies in St. Lucia.
10.011	GC	1960	Cultural assimilation in a multiracial society.
24.021	GC	1962	Negro folklore: an Africanist's view.

CRUICKSHANK, J. GRAHAM

25.017	BB	1911	Negro English, with reference particularly in Barbados.
25.018	BG/ BB	1916	"BLACK TALK": BEING NOTES ON NEGRO DIALECT IN BRITISH GUIANA, WITH (INEVITABLY) A CHAPTER ON THE VERNACULAR OF BARBADOS.
19.007	BG	1917	Among the "Aku" (Yoruba) in Canal No. 1, West Bank, Demerara River. *Timehri* 3d ser., 4(21), June: 70-82. [11] [AMN]
22.046	BG	1924	An African dance in the colony.
19.008	BG	1929	Negro games. *Man* 29(141), Oct.: 179-180. [14,22] [COL]
8.015	BG	1933	"Good time" in slavery days.

CUNDALL, FRANK

| 19.009 | BB | 1924 | An historic dripstone. *W I Comm Circ* 39(683), Dec. 4: 481-482. [NYP] |
| 40.043 | JM | 1939 | PLACE-NAMES OF JAMAICA. Rev. ed. |

DAM, THEODORE van

| 22.049 | GC | 1954 | The influence of the West African songs of derision in the New World. |

DARK, PHILIP J. C.

| 22.051 | SR | 1954 | BUSH NEGRO ART: AN AFRICAN ART IN THE AMERICAS. |

DAVIDS, LEO

| 9.006 | BG/ TR | 1964 | The East Indian family overseas. |

DeCAMP, DAVID

| 19.010 | JM | 1960 | Cart names in Jamaica. *Names* 8(1), Mar.: 15-23. [AGS] |

DELAFOSSE, MAURICE

| 14.003 | SR | 1925 | Survivances africaines chez les Nègres "Bosch" de la Guyane [African survivals among the Bush Negroes of Guiana]. |

DESPRES, LEO A.

| 67.003 | BG | 1964 | The implications of nationalist politics in British Guiana for the development of cultural theory. |

DOLPHIN, CELESTE

| 52.023 | BG | 1959 | Good afternoon, schools. |

DONICIE, A. C.

| 19.011 | SR | 1953 | Iets over de taal en de sprookjes van Suriname [On the language and the fairy-tales of Surinam]. *W I G* 33: 153-173. [14,24,25] [COL] |

DORAN, EDWIN BEAL, Jr.
35.013   GC   1962 The West Indian hip-roofed cottage.

DRIMMELEN, C. van
11.009   SR   1925/ De Neger en zijn cultuur geschiedenis [The Negro and his cultural
              26 history].

EGAN, CECILIA M.
23.040   MT   1943 Martinique—the isle of those who return.

ESPINET, CHARLES S.
22.058   TR   1953 Masquerade—origin and development of Trinidad's Carnival.

ESPINET, CHARLES S. & PITTS, HARRY
22.059   TR   1944 LAND OF THE CALYPSO: THE ORIGIN AND DEVELOPMENT OF TRINIDAD'S
              FOLK SONG.

FOCK, NIELS
13.022   BG   1958 Cultural aspects and social functions of the "oho" institution
              among the Waiwai.
9.007   GG   1960 South American birth customs in theory and practice.

FORTUNE, ROGER
30.025   GC   1961 Les bons plats de chez nous [Our tasty dishes].

FRAMPTON, H. M.
22.063   DM   1957 Carnival time in Dominica.

FRIED, MORTON H.
15.017   BG   1956 Some observations on the Chinese in British Guiana.

GARDNER, M. M.
22.064   TR   1954 The greatest show of its kind on earth—Trinidad's Carnival.

GARRETT, CLARA MAUDE
19.012   JM   1935 Caribbean Christmas. *Can-W I Mag* 25(1), Dec.: 22-23. [23]   [*NYP*]

GOODMAN, EILEEN
19.013   BC   1953 What's in a name?—millions! *Can-W I Mag* 43(5), May: 9, 11.   [*NYP*]

GUERIN, DANIEL
19.014   GC   1956 Un futur pour les Antilles? [A future for the Antilles?]   *Présence
              Afr* 6, Feb.-Mar.: 20-27. [23,25]   [*COL*]

HAWEIS, STEPHEN
19.015   DM   1947 The death of a basket. *Can-W I Mag* 37(3), May: 21,23. [13]   [*NYP*]

HEARNE, JOHN
19.016   JM   1963 European heritage and Asian influence in Jamaica. *In* OUR HERITAGE.
              Kingston, Dept. of Extra-mural Studies, University of the West In-
              dies, p.7-37. (Public affairs in Jamaica, no. 1.) [5]   [*RIS*]

HENRIQUES, FERNANDO
9.015   JM   1951 Kinship and death in Jamaica.

HENRY, BESSIE M.

49.042 BV 1957 English ceramics in the British Virgin Islands.

HERSKOVITS, MELVILLE JEAN

19.017 SR 1928/ Preliminary report of an ethnological expedition to Suriname, 1928.
29 *W I G* 10: 385-390. [14] [*COL*]

19.018 SR 1929 Adjiboto, an African game of the Bush-Negroes of Dutch Guiana.
Man 29(7), July: 122-127. [14,22] [*COL*]

22.072 GC 1932 Wari in the New World.

19.019 GC 1938 Les noirs du Nouveau Monde: sujet de recherches africanistes [The
New World Negroes: a subject for Africanist research]. *J Soc Afr*
8(1): 65-82. [11,67] [*AMN*]

22.073 GC 1941 El estudio de la música negra en el hemisferio occidental [The study
of Negro music in the Western Hemisphere].

22.074 GC 1941 Patterns of Negro music.

67.009 GC 1946 Problem, method and theory in Afroamerican studies.

67.010 GC 1948 The contribution of Afroamerican studies to Africanist research.

67.011 GC 1951 The present status and needs of Afroamerican research.

67.012 GC 1960 The ahistorical approach to Afroamerican studies: a critique.

HERSKOVITS, MELVILLE JEAN & FRANCES S.

22.076 SR 1930 Bush-Negro art.

14.006 SR 1934 REBEL DESTINY: AMONG THE BUSH NEGROES OF DUTCH GUIANA.

11.012 TR 1947 TRINIDAD VILLAGE.

HILL, LUKE M.

36.008 BG 1911 Nomenclature of Georgetown: its streets and districts.

HOGG, DONALD WILLIAM

23.064 JM 1956 A West Indian shepherd.

23.065 JM 1960 The Convince Cult in Jamaica.

23.067 JM 1963 JAMAICAN RELIGION: A STUDY IN VARIATIONS.

HOLMER, NILS M.

19.020 GC 1960 Indian place names in South America and the Antilles. *Names* 8(3),
Sept.: 133-149; 8(4), Dec.: 197-219;
1961 9(1), Mar.: 37-52. [13,26,40] [*RIS*]

HOROWITZ, MICHAEL M.

23.068 MT 1963 The worship of South Indian deities in Martinique.

HOROWITZ, MICHAEL M. & KLASS, MORTON

23.069 MT 1961 The Martiniquan East Indian cult of Maldevidan.

HURAULT, JEAN

19.021 FG 1960 Histoire des noirs réfugiés Boni de la Guyane Francaise [History of
the black Boni refugees of French Guiana]. *Rev Fr Hist O-M* 47
(166): 76-137. [5,14] [*RIS*]

14.007 FG 1961 Canots africains en Guyane [African canoes in Guiana].

HURSTON, ZORA NEALE

19.022 JM 1938 TELL MY HORSE. Philadelphia, J.B. Lippincott, 301p. [*AGS*]

JAMES, ERIC GEORGE

37.208   JM   1956   ADMINISTRATIVE INSTITUTIONS AND SOCIAL CHANGE IN JAMAICA, BRITISH
                          WEST INDIES—A STUDY IN CULTURAL ADAPTATION.

JUNKER, L.

14.011   SR   1924/ Godsdienst, zeden en gebruiken der Boschenegers [Religion, man-
                    25   ners and customs of the Bush Negroes].

KAHN, MORTON CHARLES

14.015   SR   1928   The Bush Negroes of Dutch Guiana.
22.084   SR   1931   Art of the Dutch Guiana Bush Negro.
14.017   SR   1931   DJUKA, THE BUSH NEGROES OF DUTCH GUIANA.
19.023   SR   1939   Africa's lost tribes in South America. *Nat Hist* 43(4),   Apr. 209-
                          215, 232. [14]   [*AGS*]
19.024   SR   1954   Little Africa in America: the Bush Negroes. *Américas* 6(10), Oct.:
                          6-8, 41-43. [14]   [*AGS*]
19.025   SR   1959   The Djukas of Surinam. *Explor J* 37(1), Feb.: 12-18. [14]   [*AGS*]

KLASS, MORTON

12.013   TR   1961   EAST INDIANS IN TRINIDAD: A STUDY OF CULTURAL PERSISTENCE.

KLERK, CORNELIS JOHANNES MARIA de

23.084   SR   1951   CULTUS EN RITUEEL VAN HET ORTHODOXE HINDOEÏSME IN SURINAME
                          [CULTS AND RITUAL OF ORTHODOX HINDUISM IN SURINAM].
50.074   SR   1953   De immigratie der Hindoestanen in Suriname [The immigration of
                          Hindus to Surinam].

KRUIJER, GERARDUS JOHANNES

23.092   NA   1953   Kerk en religie op de Bovenwindse Eilanden der Nederlandse Antil-
                          len [Church and religion of the Windward Islands of the Netherlands
                          Antilles].

KUNIKE, HUGO

19.026   GG   1912   Der Fisch als Fruchtbarkeitssymbol bei den Waldindianern Sud-
                          amerikas [The fish as a fertility symbol among the South American
                          forest Indians]. *Anthropos* 7(1-2), Jan.-Apr.: 206-229. [13, 23] [*AMN*]

LATOUR, M. D.

20.042   CU   1937/ Cuenta di Nanzi [Tales of Anansi].
                    40

LEACH, MacEDWARD

24.043   JM   1961   Jamaican duppy lore.

LEIRIS, MICHEL

19.027   FA   1950   Martinique, Guadeloupe, Haiti. *Temps Mod* 5(52), Feb.: 1345-1368.
                          [11]   [*COL*]

LEKIS, LISA

22.087   GC   1955   The dance as an expression of Caribbean folklore.

LELYVELD, TH. van

19.028   SR   1919   De kleeding der Surinaamsche bevolkingsgroepen [The way of dress-
                          ing of the Surinam population groups]. *W I G* 1(1): 247-268, 458-470;
                          1919/ 1(2): 20-34, 125-143. [10]   [*COL*]
                    20

LESCHALOUPE, CONSTANCE MARIE
22.088   TR   1953   Carnival in Trinidad—masquerades and steelbands.

LEWIS, GORDON K.
37.225   GC   1961   The Caribbean: colonization and culture.

LICHTVELD, LOU
25.069   SR   1928/ Afrikaansche resten in de Creolentaal van Suriname [African surviv-
           30   als in the Creole language of Surinam].
29.015   SR   1930/ Een Afrikaansch bijgeloof: snetji-koti [An African superstition:
           31   "snakebite cure"].
24.044   SR   1930/ Op zoek naar de spin [Looking for the spider].
           31

LIER, WILLEM F. van
14.021   SR   1921/ Bij de Aucaners [Among the Aucanians].
           23

LINDBLOM, K. G.
19.029   GC   1924   Uber eine alte ethnographische Sammlung aus dem nördlichsten Süd-
                amerika im Ethnographischen Reichsmuseum in Stockholm [On an
                old ethnographic collection from northernmost South America in the
                National Ethnographic Museum in Stockholm].   *Ymer* 44(2): 153-180.
                                                                             [*COL*]
22.089   SR   1926   EINIGE DETAILS IN DER ORNAMENTIK DER BUSCHNEGER SURINAMS [SOME
                DETAILS OF THE ORNAMENTS OF THE BUSH NEGROES OF SURINAM].

McELENEY, J. J.
19.030   JM   1953   From Jamaica to Canada.   *Can-W I Mag* 43(5), May: 5-7.   [*NYP*]

MALEFIJT, ANNEMARIE de WAAL
15.029   SR   1963   THE JAVANESE OF SURINAM: SEGMENT OF A PLURAL SOCIETY.
23.100   SR   1964   Animism and Islam among the Javanese in Surinam.

MATTHEWS, Dom BASIL
9.026   TR   1953   CRISIS OF THE WEST INDIAN FAMILY.

MAY, ARTHUR J.
35.031   BC   1933   The architecture of the West Indies.

MEIDEN, J. A. van der
23.103   SR   1960   Kerken, tempels en heiligdommen in Suriname [Churches, temples
                and sacred places in Surinam].

MERRIAM, A. P.; WHINERY, SARA & FRED, B. G.
22.098   TR   1956   Songs of a Rada community in Trinidad.

MERRILL, GORDON CLARK
19.031   BC   1961   The survival of the past in the West Indies.   *In* LOWENTHAL,
                DAVID, ed.   THE WEST INDIES FEDERATION.   New York, Columbia
                University Press, p.17-34.   [5,38,44,66]   [*RIS*]

MINTZ, SIDNEY W.

17.020   SC   1955 Puerto Rican emigration: a threefold comparison.
67.015   GC   1964 Melville J. Herskovits and Caribbean studies: a retrospective tribute.

MISCHEL, FRANCES
23.106   TR   1957 African "powers" in Trinidad: the Shango cult.

MOORE, JOSEPH GRAESSLE
23.107   JM   1953 RELIGION OF JAMAICAN NEGROES: A STUDY OF AFRO-JAMAICAN ACCUL-
                     TURATION.

MOORE, JOSEPH GRAESSLE & SIMPSON, GEORGE E.
23.108   JM   1957/ A comparative study of acculturation in Morant Bay and West Kings-
                58 ton, Jamaica.

MORPURGO, A. J.
19.032   SR   1958 Legkaart der beschaving [Mosaic of civilization]. In WALLE, J. van
                     de & WIT, H. de, eds. SURINAME IN STROOMLIJNEN. Amsterdam,
                     Wereld Bibliotheek, p.76-85.

MYERS, IRIS
13.053   BG   1944/ The Makushi of British Guiana—a study in culture contact.
                46

NAIDOO, M. B.
12.020   TR   1960 The East Indian in Trinidad—a study of an immigrant community.

NETTLEFORD, REX
19.033   JM   1963 The African connexion—the significance for Jamaica. In OUR HERI-
                     TAGE. Kingston, Dept. of Extra-mural Studies, University of the West
                     Indies, p.39-55. (Public affairs in Jamaica, no. 1.) [5, 11]   [RIS]

NIEHOFF, ARTHUR
12.023   TR   1959 The survival of Hindu institutions in an alien environment.

OLSCHKI, LEONARDO
40.134   GC   1943 The Columbian nomenclature of the Lesser Antilles.

OUDSCHANS DENTZ, FRED
19.034   SR   1955/ De naam van het land Suriname als geslachtsnaam [The name of the
                56 country Surinam as family name]. W I G 36: 65-71.   [COL]

PANHUYS, L. C. van
14.024   SR   1904 About the ornamentation in use by savage tribes in Dutch Guiana.
26.020   SR   1905 Indian words in the Dutch language and in use at Dutch Guiana.
14.025   SR   1906 Näheres über die Ornamente der Naturvölker Surinams [Details on
                     the ornaments of the primitive peoples of Surinam].
14.026   SR   1910 Mitteilungen über surinamsche Ethnographie und Kolonisations-
                     geschichte... [Notes on the ethnography and colonial history of
                     Surinam].
14.027   SR   1934 Die Bedeutung einiger Ornamente der Buschneger von Niederländ-
                     isch Guyane [The significance of some Bush Negroes' ornaments
                     from Dutch Guiana].

19.035   SR   1935/ De grondslag van de wiskunde in Suriname [The foundations of mathe-
                 36   matics in Surinam]. *W I G* 17:149-158. [25]   [COL]

PATTERSON, SHEILA
18.054   BC   1963 DARK STRANGERS: A SOCIOLOGICAL STUDY OF THE ABSORPTION OF A RE-
                     CENT WEST INDIAN MIGRANT GROUP IN BRIXTON, SOUTH LONDON.

PEARSE, ANDREW C.
22.115   TR   1956 Carnival in nineteenth century Trinidad.
67.019   BC   1956 Ethnography and the lay scholar in the Caribbean.

PENARD, F. P. & A. P.
23.120   SR   1913 Surinaamsch bijgeloof: iets over *winti* en andere natuurbegrippen
                     [Surinam superstition: about *winti* and other supernatural notions].
24.065   SR   1926/ Negro riddles from Surinam.
                 27

PHILLIPS, LESLIE H. C.
23.123   BG   1960 Kali-mai puja.

POWRIE, BARBARA E.
20.013   TR   1956 The changing attitude of the coloured middle class towards Carnival.

PROCOPE, BRUCE
22.117   TR   1956 The Dragon Band or Devil Band.
22.118   TR   1959 Ken Morris—metalworker.

RANDEL, WILLIAM
40.142   JM   1960 Survival of pre-English place names in Jamaica.

RAY, MICHAEL
19.036   BG   1934 Black Scots. *Can-W I Mag* 23(11), Oct.: 341-342.   [NYP]

REVERT, EUGENE
24.067   MT   1951 DE QUELQUES ASPECTS DU FOLK-LORE MARTINIQUAIS: LA MAGIE ANTIL-
                     LAISE [ON SOME ASPECTS OF MARTINIQUE FOLKLORE: ANTILLEAN MAGIC].

ROBERTS, HELEN H.
22.120   JM   1924 Some drums and drum rhythms of Jamaica.
22.122   JM   1926 Possible survivals of African song in Jamaica.

RODWAY, JAMES
40.145   BG   1906 The river-names of British Guiana.
45.030   BG   1911 Names of our plantations.
40.146   BG   1911 Our river names.
13.063   BG   1917 Indian charms.

ROTH, WALTER EDMUND
13.067   BG   1921 Some examples of Indian mimicry, fraud and imposture.

RUIZ, R. E.
11.024   GC   1965 A historical perspective on Caribbean Negro life.

SCHIPPER, ARY

22.130   SR   1944/ Enkele opmerkingen over Surinaamsche muziek [Some observations
                 45   about Surinam's music].

SCHWARTZ, BARTON M.

8.051   TR   1963 THE DISSOLUTION OF CASTE IN TRINIDAD.
23.141   TR   1964 Ritual aspects of caste in Trinidad.
37.362   TR   1965 Extra-legal activities of the village pandit in Trinidad.

SEAGA, EDWARD P. G.

29.023   JM   1955 Jamaica's primitive medicine.

SENIOR, CLARENCE

17.026   SC   1947 THE PUERTO RICAN MIGRANT IN ST. CROIX.

SIMMONS, HAROLD F. C.

22.136   SL   1960 Térré bois bois.

SIMPSON, GEORGE EATON

23.146   JM   1950 The acculturative process in Jamaican revivalism.
23.147   JM   1955 Culture change and reintegration found in the cults of West Kings-
                      ton, Jamaica.
23.150   JM   1956 Jamaican revivalist cults.
23.151   JM   1957 The nine night ceremony in Jamaica.
29.024   TR   1962 Folk medicine in Trinidad.
10.041   GC   1962 The peoples and cultures of the Caribbean area.
23.153   TR   1962 The shango cult in Nigeria and in Trinidad.
23.154   TR   1964 The acculturative process in Trinidadian Shango.
23.155   TR   1965 THE SHANGO CULT IN TRINIDAD.

SKINNER, ELLIOTT P.

10.043   BG   1955 ETHNIC INTERACTION IN A BRITISH GUIANA RURAL COMMUNITY: A STUDY
                      OF SECONDARY ACCULTURATION AND GROUP DYNAMICS.

SMITH, M. G.

19.037   GC   1960 The African heritage in the Caribbean. *In* RUBIN, VERA, ed. CAR-
                      IBBEAN STUDIES: A SYMPOSIUM. 2D ED. Seattle, University of Wash-
                      ington Press, p.34-53. [11,67]   [*RIS*]

SMITH, ROBERT JACK

12.032   TR   1963 MUSLIM EAST INDIANS IN TRINIDAD: RETENTION OF ETHNIC IDENTITY
                      UNDER ACCULTURATIVE CONDITIONS.

SNELLEMAN, J. F.

19.038   SR   1928/ De West-Indische zaal in het Museum van het Koloniaal Instituut
                 29   [The West Indian room in the museum of the Colonial Institute]. *WIG*
                      10:149-157. [10]   [*COL*]

SOLIEN, NANCIE L.

13.074   JM/   1959 West Indian characteristics of the Black Carib.
          BH/
          TR

SPECKMANN, JOHAN DIRK

10.050   SR   1963 The Indian group in the segmented society of Surinam.

TAYLOR, DOUGLAS C.

13.083 DM/   1950 The meaning of dietary and occupational restrictions among the
        BH   Island Carib.
40.182 DM   1954 Names on Dominica.

THOMPSON, ROBERT WALLACE

24.075 GC   1955/ The mushroom and the parasol: a West Indian riddle.
              56
19.039 GC   1956 Duckanoo—a word and a thing. *Caribbean* 9(10), May: 218-219, 229.
                                                              [*COL*]
25.102 GC   1958 Mushrooms, umbrellas, and black magic: a West Indian linguistic
                problem.

WATERMAN, RICHARD ALAN

22.145 TR   1943 AFRICAN PATTERNS IN TRINIDAD NEGRO MUSIC.

WICKHAM, JOHN

19.040 BC   1958 Growing up in the West Indies. *Shell Trin* 5(2), Mar.: 26-28.

WILLIAMS, JAMES

19.041 BG   1922 The name "Guiana." *W I Comm Circ* 37(612), Mar. 16:127; 37(613),
                Mar. 30:151; 37(614), Apr. 13:173-174. [13]   [*NYP*]
40.220 GG   1923 The name "Guiana."

WILLIAMS, JOSEPH J.

23.172 JM   1932 VOODOOS AND OBEAHS, PHASES OF WEST INDIA WITCHCRAFT.
23.173 JM   1934 PSYCHIC PHENOMENA OF JAMAICA.

WOOD, B. R.

13.093 BG   1944 Curare.

YDE, JENS

13.094 BG   1959 Resist-dyed bark costumes of the Waiwai Indians.

Chapter 20

VALUES AND NORMS

ABRAHAMS, PETER

20.001   JM   [1961?] The influence of ideas. *In* CUMPER, GEORGE, ed. REPORT OF THE CONFERENCE ON SOCIAL DEVELOPMENT IN JAMAICA. Kingston, Standing Committee on Social Services, p.98-100. [21]   [*RIS*]

ALLEYNE, MERVIN C.

25.001   SL   1961 Language and society in St. Lucia.

BAYLEY, GEORGE D.

20.002   BG   1911 Census comicalities. *Timehri* 3d ser., 1(18B), July: 86-88. [7] [*AMN*]

BELL, WENDELL

37.021   JM   1960 Images of the United States and the Soviet Union held by Jamaican elite groups.

37.022   JM   1962 Equality and attitudes of elites in Jamaica.

37.023   JM   1964 JAMAICAN LEADERS: POLITICAL ATTITUDES IN A NEW NATION.

BELL, WENDELL & OXAAL, IVAR

37.024   BC   1964 DECISIONS OF NATIONHOOD: POLITICAL AND SOCIAL DEVELOPMENT IN THE BRITISH CARIBBEAN.

BISWAMITRE, C. R.

12.004   SR   1937 Miskenning [Misjudgment].

BLAKE, JUDITH; STYCOS, J. MAYONE & DAVIS, KINGSLEY

34.006   JM   1961 FAMILY STRUCTURE IN JAMAICA: THE SOCIAL CONTEXT OF REPRODUCTION.

BLOM, F. E. A.

31.011   GC   1963 Conflicting values and cultural identifications facing the Caribbean adolescent today.

BOOY, THEODOOR de

24.009   JM   1915 Certain West Indian superstitions pertaining to celts.

BRATHWAITE, EDWARD

22.014   BC   1963 Roots.

BRAITHWAITE, LLOYD E.
32.029   BC   1958 The development of higher education in the British West Indies.
31.014   GC   1963 The changing social scene.

CHAMBERTRAND, GILBERT de
22.021   FA   1963 Mi io!

COHEN, YEHUDI A.
8.009   JM   1955 Four categories of interpersonal relationships in the family and community in a Jamaican village.

COLERIDGE, P. E.
8.010   SR   1958 Vrouwenleven in Paramaribo [Women's life in Paramaribo].

COULTHARD, G. R.
20.003   FA   1961 The French West Indian background of negritude. *Car Q* 7(3), Dec.: 128-136. [11,19]   [*RIS*]

DAVIDSON, LEWIS
66.036   JM   [1961?] Acceptance of social change.

DUKE, JAMES TAYLOR
20.004   JM   1963 EQUALITARIANISM AMONG EMERGENT ELITES IN A NEW NATION. Ph.D. disseration, University of California, Los Angeles, 265p. [8,32]

ERICKSEN, E. GORDON
7.019   BC   1962 THE WEST INDIES POPULATION PROBLEM: DIMENSIONS FOR ACTION.

ESPINET, ADRIAN
20.005   BC   1965 Honours and Paquotille. *New Wld Q* 2(1), Dead Season: 19-22.   [*RIS*]

FINKEL, HERMAN J.
20.006   SK/   1964 Attitudes toward work as a factor in agricultural planning in the
          NV   West Indies. *Car Stud* 4(1), Apr.: 49-53. [46,50]   [*RIS*]

GLASS, RUTH
21.007   JM   1962 Ashes of discontent.

GOEJE, C. H. de
20.007   GC   1943 Philosophy, initiation and myths of the Indians of Guiana and adjacent countries. *Int Archiv Ethnogr* 44:1-136. [13,23,24,29] [*AMN*]

GREEN, HELEN BAGENSTOSE
31.030   TR   1964 Socialization values in the Negro and East Indian subcultures of Trinidad.
20.008   TR   1965 Values of Negro and East Indian school children in Trinidad. *Social Econ Stud* 14(2), June: 204-216. [11,12,31,32]   [*RIS*]

HALL, DOUGLAS GORDON
6.022   BC   1962 Slaves and slavery in the British West Indies.

HERSKOVITS, MELVILLE JEAN & FRANCES S.
14.006   SR   1934 REBEL DESTINY: AMONG THE BUSH NEGROES OF DUTCH GUIANA.

HOETINK, HARRY

20.009   GC   1961 "Colonial psychology" and race. *J Econ Hist* Dec.: 629-640. [10]

                                                                                             [*RIS*]

HOYT, ELIZABETH E.

44.107   JM   1959 Changing standards of living in Jamaica.

JAMES, CYRIL LIONEL ROBERT

20.010   BC   1963 BEYOND A BOUNDARY. London, Hutchinson, 356p. [22]

JAYAWARDENA, CHANDRA

8.033   BG   1963 CONFLICT AND SOLIDARITY IN A GUIANESE PLANTATION.

JORDAN, WINTHROP D.

16.021   BC   1962 American chiaroscuro: the status and definition of mulattoes in the British Colonies.

KRUIJER, GERARDUS JOHANNES

34.009   JM   1958 Family size and family planning: a pilot survey among Jamaican mothers.

LOWENTHAL, DAVID

20.011   BC   1961 Caribbean views of Caribbean land. *Can Geogr* 5(2): 1-9. [10,21, 47,57]   [*RIS*]

37.234   BC   1962 Levels of West Indian government.

LYNCH, LOUIS

32.126   BB   1963 Parent-pupil-teacher relationships.

MAU, JAMES A.; HILL, RICHARD J. & BELL, WENDELL

20.012   JM   1961 Scale analyses of status perception and status attitude in Jamaica and the United States. *Pacif Sociol Rev* 4(1), Spring: 33-40. [8,67]

                                                                                             [*RIS*]

MENKMAN, W. R.

11.018   SR   1927/ Lanti sa pai [The country will pay for it].
             28

METRAUX, RHODA

66.101   MS   1957 Montserrat, B.W.I.: some implications of suspended culture change.

MOSKOS, CHARLES CONSTANTINE, Jr.

37.274   BC   1963 THE SOCIOLOGY OF POLITICAL INDEPENDENCE: A STUDY OF INFLUENCE, SOCIAL STRUCTURE AND IDEOLOGY IN THE BRITISH WEST INDIES.

MOSKOS, CHARLES CONSTANTINE, Jr. & BELL, WENDELL

37.275   BC   1964 Attitudes towards democracy among leaders in four emergent nations.

MOYSTON, B.

31.057   JM   1963 Problems of the Jamaican adolescent.

O'MARD, C. M.

31.058   AT   1963 Special problems of the senior school child in Antigua.

POWRIE, BARBARA E.

20.013   TR   1956 The changing attitude of the coloured middle class towards Carnival.
                      Car Q 4(3-4). Mar.-June: 224-232. [8, 11, 19]   [*RIS*]

ROTTENBERG, SIMON

20.014   AT   1952 Income and leisure in an underdeveloped economy. *J Polit Econ*
                      60(2), Apr.: 95-101.   [*COL*]

RUBIN, VERA

20.015   TR   1961 Family aspirations and attitudes of Trinidad youth. *In* CHILDREN OF
                      THE CARIBBEAN—THEIR MENTAL HEALTH NEEDS: PROCEEDINGS OF THE
                      SECOND CARIBBEAN CONFERENCE FOR MENTAL HEALTH, Apr. 10-16, 1959,
                      Saint Thomas, Virgin Islands. San Juan, P. R., Dept. of the Trea-
                      sury, Purchase and Supply Service—Printing Division, p.59-68.
                      [8, 9, 11, 12, 31, 32, 44]   [*RIS*]
31.064   TR   1963 The adolescent: his expectations and his society.
20.016   BC   1962 Culture, politics and race relations. *In* SINGHAM, A. & BRAITH-
                      WAITE, L. E., eds. Special number [of *Social Econ Stud*] on the
                      Conference of Political Sociology of the British Caribbean, Dec.
                      1961. *Social Econ Stud* 11(4), Dec.: 433-455. [8, 11, 12, 16, 37, 67]
                                                                                         [*RIS*]
9.035   GC   1965 The West Indian family retrospect and prospect.

SCROGGS, WILLIAM

20.017   JM   1961 Imprudent jurisprudence: an outline of an illegal fiction. *W I Econ*
                      4(1-2), July-Aug.: 6-7. [50]   [*RIS*]

SHERLOCK, PHILIP M

37.369   JM/   1963 Prospects in the Caribbean.
          TR

SIMPSON, GEORGE EATON

36.019   JM   1954 Begging in Kingston and Montego Bay.
10.041   GC   1962 The peoples and cultures of the Caribbean area.

SMITH, M. G.

20.018   JM   1960 Education and occupational choice in rural Jamaica. *Social Econ*
                      Stud 9(3), Sept.: 332-354. [8,32,44]   [*RIS*]

SMITH, RAYMOND THOMAS

8.061   BG   1964 Ethnic difference and peasant economy in British Guiana.

STRUMPEL, BURKHARD

44.227   1965 Consumption aspirations: incentives for economic change.

THORNE, ALFRED P.

46.220   JM   1960 An economic phenomenon.

VERIN, PIERRE MICHEL

25.105   BC/   1958 The rivalry of Creole and English in the West Indies.
          MT

WATTS, Sir FRANCIS

20.019   BC   1926 History as affecting outlook in the West Indies. *Can-W I Mag* 15(3), Jan.: 59-60. [5,51]   [*NYP*]

WELLS, HENRY

37.418   UV   1955 Outline of the nature of United States Virgin Islands politics.

WILLIAMS, ERIC EUSTACE

66.166   GC   1961 MASSA DAY DONE.

WONG, WALTER

20.020   JM   1963 The adolescent in the family. *In* CARTER, SAMUEL E., ed. THE ADOLESCENT IN THE CHANGING CARIBBEAN: PROCEEDINGS OF THE THIRD CARIBBEAN CONFERENCE FOR MENTAL HEALTH, Apr. 4-11, 1961, UCWI, Jamaica. Kingston, The Herald, p.68-71.   [*RIS*]

ZAVALLONI, MARISA

20.021   TR   1960 YOUTH AND THE FUTURE: VALUES AND ASPIRATIONS OF HIGH SCHOOL STUDENTS IN A MULTICULTURAL SOCIETY IN TRANSITION—TRINIDAD, W.I. Ph.D. dissertation, Columbia University, 141p. [10,32]   [*RIS*]

Chapter 21

CULTURAL AND NATIONAL IDENTITY

ABRAHAMS, PETER
20.001   JM   [1961?] The influence of ideas.

ANDERSON, DALE
21.001   BC   1963/The reality of a West Indian culture. *Social Sci* 2:18-20.   [*RIS*]
           64

BELL, WENDELL
37.023   JM   1964 JAMAICAN LEADERS: POLITICAL ATTITUDES IN A NEW NATION.

BRERETON, ASHTON S.
37.042   BC   1963/West Indian perspective.
           64
21.002   BC   1963/West Indians—a people with no self respect. *Social Sci* 1:5-6.
           64

BROWN, JOHN
32.032   LW   1961 The meaning of 'extra-mural' in the Leeward Islands.

BYLES, G. LOUIS
16.005   BC   1946 Way to real unity in the West Indies.

CAREW, JAN
21.003   BC   1953 British West Indian poets and their culture. *Phylon* 14(1) 1st quar-
           ter: 71-73.   [*COL*]

CHAPMAN, ESTHER
21.004   BC   1957 Matters of some importance: the West Indian. *W I Rev* new ser.,
           2(10), Oct.: 13,15.   [*NYP*]

COULTHARD, G. R.
16.007   GC   1962 RACE AND COLOUR IN CARIBBEAN LITERATURE.

CROWLEY, DANIEL JOHN
22.038   TR   1954 THE MEANINGS OF CARNIVAL.
10.010   TR   1957 Plural and differential acculturation in Trinidad.

DANIEL, GEORGE T.
50.031   BC   1957 Labor and nationalism in the British Caribbean.

DORAN, EDWIN BEAL, Jr.
21.005   GC   1958 Cultural connections in the Leeward Islands. *Caribbean* 11(12), July: 274-277.   [*COL*]

DRAYTON, ARTHUR D.
21.006   BC   1963 West Indian fiction and West Indian society. *Kenyon Rev* 25(1), Winter: 129-141.   [*COL*]

FARLEY, RAWLE
49.022   BC   1958 NATIONALISM AND INDUSTRIAL DEVELOPMENT IN THE BRITISH-CARIBBEAN.

GILLIN, JOHN P.
10.014   GC   1951 Is there a modern Caribbean culture?

GLASS, RUTH
21.007   JM   1962 Ashes of discontent. *Listener BBC Telev Rev* 67(1714), Feb. 1: 207-209. [5,8,20,37]   [*NYP*]

GRATIANT, GILBERT
37.150   MT   1961 ILE FÉDÉRÉE FRANCAISE DE LA MARTINIQUE [THE FEDERATED FRENCH ISLAND OF MARTINIQUE].

GLISSANT, EDOUARD
21.008   FC   1962 Culture et colonisation: l'équilibre antillais [Culture and colonization: the Antillean balance]. *Esprit* 30(305), Apr.: 588-595.   [*COL*]

HARTOG, JOHAN
21.009   CU   [n.d.] Cultural life in Curacao. *Car Q* 1(3): 36-38. [22]

HERSKOVITS, MELVILLE JEAN
67.009   GC   1946 Problem, method and theory in Afroamerican studies.

HILL, ERROL
22.077   BC   1955 Drama round the Caribbean.

HOCKEY, SIDNEY W.
21.010   BC   1958 An emerging culture in the British West Indies. *In* WILGUS, A. CURTIS, ed. THE CARIBBEAN: BRITISH, DUTCH, FRENCH, UNITED STATES [papers delivered at the Eighth Conference on the Caribbean held at the University of Florida, Dec. 5-7, 1957]. Gainesville, University of Florida Press, p.39-50. (Publications of the School of Inter-American Studies, ser. 1, v. 8.) [8,22]   [*RIS*]

HUNTE, GEORGE HUTCHINSON
16.019   BC   1946 West Indian unity: measures and machinery.

JACOBS, H. P.
38.057   BC   1956 This Federation.

LEBORGNE, YVON
21.011   FA   1962 Le climat social [The social environment]. *Esprit* 30(305), Apr.: 537-550. [37]   [*NYP*]

LICHTVELD, LOU
21.012   GC   1959   Cultural relations within the Caribbean. *Caribbean* 13(4), Apr.: 73-77.   [COL]

LOTAN, YAEL
21.013   JM   1964   Jamaica today.   *Freedomways* 4(3), 3d quarter, Summer: 370-374. [37]   [RIS]

LOWENTHAL, DAVID
20.011   BC   1961   Caribbean views of Caribbean land.
38.075   BC   1961   The social background of West Indian federation.
37.234   BC   1962   Levels of West Indian government.

MAHABIR, DENNIS J.
21.014   BC   1957   Cultural mosaic. *Caribbean* 10(12), July: 295-296.   [COL]

MAINBERGER, GONSALV
21.015   MT   1963   Mythe et realité de l'homme noir; à la memoir de Frantz Fanon   [Myth and reality of the Negro; in memory of Frantz Fanon]. *Presénce Afr* 18(46), 2d quarter: 211-224.   [11]   [COL]

MARSHALL, WOODVILLE
22.097   BC   1965   Gary Sobers and the Brisbane Revolution.

MATTHEWS, Dom BASIL
21.016   BC   1942   Calypso and Pan America.   *Commonweal* 37(4), Nov. 13: 91-93. [22]   [COL]

MOSKOS, CHARLES CONSTANTINE, Jr.
37.274   BC   1963   THE SOCIOLOGY OF POLITICAL INDEPENDENCE: A STUDY OF INFLUENCE, SOCIAL STRUCTURE AND IDEOLOGY IN THE BRITISH WEST INDIES.

MOSKOS, CHARLES CONSTANTINE, Jr. & BELL WENDELL
21.017   BC   1964   West Indian nationalism. *New Soc* 69, Jan. 23: 16-18. [8,37]
10.029   BG/   1965   Cultural unity and diversity in new states.
         TR

NETTLEFORD, REX
21.018   JM   1965   National identity and attitudes to race in Jamaica. *Race* 7(1): 59-72. [16]   [RIS]

NORRIS, KATRIN
21.019   JM   1962   JAMAICA: THE SEARCH FOR AN IDENTITY.   London, Oxford University Press, 103p.   [8,16,37]   [RIS]

PROUDFOOT, MARY
21.020   BC   1956   The British Caribbean—general conspectus. *Statist* Sept. 5-6.

RAMRAJ, VICTOR
21.021   BC   1963/   Satire and tradition in West Indies society. *Social Sci* 2:10-12. [RIS]
             64

SCROGGS, WILLIAM
37.363   JM   1962   Jamaicans are English.

SHERLOCK, PHILIP M.
32.180   BC   1955 The dynamic of nationalism in adult education.
21.022   BC   [1956?] Federation: let's meet the family. *Extra-Mural Reptr* 3(2), Apr. [38]
                                                                                               [*RIS*]

2.218   GC   1963 CARIBBEAN CITIZEN. 3d ed.
37.369   JM/   1963 Prospects in the Caribbean.
            TR

SMITH, M. G.
10.047   GC   1961 West Indian culture.

SMITH, RAYMOND THOMAS
21.023   BG   1958 British Guiana. *In* SUNDAY GUARDIAN OF TRINIDAD, THE WEST INDIAN
                            FEDERATION SUPPLEMENT, April 20. Port of Spain, Sunday Guardian,
                            p.25, 33, 63.   [10, 38]   [*RIS*]

SPRINGER, HUGH W.
21.024   BC   1953 On being a West Indian. *Car Q* 3(3), Dec.: 181-183.   [*RIS*]

STRUMPEL, BURKHARD
44.227   BH   1965 Consumption aspirations: incentives for economic change.

SYPHER, W.
21.025   BC   1939 The West Indian as a character in the 18th century. *Stud Philol*
                            34(3), July: 503-520.   [5]   [*COL*]

VOORHOEVE, JAN & RENSELAER, H. C. van
23.166   SR   1962 Messianism and nationalism in Surinam.

Chapter 22

MUSIC, ART AND RECREATION

ADAMS, ALTON A.

22.001   TR   1955 Whence came the calypso? *Caribbean* 8(10), May, 218-220, 230, 235.

[*COL*]

AMELUNXEN, C. P.

22.002   CU   1934/ De verdediging van Curacao bezongen [The defense of Curacao is
               35 sung (praised)]. *W I G* 16: 250-254. [5]   [*COL*]

ASPINALL, Sir ALGERNON E.

5.005   BB   1942 "Rachael Pringle of Barbadoes."

ATTAWAY, WILLIAM

22.003   BC   1957 Calypso song book. New York, McGraw-Hill, 64p.

BARBANSON, W. L. de

22.004   GD   1950 Frans-creoolse versjes van Guadeloupe [French-Creole verses of
                   Guadeloupe]. *W I G* 31(1), Apr.: 3-20. [24,25]   [*COL*]

BARKER, J. S.

22.005   BC   1963 Summer spectacular: the West Indies v. England, 1963. London,
                   Collins, 128p.

BECKWITH, MARTHA WARREN

22.006   JM   1922 Folk games in Jamaica. Poughkeepsie, N.Y., Vassar College, 79p.
                   (Field-work in folk-lore; publications of the Folklore Foundation,
                   no. 1.) [24]   [*COL*]

22.007   JM   1924 English ballad in Jamaica; a note upon the origin of the ballad form;
                   with music and texts. *Pubs Mod Lang Ass Am* 39, June: 455-483.

[*NYP*]

23.005   JM   1924 The Hussay festival in Jamaica.

24.005   JM   1924 Jamaica Anansi stories.

BECKWITH, MARTHA WARREN & ROBERTS, HELEN H.

22.008   JM   1923 Christmas mummings in Jamaica. Poughkeepsie, N.Y., Vassar Col-
                   lege, 46p. (Field-work in folk-lore; publications of the Folklore
                   Foundation, no. 2.) [19,24]   [*COL*]

BENJAMIN, ELSIE
22.009   JM   1945 Toward a native drama. *Th Arts* 29(5), May: 313-314.   [*COL*]

BENNETT, LOUISE
24.008   JM   1961 Laugh with Louise: a pot-pourri of Jamaican folklore.

BERNARD, C. M.
22.010   BG   1948 Music in British Guiana. *Timehri* 4th ser., 1(28), Dec.: 28-34.

BIRKETT, T. SYDNEY
22.011   GC   1927 RESUME OF BIG CRICKET IN THE WEST INDIES AND BRITISH GUIANA
                  SINCE THE WEST INDIES TOUR OF 1923 IN ENGLAND. [Bridgetown?] Bar-
                  bados, Advocate Co., 61p.

BOSKALJON, R.
22.012   CU   1958 HONDERD JAAR MUZIEKLEVEN OP CURACAO [HUNDRED YEARS OF MUSIC ON
                  CURACAO]. Assen, [Netherlands], VanGorcum, 188p.

BOWEN, CALVIN
22.013   JM   1954 Jamaica's John Canoe. *Car Commn Mon Inf B* 8(1), Aug.: 11-12.
                  [19,23]   [*COL*]

BRATHWAITE, EDWARD
22.014   BC   1963 Roots. *Bim* 10(37), July-Dec.: 10-21. [20]

CAMERON, N. E.
22.015   TR   1955 Harmony in steel bands. *New Commonw* British Caribbean Supple-
                  ment 30(11), Nov. 28: xviii-xix.   [*AGS*]

CAPLE, S. CANYNGE
22.016   BC   1957 ENGLAND V. THE WEST INDIES 1895-1957. Worcester, Littlebury, 206p.
                  [5]

CARR, ANDREW T.
22.017   TR   1954 Trinidad calypso is unique folk culture. *Car Commn Mon Inf B* 7(7),
                  Feb.: 162-164. [24]   [*COL*]
22.018   TR   1956 Pierrot Grenade. *Car Q* 4(3-4), Mar.-June: 281-314. [19,25]   [*RIS*]

CASTAGNE, PATRICK
22.019   TR   1962 This is calypso! *Chron W I Comm* 77(1377): Oct.: 518-519.   [*NYP*]

CECIL, C. H.
22.020   BC   1937 I—you, and the Devil take the loser! *Can-W I Mag* 26(12), Dec.:
                  25-26. [19]   [*NYP*]

CHAMBERTRAND, GILBERT de
22.021   FA   1963 Mi 10! New ed. by Bettino Lara & Roger Fortuné. [Basse-Terre]
                  Guadeloupe, Impr. officielle, 94p. [20,25]   [*RIS*]

CHANG, CARLISLE
22.022   TR   [1963?] Painting in Trinidad. *In* HILL, ERROL, ed. THE ARTIST IN WEST

INDIAN SOCIETY: A SYMPOSIUM [seminars held in Port of Spain, Trinidad, May-June 1963, and in Jamaica, Oct. 1962- Jan. 1963]. [Mona?] Dept. of Extra-mural Studies, University of the West Indies, p.25-37.
[*RIS*]

CLARKE, JOHN

| 22.023 | BC | 1963 CRICKET WITH A SWING: THE WEST INDIES TOUR, 1963. London, Stanley Paul, 200p. |

COLLIER, H. C.

22.024	BC	1935 "Warri," an African game transplanted to the West Indies. *Can-W I Mag* 24(6), May: 23-24. [19] [*NYP*]
22.025	JM	1937 Cristallized poetry. *Can-W I Mag* 26(12): Dec.: 28-30. [*NYP*]
22.026	TR	1939 Trinidad fantasia. *Can-W I Mag* 28(2), Feb.: 7-11. [19] [*NYP*]
22.027	JM	1940 The sculptural art of Edna Manley. *Can-W I Mag* 29(1), Feb.: 24-26. [*NYP*]
22.028	TR	1940 Tropical trove. *Can-W I Mag* 29(6), June: 21-23. [*NYP*]
22.029	BG	1941 Arts and crafts in British Guiana. *Can-W I Mag* 30(4), Apr.: 21-23. [*NYP*]
22.030	TR	1943 Carnival capers in calypso land. *Can-W I Mag* 32(1), Jan.: 19-22. [19] [*NYP*]

COMVALIUS, TH. A. C.

22.031	SR	1935/36 Het Surinaamsche Negerlied: de banja en de doe [The Surinam Negro song: the banja and the doe]. *W I G* 17:213-230. [14] [*COL*]
22.032	SR	1938 Twee historische liederen in Suriname [Two historical songs in Surinam]. *W I G* 20:291-295. [5] [*COL*]
22.033	SR	1939 Een der vormen van het Surinaamsche lied na 1863 [One of the types of the Surinam song after 1863]. *W I G* 21:355-360. [*COL*]
22.034	SR	1946 Oud-Surinaamsche rhythmische dansen in dienst van de lichamelijke opvoeding [Old Surinamese rhythmic dances in the service of physical education]. *W I G* 27:97-103. [19,32] [*COL*]

CONNELL, NEVILLE

23.026	BB	1953 St. George's Parish Church, Barbados.
22.035	BB	1954 Church plate in Barbados. *Connoisseur* 134(539), Aug.: 8-13. [23]
22.036	GC	1957 Caribbean artists paint action and colour. *Studio* 153(770), May: 129-135.

CONNOR, EDRIC

| 22.037 | TR | 1958 SONGS FROM TRINIDAD. London, Oxford University Press, 76p. |

COOK, MERCER

| 37.067 | FA | 1940 The literary contribution of the French West Indian. |

CROWLEY, DANIEL JOHN

12.005	TR	1954 East Indian festivals in Trinidad life.
22.038	TR	1954 THE MEANINGS OF CARNIVAL. Port of Spain, 3p. (mimeo.) [19,21] [*RIS*]
22.039	BG	1956 Bush Negro combs: a structural analysis. *Vox Guy* 2(4), Dec.: 145-161. [14] [*RIS*]
22.040	TR	1956 The midnight robbers. *Car Q* 4(3-4), Mar.-June: 263-274. [19] [*RIS*]

| 22.041 | TR | 1956 The traditional masques of Carnival. *Car Q* 4(3-4), Mar.-June: 194-223. [5,19] | [RIS] |

22.041 TR 1956 The traditional masques of Carnival. *Car Q* 4(3-4), Mar.-June: 194-223. [5,19] [RIS]

22.042 SL 1957 Song and dance in St. Lucia. *Ethnomusicology* 9, Jan.: 4-14 [19] [RIS]

22.043 TR 1958 Calypso: Trinidad Carnival songs and dances. *Dance Notat Rec* 9(2), Summer: 3-7. [RIS]

22.044 BB/ 1958 The shak-shak in the Lesser Antilles. *Ethnomusicology* 2(3), Sept.:
TR/ 112-115. [RIS]
WW

22.045 TR 1959 Toward a definition of "calypso." *Ethnomusicology* 3(2), May: 57-66; 3(3), Sept.: 117-124. [RIS]

CRUICKSHANK, J. GRAHAM

22.046 BG 1924 An African dance in the colony. *W I Comm Circ* 39(662, suppl.), Feb. 14: 8-9. [11,19] [NYP]

19.008 BG 1929 Negro games.

CUNDALL, FRANK

22.047 JM 1907 Sculpture in Jamaica. *Art J* 69, Mar.: 65-70. [COL]

22.048 JM 1924 Pine's painting of Rodney and his officers. *W I Comm Circ* 39(670), June 5: 219; 39(671), June 19: 242-243. [5] [NYP]

DAM, THEODORE van

22.049 GC 1954 The influence of the West African songs of derision in the New World. *Afr Mus* 1(1): 53-56. [19] [NYP]

DARK, PHILIP J.C.

22.050 SR 1951 Some notes on the carving of calabashes by the Bush Negroes of Surinam. *Man* 51(97), May: 57-60. [14] [COL]

22.051 SR 1954 BUSH NEGRO ART: AN AFRICAN ART IN THE AMERICAS. London, Alec Tiranti, 65p. [14,19] [NYP]

DOLPHIN, CELESTE

22.052 BG 1946 Arawak rhythm. *Can-W I Mag* 36(8), Oct.: 19-22. [13] [NYP]

ELDER, J. D.

22.053 TR 1961 SONG-GAMES OF TRINIDAD AND TOBAGO. Delaware, Ohio, Cooperative Recreation Service, 15p. [RIS]

22.054 BC [1963?] The future of music in the West Indies. (i) Folk music. *In* HILL, ERROL, ed. THE ARTIST IN WEST INDIAN SOCIETY; A SYMPOSIUM [seminars held in Port of Spain, Trinidad, May-June 1963, and in Jamaica Oct. 1962-Jan. 1963]. [Mona?] Dept. of Extra-mural Studies, University of the West Indies, p.38-45. [RIS]

22.055 TR 1964 Color, music and conflict: a study of aggression in Trinidad with reference to the role of traditional music. *Ethnomusicology* 8(2), May: 128-136. [5,16] [RIS]

22.056 TR 1965 Song-games from Trinidad and Tobago. *Pubs Am Folk Soc*, Bibliographical and special series, 16(119p.) [RIS]

ELLAM, PATRICK

3.092 GC 1957 THE SPORTSMAN'S GUIDE TO THE CARIBBEAN.

ESPINET, CHARLES S.

22.057   TR   [1951?] Trinidad's tinpany. *Esso Ant* 1(5), [Sept.?].   [*RIS*]

22.058   TR   1953 Masquerade—origin and development of Trinidad's Carnival. *Can-W I Mag* 43(13), Jan.: 22-23,25. [19]   [*NYP*]

ESPINET, CHARLES S. AND PITTS, HARRY

22.059   TR   1944 LAND OF THE CALYPSO: THE ORIGIN AND DEVELOPMENT OF TRINIDAD'S FOLK-SONG. Port of Spain, Guardian Commercial Printery, 74p. [5,19]   [*COL*]

EVANS, VERNON

22.060   TR   [1963?] The future of music in the West Indies. (ii) Art music. *In* HILL, ERROL, ed. THE ARTIST IN WEST INDIAN SOCIETY: A SYMPOSIUM [seminars held in Port of Spain, Trinidad, May-June 1963, and in Jamaica Oct. 1962-Jan. 1963]. [Mona?] Dept. of Extra-mural Studies, University of the West Indies, p.46-50. [32]   [*RIS*]

EYTLE, ERNEST

22.061   BC   1963 FRANK WORRELL. London, Hodder and Stoughton, 192p.

FLAGLER, J. M.

22.062   BC   1954 A reporter at large: Well caught, Mr. Holder! *New Yorker* 30, Sept. 25: 65-85.

FRAMPTON, H. M.

22.063   DM   1957 Carnival time in Dominica. *Can-W I Mag* 47(5), May: 9,11. [19] [*NYP*]

GARDNER, M. M.

22.064   TR   1954 The greatest show of its kind on earth—Trinidad's Carnival. *Can-W I Mag* 44(5), May: 26-27, 29-31. [19]   [*NYP*]

GILCHRIST, ROY

22.065   BC   1963 HIT ME FOR SIX. London, Stanley Paul, 126p.

GOEJE, C. H. de

22.066   CU   1948 De wiri-wiri, een muziek-instrument van Curacao [The wiri-wiri, a musical instrument of Curacao]. *W I G* 29:225-228.   [*COL*]

22.067   GC   1950 Verwanten van de Curacaose wiri [Relatives of the Curacao wiri]. *W I G* 31:180. [13]   [*COL*]

GRIMES, JOHN

22.068   GC   1964 Caribbean music and dance. *Freedomways* 4(3), Summer: 426-434.   [*RIS*]

GUGGENHEIM, HANS & CARR, ANDREW T.

23.060   TR   1965 Tribalism in Trinidad.

HANSON, DONALD R. AND DASH, ROBERT

22.069   TR   1955 The saga of the steelband. *Caribbean* 8(8), Mar.: 173, 176-177, 184.   [*COL*]

HARRISON, JOHN

22.070   BC   [1950?] Art for West Indian children. *Car Q* 1(3): 19-31.   [32]

22.071   BC   1952 Last thoughts on art in the British West Indies. *J Barb Mus Hist Soc* 19(2), Feb.: 53-57.   [*AMN*]

HARTOG, JOHAN

21.009   CU   [n.d.] Cultural life in Curacao.

HERSKOVITS, MELVILLE JEAN

19.018   SR   1929 Adjiboto, an African game of the Bush-Negroes of Dutch Guiana.

22.072   GC   1932 Wari in the New World. *J Roy Anthrop Inst Gr Br Ire* 62, Jan.-June: 23-37.   [19]   [*AGS*]

22.073   GC   1941 El estudio de la música negra en el hemisferio occidental [The study of Negro music in the Western Hemisphere]. *Boln Latam Mus Inst Inter-Amer Music* 5, Oct.: 133-142.   [11,19]   [*COL*]

22.074   GC   1941 Patterns of Negro music. *Trans Ill St Acad Sci* 34(1), Sept.: 19-23. [11,19]   [*NYP*]

22.075   SR   1949 Afro-American art. *In* WILDER, ELIZABETH, ed. STUDIES IN LATIN AMERICAN ART. Proceedings of a conference held in the Museum of Modern Art, New York, 28-31 May 1945. Washington, D.C., American Council of Learned Societies, p.58-64.   [14]   [*SCH*]

HERSKOVITS, MELVILLE JEAN & FRANCES S.

22.076   SR   1930 Bush-Negro art. *Arts* 17(1), Oct.: 25-37; 48-49.   [14,19]   [*COL*]

24.032   SR   1936 SURINAME FOLK-LORE (with transcriptions and Suriname songs and and musicological analysis by Dr. M. Kolinski).

HILL, ERROL

22.077   BC   1955 Drama round the Caribbean. *Car Commn Mon Inf B* 8(6), Jan.: 112-113, 120-121.   [21]   [*COL*]

22.078   BC   [1963?] West Indian drama. *In* HILL, ERROL, ed. THE ARTIST IN WEST INDIAN SOCIETY: A SYMPOSIUM [seminars held in Port of Spain, Trinidad, May-June 1963, and in Jamaica Oct. 1962-Jan. 1963]. [Mona?] Dept. of Extra-mural Studies, University of the West Indies, p.7-24.   [*RIS*]

HILL, ERROL, ed.

22.079   BC   [1963?] THE ARTIST IN WEST INDIAN SOCIETY: A SYMPOSIUM [seminars held in Port of Spain, Trinidad, May-June 1963, and in Jamaica Oct. 1962-Jan. 1963]. [Mona?] Department of Extra-mural studies, University of the West Indies, 79p.   [*RIS*]

HOCKEY, SIDNEY W.

21.010   BC   1958 An emerging culture in the British West Indies.

IM THURN, EVERARD F.

22.080   BG   1901 Games of the red-men of Guiana. *Folk-Lore* 12(2), June: 132-161. [13]   [*COL*]

JACOBS, H. P.

24.037   JM   1948 An early dialect verse.

JAMES, CYRIL LIONEL ROBERT
20.010   BC   1963 BEYOND A BOUNDARY.

JEKYLL, WALTER
24.038   JM   1907 Jamaican song and story.

JEPHCOTT, PEARL
33.017   BG   1956 REPORT ON THE NEEDS OF THE YOUTH OF THE MORE POPULATED COASTAL
                 AREAS OF BRITISH GUIANA: WITH PARTICULAR REFERENCE TO THE RE-
                 CREATION AND INFORMAL EDUCATION OF THOSE AGED 13-19.

JOHNSON, ROBERT
22.081   JM/   1939 Imperial Bisley, 1939—how Jamaica and Trinidad shot. *W I Comm*
          TR   *Circ* 54(1065), July 27: 325-326.   [*NYP*]

JOHNSTONE, ROBERT
22.082   BC   1955 Rifle shooting in the West Indies. *W I Comm Circ* 70(1288), Apr.:
                 109-110.   [*NYP*]

JOURDAIN, ELODIE
22.083   TR/   1954 Trinidad calypso *not* unique. *Car Commn Mon Inf B* 7(10), May: 221-
          FA   222,232.   [*COL*]

KAHN, MORTON CHARLES
22.084   SR   1931 Art of the Dutch Guiana Bush Negro. *Nat Hist* 31(2), Mar.-Apr.:
                 155-168. [14,19]   [*AGS*]

KALFF, S.
22.085   SR   1922/ Vroegere kunst in West-Indie [Early art in West India]. *W I G* 4:353-
          23   372.   [*COL*]

KRUIJER, GERARDUS JOHANNES
32.113   JM   1952 De 4-H Clubs van Jamaica
17.014   NW   1953 Enquête onder de Bovenwinders op Curacao en Aruba (Juli-Augustus
                 1951) [Investigation among Windward Islanders on Curacao and Aru-
                 ba (July-August 1951)].

LEAF, EARL
22.086   GC   1948 ISLES OF RHYTHM. New York, A.S. Barnes, 211p. [23]

LEKIS, LISA
22.087   GC   1955 The dance as an expression of Caribbean folklore. *In* WILGUS, A.
                 CURTIS, ed. THE CARIBBEAN: ITS CULTURE [papers delivered at the
                 Fifth Conference on the Caribbean held at the University of Florida,
                 Dec. 2-4, 1954]. Gainesville, University of Florida Press, p.43-73.
                 (Publications of the School of Inter-American Studies, ser. 1, v. 5.)
                 [13,19]   [*RIS*]

LESCHALOUPE, CONSTANCE MARIE
22.088   TR   1953 Carnival in Trinidad—masquerades and steelbands. *Can-W I Mag*
                 43(10), Oct.: 11, 13-14. [19]   [*NYP*]

LICHTVELD, LOU

35.030   SR   1960 Native arts in modern architecture.

LINDBLOM, K. G.

22.089   SR   1926 EINIGE DETAILS IN DER ORNAMENTIK DER BUSCHNEGER SURINAMS [SOME
DETAILS OF THE ORNAMENTS OF THE BUSH NEGROES OF SURINAM]. Stock-
holm, 12p.(Riksmuseets Etnografiska Avdelning, no. 1). [14,19] [*COL*]

LUQUET, G.-H.

22.090   SR   1933 Exposition d'ethnographie guyanaise au Trocadéro [Exhibit of Guianese ethnography at the Trocadéro]. *Nature* 61(2896, pt. 1), Jan. 1:
30-32. [14]   [*COL*]

LUTZ, FRANKE

22.091   BG   1912 String-figures from the upper Potaro. *Timehri* 3d ser., 2(19A), July:
117-127. [13]   [*AMN*]

McBURNIE, BERYL

22.092   TR   1958 The Belaire. *Shell Trin* 5(2), Mar.: 12-15.
22.093   BG   [1963?] West Indian dance. *In* HILL, ERROL, ed. THE ARTIST IN WEST IN-
DIAN SOCIETY: A SYMPOSIUM [seminars held in Port of Spain, Trinidad,
May-June 1963, and in Jamaica Oct. 1962-Jan. 1963]. [Mona?] Dept.
of Extra-mural Studies, University of the West Indies, p.51-54.   [*RIS*]

McKAY, CLAUDE

22.094   JM   1912 SONGS OF JAMAICA. Kingston, Aston W. Gardner, 140p. [25]   [*NYP*]

McNAMARA, ROSALIND

22.095   GC   1960 Music in the Caribbean. *Caribbean* 14(3), Mar.: 45-49; 14(4), Apr.:
69-70, 84-85, 100.   [*COL*]

McWHINNIE, HAROLD J.

32.129   GR   1962 Teaching art in Grenada.

MALLETT, R. H.

22.096   BC   1923 The West Indies cricket tour: critical survey and a retrospect. *W I
Comm Circ* 38(656), Nov. 22:501-502; 38(657), Dec. 6: 520-521
1924 39(659), Jan. 3:12-13; 39(660), Jan. 17:32-33.   [NYP]

MARSHALL, WOODVILLE

22.097   BC   1965 Gary Sobers and the Brisbane Revolution.   *New Wld Q* 2(1), Dead
Season: 35-42. [21]   [*RIS*]

MATTHEWS, Dom BASIL

21.016   BC   1942 Calypso and Pan America.

MERRIAM, A. P.; WHINERY, SARA & FRED, B. G.

22.098   TR   1956 Songs of a Rada community in Trinidad. *Anthropos* 51(1-2): 157-174.
[19]   [*COL*]

MIDAS, ANDRE
22.099   BC   1958 Festival of arts in retrospect. *Caribbean* 11(12), July: 266-270. [*COL*]

MIGHTY SPARROW
22.100   TR   1963 ONE HUNDRED AND TWENTY CALYPSOES TO REMEMBER. [Port of Spain,
                      Trinidad, National Recording Co.] 92p.   [*RIS*]

MOERHEUVEL, L. H.
52.063   NC   1937 De PHOHI in de West [The PHOHI in the West].

MURRAY, TOM
22.101   JM   1951 FOLK SONGS OF JAMAICA. London, Oxford University Press, 59p. [*RIS*]

NICOLE, CHRISTOPHER
22.102   BC   1957 WEST INDIAN CRICKET. London, Phoenix Sports Books, 256p. [5]

NORTH, LIONEL
22.103   GC   1932 Songs of the Afro-Indian. *Can-W I Mag* 21(3), Feb.: 96-98. [11] [*NYP*]

OUDSCHANS DENTZ, FRED
25.083   SR   1937 De plaats van de Creool in de literatuur van Suriname [The place of
                      Creole in the literature of Surinam].
22.104   SR   1943 De loopbaan van Krayenhoff van Wickera in Suriname [The career of
                      Krayenhoff van Wickera in Surinam]. *W I G* 25:117-121. [5] [*COL*]
22.105   SR   1949 Geschiedkundige aantekeningen over het cultureele leven in Suri-
                      name [Historical annotation about the cultural life in Surinam]. *W I G*
                      30:42-50. [32]   [*COL*]

PANHUYS, L. C. van
22.106   SR   1905 About the ornamentation in use by savage tribes in Dutch Guiana
                      and its meaning. *In* PROCEEDINGS OF THE INTERNATIONAL CONGRESS
                      OF AMERICANISTS, 13th Session, New York, Oct. 1902. Easton, Pa.,
                      Eschenbach Print. Co., p.209-212. [14]   [*AGS*]
22.107   SR   1912 Les chansons et la musique de la Guyane Néerlandaise [The songs
                      and music of Dutch Guiana]. *J Soc Am* new ser., 9:27-39.   [*AGS*]
22.108   SR   1913 Development of ornament amongst the Bush Negroes in Suriname. *In*
                      PROCEEDINGS OF THE INTERNATIONAL CONGRESS OF AMERICANISTS,
                      XVIII Session, London, 1912. London, Harrison, pt. 2, p.380-381.
                      [14]   [*AGS*]
22.109   SR   1930 Ornaments of the Bush Negroes in Dutch Guiana; a further contribu-
                      tion to research in Bush-Negro art. *In* PROCEEDINGS OF THE 23rd IN-
                      TERNATIONAL CONGRESS OF AMERICANISTS, New York, 1928. New
                      York, p.728-735. [14]   [*AGS*]
22.110   SR   1931/ Boschnegerkunst [Bush Negro art]. *W I G* 13:153-162. [14] [*COL*]
                 32
24.057   SR   1934/ Het kikvorschmotief in Suriname en elders [The frog motif in Suri-
                 35   nam and elsewhere].
22.111   SR   1934 Quelques chansons et quelques danses dans la Guyane Neerland-
                      aise [A few songs and dances of Dutch Guiana]. *In* VERHANDLUNGEN
                      DES XXIV INTERNATIONALEN AMERIKANISTEN-KONGRESSES, Hamburg,
                      1930. Hamburg, Friederichsen, de Gruyter, p.207-211. [25, 26] [*AGS*]

24.059	SR	1935/ Surinaamsche folklore (liederenverzameling Van Vliet) [Folklore of
		36 of Surinam (Song collection of Van Vliet)].
22.112	SR	1936/ Aard en karakter van Surinaamsche liederen [Nature and character
		37 of Surinam songs]. *W I G* 18:1-12. [*COL*]

PASS, Mrs. E. A. de
8.047   TR   1929 The West Indies Boy Scouts.

PATTERSON, MASSIE & BELASCO, LIONEL
22.113   GC   1943 Calypso songs of the West Indies. New York, M. Baron, 25p. [*NYP*]

PEARSE, ANDREW C.
22.114   GR/   1955 Aspects of change in Caribbean folk music.   *J Int Folk Music Coun*
            CR/   8:29-36.   [*RIS*]
            TR
22.115   TR   1956 Carnival in nineteenth century Trinidad.   *Car Q* 4(3-4), Mar.-June:
                          250-262.   [5,19,24]   [*RIS*]
67.019   BC   1956 Ethnography and the lay scholar in the Caribbean.

PEBERDY, P. STORER
4.104   BG   1948 Discovery of Amerindian rock-paintings in British Guiana.

PELAGE, AL.
2.180   GD   [n.d.] La Guadeloupe vue par Al. Pelage: gravures et dessins humor-
                          istiques [Guadeloupe as seen by Al. Pelage: humorous prints and
                          drawings.

PENARD, THOMAS E. & ARTHUR P.
22.116   SR   1925/ Four Arawak Indian songs. *W I G* 7:497-500.   [13]   [*COL*]
                          26

PROCOPE, BRUCE
22.117   TR   1956 The Dragon Band or Devil Band.   *Car Q* 4(3-4), Mar.-June: 275-280.
                          [19]   [*RIS*]
22.118   TR   1959 Ken Morris—metalworker. *Shell Mag* 5(9), Christmas: 10-12.   [19]
38.092   BC   1960 The Temporary Federal mace.

PUNCH, L. D. "LULLY"
32.160   TR   [n.d.] Scouting memories.

RAY, MICHAEL
22.119   BG   1940 Sugar cane cricket.   *Can-W I Mag* 29(12), Dec.: 23-24, 28.   [*NYP*]

ROBERTS, HELEN H.
22.120   JM   1924 Some drums and drum rhythms of Jamaica. *Nat Hist* 24(2), Mar.-Apr.
                          241-251.   [19]   [*AGS*]
22.121   JM   1925 A study of folk song variants based on field work in Jamaica., *J Am*
                          Folk-Lore 38(148), Apr.-June: 149-216.   [*COL*]
22.122   JM   1926 Possible survivals of African song in Jamaica. *Mus Q* 12(3), July:
                          340-358.   [19]   [*COL*]

ROBERTS, L. D.

22.123   BC   1961 CRICKET'S BRIGHTEST SUMMER. Kingston, United Printers, 158p.

ROBINSON, ALBAN

22.124   BG   1918 Some figures in string from the Makushis on the Ireng and Takutu Rivers. *Timehri* 3d ser., 5(22), Aug.: 140-152. [13]   [*AMN*]

ROOY, RENE de

22.125   CU   1954/ Letterkundig leven op Curacao [Literary life on Curacao]. *Vox Guy* 55   1(4-5), Nov.-Jan.: 17-24.

ROSS, ALAN

22.126   BC   1960 THROUGH THE CARIBBEAN: THE M.C.C. TOUR OF THE WEST INDIES 1959-60. London, Hamish Hamilton, 296p.

ROTH, VINCENT, ed.

22.127   BG   1949 GRAPHIC ART IN BRITISH GUIANA: A COLLECTION OF WORK BY LOCAL ARTISTS 1944-1948. Georgetown, Daily Chronicle, 54p.

ROTH, WALTER EDMUND

13.069   BG   1929 ADDITIONAL STUDIES OF THE ARTS, CRAFTS, AND CUSTOMS OF THE GUIANA INDIANS, WITH SPECIAL REFERENCE TO THOSE OF SOUTHERN BRITISH GUIANA.

ROUSSIER, PAUL

22.128   MT   1935 Fêtes d'autrefois à la Martinique [Festivals of the past in Martinique]. *In* DENIS, SERGE, ed. NOS ANTILLES. Orleans, Luzeray, p.217-220. [5]   [*AGS*]

SAMSON, PH. A.

22.129   SR   1954 Aantekeningen over kunst en vermaak in Suriname voor 1900 [Notes on art and entertainment in Surinam prior to 1900]. *W I G* 35:154-165. [5]   [*RIS*]

37.357   SR   1956/ Iets over de Surinaamsche Scherpschuttersvereeniging [About the 57   Rifle-Club in Surinam].

SATTERTHWAITE, LINTON, Jr.

4.135   BH   1954 A modified interpretation of the "giant glyph" altars at Caracol, British Honduras.

4.136   BH   1954 Sculptured monuments from Caracol, British Honduras.

SCHIPPER, ARY

22.130   SR   1944/ Enkele opmerkingen over Surinaamsche muziek [Some observations 45   about Surinam's music]. *W I G* 26:209-221. [19]   [*COL*]

SEALY, CLIFFORD

22.131   TR   [1963?] Art and the community. *In* HILL, ERROL, ed. THE ARTIST IN WEST INDIAN SOCIETY: A SYMPOSIUM [seminars held in Port of Spain, Trinidad, May-June 1963, and in Jamaica, Oct. 1962-Jan. 1963]. [Mona?] Dept. of Extra-mural Studies, University of the West Indies, 68.   [*RIS*]

SEEGER, PETER

22.132   TR   1958 The steel drum: a new folk instrument. *J Am Folk-Lore* 71:52-57.
[*COL*]

22.133   TR   1961 THE STEEL DRUMS OF KIM LOY WONG: AN INSTRUCTION BOOK. New York, Oak Publications, 40p. [49]   [*SCH*]

SHARP, STANLEY

22.134   BH   [1952?] Art in British Honduras. *Car Q* 2(2): 30-31.   [*RIS*]

SHERLOCK, PHILIP M.

22.135   JM   1943 Art in Jamaica. *Can-W I Mag* 32(7), July: 19-20.   [*NYP*]

SIMMONS, HAROLD F. C.

22.136   SL   1960 Térré bois bois. *Car Q* 6(4): 282-285. [19]   [*RIS*]

SIMPSON, GEORGE EATON

23.153 TR   1962 The shango cult in Nigeria and in Trinidad.

SMITH, LLOYD SIDNEY

22.137   BC   1922 WEST INDIES CRICKET HISTORY AND CRICKET TOURS TO ENGLAND, 1900, 1906, 1923. Port of Spain, Yuille's Printerie, 240p.

STANFORD, OLLY N.

32.192 TR   1945 The 4-H clubs movement.

SWANTON, E. W.

22.138   BC   1960 WEST INDIES REVISITED: THE M.C.C. TOUR 1959-60. London, Heinemann, 288p.

VIEIRA, PHILIP I.

22.139   TR   1941 Songs of the West. *Can- W I Mag* 30(8), Aug.: 21-23.   [*NYP*]
22.140   BC   1958 The West Indies Festival of Arts, 1958. *Caribbean* 11(8), Mar.: 177-179.   [*COL*]

VINCKE, GASTON

3.317   FG   1935 AVEC LES INDIENS DE LA GUYANE [WITH THE INDIANS OF GUIANA].

VRIES-HAMBURGER, L. de

22.141   SR   1959 Volkskunst en huisnijverheid [Folk art and handicrafts]. *Schakels* S-35: 13-16.

WAART, P. de

52.092 NC   1937 De West en de KRO [The West and the Catholic Broadcasting Corporation].

WALCOTT, CLYDE

22.142   BC   1958 ISLAND CRICKETERS. London, Hodder and Stoughton, 188p.

WALKE, OLIVE

22.143   TR   1959 Christmas music of Trinidad. *Shell Mag* 5(9), Christmas: 5-6. [23]

WALLE, J. van de
22.144   CU   1954   Walsen, danza's en tuma's der Antillen [*Walsen, danzas and tumas of the Antilles*]. *Oost West* 47(5): 11-12.

WATERMAN, RICHARD ALAN
22.145   TR   1943   AFRICAN PATTERNS IN TRINIDAD NEGRO MUSIC. Ph.D. dissertation, Northwestern University, 261p. [11, 19]

WEATHERHEAD, BASIL
22.146   BB   1954   Inter-colonial tournament. *Can-W I Mag* 44(10), Oct.: 19-20. [*NYP*]

WOOD, SYDNEY MAKEPEACE
57.073   JM   1961   Coastal erosion and its control.

WORREL, FRANK
22.147   BC   1959   CRICKET PUNCH. London, Stanley Paul, 144p.

WRIGHT, RICHARDSON
22.148   JM   1937   REVELS IN JAMAICA, 1682-1838. New York, Dodd, Mead, 378p. [5]
[*COL*]

YVANDOC, C.
25.120   GD   1962   Aporta a Feri.

Chapter 23

RELIGION, CULTS AND MAGIC

ABBENHUIS, M. F.

6.001   CU/   1953   De requesten van Pater Stöppel en Perfect Wennekers in 1817 en
       SR   1819 [The petitions of Father Stöppel and Perfect Wennekers in
                        1817 and 1819].

ADAMS-GORDON, VENETA H.

23.001   UV   1963   The history of the African Methodist Episcopal Church in the
                        Virgin Islands. *Vc Miss* 64 [i.e. 65] (2), Feb.: 10-11.   [*NYP*]

ALLAND, ALEXANDER

15.001   ST   1940   The Jews of the Virgin Islands; a history of the islands and candid
                        biographies of outstanding Jews born there.

ANDRADE, JACOB A. P. M.

15.002   JM   1941   A RECORD OF THE JEWS IN JAMAICA FROM THE ENGLISH CONQUEST TO
                        THE PRESENT TIME.

ANTHON, MICHAEL

23.002   BG   1957   The Kanaima. *Timehri* 4th ser., 1(36), Oct.: 61-65.   [13]

APPLETON, S. E.

5.002   TR   1938   Old Tobago—some notes based on a perusal of the church registers.

ASBECK, W. D. H. van

23.003   SR   1919   De Evangelische of Moravische Broeder-Gemeente in Suriname [The
                        Evangelical or Moravian Brethern in Surinam]. *W I G* 1(1): 197-207.
                        [5, 32, 66]   [*COL*]

BARBANSON, W. L. de

7.005   SB   1958   Grafschriften op Saint Barthélémy [Gravestone inscriptions on St.
                        Barthelemy].

BECKWITH, MARTHA WARREN

23.004   JM   1923   Some religious cults in Jamaica. *Am J Psychol* 34(1), Jan.: 32-45.
                                                            [*COL*]

23.005   JM   1924 THE HUSSAY FESTIVAL IN JAMAICA. Poughkeepsie, N.Y., Vassar
                  College, 17p. (Field-work in folk-lore; (Publications of the Folk-
                  lore Foundation, no. 4)).   [12, 19, 22]

           BENNETT, J. HARRY, Jr.
23.006   BB   1951 The S.P.G. and Barbadian politics, 1710-1720. *Hist Mag Prot
                  Epsc Ch* 20(2), June: 190-206.   [5, 37]   [COL]

           BETHENCOURT, CARDOZO de
15.003   GC   1925 Notes on the Spanish and Portuguese Jews in the United States,
                  Guiana, and the Dutch and British West Indies during the seven-
                  teenth and eighteenth centuries.

           BIJLSMA, R.
15.004   SR   1920/ De stichting van de Portugeesch-Joodsche gemeente en synagoge
            21   in Suriname [The founding of the Portuguese-Jewish community and
                  synagogue in Surinam].

           BOWEN, CALVIN
22.013   JM   1954 Jamaica's John Canoe.

           BRAITHWAITE, LLOYD E.
38.023   BC   1957 'Federal' associations and institutions in the West Indies.

           BROU, ALEXANDRE
23.007   BC/   1935 CENT ANS DE MISSIONS 1815-1934: LES JÉSUITES MISSIONAIRES AU
           FG   XIXe ET AU XXe SIÈCLES [ONE HUNDRED YEARS OF MISSION WORK. 1815-
                  1934: THE JESUIT MISSIONARIES IN THE 19TH AND 20TH CENTURIES].
                  Paris, Editions Spes, 312p.   [5]   [NYP]

           BURKHARDT, W.
23.008   SR   1927 Surinam. *Int Rev Miss* 16(63), July: 415-424.   [10]   [NYP]

           BUTT, AUDREY J.
23.009   BG   1953 "The burning fountain whence it came;" a study of the beliefs of
                  the Akawaio. *Social Econ Stud* 2(1), Sept.: 102-116.   [13]   [RIS]
23.010   BG   1954 The burning fountain from whence it came (a study of the system of
                  beliefs of the Carib-speaking Akawaio of British Guiana). *Timehri*
                  4th ser., 1(33), Oct.: 48-60.   [13]
23.011   BG   1959 The birth of a religion (the origins of 'Hallelujah' the semi-Christian
                  religion of the Carib-speaking peoples of the borderlands of British
                  Guiana, Venezuela and Brazil.) *Timehri* 4th ser., no. 38, Sept.: 37-48;
                  1960 4th ser., no. 39, Sept.: 37-48.   [5, 13]   [AMN]
23.012   BG   1961/ Symbolism and ritual among the Akawaio of British Guiana. *N W I G*
            62   41:141-161.   [4, 13, 26]   [COL]

           CABON, A.
23.013   FG   1950 La clergé de la Guyane sous la Révolution [The Guiana clergy
                  during the Revolution]. *Rev Hist Colon Fr* 37(3-4): 173-202.   [5]
                                                                                       [NYP]

CADBURY, HENRY J.

23.014	BB	1940 Quakers, Jews and freedom of teaching in Barbados, 1686. *B Friends Hist Ass* 29(2), Autumn: 97-106. [5,15]
23.015	BB	1941 Barbados Quakers—1683 to 1761: Preliminary list. *J Barb Mus Hist Soc* 9(1), Nov.: 29-31. [5] [AMN]
23.016	BB	1942 186 Barbados Quakeresses in 1677. *J Barb Mus Hist Soc* 9(4), Aug.: 195-197. [5] [AMN]
3.043	Bb	1943 A Quaker account of Barbados in 1718.
23.017	BB	1946/ Witnesses of a Quaker marriage in 1689. *J Barb Mus Hist Soc* 14(1-2), 47 Nov.-Feb.: 8-10. [5] [AMN]
23.018	BB	1948/ Further lists of early clergy. *J Barb Mus Hist Soc* 16(1-2), Nov.-Feb.: 49 21-24. [5] [AMN]
23.019	BB	1948 Clergymen licensed to Barbados, 1694-1811. *J Barb Mus Hist Soc* 15(2), Feb.: 62-69. [5] [AMN]
23.020	BB	1953 Glimpses of Barbados Quakerism 1676-9. *J Barb Mus Hist Soc* 20(2), Feb.: 67-70. [5] [AMN]

CAINE, W. RALPH HALL

3.044	JM	1908 THE CRUISE OF THE PORT KINGSTON.

CAIRES, H. S. de

23.021	BG	1941 The Jesuits in British Guiana. *Month* 177(923), Sept.-Oct.: 455-462. [NYP]

CALLEY, MALCOLM J. C.

18.007	BC	1962 Pentecostal sects among West Indian migrants.

CARR, ANDREW T.

19.004	TR	1953 A Rada community in Trinidad.

CASE, HENRY W.

3.049	BB	1910 ON SEA AND LAND, ON CREEK AND RIVER.
	BG	

CLEGHORN, ROBERT

23.022	BH	1939 A SHORT HISTORY OF BAPTIST MISSIONARY WORK IN BRITISH HONDURAS 1822-1939. London, Kingsgate Press, 71p. [5] [UTS]

COLLIER, H. C.

23.023	BC	1939 Duppy-hunting in paradise. *Can-W I Mag* 28(10), Nov.: 22-24. [NYP]
23.024	BC	1939 Poltergeist—or "duppy 'pon de 'ouse." *Can-W I Mag* 28(7), Aug.: 11-13. [NYP]
23.025	BC	1941 Obeah—the witchcraft of the West Indies—plain bugaboo between me and you. *Can-W I Mag* 30(8), Aug.: 24-25. [NYP]

COLLINS, Rev.

32.047	JM	1907 An agricultural and industrial experiment.

CONNELL, NEVILLE

23.026	BB	1953 St. George's Parish Church, Barbados. *J Barb Mus Hist Soc* 20(3), May: 133-136. [5, 22, 35] [AMN]
22.035	BB	1954 Church plate in Barbados.
3.066	BB	1957 Father Labat's visit to Barbados in 1700.

CRABB, J.A., ed.
23.027   JM   1951 CHRIST FOR JAMAICA. Kingston, The Pioneer Press, 102p.   [5]

CROWLEY, DANIEL JOHN
23.028   SL   1955 Festivals of the calendar in St. Lucia. *Car Q* 4(2), Dec.: 99-121.
                  [19]
                                                                                          [RIS]
23.029   SL   1955 Supernatural beings in St. Lucia. *Caribbean* 8(11-12), June-July:
                  241-244, 264-265.
                                                                                          [RIS]

CUNDALL, FRANK
23.030   JM   1930 Three fingered Jack. *W I Comm Circ* 45(816), Jan. 9: 9-10; 45(817),
                  Jan. 23: 36-37; 45(818), Feb. 6: 55-56.   [5, 11, 24]   *[NYP]*
23.031   JM   1931 A BRIEF HISTORY OF THE PARISH CHURCH OF ST. ANDREW, JAMAICA.
                  Kingston, Institute of Jamaica, 75p.   [5]   *[NYP]*

CUNDALL, FRANK; DAVIS, N. DARNELL & FRIEDENBERG, ALBERT M.
15.009   JM/   1915 Documents relating to the history of the Jews in Jamaica and
           BB   Barbados in the time of William III.

DAVIDSON, LEWIS
23.032   JM   1945 FIRST THINGS FIRST: A STUDY OF THE PRESBYTERIAN CHURCH IN
                  JAMAICA. Edinburgh, William Blackwood, 46p.   [66]   *[UTS]*

DAVIS, J. MERLE
23.033   JM   1942 THE CHURCH IN THE NEW JAMAICA: A STUDY OF THE ECONOMIC , AND
                  SOCIAL BASIS OF THE EVANGELICAL CHURCH IN JAMAICA. New York,
                  International Missionary Council, Dept. of Social and Economic
                  Research & Counsel, 100p.   [66]   *[UTS]*

DAVIS, N. DARNELL
15.010   BB   1909 Notes on the history of the Jews in Barbados.

DELANY, FRANÇIS X.
23.034   JM   1930 A HISTORY OF THE CATHOLIC CHURCH IN JAMAICA B.W.I., 1494 TO
                  1929. New York, Jesuit Mission Press, 292p.   [5]   *[UTS]*

DEVAS, RAYMUND P.
23.035   GR   1927 The Catholic Church in Grenada, B.W.I. (1650-1927) by R.C. Devas,
                  Ir Eccles Rec 5th ser., 30, Aug.: 188-199; 30, Sept.: 288-307;
                  1928 5th ser., 31, May: 474-481; 32, July: 51-56.   [5]   *[NYP]*
23.036   GR   1932 CONCEPTION ISLAND; OR, THE TROUBLED STORY OF THE CATHOLIC
                  CHURCH IN GRENADA. London, Sands, 436p.   [5]   *[RIS]*

DIX, JABEZ
23.037   SL   1933 Adolphe—one of the most terrible of Obeah-men. *Can-W I Mag* 22(2),
                  Jan.: 53-55.   *[NYP]*

DONICIE, A. C.
23.038   SR   1948 Sterfhuis en begrafenis bij de Saramakkanen [House of the deceased
                  and funeral among the Saramaccans]. *W I G* 29:175-182. [14] *[COL]*

EASTON, WILFRED
23.039   GC   1956 WEST INDIES: WHAT OF THE CHURCH? London, Edinburgh House Press,
                  24p.
                                                                                  [UTS]

EGAN, CECILIA M.

23.040   MT   1943   Martinique—the isle of those who return. *Nat Hist* 52(2), Sept.: 52-53, 96. [11,19]   [*COL*]

ELLIS, J. B.

23.041   BH/   1913   The Diocese of Jamaica: a short account of its history, growth,   JM   and organisation. London, Society for Promoting Christian Knowledge, 237p. [5]   [*NYP*]

EMMANUEL, ISAAC S.

15.011   GC   1955   New light on early American Jewry.

23.042   CU   1957   Precious stones of the Jews of Curacao; Curacaon Jewry 1656-1957. New York, Bloch, 584p. [5,15]   [*NYP*]

ESSED, W. F. R.

28.147   SR   1930/ Eenige opmerkingen naar aanleiding van de artikelen over treef en   31   lepra in dit tijdschrift verschenen [Some remarks in connection with the articles about treyf and leprosy that appeared in this magazine].

EUWENS, P. A.

15.012   CU   1930/ De eerste Jood op Curacao [The first Jew on Curacao].   31

23.043   CU   1934/ De Joodsche Synagoge op Curacao [The Jewish Synagogue on   35   Curacao]. *W I G* 16:222-231. [15]   [*COL*]

FARRAR, P. A.

23.044   BB   1935   Christ church. *J Barb Mus Hist Soc* 2(3), May: 143-154.   [5,35]   [*AMN*]

15.013   BB   1942   The Jews in Barbados.

FINDLAY, G. G. & HOLDSWORTH, W. W.

23.045   BC   1921   The history of the Wesleyan Methodist Missionary Society, v. 2. London, Epworth Press, 534p. [5,6,66]   [*UTS*]

FISHER, RUTH ANNA

15.015   JM   1943   Note on Jamaica.

FOCK, NIELS

23.046   BG   1963   Waiwai: religion and society of an Amazonian tribe. Copenhagen, National Museum, 548p. [13]   [*COL*]

FORT, Rev.

23.047   DM/   1903   La Dominique et Sainte Lucie [Dominica and St. Lucia]. *In* PIOLET,   SV   J.-B., ed. La France au dehors: les missions catholiques françaises au XIXe siècle. Vol. 6: Missions d'Amérique. Paris, Librairie Armand Colin, 331-352. [5]   [*NYP*]

FRANKLIN, C. B.

23.048   TR   1934   A century and a quarter of Hanover Methodist Church history 1809-1934. Port of Spain, 32p. [5]

FROIDEVAUX, HENRI

3.115   FG   1901   Les "lettres édifiantes" et la description de la mission de Kourou [The "edifying letters" and a description of the Kourou mission].

GAAY FORTMAN, B. de

23.049   CU   1941 Lutherschen op Curacao [Lutherans on Curacao]. *W I G* 23:280-288. [7]
    [COL]

23.050   BG/   1941 Lutherschen op St. Eustatius en in Essequebo [Lutherans on St.
    SE   Eustatius and in Essequibo]. *W I G* 23:346-352. [7]   [COL]

23.051   BG   1942 De geschiedenis der Luthersche gemeente in Berbice [The history of the Lutheran congregation in Berbice]. *W I G* 24:20-27, 51-62, 65-89. [5]
    [COL]

GALTON, C. T., Bp.

32.069   BG   1912 Elementary education in British Guiana.

GARRETT, CLARA MAUDE

19.012   JM   1935 Caribbean Christmas.

GOEJE, C. H. de

23.052   SR   1929/ A. Ph. Penard over inwijding en wereld-beschouwing der Karaïben
               30 [A. Ph. Penard on initiation and worldview of the Caribs]. *W I G* 11:275-286. [13]
    [COL]

23.053   SR   1942 De inwijding tot medicijnman bij de Arawakken (Guyana) in tekst en mythe [The initiation of medicinemen among the Arawaks (Guiana) in word and myths]. *Bijd Volk* 101:211-276. [13]

20.007   GC   1943 Philosophy, initiation and myths of the Indians of Guiana and adjacent countries.

23.054   SR   1947 Negers in Amerika [Negroes in the Americas]. *W I G* 28:217-221. [14]
    [COL]

23.055   SR   1948 Zondvloed en Zondeval bij de Indianen van West-Indie [The Deluge and the Fall among the Indians of the West Indies]. Amsterdam, Indisch Instituut, 64p. (Mededeling no. 79, Afdeling Volkenkunde no. 28.)   [13]
    [NYP]

23.056   GC   1952 The physical world, the world of magic, and the moral world of Guiana Indians. *In* TAX, SOL, ed. Indian tribes of aboriginal America: Selected papers of the XXIXth International Congress of Americanists. Chicago, University of Chicago Press, 266-270. [13, 24]
    [AGS]

23.057   NA   1956/ Enkele beschouwingen over de Indianen der Nederlandse Antillen en
               57 hun geestesleven [Some observations about the Indians in the Netherlands Antilles and their spiritual life]. *W I G* 37:41-50. [13] [COL]

GOSLINGA, C. CH.

23.058   GC   1956 Kerk, Kroon en Cariben [Church, crown and Caribs]. *W I G* 36:147-161. [5, 13, 37]
    [COL]

GUASCO, ALEXANDRE

23.059   FG   1903 La Guyane francaise [French Guiana]. *In* PIOLET, J.-B., ed. La France au dehors: les missions catholiques francaises au XIXe siècle, Vol. 6: Missions d'Amérique. Paris, Librairie Armand Colin, 395-415. [5]
    [NYP]

GUERIN, DANIEL

19.014   GC   1956 Un futur pour les Antilles? [A future for the Antilles?]

GUGGENHEIM, HANS & CARR, ANDREW T.
23.060   TR   1965 Tribalism in Trinidad. *Med Newsmag* 9(2), Feb.: 138-143.   [22]
                                                                                  [*RIS*]

HARTOG, JOHAN
23.061   NL   1947 De godsdiensten in Curacao [The religions of Curacao].*W I G* 28:1-8.
                                                                                  [*COL*]
23.062   AR   1952 Aruba's oudste kerk 1750-1816-1952 [Aruba's oldest church 1750-
                1816-1952]. *W I G* 33:191-198.   [5,66]   [*COL*]

HENDRICK, S. PURCELL
23.063   JM   1911 A SKETCH OF THE HISTORY OF THE CATHEDRAL CHURCH OF ST. JAGO DE
                LA VEGA, SPANISH TOWN IN THE PARISH OF ST. CATHERINE, JAMAICA.
                Kingston, Jamaica Times, 52p.   [5, 35]   [*NYP*]

HENFREY, COLIN
13.035   BG   1964 THE GENTLE PEOPLE: A JOURNEY AMONG THE INDIAN TRIBES OF GUIANA.

HENRY, FRANCES
8.028   TR   1965 Social stratification in an Afro-American cult.

HILFMAN, P. A.
15.019   SR   1909 Notes on the history of the Jews in Surinam.

HILL, CLIFFORD S.
18.028   BC   1963 WEST INDIAN MIGRANTS AND THE LONDON CHURCHES.

HOGG, DONALD WILLIAM
23.064   JM   1956 A West Indian shepherd. *In Context* 4(2), Mar.: 12-15.   [19]   [*RIS*]
23.065   JM   1960 The Convince Cult in Jamaica. *In* MINTZ, SIDNEY W., comp.
                PAPERS IN CARIBBEAN ANTHROPOLOGY. New Haven, Dept. of Anthro-
                pology, Yale University, no. 58 (24p.). (Yale University publications
                in anthropology, no. 57-64.)   [19]   [*RIS*]
23.066   JM   1961 Magic and "science" in Jamaica. *Car Stud* 1(2), July: 1-5.   [*RIS*]
23.067   JM   1963 JAMAICAN RELIGION: A STUDY IN VARIATIONS. Ph. D. dissertation, Yale
                University, 474p.   [19]

HOROWITZ, MICHAEL M.
23.068   MT   1963 The worship of South Indian deities in Martinique. *Ethnology* 2(3),
                July: 339-346.   [12, 19]   [*RIS*]

HOROWITZ, MICHAEL M. & KLASS, MORTON
23.069   MT   1961 The Martiniquan East Indian cult of Maldevidan. *Social Econ Stud*
                10(1), Mar.: 93-100.   [12, 19]   [*RIS*]

HOSTER, WILLIAM
23.070   UV   1926 Our mission work in Porto Rico and the Virgin Islands. *Sp Miss*
                91(1), Jan.: 19-26.   [*NYP*]

HOUTZAGER, J. C.
23.071   CU   1939 Het Gereformeerd kerkelijk leven in Curacao [The Reformed Church
                on Curacao]. *W I G* 21:43-47.   [*COL*]

HUGHES, H. B. L.

23.072   JM   1945 The Impact on Jamaica of the Evangelical Revival. *Jam Hist Rev*
                          1(1), June: 7-23. [5]   [*AMN*]

HURWITZ, SAMUEL J. & EDITH

15.020   JM   1965 The New World sets an example for the old: the Jews of Jamaica
                          and political rights 1661-1831.

HUTCHINSON, FRANK L.

33.014   JM   1956 Hunger and help in the Caribbean: Jamaica, Puerto Rico, Haiti.

HUTTON, J. E.

23.073   GC   1922 A HISTORY OF MORAVIAN MISSIONS. London, Moravian Publ. Office,
                          550p. [5, 66]   [*UTS*]

JENKINS, CHARLES FRANCIS

23.074   TT   1923 Tortola, the chief of the British Virgin Islands. *B Geogr Soc Phila*
                          21(1), Jan.: 1-20. [5]   [*AGS*]

JESSE, C.

23.075   FA   1960 Religion among the early slaves in the French Antilles.   *J Barb*
                          Mus Hist Soc 28(1), Nov.: 4-10. [5, 6]   [*AMN*]

JORDAN, W. F.

3.161   FC   1922 CRUSADING IN THE WEST INDIES.

JOSA, F. P. LUIGI

23.076   BC   1910 ENGLISH CHURCH HISTORY OF THE WEST INDIAN PROVINCE. Georgetown,
                          Argosy Co., 143p. [5]   [*SCH*]

JUDAH, GEORGE FORTUNATUS

15.022   JM   1909 The Jews' tribute in Jamaica.

JUNKER, L.

23.077   SR   1925/ De godsdienst der Boschnegers [The religion of the Bush Negroes].
                          26 *W I G* 7:81-95, 127-137, 153-164. [14]   [*COL*]

KALFF, S.

10.022   CU   1926/ Joden op het eiland Curacao [Jews on the island of Curacao].
                          27

23.078   SR/   1928/ Westindische predikanten [West Indian preachers]. *W I G* 10:413-416,
          CU   29   465-476.   [*COL*]

KAYSERLING, M.

15.024   JM   1900 The Jews in Jamaica and Daniel Israel Lopez Laguna.

KESLER, C. K.

23.079   SR   1923/ Nils Otto Tank (1800-1864). *W I G* 5:65-76. [5]   [*COL*]
                          24

23.080   NC/   1933/ Graaf von Zinzendorf in Holland [Count von Zinzendorf in Holland].
          ST   34   *W I G* 15:1-10. [5]   [*COL*]

23.081   SR   1939 Een Moravische Zuster uit de 18e eeuw: Anna Maria Kersten geb.
                          Tonn 1723-1807 [A Moravian Sister from the 18th century: Anna
                          Maria Kersten neé Tonn, 1723-1807]. *W I G* 21:206-217. [5]   [*COL*]

23.082   BG   1942 Moeilijkheden met betrekking tot eedsaflegging en het dragen van wapenen in Berbice in de 18de eeuw [Problems about oath-taking and carrying of weapons in Berbice in the 18th century]. *W I G* 24: 129-142. [5]   [COL]

KIEMEN, MATHIAS C.

32.111   GC   1960 Catholic schools in the Caribbean.

KIEV, ARI

31.042   JM   1963 Beliefs and delusions of West Indian immigrants to London.

18.032   BC   1964 Psychotherapeutic aspects of Pentecostal sects among West Indian immigrants to England.

KING, R. O. C.

23.083   BC   1948 The church in the British West Indies. *Int Rev Miss* 37(145), Jan.: 80-85.   [NYP]

KLERK, CORNELIS JOHANNES MARIA de

23.084   SR   1951 CULTUS EN RITUEEL VAN HET ORTHODOXE HINDOEÏSME IN SURINAME [CULTS AND RITUAL OF ORTHODOX HINDUISM IN SURINAM]. Amsterdam, Urbi et Orbi, 292p. [12, 19]   [RIS]

23.085   SR   1963 Over de religie der Surinaamse Hindostanen [On the religion of the Hindustanis in Surinam]. *In* LUTCHMAN, W. I., ed. VAN BRITS-INDISCH EMIGRANT TOT BURGER VAN SURINAME. The Hague, Drukkerij Wieringa, p.61-80. [12]

KLEYNTJENS, J.

23.086   NA   1931/ Het apostolische vicariaat van Curacao [The apostolic vicariate 32 of Curacao]. *W I G* 13:123-137.   [COL]

KLINGBERG, FRANK J.

32.112   BC   1939 The Lady Mico Charity Schools in the British West Indies, 1835-1842.

6.038   JM   1942 As to the state of Jamaica in 1707.

KNAPPERT, L.

23.087   CU   1925/ Koning Willem I en de Protestantsche gemeente op Curacao [King 26 William the first and the Protestant community on Curacao]. *W I G* 7:193-206. [5]   [COL]

23.088   SR   1926/ De Labadisten in Suriname [The Labadists in Surinam]. *W I G* 8: 27 193-218.   [COL]

23.089   SM   1928/ Een heksenproces op Sint Maarten [A witch trial on St. Maarten]. 29 *W I G* 10:241-264. [5, 37]   [COL]

23.090   CU   1939 Wigboldt Rasvelt en zijne gemeente op Curacao, 1730-1757 [Wigboldt Rasvelt and his congregation on Curacao]. *W I G* 21:1-11, 33-42. [5, 66]   [COL]

KOCH, L.

23.091   UV   1905 Den danske mission i Vestindien [The Danish mission in the West Indies]. *Kirk Saml* 5th ser., 3(1): 144-180. [5]   [NYP]

KRUIJER, GERARDUS JOHANNES

23.092   NA   1953 Kerk en religie op de Bovenwindse Eilanden der Nederlandse Antil-
                 len [Church and religion of the Windward Islands of the Netherlands
                 Antilles]. *W I G* 34(4): 238-251.   [19]   [*RIS*]
43.089   JM   1956 Met bulldozers en sociologie de bergen in [Trip into the mountains
                 with bulldozers and sociology].

KUNIKE, HUGO

19.026   GG   1912 Der Fisch als Fruchtbarkeitssymbol bei den Waldindianern Sud-
                 Amerikas [The fish as a fertility symbol among the South American
                 Forest Indians].

LARSEN, JENS P. M.

23.093   UV   1950 VIRGIN ISLANDS STORY: A HISTORY OF THE LUTHERAN STATE CHURCH,
                 OTHER CHURCHES, SLAVERY, EDUCATION AND CULTURE IN THE DANISH
                 WEST INDIES, NOW THE VIRGIN ISLANDS. Philadelphia, Muhlenberg
                 Press, 250p.   [*COL*]

LAWRENCE, GEORGE E.

23.094   MS   1956 THOMAS O'GARRA: A WEST INDIAN LOCAL PREACHER. London, Epworth
                 Press, 59p.

LEACH, MacEDWARD

24.043   JM   1961 Jamaican duppy lore.

LEAF, EARL

22.086   GC   1948 ISLES OF RHYTHM.

LEVY, BABETTE M.

23.095   BC   1960 The West Indies and Bahamas: Puritanism in conflict with tropical
                 island life. *In* PROCEEDINGS OF THE AMERICAN ANTIQUARIAN SOCIETY,
                 vol. 70. Worcester, Mass., p.278-348.   [5]   [*COL*]

LIER, WILLEM F. van & GOEJE, C. H. de

23.096   SR   1940 Aantekeningen over het geestelijk leven en de samenleving der
                 Djoeka's in Suriname [Notes on the spiritual life and society of
                 the Djukas in Surinam]. *Bijd Volk* 99(2): 129-294.   [14]

LINDE, J. M. van der

6.043   SR   1953 De emancipatie der Negerslaven in Suriname en de zendingsarbeid
                 der Moravische Broeders [The emancipation of the Negro slaves in
                 Surinam and the missionary work of the Moravian Brethren].

LIVINGSTON, Sir NOEL B.

23.097   JM   1946 Records of the Kingston vestry. *Jam Hist Rev* 1(2), Dec.: 181-186.
                 [5]   [*COL*]

LYNDEN, J. W. van

23.098   SR   1939 De Evangelische Broedergemeente in Suriname [The United Brethren
                 in Surinam]. *W I G* 221: 161-172.   [5]   [*COL*]

McNEILL, GEORGE

23.099   JM   1911 THE STORY OF OUR MISSIONS: THE WEST INDIES. Edinburgh, Foreign
                Mission Committees at the Offices of the United Free Church of
                Scotland, 93p. [5, 66]   [*UTS*]

McTURK, MICHAEL

5.130   BG   1912 Some old graves in the Colony.

MAKIN, WILLIAM J.

3.187   JM   1939 CARIBBEAN NIGHTS.

MALEFIJT, ANNEMARIE de WAAL

23.100   SR   1964 Animism and Islam among the Javanese in Surinam. *Anthrop Q*
                37(3), July: 149-155. [10, 19]   [*RIS*]

MARCUS, JACOB RADER

15.031   GC   1953 The West India and South America expedition of the American
                Jewish Archives.

MARTIN, KINGSLEY

23.101   JM   1961 The Jamaican volcano. *New Stsm* 61(1566), Mar. 17: 416-418.
                [11, 16, 37]   [*RIS*]

MAY, FRED

23.102   BG   1918 The Lutherans of Berbice. *Timehri* 3d ser., 5(22), Aug.: 74-77. [5]
                                                                               [*AMN*]

MEIDEN, J. A. van der

23.103   SR   1960 Kerken, tempels en heiligdommen in Suriname [Churches, temples
                and sacred places in Surinam]. *Schakels* S-38: 17-22. [19]

MENKMAN, W. R.

23.104   SM/   1958 St. Maarten en St. Barthélemy, 1911-1951. *WIG* 38:151-162.   [5,66]
          SB   [*COL*]

MERRILL, GORDON CLARK

15.032   GC   1964 The role of Sephardic Jews in the British Caribbean area during the
                seventeenth century.

METRAUX, A.

23.105   FG   1928 LA RELIGION DES TUPINAMBA ET SES RAPPORTS AVEC CELLE DES AUTRES
                TRIBUS TUPI-GUARANI [THE RELIGION OF THE TUPINAMBA AND ITS RE-
                LATIONSHIP TO THAT OF THE OTHER TUPI-GUARANI TRIBES]. Paris,
                Librairie Ernest Leroux, 260p. [13]   [*COL*]

MEYER, J.

7.047   SR   1954 PIONEERS OF PAUROMA, CONTRIBUTION TO THE EARLIEST HISTORY OF
                THE JEWISH COLONIZATION OF AMERICA.

MISCHEL, FRANCES

23.106   TR   1957 African "powers" in Trinidad: the Shango cult. *Anthrop Q* 30(2),
                Apr.: 45-59. [11, 19]   [*RIS*]

MISCHEL, WALTER & FRANCES
31.056   TR   1958 Psychological aspects of spirit possession.

MOORE, JOSEPH GRAESSLE
23.107   JM   1953 Religion of Jamaican Negroes: a study of Afro-Jamaican accul-
                      turation. Ph.D. dissertation, Northwestern University, 284p. [11,19]

MOORE, JOSEPH GRAESSLE & SIMPSON, GEORGE E.
23.108   JM   1957 A comparative study of acculturation in Morant Bay and West
                      Kingston, Jamaica. *Zaire* 9-10: 979-1019;
                      1958 11: 65-87.   [19]   [*RIS*]

MORSINK, F.
14.022   SR   1934/ Nogmaals: de dood van Jankosoe. En: nog niet het einde van een
             35 dynastie [Once again: the death of Jankosoe. And: not yet the end
                      of a dynasty].

MOTHON, R. P.
23.109   TR   1903 La Trinidad. *In* PIOLET, J.-B., ed. La France au dehors: les
                      missions catholiques francaises au XIXᵉ siècle. Vol. 6: missions
                      d'Amérique. Paris, Librairie Armand Colin, p.353-382.   [5] [*NYP*]

MULLER, KARL
23.110   GC   1931 Westindien. Suriname [West Indies. Surinam]. *In his* 200 Jahre
                      Brüdermission. Herrnhut [Ger.], Missionsbuchhandlung, p.19-109.
                      [5]   [*NYP*]

NIEHOFF, ARTHUR
23.111   TR   1959 The spirit world of Trinidad. *Shell Trin* 5(7), June: 17-19.

NOUSSANNE, HENRI de
23.112   FA/   1936 La France missionnaire aux Antilles: Guadeloupe, Martinique,
          TR   Trinidad [French missionaries in the West Indies: Guadeloupe,
                      Martinique, Trinidad]. Paris, P. Lethielleux, 173p. [5]   [*NYP*]

OLIVER. VERE LANGFORD
23.113   BB   1915 The monumental inscriptions in the churches and churchyards
                      of the island of Barbados, British West Indies. London, Mitchell
                      Hughes and Clarke, 223p.   [5]   [*NYP*]

OPPENHEIM, SAMUEL
15.033   GG/   1907 An early Jewish colony in Western Guiana 1658-1666: and its rela-
          TB   tion to the Jews in Surinam, Cayenne and Tobago.
15.034   BG   1908 An early Jewish colony in Western Guiana: supplemental data.

OUDSCHANS DENTZ, FRED
28.406   SR   1930/ Dr. Constantin Hering en Christiaan Johannes Hering.
             31
23.114   SR   1948 Wat er overbleef van het kerkhof en de synagoge van de Joden-
                      Savanne in Suriname [What is left of the cemetery and the synagogue
                      of the Jewish-Savannah in Surinam]? *W I G* 29:210-224.   [3, 7,15]
                                                                                [*COL*]

23.115   SR   1949 De Hervormde Kerk in Suriname in Haar begintijd [The Dutch Re-
                        formed Church in Surinam in her early years]. *W I G* 30:353-361. [5]
                        [*COL*]

PANHUYS, L. C. van
23.116   SR   1913 The heathen religion of the Bush Negroes in Dutch Guiana. *In*
                        ACTES DU IVᵉ CONGRÈS INTERNATIONAL D'HISTOIRE DES RELIGIONS,
                        Leide, Sept. 1912. Leiden, E. J. Brill, p.53-57. [14]   [*NYP*]
23.117   SR   1936/ De opoffering van een R. K. priester in Suriname [The sacrifice of a
                  37   Roman Catholic priest in Surinam]. *W I G* 18:200-206. [28]   [*COL*]

PAYNE, ERNEST A.
23.118   JM   1946 FREEDOM IN JAMAICA; SOME CHAPTERS IN THE STORY OF THE BAPTIST
                        MISSIONARY SOCIETY. 2d ed. London, Carey Press, 112p. [5, 6, 66]
                        [*UTS*]

PENARD, A.
23.119   SR   1928 Het pujai-geheim der Surinaamsche Caraiben [The pujai-secret of
                        the Caribs of Surinam]. *Bijd Volk Ned-Indie* 84:625-671. [13]

PENARD, F. P. & A. P.
23.120   SR   1913 Surinaamsch bijgeloof: iets over *winti* en andere natuurbegrippen
                        [Surinam superstition: about *winti* and other supernatural notions].
                        Bijd Volk Ned-Indie 67:157-183.   [10, 19]

PEROWNE, STEWART
23.121   BB   1952 Monuments in Barbados. *Ctry Life* 110(2864), Dec. 7: 1939-1942.

PETERS, FRED E.
35.035   MS   1931 SAINT ANTHONY'S CHURCH, MONTSERRAT, WEST INDIES.

PETITJEAN-ROGET, JACQUES
23.122   MT   1956 Les protestants à la Martinique sous l'ancien régime [The Protes-
                        tants in Martinique under the old regime]. *Rev Hist Colon* 40(3):
                        220-265. [5]   [*RIS*]

PHILLIPS, LESLIE H. C.
23.123   BG   1960 Kali-mai puja. *Timehri* 4th ser., no. 39, Sept.: 37-46. [12, 19] [*AMN*]

PILKINGTON, FREDERICK
23.124   JM   1950 DAYBREAK IN JAMAICA. London, Epworth Press, 220p. [3] [*SCH*]

PITMAN, FRANK WESLEY
6.056   BC   1926 Slavery on the British West India plantations in the eighteenth
                        century.

PRICE, RICHARD
56.045   MT   1964 Magie et pêche à la Martinique [Magic and fishing in Martinique].

PRINS, J.
23.125   BB   1961/ De Islam in Suriname: een Oriëntatie [Islam in Surinam: an orienta-
                  62   tion]. *N W I G* 41(1): 14-37. [12, 15]   [*COL*]

REECE, J. E. & CLARK-HUNT, C. G., eds.
23.126   BB   1925 BARBADOS DIOCESAN HISTORY. London, West India Committee, 136p. [5]

RENNARD, J.
23.127   FA   1935 Organisation des paroisses [The parish organization]. *In* DENIS, SERGE, ed. NOS ANTILLES. Orleans, Luzeray, 131-159. [5] [*AGS*]
23.128   MT   1951 LA MARTINIQUE HISTORIQUE DES PAROISSES: DES ORIGINES À LA SEPARATION [PARISH HISTORY OF MARTINIQUE: FROM CONTACT TO SEPARATION]. Thonon-les-Bains (Haute-Savoie), Société d'édition savoyarde, 349p. [5] [*RIS*]

RENS, L. L. E.
15.035   SR   1954 Analysis of annals relating to early Jewish settlement in Surinam.

REVERT, EUGENE
24.067   MT   1951 DE QUELQUES ASPECTS DU FOLK-LORE MARTINIQUAIS: LA MAGIE ANTILLAISE [ON SOME ASPECTS OF MARTINIQUE FOLK-LORE: ANTILLEAN MAGIC].

RIJNDERS, B. J. C.
23.129   SR   1947 Het werk van de Evangelische Broedergemeente in Suriname [The work of the United Brethren in Surinam]. *W I G* 28:300-311. [66] [*COL*]

ROOS, J. S.
15.036   SR   1905 Additional notes on the history of the Jews in Surinam.

ROTH, HENRY D.
23.130   BG   1950 The kanaima. *Timehri* 4th ser., 1(29), Aug.: 25-26. [13]

ROTH, WALTER EDMUND
23.131   BG   1915 An inquiry into the animism and folklore of the Guiana Indians. *In* THIRTIETH ANNUAL REPORT, BUREAU OF AMERICAN ETHNOLOGY, 1908-1909. Washington, U. S. Govt. Print. Off., p.103-453. [13, 24, 29] [*NYP*]

ROUSSIER, PAUL
32.169   MT   1930 Une maison d'éducation pour les jeunes personnes à la Martinique au temps où l'impératrice Joséphine était enfant [An educational institution for young ladies in Martinique at the time when Empress Josephine was a child].

RYCROFT, W. STANLEY
23.132   GC   1955 The contribution of Protestantism in the Caribbean. *In* WILGUS, A. CURTIS, ed. THE CARIBBEAN: ITS CULTURE [papers delivered at the Fifth Conference on the Caribbean held at the University of Florida, Dec. 2-4, 1954]. Gainesville, University of Florida Press, 158-168. (Publications of the School of Inter-American Studies, ser. 1, v. 5.) [*RIS*]

SAMSON, PH. A.
7.074   SR   1939 Uit het verleden van Suriname [From Surinam's past].

| 23.133 | SR | 1940 De oplossing van het eedsvraagstuk in Suriname [The solution of the problem of oath-taking in Surinam]. *W I G* 22:284-286. [37] [*COL*] |

23.133 SR 1940 De oplossing van het eedsvraagstuk in Suriname [The solution of the problem of oath-taking in Surinam]. *W I G* 22:284-286. [37]
[*COL*]

23.134 SR 1946 Afgoderij als strafbaar feit [Idolatry as a penal offense]. *W I G* 27:378-381. [37] [*COL*]

23.135 SR 1946 Bijgeloof in de rechtszaal [Superstition in the courtroom]. *W I G* 27:141-146. [*COL*]

SAMUEL, WILFRED S.
15.037 BB 1936 A REVIEW OF THE JEWISH COLONISTS IN BARBADOS IN THE YEAR 1680.

SCHOELCHER, VICTOR
6.061 GD 1935 LETTRES INÉDITES À VICTOR SCHOELCHER (1848-1851) [UNPUBLISHED LETTERS TO VICTOR SCHOELCHER (1848-1851)].

SCHULZE, ADOLF
23.136 GC 1931/ 200 Jahre Brüdermission [200 years of the Brothers' missions].
32 Herrnhut, [Ger.], Verlag der Missionsbuchhandlung, 2v. [5,66]
[*COL*]

SCHUTZ, H.
23.137 SR 1934/ Herrnhutter nederzetting leiding 7B [The Moravian settlement Line
35 7B]. *W I G* 16:273-281. [66] [*COL*]

23.138 SR 1935/ Sporen van tweehonderd jaar Herrnhutterzending [Traces of two
36 hundred years of Moravian missionary work]. *W I G* 17:221-227. [66]
[*COL*]

SCHUTZ, JOHN A.
23.139 BB 1946 Christopher Codrington's will: launching the S. P. G. into the Barbadian sugar business. *Pacif Hist Rev* 15(2), June: 192-200. [5, 45]
[*COL*]

SCHUTZ, JOHN A. & O'NEIL, MAUD E., eds.
23.140 BB 1946 Arthur Holt, Anglican clergyman, reports on Barbados, 1725-1733.
J Negro Hist 31(4), Oct.: 444-469. [5, 11] [*COL*]

SCHWARTZ, BARTON M.
23.141 TR 1964 Ritual aspects of caste in Trinidad. *Anthrop Q* 37(1), Jan.: 1-15.
[8, 12, 19] [*RIS*]

SERENO, RENZO
23.142 GC 1948 Obeah: magic and social structure in the Lesser Antilles. *Psychiatry* 11(1), Feb.: 15-31. [28, 31] [*COL*]

SHERLOCK, PHILIP M.
24.070 JM 1924 Jamaica superstitions.

SHILSTONE, E. M.
23.143 BB 1936 Parish churches in Barbados. *J Barb Mus Hist Soc* 4(1), Nov.: 5-8.
[5] [*AMN*]

23.144 BB 1958 MONUMENTAL INSCRIPTIONS IN THE BURIAL GROUND OF THE JEWISH
SYNAGOGUE AT BRIDGETOWN, BARBADOS. London, Jewish Historical
Society of England, University College London. [5,15] [*COL*]

SHORROCKS, FRANCIS

23.145   BB   1958 History of the Catholic Church in Barbados during the 19th century. *J Barb Mus Hist Soc* 25(3), May: 102-122. [5]   [*AMN*]

SIMPSON, GEORGE EATON

23.146   JM   1950 The acculturative process in Jamaican revivalism. *In* WALLACE, ANTHONY F.C., ed. MEN AND CULTURES: SELECTED PAPERS OF THE FIFTH INTERNATIONAL CONGRESS OF ANTHROPOLOGICAL AND ETHNOLOGICAL SCIENCES, Philadelphia, Sept. 1-9, 1956. Philadelphia, University of Pennsylvania Press, p.332-341. [19]   [*RIS*]

23.147   JM   1955 Culture change and reintegration found in the cults of West Kingston, Jamaica. *Proc Am Phil Soc* 99(2), Apr. 15: 89-92. [11, 16, 19, 37] [*RIS*]

23.148   JM   1955 Political cultism in West Kingston, Jamaica. *Social Econ Stud* 4(2), June: 133-149. [11, 16, 37]   [*RIS*]

23.149   JM   1955 The Ras Tafari movement in Jamaica: a study of race and class conflict. *Social Forces* 34(2), Dec.: 167-170. [11, 16, 37] [*RIS*]

23.150   JM   1956 Jamaican revivalist cults. *Social Econ Stud* 5(4), Dec. (iv, 442, v-xi p.) [19]   [*RIS*]

23.151   JM   1957 The nine night ceremony in Jamaica. *J Am Folk* 70(278), Oct.-Dec.: 329-335. [19]   [*RIS*]

23.152   JM   1962 The Ras Tafari movement in Jamaica in its millennial aspect. *In* THRUPP, SYLVIA L., ed. MILLENNIAL DREAMS IN ACTION: ESSAYS IN COMPARATIVE STUDY. The Hague, Mouton, p.160-165. (Comparative studies in society and history, Supplement 2.) [11, 16, 37] [*RIS*]

23.153   TR   1962 The shango cult in Nigeria and in Trinidad. *Am Anthrop* 64(6), Dec.: 1204-1219. [11, 19]   [*RIS*]

23.154   TR   1964 The acculturative process in Trinidadian Shango. *Anthrop Q* 37(1), Jan.: 16-27. [11, 19]   [*RIS*]

23.155   TR   1965 THE SHANGO CULT IN TRINIDAD. Rio Piedras, University of Puerto Rico, 140p. (Institute of Caribbean Studies, Caribbean monograph series no. 2.) [11, 19]   [*RIS*]

SLOMAN, E.

35.041 BG   1912 St. George's Cathedral.

SMITH, Rev. G.W.

23.156   GC   [1939?] Conquests of Christ in the West Indies: a short history of Evangelical missions. Brown's Town, St. Ann, Jamaica, Evangelical Book-Room, 125p. [5, 66]   [*UTS*]

SMITH, M.G.

23.157   GR   1963 DARK PURITAN. Kingston, Dept. of Extra-mural Studies, University of the West Indies, 139p. [11]   [*RIS*]

SMITH, M.G.; AUGIER, ROY & NETTLEFORD, REX

23.158   JM   1960 THE RAS TAFARI MOVEMENT IN KINGSTON, JAMAICA. Kingston, University of the West Indies, 54p. [11,16,37,66]   [*RIS*]

SMITH, RAYMOND THOMAS

12.031 BG   1959 Some social characteristics of Indian immigrants to British Guiana.

SMITH, ROBERT WORTHINGTON

23.159   BC   1950   Slavery and Christianity in the British West Indies. *Ch Hist* 19(3), Sept.: 171-186.   [COL]

STAEHELIN, F.

23.160   SR/   [1912?] Die Mission der Brüdergemeine in Suriname und Berbice im acht-
         BG   zehnten Jahrhundert [The Moravian Brethren mission in Surinam and Berbice in the 18th century]. Paramaribo, Verlag von C. Kersten & Co. in Kommission bei der Missionsbuchhandlung in Herrnhut und für den Buchhandel bei der Unitätsbuchhandlung in Gnadau, 7 pts. in 3v. [5, 13, 14, 66]   [SCH]

STYCOS, J. MAYONE & BACK, KURT

34.019   JM   1958   Contraception and Catholicism in Jamaica.

SUMMIT, ALPHONS

15.039   SR   1940   The Jews of Surinam.

SWELLENGREBEL, N. H. & KUYP, E. van der

28.511   SR   1940   HEALTH OF WHITE SETTLERS IN SURINAM.

TANNENBAUM, FRANK

6.070   GC   1947   SLAVE AND CITIZEN; THE NEGRO IN THE AMERICAS.

TAYLOR, DOUGLAS C.

23.161   DM   1945   Carib folk beliefs and customs from Dominica, B. W. I. *Sw J Anthrop* 1(4), Winter: 507-530. [13, 29]

THOMPSON, E. W.

23.162   BC   1940   The return of the West Indies. *Int Rev Miss* 29(116), Oct.: 452-462. [33]   [NYP]

23.163   GC   1943   Eyes on the West Indies. *Int Rev Miss* 32(127), July: 293-300. [33]   [NYP]

TUCKER, LEONARD, comp.

23.164   JM   1914   "GLORIOUS LIBERTY": THE STORY OF A HUNDRED YEARS' WORK OF THE JAMAICA BAPTIST MISSION. London, Baptist Missionary Society, 168p. [5, 66]   [UTS]

VANDERCOOK, JOHN WOMACK

23.165   SR   1925   White magic and black, the jungle science of Dutch Guiana. *Harper's Mag* 151, Oct.: 548-554. [29]   [COL]

15.040   SR   1928   Jungle Jews.

VEERASAWMY, J. A.

37.404   BG   1919   The Noitgedacht murder.

VOORHOEVE, JAN

25.108   SR   1957   Missionary linguistics in Surinam.

VOORHOEVE, JAN & RENSELAER, H. C. van

23.166   SR   1962   Messianism and nationalism in Surinam. *Bijd Volk* 118:193-216. [21]

VOULLAIRE, R.

23.167   SR   1907 A journey among the bush men of Surinam. *Miss Rev Wld* new ser.,
                    20(11), Nov.: 815-819. [14]   [*NYP*]

VOULLAIRE, W. R.

23.168   SR   1926 SURINAM: LE PAYS, LES HABITANTS ET LA MISSION MORAVE [SURINAM:
                    THE LAND, THE INHABITANTS, AND THE MORAVIAN MISSION]. Lausanne,
                    Impr. La Concorde, 94p. [5, 66]   [*AGS*]

WALKE, OLIVE

22.143 TR   1959 Christmas music of Trinidad.

WEISS, H.

23.169   SR   1919 Het zendingswerk der Herrnhutters in de Oerwouden van de Boven-
                    Suriname [Missionary work of the Moravian Brethren in the jungles
                    of the Upper-Surinam River]. *W I G* 1(1):102-110. [5, 66]   [*COL*]

23.170   SR   1920/ De zending der Hernhutters onder de Indianen in Berbice en Surinam,
            21 1738-1816 [The mission of the Moravians among the Indians in
                    Berbice and Surinam, 1738-1816]. *W I G* 2:36-44, 109-121, 187-197,
                    249-264. [5, 66]   [*COL*]

WESLEY, CHARLES H.

32.212 BC   1932/ Rise of Negro education in the British Empire.
            33

WHITE, RALPH J.

23.171   BG   1919 The Berbice Lutheran Church. *Timehri* 3d ser., 6(23), Sept.: 196-
                    201. [5]   [*AMN*]

WHITE, WALTER GRAINGE

3.331   BG   [n.d.] AT HOME WITH THE MACUCHI.
26.061 BG   1917 Fringes of Makuchi.

WILLIAMS, JOSEPH J.

23.172   JM   1932 VOODOOS AND OBEAHS, PHASES OF WEST INDIA WITCHCRAFT. New York,
                    Dial Press, 257p. [5, 19]   [*RIS*]

23.173   JM   1934 PSYCHIC PHENOMENA OF JAMAICA. New York, Dial Press, 309p. [19]
                                                                                   [*AMN*]

YARNLEY, J. R.

23.174   JM   1939 Behind the cactus hedge. *Can-W I Mag* 28(6), July: 7-10.   [*NYP*]

ZERRIES, OTTO

23.175   GC   1961 Die Religionen der Naturvölker Südamerikas und Westindiens. *In*
                    KRICKEBERG, WALTER, ed. DIE RELIGIONEN DES ALTEN AMERIKA
                    [THE RELIGIONS OF THE PRIMITIVE PEOPLES OF SOUTH AMERICA AND
                    THE WEST INDIES]. Stuttgart, W. Kohlhammer, p.269-376. (Die Re-
                    ligionen des Menschheit, v. 7.) [13]   [*NYP*]

ZWARTS, JAC

15.045 SR   1927/ Een episode uit de Joodsche kolonie van Guyana, 1660 [An episode
            28 from the Jewish colony of Guiana, 1660].

Chapter 24

FOLKLORE

ABBENHUIS, F. R. M.

24.001   SR   1935/ Nog eens: folklore in Suriname [Once again: folklore in Surinam].
36   *W I G* 17:367-373.   [*COL*]

ANDERSON, IZETT & CUNDALL, FRANK, comps.

24.002   JM   1910 JAMAICA NEGRO PROVERBS AND SAYINGS, COLLECTED AND CLASSIFIED
ACCORDING TO SUBJECTS. Kingston, Institute of Jamaica, 48p. [11,25]
[*NYP*]

ARCHER, A. CLIFFORD

24.003   BB   1937 "Bugaboo in Barbados." *Can-W I Mag* 26(5), May: 24-26; 26(6), June:
27-29.   [*NYP*]

ASPINALL, Sir ALGERNON E.

5.004   BC   1912 WEST INDIAN TALES OF OLD

BANKS, E. P.

24.004   GC   1955 Island Carib folk tales. *Car Q* 4(1), Jan.: 32-39.   [13]   [*RIS*]

BARBANSON, W. L. de

22.004   GD   1950 Frans-creoolse versjes van Guadeloupe [French-Creole verses of
Guadeloupe].

BECKWITH, MARTHA WARREN

22.006   JM   1922 FOLK GAMES IN JAMAICA.

24.005   JM   1924 JAMAICA ANANSI STORIES. New York, American Folk-lore Society,
295p. (Memoirs of the American Folk-lore Society, v. 17.) [22]

24.006   JM   1928 JAMAICA FOLK-LORE. New York, American Folk-lore Society, 95,67,
137,47p. (Memoirs of the American Folk-lore Society, v. 21.)   [*COL*]

11.004   JM   1929 Black roadways: a study of Jamaican folk life.

BECKWITH, MARTHA WARREN & ROBERTS, HELEN H.

22.008   JM   1923 CHRISTMAS MUMMINGS IN JAMAICA.

BENNETT, LOUISE

24.007   JM   1957 ANANCY STORIES AND DIALECT VERSE. (New series.) Kingston, Pioneer Press, 94p. [25]   [*NYP*]

24.008   JM   1961 Laugh with Louise: a pot-pourri of Jamaican folklore. Kingston, City Printery, 56p. [22]   [*RIS*]

BLACK, CLINTON VANE de BROSSE

5.016   JM   1952 TALES OF OLD JAMAICA.

BOOY, THEODOOR de

24.009   JM   1915 Certain West-Indian superstitions pertaining to celts. *J Am Folk* 28(107), Jan.-Mar., 78-82. [4,20]   [*COL*]

BRETT, WILLIAM HENRY & LAMBERT, LEONARD, eds.

24.010   BG   1931 GUIANA LEGENDS. London, Society for the Propagation of the Gospel in Foreign Parts, 49p. [13]   [*NYP*]

CAPPELLE, H. van

24.011   SR   1916 Surinaamsche Negervertellingen [Folktales of the Surinam Negroes]. *Bijd Volk Ned-Indie* 72:233-379. [14]

24.012   SR   1926 MYTHEN EN SAGEN UIT WEST-INDIË (MYTHS AND LEGENDS FROM THE WEST INDIES]. Zutphen, W.J. Thieme, 416p. [10]   [*NYP*]

CARR, ANDREW T.

22.017   TR   1954 Trinidad calypso is unique folk culture.

CASSIDY, FREDERIC G.

25.011   JM   [1953?] Language and folklore.

CHAMBERTRAND, GILBERT de

24.013   FA   1935 Manzè Elodie. *In* DENIS, SERGE, ed. NOS ANTILLES. Orléans, Luzeray, p.307-317. [25]   [*AGS*]

24.014   FA   1935 Proverbes et dictons antillais [Proverbs and sayings of the [French] Antilles]. *In* DENIS, SERGE, ed. NOS ANTILLES. Orléans, Luzeray, p.289-304. [25]   [*AGS*]

COLLIER, H. C.

24.015   BG   1938 The woman who stuck in the sky. *Can-W I Mag* 27(12), Dec.: 4-8. [13]   [*NYP*]

COOKSEY, C.

24.016   BG   1921 Warao stories. *Timehri* 3d ser., 7(24), Aug.: 90-97. [13]   [*AMN*]

CROOKS, KENNETH B. M.

24.017   JM   1933 Forty Jamaican proverbs: interpretations and inferences. *J Negro Hist* 18(2), Apr.: 132-143. [25]

CROWLEY, DANIEL JOHN

24.018   SL   1955 'The good child and the bad" in the West Indies. *Extra-Mural Reptr* 2(1), Feb.: 27-29; 2(2), Apr.: 17-20.   [*RIS*]

24.019   TR   1955 A Trinidad Hindi riddle tale. *Caribbean* 9(2), Sept.: 28-29, 41. [12]
                                                                           [*COL*]

24.020   SL   1958 La Rose and La Marguerite Societies in St. Lucia. *J Am Folk* 71
                     (282), Oct.-Dec.: 541-552. [8,19]   [*RIS*]
24.021   GC   1962 Negro folklore: an Africanist's view. *Tex Q* autumn: 65-71. [11,19]
                                                                               [*RIS*]

CRUICKSHANK, J. GRAHAM
24.022   BC   1918 "B'ru Nansi." *W I Comm Circ* 33(504), Jan. 24: 34-35; 33(505),
                     Feb. 7:53-54.   [*NYP*]

CUNDALL, FRANK
23.030 JM   1930 Three fingered Jack.

DAMAS, L.-G.
24.023   FG   1943 VEILLÉS NOIRES [BLACK EVENINGS].   Paris, Editions Stock, 220p.
                                                                               [*NYP*]

DELMOND, STANY
25.020 MT   1935 Langage et folklore martiniquais [Language and folklore of Martin-
                     ique]. *Mercure Fr* 264(898), Nov. 15: 83-95.

DILLARD, J. L.
24.024   GC   1962 Some variants in concluding tags in Antillean folk tales. *Car Stud*
                     2(3), Oct.: 16-25.   [*RIS*]
24.025   GC   1963 Beginning formulas for Antillean folk tales, etc. *Car Stud* 3(3),
                     Oct.: 51-55.

DONICIE, A. C.
19.011 SR   1953 Iets over de taal en de sprookjes van Suriname [On the language
                     and the fairy-tales of Surinam].

ENGELS, C. J. H.
24.026   CU   1954 De culturele plaats van de Antillen in het Koninkrijk [The cultural
                     position of the Antilles in the Kingdom]. *Vox Guy* 1(4-5), Nov.-Jan.:
                     25-28. [3]

FRANCK, HARRY A.
24.027   JM   1921 Jamaica proverbs. *Dial Notes* 5(4): 98-108. [25]   [*COL*]

FUNK, HENRY ELWELL
25.028 MT   1953 THE FRENCH CREOLE DIALECT OF MARTINIQUE: ITS HISTORICAL BACK-
                     GROUND, VOCABULARY, SYNTAX, PROVERBS AND LITERATURE WITH A GLOS-
                     SARY.

GOEJE, C. H. de
26.009 GG   1934/ Curiositeiten uit Guyana [Curiosities from Guiana].
                35
20.007 GC   1943 Philosophy, initiation and myths of the Indians of Guiana and adja-
                     cent countries.
24.028   SR   1947 Anansi, l'araignée rusée [Anansi, the wily spider]. *Revta Mus Paul*
                     new ser., 1: 125-126. [11]   [*AMN*]
23.056 GC   1952 The physical world, the world of magic, and the moral world of Gui-
                     ana Indians.

HENRIQUEZ, P. COHEN & HESSELING D. C.

24.029   CU/   1935/ Papiamentse en Negerengelse spreekworden [Papiamento and Negro-
          SR   36   English proverbs]. *W I G* 17:161-172.   [25]   [*COL*]
24.030   CU   1936/ Nog enige Papiamentse spreekwoorden [Some more Papiamento prov-
                   37   erbs]. *W I G* 18:82-84.   [25]   [*COL*]

HERSKOVITS, MELVILLE JEAN

24.031   TR   1945 Trinidad proverbs ("Old time saying so"). *J Am Folk* 58(299), July-
                        Sept.: 195-207.   [*COL*]

HERSKOVITS, MELVILLE JEAN & FRANCES S.

24.032   SR   1936 SURINAME FOLK-LORE (with transcriptions and Suriname songs and
                        musicological analysis by Dr. M. Kolinski). New York, Columbia
                        University Press, 766p.   [11,14,22,25,32]   [*RIS*]

HILLS, THEO L.

43.067 BG   1961 The interior of British Guiana and the myth of El Dorado.

HOLDER, GEOFFREY & HARSHMAN, TOM

24.033   TR   1959 BLACK GODS, GREEN ISLANDS. Garden City, N.Y., Doubleday, 235p.

HOROWITZ, MICHAEL M.

24.034   MT   1959 Humor and riddles in Martiniquan folk literature. *Midwest Folk* 9(3):
                        149-154.   [25]   [*RIS*]

IREMONGER, LUCILLE

24.035   BC   1956 WEST INDIAN FOLK TALES: ANANSI STORIES, TALES FROM WEST INDIAN
                        FOLKLORE RETOLD FOR ENGLISH CHILDREN. London, George G. Harrap,
                        64p.

JACOBS, H. P.

24.036   JM   1945 The untapped sources of Jamaican history. *Jam Hist Rev* 1(1), June:
                        92-98.   [*AMN*]
24.037   JM   1948 An early dialect verse. *Jam Hist Rev* 1(3), Dec.: 274-288.   [*COL*]

JEKYLL, WALTER

24.038   JM   1907 JAMAICAN SONG AND STORY. London, David Nutt, 288p. (Publication
                        of the Folk-Lore Society 55.)   [22]   [*COL*]

JOHNSON, JOHN H.

24.039   AT   1921 Folklore from Antigua, British West Indies.   *J Am Folk* 34(131),
                        Jan.-Mar.: 40-88.   [*COL*]

JOSSELIN de JONG, J. P. B. de

24.040   SR   1938 Folklore van Suriname [Folklore of Surinam]. *W I G* 20:1-8.   [*COL*]

JOURDAIN, ELODIE

24.041   MT   1954 Story-tellers of Martinique. *Car Commn Mon Inf B* 7(12), July: 265-
                        266, 268.   [*COL*]

KESLER, C. K.

25.056 NA   1926/ De naam Antillen [The name "Antilles"].
                   27

LATOUR, M. D.

24.042   CU   1937 Cuenta di Nanzi [Tales of Anansi]. *W I G* 19:33-43;
1938 20:9-18, 103-108, 143-147, 296-305;
1940 22:47-52, 86-91, 134-140. [19]   *[COL]*

LEACH, MacEDWARD

24.043   JM   1961 Jamaican duppy lore. *J Am Folk* 74(293), July-Sept.: 207-215. [11, 19,23]   *[RIS]*

LICHTVELD, LOU

24.044   SR   1930/ Op zoek naar de spin [Looking for the spider]. *W I G* 12: 209-230,
31   305-324. [19]   *[COL]*

McLELLAN, G. H.

24.045   BG   1943 OLD TIME STORY: SOME OLD GUIANESE YARNS RE-SPUN. 2d ed. George-town, Daily Chronicle, 266p.   *[RIS]*

McTURK, MICHAEL

24.046   BG   1949 ESSAYS AND FABLES IN THE VERNACULAR. Georgetown, Daily Chron-icle, 97p. [25]   *[RIS]*

MEADE, FLORENCE O.

24.047   UV   1932 Folk tales from the Virgin Islands. *J Am Folk* 45(177), July-Sept.: 363-371.   *[COL]*

MEIKLE, H. B.

24.048   TR   1958 Mermaids and fairymaids or water gods and goddesses of Tobgao. *Car Q* 5(2), Feb.: 103-108.   *[RIS]*

MENKMAN, W. R.

24.049   GC   1937 Nog eens het eiland der reuzen [Once again the island of the giants]. *W I G* 19: 85-86. [5]   *[COL]*

MORPURGO, A. J.

24.050   SR   1935/ Folklore in Suriname. *W I G* 17: 116-125. [14]   *[COL]*
36

OTTLEY, CARLTON ROBERT

24.051   TR   1950 TOBAGO LEGENDS AND WEST INDIAN LORE. Georgetown, Daily Chron-icle, 137p.   *[RIS]*
24.052   TR   1962 LEGENDS: TRUE STORIES AND OLD SAYINGS FROM TRINIDAD AND TOBAGO. Port of Spain, College Press, 71p.   *[RIS]*

PANHUYS, L. C. van

24.053   NC   1932/ Folklore in Nederlandsch West-Indië [Folklore in the Netherlands
33   West Indies]. *W I G* 14:124-130. [11]   *[COL]*
24.054   NC   1933/ Aanvulling Folklore in Nederlandsch West Indië [Addition to folk-
34   lore in the Netherlands West-Indies]. *WIG* 15:16-17. [11] *[COL]*
24.055   BN   1933/ Folklore van Bonaire [Folklore of Bonaire]. *W I G* 15: 97-101;
34
1934/ 16: 65-71; 318-320.   *[RIS]*
35

24.056   SR   1934/ Folklore in Suriname. *W I G* 16: 17-32.   [14]   [*COL*]
                 35
24.057   SR   1934/ Het kikvorschmotief in Suriname en elders [The frog motif in Suri-
                 35   nam and elsewhere]. *W I G* 16: 361-366.   [13,22]   [*COL*]
24.058   SR   1934/ Surinaamsche folklore [Surinam folklore]. *W I G* 16: 315-317.   [*COL*]
                 35
24.059   SR   1935/ Surinaamsche folklore (liederenverzameling Van Vliet) [Folklore of
                 36   Surinam (Song collection of Van Vliet)]. *W I G* 17: 282-289   [14,22]
                                                                                          [*COL*]

         PARSONS, ELSIE CLEWS
24.060   BB   1925 Barbados folklore. *J Am Folk* 38(148), Apr.: 267-292.   [*COL*]
24.061   GC   1933/ FOLK-LORE OF THE ANTILLES, FRENCH AND ENGLISH. New York, Amer-
                 43   ican Folk-lore Society, 3v.   (Memoirs of the American Folk-lore
                      Society, v. 26.)   [*COL*]

         PEARSE, ANDREW C.
22.115 TR   1956 Carnival in nineteenth century Trinidad.
67.019 BC   1956 Ethnography and the lay scholar in the Caribbean.
                       May: 133-146.

         PENARD, A. P.
24.062   SR   1924 Surinaamsche volksvertellingen [Surinam folktales]. *Bijd Volk Ned-
                       Indie* 80: 325-363;
                 1926 82: 48-94.

         PENARD, A. P. & T. E.
24.063   SR   1917 Popular notions pertaining to primitive stone artifacts in Surinam.
                       J Am Folk 30(116): Apr.-June: 251-261.   [*COL*]
24.064   SR   1917 Surinam folk-tales. *J Am Folk* 30(116), Apr.-June: 239-250.   [*COL*]

         PENARD, F. P. & A. P.
24.065   SR   1926/ Negro riddles from Surinam. *W I G* 7: 411-432.   [14,19]   [*COL*]
                 27

         PENARD, THOMAS E. & ARTHUR P.
24.066   SR   1928/ Popular beliefs pertaining to certain places in Suriname. *W I G* 10:
                 29   17-33.   [*COL*]

         REVERT, EUGENE
24.067   MT   1951 DE QUELQUES ASPECTS DU FOLK-LORE MARTINIQUAIS: LA MAGIE ANTIL-
                       LAISE [ON SOME ASPECTS OF MARTINIQUE FOLKLORE: ANTILLEAN MAGIC].
                       Paris, Editions Bellenand, 201p.   [19,23,29]   [*RIS*]

         ROTH, WALTER EDMUND
23.131 BG   1915 An inquiry into the animism and folklore of the Guiana Indians.

         ROWE, CHARLES G. & HORTH, AUGUSTE
24.068   FG   1951 'Dolos': Creole proverbs of French Guiana. *J Am Folk* 64(253),
                       July-Sept.: 253-264.   [25]   [*COL*]

SCHONT, Mme.

24.069   GD   1935 QUELQUES CONTES CRÉOLES [CREOLE TALES]. Basse-Terre, Impr. catholique, 110p. [25]   [*NYP*]

SHERLOCK, PHILIP M.

24.070   JM   1924 Jamaica superstitions. *Liv Age* 423(4169), Dec. 6: 529-534.

24.071   JM   1956 ANANSI THE SPIDER MAN: JAMAICA FOLK TALES. London, Macmillan, 85p.   [*NYP*]

SINGHAM, ARCHIE

37.375   BG/   1965 Three cases of constitutionalism and cuckoo politics: Ceylon, British Guiana and Grenada.
    GR

SPEIRS, JAMES

24.072   BG   1902 THE PROVERBS OF BRITISH GUIANA WITH AN INDEX OF PRINCIPAL WORDS, AN INDEX OF SUBJECTS, AND A GLOSSARY. Demerara, Argosy, Co., 88p. [25]   [*NYP*]

TAYLOR, DOUGLAS C.

24.073   DM   1946 Notes on the star lore of the Caribbees. *Am Anthrop* new ser., 48(2), Apr.-June: 215-222. [13]   [*COL*]

24.074   DM   1952 Tales and legends of the Dominica Caribs. *J Am Folk* 65(257), July-Sept.: 267-279. [13]   [*COL*]

THOMPSON, ROBERT WALLACE

24.075   GC   1955/ The mushroom and the parasol: a West Indian riddle. *W I G* 35-36 56 (2-4): 162-164. [19]   [*COL*]

TURENNE des PRES, F.

24.076   JM   1952 The tale—a West Indian folk story. *Phylon* 13(4): 293-297.   [*COL*]

VERIN, PIERRE MICHEL

24.077   SL   1960 Une histoire de diablesse [A she-devil]. *Rev Guad* 39, Jan.-Mar.: 42-43.   [*RIS*]

24.078   SL   1961 Littérature orale de l'île de Sainte-Lucie. [Oral literature of the island of St. Lucia]. *Rev Guad* 45,3-4 trimesters: 23-26. [25]   [*RIS*]

WHITEHEAD, HENRY S.

25.118   UV   1932 Negro dialect of the Virgin Islands.

YVANDOC, C.

24.079   FA   1962 On ti coutt langue. *Rev Guad* 13(48), 3d trimester: 35. [25]   [*RIS*]

Chapter 25

CREOLE LANGUAGES

ALLEYNE, MERVIN C.

25.001   SL   1961 Language and society in St. Lucia. *Car Stud* 1(1), Apr.: 1-10.
[8,20]   *[RIS]*

37.003   JM   1963 Communication and politics in Jamaica.

ALLSOPP, RICHARD

25.002   BG   1958 The English language in British Guiana. *Engl Lang Tch* 12(2), Jan.-Mar.: 59-66.   *[TCL]*

ANDERSON, BETTY

32.013   SL   1962 Literacy teaching.

ANDERSON, IZETT & CUNDALL, FRANK, comps.

24.002   JM   1910 JAMAICA NEGRO PROVERBS AND SAYINGS, COLLECTED AND CLASSIFIED ACCORDING TO SUBJECTS.

ARMSTRONG, PERCY E.

25.003   BC   1941 English as she is spoke. *Can-W I Mag* 30(5), May: 25-27.   *[NYP]*

BAILEY, BERYL LOFTMAN

25.004   JM   1962 A LANGUAGE GUIDE TO JAMAICA. New York, Research Institute for the Study of Man, 74p.   *[RIS]*

25.005   GC   1962 Language studies in the independent university. *Car Q* 8(1): 38-42.
[66,67]   *[RIS]*

32.016   JM   1963 Teaching of English noun-verb concord in primary schools in Jamaica.

BALEN, W. J. van

25.006   CU   1940 Papiamentoe en Portugeesch [Papiamento and Portuguese]. *W I G* 22:371-376.   *[COL]*

BARBANSON, W. L. de

22.004   GD   1950 Frans-creoolse versjes van Guadeloupe [French-Creole verses of Guadeloupe].

BARNETT, A. G.

25.007   SR   1932 Colonial survivals in Bush-Negro speech. *Am Speech* 7(6), Aug.: 393-397.   [*COL*]

BENNETT, LOUISE

24.007   JM   1957 Anancy stories and dialect verse. (New series.)

BENTZ, DOROTHY

25.008   BB   1938 American English as spoken by the Barbadians. *Am Speech* 13(4), Dec.: 310-312. [18]   [*COL*]

BOHEEMEN, H. van

32.026   SR   1951 Surinaamse onderwijszorgen [Education problems in Surinam].

BONNE, C.

25.009   SR   1920/ Het Boschnegerschrift van Afaka [The Bush Negro writing system 21 of Afaka]. *W I G* 2:391-396. [14]   [*COL*]

BOYCE, Sir RUBERT W.

28.052   BC   1910 Health progress and administration in the West Indies.

BRUNOT, FERDINAND

25.010   FA   1935 Le francais hors d'Europe [French outside of Europe]. *In his* Histoire de la langue francaise des origines à 1900. Paris, Librairie A. Colin, v. 8, pt. 3, p.1037-1194. [5]   [*TCL*]

BRUTON, J. G.

19.002   JM   1945 Influencias españoles sobre el inglés de Jamaica [Spanish influences on Jamaican English].

BUNEL, FRANCOIS

19.003   GD   [1962?] Recueil de scènes vécues à la Guadeloupe [True episodes of Guadeloupe—a miscellany].

CARR, ANDREW T.

22.018   TR   1956 Pierrot Grenade.

CASSIDY, FREDERIC G.

25.011   JM   [1953?] Language and folklore. *Car Q* 3(1): 4-12. [24]   [*RIS*]
25.012   JM   1957 Iteration as a word-forming device in Jamaican folk speech. *Am Speech* 32(1), Feb.: 49-53. [19]   [*COL*]
25.013   GC   1959 English language studies in the Caribbean. *Am Speech* 34(3), Oct.: 163-171. [67]   [*COL*]
25.014   JM   1961 Jamaica talk: three hundred years of the English language in Jamaica. London, Macmillan, 468p.   [*RIS*]
25.015   JM   1961 Some footnotes on the "junjo" question. *Am Speech* 36(2), May: 101-103. [19]   [*COL*]

CHAMBERTRAND, GILBERT de

24.013   FA   1935 Manzè Elodie.
24.014   FA   1935 Proverbes et dictons antillais [Proverbs and sayings of the [French] Antilles].
22.021   FA   1963 Mi io!

COLLYMORE, FRANK A.
25.016   BB   1955 NOTES FOR A GLOSSARY OF WORDS AND PHRASES OF BARBADIAN DIALECT.
                       Bridgetown, Advocate Co., 80p.   [RIS]

CROOKS, KENNETH B. M.
24.017   JM   1933 Forty Jamaican proverbs: interpretations and inferences.

CRUICKSHANK, J. GRAHAM
25.017   BB   1911 Negro English, with reference particularly to Barbados. Timehri
                       3d ser., 1(18B), July: 102-106. [11,19]   [AMN]
25.018   BG/   1916 "BLACK TALK": BEING NOTES ON NEGRO DIALECT IN BRITISH GUIANA,
          BB   WITH (INEVITABLY) A CHAPTER ON THE VERNACULAR OF BARBADOS. Dem-
                       erara, Argosy Co., 76p. [11,19]   [SCH]

DeCAMP, DAVID
25.019   JM   1961 Social and geographical factors in Jamaican dialects. In Le PAGE,
                       R.B., ed. PROCEEDINGS OF THE CONFERENCE ON CREOLE LANGUAGE
                       STUDIES. London, Macmillan, p.61-84. (Creole language studies,
                       no. 2.) [5,43]   [RIS]

DELMOND, STANY
25.020   MT   1935 Langage et folklore martiniquais [Language and folklore of Martin-
                       ique]. Mercure Fr 264(898), Nov. 15: 83-95. [24]   [NYP]

DENIS, SERGE
25.021   NA   1935 Notre créole [Our Creole language]. In DENIS, SERGE, ed. Nos
                       ANTILLES. Orléans, Luzeray, p.325-376.   [AGS]

DILLARD, J. L.
25.022   GC   1962 Purism and prescriptivism as applied to the Caribbean Creoles—a
                       tentative classification. Car Stud 1(4), Jan.: 3-10. [66]   [RIS]
25.023   GC   1964 The writings of Herskovits and the study of the language of the
                       Negro in the New World. Car Stud 4(2), July: 35-41. [11]   [RIS]

DONICIE, A. C.
19.011   SR   1953 Iets over de taal en de sprookjes van Suriname [On the language
                       and the fairy-tales of Surinam].
25.024   SR   1953 Kanttekeningen bij "De klanken van het Neger-Engels" [Notes
                       about "The sounds of Negro-English"]. Taal Tong 5:4-7.
25.025   SR   1955 De partikels sa en (de)go in de Creolentaal van Suriname [The par-
                       ticles sa and (de)go in the Creole language of Surinam]. W I G 36:
                       183-191.   [COL]

DOOB, LEONARD WILLIAM
31.024   JM   1958 The effect of the Jamaican patois on attitude and recall.

DORAN, EDWIN BEAL, Jr.
25.026   CM   1954 Notes on an archaic island dialect. Am Speech 29(1), Feb.: 82-85.
                                                                               [COL]

ECHTELD, J. J. M.

25.027   SR   1962 The English words in Sranan (Negro-English of Surinam). Gronin-gen, J. B. Wolters, 219p. (Ph.D. dissertation, University of Amsterdam, September 1961).   [COL]

FRANCK, HARRY A.

24.027   JM   1921 Jamaica proverbs.

FUNK, HENRY ELWELL

25.028   MT   1953 The French Creole dialect of Martinique: its historical background, vocabulary, syntax, proverbs and literature with a glossary. Ph.D. dissertation, University of Virginia, 294p.   [24]

GOBL, L.

25.029   FA   1933 Problemi di sostrato nel creolo-francese [Problems of the linguistic substratum in French Creole]. *Rev Ling Rom* 9(35-36), July-Dec.: 336-345.   [NYP]

GOBL-GALDI, L.

25.030   FC   1934 Esquisse de la structure grammaticale des patois francais-creoles [Outline of the grammatical structure of the Creole French dialects]. *Z Franz Spr* 58(5-6): 257-295.   [COL]

GOILO, E. R.

25.031   CU   1951 Papiaments leerboek [papiamento grammar]. Willemstad, Curacao, 168p.   [NYP]

GONGGRIJP, J. W.

25.032   SR   1960 The evolution of a Djuka-script in Surinam, by J.W. Gonggryp. *N W I G* 40:63-72. [14]   [RIS]

GONGGRIJP, J. W. & DUBELAAR, C.

25.033   SR   1960 Pater Morssink en Afaka [Pater Morssink and Afaka]. *Opbouw* Christmas: 11p. [14]   [RIS]

25.034   SR   1963 De geschriften van Afaka in zijn Djoeka-schrift [The papers of Afaka in Djuka script], [by] J.W. Gonggryp & C. Dubelaar. *N W I G* 42(3), May: 213-254. [14]   [RIS]

GOODMAN, MORRIS F.

25.035   TR   1958 On the phonemics of French Creole of Trinidad. *Word* 14(2-3), Aug.-Dec.: 208-212.   [RIS]

25.036   GC   1964 A comparative study of Creole French dialects. The Hague, Mouton, 281p.   [RIS]

GRANT, D. R. B.

32.081   JM   1964 Some problems in the teaching of English.

GRAY, CECIL

32.082   BC   1963 Teaching English in the West Indies.

GUERIN, DANIEL

19.014   GC   1956 Un futur pour les Antilles? [A future for the Antilles?]

HALL, ROBERT A., Jr.

25.037   SR   1948 The linguistic structure of Taki-Taki. *Language* 24:92-116.   [*COL*]

25.038   GC   1952 Pidgin English and linguistic change.   *Lingua* 3, Feb.: 138-146.
                                                                                    [*COL*]

25.039   GC   1958 Creolized languages and "genetic relationships." *Word* 14(2-3),
                     Aug.-Dec.: 367-373.   [*RIS*]

HELLINGA, W. GS.

25.040   NC   1951 De waarde van de z.g. Mengtalen in de West [The value of the so-
                     called mixed language in the West]. *Taal Tong* 3:133-137.

32.095   SR   1955 LANGUAGE PROBLEMS IN SURINAM: DUTCH AS THE LANGUAGE OF THE
                     SCHOOLS.

25.041   SR   1958 Kansen voor het Nederlands in Suriname [Changes for the Dutch
                     language in Surinam]. *In* ALBUM EDGARD BLANQUAERT. Tongeren,
                     [Belgium], George Miciels.

HENRIQUES, P. COHEN & HESSELING, D. C.

24.029   CU/ 1935/ Papiamentse en Negerengelse spreekwoorden [Papiamento and Negro-
         SR   36   English proverbs].

24.030   CU   1936/ Nog enige Papiamentse spreekwoorden [Some more Papiamento
              37   proverbs].

HERSKOVITS, MELVILLE JEAN

25.042   SR   1930/ On the provenience of the Portuguese in Saramacca Tongo. *W I G*
              31   12:545-557.   [*COL*]

HERSKOVITS, MELVILLE JEAN & FRANCES S.

24.032   SR   1936 Suriname folk-lore (with transcriptions and Suriname songs and
                     musicological analysis by Dr. M. Kolinski).

HESSELING, D. C.

25.043   UV   1905 HET NEGERHOLLANDS DER DEENSE ANTILLEN: BIJDRAGE TOT DE GESCHIE-
                     DENIS DER NEDERLANDSE TAAL IN AMERIKA [THE NEGRO-DUTCH OF THE
                     DANISH ANTILLES: CONTRIBUTION TO THE HISTORY OF THE DUTCH LAN-
                     GUAGE IN AMERICA]. Leiden, A.W. Sijthoff, 290p.   [*COL*]

HOROWITZ, MICHAEL M.

24.034   MT   1959 Humor and riddles in Martiniquan folk literature.

HOUTE, I. C. van

25.044   SR   1963 Het bilinguisme van de Hindostaanse kinderen in Suriname [Bilin-
                     gualism of Hindustani children in Surinam]. *In* LUTCHMAN, W.I., ed.
                     VAN BRITS-INDISCH EMIGRANT TOT BURGER VAN SURINAME. The Hague,
                     Drukkerij Wieringa, p.90-98.   [12, 32]

HOYER, W. M.

25.045   NA   1922 WOORDENLIJST EN SAMENSPRAAK, HOLLANDSCH-PAPIAMENTSCH-SPAANSCH
                     [VOCABULARY AND CONVERSATION, DUTCH-PAPIAMENTO-SPANISH]. [Wil-
                     lemstad?] Curacao, Librería Bethencourt, 74p.   [*NYP*]

2.104   AR   1945 A BRIEF HISTORICAL DESCRIPTION OF THE ISLAND OF ARUBA IN ENGLISH
                     AND PAPIAMENTO.

ISAAC, EMILE

25.046   FA   1961 Rapport sur les envois en langue créole [Notes on envois in the Creole language]. *Rev Guad* 43, Jan.-Mar.: 33-37.   [*RIS*]

JACOBS, H. P.

24.037   JM   1948 An early dialect verse.

JANSEN, G. P.

25.047   CU   1945 DICCIONARIO PAPIAMENTU-HOLANDÉS [PAPIAMENTO-DUTCH DICTIONARY]. 2d ed. [Willemstad? Curacao, St. Vincentiusgesticht?] 166 p. [*AGS*]

JOSSELIN de JONG, J. P. B. de

25.048   ST/   1924 HET NEGERHOLLANDSCH VAN ST. THOMAS EN ST. JAN [THE NEGRO-DUTCH
        SJ   OF ST. THOMAS AND ST. JOHN]. Amsterdam, Noord-Hollandsche Uitg. Mij., (Mededeelingen der Koninklijke Akademie van Wetenschappen, Afdeeling Letterkunde, ser. A, v. 57, no. 3.)   [*AMN*]

25.049   NC   1926 HET HUIDIGE NEGERHOLLANDSCH (TEKSTEN EN WOORDENLIJST) [THE PRESENT-DAY NEGRO DUTCH (TEXTS AND VOCABULARY)]. Amsterdam, 124p. (Verhandelingen der Koninklijke Akademie van Wetenschappen, Afdeeling Letterkunde, new ser., v.26, no.1)   [*NYP*]

JOURDAIN, ELODIE

25.050   GC   [1953?] Creole—a folk language. *Car Q* 3(1): 24-30.   [*RIS*]

25.051   FA   1954 Is Creole a key to education? *Car Commn Mon Inf B* 7(11), June: 243-244, 246, 249. [32]   [*COL*]

25.052   FA   1954 Notes on Creole speech. *Car Commn Mon Inf B* 8(2), Sept.: 42-44, 46.   [*COL*]

25.053   MT   1954 Le verbe en créole martiniquais [The verb in the Creole language of Martinique]. *W I G* 35(1-2), Apr.: 39-58.   [*RIS*]

25.054   FA   1956 DU FRANCAIS AUX PARLERS CRÉOLES [FROM FRENCH TO THE CREOLE LANGUAGES]. Paris, Librairie C. Klincksieck, 334p.   [*RIS*]

25.055   FA   1956 LE VOCABULAIRE DU PARLER CRÉOLE DE LA MARTINIQUE [THE VOCABULARY OF THE CREOLE LANGUAGE OF MARTINIQUE]. Paris, Librairie C. Klincksieck, 303p.   [*RIS*]

KARSTEN, RUDOLF

12.012   SR   1930 DE BRITSCH-INDIERS IN SURINAME, BENEVENS EEN HANDLEIDING VAN DE BEGINSELEN VAN HET HINDOESTAANS [THE BRITISH INDIANS IN SURINAM, AND A MANUAL OF THE PRINCIPLES OF THE HINDUSTANI LANGUAGE].

KESLER, C. K.

25.056   NA   1926/ De naam Antillen [The name "Antilles"]. *W I G* 8:567-569. [5,
             27 24]   [*COL*]

LATOUR, M. D.

25.057   CU   1935/ Oorsprong en betekenis van het woord *macamba* [Origin and meaning
             36 of the word *macamba*]. *W I G* 17:256-260.   [*COL*]

25.058   NL   1935/ Vreemde invloeden in het Papiamento [Foreign influences on Papia-
             36 mento]. *W I G* 17:387-396.   [*COL*]

25.059   CU   1936/ De taal van Curacao [The language of Curacao]. *W I G* 18:231-239.
             37   [*COL*]

25.060   CU   1937 Portuguese taalresten in het Papiamento [Portuguese language survivals in Papiamento]. *W I G* 19:212-214. [COL]

25.061   NL   1940 Het Papiamento [Papiamento]. *W I G* 22:220-225. [COL]

LENZ, RUDOLFO

25.062   CU   1926 El papiamento, la lengua criolla de Curazao (la gramática más sen-
cilla) [Papiamento, the Creole language of Curacao (the simplest
grammar)]. *An Univ Chile* 2d ser., 4(3): 695-768; 4(4): 1021-1090;
1927 5(1):287-327; 5(2):365-412; 5(4):889-990. [NYP]

Le PAGE, R. B.

25.063   BC   1952 A Survey of dialects in the British Caribbean. *Car Q* 2(3):49-51.
[66] [RIS]

25.064   BC   1955 The language problem of the British Caribbean. *Car Q* 4(1), Jan.:
40-49. [10,66] [RIS]

Le PAGE, R. B., ed.

25.065   GC   1961 PROCEEDINGS OF THE CONFERENCE ON CREOLE LANGUAGE STUDIES held
at the University College of the West Indies, Mar. 28-Apr. 4, 1959.
London, Macmillan, 130p. (Creole language studies, no. 2.) [RIS]

Le PAGE, R. B. & CASSIDY, F. G.

25.066   JM   1961 Lexicographic problems of "The dictionary of Jamaican English."
In Le PAGE, R. B. ed. PROCEEDINGS OF THE CONFERENCE ON CREOLE
LANGUAGE STUDIES, held at the University College of the West
Indies, Mar. 28-Apr. 4, 1959. London, Macmillan, p.17-36. (Creole
language studies, no. 2.) [RIS]

Le PAGE, R. B. & DeCAMP, DAVID

25.067   JM   1960 JAMAICAN CREOLE: AN HISTORICAL INTRODUCTION TO JAMAICAN CREOLE
BY R.B. LE PAGE, AND FOUR JAMAICAN CREOLE TEXTS, WITH INTRODUC-
TION, PHONEMIC TRANSCRIPTIONS AND GLOSSES BY DAVID DECAMP. Lon-
don, Macmillan, 182p. (Creole language studies, no. 1.) [5] [RIS]

LETANG, CASIMIR

25.068   GD   [n.d.] NOUS BITACO: POÈMES CRÉOLES ["NOUS BITACO." CREOLE POEMS].
Pointe-a-Pitre, Guad., Impr. Paran. [RIS]

LICHTVELD, LOU

25.069   SR   1928/ Afrikaansche resten in de Creolentaal van Suriname [African surviv-
           29 als in the Creole language of Surinam]. *W I G* 10:391-402, 507-526;
1929/ 11:72-84, 251-262. [19] [COL]
30

32.124   SR   1950 Educational problems in bilingual countries in the Caribbean.

25.070   GC   1954 Enerlei Creools [One kind of Creole]. *W I G* 35(1-2), Apr.: 59-71.
[67] [RIS]

LITTMAN, JEROME

25.071   CU   1945 The wind-blown language: Papiamento. *Hispania* 20(1), Feb.: 50-59.
[COL]

LOFTMAN, BERYL I.

25.072   GC   1953 CREOLE LANGUAGES OF THE CARIBBEAN AREA. M.A. thesis, Columbia
                University, 79p.   [COL]

McKAY, CLAUDE

22.094   JM   1912 SONGS OF JAMAICA.

McTURK, MICHAEL

24.046   BG   1949 ESSAYS AND FABLES IN THE VERNACULAR.

MARCKWARDT, ALBERT H.

25.073   JM   1962 Applied linguistics. *Car Q* 8(2), June: 111-120.   [32, 66]   [RIS]

MEIKLE, H. B.

25.074   TR   1955 Tobago villagers in the mirror of dialect. *Car Q* 4(2), Dec.: 154-160.
                                                                                   [RIS]

MENKMAN, W. R.

25.075   SR   1932/ De Surinaamsche taaltuin [The Surinam language and idiom]. *W I G*
                33   14: 244-252.   [COL]
25.076   CU   1936/ Curacao, zijn naam en zijn taal [Curacao, its name and its lan-
                37   guage]. *W I G* 18: 38-50. [2, 5]   [COL]
25.077   SR   1937 Surinaamsche taaltuin [Surinam language and idiom]. *W I G* 19: 243-
                246.   [COL]

MORGAN, RALEIGH, Jr.

25.078   SM   1959 Structural sketch of St. Martin Creole. *Anthrop Ling* 1(8), Nov.: 20-
                24, 24a-24f.   [COL]
25.079   SM   1960 The lexicon of St. Martin Creole. *Anthrop Ling* 2(1), Jan.: '7-29.
                                                                                    [COL]

MORPURGO, A. J.

25.080   SR   1932/ Eenige opmerkingen over de Surinaamsche Negertaal [A few remarks
                33   about the Surinam Negro-language]. *W I G* 14: 397-408.   [COL]

NAVARRO, TOMAS

25.081   CU   1953 Observaciones sobre el papiamento [Notes on Papiamento]. *Nueva
                Revta Filol Hispan* 7: 183-189.   [COL]

OTTLEY, CARLTON ROBERT, ed.

25.082   TR   1965 TRINIDADIANESE: HOW TO OLD TALK IN TRINIDAD. [Port of Spain?]
                Trinidad, Granderson, 32p.   [RIS]

OUDSCHANS DENTZ, FRED

25.083   SR   1937 De plaats van de Creool in de literatuur van Suriname [The place of
                Creole in the literature of Surinam]. *WIG* 19:208-211. [11,22] [COL]

PANHUYS, L. C. van

22.111   SR   1934 Quelques chansons et quelques danses dans la Guyane Neerlandaise
                [A few songs and dances of Dutch Guiana].
19.035   SR   1935/ De grondslag van de wiskunde in Suriname [The foundations of math-
                36   ematics in Surinam].

PEE, WILLEM, et al.

25.084 SR 1951 Opstellen over het Surinaams [Essays about the Surinam language]. *Taal Tong* 3: 130-192;
1953 5: 4-19.

PEE, WILLEM; HELLINGA, W. GS. & DONICIE, A.

25.085 SR 1951 Het Neger-Engels van Suriname [Negro-English of Surinam]. *Taal Tong* 3: 130-192.

25.086 SR 1953 Voorstellen tot een nieuwe systematische spelling van het Surinaams (Neger-Engels) op linguistische grondslag [Proposals for a new and systematic spelling of the Surinam language (Negro English) on a linguistic basis]. *Taal Tong* 5(1), Mar. 1: 8-19. [*COL*]

PELAGE, AL.

2.180 GD [n.d.] La Guadeloupe vue par Al. Pelage: gravures et dessins humoristiques [Guadeloupe as seen by Al. Pelage: humorous prints and drawings].

PENARD, THOMAS E.

25.087 TR 1927/ Remarks on an old vocabulary from Trinidad. *WIG* 9:265-270. [13]
28 [*COL*]

PRINCE, JOHN DYNELEY

25.088 SR 1934 Surinam Negro-English. *Am Speech* 9(3), Oct.: 181-186. [*COL*]

RATELBAND, K.

25.089 SR 1944/ Een Boschnegerschrift van West-Afrikaanschen oorsprong [A Bush
45 Negro system of writing of West African origin]. *W I G* 26:193-208.
[14] [*COL*]

REINECKE, JOHN E.

25.090 GC 1938 Trade jargons and Creole dialects as marginal languages. *Social Forces* 17(1), Oct.: 107-118. [*COL*]

RENS, L. L. E.

25.091 SR 1953 The historical and social background of Surinam's Negro-English. Amsterdam, North-Holland Pub. Co., 155p. [*COL*]

ROWE, CHARLES G. & HORTH, AUGUSTE

24.068 FG 1951 'Dolos': Creole proverbs of French Guiana.

RUBIN, JOAN

1.039 GC 1963 A bibliography of Caribbean Creole languages.

SCHONT, Mme.

24.069 GD 1935 Quelques contes créoles [Creole tales].

SCHUCHARDT, HUGO

25.092 SR 1914 Die sprache der Saramakkaneger in Surinam [The language of the Saramacca Negroes of Surinam], Amsterdam, Noord-Hollandsche Uitg. Mij., 120. (Verhandelingen der Koninklijke Akademie van Wetenschappen te Amsterdam, Afdeeling Letterkunde, new ser., v. 14, no. 6.) [11] [*NYP*]

25.093   ST   1914 Zum Negerholländischen von St. Thomas [Concerning the Negro-
                        Dutch of St. Thomas]. *Tijdschr Ned Taalen Lettk* new ser., 33(25):
                        123-135.   [COL]

SIMONS, R. D.
25.094   SR   1954 Het partikel 'sa' in het Surinaams [The particle 'sa' in the Surinam
                        language]. *W I G* 35(3), Oct.: 167-170.   [RIS]

SPEIRS, JAMES
24.072   BG   1902 THE PROVERBS OF BRITISH GUIANA WITH AN INDEX OF PRINCIPAL WORDS,
                        AN INDEX OF SUBJECTS, AND A GLOSSARY.

TAYLOR, DOUGLAS C.
25.095   GC   1945 Certain Carib morphological influences on Creole. *Int J Am Ling*
                        11(3), July: 140-155. [26]   [COL]
25.096   DM   1947 Phonemes of Caribbean Creole. *Word* 3(3), Dec.: 173-179.   [COL]
40.182   DM   1954 Names on Dominica.
25.097   DM   1955 Phonic interference in Dominican Creole. *Word* 11(1), Apr.:45-52.[COL]
26.033   GC   1956 Language contacts in the West Indies.
25.098   GC   1958 Use and disuse of languages in the West Indies. *Car Q* 5(2), Feb.:
                        67-77.   [RIS]
25.099   GC   1960 Language shift or changing relationships? *Int J Am Ling* 26(2),
                        Apr.: 155-161.
25.100   DM   1961 Some Dominican-Creole descendants of the French definite article.
                        In Le PAGE, R. B., ed. PROCEEDINGS OF THE CONFERENCE ON CREOLE
                        LANGUAGE STUDIES held at the University College of the West Indies,
                        Mar. 28-Apr. 4, 1959. London, Macmillan, p.85-90. (Creole language
                        studies, no. 2.)   [RIS]
25.101   MT/   1963 The origin of West Indian Creole languages: evidence from gramma-
          SR   tical categories. *Am Anthrop* 65(4), Aug.: 800-814.   [RIS]

THOMPSON, ROBERT WALLACE
25.102   GC   1958 Mushrooms, umbrellas and black magic: a West Indian linguistic
                        problem. *Am Speech* 33(3), Oct.: 170-175. [19]   [COL]
25.103   GC   1961 A note on some possible affinities between the Creole dialects of
                        the Old World and those of the New. *In* Le PAGE, R.B. ed. PRO-
                        CEEDINGS OF THE CONFERENCE ON CREOLE LANGUAGE STUDIES held at
                        the University College of the West Indies, Mar. 28-Apr. 24, 1959.
                        London, Macmillan, p.107-113. (Creole language studies, no. 2.)
                                                                                      [RIS]

VALKHOFF, MARIUS
25.104   GC   1960 Contributions to the study of Creole. I. Contributions to the study
                        of Creole. III. Some notes on Creole French. *Afr Stud* 19(2): 77-87;
                        19(4): 230-244. [1]   [COL]

VERIN, PIERRE MICHEL
25.105   BC/   1958 The rivalry of Creole and English in the West Indies. *W I G* 38(3-4):
          MT   163-167. [20,32]   [RIS]
24.078   SL   1961 Littérature orale de l'île de Sainte-Lucie [Oral literature of the
                        island of St. Lucia].

VOORHOEVE, JAN

25.106   SR   1952 De studie van het Surinaams [The study of the Surinam language]. *W I G* 33: 175-182.   [*COL*]

25.107   SR   1953 VOORSTUDIES TOT EEN BESCHRIJVING VAN HET SRANAN TONGO (NEGER-ENGELS VAN SURINAME) [PRELIMINARY STUDIES OF SRANAN TONGO (SUR-INAM NEGRO ENGLISH)]. Amsterdam, North Holland Pub. Co., 108p.   [*COL*]

25.108   SR   1957 Missionary linguistics in Surinam. *Bib Transl* 8(4), Oct.: 179-190. [23]   [*NYP*]

25.109   SR   1957 Spellingsmoeilijkheden in het Sranan [Spelling difficulties in Sranan]. *Taal Tong* 9: 147-158.

25.110   SR   1957 Structureel onderzoek van het Sranan [Structural analysis of Sranan]. *W I G* 37: 189-211.   [*COL*]

25.111   SR   1957 The verbal system of Sranan. *Lingua* 6(4), July: 374-396.   [*COL*]

25.112   SR   1959 An orthography for Saramaccan. *Word* 15(3), Dec.: 436-445.   [*COL*]

25.113   SR   1961 A project for the study of Creole language history in Surinam. *In* Le PAGE, R.B., ed. PROCEEDINGS OF THE CONFERENCE ON CREOLE LANGUAGE STUDIES held at the University College of the West Indies. Mar. 28-Apr. 4, 1959. London, Macmillan, p.99-106. (Creole language studies, no. 2.) [67]   [*RIS*]

25.114   SR   1961 Spelling difficulties in Sranan. *Bib Transl* 12, Jan.: 1-11.

25.115   SR   1961 Le ton et la grammaire dans le Saramaccan [Pitch and grammar in Saramaccan]. *Word* 12(2), Aug.: 146-163.   [*COL*]

25.116   SR   1962 SRANAN SYNTAX. Amsterdam, North-Holland Pub. Co., 91p.

VOSKUIL, J. J.

25.117   SR   1956 HET NEDERLANDS VAN HINDOESTAANSE KINDEREN IN SURINAME: ONDERZOEK NAAR DE INVLOED VAN DE MOEDERTAAL BIJ HET AANLEREN VAN EEN VREEMDE CULTUURTAAL [THE DUTCH OF THE HINDUSTANI CHILDREN IN SURINAM: STUDY OF THE INFLUENCE OF THE MOTHER LANGUAGE ON THE LEARNING OF A FOREIGN LANGUAGE]. Amsterdam, Noord-Hollandsche Uitg. Mij., 138p.   [*NYP*]

WHITEHEAD, HENRY S.

25.118   UV   1932 Negro dialect of the Virgin Islands. *Am Speech* 7(3), Feb.: 175-179. [24]   [*COL*]

WIJK, H. L. A. van

25.119   CU   1958 Orígenes y evolución del papiamentu [Origins and development of Papiamento]. *Neophilologues* 42, July: 169-182.   [5]

YVANDOC, C.

24.079   FA   1962 On ti coutt langue.

25.120   GD   1962 Aporta a Feri. *Rev Guad* 46, Jan.-Mar.: 26-27.

Chapter 26

AMERINDIAN LANGUAGES

ADAM, LUCIEN

26.001   WW   1906   Le caraïbe du Honduras et le caraïbe des îles [The Carib [language] of Honduras and the Carib of the islands]. *In* INTERNATIONALER AMER-IKANISTEN-KONGRESS, 14th SESS., Stuttgart, 1904. [PROCEEDINGS.] Berlin, W. Kohlhammer, pt. 2, p.357-371.

BUTT, AUDREY J.

23.012   BG   1961/   Symbolism and ritual among the Akawaio of British Guiana.
             62

CARY-ELWES, C. I.

26.002   BG   1917   On the correct method of spelling the Indian languages. *Timehri* 3d ser., 4(21), June: 87-97.   [*AMN*]

FANSHAWE, D. B.

41.083   BG   1947   Arawak Indian plant names.
41.085   BG   1953   Akawaio Indian plant names.

GOEJE, C. H. de

26.003   GG   1909   ETUDES LINGUISTIQUES CARAÏBES [CARIB LINGUISTIC STUDIES]. [Part 1.] Amsterdam, Noord-Hollandsche Uitg. Mij., 307p. (Verhandelingen der Koninklijke Akademie van Wetenschappen, Afdeeling Letter-kunde, new ser., v. 10, no. 3.) [13]   [*COL*]

13.029   GG   1924/   Karaïben en Guiana [Caribs and Guyana].
             25

13.030   GG   1924   Guayana and Carib tribal names.

26.004   BG/   1928   THE ARAWAK LANGUAGE OF GUIANA. Amsterdam, Noord-Hollandsche
         SR   Uitg. Mij., 309p. (Verhandelingen der Koninklijke Akademie van Wetenschappen te Amsterdam, Afdeeling Letterkunde, new ser., v. 28, no. 2.) [13]   [*COL*]

26.005   SR   1929/   Het merkwaardige Arawaksch [The remarkable Arawak (language)].
             30   *W I G* 11:11-28.   [*COL*]

26.006   BG/   1930/   Het merkwaardige Warau [The remarkable Warau (language)]. *W I G*
         SR   31   12:1-16.   [*COL*]

26.007   BG/   1930   The inner structure of the Warrau language of Guiana. *J Soc Am*
         SR   *Paris* new ser., 22:33-72.   [*AGS*]

26.008   SR   1932/ Het merkwaardige Karaïbisch [The remarkable Caribbean language].
                33   *W I G* 14:99-123.   [*COL*]
26.009   GG   1934/ Curiositeiten uit Guyana [Curiosities from Guiana]. *W I G* 16:72-76.
                35
26.010   GC   1935/ Het merkwaardige Eiland-Karaïbisch [The remarkable Island-Carib
                36   language]. *W I G* 17:241-249.   [*COL*]
26.011   GC   1935 Fünf Sprachfamilien Südamerikas [Five South American linguistic
                     families]. *Meded Kon Akad Wetensch Afd Lettk* ser. A, 77(5): 149-
                     177. [13]   [*COL*]
26.012   GG   1937 Laut und Sinn in Karibischen Sprachen [Sound and meaning in Carib
                     languages]. *In* MÉLANGES DE LINGUISTIQUE ET DE PHILOLOGIE OFFERTS
                     À JACQUES VAN GINNEKEN. Paris, Librairie C. Klincksieck, p.335-339.
                                                                                    [*AMN*]
26.013   GC   1939 Nouvel examen des langues des Antilles avec notes sur les langues
                     arawak-maipure et caribes et vocabulaires shebayo et guayana
                     (Guyane) [A new examination of Caribbean languages, with notes on
                     the Arawak-Maypure and Carib languages and on Shebayo [?] and
                     Guiana vocabularies]. *J Soc Am* new ser., 31:1-120.   [*AGS*]
26.014   GG   1946 ETUDES LINGUISTIQUES CARIBES [CARIB LINGUISTIC STUDIES]. [Part 2.]
                     Amsterdam, Noord-Hollandsche Uitg. Mij., 274p. (Verhandelingen
                     der Koninklijke Nederlandsche Akademie van Wetenschappen, Af-
                     deeling Letterkunde, new ser., v. 49, no. 2.)   [*NYP*]

HOFF, B. J.
26.015   SR   1955 The languages of the Indians of Surinam and the comparative study
                     of the Carib and Arawak languages. *Bijd Vǫlk* 111(4):325-355. [*RIS*]
26.016   SR   1961 Dorsal phonemes, with special reference to Carib. *Lingua* 10(4):
                     403-419.   [*RIS*]
26.017   SR   1962 The nominal word-groups in Carib; a problem of delimitation of
                     syntax and morphology. *Lingua* 11:157-164.   [*RIS*]

HOLMER, NILS M.
19.020   GC   1960/ Indian place names in South America and the Antilles.
                  61

NORDENSKIOLD, ERLAND
26.018   GG   1922 DEDUCTIONS SUGGESTED BY THE GEOGRAPHICAL DISTRIBUTION OF SOME
                     POST-COLUMBIAN WORDS USED BY THE INDIANS OF AMERICA. Göteberg,
                     Sweden; Elanders boktr. aktiebolag, 176p. (Comparative ethno-
                     graphical studies, v. 5.) [13]   [*COL*]

PANHUYS, L. C. van
26.019   SR   1904 Indian words in the Dutch language. *Bijd Volk Ned-Indie* 56:611-614.
26.020   SR   1905 Indian words in the Dutch language and in use at Dutch Guiana. *In*
                     PROCEEDINGS OF THE INTERNATIONAL CONGRESS OF AMERICANISTS,
                     13th Session, New York, Oct. 1902. Easton, Pa., Eschenbach Print.
                     Co., p.205-208.   [*AGS*]
26.021   SR   1913 A few observations on Carib numerals. *In* PROCEEDINGS OF THE INTER-
                     NATIONAL CONGRESS OF AMERICANISTS, XVIII Session, London, 1912.
                     London, Harrison, pt. 1, p.109-110.   [*AGS*]
22.111   SR   1934 Quelques chansons et quelques danses dans la Guyane Neerlandaise
                     [A few songs and dances of Dutch Guiana].

PENARD, THOMAS E.

26.022   SR   1926/ Note on words used by South American Indians for banana. *W I G* 27 8:375-377.   [*COL*]

PENARD, THOMAS E. & ARTHUR P.

26.023   SR   1926/ European influence on the Arawak language of Guiana. *W I G* 7:165- 27 176.   [*COL*]

PETITJEAN-ROGET, JACQUES

4.106   DM/   1963 The Caribs as seen through the dictionary of the Reverend Father GD   Breton.

RIVET, P. & REINBURG, P.

26.024   FG   1921 Les Indiens Marawan [The Marawan Indians]. *J Soc Am Paris* new ser., 13:103-118.   [*AGS*]

ROCHEFORT, CESAR de

26.025   GC   1941 Remarques sur la langue caraïbe [Observations on the Carib language]. *Rev Soc Hist Geogr Haiti* 12(41), Apr.: 13-16.   [*AGS*]

RODWAY, JAMES

40.145   BG   1906 The river-names of British Guiana.
40.146   BG   1911 Our river names.

SIMONS, R. D. & VOORHOEVE, J.

26.026   SR   1955/ Ontleningen van Nederlandse samenstellingen in het Surinaams 56   [Adoption of Dutch compounds in the Surinam language]. *W I G* 36:61-64.   [*COL*]

SOLIEN, NANCIE L.

9.050   BH   1960 Changes in Black Carib kinship terminology.

TAYLOR, DOUGLAS C.

13.079   DM   1935 The Island Caribs of Dominica.
13.080   DM   1936 Additional notes on the Island Carib of Dominica, B.W.I.
25.095   GC   1945 Certain Carib morphological influences on Creole.
26.027   DM   1946 Loan words in Dominica Island Carib. *Int J Am Ling* 12(4), Oct.: 213-216.   [*COL*]
40.182   DM   1954 Names on Dominica.
26.028   DM   1955/ Names on Dominica. *W I G* 36:121-124. [7]   [*COL*] 56
26.029   GC   1955 On the etymology of some Arawakan words for three. *Int J Am Ling* 21(2), Apr.: 185-187.   [*COL*]
26.030   BH   1955 Phonemes of the Hopkins (British Honduras) dialect of Island Carib. *Int J Am Ling* 21(3), July: 233-241.   [*COL*]
26.031   GC   1956 Island Carib II: Word-classes, affixes, nouns, and verbs. *Int J Am Ling* 22(1), Jan.: 1-44.   [*COL*]
26.032   GC   1956 Island Carib morphology III: Locators and particles. *Int J Am Ling* 22(2), Apr.: 138-150.   [*COL*]
26.033   GC   1956 Language contacts in the West Indies. *Word* 12(3), Dec.: 399-414. [25]   [*COL*]
26.034   GC   1956 Languages and ghost-languages of the West Indies. *Int J Am Ling* 22(2), Apr.: 180-183.   [*COL*]

26.035	GC	1956	Spanish Huracán and its congeners. *Int J Am Ling* 22(4), Oct.: 275-276. [COL]
26.036	GC	1957	Ballyhoo. *Int J Am Ling* 23(4), Oct.: 302-303. [COL]
26.037	GC	1957	Languages and ghost-languages of the West Indies: a postscript. *Int J Am Ling* 23(2), Apr.: 114-116. [COL]
9.055	GC	1957	Marriage, affinity, and descent in two Arawakan tribes: a sociolinguistic note.
26.038	GC	1957	A note on some Arawakan words for *man*, etc. *Int J Am Ling* 23(1), Jan.: 46-48. [9] [COL]
26.039	GC	1957	On the affiliation of "Island Carib." *Int J Am Ling* 23(4), Oct.: 297-302. [COL]
26.040	GC	1957	Spanish Canoa and its congeners. *Int J Am Ling* 23(3), July: 242-244. [COL]
26.041	GC	1957	Spanish Hamaca and its congeners. *Int J Am Ling* 23(2), Apr.: 113-114. [COL]
26.042	GC	1958	Carib, Caliban, Cannibal. *Int J Am Ling* 24(2), Apr.: 156-157. [COL]
26.043	GC	1958	A case of reconstitution. *Int J Am Ling* 24(4), Oct.: 323-324. [COL]
26.044	GC	1958	Compounds and comparison. *Int J Am Ling* 24(1), Jan.: 77-79. [COL]
26.045	GC	1958	Corrigenda to Island Carib I-IV. *Int J Am Ling* 24(4), Oct.: 325-326. [COL]
26.046	GC	1958	Island Carib IV: Syntactic notes, texts. *Int J Am Ling* 24(1), Jan.: 36-60. [COL]
26.047	GC	1958	Iwana-Yuana *iguana*. *Int J Am Ling* 24(2), Apr.: 157-158. [COL]
26.048	GC	1958	Lines by a Black Carib. *Int J Am Ling* 24(4), Oct.: 324-325. [COL]
26.049	SV	1958	Names on Saint Vincent. *W I G* 38:97-105. [7] [COL]
26.050	GC	1958	The place of Island Carib within the Arawakan family. *Int J Am Ling* 24(2), Apr.: 153-156. [COL]
26.051	GC	1958	Some problems of sound correspondence in Arawakan. *Int J Am Ling* 24(3), July: 234-239. [COL]
26.052	GC	1959	Homophony or polysemy. *Int J Am Ling* 25(2), Apr.: 134-135. [COL]
26.053	GC	1959	On dialectal divergence in Island Carib. *Int J Am Ling* 25(1), Jan.: 62-67. [COL]
26.054	GC	1960	Compounds and comparison again. *Int J Am Ling* 26(3), July: 252-256. [COL]
26.055	GC	1960	On consonantal correspondences in three Arawakan languages. *Int J Am Ling* 26(3), July: 244-252. [COL]
26.056	GC	1960	On the history of Island-Carib consonantism. *Int J Am Ling* 26(2), Apr.: 146-155. [COL]
26.057	GC	1960	Some remarks on the spelling and formation of Taino words. *Int J Am Ling* 26(4), Oct.: 345-348. [COL]
26.058	GC	1961	Arawakan for *path, bone, hand:* a semantic problem of reconstruction. *Int J Am Ling* 27(4), Oct.: 365-367. [COL]
26.059	GC	1961	A problem in relationship. *Int J Am Ling* 27, July: 284-286. [COL]
9.056	GC	1961	Some remarks on teknonymy in Arawakan.
26.060	SR	1962	Surinam Arawak as compared with different dialects of Island Carib. *Bijd Volk* 118:362-372.

TAYLOR, DOUGLAS C. & ROUSE, IRVING

| 4.144 | GC | 1955 | Linguistic and archeological time depth in the West Indies. |

THOMPSON, ROBERT WALLACE

| 40.186 | TR | 1959 | Pre-British place-names in Trinidad. |

WHITE, WALTER GRAINGE
26.061	BG	1917	Fringes of Makuchi. *Timehri* 3d ser., 4(21), June: 98-106. [*AMN*]
26.062	BG	1918	Articles on Indian languages. *Timehri* 3d ser., 5(22), Aug.: 98-103. [*AMN*]

WILLIAMS, JAMES
1.048	BG	1917	Indian languages.
40.220	GG	1923	The name "Guiana."
1.049	GG	1924	The Arawak Indians and their language.
26.063	BG	1932	GRAMMAR NOTES AND VOCABULARY OF THE LANGUAGE OF THE MAKUCHI INDIANS OF GUIANA. St. Gabriel-Mödling bei Wien, Verlag der Internationalen Zeitschrift "Anthropos", 413p. (Linguistische Anthroposbibliothek, v. 8.) [*AMN*]

HEALTH,
EDUCATION
AND
WELFARE

PHYSICAL ANTHROPOLOGY

ARNEAUD, JOHN D. & YOUNG, OSWALD

27.001   TR   1955   A preliminary survey of the distribution of A B O and Rh blood groups in Trinidad, B.W.I. *Docum Med Geogr Trop* 7(4), Dec.: 375-378. **[10]**   *[COL]*

BENOIST, JEAN

27.002   MT   1957   Stature et corpulence à la Martinique: données anthropométriques globales et incidence des conditions sociales [Height and weight in Martinique: overall anthropometric data and incidence of social factors]. *Biotypologie* 18(4):237-246.   *[RIS]*

27.003   MT   [1958?]   DONNÉES COMPARATIVES SUR LA CROISSANCE SOMATIQUE DES ENFANTS DE COULEUR ET DES ENFANTS DE RACE BLANCHE NÉS ET ÉLEVÉS À LA MARTINIQUE [COMPARATIVE DATA ON THE SOMATIC GROWTH OF COLORED CHILDREN AND WHITE CHILDREN BORN AND BRED IN MARTINIQUE]. Société des Africanistes, p.[7-9]. **[10]**   *[RIS]*

27.004   MT   1959   Notes pour l'étude de la croissance chez les enfants martiniquais: étude préliminaire chez les enfants du sexe masculin de Fort-de-France [Notes for the study of growth among Martinique children. Preliminary study among the male children of Fort-de-France]. *Archs Inst Past Mart* 12(1-2), Jan.-Apr.: 43-46.   *[RIS]*

27.005   MT   1961   L'étude de la structure génétique d'une population métissée [Study of the genetic structure of a hybrid population]. *Anthropologica* new ser., 3(1): 55-64.   *[COL]*

27.006   MT   1963   Les Martiniquais: anthropologie d'une population métissée [The people of Martinique: the anthropology of a hybrid population]. *B Mem Soc Anthrop Paris* II. ser., 4(2), Apr.-June: 241-432. **[10]**   *[RIS]*

27.007   FA   1964   Quelques facteurs sociaux de la différenciation raciale aux Antilles Francaises [Some social aspects of racial differentiation in the French Antilles]. *In* ACTAS Y MEMORIAS, XXXV CONGRESO INTERNACIONAL DE AMERICANISTAS, México, 1962. México, p.87-94. **[10]**   *[RIS]*

27.008   SB   1964   Saint-Barthélemy: physical anthropology of an isolate. *Am J Phys Anthrop* new ser., 22(4), Dec.: 473-487.   *[RIS]*

BULLBROOK, JOHN ALBERT
4.019   TR   1953 On the excavation of a shell mound at Palo Seco, Trinidad, B.W.I.

BUTTS, DONALD C. A.
27.009   SR   1955 Blood groups of the Bush Negroes of Surinam. *Docum Med Geogr Trop* 7(1), Mar.: 43-49. [14]   [*COL*]

BUXTON, L. H. DUDLEY; TREVOR, J. C. & JULIEN, ALVAREZ H.
27.010   ST   1938 Skeletal remains from the Virgin Islands. *Man* 38(47), Apr.: 49-51.
                                                                              [*COL*]

BYAS, VINCENT W.
27.011   MT   1943 Ethnologic aspects of the Martinique Creole. *J Negro Hist* 28(3), July: 261-283.   [*COL*]

COLLIER, W. A.
27.012   SR   1955 The M-N blood-groups in the Arawaks of Matta, Surinam. *Docum Med Geogr Trop* 7(4), Dec.: 359-360. [13]   [*COL*]

COLLIER, W. A.; FROS, J. & SCHIPPER, J. F. A.
27.013   SR   1952 Blood groups of some American Indian settlements. *Docum Med Geogr Trop* 4(3), Sept.: 225-226. [13]   [*COL*]

COLLIER, W. A. & La PARRA, D. A. de
27.014   SR   1952 Sickle-cell trait in Surinam Creoles. *Docum Med Geogr Trop* 4(3), Sept.: 223-225. [10]   [*COL*]

COLLIER, W. A.; WOLFF, A. E. & ZAAL, A. E. G.
27.015   SR   1952 Contributions to the geographical pathology of Surinam. I: Blood groups of the Surinam population. *Docum Med Geogr Trop* 4(1), Mar.: 92-95. [10]   [*COL*]

DAVENPORT, C. B.
27.016   JM   1928 Race crossing in Jamaica. *Scient Mon* 27(3), Sept.: 225-238.   [*AGS*]

DAVENPORT, C. B. & STEGGERDA, MORRIS
27.017   JM/   1929 Race crossing in Jamaica. Washington, D. C., Carnegie Institution
           CM   of Washington, 516p. [10]   [*RIS*]

DORAN, EDWIN BEAL, Jr.
27.018   CM   1952 Inbreeding in an isolated island community. *J Hered* 43(6), Nov.-Dec.: 263-266. [7, 28]   [*RIS*]

DROOGLEEVER FORTUYN, A. B.
27.019   SR   1946 Some data on the physical anthropology of Oajana Indians. Amsterdam, Koninklijke Vereeniging Indisch Instituut, 24p. (Mededeeling no. 69, Afdeeling Volkenkunde no. 22.) [13]   [*COL*]
27.020   SR   1952 Age, stature, and weight in Surinam conscripts. Amsterdam, Koninklijk Instituut voor de Tropen, 126p. (Mededeling no. 101, Afdeling Culturele en physische anthropologie no. 44.) [10] [*SCH*]

FERGUSON, J. E. A.
28.151   BG   1906 The climate of the Peter's Hall District and its effects on the inhabitants.

FIRSCHEIN, I. LESTER
27.021   BH   1961 Population dynamics of the sicle-cell trait in the Black Caribs of British Honduras, Central America. *Am J Hum Gntcs* 13(2), June: 233-254. [13]   [COL]

FLOCH, HERVE ALEXANDRE & LAJUDIE, P. de
27.022   FG   1947 Répartition des groupes sanguins en Guyane Francaise [Distribution of blood groups in French Guiana]. *Inst Past Guy Ter L'In* 145, Jan.: 3p. [10]   [ACM]

GARROW, J. S.
27.023   JM   1954 Some haematological and serum protein values in normal Jamaicans. *W I Med J* 3(2), June: 104-107.   [COL]

GIBBS, W. N.
27.024   JM   1963 Abo and Rh blood group distribution in a rural Jamaican community. *W I Med J* 12(2), June: 103-108.   [COL]

GOYHENECHE, E. & NICOLAS, MAURICE
5.071   FA   1956 DES ÎLES ET DES HOMMES [THE ISLANDS AND THE PEOPLE].

GRINDER, ROBERT E.
27.025   JM   1964 Negro-white differences in intellectual performance: a receding controversy. *Int Ment Heal Res Newsl* 6(4), Winter: 2, 5-6. [16, 31, 67]   [RIS]

HAMBLY, WILFRID D.
27.026   BH   1937 SKELETAL MATERIAL FROM SAN JOSÉ RUIN, BRITISH HONDURAS. Chicago, Field Museum of Natural History, 19p. (Publication no. 380, Anthropological series, v. 25, no. 1.)   [AGS]

HARPER, W. F.
27.027   JM   1959 Cranial vault sutures in the Jamaica Negro. *W I Med J* 8(4), Dec.: 267-271. [11]   [COL]
27.028   JM   1962 Aboriginal Amerindian skulls of Jamaica. *Inf B Scient Res Coun* 2(4), Mar.: 66-69.   [RIS]

HENRY, M. U.
28.275   TR   1963 The haemoglobinopathies in Trinidad.

LIACHOWITZ, CLAIRE, et al.
28.339   SR   1958 Abnormal hemoglobins in the Negroes of Surinam.

MacIVER, J. E. & WENT, L. N.
28.344   JM   1958 Further observations on abnormal haemoglobins in Jamaica.

MILLER, COLIN G.
27.029   JM   1960 Observations on liver size in Healthy Jamaican Children Hermitage Survey. *W I Med J* 9(2): 124-130.   [COL]

MONTESTRUC, ETIENNE & BERDONNEAU, ROBERT

27.030   MT   1957 Premier cas d'hémoglobinose C, S à la Martinique [First instance of hemoglobinosis C, S in Martinique]. *B Soc Path Exot Fil* 50(1), Jan.-Feb.: 94-95.   [*ACM*]

27.031   MT   1958 Quelques considérations sur les groupes sanguins A, B, O et sur le facteur *Rhesus* chez le Martiniquais [Some comments on blood groups A, B, O, and on the Rh factor among the people of Martinique]. *B Soc Path Exot Fil* 51(6), Nov.-Dec.: 917-920.   [*ACM*]

MONTESTRUC, ETIENNE; BERDONNEAU, ROBERT; BENOIST, JEAN & COLLET, ANDRE

27.032   MT   1959 Hémoglobines anormales et groupes sanguins A, B, O, chez les Martiniquais [Abnormal hemoglobins and blood groups A, B, O, among the people of Martinique]. *B Soc Path Exot Fil* 52(2), Mar.-Apr.: 156-158. [10]   [*ACM*]

NEHAUL, B. B. G.

27.033   BG   1947 Physical measurements of East Indian boys in Leguan, British Guiana. *Br Gui Med Annual* 152-161. [12]   [*RIS*]

PANHUYS, L. C. van

27.034   FG   1905 Are there pygmies in French Guiana? *In* PROCEEDINGS OF THE INTERNATIONAL CONGRESS OF AMERICANISTS, 13th Session, New York, Oct. 1902. Easton, Pa., Eschenbach Print. Co., p.131-133. [13] [*AGS*]

RICKETSON, OLIVER, Jr.

27.035   BH   1931 Excavations at Baking Pot, British Honduras. *In* CARNEGIE INSTITUTION OF WASHINGTON, PUBLICATION NO. 403; CONTRIBUTIONS TO AMERICAN ARCHAEOLOGY, Washington, D.C., v.1, no.1, p.3-27. [4] [*AGS*]

STAFFORD, J. L.; HILL, K. R. & ARNEAUD, J. D.

27.036   GC   1955 Rhesus factor distribution in the Caribbean: preliminary communication. *W I Med J* 4(2), June: 119-125. [10]   [*COL*]

STANDARD, KENNETH L.

27.037   BB   1964 Weights and heights of children in Barbados, West Indies, 1961. *W I Med J* 13(2), June: 77-83. [30]   [*COL*]

STEGGERDA, MORRIS

27.038   JM   1928 Physical development of Negro-white hybrids in Jamaica, British West Indies. *Am J Phys Anthrop* 12(1), July: 121-138.   [*COL*]

STEWART, T. D.

27.039   GC   1939 Negro skeletal remains from Indian sites in the West Indies. *Man* 39(52), Apr.: 49-51. [11]

SWELLENGREBEL, N. H.

17.028   SR   1940 Over de vraag of een proefneming tot vestiging van politieke uitgewekenen in Suriname hygienisch te verantwoorden is [On the question whether an attempt to settle political refugees in Surinam is advisable from a hygienic viewpoint].

TACOMA, J.

27.040   AR   1959 Indian skeletal remains from Aruba. *W I G* 39:95-112.   [13]   [*RIS*]

27.041   AR   1964 Kunstmatige schedeldeformatie in Aruba [Artificial skull deformation in Aruba]. *N W I G* 43(3), May: 211-222.   [13]   [*RIS*]

THOMPSON, J. ERIC S.

4.146   BH   1939 EXCAVATIONS AT SAN JOSE, BRITISH HONDURAS.

VERRILL, ALPHEUS HYATT

4.151   BG   1918 Prehistoric mounds and relics of the north west district of British Guiana.

WAGENAAR HUMMELINCK, P.

27.042   AR/   1959 Indiaanse skeletvondsten op Aruba en Curacao [Indian skeletal
       CU   discoveries in Aruba and Curacao]. *W I G* 39:72-94.   [13]   [*RIS*]

WELLS, A. V.

27.043   BB   1963 Study of birthweights of babies born in Barbados, West Indies. *W I Med J* 12(3), Sept.: 194-199.   [*COL*]

WENT, L. N. & Mac IVER, J. E.

28.584   JM   1956 Investigation of abnormal haemoglobins in Jamaica: a preliminary survey.

ZANEN, GEORGE EDUARD van

27.044   CU   1962 EXPRESSION OF THE HAEMOGLOBIN S GENE ON THE ISLAND OF CURACAO. Amsterdam, Drukkerij J. Ruysendaal, 113p. (Ph.D. thesis, University of Groningen, 1962.)   [*RIS*]

Chapter 28

HEALTH AND PUBLIC HEALTH

ABONNENC, E.
7.002 FG 1948/Aspects demographiques de la Guyane Francaise [Demographic
49 aspects of French Guiana].

ACHARD, CH.
28.001 FG 1939 Mission en Guyane [Guiana expedition]. *B Acad Med* 3d ser. 122(32),
Nov.: 401-411. [17, 66]   [*ACM*]

ADAMSON, A. M.
41.002 TR 1941 Observations on biting sandflies (*Ceratopogonidae*) in Trinidad,
British West Indies.

AITKEN, THOMAS H. G.
28.002 TR 1957 Virus transmission studies with Trinidadian mosquitoes. *W I Med J*
6(4), Dec.: 229-232.   [*COL*]
28.003 GC 1961 The public health importance of *Culex quinquefasciatus say* in the
West Indies. *W I Med J* 10(4), Dec.: 264-268.   [*COL*]

AITKEN, THOMAS H. G. & SPENCE, LESLIE
28.004 TR 1963 Virus transmission studies with Trinidadian mosquitoes pt. III:
Cache Valley virus. *W I Med J* 12(2), June: 128-132.   [*COL*]

ALCALA, V. O.
28.005 GC 1959 Instructional material for healthy living. *Caribbean* 13(2), Feb.:
34-35, 44. [1]   [*COL*]

ANDERSON, CHARLES R.
28.006 TR 1957 St. Louis virus in Trinidad. *W I Med J* 6(4), Dec.: 249-253.   [*COL*]

ANDERSON, M. F.
28.007 JM 1962 Haemoglobinopathies in pregnancy. *W I Med J* 11(4), Dec.: 265-274.
[*COL*]

ANDUZE, ROY
28.008 UV 1955 Health in the Virgin Islands. *Caribbean* 9(2), Sept.: 37-39.   [*COL*]

ANNAMUNTHODO, H.
28.009 JM 1958 Observations on carcinoma of the breast in Jamaica. *W I Med J* 7(2),
June: 93-108.   [*COL*]

28.010   JM   1958 Surgical treatment of chronic peptic ulcer in Jamaica. *W I Med J* 7(1), Mar.: 53-67.   [COL]
28.011   JM   1959 Carcinoma of penis. *W I Med J* 8(3), Sept.: 149-160.   [COL]
28.012   JM   1959 Observations on cancer of the oesophagus in Jamaica. *W I Med J* 8(2), June: 92-100.   [COL]
28.013   JM   1959 Observations on cancer of the stomach in Jamaica. *W I Med J* 8(1), Mar.: 17-32.   [COL]
28.014   JM   1962 Rectal lymphogranuloma venereum in Jamaica. *W 1 Med J* 11(2), June: 73-85.   [COL]

ASHCROFT, M. T.
28.015   BG   1962 The morbidity and mortality of enteric fever in British Guiana. *W I Med J* 11(1), Mar.: 62-71. [5, 7, 10]   [COL]

ASHCROFT, M. T.; NICHOLSON, C. C. & STUART, C. A.
28.016   BG   1963 Typhoid antibodies in British Guiana school children. *W I Med J* 12(4), Dec.: 247-252.   [COL]

ASIN, H. R. G. & THIEL, P. H. van
28.017   SR   1963 On intestinal protozoa in the urban and bushland population in Surinam. *Trop Geogr Med* 15(2), June: 108-120.   [COL]

ASREGADOO, E. R.
28.018   BG   1964 Congenital cataracts associated with rubella. *W I Med J* 13(1), Mar.: 22-24.   [COL]

BACK, E. H. & BROOKS, S. E. H.
28.019   JM   1962 The pattern of infantile gastro-enteritis in Jamaica. *W I Med J* 11(3), Sept.: 179-187.   [COL]

BACK, E. H. & DePASS, E. E.
28.020   JM   1957 Acute rheumatic fever in Jamaican children. *W I Med J* 6(2), June: 98-104.   [COL]

BACK, E. H. & HILL, K. R.
28.021   JM   1956 A case of glycogen storage disease in a West Indian infant. *W I Med J* 5(1), Mar.: 59-64.   [COL]

BACK, E. H. & WARD, E. E.
28.022   JM   1962 Electrolyte and acid-base disturbances occurring in infantile gastro-enteritis in Jamaica. *W I Med J* 11(4), Dec.: 228-234.   [COL]

BAILEY, C. E. STANLEY
28.023   LW   1944 Tuberculosis in the Leeward Islands colony. *Car Med J* 6(3): 178-182.   [COL]
28.024   AT   1960 Tuberculosis in Antigua. *Car Med J* 22(1-4): 93-95.   [COL]

BAUCKHAM, JOHN F.
28.025   SL   1960 Tuberculosis in St. Lucia. *Car Med J* 22(1-4): 118-119.   [COL]

BAYLEY, H. H.
28.026   BB   1939 An investigation of the infectious jaundice of Barbados. *Car Med J* 1(2): 135-142.   [COL]

BEADNELL, H. G.
28.027   BG   1962 Industrial injuries in the sugar industry of British Guiana. *W I Med J*
11(1), Mar.: 15-21.   [50, 58]   [*COL*]

BEAUBRUN, MICHAEL H.
28.028   TR   1962 Huntington's chorea in Trinidad. *Car Med J* 24(1-4):45-50.   [31]
[*COL*]
28.029   TR/   1963 Huntington's chorea in Trinidad. *W I Med J* 12(1), Mar. 39-46. [*COL*]
GR

BEEN, T. W.; CLARK, B. M.; GRANT, L. S. & BROOM, J. C.
28.030   JM   1960 Leptospira kremastos infection in Jamaica, West Indies. *W I Med J*
9(1), Mar.: 25-30.   [*COL*]

BEIJERING, J.
28.031   CU   1950 Het vraagstuk van het behoud van het water op Curacao [The problem
of water conservation on Curacao]. *W I G* 31:65-79.   [40]   [*COL*]

BELLE, EDWARD A.; GRANT, LOUIS S.; THOMAS, KENDRICK J. &
MINOTT, OWEN S.
28.032   JM   1964 Laboratory investigation of the 1963 influenza epidemic in Jamaica,
West Indies. *W I Med J* 13(1), Mar.: 63-69.   [*COL*]

BENNETT, C. V.
31.008   BB   1965 Nursing and mental health in the family.

BEVIER, GEORGE
28.033   GC   1943 Some international aspects of yellow fever control. *Br Gui Med
Annual 1943* 26:13-31.   [*ACM*]

BHATTACHARYA, B. P.
28.034   BG   1962 Clinical aspects of the problem of multiparity in British Guiana.
Car Med J 24(1-4):72-75.   [*COL*]

BLAINE, GEORGE
28.035   JM   1957 Tropical phagaedenic ulcer in Jamaica: evaluation of new ambula-
tory methods of treatment. *W I Med J* 6(4), Dec.: 285-296.   [*COL*]

BLIN, G.
28.036   FG   1914 L'uncinariose chez les chercheurs d'or et les forcats du Maroni
[Uncinariasis among the gold prospectors and convicts of Maroni].
Ann Hyg Med Colon 17(1), Jan.-Mar.: 149-176.   [37]   [*ACM*]

BLUMBERG, B.; McGIFF, J. & GUICHERIT, I.
28.037   SR   1951 Filariasis in Moengo (Surinam) in 1950. *Docum Ned Indo Morbis Trop*
3(4), Dec.: 368-372.   [10]   [*RIS*]
28.038   SR   1952 Malaria survey among the Bush Negroes of Marowyne District,
Surinam, S. A. in 1950. *Docum Med Geogr Trop* 4(1), Mar.: 2-4.   [14]
[*COL*]
28.039   SR   1953 A survey of intestinal parasites in the school children of Moengo,
Surinam, 1950. *Docum Med Geogr Trop* 5(2), June: 137-140.   [9, 10]
[*RIS*]

BODKIN, G. E.
28.040   BG   1921 Some recent entomological surveys bearing on malarial incidence
                in British Guiana. *J Bd Agric Br Gui* 14(4), Oct.: 226-229.   [41]
                                                                              [*AMN*]

BOLTEN, D. G. J.
28.041   SR   1925/Muggenbestrijding [The fight against gnats]. *W I G* 7:567-570.   [33]
                26
                                                                              [*COL*]
28.042   SR   1926/Eene waterleiding voor Paramaribo [Waterworks for Paramaribo].
                27 *W I G* 8:119-124.   [*COL*]

BONNE, C.
28.043   SR   1919 De maatschappelijke beteekenis der Surinaamsche ziekten [The
                social implications of the Surinam diseases]. *W I G* 1(1): 291-310.
                                                                              [*COL*]
28.044   SR   1923/Hygienische ervaring te Moengo [Hygienic experience in Moengo].
                24 *W I G* 5:394-404.   [3, 15]   [*COL*]
28.045   SR   1923/Organizatie van den geneeskundigen dienst in Suriname[Organiza-
                24 tion of the medical services in Surinam]. *W I G* 5:289-294.   [33]
                                                                              [*COL*]
28.046   SR   1925/De opleiding en de positie van den districtsgeneesheer in Suriname
                26 [The training and the position of the district medical officer in
                Surinam]. *W I G* 7:432-439.   [33]   [*COL*]

BOOLS, MARY M.
28.047   BB   1960 Sensitivity tests on *Tubercle bacilli* in Barbados. *Car Med J* 22(1-4):
                96-99.   [*COL*]

BORGHANS-DELVAUX, J. M.; BORGHANS, J. G. A. & VINKE, B.
28.048   NA   1959 Q-Fever in the Netherlands Antilles. *Trop Geogr Med* 11(3), Sept.:
                253-258.   [*COL*]

BOUCAUD, J. E. A.
28.049   TR   1942 Treatment of war casualties in Trinidad. *Car Med J* 4(2): 49-57.
                                                                              [*COL*]
28.050   BC   1962 The practice of medicine in the British West Indies 1814-1953. *Car
                Med J* 24(1-4): 40-44.   [5]   [*COL*]

BOWER, B. D.
28.051   JM   1958 Tay-Sach's disease in a West Indian of African origin. *W I Med J*
                7(1), Mar.: 68-70.   [11]   [*COL*]

BOYCE, Sir RUBERT W.
28.052   BC   1910 HEALTH PROGRESS AND ADMINISTRATION IN THE WEST INDIES. New
                York, Dutton, 328p.   [25]   [*AGS*]

BOYD, MARK F. & ARIS, F. W.
28.053   JM   1929 A malarial survey of the island of Jamaica, B.W.I. *Am J Trop Med*
                9(5), Sept.: 309-399.   [43]   [*COL*]

BRAAKSMA, H. E.
28.054   SR   1957 Myiasis caused by dermatobia cyaniventris in Surinam. *Docum Med
                Geogr Trop* 9(1), Mar.: 97-99.

BRAHMAN, A. P.

28.055   BG   1961 A report of three fatal cases of human paralytic rabies occurring in one family from British Guiana (1960). *W I Med J* 10(3), Sept.: 149-155.   [*COL*]

BRAND, C. A.

28.056   SL   1958 An outbreak of typhoid fever in St. Lucia (summer, 1957). *W I Med J* 7(2), June: 142-148.   [*COL*]

BRANDAY, WILLIAM JOSEPH

28.057   JM   1944 Tuberculosis in Jamaica. *Car Med J* 6(3): 153-169.   [*COL*]
28.058   TR   1951 Tuberculosis in Trinidad. *Car Med J* 13(3-4): 119-127.   [*COL*]
28.059   TR   1960 Tuberculosis in Trinidad. *Car Med J* 22(1-4):41-48.   [*COL*]
28.060   TR   1961 Notes on X-ray campaign in Port-of-Spain. *Car Med J* 23(1-4): 71-73.   [*COL*]

BRANDAY, WILLIAM JOSEPH; DASENT, L. E.; PIERRE, Sir HENRY & RICHARDSON, K. R.

28.061   TR   1958 Results of 200 resections for pulmonary tuberculosis. *W I Med J* 7(2), June: 149-156.   [*COL*]

BRAS, G., et al.

28.062   JM   1959 Medical Research Society of the University College of the West Indies: proceedings of the second meeting held at the University College of the West Indies on 6th June, 1959. *W I Med J* 8(3), Sept.: 218-220.   [*COL*]

BRAS, G.; BROOKS, S. E. H. & DePASS, E. E.

28.063   JM   1955 Data about malignant neoplasms and the incidence of cirrhosis of the liver in Jamaica. *W I Med J* 4(3), Sept.: 173-181.   [*COL*]

BRAS, G. & CLEARKIN, K. P.

28.064   JM   1954 Histopathology of the pancreas in Jamaican infants and children. *Docum Med Geogr Trop* 6(4), Dec.: 327-330.   [*COL*]

BRAS, G.; JELLIFFE, D. B. & STUART, K. L.

28.065   JM   1954 Histological observations on hepatic disease in Jamaican infants and children. *Docum Med Geogr Trop* 6(1), Mar.: 43-60.   [*COL*]

BRAS, G.; STEWART, D. B. & ANTROBUS, A. C. K.

28.066   JM   1956 Observations on carcinoma of the cervix in Jamaica. Pt. I: Incidence and morbid anatomical data. *W I Med J* 5(1), Mar.: 1-9. [*COL*]

BRAS, G. & WATLER, D. C.

28.067   JM   1955 Further observations on the morphology of veno-occlusive disease of the liver in Jamaica. *W I Med J* 4(4), Dec.: 201-211.   [*COL*]

BREMONT, E.

28.068   FG   1918 La syphilis à la Guyane Francaise [Syphilis in French Guiana]. *B Soc Path Exot* 11(9), Nov.: 784-788.   [*ACM*]

BROWN, JOHN

32.033   SL   1962 Education and development of St. Lucia.

BROWNE, J. A.

28.069   BG   1933 The common causes of blindness in British Guiana. *Br Gui Med Annual 1932* 25:25-34.   [*ACM*]

28.070   BG   1939 Three every-day eye diseases in British Guiana. *Car Med J* 1(3): 218-222.   [*COL*]

BRUIJNING, C. F. A.

28.071   SR   1952 Some observations on the distribution of *A. Darlingi* root in the Savannah region of Surinam, by C. F. A. Bruyning. *Docum Med Geogr Trop* 4(2), June: 171-174. [41]   [*COL*]

28.072   SR/   1957 Man-biting sandflies *(Phlebotomus)* in the endemic Leishmaniasis
          FG   area of Surinam. *Docum Med Geogr Trop* 9(3), Sept.: 229-236. [14, 41]   [*COL*]

28.073   SR   1957 Notes on the common species of Culicoides *(Diptera*: Ceratopogonidae) from Surinam in relation to Ozzardi-Filariasis. *Docum Med Geogr Trop* 9(2), June: 169-172.   [*COL*]

BURKE, L. M.

28.074   JM   1962 The acute phase of poliomyelitis. *W I Med J* 11(2), June: 123-128.
                                                                                         [*COL*]

BURROWES, J. T.

28.075   JM   1951 Hysterectomy in Jamaica. *W I Med J* 1(1), Sept.: 26-32.   [*COL*]

BUTCHER, LEONARD V.

28.076   TR   1958 The present status of paralytic rabies (bat-transmitted in Trinidad). *W I Med J* 7(1), Mar.: 17-20.   [*COL*]

BUTLER, C. S. & HAKANSSON, E. G.

28.077   UV   1917 Some first impressions of the Virgin Islands, medical, surgical and epidemiological. *U S Navl Med B* 11(4), Oct.: 465-475. [29]   [*ACM*]

BYER, M. A.

28.078   TR   1952 Hookworm disease in county Caroni. *Car Med J* 14(3-4): 87-89.
                                                                                         [*COL*]

28.079   BB   1957 Public health problems encountered during the first two and a half years at the Health Centre at Speightstown, Barbados. *Car Med J* 19(1-2): 40-52.   [*COL*]

CAIRES, P. F. de

28.080   BG   1947 Yellow fever service in British Guiana. *Br Gui Med Annual* 188-200.
                                                                                         [*RIS*]

28.081   GC   1951 The international yellow fever problem in the Caribbean islands. *W I Med J* 1(1), Sept.: 3-14. [66]   [*COL*]

CAREY, ELLEN

28.082   BG   1961 Health for British Guiana's children. *Corona* 13(7), July: 257-260.
                                                                                         [*AGS*]

CARLEY, MARY MANNING

28.083   JM   1943 MEDICAL SERVICES IN JAMAICA. Kingston, Institute of Jamaica with the assistance of Jamaica Welfare, 19p. (Social survey series, no. 2.) [30, 66]   [*COL*]

CARNEGIE, A. L.

28.084 JM 1963 Poisoning by barracuda fish. *W I Med J* 12(4), Dec.: 217-224.
[41, 56] [*COL*]

CARPENTER, REGINALD & ANNAMUNTHODO, HARRY

28.085 JM 1962 Ano rectal carcinoma in Jamaica. *W I Med J* 11(3), Sept.: 188-198.
[*COL*]

CAZANOVE, Dr.

28.086 FC 1935 Les épidémies de fièvre jaune aux Antilles et à la Guyane Française [Yellow fever epidemics in the Antilles and in French Guiana]. *In* DENIS, SERGE, ed. Nos ANTILLES. Orléans, Luzeray, 179-213. [5] [*AGS*]

CECIL, C. H.

28.087 TR 1942 Health and hygiene in Trinidad. *Can-W I Mag* 31(3), Mar.: 9-12.
[*NYP*]

CHAMBERS, H. D.

28.088 JM 1953 The syndrome called "vomiting sickness." *W I Med J* 2(1), Mar.: 37-42. [*COL*]
28.089 JM 1960 A clinical type of hypertension observed in Jamaica – illustrated by the most outstanding of the cases observed. *W I Med J* 9(1), Mar.: 67-72. [*COL*]
28.090 JM 1962 Malignant lymphocytic lymphoma. *W I Med J* 11(1), Mar.: 27-29. [*COL*]

CHARLES, E. D. B. & GRANT, L. S.

28.091 JM 1962 Poliomyelitis in Jamaica, W.I. *W I Med J* 11(3), Sept.: 203-212. [*COL*]

CHARLES, L. J.

28.092 LW/ 1952 Malaria in Leeward and Windward Islands, British West Indies. *Am*
WW *J Trop Med Hyg* 1(6), Nov.: 941-961. [*COL*]
28.093 BG 1953 Re-infestation problems in an *Aedes Aegypit*-free area in British Guiana. *W I Med J* 2(1), Mar.: 1-10. [66] [*COL*]

CLARAC,

28.094 FG 1902 La Guyane Francaise: notes de géographie médicale, d'ethnographie et de pathologie [French Guiana: medical geography, ethnography, and pathology]. *Ann Hyg Med Colon* 5:5-108. [7] [*ACM*]

CLARKE, F. J.

28.095 SL 1962 Adult education and the health of the community. *In* BROWN, JOHN, ed. AN APPROACH TO ADULT EDUCATION. Castries, St. Lucia, Govt. Print. Off., 15-19. [32] [*RIS*]

CLARKE, T. L. E.

28.096 BV 1918 Some observations on fish poisoning in the British Virgin Islands. *W I B* 17(2): 56-67. [41, 56] [*AMN*]

CLEARE, L. D.

41.062 BG 1919 Some parasites of man and animals in British Guiana.

COCHRANE, E.

28.097   GR   1941 Is *A. argyritarsis* a malarial vector in Grenada? *Car Med J* 3(4): 193-195.   [*COL*]

28.098   GR   1942 Notes on *A. argyritarsis* and *A. pseudopunctipennis* in Grenada. *Car Med J* 4(3): 97-100.   [*COL*]

COCHRANE, E. & STUART, K. L.

28.099   BB   1963 Cardiovascular disorders in Barbados. *W I Med J* 12(4), Dec.: 275-284.   [*COL*]

COIA, A. G.

28.100   BG   1933 Nephritis in British Guiana. *Br Gui Med Annual 1932* 25:45-50. [*ACM*]

28.101   BG   1933 Some racial statistics of uterine fibroids in British Guiana. *Br Gui Med Annual 1932* 25:106-109.   [10]   [*ACM*]

COLLIER, H. C.

42.008   BG   1942 Climate and health in British Guiana.

COLLIER, W. A.; COLLIER, E. E. & TJONG A HUNG, T.

28.102   SR   1956 Serological research on encephalitis in Surinam. *Docum Med Geogr Trop* 8(1), Mar.: 39-44.   [*COL*]

COLLIER, W. A. & FUENTE, A. A. de la

28.103   SR   1953 The histoplasmine test in Surinam. *Docum Med Geogr Trop* 5(2), June: 103-108.   [10]   [*COL*]

COLLIER, W. A. & TIGGELMAN-VAN KRUGTEN, V. A. H.

28.104   SR   1955 De vleermuizenlyssa in Suriname [The lyssa virus carried by bats in Surinam]. *Vox Guy* 1(6): 149-159.

COLLIER, W. A. & TJONG A HUNG, T.

28.105   SR   1953 Serological brucella tests in Surinam. *Docum Med Geogr Trop* 5(4), Dec.: 321-322.   [*COL*]

COLLIER, W. A.; WINCKEL, W. E. F. & BLOM, F. A. E.

28.106   SR   1953 Two cases of St. Louis encephalitis in Surinam. *Docum Med Geogr Trop* 5(3), Sept.: 225-234.   [*COL*]

COLLIER, W. A.; WINCKEL, W. E. F. & KAFILUDDI, S.

28.107   SR   1954 Coxsackie infections (pseudopoliomyelitis) in Surinam. *Docum Med Geogr Trop* 6(2), June: 97-105.   [*COL*]

COOK, MARTIN J.

28.108   TR   1945 Sulfonamide failures in the treatment of gonorrhea in Trinidad, B.W.I. *Car Med J* 7(2-3): 88-94.   [*COL*]

COOL, P.

28.109   SR   1923/ De Geneeskundige Dienst in Suriname [The Medical Service in
            24 Surinam]. *W I G* 5:653-657.   [*COL*]

28.110   SR   1924/ De nieuwe afdeling van het militaire hospitaal te Paramaribo voor
            25 besmettelijke ziekten [The new section for contagious diseases in the military hospital in Paramaribo]. *W I G* 6:433-440.   [66]   [*COL*]

CORY, RICHARD A. S.
28.111   JM   1960 Surgical treatment of respiratory tuberculosis over a quarter of a
               century in Jamaica, West Indies. *Car Med J* 22(1-4): 75-80.   [*COL*]

CRAIGEN, A. J.
28.112   BG   1912 Practice of midwifery at the Public Hospital, Georgetown. *Br Gui
               Med Annual 1910* 17:25-33.   [*ACM*]

CRANE, ALFRED V.
28.113   BG   1924 The Georgetown sewerage scheme. *W I Comm Circ* 39(671), June 19:
               237-238.   [36]   [*NYP*]

CRUICKSHANK, E. K.
28.114   JM   1952 The University College Hospital of the West Indies. *W I Med J* 1(3),
               Oct.: 274-280.   [32]   [*COL*]
28.115   JM   1956 A neuropathic syndrome of uncertain origin: review of 100 cases.
               W I Med J 5(3), Sept.: 147-159.   [*COL*]

CRUICKSHANK, E. K., et al.
28.116   JM   1955 Sickle cell anaemia: symposium at the University College of the West
               Indies, May 26th, 1954. *W I Med J* 4(1), Mar.: 25-37.   [10]   [*COL*]

CRUICKSHANK, E. K. & MONTGOMERY, R. D.
28.117   JM   1961 Multiple sclerosis in Jamaica. *W I Med J* 10(3), Sept.: 211-214. [*COL*]

DAN, M.
28.118   TR   1960 A study of P.A.S. intake of patients in South Trinidad. *Car Med J*
               22(1-4): 38-40.   [*COL*]

DANIELS, C. W.
28.119   BG   1902 Notes on malaria and other tropical diseases. *Br Gui Med Annual*
               [12]:40-46.   [*ACM*]

DAUTHEUIL,
28.120   FG   1936 Comment on devenait médecin au XVIIe siécle "en l'isle de
               Cayenne" [How one became a physician in the 17th century on
               "Cayenne island"]. *Chron Med* 43(9), Sept. 1:227-230.   [5]   [*COL*]

DAVIS, N. DARNELL
28.121   NV   1911 Nevis as West Indian health resort. *Timehri* 3d ser., 1(18C), Dec.:
               285-294.   [5]   [*AMN*]

DEANE, C. G.
30.008   TR   1938 Deficiency diseases in East Indians of the labouring class.

DEGAZON, D. W.
28.122   JM   1952 Primary glaucoma: pathogenesis and Jamaican aspects. *W I Med J*
               1(2), Apr.: 178-194.   [*COL*]

DePASS, E. E.
28.123   JM   1962 Some effects in rats of the administration of Crotalaria fulva ex-
               tract by mouth. *W I Med J* 11, Mar.: 12-14.   [*COL*]

DIAS, EMMANUEL

28.124   GG   1952 Doenca de chagas nas Américas. IV: Colômbia, Venezuela e Guianas
              [Running sores in the Americas. IV: Colombia, Venezuela, and
              the Guianas]. *Revta Brasil Mala Do Trop* 4(3), July: 255-280.   [41]
                                                                            [*COL*]

DOLLY, REYNOLD CARTWRIGHT

28.125   TR   1961 Some aspects of industrial medicine as seen in the oil industry.
              Car Med J 23(1-4) 59-63.   [49]   [*COL*]

DONOVAN, ANTHONY

28.126   BG   1939 Health aspects of the proposed large-scale settlement in British
              Guiana of European refugees. *In* REPORT OF THE BRITISH GUIANA
              COMMISSION TO THE PRESIDENT'S ADVISORY COMMITTEE ON POLITICAL
              REFUGEES. Washington, D. C., [no. 2] (39p.)   [*AGS*]

DORAN, EDWIN BEAL, Jr.

27.018   CM   1952 Inbreeding in an isolated island community.

DOWNS, W. G. & ANDERSON, C. R.

28.127   BC   1958 Distribution of immunity to Mayaro virus infection in the West Indies.
              W I Med J 7(3), Sept.: 190-194.   [*COL*]
28.128   GR   1959 Arthropod-borne encephalitic viruses in the West Indies area. Part
              I: A serological survey of Grenada, W.I. *W I Med J* 8(2), June:
              101-109.   [*COL*]

DOWNS, W. G.; ANDERSON, C. R.; AITKEN, T. H. G. & DELPECHE, K. A.

28.129   TR   1956 Notes on the epidemiology of ilhéus virus infection in Trinidad,
              B. W. I. *Car Med J* 18(3-4): 74-79.   [*COL*]

DOWNS, W. G.; ANDERSON, C. R.; DELPECHE, K. A. & BYER, M. A.

28.130   BB   1962 Arthropod-borne encephalitis viruses in the West Indies area. Pt. II:
              A serological survey of Barbados, W.I. *W I Med J* 11(2), June:
              117-122.   [*COL*]

DOWNS, W. G., DELPECHE, K. A. & UTTLEY, K. H.

28.131   AT   1963 Arthropod-borne encephalitis viruses in the West Indies area. Pt. IV:
              A serological survey of Antigua, W.I. *W I Med J* 12(2) June: 109-
              116.   [*COL*]

DOWNS, W. G. & GRANT, L. S.

28.132   JM   1962 Arthropod-borne encephalitis viruses in the West Indies area. Pt. III:
              A serological survey of Jamaica, W.I. *W I Med J* 11(4), Dec.: 253-
              264.   [*COL*]

DOWNS, W. G. & SPENCE, L.

28.133   SV   1963 Arthropod-borne encephalitis viruses in the West Indies area. Pt. VI:
              A serological survey of St. Vincent, W.I. *W I Med J* 12(3), Sept.:
              148-155.   [*COL*]
28.134   SL   1964 Arthropod-borne encephalitis viruses in the West Indies area. Pt. VII:
              A serological survey of St. Lucia, W.I. *W I Med J* 13(1), Mar.:
              25-32.   [*COL*]

DOWNS, W. G.; SPENCE, L.; AITKEN, T. H. G. & WHITMAN, L.

28.135   TR   1961 Cache Valley virus, isolated from a Trinidadian mosquito, *Aedes scapularis. W I Med J* 10(1), Mar.: 13-15.   [*COL*]

DOWNS, W. G.; SPENCE, L. & BORGHANS, J. G. A.

28.136   CU   1963 Arthropod-borne encephalitis viruses in the West Indies area. Pt. V: A serological survey of Curacao, N.W.I. *Trop Geogr Med* 15(3), Sept.: 237-242.   [*COL*]

DOWNS, W. G.; TURNER, L. H. & GREEN, A. E.

28.137   TR   1962 Leptospirosis in Trinidad: a preliminary report. *W I Med J* 11(1), Mar.: 51-54.   [*COL*]

DUFOUGERE, W.

28.138   FG   1920 Ankylostomiase et béribéri en Guyane Francaise [Ankylostomiasis and beriberi in French Guiana]. *B Soc Path Exot* 13(7), July: 603-617. [30]   [*ACM*]

37.101   FG   1921 De l'utilisation rationnelle de la main-d'oeuvre pénale en Guyane [On the rational use of forced labor in Guiana].

DUNCAN, W. J.

7.015   BG   1916 The public health statistics of the colony.

7.016   BG   1919 The public health and medical statistics of the colony.

EARLE, K. VIGORS

28.139   BC   1939 Esthiomène as seen in the West Indies. *Car Med J* 1(4): 310-320.   [*COL*]

28.140   TR   1939 Notes on the dengue epidemic at Point Fortin. *Car Med J* 1(3): 245-249.   [*COL*]

28.141   TR   1941 Infectious mononucleosis: some cases observed in Trinidad. *Car Med J* 3(2): 94-101.   [*COL*]

EDDEY, L. G.

28.142   BG   1947 An example of effective disease control in a tropical mining community. *Br Gui Med Annual,* 162-181.   [*RIS*]

EDGE, P. GRANVILLE

7.017   BC   1944 Infant mortality in British West Indies.

28.143   BC   1944 Malaria and nephritis in the British West Indies. *Car Med J* 6(1): 32-43.   [*COL*]

EDGHILL, H. B.

28.144   BG   1961 Filariasis at Port Mourant and its environs Corentyne coast, British Guiana. *W I Med J* 10(1), Mar.: 44-54. [10]   [*COL*]

ELLINGTON, E. V.

28.145   JM   1961 Estimation of hypoglycin "A" in *Blighia sapida*: (ackee). *W I Med J* 10(3), Sept.: 184-188. [60]   [*COL*]

ENGLISH, E. W. F., et al.

7.018   BG   1907 Report of the Mortality Commission.

ESDRAS, MARCEL
28.146   FA   1960 Les congrès des médecins de langue francaise de l'hémisphere
                Américain [Congresses of French-speaking physicians in the
                Western Hemisphere]. *Rev Guad* 39, Jan.-Mar.: 35-39. [66]   [*RIS*]

ESSED, W. F. R.
28.147   SR   1930/ Eenige opmerkingen naar aanleiding van de artikelen over treef en
          31   lepra in dit tijdschrift verschenen [Some remarks in connection with
                the articles about treyf and leprosy that appeared in this magazine].
                W I G 12:257-267. [14, 23]   [*COL*]

FAIRFIELD, LETITIA D.
28.148   BC   1921 Venereal diseases—the West Indian Commission. *W I Comm Circ*
                36(596), Aug. 4: 321-322.   [*NYP*]

FAWKES, M. A.
28.149   TR   1949 Acute gonorrhoea in the male—analysis of 500 cases. *Car Med J*
                11(2): 64-69.   [*COL*]
28.150   TR   1957 A short history of yaws in Trinidad. *W I Med J* 6(3), Sept.: 189-204.
                [5]   [*COL*]

FERGUSON, J. E. A.
28.151   BG   1906 The climate of the Peter's Hall District and its effects on the
                inhabitants. *Br Gui Med Annual 1905* 14:84-114. [42]   [*ACM*]
28.152   BG   1916 The treatment of anchylostomiasis in the Peter's Hall Medical
                District. *Br Gui Med Annual 1915* 21:43-48.   [*ACM*]

FERNANDES, H. P.
28.153   BG   1951 Streptomycin in the treatment of tuberculosis in British Guiana.
                Car Med J 13(1-2): 52-78. [10]   [*COL*]

FIELD, F. E.
28.154   BG   1913 Observations on dysentery, with special reference to its treatment
                by hypodermic injections of emetine. *Br Gui Med Annual 1912*
                19:1-7. [10]   [*ACM*]
28.155   BG   1916 Report on the amelioration and control of ankylostomiasis in the
                Belle Vue (West Bank) District of British Guiana. *Br Gui Med
                Annual 1915* 21:49-95. [10]   [*ACM*]

FIELDS, D. N.; SELLY, G. W. & GUICHERIT, I. D.
28.156   SR   1956 The treatment of ascariasis with piperazine. *Docum Med Geogr Trop*
                8:80-84.   [*RIS*]

FISTEIN, BORIS
28.157   TR   1960 Toxic hypoglycaemia (Jamaican vomiting sickness): first case
                reported from the territory of Trinidad and Tobago. *W I Med J* 9(1),
                Mar.: 62-66.   [*COL*]

FITZMAURICE, L. W., et al.
28.158   JM   1953 The vomiting sickness of Jamaica: symposium at the University
                College of the West Indies, Mar. 27th, 1953. *W I Med J* 2(2), June:
                93-124.   [*COL*]

FLOCH, HERVE ALEXANDRE

28.159	GD	1942	Apercu de pathologie médicale rurale en Guadeloupe [Sketch of the rural medical pathology in Guadeloupe]. *Inst Past Guy Ter L'In* 50, July (15p.)
28.160	FG	1944	L'endémie palustre dans les communes rurales et l'intérieur de la Guyane Francaise [Endemic malaria in the rural communities and the interior of French Guiana]. *Inst Past Guy Ter L'In* 78, June (5p.)
28.161	FG	1947	L'endémo-epidémie palustre en Guyane Francaise [Endemo-epidemic malaria in French Guiana]. *Inst Past Guy Ter L'In* 163, Oct. (12p.)
28.162	FG	1948	La pathologie humaine en Guyane Francaise [Human pathology in French Guiana]. *Rev Med Fr* 29(7), July: 99-100, 102. [*ACM*]
28.163	FG	1949	Particularités épidémiologiques de la lèpre en Guyane Francaise [Epidemiological characteristics of leprosy in French Guiana]. *Inst Past Guy Ter L'In* 189, Apr. (7p.)
28.164	FG	1950	Lutte antiamarile et lutte antipaludique en Guyane Francaise [Fight against yellow fever and malaria in French Guiana]. *Inst Past Guy Ter L'In* 213 (105p.)
28.165	FG	1951	L'assistance sociale aux lépreux et à leurs familles [Social welfare for the lepers and their families]. *Archs Ins Past Guy* 241, Sept. (6p.) [*33*]
28.166	FG	1952 1953	La fièvre jaune en Guyane Francaise [Yellow fever in French Guiana]. I: Rappel historique [Historical view]. II: Résultats de l'enquête épidémiologique de 1951 [Results of the 1951 epidemiological survey]. *Archs Inst Past Guy* 266, July; 278, Feb. (19p.) [*5*] [*ACM*]
28.167	FG	1954	La cinquième campagne de pulvérisations d'insecticides à effet remanent dans les habitations en Guyane Francaise [The fifth campaign of residual insecticide spraying of dwellings in French Guiana]. *Archs Inst Past Guy* 317, Feb. (68p.)
28.168	FG	1954	Evolution de la lutte antipaludique en Guyane Francaise de 1950 à 1954 [Development of the fight against malaria in French Guiana from 1950 to 1954]. *Archs Inst Past Guy* 345, Nov. (8p.)
28.169	FG	1954	Salmonellosis in French Guiana. *W I Med J* 3(4), Dec.: 277-278. [*COL*]
28.170	FG	1955 1956	La lutte antipaludique en Guyane Francaise [The fight against malaria in French Guiana]. I. La septième campagne de "dedetisation" [The seventh campaign of DDT spraying]. II. Notre huitième campagne de pulverisations d'insecticides à effet remanent dans les habitations [Our eighth campaign of residual insecticide spraying of dwellings]. *Archs Inst Past Guy* 369, Aug. (75p.); 404, Aug. (80p.)
30.011	FG	1955	Aspects nutritionnels de problèmes de pathologie guyanaise [Nutritional factors in the problems of Guianese pathology].
28.171	FG	1955	Yellow fever control in French Guiana. *Caribbean* 8(9), Apr.: 196-197, 208. [*COL*]
28.172	FG	1956	French Guiana malaria control. *Caribbean* 9(12), July: 270-271, 276. [*COL*]
28.173	FG	1956	Influence de la lutte antipaludique sur la natalité, la mortinatalité et la mortalité infantile en Guyane Francaise [Influence of the fight against malaria on birthrate, stillbirth rate, and infantile mortality in French Guiana]. *B Soc Path Exot* 49(4), July-Aug.: 647-651. [*7*] [*ACM*]

7.021   FG   1956 Influence du paludisme sur la natalité, mortinatalité et mortalité
                       infantile [The influence of malaria on the birthrate, stillbirth rate,
                       and infantile mortality].
28.174   FG   1956 Natalité, mortinatalité, mortalité infantile et paludisme [Birthrate,
                       stillbirth rate, infantile mortality, and malaria]. *Archs Inst Past Guy*
                       408, Sept. (5p.) [7]
30.014   FG   1956 Sur l'avitaminose PP en Guyane Francaise [On avitaminosis PP in
                       French Guiana].
28.175   FG   1956 Le traitement suppressif du paludisme chez les immigrants en
                       Guyane Francaise [Medical control of malaria among the immigrants
                       in French Guiana]. *Archs Inst Past Guy* 17(397), June (4p.)   [18]
                                                                                          [*ACM*]

FLOCH, HERVE ALEXANDRE & ABONNENC, E.
28.176   FG   1946 Sur la lèpre en Guyane Francaise [Concerning leprosy in French
                       Guiana]. III: Influence du traitement par l'huile de chaulmoogra
                       [Results of chaulmoogra oil treatment].   *Inst Past Guy Ter L'In*
                       135, Sept. (11p.) (See also 28.183)   [*ACM*]

FLOCH, HERVE ALEXANDRE & CAMAIN, R.
28.177   FG   1947 Maladies vénériennes autres que la syphilis en Guyane Francaise
                       [Venereal diseases other than syphilis in French Guiana]. *Inst
                       Past Guy Ter L'In* 165, Dec. (4p.)   [*ACM*]

FLOCH, HERVE ALEXANDRE & CORNU, G.
35.016   FG   1956 Problèmes de l'habitat à Cayenne. Le casier sanitaire des immeubles
                       [Housing problems in Cayenne. A sanitation register of the property].

FLOCH, HERVE ALEXANDRE; DURIEUX C. & KOERBER, R.
28.178   FG   1953 Enquête épidémiologique sur la fièvre jaune en Guyane Francaise
                       [Epidemiological survey of yellow fever in French Guiana]. *Annls
                       Inst Past* 84(3), Mar.: 495-508. [10]   [*ACM*]

FLOCH, HERVE ALEXANDRE & FAURAN, P.
28.179   FG   1954 Lutte antipaludique et lutte antiamarile en Guyane Francaise. Les
                       moustiques vecteurs du virus de la fièvre jaune en Guyane Fran-
                       caise [The fight against malaria and yellow fever in French Guiana.
                       Mosquito vectors of the yellow fever virus in French Guiana]. *Archs
                       Inst Past Guy* 322, Apr. (67p.) [41]

FLOCH, HERVE ALEXANDRE & LAJUDIE, P. de
28.180   FG   1942 Sur le paludisme à la Guyane Francaise et spécialement à Cayenne
                       [On malaria in French Guiana, particularly in Cayenne]. *Inst Past
                       Guy Ter L'In* 47, July (8p.)
28.181   FG   1945 L'endémo-épidémie typhoïdique en Guyane Francaise. Sur le niveau
                       moyen des agglutinines naturelles [Endemo-epidemic typhoid in
                       French Guiana. On the standard method of natural agglutination].
                       Inst Past Guy Ter L'In 105, May (8p.)
28.182   FG   1945 Sur la filariose à *W. bancrofti* en Guyane Francaise, la lymphangite
                       endémique et l'éléphantiasis des pays chauds [On *W. bancrofti*
                       filariasis in French Guiana, endemic lymphangitis and elephantiasis
                       in tropical countries]. *Inst Past Guy Ter L'In* 109, Aug. (17p.)

28.183   FG   1946   Sur la lèpre en Guyane Francaise [Regarding leprosy in French Guiana]. I. Généralités. Répartition par âge. Dépistage. Contamination [Generalities. Distribution by age. Case findings. Contamination]. II. Incubation. Symptôme initial. Formes cliniques. Diagnostic. Evolution et pronostic. Syphilis et lèpre. Cause des décès [Incubation. Initial symptom. Clinical forms. Diagnosis. Evolution and prognosis. Syphilis and leprosy. Cause of decease]. *Inst Past Guy Ter L'In* 131, July (6p.); 133, Aug. (10p.)   **[10]**   *[ACM]*

28.184   FG   1946   Sur la syphilis en Guyane Francaise [Regarding syphilis in French Guiana]. *Inst Past Guy Ter L'In* 123, Mar. (4p.)   *[ACM]*

FLOCH, HERVE ALEXANDRE; RIVIEREZ, E. & SUREAU, P.

30.023   FG   1952   Pellagre et vitamine PP en Guyane Francaise [Pellagra and Vitamin PP in French Guiana].

FLU, P. C.

3.103   SR   1922/ Sanitaire verhoudingen in Suriname [Sanitary situations in Surinam]. 23

FORDE, H. McD. & WILLIAMS, H. M.

28.185   BB   1960   Tetanus in Barbados. *W I Med J* 9(1), Mar.: 9-13.   *[COL]*

FRANCIS, A. G.

28.186   TR   1938   A brief summary of common diseases in Trinidad. *Car Med J* 1(1): 55-62.   *[COL]*

28.187   TR   1939   Some cases of interest. *Car Med J* 1(3): 234-244.   *[COL]*

FRANCIS, OLIVER M.

28.188   BG   1943   Social, economic and dietetic features of tuberculosis in British Guiana. *Br Gui Med Annual 1943* 26:43-71.   **[10, 35, 44]**   *[ACM]*

28.189   BG   1943   Tuberculin tests in British Guiana. *Br Gui Med Annual 1943* 26: 72-82.   **[10]**   *[ACM]*

28.190   BG   1944   Tuberculosis in British Guiana. *Car Med J* 6(3): 183-190.   **[10]**   *[COL]*

28.191   BG   1947   Comments on the state of the public health of British Guiana. *Br Gui Med Annual* 1-12.   *[RIS]*

FRAZER, A. C., et al.

28.192   BC   1957   Proceedings of the Second Annual Scientific Meeting of the Caribbean Medical Research Committee, held in Trinidad on Apr. 6th, 7th, 1957. *W I Med J* 6(2), June: 133-140.   *[COL]*

28.193   BC   1958   Standing Advisory Committee for Medical Research in the British Caribbean: proceedings of the Scientific Meeting Apr. 12th and 13th, 1958. *W I Med J* 7(2), June: 157-165.   *[COL]*

FREITAS, Q. B. de

28.194   BG   1904   Notes on and classification of malarial fever cases treated in the Public Hospital, Georgetown. *Br Gui Med Annual* 13:75-82. *[ACM]*

28.195   BG   1909   Record of the work of the maternity ward of the Public Hospital, Georgetown, from June, 1905, to March, 1906, and January, 1908, to May, 1908. *Br Gui Med Annual 1908* 16:26-28.   *[ACM]*

28.196   BG   1933   Former contributors to the British Guiana Annual. *Br Gui Med Annual 1932* 25:1-5.   *[ACM]*

28.197   BG   1933 Notes on cardiac dilation. *Br Gui Med Annual* 1932 25:70-73.   [11, 12]   [*ACM*]
28.198   BG   1936 A retrospect of medical practice in British Guiana, 1900-1935. *Br Gui Med Annual 1936* 26:148-152.   [*ACM*]
28.199   BG   1940 Return of post mortem examinations made on coroner's order and classification of death from 1933 to 1935 in British Guiana. *Car Med J* 2(4): 191-192.   [*COL*]
37.118   BG   1941 Notes on the trial of a nurse-midwife on the charge of murder held in the Criminal Court of Georgetown, Demarara, from 22nd April to 5th May, 1941.
28.200   BG   1942 Some observations on the proposed scheme for British Guiana for the improvement of public health and sanitary measures. *Car Med J* 4(2): 58-61. [66]   [*COL*]
28.201   BG   1943 Progress of the Medical and Public Health Services in British Guiana. *Br Gui Med Annual 1943* 26:172-180.   [*ACM*]
28.202   BG   1944 Review of the salient stages in the medical history of the colony from 1900-1944. *Timehri* 4th ser., 1(26), Nov.: 61-65.   [*AMN*]
3.114   BG   1948 Early experiences of a government and medical officer in British Guiana.
28.203   BG   1940 Report of the Sub-committee of the Infant Welfare and Maternity League of British Guiana. *Car Med J* 2(4): 174-185. [66]   [*COL*]

FROS, J.
28.204   SR   1954 Filariasis in Suriname. *Vox Guy* 1(1), May: 39-47.   [*RIS*]
28.205   SR   1956 Filariasis in South-American Indians in Surinam. *Docum Med Geogr Trop* 8(1), Mar.: 63-69. [13]   [*COL*]

FUNG-KEE-FUNG, C. O.
28.206   BG   1962 Observations on endometrioses in British Guiana and a suggested origin. *Car Med J* 24(1-4): 56-71. [10]   [*COL*]

GAIKHORST, G.
28.207   AR   1960 The presence of *Trypanosoma cruzi* on the island of Aruba and its importance to man. *Trop Geogr Med* 12(1), Mar.: 59-61.   [*COL*]

GARDNER, C. C.
28.208   JM   1956 The principle of central sterile supply and its application in the University College Hospital of the West Indies. *W I Med J* 5(4), Dec.: 231-239.   [*COL*]
28.209   JM   1956 The surgical treatment of chronic duodenal ulcer in Jamaica. *W I Med J* 5(2), June: 90-96.   [*COL*]

GENTLE, G. H. K.
28.210   TR   1956 Yellow fever vaccination programme: Trinidad, B. W. I.—1954/1955. *Car Med J* 18(1-2): 13-18.   [*COL*]
28.211   TR   1957 The significance of asymptomatic serum-positivity in Trinidad and Tobago with special reference to yaws. *W I Med J* 6(4), Dec.: 217-224.   [*COL*]

GIBSON, EUNICE
28.212   BB   1945 The Barbados Nurses Association. *Am J Nurs* 45(1), Jan.: 16-17.
                                                                      [*COL*]

GIGLIOLI, GEORGE

28.213 BG 1923 Ankylostome inspection in Mackenzie, Rio Demerara (Report on carbon tetrachloride in the treatment of hook worm). *Br Gui Med Annual 1923* 23:151-173.   [*ACM*]

28.214 BG 1926 Report on hookworm survey carried out at Mackenzie and Akyma. *Br Gui Med Annual 1925* 24:34-36.   [*ACM*]

28.215 BG 1933 Statistical data on the incidence of various malarial parasites in the river areas of the interior. *Br Gui Med Annual 1932* 25:98-102. [41]   [*ACM*]

28.216 BG 1939 Notes on health conditions on the southern Rupununi savannahs. *In* REPORT OF THE BRITISH GUIANA COMMISSION TO THE PRESIDENT'S ADVISORY COMMITTEE ON POLITICAL REFUGEES. Washington, D.C., [no. 6] (10p.) [66]   [*AGS*]

28.217 BG 1941 Malaria in British Guiana. *Car Med J* 3(1): 49-51.   [*COL*]

28.218 BG 1946 Malaria and agriculture in British Guiana. *Timehri* 4th ser., 1(27), July: 46-52. [46, 66]

28.219 BG 1948 Immediate and long-term economic effects accruing from the control of mosquito-transmitted diseases in British Guiana. *Timehri* 4th ser., 1(28), Dec.: 5-8. [66]

28.220 BG 1951 The influence of geological formation and soil characteristics on the distribution of malaria and its mosquito carrier in British Guiana. *Timehri* 4th ser., 1(30), Nov.: 48-56. [40, 41]

28.221 BG 1956 Medical services on the sugar estates of British Guiana. *Timehri* 4th ser., 1(35), Oct.: 7-31. [10, 45, 46]

28.222 BG 1958 The mosquito and sand-fly nuisance in Georgetown and its suburbs. *Timehri* 4th ser., no. 37, Sept.: 7-11. [41]   [*AMN*]

30.028 BG 1958 An outline of the nutritional situation on the sugar estates of British Guiana in respect to the eradication of malaria: recent developments in the production of green vegetables and fruit by individual units.

28.223 BG 1958 Post-mortem and histo-pathological notes on twenty fatal cases of *Bact. Paratyphosum C* infection in British Guiana. *W I Med J* 7(1), Mar.: 29-38.   [*COL*]

28.224 BG 1962 Trends in the incidence of hookworm and ascaris infestation in British Guiana. *W I Med J* 11(1), Mar.: 30-39.   [*COL*]

GILKES, C. D.; KELLETT, F. R. S. & GILLETTE, H. P. S.

28.225 TR 1956 Yellow fever in Trinidad and the development of resistance in Aedes Aegypti Linn, to D.D.T. formulations. *W I Med J* 5(2), June: 73-89.   [*COL*]

GILLETTE, H. P. S.

28.226 TR 1945 The progress of malaria control measures in Trinidad and Tobago with special references to county St. David. *Car Med J* 4-6: 212-230.   [*COL*]

28.227 TR 1949 A short review of DDT residual house spraying for malaria control in Trinidad 1945-1948. *Car Med J* 11(1): 6-26.   [*COL*]

28.228 BC 1960 Comments on Dr. Thomas's report of the chest service for the Federation of the West Indies. *Car Med J* 22(1-4): 16-19. [38, 66]   [*COL*]

GILMOUR, W. SANTON

28.229 BB [n.d.] TUBERCULOSIS SURVEY AND RECOMMENDATIONS. [Bridgetown?] Barbados. Advocate Co., 19p. [66]   [*RIS*]

28.230   BC   1944 Tuberculosis survey in the British West Indies. *Car Med J* 6(3):
                171-177.   [*COL*]

GODFREY, J. E.

28.231   BG   1904 A few introductory remarks on the regulations passed by the recent
                Quarantine Conference. *Br Gui Med Annual* 13:1-23. [37, 52] [*ACM*]

28.232   BG   1913 Tuberculosis in British Guiana. *Br Gui Med Annual 1912* 19:65-74.
                                                                           [*ACM*]

GOERKE, HEINZ

28.233   JM   1956 The life and scientific works of Dr. John Quier, practitioner of
                physic and surgery, Jamaica: 1738-1822. *W I Med J* 5(1), Mar.: 23-
                27. [5]   [*COL*]

GOLDBERG, J. & SUTHERLAND, E. S.

28.234   JM   1963 Studies on Gonorrhoea. I: Some social and sexual parameters of male
                patients in Kingston, Jamaica. *W I Med J* 12(4), Dec.: 228-246. [37]
                                                                           [*COL*]

GOLDING, J. S. R. & STAFORD, J. L.

28.235   JM   1955 Christmas disease (haemophilia B.). *W I Med J* 4(3), Sept.: 188-192.
                                                                           [*COL*]

GOLDING, J. S. R. & WESTON, PETER M.

28.236   JM   1958 Skeletal tuberculosis in Jamaica. *W I Med J* 7(1): 21-28.   [*COL*]

GOLDING, JOHN

28.237   JM   1961 The problem of treating the disabled child. *W I Med J* 10(3), Sept.:
                172-174.   [*COL*]

GOMES, G. A.

28.238   BG   1934 Some medical worthies of the past in the Colony: notes and reminis-
                cences. *Timehri* 4th ser., no. 25, Dec.: 31-37. [5]   [*RIS*]

GORDON, C. C. & GRANT, L. S.

28.239   JM   1954 A preliminary survey of fungus infections in Jamaica. *W I Med J*
                3(2), June: 95-97.   [*COL*]

GORE, DON

28.240   JM   1962 Hidradenitis suppurativa. *W I Med J* 11(4), Dec.: 249-252.   [*COL*]

GOSDEN, MINNIE

28.241   TR   1938 An account of tuberculosis lesions found in post mortem examina-
                tions on children in Trinidad. *Car Med J* 1(1): 88-95.   [*COL*]

GOURLAY, ROBERT JOHN

28.242   JM   [1961?] The importance of health in a developing community. *In* CUMPER,
                GEORGE, ed. REPORT OF THE CONFERENCE ON SOCIAL DEVELOPMENT IN
                JAMAICA. Kingston, Standing Committee on Social Services, p.101-
                104. [31]   [*RIS*]

GRACE, A. W. & GRACE, FEIGA BERMAN

28.243   BG/   1931 RESEARCHES IN BRITISH GUIANA, 1926-1928 ON THE BACTERIAL COM-
        SK   PLICATIONS OF FILARIASIS AND THE ENDEMIC NEPHRITIS; WITH A
                    CHAPTER ON EPIDEMIC ABSCESS AND CELLULITIS IN ST. KITTS, BRITISH
                    WEST INDIES. London, London School of Hygiene and Tropical
                    Medicine, 75p. (Memoir series no. 3.)   [AGS]

GRANT, LOUIS STRATHMORE

28.244   JM   1956 An analysis and interpretation of some public health laboratory
                    reports, Jamaica, B. W. I. (1940-1954). *W I Med J* 5(2), June: 97-112.
                                                [COL]

28.245   JM   1956 Modern trends in preventive medicine in the Caribbean: a review.
                    W I Med J 5(1), Mar.: 44-58. [66]   [COL]

28.246   JM   1958 A bacteriological analysis of urinary infections (University College
                    Hospital of the West Indies). *W I Med J* 7(4), Dec.: 285-290. [COL]

28.247   JM   1961 A serological survey for Q. fever antibodies in man and animals in
                    Jamaica, West Indies. *W I Med J* 10(4), Dec.: 234-239.   [COL]

GRANT, LOUIS STRATHMORE & ANDERSON, S. E.

28.248   BC   1955 Medical care insurance. Pt. I: The approach in developing a pro-
                    gramme for the Caribbean. Pt. II: The approach in developing a
                    health insurance plan in the Caribbean. *W I Med J* 4(2), June: 109-
                    118; 4(3), Sept.: 169-172. [53]   [COL]

28.249   BC   1955 The problem of medical care in the Caribbean. *W I Med J* 4(2), June:
                    105-108. [33]   [COL]

GRANT, LOUIS STRATHMORE; BECK, J. W.; CHEN, W. N. & BELLE, E. A.

28.250   JM   1963 A survey of parasitic infection in two communities in Jamaica and a
                    drug trial on positive cases. *W I Med J* 12(3), Sept.: 185-193. [COL]

GRANT, LOUIS STRATHMORE & BRAS, G.

28.251   JM   1957 Leptospirosis in Jamaica. *W I Med J* 6(2), June: 129-132.   [COL]

GRANT, LOUIS STRATHMORE & CASELITZ, F.-H.

28.252   JM   1954 Preliminary survey of Salmonella types in Jamaica. *W I Med J* 3(3),
                    Sept.: 201-206.   [COL]

28.253   JM   1954 A preliminary survey of the occurrence of typhoid vi-phage types
                    and biochemical types in the British Caribbean territories with
                    special reference to Jamaica. *W I Med J* 3(3), Sept.: 145-152. [COL]

GRANT, LOUIS STRATHMORE; CHEN, W. N. & URQUHART, A.

28.254   JM   1964 The epidemiology of leptospirosis in Jamaica (preliminary findings).
                    W I Med J 13(2), June: 90-96.   [COL]

GRANT, LOUIS STRATHMORE; GRACEY, L. & CLARK, BETTY M.

28.255   JM   1957 The prevalence of salmonella, shigella and typhoid phage types in
                    Jamaica. *W I Med J* 6(4), Dec.: 233-236.   [COL]

GRANT, LOUIS STRATHMORE & PEAT, A. A.

28.256   JM   1957 The epidemiology of the first poliomyelitis epidemic (Jamaica) 1954.
                    W I Med J 6(4), Dec.: 257-271.   [COL]

GREWAL, N.

28.257   BG   1959 Surgical treatment of peptic ulcer in British Guiana. *W I Med J* 8(4),
                    Dec.: 262-266.   [10]   [*COL*]

GRIFFIN, PHILIP NORMAN

28.258   MS   1960 Tuberculosis in Montserrat. *Car Med J* 22(1-4): 114-115.   [*COL*]

GUILBRIDE, P. D. L.

28.259   GC   1952 Veterinary public health: the importance of animal disease to public
                    health in the Caribbean with special reference to Jamaica. *W I Med J*
                    I. Tuberculosis and brucellosis, 1(2), Apr.: 105-137; II. Anthrax;
                    tetanus leptospirosis (Weil's disease) 1(3), Sept.: 291-316;
              1953 III. Virus infections. Rabies and paralytic rabies. 2(1), Mar.: 11-36;
                    IV. Fungus infections. Sylvatic plague and salmonellosis. 2(2),
                    June: 135-154; V. Parasitic Infections. 2(3), Sept.: 205-223; VI. Milk-
                    borne Diseases. Other Zoonoses. General Summary. Additions. 2(4),
                    Dec.: 259-268.   [65]   [*COL*]

GUPPY, P. LECHMERE

56.027 TR   1922 A naturalist in Trinidad and Tobago.

HABIB, GEORGE G.

28.260   TR   1962 Aseptic meningitis and acute encephalitis in Trinidad, West Indies.
                    W I Med J 11(1), Mar.: 4-11.   [*COL*]
28.261   TR   1962 Neurosyphilis (clinical experience in the diagnosis and treatment).
                    W I Med J 11(2), June: 100-116.   [*COL*]
28.262   TR   1964 Nutritional vitamin B12 deficiency among Hindus. *Trop Geogr Med*
                    16(3), Sept.: 206-215.   [12, 30]   [*COL*]

HALL, J. A. S.

28.263   JM   1961 The role of infection in myelomatosis. *W I Med J* 10(4), Dec.: 240-
                    246.   [*COL*]
28.264   JM   1963 Diphtheritic pseudo-tabes. *W I Med J* 12(1), Mar.: 47-49.   [*COL*]
28.265   JM   1963 Plasma fibrinogen in cerebral catastrophes: a preliminary report.
                    W I Med J 12(2), June: 124-127.   [*COL*]

HAMILTON, GERTRUDE

28.266   JM   1960 The University College Hospital Domiciliary Midwifery Service.
                    Pt. I: A follow-up survey of eighty patients. *W I Med J* 9(1), Mar.:
                    17-21.   [*COL*]

HARKNESS, J. W. P.

28.267   BC   1949 Montego Bay Conference report. E: Report of the Fourth Conference
                    of Heads of British West Indian Medical Departments. *Car Med J*
                    11(2): 77-94.   [66]   [*COL*]
28.268   BC   1950 Some aspects of public health progress in the British Caribbean
                    territories during the period 1947-50. *Car Med J* 12(5): 178-189.
                    [66]   [*COL*]

HARRISON, Sir JOHN B.

28.269   BG   1926 A report on the working of septic tanks at various properties in
                    Georgetown as indicated by the chemical examination of their
                    effluents. *Br Gui Med Annual 1925* 24:1-28.   [*ACM*]

HARRY, G. V.

28.270   JM   1947 Gastro-enterostomy from the economic viewpoint: a plea for its
                        more extensive use, with a review of 104 cases. *Car Med J* 9(1-2):
                        21-31.   [COL]

HARTZ, PHILIP H.

28.271   CU   1950 The incidence of sarcoma, leucaemia and allied diseases in the
                        native population of Curacao, N.W.I. *Docum Ned Indo Morbis Trop*
                        2(2), June: 159-165.   [COL]

HARTZ, PHILIP H. & SAR, ARY van der

28.272   CU   1946 Occurrence of rheumatic carditis in the native population of Cura-
                        cao, Netherlands West Indies. *Archs Path* 41(1), Jan.: 32-36. [COL]

HASSALL, C. H. & REYLE, K.

28.273   JM   1955 The toxicity of the ackee (*Blighia sapida*) and its relationship to
                        the vomiting sickness of Jamaica. *W I Med J* 4(2), June: 83-90. [60]
                                                                                        [COL]

HAYES, J. A. & SUMMERELL, JOAN

28.274   JM   1963 Emphysema in Jamaica: a preliminary report. *W I Med J* 12(1), Mar.:
                        34-38.   [COL]

HENRY, M. U.

28.275   TR   1963 The haemoglobinopathies in Trinidad. *Car Med J* 25(1-4): 26-40.
                                                                          [27]   [COL]

HENRY, M. U. & POON-KING, T.

28.276   TR   1961 Blood groups in diabetes (a preliminary survey in South Trinidad).
                        W I Med J 10(3), Sept.: 156-160.   [10]   [COL]

HILL, A. EDWARD

28.277   TR   1956 Dengue and related fevers in Trinidad and Tobago. *Car Med J*
                        18(3-4): 80-85.   [COL]

HILL, KENNETH R.

28.278   JM   1952 The vomiting sickness of Jamaica: a review. *W I Med J* 1(3), Oct.:
                        243-264.   [COL]
28.279   JM   1953 Non-specific factors in the epidemiology of yaws. *W I Med J* 2(3),
                        Oct.: 155-183.   [COL]

HILL, KENNETH R.; BRAS, G. & CLEARKIN, K. P.

28.280   JM   1955 Acute toxic hypoglycaemia occurring in the vomiting sickness of
                        Jamaica: morbid anatomical aspects. *W I Med J* 4(2), June: 91-104.
                                                                                        [COL]

HILL, KENNETH R.; RHODES, KATERINA; STAFFORD, J. L. & AUB, R.

28.281   JM   1951 Liver disease in Jamaican children (serous hepatosis). *W I Med J*
                        1(1), Sept.: 49-63.   [COL]

HILL, ROLLA B.

28.282   GC   1947 The International Health Division of the Rockefeller Foundation in
                        the Caribbean. *Car Commn Mon Inf B* 1(3), Oct.: 18-19. [66] [COL]

HILL, VINCENT G.

28.283   JM   1962 Sewage stabilization ponds and their application to Jamaica. *Inf B Scient Res Coun* 2(4), Mar.: 78-80.   [*RIS*]

HUNTE, K. R.

44.114   BB   1961 To work together in unity: for the economic betterment of the West Indies Federation.

HURST, E. WESTON & PAWAN, J. L.

28.284   TR   1959 A further account of the Trinidad outbreak of acute rabic myelitis: histology of the experimental disease. *Car Med J* 21(1-4): 25-45.   [*COL*]

28.285   TR   1959 An outbreak of rabies in Trinidad without history of bites, and with the symptoms of acute ascending myelitis. *Car Med J* 21(1-4): 11-24.   [*COL*]

HYRONIMUS, R.

28.286   FC   1958 Maintaining health standards in the French Caribbean Departments. *Caribbean* 11(8), Mar.: 170-173.   [*COL*]

IRVINE, R. A. & TANG, K.

28.287   JM   1957 Datura poisoning; a case report. *W I Med J* 6(2), June: 126-128. [29]   [*COL*]

JACOBSON, F. W.

28.288   JM   1951 Ringworm disease in Jamaican schoolchildren. *W I Med J* 1(1), Sept.: 64-74.   [*COL*]

JACOBSON, F. W.; CLEARKIN, K. P. & ANNAMUNTHODO, H.

28.289   JM   1954 Chromomycosis: report of four more cases in Jamaica. *W I Med J* 3(3), Sept.: 153-158.   [*COL*]

JEAN, SALLY LUCAS

28.290   UV   1933 Virgin Islands: school health program—utilization of existing facilities. *Education* 54(4), Dec.: 205-209.   [30, 32, 66]   [*TCL*]

JELLIFFE, D. B.

31.036   JM   1954 Mongolism in Jamaican children.

JELLIFFE, D. B.; WYNTER-WEDDERBURN, L. E.; YOUNG, V. M.; GRANT, L. S. & CASELITZ, F. H.

28.291   JM   1954 Salmonellosis in Jamaican children. *Docum Med Geogr Trop* 6(4), Dec.: 315-326.   [*COL*]

JENNY WEYERMAN, J. W.

28.292   SR   1923/ Eene waterleiding voor Paramaribo [Water works for Paramaribo].
                   24   *W I G* 5:295-309, 648-652. [66]   [*COL*]
28.293   SR   1927/ Van waar moet het water komen voor eene waterleiding te Para-
                   28   maribo? [From where do we get the water for waterworks in Para-
                        maribo]? *W I G* 9:271-286. [66]   [*COL*]

JOHNSON, J. T. C.

28.294   BB   1926 A REPORT TO THE PUBLIC HEALTH COMMISSIONERS ON THE ORGANIZATION OF THE MEDICAL AND SANITARY SERVICES OF THE COLONY OF BARBADOS, WITH RECOMMENDATIONS. [Bridgetown?] Barbados, Cole's Printery, [66]

JONES, C. R.

28.295   BG   1954 The health of the Amerindian. *Timehri* 4th ser., 1(33), Oct.: 23-27. [13]

28.296   BG   1954 Tuberculosis amongst the Amerindians of British Guiana. *W I Med J* 3(2), June: 77-87. [13]   [*COL*]

JONES, T. R.

28.297   BG   1960 Tuberculosis in British Guiana. *Car Med J* 22(1-4): 105-111. [*COL*]

JONKERS, A. H.; DOWNS, W. G.; AITKEN, T. H. G. & SPENCE, L.

28.298   SR   1964 Arthropod-borne encephalitis viruses in northeastern South America. Part I: A serological survey of northeastern Surinam. *Trop Geogr Med* 16(2): 135-145. [10]   [*COL*]

JUNKER, L.

28.299   SR   1941 Malaria in Suriname [Malaria in Surinam]. *W I G* 23:23-30.   [*COL*]

KAHN, MORTON CHARLES

3.164   SR   1936 Where black man meets red.

KELLETT, F. R. S. & OMARDEEN, T. A.

28.300   TR   1957 Tree hole breeding of *Aedes Aegypti* (Linn) in Arima, Trinidad, B. W. I. *W I Med J* 6(3), Sept.: 179-188.   [*COL*]

KELLY, F. JAMES

42.019   BG   1933 Climate and health in British Guiana.

KELLY, P. J., et al.

28.301   BG   1926 Leprosy in British Guiana (report of a Departmental Medical Conference held in Georgetown, September, 1924–May, 1925). *Br Gui Med Annual 1925* 24:86-105.   [*ACM*]

KENNARD, C. P.

28.302   BG   1902 Fever cases. *Br Gui Med Annual* [12?]: 10-25. [42]   [*ACM*]

28.303   BG   1906 Acute anaemia. *Br Gui Med Annual 1905* 14:49-60.   [*ACM*]

28.304   BG   1906 Typhoid fever. *Br Gui Med Annual 1905* 14:74-83.   [*ACM*]

28.305   BG   1909 Continuous fever—with special reference to the typhoid group. *Br Gui Med Annual 1908* 16:54-87.   [*ACM*]

28.306   BG   1911 Rice fields and malaria. *Timehri* 3d ser., 1(18C), Dec.: 280-284. [62] [*AMN*]

KESLER, C. K.

28.307   BG   1929/ Een Duitsch medicus in Essequebo in de laatste jaren der 18e 30 eeuw [A German medical doctor in Essequibo during the last years of the 18th century]. *W I G* 11:241-250. [5,6]   [*COL*]

28.308   SR   1931/ Een paar opmerkingen [A few remarks]. *W I G* 13:534-536. [66] [*COL*] 32

KING, S. D. & GRANT, L. S.

28.309   JM   1963 A review of salmonella, shigella, pathogenic escherichia coli and
                        typhoid phage types. *W I Med J* 12(2), June: 90-97.   [*COL*]

KOL, H. van

28.310   NC   1919 De Volksgezonheid in onze West-Indische kolonien [Public health in
                        our West-Indian colonies]. *W I G* 1(1): 269-290.   [*COL*]

KROGH, A. L.

28.311   TR   1944 Social medicine in Trinidad. *Car Med J* 6(2): 75-86.   [*COL*]

KUYP, EDWIN van der

28.312   SR   1950 CONTRIBUTION TO THE STUDY OF THE MALARIAL EPIDEMIOLOGY IN
                        SURINAM. Amsterdam, Koninklijke Vereeniging Indisch Instituut,
                        146p. (Mededeling no. 89, Afdeling Tropische hygiëne no. 18.)
                                                                                        [*AGS*]
28.313   SR   1950 Iets over de malaria in Suriname [About malaria in Surinam]. *W I G*
                        31:181-192.   [*COL*]
28.314   SR   1951 Yellow fever in Surinam. *Trop Geogr Med* 10(2), June: 181-194.
                        [10]   [*COL*]
28.315   SR   1954 Malaria in Nickerie (Surinam). *Docum Med Geogr Trop* 7(3), Sept.:
                        259-262.   [*COL*]
28.316   SR   1961 Schistosomiasis in the Surinam district of Surinam. *Trop Geogr Med*
                        13(4), Dec.: 357-373. [10]   [*COL*]
1.026   SR   1962 Literatuuroverzicht betreffende de voeding en de voedingsgewoonten
                        van de Bosland creool in Suriname (Bibliography about nutrition and
                        food habits of the Bush Negroes in Surinam].
28.317   SR   1964 Report on malaria eradication in Surinam. *Trop Geogr Med* 16(2):
                        172-173.   [*COL*]

La FRENAIS, A. C. L.

28.318   BG   1907 Some remarks on nervous diseases of British Guiana. *Br Gui Med
                        Annual 1906* [15:] 85-97.   [*ACM*]

LAMPE, P. H. J.

28.319   SR   1926/ Enkele opmerkingen over den sociaal-hygienischen toestanden en
          27   de geneeskundige verzorging van Suriname [Some remarks about the
                        social-hygienic conditions and medical care in Surinam]. *W I G*
                        8:249-276. [35]   [*COL*]
28.320   SR   1927/ Suriname, sociaal-hygienische beschouwingen [Suriname, social-
          28   hygienic observations]. *W I G* 9:465-487. [15]   [*COL*]
28.321   SR   1927 SURINAME, SOCIAAL-HYGIENISCHE BESCHOUWINGEN [SURINAM, SOCIAL-
                        HYGIENIC OBSERVATIONS]. Amsterdam, de Bussy, 590p. (Kolonial
                        Instituut, Afdeling Tropische hygiene, no. 14.) [7]
28.322   SR   1950 Study on filariasis in Surinam. *Docum Ned Indo Morbis Trop* 2(3),
                        Sept.: 193-208.   [*COL*]
35.027   GC   1951 Housing and health in the Caribbean.

LANJOUW, J. & UITTIEN, H.

41.156   SR   1935/ Surinaamsche geneeskruiden in den tijd van Linnaeus [Surinam's
          36   medicinal herbs during the age of Linnaeus].

LASSALLE, C. F.

28.323   TR   1915   Malaria. *Proc Agric Soc Trin Tob* 15(3), Mar.: 69-73.   [*AMN*]

41.157   TR   1921   A mosquito survey of Trinidad.

LATOUR, M. D.

28.324   CU   1955/ Het Sint Elisabeths Gasthuis op Curacao 1855-1955   [The St. 56   Elisabeths Hospital on Curacao, 1855-1955]. *W I G* 36:46-52.   [5]
                [*COL*]

LAURENCE, STEPHEN M.

28.325   TR   1938   Quarantine as part of the colony's public health service. *Car Med J*
                      1(1): 106-110.   [*COL*]

28.326   TR   1941   The evolution of the Trinidad midwife. *Car Med J* 3(4): 204-208. [5]
                [*COL*]

LEE, C. U.

28.327   BG   1923   A preliminary report on the incidence of filarial infection amongst
                      Chinese, East Indians, Portuguese, blacks and mixed races in
                      Georgetown. *Br Gui Med Annual 1923* 23:32-34.   [10]   [*ACM*]

LEES, RONALD E. M. & DeBRUIN, A. M.

28.328   SL   1963   Review of yaws in St. Lucia five years after an eradication cam-
                      paign. *W I Med J* 12(2), June: 98-102.   [*COL*]

28.329   SL   1963   Skin disease in school children in St. Lucia. *W I Med J* 12(4), Dec.:
                      265-267.   [*COL*]

LEEUWIN, R. S.

18.040   SR   1962   Microfilaraemia in Surinamese living in Amsterdam.

LEGER, MARCEL

28.330   FG   1917   La lèpre à la Guyane Francaise et ses réglementations successives
                      [Leprosy in French Guiana and successive regulations about it].
                      B Soc Path Exot 10(8), Oct.: 733-749.   [5]   [*ACM*]

28.331   FG   1917   Le paludisme à la Guyane Francaise: index endémique des diverses
                      localités[Malaria in French Guiana:Endemic indices for the various
                      localities]. *B Soc Path Exot* 10(8), Oct.: 749-756.   [*ACM*]

28.332   FG   1917   Parasitisme intestinal à la Guyane Francaise dans la population
                      locale et dans l'élément pénal [Intestinal parasitism in French
                      Guiana, among the local population and among the penal element].
                      B Soc Path Exot 10(7), July: 557-560.   [37]   [*ACM*]

28.333   FG   1918   La lèpre à la Guyane Francaise dans l'élément pénal: documents
                      statistiques [Leprosy in French Guiana among the penal element:
                      statistical documentation]. *B Soc Path Exot* 11(9), Nov.: 793-799.
                      [37]   [*ACM*]

28.334   FG   1920   La Guyane Francaise: questions de salubrité et de réglementations
                      sanitaires [French Guiana: matters of sanitation and, public health
                      regulations]. *B Soc Path Exot* 13(3), Mar.: 199-204.   [*ACM*]

28.335   FG   1921   Parasitisme intestinal chez les enfants à la Guyane Francaise: sa
                      relation avec la pureté des eaux de boisson [Intestinal parasitism
                      among the children of French Guiana: its relation to the purity of
                      drinking waters]. *B Soc Path Exot* 14(2), Feb.: 85-89.   [*ACM*]

LESCENE, G. T.
28.336   JM   1955 Brief historical retrospect of the medical profession in Jamaica.
                W I Med J 4(4), Dec.: 217-240. [5]   [*COL*]

LEWIS, L. F. E.
28.337   SL   1943 Chemotherapy of pneumonia in district practice. *Car Med J* 5(2):
                55-61.   [*COL*]

LEWTHWAITE, R.
28.338   BC   1956 Address to the inaugural meeting of the Caribbean Research
                Committee. *W I Med J* 5(2), June: 129-134.   [*COL*]

LIACHOWITZ, CLAIRE, et al.
28.339   SR   1958 Abnormal hemoglobins in the Negroes of Surinam. *Am J Med* 24(1),
                Jan.: 19-24. [14, 27]   [*RIS*]

LOSONCZI, E.
28.340   BH   1956 Report on the BCG campaigns in British Honduras. *W I Med J* 5(4),
                Dec.: 271-283.   [*COL*]

LOWE, A.
28.341   SV   1960 Tuberculosis in St. Vincent. *Car Med J* 22(1-4): 120-122.   [*COL*]

LUYKEN, R.
30.037   SR   1962/ Voedingsfysiologisch onderzoek in Suriname [Research in nutri-
                63   tional physiology in Surinam].

McCULLOCH, W. E.
28.342   GC   1955 YOUR HEALTH IN THE CARIBBEAN. Kingston, Pioneer Press, 149p.
                [30]

McDOWALL, M. F.
28.343   TR   1964 The care of the child in health and disease. *In* REPORT OF CON-
                FERENCE ON CHILD CARE IN TRINIDAD AND TOBAGO [HELD BY]
                TRINIDAD AND TOBAGO ASSOCIATION FOR MENTAL HEALTH, SUB-COMMITTEE
                ON CHILDREN AND YOUTH, Community Education Centre, St. Ann's
                Apr. 18th, 1964. [Port of Spain?] Government Printery, 11-13. [*RIS*]

MacIVER, J. E. & WENT, L. N.
28.344   JM   1958 Further observations on abnormal haemoglobins in Jamaica. *W I Med
                J* 7(2), June: 109-122. [27]   [*COL*]

McKENZIE, H. I.
28.345   JM   1963 A new health programme in Lawrence Tavern. *Car Q* 9(4), Dec.: 3-9.
                                                                                   [*RIS*]

McSHINE, L. A. H.
28.346   TR   1961 Cardiac surgery in Trinidad with an analysis of my first 25 cases.
                Car Med J 23(1-4): 49-54.   [*COL*]

MAPP, LIONEL McHENRY
28.347   TR   1952 Midwives versus middies in a rural community. *Car Med J* 14(3-4):
                139-144.   [*COL*]

MARCANO, RODERICK G.

28.348   TR   1960 Rehabilitation in Trinidad. *Car Med J* 22(1-4): 53-58.   [*COL*]
28.349   TR   1963 Twenty-five years of public health in the city of Port-of-Spain. *Car Med J* 25(1-4): 10-25. [66]   [*COL*]

MARKOWSKI, B.

28.350   BH   1959 Ruptured ectopic pregnancy: analysis of 100 operated cases in British Honduras, Central America. *W I Med J* 8(4), Dec.: 229-234.   [*COL*]

MASON, G. B.

28.351   BC   1922 The British West Indies medical services. *United Emp* new ser., 13(11), Nov.: 692-698. [33, 66]   [*AGS*]

MASSON, GEORGE H.

28.352   TR   1910 Indentured labour and preventable diseases. *Proc Agric Soc Trin Tob* 10(6), June: 209-219. [12, 66]   [*AMN*]
28.353   TR   1913 Tuberculosis. *Proc Agric Soc Trin Tob* 13(10), Oct.: 501-508. [*AMN*]
28.354   TR   1922 The treatment of ankylostomiasis on the high seas by the intensive method of thymol administration. *Proc Agric Soc Trin Tob* 22(7), July: 563-569. [12, 17]   [*AMN*]

MAUZE, J. & PILIN, E.

28.355   GD   1948 Les fièvres typho-exanthématiques en Guadeloupe [Typho-exanthematous fevers in Guadeloupe]. *B Soc Path Exot Fil* 41(7-8), July-Aug.: 442-445.   [*ACM*]

MAUZE, J.; RUGGIERO, D. & PILIN, E.

28.356   GD   1948 Le typhus tropical en Guadeloupe [Tropical typhus in Guadeloupe]. *B Soc Path Exot Fil* 41(7-8), July-Aug.: 563-564   [*ACM*]

MAY, T.

28.357   SR   1926/ De lepra, haar voorkomen, verspreiding, en bestrijding, in 'tbij-
         27   zonder in Suriname [The occurrence of leprosy, its spread, and the fight against it, specifically in Surinam]. *W I G* 8:546-556;
              1927/ 9:17-37.   [*COL*]
              28

MEETEREN, N. van

28.358   CU   1950 Grondwaterpeil en watervoorziening op Curacao voorheen en thans [The level of groundwater and the water supply on Curacao in the past and at present]. *W I G* 31:129-169. [40]   [*COL*]

MELNICK, JOSEPH L.

28.359   BC   1959 Studies on the serological epidemiology of poliomyelitis as an index of immunity in certain Caribbean islands, British Guiana, and Ecuador. *W I Med J* 8(4), Dec.: 275-298.   [*COL*]

MENKMAN, W. R.

7.044   SR   1949 Een buitengewoon Surinaams verslag [A special report on Surinam].

METIVIER, VIVIAN M.

28.360   TR   1939 Notes on ocular tuberculosis in Trinidad. *Car Med J* 1(2): 184-191.
                                                                            [*COL*]
28.361   TR   1940 Intra-ocular foreign bodies in Trinidad and Tobago. *Car Med J* 1(3):
                  110-115.   [*COL*]
28.362   TR   1941 Prevention of blindness in Trinidad and Tobago—ophthalmia neo-
                  natorum: babies' sore eyes. *Car Med J* 3(2): 91-93.   [*ÇOL*]

METSELAAR, D.; WILTERDINK, J. B. & VERLINDE, J. D.

28.363   SR   1964 Virological and serological observations made during the develop-
                  ment and control of an outbreak of poliomyelitis in Surinam. *Trop
                  Geogr Med* 16(2):129-134.   [*COL*]

MIALL, W. E. & RERRIE, J. I.

28.364   JM   1962 The prevalence of pulmonary tuberculosis in a rural population in
                  Jamaica. *W I Med J* 11(3), Sept.: 145-156.   [*COL*]

MILES, R. P. M.

28.365   JM   1956 Rectal lymphogranuloma venereum in Jamaica. *W I Med J* 5(3),
                  Sept.: 183-188.   [*COL*]

MILLER, COLIN G.; GRANT, L. S. & IRVINE, R. A.

28.366   JM   1961 Typhoid fever. *W I Med J* 10(3), Sept.: 189-197.   [*COL*]

MILLER, COLIN G. & SUE, S. LIM

28.367   JM   1964 The clinical estimation of neonatal jaundice in Jamaica. *W I Med J*
                  13(1), Mar.: 59-62.   [*COL*]

MINETT, E. P.

28.368   BG   1912 Mosquito prophylaxis. *Timehri* 3d ser., 2(19A), July: 172-178.   [41]
28.369   BG   1912 Three cases of anthrax infection in man from the Public Hospital,
                  Georgetown. *Br Gui Med Annual 1910* 17:100-106.   [*ACM*]
28.370   BG   1913 The frequency of bacillus violaceous in the water and milk supplies
                  of British Guiana. *Br Gui Med Annual 1911* 18:44-46.   [*ACM*]
28.371   BG   1913 The treatment of leprosy by nastin and benzoyl chloride. *Br Gui
                  Med Annual 1911* 18:24-33. [10]   [*ACM*]
28.372   BG   1914 The progress of village sanitation. *Br Gui Med Annual 1913* 20:90-98.
                                                                            [*ACM*]
28.373   BG   1920 Health problems in British Guiana. *J Bd Agric Br Gui* 13(1), Jan.:
                  20-24.   [*AMN*]
28.374   BG   1921 Agriculture versus malaria. *J Bd Agric Br Gui* 14(4), Oct.: 289-291.
                  [62]   [*AMN*]
7.048   BG   1923 Brief review of the public health statistics of the colony.

MOLENGRAAFF, G. J. H.

28.375   CU   1930/ Korte uiteenzetting van de destijds door den mijnbouwkundigen
          31   dienst opgestelde plannen tot waterverzorging van de haven van
                  Willemstad en van die stad zelve op het eiland Curacao [Short
                  explanation of the former plans of the mining department for the
                  water supply of the port of Willemstad and of that city itself on the
                  island Curacao]. *W I G* 12:25-30. [5]   [*COL*]

MONEKOSSO, G. L.
28.376   JM   1962 A clinical comparison of obscure myelopathies in Jamaica and western Nigeria. *W I Med J* 11(4), Dec.: 240-248.   [*COL*]

MONTAIGNE, E. L. de
28.377   JM   1953 Leprosy in Jamaica. *W I Med J* 2(2), June: 125-133.   [*COL*]

MONTAIGNE, E. L. de & HILL, KENNETH R.
28.378   JM   1958 A study of the blood in leprosy: cytology and clotting. *W I Med J* 7(3), Sept.: 195-199.   [*COL*]

MONTESTRUC, ETIENNE
28.379   MT   1949 La géographie médicale de la Martinique [The medical geography of Martinique]. *Cah O-M* 2(5), Jan.-Mar.: 54-62.   [*AGS*]

MONTGOMERY, R. D.
28.380   JM   1959 Some observations on medical outpatient practice at the University College Hospital of the West Indies. *W I Med J* 8(2), June: 119-123.   [*COL*]
28.381   GC   1964 Observations on the cyanide content and toxicity of tropical pulses. *W I Med J* 13(1), Mar.: 1-11.   [*COL*]

MOODY, L. M., et al.
28.382   JM   1954 Salmonellosis in Jamaica: symposium at the University College of the West Indies, February 10th 1954. *W I Med J* 3(2), June: 108-136.   [*COL*]

MOSER, C. A.
44.158   JM   1957 THE MEASUREMENT OF LEVELS OF LIVING WITH SPECIAL REFERENCE TO JAMAICA.

MUIR, ERNEST
28.383   TR   1941 Leprosy. *Car Med J* 3(1): suppl. (25p.)   [*COL*]
28.384   TR   1942 Leprosy control in Trinidad. *Car Med J* 4(3): 83-91.   [*COL*]
28.385   BC   1944 Leprosy in the British West Indies and British Guiana. *Car Med J* 6(1): 17-31.   [*COL*]

MURRAY, WM. C. G. & ASREGADOO, E. R.
28.386   BG   1959 Some common eye diseases in British Guiana. *W I Med J* 8(4), Dec.: 225-228.   [*COL*]

NEHAUL, B. B. G.
28.387   BG   1943 Report on the physical development and health of a sample of school children in the Island of Leguan, British Guiana, 1941. *Br Gui Med Annual 1943* 26:95-113. [10, 30]   [*ACM*]
28.388   BG   1951 Cancer in British Guiana—pathological studies. *Car Med J* 13(3-4): 90-94.   [*COL*]
28.389   BG   1951 A short history of the British Guiana Branch of the British Medical Association. *Timehri* 4th ser., 1(30), Nov.: 60-63.
28.390   BG   1954 Village administration and sanitation. *Timehri* 4th ser., 1(33), Oct.: 45-47.
28.391   BG   1955 Datura poisoning in British Guiana. *W I Med J* 4(1), Mar.: 57-59. [29]   [*COL*]

28.392   BG   1955 History of the British Guiana Branch of the British Medical Associa-
                tion. *Car Med J* 17(1-2): 31-38. [5]   [*COL*]
28.393   BG   1955 Influence of Indian immigration. *Timehri* 4th ser., 1(34), Sept.:
                35-40. [12, 17]
28.394   BG   1956 Filariasis in British Guiana: clinical manifestations of filariasis
                due to *Wuchereria Bancrofti*. *W I Med J* 5(3), Sept.: 201-206. [*COL*]
28.395   BG   1956 Some public health legislation of British Guiana in the nineteenth
                century. *Timehri* 4th ser., 1(35), Oct.: 76-81. [5]
28.396   BG   1958 Serum protein levels in a group of East Indians in a hospital. *W I
                Med J* 7(3), Sept.: 228-231. [12]   [*COL*]
28.397   BG   1960 Infantile diarrhoea in British Guiana; bacteriological findings.
                W I Med J 9(1), Mar.: 51-54.   [*COL*]

NEHAUL, B. B. G., et al.
28.398   BG   1962 Conference of the Council of Caribbean Branches of the British
                Medical Association. *Car Med J* 24(1-4): 11-39. [66]   [*COL*]

NEWBOLD, C. E. & GILLETTE, H. P. S.
28.399   TR   1949 Self-clearing sea heads for low drainage through surf and conse-
                quent effects on the incidence of malaria. *Car Med J* 11(4): 137-153.
                [40, 66]   [*COL*]

NICHOLSON, C. C.
30.043   BG   1947 Nutritional survey of pupils of elementary schools, Mahaicony
                District, February-March, 1947.
28.400   GC   1957 Observations on the incidence, aetiology and prevention of typhoid
                fever and the diarrhoeal diseases in British Guiana. *Car Med J*
                19(1-2): 24-39.   [*COL*]

NORRIS, J. R. & CUNNINGHAM, K.
28.401   JM   1963 Idiopathic hypoparathyroidism and pseudohypoparathyroidism: case
                reports and review of the literature. *W I Med J* 12(1), Mar.: 13-22.
                                                                                   [*COL*]

OGILVIE, J. A.
28.402   BC   1930 A peep into West Indian medical history. *Am J Publ Heal* 20(11),
                Nov.: 1207-1208. [66]   [*COL*]

OMARDEEN, T. A.; KELLETT, F. R. S. & GILLETTE, H. P. S.
28.403   TR   1957 Precipitin studies on *Anopheles aquasalis* Curry, the coastal
                vector of malaria in Trinidad, B. W. I. *W I Med J* 6(3), Sept.: 205-
                214.   [*COL*]

OSSENFERT, W. F.
28.404   AR/   1950 Health conditions in Aruba and Curacao. *Car Commn Mon Inf B*
          CU   4(3), Oct.: 529-530.   [*COL*]

OTTLEY, J.
28.405   BG   1909 A short account of the diseases which appear to be prevalent in
                the Puruni district, and particularly at the Peters' Mine. *Br Gui
                Med Annual 1908* 16:103-110.   [*ACM*]

OUDSCHANS DENTZ, FRED
28.406   SR   1930/ Dr. Constantin Hering en Christiaan Johannes Hering. *W I G* 12:
                31   147-160. [5, 23]   [*COL*]

OVENS, GERALD H. C.

32.150 JM 1955 A colonial medical school.

OZZARD, A. T.

28.407 BG 1902 The mosquito and malaria. *Br Gui Med Annual* [12?]: 26-39. [41]
[*ACM*]

28.408 BG 1904 Notes on the tropical diseases of British Guiana. *Br Gui Med Annual* 13:43-49.
[*ACM*]

28.409 BG 1911 Some of the preventable diseases of British Guiana and what we can do to prevent them. *Timehri* 3d ser., 1(18B), July: 136-148. [*AMN*]

28.410 BG 1912 Village sanitation in British Guiana. *Br Gui Med Annual 1910* 17: 34-42.
[*ACM*]

28.411 BG 1914 Enteric fever in the Public Hospital, Georgetown. *Br Gui Med Annual 1913* 20:75-86. [10]
[*ACM*]

28.412 BG 1916 Rural sanitation in British Guiana. *Br Gui Med Annual 1915* 21: 17-23.
[*ACM*]

PANHUYS, L. C. van

28.413 SR 1913 Recent discoveries in Dutch Guiana. *In* PROCEEDINGS OF THE INTERNATIONAL CONGRESS OF AMERICANISTS, XVIII. SESSION, London, 1912. London, Harrison, pt. 2, p.376-379. [10]
[*AGS*]

23.117 SR 1936/ De opoffering van een R. K. priester in Suriname [The sacrifice of
37 a Roman Catholic priest in Surinam].

28.414 SR 1943 Malaria het beletsel voor Suriname's bloei [Malaria, the obstacle to Surinam's advancement]. *W I G* 25:303-319.
[*COL*]

PARKER, M. MURRAY & GOSDEN, MINNIE

28.415 TR 1941 An account of cases of congenital urethral obstruction in male infants and children. *Car Med J* 3(2):61-67.
[*COL*]

PAUL, GEORGE P.

28.416 BB 1917 REPORT ON ANKYLOSTOMIASIS INFECTION SURVEY OF BARBADOS FROM SEPTEMBER 4, TO NOVEMBER 16, 1916. New York, Rockefeller Foundation, International Health Board, 54p.

PAWAN, J. L.

28.417 TR 1959 The transmission of paralytic rabies in Trinidad by the vampire bat (*Desmodus rotundus murinus* Wagner, 1840). *Car Med J* 21(1-4): 110-136.
[*COL*]

PAYNE, GEORGE C.

28.418 TR 1919 Ankylostomiasis and the planter. *Proc Agric Soc Trin Tob* 19(4), Apr.: 81-87. [50]
[*AMN*]

PENNEC, Dr.

28.419 GD 1957 The new leprosarium at Pointe Noire, Guadeloupe. *Caribbean* 10(9), Apr.: 222-225.
[*COL*]

PERRONETTE, H.

28.420 MT 1948 Public health services in Martinique have been reorganised. *Car Commn Mon Inf B* 1(12), July: 15-16. [66]
[*COL*]

PETERSON, E.
28.421   ST/   1919 Infectious and contagious diseases on the islands of St. Thomas and
          SJ   St. John, Virgin Islands of the United States, March-September 1918.
                      U S Navl Med B 13(4), Oct.: 682-706.   [33]   [*ACM*]

PICKERING, Sir GEORGE, et al.
28.422   BC   1959 Standing Advisory Committee for Medical Research in the British
                      Caribbean: [report]. *In* PROCEEDINGS OF THE FOURTH SCIENTIFIC
                      MEETING Apr. 5th and 6th, 1959, held at Georgetown, British Guiana.
                      W I Med J 8(2), June: 135-143.   [*COL*]

PINEAU, A.
28.423   GD   1960 Médecine et psychiatrie rurale en Guadeloupe [Rural medicine and
                      psychiatry in Guadeloupe]. *Concours Méd* 82(4), Jan. 23: 413-416;
                      82(5), Jan. 30: 533-544.   [30, 31]   [*COL*]

PINKERTON, J. H. M. & MILLER, C.
28.424   JM   1956 Observations on carcinoma of the cervix. Pt. II: A report on 73
                      consecutive cases of carcinoma of the cervix uteri seen at the
                      University College Hospital of the West Indies. *W I Med J* 5(1),
                      Mar.: 10-18.   [*COL*]

PITT, D. T.
28.425   BC   1943 Comment on medical section of Sir F. Stockdale's report. *Car Med J*
                      5(3):121-127.   [66]   [*COL*]

PLOTZ, HARRY; WOODWARD, DORE E.; PHILIP, CORNELIUS B. &
BENNETT, BYRON L.
28.426   JM   1943 Endemic typhus fever in Jamaica, B. W. I. *Am J Publ Heal* 43(7),
                      July: 812-814.   [*COL*]

POT, A. W.; RAALTE, S. W. G. van & SAR, A. van der
28.427   NA   1942 Bijdrage tot de kennis der bacillaire dysenterie op Curacao [Con-
                      tribution to the knowledge about amoebic dysentery on Curacao].
                      Geneesk Tijdschr Ned-Indie 82(6): 234-250.

PYKE, D. A. & WATTLEY, G. H.
28.428   TR   1962 Diabetes in Trinidad. *W I Med J* 11(1), Mar.: 22-26.   [*COL*]

RAMKEESOON, GEMMA
33.036   TR   1964 Voluntary welfare services for the child.

RAMKISSOON, R.
28.429   TR   1963 Gastroenteritis at the General Hospital, Port-of-Spain. *Car Med J*
                      25(1-4): 69-74.   [*COL*]

RAMSEY, FRANK C.
28.430   BB   1962 Scarlet fever in Barbados. *W I Med J* 11(3), Sept.: 199-202. [*COL*]
28.431   JM   1962 Trichuris dysentery syndrome. *W I Med J* 11(4), Dec.: 235-239. [*COL*]
28.432   JM   1963 Organic phosphorus insecticide poisoning in infants. *W I Med J*
                      12(1), Mar.: 50-52.   [*COL*]

REIJENGA, T. W.; VAS, I. E. & WIERSEMA, J. P.

28.433   SR   1962 On injuries caused by predatory salmon (*Serrasalmo rhombeus L.*) in the rivers of Surinam. *Trop Geogr Med* 14(2), June: 105-110. [41, 56]   [*COL*]

RERRIE, I. J.

28.434   JM   1960 Review of adult tuberculosis in Jamaica. *Car Med J* 22(1-4): 64-69.   [*COL*]

28.435   JM   1960 Review of childhood type tuberculosis in Jamaica. *Car Med J* 22(1-4): 70-74.   [*COL*]

RHODES, KATERINA

30.046   JM   1957 Two types of liver disease in Jamaican children.

ROBERTSON, E. L. S.

28.436   TR   1964 The care of the physically handicapped child. *In* REPORT OF CONFERENCE ON CHILD CARE IN TRINIDAD AND TOBAGO [HELD BY] TRINIDAD AND TOBAGO ASSOCIATION FOR MENTAL HEALTH, SUB-COMMITTEE ON CHILDREN AND YOUTH, Community Education Centre, St. Ann's, Apr. 18th, 1964. [Port of Spain?] Government Printery, p.19-21.   [*RIS*]

ROBERTSON, W. B.

28.437   JM   1961 Some factors influencing the development of atherosclerosis: a survey in Jamaica, West Indies. *W I Med J* 10(4), Dec.: 269-275.   [*COL*]

RODGERS, P. E. B. & CRUICKSHANK, E. K.

28.438   JM   1962 Spinal arachnoiditis. *W I Med J* 11(3), Sept.: 164-170.   [*COL*]

ROMBOUTS, H. E.

28.439   SR   1939 Medische notities over de grens-expedities [Medical notes about the border expeditions]. *Tijdschr Ned Aar Genoot* 2d ser., 56(6), Nov.: 876-882.   [*AGS*]

ROMER, R.

28.440   SR   [1919/ Sanitaire beschouwing in verband met immigraties van werkrachten 20] in Suriname [Essay on sanitation in connection with the immigration of labor forces into Surinam]. *W I G* 1(2): 101-124, 214-240, 380-400, 436-485. [17]   [*COL*]

ROMITI, CESARE

28.441   BG   1933 Rare hernias in aboriginal Indians of British Guiana. *Br Gui Med Annual 1932* 25:6-24. [13]   [*ACM*]

28.442   BG   1933 Three cases of pleuricystic adamantinomata of the jaw, observed in Negroes. *Br Gui Med Annual 1932* 25:51-66. [11]   [*ACM*]

28.443   BG   1936 Filariasis in British Guiana. *Br Gui Med Annual 1936* 26:54-65.   [*ACM*]

28.444   BG   1957 Post-operative malaria. *W I Med J* 6(4), Dec.: 272-284.   [*COL*]

28.445   BG   1957 Statistical report on the incidence of fibroids and malignant tumors of the uterus in British Guiana. *W I Med J* 6(4), Dec.: 243-248. [11, 12]   [*COL*]

ROSE, F. G.
28.446   BG   1919 An investigation into the causes of still-birth and abortion in the
                    city of Georgetown. *Br Gui Med Annual 1919* 22:33-47. [10] [*ACM*]
28.447   BG   1921 The progress of sanitation in British Guiana. *Timehri* 3d ser.,
                    7(24), Aug.: 61-64. [66]   [*AMN*]
28.448   BG   1926 Leprosy statistics and legislation in British Guiana. *Br Gui Med
                    Annual 1925* 24:118-121. [10, 37]   [*ACM*]
28.449   BG   1933 Six years of leprosy work in British Guiana. *Br Gui Med Annual
                    1932* 25:35-44.   [*ACM*]

ROSE, F. G. & CHOW, J. E.
28.450   BG   1923 A resume of the scientific work published by medical men in British
                    Guiana from 1769 to the present day. *Br Gui Med Annual 1923*
                    23:53-62. [1, 5]   [*ACM*]

ROWLAND, E. D.
28.451   BG   1912 Remarks on sixty-four cases of enteric fever treated in the Public
                    Hospital, Georgetown, from December, 1908, to June, 1910. *Br Gui
                    Med Annual 1910* 17:1-24. [10]   [*ACM*]
28.452   BG   1913 Enteric fever in the Public Hospital, Georgetown. *Br Gui Med
                    Annual 1912* 19:8-53. [10]   [*ACM*]
28.453   BG   1914 Pneumonia in British Guiana. *Br Gui Med Annual 1913* 20:38-74.
                    [10]   [*ACM*]

ROYES, KENNETH
28.454   JM   1948 Infantile hepatic cirrhosis in Jamaica. *Car Med J* 10(1-2): 16-48.
                                                                                   [*COL*]

ST. HENLEY, A.
28.455   BG   1960 Cancer of the stomach in British Guiana: a review of cases admitted
                    to the Georgetown Hospital 1956-1959. *W I Med J* 9(4), Dec.: 236-
                    243.   [*COL*]

SALMOND, R. W. A.
28.456   BB   1941 The new X-ray department at the General Hospital, Barbados.
                    Car Med J 3(3): 149-150.   [*COL*]

SAMPATH, MARTIN
28.457   TR   1953 The influence of socio-anthropological factors on the incidence of
                    syphilis in a heterogenous group of pregnant women in Trinidad.
                    Car Med J 15(1-2): 47-49. [9, 11, 12]   [*COL*]

SAMPATH, S. D.
28.458   TR   1960 Accidents among children. *Car Med J* 23(1-4): 64-70.   [*COL*]

SAR, A. van der
28.459   NA   1945 Lepra en las Antillas Neerlandesas [Leprosy in the Netherlands
                    Antilles]. *Revta Policl Cara* 13(76), May-June: 1-17.   [*RIS*]
28.460   CU   1951 Incidence and treatment of kwashiorkor in Curacao. *Docum Ned
                    Indo Morbis Trop* 3(1), Mar.: 25-44. [30]
28.461   CU   1955 The agranulocytoid type of bacillary dysentery. *W I Med J* 4(1),
                    Mar.: 49-54.   [*COL*]

28.462 CU 1962 Sur l'étiologie de l'éosinophilie tropicale à Curacao [On the etiology of tropical eosinophilia in Curacao]. *B Soc Path Exot* 55(4), July-Aug.: 646-655. *[RIS]*

SAR, A. van der & KROON, T. A. J.
28.463 CU 1957 The incidence of scarlet fever in Curacao (with a report on a Dick test survey). *J Trop Ped* 2(4), Mar.: 203-207. *[COL]*

SAR, A. van der & WINKEL, C. A.
28.464 CU 1959 Non-specific spondylitis in Negroid children in Curacao. *Trop Geogr Med* 11(3), Sept.: 263-275. [11] *[COL]*

SAUSSE, ANDRE
28.465 FG 1951 Pathologie comparée des populations primitives noires et indiennes de la Guyane Francaise [Comparative pathology of the primitive Negro and Indian populations of French Guiana]. *B Soc Path Exot* 44(7-8), July: 455-460. [13, 14] *[ACM]*
13.071 FG 1951 POPULATIONS PRIMITIVES DU MARONI (GUYANE FRANCAISE) [PRIMITIVE PEOPLES OF THE MARONI (FRENCH GUIANA)].

SAUTET, JACQUES
28.466 GD/ DS 1951 Les traitements modernes doivent-ils faire abandonner la ségréga-tion des lépreux et amener une refonte totale de la prophylaxie de la lèpre? [Will modern therapy lead to the abandonment of the segre-gation of lepers and to a complete change in the treatment of lepro-sy?] *Presse Med* 63(17), Mar. 5: 339-441. *[ACM]*
28.467 GC 1953 Health of the worker and industrial medicine. *Car Econ Rev* 5(1-2), Dec.: 145-157. [50, 66] *[RIS]*
28.468 FC/ TR 1955 L'épidémie de fièvre jaune de Trinidad menace-t-elle dans l'immédiat nos Départements américains? [Does the yellow fever epidemic in Trinidad represent an immediate threat to our American territories?] *Presse Med* 63(17), Mar. 5: 339-441. *[ACM]*

SAWARD, E. JOYCE
28.469 JM 1960 Rehabilitation in Jamaica. *Car Med J* 22(1-4): 81-83. *[COL]*

SCHAAD, J. D. G.
28.470 SR 1960 Epidemiological observations in Bush Negroes and Amerindians in Surinam. *Trop Geogr Med* 12(1), Mar.: 38-46. [13, 14] *[RIS]*

SCHUITEMAKER, F. S.
28.471 FG 1929/ 30 Bezoek aan St. Louis, het leprozen eiland in de Marowijne; Melaat-schen etablissement van de Fransche strafkolonie St. Laurent, Fransch-Guyana [Visit to St. Louis, the leper island in the Marowijne river; leper asylum of the French penal colony St. Laurent, French Guiana]. *W I G* 11:177-186. *[COL]*

SCOTT, HENRY HAROLD
28.472 JM 1913 Fulminating cerebro-spinal meningitis in Jamaica. *Ann Trop Med Paras* 7(1), Mar. 31: 165-181. *[COL]*
28.473 JM 1915 An investigation into the causes of the prevalence of enteric fever in Kingston, Jamaica; with special reference to the question of un-recognised carriers. *Ann Trop Med Paras* 9(2), June 30:239-284. *[COL]*

28.474   JM   1916 On the "vomiting sickness" of Jamaica. *Ann Trop Med Paras* 10(1),
                      Apr. 29: 1-78.   [*COL*]
28.475   JM   1917 The vomiting sickness of Jamaica. *Trans Roy Soc Trop Med Hyg*
                      10(3), Jan.: 47-66.   [*ACM*]
28.476   JM   1918 An investigation into an acute outbreak of "central neuritis." *Ann
                      Trop Med Paras* 12(2), Oct. 31: 109-196.   [*COL*]

SEAFORTH, COMPTON E.
28.477   GC   1962 Drugs from the West Indies. *Car Q* 7(4), Apr.: 198-202. [57, 66] [*RIS*]

SEHEULT, R.
28.478   TR   1938 A historical review of ankylostomiasis in Trinidad. *Car Med J* 1(1):
                      46-54.   [*COL*]
28.479   TR   1940 A brief historical survey of the surgeons-general of Trinidad. *Car
                      Med J* 2(3): 105-109. [5]   [*COL*]
28.480   TR   1940 A short historical survey of three notable medical men of the past
                      century. *Car Med J* 2(4): 157-163. [5]   [*COL*]
28.481   GC   1944 A brief sketch of the history of yellow fever in the West Indies.
                      Car Med J 6(3): 132-139. [5]   [*COL*]
28.482   TR   1945 Observations on the incidence of cancer in Trinidad. *Car Med J*
                      7(2-3): 72-79.   [*COL*]
28.483   TR   1946 A review of the evolution of health services in Trinidad—1814-
                      1934. *Car Med J* 8(2): 41-47. [5]   [*COL*]

SEIDELIN, HARALD
28.484   JM   1913 On "vomiting sickness" in Jamaica. *Ann Trop Med Paras* 7(3B),
                      Nov. 7: 377-478.   [*COL*]

SENIOR, CLARENCE
35.040 GC   1954 Housing and sanitation in the Caribbean.

SERENO, RENZO
23.142 GC   1948 Obeah: magic and social structure in the Lesser Antilles.

SHAFFER, ALICE
28.485   GC   1952 UNICEF in the Caribbean. *Car Med J* 14(1-2): 51-53. [66]   [*COL*]

SHAW, G. INGRAM
28.486   KNA   1960 Tuberculosis in St. Kitts-Nevis-Anguilla. *Car Med J* 22(1-4): 116-
                      117.   [*COL*]

SIMONS, R. D. G. PH.
28.487   SR   1932/ De maatschappelijke betekenis der Surinaamsche ziekten (van 1919
                33   tot 1931) [The social significance of the Surinam diseases (from
                      1919 to 1931)]. *W I G* 14:429-439.   [*COL*]

SNEATH, P. A. T.
7.076   BG   1941 A study of crude birth/death ratio (vital index) in British Guiana.
28.488   BG   1943 Contemporary facts on the incidence of tuberculosis in British
                      Guiana. *Br Gui Med Annual* 26:32-42. [10]   [*ACM*]

SOPER, FRED L.

28.489   GC   1952 Yellow fever in the Caribbean. *In* WILGUS, A. CURTIS, ed. THE CARIBBEAN; PEOPLES, PROBLEMS AND PROSPECTS [papers delivered at the Second Annual Conference on the Caribbean, held at the University of Florida, Dec. 1951]. Gainesville, University of Florida Press, p.13-17. (Publications of the School of Inter-American Studies, ser. 1, v. 2.)   *[RIS]*

SPENCE, L.; ANDERSON, C. R. & DOWNS, W. G.

28.490   TR   1957 The isolation of influenza virus during an epidemic in Trinidad, British West Indies. *Car Med J* 19(3-4): 174-179.   *[COL]*

SPENCE, L.; DOWNS, W. G. & AITKEN, T. H. G.

28.491   BG   1961 Eastern equine encephalitis virus in the West Indies and British Guiana. *W I Med J* 10(4), Dec.: 227-229.   *[COL]*

SPENCE, L.; DOWNS, W. G. & ANDERSON, C. R.

28.492   TR   1959 The isolation of Coxsackie viruses from human beings in Trinidad, *W I Med J* 8(4), Dec.: 235-237.   *[COL]*

SPENCE, L.; DOWNS, W. G.; BOYD, C. & AITKEN, T. H. G.

28.493   TR   1960 Description of human yellow fever cases seen in Trinidad in 1959. *W I Med J* 9(4), Dec.: 273-277.   *[COL]*

SPENCE, L.; McDOWALL, M. & BARRAT, N.

28.494   TR   1963 Prevalence of enteroviruses in children at the General Hospital, Port-of-Spain, Trinidad, in 1960. *W I Med J* 12(3), Sept.: 183-187.   *[COL]*

STAFFORD, J. L.; HILL, K. R. & DeMONTAIGNE, E. L.

28.495   TK   1955 Microfilariasis in the Turks Islands. *W I Med J* 4(3), Sept.: 183-187.   *[COL]*

STAGE, H. H. & GIGLIOLI, G.

28.496   BG   1947 Observations on mosquito and malaria control in the Caribbean area. Part II: British Guiana. *Mosq News* 7(2), June: 73-76. [66] *[COL]*

STAMM, H.

28.497   JM   1952 Clinical analysis of a general practice in a West Indian town. *W I Med J* 1(3), Oct.: 281-290.   *[COL]*

28.498   JM   1955 Calls after hours. *W I Med J* 4(4), Dec.: 212-216.   *[COL]*

STEVEN, GEORGE H.

28.499   BG   1933 Pathological notes on cases resembling wet beriberi occurring in British Guiana. *Br Gui Med Annual 1932* 25:84-91.   *[ACM]*

28.500   BG   1936 Post-mortem notes on the spleen in various races of British Guiana: a comparison with 1893. *Br Gui Med Annual 1936* 26:137-143. [10] *[ACM]*

STEWART, D. B.

28.501   JM   1960 The University College Hospital domiciliary midwifery services. Part II: A comment on domiciliary midwifery services. *W I Med J* 9(1), Mar.: 22-24.   *[COL]*

32.195   JM   1962 A developing medical school in the tropics.

STIRLING, G. A.
28.502   JM   1960 The adrenals in hypertensive Jamaicans. *Trop Geogr Med* 12(2),
                          June: 114-118.   [*COL*]

STIRLING, G. A. & CASTOR, URSULA S.
28.503   JM   1962 Tubal pregnancy in Jamaicans. *W I Med J* 11(1), Mar.: 45-47. [*COL*]

STOCKDALE, Sir FRANK A.
28.504   BC   1943 Development and welfare in the West Indies 1940-1942. *Car Med J*
                          5(1): 8-30. [66]   [*COL*]

STOEHL, G.
28.505   NC   1937 Over de veelvuldigheid van kanker [On the frequency of cancer].
                          Geneesk Tijdschr Ned-Indie 77:2292-2304.

STOLNITZ, GEORGE J.
28.506   GC   1958 The revolution in death control in nonindustrial countries. *Ann Am*
                          Acad Polit Social Sci 316, Mar.: 94-101. [7, 66]   [*RIS*]

STOLZE, E.
28.507   SR   1958 Histological report on 152 post-mortem liver punctures in Surinam.
                          Trop Geogr Med 10(3), Sept.: 272-276.   [*COL*]

STOUT, ROBERT J.
28.508   JM   1963 Some clinical evidence for a quantitative relationship between dose
                          of relaxant and plasma protein. *W I Med J* 12(4), Dec.: 256-264. [*COL*]

SWELLENGREBEL, N. H.
28.509   SR   1940 The efficient parasite. *Science* new ser., 92(2395), Nov. 22:465-469.
                          [11]   [*AGS*]
17.028   SR   1940 Over de vraag of een proefneming tot vestiging van politieke uit-
                          gewekenen in Suriname hygienisch te verantwoorden is [On the
                          question whether an attempt to settle political refugees in Surinam
                          is advisable from a hygienic viewpoint].
28.510   NC   1952 De Pan Amerikaanse Sanitare Organisatie (P.A.S.O.) in verband
                          met Suriname en de Nederlandse Antillen [The Pan-American Sani-
                          tary Organisation (P.A.S.O.) in relation to Surinam and the Dutch
                          Antilles]. *W I G* 33:1-11.   [*COL*]

SWELLENGREBEL, N. H. & KUYP, E. van der
28.511   SR   1940 HEALTH OF WHITE SETTLERS IN SURINAM. Amsterdam, 118p. (Colonial
                          Institute at Amsterdam, Special publication no. 53, Dept. of Tropical
                          Hygiene no. 16.) [15, 23]   [*AMN*]

SYMONDS, BRUCE
28.512   TR   1956 Fatty liver disease in South Trinidad. *Car Med J* 18(1-2): 9-12. [30]
                                                                                          [*COL*]

SYMONDS, BRUCE & MOHAMMED, I.
30.053   TR   1956 "Sugar babies" in South Trinidad.

TEIXEIRA, J.

28.513   BG   1904 The recent epidemic of small-pox. *Br Gui Med Annual* 13:24-31. [10]
                                                                                    [*ACM*]

28.514   BG   1906 Report on smallpox treated at the Isolation Hospital at the "Best".
                        Br Gui Med Annual 1905 14:39-48.   [10]   [*ACM*]

THEZE, J.

28.515   FG   1916 Pathologie de la Guyane Francaise [Pathology of French Guiana].
                        I. Paludisme. Fièvres continues et eaux de Cayenne. Dysenterie.
                        Helminthiase intestinale [Malaria. Continuous fevers and the waters
                        of Cayenne. Dysentery. Intestinal helminthiasis]. II. Lèpre,
                        filariose, etc. [Leprosy, filariasis, etc.) *B Soc Path Exot* 9(6),
                        June: 376-402; 9(7), July: 449-469.   [10]   [*ACM*]

THOMAS, J. H.

28.516   BC   1960 Respiratory tuberculosis in the Caribbean. *Car Med J* 22(1-4): 20-23.
                        [10]   [*COL*]

THOMSON, DAVID

28.517   BG/   1913 Sanitation on the Panama Canal Zone, Trinidad and British Guiana.
          TR   *Ann Trop Med Paras* 7(1), Mar. 31: 125-152.   [*COL*]

TIGGELMAN-van KRUGTEN, V. A. H. & COLLIER, W. A.

28.518   SR   1955 The search for antibodies to the parapoliomyelitis group in human
                        and animal sera in Surinam. *Docum Med Geogr Trop* 7(3), Sept.:
                        270-272.   [*COL*]

TIROLIEN, CAMILLE

55.038   GD   1961 Thermalisme [Mineral springs].

TJON SIE FAT, HOWARD CYRIL

28.519   NW   1954 ONDERZOEK NAAR DE SOCIAAL-HYGIENISCHE TOESTAND OP DE BOVEN-
                        WINDSE EILANDEN DER NEDERLANSE ANTILLEN [INVESTIGATION OF
                        SOCIAL-HYGIENIC CONDITIONS ON THE WINDWARD ISLANDS OF THE
                        NETHERLANDS ANTILLES]. Amsterdam, Uitgeverij Argus, 176p.   [7]
                                                                                     [*RIS*]

TULLOCH, J. A.

28.520   JM   1958 Heart disease in Jamaica. *W I Med J* 7(3), Sept.: 169-181.   [*COL*]
28.521   JM   1958 Myocardial infarction in Jamaica: the clinical features. *W I Med J*
                        7(4), Dec.: 244-250.   [*COL*]
30.055   JM   1958 Some aspects of myocardial infarction in Jamaica.

TULLOCH, J. A. & DOUGLAS, C. P.

28.522   JM   1963 A study of pregnancy in relation to the prediabetic state. *W I Med J*
                        12(2), June: 133-136.   [*COL*]

TULLOCH, J. A. & GAY K.

28.523   JM   1956 An analysis of the admissions to a male and female medical ward of
                        the University College Hospital of the West Indies during 1955.
                        W I Med J 5(3), Sept.: 207-211.   [*COL*]

TULLOCH, J. A.; GAY, K. & IRVINE, R. A.

28.524   JM   1956 Some aspects of diabetes in Jamaica. *W I Med J* 5(4), Dec.: 256-264.
                                                                                          [*COL*]

TULLOCH, J. A. & JOHNSON, H. M.

28.525   JM   1958 A pilot survey of the incidence of diabetes in Jamaica. *W I Med J*
                      7(2), June: 134-136.   [*COL*]

TULLOCH, J. A. & LUCK, D. E.

28.526   JM   1959 The problem of diabetic control in the Caribbean. *W I Med J* 8(3),
                      Sept.: 179-188.   [*COL*]

TURK, D. C. & WYNTER, H. H.

28.527   JM   1961 Meningitis in Jamaica, 1958-1960. *W I Med J* 10(2), June: 118-131.
                                                                                          [*COL*]

UTTLEY, K. H.

28.528   AT   1958 The mortality from erysipelas over the last hundred years in Antigua,
                      the West Indies. *W I Med J* 7(4), Dec.: 276-280. [5]   [*COL*]

28.529   AT   1959 The epidemiology of tetanus in the Negro race over the last hundred
                      years in Antigua, the West Indies. *W I Med J* 8(1), Mar.: 41-49.
                      [5, 11]   [*COL*]

28.530   AT   1959 The mortality and epidemiology of filariasis over the last hundred
                      years in Antigua, British West Indies. *W I Med J* 8(4), Dec.: 238-
                      248. [5]   [*COL*]

28.531   AT   1960 The epidemiology and mortality of whooping cough in the Negro
                      over the last hundred years in Antigua, British West Indies. *W I
                      Med J* 9(2), June: 77-95. [5, 11]   [*COL*]

28.532   AT   1960 The mortality and epidemiology of diptheria since 1857 in the
                      Negro population of Antigua, British West Indies. *W I Med J* 9(3),
                      Sept.: 156-163. [5, 11]   [*COL*]

28.533   AT   1960 The mortality and epidemiology of typhoid fever in the coloured
                      inhabitants of Antigua, West Indies, over the last hundred years.
                      W I Med J 9(2), June: 114-123. [5,11]   [*COL*]

28.534   AT   1960 The mortality of yellow fever in Antigua, West Indies, since 1857.
                      W I Med J 9(3), Sept.: 184-188. [5]   [*COL*]

28.535   AT   1960 Smallpox mortality in the Negro population of Antigua, West Indies;
                      a historical note. *W I Med J* 9(3), Sept.: 169-171. [5,11]   [*COL*]

28.536   AT   1961 Epidemiology and mortality of malaria in Antigua, BWI, 1857-1956.
                      Am J Publ Heal 51(4), Apr.: 577-585. [5]   [*COL*]

28.537   AT   1961 The epidemiology of puerperal fever and maternal mortality in
                      Antigua, West Indies, over the last hundred years, including a
                      comparison with recent trends in neighbouring territories. *W I Med J*
                      10(1), Mar.: 63-71. [5]   [*COL*]

28.538   AT   1961 Tuberculosis mortality in the Negro population of Antigua, British
                      West Indies, over the last hundred years. *Tubercle* 42(4), Dec.: 444-
                      456. [11]   [*COL*]

VERTEUIL, ERIC de

28.539   TR   1934 Agriculture and health. *Proc Agric Soc Trin Tob* 34(8), Aug.: 307-
                      314. [46]   [*AMN*]

28.540   TR   1941 Trinidad malaria in prospect and retrospect. *Car Med J* 3(3). 139-
                      147. [5]   [*COL*]

28.541 TR 1943 The urgent need for a medical and health policy for Trinidad. *Car Med J* 5(3): 107-119. [66] [COL]

VERTEUIL, ERIC de & URICH, F. W.
28.542 TR 1959 The study and control of paralytic rabies transmitted by bats in Trinidad, British West Indies. *Car Med J* 21(1-4): 85-109. [COL]

VINKE, B. & JANSEN, W.
28.543 CU 1960 Comparison of an intradermal test for *Schistosoma Mansoni* with the results of faecal examinations in Curacao. *Trop Geogr Med* 12(2), Sept.: 217-221. [COL]

VINKE, B.; SAR, A. van der; FABER, J. G. & VRIES, J. A. de
30.059 CU 1960 Penicillin in nutritional megaloblastic anaemia in Curacao.
30.060 CU 1960 Serum vitamin B12 levels and response to the treatment of megaloblastic anaemia in Curacao.

VYSE, H. G.
28.544 JM 1952 Comprehensive medical services in Jamaica. *Car Med J* 14(3-4): 119-121. [COL]
28.545 JM 1953 The incidence of diphtheria in Jamaica. *W I Med J* 2(1), Mar.: 67-79. [COL]

WAGENAAR HUMMELINCK, P.
41.254 SR 1942 Studies over de patatta-luis [Studies of the patatta louse].
28.546 CU 1947 Medisch werk op Curacao in 1939-1946 [Medical work on Curacao]. *W I G* 28:329-334. [COL]

WALLBRIDGE, J. S.
7.083 BG 1907 Remarks on the Mortality Commission Report.

WARD, E. E.
28.547 JM 1963 Serum gamma globulins and infection in Jamaica. *W I Med J* 12(1), Mar.: 59-62. [COL]

WARNER, HENRY
28.548 TR 1919 Water supply and sanitary reform. *Proc Agric Soc Trin Tob* 19(5), May: 110-122. [46, 47] [AMN]

WASHBURN, B. E.
32.207 JM 1929 JAMAICA HEALTH STORIES AND PLAYS.
28.549 JM 1933 An epidemic of malaria at Falmouth, Jamaica, British West Indies. *Am J Hyg* 17(3), May: 656-665. [COL]
28.550 BG/ 1960 AS I RECALL. New York, Rockefeller Foundation, 183p. [11, 12]
       TR   [COL]

WATERLOW, J. C.
28.551 JM 1961 The Tropical Metabolism Research Unit. *Inf B Scient Res Coun* 2(1), June: 5-7. [RIS]

WATERMAN, I. D.
28.552 TR 1958 A century of service. *Car Med J* 20(1-4): 36-41. [5] [COL]

WATERMAN, JAMES A.

28.553   TR   1938 Some notes on maternal mortality in Trinidad with a note on the
                        maternity department and the training of midwives at the Colonial
                        Hospital, Port-of-Spain. *Car Med J* 1(1): 74-81.   [*COL*]
28.554   TR   1940 A statistical analysis of eclampsia cases treated at the Colonial
                        Hospital, Port-of-Spain, from 1924 to 1938. *Car Med J* 2(3): 137-146.
                                                                                      [*COL*]
28.555   TR   1941 Haemophilia in the Afro-West Indian. *Car Med J* 3(3): 167-171.   [11]
                                                                                      [*COL*]
28.556   BC   1942 A suggested maternity scheme for the West Indies. *Car Med J* 4(4):
                        140-147. [66]   [*COL*]
28.557   TR   1943 Acute rheumatic fever and rheumatic carditis in the tropics with
                        special reference to Trinidad. *Car Med J* 5(4): 204-232.   [*COL*]
28.558   TR   1943 The disorders of cardiac rhythm confirmed by electrocardiography
                        as seen in Trinidad. *Car Med J* 5(4): 233-247.   [*COL*]
28.559   TR   1944 A national health service with special reference to Trinidad. *Car
                        Med J* 6(4): 304-309. [66]   [*COL*]
28.560   TR   1944 Notes on tuberculosis in Trinidad. *Car Med J* 6(3): 204-215. [*COL*]
28.561   TR   1948 Peroneal palsy complicating labour and the puerperium. *Car Med J*
                        10(3-4): 88-108.   [30]   [*COL*]
28.562   TR   1957 Some notes on scorpion poisoning in Trinidad. *Car Med J* 19(1-2):
                        113-128.   [*COL*]
28.563   BC   1958 The impact of federation on medicine in the West Indies. *Car Med J*
                        20(1-4): 42-48. [38]   [*COL*]
28.564   TR   1959 The history of the outbreak of paralytic rabies in Trinidad trans-
                        mitted by bats to human beings and the lower animals from 1925.
                        Car Med J 21(1-4): 1-6.   [*COL*]

WATERMAN, JAMES A., et al.

28.565   TR   1963 Voluntary pre-payment health insurance scheme. *Car Med J* 25(1-4):
                        41-69. [53]   [*COL*]

WATERMAN, N.

28.566   CU   1919/ De geneeskundige organisatie in de kolonie Curacao [The medical
                   20   organization in the colony of Curacao]. *W I G* 1(2): 35-47.   [*COL*]

WATLER, D. C.

28.567   JM   1958 Leukaemia in Jamaica: a statistical survey of seventy cases.
                        W I Med J 7(4), Dec.: 267-275.   [*COL*]
28.568   JM   1960 Congenital heart disease in Jamaica (observation on post mortem
                        incidence, with a report of an unusual case of *cor triloculare
                        biatriatum*). *W I Med J* 9(3), Sept.: 194-200.   [*COL*]

WATLER, D. C.; BRAS, G. & McDONALD, H. G.

28.569   JM   1959 The incidence of malignant neoplasms in Jamaica. *W I Med J* 8(4),
                        Dec.: 249-261.   [*COL*]

WATLER, D. C.; BURROWES, A. S. & BRAS, G.

28.570   JM   1960 Analysis of 136 consecutive cases of malignant neoplasm of the
                        stomach. *W I Med J* 9(3), Sept.: 164-168.   [*COL*]

WATLER, D. C.; McNEIL-SMITH, E. & WYNTER, L.

28.571   JM   1958 Haemophilia in Jamaica. *W I Med J* 7(1), Mar.: 1-16.   [*COL*]

WATTLEY, GEORGE H.

28.572   TR   1959 Myocardial infarction in south Trinidad. *W I Med J* 8(1), Mar.: 33-40.
[10]   [*COL*]

28.573   TR   1959 The pattern of skin disease in south Trinidad. *W I Med J* 8(3), Sept.:
199-202.   [*COL*]

28.574   TR   1960 Heart disease in Trinidad. *W I Med J* 9(3), Sept.: 189-193.   [*COL*]

WATTY, E. I.

28.575   DM   1960 Tuberculosis in Dominica. *Car Med J* 22(1-4): 112-113.   [*COL*]

WAYS, P.; BRYANT, J. & GUICHERIT, I. D.

28.576   SR   1956 Histoplasmin sensitivity among the Bush Negroes of Surinam.
Docum Med Geogr Trop 8(4), Dec.: 383-391.   [14]   [*COL*]

WEINSTEIN, B.

28.577   BG   1962 Diabetes: a regional survey in British Guiana (preliminary report).
W I Med J 11(2), June: 88-93.   [11, 12]   [*COL*]

WELLER, THOMAS H.

28.578   GC   1961 Research in the health services in the Caribbean. *W I Med J* 10(2),
June: 73-75.   [66]   [*COL*]

WELLIN, EDWARD, et al.

28.579   GC   1960 Sociocultural factors in public health. *In* RUBIN, VERA, ed. CULTURE,
SOCIETY AND HEALTH. New York, New York Academy of Sciences,
p.1044-1060. (Annals of the New York Academy of Sciences, v. 84,
art. 17.)   [*RIS*]

WELLS, A. V.

28.580   SL   1959 Antibodies to poliomyelitis viruses in St. Lucia. *W I Med J* 8(3),
Sept.: 161-170.   [*COL*]

28.581   SL   1961 Malaria eradication in St. Lucia, West Indies. *W I Med J* 10(2),
June: 103-111.   [66]   [*COL*]

WENGER, O. C.

28.582   TR   1944 The role of the private practitioner in a modern venereal disease
control programme. *Car Med J* 6(3): 87-94.   [*COL*]

28.583   TR   1946 CARIBBEAN MEDICAL CENTER. Washington, Caribbean Commission,
74p.   [66]   [*COL*]

WENT, L. N. & MacIVER, J. E.

28.584   JM   1956 Investigation of abnormal haemoglobins in Jamaica: a preliminary
survey. *W I Med J* 5(4), Dec.: 247-255.   [27]   [*COL*]

WESTON, P. M.

28.585   JM   1961 Carcinoma of the urinary bladder in Jamaica. *W I Med J* 10(2),
June: 112-117.   [*COL*]

WHITE, SENIOR

28.586   TR   1947 Malaria work in Trinidad. *Car Commn Mon Inf B* 1(4), Nov.: 14-16.
[66]   [*COL*]

WHITELOCKE, H. I., et al.

28.587   JM   1954 Peptic ulcer in Jamaica: symposium at the University College of the
West Indies, March 3rd, 1954. *W I Med J* 3(3), Sept.: 166-184.   [*COL*]

WIERSEMA, J. P. & BARROW, R. S.

28.588   SR   1961 Cancer, especially of the cervix uteri, in Surinam. *Trop Geogr Med* 13(4), Dec.: 347-350. [10]

WILDERVANCK, A.; COLLIER, W. A. & WINCKEL, W. E. F.

28.589   SR   1953 Two cases of histoplasmosis on farms near Paramaribo (Surinam): investigations into the epidemiology of the disease. *Docum Med Geogr Trop* 5(2), June: 108-115.   [*COL*]

WILLIAMS, CICELY D.

28.590   JM   1952 Vomiting in children. *W I Med J* 1(3), Oct.: 265-273.   [*COL*]

WILLIAMS, F. M. W.; HAMILTON, H. F.; SINGH, BALWANT & HERLINGER, R.

28.591   BG   1960 Tropical eosinophilia in British Guiana; a preliminary report. *W I Med J* 9(3), Sept.: 149-155.   [*COL*]

WILSON, JOHN F.

28.592   BC   1954 Blindness in the British Caribbean territories. *W I Comm Circ* 69(1281), Sept.: 245-246.   [*NYP*]

WILTERDINK, J. B.; METSELAAR, D.; KUYP, E. van der & VERLINDE, J. D.

28.593   SR   1964 Poliomyelitis in Surinam. *Trop Geogr Med* 16(2), June: 120-128. [10]
                                                                             [*COL*]

WINCKEL, W. E. F. & AALSTEIN, M.

28.594   SR   1953 Contribution to the geographical pathology of Surinam: first case of kala-azar in Surinam. *Docum Med Geogr. Trop* 5(4), Dec.: 339-342.
                                                                             [*COL*]

WISE, K. S.

28.595   BG   1907 Acute anaemia. *Br Gui Med Annual 1906* 15:103-117.   [*ACM*]
65.084   BG   1907 Observations on the milk supply of Georgetown.
28.596   BG   1909 *Filaria bancroftii. Br Gui Med Annual 1908* 16:35-50. [10] [*ACM*]
7.085   BG   1912/ The public health, statistics, and medical institutions of the
               13 Colony.
28.597   BG   1912 The nastin treatment of leprosy in British Guiana. *Br Gui Med Annual 1910* 17:45-99. [10]   [*ACM*]
41.267   BG   1914 A list of the commoner invertebrate animals of medical interest identified in British Guiana.
28.598   BG   1914 The pathological effects of *Filaria bancroftii* with reference to ·septic complications. *Br Gui Med Annual 1913* 20:1-27. [10] [*ACM*]
28.599   BG   1919 Malaria, the problem of British Guiana. *Br Gui Med Annual 1919* 22:1-28.   [*ACM*]

WISE, K. S. & MINETT, E. P.

28.600   BG   1912 Drinking water supplies: a chemical and bacteriological study of the drinking water supplies on estates from a hygienic point of view. *Timehri* 3d ser., 2(19B), Dec.: 247-254. [41, 45]   [*AMN*]

28.601 BG 1913 Review of the milk question in British Guiana. *Br Gui Med Annual 1911* 18:47-59. [65] [*ACM*]

WISHART, W. de W.
7.086 BG 1902 The influence of rainfall on death-rate in the tropics.
28.602 BG 1923 Infant welfare work in Georgetown: past, present and future. *Br Gui Med Annual 1923* 28:35-42. [*ACM*]
28.603 BG 1923 Some aspects of the sanitary and public health problems of Georgetown. *Br Gui Med Annual 1923* 23:43-52. [*ACM*]
28.604 BG 1926 Recommendations for mosquito prophylaxis in Georgetown. *Br Gui Med Annual 1925* 24:29-33. [*ACM*]
7.087 BG 1943 The Georgetown vital index as related to rainfall.

WOLFF, J. W.; COLLIER, W. A.; BOOL, P. H. & BOHLANDER, H.
28.605 SR 1958 Investigations on the occurrence of leptospirosis in Surinam. *Trop Geogr Med* 10(4), Dec.: 341-346. [*COL*]

WOLFF, J. W.; COLLIER, W. A.; ROEVER-BONNET, H. de & HOEKSTRA, J.
28.606 SR 1958 Yellow fever immunity in rural population groups of Surinam (with a note on other serological investigations). *Trop Geogr Med* 10(4), Dec.: 325-331. [10] [*COL*]

WRIGHT, H. B. & TAYLOR, BELLE
28.607 TR 1958 The incidence of diabetes in a sample of the adult population in south Trinidad. *W I Med J* 7(2), June: 123-133. [10] [*COL*]

WYLIE, A.
28.608 BG 1906 On cataract disease in British Guiana. *Br Gui Med Annual 1905* 14:65-69. [*ACM*]

ZAAL, G. PH.
28.609 SR 1937 Het drinkwatervraagstuk in Suriname en het stadium zijner oplossing [The problem of drinking water in Surinam and the stage of its solution]. *W I G* 19:65-79. [66] [*COL*]

Chapter 29

ETHNOHEALTH AND ETHNOMEDICINE

ABRAHAM, E. A. V.

29.001   BG   1912 Materia medica Guian. Britt. *Timehri* 3d ser. 2(19a), July: 179-196. [13,41]   [*AMN*]

ASPREY, G. F. & THORNTON, PHYLLIS

29.002   JM   1953 Medicinal plants of Jamaica. Pts. 1-4. *W I Med J* 2(4), Dec.: 233-252; 1954 3(1), Mar.: 17-41; 1955 4(2), June: 69-82; 4(3), Sept.: 145-168. [41]   [*COL*]

BAYLEY, IRIS

29.003   BB   1949 The bush-teas of Barbados. *J Barb Mus Hist Soc* 16(3), May: 103-109. [41]

BECKWITH, MARTHA WARREN

29.004   JM   1927 NOTES ON JAMAICAN ETHNOBOTANY. Poughkeepsie, N.Y., Vassar College, 47p. (Field-work in folk-lore; Publications of the Folklore Foundation no. 8. [30, 41]   [*COL*]

BENJAMINS, H. D.

29.005   SR   1929/ "Sneki-koti", inenting tegen de beet van vergiftige slangen ["Snake-
           30 bite cure", inoculation against the biting of poisonous snakes]. *W I G* 11:497-512;
           1931/ 13:3-23, 317-324.   [*COL*]
           32

29.006   SR   1929/ Treef en lepra in Suriname [Treyf and leprosy in Surinam]. *W I G*
           30 11:187-218. [5,14]   [*COL*]

BUCHLER, IRA R.

29.007   CM   1964 Caymanian folk medicine: a problem in applied anthropology. *Hum Org* 23(1), Spring: 48-49. [67]   [*RIS*]

BUTLER, C. S. & HAKANSSON, E. G.

28.077   UV   1917 Some first impressions of the Virgin Islands, medical, surgical and epidemiological.

BUTT, AUDREY J.
29.008   BG   1956 Ritual blowing: taling—a causation and cure of illness among the
                Akawaio. *Man* 56(48), Apr.: 49-55.   [13]   [*COL*]

COLLIER, H. C.
29.009   BC   1941 Nature, her own apothecary. *Can-W l Mag* 30(1), Jan.: 8-10.   [41]
                                                                                  [*NYP*]
29.010   BG   1942 Copper skin's secret. *Can-W l Mag* 31(4), Apr.: 19-22. [13]   [*NYP*]
29.011   BG   1946 Jungle dope. *Can-W l Mag* 36(1), Feb.: 21-24.   [13]   [*NYP*]
29.012   BG   1948 Curare—the story of a reformation. *Can-W l Mag* 38(3), Mar.: 7-10.
                                                                                  [*NYP*]

FENG, P. C.
29.013   BG   1956 A preliminary survey of the medicinal plants of British Guiana. *W l
                Med J* 5(4), Dec.: 265-270.   [41]   [*COL*]

GOEJE, C. H. de
20.007   GC   1943 Philosophy, initiation and myths of the Indians of Guiana and adja-
                cent countries.

IRVINE, R. A. & TANG, K.
28.287   JM   1957 Datura poisoning; a case report.

LAMPE, P. H. J.
29.014   SR   1928/ "Het Surinaamsche treefgeloof", een volksgeloof betreffende het
                29 ontstaan van de melaatschheid ["The treyf belief in Surinam" a
                    superstition about the cause of leprosy]. *W l G* 10:545-568.   [14]
                                                                                  [*COL*]

LICHTVELD, LOU
29.015   SR   1930/ Een Afrikaansch bijgeloof: snetji-koti [An African superstition:
                31 "snakebite cure"]. *W l G* 12: 49-52.   [14, 19]   [*COL*]
29.016   SR   1932/ Een oude getuigenis over de genezing van slangenbeet en aardeten
                    [An old testimony about the cure of snakebite and the eating of
                    earth]. *W l G* 14:1-7.   [14]   [*COL*]

MISCHEL, FRANCES
29.017   TR/   1959 Faith healing and medical practice in the southern Caribbean. *Sw J
          GR   Anthrop* 15(4), Winter: 407-417.   [11]   [*COL*]

NEHAUL, B. B. G.
28.391   BG   1955 Datura poisoning in British Guiana.

PANHUYS, L. C. van
29.018   SR   1924 About the "trafe" superstition in the colony of Surinam. *Janus*
                28: 357-368.   [*NYP*]
29.019   SR   1924 The trafe-superstition in Surinam. *In* PROCEEDINGS OF THE TWENTY-
                FIRST INTERNATIONAL CONGRESS OF AMERICANISTS, [1st SESS.,] The
                Hague, Aug. 12-16, 1924. The Hague, p.182-185.   [14]   [*AGS*]

29.020   SR   1935/ Opvattingen van Zuid-Amerikaansche Indianen nopens ziekten en
          36   geneeswijzen [South American Indian ideas about illness and cures].
                W I G 17:51-57. [13]   [*COL*]

29.021   SR   1943 "Sneki-koti," inenting tegen den bijt van vergiftige slangen ["Sneki-
                koti," immunization against the bite of poisonous snakes]. *W I G*
                25:122-128. [14]   [*COL*]

REVERT, EUGENE

24.067   MT   1951 DE QUELQUES ASPECTS DU FOLK-LORE MARTINIQUAIS: LA MAGIE ANTIL-
                LAISE [ON SOME ASPECTS OF MARTINIQUE FOLKLORE: ANTILLEAN MAGIC].

ROTH, WALTER EDMUND

13.066   BG   1913 The narcotics and stimulants of the Guianese Indian.
23.131   BG   1915 An inquiry into the animism and folklore of the Guiana Indians.
29.022   BG   1919 A few notes on the medical practises of the Guiana Indians. *Br Gui
                Med Annual 1919* 22:48-57. [13]   [*ACM*]

SEAGA, EDWARD P. G.

29.023   JM   1955 Jamaica's primitive medicine. *Tomorrow* 3(3): 70-78. [19]   [*RIS*]

SIMPSON, GEORGE EATON

29.024   TR   1962 Folk medicine in Trinidad. *J Am Folk* 75(298), Oct.-Dec.: 326-340.
                [8, 19]   [*RIS*]

STEGGERDA, MORRIS

29.025   JM   1929 Plants of Jamaica used by natives for medicinal purposes. *Am
                Anthrop* new ser., 31(3), July-Sept.: 431-434.   [*COL*]

TAYLOR, DOUGLAS C.

23.161   DM   1945 Carib folk beliefs and customs from Dominica, B. W. I.

VANDERCOOK, JOHN WOMACK

23.165   SR   1925 White magic and black, the jungle science of Dutch Guiana.
29.026   SR   1927 Magic is the jungle science: the black tribes of Guiana do not be-
                lieve in death. *Mentor* 14(12, serial no. 287), Jan.: 18+. [14] [*NYP*]

Chapter 30

NUTRITION

AIKEN, JAMES

30.001   BG   1912 Food and labour. *Timehri* 3d ser., 2(19B), Dec.: 287-291. [44] [*AMN*]

BACK, E. H.

30.002   JM   1956 A nutritional survey of small farmers in Jamaica in 1955. *W I Med J* 5(3), Sept.: 189-195. [8]   [*COL*]

30.003   JM   1961 The dietary of small farmers in Jamaica. *W I Med J* 10(1), Mar.: 28-43. [8]   [*RIS*]

BECKWITH, MARTHA WARREN

29.004   JM   1927 NOTES ON JAMAICAN ETHNOBOTANY.

BRAS, G.; WATERLOW, J. C. & DePASS, E.

30.004   JM   1957 Further observations on the liver, pancreas and kidney in malnourished infants and children. *W I Med J* 6(1), Mar.: 33-42.   [*COL*]

BROWNE, J. A.

28.070   BG   1939 Three every-day eye diseases in British Guiana.

CAMPBELL, BETTY

30.005   TR   1948 Malnutrition and allied problems in Trinidad and Tobago. *Car Commn Mon Inf B* 1(10), May: 17-19. [66]   [*COL*]

CARLEY, MARY MANNING

28.083   JM   1943 MEDICAL SERVICES IN JAMAICA.

CHRISTIAN, H. L.

30.006   DM   1953 The La Plaine 3-F Campaign. *Community Dev B* 5(1), Dec.: 20-22.   [*NYP*]

COCHRANE, E.

30.007   GC   1943 The diet of the mental worker in the tropics. *Car Med J* 5(3): 128-135.   [*COL*]

CONNELL, NEVILLE

19.005   BC   1957 Punch drinking and its accessories.

DEANE, C. G.

30.008   TR   1938 Deficiency diseases in East Indians of the labouring class. *Car Med J* 1(1): 34-45. [12, 28]   [*COL*]

DEBIEN, GABRIEL

30.009   FC   1964 La nourriture des esclaves sur les plantations des Antilles Francaises aux XVIIè et XVIIIè siècles [The diet of slaves on the plantations of the French Antilles in the 17th and 18th centuries]. *Car Stud* 4(2), July: 3-27. [5,6,45]   [*RIS*]

DUFOUGERE, W.

28.138   FG   1920 Ankylostomiase et béribéri en Guyane Francaise [Ankylostomiasis and beriberi in French Guiana].

37.101   FG   1921 De l'utilisation rationnelle de la main-d'oeuvre pénale en Guyane [On the rational use of forced labor in Guiana].

ENGLISH, E. W. F., et al.

7.018   BG   1907 Report of the Mortality Commission.

FLOCH, HERVE ALEXANDRE

30.010   FG   1953 Etude du problème de l'alimentation en Guyane Francaise [Study of the nutritional problem in French Guiana]. *Archs Inst Past Guy* 298, Oct. 10:1-7.

65.015   FG   1955 A propos d'alimentation en Guyane Francaise. Elevage de porcs et et arbre à pain [On nutrition in French Guiana. Pig-raising and the breadfruit tree].

30.011   FG   1955 Aspects nutritionnels de problèmes de pathologie guyanaise [Nutritional factors in the problems of Guianese pathology]. *Archs Inst Past Guy* 379, Oct. (5p.) [28]

30.012   FG   1956 Dosage des carotenes (Provitamines A) dans les fruits guyanais. Intérêt du fruit de l' "aouara" *astrocaryum vulgare* (Amount of carotenes (Provitamins A) in Guianese fruit. Relevance of the fruit "aouara" *astrocaryum vulgare*]. *Archs Inst Past Guy* 413, Nov. (8p.)
                                                                                                                [60]

30.013   FG   1956 Dosage des carotenes (Provitamines A) dans les legumes guyanais. Intérêt de l'"épinard de Cayenne" *basella cordifolia* [Proportion of carotene (Provitamins A) in the Guianese vegetables. Relevance of "Cayenne spinach" *basella cordifolia*]. *Archs Inst Past Guy* 414, Nov. (5p.) [63]

30.014   FG   1956 Sur l'avitaminose PP en Guyane Francaise [On avitaminosis PP in French Guiana]. *Archs Inst Past Guy* 411, Oct.: (6p.)   [28]

FLOCH, HERVE ALEXANDRE & GELARD, A.

30.015   FG   1954 Dosage de l'acide ascorbique dans des fruits guyanais [Amount of ascorbic acid in Guianese fruits]. *Archs Inst Past Guy* 337, Aug. (6p.) [60]

30.016   FG   1954 Etablissement des standards alimentaires adaptés aux conditions spéciales de notre Département guyanais [The setting of nutritional standards adapted to the specific conditions of our Guianese *Département*]. *Archs Inst Past Guy* 347, Dec. 5: (16p.)

30.017   FG   1954 Valeur alimentaire de produits guyanais [Nutritional value of Guianese produce]. *Archs Inst Past Guy* 335, Aug. (7p.)

30.018 FG 1955 "La cerise ronde de Cayenne", *malpighia punicifolia L.* Sa richesse exceptionnelle en vitamine C [The "round cherry of Cayenne," *malpighia punicifolia L.* Its exceptional richness in vitamin C]. *Archs Inst Past Guy* 368, July (6p.)   [60]

30.019 FG 1955 Sur quelques points touchant l'alimentation-nutrition en Guyane Francaise ayant des possibilités d'amélioration rapide [Regarding some aspects of diet and nutrition in French Guiana which are amenable to quick improvement]. *Archs Inst Past Guy* 16(358), Apr.: (6p.)   [RIS]

FLOCH, HERVE ALEXANDRE & LECUILLER, A.

30.020 FG 1951 Sur l'alimentation en Guyane [On nutrition in Guiana]. *Archs Inst Past Guy* 242, Sept. (7p.)

30.021 FG 1951 Sur les levures alimentaires et leur utilisation éventuelle en Guyane Francaise [On food yeasts and their possible utilization in French Guiana]. *Archs Inst Past Guy* 239, Sept. (6p.)

30.022 FG 1953 Enquête sur la consommation alimentaire réelle et la valeur alimentaire de la ration guyanaise [Survey of the actual food intake and the food value of the Guianese diet]. I. [Enquête]. II. Discussion. III. Analyses de produits alimentaires guyanais [Analyses of Guianese food products]. *Archs Inst Past Guy* 277, Jan.(10p.); 285; June (8p.); 286, June (6p.)

FLOCH, HERVE ALEXANDRE, RIVIEREZ, E. & SUREAU, P.

30.023 FG 1952 Pellagre et vitamine PP en Guyane Francaise [Pellagra and vitamin PP in French Guiana]. *Archs Inst Past Guy* 267, July (8p.) [28]

FLOCH, HERVE ALEXANDRE; RIVIEREZ, MAURICE & SUREAU, PIERRE

30.024 FG 1953 Sur la pellagre en Guyane Francaise [Concerning pellagra in French Guiana]. *B Soc Path Exot* 46(2): 245-252.   [ACM]

FORTUNE, ROGER

30.025 GC 1961 Les bons plats de chez nous [Our tasty dishes]. *Rev Guad* 3-4 trimesters (45): 27-29. [19]   [RIS]

FRANCIS, OLIVER M.

30.026 BG 1947 Nutritional aspects of cost of living survey, 1942. *Bri Gui Med Annual* 207-217. [44]   [RIS]

GARROW, J. S.; PICOU, D. & WATERLOW, J. C.

30.027 JM 1962 The treatment and prognosis of infantile malnutrition in Jamaican children. *W I Med J* 11(4), Dec.: 217-227.   [COL]

GIGLIOLI, GEORGE

30.028 BG 1958 An outline of the nutritional situation on the sugar estates of British Guiana in respect to the eradication of malaria: recent developments in the production of green vegetables and fruit by individual units. *W I Med J* 7(4), Dec.: 251-256. [12,28,45,58]   [COL]

GOODING, H. J.

30.029   BC   1958 Some problems of food crop improvement in Caribbean, with special reference to starchy tubers. *W I Med J* 7(4), Dec.: 257-266.   [*COL*]

GOURLAY, ROBERT JOHN

30.030   JM   1963 Haemoglobin levels in relation to dietary iron and protein in a semi-urban community in Jamaica. *W I Med J* 12(1), Mar.: 28-33.   [*COL*]

GREEN, LENA

41.109   JM   1962 Some seaweeds of economic importance growing in Jamaican waters.

GREENWOOD-BARTON, L. H.

30.031   JM   1957 The establishment and administration of food standards in Jamaica. *Chem Indus* 2, Jan. 12: 34-40. [37, 49]   [*COL*]

HABIB, GEORGE G.

28.262   TR   1964 Nutritional vitamin B_{12} deficiency among Hindus.

HARNEY, LENORE

30.032   KNA   1958 The effect of additional dietary skimmed milk on the nutrition of children of the colony of St. Kitts Nevis Anguilla using deaths from malnutrition in the age-group 1-4 years as indicator. *W I Med J* 7(3), Sept.: 211-214.   [*COL*]

HARRIS, DONALD J.

44.098   JM   1964 Econometric analysis of household consumption in Jamaica.

HARRISION, Sir JOHN B. & BANCROFT, C. K.

63.026   BG   1917 Food plants of British Guiana.
46.087   BG   1926 Food plants of British Guiana.

HEESTERMAN, J. E.

30.033   GC   1953 Standardising milk fat content. *Car Commn Mon Inf B* 6(12), July: 273-274. [66]   [*AGS*]

JEAN, SALLY LUCAS

28.290   UV   1933 Virgin Islands school health program—utilization of existing facilities.

KRUIJER, GERARDUS JOHANNES

8.037   JM   1957 The impact of poverty and undernourishment on man and society in rural Jamaica.

KUYP, EDWIN van der

1.026   SR   1962 Literatuuroverzicht betreffende de voeding en de voedingsgewoonten van de Boslandcreool in Suriname [Bibliography about nutrition and food habits of the Bush Negroes in Surinam].

LEES, RONALD E. M.

30.034   SL   1964 Malnutrition: the pattern and prevention in St. Lucia. *W I Med J* 13(2), June: 97-102.   [*COL*]

LOSONCZI, E.

30.035   BH   1958 Social anthropology in health education with particular reference to nutrition. *W I Med J* 7(3), Sept.: 206-210. [8, 10]   [*COL*]

LUYKEN, R.

30.036   NW   1958 Over voedingsproblemen in de tropen in verband met het voedings-onderzoek op de Bovenwindse Eilanden [On problems of nutrition in the tropics in relationship to the nutritional research on the Windward Islands]. *W I G* 38: 86-96.   [*COL*]

30.037   SR   1962/ Voedingsfysiologisch onderzoek in Suriname [Research in nutritional 63 physiology in Suriname]. *N W I G* 42:190-200. [28]   [*RIS*]

LUYKEN, R. & LUYKEN-KONING, F. W. M.

30.038   NW   1959 Nutrition research on the Windward Islands (Netherlands Antilles). *Trop Geogr Med* 11(2), June: 103-114.   [*COL*]

30.039   SR   1960 Studies on the physiology of nutrition in Surinam. *Trop Geogr Med* I. General remarks: 12(3): 229-232; II. Serum protein levels: 12(3): 233-236; III. Urea excretions: 12(3): 237-242; IV. Nitrogen balance studies: 12(4): 303-307; V. Amylase, lipase and cholinesterase activity of the serum of diverse population growth: 12(4): 308-312; VI. Cholesterol content of the blood serum: 12(4): 313-314;

              1961 VII. Serum iron: 13(1): 42-45; VIII. Metabolism of calcium: 13(1): 46-54; IX. Somatometrical data: 13(2): 123-130. [10]   [*COL*]

LUYKEN, R.; LUYKEN-KONING, F.W.M. & DAM-BAKKER, A.W.I. van

30.040   NW   1959 Nutrition survey on the Windward Islands (Netherlands Antilles). *Trop Geogr Med* 11(1), Mar.: 49-56. [10]   [*COL*]

McCULLOCH, W. E.

28.342   GC   1955 YOUR HEALTH IN THE CARIBBEAN.

30.041   BC   1958 Thirty-five years' experience of colonial nutrition. *W I Med J* 7(3), Sept.: 200-205.   [*COL*]

MOSER, C. A.

44.158   JM   1957 THE MEASUREMENT OF LEVELS OF LIVING WITH SPECIAL REFERENCE TO JAMAICA.

MURRAY, WM. C. G.

30.042   SV   1942 Infant feeding and nutrition in St. Vincent. *Car Med J* 4(3): 92-96.   [*COL*]

NEHAUL, B. B. G.

28.387   BG   1943 Report on the physical development and health of a sample of school children in the Island of Leguan, British Guiana, 1941.

NEUMARK, S. DANIEL

46.150   GC   1951 The importance of agriculture in Caribbean economy.

NICHOLSON, C. C.

30.043   BG   1947 Nutritional survey of pupils of elementary schools, Mahaicony District, February-March, 1947. *Br Gui Med Annual* 141-151. [10, 28] [*RIS*]

30.044   BG   1956 Assessment of the nutritional status of elementary school children

of British Guiana by periodic sampling surveys, and evaluation of
the beneficial effects of supplementary feeding. *W I Med J* 5(4),
Dec.: 240-246.   [10]   [*COL*]

PINEAU, A.
28.423   GD   1960 Médecine et psychiatrie rurale en Guadeloupe [Rural medicine and
psychiatry in Guadeloupe].

PLATT, B. S.
30.045   BC   1946 NUTRITION IN THE BRITISH WEST INDIES.   London, H.M.S.O., 38p.
(Colonial no. 195.)   [66]   [*COL*]

RHODES, KATERINA
30.046   JM   1957 Two types of liver disease in Jamaican children.   *W I Med J* 6(1),
Mar.: 1-29; 6(2), June: 73-93; 6(3), Sept.: 145-178.   [28]   [*COL*]

ROBERTS, LYDIA J.
33.041   GC   1952 First Caribbean Conference on Home Economics and Education in
Nutrition.

ROBINSON, C. K.
46.185   GC   1952 Food crops for local consumption.
46.186   TR   1953 The food production programme of Trinidad and Tobago.

ROBINSON, J. B. D. & PARRY, JOAN M.
30.047   BB   1949 Ascorbic acid content of some local Barbados foods.   *Nature* 164
(4169), Sept. 24: 531-532.

RODWAY, JAMES & AIKEN, JAMES
41.198   BG   1913 Some of our food fishes.

ROTH, WALTER EDMUND
30.048   BG   1912 On the native drinks of the Guianese Indian. *Timehri* 3d ser., 2(19A),
July: 128-134.   [13]   [*AMN*]

SAR, A. van der
28.460   CU   1951 Incidence and treatment of kwashiorkor in Curacao.

SAR, A. van der & KROON, T. A. J.
30.049   CU   1956 Avitaminosis A and subclinical vitamin C deficiency in Curacao.
Docum Med Geogr Trop 8(2), June: 144-150.   [*COL*]

SEAFORTH, COMPTON E.
60.073   JM   1962 The ackee—Jamaica's national fruit.

SESSLER, WA. M. & SPOON, W.
41.212   NL   1952 Over het gebruik van wilde salie op de Benedenwindse Eilanden [On
the use of wild sage in the Leeward Islands].

SHAW, EARL BENNETT
46.199   JM   1943 The food front in the Greater Antilles.

STANDARD, KENNETH L.

30.050   JM   1958 A pilot nutrition survey in five low-income areas in Jamaica. *W I Med J* 7(3), Sept.: 215-221.   [*COL*]

27.037   BB   1964 Weights and heights of children in Barbados, West Indies, 1961.

STRAW, K. H.

30.051   BB   1954 Household budgets and nutritional analysis of food consumption in Barbados. *Social Econ Stud* 3(1), June: 5-38. [9,44]   [*RIS*]

STRONG, M. S.

30.052   JM   1959 Jamaicans change their eating habits. *Caribbean* 13(12), Dec.: 234-235.   [66]   [*COL*]

SYMONDS, BRUCE

28.512   TR   1956 Fatty liver disease in South Trinidad.

SYMONDS, BRUCE & MOHAMMED, I.

30.053   TR   1956 "Sugar babies" in South Trinidad. *W I Med J* 5(3), Sept.: 159-166. [28]   [*COL*]

TAITT, D. J.

30.054   BG   1943 Malnutrition at No. 1 Government Dispensary, Georgetown, B.G., 1943. *Br Gui Med Annual* 26: 114-124.   [*ACM*]

TULLOCH, J. A.

30.055   JM   1958 Some aspects of myocardial infarction in Jamaica. *W I Med J* 7(4), Dec.: 235-243.   [28]   [*COL*]

USBORNE, VIVIAN

30.056   SV   1963 The home treatment of infant malnutrition in a rural district of St. Vincent. *W I Med J* 12(4), Dec.: 253-255.   [*COL*]

VERTEUIL, ERIC de

30.057   TR   1943 Radio talk on "Food problems during war time." *Car Med J* 5(2): 82-86.   [*COL*]

VINKE, B. & SAR, A. van der

30.058   CU   1956 Megaloblastic nutritional anaemia in Curacao. *Docum Med Geogr Trop* 8(2), June: 151-163.   [*COL*]

VINKE, B.; SAR, A. van der; FABER, J. G. & VRIES, J. A. de

30.059   CU   1960 Penicillin in nutritional megaloblastic anaemia in Curacao. *Trop Geogr Med* 12(1), Mar.: 26-30.   [28]   [*COL*]

30.060   CU   1960 Serum vitamin B_{12} levels and response to the treatment of megaloblastic anaemia in Curacao. *Trop Geogr Med* 12(1), Mar.: 31-37. [28]   [*COL*]

WABY, Mrs. J. F.

30.061   BG   1917 War cookery: the preparation and cooking of locally grown vegetable foodstuffs. *J Bd Agric Br Gui* 10(3-4), Apr.-July: 178-197.   [*AMN*]

30.062   BG   1925 The preparation and cooking of locally grown vegetable foodstuffs. *J Bd Agric Br Gui* 18(4), Oct.: 52-70.   [*AMN*]

WATERLOW, J. C.

28.551   JM   1961 The Tropical Metabolism Research Unit.

WATERMAN, JAMES A.

30.063   TR   1945 Nutrition in Trinidad, with special reference to milk during pregnan-
                          cy and infancy. *Car Med J* 7(2-3): 95-112.   [*COL*]

28.561   TR   1948 Peroneal palsy complicating labour and the puerperium.

WENT, L. N.; CHANNER, D. M.; HARDING, R. Y.; & CLUNES, B. E.

30.064   JM   1960 The effect of iron and protein supplementations on the haemoglobin
                          level of healthy female students. *W I Med J* 9(3), Sept.: 209-213.
                                                                                          [*COL*]

YDE, JENS

46.244   BG   1960 Agriculture and division of work among the Waiwai.

Chapter 31

PERSONALITY AND MENTAL HEALTH

ABEL, THEODORA M.

31.001 MS 1960 Differential responses to projective testing in a Negro peasant community: Montserrat, B.W.I. *Int J Social Psych* 6(3-4), autumn: 218-224. [11] [*RIS*]

31.002 MS 1962 Mental health and cross-cultural evaluations. *Int Ment Heal Res Newsl* 4(3-4), fall-winter: 1,4-5. [*RIS*]

ABEL, THEODORA M. & METRAUX, RHODA

31.003 MS 1959 Sex differences in a Negro peasant community; Montserrat, B.W.I. *J Proj Tech* 23(2): 127-133. [11] [*RIS*]

ARONOFF, JOEL

31.004 SK 1965 THE INTER-RELATIONSHIP OF PSYCHOLOGICAL AND CULTURAL SYSTEMS: A CASE STUDY OF A RURAL WEST INDIAN VILLAGE. Ph.D. dissertation, Brandeis University, 370p. [56,58,67] [*RIS*]

BEAUBRUN, MICHAEL H.

28.028 TR 1962 Huntington's chorea in Trinidad.

31.005 TR 1963 The role of father in Trinidad adolescence. *In* CARTER, SAMUEL E., ed. THE ADOLESCENT IN THE CHANGING CARIBBEAN: PROCEEDINGS OF THE THIRD CARIBBEAN CONFERENCE FOR MENTAL HEALTH, April 4-11, 1961, UCWI, Jamaica. Kingston, The Herald, p.75-77. [9] [*RIS*]

31.006 TR 1964 Care of the mentally retarded in Trinidad and Tobago: review of ten years progress, and plans for the future. *In* REPORT OF CONFERENCE ON CHILD CARE IN TRINIDAD AND TOBAGO [HELD BY] TRINIDAD AND TOBAGO ASSOCIATION FOR MENTAL HEALTH, SUB-COMMITTEE ON CHILDREN AND YOUTH, Apr. 18, 1964. Port of Spain, Government Printer, p. 16-18. [*RIS*]

31.007 GC [1965] Keynote address. *In* FAMILY RELATIONSHIPS: [PROCEEDINGS OF THE] FOURTH CARIBBEAN CONFERENCE FOR MENTAL HEALTH, Curacao, April 16-23, 1963, Netherlands Antilles. [Willemstad? Boek- en Offset Drukkerij "De Curacaosche Courant"], p.27-35. [9] [*RIS*]

389

BENNETT, C. V.

31.008   BB   [1965] Nursing and mental health in the family. *In* FAMILY RELATIONSHIPS: [PROCEEDINGS OF THE] FOURTH CARIBBEAN CONFERENCE FOR MENTAL HEALTH, Curacao, Apr. 16-23, 1963, Netherlands Antilles. [Willemstad? Boek- en Offset Drukkerij "De Curacaosche Courant"] p.124-128. [28]   [RIS]

BENOIT, GUY

31.009   GD   1963 Attitudes and problems of adolescents in Guadeloupe. *In* CARTER, SAMUEL E., ed. THE ADOLESCENT IN THE CHANGING CARIBBEAN: PROCEEDINGS OF THE THIRD CARIBBEAN CONFERENCE FOR MENTAL HEALTH, April 4-11, 1961, UCWI, Jamaica. Kingston, The Herald, p.35-37. [9]   [RIS]

31.010   GD   [1965] Essai sur la structure familiale vecue en Guadeloupe [Essay on family structure in Guadeloupe]. *In* FAMILY RELATIONSHIPS: [PROCEEDINGS OF THE] FOURTH CARIBBEAN CONFERENCE FOR MENTAL HEALTH, Curacao, Apr. 16-23, 1963, Netherlands Antilles. [Willemstad? Boek- en Offset Drukkerij "De Curacaosche Courant"], p.142-150. [9]   [RIS]

BLOM, F. E. A.

31.011   GC   1963 Conflicting values and cultural identifications facing the Caribbean adolescent today. *In* CARTER, SAMUEL E., ed. THE ADOLESCENT IN THE CHANGING CARIBBEAN: PROCEEDINGS OF THE THIRD CARIBBEAN CONFERENCE FOR MENTAL HEALTH, April 4-11, 1961, UCWI, Jamaica. Kingston, The Herald, p.33-34. [20]   [RIS]

BOLES, GLEN

31.012   GC   [1965] Children's drawings from seven Caribbean islands. *In* FAMILY RELATIONSHIPS: [PROCEEDINGS OF THE] FOURTH CARIBBEAN CONFERENCE FOR MENTAL HEALTH, Curacao, Apr. 16-23, 1963, Netherlands Antilles. [Willemstad? Boek- en Offset Drukkerij "De Curacaosche Courant"], p.88-106.   [RIS]

BRAITHWAITE, LLOYD E.

31.013   GC   1961 Social and economic changes in the Caribbean. *In* CHILDREN OF THE CARIBBEAN—THEIR MENTAL HEALTH NEEDS: PROCEEDINGS OF THE SECOND CARIBBEAN CONFERENCE FOR MENTAL HEALTH, Apr. 10-16, 1959, Saint Thomas, Virgin Islands, San Juan, P.R., Dept. of the Treasury, Purchase and Supply Service—Print. Division, p.50-58. [9,66] [RIS]

31.014   GC   1963 The changing social scene. *In* CARTER, SAMUEL E., ed. THE ADOLESCENT IN THE CHANGING CARIBBEAN: PROCEEDINGS OF THE THIRD CARIBBEAN CONFERENCE FOR MENTAL HEALTH, Apr. 4-11, 1961, UCWI, Jamaica. Kingston, The Herald, p.18-24. [16,20,66]   [RIS]

CAMPBELL, ALBERT A.

31.015   ST   1943 St. Thomas Negroes—a study of personality and culture. *Psychol Monogr* 55(5): 1-90. [11]   [COL]

CAMPBELL, THELMA P.

31.016   GC   1963 The role of youth clubs in preparing for maturity. *In* CARTER, SAMUEL., ed. THE ADOLESCENT IN THE CHANGING CARIBBEAN: PROCEEDINGS OF THE THIRD CARIBBEAN CONFERENCE FOR MENTAL HEALTH, Apr. 4-11, 1961, UCWI, Jamaica. Kingston, The Herald, p.190-193. [66]   [*RIS*]

CARTER, SAMUEL E., ed.

31.017   GC   1963 THE ADOLESCENT IN THE CHANGING CARIBBEAN: PROCEEDINGS OF THE THIRD CARIBBEAN CONFERENCE FOR MENTAL HEALTH, Apr. 4-11, 1961, UCWI, Jamaica. Kingston, The Herald, 250p.   [*RIS*]

CLARK, ISOBEL

32.046   UV   1963 The insular training school programme for dependent, neglected and delinquent children in the Virgin Islands.

CLOSE, KATHRYN

31.018   GC   1961 Youth in the Caribbean—reaching for maturity. *Children* 8(4), July-Aug.: 123-129. [9]   [*RIS*]

COHEN, YEHUDI A.

8.007   JM   1953 A STUDY OF INTERPERSONAL RELATIONS IN A JAMAICAN COMMUNITY.

31.019   JM   1955 Character formation and social structure in a Jamaican community. *Psychiatry* 18(3), Aug.: 275-296. [8, 9]   [*RIS*]

31.020   JM   1955 A contribution to the study of adolescence: adolescent conflict in a Jamaican community. *J Indn Psychoan Inst* 9:139-172. [8, 9]

31.021   JM   1956 Structure and function: family organization and socialization in a Jamaican community. *Am Anthrop* 58(4), Aug.: 664-686. [8, 9] [*RIS*]

CROMWELL, LETA

32.051   UV   1963 Project for discovering and assisting the mentally retarded child in the school.

CURTI, MARGARET WOOSTER

31.022   CM   1960 Intelligence tests of white and colored school children in Grand Cayman. *J Psychol* 49(1), Jan.: 13-27. [10]   [*COL*]

DAVIDSON, LEWIS

31.023   JM   1963 The adolescent's struggle for emancipation. *In* CARTER, SAMUEL, E., ed. THE ADOLESCENT IN THE CHANGING CARIBBEAN: PROCEEDINGS OF THE THIRD CARIBBEAN CONFERENCE FOR MENTAL HEALTH, Apr. 4-11, 1961, UCWI, Jamaica. Kingston, The Herald, p.165-169. [67]   [*RIS*]

DOOB, LEONARD WILLIAM

31.024   JM   1958 The effect of the Jamaican patois on attitude and recall. *Am Anthrop* 60(3), June: 574-575. [25]   [*RIS*]

FILL, J. HERBERT

31.025   UV   1963 The sexual dilemma of the Caribbean adolescent. *In* CARTER, SAMUEL E., ed. THE ADOLESCENT IN THE CHANGING CARIBBEAN: PROCEEDINGS OF THE THIRD CARIBBEAN CONFERENCE FOR MENTAL HEALTH, Apr. 4-11, 1961, UCWI, Jamaica. Kingston, The Herald, p.170-178. [9]   [*RIS*]

31.026   UV   [1965] Teacher-child-parent inter-relationships in the U.S. Virgin Islands. *In* FAMILY RELATIONSHIPS: [PROCEEDINGS OF THE] FOURTH CARIBBEAN CONFERENCE FOR MENTAL HEALTH, Curacao, Apr. 16-23, 1963, Netherlands Antilles. [Willemstad? Boek- en Offset Drukkerij "De Curacaosche Courant"], p.114-123.   [32]   [*RIS*]

GOURDON, J.
31.027   GD   [1965] Hygiène mentale et relations familiales [Mental health and family relations]. *In* FAMILY RELATIONSHIPS: [PROCEEDINGS OF THE] FOURTH CARIBBEAN CONFERENCE FOR MENTAL HEALTH, Curacao, Apr. 16-23, 1963, Netherlands Antilles. [Willemstad? Boek- en Offset Drukkerij "De Curacaosche Courant"] p.136-141.   [9]   [*RIS*]

GOURLAY, ROBERT JOHN
28.242   JM   [1961?] The importance of health in a developing community.

GOURLAY, ROBERT JOHN, et al.
31.028   JM   1961 Aggressive behaviour in a small rural community in Jamaica: the report of a cooperative epidemiological study. *W I Med J* 10(3), Sept.: 175-183.   [*COL*]

GREEN, HELEN BAGENSTOSE
31.029   JM   1960 Comparison of nurturance and independence training in Jamaica and Puerto Rico with consideration of the resulting personality structure and transplanted social patterns. *J Social Psychol* 51(1), Feb.: 27-63.   [*COL*]
31.030   TR   1964 Socialization values in the Negro and East Indian subcultures of Trinidad. *J Social Psychol* 64(1), Oct.: 1-20. [11, 12, 20]   [*RIS*]
20.008   TR   1965 Values of Negro and East Indian school children in Trinidad.

GRINDER, ROBERT E.
27.025   JM   1964 Negro-white differences in intellectual performance: a receding controversy.

GRINDER, ROBERT E.; SPOTTS, WENDY S.; & CURTI, MARGARET WOOSTER
31.031   JM   1964 Relationships between Goodenough draw-a-man test performance and skin color among preadolescent Jamaican children. *J Social Psychol* 62: 181-188. [11]   [*RIS*]

HADLEY, C. V. D.
31.032   BC   1949 Personality patterns, social class, and aggression in the British West Indies. *Hum Rel* 2(4): 349-362. [8]   [*COL*]

HAGERTY, T. F.
31.033   AR   1963 The Junior Achievement Programme in Aruba. *In* CARTER, SAMUEL E., ed. THE ADOLESCENT IN THE CHANGING CARIBBEAN: PROCEEDINGS OF THE THIRD CARIBBEAN CONFERENCE FOR MENTAL HEALTH, Apr. 4-11, 1961, UCWI, Jamaica. Kingston, The Herald, p.187-189. [44, 66]   [*RIS*]

HENRIC, S.

9.013　　GD　　1965　La famille guadeloupéenne [The Guadeloupe family].

HERSKOVITS, MELVILLE JEAN

31.034　　GC　　1952　Some psychological implications of Afroamerican studies. *In* TAX, SOL, ed. ACCULTURATION IN THE AMERICAS: PROCEEDINGS AND SELECTED PAPERS OF THE XXIXth INTERNATIONAL CONGRESS OF AMERICANISTS. Chicago, University of Chicago Press, p.152-160.　[11, 14, 67]　　　　　　　　　　　　　　　　　　　　[*AGS*]

HEWITT, W.

31.035　　JM　　1963　The attitudes of courts towards young offenders: the juvenile courts in Jamaica. *In* CARTER, SAMUEL E., ed. THE ADOLESCENT IN THE CHANGING CARIBBEAN: PROCEEDINGS OF THE THIRD CARIBBEAN CONFERENCE FOR MENTAL HEALTH, Apr. 4-11, 1961, UCWI, Jamaica. Kingston, The Herald, p.147-149.　[37]　　　　　　　[*RIS*]

HOETINK, HARRY

9.018　　GC　　[1965]　Contemporary research: the Caribbean family and its relation to the concept of mental health.

JELLIFFE, D. B.

31.036　　JM　　1954　Mongolism in Jamaican children. *W I Med J* 3(3), Sept.: 164-165. [28]　　　　　　　　　　　　　　　　　　　　　　　　[*COL*]

JOSEPH, A.

31.037　　TR　　1963　Problems of the Trinidad adolescent. *In* CARTER, SAMUEL E., ed. THE ADOLESCENT IN THE CHANGING CARIBBEAN: PROCEEDINGS OF THE THIRD CARIBBEAN CONFERENCE FOR MENTAL HEALTH, Apr. 4-11, 1961, UCWI, Jamaica. Kingston, The Herald, p.38-40.　　　　　　　[*RIS*]

KENDALL, W. E., ed.

31.038　　GC　　1957　Constructive mental hygiene in the Caribbean. PROCEEDINGS OF THE FIRST CARIBBEAN CONFERENCE ON MENTAL HEALTH, March 14-19, 1957, Aruba, Netherlands Antilles, Assen, Netherlands, Royal Van Gorcum, 176p.　　　　　　　　　　　　　　　　　　　　[*RIS*]

KERR, MADELINE

31.039　　JM　　1953　Some areas in transition: Jamaica. *Phylon* 14(4), Dec.: 410-412. [16]　　　　　　　　　　　　　　　　　　　　　　　　[*COL*]

31.040　　JM　　1955　The study of personality deprivation through projection tests. *Social Econ Stud* 4(1), Mar.: 83-94.　　　　　　　　　　　[*RIS*]

31.041　　JM　　1963　PERSONALITY AND CONFLICT IN JAMAICA. 2d ed. London, Collins, 221p.　　　　　　　　　　　　　　　　　　　　　　　[*RIS*]

KIEV, ARI

31.042　　JM　　1963　Beliefs and delusions of West Indian immigrants to London. *Br J Psych* 109(460), May: 356-363. [18, 23]　　　　　　　[*RIS*]

31.043　　BC　　1964　Psychiatric illness among West Indians in London. *Race* 5(3), Jan.: 48-54. [18]　　　　　　　　　　　　　　　　　　　　[*RIS*]

18.032　　BC　　1964　Psychotherapeutic aspects of Pentecostal sects among West Indian immigrants to England. *Br J Social* 15(2), June: 129-138. [23, 31] [*RIS*]

18.033   BC   1965 Psychiatric morbidity of West Indian immigrants in an urban group
                  practice.

KRUIJER, GERARDUS JOHANNES
31.044   SM/   1953 St. Martin and St. Eustatius Negroes as compared with those of St.
          SE/   Thomas: a study of personality and culture. *W I G* 34(4): 225-237.
          ST   [11]   [*RIS*]
8.037   JM   1957 The impact of poverty and undernourishment on man and society in
                  rural Jamaica.

LEVY, ROY
31.045   GC   1963 The doctor looks at the adolescent. *In* CARTER, SAMUEL E., ed.
                  THE ADOLESCENT IN THE CHANGING CARIBBEAN: PROCEEDINGS OF THE
                  THIRD CARIBBEAN CONFERENCE FOR MENTAL HEALTH, Apr. 4-11, 1961,
                  UCWI, Jamaica. Kingston, The Herald, p.43-44.   [*RIS*]

LEWIS, L. F. E.
31.046   TR   1953 Psychiatry in relation to the general practitioner. *Car Med J* 15(1-2):
                  40-46.   [*COL*]
31.047   TR   1956 The use of chlorpromazine and of serpasil in the treatment of psy-
                  chotic patients. *Car Med J* 18(1-2): 51-66.   [*COL*]
31.048   GC   1957 Lecture on First Caribbean Conference on Mental Health held at
                  Aruba on 14th-19th March, 1957. *Car Med J* 19(1-2): 53-59.   [*COL*]

LLOYD-STILL, R. M.
31.049   BB   1955 Folie à deux: report of two cases. *W I Med J* 4(2), June: 129-131.
                                                                                   [*COL*]
31.050   BC   1955 The mental hospital. *Car Med J* 17(3-4); 135-138. [5]   [*COL*]

MAHABIR, RODNEY
31.051   TR   1964 The care of the emotionally disturbed child—a brief survey. *In* RE-
                  PORT OF CONFERENCE ON CHILD CARE IN TRINIDAD AND TOBAGO [HELD
                  BY] TRINIDAD AND TOBAGO ASSOCIATION FOR MENTAL HEALTH, SUB-
                  COMMITTEE ON CHILDREN AND YOUTH, COMMUNITY EDUCATION CENTRE,
                  ST. ANN's, Apr. 18th, 1964. [Port of Spain?] Government Printery,
                  p.14-15.   [*RIS*]

METRAUX, RHODA & ABEL, THEODORA M.
31.052   MS   1957 Normal and deviant behavior in a peasant community: Montserrat,
                  B. W. I. *Am J Orth-Psych* 27(1), Jan.: 167-184. [67]

MISCHEL, WALTER
31.053   TR   1961 Delay of gratification, need for achievement and acquiescence in
                  another culture. *J Ab Social Psychol* 62(3), May: 543-552.   [*RIS*]
31.054   TR   1961 Father-absence and delay of gratification: cross-cultural compari-
                  sons. *J Ab Social Psychol* 63(1), July: 116-124.   [*RIS*]
31.055   TR   1961 Preference for delayed reinforcement and social responsibility. *J Ab
                  Social Psychol* 62(1): 1-7.   [*RIS*]

MISCHEL, WALTER & FRANCES
31.056   TR   1958 Psychological aspects of spirit possession. *Am Anthrop* 60(2, pt. 1),
                  Apr.: 249-260. [23]   [*COL*]

MOYSTON, B.

31.057   JM   1963 Problems of the Jamaican adolescent. *In* CARTER, SAMUEL E., ed. THE ADOLESCENT IN THE CHANGING CARIBBEAN: PROCEEDINGS OF THE THIRD CARIBBEAN CONFERENCE FOR MENTAL HEALTH, Apr. 4-11, 1961, UCWI, Jamaica. Kingston, The Herald, p.41-42. [20]   [*RIS*]

O'MARD, C. M.

31.058   AT   1963 Special problems of the senior school child in Antigua. *In* CARTER, SAMUEL E., ed. THE ADOLESCENT IN THE CHANGING CARIBBEAN: PROCEEDINGS OF THE THIRD CARIBBEAN CONFERENCE FOR MENTAL HEALTH, Apr. 4-11, 1961, UCWI, Jamaica. Kingston, The Herald, p.117-120. [20,32]   [*RIS*]

OWEN, G. H.

31.059   JM   1963 Vocational guidance and education for adolescents. *In* CARTER, SAMUEL E., ed. THE ADOLESCENT IN THE CHANGING CARIBBEAN: PROCEEDINGS OF THE THIRD CARIBBEAN CONFERENCE FOR MENTAL HEALTH, Apr. 4-11, 1961, UCWI, Jamaica. Kingston, The Herald, p.181-183. [32,44,66]   [*RIS*]

PINEAU, A.

28.423   GD   1960 Médecine et psychiatrie rurale en Guadeloupe [Rural medicine and psychiatry in Guadeloupe].

PINTO, HEATHER

31.060   TR   [1965] Group therapy among alcoholics. *In* FAMILY RELATIONSHIPS [PROCEEDINGS OF THE] FOURTH CARIBBEAN CONFERENCE FOR MENTAL HEALTH, CURACAO, Apr. 16-23, 1963, Netherlands Antilles. [Willemstad? Boek- en Offset Drukkerij "De Curacaosche Courant"] p.169-176. [10]   [*RIS*]

RIBSTEIN, MICHEL

31.061   MT   1963 Juvenile delinquency in Martinique. *In* CARTER, SAMUEL E., ed. THE ADOLESCENT IN THE CHANGING CARIBBEAN: PROCEEDINGS OF THE THIRD CARIBBEAN CONFERENCE FOR MENTAL HEALTH, Apr. 4-11, 1961, UCWI, Jamaica. Kingston, The Herald, p.150-152.   [*RIS*]

ROWE, RICHARD R. & THORNDIKE, ROBERT L.

31.062   UV   1963 VIRGIN ISLANDS INTELLIGENCE TESTING SURVEY. New York, Institute of Psychological Research, Teachers College, Columbia University, 104p.   [32,67]   [*TCL*]

ROYES, KENNETH

31.063   JM   1963 Adolescents seeking psychiatric advice. *In* CARTER, SAMUEL E., ed. THE ADOLESCENT IN THE CHANGING CARIBBEAN: PROCEEDINGS OF THE THIRD CARIBBEAN CONFERENCE FOR MENTAL HEALTH, Apr. 4-11, 1961, UCWI, Jamaica. Kingston, The Herald, p.145-146.   [*RIS*]

RUBIN, VERA

10.039   TR   1959 Approaches to the study of national characteristics in a multicultural society.

20.015   TR   1961 Family aspirations and attitudes of Trinidad youth.

31.064   TR   1963 The adolescent: his expectations and his society. *In* CARTER,
SAMUEL E., ed. THE ADOLESCENT IN THE CHANGING CARIBBEAN: PRO-
CEEDINGS OF THE THIRD CARIBBEAN CONFERENCE FOR MENTAL HEALTH,
Apr. 4-11, 1961, UCWI, Jamaica. Kingston, The Herald, p.56-67.
[9,20,32,66]   [*RIS*]

31.065   GC   1963 Report on the census of Caribbean mental hospitals. *In* CARTER,
SAMUEL E., ed. THE ADOLESCENT IN THE CHANGING CARIBBEAN: PRO-
CEEDINGS OF THE THIRD CARIBBEAN CONFERENCE FOR MENTAL HEALTH,
Apr. 4-11, 1961, UCWI, Jamaica. Kingston, The Herald, p.224-228.
[*RIS*]

9.035   GC   1965 The West Indian family retrospect and prospect.

SCHAFFNER, BERTRAM

31.066   GC   1959 Progress in mental health in the Caribbean. *Caribbean* 13(2), Feb.:
26-29, 44.   [*COL*]

31.067   GC   1963 Special problems in setting up a mental health programme in an international region: the Caribbean. *Wld Ment Heal* 15(2): 80-90.   [66]
[*RIS*]

SCOTT, JOHN P.

31.068   UV   1963 Recreation programs for adolescents in the Virgin Islands. *In* CAR-
TER, SAMUEL E., ed. THE ADOLESCENT IN THE CHANGING CARIBBEAN:
PROCEEDINGS OF THE THIRD CARIBBEAN CONFERENCE FOR MENTAL HEALTH,
Apr. 4-11, 1961, UCWI, Jamaica. Kingston, The Herald, p.124-125.
[66]   [*RIS*]

SERENO, RENZO

23.142   GC   1948 Obeah: magic and social structure in the Lesser Antilles.

TANCOCK, CATHERINE BRIDGET

18.067   BB   1961 A STUDY OF HOUSEHOLD STRUCTURE AND CHILD TRAINING IN A LOWER.
CLASS BARBADIAN GROUP.

WALTERS, ELSA H.

32.204   GC   1963 Training the teacher to work with adolescents.

WEBB, R. A. J.

31.069   BB   1961 Characteristics of first admissions to a mental hospital: a preliminary report. *W I Med J* 10(4), Dec.: 276-279.   [*COL*]

WEINSTEIN, HELEN S. & EDWIN A.

31.070   UV   [1965] Gender role and family relationships. *In* FAMILY RELATIONSHIPS: [PRO-
CEEDINGS OF THE] FOURTH CARIBBEAN CONFERENCE FOR MENTAL HEALTH,
Curacao, Apr. 16-23, 1963, Netherlands Antilles. [Willemstad?
Boek- en Offset Drukkerij "De Curacaosche Courant"] p.107-113.
[*RIS*]

WELSH, BRONTE

31.071   KNA   [1965] Paper on mental health and family relationship. *In* FAMILY RELA-
TIONSHIPS: [PROCEEDINGS OF THE] FOURTH CARIBBEAN CONFERENCE FOR
MENTAL HEALTH, Curacao, Apr. 16-23, 1963, Netherlands Antilles.
[Willemstad? Boek- en Offset Drukkerij "De Curacaosche Courant"]
p.177-180. [9]   [*RIS*]

Chapter 32

EDUCATION

ABELL, HELEN C.

32.001   BC   1956 Home economics—report on a course. *Caribbean* 9(10), May: 220, 229. [33]   [*COL*]

AETH, H. R. X. d'

32.002   BC   1956 SECONDARY SCHOOLS IN THE BRITISH CARIBBEAN: AIMS AND METHODS. London, Longmans Green, 119p.   [*UNL*]

AETH, RICHARD d'

32.003   BC   1961 The growth of the University College of the West Indies. *Br J Educ Stud* 9(2), May: 99-116.   [*TCL*]

AIKEN, JAMES

32.004   BG   1913 Some axioms of corporate education. *Timehri* 3d ser., 3(20A), Sept.: 51-62.   [*AMN*]

ALCALA, V. O.

32.005   GC   1952 Trade and industrial education. *Car Commn Mon Inf B* 6(4), Nov.: 81-83. [49]   [*AGS*]

32.006   GC   1953 Agricultural training. *Car Commn Mon Inf B* 6(8), Mar.: 176-178. [46]   [*AGS*]

50.004   GC   1953 Apprenticeship and on-the-job training.

32.007   GC   1953 Business education. *Car Commn Mon Inf B* 6(10), May: 223-224, 230. [44]   [*COL*]

32.008   GC   1953 Home economics education in the Caribbean. *Car Commn Mon Inf B* 6(9), Apr.: 199-201. [33]   [*AGS*]

32.009   GC   1953 Services and benefits of guidance. *Car Commn Mon Inf B* 7(5), Dec.: 103-104. [44]   [*COL*]

32.010   GC   1953 Survey of existing facilities for vocational training in the Caribbean. *In* DEVELOPMENT OF VOCATIONAL EDUCATION IN THE CARIBBEAN. Port of Spain, Caribbean Commission, p.5-24. [46]   [*RIS*]

32.011   GC   1954 Caribbean education. *Car Commn Mon Inf B* 8(3), Oct.: 54-55, 58-60.   [*COL*]

32.012   FA   1954 French Caribbean education. *Car Commn Mon Inf B* 7(10), May: 217-218, 235.   [*COL*]

ALFREY, PHYLLIS SHAND
33.001   BC   1963 Social education in the West Indies.

ANDERSON, BETTY
32.013   SL   1962 Literacy teaching. *In* BROWN, JOHN, ed. An approach to adult
                        education. Castries, St. Lucia, Govt. Print. Off., p.20-23.   [25]
                                                                                       [*RIS*]

ASBECK, W. D. H. van
23.003   SR   1919 De Evangelische of Moravische Broeder-Gemeente in Suriname [The
                        Evangelical or Moravian Brethren in Surinam].
32.014   SR   1921/ Negers en onderwijs in de Vereenigde Staten van America [Negroes
                22   and education in the U.S.A.]. *W I G* 3:650-664.   [11]   [*COL*]

ASQUITH, JUSTICE, et al.
32.015   BC   1945 Report of the Commission on Higher Education in the Colonies.
                        London, H.M.S.O. 119p. (Cmd. 6647.)   [66]   [*COL*]

BAILEY, BERYL LOFTMAN
32.016   JM   1963 Teaching of English noun-verb concord in primary schools in
                        Jamaica. *Car Q* 9(4), Dec.: 10-14.   [25]   [*RIS*]

BANCROFT, C. K.
49.001   BG/   1917 The making of panama hats: a suitable industry for British Guiana.
           SR

BANNISTER, A. A.
32.017   BG   1951 Amerindian education in British Guiana. *Timehri* 4th ser., 1(30),
                        Nov.: 57-59.   [13]

BARON van LYNDEN, W.E.K.
46.007   SR   1932/ Landbouwvoorlichting en landbouwonderwijs in Suriname [Agricul-
                33   tural guidance and agricultural education in Surinam].

BENNETT, J. HARRY, Jr.
32.018   BB   1950 Sir John Gay Alleyne and the Mansion School, Codrington College,
                        1775-1797. *J Barb Mus Hist Soc* 17(2-3), Feb.-May: 63-78. [5][*AMN*]

BENT, RUPERT
32.019   JM   1963 Provision for the education of the adolescent in Jamaica. *In*
                        CARTER, SAMUEL E., ed. The adolescent in the changing Carib-
                        bean: proceedings of the Third Caribbean Conference for Mental
                        Health, April 4-11, 1961; UCWI, Jamaica. Kingston, The Herald,
                        p.113-116.   [*RIS*]

BINDLEY, T. HERBERT
32.020   BB   1910 The evolution of a colonial college. *Natn Rev* 55(329), July: 847-
                        857.   [5]   [*NYP*]

BISHOP, G. D.
32.021   JM   1962 The shortage of science teachers in underdeveloped territories.
                        Car Q 8(4), Dec.: 42-44.   [66]   [*RIS*]
32.022   BC   1964 The practice of education. *Car Q* 10(1), Mar.: 31-37.   [*RIS*]

BLACKMAN, J. E.

43.017   GC   1919 AN OUTLINE OF THE GEOGRAPHY OF THE WEST INDIES.

BLAIR,

32.023   BG   1901 The system of education in British Guiana. *In* EDUCATIONAL SYSTEMS
OF THE CHIEF COLONIES OF THE BRITISH EMPIRE. London, H.M.S.O.,
p.751-795. (Dominion of Canada, Newfoundland, West Indies. Board
of Education. Special reports on educational subjects, v. 4.) [5]
[*NYP*]

BLAUCH, LLOYD E. & REID, CHARLES F.

32.024   UV   1939 Education in the Virgin Islands. *In* PUBLIC EDUCATION IN THE TERR-
TORIES AND OUTLYING POSSESSIONS. Washington, U.S. Govt. Print.
Off., p.133-163. (Advisory Committee on Education, Staff study
no. 16.)   [*NYP*]

BOHEEMEN, H. van

32.025   SR   1947 Onderwijshervorming in Suriname [School reform in Surinam]. *W I G*
28:353-367. [66]   [*COL*]

32.026   SR   1951 Surinaamse onderwijszorgen [Education Problems in Surinam].
W I G 32:65-91. [25]   [*COL*]

BONE, LOUIS W.

32.027   GG   1962 SECONDARY EDUCATION IN THE GUIANAS. Chicago, University of
Chicago, 70p. (Comparative Education Center, Comparative education monographs, no. 2.) [8, 44, 66]   [*TCL*]

BOOTH, NORMAN H.

32.028   TR   1958 West Indian Island. *Adult Educ* 30(4), Spring: 263-270.   [*NYP*]

BRAITHWAITE, LLOYD E.

38.023   BC   1957 'Federal' associations and institutions in the West Indies.

32.029   BC   1958 The development of higher education in the British West Indies.
Social Econ Stud 7(1), Mar.: 1-64. [8, 20, 46]   [*RIS*]

32.030   BC   1965 The role of the university in the developing society of the West
Indies. *Social Econ Stud* 14(1), Mar.: 76-87.   [*RIS*]

BROADWAY, W. E.

32.031   TR   1934 School gardens in Trinidad and Tobago. *Proc Agric Soc Trin Tob*
34(6), June: 217-220. [46]   [*AMN*]

BROWN, JOHN

32.032   LW   1961 The meaning of 'extra-mural' in the Leeward Islands. *In* BROWN,
JOHN, ed. LEEWARDS: WRITINGS, PAST AND PRESENT, ABOUT THE
LEEWARD ISLANDS. [Bridgetown?] Barbados, Dept. of Extra-Mural
Studies, Leeward Islands, University College of the West Indies,
p.5-11. [21]   [*RIS*]

32.033   SL   1962 Education and development of St. Lucia. *In* BROWN, JOHN, ed.
AN APPROACH TO ADULT EDUCATION. Castries, St. Lucia, Govt. Print.
Off., p.44-59. [28, 46, 66]   [*RIS*]

32.034   SL   1962 Lines of approach to adult education. *In* BROWN, JOHN, ed. AN
APPROACH TO ADULT EDUCATION. Castries, St. Lucia, Govt. Print.
Off., p.1-14. [66]   [*RIS*]

BROWN, JOHN, ed.

32.035   SL   1962 AN APPROACH TO ADULT EDUCATION. Castries, St. Lucia, Govt. Print. Off., 59p.   [66]   [RIS]

BULLEN, JEAN & LIVINGSTONE, HELEN F.

32.036   BB   1949 Of the state and advancement of the College. In KLINGBERG, FRANK J., ed. CODRINGTON CHRONICLE: AN EXPERIMENT IN ANGLICAN ALTRUISM ON A BARBADOS PLANTATION, 1710-1834. Berkeley and Los Angeles, University of California Press, p.107-122. (Publications in history no. 37.) [45]   [COL]

CADBURY, GEORGE

32.037   JM   1960 Planned education in Jamaica. *Venture* 12(4), Apr.: 4-5.   [COL]

CAMERON, NORMAN E.

32.038   BG   1955 Thoughts on agricultural education in British Guiana. *Timehri* 4th ser., 1(34), Sept.: 55-61. [46]

32.039   BG   1961 Chronology of educational development in British Guiana from 1808 to 1957. *Timehri* 4th ser., no. 40, Oct.: 57-60. [5]   [AMN]

CAMPBELL, J. S.

32.040   TR   1962 School gardening: an integral part of primary school education in Trinidad and Tobago. *J Agric Soc Trin Tob* 62(2), June: 169-176. [46]   [AMN]

CAPPER, T.

32.041   JM   1901 The system of education in Jamaica. In EDUCATIONAL SYSTEMS OF THE CHIEF COLONIES OF THE BRITISH EMPIRE. London, H.M.S.O., p.575-749. (Dominion of Canada, Newfoundland, West Indies. Board of Education. Special reports on educational subjects, v. 4.)   [5] [NYP]

32.042   JM   1901 Teaching the principles of agriculture in elementary schools. *W I B* 2(1): 61-72. [46]   [AMN]

32.043   JM   1907 Agriculture in elementary schools of Jamaica. *W I B* 8(3): 297-301. [46]   [AMN]

CARLEY, MARY MANNING

32.044   JM   1942 EDUCATION IN JAMAICA. Kingston, Institute of Jamaica with the assistance of Jamaica Welfare, Ltd., 30p. (Social survey series, no. 1.)   [COL]

CARTER, E. H.; DIGBY, G. W. & MURRAY, R. N.

5.029   GC   1959 HISTORY OF THE WEST INDIAN PEOPLES; BOOK III: FROM EARLIEST TIMES TO THE 17th CENTURY.

CESPEDES, FRANCISCO S.

32.045   GC   1960 Public elementary education in the Caribbean. In WILGUS, A. CURTIS, ed. THE CARIBBEAN: CONTEMPORARY EDUCATION. Gainesville, University of Florida Press, p.51-64.   [RIS]

CLARKE, F. J.

28.095   SL   1962 Adult education and the health of the community.

CLARK, ISOBEL

32.046 UV 1963 The insular training school programme for dependent, neglected and delinquent children in the Virgin Islands. *In* CARTER, SAMUEL E., ed. THE ADOLESCENT IN THE CHANGING CARIBBEAN: PROCEEDINGS OF THE THIRD CARIBBEAN CONFERENCE FOR MENTAL HEALTH, Apr. 4-11, 1961, UCWI, Jamaica. Kingston, The Herald, p.153-157. [31, 33]   [*RIS*]

COLLINS, Rev.

32.047 JM 1907 The agricultural and industrial experiment. *W-I B* 8(3):305-307. [23, 46]   [*AMN*]

COLLINS, SYDNEY

8.011 JM 1956 Social mobility in Jamaica, with reference to rural communities and the teaching profession.

8.012 JM 1960 The school teacher in his role as leader in West Indian and African societies.

COMVALIUS, TH. A. C.

22.034 SR 1946 Oud-Surinaamsche rhythmische dansen in dienst van de lichamelijke opvoeding [Old Surinamese rhythmic dances in the service of physical education].

COOK, KATHERINE M.

32.048 UV 1934 PUBLIC EDUCATION IN THE VIRGIN ISLANDS. Washington, U.S. Govt. Print. Off., 31p. (U.S. Dept. of the Interior, Office of Education, Pamphlet no. 50.)   [*COL*]

COOPER, JOHN IRWIN

32.049 BC 1949 The West Indies, Bermuda, and the American mainland colleges. *Jam Hist Rev* 2(1), Dec.: 1-6. [5]   [*COL*]

COUSINS, HERBERT H.

32.050 JM 1907 Some problems of agricultural education at Jamaica. *W I B* 8(3): 288-292. [46]   [*AMN*]

CROMWELL, LETA

32.051 UV 1963 Project for discovering and assisting the mentally retarded child in the school. *In* CARTER, SAMUEL E., ed. THE ADOLESCENT IN THE CHANGING CARIBBEAN: PROCEEDINGS OF THE THIRD CARIBBEAN CONFERENCE FOR MENTAL HEALTH, Apr. 4-11, 1961, UCWI, Jamaica. Kingston, The Herald, p.121-123. [31]   [*RIS*]

CRUICKSHANK, E. K.

28.114 JM 1952 The University College Hospital of the West Indies.

CUNDALL, FRANK

32.052 JM 1914 THE MICO COLLEGE JAMAICA. Kingston, Gleaner Co., 98p. [5]   [*NYP*]

CUTTERIDGE, J. O.

43.033 GC 1951 GEOGRAPHY OF THE WEST INDIES AND ADJACENT LANDS. Rev. ed.

DALTON, H. A.

32.053   BB   1907 Agricultural education in secondary schools at Barbados. *W I B*
                8(3):286-288. [46]   [*AMN*]

DAY, GLEN A.

32.054   JM   1964 Reflections on our local examinations. *Torch* 14(2), June: 8-14.
                                                                                 [*TCL*]

DEIGHTON, HORACE, et al.

32.055   BC   1905 Teaching the principles of agriculture in colleges and schools in
                the West Indies. *W I B* 6(2):197-216. [46]   [*AMN*]

DICKINSON, THOMAS H., et al.

32.056   UV   1929 REPORT OF THE EDUCATIONAL SURVEY OF THE VIRGIN ISLANDS. Hampton,
                Va., The Press of the Hampton Normal and Agricultural Institute,
                69p. [66]   [*COL*]

DILLON, A. BARROW

43.043   BH   1923 GEOGRAPHY OF BRITISH HONDURAS.

DOLLY, REYNOLD CARTWRIGHT

49.020   TR   1963 The adolescent in industry.

DOLPHIN, CELESTE

52.023   BG   1959 Good afternoon, schools.

DROOGLEEVER FORTUYN, A. B.

32.057   SR   1947 Middelbaar onderwijs in Suriname [Middle education in Surinam].
                W I G 28:97-106.   [*COL*]

DUKE, JAMES TAYLOR

20.004   JM   1963 EQUALITARIANISM AMONG EMERGENT ELITES IN A NEW NATION.

EADIE, HAZEL BALLANCE

32.058   TT   1930 A school in Treasure Island. *Hibbert J* 28(4), July: 684-698. [*COL*]

EINAAR, J. F. E.

32.059   FA/   1946 Education in the Netherlands and French West Indies. *J Negro Educ*
          NC   15(3), Summer: 444-461.   [*COL*]

EMBRA, SHIRLEY

18.018   BC   1959 Caribbean students club.

EVANS, VERNON

22.060   TR   [1963?] The future of music in the West Indies. (ii) Art music.

EYRE, ALAN

43.049   GC   1962 A NEW GEOGRAPHY OF THE CARIBBEAN.

FAGAN, S. W.

32.060   JM   1959 THE EXPERIMENT IN SECONDARY EDUCATION IN THE KINGSTON SENIOR
                SCHOOL. *Torch* 10(1), May: 26-29.   [*TCL*]

FARLEY, RAWLE

32.061　BC　1957　The role of the university in industrial relations. *Caribbean* 10(11), June: 264-265, 268. [50]　　　　　　　　　　　　　　[*COL*]

50.048　BC　1958　TRADE UNION DEVELOPMENT AND TRADE UNION EDUCATION IN THE BRITISH CARIBBEAN.

32.062　BC　1958　UNIVERSITIES AND THE EDUCATION OF WORKING PEOPLE. Georgetown, Daily Chronicle, 39p.　　　　　　　　[5, 8, 50]　　　　[*RIS*]

FARLEY, RAWLE, ed.

32.063　BC　[n.d.]　LABOUR EDUCATION IN THE BRITISH CARIBBEAN: REPORT OF A LABOUR EDUCATION SURVEY CONDUCTED JUNE-JULY, 1959, AND OF THE CONFERENCE HELD AT THE UNIVERSITY OF THE WEST INDIES, MONA, JAMAICA, AUG. 4th-9th, 1959. Georgetown: "Daily Chronicle", 119p. (Department of Extra-mural Studies, University of the West Indies.) [50]
　　　　　　　　　　　　　　　　　　　　　　　　　　[*RIS*]

FERRIER, J. H. E.

32.064　SR　1954　The organisation of education in Surinam. *Car Commn Mon Inf B* 7(6), Jan.: 125-127.　　　　　　　　　　　　　　[*COL*]

FIGUEROA, JOHN JOSEPH

32.065　BC　1964　STAFFING AND EXAMINATIONS IN BRITISH CARIBBEAN SECONDARY SCHOOLS. London, Evans, 21p.　　　　　　　　　　　　[*RIS*]

FILL, J. HERBERT

31.026　UV　1965　Teacher-child-parent inter-relationships in the U.S. Virgin Islands.

FOX, ROBERT

32.066　JM　1963　New courses: business studies at the College of Arts, Science and Technology. *Torch* 13(3), Sept.: 12-15.　　　　　[*TCL*]

FREDHOLM, A.

32.067　TR　1912　Agricultural education in Trinidad—past, present and future. *Proc Agric Soc Trin Tob* 12(4), Apr.: 96-103. [46, 66]　　　[*AMN*]

FROIDEVAUX, HENRI

32.068　FC　1900　L'OEUVRE SCOLAIRE DE LA FRANCE DANS NOS COLONIES [THE FRENCH EDUCATIONAL TASK IN THE COLONIES]. Paris, Librairie maritime et coloniale, 356p. [5]　　　　　　　　　　　　　[*COL*]

GALTON, C. T., Bp.

32.069　BG　1912　Elementary education in British Guiana. *Timehri* 3d ser., 2(19A), July: 106-112. [23]　　　　　　　　　　　　[*AMN*]

GORDON, SHIRLEY C.

32.070　TR　1962　The Keenan report, 1869. Part I: The elementary school system in Trinidad. *Car Q* 8(4), Dec.: 3-16. [5, 66]　　　　　[*RIS*]

32.071　BC　1963　A CENTURY OF WEST INDIAN EDUCATION. London, Longmans, 312p. [5]　　　　　　　　　　　　　　　　[*RIS*]

32.072　BB　1963　Documents which have guided educational policy in the West Indies: the Mitchinson report, Barbados 1875. *Car Q* 9(3), Sept.: 33-43. [5]
　　　　　　　　　　　　　　　　　　　　　　　　　　[*RIS*]

32.073　JM　1963　Documents which have guided educational policy in the West Indies— no. 5. Report upon the condition of the juvenile population of Jamaica, 1879. *Car Q* 9(4), Dec.: 15-24. [5]　　　　[*RIS*]

32.074   TR   [1963] Documents which have guided educational policy in the West
                      Indies—3: Patrick Joseph Keenan's report 1869—Pt. II: Secondary
                      and higher education. *Car Q* 9(1-2):11-25 [5, 66]   [*RIS*]

32.075   TR   1964   Documents which have guided educational policy in the West Indies:
                     Education Commission report, Trinidad, 1916. *Car Q* 10(2), June:
                     19-39.   [*RIS*]

32.076   JM   1964   Documents which have guided educational policy in the West Indies:
                     the Lumb report, Jamaica, 1898. *Car Q* 10(1), Mar.: 12-24.   [5]
                                                                                    [*RIS*]

32.077   BG   1964   Documents which have guided educational policy in the West Indies:
                     report of the Commissioner of Education, British Guiana, 1925.
                     Car Q 10(3), Sept.: 34-40.   [*RIS*]

32.078   BC   1964   Documents which have guided educational policy in the West Indies,
                     No. 8: report of the Commissioners Mayhew and Marriott on secondary
                     and primary education in Trinidad, Barbados, Leeward Islands and
                     Windward Islands, 1931-32. *Car Q* 10(4), Dec.: 3-32. [66]   [*RIS*]

GOSLINGA, W. J.

32.079   NA   1948   Netherlands educational system used in Caribbean. *Car Commn Mon
                     Inf B* 2(3), Oct.: 67-68.   [*COL*]

GRAHAM, J. W.

32.080   JM   1938   A century of education in Jamaica. *Can-W I Mag* 27(7), July: 7-9.
                     [5]   [*NYP*]

GRANT, D. R. B.

32.081   JM   1964   Some problems in the teaching of English. *Torch* 14(2), June: 1-7.
                     [25]   [*TCL*]

GRAY, CECIL

32.082   BC   1963   Teaching English in the West Indies. *Car Q* 9(1-2): 67-77. [25] [*RIS*]

GREEN, HELEN BAGENSTOSE

20.008   TR   1965   Values of Negro and East Indian school children in Trinidad.

GRIFFITHS, V. L.

32.083   BC   1955   EXTERNAL TEACHER TRAINING: A STUDY OF THE PROBLEM OF THE PUPIL-
                     TEACHER AND PROBATIONARY TEACHER SYSTEMS IN THE BRITISH
                     CARIBBEAN. [Mona?] Centre for the Study of Education, University
                     College of the West Indies, 33p.   [*RIS*]

HAGLUND, ELSA

32.084   GC   1953   Home economics in the Caribbean. *Car Commn Mon Inf B* 6(12),
                     July: 275, 280. [33]   [*AGS*]

32.085   GC   1954   The Caribbean training course in home economics. *Car Commn
                     Mon Inf B* 7(6), Jan.: 128-130. [33]   [*COL*]

HAMMOND, S. A.

32.086   BC   1945   COST OF EDUCATION. [Bridgetown?] Barbados, Advocate Co., 32p.
                     (Development and welfare bulletin, no. 15.) [66]   [*RIS*]

32.087   BC   1946   Education in the British West Indies. *J Negro Educ* 15(3), Summer:
                     427-449.   [*COL*]

HARBIN, JOHN

32.088 GR/ 1905 Agriculture in the elementary schools of Grenada and St. Vincent,
      SV   1902-4. *W I B* 6(2): 223-227. [46]   *[AMN]*

HARRIGAN, NORWELL

32.089 BV 1961 Education in the British Virgin Islands. *In* BROWN, JOHN, ed.
      LEEWARDS: WRITINGS, PAST AND PRESENT ABOUT THE LEEWARD ISLANDS.
      [Bridgetown?] Barbados, Dept. of Extra-Mural Studies, Leeward
      Islands, University College of the West Indies, p.18-23.   *[RIS]*

HARRIS, Sir JOHN

32.090 BC 1936 The vicissitudes of a legacy. *Spectator* 157(5642), Aug. 14: 265-
      266. [5]   *[NYP]*

HARRISON, JOHN

22.070 BC [1950?] Art for West Indian children.

HASKELL, H. N.

32.091 BB 1941 Some notes on the foundation and history of Harrison College.
      J Barb Mus Hist Soc 8(4), Aug.: 187-193; 9(1), Nov.: 3-16;
      1942 9(2), Feb.: 59-81;
      1952 19(2), Feb.: 74-80; 19(3), May: 112-120; 19(4), Aug.: 153-163. [5]
      [AMN]

HAUCH, CHARLES C.

32.092 GC 1960 College and university public education in the Caribbean. *In*
      WILGUS; A. CURTIS, ed. THE CARIBBEAN: CONTEMPORARY EDUCATION
      [Papers delivered at the Tenth Conference on the Caribbean held
      at the University of Florida, Dec. 3-5, 1959]. Gainesville, Univer-
      sity of Florida Press, p.65-88. (Publications of the School of Inter-
      American Studies, ser. 1, v.10.)   *[RIS]*

32.093 GC 1960 EDUCATIONAL TRENDS IN THE CARIBBEAN: EUROPEAN AFFILIATED AREAS.
      Washington, U.S. Govt. Print. Off., 153p. (Bulletin no. 26.)

HAYDEN, HOWARD

32.094 BB [1945?] A POLICY FOR EDUCATION. [Bridgetown?] Barbados: Advocate Co.,
      49p. [66]   *[RIS]*

HELLINGA, W. GS.

32.095 SR 1955 LANGUAGE PROBLEMS IN SURINAM: DUTCH AS THE LANGUAGE OF THE
      SCHOOLS. Amsterdam, North-Holland Pub. Co., 123p. [25]

HENDRICKSEN, H. E.

32.096 TR 1912 Agricultural education. *Proc Agric Soc Trin Tob* 12(5), May: 131-
      135. [46, 66]   *[AMN]*

HERKLOTS, G. A. C.

32.097 BC 1955 The Imperial College of Tropical Agriculture. *New Commonw*, Br
      Car Suppl 30(11), Nov. 28: xv-xvii. [46]   *[AGS]*

HOLDSWORTH, H.

1.025 JM 1953 The Library of the University College.

HOTCHKISS, J. C.

32.098   BC   1952 Eastern Caribbean Farm Institute. *Car Commn Mon Inf B* 5(8), Mar.:
                       233-234. [46]   [*AGS*]

32.099   GC   1953 Progress of the Eastern Caribbean Farm Institute. *Car Commn Mon
                       Inf B* 7(1), Aug.: 13-14, 24. [46]   [*AGS*]

HOTCHKISS, J. C. & Mrs. J. C.

46.092 BC   1954 The education of the small scale farmer and his family for better
                       farm and home living in the British Caribbean.

HOUTE, I. C. van

25.044 SR   1963 Het bilinguisme van de Hindostaanse kinderen in Suriname [Bi-
                       lingualism of Hindustani children in Surinam].

HOWES, H. W.

32.100   GC   1955 FUNDAMENTAL, ADULT, LITERACY AND COMMUNITY EDUCATION IN THE
                       WEST INDIES. [Paris?] UNESCO Education Clearing House, 79p.
                       (Educational studies and documents no. 15.) [66]   [*NYP*]

HOYOS, F. A.

32.101   BB   1945 TWO HUNDRED YEARS: A HISTORY OF THE LODGE SCHOOL. [Bridgetown?]
                       Advocate Co., 111p. [5]

32.102   BB   1948 Barbados aims at high level education. *Car Commn Mon Inf B* 2(5),
                       Dec.: 115-116. [66]   [*COL*]

5.091   BB   1953 OUR COMMON HERITAGE.

HUGGINS, H. D.

32.103   BC   1949 Institute of Social and Economic Research at U.C.W.I. *Car Commn
                       Mon Inf B* 3(4), Nov.: 129-130. [66]   [*COL*]

HUGILL, J. A. C.

50.069 JM   1957 Jamaica's shortage of mechanics and artisans.

HUTTON, A. B.

32.104   AT   1929 A good report. *Morav Miss* 27(5), May: 36-37.   [*NYP*]

IRVINE, JAMES, et al.

32.105   BC [1945?] REPORT OF THE WEST INDIES COMMITTEE OF THE COMMISSION ON
                       HIGHER EDUCATION IN THE COLONIES. London, H.M.S.O., 81p. [66]
                                                                                        [*COL*]

JAMES, S. A.

32.106   SL   1962 Adult education and community development. *In* BROWN, JOHN, ed.
                       AN APPROACH TO ADULT EDUCATION. Castries, St. Lucia, Govt. Print.
                       Off., p.33-38. [8, 66]   [*RIS*]

JARVIS, JOSE ANTONIO

32.107   UV   1929 A brief survey of education in the Virgin Islands. *Opportunity* 7(1),
                       Jan.: 16-18.   [*COL*]

JEAN, SALLY LUCAS

28.290 UV   1933 Virgin Islands, school health program—utilization of existing
                       facilities.

JOURDAIN, ELODIE

25.051   FA   1954 Is Creole a key to education?

JUGLALL, W. E.

32.108   SR   1963 Het onderwijs aan nakomelingen van Brits-Indische immigranten in Suriname [The education of descendants of British Indian immigrants in Surinam]. *In* LUTCHMAN, W. I., ed. VAN BRITS-INDISCH EMIGRANT TOT BURGER VAN SURINAME. The Hague, Drukkerij Wieringa, p. 83-89. [12]

KANDEL, I. L., et al.

32.109   JM   [1943?] REPORT OF THE COMMITTEE APPOINTED TO ENQUIRE INTO THE SYSTEM OF SECONDARY EDUCATION IN JAMAICA. Kingston [Govt. Printer?], 26p. [66]   [*TCL*]

KIDD, J. R.

32.110   BC   1958 ADULT EDUCATION IN THE CARIBBEAN. [Kingston?] Jamaica, Extra-Mural Dept. of the University College of the West Indies, 293p. [*RIS*]

KIEMEN, MATHIAS C.

32.111   GC   1960 Catholic schools in the Caribbean. *In* WILGUS, A. CURTIS, ed. THE CARIBBEAN: CONTEMPORARY EDUCATION [papers delivered at the Tenth Conference on the Caribbean held at the University of Florida, Dec. 3-5, 1959]. Gainesville, University of Florida Press, p.51-64. (Publications of the School of Inter-American Studies, ser. 1, v.10.) [23]   [*RIS*]

KLINGBERG, FRANK J.

6.037   BB   1938 British humanitarianism at Codrington.
32.112   BC   1939 The Lady Mico Charity Schools in the British West Indies, 1835-1842. *J Negro Hist* 24(3), July: 291-344. [5, 11, 23]   [*COL*]

KRUIJER, GERARDUS JOHANNES

32.113   JM   1952 De 4-H Clubs van Jamaica. *WIG* 33(3-4): 213-221. [8,22,46,66] [*COL*]
32.114   NA   1953 Sociologische fundamenten van het onderwijs [Sociological basis of education]. *In* KRUIJER, G. J.; VEENENBOS, J.S. & WESTER-MANN, J. H., comps. BOVENWINDENRAPPORT. Amsterdam, Voorlichtingsinstituut voor het Welvaartsplan Nederlandse Antillen, 18p.

LANDSHEERE, GILBERT L. de

32.115   JM   1962 L'éducation et la formation du personnel enseignant dans un pays en plein développement: la Jamaïque [Education and teacher training in a fast-developing country: Jamaica]. *Int Rev Educ* 8(1): 41-60.   [*COL*]

LANE, BESS B.

32.116   UV   1934 Education in the Virgin Islands. *J Negro Educ* 3(1), Jan.: 42-49.   [*COL*]

LAURIERS, L. A.

32.117   SR   1958 Geen ontwikkeling zonder onderwijs [No development without education]. *In* WALLE, J. van de & WIT, H. de, eds. SURINAME IN STROOMLIJNEN. Amsterdam, Wereld Bibliotheek, p.94-103.

LAWLEY, DAVID BAXTER

32.118   TR   1952 Trinidad's new school for the blind. *Car Commn Mon Inf B* 5(11),
                June: 301-302. [33]   [*AGS*]

LEE, FRANK F.

18.035   BC   1960 A comparative analysis of coloured grade school children: Negroes
                in the U.S. and West Indians in Britain.

LEE, ROSEMARY

18.038   BC   1965 The education of immigrant children in England.

LEECHMAN, ALLEYNE

32.119   BG   1912 Science as a school subject in British Guiana. *J Bd Agric Br Gui*
                6(2), Oct.: 62-70;
                1913 6(3), Jan.: 117-122.   [*AMN*]

LEWIS, GORDON K.

32.120   BC   1959 Technical and human resources in the Caribbean. *In* WILGUS, A.
                CURTIS, ed. THE CARIBBEAN: NATURAL RESOURCES [papers delivered
                at the Ninth Conference on the Caribbean held at the University
                of Florida, Dec. 4-6, 1958].   Gainesville, University of Florida
                Press, p.219-238. (Publications of the School of Inter-American
                Studies, ser. 1, v. 9.) [66]   [*RIS*]

LEWIS, W. ARTHUR

32.121   JM   1961 Education and economic development. *Social Econ Stud* 10(2), June:
                113-127. [44, 66]   [*RIS*]
32.122   JM   1964 Secondary education and economic structure. *Social Econ Stud* 13(2),
                June: 219-232. [44]   [*RIS*]

LEYS, J. J.

32.123   SR   1915 Agricultural instruction in Surinam. *J Bd Agric Br Gui* 9(1), Nov.:
                11-14. [46]   [*AMN*]

LICHTVELD, LOU

32.124   SR   1950 Educational problems in bilingual countries in the Caribbean. *Car
                Hist Rev* 1, Dec.: 125-132.   [25]   [*COL*]
32.125   NA   1954/ The social and economic background of education in Surinam and
                55 the Netherlands Antilles. *Vox Guy* 1(4-5), Nov.-Jan.: 35-48. [10]

LIMBURG STIRUM, O. E. G. Graaf van

37.231   SR   1926/ Voorwaardelijke veroordeeling [The probation system].
                27

LYNCH, LOUIS

32.126   BB   1963 Parent-pupil-teacher relationships. *In* CARTER, SAMUEL E., ed.
                THE ADOLESCENT IN THE CHANGING CARIBBEAN: PROCEEDINGS OF THE
                THIRD CARIBBEAN CONFERENCE FOR MENTAL HEALTH, Apr. 4-11, 1961,
                UCWI, Jamaica, Kingston, The Herald, p.111-112. [20]   [*RIS*]

MacFAYDEN, Sir ERIC

32.127   TR   1949 I.C.T.A. fills key position in British Empire. *Car Commn Mon Inf B*
                2(7), Feb.: 177-178. [46]   [*COL*]

MacPHERSON, PHYLLIS CLAIRE

32.128   JM   1961 Developing a curriculum for children and youth in Jamaica, the West Indies. Ed. D. project, Teachers College, Columbia University, 411p.   [*TCL*]

McWHINNIE, HAROLD J.

32.129   GR   1962 Teaching art in Grenada. *Oversea Educ* 34(3), Oct.: 128-131. [22]
    [*COL*]

MANLEY, DOUGLAS R.

32.130   JM   1963 Mental ability in Jamaica (an examination of the performance of children in the Jamaican common entrance examination, 1959). *Social Econ Stud* 12(1), Mar.: 51-71. [8]   [*RIS*]

MARCKWARDT, ALBERT H.

25.073   JM   1962 Applied linguistics.

MARKLE, GOWER

32.131   BC   [n.d.] Report of Labour Education Survey. *In* FARLEY, RAWLE, ed. Labour education in the British Caribbean: report of a Labour Education Survey conducted June-July, 1959, and of the Conference held at the University of the West Indies, Mona, Jamaica, Aug. 4th-9th, 1959. Georgetown, "Daily Chronicle", p.56-101. (Department of Extra-Mural Studies, University of the West Indies.) [50, 66]   [*RIS*]

MARRIOTT, F. C. & MAYHEW, ARTHUR

32.132   BC   1933 Report of a commission to consider problems of secondary and primary education in Trinidad, Barbados, Leeward Islands and the Windward Islands, 1931-32. London, H.M.S.O., 127p. (Colonial no. 79.) [66]   [*NYP*]

MARTIN, C. M.

32.133   LW   1901 Results of ten years' experience with compulsory enactments in the Leeward Islands. *W-I B* 2(1):72-78.   [*AMN*]

MASON, JOYCE

32.134   SL   1962 Adult education and family life. *In* BROWN, JOHN, ed. An approach to adult education. Castries, St. Lucia, Govt. Print. Off., p.30-33. [9]   [*RIS*]

MAYHEW, ARTHUR

32.135   BC   1938 Education in the colonial Empire. London, Longmans, Green, 290p.   [*NYP*]

MAYNARD, FITZ G. & OLGA COMMA

37.258   TR   [n.d.] The new road: a short study in citizenship.

MEEK, GEORGE

32.136   JM   1963 Jamaica's Youth Corps. *Américas* 15(4), Apr.: 13-15.   [*AGS*]

MELVILLE, EDWINA

2.152   BG   1956 This is the Rupununi.

MENKMAN, W. R.

32.137   SR   1939 Landbouwopvoeding der Surinaamsche jeugd [Agricultural education of the Surinam youth]. *W I G* 21:14-19.   [46]   [*COL*]

MERCURIUS, CECIL K. S.

32.138   BC   1963/ The role of education in developing countries. Pt. II. *Social Sci* 64 2:14-16.   [*RIS*]

MOORE, EDW. FITZ.

43.111   BG   1943 A MODERN GEOGRAPHY OF BRITISH GUIANA. [2d ed.]

MORAIS, ALLAN I.

32.139   GC   1953 Practical training for the Caribbean. *Car Commn Mon Inf B* 6(11), June: 244-246.   [67]   [*AGS*]

32.140   GC   1953 Statistical education in the Caribbean. *Car Commn Mon Inf B* 6(9), Apr.: 193-194, 196.   [66, 67]   [*AGS*]

MORSE, RICHARD M.

32.141   GC   1960 Technical and industrial education in the Caribbean. *In* WILGUS, A. CURTIS, ed. THE CARIBBEAN: CONTEMPORARY EDUCATION [papers delivered at the Tenth Conference on the Caribbean held at the University of Florida, Dec. 3-5, 1959].   Gainesville, University of Florida Press, p.162-175. (Publications of the School of Inter-American Studies, ser. 1, v. 10.)   [46, 49]   [*RIS*]

MOSE, GEORGE ELLIOTT

33.033   TR   1964 A paper prepared for the Conference on Child Care in Trinidad and Tobago.

MOSER, C. A.

44.158   JM   1957 THE MEASUREMENT OF LEVELS OF LIVING WITH SPECIAL REFERENCE TO JAMAICA.

MULFORD, H. P.

32.142   SC   1910 Our work in St. Croix: laying of the corner stone at our school at Friedensthal. *Morav Miss* 8(8), Aug.: 159-160.   [*NYP*]

NAWIJN, TJ.

32.143   SR   1913 Elementary education in Surinam. *J Bd Agric Br Gui* 6(3), Jan.: 107-112.   [*AMN*]

NETTLEFORD, REX

32.144   TR   1957 Extra-mural work in Trinidad. *Extra-Mural Reptr* 4(1), Jan.-Mar.: 1-3.   [*RIS*]

37.279   JM/   1962 Political education in the developing Caribbean.
         BG/
         BH

32.145   JM   [1961?] New goals in education. *In* CUMPER, GEORGE, ed. REPORT OF THE CONFERENCE ON SOCIAL DEVELOPMENT IN JAMAICA. Kingston, Standing Committee on Social Services, p.94-97.   [66]   [*RIS*]

NEWMAN, A. J.
2.167   JM   [1946?] JAMAICA: THE ISLAND AND ITS PEOPLE.

NICOL, J. L.
32.146   BC   1956 Education. *Statist* Sept.: 62-64. [66]

O'MARD, C. M.
31.058   AT   1963 Special problems of the senior school child in Antigua.

O'NEIL, MAUD E.
35.032   BB   1949 Of the buildings in progress with which to house the College.

OSBORNE, CHRISTOPHER
49.056   TR   1956 Handicraft in Trinidad.

OUDSCHANS DENTZ, FRED
32.147   CU/   1933/ Stichtingen en fondsen in de West [Institutions and foundations in
         SR/   34 the West]. *W I G* 15:390-406;
         BG   1934/ 16:1-6. [66]   [COL]
                35
32.148   CU   1942 De geschiedenis van het Collegium Neerlandicum, de eerste en
                  eenige middelbare onderwijsinrichting op Curacao, 1866-1871 [The
                  history of the Collegium Neerlandicum, the first and only advanced
                  education institute on Curacao, 1866-1871. *W I G* 24:269-277. [5]
                                                       [COL]
22.105   SR   1949 Geschiedkundige aantekeningen over het cultureele leven in Suriname
                  [Historical annotation about the cultural life in Surinam].
32.149   SR   1955/ Grepen uit de geschiedenis van het onderwijs in Suriname in de 17e
            56 en 18e eeuw [Aspects of the history of school education in Surinam
                  in the 17th and 18th centuries]. *W I G* 36:174-182. [5]   [COL]

OVENS, GERALD H. C.
32.150   JM   1955 A colonial medical school. *W I Med J* 4(4), Dec.: 260-263. [28]
                                                         [COL]

OWEN, G. H.
31.059   JM   1963 Vocational guidance and education for adolescents.

PADMORE, H. J.
32.151   GR   1946 Adult education in Grenada. *Oversea Educ* 18(1), Oct.: 401-403.

PAGE, H. J.
46.160   TR   1949 Agricultural research at the Imperial College of Tropical Agriculture,
                  Trinidad, B. W. I.

PALACHE, J. THOMAS
32.152   JM   1907 Agricultural instructors and their work. *W I B* 8(3):310-312. [46]
                                                         [AMN]

PASS, Mrs. E. A. de
8.047   TR   1929 The West Indies Boy Scouts.

PATTERSON, H. ORLANDO
32.153   JM   1962 The social structure of a university hall of residence. *Pelican* 9(3), Mar.: 22-39. [8]

PATTERSON, V. I.
35.033   JM   1963 New schools for a new nation.

PEARSE, ANDREW C.
32.154   TR   [1952?] Outside the walls. *Car Q* 2(4): 36-49. [66]   [*RIS*]
32.155   GC   1955 Vocational and community education in the Caribbean. *In* WILGUS, A. CURTIS, ed. THE CARIBBEAN: ITS CULTURE [papers delivered at the Fifth Conference on the Caribbean held at the University of Florida, Dec. 2-4, 1954].   Gainesville, University of Florida Press, p.118-135. (Publications of the School of Inter-American Studies, ser. 1, v. 5.) [66]   [*RIS*]

PETTER, G. S. V.; HARLOW, F. J. & MATHESON, J. A. L.
32.156   BC   1957 REPORT OF THE MISSION ON HIGHER TECHNICAL EDUCATION IN THE BRITISH CARIBBEAN. London, H.M.S.O., 30p. (Colonial report no. 336.) [66]   [*RIS*]

PHILLIPS, H. HUDSON
32.157   BC   1931 The West Indian and higher education. *W I Comm Circ* 46(843), Jan. 22:27-28.   [*NYP*]

PRESCOD, SYBIL
32.158   JM   1963 Reading retardation: a problem in some of Jamaica's senior schools. *Torch* 13(4), Dec.: 22-27.   [*TCL*]

PRESTON, ANDREW C.
32.159   GC   1960 Teacher training in the Caribbean. *In* WILGUS, A. CURTIS, ed. THE CARIBBEAN: CONTEMPORARY EDUCATION [papers delivered at the Tenth Conference on the Caribbean held at the University of Florida, Dec. 3-5, 1959].   Gainesville, University of Florida Press, p.155-161. (Publications of the School of Inter-American Studies, ser. 1, v.10.)   [*RIS*]

PUNCH, L. D. "LULLY"
32.160   TR   [n.d.] SCOUTING MEMORIES. [Port of Spain?] Ideal Printery, 123p.   [22]
                                                                         [*RIS*]

READ, MARGARET
32.161   BC   1955 EDUCATION AND SOCIAL CHANGE IN TROPICAL AREAS. London, Thomas Nelson, 130p. [66]

REECE, J. E.
32.162   BB   1907 Agricultural teaching in elementary schools of Barbados. *W I B* 8(3):302-304. [46]   [*AMN*]

REID, CHARLES FREDERICK
32.163   UV   1938 Federal support and control of education in the territories and outlying possessions. *J Negro Educ* 7(3), July: 400-412. [66] [*COL*]

32.164	UV	1941 EDUCATION IN THE TERRITORIES AND OUTLYING POSSESSIONS OF THE UNITED STATES. New York, Teachers College, Columbia University, p.443-495. [66] [*TCL*]

REID, L. H. E.

32.165	JM	1963 The common entrance examination. *Torch* 13(3), Sept.: 1-6. [*TCL*]

RICHARD, GUSTAVE

32.166	GD	1962 Propos sur la Quinzaine de l'école publique [Remarks on Public Education Fortnight]. *Rev Guad* 13(47), 2d trimester: 31-32. [*RIS*]

ROBERTS, GEORGE WOODROW & ABDULAH, N.

32.167	BC	1965 Some observations on the educational position of the British Caribbean. *Social Econ Stud* 14(1), Mar.: 144-153. [*RIS*]

ROBERTS, LYDIA J.

33.041	GC	1952 First Caribbean Conference on Home Economics and Education in Nutrition.

ROMANETTE, IRMINE

32.168	MT	1925 L'enseignement secondaire des jeunes filles à la Martinique [Secondary education for girls in Martinique]. *Rev Univ* 34(3), Mar.: 202-215. [5] [*COL*]

ROUSSIER, PAUL

32.169	MT	1930 Une maison d'éducation pour les jeunes personnes à la Martinique au temps où l'impératrice Joséphine était enfant [An educational institution for young ladies in Martinique at the time when Empress Josephine was a child]. *Rev Hist Colon Fr* 23(2), Mar.-Apr.: 137-182. [5] [*NYP*]

ROWE, RICHARD R. & THORNDIKE, ROBERT L.

31.062	UV	1963 VIRGIN ISLANDS INTELLIGENCE TESTING SURVEY.

RUBIN, VERA

20.015	TR	1961 Family aspirations and attitudes of Trinidad youth.
31.064	TR	1963 The adolescent: his expectations and his society.

RUSCOE, GORDON C.

32.170	JM	1963 DYSFUNCTIONALITY IN JAMAICAN EDUCATION. Ann Arbor, University of Michigan, 144p. (School of Education, Comparative education dissertation series no. 1.) [44, 66]

RYAN, T. E.

32.171	MS	1962 Education in Montserrat. *Corona* 14(1), Jan.: 15-18.

SAMSON, PH. A.

32.172	SR	1948 Een middelbare school in Suriname [A high school in Surinam]. *W I G* 29:289-295. [*COL*]

SCHALKWIJK, F. G.

32.173	NC	1926/ Keuze en opleiding van naar West-Indie uit te zenden rechterlijke en 27 bestuursambtenarem [Selection and training of judicial and government officials for the West Indies]. *W I G* 8:557-566. [37] [*COL*]
32.174	NC	1928/ Een Westindische leergang [A West Indian course]. *W I G* 10:320-29 322. [*COL*]

SCHOCH, C. F.

32.175   SR   1924/ Het Van Eeden Fonds [The Van Eeden Foundation]. *W I G* 6:27-29.
              25   [COL]

SEAGA, EDWARD P. G.

32.176   JM   1955 Parent-teacher relationships in a Jamaican village. *Social Econ Stud* 4(3), Sept.: 289-302. [8]   [RIS]

SHAW, FREDERICK

32.177   JM   1958 School and society in Jamaica: the Titchfield School. *J Educ Sociol* 32(3), Nov.: 107-117.   [RIS]

SHERLOCK, PHILIP M.

32.178   GC   [1950?] Education in the Caribbean area. *Car Q* 1(3): 9-18.
32.179   BC   [1952?] The extra-mural programme. *Car Q* 2(3): 4-13. [66]   [RIS]
32.180   BC   1955 The dynamic of nationalism in adult education. *Extra-Mural Reptr* 2(4-5), Oct.-Dec. [21]   [RIS]
32.181   BC   1957 Aims and priorities in education. *In* REPORT AND PROCEEDINGS [OF] HIS ROYAL HIGHNESS THE DUKE OF EDINBURGH'S STUDY CONFERENCE ON THE HUMAN PROBLEMS OF INDUSTRIAL COMMUNITIES WITHIN THE COMMONWEALTH AND EMPIRE, 9-27 JULY 1956 [OXFORD UNIVERSITY] VOL. 2: BACKGROUND PAPERS. London, Oxford University Press, p.185-190. [66]   [RIS]
32.182   BC   1957 Education in the Federation of the West Indies. *Sch Soc* 85(2120), Nov. 23: 356-358.   [COL]
32.183   BC   1957 Outside the walls. *Caribbean* 10(6-7), Jan.-Feb.: 168-170, 186.   [COL]

SIMMS, Rev. Canon WILLIAM

32.184   JM   1900 Agricultural education. *W I B* 1:77-94. [46, 66]   [AMN]
32.185   JM   1900 The proposed agricultural department and agricultural teaching in Jamaica. *W I B* 1:260-266. [46, 66]   [AMN]
32.186   JM   1901 Agricultural education and its place in general education. *W I B* 2(1): 56-61. [46]   [AMN]
32.187   JM   1907 Agricultural and scientific teaching in the secondary schools of Jamaica. *W I B* 8(3):280-281. [46]   [AMN]

SMITH, M. G.

20.018   JM   1960 Education and occupational choice in rural Jamaica.

SPECKMANN, JOHAN DIRK

32.188   SR   1962/ Enkele uitkomsten van een sociologisch onderzoek onder de Hindo-
              63 staanse leerlingen van de mulo-school in Nieuw Nickerie [Results of a sociological investigation among the Hindustani pupils of a high school in New Nickerie]. *N W I G* 42:208-211. [66]   [COL]

SPITZ, GEORGES

37.388   MT   1955 La Martinique et ses institutions depuis 1948 [Martinique and its administration since 1948].

SPRINGER, HUGH W.

32.189   BC   1960 Oriens ex occidente lux. *Car Q* 6(4):246-257.   [RIS]

| 32.190 | BC | 1962 | The historical development, hopes and aims of the University College of the West Indies. *J Negro Educ* 31(1), Winter: 8-15. [*COL*] |
| 32.191 | BC | 1963 | New ventures: the Institute of Education of the University of the West Indies. *Torch* 13(2), June: 1-5. [*TCL*] |

STANFORD, OLLY N.

| 32.192 | TR | 1945 | The 4-H clubs movement. *Proc Agric Soc Trin Tob* 45(3), Sept.: 211-221. [22, 46, 66] [*AMN*] |

STEMBRIDGE, E. C.

| 32.193 | JM | 1939 | Romance of a charity-intended marriage "dot" that benefited thousands. *W I Comm Circ* 54(1057), Apr. 6: 133-134, 141. [5] [*NYP*] |
| 32.194 | BB | 1939 | Soldier-poet who founded a college. *W I Comm Circ* 54(1064), July 13: 301-302; 54(1065), July 27: 328. [5] [*NYP*] |

STEWART, D. B.

| 32.195 | JM | 1962 | A developing medical school in the tropics. *J Med Educ* 37(9), Sept.: 1000-1011. [28] [*COL*] |

STUART, G. MOODY

| 32.196 | TR | 1919 | Agricultural college and re-organization of the Imperial Department of Agriculture. *Proc Agric Soc Trin Tob* 19(2-3), Feb.-Mar.: 36-42. [46, 66] [*AMN*] |
| 32.197 | BC | 1920 | Agricultural college for the West Indies. *Proc Agric Soc Trin Tob* 20(3), Mar.: 94-97. [46, 66] [*AMN*] |

TAYLOR, G. T.

| 56.049 | SL | 1960 | Fisheries training school in St. Lucia. |

TAYLOR, T. W. J.

| 32.198 | BC | 1952 | The University College of the West Indies. *Car Commn Mon Inf B* 5(8), Mar.: 235-238. [*AGS*] |

THOMPSON, ADOLPH A.

| 50.122 | BC | 1952 | University education in labour-management relations in British Guiana, the British West Indies and Puerto Rico in 1951-1952. |
| 50.123 | BC | [1953?] | University education in labour-management relations. |

THORNE, A. A.

| 32.199 | BG | 1911 | Education in British Guiana. *Timehri* 3d ser., 1(18B), July: 113-119; 1912 3d ser., 2(19A), July: 113-116. [5] [*AMN*] |

VERIN, PIERRE MICHEL

| 25.105 | BC/ MT | 1958 | The rivalry of Creole and English in the West Indies. |

VERNON, PHILIP E.

| 32.200 | JM | 1964 | Psychology and learning in the primary school. *Torch* 14(1), Mar.: 1-12. [*TCL*] |

WAGENAAR HUMMELINCK, P.

32.201   SR   1948 Enkele nadere gegevens betreffende den "Cursus HBS B" te Paramaribo over de periode van zijn bestaan [Some further data about
the "High School course B" in Paramaribo during the period of
its existence]. *W I G* 29:7-12.   [*COL*]

WALTERS, ELSA H.

32.202   JM   1958 LEARNING TO READ IN JAMAICA: A STUDY OF BACKGROUND CONDITIONS.
Mona, Jamaica, Centre for the Study of Education, University
College of the West Indies, 51p.   [*TCL*]

32.203   BC   1960 TEACHER TRAINING COLLEGES IN THE WEST INDIES. London, Oxford
University Press, 149p.

32.204   GC   1963 Training the teacher to work with adolescents. *In* CARTER,
SAMUEL E., THE ADOLESCENT IN THE CHANGING CARIBBEAN: PROCEED-
INGS OF THE THIRD CARIBBEAN CONFERENCE FOR MENTAL HEALTH,
Apr. 4-11, 1961, UCWI, Jamaica. Kingston, The Herald, p.106-110.
[31]   [*RIS*]

WALTERS, ELSA H. & GRANT, MARGARET

32.205   BC   1963 SCHOOL METHODS WITH YOUNGER CHILDREN: A HANDBOOK FOR TEACHERS
IN THE CARIBBEAN. London, Evans Brothers.

WARDLAW, C. W.

32.206   GC   1941 Foundations of tropical agriculture. *Nature* 147(3723), Mar. 8:
282-286. [46]   [*AGS*]

WASHBURN, B. E.

32.207   JM   1929 JAMAICA HEALTH STORIES AND PLAYS. Kingston, Govt. Print. Off.,
110p. [28]   [*COL*]

WATTS, Sir FRANCIS

32.208   BC   1910 Systems of agricultural education. *W I B* 10(4): 331-337. [46]   [*AMN*]
32.209   BC   1914 On agricultural education and its adjustment to the needs of the
students. *W I B* 14(3): 171-180. [46]   [*AMN*]

WEEVER, P. M. de

46.233 BG   1921 Our future peasantry.

WEIJTINGH, C. R.

32.210   SR   1942 Eenige aanvullingen op de Encyclopaedie van West-Indië: Het
onderwijs in Suriname [Some additions to the Encyclopedia of the
West Indies: Education in Suriname]. *W I G* 24:227-245.   [*COL*]

32.211   CU   1942 Eenige aanvullingen op de Encyclopaedie van West-Indië: Het
onderwijs op Curacao [Some additions to the Encyclopedia of the
West Indies: Education on Curacao]. *W I G* 24:289-308.   [*COL*]

WESLEY, CHARLES H.

32.212   BC   1932 Rise of Negro education in the British Empire. *J Negro Educ*
1(3-4), Oct.: 354-366;
1933 2(1), Jan.: 68-82. [5, 11, 23]   [*COL*]

WILGUS, A. CURTIS, ed.

32.213 GC 1960 THE CARIBBEAN: CONTEMPORARY EDUCATION [papers delivered at the Tenth Conference on the Caribbean held at the University of Florida, Dec. 3-5, 1959]. Gainesville, University of Florida, 290p. (Publications of the School of Inter-American Studies, ser. 1, v. 10.) [*RIS*]

WILLIAMS, C. HOLMAN B.

32.214 BC 1960 Faculty of Agriculture—University College of the West Indies. *Car Q* 6(4):243-245. [46] [*RIS*]

WILLIAMS, ERIC EUSTACE

32.215 BC 1944 Establishment of a University of the West Indies. *J Negro Educ* 13(4), Fall: 565-568. [*COL*]

32.216 BC 1945 The idea of a British West Indian University *Harv Educ Rev* 15(3), May: 182-191. [*TCL*]

32.217 GC 1946 Education in dependent territories in America. *J Negro Educ* 15(3), Summer: 534-551. [*COL*]

32.218 BC 1950 EDUCATION IN THE BRITISH WEST INDIES. [Port of Spain?] Trinidad, Teachers' Economic and Cultural Association, 167p. [66] [*RIS*]

32.219 GC 1954 In support of text books with a Caribbean flavour. *Car Commn Mon Inf B* 8(4-5), Nov.-Dec.: 69-71, 104;
     1955 8(6), Jan.: 114-115, 119. [*COL*]

38.126 BC 1956 FEDERATION: TWO PUBLIC LECTURES.

WILLIAMS, ERIC EUSTACE, ed.

32.220 GC 1953 Evaluation of existing facilities for vocational training in the Caribbean and proposals for their improvement. Prepared jointly by Lucien Dulau [et al.] and coordinated by Eric Williams. *In* DEVELOPMENT OF VOCATIONAL EDUCATION IN THE CARIBBEAN. Port of Spain, Caribbean Commission, p.25-44. [46, 66] [*RIS*]

WILLIAMS, J. R.

32.221 JM 1905 Popular agricultural education in Jamaica. *W I B* 6(2): 227-237. [46] [*AMN*]

WILSON, P. N.

32.222 BC 1961 Agricultural education in the West Indies. *J Agric Soc Trin Tob* 61(4), Dec.: 461-488. [46] [*AMN*]

32.223 TR 1963 The teaching and research programme of the Department of Agriculture (I.C.T.A.), University of the West Indies. *J Agric Soc Trin Tob* 63(3), Sept.: 285-302. [46] [*AMN*]

WORTLEY, E. J.

32.224 JM 1907 General science in elementary schools of Jamaica. *W I B* 8(3): 292-296. [46] [*AMN*]

WYNTER, H. L.

32.225 BC 1964 Some thoughts on adult education. *Car Q* 10(1), Mar.: 62-63. [*RIS*]

ZAVALLONI, MARISA

20.021 TR 1960 YOUTH AND THE FUTURE: VALUES AND ASPIRATIONS OF HIGH SCHOOL STUDENTS IN A MULTICULTURAL SOCIETY IN TRANSITION—TRINIDAD, W. I.

ABELL, HELEN C.

32.001 BC 1956 Home economics—report on a course.

ALCALA, V. O.

32.008 GC 1953 Home economics education in the Caribbean.
66.003 GC 1959 Highlights of the conference on social development in the West Indies.

ALFREY, PHYLLIS SHAND

33.001 BC 1963 Social education in the West Indies. *Chron W I Comm* 78(1380), Jan.: 20-23. [32]   [*NYP*]

BALLYSINGH, MARION C.

33.002 JM [1961?] Social services in Jamaica. a) Inter-relationship of Government and voluntary agencies and services. b) The voluntary social services of Jamaica. *In* CUMPER, GEORGE, ed. REPORT OF THE CONFERENCE ON SOCIAL DEVELOPMENT IN JAMAICA. Kingston, Standing Committee on Social Services, p.27-29, 30-37. [37]   [*RIS*]

BOLTEN, D. G. J.

28.041 SR 1925/Muggenbestrijding [The fight against gnats].
          26

BONNE, C.

28.045 SR 1923/Organizatie van den geneeskundigen dienst in Suriname [Organiza-
          24 tion of the medical services in Surinam].
28.046 SR 1925/De opleiding en de positie van den districtsgeneesheer in Suriname
          26 [The training and the position of the district medical officer in Surinam].

BORNN, ROY W.

33.003 UV 1949 Further extension of social security to Virgin Islands. *Car Commn Mon Inf B* 2(10), May: 289-291. [37, 66]   [*COL*]

BURKE, E. N.
33.004   JM   1952 Jamaica welfare. *Car Commn Mon Inf B* 6(2), Sept.: 25-28.   [*AGS*]

CALVER, W. A.
33.005   BB   [1945?] REPORTS ON THE BARBADOS POLICE FORCE AND THE BARBADOS (BRIDGE-
                TOWN) FIRE BRIGADE. [Bridgetown?] Barbados, Advocate Co., 62p.
                [66]   [*RIS*]

CHARPENTIER, S. & G.
66.028   FG   1954 An Indianist experiment in French Guiana.

CLARK, ISOBEL
32.046   UV   1963 The insular training school programme for dependent, neglected and
                delinquent children in the Virgin Islands.

COX, R. G.
33.006   BB   1948 SCHEME FOR FIRE PREVENTION AND PROTECTION, BARBADOS, B.W.I. Port
                of Spain, Fire Brigade Headquarters, 40p.   [*RIS*]

CROWLEY, DANIEL JOHN
53.007   JM/   1953 American credit institutions of Yoruba type.
          TR

DOLLY, REYNOLD CARTWRIGHT
49.020   TR   1963 The adolescent in industry.

ENSING, D.
33.007   CU   1956/ Over jeugdzorg op Curacao[About care for the youth on Curacao].
                57 *W I G* 37:212-218.   [*COL*]

FAUVEL, LUC
37.112   FA   1955 Les conséquences économiques et sociales de l'assimilation ad-
                ministrative des Antilles Francaises [The economic and social con-
                sequences of the political assimilation of the French Antilles].

FLOCH, HERVE ALEXANDRE
28.165   FG   1951 L'assistance sociale aux lépreux et à leurs familles [Social welfare
                for the lepers and their families].

FOX, ANNETTE BAKER
33.008   GC   1949 FREEDOM AND WELFARE IN THE CARIBBEAN: A COLONIAL DILEMMA. NEW
                York, Harcourt, Brace, 272p.   [37,66]   [*RIS*]

FREAN, D. E.
33.009   BG   1953 The British Council in British Guiana. *Timehri* 4th ser., 1(32),
                Nov.: 12-16.

GATES, RALPH CHARLES
66.051   GC   1961 A MONOGRAPH ON COOPERATIVE DEVELOPMENT IN THE CARIBBEAN.

GRANT, LOUIS STRATHMORE & ANDERSON, S. E.
28.249   BC   1955 The problem of medical care in the Caribbean.

HAGLUND, ELSA

32.084	GC	1953	Home economics in the Caribbean.
32.085	GC	1954	The Caribbean training course in home economics.
33.010	GC	1955	Towards better living. *Caribbean* 9(4), Nov.: 78-81. [COL]
33.011	GC	1956	Better home and family living in the Caribbean. *Afr Women* 2(1), Dec.: 1-4. [NYP]
35.019	GC	1958	HOUSING AND HOME IMPROVEMENT IN THE CARIBBEAN.

HALLEMA, A.

37.154 SR/ 1934/ Het jaar 1872 in de geschiedenis van het gevangeniswezen in de
          CU   35 West[The year 1872 in the history of the prison-system in the West].

HOCKIN, MARGARET L.

33.012 GC 1950 More bread for the Caribbean. *Car Commn Mon Inf B* 4(3), Oct.: 531-534. [COL]

HUGGINS, Sir JOHN

33.013 BC 1944 West Indies development and welfare organization. *In* FRAZIER, E.F. & WILLIAMS, E., eds. THE ECONOMIC FUTURE OF THE CARIBBEAN. Washington, D.C., Howard University Press, p.69-72. [66]

HUTCHINSON, FRANK L.

33.014 JM 1956 Hunger and help in the Caribbean: Jamaica, Puerto Rico, Haiti. *Natn Coun Outlook* 6(10), Dec.: 10-12. [23]   [NYP]

IBBERSON, DORA

33.015 JM 1953 The training of welfare officers. *Community Dev B* 5(1), Dec.: 10-13. [NYP]

33.016 BC 1956 Social welfare in the West Indies. *Statist* Sept.: 58-60.

JEPHCOTT, PEARL

33.017 BG 1956 REPORT ON THE NEEDS OF THE YOUTH OF THE MORE POPULATED COASTAL AREAS OF BRITISH GUIANA: WITH PARTICULAR REFERENCE TO THE RE-CREATION AND INFORMAL EDUCATION OF THOSE AGED 13-19. [George-town, B. G.,] Social Welfare Division, Local Government Dept., 27p. [8, 22]   [RIS]

KRUIJER, GERARDUS JOHANNES

33.018 SR 1952 "Social welfare work" in Brits West-Indie en het maatschappelijk werk in Suriname's Tienjarenplan [Social welfare work in the British West Indies and social work in Surinam's Ten Year Plan]. *W I G* 33:199-212. [66]   [COL]

KRUIJER, GERARDUS JOHANNES; VEENENBOS, J. S. & WESTERMANN, J. H.

66.086 NW 1953 Richtlijnen voor de economische en sociale ontwikkeling der Boven-windse Eilanden [Directives for the economic and social develop-ment of the Windward Islands].

LAMBERT, B.

33.019 NA 1952 Situation sociale et médicale aux Antilles Néerlandaises [The so-cial and medical situation in the Dutch West Indies]. *Civilizations* 2(3), Sept.: 407-411.   [COL]

LAWLEY, DAVID BAXTER
32.118   TR   1952 Trinidad's new school for the blind.

LAYNE, FREDERICK, et al.
33.020   BB   1964 A PLAN FOR THE IMPLEMENTATION AND ADMINISTRATION OF THE PRO-
                  POSED SOCIAL SECURITY SCHEME FOR BARBADOS. [Bridgetown?] Bar-
                  bados, Govt. Print. Off., 77p.   [37,53]

LEE, ULRIC
33.021   TR   1959 REPORT TO THE HONOURABLE THE PREMIER BY THE HONOURABLE ULRIC
                  LEE ON THE REORGANISATION OF THE PUBLIC SERVICE. [Port of Spain?]
                  Trinidad, Govt. Print. Off., 334p.   [37,44,66]   [*RIS*]

LOCHHEAD, A. V. S.
33.022   TR   [1956?] REPORT ON ADMINISTRATION OF THE SOCIAL SERVICES IN TRINIDAD AND
                  TOBAGO: WITH PARTICULAR REFERENCE TO CO-ORDINATION. [Port of
                  Spain, Govt. Print. Off.?]   [37,66]

LUKE, Sir STEPHEN
33.023   BC   [1954?] DEVELOPMENT AND WELFARE IN THE WEST INDIES 1953. London, Colo-
                  nial Office, 129p. ([Gt. Brit. Colonial Office], Development and
                  welfare in the West Indies.)   [66]   [*RIS*]
33.024   BC   [1955?] DEVELOPMENT AND WELFARE IN THE WEST INDIES 1954. [Bridgetown?]
                  Barbados, Advocate Co., 129p. ([Gt. Brit. Colonial Office], Devel-
                  opment and welfare in the West Indies.)   [66]   [*RIS*]
33.025   BC   1955 Organising development and welfare on the spot. *New Commonw,*
                  Br Car Suppl 10(10), Nov. 14:ii-iv.   [66]   [*AGS*]
33.026   BC   1956 The work of the Development and Welfare Organisation. *Statist*
                  Sept.: 11.   [66]
33.027   BC   1957 DEVELOPMENT AND WELFARE IN THE WEST INDIES, 1955-1956. London,
                  H.M.S.O. 140p. (Colonial no. 335.)   [66]
33.028   BC   1958 DEVELOPMENT AND WELFARE IN THE WEST INDIES, 1957. London,
                  H.M.S.O., 144p. (Colonial no. 337.)   [66]

MacINNES, C. M.
33.029   BC   1955 Development and welfare in the British West Indies. *In* DEVELOP-
                  MENT TOWARDS SELF-GOVERNMENT IN THE CARIBBEAN: A SYMPOSIUM
                  HELD UNDER THE AUSPICES OF THE NETHERLANDS UNIVERSITIES FOUNDA-
                  TION FOR INTERNATIONAL CO-OPERATION AT THE HAGUE, Sept. 1954.
                  The Hague, W. van Hoeve, p.224-236.   [66]   [*RIS*]

McNAMARA, ROSALIND
33.030   GC   1960 Family improvement in the Caribbean. *Caribbean* 14(2), Feb.: 28-
                  29.   [*COL*]

MacPHERSON, Sir JOHN
33.031   BC   1947 DEVELOPMENT AND WELFARE IN THE WEST INDIES, 1945-46. London,
                  H.M.S.O., 162p. [(Gt. Brit. Colonial Office], Development and wel-
                  fare in the West Indies; Colonial no. 212.)   [66]

MADDEN F.
66.096   BC   1954 Social and economic conditions of the British West Indies.

MARIER, ROGER
33.032   JM   1953 SOCIAL WELFARE WORK IN JAMAICA. Paris, UNESCO, 166p. (Monographs on fundamental education, 7.) [66]   [*RIS*]

MARSHALL, GLORIA ALBERTHA
53.028   BC   1959 BENEFIT SOCIETIES IN THE BRITISH WEST INDIES: THE FORMATIVE YEARS.

MASON, G. B.
28.351   BC   1922 The British West Indies medical services.

MOSE, GEORGE ELLIOT
33.033   TR   1964 A paper prepared for the Conference on Child Care in Trinidad and Tobago. *In* REPORT OF CONFERENCE ON CHILD CARE IN TRINIDAD AND TOBAGO [held by] Trinidad and Tobago Association for Mental Health, Sub-Committee on Children and Youth, Community Education Centre, St. Ann's, Apr. 18th, 1964. [Port of Spain?] Govt. Printer, p.26-29. [32]

MOSER, C. A.
44.158   JM   1957 THE MEASUREMENT OF LEVELS OF LIVING WITH SPECIAL REFERENCE TO JAMAICA.

NIET, M. de
33.034   SR   1935/ Overheidszorg voor de rijpere jeugd in Suriname [Government care
          36   for young adults in Surinam]. *W I G* 17:33-48.   [*COL*]

OUDSCHANS DENTZ, FRED
33.035   SR   1954 Een welvaartsplan voor Suriname in 1770 voorgesteld door Gouverneur Jan Nepveu [A welfare plan for Surinam proposed by Governor Jan Nepveu in 1770]. *W I G* 35(1-2), Apr.: 91-94. [5, 66]   [*RIS*]

PETERSON, E.
28.421   ST/   1919 Infectious and contagious diseases on the islands of St. Thomas
          SJ   and St. John, Virgin Islands of the United States, March-September 1918.

RAMKEESOON, GEMMA
33.036   TR   1964 Voluntary welfare services for the child. *In* REPORT OF CONFERENCE ON CHILD CARE IN TRINIDAD AND TOBAGO [held by] Trinidad and Tobago Association for Mental Health, Sub-Committee on Children and Youth, Community Education Centre, St. Ann's, Apr. 18th, 1964. [Port of Spain?] Govt. Printery, p.23-25. [28]   [*RIS*]

RANCE, Sir HUBERT ELVIN
33.037   BC   [1950?] DEVELOPMENT AND WELFARE IN THE WEST INDIES, 1947-49. [Bridgetown?] Advocate Co., 152p. ([Gt. Brit Colonial Office], Development and welfare in the West Indies.) [66]

RANKINE, J. D.
66.116   BB   [n.d.] A TEN YEAR DEVELOPMENT PLAN FOR BARBADOS: SKETCH PLAN OF DEVELOPMENT, 1946-56.

RICHARDSON, J. HENRY

33.038   BG   1955 REPORT ON SOCIAL SECURITY IN BRITISH GUIANA, APRIL, 1954. Georgetown, Reprinted for the Government of British Guiana by "The Ar-
gosy" Co., 17p.   [37,44,66]   [*RIS*]

33.039   BC   1956 Social security problems with special reference to the British West
Indies. *Social Econ Stud* 5(2), June: 139-169.   [37,44]   [*RIS*]

ROBERT, GERARD

33.040   GD   1935 LES TRAVAUX PUBLICS DE LA GUADELOUPE [PUBLIC WORKS IN GUADE-
LOUPE]. Paris, Librairie militaire L. Fournier, 294p.   [2]   [*AGS*]

ROBERTS, LYDIA J.

33.041   GC   1952 First Caribbean Conference on Home Economics and Education in
Nutrition. *Dep St B* 27(694), Oct. 13:576-579.   [30,32,66]   [*COL*]

ROBERTS, WALTER ADOLPHE et al.

66.120   JM   1938 WE ADVOCATE A SOCIAL AND ECONOMIC PROGRAM FOR JAMAICA.

ROYES, W. C.

33.042   JM   [1961?] Government and statutory social services in Jamaica. *In* CUMPER,
GEORGE, ed. REPORT OF THE CONFERENCE ON SOCIAL DEVELOPMENT
IN JAMAICA. Kingston, Standing Committee on Social Services, p.38-
44.   [37]   [*RIS*]

SAMLALSINGH, RUBY S.

33.043   BG   1959 Application of social welfare principles to the rural development
programme on sugar estates in British Guiana. *In* CONFERENCE ON
SOCIAL DEVELOPMENT IN THE WEST INDIES, MAR. 16-20, 1959, TRINIDAD.
Port of Spain, Ministry of Labour and Social Affairs, The West Indies,
p.44-51.   [58,66]   [*RIS*]

SEEL, Sir GEORGE

33.044   BC   [1952?] DEVELOPMENT AND WELFARE IN THE WEST INDIES, 1951. [Bridgetown,
Barbados? Printed by] Advocate Co. [for Comptroller for Develop-
ment and Welfare in the West Indies], 113p. ([Gt. Brit. Colonial Of-
fice], Development and welfare in the West Indies.) [66]   [*RIS*]

33.045   BC   [1953?] DEVELOPMENT AND WELFARE IN THE WEST INDIES, 1952. [Bridgetown,
Barbados? Printed by] Advocate Co. [for Comptroller for Develop-
ment and Welfare in the West Indies], 104p. ([Gt. Brit. Colonial Of-
fice], Development and welfare in the West Indies.) [66]   [*RIS*]

SHERLOCK, PHILIP M.

33.046   JM   [1950?] Experiment in self-help. *Car Q* 1(4): 31-34.

SIMEY, THOMAS S.

33.047   BC   1945 The welfare of the West Indies. *Geogr Mag* 18(7), Nov.: 293-301.
[*AGS*]

33.048   BC   1946 WELFARE AND PLANNING IN THE WEST INDIES. Oxford, Clarendon Press,
267p.   [2,66]   [*RIS*]

33.049   JM   1962 Sociology, social administration, and social work. *Car Q* 8(4), Dec.:
37-41.   [66]   [*RIS*]

SIMONS, R. D.
66.138   SR   1947 Suriname's ontvoogding en het welvaartsplan [Surinam's emancipation and the welfare plan].

STEHLE, HENRI & Mme.
41.233   GD   1963 Les ravets de la Guadeloupe: ces commensaux indésirables [The turnips of Guadeloupe: those undesirable table companions].

STOCKDALE, Sir FRANK A.
33.050   BC   [1943?] DEVELOPMENT AND WELFARE IN THE WEST INDIES: PROGRESS REPORT FOR 1942-1943. [Bridgetown?] Barbados, Advocate Co., 14p. (Development and welfare bulletin no. 4.) [66]   [COL]
33.051   BC   1945 The British West Indies. United Emp 36(4), July-Aug.: 135-140. [66]   [AGS]
33.052   BC   1945 DEVELOPMENT AND WELFARE IN THE WEST INDIES 1943-1944. London, H.M.S.O., 115p. ([Gt. Brit. Colonial Office]. Development and welfare in the West Indies; Colonial no. 189.) [66]   [AGS]

THOMPSON, E. W.
23.162   BC   1940 The return of the West Indies.
23.163   GC   1943 Eyes on the West Indies.

TOWERS, K. E.
33.053   BG   1952 Social welfare projects in British Guiana. Int Rev Miss 41(164), Oct.: 471-477.

VROON, L. J.
33.054   SR   1963/ Voorgeschiedenis, opzet en resultaten van het Surinaamse Tien-
              64 jarenplan [History, aim and results of the Surinam Ten-Year Welfare Plan]. N W I G 43: 25-74.   [RIS]

WELLS, A. F. & D.
53.042   BC   1953 FRIENDLY SOCIETIES IN THE WEST INDIES.

WILLIAMS, ERIC EUSTACE
33.055   BC   1947 The new British Colonial policy of development and welfare. Am Perspec 1(7), Dec.: 437-451. [66]   [COL]

WILLIAMSON, C.
37.430   BC   1952 Britain's new colonial policy: 1940-1951.

WISEMAN, H. V.
38.129   BC   1948 THE WEST INDIES, TOWARDS A NEW DOMINION?

WRIGHT, JAMES
33.056   JM   1947 Lucky Hill Community Project. Trop Agric 24(10-12), Oct.-Dec.: 137-144. [46, 66]   [AGS]

YOUNG, ALLAN
37.435   BG   1958 THE APPROACHES TO LOCAL SELF-GOVERNMENT IN BRITISH GUIANA.

Chapter 34

FERTILITY AND FAMILY PLANNING

BACK, KURT W.
34.001   JM   1963 A model of family planning experiments: the lessons of the Puerto Rican and Jamaican studies. *Marr Fam Liv* 25(1), Feb.: 14-19.
[*TCL*]

BACK, KURT W. & STYCOS, J. MAYONE
34.002   JM   1959 THE SURVEY UNDER UNUSUAL CONDITIONS: THE JAMAICA HUMAN FERTILITY INVESTIGATION. Ithaca, N.Y., Society for Applied Anthropology, Cornell University, 52p. (Monograph no. 1.) [67]   [*RIS*]

BERTRAM, G. C. L.
34.003   BG   1962 The Indians of British Guiana. *Popul Rev* 6(2), July: 114-117. [12]

BLAKE, JUDITH
34.004   JM   1955 FAMILY INSTABILITY AND REPRODUCTIVE BEHAVIOR IN JAMAICA: CURRENT RESEARCH IN HUMAN FERTILITY. New York, Milbank Memorial Fund, p.24-41. [9]   [*RIS*]
34.005   JM   1958 A reply to Mr. [Lloyd E.] Braithwaite [*Social Econ Stud* 6(4), Dec. 1957: 523-571]. *Social Econ Stud* 7(4), Dec.: 234-237. [9, 67]
[*RIS*]

BLAKE, JUDITH; STYCOS, J. MAYONE & DAVIS, KINGSLEY
34.006   JM   1961 FAMILY STRUCTURE IN JAMAICA: THE SOCIAL CONTEXT OF REPRODUCTION. Glencoe, Ill., Free Press, 262p. [8, 9, 20]   [*RIS*]

BRAITHWAITE, LLOYD E.
34.007   BC   1957 Sociology and demographic research in the British Caribbean. *Social Econ Stud* 6(4), Dec.: 523-571. [8, 9, 67]   [*RIS*]
17.003   JM   [1961?] Population, migration and urbanization.

DALE, EDMUND H.
7.013   BC   1963 The demographic problem of the British West Indies.

IBBERSON, DORA
34.008   JM   1956 A note on the relationship between illegitimacy and the birthrate. *Social Econ Stud* 5(1), Mar.: 93-99. [9]   [*RIS*]

KRUIJER, GERARDUS JOHANNES

34.009   JM   1958   Family size and family planning: a pilot survey among Jamaican mothers. *W I G* 38(3-4), Dec.: 144-150. [9, 20, 66]   [*RIS*]

LAMPE, P. H. J.

34.010   BC   1951   A study on human fertility in the British Caribbean territories. *Car Econ Rev* 3(1-2), Oct.: 93-178.   [*RIS*]

34.011   BC   1952   Human fertility in the British West Indies. *Car Commn Mon Inf B* 5(8), Mar.: 231-232, 243.   [*COL*]

MANICOM, JACQUELINE

34.012   GD   1962   A propos de la limitation des naissances en Guadeloupe [Regarding birth control in Guadeloupe]. *Rev Guad* 13(48), 3d trimester: 8-10.   [*RIS*]

MEYER, H.

7.046   SR   1961/ Suriname en het wereldbevolkingsvraagstuk [Surinam and the prob-
           62   lem of world population].

ROBERTS, GEORGE WOODROW

34.013   BC   1953   Motherhood tables of the 1946 census. *Social Econ Stud* 2(2-3), Oct.: 175-186. [9, 10]   [*RIS*]

34.014   BC   1955   Cultural factors in fertility in the British Caribbean. *In* PROCEEDINGS OF THE WORLD POPULATION CONFERENCE IN ROME, 1954. New York, United Nations, p.977-988. [9]   [*RIS*]

34.015   GC   1955   Some aspects of mating and fertility in the West Indies. *Popul Stud* 8(3), Mar.: 199-227. [9]   [*NYP*]

ROBERTS, GEORGE WOODROW & BRAITHWAITE, LLOYD

34.016   TR   1960   Fertility differentials by family type in Trinidad. *In* RUBIN, VERA, ed. CULTURE, SOCIETY, AND HEALTH. New York, New York Academy of Sciences, p.963-980. (Annals of the New York Academy of Sciences, v. 84, art. 17.) [9, 11, 12]   [*RIS*]

34.017   TR   1961   A gross mating table for a West Indian population. *Popul Stud* 14 (3), Jan.: 198-217. [9, 11]   [*RIS*]

RUSSELL, AUBREY

34.018   JM   1963   Field test of simple, foam-producing chemical contraceptive. *W I Med J* 12(1), Mar.: 23-27.   [*COL*]

STEELE, WESLEY

16.031   JM   1954   ENGULFED BY THE COLOR TIDE; STUDIES FROM JAMAICA: CONSEQUENCES OF THE SLAVE TRADE AND BRITISH COLONIALISM.

STYCOS, J. MAYONE

67.026   JM   1954   Unusual applications of research: studies of fertility in underdeveloped areas.

STYCOS, J. MAYONE & BACK, KURT

34.019   JM   1958   Contraception and Catholicism in Jamaica. *Eng Q* 5(4), Dec.: 216-220. [8, 9, 23]   [*RIS*]

TIETZE, CHRISTOPHER

34.020   BB   1957 THE FAMILY PLANNING SERVICE IN BARBADOS. New York, 14p. (United
Nations Technical Assistance Programme, Report TAA/BAR/1.)
[9,66]   [*RIS*]

34.021   BB   1958 THE EFFECTIVENESS OF THE FAMILY PLANNING SERVICE IN BARBADOS.
New York, 17p. (United Nations Technical Assistance Programme,
Report TAA/BAR/4.)   [9,66]   [*RIS*]

TIETZE, CHRISTOPHER & ALLEYNE, CHARLES

34.022   BB   1959 A family planning service in the West Indies. *Fert Ster* 10(3), May-
June: 259-271.   [9,66]   [*RIS*]

WYTHENSHAWE, Lord SIMON of

7.089   BB   1954 POPULATION AND RESOURCES OF BARBADOS.

Chapter 35

HOUSING AND ARCHITECTURE

ACWORTH, A. W.

35.001   BC   1949 Treasure in the Caribbean: a first study of Georgian buildings in the British West Indies. London, Pleiades Books, 36p.   [5]
[COL]

ATKINSON, G. ANTHONY

35.002   BC   1953 Architecture in the trade winds. *Weather* 8(10), Oct.: 313-315. [*RIS*]

BARKER, AUBREY

36.001   GC   1958 Progress, planning and people.

BROWN, AUDREY

5.021   SK   1962 Le Chateau de la Montagne, Saint Christopher.

BUENEMAN, E. R.

35.003   TB   1958 The Tobago story—example of cooperation at all levels. *Caribbean* 12(1), Aug.: 6-10. [66]   [COL]

BURGESS, CHARLES J.

35.004   GC   1951 Issues in Caribbean housing improvement. *In* Aspects of housing in the Caribbean. Port of Spain, Caribbean Commission, p.203-212. [66]   [*RIS*]

BURNS, L. V.

64.028   JM   1942 Roofing shingles in Jamaica.

BYNOE, PETER

35.005   TR   1962 The architecture of Trinidad and Tobago, 1562-1962. Port of Spain, Guardian Commercial Printery, 15p.   [*RIS*]

CHAPMAN, JOHN L.

35.006   SV   1951 Aided self-help housing in St. Vincent. *In* Aspects of housing in the Caribbean. Port of Spain, Caribbean Commission, p.98-102. [66]   [*RIS*]

CONCANNON, T. A. L.
35.007   JM   1963 Preservation of national monuments in Jamaica. *Car Q* 9(3), Sept.:
              3-9.   [*RIS*]

CONNELL, NEVILLE
23.026 BB   1953 St. George's Parish Church, Barbados.
35.008   BB   1959 18th century furniture and its background in Barbados. *J Barb Mus
              Hist Soc* 26(4), Aug.: 162-190. [5]   [*AMN*]

COSTELLO, M.
35.009   BG   1951 The possibilities of prefabrication. *In* ASPECTS OF HOUSING IN THE
              CARIBBEAN. Port of Spain, Caribbean Commission, p.63-66. [66] [*RIS*]
35.010   BG   1952 Rural housing problems: with notes on self-help housing and the
              possibilities of prefabrication. *Timehri* 4th ser., 1(31), Nov.: 16-20.
              [66]

CROSS, BERYL
35.011   BC   1954 From shack to self-help in the West Indies. *Venture* 6(5), Sept.: 8-9.
                                                                           [*COL*]

DELAWARDE, JEAN-BAPTISTE
43.038 MT   1935 Essai sur l'installation humaine dans les mornes de la Martinique
              [Essay on the human settlement on the bluffs of Martinique].

De SYLLAS, L. M.
35.012   BB   [1944?] REPORT ON PRELIMINARY HOUSING SURVEY OF TWO BLOCKS OF CHAPMAN'S
              LANE TENANTRY, BRIDGETOWN (JUNE-JULY, 1944); AND COMMENTS ON
              THE REPORT BY THE TOWN PLANNING ADVISER AND THE HOUSING
              BOARD. [Bridgetown?] Barbados, Advocate Co., 8p. [66]   [*RIS*]

DORAN, EDWIN BEAL, Jr.
35.013   GC   1962 The West Indian hip-roofed cottage. *Calif Geogr* 3:97-104. [19] [*RIS*]

DRAYTON, EVAN
35.014   BG   1955 More houses for British Guiana. *Caribbean* 8(10), May: 221-223, 236.
                                                                           [*COL*]

EBERLEIN, HAROLD DONALDSON
35.015   UV   1935 Housing in the Virgin Islands. *Architecture* 71(1), Jan.: 1-4. [36, 66]
                                                                           [*COL*]

FARRAR, P. A.
23.044 BB   1935 Christ Church.

FLOCH, HERVE ALEXANDRE & CORNU, G.
35.016   FG   1956 Problèmes de l'habitat à Cayenne. Le Casier sanitaire des im-
              meubles [Housing problems in Cayenne. A sanitation register of
              the property]. *Archs Inst Past Guy* 415, Dec. (32p.). [28]

FRANCIS, OLIVER M.
28.188 BG   1943 Social, economic and dietetic features of tuberculosis in British
              Guiana.

FRANCIS, SYBIL E.
35.017   JM   1953 A land settlement project in Jamaica. *Car Commn Mon Inf B* 7(4),
              Nov.: 83, 86. [48, 66]   [*COL*]

GOYENECHE, EUGENE

5.070   MT   1956   Historical monuments of Martinique.

GROOME, J. R.

35.018   GR   1964   Sedan-chair porches: a detail of Georgian architecture in St. George's. *Car Q* 10(3), Sept.: 31-33.   [*RIS*]

HAGLUND, ELSA

35.019   GC   1958   HOUSING AND HOME IMPROVEMENT IN THE CARIBBEAN. [Port of Spain?] Trinidad, Food and Agriculture Organization and Caribbean Commission, 216p.   [9, 33, 66]   [*RIS*]

HANSON, DONALD R.

35.020   GC   1955   Caribbean housing. *Caribbean* 8(6), Jan.: 116-119.   [66]   [*COL*]

HARTOG, JOHAN

36.007   CU/ AR   1947   De voorgenomen uitbreiding van Willemstad op Curacao, Oranjestad en St. Nicolaas op Aruba [The contemplated expansion of Willemstad in Curacao, of Oranjestad and St. Nicolaas in Aruba].

HEESTERMAN, J. E.

35.021   GC   1951   New materials and methods of construction. *In* ASPECTS OF HOUSING IN THE CARIBBEAN. Port of Spain. Caribbean Commission, p.213-217. [66]   [*RIS*]

35.022   GC   1955   Information on standardisation of milling sizes of sawn timber and of prefabricated wooden parts of houses in the Caribbean area. *In* CARIBBEAN TIMBERS, THEIR UTILISATION AND TRADE WITHIN THE AREA: report of the Timber Conference held at Kent House, Trinidad, Apr. 15-22, 1953. Port of Spain, Caribbean Commission, p.59-66.   [*RIS*]

HENDRICK, S. PURCELL

23.063   JM   1911   A SKETCH OF THE HISTORY OF THE CATHEDRAL CHURCH OF ST. JAGO DE LA VEGA, SPANISH TOWN IN THE PARISH OF ST. CATHERINE, JAMAICA.

HORN, EDWIN

35.023   BC   [n.d.]   THE WEST INDIES: REPORT OF A SURVEY ON HOUSING, NOVEMBER 1956-MAY 1957. [Bridgetown?] Barbados, Development and Welfare Organization, 16p.   [47, 66]

HOWES, J. R.

65.031   TR   1956   Livestock buildings at the college New Farm.

JOHNSTONE, H. M.

35.024   TR   1959   Queens Hall, Trinidad—the beginning of a new era of cultural development. *Can-W I Mag* 49(10), Oct.: 19-20, 22.   [*NYP*]

KADLEIGH, SERGEI

35.025   JM   [1961?]   Our housing needs. *In* CUMPER, GEORGE, ed. REPORT OF THE CONFERENCE ON SOCIAL DEVELOPMENT IN JAMAICA. Kingston, Standing Committee on Social Services, p.105-107.   [66]   [*RIS*]

LAIRD, COLIN

35.026   TR   1954   Trinidad town house. *Car Q* 3(4), Aug.: 188-198.   [*RIS*]

LAMPE, P. H. J.
28.319   SR   1926/ Enkele opmerkingen over den sociaal-hygienischen toestanden en
                  27   de geneeskundige verzorging van Suriname [Some remarks about the
                       social-hygienic conditions and medical care in Surinam].
35.027   GC   1951 Housing and health in the Caribbean. *In* ASPECTS OF HOUSING IN THE
                       CARIBBEAN. Port of Spain, Caribbean Commission, p.15-22.   [28]
                                                                                   [*RIS*]

LASHLEY, T. O.
35.028   BB   [1945?] REPORT ON A HOUSING SURVEY OF EIGHT SLUM TENANTRIES IN BRIDGE-
                       TOWN, JUNE 1944-APR. 1945. Bridgetown, Housing, Board Office,
                       47p.   [66]   [*RIS*]
35.029   BB   1953 Barbados attacks the housing problem. *Car Commn Mon Inf B* 7(5),
                       Dec.: 110-112.   [66]   [*COL*]

LICHTVELD, LOU
35.030   SR   1960 Native arts in modern architecture. *Caribbean* 14(4), Apr.: 87-89.
                       [10, 22]   [*COL*]

MAY, ARTHUR J.
35.031   BC   1933 The architecture of the West Indies. *WI Comm Circ* 48(899), Mar.16:
                       105-107; 48(900), Mar. 30: 125-126; 48(901), Apr. 13: 147-148;
                       48(902), Apr. 27: 167-168; 48(904), May 25: 207-208; 48(905), June 8:
                       227-229. [5, 19]   [*NYP*]

MINTZ, SIDNEY W.
8.043   JM   [1961?] The house and the yard among three Caribbean peasantries.

O'NEIL, MAUD E.
35.032   BB   1949 Of the buildings in progress with which to house the College. *In*
                       KLINGBERG, FRANK J., ed. CODRINGTON CHRONICLE: AN EXPERIMENT
                       IN ANGLICAN ALTRUISM ON A BARBADOS PLANTATION, 1710-1834.
                       Berkeley and Los Angeles, University of California Press, p.27-39.
                       (Publications in history no. 37.)   [5, 32, 45]   [*COL*]

OUDSCHANS DENTZ, FRED
54.051   SR   1920/ De bauxietnijverheid en de stichting van een nieuwe stad in
                  21   Suriname [The bauxite industry and the founding of a new city
                       in Surinam].

PATTERSON, V. I.
35.033   JM   1963 New schools for a new nation. *Torch* 13(4), Dec.: 12-20.   [32]
                                                                                   [*TCL*]

PEACOCKE, NORA E.
35.034   GC   1953 Building research in the Caribbean. *Car Commn Mon Inf B* 6(9),
                       Apr.: 197-198.   [66]   [*AGS*]

PETERS, FRED E.
35.035   MS   1931 SAINT ANTHONY'S CHURCH, MONTSERRAT, WEST INDIES. Bridgetown,
                       Advocate Co., 11p. [5, 23]

RANCE, Sir HUBERT ELVIN

35.036   TR   1951 Government expenditures in Trinidad and Tobago. *In* ASPECTS OF HOUSING IN THE CARIBBEAN. Port of Spain, Caribbean Commission, p.111-112. [37, 66]   *[RIS]*

ROBERTS, WALTER ADOLPHE

35.037   JM   1962 Old King's House, Spanish Town. *Chron W I Comm* 77(1372), May: 230-233. [5]   *[NYP]*

ROUX, G.

35.038   FC   1957 Housing in the French Caribbean Departments. *Caribbean* 10(6-7), Jan.-Feb.: 154-155.   *[COL]*

SAVAREY, EUNICE

35.039   SK   1954 St. Kitts housing project. *Can-W I Mag* 44(12), Dec.: 2-3.   *[NYP]*

SENIOR, CLARENCE

35.040   GC   1954 Housing and sanitation in the Caribbean. *In* WILGUS, A. CURTIS. ed. THE CARIBBEAN: ITS ECONOMY [papers delivered at the Fourth Annual Conference on the Caribbean held at the University of Florida, Dec. 3-5, 1953]. Gainesville, University of Florida Press, p.177-190. (Publications of the School of Inter-American Studies, ser. 1, v.4.) [28]   *[RIS]*

SHAW, EARL BENNETT

8.052   SC   1934 The villages of St. Croix.

SLOMAN, E.

35.041   BG   1912 St. George's Cathedral. *Timehri* 3d ser., 2(19), Dec.: 373-376. [5, 23]   *[AMN]*

SMEATHERS, R.

64.095   TR   1943 The manufacture of shingles from local woods in Trinidad and Tobago.

STEVENS, PETER

35.042   BB   1959 Planning and preservation. *J Barb Mus Hist Soc* 26(3), May: 111-119. [5]   *[AMN]*

STEVENS, PETER H. M.

36.020   BC   1957 Planning in the West Indies.

STOCKDALE, Sir FRANK A.; GARDNER-MEDWIN, R. & SYLLAS, S. M. de

35.043   BC   1948 Recent planning developments in the colonies. *J Roy Inst Br Archit* 55(4), Feb.: 140-148. [36, 66]   *[NYP]*

WATERMAN, THOMAS T.

35.044   BB   1946 Some early buildings of Barbados. *J Barb Mus Hist Soc* 13(3-4), May-Nov.: 140-148. [5]   *[AMN]*

WIGHT, Sir GERALD

35.045   TR   1951 A proposal for the future financing of public housing in Trinidad and Tobago. *In* ASPECTS OF HOUSING IN THE CARIBBEAN. Port of Spain, Caribbean Commission, p.113-119. [37, 66]   *[RIS]*

WONG, PAUL G.

35.046   SR   1953 The aided self-help housing programme in Surinam. *Car Commn Mon Inf B* 6(7), Feb.: 155-156.   [66]   [*AGS*]

WOODHOUSE, W.M.

35.047   BC   1954 Building and housing in the West Indies. *Prefabrication* 1(10), Aug.: 13-18.   [*RIS*]
35.048   BC   1955 Housing in the West Indies. *Corona* 7(6), June: 227-231. [66]   [*RIS*]
35.049   BC   1956 Housing in the West Indies. *Statist* Sept.: 66,68.
35.050   BC   1962 Developments in the local building industries of the Commonwealth. *J Roy Soc Arts* 110(5073), Aug.: 639-704.   [49]   [*RIS*]

Chapter 36

URBAN ISSUES

BARKER, AUBREY
36.001   GC   1958 Progress, planning and people. *Caribbean* 11(11), June: 251-254.
[35, 66]   [*COL*]

BRAITHWAITE, LLOYD E.
17.003   JM   [1961?] Population, migration and urbanization.

BROOM, LEONARD
36.002   BC   1953 Urban research in the British Caribbean: a prospectus. *Social Econ*
Stud 1(1), Feb.: 113-119.   [*COL*]
36.003   JM   1960 Urbanization and the plural society. *In* RUBIN, VERA, ed. SOCIAL
AND CULTURAL PLURALISM IN THE CARIBBEAN. New York, New York
Academy of Sciences, p.880-891. (Annals of the New York Aca-
demy of Sciences, v. 83, art. 5.) [10]   [*RIS*]

BRYCE, WYATT E., et al.
36.004   JM   1962 HISTORIC PORT ROYAL. Kingston, Tourist Trade Development Board,
80p. [5]   [*SCH*]

COLERIDGE, P. E.
8.010   SR   1958 Vrouwenleven in Paramaribo [Women's life in Paramaribo].

CRANE, ALFRED V.
28.113   BG   1924 The Georgetown sewerage scheme.

CRUICKSHANK, J. GRAHAM
36.005   BG   1918 "King William's people." *Timehri* 3d ser., 5(22), Aug.: 104-119.
[5, 66]   [*AMN*]

CUMPER, GEORGE E.
44.040   JM   1958 Expenditure patterns, Kingston, Jamaica, 1954.

EBERLEIN, HAROLD DONALDSON
35.015   UV   1935 Housing in the Virgin Islands.

GARDNER-MEDWIN, R. J.
36.006   BC   1948 Major problems of town planning in the West Indies. *Car Commn*
Mon Inf B 2(1), Aug.: 15-16, 18. [66]   [*COL*]

HARTOG, JOHAN

36.007   CU/   1947 De voorgenomen uitbreiding van Willemstad op Curacao, Oranjestad
          AR   en St. Nicolaas op Aruba [The contemplated expansion of Willem-
                       stad in Curacao, of Oranjestad and St. Nicolaas in Aruba]. *W I G*
                       28: 42-46.   [35,66]   [*COL*]

HILL, LUKE M.

36.008   BG   1911 Nomenclature of Georgetown: its streets and districts. *Timehri* 3d
                       ser., 1(18A), Jan.: 42-52.   [5,19]   [AMN]
36.009   BG   1915 The municipality of Georgetown. *Timehri* 3d ser., 3(20B), May: 227-
                       235.   [5,66]   [*AMN*]

IMRIE, Sir JOHN

44.117 TR   1958 Report on the finance of the three municipalities and the work-
                       ing of the county councils in Trinidad and Tobago.

KOOL, R.

44.131 SR   1956 Paramaribo; het economische leven van een stad in een tropisch
                       land [Paramaribo; economic life of a town in a tropical land].

KRUIJER, GERARDUS JOHANNES

36.010   SR   1951 Urbanisme in Suriname [Urbanism in Surinam].   *Tijdschr Ned Aar*
                       Genoot 68(1), Jan.: 31-63.   [7,10,66]   [*RIS*]

LIGHTON, G.

36.011   BG   1950 British Guiana. II: Georgetown and its trade. *Geography* 35:228-239.
                                                                                   [*AGS*]

MAUNDER, W. F.

52.056 JM   1954 Development of internal transport in Jamaica.
52.057 JM   1954 Expenditure on internal transport in Jamaica.
52.058 JM   1954 Kingston public passenger transport.

NEWLING, BRUCE E.

36.012   JM   1962 The growth and spatial structure of Kingston, Jamaica. Ph.D.
                       dissertation, Northwestern University, 195p.   [7]

OTTLEY, CARLTON ROBERT

5.155   TR   1962 The story of Port of Spain, capital of Trinidad, West Indies,
                       from the earliest times to the present day.

OUDSCHANS DENTZ, FRED

54.051 SR   1920/ De bauxietnijverheid en de stichting van een nieuwe stad in Suri-
                 21   name [The bauxite industry and the founding of a new city in Suri-
                        nam].

PAGET, HUGH

36 013   JM   1946 The founding of Mandeville. *Jam Hist Rev* 1(2), Dec.: 172-180. [5]
                                                                                   [*COL*]

PAQUETTE, ROMAIN

36.014   MT   1965 An analysis of the concentration and dispersal of settlement in
                       Martinique. M.A. thesis, McGill University, 181p.

ROBERTS, WALTER ADOLPHE, ed.

36.015   JM   1955 THE CAPITALS OF JAMAICA. Kingston, Pioneer Press, 112p. [5]

ROSE, JOHN C. & LEWIS, ANTHONY C.

36.016   SL   1949 REPORT ON THE NEW TOWN PLANNING PROPOSALS; REDEVELOPMENT OF CENTRAL AREA, CASTRIES, ST. LUCIA 1948. Castries, St. Lucia Govt., 31p.   [66]   [*RIS*]

SERTIMA, J. van

36.017   BG   1915 The municipality of New Amsterdam. *Timehri* 3d ser., 3(20B), May: 237-252.   [5,66]   [*AMN*]

66.135   BG   1921 Progress in New Amsterdam.

SHAW, EARL BENNETT

7.075   VI   1935 Population adjustments in our Virgin Islands.

SIMONS, R. D.

36.018   SR   1958 Stad en platteland [The city and the rural areas]. *In* WALLE, J. van de & WIT, H, de, eds. SURINAME IN STROOMLIJNEN. Amsterdam, Wereld Bibliotheek, p.44-58.   [8]

SIMPSON, GEORGE EATON

36.019   JM   1954 Begging in Kingston and Montego Bay. *Social Econ Stud* 3(2), Sept.: 197-211.   [8,20]   [*RIS*]

SMITH, M. G.

9.040   CR   1962 WEST INDIAN FAMILY STRUCTURE.

STEVENS, PETER H. M.

36.020   BC   1957 Planning in the West Indies. *Town Ctry Plann* 25(12), Dec.: 503-508.   [35,66]   [*COL*]

STOCKDALE, Sir FRANK A; GARDNER-MEDWIN, R. & SYLLAS, S. M. de

35.043   BC   1948 Recent planning developments in the colonies.

TEGANI, ULDERICO

3.304   CU   1929 Willemstad di Curacao [Willemstad of Curacao].

YOUNG, ALLAN

36.021   BG   1957 Some milestones in village history. [Georgetown?] British Guiana, British Guiana Village Chairmen's Conference, 22p. (A series of six radio talks.) [5, 37]

YOUNG, J. G.

36.022   JM   1946 Who planned Kingston? *Jam Hist Rev* 1(2), Dec.: 144-153. [5]   [*COL*]

POLITICAL
ISSUES

Chapter 37

POLITICAL INSTITUTIONS AND DEVELOPMENT

ABARBANEL, ALBERT
37.001   JM   1951 Bustamante of Jamaica—promises and pistols. *Reporter* 4(12), June 12: 24-26.   [*COL*]

ABBOTT, GEORGE C.
44.001   BC   1963 The future of economic co-operation in the West Indies in the light of the break-up of the Federation.

ALEXANDER, ROBERT J.
37.002   BG   1955 Communist power cracks in British Guiana. *Int Free Trade Un* 11(10), Oct.: 1p.   [*RIS*]

ALLEYNE, MERVIN C.
37.003   JM   1963 Communication and politics in Jamaica. *Car Stud* 3(2), July: 22-61. [25, 52]   [*RIS*]

ANDIC, FUAT M. & SUPHAN
44.004   FC   1965 Fiscal survey of the French Caribbean.

ANGLIN, DOUGLAS G.
37.004   BC   1961 The political development of the West Indies. *In* LOWENTHAL, DAVID, ed. The West Indies Federation. New York, Columbia University Press, p.35-62. [38]   [*RIS*]

ARCHIBALD, CHARLES H.
37.005   GC   1962 Cold war in the Caribbean. *Venture* 14(10, Nov.: 7-8.   [*COL*]
37.006   TR   1962 Trinidad: crossroads of the Caribbean. *New Commonw* 40(11), Nov.: 689-691.   [*AGS*]

ARDEN-CLARKE, CHARLES
37.007   TR   1958 Report of the Chaguaramas Joint Commission. London, H.M.S.O., 61p. (Colonial no.338.)

ARMSTRONG, W. H. R.
37.008   GC   1960 The Sea Devils of the Caribbean; an account of German U-boat activity in the West Indies during World War II. *J Barb Mus Hist Soc* 28(1), Nov.: 29-48.   [*AMN*]

443

ARNTZ, W.
66.008   SR   1925/Het Suriname vraagstuk [The Surinam problem].
                26

ASPINALL, Sir ALGERNON E.
37.009   BC   1940 British West Indian bases for the U.S.A. *Crown Colon* 10(108),
                Nov.: 491-493.   [*NYP*]
37.010   BC   1940 Constitutional changes in the British West Indies. *J Comp Leg Int
                Law* 3d ser., 22(4), Nov.: 129-135.   [*COL*]
37.011   JM   1941 New chapter in Jamaica's history. *Crown Colon* 11(114), May:
                207-209.

ASSENDERP, ANDRE L. van
37.012   NC   1957 The Netherlands Caribbean: a study in regional autonomy. *In*
                WILGUS, A. CURTIS, ed. THE CARIBBEAN: CONTEMPORARY INTER-
                NATIONAL RELATIONS [papers delivered at the Seventh Conference on
                the Caribbean held at the University of Florida, Dec. 6-8, 1956].
                Gainesville, University of Florida Press, p.69-88. (Publications of
                the School of Inter-American Studies, ser. 1, v. 7.)   [*RIS*]

AUGELLI, JOHN P.
43.002 VI   1955 The British Virgin Islands: a West Indian anomaly.

AYEARST, MORLEY
37.013   BC   1954 A note on some characteristics of West Indian political parties.
                Social Econ Stud 3(2), Sept.: 186-196.   [*RIS*]
37.014   BC   1960 The British West Indies: the search for self-government, New York,
                New York University Press, 258p.   [*RIS*]

BAILEY, SYDNEY D.
37.015   BC   1949 Constitutions of the British Colonies. I: Colonies in the western
                hemisphere. *Parl Aff* 2(2), Spring: 156-174. [38]   [*COL*]
37.016   BC   1950 Constitutions of the British colonies. London, Hansard Society,
                52p. (Hansard Society pamphlet no. 9.)   [*COL*]

BAKER, CECIL SHERMAN
37.017   UV   1935 Looking back at the turbulent Virgins: a Navy retrospect. *U S Navl
                Inst Proc* 61(9), Sept.: 1260-1276.   [*NYP*]

BAKKER, J.
37.018   SR   1928/De betuursregeling van Suriname [The governmental arrangement
                29 of Suriname]. *W I G* 11:313-319. [44]   [*COL*]

BALLYSINGH, MARION C.
33.002 JM   [1961?] Social services in Jamaica.

BARNETT, W. L.
41.028 JM   1951 GANJA.
58.006 JM   1951 NOTES ON JAMAICA RUM.

BARTELS, E.
55.002 GC   1956 Government can help.

BARTLETT, KENNETH A.
37.019   UV   1957 The U.S. Virgin Islands Corporation. *Caribbean* 10(6-7), Jan.-Feb.:
                165-167. [66]   [*COL*]

BEASLEY, CYRIL GEORGE
44.006   BB   1952 A FISCAL SURVEY OF BARBADOS.

BECKFORD, GEORGE
60.006   JM/   1965 Issues in the Windward-Jamaica banana war.
           WW

BECKLES, W. A., comp.
37.020   BB   1937 THE BARBADOS DISTURBANCES (1937); REVIEW—REPRODUCTION OF THE
                EVIDENCE AND REPORT OF THE COMMISSION. [Bridgetown?] Barbados,
                Advocate Co.

BELL, HENRY HESKETH
3.023   DM   [1946?] GLIMPSES OF A GOVERNOR'S LIFE.

BELL, WENDELL
37.021   JM   1960 Images of the United States and the Soviet Union held by Jamaican
                elite groups. *Wld Polit* 12(2), Jan.: 225-248. [8, 20]   [*COL*]
37.022   JM   1962 Equality and attitudes of elites in Jamaica. *In* SINGHAM, A. &
                BRAITHWAITE, L. E., eds. SPECIAL NUMBER [OF *Social Econ Stud*]
                ON THE CONFERENCE ON POLITICAL SOCIOLOGY IN THE BRITISH CARIB-
                BEAN, DEC. 1961. *Social Econ Stud* 11(4), Dec.: 409-432. [8, 20, 44]
                                                                                    [*RIS*]
37.023   JM   1964 JAMAICAN LEADERS: POLITICAL ATTITUDES IN A NEW NATION. Berkeley
                and Los Angeles: University of California Press, 229p. [8, 20, 21]
                                                                                    [*RIS*]

BELL, WENDELL & OXAAL, IVAR
37.024   BC   1964 DECISIONS OF NATIONHOOD: POLITICAL AND SOCIAL DEVELOPMENT IN
                THE BRITISH CARIBBEAN. Denver, University of Denver, 99p. (Mono-
                graph Series in World Affairs.) [20]

BENJAMINS, H. D.
37.025   SR   1920/De grenzen van Surinam [The borders of Surinam]. *W I G* 2:333-350.
                21   [*COL*]

BENNETT, J. HARRY, Jr.
23.006   BB   1951 The S. P. G. and Barbadian politics, 1710-1720.

BERGER, W. Y. Z.
37.026   TR   1942 "Joe" in Trinidad. *Car-W I Mag* 31(9), Sept.: 19-22.   [*NYP*]

BIJLSMA, R.
5.014   SR   1923/De brieven van Gouverneur van Aerssen van Sommelsdijck aan de
                26 Directeuren der Societeit van Surinam uit het jaar 1648 [The letters
                written by Governor van Aerssen van Sommelsdijck to the Director
                of the Society of Surinam in the year 1648].

BIRD, V. C.
50.011   AT   1950 Labour in the Leewards.

BISWAMITRE, C. R.
37.027   SR   1947 Suriname en Linggadjati [Surinam and Linggadjati]. *W I G* 28:
               321-328.   [*COL*]

BLACK, CLINTON VANE de BROSSE
1.004   BG   1955 REPORT ON THE ARCHIVES OF BRITISH GUIANA.

BLANSHARD, PAUL
37.028   GC   1947 DEMOCRACY AND EMPIRE IN THE CARIBBEAN: A CONTEMPORARY REVIEW.
               New York, Macmillan, 379p.   [44]   [*NYP*]

BLANT, ROBERT le
37.029   DS   1947 Les mauvais sujets à la Désirade, 1763-1767 [Undesirable in-
               dividuals in Desirade, 1763-1767]. *Rev Hist Colon* 33:84-95.   [5]
                                                                                          [*NYP*]

BLIN, G.
28.036   FG   1914 L'uncinariose chez les chercheurs d'or et les forcats du Maroni
               [Uncinariasis among the gold prospectors and convicts of Maroni].

BLOOD, Sir HILARY
37.030   BH   1960 British Honduras: land of opportunity. *J Roy Commonw Soc* new
               ser., 3, May-June: 83-86.   [66]   [*AGS*]
37.031   JM   1962 And now—Jamaica. *New Commonw* 40(8), Aug.: 501-504.   [*AGS*]

BOHTLINGK, F. R.
37.032   NC   1954 Les nouveaux rapports politiques entre les Pays-Bas, le Surinam
               et les Antilles Néerlandaises [The new political relations between
               the Netherlands, Surinam, and the Netherlands Antilles]. *Civilisa-
               tions* 4(3): 419-422.   [*COL*]
37.033   NC   1956 Wat moet bij rijkswet worden geregeld? [What should be regulated
               by federal law?]. *Ned Jurbl* May 12:411-415.

BOOS, W. J. & HARRIS, H. A.
50.012   TR   1959 REPORT OF THE COLONY WHITLEY COUNCIL ON THE KING COMMISSION.
               REPORT WITH COMMENTS OF THE CIVIL SERVICE ASSOCIATION ON THE
               LEE REPORT. STRUCTURE AND ORGANIZATION OF THE PUBLIC SERVICE.

BORDEWIJK, H. W. C.
37.034   CU/   1914 HANDELINGEN OVER DE REGLEMENTEN OP HET BELEID DER REGERING IN
          SR   DE KOLONIËN SURINAME EN CURACAO [PROCEEDINGS ON THE REGULATIONS
               GOVERNING THE POLICY OF THE GOVERNMENT IN THE COLONIES OF
               SURINAM AND CURACAO]. The Hague, Nijhoff, 876p.   [*NYP*]

BORNN, ROY W.
33.003   UV   1949 Further extension of social security to Virgin Islands.

BOUCLY, FELIX
37.035   FG   1932 DE LA TRANSPORTATION DES CONDAMNÉS AUX TRAVAUX FORCÉS [ON THE
               TRANSPORT OF SENTENCED CONVICTS]. Paris, Librairie Arthur
               Rousseau, 132p.   [*COL*]

BOUGH, JAMES

37.036   GC   1947 The United Nations and the Caribbean territories. *Car Commn Mon Inf B* 1(5), Dec.: 18-21.   [COL]

BOWSTEAD, WILLIAM, ed.

44.019   BC   [n.d.] THE COMMERCIAL LAWS OF THE WORLD. VOL. 17: BRITISH DOMINIONS. AND PROTECTORATES IN AMERICA.

BOYEA, SAMUEL

37.037   BG   1953 Dent in the crown: leftists win in Guiana. *Nation* 177(10), Sept. 5: 193-194.   [COL]

BOYLE, ANDREW

37.038   BG   1953 Red threat in British Guiana. *America* 90(10), Dec. 5: 261-263.

BRADLEY, C. PAUL

37.039   JM   1960 Mass parties in Jamaica: structure and organization. *Social Econ Stud* 9(4), Dec.: 375-416.   [RIS]

37.040   BG   1961 The party system in British Guiana and the general election of 1961. *Car Stud* 1(3), Oct.: 1-26.   [RIS]

37.041   BG   1963 Party politics in British Guiana. *West Polit Q* 16(2), June: 353-370.   [COL]

BRERETON, ASHTON S.

37.042   BC   1963/West Indian perspective. *Social Scient* 2:16-18. [21]   [RIS]
          64

BROWN, E. ETHELRED

37.043   JM   1937 INJUSTICES IN THE CIVIL SERVICE OF JAMAICA. New York, Jamaica Progressive League of New York, 8p. [50]   [NYP]

BROWN, G. ARTHUR

44.025   JM   1958 Economic development and the private sector.

BROWN, NOEL JOSEPH

37.044   JM   1963 JAMAICA AND THE WEST INDIES FEDERATION: A CASE STUDY ON THE PROBLEMS OF POLITICAL INTEGRATION. Ph.D. dissertation, Yale University, 472p. [38]   [COL]

BROWN, W. J.

37.045   JM   1948 Jamaica boss. *Spectator* 180(6240), Jan. 30: 127-128. [44, 66][NYP]

BRUMMER, A. F. J.

37.046   NC   1932/De titel Excellentie [The title "Excellency"]. *W I G* 14:285-286.
          33   [COL]

BRYAN, C. S.

37.047   GC   1941 Geography and the defense of the Caribbean and the Panama Canal. *Ann Ass Am Geogr* 31(2), June: 83-94.   [AGS]

BUISKOOL, J. A. E.

37.048   SR   1954 DE STAATSINSTELLINGEN VAN SURINAME, IN DE HOOFDZAKEN MEDE VERGELEKEN MET DIE VAN NEDERLAND EN DE NEDERLANDSE ANTILLEN

[THE POLITICAL INSTITUTIONS OF SURINAM, ALSO AS COMPARED WITH THOSE OF THE NETHERLANDS AND THE NETHERLANDS ANTILLES]. The Hague, Nijhoff, 659p.   [NYP]

BURNS, Sir ALAN CUTHBERT
66.022   BC   1949 Weaknesses of British West Indian administration.

BURT, ARTHUR E.
37.049   JM   1962 The first instalment of representative government in Jamaica, 1884. *Social Econ Stud* 11(3), Sept.: 241-259.   [5]   [RIS]

BYLES, G. LOUIS
37.050   JM   1948 The Jamaican experiment. *Parl Aff* 1(2), Spring: 56-69.   [COL]

CABOT, JOHN M.
37.051   GC   1953 Forces for change in the Caribbean. *Dep St B* 29(756), Dec. 21: 855-859.   [COL]

CAIRES, DAVID de
44.030   BG   1963 Regional integration.

CAMP, GEORGE
37.052   BG   1963 The "Georgetown strike"—a lie of the Western press. *Wld Trade Un Mov* 10, Oct.: 10-15.   [50]   [COL]

CAMPBELL, Sir JOCK
37.053   BC   1962 Facing up to facts in the Caribbean. *Chron W I Comm* 77(1373), June: 279-280.   [38]   [NYP]
37.054   BC   1963 The West Indies: can they stand alone? *Int Aff* 39(3), July: 335-344.   [38]   [AGS]

CAMPBELL, ROY B.
37.055   JM   1948 West Indian crisis. *America* 78(24), Mar. 13: 659-660.   [COL]

CAVASSORI, ERMES
37.056   BH   1958 L'Honduras Britannico fra Inghilterra, Guatemala e Messico [British Honduras between England, Guatemala and Mexico]. *Universo* 38(6), Nov.-Dec.: 991-1000.   [AGS]

CAZALET,
37.057   FG   1909 La Guyane et ses bagnes [Guiana and its penal colonies]. *B Soc Geogr Toul* 28:36-42.   [NYP]

CESAIRE, AIME
37.058   NA   1961 Crise dans les Départements d'Outre-Mer ou crise de la départe-mentalisation? [Crisis in the Overseas *Départements*, or crisis of departmentalization?] *Rev Guad* 43, Jan.-Mar.: 52-54.   [RIS]

CHAPMAN, ESTHER
37.059   JM   1945 Political experiment in Jamaica: a promising start. *Crown Colon* 15(166), Sept.: 599-600.   [AGS]
37.060   JM   1946 Jamaican political experiment: machinery at work. *Crown Colon* 16(170), Jan.: 15-16.   [AGS]

CHARLES, HENRI

44.034   GD   1947   La Guadeloupe: un cas d'émancipation coloniale et de rétablissement économique après la guerre [Guadeloupe: a case history of
political emancipation and economic revival after the war].

CHATELAIN, JEAN

37.061   FC   1948   Le statut des nouveaux Départements d'Outre-Mer [The status of
the new overseas territories]. *Rev Jur Polit Un Fr* 2(3), July-
Sept.: 285-316.   [*COL*]

CHILSTONE, E. M.

37.062   BB   1939   Tercentenary of the Barbados House of Assembly—growth of representative government. *W I Comm Circ* 54(1062), June 15: 251-252;
54(1063), June 29: 275-277.   [5]   [*NYP*]

CHISHOLM, HESTER DOROTHY

37.063   LW/   1938   A COLONIAL EVALUATION OF THE BRITISH LEEWARD ISLANDS AND THE
UV   VIRGIN ISLANDS OF THE UNITED STATES. M.A. thesis, Clark University,
73p.   [2]

CHRISTIAN, SYDNEY T.

37.064   LW   1955   Constitutional changes in the Leeward Islands. *New Commonw*
British Caribbean Supplement 30(10), Nov. 14: xiv-xv.   [*AGS*]

CLEMENTI, Sir CECIL

37.065   BG   1937   A CONSTITUTIONAL HISTORY OF BRITISH GUIANA. London, Macmillan,
546p.   [5]   [*NYP*]

COLLINS, B. A. N.

50.019   BG   1964   The civil service of British Guiana in the general strike of 1963.

COLLINS, BERTRAM

37.066   BG   1963   La structure constitutionnelle et administrative de la Guyane
Britannique [The constitutional and administrative structure of
British Guiana]. *Civilisations* 13(3): 294-307.   [*RIS*]

COOK, MERCER

37.067   FA   1940   The literary contribution of the French West Indian. *J Negro Hist*
25(4), Oct.: 520-530.   [22]   [*AMN*]

COORE, DAVID

37.068   JM   [1961?]   Government and the community. *In* CUMPER, GEORGE, ed. REPORT
OF THE CONFERENCE ON SOCIAL DEVELOPMENT IN JAMAICA. Kingston,
Standing Committee on Social Services, p.108-110.   [66]   [*RIS*]

CORNU, HENRI

37.069   FA   1935   UNE EXPÉRIENCE LÉGISLATIVE À LA RÉUNION, À LA MARTINIQUE ET À LA
GUADELOUPE [A LEGISLATIVE EXPERIMENT IN REUNION, MARTINIQUE,
AND GUADELOUPE]. Paris, Editions Domat-Montchrestien, 155p.   [44]
[*NYP*]

COSTA GOMEZ, F. M. da

37.070   NC   1935/   Het amendement-Marchant of art. 94 van de Grondwet van 1917 en
36 de West-Indische staatsdelen [The Marchant-amendment of article

94 of the Constitution of 1917 and the West Indian possessions].
W I G 17:374-386.   [*COL*]

COTTER. C. S.

37.071   JM   1959 Ocho Rios in Jamaican history. *Jam Hist Rev* 3(2), Mar.: 34-38. [5]
                                                                              [*COL*]

COTTER, GRAHAM

37.072   JM   1948 Toward responsible government in Jamaica. *Can Forum* 28(334),
                       Nov.: 177-178; 28(335), Dec.: 202-203.   [*COL*]

COUTINHO, D.

37.073   SR   1924/Schorsing van koloniale verordeningen [Suspension of colonial
                       25 regulations]. *W I G* 6:561-574.   [*COL*]

COX, IDRIS

37.074   BG   1963 Freedom struggle in British Guiana. *Int Aff* 9(10), Oct.: 67-70. [*COL*]

CRAIG, HEWAN

37.075   TR   1952 THE LEGISLATIVE COUNCIL OF TRINIDAD AND TOBAGO. London, Faber
                       & Faber, 195p.   [*RIS*]

CROFT, W. D.; SPRINGER, H. W. & CHRISTOPHERSON, H.S.

51.039   BC   1958 Report of the Trade and Tariffs Commission.

CROWE, HARRY J.

51.040   BC   1920 Canadian-West Indian union.
37.076   BC   1920 Separate West Indian Dominion, or confederation with Canada.
                       Can-W I Mag 8(5), Mar.: 460-461. [51]   [*NYP*]
44.039   BC   1923 Mr. Harry J. Crowe on confederation with the West Indies.
51.041   JM   1925 How Canada-West Indies federation might be achieved.
37.077   JM   1925 The political side of the question. *Can-W I Mag* 13(6), Apr.: 155-
                       157. [44, 51]   [*NYP*]

CUMMINGS, FELIX A.

37.078   BG   1964 British Guiana in transition. *Freedomways* 4(3), Summer: 392-404.
                                                                              [*RIS*]

CUMPER, GEORGE E.

44.046   BB   1962 The differentiation of economic groups in the West Indies.

CUNDALL, FRANK

37.079   BC   1906 POLITICAL AND SOCIAL DISTURBANCES IN THE WEST INDIES: A BRIEF
                       ACCOUNT AND BIBLIOGRAPHY. Published for Institute of Jamaica by
                       the Educational Supply Co., 35p. [5, 8, 16, 44]   [*NYP*]
37.080   JM   1919 Jamaica governors [some items have title: Governors of Jamaica].
                       W I Comm Circ
                       1. Edward Doyley. 34(529), Jan. 9:8; 34(530), Jan. 23:19-20;
                       2. Thomas, Seventh Baron Windsor. 34(544), Aug. 7: 208-210;
                       3. Sir Charles Lyttelton. 34(546), Sept. 4: 245-246;
                       4. Sir Thomas Modyford. 34(553), Dec. 11:333-334; 34(554), Dec.
                           25:351-352;
                  1920   35(555), Jan. 8:6; 35(556), Jan. 22:23;

5. Sir Thomas Lynch. 35(560), Mar. 18:79-80; 35(561), Apr. 1:24; 35(563), Apr. 29:124-125; 35(564), May 13:139-140; 35(566), June 10:171-172;

6. Sir Henry Morgan. 35(579), Dec. 9:378-379; 35(580), Dec. 23: 398-399;

1921   36(581), Jan. 6:13-14; 36(582), Jan. 20:31-32; 36(583), Feb. 3: 53-54; 36(584), Feb. 17:68-69;

7. John, Lord Vaughan. 36(597), Aug. 18:349-350; 36(598), Sept. 1: 368-369; 36(599), Sept. 15:396;

8. Charles, Earl of Carlisle, 36(601), Oct. 13:436-437; 36(602), Oct. 27:458-459; 36(603), Nov. 10:480-481;

1922 9. Sir Hender Molesworth. 37(607), Jan. 5:14-15; 37(608), Jan. 19: 39-40; 37(609), Feb. 2:58-59; 37(610), Feb. 16:81; 37(611), Mar. 2:104;

10. Christopher, Duke of Albemarle. 37(617), May 25:250-251; 37(618), June 8:271-273;

11. Sir Francis Watson, President. 371(624), Aug. 31:404-405; 37(625), Sept. 14:427-428;

12. William, 2nd Earl of Inchiquin. 37(626), Sept. 28:455-456; 37 (627), Oct. 12: 478-479;

13. John White, President. 37(630), Nov. 23: 542-543; 37(631), Dec. 7:570-571; 37(632), Dec. 21:593-594;

1923 14. John Bourden, President. 38(650), Aug. 30:384-385. [5]   [NYP]

37.081	BC	1920	Royal visits to the West Indies. *W I Comm Circ* 35(571), Aug. 19: 241; 35(572), Sept. 2:260-261; 35(573), Sept. 16: 276-277; 35(574), Sept. 30:290; 35(575), Oct. 14:307. [5] [NYP]
37.082	JM	1936	THE GOVERNORS OF JAMAICA IN THE SEVENTEENTH CENTURY. London, West India Committee, 177p. [5] [COL]
37.083	JM	1937	THE GOVERNORS OF JAMAICA IN THE FIRST HALF OF THE EIGHTEENTH CENTURY. London, West India Committee, 229p. [5] [COL]

CURRY, HERBERT FRANKLIN, Jr.

37.084	BH	1956	British Honduras: from public meeting to crown colony. *Americas* 13(1), July: 31-42. [5] [COL]

CURTIN, PHILIP D.

37.085	GC	1955	The United States in the Caribbean. *Curr Hist* 29(172), Dec.: 364-370. [66] [COL]

DaCOSTA, HARVEY & PHILLIPS, F. A.

37.086	BC	1960	A summary of constitutional advances. *Car Q* 6(2-3), May: 230-235. [RIS]

DALLEY, F. W.

50.030	BC	1956	The labour position: the trade unions and the political parties.

DALTON, L. C.

37.087	BG	1912	Abolition of Roman-Dutch law in British Guiana. *Timehri* 3d ser., 2(19A), July: 94-100. [AMN]
37.088	BG	1915	Some controverted points of local law with respect to leases. *Timehri* 3d ser., 3(20B), May: 215-221. [47] [AMN]

37.089   BG   1917 The civil law of British Guiana, with notes and comments. *Timehri*
                3d ser., 4(21), June: 160-243.   [*AMN*]

          DANIEL, GEORGE T.
50.031   BC   1957 Labor and nationalism in the British Caribbean.

          DARBYSHIRE, TAYLOR
37.090   BC   1937 The King in the West Indies. *W I Comm Circ* 52(1008), May 20:
                185-186.   [*NYP*]

          DAVIS, HASSOLDT
3.076   FG   1952 THE JUNGLE AND THE DAMNED.

          DAVSON, Sir EDWARD R.
37.091   BC   1919 Problems of the West Indies. *W I Comm Circ* 34(554), Dec. 25:
                suppl. (7p.) [38, 66]   [*NYP*]

          DEBROT, I. C.
37.092   NC   1960/ Een coördinerende en stimulerende cultuurpolitiek [A coordinating
          61   and stimulating cultural policy]. *N W I G* 40:185-189.   [*COL*]

          DEBROT, N.
37.093   GC   1953 Politieke aspecten in het Caraibische gebied [Political aspects in
                the Caribbean]. *W I G* 34:160-172.   [*COL*]

          DECLAREUIL, JEAN
37.094   FG   1927 LES SYSTÈMES DE TRANSPORTATION ET DE MAIN-D'OEUVRE PÉNALE AUX
                COLONIES DAN LE DROIT FRANCAIS [THE COLONIAL PENAL TRANSPORTA-
                TION AND FORCED LABOR SYSTEMS IN FRENCH LAW]. Toulouse, Impr. J.
                Fournier, 189p. (Ph.D. dissertation, University of Toulouse.)   [5]
                                                                            [*COL*]

          DENCH, MORGAN
37.095   FG   1947 The Devil's island. *Contemp Rev* 172, Oct.: 237-239.   [*COL*]

          Des FORGES, Sir CHARLES & IMRIE, J. D.
37.096   TR   1950 REPORT ON LOCAL GOVERNMENT (FINANCIAL RELATIONSHIPS). [Port of
                Spain?] Trinidad, Govt. Print. Off., 109p. [44]   [*RIS*]

          DESPRES, LEO A.
67.003   BG   1964 The implications of nationalist politics in British Guiana for the
                development of cultural theory.

          DESSARRE, EVE
2.059   JM/   1965 CAUCHEMAR ANTILLAIS [ANTILLES NIGHTMARE].
          TR/
          FA

          DEURE, A. van der
37.097   SR   1919/ Rechtszekerheid van de grondeigendommen in Surinam [Legal security
          20   of the landed properties in Surinam]. *W I G* 1(2): 193-213. [47] [*COL*]

          DIUFEAL, F.
37.098   MT   1960 Kommunisty Martiniki. *Problemy Mira Sots* 2:69.   [*COL*]

          DOMINGO, W. A.
37.099   JM   1938 Jamaica seeks its freedom. *Opportunity* 16(12), Dec.: 370-372. [*COL*]

DUFFUS, J. A. H.

37.100   JM   1963 Conduct of arbitration II—rules of procedure, of evidence, etc., in voluntary and legal arbitrations. *In* EATON, G. E., ed. PROCEEDINGS OF INDUSTRIAL RELATIONS CONFERENCE ON THE THEORY AND PRACTICE OF ARBITRATION, Nov. 1962. Mona, Institute of Social and Economic Research, University of the West Indies, p.67-81. [50]   [*RIS*]

DUFOUGERE, W.

37.101   FG   1921 De l'utilisation rationnelle de la main-d'oeuvre pénale en Guyane. [On the rational use of forced labor in Guiana]. *B Soc Path Exot* 14(5), May: 258-265. [28, 30, 50, 66]   [*ACM*]

DUNCAN, EBENEZER

37.102   BC   1947 THE POLITICAL CONSTITUTION OF THE WESTINDIAN COMMONWEALTH. Kingstown, St. Vincent, Govt. Print. Off., 23p. [38]   [*RIS*]

5.048   SV   1963 A BRIEF HISTORY OF ST. VINCENT WITH STUDIES IN CITIZENSHIP.

EINAAR, J. F. E.

37.103   SR   1934 BIJDRAGE TOT DE KENNIS VAN HET ENGELSCH TUSSCHENBESTUUR VAN SURINAME 1804-1816 [CONTRIBUTION TO KNOWLEDGE ABOUT THE ENGLISH INTERREGNUM IN SURINAM, 1804-1816]. Leiden, Dubbeldeman, 227p. (Ph.D. dissertation, Leiden, 1934.) [5]   [*NYP*]

ELLIS, J. W.; GORSIRA, M. P. & NUYTEN, F. C. J.

37.104   NA   1954 DE ZELFSTANDIGHEID DER EILANDGEBIEDEN [THE INDEPENDENCE OF THE ISLAND TERRITORIES]. Willemstad, Curacao.

EVANS, E. W.

37.105   BC   1954 Constitutional development in the British West Indies. *In* PROCEEDINGS OF THE SYMPOSIUM INTERCOLONIAL, JUNE 27–JULY 3, 1952. Bordeaux, Delmas, p.136-143.   [*RIS*]

37.106   BC   1955 A survey of the present constitutional situation in the British West Indies. *In* DEVELOPMENTS TOWARDS SELF-GOVERNMENT IN THE CARIBBEAN. A symposium held under the auspices of the Netherlands Universities Foundation for International Co-operation at The Hague, Sept. 1954. The Hague, W. van Hoeve, p.23-33.   [*RIS*]

EVANS, HARRY

50.045   BG   1962 Profsoiuzy Britanskoi Gviany na raspute [The trade unions of British Guiana in disarray], [by] Garri Evans.

EVANS, LUTHER HARRIS

5.051   UV   1945 THE VIRGIN ISLANDS: FROM NAVAL BASE TO NEW DEAL.

EVANS, SIR GEOFFREY, et al.

66.046   BG/ BH   1948 REPORT OF THE BRITISH GUIANA AND BRITISH HONDURAS SETTLEMENT COMMISSION.

EVERS, M. A.

37.107   CU   1923/ Een bezoek van den Gouverneur van Curacao aan Venezuela in 1921 24 [A visit of the Governor of Curacao to Venezuela in 1921]. *W I G* 5:318-331.   [*COL*]

FABER, MICHAEL

37.108   JM   1964 A "swing" analysis of the Jamaican election of 1962: a note. *Social Econ Stud* 13(2), June: 302-310.   [*RIS*]

FALLS, CYRIL

37.109   JM   1962 A window on the world: Jamaica moves to independence. *Illus London News* 241(6420), Aug. 18: 240. [44]   [*RIS*]

FARLEY, RAWLE

44.058   BG   1955 The economic circumstances of the British annexation of British Guiana, 1795-1815).

37.110   BG   1955 The unification of British Guiana. *Social Econ Stud* 4(2), June: 168-183. [5]   [*RIS*]

49.022   BC   1958 NATIONALISM AND INDUSTRIAL DEVELOPMENT IN THE BRITISH CARIBBEAN.

50.049   BC   1958 TRADE UNIONS AND POLITICS IN THE BRITISH CARIBBEAN.

44.059   BG   1962 Kaldor's budget in retrospect: reason and unreason in a developing area: reflections on the 1962 budget in British Guiana.

FARLEY, RAWLE & HUGHES, COLIN

37.111   BG   1952 El Dorado's new constitution. *Venture* 3(12), Jan.: 9.   [*COL*]

FAUVEL, LUC

37.112   FA   1955 Les conséquences économiques et sociales de l'assimilation adminis-trative des Antilles Francaises [The economic and social conse-quences of the political assimilation of the French Antilles]. *In* DEVELOPMENTS TOWARDS SELF-GOVERNMENT IN THE CARIBBEAN. A sym-posium held under the auspices of the Netherlands Universities Foundation for International Co-operation at The Hague, Sept. 1954. The Hague, W. van Hoeve, p.176-200. [33, 44, 46, 66]   [*RIS*]

FELHOEN KRAAL, JOHANNA L. G.

37.113   NA   1954 Notices sur les principes d'aministration des Antilles Néerland-aises et leur relation avec la situation économique et sociale [Notes on the administrative regulations of the Dutch Antilles and their relationship to the socio-economic situation]. *In* PROCEEDINGS OF THE SYMPOSIUM INTERCOLONIAL, JUNE 27-JULY 3, 1952. Bordeaux, Impr. Delmas, p.159-166.   [*RIS*]

FERDINAND. PRINCE EDGAR

37.114   TR   1964 CITIZENSHIP FOR TRINIDAD AND TOBAGO. Port of Spain, PNM Pub. Co., 182p.

FERNANDES, A. S. J.

37.115   SR   1925/Ministerieele bedreiging van de onafhankelijkheid van het opperste
          26 gerechtshof van Suriname [Ministerial threat to the independence of the highest court of justice of Surinam]. *W I G* 7:207-288.   [*COL*]

44.060   SR   1925/De Surinaamsche begrooting voor 1925 in de Staten-Generaal [The
          26 budget of Surinam for 1925 before the States-General].

FISHER, RUTH ANNA

15.015   JM   1943 Note on Jamaica.

FOOT, Sir HUGH

37.116   JM   1964 A START IN FREEDOM. London, Hodder and Stoughton, p.113-142.

FOX, ANNETTE BAKER

33.008   GC   1949 FREEDOM AND WELFARE IN THE CARIBBEAN: A COLONIAL DILEMMA.

FREITAS, G. V. de

37.117   BG   1961 British Guiana clears the decks. *New Commonw* 39(1), Jan.: 15-16. [66]   [AGS]

FREITAS, Q. B. de

37.118   BG   1941 Notes on the trial of a nurse-midwife on the charge of murder held in the Criminal Court of Georgetown, Demarara, from 22nd April to 5th May, 1941. *Car Med J* 3(2): 120-126. [28]   [COL]

GAAY FORTMAN, B. de

37.119   CU   1919 De rechtsbedeling op onze Bovenwindse Eilanden en de herziening van de rechterlijke macht en van de rechtspleging in de kolonie Curacao [The administration of justice in our Windward Islands and the revision of judiciary powers and of the judicature in the colony of Curacao]. *W I G* 1(1):85-101.   [COL]

37.120   NA   1920/ Vreendelingen [Foreigners]. *W I G* 2:315-321.   [COL]
          21

37.121   CU   1921/ Nog een staatsrechterlijke kwestie [Another constitutional-legal problem]. *W I G* 3:637-640.   [COL]
          22

37.122   NA   1921/ Een staatsrechterlijk vraagstuk [A constitutional problem]. *W I G* 3:337-341.   [COL]
          22

37.123   CU   1922/ Over de bestuursinrichting van Curacao [On the organization of the government of Curacao]. *W I G* 4:289-304, 533-551 (1922/23); 5:535-560 (1923/24); 6:385-404 (1924/25).   [COL]
          25

5.056   CU   1924/ Een bladzijde uit de geschiedenis van Curacao [A page from the history of Curacao].
          25

37.124   CU   1925/ Een aanvulling van Bordewijks ontstaan en ontwikkeling van het staatsrecht van Curacao [An addition to Bordewijk's origin and development of the constitutional law of Curacao]. *W I G* 7:505-506.   [COL]
          26

37.125   CU   1926/ De oprichting der Curacaosche shutterij [The establishment of the citizen-soldiery in Curacao]. *W I G* 8:97-118.   [COL]
          27

44.073   CU   1928/ De Curacaosche begrooting voor 1929: over den politieken toestand van Curacao [The budget of Curacao for the year 1929: about the political situation of Curacao].
          29

5.058   SR   1928/ In Suriname vóór honderd jaar [In Surinam a hundred years ago].
          29

6.015   SR   1930/ Suriname op den drempel van de afschaffing der slavernij [Surinam on the threshold of the abolition of slavery].
          31

37.126   CU   1933/ Vrijheid van drukpers en recht van vergadering [Freedom of the press and the right of assembly]. *W I G* 15:241-251. [52]   [COL]
          34

37.127   CU   1934/ Staatkundige geschiedenis van Curacao [Political history of Curacao]. *W I G* 16:209-221. [5]   [COL]
          35

44.081   CU   1935/ Staatkundige geschiedenis van Curacao: de Curacaosche begrooting voor 1935 [Political history of Curacao: the budget of Curacao for the year 1935].
          36

44.082   CU   1936/ Staatkundige geschiedenis van Curacao: de Curacaosche begrooting
                  37   voor 1936 [Political history of Curacao: the budget of Curacao for
                        the year 1936].

44.083   CU   1937 Staatkundige geschiedenis van Curacao: de Curacaosche begrooting
                        voor 1937 [Political history of Curacao: the budget of Curacao for
                        the year 1937].

44.084   CU   1938 Economische en sociale vraagstukken in Curacao [Economic and
                        social problems in Curacao].

44.085   CU   1938 Staatkundige geschiedenis van Curacao: de Curacaosche begrooting
                        voor 1938 [Political history of Curacao: the budget of Curacao for
                        the year 1938].

37.128   CU   1939 Het Plan-Jas [The proposed plan of Jas]. W I G 21:173-178.   [COL]
44.086   CU   1939 Staatkundige geschiedenis van Curacao: de Curacaosche begrooting
                        van 1939 [Political history of Curacao: the budget of Curacao for
                        the year 1939].

44.087   CU   1940 Staatkundige geschiedenis van Curacao: de Curacaosche begrooting
                        voor 1940 [Political history of Curacao: the budget of Curacao for
                        the year 1940].

37.129   CU   1942 Aanvulling van de Encyclopaedie van Nederlandsch West-Indië:
                        Bestuursregeling van Curacao [Addition to the Encyclopedia of the
                        Netherlands West Indies: Government rule of Curacao]. W I G 24:
                        214-226.   [COL]

37.130   CU   1943 Aanvulling van de Encyclopaedie van Nederlandsch West-Indië:
                        De gouverneurs van Curacao [Addition to the Encyclopedia of the
                        Netherlands West Indies: The governors of Curacao]. W I G 25:
                        380-382. [5]   [COL]

37.131   CU   1946 Politieke beschouwingen over Curacao [Political observations about
                        Curacao]. W I G 27:257-279.   [COL]

37.132   CU   1947 SCHETS VAN DE POLITIEKE GESCHIEDENIS DER NEDERLANDSCHE ANTILLEN
                        IN DE TWINTIGSTE EEUW (CURACAO) [SKETCH OF THE POLITICAL HISTORY
                        OF THE NETHERLANDS ANTILLES IN THE TWENTIETH CENTURY (CURACAO)].
                        The Hague, W. van Hoeve, 71p. [5]   [RIS]

37.133   CU   1948 Een half jaar politiek [Half a year of politics]. W I G 29:257-272.
                                                                                   [COL]

37.134   NA   1949 De ontwikkeling van den politieken toestand op de Nederlandse
                        Antillen [The development of the political situation of the Nether-
                        lands Antilles]. W I G 30:237-243.   [COL]

37.135   NA   1949 De verkiezingen in de Nederlandse Antillen [The elections in the
                        Netherlands Antilles]. W I G 30:129-135.   [COL]

7.023   NA   1959 Toelating, verblijf, vestiging, en uitzetting in de Nederlandse
                        Antillen [Admission, residence, settlement and expulsion in the
                        Netherlands Antilles].

          GAMMANS, L. D.
37.136   JM   1947 Self-governing Jamaica. Spectator 178(6189), Feb. 7:169-170.   [66]
                                                                                   [NYP]

          GARCON, MAURICE
37.137   FG   1933 Apropos de la Guyane [Concerning Guiana]. Edn Hebd J Deb 40
                        (2067), Oct. 6: 539-541.   [COL]

          GETROUW, C. F. G.
37.138   SR   1946 Suriname en de oorlog [Surinam and the War]. WIG 27:129-136. [44]
                                                                                   [COL]

GILES, WALTER I.

37.139   JM   1956 JAMAICA: A STUDY OF BRITISH COLONIAL POLICY AND THE DEVELOPMENT OF SELF-GOVERNMENT. Ph.D. dissertation, Georgetown University, 2v. (703p.) [38]

GLASS, RUTH

21.007   JM   1962 Ashes of discontent.

GLUSA, RUDOLF

37.140   GC   1962 ZUR POLITISCHEN GEOGRAPHIE WESTINDIENS [ON THE POLITICAL GEOGRAPHY OF THE WEST INDIES]. Münster, Max Kramer, 134p. (Ph.D. dissertation, Westfälischen Wilhelms-Universität zu Münster, 1962). [43]   [AGS]

GOCKING, C. V.

37.141   JM   1960 Early constitutional history of Jamaica (with special reference to the period 1838-1866). *Car Q* 6(2-3), May: 114-133. [5]   [RIS]

GODFREY, J. E.

28.231   BG   1904 A few introductory remarks on the regulations passed by the recent Quarantine Conference.

37.142   BG   1912 Village administration and local government in British Guiana. *Timehri* 3d ser., 2(19B), Dec.: 337-356. [5, 8]   [AMN]

GOLDBERG, J. & SUTHERLAND, E. S.

28.234   JM   1963 Studies on Gonorrhoea.

GOODE, RICHARD

44.090   JM   1956 Taxation and economic development in Jamaica.

GORDON, WILLIAM E.

37.143   JM   1939 Jamaicans strive for dominion status. *Crown Colon* 9(91), June: 361. [38]   [NYP]

37.144   JM   1939 A new constitution for Jamaica. *United Emp* new ser., 30(9), Sept.: 1007-1010.

37.145   JM   1942 Jamaica rejects a constitution. *Contemp Rev* 161(913), Jan.: 51-54.   [NYP]

37.146   JM   1955 Socialist planning for Jamaica. *Contemp Rev* 188(1079), Nov.: 326-329.   [COL]

44.093   JM   1957 Imperial policy decisions in the economic history of Jamaica, 1664-1934.

37.147   JM   1963 Jamaica: from colony to state. *Contemp Rev* 203, Apr.: 187-191.   [COL]

GORKOM, J. A. J. van

37.148   NC   1955 Partnership in a kingdom. *Caribbean* 8(7), Feb.: 130-133, 151-152.   [COL]

GOSLINGA, C. CH.

23.058   GC   1956 Kerk, kroon en Cariben [Church, crown and Caribs].

GRAFF, EDWARD de

37.149   BG   1962 Cheddi Jagan y el futuro de la Guayana Británica [Cheddi Jagan and the future of British Guiana]. *Cuadernos* 57, Feb.: 83-86.   [COL]

GRANT, C. H.
66.057   BG   1965 The politics of community development in British Guiana 1954-57.

GRATIANT, GILBERT
37.150   MT   1961 ILE FÉDÉRÉE FRANCAISE DE LA MARTINIQUE [THE FEDERATED FRENCH ISLAND OF MARTINIQUE]. Paris, Louis Soulanges, 110p.   [*NYP*]

GREENWOOD, THOMAS
50.054   BC   1921 East Indian emigration: the Indian government's policy.

GREENWOOD-BARTON, L. H.
30.031   JM   1957 The establishment and administration of food standards in Jamaica.

GREINER, F.
37.151   SR   1920/ Suriname en de oorzaken van de achterlijkheid dezer Nederlandsche
                            21 kolonie [Surinam and the causes for the backwardness of this Dutch
                            colony]. *W I G* 2:285-310.   [*COL*]

GRIFFITH, J. A. G.
18.022   BC   1960 Legal aspects of immigration.

GRIMBLE, JUNE A.
50.055   JM   1951 The Jamaica story.

GROOT, SILVIA W. de
14.004   SR   1963 VAN ISOLATIE NAAR INTEGRATIE: DE SURINAAMSE MARRONS EN HUN
                            AFSTAMMELINGEN OFFICIELE DOCUMENTEN BETREFFENDE DE DJOEKA'S
                            (1845-1863).[FROM ISOLATION TO INTEGRATION: THE SURINAM MAROONS
                            AND THEIR DESCENDANTS, OFFICIAL DOCUMENTS CONCERNING THE DJUKA
                            TRIBE (1845-1863)].

HAACK, OLAF
37.152   UV   1916 Dansk-vestindisk straffelovgivning [Danish-West Indian penal law].
                            Nord Tidsskr Straf 4, Jan.: 19-26.

HALLEMA, A.
37.153   CU   1934/ Eenige gegevens over oude gevangenissen, aard der gevangenisstraf,
                            35 etc. op Curacao gedurende de 17de en 18de eeuw [Some data about
                            old prisons, nature of imprisonment, etc. on Curacao during the
                            17th and 18th centuries]. *W I G* 16:192-204. [5]   [*COL*]
37.154   SR/   1934/ Het jaar 1872 in de geschiedenis van het gevangeniswezen in de
               CU   35 West [The year 1872 in the history of the prison-system in the West].
                            W I G 16:33-47, 49-64. [5, 33]   [*COL*]

HALLETT, HUGH et al.
37.155   BG   1960 REPORT OF THE BRITISH GUIANA ELECTORAL BOUNDARIES COMMISSION,
                            1960. Georgetown, Lithographic Co., printers to the Govt. of
                            British Guiana, 63p.   [*RIS*]

HALPERIN, ERNST
37.156   BG   1965 Racism and Communism in British Guiana. *J Inter-Amer Stud* 7(1),
                            Jan.: 95-134. [16]

HAMILTON, BRUCE

37.157   BB   1944 The Barbados Executive Committee: an experiment in government. *J Barb Mus Hist Soc* 11(3), May: 115-131. [5]   *[AMN]*

HAMMOND, S. A.

50.056   BB/   1952 REPORT ON AN ENQUIRY INTO THE ORGANIZATION AND SALARIES OF THE
        LW/   CIVIL SERVICE. PART 1: GENERAL.
        BV

HARLOW, VINCENT TODD

37.158   BG   1951 British Guiana and British colonial policy. *United Emp* 42(6), Nov.-Dec.: 305-309. [66]   *[RIS]*

HARPER-SMITH, JAMES W.

37.159   BG   1965 The Colonial Stock Acts and the British Guiana Constitution of 1891. *Social Econ Stud* 14(3), Sept.: 252-263. [44]   *[RIS]*

HARRIS, BRITTON

49.034   GC   1953 The role of government in industrial development in the Caribbean.

HARRIS, COLERIDGE

37.160   WW   1960 The constitutional history of the Windwards. *Car Q* 6(2-3), May: 160-176. [5]   *[RIS]*

HARTOG, JOHAN

37.161   CU   1946 Oud rechtsgebruik op Curacao herleefd: een voortvluchtige militair ingedaagd [Old legal custom on Curacao revived: a runaway soldier summoned]. *W I G* 27:137-138.   *[COL]*

HATCH, JOHN

37.162   BG   1958 Delicate balance in British Guiana. *New Stsm* 55(1407), Mar. 1: 258-260.   *[COL]*

HAYWOOD, E. J.

37.163   BG   1945 The British Guiana Regiment. *Emp Dig* 2(5), Feb.: 29-32.   *[NYP]*

HAZLEWOOD, ARTHUR

44.100   JM   1956 The Hicks Report on finance and taxation in Jamaica: a comment.

HEEMSTRA, J.

15.018   SR   1952/ De Indonesiërs in Suriname [The Indonesians in Surinam].
            53

HEIDLER, J. B.

5.082   JM   1929 The Jamaica insurrection and English men of letters.

HELSDINGEN, W. H. van

37.164   NA   1951 De zelstandigheid der eilandgebieden in de Nederlandse Antillen [The independence of the islands of the Netherlands Antilles]. *W I G* 32:193-205.   *[RIS]*

37.165   AR   1954 Aruba en de separacion [Aruba's wish to secede]. *W I G* 35(3), Oct.: 113-133.   *[RIS]*

37.166   NA   1954 Voorlopige balans over de uitvoering van de Eilandenregeling
                     Nederlandse Antillen [Preliminary assessment of the application
                     of the Netherlands Antilles Islands regulation]. *W I G* 35(1-2), Oct.:
                     72-90. [44]   [*RIS*]

37.167   NC   1955 Het Statuut voor het Koninkrijk der Nederlanden [The Statute for
                     the Kingdom of the Netherlands]. *W I G* 35:182-191.   [*COL*]

37.168   NA   1955 Voorlopige balans over de uitvoering van de Eilandenregeling
                     Nederlandse Antillen [Preliminary assessment of the application
                     of the Netherlands Antilles Islands regulation].   *W I G* 35:72-89.
                                                                              [*COL*]

37.169   NC   1956 De wetgeving betreffende Koninkrijksaangelegenheden in 1955 [The
                     legislation regarding the affairs of the Kingdom in 1955]. *Ned Jurbl*
                     Apr. 21: 334-342.   [*RIS*]

HENFREY, COLIN
37.170   BG   1961 The Amerindians of British Guiana. *Venture* 13(9), Oct.: 8-9. [13]
                                                                              [*COL*]

HENRI, EDMOND
37.171   FG   1912 Etude critique de la transportation en Guyane Francaise.
                     Réformes realisables [Critical study of transportation in
                     French Guiana. Workable improvements]. Paris, Librairie de la
                     Société du recueil Sirey, 220p. (Ph.D. dissertation, University of
                     Paris, 1912.)   [*COL*]

HERMANS, HANS G.
37.172   NC   1955 A queen calls. *Caribbean*. 9(3), Oct.: 59-61.   [*COL*]
37.173   NC   1958 Constitutional development of the Netherlands Antilles and Surinam.
                     In WILGUS, A. CURTIS, ed. The Caribbean: British, Dutch,
                     French, United States [papers delivered at the Eighth Conference
                     on the Caribbean held at the University of Florida, Dec. 5-7, 1957].
                     Gainesville, University of Florida Press, p.53-72. (Publications of
                     the School of Inter-American Studies, ser. 1, v. 8.) [5]   [*RIS*]

HEWITT, J. M.
37.174   BB   [1954] Ten years of constitutional development in Barbados. Bridge-
                     town, Barbados, Cole's Printery, 41p.
31.035   JM   1963 The attitudes of courts towards young offenders: the juvenile
                     courts in Jamaica.

HICKS, JOHN R. & URSULA K.
44.101   JM   1955 Report on finance and taxation in Jamaica.

HIGDON, E. K.
37.175   JM   1943 Democracy gains in the Caribbean. *Chr Cent* 60(43), Oct. 27: 1237,
                     1240.   [*COL*]

HIGHAM, C. S. S.
37.176   LW/   1926 The General Assembly of the Leeward Islands. *Engl Hist Rev* 41
         GR   (162), Apr.: 190-209; 41(163), July: 366-388. [5]   [*COL*]
37.177   BC   1926 Sir Henry Taylor and the establishment of crown colony government
                     in the West Indies. *Scott Hist Rev* 23(90), Jan.: 92-96. [5]   [*COL*]

HILL, L. C.

| 37.178 | JM | 1943 REPORT ON THE REFORM OF LOCAL GOVERNMENT IN JAMAICA. Kingston, Govt. Printer, 49p. [66] [NYP] |

37.178 JM 1943 REPORT ON THE REFORM OF LOCAL GOVERNMENT IN JAMAICA. Kingston, Govt. Printer, 49p. [66] [NYP]

37.179 JM 1945 Jamaica gets reform program. *Natn Munic Rev* 34(3), Mar.: 116-121. [66] [NYP]

HINDEN, RITA

44.102 JM 1941 Jamaican paradox.

37.180 BG 1954 The case of British Guiana. *Encounter* 2, Jan.: 18-22) [COL]

HOARE, SAMUEL

37.181 BH 1921 The problem of crown colony government in the Caribbean. *Nineteenth Cent After* 89(530), Apr.: 606-616. [66] [TCL]

HOLMES, Sir MAURICE, et al.

37.182 BC 1949 REPORT OF THE COMMISSION ON THE UNIFICATION OF THE PUBLIC SERVICES IN THE BRITISH CARIBBEAN AREA 1948-49. London, H.M.S.O., 75p. (Colonial no. 254.) [COL]

HOLSTEIN, CASPER

66.064 UV 1925 The Virgin Islands.

66.065 UV 1926 The Virgin Islands: past and present.

HOWIE, H. R.

44.106 BG 1945 REPORT ON INCOME TAX IN BRITISH GUIANA.

HOYOS, F. A.

37.183 BB [1947?] THE STORY OF THE PROGRESSIVE MOVEMENT: ACHIEVEMENTS OF A DECADE. [Bridgetown?] Barbados, Beacon Printery.

37.184 BB [196-?] THE ROAD TO RESPONSIBLE GOVERNMENT. [Bridgetown?] Barbados, Letchworth Press, 104p.

37.185 BC 1963 THE RISE OF WEST INDIAN DEMOCRACY: THE LIFE AND TIMES OF SIR GRANTLEY ADAMS. [Bridgetown?] Barbados, Advocate Press, 228p. [38, 50] [RIS]

HUCK, SUSAN L. M.

66.066 BH 1962 BRITISH HONDURAS: AN EVALUATION.

HUGGINS, H. D., ed.

44.110 BC 1958 [PROCEEDINGS OF THE] STUDY CONFERENCE ON ECONOMIC DEVELOPMENT IN UNDERDEVELOPED COUNTRIES [held at the University College of the West Indies, Aug. 5-15, 1957].

HUGHES, COLIN A.

37.186 BC 1953 Semi-responsible government in the British West Indies. *Polit Sci Q* 68(3), Sept.: 338-353. [COL]

37.187 JM 1955 Adult suffrage in Jamaica, 1944-1955. *Parl Aff* 8(3), Summer: 344-352. [COL]

37.188 BC 1955 Power and responsibility: a sociological analysis of the political situation in the British West Indies. *In* DEVELOPMENTS TOWARDS SELF-GOVERNMENT IN THE CARIBBEAN. A symposium held under the auspices of the Netherlands Universities Foundation for International Co-operation at The Hague, Sept. 1954. The Hague, W. van Hoeve, p.95-111. [RIS]

HULL, CHARLES H.
44.113   BC   1900 Finances in the British West Indies.

HULLU, J. de
37.189   NC   1922/ Memorie van den Amerikaanschen Raad over de Hollandsche be-
23   zittingen in West-Indie in Juli 1806 [Memorandum of the American
Council about the Dutch possessions in the West Indies in July
1806]. *W I G* 4:387-400. [5]   [*COL*]

HUMPHREYS, ROBERT ARTHUR
37.190   BH   1948 The Anglo-Guatemalan dispute. *Int Aff* 24(3), July: 387-404. [5]
[*AGS*]
37.191   BH   1961 THE DIPLOMATIC HISTORY OF BRITISH HONDURAS, 1638-1901. London,
Oxford University Press, 196p. [5]   [*RIS*]

HURWITZ, SAMUEL J. & EDITH
15.020   JM   1965 The New World sets an example for the old: the Jews of Jamaica
and political rights 1661-1831.

HUTCHINSON, LIONEL CAMPBELL
37.192   BB   1951 BEHIND THE MACE: AN INTRODUCTION TO THE BARBADOS HOUSE OF AS-
SEMBLY. Bridgetown, Advocate Co., 47p.

HUURMAN, D.
37.193   GC   1947 Nederland tezamen met Groot-Brittannie, de Vereenigde Staten van
Noord Amerika en Frankrijk in West-Indie [The Netherlands together
with Great Britain, the USA and France in the West Indies]. *W I G*
28:47-57.   [*COL*]
37.194   NC   1948 Britse federatieve voorstellen en Nederlandse federatiemogelijkheden
in West Indië [British federation proposals and Dutch federation
possibilities in the West Indies]. *W I G* 29:33-47. [38]   [*COL*]

HYDE, DOUGLAS
37.195   BG   1962 Communism in Guiana. *Commonweal* 75(19), Feb. 2: 487-489. [*COL*]

IBENE, HEGESIPPE
37.196   GD   1962 Svoboda i nezavisimost-nasha zavetnaia tsel [Freedom and independence—our sworn goal]. [By] Ezhezipp Ibene. *Partijn Zhizn*
12:65-68.   [*COL*]

IFILL, MAX B.
37.197   TR   1964 The Solomon affair: a tale of immorality in Trinidad. [Port of
Spain?] People's Democratic Society, 20p. (Citizens' series no. 1.)
[*RIS*]

IMRIE, Sir JOHN
44.117   TR   1958 REPORT ON THE FINANCE OF THE THREE MUNICIPALITIES AND THE WORK-
ING OF THE COUNTY COUNCILS IN TRINIDAD AND TOBAGO.

INGRAMS, HAROLD
37.198   BG/   1954 Our American colonies—what next? *New Commonw* 27(13), June 24:
BH   645-647.   [*AGS*]

JACOBS, H. P.

37.199   BC   1957 Centralisation and separatism in the Antilles. *W I Rev* new ser., 2(10), Oct.: 33-38.   [*NYP*]

JAGAN, CHEDDI

37.200   BG   1954 FORBIDDEN FREEDOM. New York, International Publishers, 96p. [*RIS*]

37.201   BG   1961 TOWARDS UNDERSTANDING. Washington, D.C., National Press Club, 7p.   [*RIS*]

37.202   BG   1962 Socialism and democracy. *Mon Rev* 13(10), Feb.: 461-466.   [*NYP*]

44.121   BG   1964 THE ANATOMY OF POVERTY IN BRITISH GUIANA.

37.203   BG   1964 Let it not be said that we have failed. *Mon Rev* 15(11), Mar.: 612-615. [44]   [*NYP*]

JAGAN, JANET

37.204   BG   1962 What happened in British Guiana? *Mon Rev* 13(12), Aug.: 559-567.   [*COL*]

JAMES, CYRIL LIONEL ROBERT

37.205   BC   1933 THE CASE FOR WEST INDIAN SELF-GOVERNMENT. London, Leonard & Virginia Woolf at the Hogarth Press, 32p.   [*NYP*]

37.206   TR   1962 PARTY POLITICS IN THE WEST INDIES. San Juan, Trinidad, Vedic Enterprises, 175p.   [*RIS*]

37.207   GC   1964 Parties, politics and economics in the Caribbean. *Freedomways* 4(3), Summer: 312-318.   [*RIS*]

JAMES, ERIC GEORGE

37.208   JM   1956 ADMINISTRATIVE INSTITUTIONS AND SOCIAL CHANGE IN JAMAICA, BRITISH WEST INDIES—A STUDY IN CULTURAL ADAPTATION. Ph.D. dissertation, New York University, 638p. [8, 19, 66]   [*COL*]

JAYAWARDENA, CHANDRA

8.033   BG   1963 CONFLICT AND SOLIDARITY IN A GUIANESE PLANTATION.

JOHNSON, HARRY G.; DEMAS, WILLIAM G.; MEIER, GERALD M. & BALOGH, T.

51.073   BC   1960 Symposium on the Report of the Trade and Tariffs Commission.

JONES, CHESTER LLOYD

66.074   GC   1931 CARIBBEAN BACKGROUNDS AND PROSPECTS.

JOSEPH, FRANZ M. & KOPPEL, RICHARD U.

44.122   CU   1961 Curacao organizations.

JUDAH, GEORGE FORTUNATUS

15.022   JM   1909 The Jews' tribute in Jamaica.

JUNKER, L.

14.012   SR   1932/ Het einde van een dynastie—de dood van Jankosoe [The end of a
                   33   dynasty—the death of Jankosoe].

14.013   SR   1932/ Een Staat in den Staat [A State within the State].
                   33

37.209   SR   1947 De benoeming van een grootopperhoofd der Boschnegers [The appointment of a headman of the Bush Negroes]. *W I G* 28:107-118. [14]   [*COL*]

KALFF, S.

37.210   NC   1927/Vreemdelingen in het Westindische leger [Foreigners in the West-
                28 Indian army]. *W I G* 9:161-179. [5, 16]   [*COL*]

37.211   CU   1931/Curacaosche troebelen [Troubles of Curacao]. *W I G* 13:80-94. [5]
                32   [*COL*]

KASTEEL, ANNEMARIE C. T.

37.212   NA   1956 DE STAATKUNDIGE ONTWIKKELING DER NEDERLANDSE ANTILLEN [THE
                POLITICAL EVOLUTION OF THE NETHERLANDS ANTILLES]. The Hague,
                W. van Hoeve, 351p. (Ph.D. dissertation, Rijksuniversiteit te
                Leiden.) [5]   [*COL*]

KASTELEYN, J. S. C. & KLUVERS, B. J.

44.124   SR   1919/Resumé van het rapport (1919) der studie-commissie van het Sur-
                20 naamse studie-syndicaat [Resumé of the report (1919) of the study
                committee of the Surinam study syndicate].

KELLY, JAMES B.

37.213   JM   1963 The Jamaican independence constitution of 1962. *Car Stud* 3(1),
                Apr.: 18-83.   [*RIS*]

KELSICK, CECIL A.

37.214   LW   1960 Constitutional history of the Leewards. *Car Q* 6(2-3), May: 177-209.
                [5]   [*RIS*]

KESLER, C. K.

37.215   SR   1930/Déporté's in Suriname tijdens het bewind van den Gouverneur
                31 Friderici [Deportees in Surinam during the rule of Governor Friderici].
                W I G 12:558-572.   [*COL*]

KLERK, CORNELIS JOHANNES MARIA de

50.074   SR   1953 DE IMMIGRATIE DER HINDOESTANEN IN SURINAME [THE IMMIGRATION OF
                HINDUS TO SURINAM].

KNAPPERT, L.

23.089   SM   1928/ Een heksenproces op Sint Maarten [A witch trial on St. Maarten].
                29

KNIGHT, RUDOLPH H.

37.216   BC   1960 La planificación y la política en el Caribe Británico [Economic
                planning and politics in the British West Indies]. *Revta Cienc Social*
                4(1), Mar.: 193-213. [66]

KNOX, A. D.

49.046   JM   1956 Note on pioneer industry legislation.

KNOX, GRAHAM

37.217   JM   1963 British colonial policy and the problems of establishing a free
                society in Jamaica, 1838-1865. *Car Stud* 2(4), Jan.: 3-13. [5, 8, 16]
                                                                                    [*RIS*]

KOL, H. van

37.218   SR   1919 De Koloniale Staten [The Colonial Council]. *W I G* 1(1): 5-23. [*COL*]

KOVROV, IU.

44.132   BG   1954   Proizvol angliiskikh kolonizatorov v Britanskoi Gviane [The tyranny of English colonialists in British Guiana].

KRARUP-NIELSON, A.

37.219   FG   1935   HELL BEYOND THE SEAS. London, John Lane, 259p.   [*NYP*]

LAFOND, GEORGES

37.220   BG   1954   La Guyane et Monroe [(French) Guiana and Monroe]. *Hommes Mondes* 9, Feb.: 377-388.   [*COL*]

LAGROSILLIERE, J.

37.221   MT   1903   LA QUESTION DE LA MARTINIQUE [THE QUESTION OF MARTINIQUE]. Paris, Editions du Mouvement socialiste.

LAING, MALCOLM B.

37.222   BG   [1950?]   Local government in British Guiana. *Car Q* 1(4): 35-37.

LASHLEY, L. A. G. O.

37.223   SR   1954/ Het Koninkrijk is dood, leve het Koninkrijk [The Kingdom is dead, 55   long live the Kingdom]. *Vox Guy* 1(4-5), Nov.-Jan.: 12-16.   [5, 10]

LAVIGNE, PIERRE

50.081   FC   1953   La législation industrielle dans les départements francais de la Caraïbe [Industrial legislation in the French territories of the Caribbean].

LAYNE, FREDERICK, et al.

33.020   BB   1964   A PLAN FOR THE IMPLEMENTATION AND ADMINISTRATION OF THE PROPOSED SOCIAL SECURITY SCHEME FOR BARBADOS.

LEBORGNE, YVON

21.011   FA   1962   Le climat social [The social environment].

LEDLIE, J. C.

37.224   BG   1917   Roman-Dutch law in British Guiana and a West Indian court of appeal. *J Soc Comp Leg* 17, Nov.: 210-222.

LEE, ULRIC

33.021   TR   1959   REPORT TO THE HONOURABLE THE PREMIER BY THE HONOURABLE ULRIC LEE ON THE REORGANISATION OF THE PUBLIC SERVICE.

LEGER, MARCEL

28.332   FG   1917   Parasitisme intestinal à la Guyane Francaise dans la population locale et dans l'élément pénal [Intestinal parasitism in French Guiana, among the local population and among the penal element].

28.333   FG   1918   La lèpre à la Guyane Francaise dans l'élément pénal: documents statistiques [Leprosy in French Guiana among the penal element: statistical documentation].

LEWIS, E. P.

9.024   TR   1964   Adoption and foster homes.

LEWIS, GORDON K.

37.225   GC   1961 The Caribbean: colonization and culture. *Stud Left* 1(4):26-42.
                [5, 6, 16, 19]   [*RIS*]
37.226   TR   1962 The Trinidad and Tobago general election of 1961. *Car Stud* 2(2),
                July: 2-30.   [*RIS*]

LICHTVELD, LOU

66.089   SR   1953 SURINAME'S NATIONALE ASPIRATIES (EEN AANLEIDING TOT DISCUSSIES
                OVER DE GRONDSLAGEN VAN EEN-AL-OMVATTEND ONTWIKKELINGSPLAN)
                [SURINAM'S NATIONAL ASPIRATIONS (LEADING TO DISCUSSION OF THE
                PRINCIPLES OF A GENERAL PLAN OF DEVELOPMENT)].

LIER, RUDOLF A. J. van

8.039   GC   1951 The problem of the political and social elite in the West Indies and
                the Guyana's.
8.040   NC   1955 Social and political conditions in Suriname and the Netherlands
                Antilles: Introduction.

LIMBURG, STIRUM, O. E. G., Graaf van

37.227   SR/   1923/Suriname en de Fransche strafkolonies [Surinam and the French
          FG   24 penal colonies]. *W I G* 5:95-109.   [*COL*]
54.038   SR   1923/De Surinamsche mijnwetgeving [The mining laws of Surinam].
                  24
37.228   SR/   1924/De opheffing der strafkolonie: Fransch Guyana en haar mogelijke
          FG   25 gevolgen voor Suriname [The abolition of the penal colony in French
                Guiana and its possible results for Surinam]. *W I G* 6:371-376. [66]
                                                                                   [*COL*]
37.229   SR/   1925/De strafkolonies in Fransch Guyana [The penal colonies of French
          FG   26 Guiana]. *W I G* 7:49-80, 97-120.   [*COL*]
37.230   SR   1925/De wet op de staatsinrichting van Suriname [The law about the form
                  26 of government of Surinam]. *W I G* 7:449-480.   [*COL*]
37.231   SR   1926/Voorwaardelijke veroordeeling [The probation system]. *W I G* 8:370-
                  27 374. [32]   [*COL*]

**LISTOWEL, WILLIAM FRANCIS HARE, 5th Earl of; FARLEY, RAWLE;
HINDEN, RITA & HUGHES, COLIN**

37.232   BC   1952 CHALLENGE TO THE BRITISH CARIBBEAN. London, Fabian Publications,
                37p. (Research series no. 150.) [38]

LOCHHEAD, A. V. S.

33.022   TR   [1956?] REPORT ON ADMINISTRATION OF THE SOCIAL SERVICES IN TRINIDAD AND
                TOBAGO: WITH PARTICULAR REFERENCE TO CO-ORDINATION.

LOGEMANN, J. H. A.

37.233   NC   1955 The constitutional status of the Netherlands Caribbean territories.
                In DEVELOPMENTS TOWARDS SELF-GOVERNMENT IN THE CARIBBEAN. A
                symposium held under the auspices of the Netherlands Universities
                Foundation for International Co-operation at the Hague, Sept., 1954.
                The Hague, W. van Hoeve, p.46-72.   [*RIS*]

LOTAN, YAEL

21.013   JM   1964 Jamaica today.

LOVEJOY, ROBERT M.

44.140   JM   1963 The burden of Jamaican taxation, 1958.

LOWENTHAL, DAVID

2.142   FG   1960 French Guiana: myths and realities.

37.234   BC   1962 Levels of West Indian Government. *In* SINGHAM, A. & BRAITH-WAITE, L.E., eds. SPECIAL NUMBER [of *Social Econ Stud*] ON THE CONFERENCE ON POLITICAL SOCIOLOGY IN THE BRITISH CARIBBEAN, DEC. 1961. *Social Econ Stud* 1(4), Dec.: 363-391. [20, 21]   [*RIS*]

MACAULAY, THOMAS B.

51.090   BC   1919 Canada and the West Indies—the case of commercial union.

McCOLGAN, KATHLEEN

37.235   JM   1955 Jamaica survey. *New Commonw*, British Caribbean Supplement,30(9), Oct. 31:vii-ix.   [*AGS*]

McCONNEY, E.J., comp.

17.016   BB   1963 Prisoners of the '45 rising.

McCOWAN, ANTHONY

37.236   BG   1956 British Guiana. *In* RACE AND POWER: STUDIES OF LEADERSHIP IN FIVE BRITISH DEPENDENCIES. London, The Bow Group, p.17-36. [10] [*RIS*]

McCOY, H.M.

37.237   CM   1963/The civil servant in the Cayman Islands. *Social Scient* 1:6,12. [*RIS*]
           64

MacDERMOT, T.H.

37.238   JM   1922 Jamaica, past and present. *Dalh Rev* 2(3), Oct.: 271-284. [5]   [*COL*]

37.239   JM   1922 The political constitution of Jamaica. *United Emp* new ser., 13(10), Oct.: 642-650. [5]

McFARLANE, DENNIS

37.240   BC   1964 A comparative study of incentive legislation in the Leeward Islands, Windward Islands, Barbados and Jamaica. *Social Econ Stud* 13(3), Sept.: suppl. (63p.) [49]   [*RIS*]

MacINNES, C.M.

37.241   BC   1955 Constitutional development of the British West Indies. *In* DEVELOPMENTS TOWARDS SELF-GOVERNMENT IN THE CARIBBEAN. A symposium held under the auspices of the Netherlands Universities Foundation for International Co-operation at the Hague, Sept. 1954. The Hague, W. van Hoeve, p.3-22. [5]   [*RIS*]

MACKENZIE, V. St. CLAIR, ed.

37.242   BG   1923 LAWS OF BRITISH GUIANA (1803-1921) Rev. ed. London, Waterlow, 6v. [5]   [*NYP*]

McKITTERICK, T.E.M.

37.243   BG   1962 The end of a colony. *Polit Q* 33(1), Jan.-Mar.: 30-40.   [*COL*]

McKITTERICK, TOM

37.244   BG   1957 Common sense in British Guiana. *Venture* 9(7), Dec.: 8-9.   [*COL*]

37.245   BG   1957 The political scene in British Guiana. *Venture* 8(11), Apr.: 6-7.
           [*COL*]

37.246   BG   1962 What next for British Guiana? *Venture* 14(4), Apr.: 7-8.   [*COL*]

MACMILLAN, W. M.
37.247   BC   1960 THE ROAD TO SELF RULE: A STUDY IN COLONIAL EVOLUTION. New York,
                   Frederick A. Praeger, 296p.   [5]   [*COL*]

MANVILLE, MARCEL
37.248   FC   1962 Chronique de la répression [Chronicle of repression]. *Esprit* 30(305),
                   Apr.: 551-555.   [*NYP*]

MARDEN, LUIS
37.249   BC   1942 Americans in the Caribbean. *Natn Geogr Mag* 81(6), June: 723-758.
                   [3]   [*AGS*]

MARQUAND, HILARY
37.250   BG   1956 A new step in British Guiana. *Venture* 8(2), June: 3.   [*COL*]

MARSDEN, E. J.
37.251   TR   1945 Trinidad's war effort. *Can-W l Mag* 35(5), June: 29, 31, 33.   [*NYP*]

MARSHALL, A. H.
37.252   BG   1955 REPORT ON LOCAL GOVERNMENT IN BRITISH GUIANA. Georgetown,
                   Argosy Co., 109p.

MARSHALL, ARTHUR CALDER
37.253   TR   1938 Trinidad wants to be American. *Liv Age* 355(4467), Dec.: 322-324.
                                                                                         [*COL*]

MARTIN, KINGSLEY
23.101   JM   1961 The Jamaican volcano.

MARTIN, LAWRENCE & SYLVIA
37.254   GC   1941 Outpost no. 2: the West Indies. *Harper's Mag* 182, Mar.: 359-368.
                   [66]   [*COL*]

MARTINEAU, ALFRED
37.255   FA   1935 Il y a cent ans: les droits civils et politiques, le Conseil colonial
                   [One hundred years ago: civil and political rights, the colonial
                   Council]. *In* DENIS, SERGE, ed. NOS ANTILLES. Orléans, Luzeray,
                   163-175.   [5]   [*AGS*]

MATTHEWS, Dom BASIL
37.256   GC   1943 The West Indies: bridge and laboratory of inter-Americanism.
                   Commonweal 37(19), Feb. 26: 464-467.   [*COL*]

MAUDE, Sir JOHN
37.257   BB   1949 REPORT ON LOCAL GOVERNMENT IN BARBADOS. [Bridgetown? Barbados,
                   Govt. Printer] 52p. (Supplement to Official Gazette, Nov. 28, 1949.)
                                                                                         [*UNL*]

MAYNARD, FITZ G. & OLGA COMMA
37.258   TR   [n.d.] THE NEW ROAD: A SHORT STUDY IN CITIZENSHIP. [Port of Spain?]
                   Granderson Bros. Printer, 68p.   [32]   [*RIS*]

MAZIN, E.

37.259 FA 1921 LES ANTILLES FRANCAISES: ÉTUDE JURIDIQUE ET ÉCONOMIQUE [THE FRENCH ANTILLES: A JUDICIAL AND ECONOMIC STUDY]. Toulouse, Impr. Languedocienne, 157p. (Ph.D. dissertation.) [44] [COL]

MBANEFO, Sir LOUIS; MOSES, MACDONALD & MARSHALL, OSLEY ROY

37.260 TR 1965 REPORT OF THE COMMISSION OF ENQUIRY INTO SUBVERSIVE ACTIVITIES IN TRINIDAD AND TOBAGO. [Port of Spain?] Govt. Printery, 70p. (Trinidad and Tobago, House paper no. 2 of 1965.) [RIS]

MEISLER, STANLEY

50.090 BG/ 1964 Meddling in Latin America; dubious role of AFL-CIO.
        BH

MENENDEZ VALDES, MANUEL

37.261 FG 1930 FRENCH JUSTICE: SEVEN MONTHS UNDER SENTENCE OF DEATH. London, Faber and Faber, 256p. [NYP]

MENKMAN, W. R.

44.149 SR 1928/ Eenige opmerkingen aan de hand van de Surinaamsche begrooting
        29 voor 1929 [Some remarks about the budget of Surinam for the year 1929].

37.262 NC 1929/ Moederlandsche verantwoordelijkheid en Westindische autonomie
        30 [The responsibility of the mother country and West Indian autonomy]. W I G 11:403-411. [44] [COL]

37.263 CU 1930/ Curacaosche toestanden [Curacao's conditions]. W I G 12:53-72.
        31 [44] [COL]

37.264 SR 1931/ Nederland en Suriname [The Netherlands and Surinam]. W I G 13:
        32 365-377. [44] [COL]

37.265 SR 1931/ Nederland en Suriname, een nabetrachting [The Netherlands and
        32 Surinam, in retrospect]. W I G 13:569-575. [44] [COL]

6.049 CU 1935/ Slavenhandel en rechtsbedeeling op Curacao op het einde der 17e
        36 eeuw [Slave trade and administration of justice on Curacao at the end of the 17th century].

5.139 SR 1935/ Suriname onder Engelsch bewind [Surinam under English rule].
        36

5.140 NA 1936/ De Nederlanders in de Caraïbische wateren: een nabetrachting
        37 [The Dutch in the Caribbean seas: in retrospect].

46.143 SR 1940 Landbouw-economische politiek in Suriname [Agricultural-economic policy in Surinam].

37.266 SR/ 1947 Federalisme en seperatisme in Westindië [Federalism and sepa-
        CU ratism in the West Indies]. W I G 28:368-371. [COL]

37.267 CU 1949 Curacao gedurende de oorlogsjaren [Curacao during the war years].
        W I G 30:105-115. [COL]

MICHELS, J.

37.268 SR 1954/ Suriname's binnenlands bestuur [Surinam's internal government].
        55 Vox Guy 1(4-5), Nov.-Jan.: 73-78.

MIDAS, ANDRE

37.269 BC 1957 Constitutional evolution. Caribbean 10(10), May: 236-240. [38]
        [COL]

MITCHELL, Sir HAROLD

37.270   GC   1963 Europe in the Caribbean: the policies of Great Britain, France and the Netherlands towards their West Indian territories in the twentieth century. Edinburgh, W. & R. Chambers, 211p. [44]
[*RIS*]

MITRASING, FRITS EDUARD MANGAL

37.271   SR   1959 Tien jaar Suriname: van afhankelijkheid tot gelijkgerechtigdheid [Ten years Surinam: from dependency to equality]. Leiden, Drukkerij "Luctor et Emergo," 348p.   [*NYP*]

MONTE, E.

37.272   NL   1955 Antilliaans procesrecht [Legal proceedings in the Antilles]. Schiedam, Roelants, 196p.

MOORE, RICHARD B.

37.273   GC   1964 Caribbean unity and freedom. *Freedomways* 4(3), Summer: 295-311. [5]
[*RIS*]

MORGAN, D. J.

51.105   BC   1962 Imperial preference in the West Indies and in the British Caribbean, 1929-55: a quantitative analysis.

MOSKOS, CHARLES CONSTANTINE, Jr.

37.274   BC   1963 The sociology of political independence: a study of influence, social structure and ideology in the British West Indies. Ph.D. dissertation, University of California, Los Angeles, 244p. [9, 20, 21]

MOSKOS, CHARLES CONSTANTINE, Jr. & BELL, WENDELL

37.275   BC   1964 Attitudes towards democracy among leaders in four emergent nations. *Br J Sociol* 15(4), Dec.: 317-337.   [8, 20]   [*RIS*]
21.017   BC   1964 West Indian nationalism.
10.029   BG/   1965 Cultural unity and diversity in new states.
          TR

MULLINGS, LLEWELLYN MAXIMILLIAN

44.160   JM   1964 An analysis of the economic implications of political independence for Jamaica.

MULZAC, UNA G.

37.276   BG   1963 The general strike in British Guiana. *New Wld Rev* 31(11), Dec.: 32-36.   [*COL*]

MURRAY, D. J.

37.277   BC   1965 The West Indies and the development of colonial government. Oxford, Clarendon Press, 264p.   [5]

MURRAY, GIDEON

37.278   BC   1919 Canada and the British West Indies. *United Emp* 10(2), Feb.: 54-58. [38]   [*AGS*]

MURRAY, R. N.

5.149   JM   1960 The road back—Jamaica after 1866.

NADIR, HENRI ROUSSEAU
44.161 FA 1956 Les Antilles existent [The Antilles do exist].

NETTLEFORD, REX
37.279 JM/ 1962 Political education in the developing Caribbean. *Car Q* 7(4), Apr.:
        BG/   203-212. [32, 66]   [*RIS*]
        BH

NEWMAN, PETER KENNETH
16.026 BG 1962 Racial tension in British Guiana.

NEY, ROBERT MORSE
37.280 BH/ 1938 THE COLONIAL VALUE OF BRITISH HONDURAS, BRITISH GUIANA AND
        BG/   JAMAICA. M. A. thesis, Clark University, 128p. [2]
        JM

NIGER, PAUL
37.281 FA 1962 L'assimilation, forme suprême du colonialisme [(Political) assimi-
                  lation, the supreme goal of colonialism]. *Esprit* 30(305), Apr.:
                  518-532.

NIKOLIA, A.
37.282 MT 1961 Sbrosim tsepi kolonializma! [Let us smash the chains of colonial-
                  ism!] *Partijn Zhizn* 24:60-63.   [*COL*]

NILES, BLAIR
37.283 FG 1927 Devil's Island. *Forum* 78(6), Dec.: 836-847.   [*COL*]
37.284 FG 1928 CONDEMNED TO DEVIL'S ISLAND: THE BIOGRAPHY OF AN UNKNOWN CON-
                  VICT. New York, Harcourt, Brace, 376p.   [*NYP*]

NORMAN, FRANK A.
50.092 BC 1952 WHITEHALL TO WEST INDIES.

NORRIS, KATRIN
21.019 JM 1962 JAMAICA: THE SEARCH FOR AN IDENTITY.

NUNAN, JOSEPH J.
37.285 BG 1912 Roman-Dutch law and the West Indian Appeal Court: a reply. *Timehri*
                  3d ser., 2(19A), July: 101-105.   [*AMN*]
37.286 BG 1915 West Indian law and appeals. *Timehri* 3d ser., 3(20B), May: 253-256.
                                                                         [*AMN*]
37.287 BC 1917 West Indian Appeal Court. *Timehri* 3d ser., 4(21), June: 306-315.

O'CONNOR, HARVEY
37.288 JM 1952 Jamaica: the colonial dilemma. *Mon Rev* 3(9), Jan.: 268-277; 3(10),
                  Feb.: 307-314.   [*COL*]

ODLUM, GEORGE
37.289 SL 1962 The structure of local and island government. *In* BROWN, JOHN, ed.
                  AN APPROACH TO ADULT EDUCATION. Castries, St. Lucia, Govt. Print.
                  Off., p.24-29.   [*RIS*]

OLCH, ISAIAH
37.290   GC   1940 A résumé of national interests in the Caribbean area. *U S Nvl Inst
                         Proc* 66(2), Feb.: 165-176.   [5]   [*AGS*]

OLIVIER, SYDNEY, 1st Baron RAMSDEN
37.291   BC   1938 Freedom Day, by Lord Olivier. *Contemp Rev* 872, Aug.: 154-162.
                                                                                                        [*AGS*]

O'LOUGHLIN, CARLEEN
44.174   LW/   1963/Economic problems of the Leeward and Windward Islands.
           WW   64

O'MEALLY, JAIME
37.292   JM   1938 WHY WE DEMAND SELF-GOVERNMENT. New York, Jamaica Progressive
                         League of New York, 16p.   [*NYP*]

OORSCHOT, J. W. van
37.293   SR   1919 Eene militaire beschouwing omtrent de kolonie Suriname [A military
                         viewpoint of the colony of Surinam]. *W I G* 1(1): 178-185.   [*COL*]

OTTLEY, CARLTON ROBERT
37.294   TR   1964 A HISTORICAL ACCOUNT OF THE TRINIDAD AND TOBAGO POLICE FORCE
                         FROM THE EARLIEST TIMES. [Port of Spain?] Trinidad, Published by
                         the author [printed by Robert MacLehose, University Press], 152p.
                         [5]   [*RIS*]

OUDSCHANS DENTZ, FRED
37.295   SR/   1927/Het Nederlanderschap in Suriname en Curacao [Dutch citizenship in
           CU   28 Surinam and Curacao]. *W I G* 9:131-136.   [*COL*]
37.296   SR   1928/Nogmaals het wapen van Suriname [Surinam's coat of arms once
                    29 again]. *W I G* 10:35-43. [5]   [*COL*]
37.297   NC   1932/De titel Excellentie [The title "Excellency"]. *W I G* 14:179-181.
                    33   [*COL*]
37.298   SR/   1934/Het Nederlanderschap in Suriname en Curacao [Dutch citizenship
           CU   35 in Surinam and Curacao]. *W I G* 16:205.   [*COL*]
44.181   SR   1941 Een blik op den toestand van Suriname bij den overgang van het
                         Engelsche bestuur op dat der Bataafsche Republiek in 1802 [The
                         conditions in Surinam at the time of the change from English rule
                         to that of the Batavian Republic].
37.299   SR   1943 Aanvulling van de Encyclopaedie van Nederlandsch West-Indië: De
                         Gouverneurs van Suriname [Addition to the Encyclopedia of the
                         Dutch West Indies: The Governors of Surinam]. *W I G* 25:345-348.
                         [5]   [*COL*]
37.300   SR   1948 De afzetting van het Groot-Opperhoofd der Saramaccaners Koffy in
                         1835 en de politieke contracten met de Boschnegers in Suriname
                         [The dismissal of Koffy, the headman of the Saramaccans, in 1835,
                         and the political contracts with the Bush Negroes in Surinam]. *Bijd
                         Volk* 104:33-43. [5, 14]

PANHUYS, L. C. van
37.301   SR   1924/De Gouverneur-Generaal Willem Benjamin van Panhuys [Governor-
                    25 General Willem Benjamin van Panhuys]. *W I G* 6:289-320. [5] [*COL*]

37.302	SR	1926/ De Nederlandsche Regeering tegenover de kolonie Suriname in
		27 1816 [The Dutch Government versus the colony of Surinam in 1816].
		W I G 8:463-472. [5] [*COL*]
37.303	SR	1934/ Mr. Lammers over het bestuur van Suriname in 1816 [Mr. Lammers
		35 on the government of Surinam in 1816]. *W I G* 16:151-162. [5] [*COL*]

PARES, RICHARD
5.165	GC	1936 WAR AND TRADE IN THE WEST INDIES 1739-1763.
37.304	GC	1937 Prisoners of war in the West-Indies in the eighteenth century. *J Barb*
		Mus Hist Soc 5(1), Nov.: 12-17. [5] [*AMN*]

PARKER, FRANKLIN D.
37.305	FC	1958 Political development in the French Caribbean. *In* WILGUS, A.
		CURTIS, ed. THE CARIBBEAN: BRITISH, DUTCH, FRENCH, UNITED
		STATES [papers delivered at the Eighth Conference on the Carib-
		bean held at the University of Florida, Dec. 5-7, 1957]. Gainesville,
		University of Florida Press, p.97-104. (Publications of the School
		of Inter-American Studies, ser. 1, v. 8.) [5] [*RIS*]

PARRY, JOHN HORACE
| 37.306 | BC | 1954 The Patent Offices in the British West Indies. *Engl Hist Rev* 69 |
| | | (271), Apr.: 200-225. [5] [*COL*] |

PATCHETT, K. W.
| *9.030* | BC | 1959 Some aspects of marriage and divorce in the West Indies. |

PATERSON, ALEXANDER
37.307	BC	1943 Report of Mr. Alexander Paterson on his visits to the reformatory
		and penal establishments ... of Jamaica, British Honduras, the
		Bahamas, the Leeward and Windward Islands, Barbados, Trinidad
		and Tobago, British Guiana ... 20th December, 1936—10th May, 1937.
		[Port of Spain?] Printed by A. L. Rhodes, Govt. Printer, 25p. (West
		Indian no. 234.) [*RIS*]

PATON, WALKER
| 37.308 | BB | 1944 Barbados and the war. *Can-W I Mag* 33-34(11), Nov.: 65-67. [*NYP*] |

PATTEE, RICHARD
| 37.309 | JM | 1946 Tumult in the Antilles: Jamaica. *America* 74(26), Mar. 30: 648-650. |
| | | [50] [*COL*] |

PEAN, CHARLES
| 37.310 | FG | 1953 THE CONQUEST OF DEVIL'S ISLAND. London, Max Parrish, 187p. [66] |
| | | [*SCH*] |

PENSON, LILLIAN M.
37.311	BC	1924 COLONIAL AGENTS OF THE BRITISH WEST INDIES: A STUDY IN COLONIAL
		ADMINISTRATION, MAINLY IN THE EIGHTEENTH CENTURY. London,
		University of London Press, 318p. (Ph.D. dissertation.) [5] [*COL*]
37.312	BG	1926 The making of a crown colony: British Guiana, 1803-33. *Trans Roy*
		Hist Soc 4th ser., 9:107-134. [5] [*COL*]

PERKINS, WHITNEY T.
37.313   UV   1962 DENIAL OF EMPIRE. Leyden, A. W. Sythoff, 381p.   [COL]

PHELPS, O. W.
50.096   JM   1960 Rise of the labour movement in Jamaica.

PIERRE, LENNOX & La ROSE, JOHN
37.314   TR   1955 FOR MORE AND BETTER DEMOCRACY FOR A DEMOCRATIC CONSTITUTION
                   FOR TRINIDAD AND TOBAGO. Port of Spain, West Indian Independence
                   Party of Trinidad and Tobago, 38p.

PITT, DAVID
37.315   TR   1949 Trinidad's new Constitution. Venture 1(2), Mar.: 5,8-9.   [COL]

PLATT, RAYE R.
37.316   GC   1926 A note on political sovereignty and administration in the Caribbean.
                   Geogr Rev 16(4), Oct.: 623-637.   [5]   [AGS]

PLENEL, ALAIN
37.317   FA   1963 Libération nationale et assimilation à la Martinique et à la Guade-
                   loupe [National liberation and (political) assimilation in Martinique
                   and Guadeloupe]. Temps Mod 18(205), June: 2197-2234.   [5, 44, 66]
                                                                                      [COL]

POLLAK, HARRY H.
37.318   BG   1957 What about British Guiana? Am Fed 64(7), July: 28-29. [50] [COL]

POPE-HENNESSY, JAMES
37.319   BC   1964 The Federation Riots, Barbados 1875-1876. In his VERANDAH: SOME
                   EPISODES IN THE CROWN COLONIES 1867-1889. London, George Allen
                   and Unwin, p.157-182.   [5]   [COL]

POS, H.
37.320   NA   1955 Mijmeringen naar aanleiding van het proefschrift "Antilliaans
                   procesrecht"[Contemplations on the dissertation "Legal procedures
                   in the Antilles"]. Vox Guy 1(6):185-192.

POS, R.H.
37.321   NC   1954/ De ontwikkeling der Westinidsche rijksdelen onder het Statuut voor
            55   het Koninkrijk der Nederlanden [The development of the West Indian
                   Provinces under the Constitution of the Kingdom of the Netherlands].
                   Vox Guy 1(4-5), Nov.-Jan.: 3-5.

POYER, JOHN
37.322   BB   1954 History of the administration of the Rt. Hon. Lord Seaforth, etc.,
                   etc., etc. J Barb Mus Hist Soc 21(4), Aug.: 160-174.   [5]   [AMN]

PREST, A. R.
44.190   BC   1957 A FISCAL SURVEY OF THE BRITISH CARIBBEAN.
44.191   BC   1960 Public finance.
PRINS, J.
37.323   SR   1952 Vragen inzake Bosneger-volksrecht [Questions concerning public
                   rights of the Bush Negroes]. W I G 33:53-76.   [14]   [COL]

37.324   SR   1961 De Surinaamse bevolking en haar Districtscommissarissen [The
              Surinam population and its District Commissioners]. *Mens Mij*
              36(5), Sept.-Oct.: 375-385.   [*RIS*]

9.031   SR   1963 Een Surinaams rechtsgeding over een Moslimse verstoting [A Suri-
              nam lawsuit about a Moslem divorce].

PROCTOR, JESSE HARRIS, Jr.

37.325   BC   1962 British West Indian society and government in transition 1920-1960.
              In SINGHAM, A. & BRAITHWAITE, L. E., eds. SPECIAL NUMBER [of
              Social Econ Stud] ON THE CONFERENCE ON POLITICAL SOCIOLOGY IN
              THE BRITISH CARIBBEAN, DEC. 1961. *Social Econ Stud* 11(4), Dec.:
              273-304.   [*RIS*]

QUINTUS BOSZ, A. J. A.

37.326   SR   1960/Misvattingen omtrent de staatkundige ontwikkeling van Suriname
         61   [Misunderstandings about the political development of Surinam].
              N W I G 40:3-16. [5]   [*COL*]

RABINOWITZ, VICTOR

37.327   BG   1962 Guiana rightist riots no surprise to Jagan. *Natn Guardian* 14(20),
              Feb. 26:3.   [*NYP*]

RAGATZ, LOWELL JOSEPH

45.027   BC   [1928?] ABSENTEE LANDLORDISM IN THE BRITISH CARIBBEAN 1750-1833.

RANCE, Sir HUBERT ELVIN

35.036   TR   1951 Government expenditures in Trinidad and Tobago.
44.195   TR   1953 Trinidad report.

RAWLINS, RANDOLPH

37.328   BG   1963 What really happened in British Guiana. *J Inter-Amer Stud* 5(1),
              Jan.: 140-147.   [*COL*]

RAYNER, Sir THOMAS CROSSLEY, ed.

37.329   BG   1905 Laws of British Guiana. New and rev. ed. London, Waterlow, 5v.
              [5]   [*NYP*]

REIS, CHARLES

37.330   TR   [1929?] A HISTORY OF THE CONSTITUTION OR GOVERNMENT OF TRINIDAD FROM
              THE EARLIEST TIMES TO THE PRESENT DAY, VOL. 1. Port of Spain,
              Author's Press, 291p.   [*COL*]

37.331   TR   1947 THE GOVERNMENT OF TRINIDAD AND TOBAGO: LAW OF THE CONSTITUTION.
              Port of Spain, Trinidad, Yuille's Printerie, 336p.

REVERT, EUGENE

43.129   GC   1951 Géographie politique du monde caraïbe [Political geography of the
              Caribbean].

37.332   MT   1955 Les institutions de la Martinique jusqu'à l'assimilation [The ad-
              ministration of Martinique up to the Assimilation Act of 1946].
              In DEVELOPMENTS TOWARDS SELF-GOVERNMENT IN THE CARIBBEAN. A
              symposium held under the auspices of the Netherlands Universities
              Foundation for International Co-operation at the Hague, Sept. 1954.
              The Hague, W. van Hoeve, p.34-45.   [*RIS*]

RICHARDSON, E. C.
37.333   TR   [n.d.] TRINIDAD: REVOLUTION OR EVOLUTION; A CRITICAL ANALYSIS. Port of
                Spain, Vedic Enterprises, 19p. [10]   [*RIS*]
46.183   TR   [196-] P.N.M. and its agricultural policy.

RICHARDSON, LEIGH
37.334   BH   1955 P. U. P. plan for British Honduras. *New Commonw* 29(1), Jan. 10:
                12-13. [66]   [*AGS*]

RICHARDSON, J. HENRY
33.038   BG   1955 REPORT ON SOCIAL SECURITY IN BRITISH GUIANA, APRIL, 1954.
33.039   BC   1956 Social security problems with special reference to the British West
                Indies.

RICKARDS, COLIN
37.335   GC   1963 CARIBBEAN POWER. London, Dennis Dobson, 247p.   [*RIS*]

RIEMENS, H.
37.336   NA   1960 De internationale positie van de Nederlandse Antillen [The inter-
                national position of the Netherlands Antilles]. *Int Spectator* 14(17),
                Oct. 8: 407-427.

ROBERTS, WALTER ADOLPHE
37.337   BC   1934 British West Indian aspirations *Curr Hist* 40(5), Aug.: 552-556.
                                                                                 [*COL*]
37.338   JM   1936 SELF-GOVERNMENT FOR JAMAICA. New York, Jamaica Progressive
                League of New York, 16p.   [*NYP*]
37.339   BC   1941 Caribbean headaches. *Nation* 153(12), Sept. 20:251-253.   [16, 50]
                                                                                 [*COL*]
37.340   BC   1941 Future of the British Caribbean. *Surv Graphic* 30(4), Apr.: 229-234.
                                                                                 [*COL*]
37.341   GC   1941 Strategy in the Caribbean. *Nation* 152(15), Apr. 12: 428-431. [*COL*]
37.342   BC   1944 The future of colonialism in the Caribbean: the British West Indies.
                In FRAZIER, E.F. & WILLIAMS, E., eds. THE ECONOMIC FUTURE OF
                THE CARIBBEAN. Washington, Howard University Press, p.37-39.[*COL*]
5.184   JM   1952 SIR HENRY MORGAN, BUCCANEER AND GOVERNOR., Rev. ed.
37.343   JM   1959 The Act of Havana. *Jam Hist Rev* 3(2), Mar.: 66-69.   [*COL*]

ROBERTSON, Sir JAMES
37.344   BG   1954 Report of the British Guiana Constitutional Commission 1954.
                London, H.M.S.O., 91p. (Cmd. 9274.)

ROBINSON, KENNETH
37.345   FA   1954 The end of empire: another view. *Int Aff* 30(2), Apr.: 186-195.[*AGS*]
37.346   NC/   1956 Alternatives to independence. *Polit Stud* 4(3), Oct.: 225-249.
          FC

ROCHE, JEAN CAZENAVE de la
37.347   FA   1943 Tension in the French West Indies. *For Aff* 21(3), Apr.: 560-565.
                                                                                 [*AGS*]

ROMONDT, PH. F. W.
6.059   NW   1941 Pieter Hassell.

ROMONDT, W. H. A.
37.348   SR   1922/ De ontwikkeling van het kiersrecht in Suriname [The development of
             23   suffrage in Surinam]. *W I G* 4:99-114.   [*COL*]

RORTY, JAMES
37.349   NV   1961 Independence, like it or not. *Commonweal* 74(20), Sept. 8: 491-493.
                  [38, 55]   [*RIS*]

ROSE, F. G.
28.448   BG   1926 Leprosy statistics and legislation in British Guiana.

ROTH, VINCENT
37.350   BG   1952 Amerindians and the state: a brief history of the Guiana Amerindians
                  vis-a-vis the government. *Timehri* 4th ser., 1(31), Nov.: 8-15.   [13,
                  66]

ROUSSEAU, LOUIS
37.351   FG   1925 Faillite morale et utilitaire de la transportation en Guyane: état
                  sanitaire général de la colonie pénitentiaire [The moral and practical
                  failure of the (penal) traffic to (French) Guiana: general sanitary
                  conditions in the penal colony]. *Acad Sci Colon Cr Séanc* 2:225-243.
                                                       [*NYP*]

ROYES, W. C.
33.042   JM   [1961?] Government and Statutory social services in Jamaica.

RUBIN, VERA
20.016   BC   1962 Culture, politics and race relations.

RUTTER, OWEN
37.352   TR   1941 Trinidad's contribution to the empire war effort. *Crown Colon* 11
                  (118), Sept.: 399-400.   [*AGS*]

SABLE, VICTOR
37.353   FC   1955 LA TRANSFORMATION DES ISLES D'AMÉRIQUE EN DÉPARTEMENTS FRAN-
                  CAIS [THE CONVERSION OF THE AMERICAN ISLANDS INTO FRENCH *Dé-*
                  partements]. Paris, Editions Larose, 200p.   [5]   [*AGS*]

SAMSON, PH. A.
23.133   SR   1940 De oplossing van het eedsvraagstuk in Suriname [The solution of
                  the problem of oath-taking in Surinam].
23.134   SR   1946 Afgoderij als strafbaar feit [Idolatry as a penal offense].
37.354   SR   1947 Kiesverenigingen in Suriname [Political parties in Surinam]. *W I G*
                  28:161-174.   [*COL*]
37.355   SR   1949 Uit de geschiedenis van de Surinaamse balie [From the history of
                  Surinam (judicial) bar]. *W I G* 30:172-181.   [*COL*]
52.078   SR   1950 De Surinaamse pers gedurende het Engelse tussenbestuur [The
                  Surinam press during the English interregnum].
37.356   SR   1951 Koninklijke besluiten in Surinam [Royal Government decisions in
                  Surinam]. *W I G* 32:129-142.   [*COL*]
52.079   SR   1951 Persdelicten in Suriname[Legal actions against the press in Suriıam].
37.357   SR   1956/ Iets over de Surinaamsche Scherpschuttersvereeniging [About the
                  57 Rifle-Club in Surinam]. *W I G* 37:219-222.   [22]   [*COL*]

SANJURJO, MARIA ANTONINA
37.358   FC   1938 AN APPROACH TO THE COLONIAL EVALUATION OF THE FRENCH WEST
                INDIES AND FRENCH GUIANA. M. A. thesis, Clark University, 137p.
                [2]

SAUL, SAMUEL BERRICK
44.207   BC   1957 The economic significance of "constructive imperialism."
44.208   BC   1958 The British West Indies in depression.

SCHALKWIJK, F. G.
37.359   CU   1924/ De reorganisatie van de rechterlijke macht en van de rechtspleging
               25   der kolonie Curacao in de praktijk [The reorganization of the
                    judiciary power and the administration of justice in the colony of
                    Curacao in practice]. *W I G* 6:609-624.   [*COL*]
32.173   NC   1926/ Keuze en opleiding van naar West-Indie uit te zenden rechterlijke
               27   en bestuursambtenarem [Selection and training of judicial and
                    government officials for the West Indies].

SCHROEDER, HERBERT
37.360   LW   1949 Sturm um die Inseln Unterm Wind [Storm over the Leeward Islands].
                    Dt Rdsch 75(6), June: 504-509.   [*COL*]

SCHUYLER, ROBERT LIVINGSTON
37.361   BC   1925 The constitutional claims of the British West Indies; the contro-
                    versy over the slave registry bill of 1815. *Polit Sci Q* 40(1), Mar.:
                    1-36. [6]   [*COL*]

SCHWARTZ, BARTON M.
37.362   TR   1965 Extra-legal activities of the village pandit in Trinidad. *Anthrop Q*
                    38(2), Apr.: 62-71. [12, 19]   [*RIS*]

SCHWARZ, ERNST
66.130   JM   1955 Progressive government in Jamaica: the Manley Plan.

SCOTT, WINTHROP R.
44.209   GG   1943 War economy of the Guianas.

SCROGGS, WILLIAM
37.363   JM   1962 Jamaicans are English. *W I Econ* 4(7), Jan.: 11-12. [5, 21]   [*RIS*]
37.364   JM   1962 Political pluralism. *W I Econ* 4(12), June: 2.   [*RIS*]

SEGGAR, W. H.
37.365   BG   1959 Amerindian local authority elections: upper Mazaruni Amerindian
                    district. *Timehri* 4th ser., 38, Sept.: 86-88. [13]   [*AMN*]

SEMMEL, BERNARD
16.029   JM   1962 The issue of "race" in the British reaction to the Morant Bay
                    Uprising of 1865.

SEPPEN, G.
37.366   CU   1947 Enkele maritieme gedachten over de defensie van Curacao [Some
                    maritime thoughts about the defense of Curacao]. *W I G* 28:65-73.
                                                                                  [*COL*]

SHAW, EARL BENNETT

37.367   BC   1941 Our new Atlantic defenses. *J Geogr* 40(2), Feb.: 41-56.   [*AGS*]

SHENFIELD, A. A.

66.136   BC   1958 Economic advance in the West Indies.

SHERE, LOUIS

44.216   GC   1952 SUGAR TAXATION IN THE CARIBBEAN AND CENTRAL AMERICAN COUNTRIES.

SHERLOCK, PHILIP M.

37.368   JM/   1962 Nouvelles nations dans les Antilles [New nations in the Caribbean].
          TR   *Civilisations* 12(3): 404-406. [5, 38]   [*RIS*]
37.369   JM/   1963 Prospects in the Caribbean. *For Aff* 41(4), July: 744-756. [16, 20, 21]
          TR   [*RIS*]

SHILSTONE, E. M.

37.370   BB   1934 The evolution of the general assembly of Barbados. *J Barb Mus
                      Hist Soc* 1(4), Aug.: 187-191. [5]   [*AMN*]
37.371   BB   1935 The thirteen Baronets. *J Barb Mus Hist Soc* 2(2), Feb.: 89-92. [5]
                                                                                  [*AMN*]

SILBERMAN, LEO

37.372   BH   1954 Trouble in British Honduras. *Contemp Rev* 186, July: 21-25. [*COL*]

SIMEY, THOMAS S.

37.373   BC   [1944?] PRINCIPLES OF PRISON REFORM. Bridgetown, Advocate Co., 26p.
                      (Development and welfare bulletin no. 10.) [66]   [*COL*]

SIMPSON, GEORGE EATON

23.147   JM   1955 Culture change and reintegration found in the cults of West King-
                      ston, Jamaica.
23.148   JM   1955 Political cultism in West Kingston, Jamaica.
23.149   JM   1955 The Ras Tafari movement in Jamaica: a study of race and class
                      conflict.
23.152   JM   1962 The Ras Tafari movement in Jamaica in its millennial aspect.

SINGH, JAI NARINE

37.374   BG   1954 GUAYANA: HACIA LA LIBERTAD [GUIANA: TOWARD FREEDOM]. Caracas,
                      Tip. Vargas, 63p.   [*COL*]

SINGHAM, ARCHIE

37.375   BG/   1965 Three cases of constitutionalism and cuckoo politics: Ceylon,
          GR   British Guiana and Grenada. *New Wld Q* 2(1), Dead Season: 23-33.
                      [24]   [*RIS*]

SINGHAM, ARCHIE & BRAITHWAITE, LLOYD E., eds.

37.376   BC   1962 SPECIAL NUMBER ON THE CONFERENCE ON POLITICAL SOCIOLOGY IN THE
                      BRITISH CARIBBEAN, Dec. 1961. *Social Econ Stud* 11(4), Dec. (456p.)
                                                                                  [*RIS*]

SIRES, RONALD VERNON

5.202   JM   1936 JAMAICA IN DECLINE, 1834-1856.
37.377   JM   1940 Constitutional change in Jamaica, 1834-60. *J Comp Leg Int Law*
                      3d ser., 22(4): 178-190. [5]
37.378   JM   1953 Governmental crisis in Jamaica, 1860-1866. *Jam Hist Rev* 2(3),
                      Dec.: 1-26. [5]   [*RIS*]

37.379   BG   1954 British Guiana: the suspension of the constitution. *Polit Q* 7(4),
                 Dec.: 554-569.   [*RIS*]
37.380   JM   1954 The Jamaica Constitution of 1884. *Social Econ Stud* 3(1), June:
                 64-81. [5]   [*RIS*]
37.381   JM   1955 The experience of Jamaica with a modified crown colony govern-
                 ment. *Social Econ Stud* 4(2), June: 150-167. [5]   [*RIS*]
37.382   BC   1957 Government in the British West Indies: an historical outline. *Social
                 Econ Stud* 6(2), June: 108-132. [5]   [*RIS*]

SKINNARD, FREDERICK W.
37.383   JM   1946 Evolving Jamaica. *Spectator* 177(6175), Nov. 1: 443-444. [50] [*NYP*]

SKINNER, ELLIOTT P.
8.055   BG   1960 Group dynamics and social stratification in British Guiana.

SLEPNEVA, G.
37.384   BG   1959 Britanskaia Gviana [British Guiana]. *Mezhdunarodnaia Zhizn* 7:139-
                 141.   [*COL*]

SMITH, M. G.
37.385   BC   1962 Short-range prospects in the British Caribbean. *In* SINGHAM, A. &
                 BRAITHWAITE, L. E., eds. SPECIAL NUMBER [of *Social Econ Stud*]
                 ON THE CONFERENCE ON POLITICAL SOCIOLOGY IN THE BRITISH CARIB-
                 BEAN, DEC. 1961. *Social Econ Stud* 11(4), Dec.: 392-408. [10, 38, 66]
                                                                           [*RIS*]
8.060   GR   1965 Structure and crisis in Grenada, 1950-1954.

SMITH, M. G.; AUGIER, ROY & NETTLEFORD, REX
23.158 JM   1960 THE RAS TAFARI MOVEMENT IN KINGSTON, JAMAICA.

SMITH, RAYMOND THOMAS
37.386   BG   1963 British Guiana's prospects. *New Soc* 44, Aug. 1: 6-8. [10]   [*RIS*]

SMITH, ROBERT WORTHINGTON
6.066   JM   1945 The legal status of Jamaican slaves before the anti-slavery
                 movement.

SMITH, T. E.
37.387   JM/   1960 ELECTIONS IN DEVELOPING COUNTRIES: A STUDY OF ELECTORAL PRO-
          TR/   CEDURES USED IN TROPICAL AFRICA, SOUTH-EAST ASIA AND THE BRITISH
          BG   CARIBBEAN. London, Macmillan, 278p.   [*RIS*]

SPITZ, GEORGES
37.388   MT   1955 La Martinique et ses institutions depuis 1948 [Martinique and its
                 administration since 1948]. *In* DEVELOPMENTS TOWARDS SELF-GOVERN-
                 MENT IN THE CARIBBEAN. A symposium held under the auspices of the
                 Netherlands Universities Foundation for International Co-operation
                 at the Hague, Sept. 1954. The Hague, W. van Hoeve, p.112-124.
                 [32, 44]   [*RIS*]

SPURDLE, FREDERICK G.
37.389   BB/   [n.d.] Early West Indian government, showing the progress of government
          JM/   in Barbados, Jamaica and the Leeward Islands, 1660-1783. [Well-
          LW   ington?] New Zealand, Published by the author, 275p. [5]   [*NYP*]

STAAL, G. J.

37.390 SR   1921/ De grondwetsherziening en Suriname [The revision of the Consti-
         22   tution in Surinam]. *W I G* 3:545-564.   [COL]

37.391 SR   1921/ Het voorspel der installatie van den posthouder bij de Aucaners
         22   [The prelude to the installation of the representative among the
              Aucaner]. *W I G* 3:630-636.   [14, 16]   [COL]

37.392 SR   1926/ De wet op de staatsinrichting van Suriname [The law about the form
         27   of government of Surinam]. *W I G* 8:85-91.   [COL]

STORY, CHRISTOPHER

37.393 BG   1963 Political development in British Guiana. *Q Rev* 301(635), Jan.: 77-
              88.   [COL]

SWING, RAYMOND GRAM

37.394 UV   1935 Justice in the Virgin Islands. *Nation* 40(3629), Jan. 23: 95-96. [COL]
37.395 UV   1935 Storm over the Virgin Islands. *Nation* 141(3655), July 24: 95-96.
                                                                               [COL]

TANSILL, C. C.

37.396 UV   1932 THE PURCHASE OF THE DANISH WEST INDIES. Baltimore, Johns Hopkins
              Press, 548p.   [5]   [COL]

TAYLOR, S. A. G.

37.397 JM   1949 Military operations in Jamaica 1655-1660: an appreciation. *Jam Hist
              Rev* 1(2), Dec.: 7-25.   [5]   [COL]

THAMAR, MAURICE

37.398 FG   1935 LES PEINES COLONIALES ET L'EXPÉRIENCE GUYANAISE [COLONIAL PENAL
              SENTENCES AND THE GUIANA EXPERIMENT]. Paris, Impr. Georges
              Subervie, 202p. (Ph. D. dissertation, University of Paris.)   [5]

THOMAS, R. D.

44.230 JM   1963 Local government financing in Jamaica, 1944-59.

THORNE, ALFRED P.

44.233 JM   1956 Some general comments on the Hicks Report.

TOLEDANO, LUIS

37.399 JM   1947 Tropical Gilbert and Sullivan. *New Stsm Natn* 33(831), Jan. 25: 68.

TOMASEK, ROBERT D.

37.400 BG   1959 British Guiana: a case study of British colonial policy. *Polit Sci Q*
              74(3), Sept.: 393-411.   [AGS]

TOOKE, CHARLES W.

44.236 UV   1900 The Danish colonial fiscal system in the West Indies.

TURGEON, MAURICE

37.401 MT   1943 "Vichy" in Martinique. *Can-W I Mag* 32(4), Apr.: 9-10.   [NYP]

TUYL SCHUITEMAKER–van STEENBERGEN, E.

37.402 SR   1951 Politieke ontwikkeling in Suriname na de inwerkingtreding der
              Interim-Regeling [Political development in Surinam after the intro-
              duction of the Interim-Rule]. *W I G* 32:154-167.   [COL]

VANDENBOSCH, AMRY

37.403   AR/   1931 Dutch problems in the West Indies. *For Aff* 9(2), Jan.: 350-352.
         CU   [44]   [*AGS*]

VEERASAWMY, J. A.

37.404   BG   1919 The Noitgedacht murder. *Timehri* 3d ser., 6(23), Sept.: 116-132. [23]
                                                                              [*AMN*]

VIGNON, ROBERT

2.242   FG   1954 La Guyane Francaise au sein de la Communauté Francaise (situ-
                     ation politique, juridique et économique) [French Guiana at the
                     heart of the French Community].

VILLARONGA, MARIANO

37.405   BG   1962 Quién es Cheddi Jagan: patriota, demagogo, comunista?... [Who is
                     Cheddi Jagan: patriot, demagogue, Communist?] *Boricua* 1(6), May:
                     50-51, 90.   [*NYP*]

VOLLENHOVEN, C. van

5.212   SR   1916 Politieke contracten met de Boschnegers in Suriname [Political
                     contracts with the Bush Negroes of Surinam].

VRIES, F. P. de

37.406   NA   1955/ Enige aspecten der ontwikkeling van de Nederlands-Antilliaanse
               56   vertegenwoordiging in Nederland [Some aspects of the development
                     of the Dutch-Antillean representation in the Netherlands]. *W I G*
                     36:165-173.   [*COL*]

WAARD, J. de

44.241   SR   1954/ De economische bepalingen van het Statuut [The economic provi-
               55   sions of the Constitution].

WADDELL, DAVID A. G.

37.407   BH   1957 British Honduras and Anglo-American relations. *Car Q* 5(1), June:
                     50-59. [5]   [*RIS*]
37.408   BH   1959 British Honduras and Anglo-American relations: a correction. *Car Q*
                     5(4), June: 292. [5]   [*RIS*]
37.409   BH   1959 Great Britain and the Bay Islands 1821-61. *Hist J* 2(1): 59-77. [5]
                                                                              [*RIS*]
37.410   BH   1961 Developments in the Belize question 1946-1960. *Am J Int Law*
                     55(2), Apr.: 459-469.   [*RIS*]

WALKER, H. De R.

3.320   BC   1902 THE WEST INDIES AND THE EMPIRE: STUDY AND TRAVEL IN THE WINTER
                     OF 1900-1901.

WALLE, J. van de

37.411   CU   1946 De internationale ontwikkeling in West Indië gedurende den oorlog
                     [The international development in West India during the war]. *W I G*
                     27:1-17.   [*COL*]
37.412   JM   1947 Rondom de nieuwe Constitutie van Jamaica [About the new Consti-
                     tution of Jamaica]. *W I G* 28:129-144.   [*COL*]

WEATHERHEAD, BASIL
37.413   BB   1956 The Barbados police force: the Barbados regiment. *Can-W l Mag*
               46(1), Jan.: 11, 13, 15, 17.   [*NYP*]

WEEVER, GUY E. L. de
37.414   BG   1933 The British Guiana Constitution. *Natn Rev* 101(606), Aug.: 209-214.
                                                                              [*NYP*]

WEIJTINGH, C. R.
37.415   SR   1938 Eenige aanvullingen op de Encyclopaedie van West-Indië: De krijgs-
               macht in Suriname [Some additions to the Encyclopedia of the West
               Indies: The power of the Army in Surinam]. *W I G* 20:276-281, 372-
               374.   [*COL*]
44.243   SR   1940 Eenige aanvullingen op de Encyclopaedie van West-Indië: De
               belastingen in Suriname [Some additions to the Encyclopedia of the
               West Indies: The taxes in Surinam].
44.246   CU   1941 Eenige aanvullingen op de Encyclopaedie van West-Indië: De
               belastingen in Curacao [Some additions to the Encyclopedia of the
               West Indies: The taxes in Curacao].

WEITJENS, W. M. A.
37.416   NW/   1931/ Het bestuur van de Bovenwindsche Eilanden [The government of
         CU   32   the Windward Islands]. *W I G* 13:231-239.   [*COL*]

WELLE, M.
44.247   SR   1928/ De Surinaamsche begrooting voor 1929 in de Tweede Kamer [The
               29   Surinam budget for 1929 in the "House of Representatives"].

WELLS, HENRY
37.417   UV   1955 Outline of the constitutional development of the United States
               Virgin Islands. *In* DEVELOPMENTS TOWARDS SELF-GOVERNMENT IN
               THE CARIBBEAN. A symposium held under the auspices of the Nether-
               lands Universities Foundation for International Co-operation at the
               Hague, Sept. 1954. The Hague, W. van Hoeve, p.86-92.   [5]   [*RIS*]
37.418   UV   1955 Outline of the nature of United States Virgin Islands politics. *In*
               DEVELOPMENTS TOWARDS SELF-GOVERNMENT IN THE CARIBBEAN. A
               symposium held under the auspices of the Netherlands Universities
               Foundation for International Co-operation at the Hague, Sept. 1954.
               The Hague, W. van Hoeve, p.145-147.   [16, 20]   [*RIS*]
37.419   UV   1955 Outline of the possibilities for future constitutional development in
               the United States Virgin Islands. *In* DEVELOPMENTS TOWARDS SELF-
               GOVERNMENT IN THE CARIBBEAN. A symposium held under the auspices
               of the Netherlands Universities Foundation for International Co-
               operation at the Hague, Sept. 1954. The Hague, W. van Hoeve,
               p.222-223.   [*RIS*]

WESTRA, P.
37.420   SR   1919 De Koloniale Staten van Suriname [The Colonial Council of Surinam].
               W I G 1(1): 208-215.   [5]   [*COL*]

WHITE, A. D. M.
37.421   BG   1929 Bush rum in British Guiana. *Pol J* 2:211-217.   [*COL*]

WHITEHEAD, HENRY S.

37.422   UV   1926 The grievance of the Virgin Islands. *Independent* 117(3979), Sept. 4:
                     271-273, 280.   [44]

WHITSON, AGNES M.

37.423   JM   1929 THE CONSTITUTIONAL DEVELOPMENT OF JAMAICA, 1660 TO 1729. Man-
                     chester, Manchester University Press, 182p. (Publications of the
                     University of Manchester [no. 190] Historical series, no. 52.)   [5]
                                                                              [*RIS*]

WIGHT, Sir GERALD

35.045   TR   1951 A proposal for the future financing of public housing in Trinidad
                     and Tobago.

WIGHT, MARTIN

37.424   BC   1946 THE DEVELOPMENT OF THE LEGISLATIVE COUNCIL, 1606-1945. London,
                     Faber and Faber, 187p.   [*COL*]

WILKIN, H. C.

37.425   TR   1945 Military activities in Trinidad. *Can-W I Mag* 35(5), June: 60-65.
                                                                              [*NYP*]

WILLIAMS, DOUGLAS

37.426   BC   1958 Constitutional developments in the British West Indies. *In* WILGUS,
                     A. CURTIS, ed. THE CARIBBEAN: BRITISH, DUTCH, FRENCH, UNITED
                     STATES [papers delivered at the Eighth Conference on the Carib-
                     bean held at the University of Florida, Dec. 5-7, 1957]. Gainesville,
                     University of Florida Press, p.3-10. (Publications of the School of
                     Inter-American Studies, ser. 1, v. 8.)   [38]   [*RIS*]

WILLIAMS, ERIC EUSTACE

37.427   GC   1942 Crossways of the Caribbean. *Surv Graphic* 31(11), Nov.: 510-514,564.
                     [16]   [*COL*]
58.128   BC   1943 Laissez-faire, sugar and slavery.
6.080   BC   1954 THE BRITISH WEST INDIES AT WESTMINSTER. PART I: 1789-1823.
37.428   TR   1955 THE CASE FOR PARTY POLITICS IN TRINIDAD AND TOBAGO. Port of Spain,
                     Teachers Economic and Cultural Association, 24p. (Public Affairs
                     pamphlet no. 4.)   [66]   [*RIS*]
37.429   TR   1955 CONSTITUTION REFORM IN TRINIDAD AND TOBAGO. Port of Spain,
                     Teachers Economic and Cultural Association. (Public affairs pam-
                     phlets no. 2.)   [66]
38.126   BC   1956 FEDERATION: TWO PUBLIC LECTURES.
66.165   TR   1960 PERSPECTIVES FOR THE WEST INDIES.
16.036   GC   1960 Race relations in Caribbean society.
2.264   TR   1964 Trinidad and Tobago: international perspectives.
50.126   TR   1965 Reflections on the Industrial stabilisation bill.

WILLIAMSON, C.

37.430   BC   1952 Britain's new colonial policy: 1940-1951. *S Atlan Q* 51, July: 366-
                     373.   [33, 66]   [*COL*]

WISEMAN, H. V.

38.129   BC   1948 THE WEST INDIES, TOWARDS A NEW DOMINION?

WIT, H. de

37.431   SR   1958   Baas in eigen huis [Master in one's own house]. *In* WALLE, J. van de & WIT, H. de, eds. SURINAME IN STROOMLIJNEN. Amsterdam, Wereld Bibliotheek, p.117-133.

WOODING, H. O. B.

37.432   TR   1960   The constitutional history of Trinidad and Tobago. *Car Q* 6(2-3), May: 143-159.   [5]   [*RIS*]

WORSWICK, G. D. N.

44.253   JM   1956   Financing development.

WOUW, J. J. van

46.242   SR   1949   Het departement van landbouw-economische zaken in Suriname in 1945 [The department of agricultural-economic affairs in Surinam in 1945].

WRONG, HUME

37.433   BC   1923   GOVERNMENT OF THE WEST INDIES. Oxford, Clarendon Press, 190p. [5]   [*NYP*]

WYTEMA, H. J.

37.434   CU/   1931   OPPERBESTUUR EN ALGEMEEN BESTUUR OVER NEDERLANDSCH INDIE,
           SR   SURINAME EN CURACAO [SOVEREIGN RULE AND GENERAL RULE OVER THE DUTCH EAST INDIES, SURINAM, AND CURACAO]. Groningen, Wolters, 92p.

YOUNG, ALLAN

36.021   BG   1957   Some milestones in village history.
37.435   BG   1958   THE APPROACHES TO LOCAL SELF-GOVERNMENT IN BRITISH GUIANA. London, Longmans, Green, 246p.   [5, 8, 10, 33]   [*RIS*]

YOUNG, J. G.

37.436   JM   1945   The beginnings of civil government in Jamaica. *Jam Hist Rev* 1(1), June: 49-65.   [*NYP*]
52.095   JM   1959   Old road laws of Jamaica.

ZAAL, G. PH.

53.043   SR   1938   Loterijen in Suriname [Lotteries in Surinam].

ZEIDENFELT, ALEX

52.096   GC   1950   Transportation in the Caribbean during World War II.
37.437   JM   1952   Political and constitutional developments in Jamaica. *J Polit* 14(3), Aug.: 512-540.

ZEIDLER, GERHARD

37.438   FG   1940   CAYENNE—HELL LET LOOSE! Berlin, German Information Service, 81p. [66]   [*COL*]

Chapter 38

THE BRITISH WEST INDIES FEDERATION

ABBOTT, GEORGE C.
44.001   BC   1963 The future of economic co-operation in the West Indies in the light of the break-up of the Federation.

ADAMS, F. CUNNINGHAM
38.001   BC   1961 Nations, like men, have their infancy. *In* BROWN, JOHN, ed. LEE-WARDS: WRITINGS, PAST AND PRESENT, ABOUT THE LEEWARD ISLANDS. [Bridgetown?] Barbados, Dept. of Extra-Mural Studies, Leeward Islands, University College of the West Indies, p.71-73.   [*RIS*]

ANGLIN, DOUGLAS, G.
37.004   BC   1961 The political development of the West Indies.

ARCHIBALD, CHARLES H.
38.002   BC   1956 British Caribbean Federation. *Venture* 7(11), Apr.: 6-7.   [*COL*]
38.003   BC   1958 First steps in West Indies Federation. *New Commonw* 35(11), May 26: 509-510.   [*AGS*]
38.004   BC   1959 West Indian Federation: federal and territorial conflict. *Venture* 10(8), Jan.: 6-7.   [*COL*]
38.005   BC   1961 Adrift in the Caribbean. *Venture* 13(10), Nov.: 5.   [*COL*]
38.006   BC   1961 Question-mark over the Caribbean. *New Commonw* 39(7), Aug.: 505-508.   [10]   [*AGS*]
38.007   BC   1962 The failure of the West Indies Federation. *Wld Today* 18(6), June: 233-242.   [*COL*]

ARMSTRONG, PERCY E.
38.008   BC   1945 British West Indies' approach to federation. *Crown Colon* 15(167), Oct.: 677-678.   [*AGS*]

ASPINALL, Sir ALGERNON E.
38.009   BC   1919 West Indian Federation: its historical aspect. *United Emp* new ser., 10(2), Feb.: 58-63.   [5]   [*AGS*]

AYEARST, MORLEY
38.010   BC   1957 Political aspects of Federation. *Social Econ Stud* 6(2), June: 247-261.   [*RIS*]

BAILEY, SYDNEY D.

37.015   BC   1949 Constitutions of the British Colonies. I: Colonies in the western hemisphere.

38.011   BC   1952 A British Caribbean Federation. *Fortnightly* new ser., 1028, Aug.: 84-89.   [*NYP*]

BALOGH, THOMAS

51.004   BC   1960 Making of a customs union.

BELL, WENDELL

38.012   JM   1960 Attitudes of Jamaican elites toward the West Indies Federation. *In* RUBIN, VERA, ed. SOCIAL AND CULTURAL PLURALISM IN THE CARIBBEAN. New York, New York Academy of Sciences, p.862-879. (Annals of the New York Academy of Sciences, v. 83, art. 5.) [8]   [*RIS*]

BEST, LLOYD

38.013   TR   1965 Chaguaramas to slavery? *New Wld Q* 2(1), Dead Season: 43-70.   [*RIS*]

BIRCH, A. H.

38.014   BC   1950 A British Caribbean Federation: the next dominion? *Parl Aff* 14(1), Winter: 152-162.   [*COL*]

BLANSHARD, PAUL

38.015   BC   1949 Twilight of Caribbean imperialism. *Nation* 168(4), Jan. 22: 92-94.   [*COL*]

BLOOD, Sir HILARY

38.016   BC   1955 The birth of a new nation. *Listener* 54(1400), Dec. 29: 1109-1110.   [*COL*]

38.017   BC   1956 Federation in the Caribbean. *Corona* 8(5), May: 166-169.   [*AGS*]

38.018   BC   1957 The West Indian Federation. *J Roy Soc Arts* 105(5009), Aug. 2:746-757.   [*AGS*]

38.019   BC   1958 British Caribbean Federation. *J Roy Commonw Soc* 1(2), July-Aug.: 158-162.   [*AGS*]

38.020   BC   1958 Final stages in the West Indies. *Corona* 10(5), May: 166-168.   [*AGS*]

BLOOMFIELD, ARTHUR

53.004   BC   [n.d.] CENTRAL BANKING ARRANGEMENTS FOR THE WEST INDIAN FEDERATION.

BOLT, ANNE

2.019   BC   1961 A diversity of islands: The West Indian Federation.

BRADSHAW,

44.021   BC   1958 Financial problems of the Federation.

BRADY, ALEXANDER

38.021   BC   1958 THE WEST INDIES: A NEW FEDERATION. Toronto, Canadian Institute of International Affairs, 16p. (Behind the headlines, v. 17, no. 5.)   [*RIS*]

BRAINE, BERNARD

38.022   BC   1953 To be or not to be...? in the West Indies. *New Commonw* 25(7), Mar. 30: 324-325.   [*AGS*]

BRAITHWAITE, LLOYD E.

38.023   BC   1957 'Federal' associations and institutions in the West Indies. *Social Econ Stud* 6(2), June: 286-328.   [8, 23, 32, 44, 66]   [*RIS*]

38.024   BC   1957 Progress toward Federation, 1938-1956.   *Social Econ Stud* 6(2), June: 133-184.   [5, 44]   [*RIS*]

BROWN, NOEL JOSEPH

37.044   JM   1963 JAMAICA AND THE WEST INDIES FEDERATION: A CASE STUDY ON THE PROBLEMS OF POLITICAL INTEGRATION.

BUCKMASTER, MICHAEL H.

38.025   BC   1962 What prospect for the Windwards? *New Commonw* 40(2), Feb.: 89-92.

BURNS, Sir ALAN CUTHBERT

38.026   BC   1955 Towards a Caribbean Federation. *For Aff* 34(1), Oct.: 128-140. [*AGS*]

CAHNMAN, WERNER J.

38.027   BC   1948 The West-Indian Federation. *Jew Fron* 15(1), Jan.: 16-18.   [*COL*]

CAIRES, DAVID de

44.030   BG   1963 Regional integration.

CAMPBELL, Sir JOCK

37.053   BC   1962 Facing up to facts in the Caribbean.
37.054   BC   1963 The West Indies: can they stand alone?

CARSTAIRS, C. Y.

38.028   BC   1950 Federation. *J Barb Mus Hist Soc* 17(2-3), Feb.-May: 84-92.   [*AMN*]

COON, F. SEAL

38.029   BG   1951 British Guiana's attitude towards Federation. *New Commonw* 22(6), Dec.: 474.

COZIER, EDWARD L.

38.030   BC   1957 Foreshadows of Federation. *Caribbean* 10(10), May: 241-244. [5] [*COL*]

CRABOT,

43.028   BC   1959 Naissance d'une nation: la Federation des Antilles Britanniques [Birth of a nation: the British West Indies Federation].

CROFT, W. D.; SPRINGER, H. W. & CHRISTOPHERSON, H. S.

51.039   BC   1958 Report of the Trade and Tariffs Commission.

CROWE, HARRY J.

38.031   BC   1920 Political union between Canada and the West Indies. *Can-W I Mag* 8(9), July: 576-577.   [51]   [*NYP*]

38.032   BC   1921 The future relations of Canada and Jamaica. *Can-W I Mag* 9(4), Feb.: 96-97.   [51]   [*NYP*]

CUMPER, GEORGE E., ed.

44.048   BC   1960   ECONOMY OF THE WEST INDIES.

CURRY, HERBERT FRANKLIN, Jr.

38.033   BC   1958 THE MOVEMENT TOWARDS FEDERATION OF THE BRITISH WEST INDIAN
                COLONIES, 1634-1945. Ph.D. dissertation, University of Wisconsin,
                306p. [5]   [NYP]

DALE, EDMUND H.

38.034   BC   1961 The West Indies: a Federation in search of a capital. Can Geogr
                5(2), Summer: 44-52.

38.035   BC   1962 The state-idea: missing prop of the West Indies Federation. Scott
                Geogr Mag 78(3), Dec.: 166-176.   [COL]

DAVSON, Sir EDWARD R.

37.091   BC   1919 Problems of the West Indies.

DEMAS, WILLIAM G.

51.045   BC   1960 The economics of West Indies customs union.

DOMINGO, W. A.

38.036   BC   1956 BRITISH WEST INDIAN FEDERATION: A CRITIQUE.   Kingston, Gleaner
                Co., 19p.

DRUMMOND, ANDREW T.

38.037   BC   1917 The future of the West Indies. WI Comm Circ 32(448), June 14: 224-
                228.   [44]   [NYP]

DUNCAN, EBENEZER

37.102   1947 THE POLITICAL CONSTITUTION OF THE WESTINDIAN COMMONWEALTH.

ELIAS, TASLIM OLAWALE

38.038   BC   1960 FEDERATION VS. CONFEDERATION AND THE NIGERIAN FEDERATION. Port
                of Spain, Office of the Premier of Trinidad and Tobago, 50p. [RIS]

ETZIONI, AMITAI

38.039   BC   1965 A union that failed: the Federation of the West Indies (1958-1962).
                In his POLITICAL UNIFICATION: A COMPARATIVE STUDY OF LEADERS AND
                FORCES. New York, Holt, Rinehart and Winston, p.138-183.   [RIS]

FERTIG, NORMAN ROSS

38.040   BC   1958 THE CLOSER UNION MOVEMENT IN THE BRITISH WEST INDIES. Ph.D. dis-
                sertation, University of Southern California, 316p. [5]   [NYP]

FOOT, Sir HUGH

38.041   BC   1957 Great Britain and the building of a new self-governing nation in the
                Caribbean. In WILGUS, A. CURTIS, ed. THE CARIBBEAN: CONTEMPO-
                RARY INTERNATIONAL RELATIONS [papers delivered at the Seventh
                Conference on the Caribbean held at the University of Florida,
                Dec. 6-8, 1956]. Gainesville, University of Florida Press, p.53-58.
                (Publications of the School of Inter-American Studies, ser. 1, v. 7.)
                                                                             [RIS]

FREITAS, G. V. de

38.042   BC   1956 Wanted—a federal capital. New Commonw 32(3), Aug.: 118-119. [AGS]

GILES, WALTER I.

37.139 JM 1956 JAMAICA: A STUDY OF BRITISH COLONIAL POLICY AND THE DEVELOPMENT
           OF SELF-GOVERNMENT.

GILLETTE, H. P. S.

28.228 BC 1960 Comments on Dr. Thomas's report of the chest service for the Fed-
           eration of the West Indies.

GOBAN, M. O.

38.043 BC 1951 Federation in the West Indies? *Contemp Rev* 180, Sept.: 145-148.
                                  [*COL*]

GOMES, ALBERT

38.044 BC 1959 The ides of September—for the W. I. Federation. *Can-W I Mag* 49(9),
           Sept.: 1-2.   [*NYP*]

GORDON, GARNET H.

38.045 BC 1961 The West Indies before and after Jamaica's quitvote. *Commonw J*
           4(6), Nov.-Dec.: 274-279.   [*COL*]

GORDON, WILLIAM E.

37.143 JM 1939 Jamaicans strive for dominion status.

GREENIDGE, C. W. W.

38.046 BC 1950 The British Caribbean Federation. *Wld Aff* 4(3), July: 321-334. [*AGS*]
38.047 BC 1952 West Indian Federation. *W I Comm Circ* 68(1266), June: 145-146.
                                  [*NYP*]
38.048 BB 1956 Barbados and the Pope Hennessy riots. *W I Comm Circ* 71(1303),
           July: 183-184.   [5]   [*NYP*]

HAMILTON, BRUCE

38.049 BB 1950 Barbados and British West Indian Confederation, 1871-1885. *Car His*
           Rev 1, Dec.: 80-109;
           1951 2, Dec.: 47-78. [5]   [*RIS*]
38.050 BB 1956 BARBADOS AND THE CONFEDERATION QUESTION, 1871-1885. London,
           Crown Agents for Overseas Governments & Administrations, 149p. [5]

HAREWOOD, JACK

50.060 JM/ 1960 Overpopulation and underemployment in the West Indies.
     TR

HATCH, JOHN

38.051 BC 1958 Birth of a nation. *Venture* 9(10), Mar.: 4.   [*COL*]
38.052 BC 1958 DWELL TOGETHER IN UNITY. London, Fabian Society, 40p. (Fabian
           tract 313.)   [*COL*]

HEWITT-MYRING, PHILIP

38.053 BC 1949 West Indian future. *Spectator* 182(6298), Mar. 11: 317-318. [*NYP*]
38.054 BC 1955 British Caribbean Federation. *Parl Aff* 8(4), Autumn: 436-444. [*COL*]

HINDEN, RITA

38.055 BC 1953 Federating the West Indies. *Corona* 5(3), Mar.: 97-100. [*AGS*]

HOYOS, F. A.

37.185   BC   1963 THE RISE OF WEST INDIAN DEMOCRACY; THE LIFE AND TIMES OF SIR
                    GRANTLEY ADAMS.

HUGHES, COLIN A.

38.056   BC   1958 Experiments towards closer union in the British West Indies. *J Ne-
                    gro Hist* 43(2), Apr.: 85-104.   [5]   [*COL*]

HUNTE, GEORGE HUTCHINSON

16.019   BC   1946 West Indian unity: measures and machinery.
55.016   BC   1957 Tourism: a federal approach.

HUURMAN, D.

37.194   NC   1948 Britse federatieve voorstellen en Nederlandse federatie-mogelijk-
                    heden in West Indië [British federation proposals\and Dutch federa-
                    tion possibilities in the West Indies].

JACOBS, H. P.

38.057   BC   1956 This Federation. *Pepperpot* [6]: 21-23.
38.058   BC   1957 The Federal constitution: its mechanism and meaning. *W I Rev* new
                    ser., 2(10), Oct.: 19, 21, 111.   [*NYP*]

JAMES, CYRIL LIONEL ROBERT

38.059   BC   1962 FEDERATION: "WE FAILED MISERABLY"; HOW AND WHY. San Juan,
                    Trinidad, Vedic Enterprises, 32p.   [*RIS*]

JANDRAY, FREDERICK

38.060   BC   1958 The new Federation of the West Indies. *Dep St B* 38(985), May 12:
                    768-769.   [*COL*]

JONES, A. CREECH

38.061   BC   1958 Salute to Federation. *W I Comm Circ* 73(1324), Apr.: 99-100. [*NYP*]
38.062   BC   1958 A visit to the West Indies. *Venture* 10(2), June: 4.   [*COL*]

KEIRSTEAD, B. S. & LEVITT, KARI

52.043   BC   [n.d.] INTER-TERRITORIAL FREIGHT RATES AND THE FEDERAL SHIPPING SERV-
                    ICE.

KELLY, JAMES B.

38.063   BC   1962 The end of Federation: some constitutional implications. *W I Econ*
                    4(9), Mar.: 11-26.

KNAPLUND, PAUL

38.064   BC   1962 Introduction to Federation of the West Indies. *Social Econ Stud*
                    6(2), June: 99-108.   [5]   [*RIS*]

KNOX, A. D.

51.079   BC   1960 Trade and customs union in the West Indies.

LEVO, EDITH MIRIAM

38.065   BC   1957 THE FEDERATION OF THE BRITISH WEST INDIES: DEVELOPMENT AND
                    PROSPECTS. M. A. thesis, Clark University, 108p.

LEVY, CLAUDE

38.066   BC   1950   PROBLEMS IN BRITISH WEST INDIAN FEDERATION. Ph.D. dissertation, University of Colorado, 266p.   [5]

LEWIS, Sir ARTHUR

38.067   BC   1965   THE AGONY OF THE EIGHT. [Bridgetown?] Barbados, Advocate Commercial Printery.   [*RIS*]

LEWIS, GORDON K.

38.068   BC   1957   The British Caribbean Federation: the West Indian background. *Polit Q* 28(1), Jan.-Mar.: 49-65.   [*COL*]

38.069   BC   1957   La Federación Británica del Caribe; el trasfondo de las Indias Occidentales [The British Caribbean Federation: the West Indian background]. *Revta Cienc Social* 1(1), Mar.: 139-171.   [*AGS*]

38.070   BC   1957   West Indian Federation: the constitutional aspects. *Social Econ Stud* 6(2), June: 215-246.   [*RIS*]

LEWIS, W. ARTHUR

38.071   BC   1962   PROPOSALS FOR AN EASTERN CARIBBEAN FEDERATION, COMPRISING THE TERRITORIES OF ANTIGUA, BARBADOS, DOMINICA, GRENADA, MONTSERRAT, ST. KITTS-NEVIS-ANGUILLA, ST. LUCIA AND ST. VINCENT. Port of Spain, Government of the West Indies, 8p.   [*RIS*]

LISTOWEL, WILLIAM FRANCIS HARE, 5th Earl of; FARLEY, RAWLE; HINDEN, RITA & HUGHES, COLIN

37.232   BC   1952   CHALLENGE TO THE BRITISH CARIBBEAN.

LOGAN, RAYFORD W.

38.072   BC   1944   The possibilities of a Caribbean Federation. *In* FRAZIER, E. F. & WILLIAMS E., eds. THE ECONOMIC FUTURE OF THE WEST INDIES. Washington, D.C., Howard University Press, p.55-58.

LOWENTHAL, DAVID

38.073   BC   1957   Two federations. *Social Econ Stud* 6(2), June: 185-196. [5]   [*RIS*]

38.074   BC   1958   The West Indies chooses a capital. *Geogr Rev* 48(3): 336-364.   [10]   [*RIS*]

38.075   BC   1961   The social background of West Indian Federation. *In* LOWENTHAL, DAVID, ed. THE WEST INDIES FEDERATION. New York, Columbia University Press, p.63-96.   [21]   [*RIS*]

38.076   BC   1961   THE WEST INDIES FEDERATION. New York, Columbia University Press, 142p.   [*RIS*]

LUSAKA, PAUL JOHN FIRMINO

38.077   BC   1964   THE DISSOLUTION OF THE WEST INDIES FEDERATION. M. A. thesis, McGill University, 215p.

McCOLL, E. KIMBARK

38.078   BC   1951/ Poverty and politics in the Caribbean. *Int J* 7(1), Winter: 12-22. [*AGS*]
             52

McCOWAN, ANTHONY

38.079   BG   1957   British Guiana and Federation. Corona 9(3), Mar.: 85-88.   [*AGS*]

McDERMOTT, T. W. L.

38.080   BC   1933 Federation of the West Indies: Is it desirable? *Can-W I Mag* 22(8),
                July: 239-240.   [5]   [*NYP*]

MacINNES, C. M.

38.081   BC   1955 British Caribbean Federation. *In* DEVELOPMENTS TOWARDS SELF-
                GOVERNMENT IN THE CARIBBEAN. A symposium held under the aus-
                pices of the Netherlands Universities Foundation for International
                Co-operation at the Hague, Sept. 1954. The Hague, W. van Hoeve,
                p.151-175.   [*RIS*]

MAHABIR, DENNIS J.

38.082   BC   1957 The Caribbean Federation. *India Q* 13(1), Jan.-Mar.: 32-40.   [*AGS*]

MANLEY, NORMAN

38.083   BC   1951 Political future of British West Indies. *Venture* 3(2), Mar.: 4-5. [*COL*]

MEIER, GERALD M.

51.094   BC   1960 Effects of a customs union on economic development.

MEIKLE, LOUIS S.

38.084   BC   1912 CONFEDERATION OF BRITISH WEST INDIES VERSUS ANNEXATION TO THE
                UNITED STATES OF AMERICA. London, Sampson, Low, Marston & Co.,
                279p.   [5]   [*NYP*]

MERRILL, GORDON CLARK

2.155   BC   1958 The British West Indies—the newest Federation of the Commonwealth.
19.031   BC   1961 The survival of the past in the West Indies.

MIDAS, ANDRE

37.269   BC   1957 Constitutional evolution.

MITCHELL, Sir HAROLD

44.156   BC   1957 Finance and federation.

MITCHELL, Sir PHILIP

38.085   BC   1950 A federal plan for the British Caribbean. *Corona* 2(5), May:175-178.

MORGAN, D. J.

51.105   BC   1962 Imperial preference in the West Indies and in the British Caribbean,
                1929-55: a quantitative analysis.

MUDIE, Sir FRANCIS, et al.

38.086   BC   1956 REPORT OF THE BRITISH CARIBBEAN FEDERAL CAPITAL COMMISSION.
                London, H.M.S.O., 44p. (Colonial no. 328.)   [*AGS*]

MULLINGS, LLEWELLYN MAXIMILLIAN

44.160   JM   1964 AN ANALYSIS OF THE ECONOMIC IMPLICATIONS OF POLITICAL INDEPEND-
                ENCE FOR JAMAICA.

MURKLAND, HARRY B.

38.087   BC   1958 The West Indies unite: British colonies take first step toward inde-
                pendence. *Americas* July: 3-9.   [*AGS*]

MURRAY, C. GIDEON

38.088 BC   1912 A UNITED WEST INDIES. London, West Strand Pub. Co., 127p.   [5]
                                                                          [*NYP*]

MURRAY, GIDEON

37.278 BC   1919 Canada and the British West Indies.

OLIVIER, SYDNEY, 1st Baron RAMSDEN

38.089 BC   1937 The future in the West Indies, by Lord Olivier. *Crown Colon* 7(66),
                    May: 196.   [*NYP*]

O'LOUGHLIN, CARLEEN

44.174 LW/ 1963/ Economic problems of the Leeward and Windward Islands.
          WW   64

OSBORNE, WILLIAM ADOLPHUS

38.090 BC   1956 SOME PROBLEMS OF FEDERATION IN THE BRITISH CARIBBEAN. Ph.D.
                    dissertation, Clark University, 291p.

PAGET, HUGH

38.091 BC   1950 The West Indies. *United Emp* 41(3), May-June: 164-167.

PROCOPE, BRUCE

38.092 BC   1960 The temporary federal mace. *Car Q* 6(2-3), May: 142. [22]   [*RIS*]

PROCTOR, JESSE HARRIS, Jr.

38.093 BC   1955 The development of the idea of Federation of the British Caribbean
                    territories. *Revta Hist Am* 39, June: 61-105.   [*RIS*]
38.094 BC   1955 THE EFFORT TO FEDERATE THE BRITISH CARIBBEAN TERRITORIES, 1945-
                    1953.   Ph.D. dissertation, Harvard University, 618p.   [*RIS*]
38.095 BC   1956 Britain's pro-Federation policy in the Caribbean: an inquiry into mo-
                    tivation. *Can J Econ Polit Sci* 22(3), Aug.: 319-331.   [*RIS*]
38.096 BC   1956 The functional approach to political union: lessons from the effort
                    to federate the British Caribbean territories. *Int Org* 10(1): 35-48.
                                                                          [*RIS*]
38.097 BC   1957 The international significance of the Federation of British Caribbean
                    territories. *In* WILGUS, A. CURTIS, ed. THE CARIBBEAN: CONTEMPO-
                    RARY INTERNATIONAL RELATIONS [papers delivered at the Seventh Con-
                    ference on the Caribbean held at the University of Florida, Dec. 6-8,
                    1956]. Gainesville, University of Florida Press, p.59-68. (Publica-
                    tions of the School of Inter-American Studies, ser. 1, v. 7.)   [*RIS*]
38.098 TR   1961 East Indians and the Federation of the British West Indies. *India Q*
                    17(4), Oct.-Dec.:370-395.   [10,12]   [*RIS*]

PYE, NORMAN

38.099 BC   1935 The geographical factors involved in the problem of British West
                    Indian federation. *Globe* 15, May: 6-11.   [40]   [*AGS*]

RAMPHAL, S. S.

38.100 BC   1959 The West Indies—constitutional background to Federation. *Publ Law*
                    Summer: 128-151.   [5]   [*COL*]
38.101 BC   1960 Federalism in the West Indies. *Car Q* 6(2-3), May: 210-229.   [5]
                                                                          [*RIS*]

RANCE, Sir HUBERT ELVIN

38.102   BC   1953 Towards a Federation of the British West Indies. *In* WILGUS, A.
               CURTIS, ed. THE CARIBBEAN: CONTEMPORARY TRENDS [papers del-
               ivered at the Third Annual Conference on the Caribbean held at
               the University of Florida, Dec. 18-20, 1952]. Gainesville, Uni-
               versity of Florida Press, p.241-256. (Publications of the School of
               Inter-American Studies, ser. 1, v. 3.)   [*RIS*]

38.103   BC   1954 Towards a Federation of the British West Indies. *Car Hist Rev* 3-4,
               Dec.: 1-12.   [*RIS*]

RAWLINS, RANDOLPH

38.104   GC   1958 Federation and confederation. *Corona* 10(3), Mar.: 98-100.   [*AGS*]

RICHARDSON, W. A.

38.105   TR   1959 Trinidad—the Federal Capital. *Can-W I Mag* 49(10), Oct.: 13-16. [*NYP*]

RIESGO, RAYMOND R.

51.121   BC   1961 The Federation of the West Indies.

ROBERTS, GEORGE WOODROW

38.106   BC   1957 Some demographic considerations of West Indian federation. *Social
               Econ Stud* 6(2), June: 262-285.   [5,7]   [*RIS*]

RORTY, JAMES

37.349   NV   1961 Independence, like it or not.

SCHNEIDER, FRED D.

38.107   BC   1959 British policy in West Indian Federation. *Wld Aff Q* 30(3), Oct.:
               241-265.

SEEL, G. F.

44.210   BC   [1953?] FINANCIAL ASPECTS OF FEDERATION OF THE BRITISH WEST INDIAN TER-
               RITORIES.

SEEL, Sir GEORGE

38.108   BC   1956 Federation. *Statist* Sept.: 7-9.

38.109   BC   1957 Some Federation memories. *W I Rev* new ser., 2(10), Oct.: 23-25.
                                                                                   [*NYP*]

SEERS, DUDLEY

38.110   BC   1957 Federation of the British West Indies: the economic and financial
               aspects. *Social Econ Stud* 6(2), June: 197-214. [44,66]   [*RIS*]

SHENFIELD, A. A.

66.136   BC   1958 Economic advance in the West Indies.

SHEPHEARD, WALWYN P. B.

38.111   BC   1900 The West Indies and confederation. *J Soc Comp Leg* new ser., 2(2):
               224-232.   [5]   [*NYP*]

SHERLOCK, PHILIP M.

21.022   BC   [1956?] Federation: let's meet the family.

37.368   JM/   1962   Nouvelles nations dans les Antilles [New nations in the Caribbean].
           TR

38.112   BC   1963   Une fédération restreinte? [A limited federation?] *Civilisations* 13
                       (1-2): 212-213.   [*RIS*]

SIMEY, THOMAS S.

38.113   BC   1957   A new capital for the British West Indies. *Town Plann Rev* 28(1),
                       Apr.: 63-70.   [*AGS*]

SMITH, GERALD GROGAN

38.114   BC   1955   THE PROPOSED BRITISH CARIBBEAN FEDERATION. Ph.D. dissertation,
                       Syracuse University, 250p.   [*NYP*]

SMITH, M. G.

37.385   BC   1962   Short-range prospects in the British Caribbean.

SMITH, R. G. C.

51.128   BC   1959   The West Indies.

SMITH, RAYMOND THOMAS

21.023   BG   1958   British Guiana.

SPRINGER, HUGH W.

38.115   BC   1961   The West Indies emergent: problems and prospects. *In* LOWEN-
                       THAL, DAVID, ed. THE WEST INDIES FEDERATION. New York, Col-
                       umbia University Press, p.1-16. [44, 46, 66]   [*RIS*]

38.116   BC   1962   Federation in the Caribbean: an attempt that failed. *Int Org* 16(4),
                       Autumn: 758-775.

38.117   BC   1962   REFLECTIONS ON THE FAILURE OF THE FIRST WEST INDIAN FEDERATION.
                       Cambridge, Center for International Affairs, Harvard University, 66p.
                       (Occasional papers in international affairs, no. 4.)

**STERN, PETER M.; AUGELLI, JOHN P.; LOWENTHAL, DAVID &
ALEXANDER, LEWIS M.**

38.118   BC   1956   British Caribbean Federation. *Focus* 7(1), Sept. (6p.)   [*AGS*]

STEWART, ALICE R.

38.119   BC   1950   Canadian-West Indian union, 1884-1885. *Can Hist Rev* 31(4), Dec.:
                       369-389. [5]   [*COL*]

38.120   BC   1951   Documents on Canadian-West Indian relations, 1883-1885. *Car Hist
                       Rev* 2, Dec.: 100-133. [5]

THOMPSON, GEORGE

38.121   BC   1960   The West Indies Federation. *Venture* 12(8), Sept.: 5-6.   [*COL*]

WALKER, P. C. GORDAN

38.122   BC   1955   No easy path for Caribbean federation. *New Commonw* 30(8), Oct.
                       17: 364-365.   [*AGS*]

WALLACE, ELISABETH

38.123   BC   1961   The West Indies: improbable Federation? *Can J Econ Polit Sci* 27
                       (4), Nov.: 444-459.

38.124   BC   1962 The West Indies Federation: decline and fall. *Int J* 17(3), Summer:
                        269-288.

           WASHINGTON, S. WALTER
38.125   BC   1960 Crisis in the British West Indies. *For Aff* 38(4), July: 646-655. [*RIS*]

           WATERMAN, JAMES A.
28.563   BC   1958 The impact of federation on medicine in the West Indies.

           WILGUS, A. CURTIS, ed.
2.258   GC   1957 The Caribbean: contemporary international relations.

           WILLIAMS, DOUGLAS
37.426   BC   1958 Constitutional developments in the British West Indies.

           WILLIAMS, ERIC EUSTACE
38.126   BC   1956 Federation: two public lectures. [Port of Spain?] Trinidad, Peo-
                        ple's National Movement, 60p.   [32, 37]   [*RIS*]
66.165   TR   1960 Perspectives for the West Indies.
38.127   BC   1963 The future of the West Indies and Guyana. Address delivered at
                        Queens College, Georgetown, Guyana, under the auspices of the
                        Extra-mural Department, University of the West Indies, 13th March
                        1963. Port of Spain, Govt. Print. Off., 39p. [5]   [*RIS*]

           WILLIAMS, ERIC EUSTACE, ed.
38.128   BC   1954 The historical background of the British West Indian Federation:
                        select documents. *Car Hist Rev* 3-4, Dec.: 13-69.. [5]   [*RIS*]

           WISEMAN, H. V.
38.129   BC   1948 The West Indies, towards a new dominion? London, Fabian Publi-
                        cations, 45p. (Research series no. 130.) [33, 37, 44, 46]   [*RIS*]

Chapter 39

EXTERNAL BOUNDARY ISSUES

ALVARADO, RAFAEL
39.001 BH   1958 La cuestión de Belice [The Belize question]. [Guatemala City?]
              Guatemala, Secretaría de Información de la Presidencia de la Re-
              publica, 60p.   [5]   [AGS]

ARROYO, MANUEL
39.002 BH   1947/ A questão de Belice, Honduras Britânicas [The question of Belize,
              48   British Honduras]. Revta Soc Brasil Geogr 54:23-41. [5]   [AGS]

ASTURIAS, FRANCISCO
39.003 BH   1941 Belice. 2d ed. enl. [Guatemala City?] Guatemala: Tipografía Na-
              cional de Guatemala, Publicaciones de la Revista de la Facultad de
              Ciencias Jurídicas y Sociales, 177p. [5]   [AGS]

AZEVEDO COSTA, J. A. de
39.004 FG   1945 Litígio entre o Brasil e a Franca—a questão do Território de Am-
              apá [Litigation between Brazil and France—the question of the Ter-
              ritory of Amapá]. Revta Soc Geogr Rio Jan 52: 92-100. [5]   [AGS]

BAKER, MARCUS
39.005 BG   1900 Anglo-Venezuelan boundary dispute. Natn Geogr Mag 11(4), Apr.:
              129-144.   [5]   [AGS]

BENJAMINS, H. D.
39.006 SR   1921/ Suriname's westgrens und kein Ende [Surinam's western borderline
              22   ad infinitum]. W I G 3:393-401.   [COL]
39.007 SR   1922/ Nogmaals Suriname's westgrens [Surinam's westerly border once
              23   again]. W I G 4:401-420.   [COL]
39.008 SR   1923 Minister de Graaff en de Corantijn kwestie [Minister de Graaff and
              the Courantyne problem]. W I G 6:259-276.   [COL]
39.009 SR   1924/ De Corantijnkwestie twee stappen vooruit [The Courantyne problem:
              25   two steps in the right direction]. W I G 6:338-365.   [COL]
39.010 SR   1925/ Een nieuw geluid in de Corantijn kwestie [A new possibility in the
              26   Courantyne problem]. W I G 7:311-345.   [COL]

39.011   SR   1926/ De Corantijnsche kwestie op den goeden weg? [Is the Courantyne
                27   problem going in the right direction?] *W I G* 8:293-314.   [*COL*]

39.012   SR   1927/ Hoe staat het thans met de Corantijn kwestie? [What is the present
                28   situation of the Courantyne problem?] *W I G* 9:389-416.   [*COL*]

39.013   SR   1928/ De Courantijnkwestie bij Buitenlandsche Zaken [The Courantyne
                29   problem before the Ministry of Foreign Affairs]. *W I G* 10:571-584.
                                                                                     [*COL*]

39.014   SR   1930/ Surinaamsche grenskwesties, het einde in zicht [Surinam's border
                31   problems; the end is in sight]. *W I G* 11:367-388.   [*COL*]

39.015   SR   1931/ De Corantijnkwestie: nieuw licht op oude bescheiden [The Couran-
                32   tyne problem: new light upon old documents]. *W I G* 13:49-62. [*COL*]

          BERNARD, AUGUSTIN
39.016   FG   1901 Le contesté franco-brésilien [The Franco-Brazilian [boundary] dis-
                pute]. *Quest Diplom Colon* 11, Jan.: 31-37.   [*COL*]

          BIANCHI, WILLIAM J.
39.017   BH   1959 BELIZE: THE CONTROVERSY BETWEEN GUATEMALA AND GREAT BRITAIN
                OVER THE TERRITORY OF BRITISH HONDURAS IN CENTRAL AMERICA. New
                York, Las Américas Pub. Co., 142p. [5]   [*AGS*]

          BLOOMFIELD, L. M.
39.018   BH   1953 THE BRITISH HONDURAS-GUATEMALA DISPUTE. Toronto, Carswell Co.,
                231p. [5]   [*COL*]

          BURR, GEORGE LINCOLN
39.019   BG   1900 The Guiana boundary: a postscript to the work of the American Com-
                mission. *Am Hist Rev* 6(1), Oct.: 49-64.   [5]   [*COL*]

          CALDERON QUIJANO, JOSE ANTONIO
39.020   BH   1944 BELICE 1663(?)-1821: HISTORIA DE LOS ESTABLECIMIENTOS BRITÁNICOS
                DEL RÍO VALIS HASTA LA INDEPENDENCIA DE HISPANOAMÉRICA [BELIZE
                1663(?)-1821: HISTORY OF THE BRITISH SETTLEMENTS OF THE VALIS
                RIVER UNTIL THE INDEPENDENCE OF SPANISH AMERICA]. Seville, Vic-
                toria-Artes Gráficas, 503p. (Publicaciones de la Escuela de Estu-
                dios Hispanoamericanos de la Universidad de Sevilla, general no. 5,
                2nd ser., no. 1.)   [5]   [*AGS*]

          CANALES SALAZAR, FELIX
39.021   BH   1946 DERECHOS TERRITORIALES DE LA REPÚBLICA DE HONDURAS SOBRE HON-
                DURAS BRITANICA O BELICE, ISLAS DEL CISNE Y COSTAS DE LOS INDIOS
                MOSQUITOS [TERRITORIAL RIGHTS OF THE REPUBLIC OF HONDURAS OVER
                BRITISH HONDURAS OR BELIZE, SWAN ISLANDS, AND THE MOSQUITO IN-
                DIAN COAST]. México, 91p. [5]   [*AGS*]

          CLEGERN, WAYNE M.
39.022   BH   1958 New light on the Belize dispute. *Am J Int Law* 52(2), Apr.: 280-297.
                                                                                     [*AGS*]
39.023   BH   1962 British Honduras and the pacification of Yucatán. *Americas* 18(3),
                Jan.: 243-254.   [*COL*]

          COLLIER, H. C.
39.024   BH   1947 Selling British Honduras short. *Can-W I Mag* 36(11), Jan.: 11-12. [*NYP*]

EDMUNDSON, GEORGE

39.025   BG   1923 The relations of Great Britain with Guiana.   *Trans Roy Hist Soc* 4th ser., 6:1-21.   [5]   [*COL*]

ESCALONA RAMOS, ALBERTO

39.026   BH   1940 Belice pertenece a México o a Guatemala? [Does Belize belong to Mexico or to Guatemala?]. *Revta Mex Geogr* 1(1), July-Sept.: 33-60. [5]   [*AGS*]

FAUCHILLE, PAUL

39.027   BG   1905 LE CONFLIT DE LIMITES ENTRE LE BRÉSIL ET LA GRANDE-BRETAGNE ET LA SENTENCE ARBITRALE DU ROI D'ITALIE [THE BOUNDARY DISPUTE BE-TWEEN BRAZIL AND GREAT BRITAIN AND THE ARBITRATION RULING OF THE KING OF ITALY]. Paris, A. Pedone, 131p.   [5]   [*NYP*]

FOSSUM, PAUL R.

39.028   BG   1928 The Anglo-Venezuelan boundary controversy.   *Hispan Am Hist Rev* 8(3), Aug.: 299-329.   [5]   [*COL*]

HERMES, JOAO SEVERIANO da FONSECA

39.029   BH   1939 Questão de limites entre Guatemala e Honduras Ingleza [Boundary controversy between Guatemala and British Honduras].   *Revta Soc Geogr Rio Jan* 46: 13-30.   [5]   [*AGS*]

HURTADO AGUILAR, LUIS A.

39.030   BH   [1958?] BELICE ES DE GUATEMALA: TRATADOS, SITUACIÓN JURÍDICA, ACTUA-CIONES, OPINIONES [BELIZE BELONGS TO GUATEMALA: TREATIES, JURIDI-CAL SITUATION, PROCEEDINGS, RULINGS].   [Guatemala City?] Guate-mala, Secretaría de Información de la Presidencia de la República, 128p.   [5]   [*AGS*]

IRELAND, GORDON

39.031   GG   1938 BOUNDARIES, POSSESSIONS, AND CONFLICTS IN SOUTH AMERICA.   Cam-bridge, Harvard University Press, 345p.   [*COL*]

KUNZ, JOSEF L.

39.032   BH   1946 Guatemala vs. Great Britain: in re Belice.   *Am J Int Law* 40(2), Apr.: 383-390.   [5]   [*AGS*]

LORD, W. T.

39.033   BG   1961 Experiences of a government surveyor.   *Timehri* 4th ser., no. 40, Oct.: 61-75.   [*AMN*]

MARCOS LOPEZ, FRANCISCO

39.034   BH   [n.d.] QUIEBRA Y REINTEGRACIÓN DEL DERECHO DE GENTES: GIBRALTAR, BELICE, LAS MALVINAS [THE BREAKING AND RESTORATION OF INTERNATIONAL LAW: GIBRALTAR, BELIZE, LAS MALVINAS].   [Guatemala City?] Guate-mala, Talleres de Impr. Hispania, 78p.   [5]   [*AGS*]

MENDOZA, JOSE LUIS

39.035   BH   1942 INGLATERRA Y SUS PACTOS SOBRE BELICE [GREAT BRITAIN AND ITS

TREATIES ON BELIZE]. [Guatemala City?] Guatemala, Secretaría de Relaciones Exteriores, 287p. [5]   [*AGS*]

RODWAY, JAMES

39.036   BG   1911 Our boundary war scare. *Timehri* 3d ser., 1(18C), Dec.: 239-247.
[5]   [*AMN*]

SANTISO GALVEZ, GUSTAVO

39.037   BH   1941 EL CASO DE BELICE A LA LUZ DE LA HISTORIA Y EL DERECHO INTERNACIONAL [THE BELIZE QUESTION IN THE LIGHT OF HISTORY AND INTERNATIONAL LAW]. [Guatamela City?] Guatemala, Tip. Nacional, 346p. (Thesis, University of Mexico.)   [5]   [*AGS*]

SCHOENRICH, OTTO

39.038   BG   1949 The Venezuela-British Guiana boundary dispute. *Am J Int Law* 43 (3), July: 523-530.   [5]   [*AGS*]

SLOAN, JENNIE A.

39.039   BG   1938 Anglo-American relations and the Venezuelan boundary dispute. *Hisp Am Hist Rev* 18(4), Nov.: 486-506.   [5]   [*COL*]

SLUITER, ENGEL

39.040   SR   1933 Dutch Guiana: a problem in boundaries. *Hisp Am Hist Rev* 13(1), Feb.: 2-22.   [5]   [*AGS*]

SMITH, H. CARINGTON

3.284   BG   1938 On the frontier of British Guiana and Brazil.

TORO, ELIAS

39.041   BG   1905 POR LAS SELVAS DE GUAYANA: DELIMITACIÓN DE VENEZUELA CON GUAYANA BRITÁNICA [THROUGH THE FORESTS OF GUIANA: THE BOUNDARY BETWEEN VENEZUELA AND BRITISH GUIANA]. Caracas, Tip. Herrera Irigoyen, 289p.   [5]   [*COL*]

UGARTE, MANUEL

39.042   BH   1940 Guatemala's claims in British Honduras. *Liv Age* 357(4480), Jan.: 438-439.   [5]

VASCO, G.

39.043   FG   1901 L'arbitrage du contesté franco-brésilien [The arbitration of the Franco-Brazilian [boundary] dispute]. *Rev Fr Etr Colon* 26(266), Feb.: 70-76.   [*NYP*]

VILLIERS, J. A. J. de

39.044   BG   1912 The boundaries of British Guiana. *United Emp* new ser., 3(6), June: 505-513.   [5]   [*AGS*]

WADDELL, DAVID A. G.

39.045   BH   1961 As Honduras Británicas e a reivindicacăo guatemalteca [British Honduras and the Guatemalan claim]. *Revta Brasil Polit Int* 4(15), Sept.: 55-71.   [*NYP*]

THE ENVIRONMENT
AND
HUMAN GEOGRAPHY

Chapter 40

GEOLOGY AND LAND FORMS

ALEXANDER, CHARLES S.

40.001   NL   1961 The marine terraces of Aruba, Bonaire and Curacao, Netherlands Antilles. *Ann Ass Am Geogr* 51(1), Mar.: 102-123.   [*RIS*]

ANDERSON, TEMPEST & FLETT, JOHN S.

40.002   MT/ 1903/ Report on the eruptions of the Soufrière, in St. Vincent, in 1902,
         SV   08   and on a visit to Montagne Pelée, in Martinique. Pts. 1-2 (pt. 2 by Tempest Anderson). *Phil Trans Roy Soc Lond* ser. A., 200: 353-553 (1903); 208: 275-303 (1908).   [*NYP*]

AUBERT de la RUE, EDGAR

40.003   FG   1951 Esquisse géologique de la Guyane méridionale [Geological sketch of Southern Guiana]. *Chron Min Colon* 19(181-182), July 15-Aug. 15: 182-186.   [*AGS*]

40.004   FG   1951 La Guyane Francaise. pt. 1: Caractères physiques [French Guiana. pt. I: Physical features]. *Nature* 79(3198), Oct.: 302-309. [For pt. II see 13.003.]   [*AGS*]

BAKER, HENRY D.

46.006   TR   1924 The asphalt lakes of Trinidad and Venezuela as natural wonders of the world.

BAKHUIS, L. A.

40.005   SR   1908 De 5de wetenschappelijke expeditie naar het binnenland van Suriname [The 5th scientific expedition into the interior of Surinam]. *Tijdschr Ned Aar Genoot* 25: 94-113.   [41,42]

BAKKER, J. P. & LANJOUW, J.

40.006   SR   1949 Indrukken van de natuurwetenschappelijke expeditie naar Suriname 1948-'49 [Impressions of the natural scientific expedition to Suriname 1948-'49]. *Tijdschr Ned Aar Genoot* 66:538-558.

BAKKER, J. P. & MULLER, H. J.

40.007   SR   1957 Zweiphasige Fluszablagerungen und Zweiphasenverwitterung in den Tropen unter besonderer Berücksichtigung von Surinam [Two-stage river sedimentation and two-stage erosion in the tropics, with special consideration of Surinam]. *Stuttgarter Geogr Stud* 69:365-397.   [*AGS*]

BARR, K. W.

| 40.008 | TR | 1953 The mud volcanoes of Trinidad. *Car Q* 3(2), Sept.: 80-85.   [*RIS*] |

40.009 GC 1958 The structural framework of the Caribbean region. Abstract. *In* RE-
PORT OF THE FIRST MEETING OF THE CARIBBEAN GEOLOGICAL CONFER-
ENCE held at Antigua, B.W.I., December 1955. Demerara [B.G.],
Argosy and Co., p.30-33.   [*RIS*]

BARRABE, L.

40.010 FA 1936 La constitution géologique des Antilles [The geological formation
of the Antilles]. *Chron Min Colon* 5(52), July: 214-227.   [*AGS*]

BARRON, C. N.

40.011 BG 1962 THE GEOLOGY OF THE SOUTH SAVANNAS DEGREE SQUARE. La Penitence,
E.B. [Demerara, B.G.] B.G. Lithographic, Ltd., 29p.   (Geological
Survey of British Guiana, Bulletin 33.)   [*AGS*]

BARRUOL, J.

40.012 FG 1960 Utilisation de la photographie aerienne pour l'établissement des
cartes géologiques et la prospection minière en Guyane Francaise
[The use of aerial photography in the making of geological maps
and in prospecting in French Guiana]. *In* TRANSACTIONS OF THE SEC-
OND CARIBBEAN GEOLOGICAL CONFERENCE, Mayagüez, P.R., January
1959. Mayagüez, P.R., University of Puerto Rico, p.40-42.   [*AMN*]

BEIJERING, J.

28.031 CU 1950 Het vraagstuk van het behoud van het water op Curacao [The problem of water conservation on Curacao].

BIJLSMA, R.

40.013 SR 1920/ Alexander de Lavaux en zijne generale kaart van Suriname 1737
        21 [Alexander de Lavaux and his general map of Surinam in 1737]. *W I G*
            2: 379-406.   [5]   [*COL*]

40.014 SR 1920/ De karteering van Suriname ten tijde van Gouverneur van Aerssen
        21 van Sommelsdijck [The surveying of Surinam at the time of Gover-
            nor van Aerssen van Sommelsdijck]. *W I G* 2:351-354. [5]   [*COL*]

BISHOPP, D. W.

40.015 BG 1955 THE BAUXITE RESOURCES OF BRITISH GUIANA AND THEIR DEVELOPMENT.
Georgetown, Daily Chronicle, 123p. (Bulletin no. 26, British Guiana Geological Survey.)   [54]   [*AGS*]

BLEACKLEY, D.

40.016 BG 1955 Artesian water supply and the coastal sediments of British Guiana.
Timehri 4th ser., 1(34), Sept.: 48-54.

40.017 BG 1956 THE GEOLOGY OF THE SUPERFICIAL DEPOSITS AND COASTAL SEDIMENTS
OF BRITISH GUIANA. Georgetown, Daily Chronicle. (British Guiana
Geological Survey, Bulletin no. 30.)

40.018 BG 1958 The coastal sediments and artesian water supply of British Guiana.
In REPORT OF THE FIRST MEETING OF THE CARIBBEAN GEOLOGICAL CON-
FERENCE held at Antigua, B.W.I., December 1955. Demerara [B.G.],
Argosy and Co., p.68-69.   [*RIS*]

BLUME, HELMUT

54.008 JM 1962 Der Bauxitbergbau auf Jamaika [The bauxite mining in Jamaica].

BOEKE, J.

40.019   CU   1919 De eilanden der kolonie Curacao in hunne verhouding tot hunne om-
                        geving [The islands of the colony of Curacao in their relationship
                        to their environment]. *W I G* 1(1): 132-141.   [*COL*]

BRACEWELL, SMITH

40.020   BG   1946 Mineral resources. *In* ROTH, VINCENT, comp. HANDBOOK OF THE
                        NATURAL RESOURCES OF BRITISH GUIANA. Georgetown, Daily Chroni-
                        cle, p. 20-43.   [54]   [*AGS*]

40.021   BG   1947 The geology and mineral resources of British Guiana. *B Imp Inst*
                        45(1), Jan.-Mar.: 47-69.   [54]   [*AGS*]

40.022   BG   1956 British Guiana. *Geol Soc Am* memoir 65: 89-98.   [*AMN*]

BUCK, EDWARD CLARK

40.023   BG   1919 Artesian wells of British Guiana. *Timehri* 3d ser., 6(23), Sept.: 104-
                        107.   [*AMN*]

BUISONJE, P. H. de & ZONNEVELD, J. I. S.

40.024   NL   1960 De kustvormen van Curacao, Aruba en Bonaire [The coasts of Cura-
                        cao, Aruba and Bonaire]. *W I G* 40: 121-144.   [*RIS*]

BUTSCH, ROBERT S.

41.055   BB   1939 The reef builders at Barbados.

BUTTERLIN, JACQUES

40.025   GC   1954 La structure général des Antilles [The overall (geological) structure
                        in the Antilles]. *In* COMPTES RENDUS DE LA DIX-NEUVIÈME SESSION,
                        CONGRÈS GÉOLOGIQUE INTERNATIONAL, ALGER, 1952, SECTION 13. Mâ-
                        con, France, Impr. Protat frères, pt. 2, fasc. 14, p.379-393.   [*AMN*]

40.026   GC   1956 LA CONSTITUTION GÉOLOGIQUE ET LA STRUCTURE DES ANTILLES.   [THE
                        GEOLOGICAL FORMATION AND STRUCTURE OF THE ANTILLES]. [Paris?]
                        Centre national de la recherche scientifique, 453p.   [*COL*]

CAPPELLE, H. van

40.027   SR   1907 ESSAI SUR LA CONSTITUTION GÉOLOGIQUE DE LA GUYANE HOLLANDAISE
                        [DISCUSSION OF THE GEOLOGICAL FORMATION OF DUTCH GUIANA]. Paris,
                        Librairie Polytechnique, 177p.   [*COL*]

40.028   SR   1919 De aanslibbingen der Surinaamsche rivieren [The alluvial deposits
                        of the rivers in Surinam]. *W I G* 1(1): 375-384.   [*COL*]

40.029   SR   1919 Het lage kustgebied van Suriname [The low-lying coastal area of
                        Surinam]. *W I G* 1(1): 48-53.   [*COL*]

40.030   SR   1919 De zand- en schulpritsen in het kustgebied van Suriname [The sand
                        and shell ridges in the coastal area of Surinam]. *W I G* 1(1): 311-
                        313.   [*COL*]

CASE, GERALD O.

40.031   BG   1944 History of the changes in the British Guiana coastline. *Timehri* 4th
                        ser., 1(26), Nov.: 92-106.   [*AMN*]

CEDERSTROM, D. J.

40.032   SC   1941 Notes on the physiography of St. Croix, Virgin Islands. *Am J Sci*
                        239(8), Aug.: 553-576.   [*AGS*]

40.033   SC   1950 GEOLOGY AND GROUND-WATER RESOURCES OF ST. CROIX VIRGIN ISLANDS:
                        GROUND-WATER RESOURCES OF A MODERATELY DRY CARIBBEAN ISLAND.
                        Washington, U.S. Govt. Print. Off., 117p. (Geological Survey, Water-
                        supply paper 1067.)   [*AGS*]

CHAPMAN, V. J.

40.034   JM   1939 Cambridge University expedition to Jamaica.   *Nature* 144(3658),
                       Dec. 9: 964-966.   [*AGS*]

CHOUBERT, BORIS

40.035   FG   1949 GÉOLOGIE ET PÉTROGRAPHIE DE LA GUYANE FRANCAISE [GEOLOGY AND
                       PETROGRAPHY OF FRENCH GUIANA]. Paris, Office de la recherche sci-
                       entifique outre-mer, 120p.   [54]   [*NYP*]

40.036   GG   1954 La carte géologique des trois Guyanes [Geological map of the three
                       Guianas]. *In* COMPTES RENDUS DE LA DIX-NEUVIÈME SESSION DU CON-
                       GRÈS GÉOLOGIQUE INTERNATIONAL, ALGER, 1952, SECTION 13. Mâcon,
                       France, Impr. Protat frères, pt. 2, fasc. 14, p.371-377. [54]   [*AMN*]

40.037   FG   1956 French Guiana. *In* JENKS, WILLIAM F., ed. HANDBOOK OF SOUTH
                       AMERICAN GEOLOGY. New York, Geological Society of America, p.63-
                       73. (Memoir 65.)   [*AMN*]

40.038   FG   1957 ESSAI SUR LA MORPHOLOGIE DE LA GUYANE [NOTES ON THE MORPHOLOGY
                       OF GUIANA]. Paris, Impr. nationale, 48p.   [*AGS*]

66.029   FG   1960 L'Institut francais d'Amérique tropicale (I.F.A.T.): pilot agency in
                       French Guiana.

CHRISTMAN, ROBERT A.

40.039   SB/   1953 Geology of St. Bartholomew, St. Martin, and Anguilla, Lesser An-
          SM/   tilles. *B Geol Soc Am* 64(1), Jan.: 65-96.   [*AGS*]
          AG

CHUBB, L. J.

40.040   GC   1960 The Antillean cretaceous geosyncline.   *In* TRANSACTIONS OF THE
                       SECOND CARIBBEAN GEOLOGICAL CONFERENCE, Mayagüez, P.R., Jan.
                       1959. Mayagüez, P.R., University of Puerto Rico, p.17-26.   [*AMN*]

COHEN, A. & EIJK, J. J. van der

40.041   SR   1953 KLASSIFICATIE EN ONTSTAAN VAN SAVANNEN IN SURINAME [CLASSIFICA-
                       TION AND ORIGINS OF THE SAVANNAHS IN SURINAM]. Paramaribo, Cen-
                       traal Bureau Luchtkaartering te Paramaribo, 214p. (Publicatie no.
                       11.)   [*AGS*]

CONOLLY, H. J. C.

40.042   BG   1925 REPORT...OF THE PRELIMINARY SURVEY OF THE MAZARUNI AND PURUNI
                       DIAMOND FIELDS, BRITISH GUIANA. London, Crown Agents for the
                       Colonies, 103p. (Economic Geological Survey, Department of Sci-
                       ence and Agriculture, pt. 1, Mar.-Dec.) [54]   [*NYP*]

CUNDALL, FRANK

40.043   JM   1939 PLACE-NAMES OF JAMAICA. Rev. ed. Kingston, Institute of Jamaica.
                       16p.   [19]   [*AGS*]

DAVIS, WILLIAM MORRIS

40.044   GC   1924 The formation of the Lesser Antilles. *Proc Natn Acad Sci* 10(6),
                       June: 205-211.   [*AGS*]

DELAITRE, P.

40.045   FG   1933 Observations géologiques en Guyane Francaise [Geological obser-
                       vations in French Guiana]. *Chron Min Colon* 2(19), Oct. 1: 446-455.
                                                                                       [*NYP*]

DEYDIER, JOSEPH

40.046   FG   1905   Trois ans à la Guyane Francaise (1901-1904) [Three years in French Guiana (1901-1904)]. *Géographie* 11(3), Mar. 15: 191-204. [41]   [*NYP*]

DINGLEY, FUGE P.

41.080   BB   1934   A note on diatoms in general.

DUNN, E. R.

41.081   GC   1934   Physiography and herpetology in the Lesser Antilles.

DIXON, C. G.

40.047   BH   [n.d.]   GEOLOGY OF SOUTHERN BRITISH HONDURAS. WITH NOTES ON ADJACENT AREAS. Belize. Govt. Printer, 85p.   [*AMN*]

DOERR, ARTHUR & HOY, DON R.

40.048   JM   1957   Karst landscapes of Cuba, Puerto Rico, and Jamaica. *Scient Mon* 85(4), Oct.: 178-187.

DONNELLY, THOMAS WALLACE

40.049   ST/   1959   GEOLOGY OF ST. THOMAS AND ST. JOHN, VIRGIN ISLANDS. Ph.D. dis-
        SJ   sertation, Princeton University, 262p.   [*COL*]

40.050   ST/   1960   The geology of St. Thomas and St. John, Virgin Islands. *In* TRANS-
        SJ   ACTIONS OF THE SECOND CARIBBEAN GEOLOGICAL CONFERENCE, Maya-
                          güez, P.R., Jan. 1959. Mayagüez, P.R., University of Puerto Rico,
                          p.153-155.   [*AMN*]

DORAN, EDWIN BEAL, Jr.

40.051   CM   1954   Land forms of Grand Cayman Island, British West Indies. *Tex J Sci* 6(4), Dec.: 360-377.   [*RIS*]

DRIMMELEN, C. van

40.052   SR   1928/   De Corantijn, de westelijke grens van Suriname, en haar rechter
                29   zijrivier de Kabalebo [The Courantyne River, the western border of Surinam, and her right tributary, the Kabalebo River]. *W I G* 10:49-64.   [*COL*]

EARLE, KENNETH W.

40.053   KNA [1922?]   REPORTS ON THE GEOLOGY OF ST. KITTS-NEVIS, B.W.I., AND THE GEOL-
                     OGY OF ANGUILLA, B.W.I. London, Crown Agents for the Colonies,
                     50p.   [54]   [*AGS*]

40.054   SL   [1923?]   THE GEOLOGY OF ST. LUCIA. Castries, Govt. Print. Off., p.107-111.
                                          [*AGS*]

40.055   GR/   1924   GEOLOGICAL SURVEY OF GRENADA AND THE (GRENADA) GRENADINES. St.
        GN   George, Govt. Print. Off., 9p.   [*AGS*]

40.056   SV/   1924   THE GEOLOGY OF SAINT VINCENT AND THE NEIGHBORING GRENADINES.
        GN   Kingstown, St. Vincent, Govt. Print. Off., 8p.   [*AGS*]

40.057   DM   1928   Geological notes on the island of Dominica, B.W.I. *Geol Mag* 65(4), Apr.: 169-187.

EIJK, J. J. van der

40.058   SR   1954   DE LANDSCHAPPEN VAN NOORD SURINAM [THE LANDSCAPES OF NORTH-
                     ERN SURINAM]. Paramaribo, Central Bureau Luchtkaartering, te Par-
                     amaribo, 22p. (Publication no. 15.)   [*AGS*]

EILERTS de HAAN, J. G. et al.

40.059   SR   1910 Verslag van de expeditie naar de Suriname-Rivier [Account of the
expedition to the Surinam River]. *Tijdschr Ned Aar Genoot* 27:403-
469, 641-701.   [3,41,42]

EUWENS, P. A.

40.060   CU   1928/ De oudste kaarten van het eiland Curacao [The oldest maps of the
29   island Curacao]. *W I G* 10: 97-126.   [5]   [COL]

FELS, G.

40.061   SK   1903 Ein Anorthitauswurfling von der Insel St. Christopher [A piece of
volcanic unorthoclase material [?] from the island of St. Christopher].
Z Kryst Miner 37:450-460.   [AMN]

FLETT, JOHN S.

40.062   SV   1908 Petrographical notes on the products of the eruption of May, 1902
at the Soufrière in St. Vincent. *Phil Trans Roy Soc Lond* ser. A,
208: 305-332.   [NYP]

FLORES, GIOVANNI

40.063   BH   1952 Geology of northern British Honduras. *B Am Ass Petrol Geol* 36(2),
Feb.: 404-409.   [AGS]

FORREST, W. R.

40.064   AT   1935 SKETCH OF PHYSICAL HISTORY AND DEVELOPMENT OF ANTIGUA.   [St.
John's?] Antigua, Govt. Print. Off., Leeward Islands, 10p.

FRANSSEN HERDERSCHEE, A.

40.065   SR   1905 Verslag van de Gonini-Expeditie [Account of the Gonini Expedi-
tion]. *Tijdschr Ned Aar Genoot* 22: 1-174.   [41,42]

GARROD, W. H. E.

40.066   BB   1952 Our water supply. *J Barb Mus Hist Soc* 19(3), May: 107-111.   [AMN]

GEIJSKES, D. C.

40.067   SR   1952 On the structure and origin of the sandy ridges in the Coastal Zone
of Surinam. *Tijdschr Ned Aar Genoot* 69(2): 225-237.

GIGLIOLI, GEORGE

28.220   BG   1951 The influence of geological formation and soil characteristics on
the distribution of malaria and its mosquito carrier in British Guiana.

GIRAUD, J.

40.068   SR   1906 Au travers des forêts vierges de la Guyane Hollandaise [Through
the virgin forests of Dutch Guiana]. *Géographie* 14(4), Oct. 15:185-
192.   [3,41]   [NYP]

GIRAUD, JEAN L.

40.069   MT   1918 ESQUISSE GÉOLOGIQUE DE LA MARTINIQUE AVEC CARTE GÉOLOGIQUE [GEO-
LOGICAL SKETCH OF MARTINIQUE WITH GEOLOGICAL MAP]. Hanoi-Hai-
phong, Impr. d'Extrême-Orient, 60p.   [AGS]

GOEJE, C. H. de

40.070   SR   1908 Verslag der Toemak Hoemak expeditie [Account of the Tumuc-Humac
expedition]. *Tijdschr Ned Aar Genoot* 25:945-1168.   [41, 42]

40.071   GC   1936/ De namen der Antillen [The names of the Antilles]. *W I G* 18:33-37.
37   [5]   [COL]

GOREAU, THOMAS F.

40.072   JM   1961 Recent investigations on the growth of coral reefs in Jamaica. *Inf B Scient Res Coun* 2(3), Dec.: 41-44.   [*AMN*]

GRANT, HERBERT T.

3.127   BH   1929 A second Cockscombs expedition in 1928.

GREEN, F. RAY H.

40.073   BG   1946 Physical characteristics. *In* ROTH, VINCENT, comp. HANDBOOK OF NATURAL RESOURCES OF BRITISH GUIANA. Georgetown, Daily Chronicle, p.10-13.   [*AGS*]

GRUTTERINK, J. A.

40.074   CU   1928 Dutch Antilles. *In* LES RÉSERVES MONDIALES EN PHOSPHATES: INFORMATION FAITE PAR INITIATIVE DU BUREAU DU XIVe CONGRÈS GÉOLOGIQUE INTERNATIONAL, Espagne, 1926. Madrid, Gráficas Reunidas, v. 2, p.663-666.   [*NYP*]

40.075   SR   1932/ Ijzerman's schets van de geologie van Suriname [Ijzerman's sketch 33   of the geology of Surinam]. *W I G* 14:145-163.   [*COL*]

GUPPY, R. J. LECHMERE

40.076   TR   1910 On a collection of fossils from Springvale near Couva, Trinidad. *Proc Agric Soc Trin Tob* 10(11), Nov.: 447-461;
               1911 11(3), Mar.: 194-203.   [41]   [*AMN*]

40.077   AT/   1911 The geology of Antigua and other West Indian islands. *Q J Geol*
          BB/   *Soc* 67, Nov.: 681-700.
          TR

40.078   GC   1912 An account of some recent geological discoveries in the West Indies. *Proc Agric Soc Trin Tob* 12(1-2), Jan.-Feb.: 22-37.   [*AMN*]

40.079   AT   1912 Note on Dr. Watts' remarks on the geology of Antigua. *Proc Agri Soc Trin Tob* 12(3), Mar.: 75-78.   [*AMN*]

40.080   AT/   1912 On the geology of Antigua and other West Indian islands with refer-
          BB/   ence to the physical history of the Caribean [sic] region. *Proc*
          TR   *Agric Soc Trin Tob* 12(6), June: 182-208.   [*AMN*]

40.081   MT/   1913 Observations on the geology of Martinique with notes on fossils
          TR   from Trinidad and Venezuela. *Proc Agric Soc Trin Tob* 13(4), Apr.: 159-163.   [*AMN*]

HALL, MAXWELL

40.082   JM   1913 NOTES ON THE GEOLOGY OF JAMAICA. Kingston, Govt. Print Off., 3p.

HARRINGTON, T. S.

40.083   BG   1946 Water supply resources. *In* ROTH, VINCENT, comp. HANDBOOK OF NATURAL RESOURCES OF BRITISH GUIANA. Georgetown, Daily Chronicle, p.196-216.   [*AGS*]

HARRISON, Sir JOHN B.

40.084   BB   1908 A popular account of the geological formation of Barbados. *W I B* 9(3): 281-289.   [*AMN*]

HENRIQUES, P. C.

66.061   CU   1962 PROBLEMS RELATING TO HYDROLOGY, WATER CONSERVATION, EROSION CONTROL, REFORESTATION AND AGRICULTURE IN CURAÇAO.

HILL, VINCENT G.

40.085   JM   1960 Hydrochemistry in the exploitation of water resources. *Inf B Scient Res Coun* 1(2), Sept.: 9-10.   [*RIS*]

HODGE, W. H.

46.091   DM   1942 Plants used by the Dominica Caribs.

HOLMER, NILS M.

19.020   GC   1960/ Indian place names in South America and the Antilles.
              61

HOSE, H. R.

40.086   JM   1950 The geology and mineral resources of Jamaica. *Colon geol Miner Rsrc* 1(1): 11-36.   [54]   [*AGS*]

HOSTOS, ADOLFO de

4.063   GC   1924 Notes on West Indian hydrography in its relation to prehistoric migrations.

HOVEY, EDMUND OTIS

40.087   FA/   1905 Volcanoes of Martinique, Guadeloupe, and Saba. *In* REPORT OF THE
         SA   EIGHTH INTERNATIONAL GEOGRAPHIC CONGRESS, held in [Washington and other cities of] the United States, 1904. Washington, U. S. Govt.
                    • Print. Off., p.447-451.   [*NYP*]

40.088   SV/   1905 Volcanoes of St. Vincent, St. Kitts, and Statia. *In* REPORT OF THE
         SK/   EIGHTH INTERNATIONAL GEOGRAPHIC CONGRESS, held in [Washington
         SE   and other cities of] the United States, 1904. Washington, U. S. Govt.
                    Print. Off., p.452-454.   [*NYP*]

40.089   SV   1909 Camping on the Soufrière of St. Vincent. *B Am Geogr Soc* 41(2): 72-83.   [*AGS*]

HOWE, OLIN J.

40.090   JM   1920 Is Jamaica part of a lost continent? *Can-W I Mag* 8(8), June: 550-551.   [41]   [*NYP*]

HOYER, W. M.

40.091   AR   1938 De naam "Aruba" [The name "Aruba"]. *W IG* 20:370-371. [5] [*COL*]
40.092   CU   1938 De naam "Curacao" [The name "Curacao"]. *W I G* 20:225-227.
                    [5]   [*COL*]

IJZERMAN, ROBERT

40.093   SR   1931 OUTLINE OF THE GEOLOGY AND PETROLOGY OF SURINAM (DUTCH GUIANA).
                    The Hague, Martinus Nijhoff, 519p.   [*NYP*]

40.094   SR   1931 Surinam [by] R. Yzerman. *In* LEIDSCHE GEOLOGISCHE MEDEDEELINGEN,
                    VOL. 5: FEESTBUNDEL UITGEGEVEN TER EERE VAN PROF. DR. K. MARTIN.
                    Leiden, Boek- en Steendrukkerij Eduard Ijdo, Uitgave van Geologie
                    en Mineralogie te Leiden, p.690-703.   [*COL*]

JACQUET, J. M.

40.095   FG   1930 La Guyane Francaise, pays minier [French Guiana, ore-bearing land].
                    B Ag Gen Colon 23(257), June: 425-436.   [54]   [*AGS*]

JAGGAR, T. A.

40.096   MT   1949 STEAM BLAST VOLCANIC ERUPTIONS: A STUDY OF MOUNT PELÉE IN MAR-
                    TINIQUE AS TYPE VOLCANO. Honolulu, Hawaiian Volcano Research
                    Association, 137p. (4th special report of the Hawaiian Volcano Ob-
                    servatory of the U. S. Geological Survey and the Hawaiian Volcano
                    Research Association.)

JAMES, PRESTON E.

54.027 TR 1925 The Pitch Lake, Trinidad.

40.097 GC 1959 Harbors and waterways of the Caribbean. *In* WILGUS, A. CURTIS, ed. THE CARIBBEAN: NATURAL RESOURCES [papers delivered at the Ninth Conference on the Caribbean held at the University of Florida, Dec. 4-6, 1958]. Gainesville, University of Florida Press, p.163-176. (Publications of the School of Inter-American Studies, ser. 1, v. 9.) [RIS]

JONKER, F. P. & WENSINK, J. J.

40.098 SR 1960 De Natuurwetenschappelijke Expeditie naar de Emmaketen in Suriname, Juli-Oktober 1959 [The Natural Science Expedition to the Emma Range in Surinam, July-October, 1959]. *Tijdschr Ned Aar Genoot* 77: 145-161.

JOOSTEN, J. H. L.

40.099 BG 1954 Agrarische problemen van Brits-Guyana [Agricultural problems of British Guiana]. *Tijdschr Ned Aar Genoot* 3d ser., 71(4), Oct.: 284-297. [46] [AGS]

KEILHACK, K.

40.100 CU 1926 Der geologische Bau und die Phosphatlager des östlichen Curacao [The geological structure and the phosphate deposit of eastern Curacao]. *Z Dt Geol Ges A Abh* 78(3), Sept. 30: 337-356. [AGS]

KEMP, JAMES F.

40.101 BV 1926 Introduction and review of the literature on the geology of the Virgin Islands. *In* NEW YORK ACADEMY OF SCIENCES. SCIENTIFIC SURVEY OF PORTO RICO AND THE VIRGIN ISLANDS. v. 4, pt. 1, p.3-69. [1] [AGS]

LACROIX, ALFRED

40.102 FG 1932 Guyane Francaise [French Guiana]. *In* LA GÉOLOGIE ET LES MINES DE LA FRANCE D'OUTRE-MER. Paris, Sociétés d'éditions géographiques maritimes et coloniales, p.485-504. [54] [AGS]

LANGEMEYER, F. S.

40.103 SM 1936/ Korte beschrijving van de Groote Baai van St. Maarten [Short description of the Great Bay of St. Maarten]. *WIG* 18:289-292. [COL]
37

40.104 NW 1943 Van drie toppen van het Antillenmassief (een orografische schets onzer Bovenwindsche Eilanden) [About three tops of the Antilles Mountains (an orografic sketch of our Windward Islands)]. *WIG* 25: 161-167. [COL]

LASSERRE, GUY

40.105 FA 1953 La cartographie des Antilles Francaises [The cartography of the French Antilles]. *Cah O-M* 6(23), July-Sept.: 293-296. [AGS]

LEBEDEFF, V.

40.106 FG 1935 Résumé des résultats d'une mission de recherches géologiques et minières en Guyane Francaise [Summary of the results of a geological research and prospecting expedition in French Guiana]. *Chron Min Colon* 4(45), Dec. 1: 394-408. [54] [AGS]

40.107 FG 1936 Une mission d'études géologiques et minières en Guyane-Inini [A geological research and prospecting expedition in Guiana-Inini]. *Ann Min* 13th ser., 9(1), Jan.: 1-22; 9(2), Feb.: 77-117; 9(3), Mar: 187-239. [54] [COL]

Le BOUCHER, LEON
3.179   GD   1931 LA GUADELOUPE PITTORESQUE: LES VOLCANS—LES RIVIÈRES DU SUD—
LES ÉTANGS [PICTURESQUE GUADELOUPE—THE VOLCANOES—THE SOUTH-
ERN RIVERS—THE PONDS].

LENOX-CONINGHAM, G. P.
40.108   MS   1937 Montserrat and the West Indian volcanoes. *Nature* 139(3526), May
29: 907-910.   [AGS]

LIGHTON, G.
40.109   BG   1950 British Guiana. I: Coastlands and interior. *Geography* 35:166-177.
                                                              [AGS]

McCONNELL, R. B.
40.110   BG   1959 Fossils in the North Savannas and their significance in the search
for oil in British Guiana; a short account of the non-metamorphic
sedimentary formations in British Guiana. *Timehri* 4th ser., no. 38,
Sept.: 65-85.   [54]   [AGS]
40.111   BG   1960 The Takutu formation in British Guiana and the probable age of the
Roraima formation. *In* TRANSACTIONS OF THE SECOND CARIBBEAN GEO-
LOGICAL CONFERENCE, Mayagüez, P.R., Jan. 1959. Mayagüez, P.R.,
University of Puerto Rico, p.163-170.   [AMN]
40.112   BG   1961 The Precambrian rocks of British Guiana. *Timehri* 4th ser., no. 40,
Oct.: 77-91.   [AMN]

McCONNELL, R. B. & DIXON, C. G.
40.113   BG   1960 A geologist map of British Guiana. *In* SIMONEN, A. & KUOVO,
J. A. O., eds. REPORT OF THE TWENTY-FIRST SESSION OF THE INTER-
NATIONAL GEOLOGICAL CONGRESS, 1960, PT. 9: PRE-CAMBRIAN STRATI-
GRAPHY AND CORRELATIONS. Copenhagen, Det Berlingske bogtr. p.39-
50.   [AGS]

MARTIN, K.
40.114   NL   1920/ Vroegere rijzingen van den bodem in Nederlandsch West-Indië [Ground
21   elevations in the Dutch West Indies which occurred in the past].
W I G 2:273-285.   [5]   [COL]

MARTIN-KAYE, P. H. A.
40.115   BV   1954 WATER SUPPLIES OF THE BRITISH VIRGIN ISLANDS. Georgetown, Lithographic Co., 69p.   [AGS]
40.116   AT   1956 WATER RESOURCES OF ANTIGUA AND BARBUDA, B.W.I. [Georgetown?]
British Guiana, B.G. Lithographic Co., 109p.   [COL]
40.117   CR   1958 The geology of Carriacou. *B Am Pal* 38(175), Oct. 15: 395-405. [COL]
40.118   AT   1958 Outline of the geology of Antigua and notes on field excursion localities. *In* REPORT OF THE FIRST MEETING OF THE CARIBBEAN GEO-
LOGICAL CONFERENCE held at Antigua, British West Indies, Dec. 1955.
Demerara [B.G.], Argosy and Co., p.17-19.   [RIS]
40.119   AT   1958 Water supply conditions in Antigua. *In* REPORT OF THE FIRST MEET-
ING OF THE CARIBBEAN GEOLOGICAL CONFERENCE held at Antigua,
B.W.I., Dec. 1955. Demerara [B.G.], Argosy and Co., p.64-67.   [RIS]
40.120   LW/   1959 REPORTS ON THE GEOLOGY OF THE LEEWARD AND BRITISH VIRGIN IS-
          BV   LANDS. Castries, Voice Pub. Co., 117p.

MARTIN-KAYE, P. H. A. & BADCOCK, J.

40.121 BB 1962 Geological background to soil conservation and land rehabilitation measures in Barbados, W.I. *J Barb Mus Hist Soc* 30(1), Nov.: 3-13. [46,66]

MATLEY, CHARLES ALFRED

40.122 CM 1926 The geology of the Cayman Islands (British West Indies) and their relation to the Bartlett Trough. *Q J Geol Soc Lond* 82 (pt. 3, no. 327), Oct. 19: 352-387. *[AGS]*

40.123 BB 1932 The old basement of Barbados; with some remarks on Barbadian geology. *Geol Mag* 69(818), Aug.: 366-373. *[AGS]*

MATLEY, CHARLES ALFRED, et al

40.124 JM 1951 GEOLOGY AND PHYSIOGRAPHY OF THE KINGSTON DISTRICT, JAMAICA. Kingston, Crown Agents of the Colonies, for Institute of Jamaica, 139p. [46] *[AGS]*

MAXWELL, J. C.

40.125 TB 1948 Geology of Tobago, British West Indies. *B Geol Soc Am* 59, Aug.: 801-854. (Ph.D. dissertation, Princeton Univ., May 1946). *[RIS]*

MEETEREN, N. van

28.358 CU 1950 Grondwaterpeil en watervoorziening op Curacao voorheen en thans [The level of groundwater and the water supply on Curacao in the past and at present].

MEYERHOFF, HOWARD A.

40.126 VI 1926/ The physiography of the Virgin Islands, Culebra and Vieques. *In*
     27 SCIENTIFIC SURVEY OF PORTO RICO AND THE VIRGIN ISLANDS. New York, New York Academy of Sciences, v. 4, pt. 1, p.71-141; pt. 2, p.145-219. *[AGS]*

54.044 JM 1941 Mineral resources of the Greater Antilles.

40.127 GC 1954 Antillean tectonics. *Trans NY Acad Sci* 16:149-155. *[RIS]*

MIDAS, ANDRE

40.128 MT 1954 Mont Pelé. *Car Commn Mon Inf B* 8(1), Aug.: 7-8,12. *[COL]*

MITCHELL, RAOUL C.

40.129 GC 1952 Nouvelles observations à propos de la position structurale de l'arc des Petites Antilles [New remarks on the structural position of the arc of the Lesser Antilles]. *B Soc Geol Fr, Notes Mem* 6th ser., 2(5): 71-75. *[AMN]*

MOLENGRAAFF, G. A. F.

40.130 NW 1931 Saba, St. Eustatius (Statia) and St. Martin. *In* LEIDSCHE GEOLOGISCHE MEDEDEELINGEN, VOL. 5: FEESTBUNDEL UITGEGEVEN TER EERE VAN PROF. DR. K. MARTIN. Leiden, Boek- en Steendrukkerij Eduard Ijdo, p.715-739. (Uitgave van geologie en mineralogie te Leiden.) *[COL]*

MOLENGRAAFF, G. J. H.

40.131 CU 1929 GEOLOGIE EN GEOHYDROLOGIE VAN HET EILAND CURACAO [GEOLOGY AND GEOHYDROLOGY OF THE ISLAND CURACAO]. Delft, Waldman, 126p *[NYP]*

40.132 CU 1931 Curacao. *In* LEIDSCHE GEOLOGISCHE MEDEDEELINGEN, VOL. 5: FEEST-BUNDEL UITGEGEVEN TER EERE VAN PROF. DR. K. MARTIN. Leiden, Boek- en Steendrukkerij Eduard Ijdo, p.673-689. (Uitgave van geologie en mineralogie te Leiden.) *[COL]*

MURRAY, ERIC

40.133   GC   1955 The first chapter in Caribbean history. *Car Q* 4(1), Jan.: 68-74. [*RIS*]

NARAINE, S. S.

66.105   BG   1961 The Public Works Department and sea defences in British Guiana.

NEWBOLD, C. E. & GILLETTE, H. P. S.

28.399   TR   1949 Self-clearing sea heads for low drainage through surf and consequent effects on the incidence of malaria.

OLSCHKI, LEONARDO

40.134   GC   1943 The Columbian nomenclature of the Lesser Antilles. *Geogr Rev* 33
(3), July: 397-414. [5]   [*AGS*]

OWER, LESLIE H.

4.103   BH   1926 The colony of British Honduras.
40.135   BH   1927 Features of British Honduras. *Geogr J* 70(4), Oct.: 372-386. [*AGS*]
40.136   BH   1928 Geology of British Honduras. *J Geol* 36(6), Aug.-Sept.: 494-509.
                                                                             [*AGS*]

PEACOCKE, M. A.

40.137   JM   1962 The effect of temperature on the water loss of Mona Reservoir. *Inf
B Scient Res Coun* 3(2), Sept.: 30-32.   [*RIS*]

PELATAN, L.

54.053   FG   1900 Les richesses minérales des colonies francaises: Guyane francaise
[The mineral resources of the French colonies: French Guiana].

PERRET, FRANK A.

40.138   MS   1939 THE VOLCANO-SEISMIC CRISIS AT MONTSERRAT 1933-1937. Washington,
D.C., Carnegie Institution of Washington, 76p. (Publication no. 512).

PIJPERS, P. J.

40.139   BN   1931 Bonaire. *In* LEIDSCHE GEOLOGISCHE MEDEDEELINGEN, VOL. 5: FEEST-
BUNDEL UITGEGEVEN TER EERE VAN PROF. DR. K. MARTIN. Leiden, Boek-
en Steendrukkerij Eduard Ijdo, p.704-708. (Uitgave van geologie en
Mineralogie te Leiden.)
40.140   CU   1931 Some remarks on the geology of the surroundings of "Ronde Klip"
(East Curacao). *In* KONINKLIJKE AKADEMIE VAN WETENSCHAPPEN TE
AMSTERDAM, PROCEEDINGS OF THE SECTION OF SCIENCES. Amsterdam,
Noord-Hollandsche Uitg. Mij., v. 34, no. 7, p.1023-1027.   [*NYP*]
40.141   BN   1933 GEOLOGY AND PALAEONTOLOGY OF BONAIRE (D.W.I.). Utrecht, Geographische en Geologische Mededeelingen, 103p. (Physiographisch-Geologische Reeks no. 8.)

POLLARD, E. R.; DIXON, C. G. & DUJARDIN, R. A.

54.058   BG   1957 DIAMOND RESOURCES OF BRITISH GUIANA.

PYE, NORMAN

38.099   BC   1935 The geographical factors involved in the problem of British West
Indian Federation.

RANDEL, WILLIAM

40.142   JM   1960 Survival of pre-English place names in Jamaica. *Names* 8(1), Mar.: 24-29.   [19]   [*AGS*]

REDFIELD, ARTHUR H.

54.061   GC   1923 Petroleum reserves of the West Indies.

ROBINSON, E.; VERSEY, H. R. & WILLIAMS, J. B.

40.143   JM   1960 The Jamaica earthquake of March 1, 1957. *In* TRANSACTIONS OF THE SECOND CARIBBEAN GEOLOGICAL CONFERENCE, Mayagüez, P.R., Jan. 1959. Mayagüez, P.R., University of Puerto Rico, p.50-57.   [*AMN*]

ROBINSON, J. H.

41.195   BB   1934 The study of the organic remains in the oceanic beds of Barbados, with special reference to the diatoms.

RODDAM, GEORGE

40.144   BB   1948 REPORTS ON THE GROUND WATER RESOURCES OF BARBADOS, B.W.I. AND THEIR UTILIZATION. [Bridgetown?] Barbados, Advocate Co., 74p. [66]

RODWAY, JAMES

40.145   BG   1906 The river-names of British Guiana. *B Am Geogr Soc* 36(7): 396-402. [19,26]   [*AGS*]

40.146   BG   1911 Our river names. *Timehri* 3d ser., 1(18A), Jan.: 53-56. [19, 26] [*AMN*]

ROSE, E.

40.147   MT   1955 La destruction de Saint-Pierre-Martinique d'après un temoin oculaire [The destruction of Saint-Pierre (Martinique) according to an eye-witness]. *Etud O-M* 38 (Feb.): 77-82.   [*NYP*]

RUSSELL, RICHARD J.

40.148   GC   1960 Preliminary notes on Caribbean beach rock. *In* TRANSACTIONS OF THE SECOND CARIBBEAN GEOLOGICAL CONFERENCE, Mayagüez, P.R., Jan. 1959. Mayagüez, P.R., University of Puerto Rico, p.43-49.   [*AMN*]

RUTTEN, L. M. R.

40.149   NL   1931/ De geologische geschiedenis der drie Nederlandsche Benedenwind-
           32   sche Eilanden [The geological history of the three Dutch Leeward Islands]. *W I G* 13:401-441.   [5]   [*COL*]

40.150   NL   1931/ Een geologische reis met Utrechtsche studenten naar de Nederland-
           32   sche Benedenwindsche Eilanden [A geological trip with Utrecht students to the Dutch Leeward Islands]. *W I G* 13:289-309.   [*COL*]

41.204   NC   1931 Our palaeontological knowledge of the Netherlands West Indies in 1930. *In* LEIDSCHE GEOLOGISCHE MEDEDEELINGEN, VOL. 5: FEESTBUNDEL UITGEGEVEN TER EERE VAN PROF. DR. K. MARTIN. Leiden, Boek- en Steendrukkerij Eduard Ijdo, p.651-672. (Uitgave van geologie en mineralogie te Leiden.)   [40]   [*COL*]

40.151   GC   1935 Uber den Antillenbogen [Over the arc of the Antilles]. *In* KONINKLIJKE NEDERLANDSE AKADEMIE VAN WETENSCHAPPEN TE AMSTERDAM, PRO-CEEDINGS OF THE SECTION OF SCIENCES. [Amsterdam?] v. 38, no. 10, p.1046-1058.   [*AMN*]

1.040   GC   1938 BIBLIOGRAPHY OF WEST INDIAN GEOLOGY.

SAINT, S. J.
40.152   BB   1934 The history of Barbados as revealed by a study of the geological strata of the island. *J Barb Mus Hist Soc* 1(2), Feb.: 57-63. [*AMN*]

SAMSON, PH. A.
40.153   SR   1940 Behoort Suriname tot West-Indië? [Is Surinam part of the West Indies?] *W I G* 22:83-85.   [*COL*]

SAPPER, KARL
40.154   BH   1934 Hydrographie des Maya-Gebirges in Britisch-Honduras [Hydrography of the Maya Mountains in British Honduras]. *Pet Mitt* 80(7-8): 218-220.   [*AGS*]

SCHAUB, H. P.
40.155   CU   1948 Geological observations on Curacao, N.W.I. *B Am Ass Petrol Geol* 32(7), July: 1275-1291.   [*AGS*]

SCHOLS, H.
40.156   SR   1956 Surinam. *In* JENKS, WILLIAM F., ed. HANDBOOK OF SOUTH AMERICAN GEOLOGY. New York, Geological Society of America, p.75-87. (Memoir 65.)   [*AMN*]

SCHUCHERT, CHARLES
40.157   GC   1929 The geological history of the Antillean region. *Science* 69(1780), Feb. 8: 139-145.   [*AGS*]
40.158   GC   1935 HISTORICAL GEOLOGY OF THE ANTILLEAN-CARIBBEAN REGION. New York, John Wiley, 811p.   [*COL*]

SCHULLER, RUDOLF
5.196   GG   1916 The Ordáz and Dortal Expeditions in search of El-Dorado, as described on sixteenth century maps.

SCHULZ, J. P.
40.159   SR   1960 ECOLOGICAL STUDIES ON RAIN FOREST IN NORTHERN SURINAM. Amsterdam, Noord-Hollandsche Uitg. Mij., 267p. (Koninklijke Nederlandse Akademie van Wetenschappen, Verhandelingen, Afdeling Natuurkunde, 2d ser., v. 53, no. 1.)   [42]   [*AGS*]

SENN, ALFRED
40.160   GC   1940 Paleogene of Barbados and its bearing on the history and structure of the Antillean Caribbean region. *B Am Ass Petrol Geol* 24(9), Sept.: 1548-1610.   [*AGS*]
40.161   BB   1944 INVENTORY OF THE BARBADOS ROCKS AND THEIR POSSIBLE UTILIZATION. [Bridgetown?] Barbados, Dept. of Science and Agriculture, 40p. (Bulletin, new ser., no. 1.)   [54]
40.162   BB   1946 Report of the British Union Oil Company Limited on geological investigations of the under-ground water resources of Barbados, B.W.I. *J Barb Mus Hist Soc* 14(1-2), Nov.-Feb.: 16-19.   [*AMN*]
                 47
40.163   BB   1946 REPORT OF THE BRITISH UNION OIL COMPANY LIMITED ON GEOLOGICAL INVESTIGATIONS OF THE GROUND-WATER RESOURCES OF BARBADOS, B.W.I. Bridgetown, Advocate Co., 109p.
40.164   BB   1947 Die Geologie der Insel Barbados, B.W.I. (Kleine Antillen) und die Morphogenese der umliegenden marinen Grossformen [The geology of the island of Barbados, B.W.I. (Lesser Antilles) and the morphogenesis of the surrounding marine macroforms]. *Ecl Geol Helv* 40(2): 199-222.   [*COL*]

SHILSTONE, E. M.
40.165   BB   1938 A descriptive list of maps of Barbados. *J Barb Mus Hist Soc* 5(2),
                      Feb.: 57-84. [1, 5]   [*AMN*]

SICCAMA H.
66.137   BG   1915 The sea defences of British Guiana.

SNELLEN, E.
54.070   SR   1935 De goudwinning in Suriname [Gold mining in Surinam].

SPENCE, R. O. H
66.142   BG   1912 Surveying and mapping in British Guiana.

SPENCER, JOSEPH WILLIAM WINTHROP
40.166   SB/   1901 On the geological and physical development of Anguilla, St. Martin,
          SM/   S. Bartholomew, and Sombrero. *Q J Geol Soc* 57 (pt. 4, no. 228),
          AG   Nov. 2:520-533.   [*AGS*]
40.167   AT   1901 On the geological and physical development of Antigua. *Q J Geol
                      Soc* 57 (pt. 4, no. 228), Nov. 2:490-505.   [*AGS*]
40.168   GD   1901 On the geological and physical development of Guadeloupe. *Q J
                      Geol Soc* 57 (pt. 4, no. 228), Nov. 2:506-519.   [*AGS*]
40.169   GC   1901 On the geological and physical development of the St. Christopher
                      Chain and Saba Banks. *Q J Geol Soc* 57 (pt. 4, no. 228), Nov. 2:
                      534-544.   [*AGS*]
40.170   BB/   1902 On the geological and physical development of Barbados; with notes
          TR   on Trinidad. *Q J Geol Soc* 58 (pt. 3, no. 231), Aug. 11:354-367. [*AGS*]
40.171   DM/   1902 On the geological and physical development of Dominica; with notes
          MT/   on Martinique, St. Lucia, St. Vincent, and the Grenadines. *Q J Geol
          WW   Soc* 58 (pt. 3, no. 231), Aug. 11:345-353.   [*AGS*]

SPIRLET, F. E.
40.172   SR   1922/ Werkzaamheden op topografisch en kadastraal gebied in Suriname
                23   van 1911-1920 [Topographical and cadastral activities in Surinam
                      from 1911-1920]. *W I G* 4:613-624, 639-652.   [*COL*]

STAHEL. GEROLD, et al.
3.290   SR   1926 De expeditie naar het Wilhelmina-Gebergte (Suriname) in 1926 [The
                      expedition to the Wilhelmina Mountains (Surinam) in 1926].

STAHEL, GEROLD & GEIJSKES, D. C.
40.173   SR   1940 Drie verkenningsvluchten boven Suriname's binnenlanden met het
                      K.L.M. vliegtuig "De Snip" [Three aerial research flights over the
                      interior regions of Surinam with the K.L.M. plane "De Snip"],
                      [by] Gerold Stahel & D.C. Geyskes. *Tijdschr Ned Aar Genoot* 2d
                      ser., 57(3), May: 441-456.   [*AGS*]
STEENHUIS, J. F.
1.042   GG/   1951 DE GEOLOGISCHE LITERATUUR OVER OF VAN BELANG VOOR NEDERLANDS
          NA   GUYANA (SURINAME) EN DE NEDERLANDSE WESTINDISCHE EILANDEN [THE
                      GEOLOGICAL LITERATURE ABOUT OR OF IMPORTANCE TO DUTCH GUIANA
                      (SURINAM) AND THE DUTCH WEST INDIAN ISLANDS].

STEERS, J. A.
40.174   JM   1940 The cays and the Palisadoes, Port Royal, Jamaica. *Geogr Rev* 30
                      (2), Apr.: 279-296.   [*AGS*]

STEERS, J.A.; CHAPMAN, V.J.; COLMAN, J. & LOFTHOUSE, J.A.

40.175   JM   1940 Sand cays and mangroves in Jamaica. *Geogr J* 96(5), Nov.: 305-328.
   [*AGS*]

STOCKLEY, G. M.

40.176   BG   1955 THE GEOLOGY OF BRITISH GUIANA AND THE DEVELOPMENT OF ITS MINERAL RESOURCES. Georgetown, 102p. (British Guiana Geological Survey, Bulletin no. 25.)   [54]   [*AGS*]

STOCKUM, A. J. van

40.177   SR   1904 Verslag van de Saramacca-Expeditie [Account of the Saramacca Expedition]. *Tijd Ned Aar Genoot* 21: 88-122; 227-310; 651-721; 822-878; 1022-1058.   [41,42]

STONE, ROBERT G.

40.178   UV   1942 METEOROLOGY OF THE VIRGIN ISLANDS. New York, New York Academy of Sciences, 138p. (Scientific survey of Porto Rico and the Virgin Islands, v. 19, pt. 1.)   [*AGS*]

SUTER, H. H.

40.179   TR   1951 The general and economic geology of Trinidad, B.W.I. *Colon Geol Miner Rsrc* 2(3): 177-217; 2(4): 271-307;
   1952 3(1): 3-51.   [54]   [*AGS*]
40.180   TR   1960 THE GENERAL AND ECONOMIC GEOLOGY OF TRINIDAD, B.W.I. [2d. ed., with revisionary appendix by G.E. Higgins.] London, H.M.S.O., 145p.   [54]   [*COL*]

SWEETING, M. M.

40.181   JM   1958 The Karstlands of Jamaica. *Geogr J* 124(2), June: 184-199.   [*AGS*]

TAYLOR, DOUGLAS C.

40.182   DM   1954 Names on Dominica. *Names* 2(1), Mar.: 31-37.   [19,25,26]   [*AGS*]

TAYLOR, S. A. G.

46.215   JM   1955 An account of the development of the water resources of the Clarendon Plains.
40.183   JM   1958 An account of the development of the water resources of the Clarendon Plains in Jamaica. *In* REPORT OF THE FIRST MEETING OF THE CARIBBEAN GEOLOGICAL CONFERENCE held at Antigua, B.W.I., Dec. 1955. Demerara [B.G.], Argosy and Co., p.57-61.   [*RIS*]

TAYLOR, S. A. G. & CHUBB, L. J.

40.184   JM   1957 The hydrogeology of the Clarendon Plains, Jamaica. *Proc Geol Ass* 68(3): 204-210.   [57, 66]   [*RIS*]

TEMPANY, Sir HAROLD A.

40.185   AT   1914 The ground waters of Antigua. *W I B* 14(4): 281-303.   [*AMN*]

THOMPSON, ROBERT WALLACE

40.186   TR   1959 Pre-British place-names in Trinidad. *W I G* 39:137-165.   [26]   [*COL*]

TIROLIEN, CAMILLE

55.038   GD   1961 Thermalisme [Mineral springs].

TRECHMANN, C. T.

40.187   SK   1932 Notes on Brimstone Hill, St. Kitts. *Geol Mag* 69(816), June: 241-258.   [*AGS*]

40.188 BB 1933 The uplift of Barbados. *Geol Mag* 70(823), Jan.: 19-47.   [*AGS*]

40.189 TB 1934 Tertiary and Quaternary beds of Tobago, West Indies. *Geol Mag* 71 (845), Nov.: 481-493.

40.190 TR 1935 Fossils from the Northern Range of Trinidad. *Geol Mag* 72(850), Apr.: 166-175.   [*AGS*]

40.191 CR 1935 The geology and fossils of Carriacou, West Indies. *Geol Mag* 72 (858), Dec.: 529-555.   [*AGS*]

40.192 BB 1937 The base and top of the coral rock in Barbados. *Geol Mag* 74(878), Aug.: 337-359.   [*AGS*]

40.193 AT 1941 Some observations on the geology of Antigua, West Indies. *Geol Mag* 78(2), Mar.-Apr.: 113-124.   [*AGS*]

40.194 GC 1945 THE WEST INDIES AND THE MOUNTAIN UPLIFT PROBLEM. West Hartlepool, Privately printed by Messrs. B.T. Ord, 25p.   [*NYP*]

VALLAUX, CAMILLE

40.195 FA 1935 L'atmosphère et la mer aux Antilles [The atmosphere and the sea in the Antilles]. *In* DENIS, SERGE, ed. NOS ANTILLES. Orléans, Luzeray, p.25-37.   [*AGS*]

VANN, J. H.

40.196 GG 1959 THE PHYSICAL GEOGRAPHY OF THE LOWER COASTAL PLAIN OF THE GUIANA COAST. [Baton Rouge,] Louisiana, 91p. (Technical report no. 1, Dept. of Geography and Anthropology, Louisiana State University.)   [*RIS*]

VAUGHAN, T. WAYLAND

40.197 AT 1914 Memorandum on the geology of the ground waters of the island of Antigua, B.W.I. *W I B* 14(4): 276-280.   [*AMN*]

40.198 UV 1923 Stratigraphy of the Virgin Islands of the United States and of Culebra and Vieques Islands and notes on eastern Porto Rico. *J Wash Acad Sci* 13(14), Aug. 19:303-317.   [*AGS*]

VERIN, PIERRE MICHEL

40.199 SL 1961 Toponymie de l'île de Sainte-Lucie [Toponymy of the island of St. Lucia]. *Rev Guad* 44, Apr.-June: 16-19.   [5]   [*RIS*]

VERLOOP, J. H.

54.078 SR 1911 A BRIEF OUTLINE OF THE SURINAM GOLD INDUSTRY: GEOLOGY, TECHNIQUE, HYGIENE; DESCRIPTION OF THE GOLD PLACER AND THE PROSPECTS AT THE GUIANA GOLD PLACER.

VERMUNT, L. W. J. & RUTTEN, M. G.

40.200 CU 1931 Some remarks on the geology of Curacoa [sic]. *In* KONINKLIJKE AKADEMIE VAN WETENSCHAPPEN TE AMSTERDAM, PROCEEDINGS OF THE SECTION OF SCIENCES. Amsterdam, Noord-Hollandsche Uitg. Mij., v. 34, no. 7, p.1028-1031.   [*NYP*]

VERSEY, H. R.

40.201 JM 1960 The hydrologic character of the white limestone formation of Jamaica. *In* TRANSACTIONS OF THE SECOND CARIBBEAN GEOLOGICAL CONFERENCE, Mayagüez, P.R., Jan. 1959. Mayagüez, P.R., University of Puerto Rico, p.59-68.   [*AMN*]

VERSEY, H. R. & PRESCOTT, G. C.

40.202   JM   1958 PROGRESS REPORT ON THE GEOLOGY AND GROUND WATER RESOURCES OF
                THE CLARENDON PLAINS, JAMAICA, W.I. Kingston, Government Printer,
                27p. (Geological Survey Department, Occasional paper no. 1.) [COL]

VINCENZ, S. A.

40.203   JM   1961 Resistivity surveys for water supply. Inf B Scient Res Coun 1(4),
                Mar.: 4-6.   [RIS]

WAGENAAR HUMMELINCK, P.

40.204   AR   1938 Over verweringsholten in dioretblokken op Aruba [About weathering
                holes in diorite rocks on Aruba]. W I G 20:264-369.   [COL]
40.205   NL   1943 Oude grotten en grottenvorming op Curacao, Aruba en Bonaire [Old
                caves and cave-formations on Curacao, Aruba and Bonaire]. W I G
                25:365-375.   [COL]
1.043   CU   1946 Literatuur betreffende het natuurwetenschappelijk onderzoek in Cur-
                acao gedurende de oorlogsjaren [Literature about natural science
                research in Curacao during the war].
1.044   SR   1946 Literatuur betreffende het natuurwetenschappelijk onderzoek in Sur-
                iname gedurende de oorlogsjaren [Literature about natural science
                research in Surinam during the war].
40.206   NL   1948 Een luchtreiziger over het landschap van de Nederlandse Beneden-
                windse Eilanden [An air traveler over the landscape of the Nether-
                lands Leeward Islands]. Tijd Ned Aar Genoot 65:683-691.

WARING, GERALD A.

40.207   TR   1926 THE GEOLOGY OF THE ISLAND OF TRINIDAD, B.W.I. Baltimore, Johns
                Hopkins University, 172p. (Studies in geology no. 7.)   [COL]

WARING, GERALD A. & CARLSON, C. G.

40.208   TR   1925 Geology and oil resources of Trinidad, British West Indies. B Am
                Ass Petrol Geol 9(6), Sept.: 1000-1008.   [54]   [AGS]

WEAVER, JOHN D.

40.209   GC   1960 Geological research in the Caribbean. Revta Cienc Social 4(1),
                Mar.: 171-178.   [AGS]

WEBBER, BENJ. N.

40.210   BG   1952 Manganese deposits in the North West District, British Guiana. In
                GEOLOGICAL SURVEY OF BRITISH GUIANA, BULLETIN NO. 23. George-
                town, Daily Chronicle, p.7-39.   [54]   [AGS]
54.079   BG   1952 Progress report on Kurupung Placers Company, Ltd., Kurupung River,
                Mazaruni River District, British Guiana.

WESTERGAARD, WALDEMAR

45.037   SC   1938 A St. Croix map of 1766: with a note on its significance in West In-
                dian plantation economy.

WESTERMANN, J. H.

40.211   AR   1931 Aruba. In LEIDSCHE GEOLOGISCHE MEDEDEELINGEN, VOL. 5: FEESTBUN-
                DEL UITGEGEVEN TER EERE VAN PROF. DR. K. MARTIN. Leiden, Boek-
                en Steendrukkerij Eduard Ijdo, p.709-714. (Uitgave van geologie en
                mineralogie te Leiden.)   [COL]

40.212   AR   1932 THE GEOLOGY OF ARUBA.   Utrecht, Geographische en Geologische
                 Mededeelingen, 129p. (Physiographisch-geologische reeks no. 7.)
                                                                          [AGS]

40.213   NA   1949 Overzicht van de geologische en mijnbouwkundige kennis der Neder-
                 landse Antillen, benevens voorstellen voor verdere exploratie [Sur-
                 vey of the geology and mining of the Netherlands Antilles; and pro-
                 posals for further exploration]. Meded Kon Veren Indisch Inst, 85
                 (35) (168p.) [54]   [AMN]

40.214   NW   1957 De geologische geschiedenis der drie Bovenwindse Eilanden St.
                 Martin, Saba en St. Eustatius [The geological history of the three
                 Windward Islands: St. Martin, Saba and St. Eustatius]. W I G 37:
                 127-168.   [RIS]

WESTERMANN, J. H. & KIEL, H.

40.215   SA/   1961 THE GEOLOGY OF SABA AND ST. EUSTATIUS, WITH NOTES ON THE GEOLOGY
          SE   OF ST. KITTS, NEVIS AND MONTSERRAT (LESSER ANTILLES). Utrecht,
                 Natuurwetenschappelijke Studiekring voor Suriname en de Neder-
                 landse Antillen, 175p. (Uitgaven, no. 24.)   [RIS]

WESTERMANN, J. H. & ZONNEVELD, J. I. S.

40.216   BN   1956 PHOTO-GEOLOGICAL OBSERVATIONS AND LAND CAPABILITY AND LAND USE
                 SURVEY OF THE ISLAND OF BONAIRE (NETHERLANDS ANTILLES). Amster-
                 dam, Koninklijk Instituut voor de Tropen, 101p. (Mededeling no.
                 123, Afdeling Tropische producten no. 47.)   [46]   [AGS]

WESTOLL, T. S.

40.217   SK   1932 Description of rock specimens from Brimstone Hill and three other
                 localities in St. Kitts, B.W.I. Geol Mag 69(816), June: 259-264.
                                                                          [AGS]

WEYL, RICHARD

40.218   GC   1963 Bau und Bild der Kleinen Antillen [Structure and appearance of the
                 Lesser Antilles]. Geogr Rdsch 15(3), Mar.: 103-107.   [NYP]

WILLIAMS, J. B.

40.219   JM   1962 Earthquakes and their incidence and measurement in Jamaica. Inf
                 B Scient Res Coun 3(2), Sept.: 21-25.   [RIS]

WILLIAMS, JAMES

40.220   GG   1923 The name "Guiana." J Soc Am new ser., 15:19-34. [19,26]

WILLMORE, P. L.

40.221   SK/   1952 The earthquake series in St. Kitts-Nevis, 1950-51: with notes on
          NV   Soufrière activity in the Lesser Antilles. Nature 169(4306), May 10:
                 770-772.   [AGS]

WILMORE, A. N.

40.222   BB   1924 Barbados—a key to the physical history of the West Indies and Carib-
                 bean regions. Georg Tchr 12(69), Summer: 357-363.   [AGS]

WOODRING, W. P.

40.223   GC   1954 Caribbean land and sea through the ages. B Geol Soc Am 65(8),
                 Aug.: 719-732.   [AGS]

40.224   GC   1960 Oligocene and Miocene in the Caribbean region. *In* TRANSACTIONS
                      OF THE SECOND CARIBBEAN GEOLOGICAL CONFERENCE, Mayagüez, P.R.,
                      Jan. 1959. Mayagüez, P.R., University of Puerto Rico, p.27-32.
                      [*AMN*]

WORTS, G. F.
40.225   BG   1958 A BRIEF APPRAISAL OF GROUND-WATER CONDITIONS AND PROPOSED PRO-
                      GRAM FOR WATER-RESOURCES INVESTIGATIONS IN THE COASTAL ARTESIAN
                      BASIN OF BRITISH GUIANA. Georgetown, 52p. (British Guiana Geolo-
                      gical Survey, Bulletin no. 31.)   [66]   [*AGS*]

ZANS, V. A.
54.087   JM   1951 ECONOMIC GEOLOGY AND MINERAL RESOURCES OF JAMAICA.
40.226   JM   [1952?] GROUND-WATER SUPPLIES BY BOREHOLE WELLS IN JAMAICA. Kingston,
                      Geological Survey, 5p. (Publication no. 6.)   [*AGS*]
54.088   JM   1952 Bauxite resources of Jamaica and their development.
40.227   JM   1958 Geology and mining in Jamaica: a brief historical review. *In* REPORT
                      OF THE FIRST MEETING OF THE CARIBBEAN GEOLOGICAL CONFERENCE
                      held at Antigua, B.W.I., Dec. 1955. Demerara, [B.G.], Argosy and
                      Co., p.39-41.   [5,54]   [*RIS*]
40.228   JM   1958 Major structural features of Jamaica. *In* REPORT OF THE FIRST MEET-
                      ING OF THE CARIBBEAN GEOLOGICAL CONFERENCE held at Antigua,
                      B.W.I., Dec. 1955. Demerara, [B.G.], Argosy and Co., p.34-36. [*RIS*]
40.229   JM   1958 THE PEDRO CAYS AND PEDRO BANK: REPORT ON THE SURVEY OF THE
                      CAYS, 1955-57. Kingston, Geological Survey Department, 47p. (Bul-
                      letin no. 3.)
40.230   JM   1958 Water supply problems in the Karstlands of Jamaica. *In* REPORT OF
                      THE FIRST MEETING OF THE CARIBBEAN GEOLOGICAL CONFERENCE held
                      at Antigua, B.W.I., Dec. 1955. Demerara, [B.G.], Argosy and Co.,
                      p.62-63.   [*RIS*]
40.231   JM   1960 Hydrogeological studies for water supply. *Inf B Scient Res Coun*
                      1(3), Dec.: 11-13.   [*RIS*]
54.089   JM   1960 Recent geological work and mining developments in Jamaica: a brief
                      review of the activities during the last decade.
40.232   JM   1961 GEOLOGY AND MINERAL DEPOSITS OF JAMAICA. Kingston, Govt. Printer,
                      11p. (Jamaica, Geological Survey Dept., Publication no. 72.)   [54]
                                                                              [*COL*]

ZONNEVELD, J. I. S.
40.233   SR   1949 SURINAME EN DE LUCHTKAARTERING [SURINAM AND GEOGRAPHICAL AIR SUR-
                      VEY]. Paramaribo, Centraal Bureau Luchtkaartering, 18p. (Publica-
                      tie no. 1.)   [*AGS*]
40.234   SR   1950 Riviervormen in de kustvlakte van Suriname [Forms of the rivers in
                      the coastal plain of Surinam]. *Tijdschr Ned Aar Genoot* 2d ser., 67
                      (5), Sept.: 605-615.   [*AGS*]
40.235   SR   1951 Enkele riviervormen in het binnenland [Some river forms in the inter-
                      ior]. *Tijdschr Ned Aar Genoot* 2d ser., 68(2), Apr.: 215-220. [*AGS*]
40.236   SR   1952 Luchtfoto-geografie in Suriname [Geography by aerial photography in
                      Surinam]. *W I G* 33:35-48.   [*COL*]
40.237   SR   1952 Watervallen in Suriname [Waterfalls in Surinam]. *Tijdschr Ned Aar*
                      Genoot 2d ser., 69(4), Oct.: 499-507.   [*AGS*]
40.238   SR   1953 Kust-veranderingen aan de mond van de Suriname-rivier [Coastal
                      changes at the mouth of the Surinam River]. *Geol Mijnb* new ser.,
                      15, June: 250-254.

67.028   GC   1953 Notes on the use of aerial photography in the Caribbean countries.
40.239   NL   1954 De Benedenwinden in vogelvlucht [A birds-eye view of the Leeward
                    Islands].   *Tijdschr Ned Aar Genoot* 2d ser., 71(3), July: 228-233.
40.240   SR   1954 Waarmemingen langs de kust van Suriname [Observations along the
                    coast of Surinam].   *Tijdschr Ned Aar Genoot* 2d ser., 71(1), Jan.:
                    18-31.   [*AGS*]
40.241   NL   1960 Een luchtfoto-onderzoek op de Benedenwindse Eilanden [Aerial
                    photographic research in Curacao, Aruba and Bonaire].   *Tijdschr
                    Ned Aar Genoot* 2d ser., 77(4), Oct.: 389-400.   [*AGS*]

Chapter 41

PLANT AND ANIMAL LIFE

ABRAHAM, E. A. V.

29.001   BG   1912   Materia medica Guian. Britt.

ADAMS, DENNIS; MAGNUS, KENNETH & SEAFORTH, COMPTON

41.001   JM   1963   POISONOUS PLANTS IN JAMAICA. Mona, University of the West Indies, Dept. of Extra-Mural Studies, 40p. (Caribbean affairs, new ser., no. 2.)   [*RIS*]

ADAMSON, A. M.

41.002   TR   1941   Observations on biting sandflies (*Ceratopogonidae*) in Trinidad, British West Indies. *Car Med J* 3(2): 69-76.   [28]   [*COL*]

ADAMSON, L.; HARRISON, R. G. & BAYLEY, IRIS

41.003   BB   1960   The development of the whistling frog *Eleutherodactylus martinicensis* of Barbados. *Proc Zool Soc Lond* 133(3), Feb.: 453-469.

AIKEN, JAMES

41.004   BG   1907   Mosquitoes of British Guiana. *Br Gui Med Annual 1906* 15:59-78.
                                                                        [*ACM*]

41.005   BG   1909   Notes on the mosquitoes of British Guiana. *Br Gui Med Annual 1908* 16:1-25.   [*ACM*]

41.006   BG   1911   Synoptical view of the mosquitoes of British Guiana. *Timehri* 3d ser., 1(18B), July: 187-204.   [*AMN*]

64.001   BG   1912   Commercial classification of Colony timbers.

41.007   BG   1914   Notes on mosquitoes of British Guiana: *Taeniorhynchus fasciolatus*. *Br Gui Med Annual 1913* 20:35-37.   [*ACM*]

AIKEN, JAMES & ROWLAND, E. D.

41.008   BG   1906   Preliminary notes on the mosquitoes of British Guiana. *Br Gui Med Annual 1905* 14:13-38.   [*ACM*]

ALEXANDER, CHARLES P.

41.009   JM   1964   The crane-flies of Jamaica. *B Inst Jam Sci* no. 14.

ALEXANDER, WILLIAM H.

41.010   SK   1901   The flora of St. Christopher. *B Am Geogr Soc* 33(3):207-219.   [*AGS*]

41.011   BC   1902 On the flora of the West Indies: with special reference to the island
               of St. Kitts. *B Am Geogr Soc* 34:223-231.   [*AGS*]

ALLAN, J. A.
41.012   BB   1957 THE GRASSES OF BARBADOS. London, H.M.S.O. (Colonial Office,
               Colonial research publications no. 23.) [65]

ALLEN, ROBERT PORTER
41.013   GC   1961 BIRDS OF THE CARIBBEAN. New York, Viking Press, 256p.

ALLSOPP, W. H. L.
41.014   BG   1958 Arapaima—its manners, morals and measurements,—"the giant fish
               of South America." *Timehri* 4th ser., no. 37, Sept.: 89-98.   [56]
                                                                              [*AMN*]

AMBARD, FRANK
41.015   TR   1959 Butterflies of Trinidad. Pts. 3, 5. *Shell Trin* 5(7), June: 13-16; 5(9),
               Christmas: 13-16.

ANDERSON, Mrs. F. C. K.
41.016   BB   1934 Some observations on the birds of Barbados. *J Barb Mus Hist Soc*
               2(2), Feb.: 53-60; 2(3), May: 135-142.   [*AMN*]

ARNOLDO, Brother
41.017   NA   1954 Gekweekte en nuttige planten van de Nederlandse Antillen [Culti-
               vated and useful plants of the Dutch Antilles]. [Willemstad?]
               Curacao, Natuurwetenschappelijke Werkgroep Nederlandse Antillen,
               149p. ([Publications] no. 3.)   [*COL*]

ASPREY, G. F.
41.018   GC   1959 Vegetation in the Caribbean area. *Car Q* 5(4), June: 245-263. [*RIS*]

ASPREY, G. F. & ROBBINS, R. G.
41.019   JM   1953 The vegetation of Jamaica. *Ecol Monogr* 23(4), Oct.: 359-412. [*COL*]

ASPREY, G. F. & THORNTON, PHYLLIS
29.002   JM   1953/Medicinal plants of Jamaica. Pts. 1-4.
               55

ATTENBOROUGH, DAVID
41.020   BG   1956 ZOO QUEST TO GUIANA. London, Lutterworth Press, 187p.   [3]

BAKER, R. E. D. & DALE, W. T.
41.021   BB/   1948 FUNGI OF BARBADOS AND THE WINDWARD ISLANDS. Kew, Surrey, Com-
         WW   monwealth Mycological Institute, 26p. (Mycological papers no. 25.)

BAKHUIS, L. A.
40.005   SR   1908 De 5de wetenschappelijke expeditie naar het binnenland   van
               Suriname [The 5th scientific expedition into the interior of Surinam].

BALLOU, H. A.
41.022   BB   1909 Millions and mosquitos. *W I B* 9(4): 382-390.   [*AMN*]

41.023   BB   1937 Notes on the insects mentioned in Schomburgk's history. *J Barb Mus Hist Soc* 4(4), Aug.: 184-188. [5]   [*AMN*]

BANCROFT, C. K.

41.024   BG   1918 Botanical aspect of the sea defence problem. *J Bd Agric Br Gui* 11(2), Apr.: 3-9. [66]   [*AMN*]

BARBOUR, THOMAS

41.025   GC   1914 A contribution to the zoögeography of the West Indies, with especial reference to amphibians and reptiles. *Mem Mus Comp Zool Harv Coll* 44(2), Mar.: 209-359.   [*AMN*]

41.026   GC   1916 Some remarks upon Matthew's "Climate and Evolution." *Ann N Y Acad Sci* 27, Jan. 25: 1-15.   [*AMN*]

41.027   GC   1935 A second list of Antillean reptiles and amphibians. *Zoologica* 19(3), June: 77-141.   [*AMN*]

BARNETT, W. L.

41.028   JM   1951 GANJA. Kingston, Printed by the Government Printer, 15p. (Department of Government Chemist [publication]).   [37]

BARTRAM, EDWIN B.

41.029   DM   1955 Mosses of Dominica, British West Indies and mosses of the Ecuadorian Andes collected by P. R. Bell. *B Br Mus* (Natural History) Botany, 2(2).

BAYLEY, IRIS

29.003   BB   1949 The bush-teas of Barbados.

41.030   BB   1950 The whistling frogs of Barbados. *J Barb Mus Hist Soc* 17(4), Aug.: 161-170.   [*AMN*]

BEARD, JOHN STEWART

41.031   GC   1942 Montane vegetation in the Antilles. *Car For* 3(2), Jan.: 61-74. [64]   [*AGS*]

41.032   GC   1944 Climax vegetation in tropical America. *Ecology* 25(2), Apr.: 127-158.   [*AMN*]

41.033   GC   1944 Provisional list of trees and shrubs of the Lesser Antilles. *Car For* 5(2), Jan.: 48-67. [64]   [*AGS*]

64.010   TR   1944 A silvicultural technique in Trinidad for the rehabilitation of degraded forest.

41.034   SV   1945 The progress of plant succession on the Soufrière of St. Vincent. *J Ecol* 33(1), Oct.: 1-9.   [*AGS*]

41.035   TR   1946 THE NATURAL VEGETATION OF TRINIDAD. Oxford, Clarendon Press, 152p. (Oxford forestry memoirs no. 20.)   [*AGS*]

41.036   GC   1949 THE NATURAL VEGETATION OF THE WINDWARD AND LEEWARD ISLANDS. Oxford, Clarendon Press, 192p. (Oxford forestry memoirs no. 21.)   [*AGS*]

41.037   GC   1953 The Savanna vegetation of northern tropical America. *Ecol Monogr* 23(2), Apr.: 149-215.

41.038   GC   1955 The classification of tropical American vegetation types. *Ecology* 36(1), Jan.: 89-100.   [*AMN*]

BECKETT, J. EDGAR
64.014   BG   1911 Rubber.

BECKWITH, MARTHA WARREN
29.004   JM   1927 Notes on Jamaican ethnobotany.

BEEBE, MARY BLAIR & BEEBE, WILLIAM
41.039   BG   1910 Our search for a wilderness [by] M.B. Beebe and C. William
                      Beebe. New York, Henry Holt, 408p.   [3]   [AGS]

BEEBE, WILLIAM
3.021   BG   1918 Jungle peace.
41.040   BG   1921 Edge of the jungle. New York, Henry Holt, 303p.   [RIS]
41.041   BG   1921 The Neotropical Research Station of the New York Zoological
                      Society. *Timehri* 3d ser., 7(24), Aug.: 110-114. [67]   [AMN]
41.042   BG   1925 Studies of a tropical jungle: one quarter of a square mile of jungle
                      at Kartabo, British Guiana. *Zoologica* 6(1), Mar. 11: 1-193.   [AGS]
41.043   TR   1958 The high world of the rain forest. *Natn Geogr Mag* 113(6), June:
                      838-855. [64]   [AGS]

BEEBE, WILLIAM; HARTLEY, G. INNESS & HOWES, PAUL G.
41.044   BG   1917 Tropical wild life in British Guiana. Vol. 1. New York, New York
                      Zoological Society, 499p.   [AGS]

BEIJERING, J.
28.031   CU   1950 Het vraagstuk van het behoud van het water op Curacao [The problem
                      of water conservation on Curacao].

BEVAN, ARTHUR
64.018   UV   1940 Possibilities for forestry in the Virgin Islands: St. Thomas, St. John,
                      St. Croix.

BODKIN, G. E.
41.045   BG   1921 The mosquitoes of British Guiana. *J Bd Agric Br Gui* 14(4), Oct.:
                      251-261.   [AMN]
28.040   BG   1921 Some recent entomological surveys bearing on malarial incidence
                      in British Guiana.

BOLDINGH, ISAAC
41.046   NA   1909/ The flora of the Dutch West Indian Islands. Vol. 1: The flora of
                      14 St. Eustatius, Saba and St. Martin. Vol. 2: The flora of Cura-
                      cao, Aruba, and Bonaire. Leyden, E.J. Brill, 2v.   [COL]

BOND, JAMES
41.047   WW/   1928 On the birds of Dominica, St. Lucia, St. Vincent, and Barbados,
          BB   B.W.I. *Proc Acad Nat Sci Phil* 80:523-545.   [COL]
41.048   GC   1947 Field guide of birds of the West Indies. New York, Macmillan,
                      257p.
41.049   GC   1950 Check-list of birds of the West Indies. Philadelphia, Academy of
                      Natural Sciences of Philadelphia, 200p.
41.050   GC   1960 Birds of the West Indies. London, Collins, 256p.

BOX, HAROLD E.

41.051   AT   1933 The birds of Antigua. *W I Comm Circ* 48(919), Dec. 21: 515-516.
[*NYP*]

BROWN, HERBERT H.

41.052   GC   1943 Productivity of the seas: some fundamental considerations and their possible application in the Caribbean area. *J Barb Mus Hist Soc* 10(2), Feb.: 45-55. [56]   [*AMN*]

BROWN, WILLIAM L.

41.053   GC   1953 Maize of the West Indies. *Trop Agric* 30(7-9), July-Sept.: 141-170.
[*AGS*]

BRUIJNING, C. F. A.

28.071   SR   1952 Some observations on the distribution of *A. Darlingi* root in the Savannah region of Surinam. By C. F. A. Bruyning.

28.072   SR/   1957 Man-biting sandflies (*Phlebotomus*) in the endemic Leishmaniasis
         FG   area of Surinam.

BUTSCH, ROBERT S.

41.054   BB   1939 A list of Barbadian fishes. *J Barb Mus Hist Soc* 7(1), Nov.: 17-31.
[56]   [*AMN*]

41.055   BB   1939 The reef builders at Barbados. *J Barb Mus Hist Soc* 6(3), May: 129-138.   [40]   [*AMN*]

41.056   BB   1939 Some observations on the snappers of Barbados. *J Barb Mus Hist Soc* 6(2), Feb.: 67-73. [56]   [*AMN*]

CAMPBELL, DOUGLASS HOUGHTON

41.057   BG/   1913 Some impressions of the flora of Guiana and Trinidad. *Pop Sci Mon*
         TR   82(1), Jan.: 19-32.   [*COL*]

CARMICHAEL, GERTRUDE

41.058   TR   1959 CALENDAR OF THE FLOWERING TREES AND PLANTS OF TRINIDAD AND TOBAGO. 2d ed. Port of Spain, Yuille's Printerie, 42p.   [*RIS*]

CARNEGIE, A. L.

28.084   JM   1963 Poisoning by barracuda fish.

CECIL, C. H.

41.059   BG   1937 In a tropic garden. *Can-W I Mag* 26(10), Oct.: 26-27.   [*NYP*]

CHAPMAN, V. J.

41.060   JM   1961/ The marine algae of Jamaica. Pt. 1. *Myxophyceae* and *Clorophyceae*.
         63   Pt. 2. *Phaeophyceae* and *Rhodophyceae*. *B Inst Jam Sci* 12(1) (1961); 12(2) (1963).

CHEESMAN, E. E.

41.061   GC   1939 The history of introduction of some well known West Indian staples. *Trop Agric* 16(5), May: 101-107. [5, 46]   [*AGS*]

CHOUBERT, BORIS
66.029   FG   1960 L'Institut francais d'Amérique tropicale (I.F.A.T.): pilot agency in French Guiana.

CLARKE, T. L. E.
28.096   BV   1918 Some observations on fish poisoning in the British Virgin Islands.

CLEARE, L. D.
41.062   BG   1919 Some parasites of man and animals in British Guiana. *Br Gui Med Annual 1919* 22:58-77. [28]   [*ACM*]

COLLIER, H. C.
41.063   BC   1934 West Indian curiosa. *Can-W I Mag* 23(5), Apr.: 146-148.   [*NYP*]
29.009   BC   1941 Nature, her own apothecary.

COLLINS, H. H., Jr.; VOOUS, K. H. & ZANEVELD, J. S.
41.064   NA   1956 BIRDS AND FISH OF THE NETHERLANDS ANTILLES. Bronxville, N. Y., Caribou Press, 18p. [56]   [*AMN*]

COOMANS, H. E.
41.065   CU   1964 De eerste schelpenfauna van Curacao, in Simons' beschrijving van dit eiland, 1868 [The oldest mollusk fauna of Curacao, in Simons' description of the island]. *N W I G* 43(3), May: 195-210.   [*RIS*]

CRADWICK, WILLIAM
41.066   JM   1936 The orchids of Jamaica. *W I Comm Circ* 51(988), Aug. 13: 339-341.
                                                                          [*NYP*]
41.067   JM   1937 Exotic orchids in Jamaica. *W I Comm Circ* 52(1018), Oct. 7: 393-394.   [*NYP*]

CRAWFORD, STANTON C.
41.068   BG   1932 Twilight and dawn in Guiana. *Nat Hist* 32(2), Mar.-Apr.: 207-214.
                                                                          [*AGS*]

DAHLGREN, B. E. & STANDLEY, PAUL C.
60.018   GC   1944 EDIBLE AND POISONOUS PLANTS OF THE CARIBBEAN REGION.

DALE, W. T.
41.069   JM   1955 A PRELIMINARY LIST OF JAMAICAN *Uredinales*. Kew, Surrey, Commonwealth Mycological Institute, 21p. (Mycological papers no. 60.)

DANFORTH, STUART T.
41.070   AT   1934 The birds of Antigua. *Auk* 51(3), July: 350-364;
                     1939 56(3), July: 304-305.   [*COL*]
41.071   SK/   1936 The birds of St. Kitts and Nevis. *Trop Agric* 13(8), Aug.: 213-217.
          NV   [*AGS*]
41.072   BB   1938 Observations on some Barbadian birds. *J Barb Mus Hist Soc* 5(3), May: 119-129.   [*AMN*]

DAVIS, WILLIAM MORRIS
41.073   LW/   1926 THE LESSER ANTILLES. New York, American Geographical Society,
          WW   207p. [3]   [*RIS*]

DAWSON, CHARLES B.

41.074   BG   1911   Some colony birds. *Timehri* 3d ser., 1(18C), Dec.: 268-279;
                 1915   3(20B), May: 311-331;
                 1917   4(21), June: 38-57.   [*AMN*]

41.075   BG   1915   The birds of British Guiana. *J Bd Agric Br Gui* 9(1), Nov.: 15-32;
                 1916   9(2), Feb.: 94-112; 9(3), May: 146-157; 9(4), July: 196-218.   [*AMN*]

DEVAS, RAYMUND P.

41.076   GR/   [n.d.]   BIRDS OF GRENADA AND ST. VINCENT AND THE GRENADINES (BRITISH
        GN/   WEST INDIES). [Bridgetown?] Barbados, Privately printed by Advocate
        SV   Co., 64p.

41.077   GC   [1952?]   Birds of the West Indies. *Car Q* 2(3): 39-43.   [*RIS*]

41.078   BH   1953   BIRDS OF BRITISH HONDURAS: NOTES ON SOME OF THE BIRDS RESIDENT
                 IN THAT PART OF CENTRAL AMERICA. Port of Spain, Yuille's Printerie,
                 79p.   [*AMN*]

DEVEZ, G.

41.079   FG   1932   Les plantes utiles et les bois industriels de la Guyane [The useful
                 plants and industrial timbers of Guiana]. *Agric Prat Pays Chauds*
                 new ser., 3(20), Feb.: 133-151; 3(22), Apr.: 303-314.   [64]   [*AGS*]

DEYDIER, JOSEPH

40.046   FG   1905   Trois ans à la Guyane Francaise (1901-1904) [Three years in French
                 Guiana (1901-1904)].

DIAS, EMMANUEL

28.124   GG   1952   Doenca de chagas nas Américas. IV: Colômbia, Venezuela e Guianas
                 [Running sores in the Americas. IV: Colombia, Venezuela, and the
                 Guianas].

DINGLEY, FUGE P.

41.080   BB   1934   A note on diatoms in general. *J Barb Mus Hist Soc* 1(2), Feb.:
                 85-89.   [40]   [*AMN*]

DUERDEN, J. E.

56.020   BC   1901   The marine resources of the British West Indies.

DUNN, E. R.

41.081   GC   1934   Physiography and herpetology in the Lesser Antilles. *Copeia* 3,
                 Oct. 31: 105-111.   [*AMN*]

EILERTS de HAAN, J.G., et al.

40.059   SR   1910   Verslag van de expeditie naar de Suriname-Rivier [Account of the
                 expedition to the Surinam River].

EUWENS, P. A.

41.082   CU/   1922/   De leguana [The iguana]. *W I G* 4:115-121.   [*COL*]
        BN   23

FAIRCHILD, DAVID

3.097   GC   1934   Hunting useful plants in the Caribbean.

FANSHAWE, D. B.

41.083   BG   1947   Arawak Indian plant names. *Car For* 8(3), July: 165-181. [26]   [*AGS*]

41.084   BG   1952 THE VEGETATION OF BRITISH GUIANA: A PRELIMINARY REVIEW. Oxford,
                University of Oxford, Holywell Press, 96p. (Imperial Forestry
                Institute, University of Oxford, Institute paper no. 29.)   [AGS]
41.085   BG   1953 Akawaio Indian plant names. *Car For* 14(3-4), July-Oct.: 120-127.
                [26]   [AGS]
41.086   BG   1954 Forest types of British Guiana. *Car For* 15(3-4), July-Oct.: 73-111.
                [64]   [AGS]

FANSHAWE, D. B. & SWABEY, C.
41.087   BG   1948 Botanical and ecological exploration in Guiana. *Timehri* 4th ser.,
                1(28), Dec.: 19-23.

FARR, THOMAS H.
41.088   JM   1961/ A national insect collection for Jamaica. *Inf B Scient Res Coun*
                62   2(3), Dec.: 54-55.   [AMN]
41.089   JM   1963 Peripatus: a zoological curiosity. *Inf B Scient Res Coun* 3(4), Mar.:
                61-63.   [RIS]
41.090   JM   1963 The robber-flies of Jamaica. Pt.1: The subfamily *Leptogastrinae*.
                B Inst Jam 13(1) (22p.)

FAWCETT, WILLIAM & RENDLE, ALFRED BARTON
41.091   JM   1914/ The flora of Jamaica, pts. III, IV, V. London, Printed by order of
                26   the trustees of the British Museum, 3v.   [COL]

FENG, P. C.
29.013 BG   1956 A preliminary survey of the medicinal plants of British Guiana.

FLOCH, HERVE ALEXANDRE & ABONNENC, E.
41.092   FG   1942 Catalogue et distribution géographique des moustiques de la Guyane
                Francaise actuellement connus [Listing and geographic distribution
                of the mosquitoes of French Guiana, known at present]. *Inst Past
                Guy Ter L'In* 43, May (10p.)
41.093   GD   1945 Les moustiques de la Guadeloupe [The mosquitoes of Guadeloupe].
                I. Genre *Anopheles*. II. Les genres *Megarhinus, Aedes, Culex,
                Deinocerites, Mansonia* et *Wyeomyia*. *Inst Past Guy Ter L'In* 108,
                July (15p.); 110, Aug. (48p.)   [ACM]
41.094   FG   1947 Distribution des *Anophèles* en Guyane Francaise [Distribution of
                Anopheles in French Guiana]. *Inst Past Guy Ter L'In* 144, Jan. (9p.)
41.095   FG   1947 Distribution des moustiques du genre *Culex* en Guyane Francaise
                [Distribution of the *Culex* genus of mosquitoes in French Guiana].
                Inst Past Guy Ter L'In 146, Jan. (9p.)
41.096   FG   1951 *Anophèles* de la Guyane Francaise [*Anopheles* of French Guiana].
                Archs Inst Past Guy 336, Aug. (91p.)
41.097   FG   1951 Sur la présence d'*Aedes aegypti* dans une région isolée au coeur de
                la Guyane Francaise [On the presence of *Aedes aegypti* in an iso-
                lated region in the heart of French Guiana]. *Archs Inst Past Guy*
                223, Jan. (4p.)

FLOCH, HERVE ALEXANDRE & FAURAN, P.
28.179 FG   1954 Lutte antipaludique et lutte antimarile en Guyane Francaise. Les
                moustiques vecteurs du virus de la fièvre jaune en Guyane Fran-
                caise [The fight against malaria and yellow fever in French Guiana.
                Mosquito vectors of the yellow fever virus in French Guiana].

FOWLER, HENRY W.

41.098   GR   1931 Fishes obtained by Mr. James Bond at Grenada, British West Indies,
                       in 1929. *Proc Acad Nat Sci Phil* 82:269-277.   [56]   [*COL*]

FRANSSEN HERDERSCHEE, A.

40.065   SR   1905 Verslag van de Gonini-Expeditie [Account of the Gonini Expedition].

GEIJSKES, D. C.

41.099   SR   1949 The natural science expedition in Surinam, by D.C. Geyskes. *Car
                       Commn Mon Inf B* 3(5), Dec.: 175-176.   [*COL*]
41.100   SR   1956/Zoogeografie van Suriname [Zoogeography of Surinam]. *W I G* 37:
                       57 18-24.   [*COL*]

GIGLIOLI, GEORGE

28.215   BG   1933 Statistical data on the incidence of various malarial parasites in
                       the river areas of the interior.
28.220   BG   1951 The influence of geological formation and soil characteristics on
                       the distribution of malaria and its mosquito carrier in British Guiana.
28.222   BG   1958 The mosquito and sand-fly nuisance in Georgetown and its suburbs.

GILLIARD, E. T. & TRUSLOW, F. K.

41.101   TB   1958 Feathered dancers of little Tobago. *Natn Geogr Mag* 114(3), Sept.:
                       428-440.   [*AGS*]

GIRAUD, J.

40.068   SR   1906 Au travers des forêts vierges de la Guyane Hollandaise [Through
                       the virgin forests of Dutch Guiana].

GOEJE, C. H. de

40.070   SR   1908 Verslag der Toemak Hoemak expeditie [Account of the Tumuc-
                       Humac expedition].
41.102   SR   1936/Voorzichtig met den bodem van Suriname! [Be careful with the
                       37 ground of Surinam!] *W I G* 18:274-275.   [44]   [*COL*]

GONGGRIJP, J. W.

41.103   SR   1949 Techniek en organisatie van het botanisch bosonderzoek in Suriname
                       [The technique and the organization of botanical forest research in
                       Surinam]. *W I G* 30:1-8.   [*COL*]

GOODING, E. G. B.

41.104   BB   1940 Facts and beliefs about Barbadian plants. *J Barb Mus Hist Soc*
                       7(4), Aug.: 170-183; 8(1), Nov.: 32-35;
                       1941 8(2), Feb.: 70-73; 8(3), May: 103-106; 8(4), Aug.: 194-197; 9(1),
                       Nov.: 17-19;
                       1942 9(2), Feb.: 84-88; 9(3), May: 126-129; 9(4), Aug.: 192-194; 10(1),
                       Nov.: 3-6.   [*AMN*]
41.105   BB   1943 Turner's Hall Wood. *J Barb Mus Hist Soc* 10(2), Feb.: 74-84. [*AMN*]

GOWDEY, C. C.

41.106   JM   1926 Catalogus insectorum Jamaicensis. Kingston, Govt. Print. Off., 3v.
                       (Department of Agriculture, Entomological bulletin no. 4, pts. 1-3.)

GRANT, CHAPMAN

41.107   CM   1940 The herpetology of the Cayman Islands. *B Inst Jam Sci* 2:65p. [*AGS*]

GREBERT, RENE

41.108   GD   1934 Les forêts de la Guadeloupe [The forests of Guadeloupe]. *B Ag
                       Econ Colon Auto Ter Afr* 27(302), May: 639-702; 27(303), June:
                       765-875; 27(304), July: 941-1015. [64]   [*AGS*]

GREEN, LENA

41.109   JM   1962 Some seaweeds of economic importance growing in Jamaican waters.
                       Inf B Scient Res Coun 3(2), Sept.: 35-36. [30, 44]   [*RIS*]

GREENHALL, ARTHUR M.

41.110   TR   1959 Check list of the bats of Trinidad and Tobago. *Car Med J* 21(1-4):
                       169-171.   [*COL*]
41.111   TR   1965 Trinidad and bat research. *Nat Hist* 74(6), June-July: 14-21.

GUNTHER, A. E.

41.112   TR   1942 The distribution and status of Mora Forest (*Mora excelsa*) in ·the
                       Ortoire Basin, Trinidad, B.W.I. *Emp For J* 21(2): 123-127   [64]
                                                                                      [*AGS*]

GUPPY, P. LECHMERE

56.027   TR   1922 Ã naturalist in Trinidad and Tobago.
41.113   TR   1926 A naturalist in Trinidad and Tobago. *W I Comm Circ* 41(730), Sept.:
                       23:363; 41(731), Oct. 7: 383; 41(732), Oct. 21: 409; 41(733), Nov.
                       4: 429; 41(734), Nov. 18:449;
                 1927 42(738), Jan. 13: 4; 42(739), Jan. 27: 27.   [*NYP*]
41.114   TB   1927 A naturalist in Tobago. *W I Comm Circ* 42(756), Sept. 22: 384-385.
                                                                                      [*NYP*]

GUPPY, R. J. LECHMERE

40.076   TR   1910/ On a collection of fossils from Springvale near Couva, Trinidad.
                 11

HAAN, J. H. de

41.115   SR   1955/ Ecologisch onderzoek ten behoeve van het Brokopondoplan in
                 56   Suriname [Ecological research on behalf of the Brokopondo Plan
                       in Surinam]. *W I G* 36:18-31.   [*COL*]

HARDY, F.

41.116   BB   1934 SOME ASPECTS OF THE FLORA OF BARBADOS. [Bridgetown?] Barbados,
                       Advocate Co., 173p.

HARGREAVES, DOROTHY & BOB

41.117   GC   1960 TROPICAL BLOSSOMS. Portland, Or., Hargreaves Industrial, 62p. [*RIS*]

HARRISON, S. G.

41.118   BG   1961 Notes on the vegetation of the coastal region of British Guiana.
                       Timehri 4th ser., no. 40, Oct.: 93-104.   [*AMN*]

HAVERSCHMIDT, F.

41.119   SR   1953 LIST OF THE BIRDS OF SURINAM. The Hague, Nijhoff, 153p.

HAYMAN, R. W.

41.120 TR 1932 A key to the bats of Trinidad. *Proc Agric Soc Trin Tob* 32(9), Sept.: 312-317. [*AMN*]

HEILPRIN, ANGELO

3.138 BG 1906 Impressions of a naturalist in British Guiana.

HEIM de BALSAC, F.; DEFORGE, A.; HEIM de BALSAC, H. & LEFEVRE, L.

41.121 FG 1929 Contribution à l'étude des écorces tannifères de la Guyane Française [Contribution to the study of the tanniferous barks of French Guiana]. *B Ag Gen Colon* 22(240), Jan.: 36-48; 22(241), Feb.: 119-137; 22(243), Apr.: 340-368. [64] [*AGS*]

HEINSDIJK, D.

41.122 SR 1953 BEGROEIING EN LUCHTFOTOGRAFIE IN SURINAME [VEGETATION AND AERIAL PHOTOGRAPHY IN SURINAM]. Paramaribo, Centraal Bureau Luchtkaartering te Paramaribo, 19p. (Publ. no. 12.)

HERKLOTS, G. A. C.

41.123 TR 1961 THE BIRDS OF TRINIDAD AND TOBAGO. London, Collins Clear-Type Press, 287p. [*RIS*]

HILL, ROLLA B. & CLAIRE McDOWELL

41.124 JM 1948 The mosquitoes of Jamaica. *B Inst Jam Sci* no. 4: 60p. [*AGS*]

HINGSTON, R. W. G.

41.125 BG 1930 In the canopy of the rain-forest. *W I Comm Circ* 45(824), May 1: 175-176. [64] [*NYP*]
3.148 BG 1930 The Oxford University Expedition to British Guiana.
41.126 BG 1932 A NATURALIST IN THE GUIANA FOREST. London, Edward Arnold, 384p. [*AMN*]
3.149 BG 1932 A new world to explore: in the tree-roof of the British Guiana forest flourishes hitherto-unknown life.

HITCHCOCK, A. S.

41.127 BG 1922 Grasses of British Guiana. *U S Natn Herb* 22(6), May 24: 439-515. [65] [*NYP*]
41.128 BG 1923 Grasses of British Guiana. *J Bd Agric Br Gui* 16(1), Jan.: 31-39. [65] [*AMN*]

HODGE, L. P.

41.129 BG 1918 Some of the constructional woods. *Timehri* 3d ser., 5(22), Aug.: 56-60. [64] [*AMN*]

HODGE, W. H.

41.130 DM 1942 A synopsis of the palms of Dominica. *Car For* 3(3), Apr.: 103-109. [64] [*AGS*]
41.131 DM 1943 The vegetation of Dominica. *Geogr Rev* 33(3), July: 349-375. [*AGS*]

HOFF, C. CLAYTON

41.132 JM 1959/ The pseudoscorpions of Jamaica. Part I. The genus *Tyrannoch-* 64 *thonius*. Part II. The genera *Pseudochthonius Paraliochthonius, lechytia*, and *Tridenchthonius*. Part III. The suborder *Diplosphyronida*. *B Inst Jan Sci* 1959: 10(1); 1963: 10(2); 1964: 10(3). [*AGS*]

HOHENKERK, L. S.

41.133   BG   1918 Botanical identifications of British Guiana trees and plants. *J Bd
                   Agric Br Gui* 11(3), July: 98-108; 11(4), Oct.: 178-185;
                   1922 15(4), Oct.: 196-199.   [64]   [*AMN*]

HOLTHUIS, L. B.

41.134   SR   1958 G. D. Collins' *Fauna surinamensis. W I G* p.38:71-85.   [*COL*]

HORST, C. J. van der

41.135   CU   1924 Narrative of the voyage and short description of localities. *Bijd
                   Dierkunde* 23:1-12.   [*AMN*]

HOUGHTON, T. R.

41.136   TR   1960 The water buffalo in Trinidad. *J Agric Soc Trin Tob* 60(3), Sept.:
                   339-356.   [65]   [*AMN*]

HOWARD, RICHARD A.

41.137   TR   1951 Botanical observations on Pitch Lake in Trinidad. *Car For* 12(4),
                   Oct.: 171-182.   [46]   [*AGS*]

41.138   GN   1952 THE VEGETATION OF THE GRENADINES, WINDWARD ISLANDS, BRITISH
                   WEST INDIES. Cambridge, Mass., Gray Herbarium of Harvard Univer-
                   sity, 129p. (Contributions from the Gray Herbarium of Harvard Uni-
                   versity, no. 174.)   [*RIS*]

41.139   SV   1954 A history of the Botanic Garden of Saint Vincent, British West
                   Indies. *Geogr Rev.* 44(3): 381-393.   [*AGS*]

41.140   MS   1961 Why Montserrat? *In* BROWN, JOHN, ed. LEEWARDS: WRITINGS, PAST
                   AND PRESENT, ABOUT THE LEEWARD ISLANDS. [Bridgetown?] Barbados,
                   Dept. of Extra-mural Studies, Leeward Islands, University College
                   of the West Indies, p.12-17.   [5]   [*RIS*]

HOWARD, RICHARD A. & PROCTOR, GEORGE R.

41.141   JM   1957 A vegetation of bauxitic soils in Jamaica. *J Arn Arb* 38(1), Jan.:
                   1-41; 38(2), Apr.: 151-169.   [54]   [*AMN*]

HOWE, OLIN J.

40.090   JM   1920 Is Jamaica part of a lost continent?

HOWE, W. N. & SINGH, RAM S.

41.142   BG   1960 Survey of the birds of Greater Georgetown. *Timehri* 4th ser., no. 39,
                   Sept.: 79-100.   [*AMN*]

HOWES, PAUL GRISWOLD

41.143   DM   1928 Anomaly island: Strange animals adapted to a unique environment
                   give the picturesque island of Dominica its peculiar local color.
                   Scient Am 139(6), Dec.: 516-518.   [*COL*]

41.144   DM   1930 Wild life in Dominica. *Nat Hist* 30(1), Jan.-Feb.: 90-103.   [*AGS*]

41.145   DM   1931 Boa constrictors and other pets. *Nat Hist* 31(3), May-June: 300-309.
                                                                           [*AGS*]

HUGHES, J. HENRY

41.146   BG   1946 Forest resources. *In* ROTH, VINCENT, comp. HANDBOOK OF NATURAL
                   RESOURCES OF BRITISH GUIANA. Georgetown, Daily Chronicle, p.46-
                   191.   [64]   [*AGS*]

HUTCHINSON, J. B.

41.147 JM 1943 The cottons of Jamaica. *Trop Agric* 20(3), Mar.: 56-58. [61] [*AGS*]

41.148 TR 1943 Notes on the native cottons of Trinidad. *Trop Agric* 20(12), Dec.: 235-238. [61] [*AGS*]

JEFFREY-SMITH, MAY

41.149 JM 1956 BIRD-WATCHING IN JAMAICA. Kingston, Pioneer Press, 160p. [*AMN*]

KAYE, WILLIAM JAMES

41.150 TR 1913 Butterflies of Trinidad and Tobago. *Proc Agric Soc Trin Tob* 13(5), May: 228-245; 13(6), June: 292-305; 13(7), July: 346-355; 13(8), Aug.: 402-415; 13(10), Oct.: 509-524; 13(11), Nov.: 575-580. [*AMN*]

41.151 TR 1914 Moths of Trinidad. *Proc Agric Soc Trin Tob* 14(2), Feb.: 58-69; 14(3), Mar.: 115-125; 14(5), May: 191-200; 14(6), June: 231-242. [*AMN*]

KINLOCH, J. B.

41.152 BH 1940 Mapping vegetational types in British Honduras from aerial photographs. *Car For* 1(2), Jan.: 1-4. [67] [*AGS*]

KOUMANS, F. P.

41.153 SR 1948 Het onderzoek van de vissen van Suriname [The study of Surinam's fish]. *W I G* 29:55-58. [*COL*]

KUYP, EDWIN van der

41.154 NA/ 1949 Annotated list of mosquitoes of the Netherlands Antilles including
   SM   French St. Martin, with a note on *Eutriatoma maculta* on Curacao and Bonaire. *Docum Ned Indo Morbis Trop* 1, Mar.-Dec.: 69-70. [*COL*]

41.155 CU 1953 Mosquitoes of Curacao. *Car Med J* 15(1-2): 37-39. [*COL*]

LANJOUW, J. & UITTIEN, H.

41.156 SR 1935/ Surinaamsche geneeskruiden in den tijd van Linnaeus [Surinam's
      36 medicinal herbs during the age of Linnaeus]. *W I G* 17:172-190. [5, 28] [*COL*]

LASSALLE, C. F.

41.157 TR 1921 A mosquito survey of Trinidad. *J Bd Agric Br Gui* 14(1), Jan.: 30-36. [28, 66] [*AMN*]

Le GALLO, C. & MONACHINO, JOSEPH

41.158 SB 1956 Additions to the flora of St. Barthelemy. *Car For* 17(1-2), Jan.-June: 12-24. [*AGS*]

LEWIS, C. BERNARD, ed.

41.159 JM 1949/ GLIMPSES OF JAMAICAN NATURAL HISTORY. Kingston, Institute of
      46 Jamaica, 2 v. (vol. 1: 2d ed.)

LEWIS, JOHN B.

41.160 BB 1960 The fauna of rocky shores of Barbados, West Indies. *Can J Zool* 38:391-435.

LINDEMAN, JAN CHRISTIAAN

41.161   SR   1953 THE VEGETATION OF THE COASTAL REGION OF SURINAME. Amsterdam, Van Eedenfonds, in cooperation with 's Lands Bosbeheer and Landbouwproefstation, Paramaribo, Suriname, 135p. (The vegetation of Surinam, v. 1, pt. 1.)

LONGSTAFF, G. B.

41.162   TB   1914 Butterflies of Tobago. *Proc Agric Soc Trin Tob* 14(1), Jan.: 27-32.
                                                                           [*AMN*]

LOVELESS, A. R.

41.163   AT   1960 The vegetation of Antigua, West Indies. *J Ecol* 48(3), Oct.: 495-527.   [*AGS*]

LUNDELL, CYRUS LONGWORTH

41.164   BH   1940 The 1936 Michigan-Carnegie botanical expedition to British Honduras. *In* CARNEGIE INSTITUTION OF WASHINGTON. PUBLICATION 522. Washington, D. C., p.3-57.   [*AGS*]

McCONNELL, R. H.

41.165   BG   1958 Introduction to the fish fauna of British Guiana. *Timehri* 4th ser., no. 37, Sept.: 25-35. [56]   [*AMN*]

McINTOSH, A. E. S.

41.166   BB   1937 Progress report on the collection of the flora of Barbados. *J Barb Mus Hist Soc* 4(3), May: 123-128.   [*AMN*]

MARIE, ERNEST

41.167   MT   1949 Notes sur les reboisements en *Swietenia macrophylla King* [Notes on reforestation with *Swietenia macrophylla King*]. *Car For* 10(3), July: 205-222. [64]   [*AGS*]

MARSHALL, R. C.

41.168   TR   1934 THE PHYSIOGRAPHY AND VEGETATION OF TRINIDAD AND TOBAGO; A STUDY IN PLANT ECOLOGY. Oxford, Clarendon Press, 56p. (Oxford forestry memoirs, no. 17.)   [*AGS*]

MILLER, GERRIT S.

4.099   JM   1932 Collecting in the caves and kitchenmiddens of Jamaica.

MILLSPAUGH, CHARLES FREDERICK

41.169   SC   1902 Flora of the island of St. Croix. *Fld Col Mus*, Botanical series, publ. 68, 1(7), Nov.: 441-546.   [*AGS*]

MINETT, E. P.

28.368   BG   1912 Mosquito prophylaxis.

MOLE, R. R.

41.170   TR   1914 Trinidad snakes. *Proc Agric Soc Trin Tob* 14(9), Sept.: 363-369.
                                                                           [*AMN*]

MONACHINO, JOSEPH

41.171   SB   1940 A check list of the Spermatophytes of St. Bartholomew. *Car For* 2(1), Oct.: 24-47;
                1941 2(2), Jan.: 49-66.   [*AGS*]

MYERS, GEORGE S.

41.172   GC   1938 Fresh-water fishes and West Indian zoogeography. *In* ANNUAL REPORT
                      OF THE SMITHSONIAN INSTITUTION FOR 1937. Washington, U. S. Govt.
                      Print. Off., p.339-364. [56]   [*AGS*]

MYERS, J.G.

59.033   BG   1934 Observations on wild cacao and wild bananas in British Guiana.

NUTTING, C. C.

41.173   BB/   1919 BARBADOS-ANTIGUA EXPEDITION. Iowa City, University of Iowa,
          AT   274p. (University of Iowa studies, 1st ser. no. 28, Studies in natural
                      history, v. 8, no. 3.)   [*AGS*]

41.174   BB   1935 Some notes on the fishes of Barbados. *J Barb Mus Hist Soc* 2(4),
                      Aug.: 187-190. [56]   [*AMN*]

41.175   BB   1936 Some notes on the crustacea of Barbados. *J Barb Mus Hist Soc*
                      3(2), Feb.: 81-86.   [*AMN*]

41.176   BB   1937 Some notes on the Echinoderms (starfish, sea-eggs) of Barbados.
                      J Barb Mus Hist Soc 4(2), Feb.: 68-71. [56]   [*AMN*]

OUDSCHANS DENTZ, FRED

41.177   SR   1942 Bananen en bacoven [Bananas and bacoven]. *W I G* 24:246-250.
                      [60]   [*COL*]

OZZARD, A. T.

28.407   BG   1902 The mosquito and malaria.

PANHUYS, L. C. van

67.018   NC   1922/ De jongste botanische en zoologische onderzoekingen van het
                 23   eiland Krakatau als een aansporing tot wetenschappelijke waarnem-
                      ingen ook in Suriname en Curacao [The latest botanical and zoological
                      research of the island Krakatoa as encouragment to scientific re-
                      search in Surinam and Curacao].

41.178   NC   1943 Natuurschoon in Nederlandsche West-Indië [The beauty of nature
                      in the Dutch West Indies]. *W I G* 25:181-191.   [*COL*]

41.179   SR/   1944/ Eenige gegevens over de dieren-en plantenwereld in West-Indië
          CU   45   [Notes about the fauna and flora in West India]. *W I G* 26:222-224.
                                                                                     [*COL*]

41.180   SR   1946 Suriname ... een paradijs [Surinam ... a paradise]. *W I G* 27:147-
                      156.   [*COL*]

PARKER, H. W.

41.181   TR   1935 The lizards of Trinidad. *Trop Agric* 12(3), Mar.: 65-70.   [*AGS*]

PARLOUR, ROGER R.

41.182   TR   1953 Monkeybones and Cascadoux. *Can-W I Mag* 43(12), Dec.: 13,15.
                                                                                     [*NYP*]

PENARD, THOMAS E.

41.183   SR   1924/ Historical sketch of the ornithology of Surinam. *W I G* 6:146-168.
                 25

PENARD, THOMAS E. & ARTHUR P.

41.184   SR   1925/ Birdcatching in Surinam. *W I G* 7:545-566.   [*COL*]
                 26

PERCIVAL, EXLEY

41.185   BG   1923 Wild flowers of Georgetown: a study in field botany for tyros. *J Bd
                        Agric Br Gui* 16(4), Oct.: 205-222;
                        1924 17(1), Jan.: 39-54.   [*AMN*]

PERTCHIK, BERNARD & HARRIET

41.186   GC   1951 FLOWERING TREES OF THE CARIBBEAN. New York, Rinehart, 125p.
                        [64]   [*RIS*]

POTTER, THOMAS I.

63.040   TR   1930 Some Trinidadian "honey plants."
41.187   TR   1931 Notes on bats in connection with agriculture. *Proc Agric Soc Trin
                        Tob* 31(11), Nov.: 429-437. [46]   [*AMN*]

PRICE, J. L.

41.188   TR   1955 A survey of the freshwater fishes of the island of Trinidad. *J Agric
                        Soc Trin Tob* 55(3), Sept.: 390-416. [56]   [*AMN*]

QUELCH, J. J.

41.189   BG   1925 Native birds of Georgetown. *J Bd Agric Br Gui* 18(1), Jan.: 30-50;
                        18(2), Apr.: 93-106.   [*AMN*]

QUESTEL, ADRIEN

41.190   SB   1941 THE FLORA OF ST. BARTHOLOMEW (FRENCH WEST INDIES) AND ITS
                        ORIGIN. Basse-Terre, Impr. Catholique, 224p.   [*AGS*]
41.191   GD   1946 Les palmiers de la 'Guadeloupe et dépendances [The palm trees
                        of Guadeloupe and her dependencies]. *Car For* 7(4), Oct.: 297-314.
                        [64]   [*AGS*]

RANKIN, JESSIE

66.115   BG   1954 A plea for national parks.

REGAN, C. TATE

41.192   GC   1916 Report on poisonous fishes of the West Indies. *Proc Agric Soc
                        Trin Tob* 16(6), June: 214-217. [56]   [*AMN*]

REICHLEN, HENRI & BARRET, PAULE

4.110   MT   1940 Contribution à l'archéologie de la Martinique: le gisement de l'anse
                        Belleville [Contribution to the archaeology of Martinique: the site
                        of Belleville Cove].

REID, LESLIE

41.193   TB   1961 Little Tobago. *Cont Rev* 200, Nov.: 598-601.   [*COL*]

REIJENGA, T. W.; VAS, I. E. & WIERSEMA, J. P.

28.433   SR   1962 On injuries caused by predatory salmon (*Serrasalmo rhombeus* L.)
                        in the rivers of Surinam.

RENAUD, MAURICE

41.194   FG   1932 Contribution à l'étude des bois de la Guyane Francaise [Contribu-
                        tion to the study of the timbers of French Guiana]. *B Ag Gen Colon*
                        25(279), June: 970-1031; 25(280), July: 1120-1177; 25(281), Aug.:
                        1265-1308; 25(282), Sept.: 1372-1434. [46]   [*AGS*]

ROBINSON, J. H.

41.195 BB 1934 The study of the organic remains in the oceanic beds of Barbados, with special reference to the diatoms. *J Barb Mus Hist Soc* 1(2), Feb.: 80-84. [40]   *[AMN]*

41.196 BB 1935 Some recent marine diatoms from the north-east coast of Barbados. *J Barb Mus Hist Soc* 2(3), May: 111-114. [56]   *[AMN]*

41.197 BB 1936 The occurrence and distribution of the diatoms in the oceanic beds of Barbados. *J Barb Mus Hist Soc* 3(3), May: 149-152; 4(1), Nov.: 9-11;
       1937 4(4), Aug.: 180-183;
       1938 5(3), May: 144-150;
       1941 8(2), Feb.: 84-86; 8(4), Aug.: 181-185.   *[AMN]*

RODWAY, JAMES & AIKEN, JAMES

41.198 BG 1913 Some of our food fishes. *Timehri* 3d ser., 3(20A). Dec.: 43-50. [30]
                           [AMN]

ROTH, HENRY D.

41.199 BG 1944 Some notes on our snakes. *Timehri* 4th ser., 1(26), Nov.: 78-91.
                           [AMN]

ROTH, VINCENT

41.200 BG 1943 NOTES AND OBSERVATIONS ON FISH LIFE IN BRITISH GUIANA 1907-1943. Georgetown, Daily Chronicle, 282p. [56]   *[AMN]*

41.201 BG 1946 Wild life resources of British Guiana. *In* ROTH, VINCENT, comp. HANDBOOK OF NATURAL RESOURCES OF BRITISH GUIANA. Georgetown, Daily Chronicle, p.223-231. (Interior Development Committee of British Guiana. [Publications].)   *[AGS]*

41.202 BG 1953 NOTES AND OBSERVATIONS ON ANIMAL LIFE IN BRITISH GUIANA. Georgetown, Daily Chronicle, 164p.

ROTH, VINCENT, comp.

41.203 BG 1946/ HANDBOOK OF NATURAL RESOURCES OF BRITISH GUIANA. Georgetown,
       47 Daily Chronicle, 2v. (243, 11p.) (Interior Development Committee of British Guiana. [Publications].)   *[RIS]*

RUTTEN, L. M. R.

41.204 NC 1931 Our palaeontological knowledge of the Netherlands West-Indies in 1930. *In* LEIDSCHE GEOLOGISCHE MEDEDEELINGEN, Vol. 5: FEESTBUNDEL UITGEGEVEN TER EERE VAN PROF. DR. K. MARTIN. Leiden, Boek- en Steendrukkerij Eduard Ijdo, p.651-672. (Uitgave van geologie en mineralogie te Leiden.) [40]   *[COL]*

SANDERSON, IVAN T.

41.205 TR/ 1939 CARIBBEAN TREASURE. New York, Viking Press, 292p.   *[NYP]*
    SR

41.206 BH/ 1941 LIVING TREASURE. New York, Viking Press, 290p.   *[AGS]*
    JM

SANDS, W. N.

41.207 SV 1914 The "tri-tri" or West Indian whitebait in St. Vincent. *W I B* 14(2): 120-122. [56]   *[AMN]*

SCHMITT, WALDO L.
41.208   GC   1938 The Smithsonian-Hartford Expedition to the West Indies, 1937. *In*
EXPLORATIONS AND FIELD WORK OF THE SMITHSONIAN INSTITUTION IN
1937. Washington, D. C., Smithsonian Institution, p.57-64.   [*AMN*]
41.209   GC   1957 A narrative of the Smithsonian-Bredin Caribbean Expedition, 1956.
In ANNUAL REPORT OF THE SMITHSONIAN INSTITUTION FOR 1956.
Washington, U. S. Govt. Print. Off., p.443-460. [56]   [*AGS*]

SENIOR-WHITE, R. A.
41.210   GC   1950 The distribution of the Culicid tribe *Anophelinae* around the Caribbean Sea. *Car Med J* 12(3-4): 67-71.   [*COL*]
41.211   TR   1951 Key to the anopheline larvae of Trinidad and Tobago. *Car Med J*
13(3-4): 151-152.   [*COL*]

SESSLER, WA. M. & SPOON, W.
41.212   NL   1952 Over het gebruik van wilde salie op de Benedenwindse Eilanden
[On the use of wild sage in the Leeward Islands]. *W I G* 33:49-52.
[30]   [*COL*]

SIMPSON, GEORGE GAYLORD
41.213   JM   1956 ZOOGRAPHY OF WEST INDIAN LAND MAMMALS. New York, American
Museum of Natural History, 28p. (American Museum Novitates, no.
1759, Mar. 8.)   [*RIS*]

SKEETE, C. C.
41.214   BB   1953 GARDEN BOOK OF BARBADOS. [Bridgetown?] Barbados [Printed for the]
Department of Science and Agriculture [by] Advocate Co., 160p.

SMELLIE, G. H.
41.215   BG   1944 Some notes on the birds of British Guiana. *Timehri* 4th ser., 1(26),
Nov.: 107-116.   [*AMN*]

SMITH, J. H. NELSON
41.216   BH   1945 Forest associations of British Honduras, parts II-III. *Car For* 6(2),
Jan.: 45-70; 6(3), Apr.: 131-158. [64]   [*AGS*]

SPOON, W.
41.217   NW   1944/ Ricinus van de Bovenwindsche eilanden [Ricinus of the Windward
45 Islands]. *W I G* 26:225-228. [63]   [*COL*]

STAHEL, GEROLD
41.218   SR   1942 DE NUTTIGE PLANTEN VAN SURINAME [THE USEFUL PLANTS OF SURINAM].
Paramaribo, 197p. (Surinam. Departement Landbouwproefstation.
Bulletin no. 57.)   [*AGS*]

STAHEL, GEROLD, et al.
3.290   SR   1926 De expeditie naar het Wilhelmina-Gebergte (Suriname) in 1926 [The
expedition to the Wilhelmina mountains in 1926].

STANDLEY, PAUL C.
41.219   BH   1932 New plants from British Honduras. Chicago, 129-142p. (Field Museum of Natural History, Publication 316, Botanical series, v. 11,
no. 4.)   [*NYP*]

STANDLEY, PAUL C. & RECORD, SAMUEL J.

41.220 BH 1936 THE FORESTS AND FLORA OF BRITISH HONDURAS. Chicago, 432p. (Field museum of Natural History, Publication 350, Botanical series, v. 12.) [64]   [AGS]

STEHLE, HENRI

41.221 GD 1936 Flore de la Guadeloupe et dépendances [Flora of Guadeloupe and subordinate islands]. Vol. I: Essai d'écologie et de géographie botanique. Basse-Terre, Impr. Catholique, 167p.   [NYP]

41.222 GD 1940 Guadeloupe—emerald of the Antilles. J N Y Bot Gdn 41(482), Feb.: 36-44.   [AGS]

41.223 FA 1941 Conditions éco-sociologiques et évolution des forêts des Antilles Francaises [Socio-ecological conditions and development of forests in the French Antilles]. Car For 2(4), July: 154-159. [64] [AGS]

41.224 MT 1941 The flora of Martinique. J N Y Bot Gdn 42(502), Oct.: 235-244. [AGS]

41.225 FA 1942 Catalogue des cryptogames vasculaires des Antilles Francaises [List of vascular cryptogams in the French Antilles]. Car For 4(1), Oct.: 35-46; 83-88.

1943 4(2), Jan.: 83-88.   [AGS]

41.226 FA 1943 Classification des arbres à latex et à secretions de gommes, resines et matières colorantes aux Antilles Francaises [Classification of latex- and gum-yielding trees, resins and dyes in the French Antilles]. Car For 4(3), Apr.: 112-123. [64]   [AGS]

41.227 FA 1943 La vegetation muscinale des Antilles Francaises et son intérêt dans la valorisation sylvicole [Mosses in the French Antilles, and their importance to sylviculture]. Car For 4(4), July: 164-182. [64] [AGS]

41.228 FA 1944 Les glumiflorées des Antilles Francaises: espèces nouvelles pour la Guadeloupe et pour la Martinique [Glumiflorae in the French Antilles: species new to Guadeloupe and Martinique]. Car For 5(4), July: 181-206.   [AGS]

41.229 GC 1945 Forest types of the Caribbean Islands. Car For 6, Oct., suppl.: 273-414. [64]   [AGS]

41.230 GC 1947 Notes taxonomiques, xylologiques et géographiques sur les châtaigniers du genre Sloanea des Petites Antilles [Taxonomic, xylologic, and geographic notes on Sloanea genus chestnut trees in the Lesser Antilles]. Car For 8(4), Oct.: 301-322. [64] [AGS]

STEHLE, HENRI & MME.

41.231 GC 1947 Liste complementaire des arbres et arbustes des Petites Antilles [Complementary list of trees and shrubs in the Lesser Antilles]. Car For 8(2), Apr.: 91-123. [64]   [AGS]

41.232 GD 1963 Quelques insectes curieux des Antilles Francaises: le scieur de long et les lucioles. [Some interesting insects of the French Antilles—scieur de long and fireflies]. B Pedag 1(6-8), Apr.-June: 41-53.   [RIS]

41.233 GD 1963 Les ravets de la Guadeloupe: ces commensaux indésirables [The turnips of Guadeloupe, those undesirable table companions]. B Pedag 1(6-8), Apr.-June: 37-40. [33]   [RIS]

STEHLE, HENRI & MARIE, E.

41.234 GC 1947 Le magnolia, Talauma dodecapetala, des Petites Antilles: mono-graphie sylvo-botanique [The magnolia Talauma dedecapetala, of the Lesser Antilles: sylvo-botanical monograph]. *Car For* 8(3), July: 183-202. [64]   [*AGS*]

STELL, F.
41.235   BG   1921 Colony birds in relation to agriculture. *J Bd Agric Br Gui* 14(1), Jan.: 52-53; 14(2), Apr.: 139-140. [46]   [*AMN*]

STEVENSON, N. S.
64.100   BH   1938 The evolution of vegetation survey and rural planning in British Honduras.
41.236   BH   1942 Forest associations of British Honduras. *Car For* 3(4), July: 164-172. [64]   [*AGS*]

STOCKDALE, Sir FRANK A.
41.237   BG   1911 The indigenous "rubber" trees of British Guiana. *Timehri* 3d ser., 1(18A), Jan.: 21-25. [64]   [*AMN*]

STOCKUM, A. J. van
40.177   SR   1904 Verslag van de Saramacca-Expeditie [Account of the Saramacca Expedition].

STOFFERS, A. L., ed.
41.238   NA   1962 FLORA OF THE NETHERLANDS ANTILLES. Vol. I: PTERIDOPHYTA. Utrecht, Natuurwetenschappelijke Studiekring voor Suriname en de Nederlandse Antillen, 84p. ([Publication] no. 25.)   [*NYP*]

STORER, DOROTHY P.
41.239   JM   1958 FAMILIAR TREES AND CULTIVATED PLANTS OF JAMAICA. London, Macmillan, 81p. [64]

SWABEY, CHRISTOPHER
64.107   JM   1945 FORESTRY IN JAMAICA.

TATE, G. H. H.
41.240   BG   1930 Notes on the Mount Roraima region. *Geogr Rev* 20(1), Jan.: 53-68.   [*AGS*]

TAYLOR, Lady R. G.
41.241   JM   1955 INTRODUCTION TO THE BIRDS OF JAMAICA. London, Macmillan and Co., 114p.

THOMPSON, G. A.
41.242   JM   1947 A list of the mosquitoes of Jamaica, British West Indies. *Mosq News* 72(2), June: 78-80.   [*COL*]

TIROLIEN, CAMILLE
55.038   GD   1961 Thermalisme [Mineral Springs].

TUCKER, R. W. E.
41.243   BB   1953 Insects of Barbados. *J Barb Mus Hist Soc* 20(4), Aug.: 155-181.   [*AMN*]

TUCKER, R.W.E., et al.
46.222   BB   1931 CONTROL OF FIELD CROP, GARDEN AND FRUIT PESTS IN BARBADOS.

UNDERWOOD, GARTH
41.244   GC   1953 West Indian reptiles. *Car Q* 3(3), Dec.: 174-180.   [*RIS*]
41.245   GC   [1962?] REPTILES OF THE EASTERN CARIBBEAN. [Mona,] Dept. of Extra-mural
                Studies, University of the West Indies, 192p. (Caribbean affairs, new
                ser., no. 1.)   [*RIS*]

URICH, F. W.
41.246   TR   1913 Mosquitoes of Trinidad. *Proc Agric Soc Trin Tob* 13(10), Oct.: 525-
                530.   [*AMN*]

VESEY-FitzGERALD, DESMOND
41.247   BG   1934 The Great Savannah district of British Guiana, with brief notes on
                the other vertebrate fauna. *Trop Agric* 11(5), May: 111-116.   [*AGS*]
41.248   TR   1936 Further notes on the food and habits of Trinidad birds with special
                reference to common cane field birds. *Trop Agric* 13(1), Jan.: 12-18.
                                                                          [*AGS*]
41.249   TR   1936 Trinidad mammals. *Trop Agric* 13(6), June: 161-165.   [*AGS*]

VINCENT, HARRY
56.053   TR   1910 THE SEA FISH OF TRINIDAD.

VOOUS, K. H.
41.250   NL   1952 Vogeltrek op de Nederlandse Benedenwindse Eilanden [Bird migra-
                tion on the Dutch Leeward Islands]. *W I G* 33:183-190.   [*COL*]
41.251   NA   1953 Enkele bekende vogels van de Nederlandse Antillen [Some well-
                known birds of the Dutch Antilles]. *W I G* 34:252-255.   [*COL*]

WABY, J. F.
41.252   GC   1921 Plants worth knowing. *J Bd Agric Br Gui* 14(4), Oct.: 247-251;
                1922 15(1), Jan.: 18-25; 15(2), Apr.: 73-77; 15(3), July: 144-147. [*AMN*]

WADSWORTH, FRANK H., et al.
41.253   GC   1960 Records of forest plantation growth in Mexico, the West Indies and
                Central and South America. *Car For* 21, Dec.: suppl. (various
                pagings.) [64]   [*AGS*]

WAGENAAR HUMMELINCK, P.
41.254   SR   1942 Studies over de patatta-luis [Studies of the patatta louse]. *W I G*
                24:309-313. [28]   [*COL*]
41.255   NL   1943 Zoögeografische opmerkingen over de Nederlandsche Benedenwind-
                sche Eilanden [Zoological-geographic remarks about the Dutch Lee-
                ward Islands]. *W I G* 25:168-180.   [*COL*]
41.256   CU   1944/ Over de namen der dieren in het boek van Hans Hass: Unter Korallen
                45   und Haien [On the names of the animals in the book of Hans Hass:
                among coral reefs and sharks]. *W I G* 26:181-192.   [*COL*]
1.043   CU   1946 Literatuur betreffende het natuurwetenschappelijk onderzoek in
                Curacao gedurende de oorlogsjaren [Literature about natural science
                research in Curacao during the war].

1.044   SR   1946 Literatuur betreffende het natuurwetenschappelijk onderzoek in
                  Suriname gedurende de oorlogsjaren [Literature about natural sci-
                  ence research in Surinam during the war].

41.257   NA   1951 Natuurwetenschappelijke belangstelling voor de Nederlandse An-
                  tillen [Scientific interest in the Netherlands Antilles]. *W I G* 32:1-
                  31.   [67]   [*RIS*]

WATERMAN, JAMES A.
41.258   BC   1950 Scorpions in the West Indies with special reference to *Tityus
                  trinitatis*. *Car Med J* 12(5): 167-177.   [*COL*]

WATKINS, JOHN V.
41.259   GC   1952 GARDENS OF THE ANTILLES. Gainsville, University of Florida Press,
                  244p.   [*COL*]

WATTS, DAVID
41.260   BB   1963 PLANT INTRODUCTION AND LANDSCAPE CHANGE IN BARBADOS 1625-1830.
                  Ph.D. dissertation, McGill University, 387p.   [5]

WEBB, C. S.
41.261   BG   1948 An account of the mammals of British Guiana. *Timehri* 4th ser.,
                  1(28), Dec.: 35-46.

WENT, F. A. F. C.
41.262   SR   1932/ De flora van Suriname. *W I G* 14:131-134.   [*COL*]
               33

WESTERMANN, J. H.
46.235   NA   1947 Natuurbescherming op de Nederlandsche Antillen, haar etische,
                  aesthetische, wetenschappelijke en economische perspectieven
                  [The protection of nature by the Dutch Antilles, its ethical, esthet-
                  ical, scientific and economic perspectives].
41.263   GC   1953 NATURE PRESERVATION IN THE CARIBBEAN. Utrecht, 106p. (Publica-
                  tions of the Foundation for Scientific Research in Surinam and the
                  Netherlands Antilles, no. 9.)   [66]   [*COL*]

WHITTON, B. A.
41.264   BG   1962 Forests and dominant legumes of the Amatuk region, British Guiana.
                  Car For 23(1): 35-57.   [64]   [*AGS*]

WICKSTEAD, J. H.
41.265   BB   1956 A note on some pelagic copepods from the West Indies. *J Barb Mus
                  Hist Soc* 24(1), Nov.: 3-28.   [*AMN*]

WILLIAMS, R. O. & R. O., Jr.
41.266   TR   1941 THE USEFUL AND ORNAMENTAL PLANTS IN TRINIDAD AND TOBAGO, Rev.
                  3d ed. Port of Spain, A. L. Rhodes, Govt. Printer, 265p.   [46]

WISE, K. S.
41.267   BG   1914 A list of the commoner invertebrate animals of medical interest
                  identified in British Guiana. *Br Gui Med Annual 1913* 20:106-108.
                  [28]   [*ACM*]

WISE, K. S. & MINETT, E. P.

28.600   BG   1912 Drinking water supplies: a chemical and bacteriological study of the drinking water supplies on estates from a hygienic point of view.

WOLSTENHOLME, G. L.

41.268   BG   1953 Jenman and the Georgetown Botanic Gardens. *Timehri* 4th ser., 1(32), Nov.: 17-27. [5]

WOOD, B. R.

13.093   BG   1944 Curare.

ZANEVELD, JACQUES S.

41.269   NA   1956/ Enige algemeen voorkomende zeevissen in de Nederlandse Antillen
               57 [Some common sea fish in the Dutch Antilles]. *W I G* 37: 5-17. [56]   [COL]

41.270   CU   1960 Probing Caribbean waters. *Caribbean* 14(4), Apr.: 65-68. [56] [COL]

Chapter 42

CLIMATE AND WEATHER

BAKER, CECIL SHERMAN

16.002   GC   1930 Climatic influences in the Caribbean.

BAKHUIS, L. A.

40.005   SR   1908 De 5de wetenschappelijke expeditie naar het binnenland van Suriname [The 5th scientific expedition into the interior of Surinam].

BLUME, HELMUT

42.001   GC   1962 Beiträge zur Klimatologie Westindiens [Contributions to West Indian climatology]. *Erdkunde* 16(4): 271-289.   [*RIS*]

BRAAK, CORNELIS

42.002   NA   [1935?] HET KLIMAAT VAN NEDERLANDSCH WEST-INDIE [THE CLIMATE OF THE NETHERLANDS WEST INDIES]. The Hague, Rijksuitgeverij, 120p. (Koninklijk Nederlandsch Meteorologisch Instituut, Mededeelingen en verhandelingen, no. 36.)   [AGS]

BRENNAN, T. F.

42.003   JM   1937 Climate in Jamaica. *Can-W I Mag* 26(3), Mar.: 7-8.   [*NYP*]
42.004   JM   1938 The climatic "Why" of Jamaica. *Can-W I Mag* 27(11), Nov.: 10-12.
                                                                        [*NYP*]

BURRA, J. A. N.

42.005   JM   1961 The forest and climate. *Inf B Scient Res Coun* 2(3), Dec.: 51-53.
                    [64]   [*COL*]
42.006   JM   1962 The forest and watershed control. *Inf B Scient Res Coun* 2(4), Mar.: 73-75.   [57, 64, 66]   [*RIS*]

CHANNON, J. A.

42.007   GC   1962 The forecasting of hurricanes. *Inf B Scient Res Coun* 3(1), June 1-5.
                                                                        [*RIS*]

COLLIER, H. C.

42.008   BG   1942 Climate and health in British Guiana. *Can-W I Mag* 31(2), Feb.: 7-10.
                    [28]   [*NYP*]
42.009   JM   1950 Jamaica year-round climate. *Can-W I Mag* 40(1), Jan.: 7-10.   [*NYP*]

DONN, WILLIAM L. & McGUINNESS, WILLIAM T.

42.010   BB   1959 Severe sea surges at Barbados (Barbados storm swell) *J Geogr Res*
                        64(12), Dec.: 2341-2349.   [*COL*]

EILERTS de HAAN, J. G., et al.

40.059   SR   1910 Verslag van de expeditie naar de Suriname-Rivier [Account of the
                        expedition to the Surinam River].

FERGUSON, J. E. A.

28.151   BG   1906 The climate of the Peter's Hall District and its effects on the
                        inhabitants.

FRANSSEN HERDERSCHEE, A.

40.065   SR   1905 Verslag van de Gonini-Expeditie [Account of the Gonini Expedition].

GIGLIOLI, GEORGE

28.220   BG   1951 The influence of geological formation and soil characteristics on
                        the distribution of malaria and its mosquito carrier in British Guiana.

GOEJE, C. H. de

40.070   SR   1908 Verslag der Toemak Hoemak expeditie [Account of the Tumuc Humac
                        expedition].

GUERNSEY, JACKSON EDWIN

42.011   JM   1941 CLIMATE OF JAMAICA. Ph. D. dissertation, Clark University, 270p.
                                                                                     [*COL*]

HALL, MAXWELL

42.012   JM   1904 THE METEOROLOGY OF JAMAICA. Kingston, Institute of Jamaica.
                                                                                     [*AMN*]

42.013   JM   1923 THE RAINFALL OF JAMAICA FROM ABOUT 1870 TO END OF 1919. Jamaica,
                        Govt. Print. Off., 21p.   [*COL*]

HARRISON, Sir JOHN B.

42.014   BG   1926 The climate of British Guiana. *J Bd Agric Br Gui* 19(2), Apr.:
                        116-126. [5]   [*AMN*]

HUTCHINSON, MARY CURTIS

42.015   JM   1937 THE CLIMATIC REGIONS OF JAMAICA. M. A. thesis, Clark University,
                        95p.   [*AGS*]

JACOBS, H. P.

42.016   JM   1951 Jamaica after the hurricane. *W I Comm Circ* 66(1247), Nov.: 257-
                        258. [66]   [*NYP*]

42.017   JM   1951 The Jamaica hurricane. *W I Comm Circ* 66(1245), Sept.: 209-210.
                                                                                     [*NYP*]

JAMES, PRESTON E.

42.018   TR   1925 The climate of Trinidad, B.W.I. *Mon Weath Rev* 53(2), Feb.: 71-75.
                                                                                     [*AGS*]

KELLY, F. JAMES

42.019   BG   1933 Climate and health in British Guiana. *Can-W I Mag* 22(10), Sept.:
                        299-300. [28]   [*NYP*]

KENNARD, C. P.

28.302   BG   1902   Fever cases.

KIRBY, A. H.

42.020   NV/   1910   The rainfall of Nevis and Antigua. *W I B* 10(3): 273-284.   [*AMN*]
        AT

LANGEMEYER, F. S.

3.170   NW   1934/ Het klimaat en de natuurverschijnselen op onze Bovenwindsche
             35   Eilanden [The climate and the natural phenomena on our Windward
                  Islands].

McDONALD, J. A.

42.021   TR   1959   The 1959 drought compared with previous drought years in Trinidad
                  and Tobago. *J Agric Soc Trin Tob* 59(2), June: 243-249.   [*AMN*]

MEADE, J. H. ARNOLD

42.022   MS   1928   ON GOING SOUTH: IMPRESSIONS OF THE HURRICANE IN MONTSERRAT
                  SEPTEMBER 1928. [n.p.,] 6p.

MORAIS, ALLAN I.

2.161   GR   1955   This is Grenada.

NANCOO, M. E.

42.023   JM   1961   Jamaica helps to produce its rainfall. *Inf B Scient Res Coun* 2(2),
                  Sept.: 38-39.   [*AMN*]

OGUNTOYINBO, JULIUS SUNDAY

42.024   BB   1964   RAINFALL, EVAPORATION AND SUGARCANE YIELDS IN BARBADOS. M.Sc.
                  thesis, McGill University, 72p.   [58]

PAGNEY, PIERRE

42.025   GC   1957   Un cyclone dans la mer Caraïbe: le cyclone Janet (septembre 1955)
                  [A hurricane in the Caribbean: hurricane Janet (September 1955)].
                  Cah O-M 10(37), Jan.-Mar.: 65-91.   [*RIS*]

PETERS, FRED E.

42.026   MS   1928   MONTSERRAT: HER DISASTERS; A SOUVENIR OF THE GREAT HURRICANE OF
                  SEPTEMBER 12th-13th, 1928. New York, Steber Press, 51p.

ROUSE, WAYNE ROBERT

42.027   BB   1962   THE MOISTURE BALANCE OF BARBADOS AND ITS INFLUENCE UPON SUGAR
                  CANE YIELD. M.Sc. thesis, McGill University, 60p.   [58]

SANSON, J.

42.028   FC   1931   Introduction à la climatologie agricole coloniale. III: Climatologie
                  des colonies américaines [Introduction to colonial agricultural
                  climatology. III. Climatology of the American colonies]. *Agric Prat
                  Pays Chauds* new ser., 2(7), Jan.: 24-32.   [*AGS*]

SCHULZ, J. P.

40.159   SR   1960   ECOLOGICAL STUDIES ON RAIN FOREST IN NORTHERN SURINAM.

SKEETE, C. C.

42.029   GC   1931 West Indian hurricanes. *Trop Agric* 8(7), July: 178-185; 8(8), Aug.:
                   206-210.   [*AGS*]

42.030   BB   1934 Weather observations and records in Barbados. *J Barb Mus Hist Soc*
                   1(3), May: 115-136.   [*AMN*]

42.031   BB   1944 NOTES ON WEST INDIAN HURRICANES WITH SPECIAL REFERENCE TO
                   BARBADOS. [Bridgetown?] Barbados, Advocate Co., 17p. (Department
                   of Science and Agriculture, Bulletin no. 3, new series.) [66] [*NYP*]

42.032   BB   1963 A DESCRIPTION OF THE WEATHER OF THE ISLAND OF BARBADOS, W.I.
                   Woods Hole, Mass., Woods Hole Oceanographic Institution, 284p.
                   (Reference no. UM 63-19.)   [*RIS*]

SMITH, SAMUEL IVAN

42.033   GC   1963 CLIMATIC CONTROL OF DISTRIBUTION AND CULTIVATION OF SUGAR CANE.
                   Ph.D. dissertation, McGill University, 206p.   [58]

STAHEL, GEROLD, et al.

3.290   SR   1926 De expeditie naar het Wilhelmina-Gebergte (Suriname) in 1926 [The
                   expedition to the Wilhelmina Mountains (Surinam) in 1926].

STOCKUM, A. J. van

40.177   SR   1904 Verslag van de Saramacca-Expeditie [Account of the Saramacca
                   Expedition].

STODDART, D. R.

42.034   BH   1962 Catastrophic storm effects on the British Honduras reefs and cays.
                   Nature 196(4854), Nov. 10: 512-515.

TANNEHILL, IVAN RAY

42.035   GC   1938 HURRICANES: THEIR NATURE AND HISTORY, PARTICULARLY THOSE OF THE
                   WEST INDIES AND THE SOUTHERN COASTS OF THE UNITED STATES.
                   Princeton, Princeton University Press, 257p.   [*AGS*]

VINK, G. J.

17.029   SR   1941 Over de mogelijkheid van kolonisatie van blanken in Suriname [On
                   the possibility of colonization of whites in Surinam].

WARD, ROBERT DeC. & BROOKS, CHARLES F.

42.036   GC   1934 Westindien: Climatology of the West Indies. *In* KOPPEN, W. &
                   GEIGER, R., eds. HANDBUCH DER KLIMATOLOGIE. Berlin, Borntraeger,
                   v. 2, pt. 1 (47p.)   [*AGS*]

WISHART, W. de W.

7.086   BG   1902 The influence of rainfail on death-rate in the tropics.
7.087   BG   1943 The Georgetown vital index as related to rainfall.

ZUYLEN, G. F. A. van

42.037   NA   1962 De neerslag op de Nederlandse Antillen [Rainfall of the Dutch
                   Antilles]. *Geogr Tijdschr* 15(5), Oct.: 203-208.

Chapter 43

HUMAN GEOGRAPHY

AHSAN, SYED REZA

12.002   TR   1963 East Indian agricultural settlements in Trinidad; a study in cultural geography.

AUBERT de la RUE, EDGAR

43.001   GC   1935 L'homme et les îles [The people and their islands]. Paris, Gallimard, 194p. (Collection Geographie humaine.)   *[AGS]*

AUGELLI, JOHN P.

43.002   VI   1955 The British Virgin Islands: a West Indian anomaly. *Geogr Rev* 66(1): 43-58. [37, 44, 46]   *[RIS]*

43.003   GD   1962 Land use in Guadeloupe. *Geogr Rev* 52(3): 436-438. [46, 47] *[RIS]*

43.004   GC   1962 The rimland-mainland concept of culture areas in Middle America. *Ann Ass Am Geogr* 52(2), June: 119-129. [67]   *[AGS]*

BAGUET, HENRI

43.005   FA   1905 Du régime des terres et la condition des personnes aux Antilles françaises avant 1789 [Land administration and the condition of people in the French Antilles prior to 1789]. Paris, Panvert, 229p. (Ph.D. dissertation, University of Paris.) [5]   *[COL]*

BAKER, CECIL SHERMAN & THOMPSON, WALLACE

43.006   GC   1930 Climatic influences in the Caribbean. *Curr Hist* 31(5), Feb.: 908-918.   *[COL]*

BALLOU, H. A.

43.007   NL   1934 The Dutch Leeward Islands. *Trop Agric* 11(12), Dec.: 317-320.   *[AGS]*

BARRE, PAUL

43.008   FG/   1907 La Guyane Francaise [French Guiana]. *Rev Fr Etr Colon* 32(344),
        BG   Aug.: 449-458.   *[NYP]*

BEEBE, WILLIAM

43.009   TR   1952 Introduction to the ecology of the Arima Valley, Trinidad, B.W.I. *Zoologica* 37(4), Dec.: 157-183. [57]   *[RIS]*

BELLET, DANIEL

43.010   JM   [n.d.] LES GRANDES ANTILLES: ÉTUDE DE GÉOGRAPHIE ECONOMIQUE [THE
                GREATER ANTILLES: STUDY OF ECONOMIC GEOGRAPHY]. Paris, Librairie
                orientale et américaine, 315p.   [COL]

BERGER, ROLF

43.011   UV   1934 DIE INSELN ST. THOMAS UND ST. CROIX: EINE VERGLEICHENDE WIRT-
                SCHAFTSGEOGRAPHISCHE UNTERSUCHING AUF LANDSCHAFTSKÜNDLICHER
                GRUNDLAGE [THE ISLANDS OF ST. THOMAS AND ST. CROIX: A COMPARA-
                TIVE ECONOMIC GEOGRAPHICAL STUDY BASED ON REGIONAL GEOGRAPHY].
                Wandsbeck, Hamburg, J. G. Bitter, 130p.   [AGS]

BERGMANN, JOHN F. & NELSON, J. GORDON

43.012   JM   1964 Jamaica: prospects for a new nation. J Geogr 63(3), Mar.: 116-123.
                                                                              [COL]

BERINGUIER, CHRISTIAN

43.013   MT   1964 L'ESPACE RÉGIONAL MARTINIQUAIS [THE REGIONAL SPACE OF
                MARTINIQUE]. [Fort-de-France, Martinique,] CERAG, 2v. (192p.)
                (Les Cahiers du Centre d'études régionales Antilles-Guyane, no. 3.)
                                                                              [RIS]

BERNISSANT, P.

43.014   FA   1916 ETUDE SUR LE RÉGIME AGRICOLE DES ANTILLES FRANCAISES [STUDY OF
                AGRICULTURAL CONDITIONS IN THE FRENCH ANTILLES]. Paris, Girard et
                Brière, 195p. (Ph.D. dissertation, University of Paris.) [5] [COL]

BIJLSMA, R.

43.015   SR   1921/ Surinaamsche plantage-inventarissen van het tijdperk 1713-1742
          22   [Surinam plantation inventories of the years 1713-1742]. W I G
                3:325-336. [5, 8, 45]   [COL]

BILLMYER, JAMES H. S.

43.016   CM   1946 The Cayman Islands. Geogr Rev 36(1), Jan.: 29-43.   [AGS]

BLACKMAN, J. E.

43.017   GC   1919 AN OUTLINE OF THE GEOGRAPHY OF THE WEST INDIES. Oxford, B. H.
                Blackwell, 110p. [32]   [AGS]

BLAUT, JAMES M.

43.018   GC   1959 The ecology of tropical farming systems. In RUBIN, VERA, ed.
                PLANTATION SYSTEMS OF THE NEW WORLD. Washington, D. C., Re-
                search Institute for the Study of Man and Pan American Union,
                p.83-103. (Social science monographs, 7.) [45, 46, 57]   [RIS]

BLAUT, JAMES M. & RUTH P.; HARMAN, NAN & MOERMAN, MICHAEL

43.019   JM   1959 A study of cultural determinants of soil erosion and conservation
                in the Blue Mountains of Jamaica. Social Econ Stud 8(4), Dec.:
                403-420. [57]   [RIS]

BOOY, THEODOOR de

43.020   UV   1917 The Virgin Islands of the United States. Geogr Rev 4(5), Nov.:
                359-373.   [AGS]

43.021 TC 1918 The Turks and Caicos Islands, British West Indies. *Geogr Rev* 6(1), July: 37-51. [*AGS*]

BOYD, MARK F. & ARIS, F.W.
28.053 JM 1929 A malarial survey of the island of Jamaica, B.W.I.

BROUSSEAU, GEORGES
43.022 FG 1901 LES RICHESSES DE LA GUYANE FRANCAISE ET DE L'ANCIEN CONTESTÉ FRANCO-BRÉSILIEN [THE NATURAL RESOURCES OF FRENCH GUIANA AND THE BOUNDARY DISPUTE BETWEEN FRANCE AND BRAZIL]. Paris, Société d'éditions scientifiques, 248p. [*AGS*]

BRULEY, EDOUARD
43.023 FA 1935 Apercu géographique [Geographical survey]. *In* DENIS, SERGE, ed. NOS ANTILLES. Orléans, Luzeray, p.41-57. [*AGS*]

BUREAU, GABRIEL
43.024 FG 1936 LA GUYANE MÉCONNUE [MISUNDERSTOOD GUIANA]. Paris, Fasquelle, 170p. [*NYP*]

CHEMIN DUPONTES, P.
43.025 GC [1909?] LES PETITES ANTILLES: ÉTUDE SUR LEUR ÉVOLUTION ÉCONOMIQUE [THE LESSER ANTILLES: STUDY OF THEIR ECONOMIC DEVELOPMENT]. Paris, Librairie orientale & américaine, 362p. [*NYP*]

CORFIELD, GEORGE SIBLEY
43.026 AR 1931 ARUBA: A STUDY OF HUMAN ADJUSTMENT TO A TROPICAL ARID ISLAND ENVIRONMENT. M.A. thesis, Clark University, 201p. [*AGS*]
43.027 NA 1941 Netherlands West Indies: life and work. *J Geogr* 40(8), Nov.: 281-290. [*AGS*]

CRABOT,
43.028 BC 1959 Naissance d'une nation: la Federation des Antilles Britanniques [Birth of a nation: the British West Indies Federation]. *Inf Geogr* 23(2), Mar.-Apr.: 47-57. [38] [*AGS*]

CREDNER, WILHELM
43.029 JM 1940 Probleme der Landnutzung auf den Grossen Antillen [Problems of land use in the Greater Antilles]. *Z Ges Erdk Berl* 7-8, Oct.: 287-302. [*AGS*]

CRIST, RAYMOND E.
43.030 SK/ 1949 Static and emerging cultural landscapes in St. Kitts and Nevis,
NV British West Indies. *Econ Geogr* 25(2): 133-145. [5] [*RIS*]
43.031 AT 1953 Paisajes culturales de Antigua. [Cultural landscapes of Antigua]. *Revta Geogr Am* 35(209), Feb.: 81-87. [*AGS*]
43.032 AT 1954 Changing cultural landscapes in Antigua, B.W.I. *Am J Econ Sociol* 13(3), Apr.: 225-232. [5] [*RIS*]

CUTTERIDGE, J. O.
43.033 GC 1951 GEOGRAPHY OF THE WEST INDIES AND ADJACENT LANDS. Rev. ed. London, Thomas Nelson, 326p. [32]

DAHLBERG, H. N.
43.034 SR 1956 SURINAME IN DE AARDRIJKSKUNDE [GEOGRAPHY OF SURINAM]. Para-maribo, C. Kerstem, 224p. [*AGS*]

DAMBAUGH, LUELLA N.

43.035   JM   1953 Jamaica: an island in transition. *J Geogr* 52(2), Feb.: 45-57.   [44,
              46, 47]   [*RIS*]

DARQUITAIN, VICTOR

43.036   FG   1911 NOTICE SUR LA GUYANE FRANCAISE [REPORT ON FRENCH GUIANA].
              Paris, Augustin Challamel, 62p.

De CAMP, DAVID

25.019 JM   1961 Social and geographical factors in Jamaican dialects.

DELAWARDE, JEAN-BAPTISTE

43.037   MT   1935 Les défricheurs et les petits colons de la Martinique aux XVIIᵉ
              siècle [Settlers and small land holders in Martinique in the 17th
              century]. Paris, R. Buffault, 181p.   [5]   [*NYP*]

43.038   MT   1935 ESSAI SUR L'INSTALLATION HUMAINE DANS LES MORNES DE LA MAR-
              TINIQUE [ESSAY ON THE HUMAN SETTLEMENT ON THE BLUFFS OF MAR-
              TINIQUE]. Fort-de-France, Impr. du Gouvernement, 40p. [35]   [*AGS*]

43.039   MT   1936 LE PRÊCHEUR: HISTOIRE D'UN ÉTABLISSEMENT HUMAIN SUR LES PENTES
              DE LA PELÉE [PRÊCHEUR: HISTORY OF A HUMAN SETTLEMENT ON THE
              SLOPES OF MT. PELÉE]. Paris, R. Buffault, 102p.   [*NYP*]

43.040   MT   1937 LA VIE PAYSANNE À LA MARTINIQUE: ESSAI DE GÉOGRAPHIE HUMAINE
              [PEASANT LIFE IN MARTINIQUE: A STUDY IN HUMAN GEOGRAPHY]. Fort-
              de-France, Impr. officielle, 226p. (Ph.D. dissertation, University
              of Clermont.)

DEVEZ, G.

43.041   FG   1931 La Guyane Francaise [French Guiana]. *In* GUADELOUPE, GUYANE,
              MARTINIQUE, SAINT-PIERRE ET MIQUELON. Paris, Société d'editions
              geographiques, maritimes et coloniales, 70p. (Exposition coloniale
              internationale de Paris.)   [*NYP*]

DEYDIER, JOSEPH

43.042   FG   1905 La Guyane Francaise en 1904: son avenir économique [French
              Guiana in 1904: its economic future]. *B Soc Geogr Comml Paris*
              27:126-143.   [*NYP*]

DILLON, A. BARROW

43.043   BH   1923 GEOGRAPHY OF BRITISH HONDURAS. London, Waterlow, 39p.   [32]
                                                                           [*AGS*]

DORAN, EDWIN BEAL, Jr.

43.044   CM   1953 A PHYSICAL AND CULTURAL GEOGRAPHY OF THE CAYMAN ISLANDS.
              Ph.D. dissertation, University of California, Northern section,
              475p.   [*COL*]

DUCHESNE-FOURNET, JEAN

43.045   GG   1905 LA MAIN-D'OEUVRE DANS LES GUYANES [MANPOWER IN THE GUIANAS].
              Paris, Plon-Mourrit, 199p.   [5]   [*SCH*]

DUNLOP, W. R.

44.053 BG   1925 Economic research in tropical development, with special reference
              to British Guiana and British Malaya.

43.046   JM   1926 Queensland and Jamaica: a comparative study in geographical economics. *Geogr Rev* 16, Oct.: 548-567.   [*AGS*]

EASTON, DAVID K.
43.047   GG   1957 The Guianas. *Focus* 8(3), Nov.: 1-6.   [*AGS*]

EDWARDS, DAVID T.
43.048   JM   1954 The Jamaican economic situation. *In* THE FARMER'S GUIDE, APPENDIX B. Glasgow, University Press, p.746-749.   [*NYP*]

EYRE, ALAN
43.049   GC   1962 A NEW GEOGRAPHY OF THE CARIBBEAN. London, George Philip, 162p. [32]

FARNWORTH, CONSTANCE H.
43.050   BH   1946 Agriculture of British Honduras. *For Agric* 10(4), Apr.: 55-64. [*AGS*]

FENTEM, ARLIN D.
43.051   DM   1960 COMMERCIAL GEOGRAPHY OF DOMINICA. Bloomington, Indiana University, 18p. (Office of Naval Research technical report no. 5.)   [*RIS*]
43.052   AT   1961 COMMERCIAL GEOGRAPHY OF ANTIGUA. Bloomington, Indiana University, 24p. (Office of Naval Research technical report no. 11.)
43.053   SV   1961 COMMERCIAL GEOGRAPHY OF ST. VINCENT. Bloomington, Indiana University, 19p. (Office of Naval Research technical report no. 10.)   [52,66]   [*RIS*]

FISHER, NORMAN
43.054   GC   1953 Caribbean problem: education, food, and human resources. *Car Commn Mon Inf B* 7(2), Sept.: 33-34.   [66]   [*COL*]

FOSTER, ALICE
43.055   BB   1923 Barbados: a geographical study of the densely populated island in tropical America. *J Geogr* 22(6), Sept.: 205-216.   [*AGS*]

FOX, DAVID J.
43.056   BH   1962 Recent work on British Honduras. *Geogr Rev* 52(1), Jan.: 112-117.   [*RIS*]

GEISERT, HAROLD L.
43.057   JM/   1960 THE CARIBBEAN: POPULATION AND RESOURCES. Washington, D.C.,
        TR   George Washington University, Population Research Project, 48p.   [*AGS*]

GERLING, WALTER
43.058   JM   1938 WIRTSCHAFTSENTWICKLUNG UND LANDSCHAFTSWANDEL AUF DEN WEST-INDISCHEN INSELN JAMAIKA, HAITI UND PUERTO RICO [ECONOMIC DEVELOPMENT AND CHANGES IN LANDSCAPE IN THE WEST INDIAN ISLANDS OF JAMAICA, HAITI AND PUERTO RICO]. Freiburg i. Br., Carl Sintermann, 262p.   [46]   [*COL*]

GIGLIOLI, GUIDO RENZO
43.059   BG   1934 CONSIDERAZIONE AGRARIE ED ECONOMICHE SULLA GUIANA BRITTANNICA
                [AGRARIAN AND ECONOMIC CONSIDERATIONS ABOUT BRITISH GUIANA].
                Florence, Istituto agricole coloniale italiano, 43p. (Relazioni e
                monografie agrario-coloniali, no. 32.)   [*AGS*]

GLUSA, RUDOLF
37.140   GC   1962 ZUR POLITISCHEN GEOGRAPHIE WESTINDIENS [ON THE POLITICAL GEO-
                GRAPHY OF THE WEST INDIES].

GOMMERSBACH, WILHELM
43.060   TR   1907 GESCHICHTE, GEOGRAPHIE UND BEDEUTUNG DER INSEL TRINIDAD
                [HISTORY, GEOGRAPHY AND THE SIGNIFICANCE OF THE ISLAND OF TRINIDAD].
                Bonn, Bonner Kunstdruckerei Arthur Brock, 97p. (Ph.D.dissertation,
                Fakultät der Rheinischen Friederich-Wilhelms-Universitäts.) [*AGS*]

GOTTMANN, JEAN
43.061   GD   1945 The Isles of Guadeloupe. *Geogr Rev* 35(2): 182-203.   [*RIS*]

GUIEYSSE, MARCEL
43.062   MT   1924 La Martinique. *In* LES COLONIES FRANCAISES D'AMÉRIQUE. Paris,
                Notre domaine coloniale, p.65-93.   [*NYP*]

HANRATH, JOHANNES, J.
43.063   SR   1956 The economic-geographical structure of Surinam. *Tijdschr Econ
                Social Geogr* 47(6-7), June-July: 165-166. [44, 66]   [*RIS*]

HARRISON, LUCIA CAROLYN
43.064   DM   1935 Dominica: a wet tropical human habitat. *Econ Geogr* 11(1), Jan.:
                62-76.   [*AGS*]

HENSHALL, JANET DAPHNE
43.065   BB   1964 THE SPATIAL STRUCTURE OF BARBADIAN PEASANT AGRICULTURE AND
                SETTLEMENT. M.Sc. thesis, McGill University, 143p.

HEYREL, JEAN
43.066   MT   1957 LA MARTINIQUE ET SON AVENIR [MARTINIQUE AND ITS FUTURE]. Paris,
                Les Editions francaises, 105p.   [*NYP*]

HILLS, THEO L.
43.067   BG   1961 The interior of British Guiana and the myth of El Dorado. *Can Geogr*
                2:30-43. [24]   [*RIS*]

HODGE, W. H.
43.068   DM   1944 A botanist's Dominica diary. I: In and about Roseau. II. Off the
                beaten path. *Scient Mon* 58(3), Mar.: 185-194; 58(4), Apr.: 281-291.
                                                                                   [*AGS*]

HOETINK, HARRY
43.069   GC   1961 Enkele sociaal-geografische kenmerken van het Caribische gebied
                [Some socio-geographic characteristics of the Caribbean area].
                Geogr Tijdschr 14, May-June: 145-156. [57]   [*RIS*]

HOLDRIDGE, DESMOND

43.070   BH   1940 Toledo: a tropical refugee settlement in British Honduras. *Geogr Rev* 30(3), July: 376-393. [*AGS*]

HURAULT, JEAN

13.037   FG   1962/ Les Indiens de Guyane et le milieu géographique [The Indians of
             63   Guiana and the geographical environment].

43.071   FG   1965 LA VIE MATÉRIELLE DES NOIRS RÉFUGIÉS BONI ET DES INDIENS WAYANA DU HAUT-MARONI (GUYANE FRANCAISE): AGRICULTURE, ÉCONOMIE ET HABITAT [THE MATERIAL LIFE OF THE BLACK BONI REFUGEES AND THE WAIYANA INDIANS OF THE UPPER MARONI (FRENCH GUIANA): AGRICULTURE, ECONOMY AND HABITAT]. Paris, Office de la Recherche scientifique et technique Outre-Mer, 142p. [11, 13] [*RIS*]

HURAULT, JEAN & FRIBOURG-BLANC, ANDRE

43.072   FG   1949 MISSION ASTRO-GÉODESIQUE DE L'OYAPOC (GUYANE FRANCAISE) JUILLET À NOVEMBRE 1947 [ASTRO-GEODETIC EXPEDITION TO THE OYAPOC (FRENCH GUIANA) JULY TO NOVEMBER 1947]. Paris, Impr. de l'Institut géographique national, 131p. [13] [*AGS*]

ISNARD, HILDEBERT

43.073   MT   1956 La Réunion et la Martinique [Reunion and Martinique]. *Cah O-M* 9(33), Jan.-Mar.: 58-69. [*RIS*]

JACOB, LEON

43.074   FG   1924 La Guyane. *In* LES COLONIES FRANCAISES D'AMÉRIQUE. Paris, Notre domaine coloniale, p.97-126. [*NYP*]

JAMES, PRESTON E.

43.075   TR   1926 Some geographic relations in Trinidad. *Scott Geogr Mag* 42(2), Mar. 15:84-96. [*AGS*]

43.076   TR   1927 A geographic reconnaissance of Trinidad. *Econ Geogr* 3(1), Jan.: 87-109. [*AGS*]

43.077   TR   1927 Notes on the geography of Trinidad. *J Geogr* 26(4), Apr.: 130-142. [*AGS*]

43.078   TR   1957 Changes in the geography of Trinidad. *Scott Geogr Mag* 73(3), Dec.: 158-166. [*AGS*]

43.079   GC   1960 Man-land relations in the Caribbean area. *In* RUBIN, VERA, ed. CARIBBEAN STUDIES: A SYMPOSIUM. Seattle, University of Washington Press, p.14-21. [57, 66] [*RIS*]

KEUR, JOHN Y.

43.080   NW   1962 Land utilization in the Netherlands Windward Islands (St. Maarten, St. Eustatius and Saba). *In* AKTEN DES 34. INTERNATIONALEN AMERIKANISTENKONGRESSES, Wien, 1960. Vienna, Ferdinand Berger, p.835-839. [*AGS*]

KEUR, JOHN Y. & DOROTHY L.

43.081   NW   1960 WINDWARD CHILDREN: A STUDY IN HUMAN ECOLOGY OF THE THREE DUTCH WINDWARD ISLANDS IN THE CARIBBEAN. Assen, Netherlands, Van Gorcum, 299p. [*RIS*]

KINGSBURY, ROBERT C.

43.082   CR   1960   Carriacou: an old world in the new. *J Geogr* 59(9), Dec.: 399-409.
                      [5]   [*RIS*]

43.083   GR   1960   COMMERCIAL GEOGRAPHY OF GRENADA. Bloomington, Indiana Univers-
                      ity, 26p. (Office of Naval Research, Technical report no. 3.) [52, 66]
                                                                                  [*RIS*]

43.084   BV   1960   COMMERCIAL GEOGRAPHY OF THE BRITISH VIRGIN ISLANDS. Blooming-
                      ton, Indiana University, 25p. (Office of Naval Research, Technical
                      report no. 2.)   [52, 66]   [*RIS*]

43.085   GN   1960   COMMERCIAL GEOGRAPHY OF THE GRENADINES. Bloomington, Indiana
                      University, 39p. (Office of Naval Research, Technical report no. 1.)
                      [52, 66]   [*RIS*]

43.086   TR   1960   COMMERCIAL GEOGRAPHY OF TRINIDAD AND TOBAGO. Bloomington,
                      Indiana University, 44p. (Office of Naval Research, Technical
                      report no. 4.)   [52, 66]   [*RIS*]

KRUIJER, GERARDUS, JOHANNES

43.087   SR   1949   Enkele sociaal geografische indrukken van een verkenningsvlucht
                      boven Suriname [Some socio-geographic impressions from a recon-
                      naissance flight over Surinam]. *Tijdschr Ned Aar Genoot* 66(5):
                      625-630.   [*RIS*]

43.088   NW   1953   De Bovenwindse Eilanden geografisch [The Windward Islands,
                      geographically speaking]. *In* KRUIJER, G. J.; VEENENBOS, J. S.
                      & WESTERMANN, J. H., comps. BOVENWINDENRAPPORT. Amsterdam,
                      Voorlichtingsinstituut voor het Welvaartsplan Nederlandse Antillen,
                      27p.

43.089   JM   1956   Met bulldozers en sociologie de bergen in [Trip into the mountains
                      with bulldozers and sociology]. *Folia Civ* 10(2), Sept. 15: 1-2.
                      [3, 23]   [*RIS*]

KUCHLER, A. WILHELM

43.090   JM   1936   Jamaica: eine Passatinsel [Jamaica: a trade-wind island]. *In*
                      DRYGALSKI, ERICH von, ed.   AMERIKANISCHE LANDSCHAFT: ENT-
                      STEHUNG UND ENTWICKLUNG IN EINZELBILDERN. Berlin, W. de Gruyter,
                      p.347-459.   [*AGS*]

LAIGRET, CHRISTIAN

43.091   MT   1954   Martinique: its resources and problems. *Car Commn Mon Inf B*
                      7(8), Mar.: 189-182.   [*COL*]

LAMARCHE,

43.092   FG   1921   La Guyane Francaise [French Guiana]. *Colon Mar* 5(38), Oct.:
                      677-686.   [*NYP*]

LASSERRE, GUY

43.093   MG   1950   Marie-Galante. *Cah O-M* 3(10), Apr.-June: 123-152.   [*RIS*]
43.094   GD   1953   Les Indiens de la Guadeloupe [The Indians of Guadeloupe]. *Cah
                      O-M* 6(22), Apr.-May: 128-158.   [12]   [*RIS*]
43.095   DS   1957   La Désirade: une petite île Guadeloupéenne [Désirade: a small
                      Guadeloupean island]. *Cah O-M* 10(40), Oct.-Dec.: 325-366. [*RIS*]
43.096   GD   1961   LA GUADELOUPE: ÉTUDE GÉOGRAPHIQUE. (VOL. 1: LE MILIEU NATUREL;
                      L'HÉRITAGE DU PASSÉ. VOL. 2: LES RÉGIONS GÉOGRAPHIQUES; LES
                      PROBLÈMES GUADELOUPÉENS) [GUADELOUPE: A GEOGRAPHIC STUDY. VOL.

1: THE NATURAL ENVIRONMENT; THE HERITAGE OF THE PAST. VOL. 2: THE GEOGRAPHICAL REGIONS; GUADELOUPEAN PROBLEMS]. Bordeaux, Union francaise d'impression, 2v.   [2]   [*RIS*]

LOWENTHAL, DAVID

43.097   BB   1957 The population of Barbados. *Social Econ Stud* 6(4), Dec.: 445-501.

43.098   JM   1958 Population and production in Jamaica. *Geogr Rev* 48(4): 568-571. [7, 66]   [*RIS*]

43.099   JM   1959 Economy and society in Jamaica. *Geogr Rev* 49(2), Apr.: 259-261. [46, 47, 66]   [*RIS*]

43.100   BC   1960 Physical resources. *In* CUMPER, G.E., ed. THE ECONOMY OF THE WEST INDIES. Kingston, Institute of Social and Economic Research, University College of the West Indies, p.48-94.   [*RIS*]

43.101   GG   1960 Population contrasts in the Guianas. *Geogr Rev* 50(1), Jan.: 41-58. [7, 10, 57]   [*RIS*]

LOWENTHAL, DAVID & COMITAS, LAMBROS

43.102   MS   1962 Emigration and depopulation: some neglected aspects of population geography. *Geogr Rev* 52(2): 195-210.   [17]   [*RIS*]

LUCAS, Sir CHARLES PRESTWOOD

43.103   BC   1905 HISTORICAL GEOGRAPHY OF THE BRITISH COLONIES. VOL. II: THE WEST INDIES. Oxford, Clarendon Press, 343p.   [5]   [*COL*]

MacPHERSON, JOHN

43.104   GC   1963 CARIBBEAN LANDS; A GEOGRAPHY OF THE WEST INDIES. London, Longmans, 180p.

MAI, WOLFGANG

43.105   BC   1962 WESTINDIEN UND ENGLAND: BEZIEHUNGEN UND VERFLECHTUNGEN EINES KOLONIALGEBIETES MIT SEINEM MUTTERLAND [THE WEST INDIES AND ENGLAND: TIES AND INTERRELATIONSHIPS OF A COLONIAL TERRITORY WITH ITS MOTHER COUNTRY]. Münster, Max Kramer, 124p. (Ph.D. dissertation, Westfälischen Wilhelms-Universität zu Münster.)

MAY, LOUIS-PHILIPPE

43.106   MT   1930 HISTOIRE ÉCONOMIQUE DE LA MARTINIQUE (1635-1763) [ECONOMIC HISTORY OF MARTINIQUE (1635-1763)]. Paris, Les Presses Modernes, 334p. (Ph.D. dissertation, University of Paris.)   [5]   [*COL*]

MERRILL, GORDON CLARK

43.107   SK/ 1958 THE HISTORICAL GEOGRAPHY OF ST. KITTS AND NEVIS, THE WEST INDIES.
         NV   Mexico, Instituto Panamericano de Geografía e Historia, 145p. (Publicación no. 232.)   [*RIS*]

46.144   GC   1958 The historical record of man as an ecological dominant in the Lesser Antilles.

43.108   BG   1961 Recent land developments in coastal British Guiana. *Can Geogr* 5(2), Summer: p.24-29.   [*AGS*]

MIGNARD, NADIR

43.109   GD   1921 Les Antilles Francaises (la Guadeloupe) [The French Antilles (Guadeloupe)]. *B Soc Geogr* 63, July-Aug.: 167-188.   [*AGS*]

MILSTEAD, HARLEY PORTER
43.110   GR   1933 GRENADA: A GEOGRAPHICAL STUDY OF A HUMID TROPICAL ISLAND. Ph.D.
                dissertation, Clark University, 230p.   [AGS]

MOORE, EDW. FITZ.
43.111   BG   1943 A MODERN GEOGRAPHY OF BRITISH GUIANA. [2d ed.] Georgetown,
                "Argosy" Co., 127p. [32]

NIDDRIE, DAVID L.
43.112   TB   1961 LAND USE AND POPULATION IN TOBAGO: AN ENVIRONMENTAL STUDY.
                Bude, Eng., Geographical Publications, 59p.   [7]   [RIS]

NORDLOHNE, EDGAR
43.113   NL   1951 DE ECONOMISCH-GEOGRAFISCHE STRUCTUUR DER NEDERLANDSE BENEDEN-
                WINDSE EILANDEN [THE ECONOMIC-GEOGRAPHICAL STRUCTURE OF THE
                DUTCH LEEWARD ISLANDS]. Haarlem, Joh. Enschede, 125p.   [COL]
43.114   NA   1956 The Netherlands Antilles. *Tijdschr Econ Social Geogr* 47(6-7),
                June-July: 167-170.   [RIS]

NYSTROM, J. WARREN
43.115   SR   1942 SURINAM: A GEOGRAPHICAL STUDY. New York, Netherlands Information
                Bureau, 110p. (Booklet no. 6.)

OLIPHANT, J. N. & STEVENSON, DUNCAN
3.228   BH   1929 An expedition to the Cockscomb Mountains, British Honduras, in
                March 1928.

PAGET, E.
43.116   JM   1956 Land use and settlement in Jamaica. *In* STEEL, R. W. & FISHER,
                C.A., eds. GEOGRAPHICAL ESSAYS ON BRITISH TROPICAL LANDS. London,
                George Philip, p.181-223.

PANHUYS, L. C. van
43.117   SR   1921/ Het aantal en de woonplaatsen van de Boschnegers en Indianen in
          22   Suriname [The numbers and the settlements of the Bush-Negroes and
                Indians in Surinam]. *W I G* 3:83-99.   [COL]
43.118   SR   1921/ Na drie-kwart eeuw [After three quarters of a century]. *W I G* 3:303-
          22   309.   [COL]

PAPY, LOUIS
43.119   FG   1955 La Guyane Francaise [French Guiana]. *Cah O-M* 8(31), July-Sept.:
                209-232; 8(32), Oct.-Dec.: 369-400.   [RIS]

PEARCY, G. ETZEL
43.120   GC   1965 THE WEST INDIAN SCENE. Princeton, N.J., Van Nostrand, 136p.
                (Van Nostrand Searchlight books.)   [RIS]

PLATT, RAYE R.; WRIGHT, JOHN K.; WEAVER, JOHN C. &
FAIRCHILD, JOHNSON
43.121   GC   1941 THE EUROPEAN POSSESSIONS IN THE CARIBBEAN AREA. New York,
                American Geographical Society, 112p.   [COL]

PLATT, ROBERT S.

43.122   BG   1939 Reconnaissance in British Guiana, with comments on microgeography. *Ann Ass Am Geogr* 29(2), June: 105-126. [45]   [*AGS*]

PRICE A. GRENFELL

43.123   GC   1939 WHITE SETTLERS IN THE TROPICS. New York, American Geographical Society, 311p. (Special publication no. 23.)   [*AGS*]

PRICE, EDWARD T.

43.124   BB   1962 Notes on the geography of Barbados. *J Barb Mus Hist Soc* 29(4), Aug.: 119-154.

RAPPENECKER, CASPAR

43.125   JM   1936 THE REGIONAL AND ECONOMIC GEOGRAPHY OF JAMAICA, B.W.I. Ph.D. dissertation, Cornell University.   [*AGS*]

REIZLER, S.

43.126   FG   1922 La Guyane Francaise [French Guiana]. *Presse Med* 99, Dec. 13: 2069-2075.

REVERT, EUGENE

43.127   MT   1949 LA MARTINIQUE: ÉTUDE GÉOGRAPHIQUE ET HUMAINE [MARTINIQUE: A GEOGRAPHIC AND HUMAN STUDY]. Paris, Nouvelles éditions latines, 559p. (Ph.D. dissertation, University of Lyons.)   [*RIS*]

43.128   FA   1950 Problèmes de géographie antillaise [Problems in Antillean geography]. *Cah O-M* 3(9), Jan.-Mar.: 1-27.   [*AGS*]

43.129   GC   1951 Géographie politique du monde caraïbe [Political geography of the Caribbean]. *Ann Geogr* 60(318), Jan.-Feb.: 34-47. [37]   [*COL*]

ROBEQUAIN, CHARLES

43.130   SB   1949 Saint-Barthélémy terre francaise [St. Barthélémy, French land]. *Cah O-M* 2(5), Jan.-Mar.: 14-37.   [*AGS*]

ROBERTS, WALTER ADOLPHE, ed.

2.198   JM   1960 THE GLEANER GEOGRAPHY AND HISTORY OF JAMAICA. (Rev.)

ROSE, FRIEDRICH

43.131   UV   1930 Landeskundliche Untersuchung der Jungfern-Inseln (Virgin Islands) [Cultural geographical study of the Virgin Islands]. Engelsdorf-Leipzig, C. und E. Vogel, 91p. (Ph.D. dissertation, University of Leipzig.)   [*COL*]

ROSS, WILLIAM GILLIES

5.189   AT   1960 THE HISTORICAL GEOGRAPHY OF ANTIGUA.

SAINT-LUCE-BANCHELIN,

43.132   GD   1924 La Guadeloupe. *In* LES COLONIES FRANCAISES D'AMÉRIQUE. Paris, Notre domaine coloniale, p.31-62.   [*NYP*]

SAUER, CARL O.

43.133   GC   1954 Economic prospects of the Caribbean. *In* WILGUS, A. CURTIS, ed. THE CARIBBEAN: ITS ECONOMY [papers delivered at the Fourth Annual Conference on the Caribbean held at the University of

Florida. Dec. 3-5, 1953]. Gainesville, University of Florida Press,
p.15-27. (Publications of the School of Inter-American Studies, ser. 1.
v. 4.)   [57]   [*RIS*]

SHAW, EARL BENNETT

43.134   UV   1933   GEOGRAPHIC STUDIES ON THE VIRGIN ISLANDS OF THE UNITED STATES.
                     Ph.D. dissertation, Clark University, 401p.   [*AGS*]
43.135   BG   1940   The Rupununi savannahs of British Guiana. *J Geogr* 39(3), Mar.:
                     89-104. [66]   [*AGS*]
43.136   UV   1940   The Virgin Islands of the United States. *In* HAAS, WILLIAM H., ed.
                     THE AMERICAN EMPIRE. Chicago, University of Chicago Press, p.92-
                     122.   [*AGS*]

SKUTSCH, ILSE

43.137   TR   1929   DIE INSELN TRINIDAD AND TOBAGO: LANDESKUNDLICHE DARSTELLUNG
                     EINER BRITISCHEN KOLONIE [THE ISLANDS OF TRINIDAD AND TOBAGO:
                     DESCRIPTION OF THE CULTURAL GEOGRAPHY OF A BRITISH COLONY]. Leip-
                     zig, C. & M. Vogel, 198p. (Ph.D. dissertation, University of Leipzig.)
                                                                                     [*NYP*]

STARKEY, OTIS P.

43.138   BB   1939   THE ECONOMIC GEOGRAPHY OF BARBADOS. New York, Columbia Uni-
                     versity Press, 228p.   [*COL*]
43.139   MS   1960   COMMERCIAL GEOGRAPHY OF MONTSERRAT. Bloomington, Indiana
                     University, 18p. (Office of Naval Research, Technical report no. 6.)
                     [52, 66]   [*RIS*]
43.140   BB   1961   COMMERCIAL GEOGRAPHY OF BARBADOS. Bloomington, Indiana Uni-
                     versity, 32p. (Office of Naval Research, Technical report no. 9.)
                     [52, 66]   [*RIS*]
43.141   SK/ 1961   COMMERCIAL GEOGRAPHY OF ST. KITTS-NEVIS. Bloomington, Indiana
         NV   University, 16p. (Office of Naval Research, Technical report no. 7.)
                     [52, 66]   [*RIS*]
43.142   SL   1961   COMMERCIAL GEOGRAPHY OF ST. LUCIA. Bloomington, Indiana Uni-
                     versity, 15p. (Office of Naval Research, Technical report no. 8.)
                     [52, 66]   [*RIS*]
43.143   BC   1961   COMMERCIAL GEOGRAPHY OF THE EASTERN BRITISH CARIBBEAN. Bloom-
                     ington, Indiana University, 18p. (Office of Naval Research, Technical
                     report no. 12.) [66]   [*AGS*]

SUMNER, ALFRED ROCKWELL

43.144   JM   1933   LAND UTILIZATION IN ST. CATHERINE, JAMAICA. M. A. thesis, Clark
                     University, 57p.   [*AGS*]

THOMAS, LEON

43.145   DM   1955   La Dominique, asile des derniers autochtones antillais [Dominica,
                     haven of the last Caribbean aborigines]. *Nature* 3246, Oct.: 382-388.
                     [13]   [*COL*]

TROLL, CARL

43.146   CU/ 1930   Curacao, Trinidad and Tobago. *In* KLUTE, FRITZ, ed. HANDBUCH
         TR   DER GEOGRAPHISCHEN WISSENSCHAFT: SÜD-AMERIKA IN NATUR, KULTUR
                     UND WIRTSCHAFT. Wildpark-Potsdam, Akademische Verlagsgesell-
                     schaft Athenaion, p.463-467.   [*AGS*]

VERIN, PIERRE MICHEL

43.147   SL   1963 La Pointe Caraibe (Sainte-Lucie). M.A. thesis, Yale University, 294p. [56]   [*RIS*]

WAAL, L. de

43.148   SR   1927/Kolonies in Suriname [Colonies in Surinam]. *W I G* 9:297-308. [*COL*] 28

WADDELL, ERIC WILSON

43.149   BG   1963 The anthropic factor in a savanna environment: an analysis of the changing relations between man and the physical environment ... in the Rupununi District of British Guiana. M.A. thesis, McGill University, 207p.

WALKER, FREDERICK

43.150   SV   1937 Economic progress of St. Vincent, B.W.I., since 1927. *Econ Geogr* 13(3), July: 217-234.   [*AGS*]

WHITBECK, R. H.

43.151   JM   1932 The agricultural geography of Jamaica. *Ann Ass Am Geogr* 22(1), Mar.: 13-27.   [*AGS*]

WINKLER, OTTO

43.152   NA   1926 Niederländisch-Westindien (eine länderkundliche Skizze) [The Netherlands West Indies (a cultural geographical outline)]. *In* Mitteilungen der Gesellschaft für Erdkunde zu Leipzig für 1923-1925. Leipzig, p.87-137.   [*AGS*]

WOELK, G.

43.153   JM   1936 Die wirtschaftsgeographische Bedeutung Jamaikas [The economic-geographical significance of Jamaica]. *In* SCHEU, ERWIN, ed. Wirtschaftsgeographische Probefahrten. Breslau, Ferdinand Hirt, p.88-89. (Wirtschaftsgeographische Arbeiten, v. 1.)   [*AGS*]

WRIGHT, G.

43.154   SV   1929 Economic conditions in St. Vincent, B.W.I. *Econ Geogr* 5(3), July: 236-259.   [*AGS*]

WUNSCHE, BRUNO

43.155   JM   1936 Die wirtschaftliche Entwicklung und Gliederung der Insel Jamaika: eine wirtschaftsgeographische Untersuchung auf landschaftskundlicher Grundlage [The economic development and organization of the island of Jamaica: an economic-geographical study based on regional geography]. Hamburg, Paul Evert, 66p.   [*AGS*]

WYLIE, KATHRYN H.

43.156   JM   1942 The agriculture of Jamaica. *For Agric* 6(4), Apr.: 121-146.   [*AGS*]

SOCIOECONOMIC ACTIVITIES AND INSTITUTIONS

Chapter 44

GENERAL ECONOMIC STUDIES

ABBOTT, GEORGE C.

44.001   BC   1963 The future of economic co-operation in the West Indies in the light of the break-up of the Federation. *Social Econ Stud* 12(2), June: 160-178.   [37,38,46]   [*RIS*]

ABENDANON, E. C.

44.002   SR   1919 Economische waardebepaling van Suriname [Economic evaluation of Surinam]. *W I G* 1(1): 165-174.   [*COL*]

ADHIN, J. H.

50.001   SR   1963 De economisch-historische betekenis van de Hindostaanse immigratie voor Suriname [The economic-historical value of the Hindustani immigration for Surinam].

AHIRAM, E.

44.003   JM   1964 Income distribution in Jamaica, 1958. *Social Econ Stud* 13(3), Sept.: 333-369.   [*RIS*]

AIKEN, JAMES

30.001   BG   1912 Food and labour.

ALCALA, V. O.

32.007   GC   1953 Business education.
32.009   GC   1953 Services and benefits of guidance.

AMSTEL, J. E. van

51.002   SR   1924/ Nog eenige opmerkingen over Surinaamsche Liberia-koffie en de 25 mogelijkheid tot verbetering der reputatie er van [Some added remarks about the Surinam Liberia-coffee and the possibilities of improving its reputation].

ANDIC, FUAT M. & SUPHAN

44.004   FC   1965 Fiscal survey of the French Caribbean. Rio Piedras, Institute of Caribbean Studies, University of Puerto Rico, 108p. (Special study no. 2.)   [37]   [*RIS*]

ARMSTRONG, ERIC

44.005   TR   1963 Projections of the growth of the economy of Trinidad and Tobago.
                         Social Econ Stud 12(3), Sept.: 283-306.   [*RIS*]

AUGELLI, JOHN P.

43.002   VI   1955 The British Virgin Islands: a West Indian anomaly.

AUGELLI, JOHN P. & TAYLOR, HARRY W.

7.004   TR   1960 Race and population patterns in Trinidad.

BAKKER, J.

37.018   SR   1928/ De betuursregeling van Suriname [The governmental arrangement of
                    29   Surinam].

BEASLEY, CYRIL GEORGE

44.006   BB   1952 A FISCAL SURVEY OF BARBADOS. Barbados, Printed for the Govt. of
                         Barbados by Cole's Printery, 107p.   [37]   [*RIS*]
44.007   BC   1956 Prospects and obstacles to economic development. *Statist* Sept.:
                         15.   [66]

BELL, WENDELL

37.022   JM   1962 Equality and attitudes of elites in Jamaica.

BENHAM, FREDERIC. C.

44.008   BB   [n.d.] THE NATIONAL INCOME OF BARBADOS, 1942.   Bridgetown, Advocate
                         Co., 24p. (Development and welfare bulletin no. 9.)   [*COL*]
44.009   BG   [n.d.] THE NATIONAL INCOME OF BRITISH GUIANA, 1942. Bridgetown, Advo-
                         cate Co., 28p. (Development and welfare bulletin no. 17.)   [*COL*]
44.010   GR   [n.d.] THE NATIONAL INCOME OF GRENADA, 1942. Bridgetown, Advocate Co.,
                         7p. (Development and welfare bulletin no. 12.)   [*COL*]
44.011   JM   [n.d.] THE NATIONAL INCOME OF JAMAICA, 1942. Bridgetown, Advocate Co.,
                         29p. (Development and welfare bulletin no. 5.)   [*COL*]
44.012   SV   [n.d.] THE NATIONAL INCOME OF ST. VINCENT, 1942. Bridgetown, Advocate
                         Co., 6p. (Development and welfare bulletin no. 8.)   [*COL*]

BERRILL, KENNETH

44.013   BG   1961 A comment [on "The economic future of British Guiana" by Peter
                         Newman, in *Social Econ Stud* 9(3)]. *Social Econ Stud* 10(1), Mar.:
                         1-5.   [66]   [*RIS*]

BEST, ETHEL

50.010   UV   1936 ECONOMIC PROBLEMS OF THE WOMEN OF THE VIRGIN ISLANDS OF THE
                         UNITED STATES.

BETHEL, JEANETTE

44.014   BB   1960 A national accounts study of the economy of Barbados. *Social Econ
                         Stud* 9(2), June: 123-252.   [*RIS*]
44.015   JM   1961 Some national income aggregates for Jamaica at constant prices.
                         Social Econ Stud 10(2), June: 128-155.   [67]   [*RIS*]

BLANSHARD, PAUL

37.028   GC   1947 DEMOCRACY AND EMPIRE IN THE CARIBBEAN: A CONTEMPORARY REVIEW.

BONE, LOUIS W.
32.027 GG 1962 SECONDARY EDUCATION IN THE GUIANAS.

BONNETT, R. L.
44.016 BB 1956 The national income and national accounts of Barbados. *Social Econ Stud* 5(3), Sept.: 213-259. [*RIS*]

BOULDING, K. E.
66.019 BG 1961 Social dynamics in West Indian society [cf. Newman's article in *Social Econ Stud* 9(3)].

BOSMAN, H. W. J.
44.017 SR 1948 De betalingsbalans en het geldwezen van Suriname tijdens de tweede Wereldoorlog [The balance of payment and the financial situation of Surinam during the second World War]. *W I G* 29:48-54. [*COL*]

BOVEN, J. H. van
44.018 CU 1944 Culture and commerce in Curacao. *Can-W I Mag* 33-34(4), Apr.: 9-11. [*NYP*]

BOWSTEAD, WILLIAM, ed.
44.019 BC [n.d.] THE COMMERCIAL LAWS OF THE WORLD. VOL. 17: BRITISH DOMINIONS AND PROTECTORATES IN AMERICA. Boston, Boston Book Co., 1160p. [37] [*NYP*]

BRADLEY, DAVID H.
44.020 BH 1944 British Honduras under war economy. *Can-W I Mag* 33-34(1), Jan.: 20-21,23. [*NYP*]

BRADSHAW,
44.021 BC 1958 Financial problems of the federation. *W I Comm Circ* 73(1329), Sept.: 251-252. [38] [*NYP*]

BRAITHWAITE, LLOYD E.
38.023 BC 1957 'Federal' associations and institutions in the West Indies.
38.024 BC 1957 Progress toward federation, 1938-1956.

BRANDON, H. G.
44.022 SR 1924/ Het Suriname vraagstuk [The problem of Surinam]. *W I G* 6:481-560. 25 [17] [*COL*]

BREEVELD, F.
44.023 SR 1958 Electriciteit in het oerwoud [Electricity in the primeval forest]. *In* WALLE, J. van de & WIT, H.D., eds. SURINAME IN STROOMLIJNEN. Amsterdam, Wereld Bibliotheek, p.36-43. [57,66]

BROCK, H. G.; SMITH, PHILIP S. & TUCKER, W. A.
44.024 UV 1917 THE DANISH WEST INDIES, THEIR RESOURCES AND COMMERCIAL IMPORTANCE. Washington, U.S. Govt. Print. Off., 68p. (U.S., Dept. of Commerce, Bureau of Foreign and Domestic Commerce, Special agents series no. 129.) [*AGS*]

BROWN, G. ARTHUR

44.025   JM   1958 Economic development and the private sector. *In* HUGGINS, H.D.,
ed. [PROCEEDINGS OF THE] STUDY CONFERENCE ON ECONOMIC DEVELOP-
MENT IN UNDERDEVELOPED COUNTRIES [held at the University College of the West Indies, Aug. 5-15, 1957]. *Social Econ Stud* 7(3),
Sept.: 103-119.   [37,66]   [*RIS*]

44.026   JM   [1961?] Economic development and trends in Jamaica (1950-1960). *In* CUM-
PER, GEORGE, ed. REPORT OF THE CONFERENCE ON SOCIAL DEVEL-
OPMENT IN JAMAICA. Kingston, Standing Committee on Social Serv-
ices, p.12-22.   [*RIS*]

44.027   JM   [1961?] Economic factors in social development. *In* CUMPER, GEORGE,
ed. REPORT OF THE CONFERENCE ON SOCIAL DEVELOPMENT IN JAMAICA.
Kingston, Standing Committee on Social Services, p.83-86.   [*RIS*]

BROWN, HEADLEY A.

44.028   JM   1963/ The Jamaican economy and international liquidity. *Social Scient*
64 1:10.

BROWN, W. J.

37.045   JM   1948 Jamaica boss.

BRUCE, GEORGE

44.029   JM   1961 Jamaica's 10-year miracle. *New Commonw* 39(4), Apr.: 220-222.
[66]

CAINE, W. RALPH HALL

3.044   JM   1908. The CRUISE OF THE PORT KINGSTON.

CAIRES, DAVID de

44.030   BG   1963 Regional integration. *New Wld Q* Mar.: 82-86.   [37,38]   [*RIS*]

CAREY-JONES, N. ·S.

44.031   BH   1953 THE PATTERN OF A DEPENDENT ECONOMY: A STUDY OF THE NATIONAL IN-
COME OF BRITISH HONDURAS. Cambridge, Cambridge University Press,
162p.   [66]   [*RIS*]

CASE, GERALD O.

44.032   BG   1946 Power resources of British Guiana. *In* ROTH, VINCENT, comp.
HANDBOOK OF NATURAL RESOURCES OF BRITISH GUIANA. Georgetown,
Daily Chronicle, p.218-221.   [66]   [*AGS*]

CHARDON, CARLOS E.

44.033   GC   1949 The Caribbean island economy. *Scient Mon* 69(3), Sept.: 169-172.
[*AGS*]

CHARLES, HENRI

44.034   GD   1947 La Guadeloupe: un cas d'émancipation coloniale et de rétablissement
économique après la guerre [Guadeloupe: a case history of political
emancipation and economic revival after the war]. *Etudes* 80(254),
July-Sept.: 205-216.   [37,66]   [*NYP*]

CLARKE, S. St. A.

44.035   JM   1962 Overseas investment in Jamaica. *W I Econ* 4(12), June: 5-8.   [*RIS*]

COHEN, YEHUDI A.

8.009   JM   1955 Four categories of interpersonal relationships in the family and community in a Jamaican village.

COLLINS, DOREEN

44.036   TC   1961 Turks and Caicos: unknown islands in the sun. *New Commonw* 39 (6), June: 377-378.   [AGS]

COMVALIUS, TH. A. C.

44.037   SR   1927/ Economisch Suriname en het loonstelsel [The economy of Surinam
               28   and the wage system]. *WIG* 9:449-454.   [50]   [COL]
44.038   SR   1931/ Economisch Suriname [Economics of Surinam].   *W I G* 13:144-146.
               32   [COL]

CORNU, HENRI

37.069   FA   1935 Une expérience législative à la Réunion, à la Martinique et à la Guadeloupe [A legislative experiment in Reunion, Martinique, and Guadeloupe].

CROWE, HARRY J.

44.039   BC   1923 Mr. Harry J. Crowe on confederation with the West Indies. *Can-W I Mag* 11(4), Feb.: 96-98.   [37]   [NYP]
37.077   JM   1925 The political side of the question.

CUMPER, GEORGE E.

46.043   JM   1953 Two studies in Jamaican productivity.
44.040   JM   1958 Expenditure patterns, Kingston, Jamaica, 1954. *Social Econ Stud* 7(2), June: 165-177.   [36]   [RIS]
44.041   BC   1960 The development of the West Indies. *In* CUMPER, G.E., ed. THE ECONOMY OF THE WEST INDIES. Kingston, Institute of Social and Economic Research, University College of the West Indies, p.1-23.
                                                                                  [RIS]
44.042   BC   1960 Personal consumption in the West Indies. *In* CUMPER, G.E., ed. THE ECONOMY OF THE WEST INDIES. Kingston, Institute of Social and Economic Research, University College of the West Indies, p.126-151.   [RIS]
44.043   BB   1960 West Indian household budgets. *Social Econ Stud* 9(3), Sept.: 355-365.   [9]   [RIS]
44.044   BB   1961 Household and occupation in Barbados. *Social Econ Stud* 10(4), Dec.: 386-419.   [8,9]   [RIS]
44.045   JM/   1961 Investment criteria: a comment [on Newman's article in *Social Econ
         BG   Stud* 9(3)]. *Social Econ Stud* 10(1), Mar.: 18-24.   [66]   [RIS]
44.046   BB   1962 The differentiation of economic groups in the West Indies. *In* SINGHAM, A. & BRAITHWAITE, L.E., eds. SPECIAL NUMBER [OF *Social Econ Stud*] ON THE CONFERENCE ON POLITICAL SOCIOLOGY IN THE BRITISH CARIBBEAN, Dec. 1961. *Social Econ Stud* 11(4), Dec.: 319-332.   [7,8,37]   [RIS]
44.047   JM   1963/ Price control in Jamaica. *Social Scient* 2:24-27.   [RIS]
               64

CUMPER, GEORGE E., ed.

44.048   BC   1960 ECONOMY OF THE WEST INDIES. Kingston, Institute of Social & Economic Research, University College of the West Indies, 273p.   [38]   [RIS]

CUNDALL, FRANK
37.079   BC   1906 POLITICAL AND SOCIAL DISTURBANCES IN THE WEST INDIES: A BRIEF AC-
                  COUNT AND BIBLIOGRAPHY.

DAMBAUGH, LUELLA N.
43.035   JM   1953 Jamaica: an island in transition.

DAVENPORT, WILLIAM HUNT
8.019   JM   1956 A COMPARATIVE STUDY OF TWO JAMAICAN FISHING COMMUNITIES.

DAVIDSON, H. K. & MINKES, A. L.
66.035   JM   1954 Social factors in the economic problems of Jamaica.

DELOBEZ, A.
44.049   MT   1963 La population et l'économie de la Martinique en 1960 [The popula-
                  tion and economy of Martinique in 1960]. *Inf Geogr* 27(1), Jan.-Feb.:
                  22-26.   [7]   [*AGS*]

DENHAM, Sir EDWARD
44.050   BG   1931 British Guiana's financial situation. *Can-W I Mag* 20(12), Nov.: 420-
                  422.   [*NYP*]

Des FORGES, Sir CHARLES & IMRIE, J. D.
37.096   TR   1950 REPORT ON LOCAL GOVERNMENT (FINANCIAL RELATIONSHIPS).

DICKINSON, THOMAS H.
44.051   UV   1927 Economic crisis in the Virgin Islands. *Curr Hist* 27(3), Dec.: 378-
                  381.   [66]   [*COL*]

DOUGLAS, CH.
46.055   SR   1927/ Aanteekeningen over den landbouw in Suriname [Notes about agri-
                  28   culture in Surinam].

DOWNIE, JACK
44.052   BH   1959 AN ECONOMIC POLICY FOR BRITISH HONDURAS. Belize, 25p. [66] [*COL*]

DUNLOP, W. R.
44.053   BG   1925 Economic research in tropical development, with special reference
                  to British Guiana and British Malaya. *J Roy Soc Arts* 73(3770),
                  Feb. 20: 312-334.   [43,66]   [*AGS*]

DRUMMOND, ANDREW T.
38.037   BC   1917 The future of the West Indies.

EARLE, A. F.
44.054   JM   1953 Incentives to private investment as an aspect of development pro-
                  grammes. *Social Econ Stud* 1(3), July: 141-150.   [66]   [*RIS*]

EASTMAN, P. T.
44.055   BC   1959 British eastern Caribbean. *Can-W I Mag* 49(1), Jan.: 15-16.   [*NYP*]

EDWARDS, DAVID T.
46.061   JM   1961 An economic view of agricultural research in Jamaica.

EISNER, GISELA

44.056   JM   1961 JAMAICA, 1830-1930: A STUDY IN ECONOMIC GROWTH. Manchester, Manchester University Press, 399p.   [5,46]   [*RIS*]

EYK, W. van

44.057   CU   1947 De Curacaosche begrooting voor 1948 [The budget of Curacao for the year 1948]. *W I G* 28: 269-283.   [*COL*]

FALLS, CYRIL

37.109   JM   1947 A window on the world: Jamaica moves to independence.

FARLEY, RAWLE

44.058   BG   1955 The economic circumstances of the British annexation of British Guiana (1795-1815). *Revta Hist Am* 39, June: 21-59. [5,37]   [*NYP*]

44.059   BG   1962 Kaldor's budget in retrospect: reason and unreason in a developing area: reflections on the 1962 budget in British Guiana. *Inter-Am Econ Aff* 16(3): 25-63.   [37,66]   [*COL*]

FAUVEL, LUC

37.112   FA   1955 Les conséquences économiques et sociales de l'assimilation administrative des Antilles Francaises [The economic and social consequences of the political assimilation of the French Antilles].

FERNANDES, A. S. J.

44.060   SR   1925/ De Surinaamsche begrooting voor 1925 in de Staten-Generaal [The
                  26   budget of Surinam for 1925 before the States-General]. *W I G* 7:289-310.   [37]   [*COL*]

FINCH, KENNETH W.

49.023   TR   1962 A commercial approach to rural electrification.

FISHER, RUTH ANNA

15.015   JM   1943 Note on Jamaica.

FRANCIS, OLIVER M.

28.188   BG   1943 Social, economic and dietetic features of tuberculosis in British Guiana.

30.026   BG   1947 Nutritional aspects of cost of living survey, 1942.

FRAZIER, E. FRANKLIN & WILLIAMS, ERIC, eds.

2.080   GC   1944 THE ECONOMIC FUTURE OF THE CARIBBEAN.

GAAY FORTMAN, B. de

44.061   CU   1919 Curacao tegen het einde der West-Indische Compagnie [Curacao's position during the final years of the West Indian Company]. *W I G* 1(1): 441-457.   [5]   [*COL*]

44.062   CU   1919 De Curacaosche begrooting voor 1919 [The budget of Curacao for the year 1919]. *W I G* 1(1): 186-196.   [*COL*]

44.063   CU   1920/ De Curacaosche begrooting voor 1920 [The Curacao budget for the
                  21   year 1920]. *W I G* 2:45-57.   [*COL*]

44.064   CU   1921/ Curacao: De voorstellen van den Gouverneur in het belang van de
                  22   economische opheffing der kolonie [The suggestions of the Governor toward the economic development of the colony]. *W I G* 3:197-204.
                         [66]   [*COL*]

44.065   CU   1921/ De Curacaosche begrooting voor 1921 [The budget of Curacao for
              22   the year 1921]. *W I G* 3:189-196.   [*COL*]
44.066   CU   1922/ De Curacaosche begrooting voor 1922 [The budget of Curacao for
              23   the year 1922]. *W I G* 4:159-166.   [*COL*]
44.067   CU   1923/ De Curacaosche begrooting voor 1923 [The budget of Curacao for
              24   the year 1923]. *W I G* 5:177-184.   [*COL*]
44.068   CU   1924/ De Curacaosche begrooting voor 1924 [The budget of Curacao for
              25   the year 1924]. *W I G* 6:321-329.   [*COL*]
44.069   CU   1925/ De Curacaosche begrooting voor 1925 [The budget of Curacao for
              26   the year 1925]. *W I G* 7:241-251.   [*COL*]
44.070   CU   1926/ De Curacaosche begrooting voor 1926 [The budget of Curacao for
              27   the year 1926]. *W I G* 8:277-282.   [*COL*]
2.081 CU   1927/ Curacao en onderhorige eilanden [Curacao and subordinate islands].
              29
44.071   CU   1927/ De Curacaosche begrooting voor 1927 [The budget of Curacao for
              28   the year 1927]. *W I G* 9:199-202.   [*COL*]
44.072   CU   1928/ De Curacaosche begrooting voor 1928 [The budget of Curacao for
              29   the year 1928]. *W I G* 10:158-164.   [*COL*]
44.073   CU   1928/ De Curacaosche begrooting voor 1929: over den politieken toestand
              29   van Curacao [The budget of Curacao for the year 1929: about the
                   political situation in Curacao]. *W I G* 10:289-299. [37]   [*COL*]
44.074   CU   1929/ De Curacaosche begrooting voor 1929 [The budget of Curacao for
              30   the year 1929]. *W I G* 11:85-88.   [*COL*]
44.075   CU   1929/ De Curacaosche begrooting voor 1930 [The budget of Curacao for
              30   the year 1930]. *W I G* 11:545-553.   [*COL*]
44.076   NA   1929/ De West-Indische Maatschappij [The West Indian Company]·   [5]
              30   [*COL*]
44.077   CU   1931/ De Curacaosche begrooting voor 1931 [The budget of Curacao for
              32   the year 1931]. *W I G* 13:72-79.   [*COL*]
44.078   CU   1932/ De Curacaosche begrooting voor 1932 [The budget of Curacao for
              33   the year 1932]. *W I G* 14:69-75.   [*COL*]
44.079   CU   1933/ De Curacaosche begrooting voor 1933 [The budget of Curacao for
              34   the year 1933]. *W I G* 15:124-130.   [*COL*]
44.080   CU   1934/ De Curacaosche begrooting voor 1934 [The budget of Curacao for
              35   the year 1934]. *W I G* 16:7-16.   [*COL*]
44.081   CU   1935/ Staatkundige geschiedenis van Curacao: de Curacaosche begrooting
              36   voor 1935 [Political history of Curacao: the budget of Curacao for
                   the year 1935]. *W I G* 17:135-148.   [5,37]   [*COL*]
44.082   CU   1936/ Staatkundige geschiedenis van Curacao: de Curacaosche begrooting
              37   voor 1936 [Political history of Curacao: the budget of Curacao for
                   the year 1936]. *W I G* 18:85-115.   [5,37]   [*COL*]
44.083   CU   1937 Staatkundige geschiedenis van Curacao: de Curacaosche begrooting
                   voor 1937 [Political history of Curacao: the budget of Curacao for
                   the year 1937]. *W I G* 19:129-146.   [5,37]   [*COL*]
44.084   CU   1938 Economische en sociale vraagstukken in Curacao [Economic and so-
                   cial problems in Curacao]. *W I G* 20:329-341.   [37,66]   [*COL*]
44.085   CU   1938 Staatkundige geschiedenis van Curacao: de Curacaosche begrooting
                   voor 1938 [Political history of Curacao: the budget of Curacao for
                   the year 1938]. *W I G* 20:234-246.   [5,37]   [*COL*]
44.086   CU   1939 Staatkundige geschiedenis van Curacao: de Curacaosche begrooting
                   van 1939 [Political history of Curacao: the budget of Curacao for
                   the year 1939]. *W I G* 21:337-354.   [5,37]   [*COL*]

44.087   CU   1940 Staatkundige geschiedenis van Curacao: de Curacaosche begrooting voor 1940 [Political history of Curacao: the budget of Curacao for the year 1940]. *W I G* 22:303-313, 321-333. [5,37]   [*COL*]

GETROUW, C. F. G.
37.138   SR   1946 Suriname en de oorlog [Surinam and the War].

GOEJE, C. H. de
41.102   SR   1936/ Voorzichtig met den bodem van Suriname! [Be careful with the 37 ground of Surinam!]

GOODE, J. L. WILSON
44.088   BC   1931 ECONOMIC CONDITIONS IN THE BRITISH WEST INDIES AND CONTIGUOUS BRITISH TERRITORIES. London, H.M.S.O., 94p. ([Publications of the] Dept. of Overseas Trade.)   [*COL*]
44.089   BC   1932 ECONOMIC CONDITIONS IN THE BRITISH WEST INDIES AND CONTIGUOUS BRITISH TERRITORIES. London, H.M.S.O., 107p. ([Publications of the] Dept. of Overseas Trade, no. 510.)   [*COL*]

GOODE, RICHARD
44.090   JM   1956 Taxation and economic development in Jamaica. *In* SYMPOSIUM ON THE HICKS REPORT. *Social Econ Stud* 5(1), Mar.: 19-26. [37,66] [*RIS*]

GOODMAN, EILEEN
44.091   JM   1962 Canada in Jamaica. *New Commonw* 40(12), Dec.: 729-731.   [*AGS*]

GORDON, GARNET H.
44.092   BC   1955 British Caribbean offers investment opportunities. *New Commonw,* Br Car Suppl 30(11), Nov. 28: ii-iii.   [*AGS*]

GORDON, WILLIAM E.
44.093   JM   1957 Imperial policy decisions in the economic history of Jamaica, 1664-1934. *Social Econ Stud* 6(1), Mar.: 1-28. [5,37]   [*RIS*]

GREEN, LENA
41.109   JM   1962 Some seaweeds of economic importance growing in Jamaican waters.

GREENFIELD, SIDNEY M.
9.010   BB   1961 Socio-economic factors and family form: a Barbadian case study.

GREINER, F.
44.094   SR   1927/ Het Suriname probleem [The Surinam problem]. *W I G* 9:531-541 29 (1927/28); 10:355-368 (1928/29).   [*COL*]

GRIFFIN, CORNELIUS J.
44.095   GC   1958 Energy in Caribbean progress. *In* WILGUS, A. CURTIS, ed. THE CARIBBEAN: BRITISH, DUTCH, FRENCH, UNITED STATES [papers delivered at the Eighth Conference on the Caribbean held at the University of Florida, Dec. 5-7, 1957].   Gainesville, University of Florida Press, p.225-232. (Publications of the School of Inter-American Studies, ser. 1, v. 8).   [57]   [*RIS*]

HAGERTY, T. F.

31.033   AR   1963 The Junior Achievement Programme in Aruba.

HALL, DOUGLAS GORDON

44.096   JM   1959 FREE JAMAICA, 1838-1865: AN ECONOMIC HISTORY. New Haven, Yale
University Press, 290p.   [5]   [*RIS*]

HALLEMA, A.

6.024   NC   1939 Koloniale vraagstukken ten opzichte van onze West anderhalve eeuw
geleden [Colonial problems in connection with our West one and a
half centuries ago].

HANRATH, JOHANNES J.

43.063   SR   1956 The economic-geographical structure of Surinam.

HAREWOOD, JACK

50.058   BC   1956 A system of labour force statistics.

HARNARINE, HAROLD

44.097   BC   1963/ Business enterprise and Asiatic groups in the West Indies. *Social*
64 *Scient* 2:2-4.   [8,10]   [*RIS*]

HARPER-SMITH, JAMES W.

37.159   BG   1965 The Colonial Stock Acts and the British Guiana Constitution of 1891.

HARRIS, DONALD J.

44.098   JM   1964 Econometric analysis of household consumption in Jamaica. *Social*
Econ Stud 13(4), Dec.: 471-487.   [30]   [*RIS*]

HARRISON, Sir JOHN B.

44.099   BG   1918 Now and then: or, notes on the Society and its work in 1897 and in
1918. *Timehri* 3d ser., 5(22), Aug.: vii-lxxxi.   [66]   [*AMN*]

HAZELWOOD, ARTHUR

44.100   JM   1956 The Hicks Report on finance and taxation in Jamaica: a comment.
In SYMPOSIUM ON THE HICKS REPORT. *Social Econ Stud* 5(1), Mar.:
27-31.   [37,66]   [*RIS*]

HELSDINGEN, W. H. van

37.166   NA   1954 Voorlopige balans over de uitvoering van de Eilandenregeling Nederlandse Antillen [Preliminary assessment of the application of the
Netherlands Antilles Islands regulation].

HENRIQUEZ, P. COHEN

49.041   CU   1938 Zeewaterverwerking [The processing of sea water].

HESSLING, H. A.

7.031   AR   1933/ Beeld van Aruba in cijfers [Statistical picture of Aruba].
34

HICKS, JOHN R. & URSULA K.

44.101   JM   1955 REPORT ON FINANCE AND TAXATION IN JAMAICA. Kingston, Government
Printer, 171p.   [37,66]   [*NYP*]

HINDEN, RITA

44.102   JM   1941 Jamaican paradox. *New Stsm Natn* 21(527), Mar. 29:319-320.   [37]

HISS, PHILIP HANSON
5.088   NA   1943 NETHERLANDS AMERICA: THE DUTCH TERRITORIES IN THE WEST.

HOETINK, HARRY
44.103   CU   1956 Curacao en Thorstein Veblen. *Mens Mij Twee Tijdschr* 31, Jan.-
                Feb.: 40-46.   [*RIS*]

HOFFMAN, H. THEODORE
44.104   BG   1946 Economic situation in British Guiana 1945. *Int Ref Serv* 3(40), Sept.:
                4p.   [*AGS*]
44.105   SR   1946 Economic situation in Surinam 1945. *Int Ref Serv* 3(31), Aug.: 4p.
                                                                        [*AGS*]

HOWIE, H. R.
44.106   BG   1945 REPORT ON INCOME TAX IN BRITISH GUIANA. Georgetown, Daily Chron-
                icle, 23p. (Legislative Council paper no. 12.)   [37]   [*COL*]

HOYT, ELIZABETH E.
44.107   JM   1959 Changing standards of living in Jamaica. *Caribbean* 13(7), July:
                132-133.   [20,66]   [*RIS*]
50.066   JM   1960 Voluntary unemployment and unemployability in Jamaica with spe-
                cial reference to the standard of living.

HOYTE, CLYDE, ed.
44.108   JM   [n.d.] THE YEARBOOK OF INDUSTRY AND AGRICULTURE IN JAMAICA 1957. Kings-
                ton, City Printery, 344p.

HUGGINS, H. D.
44.109   JM   1953 Employment, economic development and incentive financing in Ja-
                maica. *Social Econ Stud* 1(1), Feb.: 3-60.   [66]   [*COL*]

HUGGINS, H. D., ed.
44.110   BC   1958 [PROCEEDINGS OF THE] STUDY CONFERENCE ON ECONOMIC DEVELOPMENT
                IN UNDERDEVELOPED COUNTRIES [held at the University College of
                the West Indies, Aug. 5-15, 1957].   *Social Econ Stud* 7(3), Sept.:
                139p.   [7,37,46,66]   [*RIS*]

HUGGINS, H. D. & CUMPER, G. E.
44.111   JM/   1958 Economic development in a context of low population pressure. *In*
         BG   HUGGINS, H.D., ed. [PROCEEDINGS OF THE] STUDY CONFERENCE ON
                ECONOMIC DEVELOPMENT IN UNDERDEVELOPED COUNTRIES [held at the
                University College of the West Indies, Aug. 5-15, 1957].   *Social
                Econ Stud* 7(3), Sept.: 54-74.   [7,66]   [*RIS*]

HUGHES, COLIN A.
44.112   BH   1953 A dependent economy. *Venture* 5(4), June: 8-9.   [*COL*]

HUGILL, J. A. C.
58.058   TR   1963 Trinidad's sugar markets.

HUIZINGA, D. S.
50.070   SR   1927/ De Surinaamsche loonsverhoging van 1920 [The wage increase of
         28   1920, in Surinam].

HULL, CHARLES H.
44.113   BC   1900 Finances in the British West Indies. *In* ESSAYS IN COLONIAL FINANCE.
                Publs Am Econ Ass 1(3): 168-188.   [37]   [*COL*]

HUNTE, K. R.

44.114   BB   1961 To work together in unity: for the economic betterment of the
                West Indies Federation. [Bridgetown?] Barbados, Advocate Co.,
                67p. [28]

IFILL, MAX B., ed.

44.115   BC   1962 Caribbean economic almanac 1962. [Port of Spain?] Trinidad, Eco-
                nomic and Business Research Information and Advisory Service,
                94p.   [*RIS*]

44.116   GC   1964 Caribbean economic almanac 1964-1966. Port of Spain, Economic
                and Business Research Information and Advisory Service, 270p. [*RIS*]

IMRIE, Sir JOHN

44.117   TR   1958 Report on the finance of the three municipalities and the work-
                ing of the county councils in Trinidad and Tobago. Port of Spain,
                Govt. Print. Off., 90p.   [36,37,66]

INTERNATIONAL BANK FOR RECONSTRUCTION AND DEVELOPMENT

66.069   JM   1952 The economic development of Jamaica.
66.070   SR   1952 Surinam; recommendations for a ten year development program.
66.071   BG   1953 The economic development of British Guiana.

JACKSON, MELVIN H.

44.118   FC   1958 The economy of the French Caribbean. *In* WILGUS, A. CURTIS, ed.
                The Caribbean: British, Dutch, French, United States [papers
                delivered at the Eighth Conference on the Caribbean held at the
                University of Florida, Dec. 5-7, 1957]. Gainesville, University of
                Florida Press, p.97-124. (Publications of the School of Inter-Ame-
                rican studies, ser. 1, v. 8.)   [*RIS*]

JACOBS, H. P.

44.119   JM   1954 New economic pattern. *Pepperpot* 4:25-32.
44.120   JM   1955 Production pattern. *Pepperpot* 5:41-43. [66]

JAGAN, CHEDDI

44.121   BG   1964 The anatomy of poverty in British Guiana. Georgetown, People's
                Progressive Party, 65p. [37]

37.203   BG   1964 Let it not be said that we have failed.

JAYAWARDENA, CHANDRA

9.021   BG   1962 Family organisation in plantations in British Guiana.

JOSEPH, FRANZ M. & KOPPEL, RICHARD U.

44.122   CU   1961 Curacao organizations. *Taxes* 39(6), June: 485-507. [37]   [*RIS*]

JOUANDET-BERNADAT, ROLAND

44.123   MT   1964 Note sur les revenus en Martinique [Revenues in Martinique]. *Car
                Stud* 4(3), Oct.: 14-31.   [*RIS*]

KASTELEYN, J. S. C. & KLUVERS, B. J.

44.124   SR   1919/ Resumé van het rapport (1919) der studie-commissie van het Suri-
                20   naamse studie-syndicaat [Resumé of the report (1919) of the study
                committee of the Surinam study syndicate]. *WIG* 1(2): 287-316. [37]
                                                                                 [*COL*]

KERVEGANT, D.

46.125   MT   1954 L'agronomie aux Antilles [Agronomy in the Antilles].

KESLER, C. K.

51.078   SR   1926/ Amsterdamsche bankiers en de West in de 18de eeuw [Amsterdam
            27   bankers and the West in the 18th Century].

KIELSTRA, J. C.

44.125   SR   1925 WIRTSCHAFTLICHE UND SOZIALE PROBLEME IN NIEDERLÄNDISCH-WEST-
            INDIEN [ECONOMIC AND SOCIAL PROBLEMS IN THE DUTCH WEST INDIES].
            Jena, Kommissionsverlag von Gustav Fischer, 24p. (Kieler Vör-
            trage, no. 13.)   [6]   [COL]

KITTERMASTER, Sir HAROLD

44.126   BH   1933 British Honduras faces forward. *Can-W I Mag* 22(8), July: 235-236.
            [66]   [NYP]

KLAASESZ, J.

44.127   SR   1952 The Surinam Development Fund and the small man. *Car Commn Mon
            Inf B* 5(11), June: 303.   [66]   [COL]

KLEIN, W. C.

44.128   GG   1940 Economische binnenland-penitratie in de vier Guyana's [Penetra-
            tion into the interior regions of the four Guianas for economic rea-
            sons]. *W I G* 22:1-11.   [66]   [COL]

KLUVERS, B. J.

44.129   SR   1921/ Het Suriname vraagstuk [The problem of Surinam]. *W I G* 3:521-543.
            22   [COL]

KNOWLES, WILLIAM H.

66.081   JM   1956 Social consequences of economic change in Jamaica.

KOOL, R.

44.130   NC   1955/ Economische samenwerking binnen het Koninkrijk nieuwe stijl [Eco-
            56   nomic cooperation within the Kingdom in a new style].   *W I G* 36:
            32-45.   [COL]

44.131   SR   1956 Paramaribo; het economische leven van een stad in een tropisch
            land [Paramaribo; economic life of a town in a tropical land]. *Tijdschr
            Econ Social Geogr* 47(11), Nov.: 276-288.   [36,66]   [AGS]

KOVROV, IU.

44.132   BG   1954 Proizvol angliiskikh kolonizatorov v Britanskoi Gviane [The tyranny
            of English colonialists in British Guiana]. *Vopr Ekon* 4:98-103.
            [37]   [COL]

KRUIJER, GERARDUS JOHANNES

46.128   NW   1953 Notities over de bestaansmiddelen op de buureilanden van St. Maar-
            ten, St. Eustatius en Saba [Notes on the subsistence possibilities
            on the neighboring islands St. Maarten, St. Eustatius, and Saba.

44.133   NW   1953 Notities over de niet-agrarische bestaansmiddelen [Notes on non-
            agrarian means of subsistence]. *In* KRUIJER, G. J.; VEENENBOS,
            J.S. & WESTERMANN, J.H., comps. BOVENWINDENRAPPORT. Amster-
            dam, Voorlichtingsinstituut voor het Welvaartsplan Nederlandse An-
            tillen, 20p.

KUNDU, A.

44.134   BG   1963 The economy of British Guiana: 1960-1975. *Social Econ Stud* 12(3),
                      Sept.: 307-380.   [*RIS*]

44.135   BG   1963 Inter-industry table for the economy of British Guiana, 1959, and na-
                      tional accounts, 1957-60.   *Social Econ Stud* 12(1), Mar.: suppl.
                      (43p.)   [52]   [*RIS*]

LAMBERT, B.

44.136   SR   1952 Suriname (Guyane Néerlandaise) [Surinam (Dutch Guiana)]. *Civilisa-
                      tions* 2(1): 125-130.   [*COL*]

LAMBIE, W. D. & PICKTHALL, C. M.

44.137   BC   1937 REPORT ON ECONOMIC AND COMMERCIAL CONDITIONS IN THE BRITISH
                      WEST INDIES, BRITISH GUIANA, BRITISH HONDURAS AND BERMUDA. Lon-
                      don, H.M.S.O., 126p. ([Reports of the] Dept. of Overseas Trade, no.
                      688.)   [*COL*]

LANGEMEYER, F. S.

51.081   SM   1922/ Het zoutbedrijf op St. Martin [The salt industry on St. Martin].
                23

LEE, ULRIC

33.021   TR   1959 REPORT TO THE HONOURABLE THE PREMIER BY THE HONOURABLE ULRIC
                      LEE ON THE REORGANISATION OF THE PUBLIC SERVICE.

LEWIS, W. ARTHUR

44.138   JM   1944 An economic plan for Jamaica. *Agenda* 3(4), Nov.: 154-163. [66] [*AGS*]
32.121   JM   1961 Education and economic development.
44.139   BC   1962 Competition and regulation in the West Indies. *In* HOOVER, CAL-
                      VIN, B., ed. ECONOMIC SYSTEMS OF THE COMMONWEALTH. Durham,
                      N.C., Duke University Press, p.501-518.   [*NYP*]
32.122   JM   1964 Secondary education and economic structure.

LIER, RUDOLF A. J. van

66.092   SR   1954 Le plan de développement de Surinam [The development plan for
                      Surinam] [by] R.A.L. [sic] van Lier.

LOVEJOY, ROBERT M.

44.140   JM   1963 The burden of Jamaican taxation, 1958. *Social Econ Stud* 12(4),
                      Dec.: 442-458.   [37]   [*RIS*]

LOWENTHAL, DAVID

2.142   FG   1960 French Guiana: myths and realities.

MacKNIGHT, JESSE M.

44.141   SR   1957 ECONOMIC DEVELOPMENTS IN SURINAM, 1956. Washington, U.S. Govt.
                      Print. Off., 8p. (World Trade Information Service, Economic reports,
                      pt. 1, no. 57-78.)   [66]   [*AGS*]

MADDEN, F.

66.096   BC   1954 Social and economic conditions of the British West Indies.

MAJOR, T. GRANT

44.142   GC   1950 Effects of devaluation becoming apparent in eastern Caribbean. *Car
                      Commn Mon Inf B* 3(9), Apr.: 320-321.   [*COL*]

MALEFIJT, ANNEMARIE de WAAL
15.030   SR   1963 Het sociaal-economisch vermogen van de Javanen in Suriname [The socio-economic potential of the Javanese in Surinam].

MANNERS, ROBERT A.
44.143   BC   1965 Remittances and the unit of analysis in anthropological research. *Sw J Anthrop* 21(3), Autumn: 179-195.   [67]   [*RIS*]

MARIE-JOSEPH, E.
44.144   FC   1962 Réalités économiques [Economic facts]. *Esprit* new ser., 30(305), Apr.: 516-585.   [66]   [*NYP*]

MARRYSHOW, JULIAN A.
44.145   BC   1954 The Regional Economic Committee of the British West Indies, British Guiana and British Honduras. *Car Commn Mon Inf B* 7(1), Jan.: 131-132, 144.   [66]   [*COL*]

MARSHALL, IONE
44.146   BH   1962 The national accounts of British Honduras. *Social Econ Stud* 11(2), Mar.: 99-127.   [*RIS*]

MAZIN, E.
37.259   FA   1921 Les Antilles Francaises: étude juridique et économique [The French Antilles: a judicial and economic study].

MEEHAN, M. J.
44.147   GG   1927 Economic development of the Guianas. *Commerce Reports* 4(42), Oct. 17: 136-137.   [66]   [*AGS*]

MEISLER, STANLEY
50.090   BG/   1964 Meddling in Latin America; dubious role of AFL-CIO.
         BH

MENKMAN, W. R.
44.148   SR   1919 De handelsbetekenis van onze West [The commerical importance of our West]. (i.e. colonies in the West.) *WIG* 1(1): 56-70.   [*COL*]
52.060   CU   1923/ Scheepvaart beweging en scheepvaart wetgeving op Curacao [Shipping movement and navigation laws in Curacao].
               24
44.149   SR   1928/ Eenige opmerkingen aan de hand van de Surinaamsche begrooting voor 1929 [Some remarks about the budget of Surinam for the year 1929]. *WIG* 10:375-381.   [37]   [*COL*]
               29
44.150   CU   1929/ De havenbeweging van het eiland Curacao [The volume of trade of the island Curacao]. *WIG* 11:554-558.   [51]   [*COL*]
               30
37.262   NC   1929/ Moederlandsche verantwoordelijkheid en Westindische autonomie [The responsibility of the mother country and the autonomy of West India].
               30
37.263   CU   1930/ Curacaosche toestanden [Curacao's conditions].
               31
44.151   CU   1931/ Enkele voorloopige opmerkingen aangaande de voorloopige Curacaosche begrooting voor 1936 [Some preliminary remarks about the tentative budget of Curacao for the year 1936]. *WIG* 13:72-79. [66]   [*COL*]
               32
37.264   SR   1931/ Nederland en Suriname [The Netherlands and Surinam].
               32

37.265   SR   1931/ Nederland en Suriname, een nabetrachting [The Netherlands and
            32   Surinam, in retrospect].

66.098   SE   1932/ Sint Eustatius' gouden tijd [The golden age of Saint Eustatius].
            33

44.152   CU   1933/ De voorloopige Curacaosche begrooting voor 1934 [The preliminary
            34   budget for Curacao for the year 1934]. *W I G* 15:49-68.   [*COL*]

44.153   NA   1934 De economische beteekenis der Nederlandsche Antillen, voorheen
                  en thans [The economic importance of the Dutch Antilles, in the
                  past and present]. *Tijdschr Econ Geogr* 25(8), Aug. 15:245-254.   [5]
                                                                              [*AGS*]

44.154   CU   1947 Curacaosche gegevens op economisch gebied [Curacao data about
                  economic conditions. *W I G* 28:335-339;
                  1948 29:339-341.   [51]   [*COL*]

44.155   NA   1948 De economische ontwikkeling der Boven- en Benedenwindse Eiland-
                  en [The economic development of the Windward and Leeward Islands].
                  Tijdschr Ned Aar Genoot 2d ser., 65(4-5), July-Sept.: 669-682.   [*AGS*]

7.045   SR   1949 Het Surinaamse verslag [The Surinam report].   [52,66]

MERRILL, GORDON CLARK
19.031   BC   1961 The survival of the past in the West Indies.

MITCHELL, Sir HAROLD
44.156   BC   1957 Finance and Federation. *W I Rev* new ser., 2(10), Oct.: 27, 29.   [38]
                                                                              [*NYP*]
37.270   GC   1963 Europe in the Caribbean: the policies of Great Britain, France
                  and the Netherlands towards their West Indian territories in the
                  twentieth century.

MORGAN, D. J.
44.157   JM   1957 Finance and taxation in Jamaica.   *Econ J* 67(266), June: 347-353.
                  [66]   [*COL*]

MOSER, C. A.
44.158   JM   1957 The measurement of levels of living with special reference to
                  Jamaica. London, H.M.S.O. 106p. (Colonial research studies no.
                  24.)   [9,28,30,32,33,66,67]   [*NYP*]

MULDER, G. C. A.
44.159   SR   1960/ Suriname's economische stilstand in de vorige eeuw (Surinam's eco-
            61   nomic stagnation during the previous century. *N W I G* 40:73-76.
                  [5]   [*COL*]

MULLINGS, LLEWELLYN MAXIMILLIAN
44.160   JM   1964 An analysis of the economic implications of political independ-
                  ence for Jamaica.   Ph.D. dissertation, Clark University, 314p.
                  [37,38]

NADIR, HENRI ROUSSEAU
44.161   FA   1956 Les Antilles existent [The Antilles do exist]. *Rev Social* new ser.,
                  98, June: 85-102.   [37]

NEWMAN, PETER KENNETH
44.162   BG   1960 The economic future of British Guiana. *Social Econ Stud* 9(3): 263-
                  296.   [66]   [*RIS*]

44.163   BG   1961   Epilogue on British Guiana [reply to comments on his article in *So-cial Econ Stud* 9(3)]. *Social Econ Stud* 10(1), Mar.: 35-41. [66] [*RIS*]

16.026   BG   1962   Racial tension in British Guiana.

NORDLOHNE, EDGAR

44.164   CU   1949   Curacao's economisch perspectief [The economic perspective of Curacao]. *Tijdschr Econ Social Geogr* 40(7), July: 139-144.   [*AGS*]

NUMILE, L. G.

44.165   FG   1930   La Guyane mal exploitée [Underdeveloped Guiana]. *J Econ* 89, Nov. 15: 318-323.   [*COL*]

OCHSE, J. J.

44.166   NC   1958   Economic factors in the Netherlands Antilles and Surinam. *In* WILGUS, A. CURTIS, ed. THE CARIBBEAN: BRITISH, DUTCH, FRENCH, UNITED STATES [papers delivered at the Eighth Conference on the Caribbean held at the University of Florida, Dec. 5-7, 1957]. Gainesville, University of Florida Press, p.73-85. (Publications of the School of Inter-American Studies, ser. 1, v. 88.)   [*RIS*]

O'LOUGHLIN, CARLEEN

46.158   GC   1957   The measurement and significance of agricultural sector statistics in national accounting.

44.167   AT   1959   The economy of Antigua. *Social Econ Stud* 8(3), Sept.: 229-264. [*RIS*]

44.168   BG   1959   The economy of British Guiana, 1952-56: a national accounts study. *Social Econ Stud* 8(1), Mar. (104p.)   [*RIS*]

44.169   MS   1959   The economy of Montserrat: a national accounts study. *Social Econ Stud* 8(2), June: 147-178.   [*RIS*]

44.170   NKA   1959   The economy of St. Kitts-Nevis-Anguilla. *Social Econ Stud* 8(4), Dec.: 377-402.   [*RIS*]

44.171   AT   1961   Problems in the economic development of Antigua. *Social Econ Stud* 10(3), Sept.: 237-277.   [*RIS*]

44.172   LW/ WW   1962   Economic problems of the smaller West Indies islands. *Social Econ Stud* 11(1), Mar.: 44-56.   [*RIS*]

44.173   BV   1962   A survey of economic potential, fiscal structure and capital requirements of the British Virgin Islands. *Social Econ Stud* 11(3), Sept.: suppl.: 1-60.   [*RIS*]

44.174   LW/ WW   1963/ 64   Economic problems of the Leeward and Windward Islands. *Social Scient* 1:3-4,8. [37, 38]

44.175   JM   1963   Long-term growth of the economy of Jamaica. *Social Econ Stud* 12 (3), Sept.: 246-282.   [*RIS*]

O'LOUGHLIN, CARLEEN & BEST, L.

44.176   BC   1960   Economic structure in the West Indies. *In* CUMPER, G.E., ed. THE ECONOMY OF THE WEST INDIES. Kingston, Institute of Social and Economic Research, University College of the West Indies, p.95-125. [*RIS*]

O'NEALE, H. W.

44.177   SL   1964   The economy of St. Lucia. *Social Econ Stud* 13(4), Dec.: p.440-470. [*RIS*]

OSGOOD, THEODORE K.

44.178   SR   1963 Surinam seeks foreign investment to speed industrial development.
                Int Com 69(16), Apr. 22: 3-4.   [*NYP*]

OUDSCHANS DENTZ, FRED

44.179   SR   1927 Eenige beschouwingen over Suriname [Some observations about Sur-
                inam]. *Tijdschr Econ Geogr* 18(4), Apr. 15: 146-150; 18(6), June 15:
                214-216; 18(9), Sept. 15: 332-334.   [*AGS*]

44.180   SR   1937 Suriname in 1936. *Tijdschr Econ Geogr* 28(7-8), July 15-Aug. 15:
                189-191.   [*AGS*]

44.181   SR   1941 Een blik op den toestand van Suriname bij den overgang van het En-
                gelsche bestuur op dat der Bataafsche Republiek in 1802 [The con-
                ditions in Surinam at the time of the change from English rule to
                that of the Batavian Republic]. *WIG* 23:379-383. [5,37]   [*COL*]

OWEN, G. H.

31.059   JM   1963 Vocational guidance and education for adolescents.

PAPINEAU, O. C.

44.182   TR   1953 An economic survey of Trinidad and Tobago at the end of 1952. *J
                Agric Soc Trin Tob* 53(1), Mar.: 21-30.   [*AMN*]

PARRY, JOHN HORACE

46.165   JM   1955 Plantation and provision ground: an historical sketch of the intro-
                duction of food crops into Jamaica.

PECK, H. AUSTIN

44.183   JM   1958 Economic planning in Jamaica: a critique. *Social Econ Stud* 7(4),
                Dec.: 141-169.   [7,66]   [*RIS*]

PERCIVAL, D. A. & D'ANDRADE, W. P.

44.184   BG   [n.d.] THE NATIONAL ECONOMIC ACCOUNTS OF BRITISH GUIANA, 1948-1951.
                Georgetown, Daily Chronicle, 111p.   [*COL*]

PETER, JACQUES

44.185   FC   1964 Les effets multiplicateurs des revenus aux Antilles Francaises [The
                multiplier effects of revenues in the French West Indies]. *Cah Cent
                Etud Reg* 8, Dec. (45p.)   [*RIS*]

PLENEL, ALAIN

37.317   FA   1963 Libération nationale et assimilation à la Martinique et à la Guade-
                loupe [National liberation and (political) assimilation in Martinique
                and Guadeloupe].

POLLARD, A. E. & MASSIE-BLOMFIELD, H.

44.186   BH   1935 ECONOMIC CONDITIONS IN THE BRITISH WEST INDIES, BRITISH GUIANA,
                BRITISH HONDURAS AND BERMUDA, 1933-34. London, H.M.S.O., 124p.
                ([Reports of the] Dept. of Overseas Trade, no. 594.)   [*COL*]

POOLE, BERNARD L.

44.187   BC   1958 Economic trends in the British West Indies. *In* WILGUS, A. CURTIS,
                ed. THE CARIBBEAN: BRITISH, DUTCH, FRENCH, UNITED STATES [papers

delivered at the Eighth Conference on the Caribbean held at the University of Florida, Dec. 5-7, 1957]. Gainesville, University of Florida Press, p.11-26. (Publications of the School of Inter-American Studies, ser. 1, v. 8.) [*RIS*]

PRAKKEN, A. B. J.
44.188   CU   1923/ Een en ander over den financieelen en economischen toestand der
           24 kolonie Curacao [A few remarks about the financial and economic conditions in the colony Curacao]. *WIG* 5:21-34. [*COL*]

PREIJ, L. C.
44.189   SR   1933/ De economische toestand van Suriname [The economic conditions in
           34 Surinam] by L.C. Prey. *W I G* 15:227-240. [*COL*]

PREST, A. R.
44.190   BC   1957 A FISCAL SURVEY OF THE BRITISH CARIBBEAN. London, H.M.S.O., 136p. (Colonial research studies no. 23.) [37] [*COL*]
44.191   BC   1960 Public finance. *In* CUMPER, G.E., ed. THE ECONOMY OF THE WEST INDIES. Kingston, Institute of Social and Economic Research, University College of the West Indies, p.181-222. [37] [*RIS*]

PYTTERSEN, TJ.
44.192   SR   1919/ De waarde van Suriname [The value of Surinam]. *W I G* 1(2): 365-
           20 379. [*COL*]
44.193   SR   1928/ Kunnen wij dat zelf niet? [Can't we do that ourselves?] *W I G* 10:
           31 337-354 (1928/29); 11:142-158 (1929/31). [*COL*]

RAMPERSAD, FRANK B.
44.194   TR   1963 Growth and structural change in the economy of Trinidad and Tobago 1951-1961. *In* RESEARCH PAPERS [OF THE] CENTRAL STATISTICAL OFFICE [OF] TRINIDAD AND TOBAGO, NO. 1. Port of Spain, Central Statistical Office, p. 82-176. [*RIS*]

RANCE, Sir HUBERT ELVIN
44.195   TR   1953 Trinidad report. *Car Commn Mon Inf B* 7(3), Oct.: 57-58.[37,66] [*COL*]

REID, J. M.
44.196   BG   1920 BRITISH GUIANA COMMERCIAL HANDBOOK. Georgetown, Argosy Co., 87p. [*AGS*]

RENSELAAR, H. C. van
11.023   SR   1963 Het sociaal-economisch vermogen van de Creolen in Suriname [The socio-economic potential of the Creoles in Surinam].

REYNE, A.
44.197   SR   1920/ Suriname's economische toekomst [Surinam's economic future]. *WIG*
           21 2:467-475. [*COL*]

RICHARDSON, J. HENRY
33.038   BG   1955 REPORT ON SOCIAL SECURITY IN BRITISH GUIANA, APRIL, 1954.
33.039   BC   1956 Social security problems with special reference to the British West Indies.

RIESGO, RAYMOND R.

44.198   JM   1958 ECONOMIC DEVELOPMENTS IN JAMAICA 1957. Washington, U.S. Govt. Print. Off., 4p. (World Trade Information Service. Economic reports pt. 1, no. 58-39.)   [66]   [*AGS*]

RIPPY, J. FRED

44.199   TR   1954 Trinidad and Ceylon: two profitable British crown colonies. *Inter-Amer Econ Aff* 8(2), Autumn: 84-93.   [*COL*]

ROBERTS, WALTER ADOLPHE

5.184   JM   1952 SIR HENRY MORGAN, BUCCANEER AND GOVERNOR. REV. ED. Kingston, Pioneer Press, 165p.   [37,44]

ROBINSON, ARTHUR N. R.

44.200   TR   1965 BUDGET SPEECH 1965. [Port of Spain?] Govt. Printer, 40p.   [*RIS*]

ROSE, H.

44.201   BC   1961 Economic prospects for the West Indies. *Commonw Dev* 7(2), Jan.-Feb.: 13-16.   [66]   [*NYP*]

ROTTENBERG, SIMON

44.202   AT   1951 The economy of Antigua. *Car Commn Mon Inf B* 4(12), July: 851-855.   [*AGS*]

44.203   ST/ TT   1953 A note on economic policy in Tortola. *Car Q* 3(2), Sept.: 110-115. [46]   [*RIS*]

RUBIN, VERA

20.015   TR   1961 Family aspirations and attitudes of Trinidad youth.

RUSCOE, GORDON C.

32.170   JM   1963 DYSFUNCTIONALITY IN JAMAICAN EDUCATION.

ST. JOHNSTON, Sir REGINALD

44.204   LW   1933 The situation in the Leeward Islands. *Can-W I Mag* 22(4), Mar.: 103-104.   [*NYP*]

44.205   LW   1935 The situation in the Leeward Islands. *Can-W I Mag* 24(5), Apr.: 7-8,28.   [66]   [*NYP*]

SAMSON, PH. A.

44.206   NC   1940 Amendeering van begrootingsontwerpen [Amendments of preliminary budgets]. *W I G* 22:53-56.   [*COL*]

SAUL, SAMUEL BERRICK

44.207   BC   1957 The economic significance of "constructive imperialism." *J Econ Hist* 17(2), June: 173-192.   [5,37]   [*RIS*]

44.208   BC   1958 The British West Indies in depression. *Inter-Amer Econ Aff* 12(3), Winter: 3-25.   [37,46]   [*RIS*]

SCOTT, WINTHROP R.

44.209   GG   1943 War economy of the Guianas. *For Com Wkly* 11(3), Apr. 17: 5-9. [37]   [*AGS*]

SEEL, G. F.

44.210   BC   [1953?] FINANCIAL ASPECTS OF FEDERATION OF THE BRITISH WEST INDIAN TER-
RITORIES. [Bridgetown?] Barbados, Advocate Co., 38p.

SEERS, DUDLEY

38.110   BC   1957 Federation of the British West Indies: the economic and financial
aspects.

44.211   BC   1962 Economic programming in a country newly independent. *Social Econ
Stud* 11(1), Mar.: 34-43. [66]   [*RIS*]

SERTIMA, J. van

44.212   BG   1912 The Colony's financial position. *Timehri* 3d ser., 2(19A), July: 86-
93.   [*AMN*]

SHAW, EARL BENNETT

44.213   SJ   1933 The balanced economy of St. John Island. *Econ Geogr* 9(2), Apr.:
160-166.   [*AGS*]

SHELTON, H. S.

50.111   JM   1939 Economic conditions in Jamaica.

SHENFIELD, A. A.

44.214   BC   1955 Economic outlook—an upward trend. *New Commonw* Br Car Suppl
30(10), Nov. 14: ix-xi.   [*AGS*]

44.215   BC   1963 The economic potential of the "little eight." *Chron W I Comm* 78
(1390), Nov.: 592-593.   [*NYP*]

SHERE, LOUIS

44.216   GC   1952 SUGAR TAXATION IN THE CARIBBEAN AND CENTRAL AMERICAN COUNTRIES.
Washington [D.C.] Pan American Union, 82p. [37,58]   [*NYP*]

SHERMAN, GERTRUDE

44.217   JM   1957 A buoyant economy. *Can-W I Mag* 47(4), Apr.: 11-12.   [*NYP*]

SIFFLEET, NORA M.

44.218   BC   1953 The national income and the national accounts of Barbados; Antigua; St. Christopher, Nevis & Anguilla; Dominica; St. Lucia; St.
Vincent and Grenada. *Social Econ Stud* 1(3), July: 5-139.   [*RIS*]

SIMONS, A. J.

44.219   SR   1933/ Het verval van Suriname [The decline of Surinam]. *W I G* 15:299-308.
34   [*COL*]

SLOTHOUWER, L.

46.208   NW   1930/ Nog eens de Bovenwindsche Eilanden [The Windwards Islands once
31 again].

SMITH, E. P.

44.220   TR   1955 Trinidad...oil-agriculture-industry. *New Commonw* Br Car Suppl 30
(10), Nov. 14: v-vi. [66]   [*AGS*]

SMITH, M.G.

9.037   JM   1957 Family patterns in rural Jamaica.

20.018   JM   1960   Education and occupational choice in rural Jamaica.
8.060   GR   1965   Structure and crisis in Grenada, 1950-1954.

SMITH, RAYMOND THOMAS
8.061   BG   1964   Ethnic difference and peasant economy in British Guiana.

SPECKMANN, JOHAN DIRK
12.033   SR   1963   De positie van de Hindostaanse bevolkingsgroep in de sociale en
                        ekonomische struktuur van Suriname [The position of the Hindustani
                        population group in the social and economic structure of Surinam].

SPITZ, GEORGES
37.388   MT   1955   La Martinique et ses institutions depuis 1948 [Martinique and its
                        administration since 1948].

SPOON, W.
51.133   SR   1943   Surinaamsch hout voor fineer en triplex [Surinam lumber for veneer
                        and triplex.

SPRINGER, HUGH W.
38.115   BC   1961   The West Indies emergent: problems and prospects.

STAAL, G. J.
44.221   SR   1921/ Suriname's behoeften [Surinam's needs]. *W I G* 3:402-412, 497-506
                  23   (1921/22); 4:91-98 (1922/23).   [*COL*]

STARK, HARRY N.
44.222   FA   1943   Martinique and France's other West Indian islands. *For Com Wkly*
                        10(13), Mar. 27: 3-7, 34.   [*AGS*]
44.223   NA   1943   Peace and war in the Netherlands West Indies. *For Com Wkly* 10(9),
                        Feb. 27: 6-13,39.   [*AGS*]

STARKEY, OTIS P.
44.224   BB   1958   Increasing crops and the standard of living—a West Indian example.
                        Proc Ind Acad Sci 68:273-276.   [46]   [*COL*]

STRAW, K. H.
44.225   BB   1953   Some preliminary results of a survey of income and consumption
                        patterns in a sample of households in Barbados. *Social Econ Stud*
                        1(4), Aug.: 5-40.   [*COL*]
30.051   BB   1954   Household budgets and nutritional analysis of food consumption in
                        Barbados.

STRONG, M. S.
44.226   JM   1959   Jamaica. *Can-W I Mag* 49(1), Jan.: 16-17.   [*NYP*]

STRUMPEL, BURKHARD
44.227   BH   1965   Consumption aspirations: incentives for economic change.   *Social
                        Econ Stud* 14(2), June: 183-193.   [20]   [*RIS*]

TAYLOR, LeROY

44.228   JM   1964 CONSUMER'S EXPENDITURE IN JAMAICA. Mona, Institute of Social and
Economic Research, University of the West Indies, 148p.   [*RIS*]

TERVOOREN, E. P. M.

66.149   SR   1954/ De financiering van het Tienjarenplan en de Nederlandse bijstand
55   [The financing of the Ten Year Plan of Development and the contribution of the Netherlands].

THOMAS, C. Y.

44.229   BC   1964 Short-term improvements in Caribbean economic planning. *Car Q* 10
(4), Dec.: 55-66.   [66]   [*RIS*]

THOMAS, R. D.

44.230   JM   1963 Local government financing in Jamaica, 1944-59. *Social Econ Stud*
12(2), June: 141-159.   [37]   [*RIS*]

THOMPSON, RALPH

44.231   VI   1935 The promise of the Virgin Islands. *Curr Hist* 41(6), Mar.: 681-686.
[66]   [*COL*]

THORNE, ALFRED P.

44.232   JM   1955 Size, structure and growth of the economy of Jamaica. *Social Econ
Stud* 4(4), Dec.: suppl. (112p.)   [*RIS*]

44.233   JM   1956 Some general comments on the Hicks Report. *In* SYMPOSIUM ON THE
HICKS REPORT. *Social Econ Stud* 5(1), Mar.: 39-47. [37,66]   [*RIS*]

44.234   JM   1960 Revisions, and suggestions for deflating the gross product estimates for Jamaican-type economies. *Social Econ Stud* 9(1), Mar.:
41-58.   [*RIS*]

44.235   BG   1961 British Guiana's development programme: analysis of the Berrill report and Newman article [in *Social Econ Stud* 9(3)]. *Social Econ
Stud* 10(1), Mar.: 6-17.   [66]   [*RIS*]

TOOKE, CHARLES W.

44.236   UV   1900 The Danish colonial fiscal system in the West Indies. *In* ESSAYS
IN COLONIAL FINANCE. *Publs Am Econ Ass* 1(3): 144-167. [5,37]

TRAA, A. van

44.237   SR   1933/ De economische toestand van Suriname [The economic conditions
34   in Surinam]. *W I G* 15:338-343.   [*COL*]

TSCHEBOTAREFF, VALENTINE P.

44.238   BC   1941 New problems for the British West Indies. *Inter-Amer Q* 3(3), July:
27-37.   [*AGS*]

VANDENBOSCH, AMRY

37.403   AR/   1931 Dutch problems in the West Indies.
CU

VERZIJL, J. H. W.

44.239   CU   1939 Amendeering van begrootingsontwerpen [The amendments of budget
plans]. *W I G* 21:275-289.   [*COL*]

VIGNON, ROBERT

44.240   FG   1954 French Guiana: looking ahead. *Car Commn Mon Inf B* 7(11), June:
                        251,254.   [66]   [*COL*]

WAARD, J. de

44.241   SR   1954/ De economische bepalingen van het Statuut [The economic provi-
             55   sions of the Constitution]. *Vox Guy* 1(4-5), Nov.-Jan.: 53-60.   [37]

WEIJTINGH, C. R.

44.242   SR/   1940 Eenige aanvullingen op de Encyclopaedie van West-Indië: De be-
           CU   grootingen van Suriname en Curacao [Some additions to the Ency-
                         clopedia of the West Indies: The budgets of Surinam and Curacao].
                         W I G 22:245-249.   [*COL*]

44.243   SR   1940 Eenige aanvullingen op de Encyclopaedie van West-Indië: De be-
                        lastingen in Suriname [Some additions to the Encyclopedia of the
                        West Indies: The taxes in Surinam]. *W I G* 22:337-349; 353-370.
                        [37]   [*COL*]

44.244   CU   1940 Eenige aanvullingen op de Encyclopaedie van West-Indië: De finan-
                        cien van Curacao [Some additions to the Encyclopedia of the West
                        Indies: the finances of Curacao]. *W I G* 22:141-146.   [*COL*]

44.245   SR   1940 Eenige aanvullingen op de Encyclopaedie van West-Indië: De finan-
                        cien van Suriname [Some additions to the Encyclopedia of the West
                        Indies: The finances of Surinam]. *W I G* 22:20-26.   [*COL*]

44.246   CU   1941 Eenige aanvullingen op de Encyclopaedie van West-Indië: De be-
                        lastingen in Curacao [Some additions to the Encyclopedia of the
                        West Indies: The taxes in Curacao]. *W I G* 23:129-147; 177-185; 225-
                        233.   [37]   [*COL*]

WELLE, M.

44.247   SR   1928/ De Surinaamsche begrooting voor 1929 in de Tweede Kamer [The
             29   Surinam budget for 1929 in the "House of Representatives"]. *W I G*
                    10:495-506.   [37]   [*COL*]

WENGEN, G. D. van

15.041   SR   1963 Tajoeb, een prestige-feest bij de Javanen in Suriname [Tajub, a
                        prestige festival among the Javanese of Surinam].

WHITEHEAD, HENRY S.

37.422   UV   1926 The grievance of the Virgin Islands.

WILGUS, A. CURTIS, ed.

44.248   GC   1954 THE CARIBBEAN: ITS ECONOMY [papers delivered at the Fourth An-
                        nual Conference on the Caribbean held at the University of Florida,
                        Dec. 3-5, 1953]. Gainesville, University of Florida Press, 286p.
                        (Publications of the School of Inter-American studies, ser. 1, v. 4.)
                                                                                    [*RIS*]

WILLIAMS, ERIC EUSTACE

44.249   GC   1944 The economic development of the Caribbean up to the present. *In*
                        FRAZIER, E.F. & WILLIAMS, E., eds. THE ECONOMIC FUTURE OF
                        THE CARIBBEAN. Washington, D.C., Howard University Press, p.19-24.

6.079   BC   1944 CAPITALISM AND SLAVERY.

58.130 GC 1951 The Caribbean bookshelf: the sugar economy of the Caribbean.

44.250 TR 1955 ECONOMIC PROBLEMS OF TRINIDAD AND TOBAGO. Port of Spain, College Press for Teachers, Economic and Cultural Association, 35p. (Public affairs pamphlets no. 1.)   [66]   [*RIS*]

WILLIAMS, GERTRUDE
44.251 BC 1953 THE ECONOMICS OF EVERYDAY LIFE IN THE WEST INDIES. [Mona] Extra-Mural Dept., University College of the West Indies, 52p. (Caribbean affairs).   [7,50]   [*RIS*]

WILLOCK, G. W.
44.252 BG 1955 British Guiana... economic recovery after political misadventure. *New Commonw* Br Car Suppl 30(11), Nov. 28: x-xi. [66]   [*AGS*]

WISEMAN, H. V.
38.129 BC 1948 THE WEST INDIES, TOWARDS A NEW DOMINION?

WORSWICK, G. D. N.
44.253 JM 1956 Financing development. *In* SYMPOSIUM ON THE HICKS REPORT. *Social Econ Stud* 5(1), Mar.: 48-53.   [37,66]   [*RIS*]

WOUW, J. J. van
46.242 SR 1949 Het departement van landbouw-economische zaken in Suriname in 1945.[The department of agricultural-economic affairs in Surinam in 1945].

WRIGHT, KARL
44.254 JM 1963/ Paper written for Economics Society's Belle-vue Seminar: Some
        64 problems of capital formation in an under developed country with special reference to foreign capital. *Social Scient* 2:37-40.   [*RIS*]

Chapter 45

PLANTATION SYSTEMS

ADAMS, RICHARD N.

45.001   GC   1959 On the relations between plantation and "Creole cultures." *In* RUBIN, VERA, ed. PLANTATION SYSTEMS OF THE NEW WORLD. Washington, D.C., Research Institute for the Study of Man and Pan American Union, p.73-82. (Social science monographs, 7.)   [67]
   [*RIS*]

AIKEN, JAMES

45.002   BG   1917 A voice from the past. *Timehri* 3d ser., 4(21), June: 131-142.   [5]
   [*AMN*]

BENNETT, J. HARRY, Jr.

45.003   JM   1964 Cary Helyar, merchant and planter of seventeenth-century Jamaica. *Wm Mary Q* 21(1), Jan.: 53-76.   [5]   [*COL*]

BIJLSMA, R.

45.004   SR   1921/ Gouverneur Temmings plantage Berg en Daal bij den Parnassusberg
            22 in Suriname [Governor Temmings' plantation "Berg en Daal" near the Parnassus Mountain in Surinam]. *W I G* 3:31-34. [5]   [*COL*]

43.015   SR   1921/ Surinaamsche plantage-inventarissen van het tijdperk 1713-1742
            22 [Surinam plantation inventories of the years 1713-1742].

45.005   SR   1922/ Aanwijzingen voor plantage-ondernemingen in Surinam in 1735 [Di-
            23 rectives for plantations in Surinam in the year 1735]. *W I G* 4:53-58.
               [5]   [*COL*]

BLANCHARD, RAE

45.006   BB   1942 Richard Steele's West Indian plantation. *Mod Philol* 39(3), Feb.: 281-285. [5]   [*COL*]

BLAUT, JAMES M.

43.018   GC   1959 The ecology of tropical farming systems.

BULLEN, JEAN & LIVINGSTONE, HELEN F.

32.036   BB   1949 Of the state and advancement of the College.

597

CRUICKSHANK, J. GRAHAM
45.007   BG   1930 The wreckage of an industry. *W I Comm Circ* 45(820), Mar. 6: 87-88.
                [5]   [*NYP*]

CUMPER, GEORGE E.
58.028   JM   1954 A modern Jamaican sugar estate.

CUNDALL, FRANK
45.008   JM   1927 An historic Jamaica estate. *W I Comm Circ* 42(755), Sept. 8: 369-
                370; 42(756), Sept. 22: 389-390; 42(757), Oct. 6: 408-409; 42(758),
                Oct. 20: 428; 42(759), Nov. 3: 448; 42(760), Nov. 17: 468-469.   [5]
                                                                                 [*NYP*]

DEBIEN, GABRIEL
30.009   FC   1964 La nourriture des esclaves sur les plantations des Antilles Fran-
                caises aux XVIIè et XVIIIè siècles [The diet of slaves on the
                plantations of the French Antilles in the 17th and 18th centuries].

DRIMMELEN, C. van
45.009   SR   1923/ Een uitweg voor verzinkend Suriname [A way out for sinking
                24 Suriname]. *W I G* 5:151-167.   [66]   [*COL*]

FARLEY, RAWLE
16.010   BG   1955 The substance and the shadow—a study of the relations between
                white planters and free coloured in a slave society in British
                Guiana.

FURNESS, ALAN
5.052   JM   1962 The Jamaican coffee boom and John Mackeson.

GERLING, WALTER
58.046   JM   1954 Die Plantagenwirtschaft des Rohrzuckers auf den Grossen
                Antillen: ein Beitrag zur Agrargeographie der Tropen [The
                plantation economy of sugarcane in the Greater Antilles:
                contribution to agrarian geography in the tropics].

GIGLIOLI, GEORGE
28.221   BG   1956 Medical services on the sugar estates of British Guiana.
30.028   BG   1958 An outline of the nutritional situation on the sugar estates of
                British Guiana in respect to the eradication of malaria: recent
                developments in the production of green vegetables and fruit by
                individual units.

GREAVES, IDA C.
45.010   JM   1959 Plantations in world economy. *In* RUBIN, VERA, ed. Plantation
                systems of the New World. Washington, D.C., Research Institute
                for the Study of Man and Pan American Union, p.13-25. (Social
                Science monographs, 7.)   [46]   [*RIS*]

HALL, DOUGLAS GORDON
45.011   BC   1954 The social and economic background to sugar in slave days (with
                special reference to Jamaica). *Car Hist Rev* 3-4, Dec.: 149-169. [5]
                                                                                 [*RIS*]

HANDLER, JEROME S.

50.057   BB   1965 Some aspects of work organization on sugar plantations in Barbados.

HARES, L. G.

52.036   BG   1935 A railway enterprise in Demerara.

HARTLEY, HAZEL MORSE

46.088   BB   1949 Of the produce of the plantations.

JAYAWARDENA, CHANDRA

9.020   BG   1960 Marital stability in two Guianese sugar estate communities.
9.021   BG   1962 Family organisation in plantations in British Guiana.

KALFF, S.

7.035   SR   1929/Franschen in Suriname [French people in Surinam].
       30

KLERK, CORNELIS JOHANNES MARIA de

50.074   SR   1953 DE IMMIGRATIE DER HINDOESTANEN IN SURINAME [THE IMMIGRATION OF HINDUS TO SURINAM].

KLINGBERG, FRANK J., ed.

45.012   BB   1949 CODRINGTON CHRONICLE: AN EXPERIMENT IN ANGLICAN ALTRUISM ON A BARBADOS PLANTATION, 1710-1834. Berkeley and Los Angeles, University of California Press, 157p. (University of California Publications in history no. 37.) [6]   [*COL*]

LAMONT, Sir NORMAN

45.013   TR   1928 A Trinidad plantation: a century's vicissitudes. *Trop Agric* 5(7): 167-169.   [*RIS*]

LASSERRE, GUY

58.063   GD   1952 Une plantation de canne aux Antilles: la Sucrerie Beauport. [A sugar plantation in the Antilles: the Beauport sugar mill].

LENS, TH.

45.014   CU   1938 Deux colonisations de blancs aux Indes Occidentales (Curacao) [Two white colonies in the West Indies]. *In* COMPTES RENDUS DU CONGRÈS INTERNATIONAL DE GÉOGRAPHIE, AMSTERDAM, 1938, VOL. 2. TRAVAUX DE LA SECTION III c. Leiden, E. J. Brill, p.192-198.   [*AGS*]

LUDLOW, ANTHONY

50.086   BG   1938 Red sky at morning.

McCULLOCH, SAMUEL CLYDE & SCHUTZ, JOHN A.

45.015   BB   1949 Of the noble and generous benefaction of General Christopher Codrington. *In* KLINGBERG, FRANK J., ed. CODRINGTON CHRONICLE: AN EXPERIMENT IN ANGLICAN ALTRUISM ON A BARBADOS PLANTATION, 1710-1834. Berkeley and Los Angeles, University of California Press, p.15-24. (Publications in history no. 37.)   [*COL*]

MINTZ, SIDNEY W.

45.016   GC   1959 The plantation as a socio-cultural type. *In* RUBIN, VERA, ed.
                         PLANTATION SYSTEMS OF THE NEW WORLD. Washington, D.C., Re-
                         search Institute for the Study of Man and Pan American Union, p.42-
                         53. (Social science monographs, 7.) [8]   [*RIS*]

O'NEIL, MAUD E.

35.032   BB   1949 Of the buildings in progress with which to house the College.

OUDSCHANS DENTZ, FRED

45.017   SR   1944/ De herkomst en de beteekenis van Surinaamsche plantagenamen
                  45   [The origins and meanings of the names of the plantations in
                         Surinam]. *W I G* 26:147-180. [6, 7]   [*COL*]

PADILLA, ELENA

45.018   GC   1959 Colonization and development of plantations. *In* RUBIN, VERA, ed.
                         PLANTATION SYSTEMS OF THE NEW WORLD. Washington, D.C. Research
                         Institute for the Study of Man and Pan American Union, p.54-63.
                         (Social science monographs, 7.) [5, 6]   [*RIS*]
10.033   GC   1960 Peasants, plantations, and pluralism.

PARES, RICHARD

45.019   NV   1950 A WEST INDIA FORTUNE. London, Longmans, Green, 374p. [5]   [*RIS*]
45.020   GC   1960 MERCHANTS AND PLANTERS. Cambridge, Cambridge University Press,
                         91p. (Economic history review, supplement 4.) [5]   [*RIS*]

PHILLIPS, LESLIE, H. C.

45.021   BG   1961 Single men in barracks: some memories of sugar plantation life.
                         Timehri 4th ser., no. 40, Oct.: 23-34.   [*AMN*]

PHILLIPS, ULRICH B.

45.022   JM   1914 A Jamaica slave plantation. *Am Hist Rev* 19(3), Apr.: 543-558.   [5]
                                                                                         [*AGS*]
45.023   AT   1926 An Antigua plantation, 1769-1818. *Nth Caro Hist Rev* 3(3), July:
                         439-445. [5]   [*COL*]

PITMAN, FRANK WESLEY

6.056   BC   1926 Slavery on the British West India plantations in the eighteenth
                         century.
45.024   BC   1927 The West Indian absentee planter as a British Colonial type. *In*
                         PROCEEDINGS OF THE PACIFIC COAST BRANCH OF THE AMERICAN HIS-
                         TORICAL ASSOCIATION, [n.p.], p.113-127. [5]   [*NYP*]
45.025   BC   1931 The settlement and financing of British West India plantations in
                         the eighteenth century. *In* ESSAYS IN COLONIAL HISTORY, presented
                         to Charles McLean Andrews by his students. New Haven, Yale
                         University Press, p.252-283. [5]   [*NYP*]

PLATT, ROBERT S.

43.122   BG   1939 Reconnaissance in British Guiana, with comments on micro-
                         geography.

POTTER, THOMAS I.

46.171   TR   1932 River Estate: a brief history of the property.

RAGATZ, LOWELL JOSEPH

45.026   BC   1925 THE OLD PLANTATION SYSTEM IN THE BRITISH CARIBBEAN. London,
                         Bryan Edwards Press, 81p. [5]   [*NYP*]

51.117   BC   1927 STATISTICS FOR THE STUDY OF BRITISH CARIBBEAN ECONOMIC HISTORY,
                         1763-1833.

45.027   BC [1928?] ABSENTEE LANDLORDISM IN THE BRITISH CARIBBEAN 1750-1833. Lon-
                         don, Bryan Edwards Press, 21p. [5, 37]   [*COL*]

45.028   GC   1928 FALL OF THE PLANTER CLASS IN THE BRITISH CARIBBEAN, 1763-1833.
                         New York, Century Co., 520p. (Reprinted by Octagon Books 1963.)
                         [5, 66]   [*RIS*]

45.029   BC   1931 Absentee landlordism in the British Caribbean, 1750-1833. *Agric
                         Hist* 5(1), Jan.: 7-24. [5]   [*COL*]

RODNEY, WALTER & AUGUSTUS, EARL

6.058   GC   1964 The Negro slave.

RODWAY, JAMES

45.030   BG   1911 Names of our plantations. *Timehri* 3d ser., 1(18A), Jan.: 57-61.
                         [5, 19]   [*AMN*]

50.098   BG   1919 Labour and colonization.

RUBIN, VERA, ed.

45.031   GC   1959 PLANTATION SYSTEMS OF THE NEW WORLD. Washington, D.C., Pan
                         American Union and Research Institute for the Study of Man. (Social
                         science monographs, 7.) 212p.   [*RIS*]

SCHOCH, C. F.

45.032   SR   1924/ De Koloniale Staten en de belangen van den grooten landbouw in
                     25   the landbouw kolonie Suriname [The Colonial States and the in-
                         terests of large-scale agriculture in the agricultural colony of
                         Surinam]. *W I G* 6:625-634.   [*COL*]

SCHUTZ, JOHN A.

23.139   BB   1946 Christopher Codrington's will: launching the S.P.G. into the Bar-
                         badian sugar business.

SCHUTZ, JOHN A. & O'NEIL, MAUD E.

45.033   BB   1949 Of the plantations intire. *In* KLINGBERG, FRANK J., ed. CODRING-
                         TON CHRONICLE: AN EXPERIMENT IN ANGLICAN ALTRUISM ON A BARBADOS
                         PLANTATION, 1710-1834. Berkeley and Los Angeles, University of
                         California Press, p.43-59. (Publications in history no. 37.)   [*COL*]

STAAL, G. J.

6.069   SR   1928/ Uit den slaventijd [About the era of slavery].
                     29

TAYLOR, RONALD V.

45.034   BB   1957 Two Barbados estate plans. *J Barb Mus Hist Soc* 25(1), Nov.: 82-
                         83. [5]   [*AMN*]

TEMPANY, Sir HAROLD A.

46.216   FC   1952 The influence of introduced crops on colonial economies.

WAGENAAR HUMMELINCK, P.

45.035   SR   1947 Het dagelijksch leven op de Surinaamsche koffieplantage "Koks-
                         woud" in 1828 [Daily life on the coffee plantation "Kokswoud" in
                         1828]. *W I G* 28:33-41.   [5, 6]   [*COL*]

WAGLEY, CHARLES

45.036   GC   1960 Plantation America: a culture sphere. *In* RUBIN, VERA, ed.
                         CARIBBEAN STUDIES: A SYMPOSIUM. 2d ed. Seattle, University of
                         Washington Press, p.3-13.   [*RIS*]

WARDLAW, C. W.

46.226   SR   1930 Agriculture in Suriname.

WESTERGAARD, WALDEMAR

45.037   SC   1938 A St. Croix map of 1766: with a note on its significance in West
                         Indian plantation economy. *J Negro Hist* 23(2), Apr.: 216-228.
                         [5, 40]   [*AMN*]

WESTRA, P.

50.125   SR   1919 Plantage-arbeiders [Plantation laborers].

WILLIAMS, ERIC EUSTACE

66.166   GC   1961 MASSA DAY DONE.

WISE, K. S. & MINETT, E. P.

28.600   BG   1912 Drinking water supplies: a chemical and bacteriological study of
                         the drinking water supplies on estates from a hygienic point of view.

WOLF, ERIC R. & MINTZ, SIDNEY

45.038   GC   1957 Haciendas and plantations in Middle America and the Antilles.
                         Social Econ Stud 6(3): 380-412.   [*RIS*]

ZWARTS, JAC

15.045   SR   1927/Een episode uit de Joodsche kolonie van Guyana, 1660 [An epi-
             28   sode from the Jewish colony of Guiana, 1660].

Chapter 46

LAND USE AND AGRICULTURAL ECONOMICS

ABBOTT, GEORGE C.
44.001   BC   1963 The future of economic co-operation in the West Indies in the light of the break-up of the Federation.

ABRAHAM, A. A.
46.001   BG   1918 The agricultural development of the North Western District, during the years 1907-1918. *J Bd Agric Br Gui* 11(3), July: 107-110.   [66]
[*AMN*]

ADAM, DENIS
46.002   FG   1936 EL DORADO; LA GUYANE FRANCAISE AGRICOLE [EL DORADO; AGRICULTURE IN FRENCH GUIANA]. Paris, Larose, 84p.   [*AGS*]

ALCALA, V. O.
32.006   GC   1953 Agricultural training.
32.010   GC   1953 Survey of existing facilities for vocational training in the Caribbean.

ALTSON, R. A.
46.003   JM/   1925 Report on a visit to Jamaica, Costa Rica and Trinidad. *J Bd Agric*
TR/   *Br Gui* 18(1), Jan.: 2-19.   [*AMN*]
BG

ANDERSON, ROBERT M.
53.002   SV   1914 Report on the agricultural credit societies of St. Vincent.

ARRIENS, R. A. LINCKLAAEN & HAAN, J. H. de
46.004   BG   1953 Verslag van een reis naar Brits Guyana [Report on a trip to British Guiana]. *Sur Landb* 1(5), Sept./Oct.: 183-193.

AUCHINLECK, GILBERT; SMITH, G. WHITFIELD &
BERTRAND, WALTER
47.001   GN/   1914 Government schemes of land settlement in Grenada and the
GR   Grenadines.

AUGELLI, JOHN P.
43.002   VI   1955 The British Virgin Islands: a West Indian anomaly.
43.003   GD   1962 Land use in Guadeloupe.

603

BADCOCK, W. J.
46.005   BB   1960 The problems relative to soil conservation in the Scotland District. *J Barb Mus Hist Soc* 27(4), Aug.: 126-129. [57, 66]   [*AMN*]

BAKER, HENRY D.
46.006   TR   1924 The asphalt lakes of Trinidad and Venezuela as natural wonders of the world. *Am Cons B*, 24p. [40]   [*AGS*]

BALDWIN, RICHARD
47.003   BG   1959 The little republic.

BARON van LYNDEN, W. E. K.
46.007   SR   1932/ Landbouwvoorlichting en landbouwonderwijs in Suriname [Agri-
         33   cultural guidance and agricultural education in Surinam]. *W I G* 14:257-266. [32, 66]   [*COL*]

BAXTER, G. D.
46.008   BG   1962 Kenaf trials in British Guiana. *Trop Sci* 4(4): 205-215.   [*AGS*]

BECKETT, J. EDGAR
46.009   BG   1905 HINTS ON AGRICULTURE IN BRITISH GUIANA. Georgetown, Estate of C. K. Jardine (2d impression published by the Daily Chronicle, ⸴Georgetown, 1948), 183p. [66]   [*RIS*]
11.003   BG   1917 The black peasant proprietor.

BECKFORD, G. L. F.
46.010   TR   1965 Agriculture in the development of Trinidad and Tobago: a comment. *Social Econ Stud* 14(2), June: 217-220. [66]   [*RIS*]

BENSON, E. G.
46.011   TR   1950 Mixed farming. *Proc Agric Soc Trin Tob* 50(1), Mar.: 57-63. [*AMN*]

BEUKERING, J. A. van
46.012   SR   1952 Types of farming. *Car Econ Rev* 4(1-2), Dec.: 140-163. [5, 66] [*RIS*]

BEYLERS, H. de
17.002   FG   1951 Immigration en Guyane [Immigration into Guiana].

BLAICH, O. P.
46.013   BG   [ca. AGRICULTURE IN BRITISH GUIANA. Georgetown, B.G. Lithographic Co. 1954] 99p. (Census 1952, v. 1, no. 1.)   [*COL*]

BLAICH, O. P., comp.
46.014   BG   1954 AGRICULTURE IN BRITISH GUIANA. Georgetown, Published by author- ity of the Director of Agriculture, 20p. (British Guiana, Dept. of Agriculture, Census 1953, v. 1, no. 2.)   [*COL*]
46.015   BG   1956 AGRICULTURE IN BRITISH GUIANA. [Georgetown?] British Guiana, Dept. of Agriculture, 23p. (Census 1954, v. 1, no. 3.)

BLAUT, JAMES M.
43.018   GC   1959 The ecology of tropical farming systems.

BLOM, D. van

46.016   SR   1919   Kolonisatie met Nederlandsche boeren in Suriname [Colonization with Dutch peasants in Surinam] *W I G* 1(1): 341-359.   [*COL*]

46.017   SR   1921/   Nederlandsche boeren-kolonisatie in Suriname [Colonization with 22   Dutch farmers in Surinam]. *W I G* 3:257-266.   [*COL*]

BLUME, HELMUT

47.007   JM   1961   Die gegenwärtigen Wandlungen in der Verbreitung von Gross- und Kleinbetreiben auf den Grossen Antillen [Contemporary changes in the distribution of large- and small-holdings in the Greater Antilles].

BOND, RICHARD M.

46.018   UV   1957   The Federal experiment station in U.S. Virgin Islands. *Caribbean* 10(8), Mar.: 196-197. [66]   [*COL*]

BOONACKER, J.

46.019   SR   1931/   De tegenwoordige toestand van Suriname op het gebied van den 32   landbouw [The present agricultural situation in Surinam]. *W I G* 13:483-488.   [*COL*]

46.020   SR   1932/   Hoe kan Suriname's landbouw tot ontwikkeling komen [How can 33   Surinam's agriculture be developed]? *W I G* 14:175-178, 342-346. [66]   [*COL*]

BRACK, DAVID MELVILLE

46.021   BB   1964   PEASANT AGRICULTURE IN BARBADOS: A CASE STUDY OF A RURAL SYSTEM. M. A. thesis, McGill University, 172p.

BRAITHWAITE, LLOYD E.

32.029   BC   1958   The development of higher education in the British West Indies.

BRANDON, H. G.

46.022   SR   1936/   De proefneming van de Surinaamsche Hoeve Maatschappij [The 37   experiment of the Surinam Hoeve Company]. *W I G* 18:293-396. [*COL*]

BROADWAY, W. E.

32.031   TR   1934   School gardens in Trinidad and Tobago.

BROWN, HEADLEY & ANDERSON, ERROL

47.008   BC   1963/   Economic development in the West Indies and the peasantry. 64

BROWN, JOHN

32.033   SL   1962   Education and development of St. Lucia.

BROWNE, C. A.

46.023   GC   1927   Some historical relations of agriculture in the West Indies to that of the United States. *Agric Hist* 1(2), July: 23-33. [5]   [*AGS*]

BRYAN, VICTOR

46.024   TR   1951   Agricultural policy. *J Agric Soc Trin Tob* 51(2), June: 271-276.   [66] [*AMN*]

BUCHLER, IRA R.

46.025   CM   1963 Shifting cultivation in the Cayman Islands. *Anthropologica* 12, Dec.: 1-5.   [*RIS*]

BUIE. T. S.

46.026   BB   1956 Barbadian agriculture. *Bett Crops Pl Fd* 40(3), Mar.: 23-25, 48-50.

BURGESS, CHARLES J.

46.027   GC   1952 Some sociological factors in agricultural development in the Caribbean. *Car Commn Mon Inf B* 6(3), Oct.: 49-50, 65. [66]   [*AGS*]

BURROWES, W. D.

46.028   JM   1952 SAMPLE SURVEY OF PRODUCTION OF SELECTED AGRICULTURAL PRODUCTS, 1950. Kingston, Gleaner Co., 65p. (Department of Agriculture, Bulletin no. 48, new ser.) [67]   [*NYP*]

CAMERON, NORMAN E.

32.038   BG   1955 Thoughts on agricultural education in British Guiana.

CAMPBELL, J. S.

32.040   TR   1962 School gardening: an integral part of primary school education in Trinidad and Tobago.

CAMPBELL, L. G.

46.029   TR   1956 Preliminary studies on sprinkler irrigation at the government stock farms in Trinidad and Tobago. *J Agric Soc Trin Tob* 56(2), June: 288-292.   [*AMN*]

CAMPBELL, LEWIS

46.030   GC   1962 Production methods in West Indies agriculture. *Car Q* 8(2), June: 94-104. [66]   [*RIS*]

CAPPER, T.

32.042   JM   1901 Teaching the principles of agriculture in elementary schools.
32.043   JM   1907 Agriculture in elementary schools of Jamaica.

CARLIN, CLAIR

46.031   BQ   1936 The planting. *Can-W I Mag* 25(4), Mar.: 23-25.   [*NYP*]

CASE, GERALD O.

46.032   BG   1946 Notes on natural resources of the interior of British Guiana. *Timehri* 4th ser., 1(27), July: 39-45.

CATER, JOHN C.

46.033   TR   1939 Deforestation and soil erosion in Trinidad: deforestation and soil erosion in the foothills of the Northern Range caused by shifting cultivation. *Trop Agric* 16(10), Oct.: 230-232. [57]   [*AGS*]

CHAPMAN, T. & HERRERA, E.

1.006   TR   1961/ List of completed research work carried out at the Imperial College 62 of Tropical Agriculture on crop husbandry.

CHEESMAN, E. E.

41.061   GC   1939 The history of introduction of some well known West Indian staples.

CLARKE, S. St. A.

51.025   JM   1962 The competitive position of Jamaica's agricultural exports.

COLLIER, H. C.

46.034   BC   1936 Economic trees, plants and agricultural products of the West Indies. *Can-W I Mag* 25(7), June: 9-11; 25(8), July: 8-9, 32; 25(9), Aug.: 11-12.   [*NYP*]

46.035·   BC   1943 Economic plants and trees of the W.I. *Can-W I Mag* 32(6), June: 7-8; 32(7), July: 11, 24.   [*NYP*]

COLLINS, Rev.

32.047   JM   1907 An agricultural and industrial experiment.

COLON-TORRES, RAMON

46.036   GC   1952 Agricultural credit in the Caribbean. *Car Econ Rev* 4(1-2), Dec.: 60-112. [53]   [*RIS*]

COMITAS, LAMBROS

56.017   JM   1962 Fishermen and cooperation in rural Jamaica.

COUSINS, HERBERT H.

32.050   JM   1907 Some problems of agricultural education at Jamaica.

COZIER, EDWARD L.

46.037   WW   1955 Reporting progress in the Windward Islands. *New Commonw*, Br Car Suppl 30(10), Nov. 14: xii-xiii.   [*AGS*]

46.038   SL   1956 Agricultural progress in St. Lucia. *New Commonw* 32(2), July 23: 73-74. [66]   [*AGS*]

CRADWICK, WILLIAM

46.039   JM   1907 The small-holdings competition in Jamaica. *W I B* 8(3): 267-270.   [*AMN*]

CREDNER, WILHELM

46.040   JM   1943 Typen der Wirtschaftslandschaft auf den Grossen Antillen [Types of economic landscapes in the Greater Antilles]. *Pet Geogr Mitt* 89:1-23.   [*AGS*]

CROUCHER, H. H. & SWABEY, C.

46.041   JM   1938 SOIL EROSION AND CONSERVATION IN JAMAICA, 1937. Kingston, Govt. Print. Off., 20p. (Dept. of Science and Agriculture. Bulletin no. 17, new ser.) [57, 66]   [*AGS*]

CROUCHER, HERBERT

46.042   NV   1961 Agriculture on Nevis, Part II. *In* BROWN, JOHN, ed. LEEWARDS: WRITINGS, PAST AND PRESENT, ABOUT THE LEEWARD ISLANDS. Barbados, Dept. of Extra-Mural Studies, Leeward Islands, University College of the West Indies, p.62-64.   [*RIS*]

CUMPER, GEORGE E.

46.043   JM   1953 Two studies in Jamaican productivity. *Social Econ Stud* 1(2), June: 3-83. [44]   [*RIS*]

46.044   JM   1958 The Jamaican family: village and estate. *Social Econ Stud* 7(1), Mar.: 76-108. [8, 9]   [*RIS*]

50.021   BB   1959 Employment in Barbados.

CUSH, J. M.

46.045   BG   1920 Possibilities of farming on the banks of the Berbice River. *J Bd Agric Br Gui* 13(3), July: 169-173. [66]   [*AMN*]

DALTON, H. A.

32.053   BB   1907 Agricultural education in secondary schools at Barbados.

DAMBAUGH, LUELLA N.

43.035   JM   1953 Jamaica: an island in transition.

DARDET, VICTOR

46.046   FA   1939 ÉTUDE SUR L'ÉCONOMIE AGRICOLE DES ANTILLES FRANCAISES [STUDY ON THE AGRICULTURAL ECONOMICS OF THE FRENCH ANTILLES]. Marseille, Impr. Ant. Ged., 270p. (Ph.D. dissertation, Université d'Aix-Marseille.)   [*COL*]

DASH, J. SYDNEY

46.047   BG   1932 Agriculture in British Guiana. *Can-W I Mag* 21(11), Oct.: 357-360. [*NYP*]

46.048   BG   1943 Agriculture in British Guiana, by J. Sidney Dash. *Can-W I Mag* 32(9), Sept.: 10-11, 23-24; 32(10), Oct.: 7-9. [*NYP*]

46.049   BC   1955 Making the most of agriculture. *New Commonw*, Br Car Suppl 30 (10, Nov. 14: xviii-xx. [66]   [*AGS*]

DAVIES, F. D.

46.050   TR   1924 Crops to grow and how to grow them. *Proc Agric Soc Trin Tob* 24(3), Mar.: 121-134; 24(6), June: 260-278.   [*AMN*]

DEIBLE, C. H. von

46.051   JM   1945 A visit to Jamaica. *Proc Agric Soc Trin Tob* 45(1), Mar.: 43-49. [*AMN*]

DEIGHTON, HORACE, et al.

32.055   BC   1905 Teaching the principles of agriculture in colleges and schools in the West Indies.

DENNY, J. F.

46.052   BG   1921 The farmer's progress. *Timehri* 3d ser., 7(24), Aug.: 44-46. [66] [*AMN*]

DesBRIERE, JUANITA

46.053   AR   1938 Aruba, Cinderella of the Caribbean. *Nat Hist* 41(2), Feb.: 138-140, 148. [5]   [*AGS*]

DOBBS, P. J.

46.054   BG   1960 Water control in British Guiana. *Wld Crops* 12(12), Dec.: 457-460. [*AGS*]

DOUGLAS, CH.
46.055   SR   1927/ Aanteekeningen over den landbouw in Suriname [Notes about agri-
           28 culture in Surinam]. *W I G* 9:455-464. [44, 47]   [*COL*]

DRESDEN, D. & GOUDRIAAN, J.
66.039   CU   1947 RAPPORT WELVAARTSPLAN NEDERLANDSE ANTILLEN 1946 [REPORT ABOUT
                THE WELFARE PLAN, NETHERLANDS ANTILLES 1946].

DRIMMELEN, C. van
46.056   SR   1922/ Kolonisatie van het blanke ras in de tropen [Colonization of the
           23 white race in the tropics]. *W I G* 4:193-204.   [*COL*]

DUCLOS, B. HAVARD
46.057   GC   1957 REPORT ON AGRICULTURAL DEVELOPMENT IN THE CARIBBEAN. Port of
                Spain, Caribbean Commission, 24p. [66]

DUNLOP, W. R.
53.009   BC   1914 The West Indies and co-operative credit.

EDWARDS, DAVID T.
46.058   JM   1954 An economic study of agriculture in the Yallahs Valley area of
                Jamaica. *Social Econ Stud* 3(3-4), Dec.: 316-341. [66]   [*NYP*]
46.059   JM   1954 Remedies proposed by the International Bank Mission. *In* THE
                FARMER'S GUIDE, APPENDIX D. Glasgow, University Press, p.767-772.
                [66]   [*NYP*]
46.060   JM   1961 AN ECONOMIC STUDY OF SMALL FARMING IN JAMAICA. Kingston.
                University College of the West Indies, 370p. [47,57]   [*RIS*]
46.061   JM   1961 An economic view of agricultural research in Jamaica. *Social Econ
                Stud* 10(3), Sept.: 306-339. [44]   [*RIS*]

EDWARDS, W. H.
46.062   CM   1938 REPORT ON AN AGRICULTURAL SURVEY IN THE CAYMAN ISLANDS. [Kings-
                ton?] Jamaica, Govt. Print. Off., 40p. (Dept. of Science and Agri-
                culture, Bulletin, new ser. no. 13.)   [66]   [*AGS*]

EISNER, GISELA
44.056   JM   1961 JAMAICA, 1830-1930: A STUDY IN ECONOMIC GROWTH.

ENGLEDOW, Sir FRANK L.
46.063   BC   [n.d.] WEST INDIAN AGRICULTURE: THE AGRICULTURAL REPORT OF THE ROYAL
                COMMISSION OF 1938. Kingston, University College of the West
                Indies, Extra-Mural Department, 235p.
46.064   GC   1945 REPORT ON AGRICULTURE, FISHERIES, FORESTRY AND VETERINARY
                MATTERS [OF THE] WEST INDIA ROYAL COMMISSION. London, H.M.S.O.,
                235p. [56, 64, 65]   [*RIS*]

EVANS, Sir GEOFFREY
66.044   GC   1939 Note on the possibilities for the agricultural settlement of invo-
                luntary refugees from Central Europe in the hinterland of British
                Guiana.
46.065   BC   1942 West Indian agriculture. *Nature* 149(3788), June 6: 626-630. [66]
                                                         [*AGS*]

FAHEY, HAROLD NEAL

46.066   TR   1940 Re-adjustment of Trinidad's agriculture, its necessity, and policy
                     required for same. *Proc Agric Soc Trin Tob* 40(2), June: 137-143.
                     [66]   [*AMN*]
57.015   TR   1943 Soil fertility often a minor factor.
46.067   TR   1944 The necessity of resuscitating Trinidad's agriculture. *Proc Agric
                     Soc Trin Tob* 44(2), June: 133-135.   [66]   [*AMN*]
46.068   TR   1946 Agricultural readjustments. *Proc Agric Soc Trin Tob* 46(1), Mar.:
                     65-71.   [*AMN*]

FARFAN, FERNAND T.

46.069   TR   1942 Some reflections on a paper read by Dr. A. L. Jolly. *Proc Agric Soc
                     Trin Tob* 42(2), June: 121-128.   [*AMN*]

FARLEY, RAWLE

46.070   BG   1958 Economic and social change on a Caribbean frontier. *Caribbean*
                     11(9), Apr.: 194-199.   [50, 66]   [*COL*]
49.022   BC   1958 NATIONALISM AND INDUSTRIAL DEVELOPMENT IN THE BRITISH CARIBBEAN.

FAULKNER, O. T. & SHEPHARD, C. Y.

46.071   BC   1943 Mixed farming: the basis of a system for West Indian peasants.
                     Trop Agric 20(7), July: 136-142.   [66]   [*RIS*]

FAUVEL, LUC

37.112   FA   1955 Les conséquences économiques et sociales de l'assimilation
                     administrative des Antilles Francaises [The economic and social
                     consequences of the political assimilation of the French Antilles].

FAWCETT, WILLIAM

53.017   JM   1905 Raiffeisen agricultural banks.

FINCH, T. F.

57.017   JM   1959 SOIL AND LAND-USE SURVEYS. No. 7: Jamaica—Parish of Clarendon.
57.018   JM   1961 SOIL AND LAND-USE SURVEYS. No. 11: Jamaica—Parish of Portland.

FINKEL, HERMAN J.

20.006   SK/   1964 Attitudes toward work as a factor in agricultural planning in the
           NV   West Indies.

FLOOR, J.

46.072   SR   1948 De Surinaamse landbouw [The agriculture of Surinam]. *W I G* 29:
                     129-136.   [*COL*]

FOREMAN, R. A.

47.013   SL   1958 LAND SETTLEMENT SCHEME FOR SAINT LUCIA: BASED ON A SURVEY OF
                     THE AGRICULTURAL AND SOCIAL CONDITIONS OF THE ISLAND ON A VISIT
                     FROM 24.3.58-26.4.58.

FRAMPTON, A. de K.

46.073   BC   1954 Land problems in small scale farming. *In* SMALL SCALE FARMING
                     IN THE CARIBBEAN. [Port of Spain?] Trinidad, Caribbean Commission,
                     p.65-74.   [47, 48]

FREDHOLM, A.
32.067   TR   1912   Agricultural education in Trinidad—past, present and future.

FREEMAN, WILLIAM G.
51.052   TR   1929   The balance of trade and prosperity.

GAAY FORTMAN, B. de
47.017   CU   1936/ Twee verzoekschriften aan den koning over den landbouwpolitiek
            37   van Gouverneur van Raders in Curacao [Two petitions to the king
                 about the agricultural policy of Governor van Raders in Curacao].
46.074   NL   1948   De landbouwplannen van den Gezaghebber van Rades [The agri-
                 cultural plans of the District Commissioner van Rades]. *W I G* 29:
                 353-367.   [66]   [*COL*]

GANZERT, FREDERIC W.
51.053   GC   1958   Trade trends and prospects.

GATES, RALPH CHARLES
66.051   GC   1961   A MONOGRAPH ON COOPERATIVE DEVELOPMENT IN THE CARIBBEAN.

GEORGE, Mc.
46.075   AT   1956   Antigua peasant agriculture. *Caribbean* 9(12), July: 264-266, 275.
                 [66]   [*COL*]

GERLING, WALTER
43.058   JM   1938   Wirtschaftsentwicklung und Landschaftswandel auf den West-
                 indischen Inseln Jamaika, Haiti und Puerto Rico [Economic develop-
                 ment and changes in landscape in the West Indian islands of
                 Jamaica, Haiti and Puerto Rico].

GIGLIOLI, GEORGE
28.218   BG   1946   Malaria and agriculture in British Guiana.
28.221   BG   1956   Medical services on the sugar estates of British Guiana.

GOODING, H. J.
46.076   BC   1960   West Indian 'Dioscorea alata' cultivars. *Trop Agric* 37(1), Jan.:
                 11-30.   [*AGS*]

GORE-ORMSBY, W.
46.077   BC   1922   The progress of the West Indies. *Can-W I Mag* 10(6), Apr.: 160-161.
                 [52, 66]   [*NYP*]

GREAVES, IDA C.
45.010   JM   1959   Plantations in world economy.

GREENFIELD, SIDNEY M.
46.078   BB   1964   Stocks, bonds, and peasant canes in Barbados: some notes on the
                 use of land in an overdeveloped economy. *In* ZOLLSCHAN, G.K. &
                 HIRSCH, WALTER, eds. EXPLORATIONS IN SOCIAL CHANGE. Boston,
                 Houghton, p.619-650.   [58]

GROL, G. J. van
46.079   SE   1920/ Economische arbeid op St. Eustatius van gouvernementswege
            21   1903-1918. [Government supported economic work on St. Eustatius
                 1903-1918. *W I G* 2:151-162, 198-212.   [6]   [*COL*]

HAHN, J. H. de
46.080   SR   1953   The Lelydorp project. *Car Commn Mon Inf B* 7(3), Oct.: 53-54, 66.
                 [66]   [*COL*]

46.081   SR   1955 De landstreekontwikkeling in Suriname [Development of rural re-
                  gions in Surinam]. *Tijdschr Econ Social Geogr* 46(10), Oct.: 201-
                  210.   [66]

HAAN, J.H. de & HENDRIKS, J.A.H.
46.082   SR   1954 Lelydorp project—a pilotscheme for land-development in Surinam.
                  Neth J Agric Sci 2(2), May: 120-133. [10, 66]   [*NYP*]

HAARER, A.E.
46.083   BC   1959 Agriculture in the West Indies. *Corona* 11(3), Mar.: 99-103.   [*AGS*]

HALCROW, M. & CAVE, J.M.
46.084   BB   1947 PEASANT AGRICULTURE IN BARBADOS. [Bridgetown?] Barbados, Advo-
                  cate Co., 83p. (Department of Science and Agriculture Bulletin no.
                  11, new ser.)

HARBIN, JOHN
32.088   GR/   1905 Agriculture in the elementary schools of Grenada and St. Vincent,
          SV   1902-4.

HARDY, F.
46.085   SV   [1921?] The interpretation of results of agricultural experiments. *W I B*
                  18(4): 207-223.   [*AMN*]
57.031   BC   1951 Soil productivity in the British Caribbean region.

HARDY, F. & JORDAN, J.W.
57.036   TR   1946 Soil fertility of some peasant lands in Trinidad.

HAREWOOD, JACK
50.060   JM/   1960 Overpopulation and underemployment in the West Indies.
          TR

HARRISON, Sir JOHN B. & BANCROFT, C.K.
46.086   BG   1915 The field and forest resources of British Guiana. *Imp Inst B* 13:
                  203-33.   [*NYP*]
46.087   BG   1926 Food plants of British Guiana. *J Bd Agric Br Gui* 19:18-51.   [30]
                                                                                      [*AMN*]

HARTLEY, HAZEL MORSE
46.088   BB   1949 Of the produce of the plantations. *In* KLINGBERG, FRANK J., ed.
                  CODRINGTON CHRONICLE: AN EXPERIMENT IN ANGLICAN ALTRUISM ON A
                  BARBADOS PLANTATION, 1710-1834. Berkeley and Los Angeles, Uni-
                  versity of California Press, p.63-82. (Publications in history no.
                  37.) [5, 45]   [*COL*]

HENDRIKS, J. A. H.
46.089   SR   1956 HET LELYDORPPLAN IN SURINAME: INLEIDING TOT HET VRAAGSTUK VAN
                  DE LANDONTWIKKELING OP ARME GRONDEN IN EEN TROPISCH GEBIED [THE
                  LELYDORP PLAN IN SURINAM: INTRODUCTION TO THE PROBLEM OF LAND
                  DEVELOPMENT ON INFERIOR SOILS IN A TROPICAL AREA]. Wageningen,

Drukkerij Verweij. (Ph.D. dissertation, Landbouwhogeschool, Wageningen.) [66]

HENDRICKSEN, H. E.

32.096   TR   1912 Agricultural education.

HENRIQUEZ, P. C.

66.061   CU   1962 Problems relating to hydrology, water conservation, erosion control, reforestation and agriculture in Curacao.

HERKLOTS, G. A. C.

32.097   BC   1955 The Imperial College of Tropical Agriculture.

HERVE, P.

46.090   FG   1964 Le polder de Marie-Anne: l'aménagement des terres basses de la Guyane par la S.A.T.E.C. [The Marie-Anne polder: the utilization of the Guiana lowlands by the S.A.T.E.C.]. *Cah Cent Etud Reg Ant-Guy* Oct.: 6p.   [*RIS*]

HODGE, W. H.

46.091   DM   1942 Plants used by the Dominica Caribs. *J N Y Bot Gdn* 43(512), Aug.: 189-201. [13, 40]

HOTCHKISS, J. C.

32.098   BC   1952 Eastern Caribbean Farm Institute.
32.099   GC.   1953 Progress of the Eastern Caribbean Farm Institute.

HOTCHKISS, J. C. & Mrs. J. C.

46.092   BC   1954 The education of the small scale farmer and his family for better farm and home living in the British Caribbean. *In* SMALL SCALE FARMING IN THE CARIBBEAN. [Port of Spain?] Trinidad, Caribbean Commission, p.86-105. [32,66]

HOWARD, RICHARD A.

41.137   TR   1951 Botanical observations on Pitch Lake in Trinidad.

HOY, DON R.

46.093   GD   1961 AGRICULTURAL LAND USE OF GUADELOUPE. Washington, D.C., National Academy of Sciences, 90p. (National Research Council, Publication 884.) [5, 47, 57]   [*RIS*]
46.094   GD   1962 Changing agricultural land use on Guadeloupe, French West Indies. *Ann Ass Am Geogr* 52(4), Dec.: 441-454. [58]

HUGGINS, H. D.

50.068   JM   1953 Seasonal variation and employment in Jamaica.

HUGGINS, H. D., ed.

44.110   BC   1958 [PROCEEDINGS OF THE] STUDY CONFERENCE ON ECONOMIC DEVELOPMENT IN UNDERDEVELOPED COUNTRIES [held at the University College of the West Indies, Aug. 5-15, 1957].

HUTCHINGS, C. D.
46.095   JM   1955 Peasant farming in Jamaica. *Caribbean* 9(3), Oct.: 54-55, 65. [*COL*]

HYNAM, C. A. S.
46.096   NW   1941 Agriculture in the Dutch Windward Islands. *Trop Agric* 18(7), July: 135-138.   [*AGS*]

INNIS, DONALD Q.
46.097   JM   1961 The efficiency of Jamaican peasant land use. *Can Geogr* 5(2), Summer: 19-23.

INTERNATIONAL BANK FOR RECONSTRUCTION AND DEVELOPMENT
66.069   JM   1952 The economic development of Jamaica.
66.070   SR   1952 Surinam: recommendations for a ten year development program.
66.071   BG   1953 The economic development of British Guiana.

JERVIS, T. S.
66.073   BC   [n.d.] Robusta coffee production in the Eastern Caribbean: Report on a visit from September, 1956, to January, 1957.

JOLLY, A. L.
46.098   TR   [1945] Peasant farming in the Bejucal area of Trinidad. *Trop Agric* 22(5): 83-88.   [*RIS*]
46.099   TR   1946 Peasant agriculture: an economic survey on the La Pastora land settlement, Trinidad, May 1944-45. *Trop Agric* 23(7): 117-122; 23 (8): 137-145.   [*RIS*]
46.100   TR   1948 Peasant farming in two districts of the Oropouche Lagoon, June 1944-5. *Trop Agric* 25(1-12): 23-32. [12]   [*AGS*]
46.101   TR   1952 Peasant agriculture investigation at I.C.T.A. *J Agric Soc Trin Tob* 52(4), Dec.: 393-401.   [*AMN*]
46.102   TR   1952 Unit farms. *Trop Agric* 29(7-12), July-Dec.: 172-179. [66]   [*AGS*]
46.103   GC   1954 Financing small scale farming. *In* Small scale farming in the Caribbean. [Port of Spain?] Trinidad, Caribbean Commission, p.31-39.
46.104   TR   1954 Report on peasant experimental farms at the Imperial College of Tropical Agriculture, Trinidad, B.W.I. [Port of Spain?] Trinidad, Central Secretariat, Caribbean Commission, 117p.   [*RIS*]
46.105   BC   1954 Research into the problems of small scale farming in British Caribbean countries. *In* Small scale farming in the Caribbean. [Port of Spain?] Trinidad, Caribbean Commission, p.80-81. [66]
46.106   GC   1954 Small scale farming ... management and financing. *Car Commn Mon Inf B* 8(4-5), Nov.-Dec.: 86-94, 96. [53]   [*COL*]
46.107   GC   1954 Small scale farming management problems. *In* Small scale farming in the Caribbean. [Port of Spain?] Trinidad, Caribbean Commission, p.15-24. [66]
46.108   TR   1955 Peasant experimental farms. *Trop Agric* 32(4), Oct.: 257-273. [66]
                                                                    [*AGS*]
46.109   GC   1955 The philosophy of unit farms. *Caribbean* 8(6), Jan.: 105-108. [*COL*]
46.110   GC   1956 Agriculture. *Caribbean* 10(4), Nov.: 80-82, 97. [66]   [*COL*]
46.111   GC   1956 Can mixed farming pay? *Caribbean* 9(8), Mar.: 175-177.   [*COL*]
46.112   GC   1956 Readings in small scale farming. [Port of Spain?] Trinidad, 47p. (Memoirs of the Imperial College of Tropical Agriculture. Economic series no. 3.)

46.113	GC	1956	Small-scale farming in the West Indies. *Wld Crops* 8(5), May: 173-176, 202. [*AGS*]
46.114	TR	1957	The future of Trinidad's agriculture. *Caribbean* 11(2), Sept.: 38-41. [66] [*COL*]
46.115	GC	1958	The case for local food production in the Caribbean. *Caribbean* 12(4), Nov.: 74-76, 96. [*COL*]

JONES, G. A.

46.116	LW/ WW	1933	Recent agricultural developments in some of the Leeward and Windward Islands. *Proc Agric Soc Trin Tob* 33(6), June: 168-180. [*AMN*]
46.117	BC	1933	The state of agriculture in the West Indies. *Can-W I Mag* 22(10), Sept.: 304-306. [*NYP*]

JONES, T. A.

46.118	BC	1960	Some aspects of improved land utilisation. *Caribbean* 14(2), Feb.: 24-27, 31. [66] [*COL*]

JOOSTEN, J. H. L.

40.099	BG	1954	Agrarische problemen van Brits-Guyana [Agricultural problems of British Guiana].

JOSEF, W.

46.119	SR	1958	Tienjarenplan en Plan-Wageningen [The Ten Year Plan and the Wageningen Plan]. *In* WALLE, J. van de & WIT, H. de, eds. SURINAME IN STROOMLIJNEN. Amsterdam, Wereld Bibliotheek, p.20-35. [66]

JUMELLE, HENRI

46.120	FC	1907	LES RESSOURCES AGRICOLES ET FORESTIÈRES DES COLONIES FRANCAISES [THE AGRICULTURAL AND TIMBER RESOURCES OF THE FRENCH COLONIES]. Marseilles, Barlatier, p.365-397. [*NYP*]

JUNKER, L.

46.121	SR	1932/33	De cultuurwaarde van Suriname [The value of Surinam's cultivations]. *W I G* 14:417-428. [66] [*COL*]
46.122	SR	1940	Het irrigatievraagstuk in Suriname [The problem of irrigation in Surinam]. *W I G* 22:226-233. [*COL*]
46.123	SR	1943	Nogmaals de vruchtbaarheid van het Surinaamsche binnenland [Once again: the fertility of the interior regions of Surinam]. *W I G* 25:353-364. [*COL*]

KERVEGANT, D.

46.124	TR	1936	Notes agricoles sur la Trinité [Agricultural notes on Trinidad]. *Agron Colon* 25(223), July: 1-14; 25(224), Aug.: 44-55; 25(225), Sept.: 79-88. [*AGS*]
46.125	MT	1954	L'agronomie aux Antilles [Agronomy in the Antilles]. *In* PROCEEDINGS OF THE SYMPOSIUM INTERCOLONIAL, June 27–July 3, 1952. Bordeaux, Impr. Delmas, p.147-158. [44] [*RIS*]

KOPP, A.

46.126	GD	1929	L'agriculture à la Guadeloupe [Agriculture in Guadeloupe]. *Ann Geogr* 38(215), Sept. 15: 480-500. [58] [*AGS*]

KRUIJER, GERARDUS JOHANNES

46.127   BG/   1950   Landbouw-cooperatie onder de Aziatische bevolkingsgroepen van
         SR   Suriname en Brits Guyana [Agrarian cooperation among the Asiatic
                      population groups of Surinam and British Guiana]. *W I G* 31:209-235.
                      [12, 48]   [*COL*]

32.113   JM   1952   De 4-H Clubs van Jamaica.

46.128   NW   1953   Notities over de bestaansmiddelen op de buureilanden van St.
                      Maarten, St. Eustatius en Saba [Notes on the subsistence possibili-
                      ties on the neighboring islands of St. Maarten, St. Eustatius, and
                      Saba]. *In* KRUIJER, G. J., VEENENBOS, J. S. & WESTERMANN,
                      J. H., comps. BOVENWINDENRAPPORT. Amsterdam, Voorlichtings-
                      instituut voot het Welvaartsplan Nederlandse Antillen, 25p.   [44]
                                                                    [*RIS*]

46.129   NW   1953   Notities over de landbouw en veeteelt [Notes on agriculture and
                      cattle-breeding]. *In* KRUIJER, G. J. VEENENBOS, J. S. & WEST-
                      ERMANN, J. H., comp. BOVENWINDENRAPPORT. Amsterdam, Voorlicht-
                      ingsinstituut voor het Welvaartsplan Nederlandse Antillen, 100p.

8.037   JM   1957   The impact of poverty and undernourishment on man and society in
                      rural Jamaica.

46.130   JM   1958   Het Christianagebied; een landhervormings project in Jamaica
                      [The Christiana Area—a land reform project in Jamaica]. *Tijdschr*
                      Ned Aar Genoot 2d ser., 75(3), July: 252-269.   [66]   [*AGS*]

KRUIJER, GERARDUS JOHANNES & NUIS, A.

46.131   JM   1960   REPORT ON AN EVALUATION OF THE FARM DEVELOPMENT SCHEME: FIRST
                      PLAN: 1955-1960. Kingston, Government Printer, 46p.   [66]   [*RIS*]

LAMY, GEORGES

46.132   FG   1936   Situation économique de la Guyane [Economic status of Guiana].
                      Rev Econ Fr 58(2), Mar.-Apr.: 83-88.   [52]   [*NYP*]

LEAKE, H. MARTIN

47.025   BC   1938   Further studies in tropical land tenure: Part II: The West Indies.

LEIMS, J. A.

50.082   SR   1925/   Over den kleinen landbouw in Suriname [About small-scale agri-
                      26   culture in Surinam].

LEPPER, G. W.

54.035   BB   1949   Report on oil development policy in Barbados.

LEWIS, A. B.

46.133   GC   1951   A land improvement programme for the Caribbean. *Car Commn Mon*
                      Inf B 4(10), May: 787-792.   [66]   [*COL*]

LEWIS, W. ARTHUR

49.050   BC   1950   The industrialization of the British West Indies.

46.134   GC   1951   Issues in land settlement policy. *Car Econ Rev* 3(1-2), Oct.: 58-92.
                      [47, 66]   [*RIS*]

LEYS, J. J.

32.123   SR   1915   Agricultural instruction in Surinam.

LIDEN, CONRAD H.

66.090   BG   1956   Technical assistance in British Guiana.

LIEMS, J. A.
46.135   SR   1931/ Antwoord op "Indruk van Suriname" van Ir. Iman G.J. van den Bosch
              32 [Reply to "Impression of Surinam" of Ir. Iman G. J. van den Bosch].
              W I G 13:25-29.   [*COL*]

LIER, RUDOLF A. J. van
66.092   SR   1954 Le plan de développement de Surinam [The development plan for
              Surinam], [by] R. A. L. [sic] van Lier.

LOXTON, R. F.; RUTHERFORD, G. K. & SPECTOR, J.
57.048   BG   1958 SOIL AND LAND-USE SURVEYS. No. 2: BRITISH GUIANA–THE RUPUNUNI
              SAVANNAS.

LOWENTHAL, DAVID
55.028   AT   1955 Economic tribulations in the Caribbean: a case study in the British
              West Indies.

MacFAYDEN, Sir ERIC
32.127   TR   1949 I.C.T.A. fills key position in British Empire.

McMORRIS, C. S.
46.136   JM   1957 Small-farm financing in Jamaica. *Social Econ Stud* 6(3), Sept.:
              suppl. (128p.) [47, 53]   [*RIS*]

MADDEN, F.
66.096   BC   1954 Social and economic conditions of the British West Indies.

MADDOX, JAMES G.
46.137   GC   1952 The major land utilization problems of the Caribbean areas. *In*
              WILGUS, A. CURTIS, ed. THE CARIBBEAN: PEOPLES, PROBLEMS AND
              PROSPECTS [papers delivered at the Second Annual Conference on
              the Caribbean, held at the University of Florida, Dec. 1951].
              Gainesville, University of Florida Press, p.27-43. (Publications
              of the School of Inter-American Studies, ser. 1, v. 2.) [47, 66] [*RIS*]

MARTIN-KAYE, P. H. A. & BADCOCK, J.
40.121   BB   1962 Geological background to soil conservation and land rehabilitation
              measures in Barbados, W. I.

MASEFIELD, G. B.
46.138   BC   1950 A SHORT HISTORY OF AGRICULTURE IN THE BRITISH COLONIES. Oxford,
              Oxford University Press, 178p. [5]   [*RIS*]

MATLEY, CHARLES ALFRED, et al.
40.124   JM   1951 GEOLOGY AND PHYSIOGRAPHY OF THE KINGSTON DISTRICT, JAMAICA.

MATTHEWS, CEDRIC O. J.
46.139   GC   1951 Agricultural labour and mechanisation. *Car Econ Rev* 3(1-2), Oct.:
              48-57. [66]   [*RIS*]

MAURICE, JOSEPH
46.140   MT   1963 L'expansion de l'économie agricole de la Martinique [The expan-
              sion of Martinique's agricultural economy]. *Rev Econ Fr* 85(1):
              23-28. [66]   [*AGS*]

MBOGUA, JOHN PETER
46.141   BB   1964 PEASANT AGRICULTURE IN BARBADOS—A SAMPLE STUDY. M. A. thesis,
                   McGill University, 152p.

MENKMAN, W. R.
17.018   SR   1927/ Nog een emigratie van Nederlanders naar Suriname [Another emi-
              28   gration of Dutch people to Surinam].
46.142   SR   1937 Welke kansen biedt Suriname voor landbouwkolonisatie door blanken?
                   [What possibilities can Surinam offer for agricultural colonization
                   by whites?] W I G 19:107-117.   [7]   [COL]
32.137   SR   1939 Landbouwopvoeding der Surinaamsche jeugd [Agricultural education
                   of the Surinam youth].
46.143   SR   1940 Landbouw-economische politiek in Suriname [Agricultural-economic
                   policy in Surinam]. W I G 22:12-19.   [37, 66]   [COL]

MERRILL, GORDON CLARK
46.144   GC   1958 The historical record of man as an ecological dominant in the
                   Lesser Antilles. Can Geogr 11:17-22.   [43]   [AGS]

MILLER, H.
46.145   JM   1958 The role of surveys in planning agricultural development in Jamaica.
                   W I Med J 7(3), Sept.: 222-227.   [66]   [COL]

MORRISON, CECIL J.
46.146   BB   1951 Peasant farming in Barbados. Farmer Jan.-Mar.: 31-35.

MORSE, RICHARD M.
32.141   GC   1960 Technical and industrial education in the Caribbean.

MUIR, J. C.
46.147   TR   1954 Agriculture in Trinidad. J Agric Soc Trin Tob 54(2), June: 137-152.
                                                                                          [AMN]

MURRAY, D. B.
46.148   TR   1962 The agricultural needs of Trinidad and Tobago with independence.
                   J Agric Soc Trin Tob 62(3), Sept.: 311-327.   [66]   [AMN]

MURRAY, GIDEON
46.149   BC   1919 The British West Indies and British Guiana: their resources and
                   development. Emp Rev 33(222), July: 218-224.   [50]   [NYP]

NASH, E. F.
51.107   BC   1958 Main characteristics of West Indian trade.

NATH, DWARKA
12.022   BG   1950 A HISTORY OF THE INDIANS IN BRITISH GUIANA.

NEUMARK, S. DANIEL
46.150   GC   1951 The importance of agriculture in Caribbean economy. Car Econ Rev
                   3(1-2), Oct.: 1-47.   [30, 66]   [RIS]

NICHOLLS, H. A. ALFORD
46.151   BC   1901 Legislation to control bush fires. W I B 2(2): 79-96.   [66]   [AMN]

46.152 BC 1902 The harmfulness of bush fires. *Proc Agric Soc Trin Tob* 4:305-321. [66] [*AMN*]

OBERG, KALERVO
46.153 SR 1964 A STUDY OF FARM PRODUCTIVITY IN THE SANTO BOMA SETTLEMENT PROJECT SURINAM. Ithaca, N.Y., Cornell University, 147p. (Comparative studies of cultural change.) [10, 50]

OBERG, KALERVO & HINDORI, GEORGE
46.154 SR 1963 GROOT HENAR POLDER: POLDER SETTLEMENT STUDY NO. II. Paramaribo, Surinam-American Technical Cooperative Service, 130p. [8, 66]

OBERG, KALERVO & MAY, EDWARD
46.155 SR 1961 POLDER SETTLEMENT STUDY NO. I: LA POULE. Paramaribo, Surinam-American Technical Cooperative Service, 82p. [66]

OLIVIER, SYDNEY, 1st Baron RAMSDEN
46.156 JM 1915 Recent developments in Jamaica: internal and external, by Sir Sydney Olivier. *J Roy Soc Arts* 64(3291), Dec. 17: 78-89. [51, 66] [*AMN*]
46.157 JM 1929 The improvement of Negro agriculture, by Lord Olivier. *J Roy Soc Arts* 77(3980), Mar. 1: 396-419. [11, 47, 66] [*AGS*]
11.021 JM 1929 Progress of a Negro peasantry, by Lord Olivier.

O'LOUGHLIN, CARLEEN
46.158 GC 1957 The measurement and significance of agricultural sector statistics in national accounting. *Social Econ Stud* 6(3), Sept.: 363-379. [44, 67] [*RIS*]

PAGE, H. J.
46.159 TR 1947 Peasant agriculture investigation at the Imperial College of Tropical Agriculture. *Proc Agric Soc Trin Tob* 47(4), Dec.: 293-310. [*AMN*]
46.160 TR 1949 Agricultural research at the Imperial College of Tropical Agriculture, Trinidad, B.W.I. *Car Econ Rev* 1(1-2), Dec.: 1-13. [32, 66] [*RIS*]
46.161 GC 1951 Agricultural research in relation to Caribbean economy. *Car Commn Mon Inf B* 4(9), Apr.: 749-752. [66] [*AGS*]

PAGET, E.
46.162 BC 1961 Value, valuation and use of land in the West Indies. *Geogr J* 127(4), Dec.: 493-498. [67] [*AGS*]

PALACHE, J. THOMAS
32.152 JM 1907 Agricultural instructors and their work.

PANDAY, R. M. N.
46.163 SR 1959 AGRICULTURE IN SURINAM, 1650-1950: AN INQUIRY INTO THE CAUSES OF ITS DECLINE. Amsterdam, H. J. Paris, 226p. [5] [*AGS*]

PARISINOS, C. C.; SHEPHARD, C. Y. & JOLLY, A. L.
46.164 TR 1944 Peasant agriculture: an economic survey of the Las Lomas District, Trinidad. *Trop Agric* 21(5), May: 84-98. [*RIS*]

PARRY, JOHN HORACE
46.165 JM 1955 Plantation and provision ground: an historical sketch of the introduction of food crops into Jamaica. *Revta Hist Am* 39 (June): 1-20. [44] [*RIS*]

46.166   JM   1962 Salt fish and ackee: an historical sketch of the introduction of food
                        crops into Jamaica. *Car Q* 8(4), Dec.: 30-36.   [5]   [*RIS*]

PEACOCKE, NORA E.
46.167   GC   1953 Research in relation to extension services in the Caribbean. *Car
                        Commn Mon Inf B* 6(10), May: 229-230.   [66]   [*AGS*]

PIM, Sir ALAN
46.168   BG   1946 The West Indies. *In his* COLONIAL AGRICULTURAL PRODUCTION. London,
                        Oxford University Press, p.87-114.   [*NYP*]

PLAATS, G. van der
46.169   NW   1923/ Eenige beschouwingen over de toekomst van den landbouw op de
                  24   Bovenwindsche Eilanden [Some observations about the future of
                        agriculture on the Windward Islands]. *W I G* 5:475-490. [66] [*COL*]

POTTER, THOMAS I.
41.187   TR   1931 Notes on bats in connection with agriculture.
46.170   TR   1932 The Agricultural Society and its affiliated branches. *Proc Agric Soc
                        Trin Tob* 32(9), Sept.: 317-326.   [5]   [*AMN*]
46.171   TR   1932 River Estate: a brief history of the property. *Proc Agric Soc Trin
                        Tob* 32(3), Mar.: 86-89; 32(5), May: 172-176.   [5, 45]   [*AMN*]

POULALION, PIERRE
46.172   FG   1927 Les ressources économiques de la Guyane Francaise [The economic
                        resources of French Guiana]. *B Ag Gen Colon* 20(223), Apr.: 595-
                        600.

POUND, F. J.
46.173   TR   1946 The extension services of the Department of Agriculture. *Proc
                        Agric Soc Trin Tob* 46(4), Dec.: 301-323.   [*AMN*]

PRICE, R. W.
57.052   JM   1959 SOIL AND LAND-USE SURVEYS. NO. 8: JAMAICA—PARISH OF ST. JAMES.
57.053   JM   1960 SOIL AND LAND-USE SURVEYS. NO. 12: JAMAICA—PARISH OF HANOVER.

PYTTERSEN, TJ.
46.174   SR   1920/ De toekomst van verschillende cultures in Suriname [The future of
                  21   several agricultural products in Surinam]. *W I G* 2:177-188, 344-354,
                        507-520, 565-587.   [58]   [*COL*]
46.175   SR   1921/ De toekomst van verschillende cultures in Suriname [The future of
                  22   several agricultural products in Surinam]. *W I G* 3:445-466, 573-
                        590, 608-625.   [*COL*]
58.079   TR   1927/ Enkele beschouwingen [Some observations].
                  28
46.176   SR   1927/ Europeesche kolonies in Suriname [European colonies in Surinam].
                  28   *W I G* 9:193-198.   [7]   [*COL*]
46.177   SR   1929/ Kantteekeningen over cultures in Suriname en elders [Some marginal
                  30   notes about cultivations in Surinam and elsewhere]. *W I G* 11:49-71.
                                                                                                [*COL*]
46.178   SR   1929/ De mogelijke opleving van Suriname [The possible revival of Sur-
                  30   inam]. *W I G* 11:289-306, 337-352. [5]   [*COL*]
46.179   SR   1931/ De cultuur-waarde van Suriname [The value of Surinam's cultiva-
                  32   tions]. *W I G* 13:109-122.   [*COL*]

REECE, J. E.

32.162   BB   1907 Agricultural teaching in elementary schools of Barbados.

RENAUD, MAURICE

41.194   FG   1932 Contribution à l'étude des bois de la Guyane Francaise [Contribution to the study of the timbers of French Guiana].

REVERT, EUGENE

46.180   MT   1946 L'agriculture à la Martinique [Agriculture in Martinique]. *B Ass Geogr Fr* 179-180, May-June: 83-90.   [*AGS*]

46.181   MT   1948 L'économie martiniquaise [Martinique's economy]. *Cah O-M* 1(1), Jan.-Mar.: 28-39. [58]   [*AGS*]

46.182   FA   1955 L'économie antillaise [Antillean economy]. *Etud O-M* 38, Feb.: 63-70. [51]   [*NYP*]

RICHARDSON, E. C.

46.183   TR   [196–] P.N.M. AND ITS AGRICULTURAL POLICY. San Juan, Trinidad, Vedic Enterprises, 23p. [37]   [*RIS*]

RIGOTARD, MARCEL

46.184   GD   1930 Une vieille colonie agricole: la Guadeloupe [An old agricultural colony: Guadeloupe]. *Agric Prat Pays Chauds* new ser., 1(3), Sept.: 182-193.   [*AGS*]

ROBERTS, GEORGE WOODROW

17.023   BC   1954 Immigration of Africans into the British Caribbean.

ROBINSON, C. K.

46.185   GC   1952 Food crops for local consumption. *Car Commn Mon Inf B* 6(5), Dec.: 105-107. [30, 66]   [*AGS*]

46.186   TR   1953 The food production programme of Trinidad and Tobago. *Car Commn Mon Inf B* 6(8), Mar.: 179-184. [30, 51, 66]   [*AGS*]

RODRIQUEZ, D. W.

46.187   JM   1961 COFFEE: A SHORT ECONOMIC HISTORY WITH SPECIAL REFERENCE TO JAMAICA. Kingston, Govt. Printer, 77p. (Ministry of Agriculture and Lands, Commodity bulletin no. 2.)

ROMNEY, D. H., ed.

46.188   BH   1959 LAND IN BRITISH HONDURAS: REPORT OF THE BRITISH HONDURAS LAND USE SURVEY TEAM. London, H.M.S.O., 326p. (Colonial research publications no. 24.)   [47,57,66]   [*RIS*]

ROTTENBERG, SIMON

50.100   AT   1951 Labor force measurement in pre-industrial economy.
50.103   GR   1952 Labor relations in an underdeveloped economy.
44.203   ST/   1953 A note on economic policy in Tortola.
         TT

RUTHERFORD, G. K.

57.056   BG   1956 Soil and land use patterns in the Rupununi savannas of British Guiana.

SAMPSON, H. C.

46.189   BG   1927 REPORT ON DEVELOPMENT OF AGRICULTURE IN BRITISH GUIANA. London,
                       H.M.S.O., 26p. (Empire Marketing Board publication no. 4.)   [*AGS*]
46.190   LW/   1927 REPORT ON DEVELOPMENT OF AGRICULTURE IN THE LEEWARD AND WIND-
          WW/   WARD ISLANDS AND BARBADOS. London, H.M.S.O., 16p. (Empire
          BB   Marketing Board publications, no. 5.)   [*AGS*]

SAMSON, PH. A.

46.191   SR   1949 Een mislukte poging [An unsuccessful attempt]. *W I G* 30:16-22.
                                                                                        [*COL*]

SANDERSON, AGNES G.

46.192   GC   1965 Notes on the agricultural economies of dependent territories in the
                       Western hemisphere and Puerto Rico. Washington, U.S. Department
                       of Agriculture, 68p. (Economic Research Service, ERS Foreign 145.)
                                                                                        [*RIS*]

SANDS, W. N.

46.193   SV   1914 Method of working small holdings under the land settlement scheme,
                       St. Vincent. *W I B* 14(1): 28-34. [47, 66]   [*AMN*]

SAUL, SAMUEL BERRICK

44.208 BC   1958 The British West Indies in depression.

SCHOCH, C. F.

46.194   SR   1926/De ondernemersraad voor Suriname en zijne voorstellen betreffende
                    27 den grooten landbouw [The Council of employers for Surinam and its
                       suggestions for large-scale agriculture]. *W I G* 8:219-234. [51,66]
                                                                                        [*COL*]

SEEL, Sir GEORGE

46.195   BG   1952 Some of the problems facing British Guiana agriculture. *Car Commn
                       Mon Inf B* 5(11), June: 311-313. [66]   [*AGS*]

SHANNON, J. LIONEL

46.196   TR   1940 Mixed farming. *Proc Agric Soc Trin Tob* 40(1), Mar.: 31-34.   [*AMN*]
46.197   TB   1948 Mixed farming in Tobago. *Proc Agric Soc Trin Tob* 48(1), Mar.:
                       67-73.   [*AMN*]
46.198   TR   1951 Grow more food through mixed farming. *J Agric Soc Trin Tob* 51(2),
                       June: 238-241.   [*AMN*]

SHAW, EARL BENNETT

46.199   JM   1943 The food front in the Greater Antilles. *Econ Geogr* 19(1), Jan.:
                       55-76. [30]   [*AGS*]

SHEPHARD, C. Y.

50.112 TR   1935 Agricultural labour in Trinidad.
51.123 GC   1939 British West Indian economic history in imperial perspective.
46.200   LW/   1947 Peasant agriculture in the Leeward and Windward Islands. Part I:—
          WW   The development of peasant agriculture. *Trop Agric* 24(4-6), Apr.-
                       June: 61-71. [5, 47]   [*RIS*]
46.201   LW/   1948 Peasant agriculture in the Leewards and Windwards. *Car Commn
          WW   Mon Inf B* 1(7), Feb.: 19-21. [47]   [*COL*]

46.202	BH	1954	Agriculture in British Honduras. *Car Commn Mon Inf B* 7(9), Apr.: 194-196, 201. [*COL*]
46.203	GC	1954	Background to agricultural extension in the Caribbean. *Car Commn Mon Inf B* 8(2), Sept.: 25-28, 33-34. [66] [*COL*]
46.204	FG	1954	French Guiana: background to agriculture. *Car Commn Mon Inf B* 7(11), June: 250, 252-253, 255. [*COL*]
46.205	JM	1955	Agricultural extension. *Caribbean* 9(3), Oct.: 56-57, 65: [66] [*COL*]
46.206	JM	1955	Jamaica: report on agriculture. *Caribbean* 8(9), Apr.: 202-208. [66] [*COL*]
53.034	JM	1955	Land titles.

SIMMS, Rev. Canon WILLIAM

32.184	JM	1900	Agricultural education.
32.185	JM	1900	The proposed agricultural department and agricultural teaching in Jamaica.
32.186	JM	1901	Agricultural education and its place in general education.
32.187	JM	1907	Agricultural and scientific teaching in the secondary schools of Jamaica.

SIRES, RONALD VERNON

| *50.115* | JM | 1940 | Negro labor in Jamaica in the years following emancipation. |
| *50.116* | JM | 1940 | Sir Henry Barkly and the labor problem in Jamaica 1853-1856. |

SKEETE, C. C.

| 46.207 | BB | 1930 | THE CONDITION OF PEASANT AGRICULTURE IN BARBADOS. [Bridgetown?] Barbados, [Printed for the] Department of Science and Agriculture, Barbados [by] Advocate Co., 52p. |

SLOTHOUWER, L.

| 46.208 | NW 31 | 1930/ | Nog eens de Bovenwindsche Eilanden [The Windward Islands once again]. *W I G* 12:17-24. [44] [*COL*] |

SMITH, M. G.

| *50.117* | JM | 1956 | A report on labour supply in rural Jamaica. |

SPAULL, HEBE

| 46.209 | JM | 1962 | Jamaica plans an agricultural policy. *New Commonw* 40(10), Oct.: 621-624. [48] |

SPOON, W.

| *51.131* | SR 33 | 1932/ | Enkele Surinaamsche producten in Nederland in 1932 [Some Surinam products in the Netherlands in 1932]. |

SPRINGER, HUGH W.

| *38.115* | BC | 1961 | The West Indies emergent: problems and prospects. |

STAHEL, GEROLD

| 46.210 | SR 34 | 1933/ | De cultuurwaarde van Suriname [The value of Surinam's cultivations]. *W I G* 15:158-162. [66] [*COL*] |

STANFORD, OLLY N.

| *32.192* | TR | 1945 | The 4-H clubs movement. |

STARCK, AUBREY R.

55.036   BC   1952 British West Indies: economic and commercial conditions in the
                         eastern Caribbean.

STARK, J. et al.

57.057   BG   1959 Soil and land-use surveys. No. 5: British Guiana.

STARK, J.; RUTHERFORD, G. K.; SPECTOR, J. & JONES, T. A.

57.058   BG   1959 Soil and land-use surveys. No. 6: British Guiana.

STARKEY, OTIS P.

44.224   BB   1958 Increasing crops and the standard of living—a West Indian example.

STEHLE, HENRI

46.211   FC   1950 New agricultural research centre set up for French Caribbean
                         Departments. *Car Commn Mon Inf B* 4(4), Nov.: 571-578, 570.   [66]
                                                                                         [*COL*]

46.212   FA   1954 Research into the problems of small scale farming in the French
                         West Indies. *In* Small scale farming in the Caribbean. [Port of
                         Spain?] Trinidad, Caribbean Commission, p.75-77.   [66]

STELL, F.

41.235   BG   1921 Colony birds in relation to agriculture.

STEVENSON, N. S.

64.100   BH   1938 The evolution of vegetation survey and rural planning in British
                         Honduras.

STOCKDALE, Sir FRANK A., ed.

46.213   BB   1941 Agricultural development in Barbados: despatches from the
                         Comptroller for Development and Welfare in the West Indies
                         to His Excellency the Governor of Barbados. [Bridgetown?]
                         Barbados, Advocate Co., 32p.   [58, 66]   [*RIS*]

STUART, G. MOODY

32.196   TR   1919 Agricultural college and re-organization of the Imperial Department
                         of Agriculture.
32.197   BC   1920 Agricultural college for the West Indies.

TAYLOR, CARL C.

46.214   JM   1953 Some land situations and problems in Caribbean countries. *In*
                         WILGUS A. CURTIS, ed. The Caribbean: contemporary trends
                         [papers delivered at the Third Annual Conference held at the Uni-
                         versity of Florida, December 18-20, 1952]. Gainesville, University
                         of Florida Press, p.59-73. (Publications of the School of Inter-
                         American Studies, ser. 1, v. 3.)   [47, 66]   [*RIS*]

TAYLOR, S. A. G.

46.215   JM   1955 An account of the development of the water resources of the Claren-
                         don Plains. *Social Econ Stud* 4(3), Sept.: 216-230.   [40,66]   [*RIS*]

TEMPANY, Sir HAROLD A.

46.216   GC   1952 The influence of introduced crops on colonial economies. *Car Commn
                         Mon Inf B* 6(2), Sept.: 33-36, 38.   [45]   [*AGS*]

THAYSEN, A. C.

46.217　GC　1950　Can politics feed our millions? *Proc Agric Soc Trin Tob* 50(1), Mar.: 81-85.　[66]　　　　　　　　　　　　　　　　　*[AMN]*

THOMPSON, JOHN B.

46.218　UV　1926　GARDENING IN THE VIRGIN ISLANDS. Washington, U.S. Govt. Print. Off., 19p. (Virgin Islands Agricultural Experiment Station bulletin no. 6.)　　　　　　　　　　　　　　　　　*[NYP]*

THOMPSON, ROBERT WALLACE

46.219　JM　1959　Vázquez de Espinosa and Jamaica. *Jam Hist Rev* 3(2), Mar.: 63-65. [5]　　　　　　　　　　　　　　　　　*[COL]*

THORNE, ALFRED P.

46.220　JM　1960　An economic phenomenon. *Car Q* 6(4): 270-278.　[20]　　　*[RIS]*

TIGGELMAN, G. P.

46.221　SR　1954　Research into the problems of small scale farming in Surinam. *In* SMALL SCALE FARMING IN THE CARIBBEAN. [Port of Spain?] Trinidad, Caribbean Commission, p.78-79.　[66]

TUCKER, R. W. E. et al.

46.222　BB　1931　CONTROL OF FIELD CROP, GARDEN AND FRUIT PESTS IN BARBADOS. [Bridgetown?] Barbados, Dept. of Science and Agriculture, 8p. (Pamphlet no. 7.)　[41]

VERKADE-CARTIER van DISSEL, E. F.

7.080　SR　1937　DE MOGELIJKHEID VAN LANDBOUW-KOLONISATIE VOOR BLANKEN IN SURINAME [THE POSSIBILITY OF AGRICULTURAL SETTLEMENT FOR WHITES IN SURINAM].

VERNON, K. C.

57.063　JM　1958　SOIL AND LAND-USE SURVEYS. NO. 1: JAMAICA—PARISH OF ST. CATHERINE.
57.064　JM　1959　SOIL AND LAND-USE SURVEYS. NO. 4: JAMAICA—PARISH OF ST. ANDREW.
57.065　JM　1960　SOIL AND LAND-USE SURVEYS. NO. 10: JAMAICA—PARISH OF ST. MARY.

VERNON, K. C.; PAYNE, HUGH & SPECTOR, J.

57.066　GR/　1959　SOIL AND LAND-USE SURVEYS. NO. 9: GRENADA.
　　　　CR

VERTEUIL, ERIC de

28.539　TR　1934　Agriculture and health.

VOGT, J.

46.223　SR　1958　Surinam et Guyane Britannique [Surinam and British Guiana]. *Inf Geogr* 22(4), Sept.-Oct.: 139-148.　　　　　　　　　　*[AGS]*

WAAL, L. de

46.224　SR　1927/　Java-methoden voor Suriname [Javanese methods for Surinam]? 28　*W I G* 9:38-42.　[15]　　　　　　　　　　　　　　*[COL]*

WAKEFIELD, A. J. et al.
46.225   TR   1943 REPORT OF THE AGRICULTURAL POLICY COMMITTEE OF TRINIDAD AND
                        TOBAGO. [Port of Spain?] Trinidad, Government Printer, 2v.   [66]

WALKER, H. De R.
3.320   BC   1902 THE WEST INDIES AND THE EMPIRE: STUDY AND TRAVEL IN THE WINTER
                        OF 1900-1901.

WARDLAW, C. W.
46.226   SR   1930 Agriculture in Surinam. Trop Agric 7(2): 31-37.   [45]   [RIS]
32.206   GC   1941 Foundations of tropical agriculture.

WARNER, HENRY
28.548   TR   1919 Water supply and sanitary reform.

WATSON, J. P.; SPECTOR, J. & JONES, T. A.
57.069   SV   1958 SOIL AND LAND-USE SURVEYS. NO. 3: ST. VINCENT.

WATTS, Sir FRANCIS
32.208   BC   1910 Systems of agricultural education.
32.209   BC   1914 On agricultural education and its adjustment to the needs of the
                        students.
46.227   MS   1915 Agricultural industries of Montserrat. W I B 15(1): 14-21 [66] [NYP]
46.228   DM   1915 The development of Dominica. W I B 15(3): 198-207. [66]   [AMN]
46.229   BC   1920 Tropical departments of agriculture, with special reference to the
                        West Indies. J Roy Soc Arts 68(3509), Feb. 20: 216-225; 68(3510),
                        Feb. 27: 232-243. [5]   [AGS]
46.230   BC   1921 Tropical departments of agriculture with special reference to the
                        West Indies. W I B 18(3): 101-133. [66]   [AMN]
46.231   BC   1924 Complexities of modern agriculture. Proc Agric Soc Trin Tob 24(10),
                        Oct.: 483-497.   [AMN]
46.232   BC   1927 West Indian notes. Trop Agric 4(10), Oct.: 187-188; 4(11), Nov.:
                        208-209; 4(12), Dec.: 227-229. [5]   [AGS]

WEEVER, P. M. de
46.233   BG   1921 Our future peasantry. Timehri 3d ser., 7(24), Aug.: 107-109.
                        [8, 32, 66]   [AMN]

WENT, F. A. F. C.
46.234   NL   1902 RAPPORT OMTRENT DEN TOESTAND VAN LAND- EN OOFTBOUW OP DE
                        NEDERLANDSCHE ANTILLEN [REPORT CONCERNING THE CONDITION OF
                        AGRICULTURE AND FRUIT GROWING IN THE NETHERLANDS ANTILLES].
                        [Willemstad?] Bijlage Koloniaal Verslag Curacao.

WESTERMANN, J. H.
46.235   NA   1947 Natuurbescherming op de Nederlandsche Antillen, haar etische,
                        aesthetische, wetenschappelijke en economische perspectieven
                        [The protection of nature on the Dutch Antilles, its ethical, es-
                        thetical, scientific and economic perspectives]. W I G 28:193-216.
                        [2, 41, 66]   [COL]

WESTERMANN, J. H. & ZONNEVELD, J. I. S.

40.216   BN   1956 PHOTO-GEOLOGICAL OBSERVATIONS AND LAND CAPABILITY AND LAND USE SURVEY OF THE ISLAND OF BONAIRE (NETHERLANDS ANTILLES).

WILLIAMS, C. HOLMAN B.

46.236   BC   1954 Peasant farming in the British Caribbean. *J Agric Soc Trin Tob* 54(2), June: 226-236.   [*AMN*]

32.214   BC   1960 Faculty of Agriculture—University College of the West Indies.

WILLIAMS, ERIC EUSTACE

46.237   GC   1952 Agricultural development. *Car Commn Mon Inf B* 6(5), Dec.: 108-110. [66]   [*AGS*]

46.238   GC   1954 The importance of small scale farming in the Caribbean. *In* SMALL SCALE FARMING IN THE CARIBBEAN. [Port of Spain?] Trinidad, Caribbean Commission, p.1-14. [58]

WILLIAMS, ERIC EUSTACE, ed.

32.220   GC   1953 Evaluation of existing facilities for vocational training in the Caribbean and proposals for their improvement.

WILLIAMS, J. R.

32.221   JM   1905 Popular agricultural education in Jamaica.

WILLIAMS, R. O. & R. O., Jr.

41.266   TR   1941 THE USEFUL AND ORNAMENTAL PLANTS IN TRINIDAD AND TOBAGO, Rev. 3d ed.

WILSON, P. N.

32.222   BC   1961 Agricultural education in the West Indies.

46.239   TR   1963 Agricultural prospects for Trinidad and Tobago. *J Agric Soc Trin Tob* 63(4), Dec.: 473-494.   [*AMN*]

32.223   TR   1963 The teaching and research programme of the Department of Agriculture (I.C.T.A.), University of the West Indies.

WISEMAN, H. V.

38.129   BC   1948 THE WEST INDIES, TOWARDS A NEW DOMINION?

WITT, GORDON

46.240   TR   1959 The use of fertilisers in Trinidad agriculture. *J Agric Soc Trin Tob* 59(2), June: 175-191. [57]   [*AMN*]

WOOD, R. CECIL

46.241   TR   1938 Settled holdings in the tropics. *Trop Agric* 15(7), July: 147-153.   [*AGS*]

WORTLEY, E. J.

32.224   JM   1907 General science in elementary schools of Jamaica.

WOOD, R. CECIL; PATERSON, D. D. & SEIGNORET, E. J.

50.127   TR   1933 Labour and labour rates on the College Farm.

WOUW, J. J. van

46.242   SR   1949 Het departement van landbouw-economische zaken in Suriname in 1945 [The department of agricultural-economic affairs in Surinam in 1945]. *W I G* 30:244-249. [37, 44]   [*COL*]

WRIGHT, JAMES

33.056   **JM**   1947 Lucky Hill Community Project.

YDE, JENS

46.243   **BG**   1957 The agricultural level of the Waiwai Indians. *Timehri* 4th ser.,
                              1(36), Oct.: 23-35.   [13]

46.244   **BG**   1960 Agriculture and division of work among the Waiwai. *Folk* 2:83-97.
                              [13, 30]   [*COL*]

YOUNG, R. T.

46.245   **TR**   1929 The resources of Trinidad. *Can-W I Mag* 18(10), Aug.: 231-232.
                                                                                                         [*NYP*]

Chapter 47

LAND TENURE

AUCHINLECK, GILBERT; SMITH, G. WHITFIELD & BERTRAND, WALTER
47.001   GN/   1914   Government schemes of land settlement in Grenada and the Grena-
        GR   dines. *W I B* 14(1): 9-23.   [46,66]   [*AMN*]

AUGELLI, JOHN P.
47.002   AT   1953   Patterns and problems of land tenure in the Lesser Antilles: Anti-
                   gua, B.W.I. *Econ Geogr* 29(4), Oct.: 362-367.   [*RIS*]
43.003   GD   1962   Land use in Guadeloupe.

BALDWIN, RICHARD
47.003   BG   1959   The little republic. *Timehri* 4th ser., no. 38: 49-56.   [46]   [*AMN*]

BIJLSMA, R.
47.004   SR   1920/   De Surinaamsche grondbrieven ten tijde van Gouverneur van Aers-
              21   sen van Sommelsdijck [The land certificates of Surinam during the
                   time of Governor van Aerssen van Sommelsdijck]. *W I G* 2:593-596.
                   [5]   [*COL*]

BLECOURT, A. S. de
47.005   SR   1922/   Allodiaal eigendom en erfelijk bezit in Suriname [Allodial ownership
              23   and hereditary property in Surinam]. *W I G* 4:129-158.   [*COL*]

BLUME, HELMUT
47.006   BC   1961   Die Britischen Inseln über dem Winde (Kleine Antillen): Grundbe-
                   sitz und Betriebsformen in ihrem Einfluss auf das Bild der Kultur-
                   landschaft [The British Lesser Antilles: The influence of land ten-
                   ure and property structure on the appearance of the cultural land-
                   scape]. *Erdkunde* 15(4): 265-287.   [*RIS*]
47.007   JM   1961   Die gegenwärtigen Wandlungen in der Verbreitung von Gross- und
                   Kleinbetreiben auf den Grossen Antillen [Contemporary changes in
                   the distribution of large and small holdings in the Greater Antilles].
                   In LAUER, WILHELM, ed.   BEITRÄGE ZUR GEOGRAPHIE DER NEUEN
                   WELT. Kiel, Im Selbstverlag des Geographischen Instituts der Uni-
                   versität Kiel, p.75-123. (Schriften des Geographischen Instituts
                   der Universität Kiel, v.20.)   [46,66]   [*RIS*]

BROWN, HEADLEY & ANDERSON, ERROL
47.008   BC   1963/ Economic development in the West Indies and the peasantry. *Social*
                    64   *Scient* 2:21-24.   [46, 50, 66]   [*RIS*]

BUCKMASTER, MICHAEL H.
47.009   LW/   1965 Some aspects of land purchase and development in the Leewards
            WW   and Windwards. *Chron W I Comm* 80(1404), Jan.: 17-18. [55]   [*NYP*]

CLARKE, EDITH
47.010   JM   1953 Land tenure and the family in four communities in Jamaica. *Social*
                          Econ Stud 1(4), Aug.: 81-118.   [9]   [*RIS*]
9.003   JM   1957 MY MOTHER WHO FATHERED ME: A STUDY OF THE FAMILY IN 3 SELECTED
                          COMMUNITIES IN JAMAICA.

CUMPER, GEORGE E.
58.028   JM   1954 A modern Jamaican sugar estate.
7.011   JM   1956 Population movements in Jamaica, 1830-1950.

DALTON, L.C.
37.088   BG   1915 Some controverted points of local law with respect to leases.

DAMBAUGH, LUELLA N.
43.035   JM   1953 Jamaica: an island in transition.

DEURE, A. van der
37.097   SR   1919/ Rechtszekerheid van de grondeigendommen in Suriname [Legal se-
                    20   curity of the landed properties in Surinam].

DOUGLAS, CH.
46.055   SR   1927/ Aanteekeningen over den landbouw in Suriname [Notes about agri-
                    28   culture in Surinam].

EDWARDS, DAVID T.
46.060   JM   1961 AN ECONOMIC STUDY OF SMALL FARMING IN JAMAICA.

FABIUS, G. J.
47.011   NA/   1914 Het leenstelsel van de West-Indische Compagnie [The feudal system
            BG   of the West-Indian Company]. *Bijd Volk Ned-Indie* 70:555-593.   [5]

FINKEL, HERMAN J.
47.012   LW/   1964 Patterns of land tenure in the Leeward and Windward Islands and
            WW   their relevance to problems of agricultural development in the West
                          Indies. *Econ Geogr* 40(2), Apr.: 163-172.   [*COL*]

FOREMAN, R. A.
47.013   SL   1958 LAND SETTLEMENT SCHEME FOR SAINT LUCIA: BASED ON A SURVEY OF
                          THE AGRICULTURAL AND SOCIAL CONDITIONS OF THE ISLAND ON A VISIT
                          FROM 24.3.58-26.4.58.   Castries, St. Lucia, Government Printer.
                          [46,66]

FOSTER, BEN R.
47.014   UV   1947 Homesteading in the Virgin Islands. *Car Commn Mon Inf B* 1(4),
                          Nov.: 26-28.   [66]   [*COL*]

FRAMPTON, A. de K.

47.015   BC   1952 Land tenure in relation to the British West Indies. *Car Econ Rev* 4(1-2), Dec.: 113-139.   [66]   [*RIS*]

46.073   BC   1954 Land problems in small scale farming.

FREEMAN, L. A.

47.016   BG   1946 Land tenure in British Guiana. *In* CARIBBEAN LAND TENURE SYMPOSIUM, CARIBBEAN COMMISSION: COMMITTEE ON AGRICULTURE, NUTRITION, FISHERIES AND FORESTRY OF THE CARIBBEAN RESEARCH COUNCIL [Mayagüez, P. R., Aug. 1944]. Washington, D.C. p.357, 374.   [*RIS*]

FREILICH, MORRIS

67.005   TR   1960 Cultural models and land holdings.

GAAY FORTMAN, B. de

47.017   CU   1936/ Twee verzoekschriften aan den koning over den landbouwpolitiek 37   van Gouverneur van Raders in Curacao [Two petitions to the king about the agricultural policy of Governor van Raders in Curacao]. *W I G* 18:321-329.   [5,46]   [*COL*]

GREENFIELD, SIDNEY M.

47.018   BB   1960 Land tenure and transmission in rural Barbados. *Anthrop Q* 33(4), Oct.: 165-176.   [8,9]   [*RIS*]

GROL, G. J. van

47.019   NA   1934/ DE GRONDPOLITIEK IN HET WEST-INDISCHE DOMEIN DER GENERALITEIT: 47   EEN HISTORISCHE STUDIE [LAND POLICY IN THE WEST INDIAN DOMAIN OF THE STATES GENERAL: AN HISTORICAL STUDY]. The Hague, Algemeene Landsdrukkerij, 3v.   [*COL*]

HARRIS, MARSHALL

47.020   GC   1946 Objectives of land tenure policy. *In* CARIBBEAN LAND TENURE SYMPOSIUM, CARIBBEAN COMMISSION: COMMITTEE ON AGRICULTURE, NUTRITION, FISHERIES AND FORESTRY OF THE CARIBBEAN RESEARCH COUNCIL [Mayagüez, P. R., Aug. 1944]. Washington, D.C., p.30-57. [*RIS*]

HODNETT, G. E. & NANTON, W. R. E.

47.021   BC   1959 Definitions of a farm and a farmer in agricultural statistics in the West Indies. *Social Econ Stud* 8(2), June: 190-196. [67]   [*RIS*]

HORN, EDWIN

35.023   BC   [n.d.] THE WEST INDIES: REPORT OF A SURVEY ON HOUSING, NOVEMBER 1956- MAY 1957.

HOY, DON R.

46.093   GD   1961 Agricultural land use of Guadeloupe.

JOHNS, ROBERT

47.022   LW   1946 The British system of compensation for unexhausted improvements and penalties for dilapidations: its application to the West Indies. *In* CARIBBEAN LAND TENURE SYMPOSIUM, CARIBBEAN COMMISSION: COMMITTEE ON AGRICULTURE, NUTRITION, FISHERIES AND FORESTRY OF THE CARIBBEAN RESEARCH COUNCIL [Mayagüez, P. R., Aug. 1944]. Washington, D.C., p.81-90.   [*RIS*]

KIELSTRA, J. C.
47.023   SR   1946 Application of Netherlands Indies agrarian principles to Surinam. *In*
CARIBBEAN LAND TENURE SYMPOSIUM, CARIBBEAN COMMISSION: COM-
MITTEE ON AGRICULTURE, NUTRITION, FISHERIES AND FORESTRY OF THE
CARIBBEAN RESEARCH COUNCIL [Mayagüez, P. R., Aug. 1944].   Wash-
ington, D. C. p.335-346.   [*RIS*]

LEAKE, H. MARTIN
47.024   BC   1932 Studies in tropical land tenure. (2) The West Indies. *Trop Agric* 9
(9), Sept.: 272-276.   [5]   [*AGS*]
47.025   BC   1938 Further studies in tropical land tenure. Part II: The West Indies.
Trop Agric 15(7), July: 163-165; 15(8), Aug.: 175-178. [46]   [*AGS*]

LEWIS, W. ARTHUR
46.134   GC   1951 Issues in land settlement policy.

LIMBURG, STIRUM, O. E. G., Graaf van
47.026   SR   1923/ De Surinaamsche grondpolitiek [The land policy of Surinam] *W I G*
24   5:639-647.   [*COL*]

LOWENTHAL, DAVID
20.011   BC   1961 Caribbean views of Caribbean land.

McMORRIS, C. S.
46.136   JM   1957 Small-farm financing in Jamaica.

MADDOX, JAMES G.
46.137   GC   1952 The major land utilization problems of the Caribbean areas.

MATHIESON, WILLIAM LAW
6.047   BC   1932 BRITISH SLAVE EMANCIPATION, 1838-49.

OLIVIER, SYDNEY, 1st Baron RAMSDEN
46.157   JM   1929 The improvement of Negro agriculture, by Lord Olivier.

OTTERBEIN, KEITH F.
9.028   JM/   1964 A comparison of the land tenure systems of the Bahamas, Jamaica,
          BB   and Barbados: the implications it has for the study of social sys-
                       tems shifting from bilateral to ambilineal descent.

PADILLA, ELENA
67.017   GC   1960 Contemporary social-rural types in the Caribbean region.

QUINTUS BOSZ, A. J. A.
47.027   SR   1954/ Het recht van allodiale eigendom en erfelijk bezit in Suriname [The
          55   right of allodial property and hereditary possession in Surinam]. *Vox*
                Guy 1(4-5), Nov.-Jan.: 79-84.
47.028   SR   1954 DRIE EEUWEN GRONDPOLITIEK IN SURINAME: EEN HISTORISCHE STUDIE
VAN DE ACHTERGROND EN DE ONTWIKKELING VAN DE SURINAAMSE RECHTEN
OP DE GROND [THREE CENTURIES OF LAND POLICY IN SURINAM: AN HIS-
TORICAL STUDY OF THE BACKGROUND AND DEVELOPMENT OF LAND RIGHTS
IN SURINAM].   Assen [Netherlands] VanGorcum, 487p. [5]   [*RIS*]

ROMNEY, D. H., ed.

46.188   BH   1959 LAND IN BRITISH HONDURAS: REPORT OF THE BRITISH HONDURAS LAND USE SURVEY TEAM.

SANDS, W. N.

46.193   SV   1914 Method of working small holdings under the land settlement scheme, St. Vincent.

SHEPHARD, C. Y.

46.200   LW/   1947 Peasant agriculture in the Leeward and Windward Islands. Part I:
           WW   The development of peasant agriculture.

46.201   LW/   1948 Peasant agriculture in the Leewards and Windwards.
           WW

53.034   JM   1955 Land titles.

SMITH, M. G.

50.117   JM   1956 A REPORT ON LABOUR SUPPLY IN RURAL JAMAICA.

47.029   CR   1956 The transformation of land rights by transmission in Carriacou. *Social Econ Stud* 5(2), June: 103-138.   [9]   [*RIS*]

SMITH, RAYMOND THOMAS

47.030   BG   1955 Land tenure in three Negro villages in British Guiana. *Social Econ Stud* 4(1), Mar.: 64-82.   [8,11]   [*RIS*]

62.024   BG   1957 Economic aspects of rice production in an East Indian community in British Guiana.

TAYLOR, CARL C.

46.214   JM   1953 Some land situations and problems in Caribbean countries.

THELWELL, ARTHUR

47.031   GC   1946 Comparison of leasehold and freehold systems of land tenure. *In* CARIBBEAN LAND TENURE SYMPOSIUM, CARIBBEAN COMMISSION: COMMITTEE ON AGRICULTURE, NUTRITION, FISHERIES AND FORESTRY OF THE CARIBBEAN RESEARCH COUNCIL [Mayagüez, P. R., Aug. 1944]. Washington, D.C., p.59-71.   [*RIS*]

WARNER, HENRY

28.548   TR   1919 Water supply and sanitary reform.

WATTS, Sir FRANCIS

47.032   GR/   1914 Efforts in aid of peasant agriculture in the West Indies. *W I B* 14(1),
           CR/   1-8.   [48,53]   [*AMN*]
           SV

WILLIAMS, JAMES

47.033   BG   1936 The aborigines of British Guiana and their land. *Anthropos* 31(3-4), May-Aug.: 417-432.   [5,13]   [*NYP*]

ZONNEVELD, J. I. S. & KRUIJER, GERARDUS JOHANNES

47.034   SR   1951 Nederzettings- en occupatie-vormen in Suriname [Settlements and other forms of territorial occupation in Surinam]. *Tijdschr Ned Aar Genoot* 68(4), Oct.: 376-411.   [10]   [*RIS*]

Chapter 48

COOPERATIVES

ANDERSON, ROBERT M.
53.002   SV   1914 Report on the agricultural credit societies of St. Vincent.

BERNARD, HECTOR
56.006   FC   1949 Jamaica peasant farmers set example in cooperation.

BONNER, A.
48.001   BC   1956 Cooperation in the British West Indies. *Venture* 8(6), Nov.: 4-5. [*COL*]

BOWEN, NOEL P.
48.002   GC   1954 Cooperatives in the Caribbean. *Car Commn Mon Inf B* 7(9), Apr.:
191-193, 208, 216.   [*COL*]

BRAITHWAITE, E. A.
48.003   GC   1954 Cooperatives in the Caribbean. *Car Commn Mon Inf B* 7(10), May:
219-220,232;   7(11), June: 241-242,260;   8(1), Aug.: 20-22; 8(4-5),
Nov.-Dec.: 80-81.   [*COL*]

CHEESMAN, W. J. W.
48.004   GC   1956 HANDBOOK FOR COOPERATIVE PERSONNEL IN THE CARIBBEAN. [Port of
Spain?] Trinidad, Food and Agriculture Organization of the United
Nations and the Caribbean Commission, 252p.

CLARKE, F. J.
48.005   BB   1908 Origin and establishment of the Barbados co-operative cotton factory. W I B 9(3): 243-246.   [61]   [*AMN*]

COMITAS, LAMBROS
56.017   JM   1962 FISHERMAN AND COOPERATION IN RURAL JAMAICA.

DAVIES, E. D.
48.006   TB   1957 Cocoa co-ops. *Caribbean* 11(3), Oct.: 60-62,72. [51,59]   [*COL*]

DUNLOP, W. R.
53.009   BC   1914   The West Indies and co-operative credit.

FRAMPTON, D. de K.
46.073   BC   1954 Land problems in small scale farming.

FRANCIS, SYBIL E.
35.017   JM   1953 A land settlement project in Jamaica.

GATES, RALPH CHARLES
51.054   BC   1959 Marketing of fresh vegetables in the Caribbean islands.
66.051   GC   1961 A MONOGRAPH ON COOPERATIVE DEVELOPMENT IN THE CARIBBEAN.

GILBERT, S. M.
48.007   TR   1931 Co-operation. *Proc Agric Soc Trin Tob* 31(5), May: 185-193.   [*AMN*]

GORDON, G. C. L.
48.008   BG   1957 The development of co-operation in British Guiana.   *Timehri* 4th
                           ser., 1(36), Oct.: 55-60.

GRETTON, R. H.
48.009   GC   1957 THE ROLE OF THE COOPERATIVE MOVEMENT IN ECONOMIC DEVELOPMENT,
                           WITH SPECIAL REFERENCE TO THE AREA SERVED BY THE CARIBBEAN COM-
                           MISSION. [Port of Spain?] Caribbean Commission, 18p.

HANDLER, JEROME S.
63.025   BB   1965 The history of arrowroot production in Barbados and the Chalky
                           Mount Arrowroot Growers' Association, a peasant marketing experi-
                           ment that failed.

KRUIJER, GERARDUS JOHANNES
46.127   BG/   1950 Landbouw-cooperatie onder de Aziatische bevolkingsgroepen van
             SR   Suriname en Brits Guyana [Agrarian cooperation among the Asiatic
                           population groups of Surinam and British Guiana.

LAMONT, Sir NORMAN, et al.
48.010   TR   1918 Report of the Co-operative Sugar Factories Committee.   *Proc Agric
                           Soc Trin Tob* 18(10), Oct.: 894-902.   [58]   [*AMN*]

ROBINSON, H. E.
48.011   TR   1954 The Cooperative Citrus Growers Association: a record of coopera-
                           tion and progress. *J Agric Soc Trin Tob* 54(2), June: 153-159. [60]
                                                                                          [*AMN*]

SHEPHARD, C. Y.
51.124   GC   1954 Marketing and processing problems.
51.125   BC   1954 Organisation for the processing and marketing of the products of
                           small scale farming.
59.047   TB   1957 Cooperative cocoa fermentaries in Tobago.
48.012   TR   1957 Postscript. *Caribbean* 11(3), Oct.: 63-64.   [59,66]   [*COL*]

SHERLOCK, PHILIP M.
48.013   BC   1958 The co-operative movement in the British Caribbean. *Int Lab Rev*
                           77(4), Apr.: 325-341.   [66]   [*COL*]

SPAULL, HEBE
46.209   JM   1962 Jamaica plans an agricultural policy.

STANIFORTH, A. R.
48.014   BG/   1944 Co-operative credit societies in the South Caribbean area. *Trop*
           SV/   *Agric* 21(12), Dec.: 219-227;
           TR   1945 22(1), Jan.: 3-8.   [*AGS*]

TURNER, WM. T.
53.039   JM   1907 The Christiana People's Co-operative Bank Limited.

VILLARONGA, MARIANO
48.015   GC   1962 El cooperativismo en el Caribe [Cooperative ventures in the Carib-
                       bean]. *Boricua* 1(4), Mar.: 32-33,95.   [53]   [*NYP*]

WATTS, Sir FRANCIS
47.032   GR/   1914 Efforts in aid of peasant agriculture in the West Indies.
           CR/
           SV

WEBSTER, AIMEE
48.016   JM   1961 Small farmers' role in Jamaica's economy. *New Commonw* 39(1),
                       Jan.: 65-66.   [*AGS*]

WELLS, A. F. & D.
53.042   BC   1953 FRIENDLY SOCIETIES IN THE WEST INDIES.

WOODING, H. O. B.
48.017   JM/   1947 Co-operation and agriculture. *Proc Agric Soc Trin Tob* 47(4), Dec.:
           TR   311-317.   [*AMN*]

Chapter 49

HANDICRAFTS, INDUSTRY AND INDUSTRIALIZATION

ALCALA, V. O.
32.005   GC   1952 Trade and industrial education.

BANCROFT, C. K.
49.001   BG/   1917 The making of panama hats: a suitable industry for British Guiana.
         SR   *J Bd Agric Br Gui* 10(2), Jan.: 90-92.   [32,66]   [*AMN*]

BARRY, JOHN
49.002   JM/   1946 Mulberry planting.   *Proc Agric Soc Trin Tob* 46(2), June: 139-147.
         TR   [63,66]   [*AMN*]

BATAILLE, EMILE C.
49.003   BG   1939 Report on industrial possibilities in British Guiana and on the establishment of an industrial center. *In* REPORT OF THE BRITISH GUIANA COMMISSION TO THE PRESIDENT'S ADVISORY COMMITTEE ON POLITICAL REFUGEES. Washington, D.C., [no. 1] (7p.)   [66]   [*AGS*]
49.004   BG   1942 Possibilities for industrial enterprise in British Guiana.   *Can-W I Mag* 31(12), Dec.: 11-14.   [66]   [*NYP*]

BRAHAM, HAROLD A.
49.005   JM   1961 Jamaica's trade fair and industrial progress. *W-I Econ* 4(1-2), July-Aug.: 34-35.   [*RIS*]

BRANNAM, J. R.
49.006   BB   1948 REPORT ON A PROPOSED CLAYWORKING INDUSTRY IN BARBADOS. Bridgetown, Colonial Secretary's Office, 25p.

BRETON, B. O.
49.007   AT   1956 Antigua—industrial development. *Caribbean* 10(2), Sept.: 30-31.   [66]
                                                         [*COL*]

BURGESS, CHARLES J.
49.008   GC   1952 Prewar industrial development.   *Car Commn Mon Inf B* 6(4), Nov.: 77-78.   [66]   [*AGS*]
49.009   GC   1952 World War II and industrialisation.   *Car Commn Mon Inf B* 6(5), Dec.: 99-100.   [66]   [*AGS*]

49.010   GC   1953 The achievements of industrialisation policy in the Caribbean. *Car Commn Mon Inf B* 6(9), Apr.: 207-210; 6(10), May: 217-218.   [66]
                                                                                          [*AGS*]
49.011   GC   1953 The future of industrialisation in the Caribbean. *Car Commn Mon Inf B* 6(11), June: 247-248,250.   [66]   [*AGS*]
49.012   GC   1953 Post war industrialisation policy. *Car Commn Mon Inf B* 6(7), Feb.: 149-150.   [66]   [*AGS*]

CAMPBELL, ELLA
49.013   JM   1953 Industrial training methods and techniques. *Social Econ Stud* 2(1), Sept.: 5-101.   [*RIS*]

CASE, GERALD O.
49.014   BG   1946 Problems affecting industrialisation of the interior of British Guiana. *In* ROTH, VINCENT, comp. HANDBOOK OF NATURAL RESOURCES OF BRITISH GUIANA. Georgetown, Daily Chronicle, p.234-243. [66]
                                                                                          [*AGS*]

CASSERLEY, C. J.
49.015   JM   1962 Ten years of progress. *Chron W I Comm* 77(1375), Aug.: 397-398.
                                                                                          [*NYP*]

CHAMPION, HAROLD
49.016   JM   1955 Industrial era for Jamaica. *New Commonw* 29(3), Feb. 7: 130-133. [66]

CHILES, KENLY
49.017   ST   1961 Manufacturing industry comes to St. Thomas. *Empl Secur Rev* 28(4), Apr.: 3-7.   [*NYP*]

CLEGG, J. B.
49.018   JM   1952 Commercial and industrial prospects in Jamaica. *Car Commn Mon Inf B* 6(5), Dec.: 97-98.   [66]   [*AGS*]

CUMPER, GEORGE E.
49.019   JM   1953 Labour productivity and capital-labour ratios in Jamaican manufacturing industry: their relation to the problem of selective industrialization. *Social Econ Stud* 1(1), Feb.: 61-86.   [50]   [*RIS*]

DOLLY, REYNOLD CARTWRIGHT
28.125   TR   1961 Some aspects of industrial medicine as seen in the oil industry.
49.020   TR   1963 The adolescent in industry. *In* CARTER, SAMUEL E., ed. THE ADOLESCENT IN THE CHANGING CARIBBEAN: PROCEEDINGS OF THE THIRD CARIBBEAN CONFERENCE FOR MENTAL HEALTH, APR. 4-11, 1961, UCWI JAMAICA. Kingston, Herald, p.184-186.   [32,33]   [*RIS*]

EMLYN, ARTHUR
49.021   TR   1963 Angostura Bitters (Dr. J.G.B. Siegert & Sons) Ltd. *Chron W I Comm* 78(1381), Feb.: 101,103.   [*NYP*]

FARLEY, RAWLE
49.022   BC   1958 NATIONALISM AND INDUSTRIAL DEVELOPMENT IN THE BRITISH CARIBBEAN. Georgetown, Daily Chronicle, 58p. [8, 21, 37, 46, 66]   [*RIS*]

FINCH, KENNETH W.

49.023   TR   1962 A commercial approach to rural electrification. *J Agric Soc Trin Tob* 62(3), Sept.: 335-358.   [44,66]   *[AMN]*

49.024   BC   1963 Electricity in the eastern Caribbean. *Chron W I Comm* 78(1382), Mar.: 124-126.   *[NYP]*

FLETCHER, S. G.

49.025   JM   1963 Conduct of arbitration I—preparation and presentation of case. (An employer's point of view.) *In* EATON, G.E., ed. PROCEEDINGS OF INDUSTRIAL RELATIONS CONFERENCE ON THE THEORY AND PRACTICE OF ARBITRATION, NOV. 1962. Mona, Institute of Social and Economic Research, University of the West Indies, p.30-38.   *[RIS]*

FLOOD, E. H. S.

49.026   BC   1920 The imports of machinery into the West Indies, by F. [sic] H. S. Flood. *Can-W I Mag* 8(10), Aug.: 601.   [51]   *[NYP]*

FRASER, F. W.

49.027   JM   1944 Industrial development in Jamaica. *Can-W I Mag* 33-34(2), Feb.: 10-15.   *[NYP]*

FUTEIN-NOLTHENIUS, A.

49.028   SR   1955 Getijmolens in Suriname [Tidal water-mills in Surinam]. *W I G* 35: 219-225.   *[COL]*

GREENWOOD-BARTON, L. H.

30.031   JM   1957 The establishment and administration of food standards in Jamaica.

GRIGSBY, W.

49.029   NV   1962 The potters of Nevis. *Craft Hor* 22(2), Mar.-Apr.: 21-23.   *[NYP]*

HANDLER, JEROME S.

49.030   BB   1963 A historical sketch of pottery manufacture in Barbados. *J Barb Mus Hist Soc* 30(3), Nov.: 129-153.   *[RIS]*

49.031   BB   1963 Pottery making in rural Barbados. *Sw J Anthrop* 19(3), Autumn: 314-334.   *[RIS]*

49.032   AT   1964 Notes on pottery-making in Antigua. *Man* 64(184), Sept.-Oct.: 150-151.   *[RIS]*

HANRATH, JOHANNES J.

49.033   SR   1953 Kans op hoogovenbedrijf in Suriname verkeken? [Has the chance for a blastoven industry in Surinam gone by?] *Tijdschr Econ Social Geogr* 44(1), Jan.: 30-32.   *[AGS]*

HARRIS, BRITTON

49.034   GC   1953 The role of government in industrial development in the Caribbean. *Car Econ Rev* 5(1-2), Dec.: 118-126.   [37,66]   *[RIS]*

HEESTERMAN, J. E.

49.035   CU/   1954 Fresh water can be made from the sea. *Caribbean* 8(2), Sept.: 29-
       AR   31,34,45.   *[COL]*

49.036   JM   1955 Jamaica, report on industry. *Caribbean* 8(6), Jan.: 109-111,127-128.   *[COL]*

65.023   GC   1955 USE OF INDUSTRIAL BY-PRODUCTS AS STOCK FEED.
49.037   GC   1956 Industry. *Caribbean* 10(4), Nov.: 83-85,112.   [66]   [COL]
49.038   NA   1956 Netherlands Antilles—industrial development.   *Caribbean* 10(1),
                 Aug.: 11-12.   [COL]
49.039   TR   1957 Industrial use of natural gas. *Caribbean* 10(6-7), Jan.-Feb.: 161-
                 164.   [54]   [COL]

HENRIQUEZ, O. S.
49.040   AR   1960 Aruba depends on sea-water. *Caribbean* 14(4), Apr.: 62-64,100.
                                                                                  [COL]

HENRIQUEZ, P. COHEN
49.041   CU   1938 Zeewaterverwerking [The processing of sea water]. *W I G* 20:321-
                 328.   [44]   [COL]

HENRY, BESSIE M.
49.042   BV   1957 English ceramics in the British Virgin Islands. *Antiques* 71(6),
                 June: 547-549.   [19]   [COL]

HOPKINS, E. B.
49.043   JM   1925 The silk worm industry in Jamaica. *Can-W I Mag* 15(1), Nov.: 15.
                 [63]   [NYP]

HUGHES, JUDITH C.
49.044   BB   1961 On sailors' valentines. *J Barb Mus Hist Soc* 29(1), Nov.: 3-6. [AMN]

JOUANDET-BERNADAT, ROLAND
49.045   GC   1964 Les expériences antillaises d'industrialisation [Antillean experi-
                 ence of industrialization]. *Cah Cent Etud Reg Ant-Guy* 4, Nov.:
                 59p.   [RIS]

KNOX, A. D.
49.046   JM   1956 Note on pioneer industry legislation. *In* SYMPOSIUM ON THE HICKS
                 REPORT. *Social Econ Stud* 5(1), Mar.: 32-38.   [37,66]   [RIS]

LEIGHTON, FRED
49.047   BC   1951 REPORT ON HANDICRAFTS AND COTTAGE INDUSTRIES IN THE BRITISH
                 WEST INDIES. Kingston, Government Printer, 10p. (Development and
                 Welfare Bulletin no. 31.)   [66]   [COL]
49.048   BC   1952 Handicrafts and cottage industries in the British West Indies. *Car
                 Commn Mon Inf B* 5(7), Feb.: 207-209.   [66]   [AGS]

LEITCH, ADELAIDE
49.049   DM   1956 Handicraft mats of Dominica. *Can Geogr J* 53(4), Oct.: 152-153.
                                                                                  [AGS]

LeMAIRE, G. W.
54.034   AR   1936 Aruba, Netherlands West Indies—the history and industrial develop-
                 ment.

LEWIS, W. ARTHUR
49.050   BC   1950 The industrialization of the British West Indies. *Car Econ Rev* 2
                 (1), May: 1-61.   [7,46,66]   [RIS]

McCOLGAN, KATHLEEN
49.051 TR 1951 Trinidad's brave new world. *U N Wld* 5(2), Feb.: 66-67.   [*COL*]

McFARLANE, DENNIS
37.240 BC 1964 A comparative study of incentive legislation in the Leeward Islands, Windward Islands, Barbados and Jamaica.

McKUSICK, MARSHALL BASSFORD
4.092 GC 1960 Aboriginal canoes in the West Indies.

MENDES, D. F.
49.052 JM 1962 Sulphuric acid manufacture in Jamaica. *Inf B Scient Res Coun* 3(3), Dec.: 41-43.   [*RIS*]

MENKMAN, W. R.
49.053 SR 1949 Industrie en industrialisatie in Suriname [Industry and industrialization in Surinam]. *W I G* 30:166-171.   [66]   [*COL*]

MERRY, C. A.
49.054 TR 1962 Progress and prospects of industrial development. *Chron W I Comm* 77(1376), Sept.: 457-458.   [*NYP*]

MORAIS, ALLAN I.
49.055 GC 1955 Tide of industry. *Caribbean* 8(11-12), June-July: 245-249,270-271; 9(1), Aug.: 5-8,15.   [*COL*]

MORSE, RICHARD M.
32.141 GC 1960 Technical and industrial education in the Caribbean.

OSBORNE, CHRISTOPHER
49.056 TR 1956 Handicraft in Trinidad. *Caribbean* 10(1), Aug.: 8-10. [32,66] [*COL*]

PANHUYS, L. C. van
49.057 SR 1920/ Waterkracht in Suriname [Hydraulic power in Surinam]. *W I G* 2:385-
21   390.   [*COL*]

PERCIVAL, D. A.
49.058 GC 1953 Industrialization: historical background, existing industries and industrial potential of the Caribbean area. *Car Econ Rev* 5(1-2), Dec.: 5-19.   [5]   [*RIS*]

PIXLEY, DICK
49.059 JM 1958 Of progress and potential. *Caribbean* 12(5), Dec.: 106-108.   [*COL*]

PRINCE, J. F.
49.060 TR 1940 Paper from bamboo made in electrical mill at Trinidad. *Far East Rev* 36(2), Feb.: 78-82.   [*COL*]

ROBERTSON, FAITH
49.061 TR 1962 Outlook for independence. *W I Rev* 7(11-12), Nov.-Dec.: 31-33,35.
                                                                    [*NYP*]

ROSKILL, O. W.

49.062   WW   1951 Scope for industrial development in the Windward Islands. *Car Commn Mon Inf B* 5(4), Nov.: 128-132.   [66]   [*AGS*]

ROTH, WALTER EDMUND

13.069   BG   1929 ADDITIONAL STUDIES OF THE ARTS, CRAFTS, AND CUSTOMS OF THE GUIANA INDIANS, WITH SPECIAL REFERENCE TO THOSE OF SOUTHERN BRITISH GUIANA.

SCOTT, WALTER

58.085   GC   1950 THE INDUSTRIAL UTILISATION OF SUGAR CANE BY-PRODUCTS.

SEALY, THEODORE

49.063   JM   1962 INDUSTRIALIZATION. Kingston, Gleaner Co., 23p.

SEEGER, PETER

22.133   TR   1961 THE STEEL DRUMS OF KIM LOY WONG: AN INSTRUCTION BOOK.

SHAW, EARL BENNETT

63.049   SJ   1934 The bay oil industry of St. John.

SHENFIELD, A. A.

49.064   BC   1956 Industrialisation—and opportunities for British capital in the British West Indies. *Statist* Sept.: 25-28.   [66]

SINGH, B. G.

49.065   JM   1961 Stabilising marl with Portland cement. *Inf B Scient Res Coun* 2(1), June: 11-13.   [52]   [*COL*]

SNELLEMAN, J. F.

49.066   SR   1919/ Twijnen en spinnen [Twining and spinning]. *W I G* 1(2): 500-505.
            20   [*COL*]

STEEL, J. L. S. et al.

49.067   BC   1953 INDUSTRIAL DEVELOPMENT IN JAMAICA, TRINIDAD, BARBADOS AND BRITISH GUIANA: REPORT OF MISSION OF UNITED KINGDOM INDUSTRIALISTS, OCTOBER TO NOVEMBER 1952 [J.L.S. STEEL (LEADER)]. London, H.M.S.O., 51p. (Colonial no. 294.)   [*RIS*]

STEWART, WILLIAM FORRES

49.068   BB   1952 It's happening in Barbados. *Can-W I Mag* 42(2), Feb.: 5-6.   [*NYP*]

TAYLOR, DOUGLAS C. & MOORE, HARVEY C.

49.069   DM   1948 A note on Dominican basketry and its analogues. *Sw Anthrop* 4(3), Autumn: 328-343.   [13]

TEUNISSEN, H.

49.070   SR   1957 The Brokopondo Plan. *Caribbean* 11(1), Aug.: 12-13. [54,66]   [*COL*]

THAKUR, B. STANISLAUS

49.071   BG   1958 Where planners are preparing firm foundations. *Caribbean* 12(5), Dec.: 114-116.   [*COL*]

VOELKER, WALTER D.

49.072   BC   [n.d.] SURVEY OF INDUSTRY IN THE WEST INDIES. Mona, Institute of Social and Economic Research, University College of the West Indies, 28p. (Studies in federal economics no. 1.)   [50]   *[RIS]*

WALLE, J. van de

49.073   CU   1948 De industriële voorsprong van Curacao [The industrial headstart of Curacao]. *W I G* 29:1-6.   [66]   *[COL]*

WILLIAMS, ERIC EUSTACE

49.074   BC   1952 Industrial development. *Car Commn Mon Inf B* 6(4), Nov.: 87-89. [66]   *[AGS]*

WILLIAMS, J. B.

49.075   JM   1961 Raw material for concrete blocks in Jamaica. *Inf B Scient Res Coun* 2(3), Dec.: 36-59.   *[AMN]*

WOODHOUSE, W. M.

35.050   BC   1962 Developments in the local building industries of the Commonwealth.

WOOLLEY, Sir CHARLES CAMPBELL

49.076   BG   1950 Some aspects of British Guiana's economy. *Car Commn Mon Inf B* 3(11), June: 399-400.   [58]   *[COL]*

Chapter 50

LABOR, LABOR RELATIONS AND TRADE UNIONS

ADHIN, J. H.
50.001   SR   1963 De economisch-historische betekenis van de Hindostaanse immigratie voor Suriname [The economic-historical value of the Hindustani immigration for Surinam]. *In* LUCHTMAN, W.J., ed. VAN BRITS-
INDISCH EMIGRANT TOT BURGER VAN SURINAME. The Hague, Drukkerij
Wieringa, p.31-38.   [12, 17, 44]

AHRENS, H.
50.002   SR   1922/ Kolonisatie op particulier land in Suriname met Javanen onder
23   contract onder de thans geldende immigratie wetten [Colonization
with Javanese contract laborers on privately owned land in Surinam
under the current immigration laws]. *W I G* 4:266-273.   [15,17,66]
[*COL*]

ALCALA, V. O.
50.003   GC   1952 Guidance services. *Car Commn Mon Inf B* 6(5), Dec.: 101-102. [*AGS*]
50.004   GC   1953 Apprenticeship and on-the-job training. *Car Commn Mon Inf B* 6(7),
Feb.: 151-152, 154.   [32]   [*AGS*]

ANDREWS, C. F.
50.005   BG/   1930 "India's emigration problem." *For Aff* 8(3), Apr.: 430-441.   [12, 17]
TR   [*AGS*]

ARONSON, ROBERT L.
50.006   JM   1961 Labour commitment among Jamaican bauxite workers: a case study.
Social Econ Stud 10(2), June: 156-182.   [8]   [*RIS*]

ASBECK, W. D. H. van
50.007   NC   1922/ E. B. en V. B. in onze Indien [Economic Association and Free Asso-
23   ciation in our Indies]. *W I G* 4:37-41.   [*COL*]

BASCOM, F. C. S.
50.008   BG   1912 The labour question: the problem stated. *Timehri* 3d ser., 2(19B),
Dec.: 273-286.   [17, 66]   [*AMN*]

BAYLISS, F. J. & COATES, J. B.
18.006   BC   1965 West Indians at work in Nottingham.

BEADNELL, H. G.
28.027   BG   1962 Industrial injuries in the sugar industry of British Guiana.

BECKFORD, LASELLES
50.009   JM   1963 Conduct of arbitration: preparation of the case—a trade union point
                          of view. *In* EATON, G. E., ed. PROCEEDINGS OF INDUSTRIAL RELA-
                          TIONS CONFERENCE ON THE THEORY AND PRACTICE OF ARBITRATION,
                          Nov., 1962. Mona, Institute of Social and Economic Research,
                          University of the West Indies, p.39-43.   [*RIS*]

BENSON, GEORGE C.
64.017   BG   1912 The balata industry.

BERNARD, HECTOR
56.006   FC   1949 Jamaica peasant farmers set example in cooperation.

BEST, ETHEL
50.010   UV   1936 ECONOMIC PROBLEMS OF THE WOMEN OF THE VIRGIN ISLANDS OF THE
                          UNITED STATES. Washington, U.S. Govt. Print. Off. 24p. ([Publication]
                          no. 142, U. S. Dept. of Labor, Women's Bureau.) [44, 66]   [*COL*]

BIRD, V. C.
50.011   AT   1950 Labour in the Leewards. *Venture* 2(7), Aug.: 3-4. [37, 66] [*COL*]

BOOS, W. J. & HARRIS, H. A.
50.012   TR   1959 REPORT OF THE COLONY WHITLEY COUNCIL ON THE KING COMMISSION.
                          REPORT WITH COMMENTS OF THE CIVIL SERVICE ASSOCIATION ON THE
                          LEE REPORT. STRUCTURE AND ORGANIZATION OF THE PUBLIC SERVICE.
                          Port of Spain, Govt. Print. Off., 30p. [37]

BROWN E. ETHELRED
50.013   JM   1919 Labor conditions in Jamaica prior to 1917. *J Negro Hist* 4(4), Oct.:
                          349-360. [5]   [*SCH*]
37.043   JM   1937 INJUSTICES IN THE CIVIL SERVICE OF JAMAICA.

BROWN, HEADLEY & ANDERSON, ERROL
47.008   BC   1963/ Economic development in the West Indies and the peasantry.
                      64

BURN, W. L.
6.008   BC   1937 EMANCIPATION AND APPRENTICESHIP IN THE BRITISH WEST INDIES.

CAMMAERTS, E.
50.014   BC   1914 L'importation des coolies dans les Indes occidentales [The impor-
                          tation of coolies into the West Indies]. *B Colon Comp* 2, Feb. 20:
                          49-75. [12, 17]   [*NYP*]

CAMP, GEORGE
37.052   BG   1963 The "Georgetown strike"—a lie of the Western press.

CAMPBELL, J. S. & COLE, J. C.

50.015   TR   1963   A comparison of labour requirements and costs of cultivation on cocoa and coconut estates in Trinidad and Tobago. *Trop Agric* 40(1), Jan.: 25-33.   [59]   [*AGS*]

CAMPBELL, PERSIA CRAWFORD

15.006   BC   1923   Foreign competition for Chinese labour, 1845-74.

CARLEE, J. J. A.

50.016   BC   1919   Implemental tillage—how labor can be saved. *W I Comm Circ* 34(545), Aug. 21: 223-224.   [58]   [*NYP*]

CASTA-LUMIO, LUCIEN

50.017   FC   1906   ETUDE HISTORIQUE SUR LES ORIGINES DE L'IMMIGRATION RÉGLEMENTÉE DANS NOS ANCIENNES COLONIES DE LA RÉUNION, LA GUADELOUPE, LA MARTINIQUE, ET LA GUYANE [HISTORICAL STUDY ON THE ORIGINS OF REGULATED IMMIGRATION INTO OUR FORMER COLONIES OF REUNION, GUADELOUPE, MARTINIQUE, AND GUIANA]. Paris, Impr. G. Vilette, 207p. [5, 17]   [*NYP*]

CHAPMAN, ESTHER

50.018   JM   1938   The truth about Jamaica. *W I Rev* 4(10), June: 13-18.   [*NYP*]

COLLINS, B. A. N.

50.019   BG   1964   The civil service of British Guiana in the general strike of 1963. *Car Q* 10(2), June: 3-15.   [37]   [*RIS*]

COMITAS, LAMBROS

50.020   JM   1964   Occupational multiplicity in rural Jamaica. *In* GARFIELD, VIOLA & FRIEDL, ERNESTINE, ed. PROCEEDINGS OF THE AMERICAN ETHNOLOGICAL SOCIETY, 1963. Seattle, University of Washington Press, p.41-50. [8, 56]   [*RIS*]

COMVALIUS, TH. A. C.

44.037   SR   1927/ Economisch Suriname en het loonstelsel [The economy of Surinam 28   and the wage system].

CRUICKSHANK, J. GRAHAM

11.008   BG   1919   African immigrants after freedom.

CUMPER, GEORGE E.

49.019   JM   1953   Labour productivity and capital-labour ratios in Jamaican manufacturing industry: their relation to the problem of selective industrialisation.

58.027   JM   1954   Labour demand and supply in Jamaican sugar industry, 1830-1950.

50.021   BB   1959   Employment in Barbados. *Social Econ Stud* 8(2), June: 105-146. [5, 7, 46]   [*RIS*]

50.022   BB   1959   REPORT ON EMPLOYMENT IN BARBADOS. Bridgetown, Govt. Print. Off., 42p.   m   m   [66]   [*RIS*]

50.023   BC   1960   Employment and unemployment in the West Indies. *In* CUMPER, G. E., ed. THE ECONOMY OF THE WEST INDIES. Kingston Institute of Social and Economic Research, University College of the West Indies, p.152-180.   [*RIS*]

50.024   JM/   1961/Labour and development in the West Indies. *Social Econ Stud* 10(3),
          BB   62 Sept.: 278-305; 11(1), Mar.: 1-33.   [8, 9]   [*RIS*]
50.025   JM   1964 A comparison of statistical data on the Jamaican labour force,
                    1953-1961. *Social Econ Stud* 13(4), Dec.: 430-439.   [*RIS*]

CUMPSTON, I. M.
50.026   BC   1953 INDIANS OVERSEAS IN BRITISH TERRITORIES, 1834-1854. London, Ox-
                    ford University Press, 198p.   [5, 7, 12]   [*RIS*]

DAGLEISH, A.
50.027   BC   1957 Trade unionism in the West Indies. *Venture* 8(11), Apr.: 4-5.   [*COL*]

DALLEY, F. W.
50.028   TR   1947 TRADE UNION ORGANIZATION AND INDUSTRIAL RELATIONS IN TRINIDAD.
                    London, H.M.S.O. 55p.   [*RIS*]
50.029   TR   1954 GENERAL INDUSTRIAL CONDITIONS AND LABOUR RELATIONS IN TRINIDAD.
                    [Port of Spain?] Trinidad, Govt. Print. Off., 70p.   [*RIS*]
50.030   BC   1956 The labour position: the trade unions and the political parties.
                    Statist Sept.: 31-32.   [37]

DANIEL, GEORGE T.
50.031   BC   1957 Labor and Nationalism in the British Caribbean. *Ann Am Acad
                    Polit Social Sci* 310, Mar.: 162-171.   [21, 37]   [*RIS*]
50.032   BC   1957 The role of trade union leaders. *Caribbean* 10(11), June: 272-275.
                                                                                     [*COL*]

DEBIEN, GABRIEL
50.033   FC   1942 LE PEUPLEMENT DES ANTILLES FRANCAISES AU XVIIᵉ SIÈCLE: LES
                    ENGAGÉS PARTIS DE LA ROCHELLE (1683-1715). [THE SETTLEMENT OF
                    THE FRENCH ANTILLES IN THE 17th CENTURY: THE BONDED SERVANTS
                    FROM LA ROCHELLE (1683-1715)]. Caire: L'Institut francais d'arché-
                    ologie orientale du Caire, 222p.   [5, 17]   [*AGS*]
50.034   FA   1951 Les engagés pour les Antilles (1634-1715) [Bonded servants signed
                    up for the Antilles (1634-1715)]. *Rev Hist Colon Fr* 38:1-279. [*NYP*]

DEBRETAGNE, L.
50.035   MT   1935 Labour conditions in Martinique. *Int Lab Rev* 32(6), Dec.: 792-800.
                                                                                     [*AGS*]

DEERR, NOEL
50.036   GC   1938 Indian labour in the sugar industry. *Int Sug J* 40(471), Mar.: 94-98.
                    [12, 17, 58]   [*COL*]

DOLLY, JAMES O.
50.037   TR   1929 Hindrances other than diseases and pests to the successful working
                    of cocoa and coconut estates. *Proc Agric Soc Trin Tob* 29(6), June:
                    166-174.   [59, 60]   [*AMN*]

DUFFUS, J. A. H.
37.100 JM   1963 Conduct of arbitration II—rules of procedure, of evidence, etc., in
                    voluntary and legal arbitrations.

DUFOUGERE, W.

37.101   FG   1921   De l'utilisation rationnelle de la main-d'oeuvre pénale en Guyane [On the rational use of forced labor in Guiana].

DUSSELDORP, D. B. W. M. van

50.038   SR   1962   Een classificatie van de occupatievormen in Suriname [A classification of the occupations in Surinam]. *Tijdschr Ned Aar Genoot* 79(2): 128-148.

EATON, GEORGE E.

50.039   JM   [1962?] Trade union development in Jamaica (Part I) *Car Q* 8(1): 43-53.   [*RIS*]

50.040   JM   1962   Trade union development in Jamaica. (Part II) *Car Q* 8(2), June: 69-75.   [*RIS*]

50.041   JM   1963   The theory and practice of arbitration—approaches to arbitration— the functions and role of the arbitrator. *In* EATON, G. E., ed. Proceedings of Industrial Relations Conference on the Theory and Practice of Arbitration, Nov. 1962. Mona, Institute of Social and Economic Research, University of the West Indies, p.7-24. [*RIS*]

EATON, GEORGE E., ed.

50.042   JM   1963   Proceedings of Industrial Relations Conference on the Theory and Practice of arbitration, Nov. 1962. Mona, Institute of Social and Economic Research, University of the West Indies, 102p. [*RIS*]

EDWARDS, R. D.

50.043   TR   1963   The role of employers' organisations in a democratic society. *Enterprise* 1(3), July-Sept.: 20-21, 29.   [*RIS*]

ERICKSON, EDGAR L.

50.044   BC   1934   The introduction of East Indian coolies into the British West Indies. *J Mod Hist* 6(2), June: 127-146. [5, 12, 17]   [*COL*]

EVANS, HARRY

50.045   BG   1962   Profsoiuzy Britanskoi Gviany na raspute [The trade unions of British Guiana in disarray] [by] Garri Evans. *Vse Pro Dviz* 3:17-20. [10, 37]   [*COL*]

FARLEY, RAWLE

32.061   BC   1957   The role of the university in industrial relations.

50.046   GC   1958   Caribbean industrial relations. *Venture* 10(1), May: 3-4.   [*COL*]

50.047   BC   1958   Caribbean labour comes of age. *Free Lab Wld* 94, Apr.: 29-34. [66]   [*NYP*]

46.070   BG   1958   Economic and social change on a Caribbean frontier.

50.048   BC   1958   Trade union development and trade union education in the British Caribbean. British Guiana, Daily Chronicle, 64p. [32]   [*NYP*]

50.049   BC   1958   Trade unions and politics in the British Caribbean. Georgetown, Daily Chronicle, 39p. [37]   [*RIS*]

32.062   BC   1958   Universities and the education of working people.

FARLEY, RAWLE, ed.

32.063   BC   [n.d.] Labour education in the British Caribbean: Report of a Labour Education Survey conducted June-July, 1959, and of the Con-

FERENCE HELD AT THE UNIVERSITY OF THE WEST INDIES, MONA, JAMAICA, Aug. 4th–9th, 1959.

FARLEY, RAWLE; FLANDERS, ALLAN & ROPER, JOE

50.050　　BC　　1961 INDUSTRIAL RELATIONS AND THE BRITISH CARIBBEAN. London, University of London Press, 79p. [66]　　　　　　　　　　　[RIS]

FARQUHARSON, DONALD G.; ARNOLD, HUBERT; SKINNER, GEORGE & BLAKE, VIVIAN

50.051　　JM　　[1961?] The responsibilities of capital and labour. In CUMPER, GEORGE, ed. REPORT OF THE CONFERENCE ON SOCIAL DEVELOPMENT IN JAMAICA. Kingston, Standing Committee on Social Services, p.70-78.　　[RIS]

FINKEL, HERMAN J.

20.006　　SK/　　1964 Attitudes toward work as a factor in agricultural planning in the
　　　　　NV　　West Indies.

FUIJKSCHOT, F. P.

50.052　　SR/　　1949 Suriname en Curacao zoals een arbeidersleider die zag [Surinam
　　　　　CU　　and Curacao as seen by a labor leader. W I G 30:65-81.　　[COL]

GAAY FORTMAN, B. de

50.053　　CU　　1941 Het ontwerp-landsverordening tot regeling van de arbeidersovereenkomst in Curacao [The proposed land-regulations to settle the labor contracts in Curacao]. W I G 23:365-378.　　　　　　　　[COL]

GREENWOOD, THOMAS

50.054　　BC　　1921 East Indian emigration: the Indian government's policy. W I Comm Circ 36(589), Apr. 28: 167-168. [12, 17, 37]　　　　　　[NYP]

GRIMBLE, JUNE A.

50.055　　JM　　1951 The Jamaica story. U N Wld 5(2), Feb.: 70-71. [37]　　[COL]

HAMMOND, S. A.

50.056　　BB/　　1952 REPORT ON AN ENQUIRY INTO THE ORGANIZATION AND SALARIES OF THE
　　　　　LW/　　CIVIL SERVICE. Part 1: General. [Bridgetown?] Barbados, Advocate
　　　　　BV　　Co., 187p. [37]　　　　　　　　　　　　　　　　[COL]

HANDLER, JEROME S.

50.057　　BB　　1965 Some aspects of work organization on sugar plantations in Barbados. Ethnology 4(1), Jan.: 16-38. [45, 58]　　　　　　　[RIS]

HAREWOOD, JACK

50.058　　BC　　1956 A system of labour force statistics. Social Econ Stud 5(2), Mar.: 1-18. [44, 66, 67]　　　　　　　　　　　　　　[RIS]

50.059　　TR　　[196?] EMPLOYMENT IN TRINIDAD AND TOBAGO, 1960. [Mona?] Jamaica, Institute of Social and Economic Research, University of the West Indies, 81p. (1960 Population Census Research Programme, Publication no. 5.)　　　　　　　　　　　　　　　　[RIS]

50.060　　JM/　　1960 Overpopulation and underemployment in the West Indies. Int Lab Rev
　　　　　TR　　82(2), Aug.: 1-32. [7, 38, 46]　　　　　　　　　[RIS]

50.061　　TR　　1963 Employment in Trinidad and Tobago. In RESEARCH PAPERS [OF THE] CENTRAL STATISTICAL OFFICE OF TRINIDAD AND TOBAGO, No. 1, DEC. Port of Spain, Central Statistical Office, p.1-81.　　　　[RIS]

HART, RICHARD

50.062   JM   1952 THE ORIGIN AND DEVELOPMENT OF THE PEOPLE OF JAMAICA. Kingston, Education Department of the Trade Union Congress, 30p. [5] [*AGS*]

HILL, ARTHUR H.

50.063   BG   1919 Emigration from India. *Timehri* 3d ser., 6(23), Sept.: 43-52. [12, 17]   [*AMN*]

HILL, FRANK

50.064   JM   1963 Arbitration and the public interest. *In* Eaton, G. E., ed. PROCEEDINGS OF INDUSTRIAL RELATIONS CONFERENCE ON THE THEORY AND PRACTICE OF ARBITRATION, Nov. 1962. Mona, Institute of Social and Economic Research, University of the West Indies, p.45-52.   [*RIS*]

HINDEN, RITA et al.

50.065   BC   1942 Labour in the colonies. 1: Some current problems. London, Victor Gollancz, 48p. (Fabian Society, Research series no. 61.)   [*NYP*]

HOYOS, F. A.

37.185   BC   1963 THE RISE OF WEST INDIAN DEMOCRACY; THE LIFE AND TIMES OF SIR GRANTLEY ADAMS.

HOYT, ELIZABETH E.

50.066   JM   1960 Voluntary unemployment and unemployability in Jamaica with special reference to the standard of living. *Br J Sociol* 11(2), June: 129-136. [9, 44, 66]   [*RIS*]

HOYTE, RUPERT L., comp.

50.067   SL   1950 ST. LUCIA WORKERS' UNION WAGE DISPUTE: EVIDENCE AT THE PUBLIC HEARING JULY 11-13, 1950 AND REPORT OF THE ARBITRATION TRIBUNAL. Castries, The Voice Printery.

HUGGINS, H. D.

50.068   JM   1953 Seasonal variation and employment in Jamaica. *Social Econ Stud* 1(2), June: 84-115. [46]   [*RIS*]

HUGILL, J. A. C.

50.069   JM   1957 Jamaica's shortage of mechanics and artisans. *W I Comm Circ* 72(1316), Aug.: 221-222. [32]   [*NYP*]

HUIZINGA, D. S.

50.070   SR   1927/ De Surinaamsche loonsverhoging van 1920 [The wage increase of
             28 1920 in Surinam]. *W I G* 9:111-130. [44]   [*COL*]

JACOBS, H. P.

16.020   JM   1961 Reality and race: a reply to 'realism and race.'

JAYAWARDENA, CHANDRA

8.033   BG   1963 CONFLICT AND SOLIDARITY IN A GUIANESE PLANTATION.

KASTELEYN, J. S. C.

50.071   SR   1921/ Het vekrijgen van een vrije arbeidersbevolking in Suriname [The
             22 establishment of an independent labor-population in Surinam]. *W I G* 3:226-236.   [*COL*]

KESLER, C. K.
50.072   CU   1927/Het assiento [The assiento]. *W I G* 9:152-160.   [*COL*]
               28

KLERK, CORNELIS JOHANNES MARIA de
50.073   SR   1942 De Britisch-Indiërs in Suriname [The British Indians in Surinam].
                     W I G 24:97-117.   [5, 7, 12, 17]   [*RIS*]
50.074   SR   1953 DE IMMIGRATIE DER HINDOESTANEN IN SURINAME [THE IMMIGRATION OF
                     HINDUS TO SURINAM]. Amsterdam, Urbi et Orbi, 247p.   [8, 12, 17, 19,
                     37, 45, 66]   [*RIS*]
50.075   SR   1963 De komst en vestiging van de Brits-Indiërs in Suriname [The arrival
                     and settlement of the British Indians in Surinam]. *In* LUTCHMAN,
                     W. I., ed., VAN BRITS-INDISCH EMIGRANT TOT BURGER VAN SURINAME.
                     The Hague, Drukkerij Wieringa, p.15-27.   [12, 17]

KLUVERS, B. J.
53.026   SR   1919/De verzekeringskas van de firma C. Kersten en Companie te Para-
           20   maribo [The insurance funds of the firm C. Kersten and Company in
                     Paramaribo].

KNOWLES, WILLIAM H.
50.076   BC   1955 Supervision in the British West Indies: cause of industrial unrest.
                     Indus Lab Rel Rev 8(4), July: 572-580.   [*COL*]
50.077   BC   1959 TRADE UNION DEVELOPMENT AND INDUSTRIAL RELATIONS IN THE BRITISH
                     WEST INDIES. Berkeley, University of California Press, 214p.   [*RIS*]

KRUIJER, GERARDUS JOHANNES
50.078   NW   1953 Enquête onder de arbeiders- en boerenbevolking van de Bovenwindse
                     Eilanden, 1951 [Survey of the labor and farming population of the
                     Windward Islands, 1951]. *In* KRUIJER, G. J.; VEENENBOS, J.S. &
                     WESTERMANN, J. H., comps. BOVENWINDENRAPPORT. Amsterdam,
                     Voorlichtingsinstituut voor het Welvaartsplan Nederlandse Antillen,
                     20p.   [7]

LACASCADE, PIERRE
50.079   FA   1907 ESCLAVAGE ET IMMIGRATION. LA QUESTION DE LA MAIN-D'OEUVRE AUX
                     ANTILLES: LE DÉCRÉT DU 13 FÉVRIER 1852 ET LA CONVENTION ANGLAISE
                     DU 1ER JUILLET 1861. Paris, Librairie des Facultés, A. Michalon,
                     134p. (Ph.D. dissertation, University of Paris.)   [6, 17]   [*COL*]

LAMONT, Sir NORMAN et al.
50.080   TR   1918 Labour exchanges. *Proc Agric Soc Trin Tob* 18(7-8), July-Aug.:
                     801-805.   [*AMN*]

LAVIGNE, PIERRE
50.081   FC   1953 La législation industrielle dans les départements francais de la
                     Caraïbe [Industrial legislation in the French territories of the
                     Caribbean]. *Penant* Doctrine 63:57-62.   [37]   [*COL*]

LEIMS, J. A.
50.082   SR   1925/Over den kleinen landbouw in Suriname [About small-scale agri-
           26   culture in Surinam]. *W I G* 7:371-384.   [46]   [*COL*]

LEWIS, W. ARTHUR

50.083   BC   1939 LABOUR IN THE WEST INDIES: THE BIRTH OF A WORKERS' MOVEMENT. London, V. Gollancz, 44p. (Fabian Society research series no. 44.) [66]   [*NYP*]

LISSER, H. G. de

11.016   BC   1900 The Negro as a factor in the future of the West Indies.

LONG, EDWARD E.

50.084   BG   1925 British Guiana and Indian immigration. *W I Comm Circ* 40(687), Jan. 29: 50; 40(688), Feb. 12: 71-72. [12, 17]   [*NYP*]

LOPEZ, AMY K.

50.085   JM   1948 Land and labour to 1900. *Jam Hist Rev* 1(3), Dec.: 289-301. [6]   [*COL*]

LUDLOW, ANTHONY

50.086   BG   1938 Red sky at morning. *Blwd Mag* 243(1472), June: 721-735. [45]   [*COL*]

MANLEY, MICHAEL

50.087   JM   1963 Economic criteria by which arbitrators may be guided. *In* EATON, G. E., ed. PROCEEDINGS OF INDUSTRIAL RELATIONS CONFERENCE ON THE THEORY AND PRACTICE OF ARBITRATION, Nov. 1962. Mona, Institute of Social and Economic Research, University of the West Indies, p.53-63.   [*RIS*]

MARKLE, GOWER

32.131   BC   [n.d.] Report of labour education survey.

MARRIOTT, F. C.

50.088   TR   1918 Labour exchanges. *Proc Agric Soc Trin Tob* 18(6), June: 771-774. [10]   [*AMN*]

MATHIESON, WILLIAM LAW

6.047   BC   1932 British slave emancipation, 1838-49.

MAUNDER, W. F.

50.089   JM   1960 EMPLOYMENT IN AN UNDERDEVELOPED AREA: A SAMPLE SURVEY OF KINGSTON, JAMAICA. New Haven, Yale University Press, 215p. [67]   [*RIS*]

MEISLER, STANLEY

50.090   BG/   1964 Meddling in Latin America: dubious role of AFL-CIO. *Nation* 198(7),
        BH   Feb. 10: 133-138. [37, 44]   [*NYP*]

MINTZ, SIDNEY W.

58.070   JM   1959 Labor and sugar in Puerto Rico and in Jamaica, 1800-1850.

MOWATT, S. W.

50.091   JM   1963 Third party intervention in labour disputes. *In* EATON, G. E., ed. PROCEEDINGS OF INDUSTRIAL RELATIONS CONFERENCE ON THE THEORY AND PRACTICE OF ARBITRATION, Nov. 1962. Mona, Institute of Social and Economic Research, University of the West Indies, p.1-6. [*RIS*]

MURRAY, GIDEON

46.149   BC   1919 The British West Indies and British Guiana: Their resources and development.

NORMAN, FRANK A.

50.092   BC   1952 WHITEHALL TO WEST INDIES. London, The Bodley Head, 256p.   [37, 66]   [*NYP*]

OBERG, KALERVO

46.153   SR   1964 A study of farm productivity in the Santo Boma Settlement Project Surinam.

OLIVIER, SYDNEY, 1st Baron RAMSDEN

50.093   BC   1910 WHITE CAPITAL AND COLOURED LABOR, by Lord Olivier. London, Independent Labour Party, 1750. (The Socialist library.)   [16]
                                                                                [*COL*]

50.094   BC   1938 The scandal of West Indian labour conditions, by Lord Olivier. *Contemp Rev* 867, Mar.: 282-289.   [*AGS*]

ORDE-BROWNE, G.

50.095   BC   1939 LABOUR CONDITIONS IN THE WEST INDIES. London, H.M.S.O., 216p. (Cmd. 6070.)   [*AGS*]

PATTEE, RICHARD

37.309   JM   1946 Tumult in the Antilles: Jamaica.

PAYNE, GEORGE C.

28.418   TR   1919 Ankylostomiasis and the planter.

PHELPS, O. W.

50.096   JM   1960 Rise of the labour movement in Jamaica. *Social Econ Stud* 9(4), Dec.: 417-468:   [37]   [*RIS*]

POLLAK, HARRY H.

37.318   BG   1957 What about British Guiana?

PRAKKEN, A. B. J.

3.249   NW   1919 De Bovenwindsche Eilanden der kolonie Curacao [The Windward Islands of the colony Curacao].

REUBENS, EDWIN P. & BEATRICE G.

50.097   BG   1962 LABOUR DISPLACEMENT IN A LABOUR-SURPLUS ECONOMY; THE SUGAR INDUSTRY OF BRITISH GUIANA. Mona, Jamaica, Institute of Social and Economic Research, University of the West Indies, 105p.   [58]
                                                                                [*NYP*]

ROBERTS, GEORGE WOODROW

7.068   BC   1960 Movements in population and the labour force.

ROBERTS, WALTER ADOLPHE

37.339   BC   1941 Caribbean headaches.

RODWAY, JAMES

50.098   BG   1919 Labour and colonization. *Timehri* 3d ser., 6(23), Sept.: 22-42.
[5, 12, 45]   [*AMN*]

ROMUALDI, SERAFINO

50.099   GC   1953 Free labor in the Caribbean. *Am Fed* 60(4), Apr.: 14-15, 31. [*COL*]

ROTTENBERG, SIMON

50.100   AT   1951 Labor force measurement in pre-industrial economy. *So Econ J*
18(2), Oct.: 219-224. [46]   [*COL*]

50.101   AT   1951 Note on labour force measurement in a pre-industrial economy.
Car Commn Mon Inf B 5(5), Dec.: 161-163.   [*AGS*]

50.102   AT   1952 Comment on Mr. Sommermeijer's supplementary note. *Car Commn
Mon Inf B* 5(11), June: 305, 308.   [*AGS*]

50.103   GR   1952 Labor relations in an underdeveloped economy. *Econ Dev Cult Chg*
4, Dec.: 250-260. [46]   [*COL*]

ROTTENBERG, SIMON & SIFFLEET, NORA

50.104   AT   1952 UNEMPLOYMENT IN ANTIGUA: A REPORT MADE TO THE UNEMPLOYMENT
COMMITTEE APPOINTED BY THE ADMINISTRATOR OF THE PRESIDENCY OF
ANTIGUA IN THE BRITISH LEEWARD ISLANDS. Rio Piedras, Labor Re-
lations Institute, College of Social Sciences, University of Puerto
Rico, 52p.   [*UNL*]

RYLE-DAVIES, W.

50.105   JM   [1961?] Employment in a developing economy. *In* CUMPER, GEORGE, ed.
REPORT OF THE CONFERENCE ON SOCIAL DEVELOPMENT IN JAMAICA.
Kingston, Standing Committee on Social Services, p.87-90.   [66]
[*RIS*]

SAUTET, JACQUES

28.467   GC   1953 Health of the worker and industrial medicine.

SCHOCH, C. F.

50.106   SR   1924/ De Ondernemersraad van Suriname [The Council of Employers of
25   Surinam]. *W I G* 6:635-640.   [*COL*]

SCHWARZ, ERNST

50.107   GC   1954 Some observations on labor organization in the Caribbean. *In* WILGUS,
A. CURTIS, ed. THE CARIBBEAN: ITS ECONOMY [papers delivered at
the Fourth Annual Conference on the Caribbean held at the
University of Florida, Dec. 3-5, 1953]. Gainesville, University of
Florida Press, p.163-176. (Publications of the School of Inter-
American Studies, ser. 1, v. 4.)   [*RIS*]

SCROGGS, WILLIAM

20.017   JM   1961 Imprudent jurisprudence: an outline of an illegal fiction.

SEDNEY, JULES

50.108   SR   1955 Het werkgelegenheidsaspect van het Surinaamse Tienjarenplan
[The aspect of employment opportunities under the Surinam Ten

Year Plan]. Amsterdam, S. J. P. Bakker. (Ph.D. dissertation, Universiteit van Amsterdam.) [66]

SERTIMA, J. van

50.109   BG   1919 An aching industrial void. *Timehri* 3d ser., 6(23), Sept.: 68-73.
                          [12]   [*AMN*]

SHAW, EARL BENNETT

50.110   ST   1935 St. Thomas carries its coal. *J Geogr* 34(6), Sept.: 229-236.   [11, 52]
                                                                                        [*AGS*]

SHELTON, H. S.

50.111   JM   1939 Economic conditions in Jamaica. *Fortnightly* new ser., 869, May:
                          539-548. [44]   [*NYP*]

SHEPHARD, C. Y.

50.112   TR   1935 Agricultural labour in Trinidad. *Trop Agric* 12(1), Jan.: 3-9; 12(2),
                          Feb.: 43-47; 12(3), Mar.: 56-64; 12(4), Apr.: 84-88; 12(5), May:
                          126-131; 12(6), June: 153-157; 12(7), July: 187-192. [46]   [*RIS*]

50.113   BB   1946 CANE CUTTING ENQUIRY: BARBADOS. [Bridgetown?] Barbados, Advo-
                          cate Co., 48p. [58]

58.089   BB   1946 THE SUGAR INDUSTRY OF BARBADOS; 1946 CROP: REPORT ON THE NEW
                          METHOD OF REMUNERATING CANE CUTTERS.

SIMPSON, GEORGE EATON

50.114   GC   1962 Employment policy problems in a multiracial society. *Car Q* 8(2),
                          June: 105-110. [16, 66]   [*RIS*]

SIRES, RONALD VERNON

50.115   JM   1940 Negro labor in Jamaica in the years following emancipation. *J Negro
                          Hist* 25(4), Oct.: 484-497. [5, 11, 46]   [*RIS*]

50.116   JM   1940 Sir Henry Barkly and the labor problem in Jamaica 1853-1856. *J Negro
                          Hist* 25(2), Apr.: 216-235. [5, 7, 12, 15, 46]   [*RIS*]

SKINNARD, FREDERICK W.

37.383   JM   1946 Evolving Jamaica.

SMITH, M. G.

50.117   JM   1956 A REPORT ON LABOUR SUPPLY IN RURAL JAMAICA. Kingston, Govt.
                          Printer, 167p. [8, 46, 47, 66]   [*RIS*]

SOMERMEIJER, W. H.

50.118   AT   1952 A supplementary note on labour force measurement in a pre-indus-
                          trial economy. *Car Commn Mon Inf B* 5(11), June: 304, 306. [*AGS*]

STAAL, G. J.

50.119   SR   1926/ Ontwrongen bezwaren [Objections obtained by extortion]. *W I G*
                          27 8:235-248.   [*COL*]

STEMBRIDGE, E. C.

50.120   BG   1914 Indian immigration in British Guiana. *United Emp* new ser., 5(1):
                          71-78. [12, 17]   [*AGS*]

SWAYNE, Sir ERIC J. E.

50.121 BH   1910 India and British Honduras. *In* HOPKINS, J. CASTELL, ed. EMPIRE
                   CLUB SPEECHES, 1908-1909. Toronto, William Briggs, p.102-109.
                   [12, 17]   [*NYP*]

THOMPSON, ADOLPH A.

50.122 BC   1952 University education in labour-management relations in British
                   Guiana, the British West Indies and Puerto Rico in 1951-1952.
                   Timehri 4th ser., 1(31), Nov.: 4-7.   [32]

50.123 BC [1953?] University education in labour-management relations. *Car Q* 3(1):
                   57-60.   [32]   [*RIS*]

VIGNOLS, LEON

50.124 FC   1928 Les Antilles Francaises sous l'Ancien Régime: Aspects écono-
                   miques et sociaux: l'institution des engagés (1626-1774) [The
                   French Antilles under the old regime: Economic and social aspects:
                   The institution of bonded servants (1626-1774)]. *Rev Hist Econ
                   Social* 16(1): 12-45.   [5, 17]

VOELKER, WALTER D.

49.072 BC   [n.d.] Survey of industry in the West Indies.

WESTRA, P.

50.125 SR   1919 Plantage-arbeiders [Plantation laborers]. *W I G* 1(1): 438-440.   [45]
                                                                                        [*COL*]

WILLIAMS, ERIC EUSTACE

50.126 TR   1965 Reflections on the industrial stabilisation bill. Port of Spain: PNM
                   Pub. Co., [52]p.   [37]   [*RIS*]

WILLIAMS, GERTRUDE

44.251 BC   1953 The economics of everyday life in the West Indies.

WOOD, R. CECIL; PATERSON, D. D. & SEIGNORET, E. J.

50.127 TR   1933 Labour and labour rates on the College Farm. *Trop Agric* 10(12),
                   Dec.: 340-344.   [46]   [*AGS*]

WOODHAM, WARREN

50.128 JM   1962 ELEMENTS OF A MANPOWER PROGRAMME FOR A DEVELOPING COUNTRY: A
                   JAMAICAN CASE STUDY. [San Juan, P. R.?] 15p. (Human skills in the
                   decade of development: international conference on middle level
                   manpower, San Juan, P. R., October 10-11-12, 1962. TECH/7,
                   Sept. 14, 1962.)   [66]   [*RIS*]

Chapter 51

EXTERNAL TRADE AND INTERNAL MARKETING

ALLEN, W. H. van

51.001   BC   1930   The trend of Canadian-West Indian trade. *Can-W I Mag* 19(8), July: 8-12.   [*NYP*]

AMSTEL, J. E. van

51.002   SR   1924/ Nog eenige opmerkingen over Surinaamsche Liberia-koffie en de 25   mogelijkheid tot verbetering der reputatie er van [Some added remarks about the Surinam Liberia-coffee and the possibilities of improving its reputation]. *W I G* 6:271-376.   [44]   [*COL*]

ANDREWS, L. R.

64.004   BC   1937   The West Indies market for B. C. lumber.

ARMYTAGE, FRANCES

51.003   BC   1953   THE FREE PORT SYSTEM IN THE BRITISH WEST INDIES; A STUDY IN COMMERCIAL POLICY, 1766-1822. London, Longmans, 176p. [5]   [*RIS*]

BALOGH, THOMAS

51.004   BC   1960   Making of a customs union. *Social Econ Stud* 9(1), Mar.: 37-40.   [38]   [*RIS*]

BELL, HERBERT C.

51.005   BC   1916   British commercial policy in the West Indies, 1783-1793. *Engl Hist Rev* 31(123), July: 429-441.   [5]   [*COL*]

51.006   BC   1917   The West India trade before the American Revolution. *Am Hist Rev* 22(2), Jan.: 272-287.   [5]   [*COL*]

BENHAM, FREDERIC C.

51.007   BC   1945   BRITISH WEST INDIAN INTER-COLONIAL TRADE IN THE WEST INDIES. Bridgetown, Advocate Co., 42p. (Development and welfare bulletin no. 14.)   [*RIS*]

BENJAMINS, H. D.

51.008   SR   1924/ Iets over den ouden handel met de Indianen in Guiana [Some facts 25   about the old trade with the Indians in Guiana]. *W I G* 6:179-186. [5,13]   [*COL*]

BEYERINCK, F. H.

64.019   GC   1955 The value of a centralised market information service for Caribbean
                timbers.

BIGGS, H. C.

51.009   BB   1961 REPORT ON VISITS TO BARBADOS DURING 1959 AND 1960 TO ADVISE ON
                MARKETING IN BARBADOS. [Bridgetown] Barbados, Barbados Govt.
                Print. Off., 39p.

BIJLSMA, R.

51.010   SR   1919/ Suriname's handelsbeweeging 1683-1712 [Surinam's commercial de-
                20   velopment from 1683 to 1712]. *W I G* 1(2): 48-51. [5]   [*COL*]

BLAINE, J. C. D.

51.011   JM/   1957 Trade relations of the United Kingdom and the United States in the
          TR   Caribbean. *In* WILGUS, A. CURTIS, ed. THE CARIBBEAN: CONTEM-
                      PORARY INTERNATIONAL RELATIONS [papers delivered at the Seventh
                      Conference on the Caribbean held at the University of Florida,
                      Dec. 6-8, 1956]. Gainesville, University of Florida Press, p.103-
                      121. (Publications of the School of Inter-American Studies, ser. 1,
                      v. 7.)   [*RIS*]

BOISMERY, ALAIN

51.012   GC   1964 Les relations commerciales entre Marseille et les Antilles [Trade
                relations between Marseille and the Antilles]. *Cah O-M* 17(68),
                Oct.-Dec.: 386-413.   [*RIS*]

BOUCHER, MAURICE

51.013   GD   1928 Exposé du régime douanier des colonies francaises: Guadeloupe et
                dependances [Account of the customs regulations of the French col-
                onies: Guadeloupe and subordinate islands]. *B Ag Gen Colon* 21
                (236), Sept.: 917-921.   [*AGS*]
51.014   GD   1928 Exposé du régime douanier des colonies francaises: Guyane Fran-
                caise [Account of the customs regulations of the French colonies:
                French Guiana]. *B Ag Gen Colon* 21(237), Oct.: 1029-1032.   [*AGS*]
51.015   MT   1928 Exposé du régime douanier des colonies francaises: Martinique [Ac-
                count of the customs regulations of the French colonies: Martinique].
                B Ag Gen Colon 21(235), July-Aug.: 835-841.   [*AGS*]

BOUTRUCHE, ROBERT

51.016   FA   1935 Bordeaux et le commerce des Antilles Francaises au XVIIIᵉ siècle
                [Bordeaux and the French Antillean trade in the 18th century]. *In*
                DENIS, SERGE, ed. NOS ANTILLES. Orléans, Luzeray, p.83-124.
                [5]   [*AGS*]

BROAD, D. & FERGUSON, W.

51.017   BC   1956 Trade opportunities for the U.K. *Statist* Sept.: 23-24.   [66]

BURGESS, CHARLES J.

52.017   GC   1954 Problems of intra-Caribbean transportation.
51.018   BC   1956 Trade relations between the British West Indies and Canada. *Stat-
                ist* Sept.: 21-22.

CANDACE, GRATIEN

51.019   FA   1935   Les Antilles dans la prospérité des ports francais depuis trois siècles [The Antilles' share in the prosperity of French ports over the last three centuries]. *In* DENIS, SERGE, ed. Nos ANTILLES. Orléans, Luzeray, p.65-79.   [5]   [*AGS*]

CARACCIOLO, HARRY A.

51.020   TR   1924   Trade promotion and the welfare of the colony. *Proc Agric Soc Trin Tob* 24(1), Jan.: 26-31.   [*AMN*]

CASSERLY, F. L.

51.021   JM   1947   Retrospect of Canada—Jamaica trade. *Can-W I Mag* 37(3), May: 11-14.   [*NYP*]

CECIL, C. H.

51.022   BC   1943   Tips to the trader. *Can-W I Mag* 32(11), Nov.: 7-10.   [*NYP*]

CHARPENTIER, GENEVIEVE

51.023   FA   1937   LES RELATIONS ÉCONOMIQUES ENTRE BORDEAUX ET LES ANTILLES AU XVIIIᵉ SIÈCLE. [ECONOMIC RELATIONS BETWEEN BORDEAUX AND THE ANTILLES IN THE 18TH CENTURY]. Bordeaux, Impr. Bière, 176p. [5] [*SCH*]

CHRISTELOW, ALLAN

51.024   JM   1942   Contraband trade between Jamaica and the Spanish Main, and the Free Port Act of 1766. *Hispan Am Hist Rev* 22(2), May: 309-343. [5]   [*COL*]

CLARKE, S. St. A.

51.025   JM   1962   THE COMPETITIVE POSITION OF JAMAICA'S AGRICULTURAL EXPORTS. Mona, Jamaica, University of the West Indies, Institute of Social and Economic Research, 156p.   [46]   [*RIS*]

COLLIER, H. C.

51.026   JM   1932   Canada's trade with Jamaica. *Can-W I Mag* 21(2), Jan.: 51-57.   [*NYP*]

54.015   BG   1935   From Guiana bauxite to Canadian aluminum.

51.027   BB   1935   The trade of Barbados. *Can-W I Mag* 24(11), Oct.: 11-13.   [*NYP*]

51.028   BC   1938   A B.W.I. market for boots and shoes. *Can-W I Mag* 27(2), Feb.:6-7.   [*NYP*]

51.029   JM   1938   The import trade of Jamaica in 1937. *Can-W I Mag* 27(10), Oct.: 27-30.   [*NYP*]

51.030   BC   1938   Opportunity for Canadian canners in the B.W.I. *Can-W I Mag* 27(6), June: 10-11.   [*NYP*]

51.031   BC   1938   The W.I. market for shooks and staves. *Can-W I Mag* 27(4), Apr.: 6-9.   [*NYP*]

51.032   BC   1939   Canadian trade opportunities in the W.I. *Can-W I Mag* 28(11), Dec.: 19-22.   [*NYP*]

51.033   JM   1940   The changing channels of trade. *Can-W I Mag* 29(6), June: 12-13.   [*NYP*]

51.034   BC   1940   Germany's loss, Canada's opportunity in West Indies trade. *Can-W I Mag* 29(4), Apr.: 7-9.   [*NYP*]

51.035   BC   1940   Scandinavia's loss, Canada's opportunity in West Indies trade. *Can-W I Mag* 29(5), May: 7-9.   [*NYP*]

51.036   JM   1946 The trade and commerce of Jamaica. *Can-W I Mag* 36(3), May: 17-21.
                                                                                              [*NYP*]

51.037   BC   1947 Some rudiments of West Indies trade. *Can-W I Mag* 36(11), Jan.:
                       13-16.   [*NYP*]

COOK, P. W.

51.038   JM   1927 Canada's trade with Jamaica—some facts and figures. *Can-W I Mag*
                       16(5), Mar.: 113, 116.   [*NYP*]

CROFT, W. D.; SPRINGER, H. W. & CHRISTOPHERSON, H. S.

51.039   BC   1958 Report of the Trade and Tariffs Commission. Bridgetown, Govt.
                       of the West Indies, 2 pts. [37, 38, 66]

CROWE, HARRY J.

51.040   BC   1920 Canadian-West Indian union. *Can-W I Mag* 8(7), May: 515-517. [37]
                                                                                       [*NYP*]

38.031 BC   1920 Political union between Canada and the West Indies.

37.076 BC   1920 Separate West Indian Dominion, or confederation with Canada.

38.032 BC   1921 The future relations of Canada and Jamaica.

51.041   JM   1925 How Canada-West Indies federation might be achieved. *Can-W I Mag*
                       13(6), Apr.: 152-155. [37]   [*NYP*]

37.077 JM   1925 The political side of the question.

CROWELL-HORATION

51.042   BC   1928 A south for our north. *Can-W I Mag* 17(4), Feb.: 83-85.   [*NYP*]

CURTIN, PHILIP D.

51.043   BC   1954 The British sugar duties and West Indian prosperity. *J Econ Hist*
                       14, Spring: 157-164. [5, 58]   [*RIS*]

DARRELL, H. A.

51.044   TC   1931 A Turk's Island call for attention. *Can-W I Mag* 20(4), Mar.: 108-109.
                                                                                              [*NYP*]

DAVIES, E. D.

48.006 TB   1957 Cocoa co-ops.

DEMAS, WILLIAM G.

51.045   BC   1960 The economics of West Indies customs union. *Social Econ Stud*
                       9(1), Mar.: 13-28. [38]   [*RIS*]

DESBOROUGH, MAURICE

51.046   BC   1955 Trade prospects. *New Commonw* British Caribbean Supplement,
                       30(9), Oct. 31: x-xiii.   [*AGS*]

DEVENTER, S. van

51.047   CU   1921/ De handelsomzet van de kolonie Curacao [The trade volume of the
                      22 colony of Curacao]. *W I G* 3:205-214.   [*COL*]

DORAN, EDWIN BEAL, Jr.

51.048   CC   1958 The Caicos Conch Trade. *Geogr Rev* 48(3): 388-401. [8, 56]   [*RIS*]

EVANS, G.

51.049 BC 1930 The possibility of establishing a trade in fruit and vegetable produce between Canada and the British West Indies. *Proc Agric Soc
Trin Tob* 30(10), Oct.: 373-378. [60, 63]   [*AMN*]

FLOOD, E. H. S.

49.026 BC 1920 The imports of machinery into the West Indies, by F. [sic] H. S.
Flood.

51.050 BC 1922 Trade conditions in the British West Indies. *Can-W I Mag* 10(5),
Mar.: 132-133.   [*NYP*]

51.051 BC 1922 What merchants should know about trade with the West Indies.
Can-W I Mag 10(11), Sept.: 294-295.   [*NYP*]

FREEMAN, WILLIAM G.

51.052 TR 1929 The balance of trade and prosperity. *W I Comm Circ* 44(815), Dec.
26: 503-504. [46]   [*NYP*]

GANZERT, FREDERIC W.

51.053 GC 1958 Trade trends and prospects. *In* WILGUS, A. CURTIS, ed. THE CARIB-
BEAN: BRITISH, DUTCH, FRENCH, UNITED STATES [Papers delivered at
the Eighth Conference on the Caribbean at the University of Florida, Dec. 5-7, 1957]. Gainesville, University of Florida Press, p. 193-
224. (Publications of the School of Inter-American Studies, ser. 1,
v. 8.)   [46]   [*RIS*]

GATES, RALPH CHARLES

51.054 BC 1959 Marketing of fresh vegetables in the Caribbean islands. *Caribbean*
13(11), Nov.: 212-215. [48]   [*COL*]

GELLNER, MARIANNE

51.055 BC 1956 Trade relations and prospects. *Statist* Sept.: 17, 19-20.

GERVILLE-REACHE, LUCIEN

51.056 GD 1960 Possibilités d'exportation de banane vers l'U.R.S.S. [Possibilities
of banana export to the U.S.S.R.]. *Rev Guad* 39, Jan.-Mar.: 26-32.
[60]   [*RIS*]

GICK, F. J.

51.057 JM 1945 In Jamaica. *In* BRITISH WEST INDIES: REVIEW OF COMMERCIAL CONDI-
TIONS. In Trinidad, by W. D. Lambie. In Jamaica, by F. J. Gick.
Aug.-Sept. 1945. London, Published for the Dept. of Overseas
Trade by H.M.S.O. p. 23-48. (Reviews of commercial conditions.)
[*COL*]

GLASS, LESTERS

51.058 BC 1933 Canadian-West Indian trade. *Can-W I Mag* 22(2), Jan.: 58-59. [*NYP*]

GOODMAN, EILEEN

64.051 BH 1937 British Honduras—the forest colony.

GOULD, CLARENCE P.

51.059 FA 1939 Trade between the Windward Islands and the continental colonies
of the French Empire, 1683-1763. *Missi Valley Hist Rev* 25(4),
Mar.: 473-490. [5]   [*AGS*]

GRAHAM, GERALD S.

51.060   BC   1941 The origin of free ports in British North America. *Can Hist Rev*
                       22(1), Mar.: 25-34.   [5]   [*NYP*]

GRANT, WILLARD G.

51.061   BC   1959 Looking to Canada—some reflections on Canadian-West Indies trade.
                       Can-W I Mag 49(10), Oct.: 11-12.   [*NYP*]

GRUTTERINK, J. A.

54.021   SR   1919 Bauxiet [Bauxite].

HALLEMA, A.

51.062   NC   1933/ Friesland en de voormalige compagnieën voor den handel op Oost
                   34   en West [Friesland and the former companies that traded with the
                       East and the West]. *W I G* 15:81-96.   [5]   [*COL*]

6.024   NC   1939 Koloniale vraagstukken ten opzichte van onze West anderhalve
                       eeuw geleden [Colonial problems in connection with our West one-
                       and-a-half centuries ago].

HART, ANSELL

51.063   JM   1954 The banana in Jamaica: export trade. *Social Econ Stud* 3(2), Sept.:
                       212-229.   [60]   [*RIS*]

HEESTERMAN, J. E.

51.064   GC   1955 Marketing of Caribbean timbers. *Car For* 16(3-4), July-Oct.: 57-63.
                       [64]   [*AGS*]

HENDERSON, DOUG

51.065   BC   1959 The West Indies Mission. *Can-W I Mag* 49(6), June: 1-2, 4.   [*NYP*]

HILL, O. MARY

51.066   BC   1959 Canada's trade with the West Indies. *Can Geogr J* 58(1), Jan.: 2-9.
                                                                                    [*AGS*]

HINCKLEY, THEODORE C.

51.067   JM   1963 The decline of Caribbean smuggling. *J Inter-Amer Stud* 5(1), Jan.:
                       107-121.   [5]   [*COL*]

HUGHES, DAVID A.

51.068   BG   1963 British Guiana hopes to broaden markets and sources of supply.
                       Int Com 69(16), Apr. 22: 5-6.   [*NYP*]

HULLU, J. de

51.069   SE   1921/ De handel van St. Eustatius in 1786 [The commerce of St. Eustatius
                   22   in 1786]. *W I G* 3:35-52.   [5]   [*COL*]

IFILL, BARBARA

51.070   TR   1964 The richest trade centre of the Indies: a vision of Trinidad's future.
                       Car Q 10(4), Dec.: 33-45.   [*RIS*]

INGRAM, K. E.

51.071   BC   1962 The West Indian trade of an English furniture firm in the eighteenth
                       century. *Jam Hist Rev* 3(3), Mar.: 22-37.   [*COL*]

JAMESON, JOHN FRANKLIN

51.072   SE   1903 St. Eustatius in the American Revolution. *Am Hist Rev* 8(4), July: 683-708. [5]   [*COL*]

JOHNSON, HARRY G.; DEMAS, WILLIAM G.; MEIER, GERALD M. & BALOGH, T.

51.073   BC   1960 Symposium on the Report of the Trade and Tariffs Commission. *Social Econ Stud* 9(1), Mar.: 1-40. [37]   [*RIS*]

JONES, CLEMENT W. et al.

52.040   BC   1948 REPORT ON WEST INDIAN SHIPPING SERVICES.

KATZIN, MARGARET FISHER

51.074   JM   1959 HIGGLERS OF JAMAICA. Ph.D. dissertation, Northwestern University, 238p.   [*COL*]

51.075   JM   1959 The Jamaican country higgler. *Social Econ Stud* 8(4), Dec.: 421-440.   [*RIS*]

51.076   JM   1960 The business of higgling in Jamaica. *Social Econ Stud* 9(3), Sept.: 297-331.   [*RIS*]

KEIRSTEAD, B. S. & LEVITT, KARI

52.043   BC   [n.d.] Inter-territorial freight rates and the federal shipping service.

KEITH, ALICE B.

51.077   BC   1948 Relaxations in the British restrictions on the American trade with the British West Indies, 1783-1802. *J Mod Hist* 20(1), Mar.: 1-18. [5]   [*COL*]

KESLER, C. K.

51.078   SR   1926/ Amsterdamsche bankiers en de West in de 18de eeuw [Amsterdam
27   bankers and the West in the 18th century]. *W I G* 8:499-516. [5, 44]   [*COL*]

60.043   CU   1931/ Twee populaire vruchten van Curacao: oranjeappelen en pinda's
32   [Two popular fruits of Curacao: oranges and peanuts].

KLERK, J. A. de

54.031   CU   1921/ Het petroleumbedrijf op Curacao [The oil industry of Curacao].
22

KNOX, A. D.

51.079   BC   1960 Trade and customs union in the West Indies. *In* CUMPER, G. E., ed. THE ECONOMY OF THE WEST INDIES. Kingston, Institute of Social and Economic Research, University College of the West Indies, p.243-265. [38]   [*RIS*]

KUNDU, A.

62.018   BC   1964 Rice in the British Caribbean Islands and British Guiana, 1950-1975.

LAMBIE, W. D.

51.080   TR   1945 In Trinidad. *In* BRITISH WEST INDIES: REVIEW OF COMMERCIAL CONDITIONS. In Trinidad, by W.D. Lambie. In Jamaica, by F.J. Gick. Aug.-Sept. 1945. London, published for the Dept. of Overseas Trade by H.M.S.O., p.2-22. (Reviews of commercial conditions.)   [*COL*]

LANGEMEYER, F. S.

51.081   SM   1922/Het zoutbedrijf op St. Martin [The salt industry on St. Martin].
              23 *W I G* 4:241-265, 305-330.   [44]   [*COL*]

LARET, W. F. H.

51.082   SR   1949 Honderd jaren vrijhandel in Suriname [A hundred years of free trade
              in Surinam]. *W I G* 30:23-25.   [5]   [*COL*]

LE BIHAN,

51.083   GD   1951 The foreign trade of Guadeloupe from 1938-1949. *Car Commn Mon
              Inf B* 4(9), Apr.: 742-744.   [*AGS*]

LEONARD, E. R.

51.084   BC   1941 The banana trade from the West Indies to Canada. *Trop Agric* 18(12),
              Dec.: 244-246.   [*AGS*]

LICHTVELD, U. M. & VOORHOEVE, J.

51.085   SR   1958 SURINAME: SPIEGEL DER VADERLANDSE KOOPLIEDEN [SURINAM: MIRROR OF
              THE DUTCH MERCHANTS]. Zwolle [Holland] Tjeenk Willink, 301p.   [5]
                                                                         [*NYP*]

LICKFOLD, E. R.

51.086   TR   1939 Tuttle steals the show; or, Sunday market in Trinidad. *Can-W I Mag*
              28(5), June: 11-13.   [*NYP*]

LOGAN, HANCE

51.087   BC   1924 Hance Logan tells Parliament some plain truths about the West
              Indies. *Can-W I Mag* 12(5), Mar.: 128-129.   [*NYP*]
51.088   GC   1925 Hance Logan, M. P., gives Parliament account of his mission to
              West Indies. *Can-W I Mag* 13(6), Apr.: 158-163.   [3, 66]   [*NYP*]

MACAULAY, THOMAS B.

51.089   BG   1919 Canada and the West Indies. *Timehri* 3d ser., 6(23), Sept.: 108-115.
                                                                         [*AMN*]
51.090   BC   1919 Canada and the West Indies—the case of commercial union. *W I Comm
              Circ* 34(541), June 26: 156-157.   [37]   [*NYP*]
51.091   BC   1926 Canada and West Indies: the future holds much promise for Canadian
              West Indian relations. *Can-W I Mag* 15(10), Aug.: 227-229.   [52]
                                                                         [*NYP*]

MACFARLANE, JOHN J.

51.092   GC   1921 The trade of the West Indies. *Can-W I Mag* 9(11), Sept.: 300-301.
                                                                         [*NYP*]

MASCART, D.

51.093   MT   1951 The foreign trade of Martinique in 1950. *Car Commn Mon Inf B*
              5(4), Nov.: 113-116.   [*AGS*]

MEIER, GERALD M.

51.094   BC   1960 Effects of a customs union on economic development. *Social Econ
              Stud* 9(1), Mar.: 29-36.   [38]   [*RIS*]

MENKMAN, W. R.

44.150 CU   1929/ De havenbeweging van het eiland Curacao [The volume of trade
              30   of the island Curacao].

51.095 NC   1929/ Westindische handelsstatistieken [Trade statistics of West India].
              30   *W I G* 11:1-10.   [*COL*]

51.096 NC   1930/ De West en onze scheepvaart [The West and our shipping-trade].
              31   *W I G* 12:231-242, 268-278.   [52]   [*COL*]

51.097 GC   1938 Oorlog en handel in West Indië [War and trade in the West Indies].
                   W I G 20:77-88, 97-102.   [*COL*]

44.154 CU   1947/ Curacaosche gegevens op economisch gebied [Curacao data about
              48   economic conditions].

MINTZ, SIDNEY W.

51.098 JM   1955 The Jamaican internal marketing pattern. *Social Econ Stud* 4(1),
                   Mar.: 95-103.   [*RIS*]

51.099 JM   1956 The role of the middleman in the internal distribution system of a
                   Caribbean peasant economy. *Hum Org* 15(2), Summer: 18-23.   [8]
                                                                                      [*RIS*]

51.100 JM   1959 Internal market systems as mechanisms of social articulation. *In*
                   RAY, VERNE F., ed. INTERMEDIATE SOCIETIES, SOCIAL MOBILITY,
                   AND COMMUNICATION: PROCEEDINGS OF THE 1959 ANNUAL SPRING MEET-
                   ING OF THE AMERICAN ETHNOLOGICAL SOCIETY. Seattle, University of
                   Washington, American Ethnological Society, p.20-30.   [8]   [*RIS*]

51.101 JM   1964 Currency problems in eighteenth-century Jamaica and Gresham's
                   law. *In* MANNERS, ROBERT A., ed. PROCESS AND PATTERN IN
                   CULTURE: ESSAYS IN HONOR OF JULIAN J. STEWARD. Chicago, Aldine
                   Pub. Co., p.251-265.   [5]   [*RIS*]

MINTZ, SIDNEY W. & HALL, DOUGLAS

51.102 JM   1960 The origins of the Jamaican internal marketing system. *In* MINTZ,
                   SIDNEY W., comp. PAPERS IN CARIBBEAN ANTHROPOLOGY. New Haven,
                   Dept. of Anthropology, Yale University, no. 57 (58p.) (Yale Uni-
                   versity publications in anthropology, nos. 57-64.)   [5, 8]   [*RIS*]

MORAIS, ALLAN I.

51.103 GC   1952 Standardisation of Caribbean trade accounts. *Car Commn Mon Inf B*
                   6(3), Oct.: 51-52, 65.   [*AGS*]

1.030   GC   1954 SELECT BIBLIOGRAPHY OF TRADE PUBLICATIONS WITH SPECIAL REFER-
                   ENCE TO CARIBBEAN TRADE STATISTICS.

51.104 BC   1955 The present status of British Caribbean trade accounts. *Caribbean*
                   8(8), Mar.: 169-171.   [*COL*]

MORGAN, D. J.

51.105 BC   1962 Imperial preference in the West Indies and in the British Caribbean,
                   1929-55: a quantitative analysis. *Econ J* 72(285), Mar.: 104-133.
                   [37, 38]   [*COL*]

MOTTA, STANLEY

51.106 JM   1961 The role of commerce in independent Jamaica. *Spotlight News Mag*
                   22(12), Dec.: 17.   [66]   [*RIS*]

NASH, E. F.

51.107   BC   1958 Main characteristics of West Indian trade. *In* HUGGINS, H.D., ed.
[PROCEEDINGS OF THE] STUDY CONFERENCE ON ECONOMIC DEVELOPMENT
IN UNDERDEVELOPED COUNTRIES [held at the University College of the
West Indies, Aug. 5-15, 1957]. *Social Econ Stud* 7(3), Sept.: 120-139.
[46]   [*RIS*]

51.108   BC   1960 Trading problems of the British West Indies. *In* CUMPER, G. E., ed.
THE ECONOMY OF THE WEST INDIES. Kingston, Institute of Social and
Economic Research, University College of the West Indies, p.223-
242.   [*RIS*]

NEWMAN, PETER KENNETH

51.109   BC   1960 Canada's role in West Indian trade before 1912. *Inter-Amer Econ Aff*
14(1), Summer: 25-49.   [5]   [*RIS*]

OLIVIER, SYDNEY 1st Baron RAMSDEN

51.110   BC   1902 The regulation of the quality of exported fruit. *W I B* 3(2): 131-139.
[60]   [*AMN*]

46.156   JM   1915 Recent developments in Jamaica: internal and external, by Sir
Sydney Olivier.

OUDSCHANS DENTZ, FRED

51.111   SR   1942 De eerste handelsbetrekkingen van Suriname met de Amerikaansche
Republiek [The first trade relations of Surinam with the American
Republic]. *W I G* 24:193-200.   [5]   [*COL*]

PANHUYS, L. C. van

51.112   NC   1921/ De Pan-Amerikaansche Unie [The Pan-American Union]. *W I G*
22 3:53-57.   [*COL*]

PARES, RICHARD

5.165   GC   1936 WAR AND TRADE IN THE WEST INDIES 1739-1763.

51.113   GC   1956 YANKEES AND CREOLES: THE TRADE BETWEEN NORTH AMERICA AND THE
WEST INDIES BEFORE THE AMERICAN REVOLUTION. New York, Longmans,
Green, 168p.   [5]   [*RIS*]

PARLOUR, ROGER R.

51.114   TR   1953 Canada's trade with Trinidad. *Can-W I Mag* 43(13[i.e. 1], Jan.:
13-15, 17.   [*NYP*]

51.115   TR   1954 How's business in Trinidad? *Can-W I Mag* 44(7), July: 2, 38-39.
[*NYP*]

PARRY, JOHN HORACE

51.116   JM   1955 Eliphalet Fitch: a Yankee trader in Jamaica during the War of
Independence. *History* new ser., 40(138), Feb.: 84-98. [5]   [*COL*]

RAGATZ, LOWELL JOSEPH

51.117   BC   1927 STATISTICS FOR THE STUDY OF BRITISH CARIBBEAN ECONOMIC HISTORY,
1763-1833. London, Bryan Edwards Press, 25p.   [5, 45]   [*NYP*]

RAMPERSAD, FRANK B.

51.118   TR   1963 Some aspects of the external trade and payments of Trinidad and
Tobago, 1951-1959. *Social Econ Stud* 12(2), June: 101-140.   [*RIS*]

RENNARD, J.

51.119   FA   1946 LE COMMERCE AUX ANTILLES [TRADE IN THE ANTILLES]. Fort-de-France, Impr. du service de l'information, 76p.   *[NYP]*

RENNER, AGNES CECELIA

51.120   JM   1940 TRENDS IN THE TRADE OF JAMAICA. M. A. thesis, Clark University, 106p. [66]

REVERT, EUGENE

46.182   FA   1955 L'économie antillaise [Antillean economy].

RIESGO, RAYMOND R.

51.121   BC   1961 The Federation of the West Indies. 1) A bright opportunity for trade. 2) Jamaica and Trinidad, thriving markets. *For Com Wkly* 66(3), July 17: 9, 16; 66(4), July 24: 5,30. [38]   *[COL]*

ROBINSON, C. K.

46.186   TR   1953 The food production programme of Trinidad and Tobago.

ROWAAN, P. A.

63.047   SR   1941 Surinaamsche honing als exportproduct [Surinam honey as an export product].

SCHOCH, C. F.

46.194   SR   1926/ De ondernemersraad voor Suriname en zijne voorstellen betreffende 27 den grooten landbouw [The Council of employers for Surinam and its suggestions for large-scale agriculture].

SERTIMA, J. van

51.122   BG   1912 The Colony's foreign trade: a ten years' review. *Timehri* 3d ser., 2(19B), Dec.: 259-272.   *[AMN]*

SHEPHARD, C. Y.

51.123   GC   1939 British West Indian economic history in imperial perspective. *Trop Agric* 16(7), July: 151-155; 16(8), Aug.: 175-178. [5, 46]   *[RIS]*

51.124   GC   1954 Marketing and processing problems. *Car Commn Mon Inf B* 8(3), Oct.: 47-48, 61-64,68. [48]   *[COL]*

51.125   BC   1954 Organisation for the processing and marketing of the products of small scale farming. *In* SMALL SCALE FARMING IN THE CARIBBEAN. [Port of Spain?] Trinidad, Caribbean Commission, p.40-52. [48]

SHILL, A. C.

51.126   LW/ WW   1932 The fruit and vegetable industry of the Leeward and Windward Islands. *Trop Agric* 9(12), Dec.: 362-370. [63]   *[AGS]*

SIBLEY, C. LINTERN

51.127   BC   1919 Canada and the West Indies. *Can Mag* 53(5), Sept.: 358-363.   *[NYP]*

SIMMONDS, N. W.

60.079   BC   1960 The growth of post-war West Indian banana trades.

SMITH, R. G. C.

51.128   BC   1959 The West Indies. *Can-W I Mag* 49(1), Jan.: 14-15. [38]   *[NYP]*

SOMERMEIJER, W. H.

51.129   NA   1951 De paradoxen der Antillaanse economie [The paradoxes of the
                     Antillean economy]. *Tijdschr Econ Social Geogr* 42:236-251. [*AGS*]

SPENCE, ELEANOR JEAN

51.130   BB   1964 MARKETING ACTIVITIES AND HOUSEHOLD ACTIVITIES OF COUNTRY HAWKERS
                     IN BARBADOS. M.A. thesis, Department of Sociology and Anthro-
                     pology, McGill University, Montreal, 129p. [8, 9, 11]

SPOON, W.

51.131   SR   1932/ Enkele Surinaamsche producten in Nederland in 1932 [Some Surinam
            33   products in the Netherlands in 1932]. *W I G* 14:409-415.   [46, 66]
                                                                              [*COL*]
51.132   SR   1941 Surinaamsche sinaasappelen in Nederland [Surinam oranges in the
                     Netherlands]. *W I G* 23:193-202.   [*COL*]
51.133   SR   1943 Surinaamsche hout voor fineer en triplex [Surinam lumber for veneer
                     and triplex]. *W I G* 25:33-40. [44]   [*COL*]
51.134   NL   1946 Enkele opmerkingen over de afzet van het West-Indische zeezout
                     [Some remarks about the sale of West Indian seasalt]. *W I G* 27:
                     353-362.   [*COL*]
51.135   SR   1947 Toepassingen van Walaba of bijlhout [Applications for Wallaba].
                     W I G 28-289-299.   [*COL*]

SPOON, W. & SESSLER, WA. M.

51.136   SR   1948 Beoordeling van Surinaamse tabak [Appreciation of tobacco from
                     Surinam]. *W I G* 29:321-327.   [*COL*]

STANLEY, E. L.

52.088   BC   1939 Notes on advertising for West Indies markets.

STEVENS, G. R.

52.089   JM   1922 Advertising in Jamaica.

THORNTON, A. P.

51.137   TR   1954 Some statistics of West Indian produce, shipping and revenue, 1660-
                     1685. *Car Hist Rev* 3-4, Dec.: 251-280. [5]   [*RIS*]

TIDEMAN, M. C.

51.138   SR   1949 De ontwikkeling van de handel tussen Suriname en Nederland [The
                     development of trade between Surinam and the Netherlands]. *W I G*
                     30:297-310.   [*COL*]

TOUGH, JOHN

51.139   BC   1930 Some possibilities and suggestions in Canadian West Indian trade.
                     Can-W I Mag 19(11), Oct.: 111-113.   [*NYP*]

VERRILL, ALPHEUS HYATT

51.140   GC   1918 Some lands of opportunity. *Pan-Am Mag* 26(3), Jan.: 133-142. [66]
                                                                              [*COL*]

WAINWRIGHT, D. C.

51.141   JM   1940 Jamaica's trade with Canada. *Can-W I Mag* 29(3), Mar.: 7-8. [*NYP*]

WATTS, Sir FRANCIS
20.019   BC   1926 History as affecting outlook in the West Indies.

WILDE, C. NOEL
51.142   BH   1929 Import trade of British Honduras. *Can-W I Mag* 18(6), Apr.: 138-139.
            [*NYP*]

WILLIAMS, ERIC EUSTACE
51.143   GC   1954 Caribbean trade with Argentina. *Car Commn Mon Inf B* 7(1), Jan.:
            139-142.   [*COL*]

WRIGHT, G.
51.144   SV   1928 St. Vincent arrowroot. *Trop Agric* 7(7), July: 162-166. [63]   [*AGS*]

YOUNG, R. T.
51.145   BC/   1931 Points for exporters to the West Indies (eastern group) and British
        FA   Guiana. *Can-W I Mag* 20(11), Oct.: 378-379.   [*NYP*]

Chapter 52

TRANSPORTATION AND COMMUNICATION

AIKEN, JAMES

66.001   BG   1915 "Timehri" and development.

ALLEYNE, MERVIN C.

37.003   JM   1963 Communication and politics in Jamaica.

ARMSTRONG, PERCY E.

52.001   BC   1937 Foundation of closer union. *Can-W I Mag* 26(11), Nov.: 6-8.   [*NYP*]
52.002   BC   1938 The West Indies and communications. *United Emp* new ser., 29(7), July: 291-293.   [*AGS*]

ASPINALL, Sir ALGERNON E.

52.003   BC   1945 Some roads and their burdens.   *J Barb Mus Hist Soc* 12(2), Feb.: 61-66.   [5]   [*AMN*]

BAKKER, H.-B.

52.004   CU   1929 The harbour of Curacao. *B Perm Int Ass Nav Congr* 4(8), July: 80-88.   [*AGS*]

BALDWIN, RICHARD

52.005   BG   1956 The river boathand of Guiana, a disappearing character. *Timehri* 4th ser., 1(35), Oct.: 82-86.   [3]

BAYLEY, HERBERT

52.006   BB   1940 The twopenny Barbados stamp of 1859. *J Barb Mus Hist Soc* 7(3), May: 123-136.   [5]   [*AMN*]
52.007   BB   1941 The postmarks of the Barbados post offices 1852-1941. *J Barb Mus Hist Soc* 8(4), Aug.: 149.   [5]   [*AMN*]
52.008   BB   1944 Postmarks and cancelling marks used in Barbados 1841-1944. *J Barb Mus Hist Soc* 11(2), Feb.: 76-79.   [5]   [*AMN*]
52.009   BB   1952 The centenary of the Barbados Post Office: 1852-1952. *J Barb Mus Hist Soc* 19(4), Aug.: 170-177.   [5]   [*AMN*]

BELL, FRANK K.

52.010   GC   1954 Ships and shipping in the Caribbean. *In* WILGUS, A. CURTIS, ed. THE CARIBBEAN: ITS ECONOMY [Papers delivered at the Fourth Annual Conference on the Caribbean held at the University of Florida, Dec. 3-5, 1953]. Gainesville, University of Florida Press, p.117-125. (Publications of the School of Inter-American Studies, ser. 1, v. 4.   [*RIS*]

BLANCHE, LENIS

52.011   GD   1935 CONTRIBUTION À L'HISTOIRE DE LA PRESSE À LA GUADELOUPE [CONTRI-
BUTION TO THE HISTORY OF JOURNALISM IN GUADELOUPE]. Basse-Terre,
Impr. catholique, 55p. [5]   [NYP]

BOER, M. G. de

52.012   NC   1919 De oprichting van den koninklijken West-Indischen Maildienst
[The establishment of the Royal West Indian Mail Service]. *W I G*
1(1): 111-131.   [COL]

BOUMAN, L. F.

52.013   NC   1937 De West-Indische afdeeling der KLM [The West Indian department
of the KLM]. *W I G* 19:7-15.   [COL]

52.014   GC   1944 Netherlands commercial aviation in the Caribbean. *Can-W I Mag*
33-34 (4), Apr.: 31-33.   [NYP]

BRINDLEY, MAUD D.

13.008   BG   1924 The canoes of British Guiana.

BROUWER, N. C. W.

52.015   SR   1927 Suriname's herstel: de verkeersontwikkeling is van primair belang
voor den economischen opbouw van Suriname [Surinam's recovery:
development of transportation and traffic is of primary importance
for Surinam's economic growth]. *Tijdschr Econ Geogr* 18(3), Mar.
15: 79-88.   [AGS]

BUCK, EDWARD CLARK

52.016   BG   1919 Proposed railway development of the hinterland of British Guiana.
Timehri 3d ser., 6(23), Sept.: 99-103. [66]   [AMN]

BURGESS, CHARLES J.

52.017   GC   1954 Problems of intra-Caribbean transportation. *Car Commn Mon Inf B*
7(2), Feb.: 152-154. [51]   [COL]

CHAPIN, HOWARD M.

52.018   BB   1934 Barbados signal books of 1814. *J Barb Mus Hist Soc* 1(4), Aug.:
203-205. [5]   [AMN]

COBBE, H. N. G.

52.019   BG   1942 Through British Guiana's hinterland towards Brazil. *Crown Colon*
12(133), Dec.: 811-812.   [AGS]

COMBER, STAFFORD X.

52.020   BG   1919 Interior communications for British Guiana. *Timehri* 3d ser., 6(23),
Sept.: 12-21. [66]   [AMN]

CUNDALL, FRANK

52.021   JM   1926 Early printing in Jamaica. *W I Comm Circ* 41(719), Apr. 22: 150.
[5]   [NYP]

DAVIDSON, GEOFFREY

52.022   BG   1935 Route to the Rupununi Savanna. *Geogr J* 85(3), Mar.: 270-273. [AGS]

DOLPHIN, CELESTE
52.023   BG   1959   Good afternoon, schools. *Corona* 11(6), June: 219-222.   [13, 19, 32]
[*AGS*]

DORAN, EDWIN BEAL, Jr.
52.024   CC   1957   Caicos cruise. *Mot Boating* Dec.: 28-29, 63-64, 66, 68, 70. [3]

DUYMAER van TWIST, H. M. C.
52.025   SR/   1942   De ontwikkeling van het Nederlandsche civiele luchtverkeer in West-
          CU   Indië [The development of Dutch civil air-traffic in the West Indies].
                    W I G 24:181-187.   [*COL*]

EGERTON, Sir WALTER
52.026   BG   1915   A railway and hinterland development. *Timehri* 3d ser., 3(20B),
                    May: 159-167.   [66]   [*AMN*]

FENTEM, ARLIN D.
43.053   SV   1961   COMMERCIAL GEOGRAPHY OF ST. VINCENT.

FLETCHER, W. E. L.
52.027   BB   1961   The Barbados Railway. *J Barb Mus Hist Soc* 28(3), May: 86-98.   [5]
[*AMN*]

FREITAS, G. V. de
52.028   BC   1956   Press and radio. *Statist* Sept.: 69-70.

GAAY FORTMAN, B. de
37.126   CU   1933/ Vrijheid van drukpers en recht van vergadering [Freedom of the
                34   press and the right of assembly].

GILL, F. T.
52.029   JM   1937   A new link in communication. *Can-W I Mag* 26(11), Nov.: 28-30.
[*NYP*]
52.030   JM   1939   Canada Caribbean communications. *Can-W I Mag* 28(2), Feb.: 30-32.
[*NYP*]

GODFREY, J. E.
28.231   BG   1904   A few introductory remarks on the regulations passed by the recent
                    Quarantine Conference.

GOEJE, C. H. de
5.066   GC   1936/ Op den oceaan voor en na Columbus [On the ocean before and after
              37   Columbus].

GORE-ORMSBY, W.
46.077   BC   1922   The progress of the West Indies.

GRANT, ANDREW
52.031   BG   1930   Railways necessary to progress. *Can-W I Mag* 19(9), Aug.: 40-42, 44.
                    [66]   [*NYP*]
52.032   BG   1931   Railroad construction advocated. *Can-W I Mag* 20(3), Feb.: 72-73,
                    88.   [66]   [*NYP*]

GROOTE, J. F.

52.033   AR/   1950 The new harbours of Aruba and Curacao. *Dock Harb Auth* 31(356),
           CU   June: 39-45. [66]   [*AGS*]

HANRATH, JOHANNES J.

52.034   SR   1952 "Planning" met betrekking tot het binnenlandse verkeer van Suriname
                         [Planning of inland traffic of Surinam]. *Tijdschr Econ Social Geogr*
                         43(10-11), Oct.-Nov.: 233-242. [66]   [*RIS*]

52.035   SR   1952 DE ZEESCHEEPVAART VAN SURINAME; VOORSTELLEN VOOR DE TEEKOMSTIGE
                         VERKEERSONTWIKKELING VAN SURINAME [THE SEA TRAFFIC OF SURINAM:
                         PROPOSALS FOR THE FUTURE DEVELOPMENT OF TRANSPORTATION AND
                         TRAFFIC OF SURINAM]. Paramaribo, Planbureau Suriname.   [66]

HARES, L. G.

52.036   BG   1935 A railway enterprise in Demerara. *Can-W I Mag* 24(10), Sept.: 11, 20.
                         [45, 58]   [*NYP*]

HARRIS, WILLIAM H.

52.037   BC   1944 The West Indian radio newspaper. *In* FRAZIER, E. F. & WILLIAMS,
                         E., eds. THE ECONOMIC FUTURE OF THE CARIBBEAN. Washington, D. C.,
                         Howard University Press, p.75-77.

HARTOG, JOHAN

52.038   CU   1946 De pers van Curacao in Wereldoorlog II [The press of Curacao dur-
                         ing World War II]. *W I G* 27:18-22.   [*COL*]

HILL, LUKE M.

52.039   BG   1912 Railway discussion 1902: the possibilities of railway development
                         in British Guiana. *Timehri* 3d ser., 2(19A), July: 45-55. [66] [*AMN*]

HURAULT, JEAN

14.007   FG   1961 Canots africains en Guyane [African canoes in Guiana].

INTERNATIONAL BANK FOR RECONSTRUCTION AND DEVELOPMENT

66.069   JM   1952 THE ECONOMIC DEVELOPMENT OF JAMAICA.
66.070   SR   1952 SURINAM; RECOMMENDATIONS FOR A TEN YEAR DEVELOPMENT PROGRAM.
66.071   BG   1953 THE ECONOMIC DEVELOPMENT OF BRITISH GUIANA.

JONES, CLEMENT W. et al.

52.040   BC   1948 REPORT ON WEST INDIAN SHIPPING SERVICES. London, H.M.S.O., 46p.
                         ([Reports of the] Commonwealth Shipping Committee.) [51, 66] [*RIS*]

KALFF, S.

52.041   SR   1923/ Surinaamsche journalistiek [Surinam journalism]. *W I G* 5:463-474.
                   24   [*COL*]

52.042   CU   1925/ Curacaosche journalistiek [Curacao journalism]. *W I G* 7:1-6. [*COL*]
                   26

KEIRSTEAD, B. S. & LEVITT, KARI

52.043   BC   [n.d.] INTER-TERRITORIAL FREIGHT RATES AND THE FEDERAL SHIPPING SERVICE.
                         Mona, Institute of Social and Economic Research, University of the
                         West Indies, 91p. [38, 51]   [*RIS*]

KESLER, C. K.

52.044   CU   1926/De interoceanische verbinding voor 100 jaar [The inter-ocean con-
                27 nection 100 years ago]. *W I G* 8:125-139.   [5]   [*COL*]

KIENIT, H. de

52.045   CU   1960/De vaste oeververbinding over de St. Annabaai te Curacao als
                61 onderdeel van de verbetering voor land- en scheepvaartverkeer
                    [The permanent shore connections over the St. Anna Bay in Curacao
                    as part of the improvement of land and sea traffic]. *N W I G* 40:
                    221-225.   [*COL*]

KINGSBURY, ROBERT C.

43.083   GR   1960 COMMERCIAL GEOGRAPHY OF GRENADA.
43.084   BV   1960 COMMERCIAL GEOGRAPHY OF THE BRITISH VIRGIN ISLANDS.
43.085   GN   1960 COMMERCIAL GEOGRAPHY OF THE GRENADINES.
43.086   TR   1960 COMMERCIAL GEOGRAPHY OF TRINIDAD AND TOBAGO.

KLUVERS, B. J.

52.046   SR   1921/Een wegtracé door het moeras naar Coronie [A road plan for travers-
                22 ing the swamps to Coronie]. *W I G* 3:641-649.   [66]   [*COL*]

KOUSHNAREFF, SERGE G. & HYNES, KENNETH N.

52.047   GC   1954 Extra-Caribbean shipping facilities available to the countries
                      served by the Caribbean Commission. *Car Econ Rev* 6, Dec.:
                      146-168.   [*RIS*]

KRUSEMAN, J. P.

52.048   NC   1954/Het verkeerswezen [Transportation]. *Vox Guy* 1(4), Nov.-Jan.: 49-52.
                55

KUNDU, A.

44.135   BG   1963 Inter-industry table for the economy of British Guiana, 1959, and
                      national accounts, 1957-60.

LADEL, ROBERT

52.049   FG   1956 French Guiana—telecommunications. *Caribbean* 10(2), Sept.: 33-34.
                      [66]   [*COL*]

LAING, MICHAEL

52.050   BC   1955 Radio comes to the West Indies. *New Commonw* British Caribbean
                      Supplement 30(11), Nov. 28: vi-vii.   [*AGS*]

LAMY, GEORGES

46.132   FG   1936 Situation économique de la Guyane [Economic status of Guiana].

LANGEMEYER, F. S.

52.051   SM   1937 Eene reis naar Sint Maarten in oorlogstijd [A voyage to St. Maarten
                      in time of war]. *W I G* 19:225-242.   [5]   [*COL*]

LLOYD, M. V.

52.052   BC   1941 Inter-island communications. *Can-W I Mag* 30(1), Jan.: 11-12. [*NYP*]

MACAULAY, THOMAS B.

51.091   BC   1926   Canada and West Indies: the future holds much promise for Canadian
                       West Indian relations.

McMURTRIE, DOUGLAS C.

52.053   DM   1932   THE FIRST PRINTING IN DOMINICA. London, Privately printed, 8p. [5]
                                                                                      [COL]
52.054   BB   1933   EARLY PRINTING IN BARBADOS. London, Privately printed, 15p. [5]
                                                                                      [COL]
52.055   JM   1942   THE FIRST PRINTING IN JAMAICA ... Evanston, Ill., Privately printed.
                       11p.   [5]   [COL]

MAUNDER, W. F.

52.056   JM   1954   Development of internal transport in Jamaica. *Social Econ Stud*
                       3(2), Sept.: 161-185. [36]   [RIS]
52.057   JM   1954   Expenditure on internal transport in Jamaica. *Social Econ Stud*
                       3(1), June: 29-63. [36]   [RIS]
52.058   JM   1954   Kingston public passenger transport. *Social Econ Stud* 2(4), Mar.:
                       5-36. [36]   [AGS]

MEEHAN, M. J. & HERRON, C. R.

52.059   GC   1927   Travel routes and costs in Caribbean countries. Washington, U.S.
                       Govt. Print. Off., 42p. (U.S. Dept. of Commerce, Bureau of Foreign
                       and Domestic Commerce, Trade information bulletin no. 491.) [NYP]

MENKMAN, W. R.

52.060   CU   1923/ Scheepvaart beweging en scheepvaart wetgeving op Curacao [Ship-
                24   ing movement and navigation laws in Curacao]. *W I G* 15:185-196.
                       [44]   [COL]
51.096   NC   1930/ De West en onze scheepvaart [The West and our shipping-trade].
                31
5.140   NA   1936/ De Nederlanders in de Caraïbische wateren: een nabetrachting
                37   [The Dutch in the Caribbean seas: in retrospect].
44.155   NA   1948   De economische ontwikkeling der Boven- en Benedenwindse Eilanden
                       [The economic development of the Windward and Leeward Islands].

MEYER, H. A., comp.

52.061   BC   1956   COMMERCIAL BROADCASTING IN THE BRITISH WEST INDIES. London,
                       Butterworths Scientific Publications, for Central Rediffusion
                       Services, 91p.

MISCALL, LEONARD

52.062   TR   1944   Jungle roadbuilding. *Can-W I Mag* 33-34(8), Aug.: 19-22.   [NYP]

MOERHEUVEL, L. H.

52.063   NC   1937   De PHOHI in de West [The PHOHI in the West]. *W I G* 19:80-84. [22]
                                                                                      [COL]

MOSS, GUIDO

52.064   TR   1961   BUS TRANSPORTATION IN TRINIDAD AND TOBAGO [BY THE] NATIONAL
                       CITY MANAGEMENT CO., CHICAGO, ILL. [GUIDO MOSS, ENGINEER]. Port
                       of Spain, Govt. Print. Off., 22p. [66]   [RIS]

NICHOLAS, RICHARD U.

52.065   BG   1939 The development of transportation routes under the projected colonization of refugees in British Guiana. *In* REPORT OF THE BRITISH GUIANA COMMISSION TO THE PRESIDENT'S ADVISORY COMMITTEE ON POLITICAL REFUGEES. Washington, D.C. [no. 7.] (20p.)   [66] [*AGS*]

NUNAN, JOSEPH J.

52.066   BG   1915 Railways, twelve years after. *Timehri* 3d ser., 3(20B), May: 211-214. [66]   [*AMN*]

OLCH, ISAIAH

52.067   ST   1933 St. Thomas. *U S Navl Inst Proc* 59(370), Dec.: 1734-1746. [*AGS*]

OUDSCHANS DENTZ, FRED

1.032   SR   1938 Surinaamsche journalistiek [Surinam journalism].

PANHUYS, L. C. van

52.068   SR   1920/ Luchtvaart in Guyana [Air transportation in Guiana]. *W I G* p.2:321-21 332.   [*COL*]

52.069   SR   1922/ Denkbeelden en plannen nopens een kustspoorweg in Suriname 23 [Plans and ideas about a coastal railroad in Surinam]. *W I G* 4:25-36. [66]   [*COL*]

PLUMMER, HARRY CHAPIN

52.070   CU   1913 Improving a harbor of Curacao: one effect of the Panama Canal's completion. *Scient Am* 108(21), May 24: 474-475. [66]   [*COL*]

PREIJ, L. C.

52.071   SR   1934/ De waarde van vliegtuigen voor Suriname [The value of airplanes 35 for Surinam] [by] L.C. Prey. *W I G* 16:106-114.   [66]   [*COL*]

52.072   SR   1938 Suriname en het luchtverkeer [Surinam and air traffic]. *W I G* 20: 137-174. [66]   [*COL*]

52.073   SR   1939 Het vliegveld Paramaribo [The Paramaribo airport]. *W I G* 21:382-388.   [*COL*]

PYTTERSEN, TJ.

52.074   SR   1920/ Nieuwe wegen [New roads]. *W I G* 2:129-150.   [*COL*] 21

52.075   BG/   1923/ Waarom landwegen in Demarary wél en in Suriname niet noodzake-
        SR   24 lijk waren [Why country roads were necessary in Demerara and unnecessary in Surinam]. *W I G* 5:277-280.   [*COL*]

RAHR, JOHN

52.076   BC   1955 Airways—a federal link. *New Commonw* 30(9), Oct. 31: xvii-xviii.   [*AGS*]

RICHARDSON, W. A.

52.077   BC   1961 The place of radio in the West Indies, by Willy Richardson. *Car Q* 7(3), Dec.: 158-162. [66]   [*RIS*]

SAMSON, PH. A.

52.078   SR   1950 De Surinaamse pers gedurende het Engelse tussenbestuur [The
                        Surinam press during the English interregnum]. *W I G* 31:80-93.
                        [5, 37]   [COL]
52.079   SR   1951 Persdelicten in Suriname [Legal actions against the press in
                        Surinam]. *W I G* 32:32-44. [37]   [COL]
52.080   SR   1952 Preventieve maatregelen tegen de pers in Suriname [Restrictive
                        measures against the press in Surinam]. *W I G* 33:222-228.   [COL]

SCHELTEMA de HEERE, G. A. N.

3.272   SR   1947 De reis Nederland-Paramaribo in 1861 en sedert 1884 [The Nether-
                        land-Paramaribo journey in 1861 and after 1884].

SCHUTZ, H.

52.081   SR   1935/ Paramaribo luchthaven [Paramaribo airports].*W I G* 17:129-134.[COL]
                  36

SHARP, G. F.

52.082   BB   1963 The Barbados Publicity Committee (1932): its origin and history.
                        J Barb Mus Hist Soc 31(2), May: 60-71. [55]
52.083   BB   1964 The first Barbados Post Office guide 1932. *J Barb Mus Hist Soc*
                        30(4), May: 185-189.   [AMN]

SHAW, EARL BENNETT

50.110   ST   1935 St. Thomas carries its coal.

SHENFIELD, A. A.·

52.084   BC   1952 Sea transport in the West Indies. *W I Comm Circ* 67(1259), Nov.:
                        251-252.   [NYP]

SHILSTONE, E. M.

52.085   BB   1958 Some notes on early printing presses and newspapers in Barbados.
                        J Barb Mus Hist Soc 26(1), Nov.: 19-33. [5]   [AMN]

SINGH, B. G.

49.065   JM   1961 Stabilising marl with Portland cement.

SMITH, J. H. NELSON

52.086   BH   1941 Use of British Honduras woods for railway sleepers or cross ties.
                        Car For 2(2), Jan.: 75-79. [64]   [AGS]

SPURIER, CHRISTOPHER

52.087   BC   1953 The story of an airline in the West Indies. *Can-W I Mag* 43(3), Mar.:
                        5-7, 9.   [NYP]

STANLEY, E. L.

52.088   BC   1939 Notes on advertising for West Indies markets. *Can-W I Mag* 28(8),
                        Sept.: 26-27. [51]   [NYP]

STARCK, AUBREY R.

55.036   BC   1952 BRITISH WEST INDIES: ECONOMIC AND COMMERCIAL CONDITIONS IN THE
                        EASTERN CARIBBEAN.

STARKEY, OTIS P.

43.139	MS	1960	COMMERCIAL GEOGRAPHY OF MONTSERRAT.
43.140	BB	1961	COMMERCIAL GEOGRAPHY OF BARBADOS.
43.141	SK/NV	1961	COMMERCIAL GEOGRAPHY OF ST. KITTS-NEVIS.
43.142	SL	1961	COMMERCIAL GEOGRAPHY OF ST. LUCIA.

STEVENS, G. R.

52.089   JM   1922 Advertising in Jamaica. *Can-W I Mag* 10(7), May: 180-181.   [51]
[*NYP*]

SWINTON, A. J.

52.090   BC   1917 Aviation in the West Indies: possibilities of the flying boat. *W I Comm Circ* 32(498), Nov. 1: 414-419.   [*NYP*]

VERVOORT, J.

52.091   GC   1948 De KLM in West-Indie [The Royal Dutch Airlines in the West Indies]. *W I G* 29:71-75.   [*COL*]

WAART, P. de

52.092   NC   1937 De West en de KRO [The West and the Catholic Broadcasting Corporation]. *W I G* 19:16-20.   [22]   [*COL*]

WILLIAMS, A. J. & DA SILVA, C. H.

52.093   BG   1951 The development of air transport services in British Guiana. *Timehri* 4th ser., 1(30), Nov.: 30-36.

WILLIAMS, F. H. P.

52.094   BC   1957 REPORT ON ROADS AND ROAD PROBLEMS IN SOUTH EAST ASIA AND THE CARIBBEAN. London, H.M.S.O., 88p. (Colonial Research Publications no. 18.)

YOUNG, J. G.

52.095   JM   1959 Old road laws of Jamaica. *Jam Hist Rev* 3(2), Mar.: 39-51.   [5, 37]
[*COL*]

ZEIDENFELT, ALEX

52.096   GC   1950 Transportation in the Caribbean during World War II. *Inter-Amer Econ Aff* 4(3): 75-96.   [37]

Chapter 53

CURRENCY, BANKING, CREDIT AND INSURANCE

ANDERSON, CECIL G.
53.001 BC 1956 Progress of the insurance industry. *Statist* Sept.: 61-62.

ANDERSON, ROBERT M.
53.002 SV 1914 Report on the agricultural credit societies of St. Vincent. *W I B* 14(1): 75-79. [46, 48] [*AMN*]

BEST, LLOYD & McINTYRE, ALISTER
53.003 JM 1961 A first appraisal of monetary management in Jamaica. *Social Econ Stud* 10(3), Sept.: 353-363. [*RIS*]

BLOOMFIELD, ARTHUR
53.004 BC [n.d.] CENTRAL BANKING ARRANGEMENTS FOR THE WEST INDIAN FEDERATION. Mona, Institute of Social and Economic Research, University College of the West Indies, 36p. (Studies in federal economics no. 2.) [38] [*RIS*]

CALLENDER, CHARLES VICTOR
53.005 JM 1965 The development of the capital market institutions of Jamaica. *Social Econ Stud* 14(3), suppl. (174p.) [8] [*RIS*]

CLARKE, F. J.
53.006 BB 1908 Establishment and working of the Sugar Industry Agricultural Bank at Barbados. *W I B* 9(2): 133-137. [58] [*AMN*]

COLON-TORRES, RAMON
46.036 GC 1952 Agricultural credit in the Caribbean.

CROWLEY, DANIEL JOHN
53.007 JM/ 1953 American credit institutions of Yoruba type. *Man* 53(51), May: 80.
TR [10, 33] [*RIS*]

DAVSON, IVAN
53.008 BC 1920 West Indian currency reform. *W I Comm Circ* 35(575), Oct. 14:306; 35(576), Oct. 28: 324-325. [*NYP*]

DUNLOP, W. R.

53.009   BC   1914 The West Indies and co-operative credit. *W I B* 14(1): 35-74.   [46,
                  48]   [*AMN*]

EARLE, A. F.

53.010   JM   1954 Colonial monetary theory. *Social Econ Stud* 3(1), June: 97-108.
                                                                                             [*RIS*]

ETTINGER, J. van

53.011   CU   1926/De stichting van de Curacaosche Bank [The establishment of the
                  27 Bank of Curacao]. *W I G* 8:485-498.   [*COL*]

53.012   CU   1926/ Een vergeten hoofdstuk uit de geschiedenis van het Curacaosche
                  27 circulatie-bankwezen [A forgotten chapter from the history of cir-
                      culation banking on Curacao]. *W I G* 8:177-182. [5]   [*COL*]

53.013   SR   1927/ Pogingen tot oprichting van eene circulatie-bank in Suriname 1849-
                  28 1864 [Attempts to establish a circulation bank in Surinam]. *W I G*
                      9:309-322. [5]   [*COL*]

53.014   CU   1928/ Munt- en bankwezen in Curacao (1880-1905) [Money and banking in
                  29 Curacao (1880-1905)]. *W I G* 10:433-464. [5]   [*COL*]

53.015   CU   1930/ Bankwezen in Curacao 1906-1928 [Banking institutions in Curacao,
                  31 1906-1928]. *W I G* 12:453-470, 522-534. [5, 66]   [*COL*]

53.016   CU   1938 Wijziging van de regeling nopens het circulatiebankwezen van Cura-
                      cao [Modification of the rule about the circulation banking institu-
                      tions of Curacao]. *W I G* 20:175-177.   [66]   [*COL*]

FAWCETT, WILLIAM

53.017   JM   1905 Raiffeisen agricultural banks. *W I G* 6(2):129-138. [46]   [*AMN*]

FERRIER, ROBERT A.

53.018   SR   1957 Zoeklicht op de Surinaamse gulden [Searchlight on the Surinamese
                      gulden]. *Oost West* 50, Mar.: 17-19.

GAAY FORTMAN, B. de

53.019   CU   1925/ Munt- en geldmoeilijkheden op Curacao voor 1 honderd jaar [Coin
                  26 and money difficulties in Curacao 100 years ago]. *W I G* 7: 353-370.
                      [5]   [*COL*]

53.020   CU   1928/ Munt- en geldmoeilijkheden op Curacao vóór honderd jaar [Coin and
                  29 money difficulties in Curacao a hundred years ago].   *W I G* 10:
                      569-570.   [5]   [*COL*]

GRANT, LOUIS STRATHMORE & ANDERSON, S. E.

28.248 BC   1955 Medical care insurance.

GREAVES, IDA C.

53.021   BC   1951 Money and currency in the West Indies. *J Barb Mus Hist Soc* 18(3-4),
                      May-Aug.: 138-142.   [*AMN*]

53.022   BC   1952 Money and currency in Barbados. *J Barb Mus Hist Soc* 19(4), Aug.:
                      164-169; 20(1), Nov.: 3-19;
                  1953 20(2), Feb.: 53-66. [5]   [*AMN*]

HENGEL, J. W. A. van

53.023   CU   1938 De Curacaosche realen en stuivers van 1821 en 1822 [The Curacao
                      realen and *stivers* of 1821 and 1822]. *WIG* 20:228-233. [5]   [*COL*]

HOYER, W. M.
53.024   CU   1936/ De Curacaosche muntspeciën [The coins of Curacao]. *W I G* 18:
37 184-187. [5]   [*COL*]

JOLLY, A. L.
46.106   GC   1954 Small scale farming ... management and financing.

KESLER, C. K.
53.025   CU   1929/ De ontwikkeling van een modern bankbedrijf [The development of a
30 modern banking system]. *W I G* 11:461-472. [66]   [*COL*]

KLUVERS, B. J.
53.026   SR   1919/ De verzekeringskas van de firma C. Kersten en Companie te
20 Paramaribo [The insurance funds of the firm C. Kersten and Company in Paramaribo]. *W I G* 1(2): 157-162. [50]   [*COL*]

LAYNE, FREDERICK, et al.
33.020   BB   1964 A PLAN FOR THE IMPLEMENTATION AND ADMINISTRATION OF THE PRO-
POSED SOCIAL SECURITY SCHEME FOR BARBADOS.

LIGTHART, TH.
53.027   SR   1948 Suriname 1940/1946; enige opmerkingen naar aanleiding van de
jaarverslagen van de Surinaamse Bank N. V. over de jaren 1940/
1946 [Surinam 1940-1946: some remarks regarding the annual reports of the Surinam Bank in the years 1940-1946]. *Tijdschr Econ
Social Geogr* 39(4), Apr. 15: 462-465.   [*AGS*]

McMORRIS, C. S.
46.136   JM   1957 Small-farm financing in Jamaica.

MARSHALL, GLORIA ALBERTHA
53.028   BC   1959 BENEFIT SOCIETIES IN THE BRITISH WEST INDIES: THE FORMATIVE
YEARS. M.A. thesis, Columbia University, 61p. [5,8,11,33] [*COL*]

PANHUYS, L. C. van
53.029   SR   1905 Ways of paying in the New Netherlands, at Dutch Guiana, and in
the former Dutch colonies of British Guiana. *In* PROCEEDINGS OF
THE INTERNATIONAL CONGRESS OF AMERICANISTS, 13TH SESSION, New
York, Oct. 1902. Easton, Pa., Eschenbach Print. Co., p.273-275.
       [*AMN*]

PRIDMORE, F.
53.030   BB   1962 Notes on colonial coins: the Barbados issues of 1788 and 1792. Are
they coins or private tokens? *J Barb Mus Hist Soc* 30(1), Nov.:
14-19. [5]   [*AMN*]
53.031   BB   1964 Notes on colonial coins: cut money of Barbados. *J Barb Mus Hist
Soc* 30(4), May: 169-181. [5]   [*AMN*]

SCHOCH, C. F.
53.032   SR   1919 Cultuurcrediet van Suriname [Culture Credit of Surinam]. *W I G*
1(1): 24-48.   [*COL*]

SERTIMA, J. van
53.033   BG   1913 The British Guiana Bank. *Timehri* 3d ser., 3(20A), Sept.: 9-15.   [5]
                                                                                        [*AMN*]

SHEPHARD, C. Y.
53.034   JM   1955 Land titles. *Caribbean* 9(4), Sept.: 76-81, 88.   [46, 47]   [*COL*]

SWAIN, HAZEL C.
53.035   BQ   1935 Insurance in the West Indies. *Can-W I Mag* 24(12), Nov.: 19-21.
                                                                                        [*NYP*]

SWAIN, HAZEL C.
53.036   BQ   1940 Brotherly love in Bequia. *Can-W I Mag* 29(9), Sept.: 23-25.   [*NYP*]

TEWKSBURY, HOWARD H.
53.037   GC   1954 Financing and credit facilities in the Caribbean. *Car Commn Mon
              Inf B* 7(9), Apr.: 197-198, 205.   [*COL*]
53.038   GC   1954 Financing and credit facilities in the countries served by the Carib-
              bean Commission. *Car Econ Rev* 6, Dec.: 76-100.   [*RIS*]

TURNER, WM. T.
53.039   JM   1907 The Christiana People's Co-operative Bank Limited. *W I B* 8(3):
              250-253.   [48]   [*AMN*]

VILLARONGA, MARIANO
48.015   GC   1962 El cooperativismo en el Caribe [Cooperative ventures in the Carib-
              bean].

WATERMAN, JAMES A., et al.
28.565   TR   1963 Voluntary pre-payment health insurance scheme.

WATTS, Sir FRANCIS
47.032   GR/ 1914 Efforts in aid of peasant agriculture in the West Indies.
         CR/
         SV

WEIJTINGH, C. R.
53.040   CU   1939 Eenige aanvullingen op de Encyclopaedie van West-Indië: Het munt-
              wezen in Curacao [Some additions to the Encyclopedia of the West
              Indies: The money system in Curacao]. *W I G* 21:140-145.   [*COL*]
53.041   SR   1939 Eenige aanvullingen op de Encyclopaedie van West-Indië: Het munt-
              wezen in Suriname [Some additions to the Encyclopedia of the West
              Indies: The money system in Surinam]. *W I G* 21:72-77.   [*COL*]

WELLS, A.F. & D.
53.042   BC   1953 FRIENDLY SOCIETIES IN THE WEST INDIES. London, H.M.S.O., 131p.
              (Colonial research publication no. 15.)   [8,33,48,66]   [*RIS*]

ZAAL, G. PH.
53.043   SR   1938 Loterijen in Suriname [Lotteries in Surinam]. *W I G* 20:109-119. [37]
                                                                                        [*COL*]

Chapter 54

MINING AND ECONOMIC GEOLOGY

AIKEN, J. W. DONALDSON
54.001   SR   1912   The gold mining industry in Surinam. *Timehri* 3d ser., 2(19A), July: 83-85.   [*AMN*]

ANGEL, M.
54.002   FG   1956   Mining and minerals in French Guiana. *Caribbean* 10(2), Sept.: 35-37.   [*COL*]

ARMSTRONG, PERCY E.
54.003   BG   1936   There's gold in them thar hills! *Can-W l Mag* 25 (Jubilee issue), Dec.: 13-14, 19-21, 40-42.   [*NYP*]
54.004   BG   1958   Mackenzie—the town that bauxite built. *Can-W l Mag* 48(2), Feb.: 5-6.   [*NYP*]

BALOGH, THOMAS
54.005   JM   1957   A new deal in Jamaica. *Venture* 9(2), June: 5-6.   [*COL*]

BERGH, V. H. van den
54.006   CU   1935/ Petroleum, het levens-elixer voor Curacao [Petroleum, the elixer of 36   life for Curacao]. *W I G* 17:1-10.   [66]   [*COL*]

BIJLSMA, R.
54.007   SR   1919/ Het mijnwerk der Societeit van Suriname op den Van den Bempden-20   berg 1729-1743 [The mining operations of the Society of Surinam on the Van den Bempden Mountain 1729-1743]. *W I G* 1(2): 335-338.   [5]   [*COL*]

BISHOPP, D. W.
40.015   BG   1955   The bauxite resources of British Guiana and their development.

BLUME, HELMUT
54.008   JM   1962   Der Bauxitbergbau auf Jamaika [The bauxite mining in Jamaica]. *Geogr Rdsch* 14(6), June: 227-235.   [40]   [*RIS*]

BRACEWELL, SMITH
40.020   BG   1946   Mineral resources.
40.021   BG   1947   The geology and mineral resources of British Guiana.

54.009   BG   1950 The search for minerals in British Guiana. *Car Commn Mon Inf B*
                  4(4), Nov.: 568-570.   [66]   [*COL*]

BRYAN, VICTOR
54.010   TR   1935 Oilfields in a tropical garden. *Can-W I Mag* 24(9), Aug.: 7-9.   [*NYP*]
54.011   TR   1939 Trinidad's oil industry. *Can-W I Mag* 28(8), Sept.: 21-25.   [*NYP*]

CANNON, R. T.
54.012   BG   1958 THE GOLD DEPOSITS OF THE CUYUNI RIVER. Georgetown, Daily Chroni-
                  cle, 69p. (Geological Survey of British Guiana, Bulletin 27.)

CECIL, C. H.
54.013   TR   1945 Trinidad's "black gold". *Can-W I Mag* 35(5), June: 55-57.   [*NYP*]

CHOUBERT, BORIS
40.035 FG   1949 Géologie et pétrographie de la Guyane Francaise [Geology and petro-
                  graphy of French Guiana].
54.014   FG   [1952?] LA MINE D'OR SAINT-ELIE ET ADIEU-VAT EN GUYANE FRANCAISE [THE
                  GOLD MINE 'SAINT-ELIE ET ADIEU-VAT' IN FRENCH GUIANA]. Paris,
                  Publications minières et métallurgiques, 20p.
40.036 GG   1954 La carte géologique des trois Guyanes [Geological map of the three
                  Guianas].

COLLIER, H. C.
54.015   BG   1935 From Guiana bauxite to Canadian aluminum. *Can-W I Mag* 24(2),
                  Jan.: 39-40.   [51]   [*NYP*]

CONOLLY, H. J. C.
40.042 BG   1925 REPORT ... OF THE PRELIMINARY SURVEY OF THE MAZARUNI AND PURUNI
                  DIAMOND FIELDS, BRITISH GUIANA.

DANGOISE, ARTHUR & POTTEREAU, L.
2.053   FG   [n.d.] NOTES, ESSAIS ET ÉTUDES SUR LA GUYANE FRANCAISE ET LE DÉVELOP-
                  PEMENT DE SES RESSOURCES VARIÉES ET SPÉCIALEMENT DE SES RICH-
                  ESSES AURIFÈRES, FILONIÈNNES ET ALLUVIONNAIRES [NOTES, DISCUS-
                  SIONS, AND STUDIES ON FRENCH GUIANA AND THE DEVELOPMENT OF ITS
                  VARIED RESOURCES, PARTICULARLY ITS GOLD, LODE-METAL, AND ALLUVIAL
                  RESOURCES].

DUBOIS-CHABERT. A.
64.042 FG   1959 Research begins to bear fruit.

DUNBAR, ELIZABETH U.
2.069   CU   1934 What oil did to Curacao.

DUNN, W. A.
54.016   BG   1912 Gold mining industry of British Guiana. *Timehri* 3d ser., 2(19B),
                  Dec.: 243-246.   [*AMN*]

EARLE, KENNETH W.
40.053 KNA   1922 REPORTS ON THE GEOLOGY OF ST. KITTS-NEVIS, B. W. I., AND THE
                  GEOLOGY OF ANGUILLA, B. W. I.

EMORY, LLOYD T.

54.017   SR   1924 Prospecting for bauxite in Dutch Guiana. *Engng Min J* 118(2), July 12: 45-48.   [*COL*]

GARRATT, A. P.

54.018   BG   1951 Activities of the Demerara Bauxite Company, Limited. *Timehri* 4th ser., 1(30), Nov.: 11-20.

GILL, ROLAND

54.019   TR   1957 Trinidad's oil industry. *Caribbean* 11(1), Aug.: 2-6.   [*COL*]

GONGGRIJP, J. W.

54.020   SR   1948 Bijdrage tot de kennis van's lands domein in Suriname betreffende bauxiet en hout [Contribution to the knowledge of the value of Surinam's crownland in relationship to bauxite and lumber]. *W I G* 29:137-160.   [64]   [*COL*]

GRUTTERINK, J. A.

54.021   SR   1919 Bauxiet [Bauxite]. *W I G* 1(1):360-374.   [51]   [*COL*]

HALSE, G. W.

54.022   TR   1931 The Trinidad oil industry. *Can-W I Mag* 20(9), Aug.: 310-311. [*NYP*]

HEESTERMAN, J. E.

54.023   GC   1954 Bauxite. *Car Commn Mon Inf B* 7(12), July: 268-273, 280.   [*COL*]
49.039   TR   1957 Industrial use of natural gas.

HILL, VINCENT G.

54.024   JM   1961 Geochemical prospecting for nickel in the Blue Mountains. *Inf B Scient Res Coun* 1(4), Mar.: 10-11.   [*RIS*]

HOLMAN, BERNARD W.

54.025   SR   1924 The goldfields of Dutch Guiana. *Min Mag* 30(2), Feb.: 85-89. [*COL*]

HOSE, H. R.

40.086   JM   1950 The geology and mineral resources of Jamaica.

HOWARD, RICHARD A. & PROCTOR, GEORGE R.

41.141   JM   1957 Vegetation of bauxitic soils in Jamaica.

HUGGINS, H.D.

54.026   GC   1965 ALUMINIUM IN CHANGING COMMUNITIES. London, Andre Deutsch, in association with the Institute of Social and Economic Research, 309p.   [66]   [*RIS*]

JACQUET, J. M.

40.095   FG   1930 La Guyana Francaise, pays minier [French Guiana, ore-bearing land].

JAMES, PRESTON E.

54.027   TR   1925 The Pitch Lake, Trinidad. *J Geogr* 24(6), Sept.: 212-220.   [40]
                                                      [*AGS*]

JONES, D. A.
54.028   JM   1953 The truth about bauxite discovery and development in Jamaica.
              Can-W I Mag 43(3), Mar.: 25-26.   [*NYP*]

JUNKER, L.
54.029   SR   1940 Goudexploitatie in Suriname [Goldmining in Surinam] *W I G* 22:
              111-121.   [*COL*]

KILINSKI, E. A.
54.030   SR   1928 Notes on Dutch Guiana: a colony that has been of little importance
              from a mineral standpoint but promises to become an important pro-
              ducer of bauxite. *Min Metall* 9(254), Feb.: 59-61.   [*COL*]

KLERK, J. A. de
54.031   CU   1921/Het petroleumbedrijf op Curacao [The oil industry of Curacao]. *W I G*
              22 3:267-270.   [51]   [*COL*]

LACROIX, ALFRED
40.102 FG   1932 Guyane Francaise [French Guiana].

LAIRD, GEORGE A.
54.032   FG/ 1922 Gold in Dutch and French Guiana. *Min Metall* 3(190), Oct.: 11-13.
         SR   [*COL*]

LAURENT, L.
54.033   FG   1902 Guyane. *In his* L'OR DANS LES COLONIES FRANCAISES. Paris, A.
              Challamel, p.91-109.   [*SCH*]

LEBEDEFF, V.
40.106 FG   1935 Résumé des résultats d'une mission de recherches géologiques et
              minières en Guyane Francaise [Summary of the results of a geo-
              logical research and prospecting expedition in French Guiana].
40.107 FG   1936 Une mission d'études géologiques et minières en Guyane-Inini
              [A geological research and prospecting expedition in Guiana-Inini].

LeMAIRE, G. W.
54.034   AR   1936 Aruba, Netherlands West Indies—the history and industrial develop-
              ment.   *Mines Mag* 26(1), Jan.: 15-18, 39.   [5,49]   [*COL*]

LEPPER, G. W.
54.035   BB   1949 REPORT ON OIL DEVELOPMENT POLICY IN BARBADOS. [Bridgetown?]
              Barbados, Colonial Secretary's Office, 32p.   [46, 66]

LEVY, W. J. Inc.
54.036   TR   1958 THE TRINIDAD OIL ECONOMY. [Port of Spain?] Trinidad, Govt. Print.
              Off., 52p.   [*RIS*]

LEWES, M. D.
54.037   JM   1962 The mining of gypsum in Jamaica. *Inf B Scient Res Counc* 3(1),
              June: 6-9.   [*RIS*]

LIMBURG STIRUM, O. E. G., Graaf van

54.038   SR   1923/ De Surinamsche mijnwetgeving [The mining laws of Surinam]. *W I G* 24   5:385-394.   [37]   [*COL*]

LITCHFIELD, LAWRENCE, Jr.

54.039   BG/   1929   The bauxite industry of northern South America. *Engng Min J*
         SR   128(7), Aug. 17: 242-248.   [*AGS*]

54.040   BG   1929   Bauxite mining in British Guiana. *Engng Min J* 128(9), Aug. 31: 346-349.   [*AGS*]

54.041   SR   1929   Bauxite mining in Dutch Guiana. *Engng Min J* 128(12), Sept. 21: 460-464.   [*AGS*]

McCONNELL, R.B.

40.110   BG   1959   Fossils in the North Savannas and their significance in the search for oil in British Guiana; a short account of the non-metamorphic sedimentary formations in British Guiana.

McNAMARA, ROSALIND

54.042   BG   1959   British Guiana's Mackenzie story. *Caribbean* 13(3), Mar.: 46-49. [66]   [*COL*]

MARTIN-KAYE, P. H. A.

54.043   LW   1958   Mineral prospects in the Leeward Islands. *In* REPORT OF THE FIRST MEETING OF THE CARIBBEAN GEOLOGICAL CONFERENCE held at Antigua, B.W.I., Dec. 1955. Demerara [B. G.] Argosy and Co., p.43-48. [*RIS*]

MEYERHOFF, HOWARD A.

54.044   JM   1941   Mineral resources of the Greater Antilles. *Min Metall* May: 1-4. [40]   [*AGS*]

MOORHEAD, G. A.

54.045   JM   1961   Bauxite mining in Jamaica, by G. A. Moorehead. *Min Qua Engng* June.

54.046   JM   1961   Mining in Jamaica: the development of copper. *Inf B Scient Res Counc* 2(1), June: 8-10.   [*AMN*]

54.047   JM   1962   Rock ripping at Long Mountain, Jamaica, by G. A. Moorehead. *Min Qua Engng* 28(4), Apr.: 146-151.   [*NYP*]

MULDER, J. SIBINGA

54.048   TR   1937   Trinidad en zijn aardpekmeer [Trinidad and its pitch lake]. *Tijdschr Ned Aar Genoot* 2d ser., 54(1), Jan.: 88-92.   [*AGS*]

MULLINGS, LLEWELLYN MAXIMILLIAN

54.049   JM   1961   DEVELOPMENT OF JAMAICAN BAUXITE RESOURCES. M. A. thesis, Clark University, 106p.   [66]

MUNNICK, OWEN M. de

54.050   SR   1946   HET RIJKE ERTSLAND SURINAME EN ZIJN PROBLEMEN [THE RICH ORE LAND SURINAM AND ITS PROBLEMS]. Hengelo, H. L. Smit, 157p.

OUDSCHANS DENTZ, FRED

54.051   SR   1920/ De bauxietnijverheid en de stichting van een nieuwe stad in 21   Suriname [The bauxite industry and the founding of a new city in Surinam]. *W I G* 2:481-508.   [3, 35, 36, 66]   [*COL*]

PEARSON, ROSS

54.052   JM   1957   The Jamaica bauxite industry. *J Geogr* 56(8), Nov.: 377-385.   [*AGS*]

PELATAN, L.

54.053   FG   1900 Les richesses minérales des colonies francaises: Guyane Francaise [The mineral resources of the French colonies: French Guiana]. *Rev Univers Min Metall Trav Publ Sci Arts Appl Indus* 3d ser., 51, 3d trimester: 1-36. [40]

PERCIVAL, J. B.

54.054   SR   1915 Gold-bearing quartz veins in Dutch Guiana. *Engng Min J* 100(13), Sept. 25: 511-512.   [COL]

POLLARD, E. R.

54.055   BG   1953 Reports of the occurrence of iron in British Guiana. *Timehri* 4th ser., 1(32), Nov.: 32-34.

54.056   BG   1958 The bauxite resources of British Guiana [Abstract]. *In* REPORT OF THE FIRST MEETING OF THE CARIBBEAN GEOLOGICAL CONFERENCE held at Antigua, B.W.I., Dec. 1955.   Demerara, [B. G.] Argosy and Co., p.55-56.   [RIS]

54.057   BG   1958 Diamond resources and their development in British Guiana. [Abstract] *In* REPORT OF THE FIRST MEETING OF THE CARIBBEAN GEOLOGICAL CONFERENCE held at Antigua, B.W.I., Dec. 1955. Demerara, [B.G.] Argosy and Co., p.53-54.   [RIS]

POLLARD, E. R.; DIXON, C. G. & DUJARDIN, R. A.

54.058   BG   1957 DIAMOND RESOURCES OF BRITISH GUIANA. Georgetown, British Guiana Geological Survey, 45p. (Bulletin no. 28.) [40]   [AGS]

PROBERT, ALAN

54.059   GC   1954 The role of mineral resources in the economy of the Caribbean. *In* WILGUS, A. CURTIS, ed. THE CARIBBEAN: ITS ECONOMY [papers delivered at the Fourth Annual Conference on the Caribbean held at the University of Florida, Dec. 3-5, 1953]. Gainesville, University of Florida Press, p.35-59. (Publications of the School of Inter-American Studies, ser. 1, v. 4.)   [RIS]

PROCTOR, GEORGE R.

57.054   JM   1960 Studies of bauxite vegetation in Jamaica.

QUAST, J. F.

54.060   AR   1925/ Lago Oil and Transport Company Ltd. op Aruba [Lago Oil and Trans-
          26   port Company Ltd. on Aruba]. *W I G* 7:265-270.   [COL]

REDFIELD, ARTHUR H.

54.061   GC   1923 Petroleum reserves of the West Indies. *Trans Am Inst Min Metall Engn* 68:1082-1090. [46]   [AGS]

REGINALDUS DELLAERT, P.

54.062   AR   1926/ Aruba's verlaten goudvelden [Aruba's deserted goldfields]. *W I G* 27 8:539-546.   [COL]

RENO, PHILIP

54.063   JM/   1963 Aluminum profits and Caribbean people. *Mon Rev* 15(6), Oct.: 305-
          BG   315.

RIVET, P.

54.064   GC   1923   L'orfèvrerie précolombienne des Antilles, des Guyanes et du Vénézuela, dans ses rapports avec l'orfèvrerie et la métallurgie des autres régions américaines [Precolombian metal-working in the Antilles, Guianas, and Venezuela, in relation to metal-working and metallurgy in other parts of the Americas]. *J Soc Am Paris* 15: 183-213. [4]   [*AGS*]

54.065   GG   1924/   L'origine de l'industrie de l'or en Amérique [The origins of the gold
                   25   industry in America]. *W I G* 6:366-370.   [*COL*]

ROACH, E. H.

54.066   BG   1957   Bauxite, Demba, alumina and British Guiana. *Timehri* 4th ser., 1(36), Oct.: 7-22.

RUDD, R. T.

54.067   BG   1951   Bauxite, basic ore of aluminum, comes from far off British Guiana. *Can-W I Mag* 41(4), Apr.: 5-7, 9, 11.   [*NYP*]

SCOTT-HILLIARD, HUGH

54.068   TR   1937   Eighth wonder. *Can-W I Mag* 26(9), Sept.: 25-27.   [*NYP*]

SENN, ALFRED

40.161   BB   1944   INVENTORY OF THE BARBADOS ROCKS AND THEIR POSSIBLE UTILIZATION.

SHERMAN, GERTRUDE

54.069   BG/   1958   It takes teamwork to produce aluminum. *Can-W I Mag* 48(12), Dec.:
            JM/   14-15.   [*NYP*]
            TR

SNELLEN, E.

54.070   SR   1935   De goudwinning in Suriname [Gold mining in Surinam]. *Tijdschr Econ Social Geogr* 26(7), July 15: 145-156. [40]   [*AGS*]

STOCKLEY, G. M.

54.071   BG   1955   Exploration for natural oil in British Guiana. *Timehri* 4th ser., 1(34), Sept.: 31-34.

40.176   BG   1955   The geology of British Guiana and the development of its mineral resources.

54.072   BG   1958   Exploration for mineral oil in British Guiana. *In* REPORT OF THE FIRST MEETING OF THE CARIBBEAN GEOLOGICAL CONFERENCE held at Antigua, B.W.I., Dec. 1955. Demerara [B.G.] Argosy and Co., p.27-29.   [*RIS*]

54.073   BG   1958   Mineral development in the economy of British Guiana. *In* REPORT OF THE FIRST MEETING OF THE CARIBBEAN GEOLOGICAL CONFERENCE held at Antigua, B. W. I., Dec. 1955. Demerara [B. G.] Argosy and Co., p.49-52.   [*RIS*]

SUTER, H. H.

40.179   TR   1951/   The general and economic geology of Trinidad, B. W. I.
                       52

40.180   TR   1960   THE GENERAL AND ECONOMIC GEOLOGY OF TRINIDAD, B.W.I.

TEATS, E. H.

54.074   SR   1906   Notes on Dutch Guiana. *Engng Min J* 81(12), Mar. 24: 559-562.[*COL*]

TEMPANY, Sir HAROLD A.
54.075   AT   1915 Report on the island of Redonda. *W I B* 15(1): 22-25.   [*AMN*]

TEUNISSEN, H.
49.070   SR   1957 The Brokopondo Plan.

THOMPSON, A. BEEBY
54.076   TR   1917 Trinidad oilfields. *W I Comm Circ* 32(478), Jan. 25: 26-27.   [*NYP*]
54.077   BB/   1921 West Indian oil prospects. *W I Comm Circ* 36(588), Apr. 14: 143-144.
           BG/   [*NYP*]
           TR

VERLOOP, J. H.
54.078   SR   1911 A BRIEF OUTLINE OF THE SURINAM GOLD INDUSTRY: GEOLOGY, TECHNIQUE,
                        HYGIENE; DESCRIPTION OF THE GOLD PLACER AND THE PROSPECTS AT THE
                        GUIANA GOLD PLACER. Amsterdam, J. H. de Bussy, 106p. [40] [*NYP*]

WARING, GERALD A. & CARLSON, C. G.
40.208   TR   1925 Geology and oil resources of Trinidad, British West Indies.

WEBBER, BENJ. N.
40.210   BG   1952 Manganese deposits in the North West District, British Guiana.
54.079   BG   1952 Progress report on Kurupung Placers Company, Ltd., Kurupung
                        River, Mazaruni River District, British Guiana. *In* GEOLOGICAL
                        SURVEY OF BRITISH GUIANA, BULLETIN NO. 23. Georgetown, Daily
                        Chronicle, p.71-75. [40]   [*AGS*]
54.080   BG   1952 Reconnaissance of the Alex Hill and Mad Kiss mines, Cuyuni
                        goldfields, Aurora District, Cuyuni River, British Guiana. *In* GEO-
                        LOGICAL SURVEY OF BRITISH GUIANA, BULLETIN NO. 23. Georgetown,
                        Daily Chronicle, p.79-86.   [*AGS*]
54.081   BG   1952 Reconnaissance report on Kurupung diamond field, Mazaruni District,
                        British Guiana. *In* GEOLOGICAL SURVEY OF BRITISH GUIANA, BULLETIN
                        NO. 23. Georgetown, Daily Chronicle, p.49-68.   [*AGS*]

WEISZ, T.T.
57.072   JM   1962 Rehabilitation of bauxite lands.

WESTCOTT, JAMES H.
54.082   AR/   1929 What conservation means to Venezuela and the Dutch West Indies.
           CU   *Natn Petrol News* 21(35), Aug. 28: 62-63, 65-67.   [*COL*]

WESTERMANN, J. H.
40.213   NA   1949 Overzicht van de geologische en mijnbouwkundige kennis der
                        Nederlandse Antillen, benevens voorstellen voor verdere exploratie
                        [Survey of the geologic and mining of the Netherlands Antilles,
                        and proposals for further exploration].

WILHELMY, HERBERT
54.083   CU/   1954 Curacao, Aruba, Maracaibo—eine ölwirtschaftliche Symbiose [Curacao,
           AR   Aruba, Maracaibo—a symbiotic oil economy]. *In* ERGEBNISSE UND
                        PROBLEME MODERNER GEOGRAPHISCHER FORSCHUNG: HANS MORTENSEN
                        ZU SEINEM 60. GEBURTSTAG. Bremen, Walter Dorn, p.275-302. [*AGS*]

WILLIAMS, G. J.

54.084   BG   1937   Alluvial gold and diamonds in British Guiana. *Min Mag* 56(3), Mar.: 153-158.

YOUNG, ARTHUR A.

54.085   TR   1928   A Chinese pioneer of Trinidad's oil wells. *China Wkly Rev* 46(10), Nov. 3: 317.   [15]   [NYP]

YOUNGMAN, E. P.

54.086   SR   1933   MINING LAWS OF SURINAM (DUTCH GUIANA). [Washington, U.S. Govt. Print. Off.,] 14p. (U.S. Dept. of Commerce, Bureau of Mines, Information circular no. 6717.)   [NYP]

ZANS, V. A.

54.087   JM   1951   ECONOMIC GEOLOGY AND MINERAL RESOURCES OF JAMAICA. Kingston, Geological Survey Department, 61p. (Bulletin no. 1.)   [40]   [COL]

54.088   JM   1952   Bauxite resources of Jamaica and their development. *Colon Geol Miner Rsrc* 3(4): 307-33.   [40]   [AGS]

40.227   JM   1958   Geology and mining in Jamaica: a brief historical review.

54.089   JM   1960   Recent geological work and mining developments in Jamaica: a brief review of the activities during the last decade. *In* TRANSACTIONS OF THE SECOND CARIBBEAN GEOLOGICAL CONFERENCE, Mayagüez, P.R., Jan. 1959. Mayagüez, P.R., University of Puerto Rico, p.69-80. [40]   [AMN]

40.232   JM   1961   GEOLOGY AND MINERAL DEPOSITS OF JAMAICA.

Chapter 55

TOURISM

BARTELS, E.

55.001 AR 1956 Aruba moves ahead. *Caribbean* 9(9), Apr.: 192, 216. [66] *[COL]*
55.002 GC 1956 Government can help. *Caribbean* 9(9), Apr.: 190-191. [37, 66] *[COL]*

BLUME, HELMUT

55.003 GC 1963 Westindien als Fremdenverkehrsgebiet [The West Indies as a tourist area]. *Erde* 94(1): 47-72. *[RIS]*

BOUMAN, L. F.

55.004 NA 1949 Tourism in the Netherlands West Indies. *Car Commn Mon Inf B* 3(3), Oct.: 100-102. [66] *[COL]*
55.005 NW 1959 Islands to windward. *Caribbean* 13(5), May: 90-92, 89. [66] *[COL]*

BRERETON, B. O.

55.006 AT 1960 Antiguans and their visitors. *Caribbean* 14(1), Jan.: 11-12. *[COL]*

BUCKMASTER, MICHAEL H.

47.009 LW/ 1965 Some aspects of land purchase and development in the Leewards
        WW   and Windwards.

CARLE, R. BENITEZ

55.007 GC 1959 The tourist potential of the Caribbean. *Caribbean* 13(3), Mar.: 50-55. [66] *[COL]*

CARTO, W. L.

55.008 BG 1960 British Guiana moves to capture share of tourist trade. *Caribbean* 14(1), Jan.: 5-7. *[COL]*

CHARTOL, ED.

55.009 GD 1960 Vérités premières en tourisme [The basic facts of tourism]. *Rev Guad* 39, Jan.-Feb.: 22-23. *[RIS]*

COLLIER, H. C.

55.010 JM 1937 Let's go to Jamaica. *Can-W I Mag* 26(1), Jan.: 20-22, 26. *[NYP]*
55.011 BC 1938 Where the dollar goes further. *Can-W I Mag* 27(1), Jan.: 27-30; 27(2), Feb.: 23-25; 27(3), Mar.: 9-11, 36; 27(4), Apr.: 26-29. *[NYP]*

55.012   JM/   1940 Designs for living. *Can-W I Mag* 29(8), Aug.: 21-24.   [*NYP*]
          BB

CUMPER, GEORGE E.
55.013   JM   1959 Tourist expenditure in Jamaica, 1958. *Social Econ Stud* 8(3), Sept.:
                       287-310.   [*RIS*]

DESBONS, GEORGES
55.014   FA   1956 Le tourisme à la Guadeloupe et à la Martinique [Tourism in Guade-
                       loupe and Martinique]. *Rev Econ Fr* 69(4), Nov.: 7-18.   [*AGS*]

HEESTERMAN, J. E.
55.015   BN   1957 A development plan for Bonaire. *Caribbean* 10(6-7), Jan.-Feb.:
                       171-173, 178. [66]   [*COL*]

HUNTE, GEORGE HUTCHINSON
58.059 BB   1955 Barbados ... sugar and tourism.
55.016   BC   1957 Tourism: a federal approach. *Caribbean* 11(5), Dec.: 104-107. [38,
                       66]   [*COL*]
55.017   BB   1959 Barbados in the federal tourist picture. *Caribbean* 13(12), Dec.: 231-
                       233, 243. [66]   [*COL*]

ISSA, ABE
55.018   BC   [1959?] A SURVEY OF THE TOURIST POTENTIAL OF THE EASTERN CARIBBEAN:
                       WITH PARTICULAR REFERENCE TO THE DEVELOPMENT OF BEACHES, THE
                       BUILDING OF HOTELS, AND THE PROVISION OF ANCILLARY FACILITIES
                       AND AMENITIES FOR THE TOURIST INDUSTRY. Port of Spain, Released
                       by the Ministry of Trade & Industry, 40p. [66]   [*UNL*]
55.019   BC   1959 Tourism will be the biggest industry within ten years. *Caribbean*
                       13(10), Oct.: 186-189. [66]   [*COL*]

KARWICK, LEE
55.020   GC   1956 A growing industry. *Caribbean* 9(9), Apr.: 189, 191, 207. [66] [*COL*]
55.021   GC   1959 Boosting Caribbean tourism. *Caribbean* 13(7), July: 126-128. [66]
                                                                                      [*COL*]

KIES, H. E.
55.022   GC   1946 The why and the wherefore of Caribbean tourist development. *Can-
                       W I Mag* 36(8), Oct.: 11-14.   [*NYP*]
55.023   CU   1948 Toeristenindustrie [Tourist industry]. *W I G* 29:296-306.   [*COL*]

LAW, LOUIS S.
55.024   GC   1950 Survey of tourism in the Caribbean. *Car Commn Mon Inf B* 4(2),
                       Sept.: 497-499. [66]   [*COL*]
55.025   GC   1953 Promoting the Caribbean as a summer tourist resort. *Car Commn
                       Mon Inf B* 6(6), Jan.: 135-136. [66]   [*AGS*]
55.026   BC   1956 Tourism. *Statist* Sept.: 71-73.
55.027   GR   1956 Tourism matters to you. *Caribbean* 9(9), Apr.: 187-188, 203, 207.
                                                                                      [*COL*]

LOWENTHAL, DAVID
55.028   AT   1955 Economic tribulations in the Caribbean: a case study in the British
                       West Indies. *Inter-Amer Econ Aff* 9(3), Winter: 67-81. [46] [*RIS*]

McREYNOLDS, FRANCES R. P.

55.029 GC 1946 The Caribbean plans for tourists. *Dep St B* 15(382), Oct. 27: 735-738. [66] [*AGS*]

NICOLAS, MAURICE

55.030 MT 1956 Martinique: sidelights on tourism. *Caribbean* 9(12), July: 267-268, 275. [*COL*]

PEARSON, ROSS

55.031 JM 1957 The geography of recreation on a tropical island: Jamaica. *J Geogr* 56(5), Jan.: 12-22. [*AGS*]

ROBERTSON, WINDOM J.

55.032 GR 1959 A tourist "fairyland." *Can-W I Mag* 49(7), July: 7-8. [*NYP*]

RORTY, JAMES

37.349 NV 1961 Independence, like it or not.

ROTH, VINCENT

55.033 BG 1944 Development of a tourist industry in the interior. *Timehri* 4th ser., 1(26), Nov.: 146-148. [66] [*AMN*]

SEARL, D. M.

55.034 TR 1956 Tourism in Trinidad. *Caribbean* 9(9), Apr.: 214-216. [66] [*COL*]

SHARP, G. F.

52.082 BB 1963 The Barbados Publicity Committee (1932); its orgin and history.

SHELTON, H. S.

55.035 JM 1937 Jamaica and the tourist. *Contemp Rev* 864, Dec.: 729-735. [*AGS*]

STARCK, AUBREY R.

55.036 BC 1952 British West Indies: economic and commercial conditions in the eastern Caribbean. London, Published for the Board of Trade, Commercial Relations and Exports Dept., by H.M.S.O., 74p. (Overseas economic surveys.) [46, 52] [*RIS*]

STEDMAN, LOUISE

55.037 JM 1935 Holidaying in Jamaica on less. *Can-W I Mag* 24(7), June: 22-23. [*NYP*]

TIROLIEN, CAMILLE

55.038 GD 1961 Thermalisme [Mineral springs]. *Rev Guad* new ser., 45, 3d-4th trimesters: 11-13. [28, 40] [*RIS*]

VOYLES, ROBERT J.

55.039 GC 1956 The tourist industry of the Caribbean islands. Coral Gables, Fla., University of Miami, 80p. (Bureau of Business and Economic Research, University of Miami, Area development series, no. 6.) [*NYP*]

WOLFF, REINHOLD P. & MARCENARO, OSCAR

55.040 GC 1955 Caribbean tourist trade index: a comprehensive study of tourist trends in the Caribbean for the past six years. Coral Gables, Fla.,Bureau of Business and Economic Research, University of Miami, 11p. [*NYP*]

Chapter 56

FISHING

ALLSOPP, W. H. L.

56.001   BG   1952 The work of British Guiana's Fisheries Department. *Car Commn Mon Inf B* 5(10), May: 277-280.   [*AGS*]

41.014   BG   1958 Arapaima—its manners, morals and measurements—"the giant fish of South America."

56.002   BG   1958 REVIEW OF THE FISHERIES OF BRITISH GUIANA IN 1958. [Georgetown?] British Guiana, B. G. Lithographic Co., 52p. (Fisheries Division of the Agriculture Department, Bulletin 1.)

ARONOFF, JOEL

31.004   SK   1965 THE INTER-RELATIONSHIP OF PSYCHOLOGICAL AND CULTURAL SYSTEMS: A CASE STUDY OF A RURAL WEST INDIAN VILLAGE.

ASPINALL, Sir ALGERNON E.

56.003   BB   1935 The flying-fish industry. *W I Comm Circ* 50(959), July 4: 269-270.   [*NYP*]

BAIR, ROSLYN ANNETTE

56.004   BB   1962 THE DEVELOPMENT AND ECONOMIC IMPORTANCE OF A FISHING INDUSTRY IN THE TROPICS. M. A. thesis, McGill University, 86p.

BENOIST, JEAN

56.005   MT   1959 Individualisme et traditions techniques chez les pêcheurs martiniquais [Individualism and technical tradition among Martinique fishermen]. *Cah O-M* 12(47), July-Sept.: 265-285. [8, 19]   [*RIS*]

BERNARD, HECTOR

56.006   FC   1949 Jamaica peasant farmers set example in cooperation. *Car Commn Mon Inf B* 2(9), Apr.: 249-250, 252. [48, 50]   [*COL*]

BLOOD, Sir HILARY

56.007   BB   1956 The flying-fish industry in Barbados. *Times Br Colon Rev* 3d quarter: 9.

BODKIN, G. E.

3.027   BG   1918 A fishing trip on the upper waters of the Mazaruni River.

703

BOEKE, J.

56.008   CU   1907/ Rapport betreffende een voorlopig onderzoek naar den toestand
                    19   van de visscherij en de industrie van zeeproducten in de kolonie
                          Curacao [Report of a preliminary investigation of the state of
                          fisheries and the industry of sea products in the colony of
                          Curacao]. The Hague, Belinfante, 2v.   [*AGS*]
56.009   NA   1948 Eenige opmerkingen over de visscherij naar aanleiding van het
                          Rapport Welvaartsplan Nederlandsche Antillen 1946 [Some remarks
                          about fishing, inspired by the Welfare Plan Report of the Dutch
                          Antilles 1946]. *W I G* 29: 65-70.   [66]   [*COL*]

BROWN, HERBERT H.

56.010   BG   1942 The fisheries of British Guiana. [Bridgetown] Barbados, Advocate
                          Co., 69p. (Development and welfare in the West Indies, bulletin no.3.)
41.052   GC   1943 Productivity of the seas: some fundmental considerations and their
                          possible application in the Caribbean area.
56.011   LW/   1945 The fisheries of the Windward and Leeward Islands. Bridgetown,
           WW   Advocate Co., 97p. (Development and welfare in the West Indies,
                          bulletin no. 20.)   [66]   [*AGS*]

BUTSCH, ROBERT S.

41.054   BB   1939 A list of Barbadian fishes.
41.056   BB   1939 Some observations on the snappers of Barbados.

CARNEGIE, A. L.

28.084   JM   1963 Poisoning by barracuda fish.

CHASE, PHILIP P.

56.012   SL   1942 St. Lucia dug-outs. *Am Neptune* 2(1), Jan.: 71-73.   [*AGS*]

CHUCK, L. M.

56.013   JM   1963 1962 sample survey of the fishing industry in Jamaica. [Kingston?]
                          Jamaica, Division of Economics and Statistics, Ministry of Agri-
                          culture and Lands, 169p.

CLARKE, T. L. E.

28.096   BV   1918 Some observations on fish poisoning in the British Virgin Islands.

COLLIER, H. C.

56.014   BC   1938 Fish and seaman's chips. *Can-W I Mag* 27(8), Aug.: 23-26.   [*NYP*]
56.015   BC   1938 Fishing with poison. *Can-W I Mag* 27(9), Sept.: 9-11.   [*NYP*]
56.016   BG   1941 Fishing without fiction. *Can-W I Mag* 30(11), Nov.: 21-23.[13][*NYP*]

COLLINS, H. H. Jr.; VOOUS, K. H. & ZANEVELD, J. S.

41.064   NA   1956 Birds and fish of the Netherlands Antilles.

COMITAS, LAMBROS

56.017   JM   1962 Fishermen and cooperation in rural Jamaica. Ph.D. dissertation,
                          Columbia University, 364p.   [8, 19, 46, 48, 66]   [*RIS*]
50.020   JM   1964 Occupational multiplicity in rural Jamaica.

DAVENPORT, WILLIAM HUNT

67.002   JM   1960 Jamaican fishing: a game theory analysis.

CONSEIL, L. B.

56.018   MT   1926 La question de la pêche industrielle à la Martinique [The question of industrial fishing in Martinique]. Fort-de-France, Impr.
du Gouvernment, 42p. [66]   [*AMN*]

DESSOMES, P.

56.019   GD   1959 La pêche en Guadeloupe [Fishing in Guadeloupe]. *Pêche Marit*
38(978), Sept.: 549-553.   [*NYP*]

DORAN, EDWIN BEAL Jr.

51.048   CC   1958 The Caicos conch trade.

DUERDEN, J. E.

56.020   BC   1901 The marine resources of the British West Indies. *W I B* 2(2): 121-163.
[41]   [*AMN*]

DUNLOP, W. R.

56.021   BC   1915 A method of sponge cultivation and its prospects in the Lesser
Antilles: with notes on other possible shallow water fisheries.
W I B 15(2): 103-119. [66]   [*AMN*]

ENGLEDOW, Sir FRANK L.

46.064   GC   1945 Report on agriculture, fisheries, forestry and veterinary
matters [of the] West India Royal Commission.

FIEDLER, R. H. & JARVIS, N. D.

56.022   UV   1932 Fisheries of the Virgin Islands of the United States. Washington,
U. S. Govt. Print. Off., 32p. (U. S. Dept. of Commerce. Bureau of
Fisheries. Investigational report no. 14.)   [*COL*]

FOWLER, HENRY W.

41.098   GR   1931 Fishes obtained by Mr. James Bond at Grenada, British West Indies,
in 1929.

FRANK, MURRAY

56.023   GC   1944 Fisheries of the colonial West Indies and Bermuda. *For Com Wkly*
17(12), Dec. 16: 10-12, 45-50.   [*AGS*]
56.024   BG   1944 Opportunity for fisheries in British Guiana. *Can-W I Mag* 33-34(6),
June: 9-11.   [*NYP*]

GORDON, HOPETON

56.025   JM   1964 Commentary: a note on Jamaica's marine fisheries. *Car Q* 10(3),
Sept.: 41-49. [66]   [*RIS*]

GUPPY, P. LECHMERE

56.026   TB   1922 Fishing in Tobago. *Can-W I Mag* 10(10), Aug.: 271.   [*NYP*]
56.027   TR   1922 A naturalist in Trinidad and Tobago. *W I Comm Circ* 37(626), Sept.
28: 443-445; 37(627), Oct. 12: 467-468; 37(628), Oct. 26: 492-493.
[28, 41]   [*NYP*]

HALL, D. N. F.

56.028   BB   1956 Recent developments in the Barbados flying-fish fishery and
contributions to the biology of the flying-fish, *Hirundichthys*

affinis (GÜNTHER, 1866). London, H.M.S.O., 41p. (Colonial Office
fishery publications, no. 7.)

HESS, ERNEST

56.029   BB   1962 FISHERIES DEVELOPMENT PROGRAMME, 1961-1965. [Bridgetown]
Barbados, Barbados Govt. Print. Off., 41p. [66]

HICKLING, C. F.

56.030   BC   [1950?] THE FISHERIES OF THE BRITISH WEST INDIES: REPORT ON A VISIT IN
1949. Bridgetown, Cole's Printery, 41p. (Development and welfare
bulletin, no. 29.) [66]   [*COL*]

**IDYLL, CLARENCE P.; WHITELEATHER, R. T.; &
HOWARD, GERALD V.**

56.031   GC   1950 Potentialities of the Caribbean fisheries and recommendations for
their realization. *Car Commn Mon Inf B* 3(12), July: 427-428. [66]
[*COL*]

KING-WEBSTER, W. A.

56.032   TR   1956 An account of a small experimental fish weir. *J Agric Soc Trin Tob*
56(4), Dec., suppl.:637-646.   [*AMN*]
56.033   TR   1956 Carenage fishing centre—a "combined operation." *J Agric Soc
Trin Tob* 56(1), Mar.: 114-117. [66]   [*AMN*]

LEE, GUY

56.034   JM   1933 Big game fishing in Jamaica. *W I Comm Circ* 48(894), Jan. 5: 5-7.
[*NYP*]

LOBELL, MILTON J.

56.035   GC   1943 Yesterday, today, and tomorrow in the Caribbean fisheries. *B Pan
Am Un* 77(3), Mar.: 134-139.   [*NYP*]

McCONNELL, R. H.

41.165   BG   1958 Introduction to the fish fauna of British Guiana.

MANTEL, PIERRE

56.036   MT/   1936 La pêche de la langouste aux Antilles par les pêcheurs bretons
SM   [Lobster fishing in the Antilles by Breton fishermen]. *B Soc Oceanogr Fr* 16(87), Jan. 15: 1515-1520; 16(88), Mar. 15: 1528-1530;
16(89), May 15: 1547-1552.   [*AGS*]

MARSLAND, HERBERT

56.037   GR   1925 Whaling in the West Indies. *Can-W I Mag* 14(9), July: 241.   [*NYP*]

MASSON, R. K.

56.038   BH   1949 Fisheries and fishing methods of British Honduras. *Car Commn
Mon Inf B* 2(7), Feb.: 181-182.   [*COL*]

MENDES, ALEX L.

56.039   TR   1932 Around Trinidad with rod, line and harpoon. *Can-W I Mag* 22(1),
Dec.: 18-21.   [*NYP*]
56.040   TR   1937 Fisherman's paradise. *Can-W I Mag* 26(2), Feb.: 21-24.   [*NYP*]
56.041   TR   1944 Angler's paradise. *Can-W I Mag* 33-34(7), July: 21-24.   [*NYP*]

MYERS, GEORGE S.

41.172   GC   1938 Fresh-water fishes and West Indian zoogeography.

NUTTING, C. C.

41.174   BB   1935 Some notes on the fishes of Barbados.
41.176   BB   1937 Some notes on the Echinoderms (starfish, sea-eggs) of Barbados.

OBERG, KALERVO

56.042   SR   1961 Aspectos sociais da vida do pescador do Surinam [Social aspects of the life of a fisherman in Surinam]. *Sociologia* 23(3): 239-251.
[*COL*]

OBERG, KALERVO & DYK, FRANK van

56.043   SR   1960 THE FISHERMEN OF SURINAM. Paramaribo, Surinam-American Technical Cooperative Service, 58p.

PAUWELS, W. M. I. B.

56.044   SR   1903 Over de wijze van visschen met het Surinaamsche vischvergift koemaparie [On the manner of fishing with the Surinam fish-poison *Koemapari*]. *Int Archiv Ethnogr* 16:42-43.

PRICE, J. L.

41.188   TR   1955 A survey of the freshwater fishes of the island of Trinidad.

PRICE, RICHARD

56.045   MT   1964 Magie et pêche à la Martinique [Magic and fishing in Martinique]. *L'Homme* [4(2)], May-Aug.: 84-113. [23]   [*RIS*]

REGAN, C. TATE

41.192   GC   1916 Report on poisonous fishes of the West Indies.

REIJENGA, T. W.; VAS, I. E. & WIERSEMA, J. P.

28.433   SR   1962 On injuries caused by predatory salmon (*Serrasalmo rhombeus L.*) in the rivers of Surinam.

RICHARDS, A. R.

56.046   TR   1955 TRAWLFISHING IN THE SOUTH-EASTERN CARIBBEAN: A REPORT PREPARED FOR THE GOVERNMENT OF TRINIDAD AND TOBAGO AND THE CARIBBEAN COMMISSION. Port of Spain, Caribbean Commission Central Secretariat, 147p.

ROBINSON, J. H.

41.196   BB   1935 Some recent marine diatoms from the north-east coast of Barbados.

ROSE, W. V.

56.047   BB   1955 Memorandum on the Barbados fishing industry for consideration by the Marketing Committee. [Bridgetown? Govt. Printer?], 29p. [66]

ROTH, VINCENT

41.200   BG   1943 NOTES AND OBSERVATIONS ON FISH LIFE IN BRITISH GUIANA 1907-1943.

SANDS, W. N.

41.207   SV   1914 The "tri-tri" or West Indian whitebait in St. Vincent.

SCHMITT, WALDO L.

41.209   GC   1957 A narrative of the Smithsonian-Bredin Caribbean Expedition, 1956.

SHAW, EARL BENNETT

56.048   UV   1933 The fishing industry of the Virgin Islands of the United States.
                         B Geogr Soc Phila 31(2), Apr.: 61-72. [66]   [*AGS*]

TAYLOR, G. T.

56.049   SL   1960 Fisheries training school in St. Lucia. *Caribbean* 3, Mar.: 51-52.
                         [32, 66]   [*COL*]

THOMPSON, ERNEST F.

56.050   BH   [n.d.] THE FISHERIES OF BRITISH HONDURAS. [Bridgetown?] Barbados,
                         Advocate Co., 32p.   [*RIS*]
56.051   JM   1945 THE FISHERIES OF JAMAICA. Bridgetown, Advocate Co., 103p. [66]
                                                                                         [*AGS*]
56.052   CM   [1946?] THE FISHERIES OF CAYMAN ISLANDS. Bridgetown, Advocate Co.,
                         33p. (Development and welfare in the West Indies, bulletin no. 22.)
                         [66]   [*AGS*]

VERIN, PIERRE-MICHEL

43.147   SL   1963 LA POINTE CARAÏBE (SAINTE-LUCIE).

VINCENT, HARRY

56.053   TR   1910 THE SEA FISH OF TRINIDAD. New York, [Printed by] Press of J. J.
                         Little & Ives Co., 97p. [3,41]   [*NYP*]

WEMPE, A.

56.054   SR   1938 Visscherij aan de Coppenamepunt in het district Saramacca [Fishing
                         in the Coppename River in the Saramacca district]. *Tijdschr Econ
                         Social Geogr* 29(7-8), July 15—Aug. 15: 163-166.   [*AGS*]

WHITELEATHER, RICHARD T. & BROWN, HERBERT H.

56.055   TR/   1945 AN EXPERIMENTAL FISHERY SURVEY IN TRINIDAD, TOBAGO AND BRITISH
           BG   GUIANA. Washington, D. C., Anglo-American Caribbean Commission,
                         130p. [66]   [*RIS*]

WILES, DUDLEY W.

56.056   BB   1949 The fisheries of Barbados and some of their problems. *Car Commn
                         Mon Inf B* 2(6), Jan.: 145-147.   [*COL*]
56.057   BB   1952 Flying fish research in Barbados. *Car Commn Mon Inf B* 6(1), Aug.:
                         3-4.   [*AGS*]

ZANEVELD, JACQUES S.

41.269   NA   1956/Enige algemeen voorkomende zeevissen in de Nederlandse Antillen
                         57 [Some common sea fish in the Dutch Antilles].
41.270   CU   1960 Probing Caribbean waters.

SOILS, CROPS
AND
LIVESTOCK

Chapter 57

SOILS AND SOIL SURVEYS

AHMAD, N.

57.001   BG   1963 The potassium status of the inorganic coastal soils of British Guiana. *Trop Agric* 40(3), July: 197-203.   [*AGS*]

BADCOCK, W. J.

46.005   BB   1960 The problems relative to soil conservation in the Scotland District.

BAXTER, G. D.

57.002   BG   1959 Some problems of jute cultivation on the coastland soils of British Guiana. *Trop Sci* 1(2): 73-84.   [63]   [*AGS*]

BEARD, JOHN STEWART

57.003   TR   1941 Land-utilization survey of Trinidad. *Car For* 2(4), July: 182-187.
                                                                                [*AGS*]

BEEBE, WILLIAM

43.009   TR   1952 Introduction to the ecology of the Arima Valley, Trinidad, B.W.I.

BIJLSMA, R.

58.010   SR   1922/ Over bodemgesteldheid en suikerplantage-exploitatie in Suriname,
          23   1765 [On soil conditions and sugar-plantation exploitation in Surinam, 1765].

BIRD, MAURICE

58.011   BG   1922 Concerning yield deterioration in the older sugar countries.
57.004   BG   1924 Deep ploughing in relation to soil water in British Guiana. *J Bd Agric Br Gui* 17(3), July: 176-178.   [58]   [*AMN*]
57.005   BG   1929 Guiana's sugar soils. *W I Comm Circ* 44(799), May 16: 188-189.
                 [58]   [*NYP*]

BIRSE, E. L. & WATSON, J. P.

57.006   BG   1954 REPORT ON A RECONNAISSANCE SOIL SURVEY OF AN AREA OF THE NORTH WEST DISTRICT, BRITISH GUIANA. [Georgetown] "The Argosy" Co., 28p.

BLAUT, JAMES M.

43.018   GC   1959 The ecology of tropical farming systems.

BLAUT, JAMES M. & RUTH P.; HARMAN, NAN & MOERMAN, MICHAEL

43.019   JM   1959 A study of cultural determinants of soil erosion and conservation in the Blue Mountains of Jamaica.

BOYE, MARC

64.020   FG   1962 Les paletuviers du littoral de la Guyane Francaise: ressources et problemes d'exploitation [The mangroves of coastal French Guiana: potential and problems of exploitation].

BREEVELD, F.

44.023   SR   1958 Electriciteit in het oerwoud [Electricity in the primeval forest].

BUIE, T. S.

57.007   BB   1955 REPORT OF STUDY OF THE SCOTLAND DISTRICT, BARBADOS, B.W.I., WITH RECOMMENDATIONS FOR A SOIL CONSERVATION PROGRAM.   [Bridgetown?] Barbados, 11p. (Supplement to the Official Gazette, Jan. 31.) [66]

BURRA, J. A. N.

42.006   JM   1962 The forest and watershed control.

CATER, JOHN C.

46.033   TR   1939 Deforestation and soil erosion in Trinidad: deforestation and soil erosion in the foothills of the Northern Range caused by shifting cultivation.

CHENERY, E. M.

57.008   TR   1938 The soil-types of east Trinidad. *Proc Agric Soc Trin Tob* 38(5), May: 139-152.   [*AMN*]

CHENERY, E. M. & HARDY, F.

57.009   TR   1945 The moisture profile in some Trinidad forest and cacao soils. *Trop Agric* 22(6), June: 100-115.   [59]   [*AGS*]

CHOUBERT, BORIS

66.029   FG   1960 L'Institut francais d'Amerique tropicale (I.F.A.T.) (Pilot agency in French Guiana].

CROUCHER, H. H. & SWABEY, C.

46.041   JM   1938 SOIL EROSION AND CONSERVATION IN JAMAICA, 1937.

DUTHIE, D. W.

65.014   BG   1939 Mineral deficiency and cattle raising in British Guiana.

57.010   BG   1939 Report on the soils of British Guiana south of the 5th parallel, and of the North-West district. *In* REPORT OF THE BRITISH GUIANA COMMISSION TO THE PRESIDENT'S ADVISORY COMMITTEE ON POLITICAL REFUGEES. Washington, D.C. [no. 3] (19p.)   [*AGS*]

57.011   BG   1939 Soil notes complementary to Sir Geoffrey Evans' Report on the agricultural possibilities for the hinterland of British Guiana. *In* REPORT OF THE BRITISH GUIANA COMMISSION TO THE PRESIDENT'S ADVISORY COMMITTEE ON POLITICAL REFUGEES. Washington, D.C. [no. 4] (7 p.)   [*AGS*]

57.012   BG   1939 Soils of British Guiana south of the 5th parallel and of the North-
              West District. *Agric J Br Gui* 10(4): 173-193.   [*AGS*]

EDWARDS, DAVID T.
46.060   JM   1961 AN ECONOMIC STUDY OF SMALL FARMING IN JAMAICA.

EIJK, J. J. van der & HENDRIKS, J. A. H.
57.013   SR   1953 Bodem- en landclassificatie in de oude kustvlakte [Soil and land
              classification in the older coastal area]. *Sur Landb* 1(5), Sept.-Oct.:
              200-223.
57.014   SR   1953 Soil- and land classification in the old coastal plain of Surinam.
              Neth J Agric Sci 1(4), Nov.: 278-298.

FAHEY, HAROLD NEAL
57.015   TR   1943 Soil fertility often a minor factor. *Proc Agric Soc Trin Tob* 43(3),
              Sept.: 207-211.   [46]   [*AMN*]

FINCH, T. F.
57.016   JM   1954 Soil survey of the area administered by the Yallahs Valley Land
              Authority. *In* THE FARMER'S GUIDE, Appendix F. Glasgow, Univer-
              sity Press, p.778-803.   [*NYP*]
57.017   JM   1959 SOIL AND LAND-USE SURVEYS. NO. 7: JAMAICA—PARISH OF CLARENDON.
              [Port of Spain?] Trinidad, Regional Research Centre, Imperial Col-
              lege of Tropical Agriculture, 33p.   [46,66]   [*RIS*]
57.018   JM   1961 SOIL AND LAND-USE SURVEYS. NO. 11: JAMAICA—PARISH OF PORTLAND.
              [Port of Spain?] Trinidad, Regional Research Centre, Imperial Col-
              lege of Tropical Agriculture, 32p.   [46,66]   [*RIS*]

FREILICH, MORRIS
67.005   TR   1960 Cultural models and land holdings.

GRIFFIN, CORNELIUS J.
44.095   GC   1958 Energy in Caribbean progress.

GUYADEEN, K. D.
57.019   SV   1957 A note on soil conservation work in St. Vincent, B.W.I. *J Agric Soc
              Trin Tob* 57(1), Mar.: 98-107.   [66]   [*AMN*]

HARDY, F.
57.020   DM   1921 Studies in West Indian soils. (I)-The soils of Dominica, their gene-
              sis and fertility considered in relation to reaction. *W I B* 19(1),
              Sept. 30: 86-123.   [*RIS*]
57.021   MS   1922 Studies in West Indian soils. (II)-The soils of Montserrat, their na-
              tural history and chief physical properties, and the relationship of
              these to the problem of die-back of lime trees. *W I B* 19(2), Mar. 31:
              189-213.   [63]   [*RIS*]
58.052   TR   1933 Root distribution of sugar-cane in different soils in Trinidad: em-
              bodying some results obtained by a soil-core method.
57.022   TR   1934 The chief soil-types of Trinidad. *Proc Agric Soc Trin Tob* 34(11),
              Nov.: 443-458.   [*AMN*]
57.023   TR   1936 Some aspects of Cacao soil fertility in Trinidad. *Trop Agric* 13(12),
              Dec.: 315-317.   [59]   [*AGS*]
1.023   BC   1936 Studies in West Indian soils.

57.024   SV   1939 Soil erosion in St. Vincent, B.W.I. *Trop Agric* 16(3), Mar.: 58-65.
                                                                                    [*RIS*]
57.025   TR   1940 A provisional classification of the soils of Trinidad. *Trop Agric*
                      17(8), Aug.: 153-158.   [*AGS*]
57.026   TR   1942 Soil erosion in Trinidad and Tobago. *Trop Agric* 19(2), Feb.: 29-35.
                                                                                    [*AGS*]
57.027   TR   1943 Studies on aeration and water supply in some cacao soils of Trini-
                      dad. *Trop Agric* 20(5), May: 89-104.   [59]   [*AGS*]
57.028   GC   1946 The need for soil surveys in the Caribbean region. *Trop Agric* 23
                      (11), Nov.: 197-200.   [*AGS*]
57.029   BC   1949 Soil classification in the Caribbean region (a review). PROCEEDINGS
                      OF THE FIRST COMMONWEALTH CONFERENCE ON TROPICAL AND SUB-
                      TROPICAL SOILS, 1948. Harpenden, Eng., Commonwealth Bureau of
                      Soil Science, p.64-75. (Technical communication, no. 46.)
57.030   BC   1950 The present state of soil knowledge in the British Caribbean region.
                      Car Commn Mon Inf B 4(4), Nov.: 561-563.   [*COL*]
57.031   BC   1951 Soil productivity in the British Caribbean region. *Trop Agric* 28
                      (1-6), Jan.-June: 3-25.   [46]   [*AGS*]
57.032   TR   1953 The productivity of cacao soils and its improvement. *Trop Agric*
                      30(7-9), July-Sept.: p.135-138.   [59]   [*AGS*]

                HARDY, F.; AKHURST, C. G. & GRIFFITH, G.
57.033   TB   1931 Studies in West Indian soils. (III)-The cacao soils of Tobago. *Trop
                      Agric* Feb.: suppl. (22p.)   [59]   [*RIS*]

                HARDY, F. & CRIPPS, E. G.
57.034   SV   1944 Subsoil fertility of eroded volcanic ash in St. Vincent, B.W.I. *Trop
                      Agric* 21(2), Feb.: 30-39.   [*AGS*]

                HARDY, F. & DERRAUGH, L. F.
58.053   TR   1947 The water and air relations of some Trinidad sugar-cane soils.

                HARDY, F.; DUTHIE, D. W. & RODRIGUEZ, G.
57.035   TR   1936 STUDIES IN WEST INDIAN SOILS. (X)-THE CACAO AND FOREST SOILS OF
                      TRINIDAD. (B)-SOUTH-CENTRAL DISTRICT. [Port of Spain?] Trinidad,
                      Imperial College of Tropical Agriculture, 56p.   [59,64]   [*RIS*]

                HARDY, F. & JORDAN, J. W.
57.036   TR   1946 Soil fertility of some peasant lands in Trinidad. *Trop Agric* 23(1),
                      Jan.: 12-19.   [46]   [*AGS*]

                HARDY, F.; McDONALD, J. A. & RODRIGUEZ, G.
57.037   GR   1932 Studies in West Indian soils. (IV)-The cacao soils of Grenada: their
                      origin, formation and chief characters. *Trop Agric* Dec.: suppl.
                      (28p.)   [59]   [*RIS*]
57.038   AT   1933 STUDIES IN WEST INDIAN SOILS. (V)-THE SUGAR-CANE SOILS OF ANTI-
                      GUA. [Port of Spain?] Trinidad, Imperial College of Tropical Agri-
                      culture, 50p.   [58,66]   [*RIS*]

                HARDY, F.; ROBINSON, C. K. & RODRIGUEZ, G.
57.039   SV   1934 STUDIES IN WEST INDIAN SOILS. (VIII)-THE AGRICULTURAL SOILS OF ST.
                      VINCENT. [Port of Spain?] Trinidad, Imperial College of Tropical
                      Agriculture, 43p.   [66]   [*RIS*]

HARDY, F. & RODRIGUEZ, G.

60.033   TR   1935 Grapefruit investigations in Trinidad.

HARDY, F. & RODRIGUES, G.

57.040   SL   1947 STUDIES IN WEST INDIAN SOILS. (XII)-THE AGRICULTURAL AND FOREST SOILS OF ST. LUCIA. [Port of Spain?] Trinidad, Imperial College of Tropical Agriculture, 48p.   [64]   [*RIS*]

57.041   SK/   1947 STUDIES IN WEST INDIAN SOILS. (XIII)-THE AGRICULTURAL SOILS OF ST.
    NV/   KITTS-NEVIS WITH NOTES ON STATIA (DUTCH). [Port of Spain?] Trini-
    SE   dad, Imperial College of Tropical Agriculture, 45p.   [*RIS*]

HARDY, F.; RODRIGUES, G. & NANTON, W. R. E.

57.042   MS   [1949?] STUDIES IN WEST INDIAN SOILS. (XI)-THE AGRICULTURAL SOILS OF MONT-SERRAT. [Port of Spain?] Trinidad, Imperial College of Tropical Agriculture, 68p.   [66]   [*RIS*]

HARDY, F.; SMART, H. P. & RODRIGUEZ, G.

57.043   BH   1935 STUDIES IN WEST INDIAN SOILS. (IX)-SOME SOIL-TYPES OF BRITISH HONDURAS, CENTRAL AMERICA. [Port of Spain?] Trinidad, Imperial College of Tropical Agriculture, 56p.   [66]   [*RIS*]

HARRISON, Sir JOHN B.

57.044   BB   [1921?] The genesis of a fertile soil. *W I B* 18(3): 77-98.   [*AMN*]

HAVORD, G.

57.045   TR   1961 SOIL AND LAND-USE SURVEYS. NO. 13: A DETAILED SOIL AND LAND CA-PABILITY SURVEY OF A CACAO AREA IN TRINIDAD. [Port of Spain?] Trinidad, Regional Research Centre, Imperial College of Tropical Agriculture, 59p.   [59,66]   [*RIS*]

HENIN, S.

57.046   FG   1954 Les sols et les possibilités de la Guyane Francaise [The soils and the possibilities of French Guiana]. *In* PROCEEDINGS OF THE SYM-POSIUM INTERCOLONIAL, JUNE 27-JULY 3, 1952. Bordeaux, Impr. Del-mas, p.213-220.   [*RIS*]

HENRIQUEZ, P. C.

66.061   CU   1962 PROBLEMS RELATING TO HYDROLOGY, WATER CONSERVATION, EROSION CONTROL, REFORESTATION AND AGRICULTURE IN CURACAO.

HOETINK, HARRY

43.069   GC   1961 Enkele sociaal-geografische kenmerken van het Caribische gebied [Some socio-geographic characteristics of the Caribbean area].

HOOCK, J.

57.047   FG   1960 The reclamation of dry savannahs in French Guiana. *Caribbean* 14 (4), Apr.: 82-83, 100.   [*COL*]

HOY, DON R.

46.093   GD   1961 Agricultural land use of Guadeloupe.

JAMES, PRESTON E.

43.079   GC   1960 Man-land relations in the Caribbean area.

LOWENTHAL, DAVID
43.101   GG   1960 Population contrasts in the Guianas.
20.011   BC   1961 Caribbean views of Caribbean land.

LOXTON, R. F.; RUTHERFORD, G. K. & SPECTOR, J.
57.048   BG   1958 SOIL AND LAND-USE SURVEYS. NO. 2: BRITISH GUIANA—THE RUPUNUNI
                       SAVANNAS. [Port of Spain?] Trinidad, Regional Research Centre, Im-
                       perial College of Tropical Agriculture, 33p.   [46,66]   [*RIS*]

McDONALD, J. A.; HARDY, F. & RODRIGUEZ, G.
57.049   TR   1933 STUDIES IN WEST INDIAN SOILS. (VII)-THE CACAO SOILS OF TRINIDAD:
                       (A) MONTSERRAT DISTRICT. [Port of Spain?] Trinidad, Imperial Col-
                       lege of Tropical Agriculture, 50p.   [59]   [*RIS*]

McMORRIS, C. S.
57.050   JM   1955 Rebuilding the soil in Jamaica. *Caribbean* 9(2), Sept.: 31-35. [*COL*]

PAUL, HARRY
57.051   BG   1954 Phosphorus status of peat soils in British Guiana. *Soil Sci* 77(2),
                       Feb.: 87-93.

PRICE, R. W.
57.052   JM   1959 SOIL AND LAND-USE SURVEYS. NO. 8: JAMAICA—PARISH OF ST. JAMES.
                       Trinidad, Regional Research Centre, Imperial College of Tropical
                       Agriculture, 26p.   [46,66]   [*RIS*]
57.053   JM   1960 SOIL AND LAND-USE SURVEYS. NO. 12: JAMAICA—PARISH OF HANOVER.
                       Trinidad, Regional Research Centre, Imperial College of Tropical
                       Agriculture, 25p.   [46,66]   [*RIS*]

PROCTOR, GEORGE R.
57.054   JM   1960 Studies of bauxite vegetation in Jamaica. *Inf B Scient Res Coun*
                       1(3), Dec.: 6-10.   [54]   [*RIS*]

ROBINSON, J. B. D.
57.055   BB   1952 A comparative study of some soil nutrients in the coralline sugar-
                       cane soils of Barbados. *J Soil Sci* 3(2): 182-188.   [58]

ROMNEY, D. H., ed.
46.188   BH   1959 LAND IN BRITISH HONDURAS: REPORT OF THE BRITISH HONDURAS LAND
                       USE SURVEY TEAM.

RUTHERFORD, G. K.
57.056   BG   1956 Soil and land use patterns in the Rupununi savannas of British Gui-
                       ana. *Timehri* 4th ser., 1(35), Oct.: 53-61.   [46]

SAUER, CARL O.
43.133   GC   1954 Economic prospects of the Caribbean.

SEAFORTH, COMPTON E.
28.477   GC   1962 Drugs from the West Indies.

SHEPHARD, C. Y.
59.040   TR   1932/ The cacao industry of Trinidad; some economic aspects.
                       37

STARK, J. et al.

57.057　BG　1959 Soil and land-use surveys. No. 5: British Guiana. (1) The Mahdia Valley. (2) The Bartica Triangle. (3) The Kamarang and Kukui Valleys. (4) A part of the upper Mazaruni Valley. [Port of Spain?] Trinidad, Regional Research Centre, Imperial College of Tropical Agriculture, 34p.　　[46,66]　　*[RIS]*

STARK, J.; RUTHERFORD, G. K.; SPECTOR, J. & JONES, T. A.

57.058　BG　1959 Soil and land-use surveys. No. 6. British Guiana. (1) The Rupununi savannas (continued). (2) The intermediate savannas. (3) General remarks. [Port of Spain?] Trinidad, Regional Research Centre, Imperial College of Tropical Agriculture, 23p.　　[46,66]　　*[RIS]*

STEELE, J. G.

57.059　JM　1954 A land-capability classification for the Yallahs Valley area. *In* The Farmers Guide, Appendix G. Glasgow, University Press, p.804-808.　　　　　　　　　　　　　　　　　*[NYP]*

TAYLOR, S. A. G. & CHUBB, L. J.

40.184　JM　1957 The hydrogeology of the Clarendon Plains, Jamaica.

TEMPANY, Sir HAROLD A.

57.060　AT　1915 The soils of Antigua. *W I G* 15(2): 69-102.　　　*[AMN]*

THORP, JAMES

57.061　SC　1932 Soil survey (reconnaissance) of St. Croix Island, Virgin Islands. Washington, U.S. Govt. Print. Off., 28p. (U.S. Dept. of Agriculture, Technical bulletin no. 315.)　　　　　　　　　　*[NYP]*

TURNER, P. E.

58.103　TR　1935/ Recent investigations on sugar-cane and sugar-cane soils in Trinidad.
　　　　37

TURNER, P. E.; CHARTER, C. F. & WARNEFORD, F. H. S.

58.108　AT　1936 Investigations on sugar-cane and sugar-cane soils in Antigua. I: Preliminary results of the new experimental scheme.

TURNER, P. E. & KELSICK, R. E.

58.109　SK　1936/ Recent investigations on sugar-cane and sugar-cane soils in St. Kitts. II: Experiments with varieties, with time of planting, with distance of spacing, reaped in 1936. III: Cultural, mulching and manurial experiments, reaped in 1936.

TURNER, P. E.; KELSICK, R. E. & GREGORY, G. B.

58.110　SK　1936 Recent investigations on sugar-cane and sugar-cane soils in St. Kitts. I: Preliminary results of the new experimental scheme.

TURNER, P.E.; WARNEFORD, F. H. S. & CHARTER, C. F.

58.111　AT　1937 Recent investigations on sugar-cane and sugar-cane soils in Antigua. II: Manurial experiments reaped in 1936.

VEENENBOS, J. S.

57.062   NA   1955 A SOIL AND LAND CAPABILITY SURVEY OF ST. MAARTEN, ST. EUSTATIUS
                AND SABA, NETHERLANDS ANTILLES. Utrecht, Foundation for Scien-
                tific Research in Surinam and the Netherlands Antilles, 94p. (Na-
                tuurwetenschappelijke Studiekring voor Suriname en de Nederlandse
                Antillen. Publication no. 11).   [*AGS*]

VERNON, K. C.

57.063   JM   1958 SOIL AND LAND-USE SURVEYS. NO. 1: JAMAICA—PARISH OF ST. CATHER-
                INE. [Port of Spain?] Trinidad, Regional Research Centre, Imper-
                ial College of Tropical Agriculture, 42p.   [46,66]   [*RIS*]

57.064   JM   1959 SOIL AND LAND-USE SURVEYS. NO. 4: JAMAICA—PARISH OF ST. ANDREW.
                [Port of Spain?] Trinidad, Regional Research Centre, Imperial Col-
                lege of Tropical Agriculture, 28p.   [46,66]   [*RIS*]

57.065   JM   1960 SOIL AND LAND-USE SURVEYS. NO. 10: JAMAICA—PARISH OF ST. MARY.
                [Port of Spain?] Trinidad, Regional Research Centre, Imperial Col-
                lege of Tropical Agriculture, 30p.   [46,66]   [*RIS*]

VERNON, K. C.; PAYNE, HUGH & SPECTOR, J.

57.066   GR/   1959 SOIL AND LAND-USE SURVEYS. NO. 9: GRENADA. [Port of Spain?] Trin-
          CR   dad, Regional Research Centre, Imperial College of Tropical Agri-
                culture, 42p.   [46,66]   [*RIS*]

WALKER, B.

58.113 BG   1960 The effect of soil type and soil moisture content on growth of sugar-
                cane in the east coast area of Demerara.

WALTERS, E. A.

57.067   SL   1929 St. Lucia banana lands: observations and comments on soil changes
                in relation to tropical agriculture.   *Trop Agric* 6(3), Mar.: 69-73.
                [63]   [*AGS*]

WARDLAW, C. W.

57.068   SL   1929 Soils and flora; notes on a botanical and soil inspection of the St.
                Lucia banana and forest lands.   *Trop Agric* 6(11), Nov: 304-309.
                [63,64]   [*AGS*]

WASOWICZ, T.

59.058 TR   1952 Notes on the fertility of cacao soils: (a) Diminishing fertility of suc-
                cessive soil layers. (b) Effect of drying on soil fertility.

WATSON, J. P.; SPECTOR, J. & JONES, T. A.

57.069   SV   1958 SOIL AND LAND-USE SURVEYS. NO. 3: ST. VINCENT. [Port of Spain?]
                Trinidad, Regional Research Centre, Imperial College of Tropical
                Agriculture, 70p.   [46,66]   [*RIS*]

WATTS, Sir FRANCIS

57.070   NV   1909 The soils of Nevis. *W I B* 10(1): 60-79.   [*AMN*]

WATTS, Sir FRANCIS & TEMPANY, H. A.

57.071   MS   1905 The soils of Montserrat. *W I B* 6(3): 263-284.   [*AMN*]

WEISZ, T. T.

57.072   JM   1962   Rehabilitation of bauxite lands. *Inf B Scient Res Coun* 3(1), June: 10-12.   [54]   [*RIS*]

WITT, GORDON

46.240   TR   1959   The use of fertilisers in Trinidad agriculture.

WOOD, SYDNEY MAKEPEACE

57.073   JM   1961   Coastal erosion and its control. *Inf B Scient Res Coun* 2(3), Dec.: 45-47.   [66]   [*COL*]

Chapter 58

THE SUGAR COMPLEX

ABBOTT, GEORGE C.

58.001   BC   1963 Stabilisation policies in the West Indian sugar industry. *Car Q* 9
(1-2): 53-66.   [*RIS*]

58.002   BC   1964 The West Indian sugar industry, with some long term projections of
supply to 1975. *Social Econ Stud* 13(1), Mar.: 1-37.   [*RIS*]

ALBUQUERQUE, J. P. D.

58.003   BB   1908 Sugar cane experiments in Barbados. *W I B* 9(1): 39-62.   [*AMN*]

ALKINS, H. F.

58.004   BC   1948 B. W. I. Sugar Association aims to promote industry. *Car Commn Mon
Inf B* 2(2), Sept.: 40, 42.   [*COL*]

ARONOFF, JOEL

31.004   SK   1965 The inter-relationship of psychological and cultural systems: a case
study of a rural West Indian village.

BARNES, ARTHUR C.

58.005   BC   1950 Sugar: mainstay of the British West Indies. *Wld Crops* 2(8), Aug.:
325-327; 2(9), Sept.: 365-369.   [*AGS*]

BARNETT, W. L.

58.006   JM   1951 NOTES ON JAMAICA RUM. Kingston, Jamaica, Government Printer, 8p.
(Department of Government Chemist, Bulletin no. 1)   [37]

BEACHEY, RAYMOND W.

58.007   BC   1951 The period of prosperity in the British West Indian sugar industry
and the continental bounty system, 1865-1884. *Car Hist Rev* 2,
Dec.: 79-99.   [5]   [*RIS*]

58.008   BC   1954 Sugar technology in the British West Indies in the late nineteenth
century. *Car Hist Rev* 3-4, Dec.: 170-196.   [5]   [*RIS*]

58.009   BC   1957 THE BRITISH WEST INDIES SUGAR INDUSTRY IN THE LATE 19TH CENTURY.
Oxford, Basil Blackwell, 189p.   [5]   [*RIS*]

BEADNELL, H. G.

28.027   BG   1962 Industrial injuries in the sugar industry of British Guiana.

BIJLSMA, R.

58.010   SR   1922/ Over bodemgesteldheid en suikerplantage-exploitatie in Suriname,
                23   1765 [On soil conditions and sugar-plantation exploitation in Suri-
                      nam, 1765]. *W I G* 4:341-349.   [5,57]   [*COL*]

BIRD, MAURICE

58.011   BG   1922 Concerning yield deterioration in the older sugar countries. *J Bd
                      Agric Br Gui* 15(4), Oct.: 200-203.   [57]   [*AMN*]
57.004 BG   1924 Deep ploughing in relation to soil water in British Guiana.
58.012   BG   1928 The British Guiana cane sugar industry. *Emp Prod Exp* 148, Dec.:
                      290-297.   [*NYP*]
57.005 BG   1929 Guiana's sugar soils.

BIRKETT, L. S.

58.013   BG   1947 The deterioration of cane after burning for reaping with special ref-
                      erence to British Guiana. *Trop Agric* 24(1-3), Jan.-Mar.: 28-31. [*AGS*]

BOVELL, J. R.

58.014   BB   1907 Sugar-cane experiments at Barbados. *W I B* 8(1): 51-78.   [*AMN*]
58.015   BB   1909 Comparison of the bourbon sugar-cane with the white transparent
                      and other varieties at Barbados. *W I G* 10(1): 55-59.   [*AMN*]

BROMLEY, ROBERT

58.016   BB/   1904 The muscovado sugar industry in Barbados and the Leeward Islands.
          LW   *W I B* 5(3): 195-210.   [*AMN*]

CARLEE, J. J. A.

50.016 BC   1919 Implemental tillage—how labor can be saved.

CARMODY, P.

58.017   TR   1901 Cane-farming in Trinidad. *W I B* 2(1): 33-41.   [*AMN*]
58.018   TR   1908 Further notes on cane farming in Trinidad. *Proc Agric Soc Trin
                      Tob* 8(1), Jan.: 5-8.   [*AMN*]

CHARLEY, A.

58.019   JM   1907 Selective cane reaping at Jamaica. *W I B* 8(1): 109-119.   [*AMN*]

CHINLOY, T.

58.020   JM   1961 Sugar cane research in Jamaica. *Inf B Scient Res Coun* 2(2), Sept.:
                      21-24.   [*AMN*]

CLARKE, F. J.

53.006 BB   1908 Establishment and working of the Sugar Industry Agricultural Bank
                      at Barbados.

COON, F. SEAL

58.021   JM   1958 Research in the Jamaican sugar industry. *Caribbean* 12(3), Oct.:
                      54-57; 12(4), Nov.: 77-79, 96.   [*COL*]

COOPER, St. G. C.

58.022   BG   1947 Cane-farming in British Guiana. *Trop Agric* 24(10-12), Oct.-Dec.:
                      121-126.   [*AGS*]

COUSINS, HERBERT H.

58.023   JM   1902 The prospects of the sugar industry in Jamaica. *W I B* 3(1): 46-65.
                                                                                          [*AMN*]
58.024   JM   1907 Jamaica rum. *W I B* 8(1): 120-128.   [*AMN*]
58.025   JM   1907 The rational use of manures for sugar-cane in Jamaica. *W I B* 8(1):
                       90-93.   [*AMN*]
58.026   JM   1907 Seeding canes in Jamaica. *W I B* 8(1): 26-28.   [*AMN*]

CUMPER, GEORGE E.

58.027   JM   1954 Labour demand and supply in Jamaican sugar industry, 1830-1950.
                       Social Econ Stud 2(4), Mar.: 37-86. [5, 50]   [*RIS*]
58.028   JM   1954 A modern Jamaican sugar estate. *Social Econ Stud* 3(2), Sept.: 119-
                       160. [45, 47]   [*RIS*]

CURTIN, PHILIP D.

51.043 BC   1954 The British sugar duties and West Indian prosperity.

DANKLEFSEN, MILDRED MARIE

58.029   JM   1952 RECENT TRENDS IN THE SUGAR INDUSTRY OF JAMAICA. Ph.D. disserta-
                       tion, Clark University, 171p. [66]

De CARTERET, P. E. V.

58.030   TR   1963 Trinidad. *Sug Azucar* 58(9), Sept.: 49-51.   [*RIS*]

DEERR, NOEL

50.036 GC   1938 Indian labour in the sugar industry.
58.031   BC   1946 Sugar in the West Indies. *W I Comm Circ* 61(1186), Oct.: 207-208,
                       [5]   [*NYP*]

DEVENTER, S. van

58.032   SR/   1923/ Suikercultuur in Suriname in vergelijking met die in Britsch Guyana
          BG   24   [Sugar culture in Surinam as compared with that in British Guiana].
                       W I G 5:281-285.   [*COL*]

DUNLOP, W. R.

58.033   BG   1915 A summary of the manurial experiments with sugar-cane in the West
                       Indies. *W I B* 15(4): 212-234.   [*AMN*]

EVANS, HARRY

58.034   BG   1958 Some aspects of sugar agronomy in British Guiana. *Timehri* 4th
                       ser., no. 37, Sept.: 59-73.   [*AMN*]
58.035   BG   1963 The sugar industry in British Guiana. *Sug Azucar* 58(9), Sept.: 64-
                       66.   [*RIS*]

FARLEY, RAWLE, IFILL, MAX B. & BROWN, J. C.

58.036   BB   [1964?] REPORT OF THE COMMISSION OF ENQUIRY INTO THE BARBADOS SUGAR
                       INDUSTRY 1962-1963. [Bridgetown?] Barbados, Govt. Print. Off., 88p.

FARNELL, R. G. W.

58.037   BC   1924 Sugar making in the West Indies and Guiana. *W I Comm Circ* 39
                       (668), May 8: 181-182.   [*NYP*]

FOLLETT-SMITH, R. R.

58.038   BG   1933   The flood fallowing of cane fields in British Guiana. *Trop Agric*
                       10(4), Apr.: 91-95.   [*AGS*]

58.039   BG   1958   British Guiana's industry: thirty years of progress. *Caribbean* 11
                       (10), May: 223-227.   [66]   [*COL*]

FOSTER, C. B.

58.040   BB   1946   SUGAR CANE AND ITS CULTIVATION IN BARBADOS. [Bridgetown?] Bar-
                       bados [Advocate Co.?] 19p. (Dept. of Science and Agriculture.
                       Bulletin no. 6, new ser.)

58.041   BB   1951   THE YIELD OF SUGAR CANE IN BARBADOS IN 1951. [Bridgetown?] Bar-
                       bados, Advocate Co., 15p. (Dept. of Science and Agriculture. Bul-
                       letin no. 17, new ser.)   [*RIS*]

58.042   BB   1952   THE YIELD OF SUGAR CANE IN BARBADOS IN 1952. [Bridgetown?] Bar-
                       bados, Advocate Co., 16p. (Dept. of Science and Agriculture, Bul-
                       letin no. 19, new ser.)   [*RIS*]

58.043   BB   1956   YIELD OF SUGAR CANE IN BARBADOS. Bridgetown [Printed by Advocate
                       Co.?] (Dept. of Science & Agriculture, Bulletin no. 24, new ser.)

FREEMAN, WILLIAM G.

58.044   TR   1920   The Trinidad cane farming industry: its past and suggestions for
                       its future. *Proc Agric Soc Trin Tob* 20(6-7), June-July: 177-187.
                                                                                        [*AMN*]

58.045   BC   1930   The historic Bourbon cane. *W I Comm Circ* 45(816), Jan. 9:5-6.   [5]
                                                                                        [*NYP*]

GERLING, WALTER

58.046   JM   1954   DIE PLANTAGENWIRTSCHAFT DES ROHRZUCKERS AUF DEN GROSSEN AN-
                       TILLEN: EIN BEITRAG ZUR AGRARGEOGRAPHIE DER TROPEN [THE PLANTA-
                       TION ECONOMY OF SUGAR CANE IN THE GREATER ANTILLES: A CONTRIBU-
                       TION TO AGRARIAN GEOGRAPHY IN THE TROPICS]. Würzburg: Im Selbst-
                       verlag des Geographischen Instituts der Univerität Würzburg in Ver-
                       bindung mit der Geographischen Gesellschaft Würzburg, 52p. (Würz-
                       burger geographische Arbeiten, v. 2.)   [45]   [*AGS*]

GIANETTI, G. G.

58.047   AT   1929   Sugar production in Antigua. *Trop Agric* 6(4), Apr.: 105-106.   [*AGS*]

GIGLIOLI, GEORGE

30.028   BG   1958   An outline of the nutritional situation on the sugar estates of Brit-
                       ish Guiana in respect to the eradication of malaria: recent develop-
                       ments in the production of green vegetables and fruit by individual
                       units.

GOLDENBERG, H. CARL, et al.

58.048   JM   1960   THE COMMISSION OF ENQUIRY ON THE SUGAR INDUSTRY OF JAMAICA
                       1959-1960. Kingston, Govt. Printer, 93p.

GREEMAN, W. G. & BRUNTON, L. A.

58.049   TR   1928   Trinidad seedling canes. *Proc Agric Soc Trin Tob* 28(8), Aug.:
                       337-346.   [*AMN*]

GREENFIELD, SIDNEY M.

46.078   BB   1964   Stocks, bonds, and peasant canes in Barbados: some notes on the use of land in an overdeveloped economy.

GUERRA y SANCHEZ, RAMIRO

58.050   BB   1927   AZÚCAR Y POBLACIÓN EN LAS ANTILLAS [SUGAR AND POPULATION IN THE WEST INDIES]. Havana, Cultural, 190p. [5]   [COL]

HALL, DOUGLAS GORDON

58.051   BC   1961   Incalculability as a feature of sugar production during the eighteenth century. *Social Econ Stud* 10(3), Sept.: 340-352. [5]   [RIS]

HANDLER, JEROME S.

50.057   BB   1965   Some aspects of work organization on sugar plantations in Barbados.

HARDY, F.

58.052   TR   1933   Root distribution of sugar-cane in different soils in Trinidad; embodying some results obtained by a soil-core method. *Trop Agric* 10(6), June: 165-172. [57]   [AGS]

HARDY, F. & DERRAUGH, L. F.

58.053   TR   1947   The water and air relations of some Trinidad sugar-cane soils. *Trop Agric* 24(7-9), July-Sept.: 76-87; 24(10-12), Oct.-Dec.: 111-121. [AGS]

HARDY, F.; McDONALD, J. A. & RODRIGUEZ, G.

57.038   AT   1933   STUDIES IN WEST INDIAN SOILS. (V)-THE SUGAR-CANE SOILS OF ANTIGUA.

HARDY, F. & RODRIGUES, G.

58.054   BG   [n.d.] SOME SUGAR-CANE SOIL PROFILES OF BRITISH GUIANA: PROCEEDINGS OF THE 1946 MEETING OF BRITISH WEST INDIES SUGAR TECHNOLOGISTS. Bridgetown, British West Indies Sugar Association, 14p.

HARES, L. G.

52.036   BG   1935   A railway enterprise in Demerara.

HARRISON, Sir JOHN B.

58.055   BG   1908   Varieties of sugar-cane and manurial experiments in British Guiana. *W I B* 9(1): 1-39.   [AMN]

HENRY, C. C.

58.056   JM   1938   Prime Jamaica rum. *Can-W I Mag* 27(5), May: 9-10.   [NYP]

HENZELL, L. I.

58.057   AT   1910   Five years' working of the Antigua Sugar Factory. *W I B* 10(4): 305-312.   [AMN]

HOY, DON R.

46.094   GD   1962   Changing agricultural land use on Guadeloupe, French West Indies.

HUGILL, J. A. C.

58.058   TR   1963   Trinidad's sugar markets. *Enterprise* 1(3), July-Sept.: 16-17, 31. [44]   [RIS]

HUNTE, GEORGE HUTCHINSON

58.059   BB   1955   Barbados . . . sugar and tourism. *New Commonw* British Caribbean Supplement 30(11), Nov. 28: iv-v. [55, 66]   [AGS]

JENKS, LELAND H.

58.060   GC   1944 The sugar industry of the Caribbean. *In* FRAZIER, E.F. & WIL-
                     LIAMS, E., eds. THE ECONOMIC FUTURE OF THE CARIBBEAN. Wash-
                     ington, D.C., Howard University Press, p.11-17.

JOSA, GUY

58.061   MT   1931 LES INDUSTRIES DU SUCRE ET DU RHUM À LA MARTINIQUE (1639-1931)
                     [THE SUGAR AND RUM INDUSTRIES IN MARTINIQUE (1639-1931)]. Paris,
                     Les Presses modernes, 185p.   [5]   [*COL*]

KIRKWOOD, R.L.M.

58.062   BC   1955 Sugar from the West Indies. *New Commonw* British Caribbean Sup-
                     plement 30(10), Nov. 14: vi-viii.   [*AGS*]

KOPP, A.

46.126   GD   1929 L'agriculture à la Guadeloupe [Agriculture in Guadeloupe].

LAMONT, Sir NORMAN, et al.

48.010   TR   1918 Report of the Co-operative Sugar Factories Committee.

LASSERRE, GUY

58.063   GD   1952 Une plantation de canne aux Antilles: la Sucrerie Beauport [A sugar
                     cane plantation in the Antilles: the Beauport sugar mill]. *Cah O-M*
                     5(20), Oct.-Dec.: 297-329.   [45]   [*RIS*]

LEGIER, EMILE

58.064   FA   1905 LA MARTINIQUE ET LA GUADELOUPE. Paris, Bureaux de la sucrerie
                     indigène et coloniale, 190p.   [*NYP*]

McINTOSH, A.E.S.

58.065   BC   1936 The British West Indies Central Sugar Cane Breeding Station, Bar-
                     bados, B.W.I. *Trop Agric* 13(8), Aug.: 204-212.   [*AGS*]

McKENZIE, A.F.

58.066   BB   1958 REPORT OF AN INQUIRY INTO THE SUGAR INDUSTRY OF BARBADOS.
                     [Bridgetown?] Barbados, Govt. Print. Off., 43p.

MANDEVILLE, R.G.F.

58.067   BC   1961 THE COMMONWEALTH SUGAR AGREEMENT. [Bridgetown?] Barbados,
                     Barbados Sugar Producers' Association.

58.068   BB   1963 A BRIEF NOTE ON THE HISTORY OF SUGAR IN BARBADOS. [Bridgetown?]
                     Barbados, Barbados Sugar Producers' Association.   [5]

MASSY, C.R. & PATERSON, D.D.

58.069   TR   1933 The use of the tractor in Trinidad for sugar-cane cultivation. *Trop
                     Agric* 10(10), Oct.: 280-285.   [*AGS*]

MINTZ, SIDNEY W.

58.070   JM   1959 Labor and sugar in Puerto Rico and in Jamaica, 1800-1850. *Comp
                     Stud Soc Hist* 1(3), Mar.: 273-283.   [5, 50]   [*RIS*]

MURRAY, H. E.

58.071   TR   1912   Paper on bourbon and seedling canes. *Proc Agric Soc Trin Tob* 12 (1-2), Jan.-Feb.: 9-15.   [*AMN*]

NORRIS, R.

58.072   BC   1963   Progress in the West Indies. *Sug Azucar* 58(9), Sept.: 47-48, 80. [*RIS*]

OGUNTOYINBO, JULIUS SUNDAY

42.024   BB   1964   RAINFALL, EVAPORATION AND SUGAR CANE YIELDS IN BARBADOS.

OLIVIER, SYDNEY, 1st Baron RAMSDEN, & SEMPLE, D. M.

58.073   BC   1930   REPORT OF THE WEST INDIAN SUGAR COMMISSION [pref. signed: Olivier and D. M. Semple]. London, H.M.S.O., 124p. (Cmd. 3517)   [66] [*NYP*]

PASS, E. A. de

58.074   BC   1930   The crisis in the Caribbean sugar industry. *W I Comm Circ* 45(824), May 1: 171-172.   [*NYP*]

PILE, G. LAURIE, et al.

58.075   BB   [1935?] A REPORT ON THE PRESENT CONDITION AND FUTURE OUTLOOK OF THE SUGAR INDUSTRY OF BARBADOS BY DELEGATES APPOINTED BY THE LEGISLATURE OF BARBADOS. [Bridgetown?] Barbados, 12p.   [*RIS*]

PITMAN, FRANK WESLEY

58.076   BC   1917   THE DEVELOPMENT OF THE BRITISH WEST INDIES 1700-1763. New Haven, Yale University Press, 495p.   [5]   [*COL*]

POUND, F. J.

58.077   TR   1944   The mechanisation of agricultural practices on sugar estates. *Proc Agric Soc Trin Tob* 44(2), June: 111-119.   [*AMN*]

PYTTERSEN, TJ.

58.078   SR   1920/ De toekomst van Suriname als suikerland [The future of Surinam as 21   sugar producer. *W I G* 2:17-35.   [*COL*]

46.174   SR   1920/ De toekomst van verschillende cultures in Surinam [The future of 21   several agricultural products in Surinam].

58.079   TR   1927/ Enkele beschouwingen [Some observations]. *W I G* 9:545-560.   [46] 28   [*COL*]

REUBENS, EDWIN P. & BEATRICE G.

50.097   BG   1962   LABOUR DISPLACEMENT IN A LABOUR-SURPLUS ECONOMY; THE SUGAR INDUSTRY OF BRITISH GUIANA.

REVERT, EUGENE

46.181   MT   1948   L'économie martiniquaise [Martinique's economy].

ROBERTS, W. D.

58.080   JM   1962   We should store 60,000 tons of sugar. *Spotlight* 23(2), Feb.: 11. [*RIS*]

ROBERTSON, C. J.

58.081   BC   1930 Cane sugar production in the British Empire. *Econ Geogr* 6(2), Apr.:
                       135-151.   [*AGS*]

58.082   GC   1941 Sugar as a mono-export: its development and consequences. *Int Sug
                       J* 43(507), Mar.: 73-76.   [*COL*]

ROBINSON, J. B. D.

57.055   BB   1952 A comparative study of some soil nutrients in the coralline sugar-
                       cane soils of Barbados.

ROTH, VINCENT

58.083   BG   1953 Some sugar biography. *Timehri* 4th ser., 1(32), Nov.: 45-48. [5]

ROUSE, WAYNE ROBERT

42.027   BB   1962 THE MOISTURE BALANCE OF BARBADOS AND ITS INFLUENCE UPON SUGAR
                       CANE YIELD.

RUNGE, PETER

58.084   BC   1961 The West Indian sugar industry. *J Roy Soc Arts* 109, Jan.: 91-104.
                                                                                  [*AGS*]

SAMLALSINGH, RUBY S.

33.043   BG   1959 Application of social welfare principles to the rural development
                       programme on sugar estates in British Guiana.

SCOTT, WALTER

58.085   GC   1950 THE INDUSTRIAL UTILISATION OF SUGAR CANE BY-PRODUCTS. Port of
                       Spain, Caribbean Commission, 121p.   [49]   [*RIS*]

SEAFORD, F. A.

58.086   BG   1939 The Ruimveldt bulk sugar terminal. *Timehri* 4th ser., no. 39, Sept.:
                       47-54.   [*AMN*]

SHAW, EARL BENNETT

58.087   SC   1933 St. Croix: a marginal sugar-producing island. *Geogr Rev* 23(3), July:
                       414-422.   [*AGS*]

SHEPHARD, C. Y.

58.088   BC   1929 THE SUGAR INDUSTRY OF THE BRITISH WEST INDIES AND BRITISH
                       GUIANA WITH SPECIAL REFERENCE TO TRINIDAD. [Port of Spain?] 20p.
                       (Memoirs of the Imperial College of Tropical Agriculture, Trinidad.
                       Economic series, no. 1.) [5]   [*RIS*]

50.113   BB   1946 CANE CUTTING ENQUIRY: BARBADOS.

58.089   BB   1946 THE SUGAR INDUSTRY OF BARBADOS; 1946 CROP: REPORT ON THE NEW
                       METHOD OF REMUNERATING CANE CUTTERS. [Bridgetown?] Barbados
                       Advocate Co., printers, 9p.   [50]   [*RIS*]

58.090   BB   1947 THE SUGAR INDUSTRY OF BARBADOS; A METHOD FOR CALCULATING THE
                       PRICE OF SUGAR-CANE. [Bridgetown?] Barbados, Advocate Co., prin-
                       ters, 41p.   [*RIS*]

SHERE, LOUIS
44.216 GC 1952 SUGAR TAXATION IN THE CARIBBEAN AND CENTRAL AMERICAN COUNTRIES.

SHERIDAN, RICHARD B.
6.063 BC 1961 The West India sugar crisis and British slave emancipation, 1830-1833.

SHORE, JOSEPH
58.091 JM 1902 Ratooning estates and central factories in Jamaica. *W I B* 3(1): 66-73.   [*AMN*]

SKINNER, G. C.
58.092 TR 1928 Sugar cost accounts. *Trop Agric* 5(10), Oct., suppl.: 1-26. [67] [*AGS*]

SMITH, LONGFIELD
58.093 SC 1921 SUGAR CANE IN ST. CROIX. Washington, U. S. Govt. Print. Off., 23p. (Virgin Islands Agricultural Experiment Station bulletin no. 2.) [*NYP*]

SMITH, SAMUEL IVAN
42.033 GC 1963 CLIMATIC CONTROL OF DISTRIBUTION AND CULTIVATION OF SUGAR CANE.

SOULBURY, HERWALD RAMSBOTHAM 1st Viscount, et al.
58.094 SK 1949 REPORT OF THE COMMISSION APPOINTED TO ENQUIRE INTO THE ORGANISATION OF THE SUGAR INDUSTRY OF ST. CHRISTOPHER; THE RIGHT HONORABLE LORD SOULBURY, CHAIRMAN. London, Crown Agents for the Colonies.   [66]

STARKEY, OTIS P.
58.095 BC 1942 Declining sugar prices and land utilization in the British Lesser Antilles. *Econ Geogr* 18(2), Apr.: 209-214.   [*AGS*]

STEVENSON, G. C.
58.096 BB 1937 Root-development of the sugar-cane in Barbados. *Emp J Expl Agric* 5(19), July: 239-247.
58.097 BB 1955 Barbados has unique cane breeding record, by G.S. [sic] Stevenson. *Can-W I Mag* 45(8), Aug.: 3, 5, 7, 38-39.   [*NYP*]
58.098 BB 1959 Sugar cane varieties in Barbados: an historical review. *J Barb Mus Hist Soc* 26(2), Feb.: 67-93.   [5]   [*AMN*]

STOCKDALE, Sir FRANK A., ed.
46.213 BB 1941 AGRICULTURAL DEVELOPMENT IN BARBADOS: DESPATCHES FROM THE COMPTROLLER FOR DEVELOPMENT AND WELFARE IN THE WEST INDIES TO HIS EXCELLENCY THE GOVERNOR OF BARBADOS.

STRONG, L. A. G.
58.099 BC 1954 THE STORY OF SUGAR. London, George Weidenfeld and Nicolson, 159p.   [5]   [*NYP*]

TEMPANY, Sir HAROLD A.
58.100 AT 1909 The passing of the bourbon cane in Antigua. *W I B* 10(1): 34-54.   [*AMN*]

TURNER, P. E.

58.101   TR   1932 Cultivation experiments with sugar-cane: 1) The effect of type of
                        preparatory tillage on yield of plant canes. *Trop Agric* 9(4), Apr.:
                        120-126.   [*AGS*]

58.102   TR   1933 Some manurial and cultivation experiments on sugar-cane in Trini-
                        dad 1927-32. *Proc Agric Soc Trin Tob* 33(5), May: 118-140. [*AMN*]

58.103   TR   1935 Recent investigations on sugar-cane and sugar-cane soils in Trini-
                        dad. *Trop Agric* 12(10), Oct.: 262-268; 12(11), Nov.: 293-302;
                  1936 13(11), Nov.: 299-306; 13(12), Dec.: 319-326;
                  1937 14(3), Mar.: 63-69.   [57]   [*AGS*]

58.104   AT   1940 Progress in sugar-cane agriculture in Antigua during the period
                        1933-40. *Trop Agric* 17(11), Nov.: 208-212.   [*AGS*]

58.105   SK   1940 Progress of sugar-cane agriculture in St. Kitts during the period
                        1933-40. *Trop Agric* 17(12), Dec.: 226-232.   [*AGS*]

58.106   BB   1945 REPORT ON DEVELOPMENTS IN SUGAR-CANE AGRICULTURE IN BARBADOS
                        WITH SPECIAL REFERENCE TO METHODS OF TILLAGE, DRAINAGE AND CON-
                        TOUR CULTIVATION. [Bridgetown?] Barbados, Advocate Co., 27p.   [66]

58.107   BG   1947 SECOND REPORT ON MECHANISATION OF SUGAR-CANE CULTIVATION IN
                        BRITISH GUIANA: YIELDS OF PLANT CANE AND SUGAR IN CULTIVATION EX-
                        PERIMENTS. Georgetown, 44p.

TURNER, P. E., CHARTER, C. F. & WARNEFORD, F. H. S.

58.108   AT   1936 Investigations on sugar-cane and sugar-cane soils in Antigua. I:
                        Preliminary results of the new experimental scheme. *Trop Agric*
                        13(1), Jan.: 19-24; 13(2), Feb.: 38-47.   [57]   [*AGS*]

TURNER, P. E. & KELSICK, R. E.

58.109   SK   1936 Recent investigations on sugar-cane and sugar-cane soils in St.
                        Kitts.   II: Experiments with varieties, with time of planting, and
                        with distance of spacing, reaped in 1936.   III: Cultural, mulching
                        and manurial experiments, reaped in 1936. *Trop Agric* 13(10), Oct.:
                        257-265;
                  1937 14(4), Apr.: 97-109.   [57]   [*AGS*]

TURNER, P. E.; KELSICK, R. E. & GREGORY, G. B.

58.110   SK   1936 Recent investigations on sugar-cane and sugar-cane soils in St.
                        Kitts. I: Preliminary results of the new experimental scheme. *Trop
                        Agric* 13(3), Mar.: 64-70; 13(4), Apr.: 91-97.   [57]   [*AGS*]

TURNER, P. E.; WARNEFORD, F. H. S. & CHARTER, C. F.

58.111   AT   1937 Recent investigations on sugar-cane and sugar-cane soils in Anti-
                        gua. II: Manurial experiments reaped in 1936. *Trop Agric* 14(5),
                        May: 150-155; 14(6), June: 179-188.   [57]   [*AGS*]

VLITOS, A. J. & LAWRIE, I. D.

58.112   TR   1963 Foliar diagnosis as a guide to the mineral nutrition of sugar-cane
                        in Trinidad. *Trop Agric* 40(3), July: 173-183.   [*AGS*]

WALKER, B.

58.113   BG   1960 The effect of soil type and soil moisture content on growth of sugar-
                        cane in the east coast area of Demerara. *Trop Agric* 37(3), July:
                        227-233.   [57]   [*AGS*]

WARNEFORD, F. H. S.

58.114   AT   1950 Antigua's major industries. *Can-W I Mag* 40(10), Oct.: 37,39,41. [61]   [*NYP*]

WARNER, HENRY

58.115   TR   1924 Cane farming industry: notes for the establishment of a permanent committee or board. *Proc Agric Soc Trin Tob* 24(2), Feb.: 66-69. [*AMN*]

WATSON, BARTON

58.116   BB   1954 The garden of the Caribbean—"where sugar is king." *Can-W I Mag* 44(8), Aug.: 23,25.   [*NYP*]

WATTS, Sir FRANCIS

58.117   AT   1905 The Central Sugar Factory in Antigua. *W I B* 6(1): 60-64; 1908 9(1): 79-84.   [*AMN*]

58.118   AT/ SK/ NV   1906 A review of the sugar industry in Antigua and St. Kitt's-Nevis during 1881-1905. *W I B* 6(4): 373-386.   [*AMN*]

58.119   LW   1907 Sugar-cane experiments in the Leeward Islands. *W I B* 8(1): 28-50. [*AMN*]

58.120   LW   1908 Sugar-cane experiments in the Leeward Islands. *W I B* 9(1): 63-78. [*AMN*]

58.121   BB   1909 Central factories. *W I B* 10(2): 107-117.   [*AMN*]

58.122   AT/ SK   1909 The composition of Antigua and St. Kitt's molasses. *W I B* 10(1): 29-34.   [*AMN*]

58.123   AT   1915 Review of ten years' work of the Antigua Sugar Factory (Gunthorpes). *W I B* 15(2): 47-68.   [66]   [*AMN*]

58.124   AT/ SK   1919 On the sucrose content of the canes crushed at the Antigua and St. Kitts Central Sugar Factories. *W I B* 17(3): 183-188.   [*AMN*]

58.125   AT   [1921?] The Antigua Central Sugar Factory (Gunthorpes). *W I B* 18(3): 134-155.   [*AMN*]

WIGGINS, L. F.

58.126   BC   1952 A survey of the work of the British West Indies sugar research scheme. *J Agric Soc Trin Tob* 52(4), Dec.: 415-438.   [*AMN*]

WILLIAMS, C. HOLMAN B.; HUGH, E. I. & SINGH, H. B.

58.127   BG   1942 The quality of British Guiana cane. *Sug B* 2:38-46.   [*RIS*]

WILLIAMS, ERIC EUSTACE

6.076   BC   1938 THE ECONOMIC ASPECT OF THE ABOLITION OF THE BRITISH WEST INDIAN SLAVE TRADE AND SLAVERY.

58.128   BC   1943 Laissez faire, sugar and slavery. *Polit Sci Q* 58(1), Mar.: 67-85. [5,6,37]   [*COL*]

58.129   BG   1944 The historical background of British Guiana's problems. *Timehri* 4th ser., 1(26), Nov.: 18-34.   [5]   [*AMN*]

2.262   BG   1945 The historical background of British Guiana's problems.

58.130   GC   1951 The Caribbean bookshelf: the sugar economy of the Caribbean. *Car Hist Rev* 2, Dec.: 142-152.   [44]   [*RIS*]

46.238   GC   1954 The importance of small scale farming in the Caribbean.

WILLIAMS, J. F.

58.131   BG   1950 The development of the cane sugar industry in British Guiana. *Timehri* 4th ser., 1(29), Aug.: 9-15.

58.132   BG   1951 Development of the cane sugar industry in British Guiana. *Car Commn Mon Inf B* 4(7), Feb.: 674-677.   [5]   [*AGS*]

WILSON, T. B.

58.133   TR   1954 The economics of peasant cane farming in Trinidad. *Wld Crops* 6(4), Apr.: 135-140.   [*AGS*]

WOOLLEY, Sir CHARLES CAMPBELL

49.076   BG   1950 Some aspects of British Guiana's economy.

Chapter 59

CACAG AND COFFEE

BADCOCK, W. J
59.001　　TR　　1955 The possibility of developing coffee growing in Trinidad. *J Agric Soc Trin Tob* 55(3), Sept.: 287-295.　　　　　　　　　　[*AMN*]

BAKER, R. E. D.
59.002　　TR　　1950 West Indian cacao research—a progress report. *Trop Agric* 27(7-12), July-Dec.: 227-230.　　　　　　　　　　[*AGS*]

BURLE, L.
59.003　　TR　　1955 Le cacao à la Trinidad: rapport de mission, 1955 (février-mars) [Cacao in Trinidad: commission report, 1955 (February-March)]. *Agron Trop* 10(6), Nov.-Dec.: 687-751.　　　　　　　　　　[*AGS*]

CAMPBELL, J. S. & COLE, J. C.
50.015　　TR　　1963 A comparison of labour requirements and costs of cultivation on cocoa and coconut estates in Trinidad and Tobago.

CHENERY, E. M. & HARDY, F.
57.009　　TR　　1945 The moisture profile in some Trinidad forest and cacao soils.

CLARKE, E. RADCLIFF
59.004　　TR　　1928 The present situation of cocoa. *Proc Agric Soc Trin Tob* 28(1), Jan.: 15-22.　　　　　　　　　　[*AMN*]

COLLIER, H. C.
59.005　　JM　　1938 Coffee growing in Jamaica. *Can-W I Mag* 27(5), May: 6-7.　　[*NYP*]

CRADWICK, WILLIAM
59.006　　JM　　1927 Coffee growing in Jamaica. *W I Comm Circ* 42(738), Jan. 13: 7-8.　　　　　　　　　　[*NYP*]
59.007　　JM　　1928 Jamaica's coffee crops. *W I Comm Circ* 43(786), Nov. 15: 445-446.　　　　　　　　　　[*NYP*]

DAVIES, ED.
48.006　　TB　　1957 Cocoa co-ops.

DAVIES, SAMUEL HENRY
59.008   BC   1924 Cocoa cultivation in the British tropical colonies. *J Roy Soc Arts*
                      72(3714), Jan. 25: 158-168.   [*AGS*]

DOLLY, JAMES O.
50.037   TR   1929 Hindrances other than diseases and pests to the successful working
                      of cocoa and coconut estates.

EVANS, HARRY
59.009   TR   1951 Some problems in the physiology of cacao. *J Agric Soc Trin Tob*
                      51(2), June: 277-292.   [*AMN*]

FAHEY, HAROLD NEAL
59.010   TR   1943 Sic transit gloria cacao. *Proc Agric Soc Trin Tob* 43(2), June:
                      129-135.   [*AMN*]

FREEMAN, WILLIAM G.
59.011   TR   1919 Recent experimental work on cacao. *Proc Agric Soc Trin Tob* 19(11),
                      Nov.: 253-269.   [*AMN*]
59.012   TR   1928 Some practical results from experimental work on cacao at River
                      Estate. *Proc Agric Soc Trin Tob* 28(5), May: 193-214.   [*AMN*]

GREEN, D.
59.013   TR   1934 Trinidad cocoa—its history from bean to beverage. *Can-W I Mag*
                      23(8), July: 233-234.   [*NYP*]

GULCHER, C. F.
59.014   SR   1943 Een Surinaamsch koffieplanter uit de 18de eeuw (S. L. Neale) [A
                      Surinam coffee planter from the 18th century (S. L. Neale)]. *W I G*
                      25:41-59. [5]   [*COL*]

HALL, C. J. J. van
59.015   SR   1933/ De proeven van Dr. Fernandes in de koffie-proeffabriek in Suriname
                34   [The experiments of Dr. Fernandes in the experimental coffee-
                      factory in Surinam]. *W I G* 15:163-166. [66]   [*COL*]

HARDY, F.
57.023   TR   1936 Some aspects of cacao soil fertility in Trinidad.
57.027   TR   1943 Studies on aeration and water supply in some cacao soils of Trinidad.
57.032   TR   1953 The productivity of cacao soils and its improvement.

HARDY, F.; AKHURST, C. G. & GRIFFITH, G.
57.033   TB   1931 Studies in West Indian soils. (III)—The cacao soils of Tobago.

HARDY, F.; DUTHIE, D. W. & RODRIGUEZ, G.
57.035   TR   1936 STUDIES IN WEST INDIAN SOILS. (X)—THE CACAO AND FOREST SOILS OF
                      TRINIDAD. (B)—SOUTH CENTRAL DISTRICT.

HARDY, F.; McDONALD, J. A. & RODRIGUEZ, G.
57.037   GR   1932 Studies in West Indian soils. (IV)—The cacao soils of Grenada: their
                      origin, formation and chief characters.

HART, J. H.

59.016   TR   1908 The improvement of cacao planting in the West Indies. *W I B* 9(2):
                       162-165.   [*AMN*]

HAVORD, G.

57.045   TR   1961 Soil and land-use surveys. No. 13: A detailed soil and land capa-
                       bility survey of a cacao area in Trinidad.

HOY, HARRY E.

59.017   JM   1938 Blue Mountain coffee of Jamaica. *Econ Geogr* 14(4), Oct.: 409-412.
                                                                                       [*AGS*]

JOLLY, A. L.

59.018   TR   1942 Address delivered to Agricultural Society of Trinidad and Tobago,
                       setting forth results of work with respect to cocoa investigations.
                       Proc Agric Soc Trin Tob 42(2), June: 107-119. [66]   [*AMN*]
59.019   TR   1942 Cacao industry of Trinidad. *Trop Agric* 19(7), July: 127-129. [*AGS*]
59.020   GR   1942 Factors affecting field yields of cacao in Grenada. *Trop Agric*
                       19(12), Dec.: 234-243.   [*AGS*]
59.021   GR   1942 Uniformity trials on estate cacao fields in Grenada, B.W.I. *Trop
                       Agric* 19(9), Sept.: 167-174. [66]   [*AGS*]
59.022   TR   1950 Field performance of cacao cuttings. *Proc Agric Soc Trin Tob*
                       50(3), Sept.: 239-255.
59.023   TR   1956 Cocoa farm management. *J Agric Soc Trin Tob* 56(3), Sept.: 309-
                       349; 56(4), Dec.: 479-503.   [*AMN*]
59.024   TR   1959 The prospects of Trinidad cocoa. *J Agric Soc Trin Tob* 59(4), Dec.:
                       509-524.   [*AMN*]

JONES, JOSEPH

59.025   DM   1910 Notes on some cacaos at the Dominica Botanic Station. *W I B* 10(4):
                       337-343.   [*AMN*]

KERVEGANT, D.

59.026   MT   1932 Le caféier à la Martinique [Coffee growing in Martinique]. *B Ag
                       Gen Colon* 25(284), Nov.: 1653-1686. [5]   [*AGS*]

LANDALE, W. H.

59.027   JM   1938 Jamaica Blue Mountain coffee. *Can-W I Mag* 27(9), Sept.: 23-25. [*NYP*]

McDONALD, J. A.; HARDY, F. & RODRIGUEZ, G.

57.049   TR   1933 STUDIES IN WEST INDIAN SOILS. (VII)—THE CACAO SOILS OF TRINIDAD:
                       (A) MONTSERRAT DISTRICT.

MALINS-SMITH, W.

59.028   TR   1931 The cocoa industry of Trinidad. *Proc Agric Soc Trin Tob* 31(2),
                       Feb.: 61-71.   [*AMN*]

MILSTEAD, HARLEY PORTER

59.029   GR   1940 Cacao industry of Grenada. *Econ Geogr* 16(2), Apr.: 195-203. [*AGS*]

MONTSERIN, B. G.

59.030   TR   1949 The evolution of modern trends in cocoa cultivation. *Proc Agric
                       Soc Trin Tob* 49(4), Dec.: 283-291.   [*AMN*]

59.031   JM   1961 Processing of cocoa for the market. *Inf B Scient Res Coun* 2(1),
                  June: 2-4.   [*COL*]

MOORE, DAVID
59.032   TR   1956 A forester's thoughts on cocoa plantations. *J Agric Soc Trin Tob*
                  56(3), Sept.: 351-357. [64]   [*AMN*]

MYERS, J. G.
59.033   BG   1934 Observations on wild cacao and wild bananas in British Guiana.
                  Trop Agric 11(10), Oct.: 263-267. [41]   [*AGS*]

POUND, F. J.
59.034   GR   1938 Cacao cultivation in Grenada. *Trop Agric* 15(1), Jan.: 18-19. [*AGS*]
59.035   TR   1944 Government's scheme for cacao rehabilitation. *Proc Agric Soc Trin
                  Tob* 44(3), Sept.: 183-189. [66]   [*AMN*]

PYKE, E. E.
59.036   TR/   1935 Cocoa growing in the West Indies. *W I Comm Circ* 50(966), Oct. 10:
          GR   413-414.   [*NYP*]

REYNE, A.
59.037   SR   1924/ Geschiedenis der Cacaocultuur in Suriname [History of the cultiva-
                  25 tion of cocoa in Surinam]. *W I G* 6:1-20, 49-72, 107-126, 193-216.
                  [5]   [*COL*]

SEHEULT, L.
59.038   TR   1922 Notes on cacao experimental work at River Estate. *Proc Agric Soc
                  Trin Tob* 22(12), Dec.: 812-826.   [*AMN*]

SHEPHARD, C. Y.
59.039   TR   1927 Economic survey of the cacao industry of Trinidad, British West
                  Indies. *Econ Geogr* 3(2), Apr.: 239-258.   [*AGS*]
59.040   TR   The cacao industry of Trinidad; some economic aspects. *Trop Agric*
                  1932 9(4), Apr.: 95-100; 9(5), May: 145-152; 9(6), June: 185-195; 9(7),
                  July: 200-205; 9(8), Aug.: 236-243; 9(10), Oct.: 307-317; 9(11),
                  Nov.: 334-345;
                  1936 13(11), Nov.: 285-291; 13(12), Dec.: 327-329;
                  1937 14(1), Jan.: 10-16; 14(2), Feb.: 47-49; 14(3), Mar.: 87-89; 14(4),
                  Apr.: 121-122; 14(5), May: 128-130; 14(6), June: 172-174. [5, 57]
                                                                                [*AGS*]
59.041   TR   1932 Notes ... on cocoa in Trinidad, with a table showing the exports
                  from the colony from1797 to 1931....*Proc Agric Soc Trin Tob* 32(3),
                  Mar.: 101-104.   [*AMN*]
59.042   TR   1936 Cacao economics. *Proc Agric Soc Trin Tob* 36(11), Nov.: 385-399.
                                                                                [*AMN*]
59.043   TR   1936 Some economic aspects of cacao production in Trinidad with special
                  reference to the Montserrat district. *Trop Agric* 13(4), Apr.: 85-90.
                                                                                [*AGS*]
59.044   TR   1939 The cacao industry of Trinidad; the rehabilitation of an old field:
                  a progress report. *Trop Agric* 16(11), Nov.: 247-251.   [*AGS*]
59.045   TR   1955 Looking at cacao in Trinidad. *Caribbean* 8(7), Feb.: 146-151. [*COL*]
59.046   JM   1956 Seeing coffee in Jamaica. *J Agric Soc Trin Tob* 56(4), Dec.: 511-
                  525.   [*AMN*]

| 59.047 | TB | 1957 Cooperative cocoa fermentaries in Tobago. *J Agric Soc Trin Tob* 57(3), Sept.: 321-341. [48] [*AMN*] |

48.012 TR 1957 Postscript.

SMITH, G. W.
59.048 TR 1960 Cacao in Trinidad. *Wld Crops* 12(9), Sept.: 355-357.   [*AGS*]

SPOON, W.
59.049 SR 1956 Onderzoek van Surinaamse cacao in het laboratorium [Analyses of cacao beans from Surinam]. *Sur Landb* 4(6), Nov.-Dec.: 202-207.

STAHEL, GEROLD
59.050 SR 1942 CACAO. Paramaribo, 32p. (Departement Landbouproefstation. Mededeeling no. 10.)   [*AGS*]

SUCHTELEN, N. van
59.051 SR 1964 Vijftien jaar nieuwe cacaocultuur in Suriname, 1945-1960 [Fifteen years of the cacao-growing revival in Surinam, 1945-1960]. *N W I G* 43(3), May: 175-194. [66]   [*RIS*]

TEMPANY, Sir HAROLD A.
59.052 DM 1914 A study of the results of the manurial experiments with cacao conducted at the Botanic Station, Dominica. *W I B* 14(2): 81-119. [*AMN*]

THOMAS, CLIVE Y.
59.053 JM 1964 Coffee production in Jamaica. *Social Econ Stud* 13(1), Mar.: 188-217.   [*RIS*]
59.054 GR/ 1964 Projections of cocoa output in Grenada, Trinidad and Jamaica, TR/ 1960-1975. *Social Econ Stud* 13(1), Mar.: 94-117. [66]   [*RIS*] JM

TOPPER, B. F.
59.055 JM 1960 Cocoa: its role in Jamaican agriculture. *Inf B Scient Res Coun* 1(3), Dec.: 1-3.   [*RIS*]

VERTEUIL, J. de
59.056 GR 1927 Grenada's cocoa crop. *W I Comm Circ* 42(741), Feb.: 24: 65-66; 42(742), Mar. 10: 85-86; 42(743), Mar. 24: 104.   [*NYP*]

VERTEUIL, LUDOVIC de
59.057 TR 1930 Consumption of cocoa in Trinidad. *Proc Agric Soc Trin Tob* 30(1), Jan.: 13-15.   [*AMN*]

WASOWICZ, T.
59.058 TR 1952 Notes on the fertility of cacao soils: (a) Diminishing fertility of successive soil layers. (b) Effect of drying on soil fertility. *Trop Agric* 29(7-12), July-Dec.: 156-162. [57]   [*AGS*]

WATTS, Sir FRANCIS
59.059 TR 1926 A talk about coffee. *Proc Agric Soc Trin Tob* 26(2), Feb.: 93-105.   [*AMN*]

ZUIDEN, D. S. van
59.060 SR 1921/ De oudste cacao-aanplant in Suriname [The earliest cocoa cultiva-
22 tion in Surinam]. *W I G* 3:79-82.   [*COL*]

Chapter 60

BANANAS, CITRUS AND OTHER FRUIT

ADAM, DESIRE
60.001   FG   1935 Vue d'ensemble sur le mouvement bananier en Guyane Francaise [Survey of the banana-growing movement in French Guiana]. *Agron Colon* 24(206), Feb.: 48-55.   [*AGS*]

ALLNUTT, R. B.
60.002   LW   1950 Pineapple possibilities in the Leeward Islands. *Car Commn Mon Inf B* 4(3), Oct.: 535-537.   [*COL*]

BAIN, F. M.
60.003   TR   1944 A brief account of the results of the citrus experiments at St. Augustine Station. *Proc Agric Soc Trin Tob* 44(4), Dec.: 255-276; 1945 45(1), Mar.: 51-65.   [*AMN*]

BECKETT, J. EDGAR
60.004   BG   1926 Some rough notes on coconuts. *J Bd Agric Br Gui* 19(4), Oct.: 300-303.   [*AMN*]

BECKFORD, GEORGE
60.005   JM/   1964 Commentary: 'Crisis' in the West Indian banana industry. *Car Q*
        WW   10(2), June: 16-18.   [*RIS*]
60.006   JM/   1965 Issues in the Windward-Jamaica banana war. *New Wld Q* 2(1), Dead
        WW   Season: 3-11. [37]   [*RIS*]

BOSCH REITZ, P.
60.007   SR   1931/ Ananascultuur in Suriname [Pineapple cultivation in Surinam]. *W I G*
                32 13:281-284.   [*COL*]

BOVELL, J. R.
60.008   BB   1905 The fruit industry at Barbados. *W I B* 6(2): 99-108.   [*AMN*]

BROADWAY, W. E.
60.009   TR   1917 The present position of the citrus industry in Trinidad and Tobago. *Proc Agric Soc Trin Tob* 17(7), July: 253-258.   [*AMN*]

BURKE, J. HENRY

60.010   BH/   1956 CITRUS INDUSTRY OF BRITISH HONDURAS, JAMAICA, TRINIDAD. Wash-
        JM/   ington, U.S. Govt. Print. Off., 77p. (U.S. Dept. of Agriculture.
        TR   Foreign Agricultural Service. Foreign agricultural report, no. 88.)
                                                                          [*AGS*]

CADILLAT, R. M.

60.011   FA   1955 Apercu sur la production fruitière antillaise [Outline of Antillean
                  fruit production]. *Etud O-M* 38, Feb.: i-iv.   [*NYP*]

CAMPBELL, J. S.

60.012   TR   1957 Some observations on the fruit trees of Trinidad. *J Agric Soc Trin*
                  Tob 57(2), June: 209-222.   [*AMN*]

CASTELLI, ENRICO

60.013   TR   1937 The pawpaw (*Carica papaya*) in Trinidad agriculturally and in-
                  dustrially treated. *Proc Agric Soc Trin Tob* 37(1-3), Jan.-Mar.: 61-
                  75.   [*AMN*]
60.014   TR   1939 Conclusions arrived at after thorough investigation on the cultiva-
                  tion of the pawpaw and its industrial applications. *Proc Agric Soc*
                  Trin Tob 39(1-2), Jan.-Feb.: 25-32; 39(3), Mar.: 77-85; 39(4), Apr.:
                  129-131; 39(5), May: 165-170; 39(6), June: 219-220.   [*AMN*]

COLLIER, H. C.

60.015   BC   1940 Opportunity in juice. *Can-W I Mag* 29(8), Aug.: 13-15.   [*NYP*]

COOPER, ST. G. C.

60.016   TR   1956 Citrus production in the Santa Cruz and Diego Martin valleys of
                  Trinidad. *J Agric Soc Trin Tob* 56 suppl. (4), Dec.: 612-628. [*AMN*]

COZIER, EDWARD L.

60.017   JM   1957 Banana tour in Jamaica. *Caribbean* 11(2), Sept.: 26-29.   [*COL*]

DAHLGREN, B. E. & STANDLEY, PAUL C.

60.018   GC   1944 EDIBLE AND POISONOUS PLANTS OF THE CARIBBEAN REGION. Bureau of
                  Medicine and Surgery, Navy Department. Washington, U.S. Govt.
                  Print. Off., 102p. [41, 63]   [*AGS*]

DASH, J. SYDNEY

60.019   BG   1925 Banana cultivation. *Proc Agric Soc Trin Tob* 25(5), May: 169-187.
                                                                     [*AMN*]

DOLLY, JAMES O.

50.037   TR   1929 Hindrances other than diseases and pests to the successful work-
                  ing of cocoa and coconut estates.

DOUGLAS, CH.

60.020   SR   1929/ Ananas-kultuur in Suriname [The cultivation of pineapples in Suri-
               30   nam]. *W I G* 11:34-40.   [*COL*]

DUNEGAN, JOHN C.

60.021   JM   1957 The banana demonstration tour of Jamaica. *J Agric Soc Trin Tob*
                  57(4), Dec.: 459-482.   [*AMN*]

DU PUIS, H. G.

60.022   SR   1931/ De sinaasappel-cultuur in Suriname, hare mogelijkheden en finan-
                 32   cieele perspectieven en het belang daarvan voor de kolonie [The
                      cultivation of oranges in Surinam, its possibilities and financial
                      perspectives, and the importance thereof for the colony]. *W I G*
                      13:489-493.   [*COL*]

ELLINGTON, E. V.

28.145   JM   1961 Estimation of hypoglycin "A" in *Blighia sapida:* (ackee).

EVANS, G.

51.049   BC   1930 The possibility of establishing a trade in fruit and vegetable pro-
                      duce between Canada and the British West Indies.

FAHEY, HAROLD NEAL

60.023   TR   1950 Problems of the citrus planter. *Proc Agric Soc Trin Tob* 50(3),
                      Sept.: 259-265.   [*AMN*]

FAWCETT, WILLIAM

60.024   JM   1902 The banana industry in Jamaica. *W I B* 3(2): 153-171.   [*AMN*]

FENWICK, D. W.

60.025   TB   1964 The problem of rehabilitation of coconuts in Tobago. *J Agric Soc
                      Trin Tob* 64(1), Mar.: 75-95.   [*AMN*]

FLOCH, HERVE ALEXANDRE

65.015   FG   1955 A propos d'alimentation en Guyane Francaise. Elevage de porcs et
                      arbre à pain [On nutrition in French Guiana. Pig-raising and the
                      breadfruit tree].

30.012   FG   1956 Dosage des carotenes (Provitamines A) dans les fruits guyanais.
                      Intérêt du fruit de l' "aouara" *astrocaryum vulgare* [Amount of
                      čarotenes (Provitamins A) in Guianese fruit. Relevance of the fruit
                      "aouara" *astrocaryum vulgare*].

FLOCH, HERVE ALEXANDRE & GELARD, A.

30.015   FG   1954 Dosage de l'acide ascorbique dans des fruits guyanais [Amount of
                      ascorbic acid in Guianese fruits].

30.018   FG   1955 "La cerise ronde de Cayenne", *malpighia punicifolia L.* Sa richesse
                      exceptionnelle en vitamine C [The "round cherry of Cayenne,"
                      malpighia punicifolia L. Its exceptional richness in Vitamin C].

FREEMAN, WILLIAM G.

60.026   BB   1902 The aloe industry of Barbados. *W I B* 3(2): 178-197.   [*AMN*]
60.027   BC   1903 Ground nuts in the West Indies. *W I B* 4(2): 101-110.   [*AMN*]
60.028   TR   1922 The establishment of a fruit industry in Trinidad and Tobago. *Proc
                      Agric Soc Trin Tob* 22(1-3), Jan.-Mar.: 380-393.   [*AMN*]

GERVILLE-REACHE, LUCIEN

51.056   GD   1960 Possibilitiés d'exportation de banane vers l'U.R.S.S. [Possibilities
                      of banana export to the U.S.S.R.].

GREEVES, FITZ

60.029   BG   1922 The cultivation of the avocado pear. *J Bd Agric Br Gui* 15(2),
                      Apr.: 77-81.   [*AMN*]

GREIG, W.
60.030   TR   1905 The cocoa-nut industry of Trinidad. *W I B* 6(2): 149-156.   [*AMN*]

GUPPY, JOHN LECHMERE
60.031   TR   1932 Cashew nuts: as a possible local agricultural industry. *Proc Agric Soc Trin Tob* 32(3), Mar.: 89-91. [66]   [*AMN*]

HAARER, A. E.
60.032   BC   1955 More bananas. *New Commonw,* British Caribbean Supplement, 30(11), Nov. 28: xiii-xiv.   [*AGS*]

HARDY, F. & RODRIGUEZ, G.
60.033   TR   1935 Grapefruit investigations in Trinidad. *Trop Agric* 12(8), Aug.: 205-215. [57]   [*AGS*]

HARRISON, Sir JOHN B. & BANCROFT, C. K.
60.034   BG   1915 The cultivation of limes. *J Bd Agric Br Gui* 8(4), Sept.: 135-142;
                      9(1), Nov.: 4-10;
                1916 9(3), May: 122-129; 10(1), Oct.: 6-8.   [*AMN*]

HARRISON, Sir JOHN B. & FOWLER, F.
60.035   BG   1913 The profitable planning of coconut plantations. *J Bd Agric Br Gui* 6(3), Jan.: 113-116.   [*AMN*]

HART, ANSELL
51.063   JM   1954 The banana in Jamaica: export trade.

HASSALL, C. H. & REYLE, K.
28.273   JM   1955 The toxicity of the ackee (*Blighia sapida*) and its relationship to the vomiting sickness of Jamaica.

HOY, DON R.
60.036   GD   1962 The banana industry of Guadeloupe, French West Indies. *Social Econ Stud* 11(3), Sept.: 260-266.   [*RIS*]

HOYER, W. M.
60.037   CU   1947 Oranje appelen [Oranges]. *W I G* 28:236-238.   [*COL*]

HUBBARD, L. C.
60.038   BG   1932 A new industry for British Guiana. *Can-W I Mag* 21(8), July: 259.
                                                                                            [*NYP*]

JAMES, PRESTON E.
60.039   TR   1926 Geographic factors in the Trinidad coconut industry. *Econ Geogr* 2(1), Jan.: 108-125.   [*AGS*]

JONES. T. A.
60.040   JM   1961 Consider the coconut. *Inf B Scient Res Coun* 1(4), Mar.: 1-3.   [*RIS*]

JUNKER, L.
60.041   SR   1946 De citruscultuur in Suriname [The cultivation of citrus in Surinam]. *W I G* 27:39-60.   [*COL*]

KEPNER, CHARLES D. & SOOTHILL, JAY HENRY

60.042   JM   1935 THE BANANA EMPIRE: A CASE STUDY IN ECONOMIC IMPERIALISM. New
York, Vanguard Press, 392p.   [*NYP*]

KESLER, C. K.

60.043   CU   1931/Twee populaire vruchten van Curacao: oranjeappelen en pinda's
              32 [Two popular fruits of Curacao: oranges and peanuts]. *W I G* 13:
241-248. [51]   [*COL*]

60.044   SR   1932/ Bacoven in Suriname [Bacoven in Surinam]. *W I G* 14:216-222. [66]
              33   [*COL*]

KNOWLTON, JOHN

60.045   DM   1945 Citrus gowing in Dominica. *Can-W I Mag* 35(7), Aug.-Sept.: 82-84.
                [*NYP*]

KNOWLTON, JOHN S.

60.046   DM   1932 Dominica fruit and the Canadian market. *Can-W I Mag* 21(7), June:
228.   [*NYP*]

KNOWLTON, JOHN W.

60.047   DM   1931 Citrus cultivation in Dominica. *Can-W I Mag* 20(5), Apr.: 163. [*NYP*]

LAM, A. L.

60.048   SL   1959 St. Lucia's banana industry. *Caribbean* 13(8), Aug.: 154-155. [*COL*]

LIEMS, J. A.

60.049   SR   1922/ Het klein-landbouw bedrijf en de vruchten cultuur in Suriname [Small
              23   scale agriculture and fruit cultures in Surinam]. *W I G* 4:625-638. [66]
                [*COL*]

60.050   SR   1929/ Sinaasappel-cultuur in Suriname [Cultivation of oranges in Surinam].
              31   *W I G* 11:449-460 (1929/30); 12:179-186 (1930/31).   [*COL*]

LUCAS, G. L.

60.051   GC   1907 Pine-apple growing in the West Indies. *W I B* 8(2): 151-157.   [*AMN*]

LUCIE-SMITH, M. N.

60.052   TR   1949 Modern trends in citrus cultivation. *Proc Agric Soc Trin Tob* 49(4),
Dec.: 295-309.   [*AMN*]

60.053   TR/   1950 Extracts from a report on a visit to the lime cultivations of Dominica,
        DM   B.W.I. *Proc Agric Soc Trin Tob* 50(1), Mar.: 103-109.   [*AMN*]

60.054   TR   1951 The cultivation of West Indian limes. *J Agric Soc Trin Tob* 51(2),
June: 354-366.   [*AMN*]

McFARLANE, DENNIS

60.055   BC   1964 The foundations for future production and export of West Indian
citrus. *Social Econ Stud* 13(1), Mar.: 118-156.   [*RIS*]

60.056   BC   1964 The future of the banana industry in the West Indies: an assessment
of supply prospects for 1965 and 1975. *Social Econ Stud* 13(1),
Mar.: 38-93.   [*RIS*]

MENKMAN, W. R.

60.057   SR   1930/ Heeft in Suriname een vruchtenbedrijf kans van slagen [Has fruit
              31   cultivation in Surinam a chance of success]? *W I G* 12:503-509. [66]
                [*COL*]

60.058   SR   1934/ De hervatting van de Surinaamsche bacovencultuur [The resumption
                     35 of the cultivation of bacoven in Surinam]. *W I G* 16:347-360.   [66]
                                                                                          [*COL*]

            MONTSERIN, B. G.
60.059   TR   1952 The cultivation of bananas and plantains. *J Agric Soc Trin Tob*
                     52(2), June: 243-268.   [*AMN*]
60.060   TR   1956 Banana growing in Trinidad and Tobago. *J Agric Soc Trin Tob* 56(4),
                     Dec.: 527-575.   [*AMN*]

            MURRAY, D. B.
60.061   TR   1950 Coconut growing in Trinidad and Tobago. *Proc Agric Soc Trin Tob*
                     50(2), June: 193-200.   [*AMN*]

            OLIVIER, SYDNEY, 1st Baron RAMSDEN
51.110   BC   1902 The regulation of the quality of exported fruit.

            OLLEY, PHILIP P.
60.062   JM   1926 Jamaica—for Canadian fruit growers. *Can-W I Mag* 15(10), Aug.: 233,
                     236.   [*NYP*]

            OSBORNE, R. E. & HEWITT, C. W.
60.063   JM   1963 The effect of frequency of application of nitrogen, phosphate, and
                     potash fertilizers on Lacatan bananas in Jamaica. *Trop Agric* 40(1),
                     Jan.: 1-8.   [*AGS*]

            OUDSCHANS DENTZ, FRED
41.177   SR   1942 Bananen en bacoven [Bananas and bacoven].

            PANHUYS, L. C. van
60.064   SR   1936/ De overbrenging van de banaan en de bacove uit Afrika naar tropisch
                     37 Amerika in het begin van de 16de eeuw [The importation of the
                     banana and the bacove from Africa into tropical America in the be-
                     ginning of the 16th century]. *W I G* 18:207-212.   [5]   [*COL*]

            PHILLIS, E.
60.065   TR   1946 An outline for a coconut selection scheme. *Proc Agric Soc Trin Tob*
                     46(2), June: 155-159.   [*AMN*]

            POTTER, THOMAS I.
60.066   TR   1939 Fruit: "native and imported" in the island of Trinidad, B.W.I. *Proc
                     Agric Soc Trin Tob* 39(9), Sept.: 337-342; 39(10), Oct.: 364-368;
                     39(12), Dec.: 475-500.   [*AMN*]

            POTTER, THOMAS J.
60.067   TR   1931 Citrus cultivation in Trinidad. *Can-W I Mag* 20(10), Sept.: 334, 342.
                                                                                          [*NYP*]

            POUND, F. J. et al.
60.068   TR   1949 Fruit and vegetables: report of Committee on Export Possibilities.
                     Proc Agric Soc Trin Tob 49(1), Mar.: 57-60.   [*AMN*]

POWELL, CLARK

60.069   BC   1928 West Indies grapefruit. *W I Comm Circ* 43(786), Nov. 15: 443-444.
                  [*NYP*]

60.070   TR   1928 Citrus fruit industry. *Proc Agric Soc Trin Tob* 28(6), June: 249-267.
                  [*AMN*]

ROBINSON, H. E.

48.011   TR   1954 The Cooperative Citrus Growers Association: a record of cooperation and progress.

RUDOLPH, N. A.

60.071   JM   1935 The pimento industry of Jamaica. *Can-W I Mag* 25(1), Dec.: 7-9, 32.
                  [*NYP*]

SAMSON, J. A.

60.072   SR   1956 HANDLEIDING VOOR DE CITRUSCULTUUR IN SURINAME [MANUAL ON CITRUS
CULTIVATION IN SURINAM]. [Paramaribo] Surinam, Landbouwproef-
station, 77p. (Mededeling no. 19.)

SEAFORTH, COMPTON E.

60.073   JM   1962 The ackee—Jamaica's national fruit. *Inf B Scient Res Coun* 3(3),
Dec.: 51-53. [30]   [*RIS*]

SHARP, G. G. R.

60.074   BC   1955 Caribbean citrus—second to none. *New Commonw* British Caribbean
Supplement 30(11), Nov. 28: xii-xiii.   [*AGS*]

60.075   BC   1956 Citrus fruit. *Statist* Sept.: 48-49.

SHARP, T. H.

60.076   JM   1907 How to encourage orange trees to bear early in Jamaica. *W I B* 8(2):
149-150.   [*AMN*]

SIMMONDS, N. W.

60.077   TR   1951 Prospects of banana growing in Trinidad. *J Agric Soc Trin Tob*
51(4), Dec.: 418-423.   [*AMN*]

60.078   GC   1959 BANANAS. London, Longmans, 466p.   [*AGS*]

60.079   BC   1960 The growth of post-war West Indian banana trades. *Trop Agric*
37(2), Apr.: 79-85. [51]   [*AGS*]

SMITH, W. E.

60.080   JM   1906 The fruit industry of Jamaica. *Proc Agric Soc Trin Tob* 6:18-34.
                  [*AMN*]

STOLLMEYER, A. V.

60.081   TR   1922 Trinidad's fruit growing possibilities. *Proc Agric Soc Trin Tob*
22(1-3), Jan.-Mar.: 394-405.   [*AMN*]

60.082   TR   1927 Impressions on the prospects of the fruit industry. *Proc Agric Soc
Trin Tob* 27(10), Oct.: 439-447.   [*AMN*]

60.083   TR   1929 Grape fruit industry. *Proc Agric Soc Trin Tob* 29(8), Aug.: 244-250.
                  [*AMN*]

STONE, E. F.

65.074   TR   1935 Poultry raising in citrus orchards.

TAI, EGBERT A.

60.084   TR   1953 The citrus investigation programme of the Department of Agriculture.
              J Agric Soc Trin Tob 53(4), Dec.: 387-396.   [*AMN*]

60.085   TR   1953 A quick look at Trinidad's citrus industry. *J Agric Soc Trin Tob*
              53(3), Sept.: 363-373.   [*AMN*]

TALIAFERRO, REBECCA M.

60.086   GC   1931 THE BANANA INDUSTRY OF THE CARIBBEAN. M.A. thesis, Clark Univers-
              ity, 111p.   [*AGS*]

TOMSON, C. L.

60.087   SR   1931 De beteekenis van de vruchtenteelt voor Suriname [The importance
              of fruit growing for Surinam]. *In* INDISCH GENOOTSCHAP. VERGADERING
              VAN 17 DECEMBER 1930, BLS. 135-158. The Hague, Nijhoff, p.135-
              150.   [*AGS*]

WALTERS, E. A.

60.088   SL   1928 St. Lucia's banana industry. *Trop Agric* 5(10), Oct.: 247-249; 5(11),
              Nov.: 284-286.   [*AGS*]

WATTS, Sir FRANCIS

60.089   AT   1901 Pine apple cultivation in Antigua. *W I B* 2(2): 113-121.   [*AMN*]

WHARTON, R. VERNON

60.090   TR   1930 Notes on coconut cultivation at Point Galera. *Proc Agric Soc Trin
              Tob* 30(7), July: 252-259.   [*AMN*]

WILLIAMS, R. F.

60.091   BC   1956 Bananas. *Statist* Sept.: 51.

WILLIAMS, R. O.

60.092   TR   1933 The citrus fruit industry as a substitute for cacao. *Proc Agric Soc
              Trin Tob* 33(8), Aug.: 259-264.   [*AMN*]

Chapter 61

COTTON

ABBOTT, GEORGE C.
61.001   BC   1964 The collapse of the sea island cotton industry in the West Indies. *Social Econ Stud* 13(1), Mar.: 157-187.   [*RIS*]

ASPINALL, Sir ALGERNON E.
61.002   BC   1935 The sea island cotton harvest. *W I Comm Circ* 50(961), Aug. 1: 311-312.   [*NYP*]

BALLOU, H. A.
61.003   SV   1929 St. Vincent cotton. *Trop Agric* 6(10), Oct.: 292-294.

BEASLEY, CYRIL GEORGE & SCHOUTEN, SWITHIN ADALBERT
61.004   MS   [1953?] Montserrat cotton industry enquiry. [n.p.] 66p.

BOONE, RAY C. P.
61.005   GC   1927 Le coton aux Antilles [Cotton-growing in the Antilles]. *B Ag Gen Colon* 20(224): 765-774.   [*AGS*]

BOVELL, J. R.
61.006   BB   1907 Recent results in the cultivation of cotton at Barbados. *W I B* 8(2): 173-178.   [*AMN*]
61.007   BB   1908 Recent results in the cultivation of cotton at Barbados. *W I B* 9(3): 195-201.   [*AMN*]

CLARKE, F. J.
48.005   BB   1908 Origin and establishment of the Barbados co-operative cotton factory.

COLLIER, H. C.
61.008   BG   1948 Sea Island—the world's best cotton. *Can-W I Mag* 38(8), Aug.: 10-11, 13.   [*NYP*]

GOODMAN, EILEEN
61.009   BC   1938 The sea-island cotton industry. *Can-W I Mag* 27(11), Nov.: 29-30.   [*NYP*]

HARLAND, S. C.

61.010   SV   1918 Manurial experiments with sea island cotton in St. Vincent in 1917-
                       18. *W I B* 17(2): 69-79.   [*AMN*]

61.011   BC   1919 The improvement of the yield of sea island cotton in the West Indies
                       by the isolation of pure strains. *W I B* 17(3): 145-161; 17(4): 210-
                       225.   [*AMN*]

61.012   GC   1920 Studies of inheritance in cotton. 1: The inheritance of corolla
                       colour. *W I B* 18(1-2): 13-19.   [*AMN*]

61.013   SV   [1921?] Manurial experiments with sea island cotton in St. Vincent in 1918-
                       19, with some notes on the control of certain diseases by spraying.
                       W I B 18(3): 20-33.   [*AMN*]

61.014   TR   1925 Cotton in Trinidad. *Proc Agric Soc Trin Tob* 25(3), Mar.: 92-98.
                                                                                         [*AMN*]

HARRISON, Sir JOHN B.

61.015   BG   1908 Cotton cultivation in British Guiana. *W I B* 9(3):213-214.   [*AMN*]

HUTCHINSON, J. B.

41.147 JM   1943 The cottons of Jamaica.

41.148 TR   1943 Notes on the native cottons of Trinidad.

61.016   BC   1945 West Indian sea island cotton. *Can-W I Mag* 35(1), Jan.-Feb.: 6-9.
                                                                                         [*NYP*]

HUTCHINSON, J. B. & STEPHENS, S. G.

61.017   TB   1944 Note on the "French" or "small-seeded" cotton grown in the West
                       Indies in the 18th century. *Trop Agric* 21(7), July: 123-125.   [5]
                                                                                         [*AGS*]

KELSICK, R. E.

61.018   SK   1918 Some observations on the relation of lint length to rainfall. *W I B*
                       17(2): 79-82.   [*AMN*]

MASON, T. G.

61.019   SV   [1921?] A note on some recent researches on the cotton plant in the West
                       Indies, with special reference to St. Vincent. *W I B* 18(4): 184-197.
                                                                                         [*AMN*]

MORRIS, DANIEL

61.020   BC   1903 Cotton-growing in the West Indies. *W I B* 4(1): 28-32.   [*AMN*]

MORRIS, DANIEL & BOVELL, J. R.

61.021   BC   1904 Sea island cotton in the United States and in the West Indies. *W I B*
                       4(4): 287-325.   [*AMN*]

NOWELL, W.

61.022   SK/   1914 Two physiological affections of sea island cotton in the West Indies.
         NV/   *W I B* 14(4): 304-317.   [*AMN*]
         SC

PYTTERSEN, TJ.

61.023   SR   1923/ Suriname en da katoen cultuur [Surinam and the cotton culture].
                 24   *W I G* 5:405-420.   [*COL*]

SANDS, W. N.

61.024	SV	1907 Sea island cotton cultivation at St. Vincent. *W I B* 8(2): 183-186. [*AMN*]
61.025	SV/ GN	1908 Recent results of the cultivation of sea island cotton at St. Vincent. *W I B* 9(3): 209-212. [*AMN*]
61.026	BC	1937 The sea island cotton industry. *W I Comm Circ* 52(1003), Mar. 11: 83-84; 52(1004), Mar. 25: 107-108. [*NYP*]

SHENFIELD, A. A.

61.027	BC	[n.d.] REPORT ON THE MARKETING OF SEA ISLAND COTTON. [St. John's?] Antigua, Antigua Printery, 25p.

SKEETE, C. C.

61.028	BC	1936 The West Indian Sea Island Cotton Association: its formation and work. *Proc Agric Soc Trin Tob* 36(7), July: 227-232; 36(9-10), Sept.-Oct.: 350-353. [*AMN*]

SMITH, LONGFIELD

61.029	SC	1921 SEA ISLAND COTTON IN ST. CROIX. Washington, U. S. Govt. Print. Off., 14p. (Virgin Islands Agricultural Experiment Station bulletin no. 1.) [*NYP*]

STEPHENS, S. G.

61.030	BC	1944 Cotton growing in the West Indies during the 18th and 19th centuries. *Trop Agric* 21(2), Feb.: 23-29. [5] [*AGS*]

STEVENSON, G. C.

61.031	BG	1949 Some historical notes on the cultivation of cotton in British Guiana. *Trop Agric* 26(1-6), Jan.-June: 67-68. [5] [*AGS*]

THORNTON, THOMAS

61.032	BC	1908 Progress of the sea island cotton industry in the West Indies. *W I B* 9(3):215-219. [*AMN*]

TODD, JOHN A.

61.033	BC	1929 Cotton growing in the West Indies. *W I Comm Circ* 44(811), Oct. 31: 423-424; 44(812), Nov. 14: 449. [*NYP*]
61.034	MS/ SV	1930 Sea island cotton. *Trop Agric* 7(7), July: 190-191. [*AGS*]

WARNEFORD, F. H. S.

58.114	AT	1950 Antigua's major industries.

WATTS, Sir FRANCIS

61.035	LW	1907 Cotton industry in the Leeward Islands. *W I B* 8(2): 179-182. [*AMN*]
61.036	LW	1908 The cotton industry in the Leeward Islands. *W I B* 9(3): 202-208. [*AMN*]
61.037	LW	1908 Experiments on the improvement of cotton by seed selection in the Leeward Islands. *W I B* 9(3): 220-234. [*AMN*]
61.038	LW	1909 Cotton selection in the Leeward Islands, 1907-8. *W I B* 10(1): 79-92. [*AMN*]
61.039	SV	1919 Concerning cotton in St. Vincent and the steps which must be taken to safeguard the industry. *W I B* 17(3): 167-176. [*AMN*]

Chapter 62

RICE

BAYLEY, PETER

62.001 BG 1956 Rice production and marketing in British Guiana. *Caribbean* 9(12), July: 271-272. [*COL*]

BECKETT, J. EDGAR

62.002 BG 1922 Rice *(Oryza spp.) J Bd Agric Br Gui* 15(4), Oct.: 213-215. [*AMN*]

BENSON, E. G.

62.003 TR 1951 The rice industry. *J Agric Soc Trin Tob* 51(1), Mar.: 114-117. [*AMN*]

BRAINE, BERNARD

62.004 BG/ 1953 Caribbean contribution to relief of world rice shortage. *New Com-*
        TR   *monw* 25(1), Jan. 5: 60-61. [66] [*AGS*]

BRANDON, H. G.

62.005 SR 1932/ Proefneming voor machinale hoeverijstcultuur op de plantage
            33   Guadeloup in Suriname in 1925-26 [Experiments with mechanical field-rice cultivation on the Guadeloup plantation in Surinam in 1925-26]. *W I G* 14:81-98. [66] [*COL*]

CAMPO, E. J. à

62.006 SR 1955 Het Wageningen project [The Wageningen project]. *Oost West* 48(9): 27-29. [66]

CODD, L. E. W.; PETERKIN, E. M.; FOLLETT-SMITH, R. R.
SQUIRE, F. A. & MARTYN, E. B.

62.007 BG 1933 RICE IN BRITISH GUIANA 1927-32. Georgetown, British Guiana Dept. of Agriculture, 48p. (Rice bulletin no. 1.) [*NYP*]

COYAUD, YVES

62.008 FG 1952 Les possibilités rizicoles de la Guyane Francaise [The rice-growing possibilities in French Guiana]. *Agron Trop* 7(4): 355-366. [66] [*AGS*]

DASH, J. SYDNEY

62.009 BG 1936 The rice industry of British Guiana. *Can-W I Mag* 25(9), Aug.: 7-9. [*NYP*]

FERRER, V. O.
67.004   BG   1951 Eye estimation of paddy yields in British Guiana.

FRAMPTON, A. de K.
62.010   BG   1934 The Essequibo autumn rice crop. *Agric J Br Gui* 5(3): 214-218. [*AGS*]

FREITAS, G. V. de
62.011   BH   1958 Rice—the modern way in British Honduras. *Caribbean* 12(2), Sept.:
                      34-36.   [*COL*]

GADD, HAROLD E.
62.012   BG   1951 Some problems of mechanised rice cultivation in British Guiana.
                      Timehri 4th ser., 1(30), Nov.: 41-47.

GIGLIOLI, E. G.
62.013   BG   1959 Mechanized rice production at the Mahaicony-Abary Scheme, British
                      Guiana. *Trop Agric* 36(1), Jan.: 2-14. [66]   [*AGS*]

GRIST, D. H.
62.014   BG   1954 Rice in British Guiana. *Wld Crops* 6(9), Sept.: 367-371.   [*AGS*]

HARRISON, Sir JOHN B.
62.015   BG   1908 Experiments with rice at British Guiana. *W I B* 9(3): 246-252. [*AMN*]

HUGGINS, H. D.
62.016   BG   1941 An economic. survey of rice farming in West Demerara. *Trop Agric*
                      18(2): 26-32. [8]   [*RIS*]

JONES, B. HOWELL
62.017   BG   1907 Experimental rice cultivation in British Guiana. *W I B* 8(2): 187-190.
                                                                                [*AMN*]

KENNARD, C. P.
28.306   BG   1911 Rice fields and malaria.

KUNDU, A.
62.018   BC   1954 Rice in the British Caribbean Islands and British Guiana, 1950-
                      1975. *Social Econ Stud* 13(2), June: 243-281. [51]   [*RIS*]

MINETT, E. P.
28.374   BG   1921 Agriculture versus malaria.

O'LOUGHLIN, CARLEEN
62.019   BG   1958 The rice sector in the economy of British Guiana. *Social Econ Stud*
                      7(2), June: 115-143.   [*RIS*]

OUDSCHANS DENTZ, FRED
62.020   SR   1930/ Iets uit de geschiedenis van de rijstcultuur in Suriname [Some facts
              31 from the history of rice culture in Surinam]. *W I G* 12:107-108. [5]
                                                                                [*COL*]

PORTERES, ROLAND
62.021   GG   1949 Les Guyanes, centre secondaire nouveau de variation des riz cultives

(*Oryza saliva L.*) [The Guianas, a new secondary center of experimental rice cultivation (*Oryza saliva L.*)]. *Agron Trop* 4(7-8), July-Aug.: 379-404.   [*AGS*]

ROBERTS, WALTER

62.022   BG   1959 Rice in British Guiana: a preliminary review. *Timehri* 4th ser., no. 38, Sept.: 25-34.   [66]   [*AMN*]

ROSHER, PETER H.

62.023   TR   1957 Means of increasing rice production in Trinidad. *J Agric Soc Trin Tob* 57(3), Sept.: 343-365.   [*AMN*]

SMITH, RAYMOND THOMAS

62.024   BG   1957 Economic aspects of rice production in an East Indian community in British Guiana. *Social Econ Stud* 6(4), Dec.: 502-522.   [12, 47]
                                                                                                                [*RIS*]

VERKADE-CARTIER van DISSEL, E. F.

62.025   SR   1940 De mechanische rijstcultuur in Suriname [Mechanical rice cultivation in Surinam]. *W I G* 22:166-169.   [*COL*]

VOS, L. de

62.026   SR   1956 De opslag van padi in Suriname. 3: Methoden van opslag [Storage of rough rice in Suriname. 3: Methods of storage). *Sur Landb* 4(6), Nov.-Dec.: 208-225.

WIT, THEODORUS PETRUS MARIA de

62.027   SR   1957 The Wageningen rice scheme in Suriname. *Trop Agric* 34(1), Jan.: 29-40.   [66]   [*AGS*]

62.028   SR   1960 THE WAGENINGEN RICE PROJECT IN SURINAM; A STUDY ON THE DEVELOPMENT OF A MECHANIZED RICE FARMING PROJECT IN THE WET TROPICS. The Hague, Mouton, 293p. (Thesis, Landbouwhogeschool, Wageningen.)

Chapter 63

OTHER AGRICULTURAL PRODUCTS

BARRY, JOHN

49.002 JM/   1946 Mulberry planting.
         TR

BATHGATE, H. NORMAN

63.001   BC   1940 Market possibilities for West Indian honey. *Proc Agric Soc Trin Tob*
                 40(3), Sept.: 223-226.   [*AMN*]

BAXTER, G. D.

57.002 BG   1959 Some problems of jute cultivation on the coastland soils of British
                 Guiana.

BECKETT, J. EDGAR

63.002   BG   1912 The minor industries. *Timehri* 3d ser., 2(19A), July: 71-79.   [*AMN*]

BITTER, B. A.

63.003   NA   1950 Geschiedenis van de bijenteelt op de Nederlandse Antillen [History
                 of apiculture on the Dutch Antilles]. *W I G* 31:170-174. [5]   [*COL*]

BRUCE, S. N.

63.004   BG   1926 A local industry. *J Bd Agric Br Gui* 19(3), July: 180-184. [65] [*AMN*]

CAMPBELL, J. S.

63.005   GC   1958 Commercial tomato growing in the West Indies. *J Agric Soc Trin
                 Tob* 58(2), June: 158-170.   [*AMN*]

CAMPBELL, J. S. & BHARATH, S.

63.006   TR   1960 The improvement of cultivation methods in tomato growing in Trini-
                 dad. *J Agric Soc Trin Tob* 60(4), Dec.: 443-460.   [*AMN*]

CAMPBELL, J. S. & GOODING, H. J.

63.007   TR   1962 Recent developments in the production of food crops in Trinidad.
                 Trop Agric 39(4), Oct.: 261-270.   [*RIS*]

CARR, A. B.

63.008   TR   1916 Yam cultivation as a minor industry. *Proc Agric Soc Trin Tob* 16(5),
                 May: 157-164.   [*AMN*]

CHAPMAN, T. & SQUIRE, H. A.

63.009   TR   1964 An attempt to grow the Irish potato commercially in Trinidad. *J Agric Soc Trin Tob* 64(3), Sept.: 321-329.   [*AMN*]

COLLENS, A. E.

63.010   AT/   1918 Notes on thymol content of horse-mint *(Monarda punctata)* and ajo-
          SK/   wan seed *(Carum copticum). W I B* 17(1): 50-55.   [*NYP*]
          MS

COLLIER, H. C.

63.011   JM/   1939 The economic use of cassava. *Can-W I Mag* 28(1), Jan.: 31-32. [*NYP*]
          SV

63.012   BG/   1942 East goes west in cassava. *Can-W I Mag* 31(1), Jan.: 11.13-14.   [13]
          JM/   [*NYP*]
          SV

CONNELL, ARTHUR R.

63.013   SV   1954 The world's finest arrowroot in St. Vincent. *Can-W I Mag* 44(4),
                    Apr.: 3-5.   [*NYP*]

COX, H. E.

63.014   JM   1907 Tea in Jamaica. *W I B* 8(3): 254-259.   [*AMN*]

CUNLIFFE, R. S.

63.015   TR   1914 Vegetable growing. *Proc Agric Soc Trin Tob* 14(1), Jan.: 10-22. [*AMN*]

DAHLGREN, B. E. & STANDLEY, PAUL C.

60.018   GC   1944 Edible and poisonous plants of the Caribbean region.

EMOND, E. A.

63.016   TR   1938 Report of the inspector of apiaries for the year 1937. *Proc Agric Soc Trin Tob* 38(4), Apr.: 107-111.   [*AMN*]

63.017   TR   1939 Beekeeping as an agricultural occupation. *Proc Agric Soc Trin Tob* 39(3), Mar.: 67-71.   [*AMN*]

63.018   TR   1940 Bees and beekeeping with reference to agriculture. *Proc Agric Soc Trin Tob* 40(4), Dec.: 339-343.   [*AMN*]

EVANS, G.

51.049   BC   1930 The possibility of establishing a trade in fruit and vegetable prod-
                    uce between Canada and the British West Indies.

FAWCETT, WILLIAM

63.019   JM   1907 Tobacco in Jamaica. *W I B* 8(2): 209-228.   [*AMN*]

FFRENCH-MULLEN, M. D.

63.020   BG   1959 Experiments in the cultivation, harvesting and retting of jute in
                    British Guiana. *Trop Sci* 1(4): 231-285;
                    1960 2(1-2): 1-35.   [*AGS*]

FLOCH, HERVE ALEXANDRE

30.013   FG   1956 Dosage des carotenes (Provitamines A) dans les legumes guyanais.
                    Intérêt de l'"épinard de Cayenne" *basella cordifolia* [Proportion of
                    carotene (Provitamins A) in the Guianese vegetables. Relevance of
                    "Cayenne spinach" *basella cordifolia*].

FURNESS, ALAN

5.052   JM   1962 The Jamaican coffee boom and John Mackeson.

GOODING, H. J.

63.021   BC   1960 Yields of West Indian maize. *Trop Agric* 37(4), Oct.: 257-264.   [*AGS*]

63.022   TR   1961 Irish potatoes *(Solanum tuberosum)* in Trinidad. *J Agric Soc Trin Tob* 61(2), June: 193-211.   [*AMN*]

GOULDING, ERNEST

63.023   BC   1924 Cultivation of sisal hemp (the industry in the W.I. and Guiana). *W I Comm Circ* 39(674), July 31: 303-304.   [*NYP*]

GRAHAM, HORACE D.

63.024   JM   1963 The castor oil plant: a potential minor industry? *Inf B Scient Res Coun* 3(4), Mar.: 74-76.   [*RIS*]

HANDLER, JEROME S.

63.025   BB   1965 The history of arrowroot production in Barbados and the Chalky Mount Arrowroot Growers' Association, a peasant marketing experiment that failed. *J Barb Mus Hist Soc* 31(3), Nov.: 131-152.   [48]
   [*RIS*]

HARDY, F.

57.021   MS   1922 Studies in West Indian soils. (II)-The soils of Montserrat, their natural history and chief physical properties, and the relationship of these to the problem of die-back of lime trees.

HARRISON, Sir JOHN B. & BANCROFT, C. K.

63.026   BG   1917 Food plants of British Guiana. *J Bd Agric Br Gui* 10:143-177.   [30]
   [*AMN*]

HARRISON, Sir JOHN B.; BANCROFT, C. K. & WARD, R.

63.027   BG   1916 Experiments with rice, coconuts, rubber, coffee and cacao: crops of 1914. *J Bd Agric Br Gui* 9(3):130-145.   [*AMN*]

HART, J. H.

63.028   BC   1902 The preparation of essential oils in the West Indies. *W I B* 3(2): 171-178.   [*AMN*]

63.029   TR   1904 Report on bee-keeping in Trinidad. *Proc Agric Soc Trin Tob* 5:26-30.
   [*AMN*]

HENRY, C. C.

63.030   JM   1940 Perseverance ripens the tomato in Jamaica. *Can-W I Mag* 29(5), May: 10-11.   [*NYP*]

HODNETT, G. E. & CAMPBELL, J. S.

63.031   TR   1963 Effect of spacing on yield of cabbage and lettuce in Trinidad. *Trop Agric* 40(2), Apr.: 103-108.   [*AGS*]

HOPKINS, E. B.

49.043   JM   1925 The silk worm industry in Jamaica.

JEFFERS, BERT

63.032   DM   1945 The flavourful orchid of Dominica. *Can-W I Mag* 35(7), Aug.-Sept.:
                 85-86.   [*NYP*]

JUNKER, L.

63.033   SR   1931/ Cassavecultuur in Suriname [Cassava cultivation in Surinam]. *W I G*
                 32 13:30-36.   [*COL*]

LALLA, C. D.

63.034   TR   1927 An afternoon with the honey-bee. *Proc Agric Soc Trin Tob* 27(7),
                 July: 311-323.   [*AMN*]
63.035   TR   1931 Facts about the honey bee industry. *Proc Agric Soc Trin Tob* 31(9),
                 Sept.: 331-334.   [*AMN*]
63.036   TR   1946 Bee-culture as a profitable hobby. *Proc Agric Soc Trin Tob* 46(3),
                 Sept.: 211-221.   [*AMN*]

LARTER, L. N. H.

63.037   JM   1947 Maize population and yield in Jamaica. *Trop Agric* 24(1-3), Jan.-
                 Mar.: 19-27.   [*AGS*]

MILLARD, I. S.

66.103 JM   1950 The village schoolmaster as community development leader.

MILLER, R. J.

63.038   JM   1907 Cultivation and preparation of Jamaica ginger. *W I B* 8(3): 264-
                 266.   [*AMN*]

OYELESE, JOHN OLADEJO

63.039   BB   1964 THE CULTIVATION OF FOOD CROPS IN BARBADOS. M.A. thesis, McGill
                 University, 179p.

POTTER, THOMAS I.

63.040   TR   1930 Some Trinidadian "honey plants." *Proc Agric Soc Trin Tob* 30(5),
                 May: 173-183.   [41]   [*AMN*]

POUND, F. J.

63.041   TR   1940 Adlay *(Coix lachryma-Jobi)* a useful grain crop for Trinidad. *Proc
                 Agric Soc Trin Tob* 40(2), June: 147-163.   [*AMN*]
63.042   TR   1940 A few facts about maize for the Trinidad grower. *Proc Agric Soc
                 Trin Tob* 40(3), Sept.: 241-262.   [*AMN*]
63.043   TR   1940 A survey of the possibilities of *Urena lobata* as a source of fibre in
                 Trinidad. *Proc Agric Soc Trin Tob* 40(4), Dec.: 303-321.   [*AMN*]

POWELL, DULCIE A.

63.044   JM   1963 Spices in Jamaica. *Chron W I Comm* 78(1387), Aug.: 429-431. [*NYP*]

PYTTERSEN, TJ.

63.045   SR   1920/ Oliepalmen in Suriname [Oil-producing palmtrees in Surinam]. *W I G*
                 21 2:509-512.   [*COL*]

ROMNEY, D. H.

63.046   JM   1962 Copra quality and moisture content. *Inf B Scient Res Coun* 3(3),
                 Dec.: 54-57.   [*RIS*]

ROWAAN, P. A.

63.047   SR   1941 Surinaamsche honing als exportproduct [Surinam honey as an export product]. *W I G* 23:289-293.   [51,66]   [*COL*]

SANDS, W. N.

63.048   AT   1901 The cultivation of onions at Antigua. *W I B* 2(2): 163-166.   [*AMN*]

SHAW, EARL BENNETT

63.049   SJ   1934 The bay oil industry of St. John. *Econ Geogr* 10(2), Apr.: 143-146. [49]   [*AGS*]

SHILL, A. C.

51.126   LW/ WW   1932 The fruit and vegetable industry of the Leeward and Windward Islands.

SPOON, W.

41.217   NW   1944/ Ricinus van de Bovenwindsche eilanden [Ricinus of the Windward 45 Islands].

SPOON, W. & SESSLER, WA. M.

63.050   CU   1950 Kwaliteit van de honing van Curacao [Quality of the honey from Curacao]. *W I G* 31:175-179.   [*COL*]

TEMPANY, Sir HAROLD A.

63.051   GC   1915 Bay oil, and the cultivation of the bay tree as a crop plant. *W I B* 15(3): 176-197.   [*AMN*]

THOMPSON, JOHN B.

63.052   UV   1926 Production of sweet-potato seedlings at the Virgin Islands Experiment Station. Washington, U.S. Govt. Print. Off., 14p. (Virgin Islands Agricultural Experiment Station Bulletin no. 5.)   [*NYP*]

WABY, J. F.

63.053   BG   1914 The cultivation of vegetables. *J Bd Agric Br Gui* 7(4), Apr.: 178-180; 8(1-2), July-Oct.: 13-19;

            1915 9(1), Nov.: 33-35;

            1916 9(3), May: 158-161.   [*AMN*]

WALTERS, E. A.

57.067   SL   1929 St. Lucia banana lands: observations and comments on soil changes in relation to tropical agriculture.

WARDLAW, C. W.

57.058   SL   1929 Soils and flora; notes on a botanical and soil inspection of the St. Lucia banana and forest lands.

WATTS, Sir FRANCIS & TEMPANY, H. A.

63.054   BC   1908 Lemon grass, bay leaf, and camphor. *W I B* 9(3): 265-277.   [*AMN*]

WEEVER, P. M. de

63.055   BG   1918 Bee-keeping in British Guiana. *J Bd Agric Br Gui* 11(3), July: 86-96.   [*AMN*]

WHITAKER, CHARLES H.

63.056   GR   1947 Nutmegs from Grenada. *Agric Am* 7(3), Mar.: 50-53.   [*AGS*]

WILLIAMS, R. O.

63.057   TR   1922 Kitchen gardening with special reference to cabbage, tomatoes and beans. *Proc Agric Soc Trin Tob* 22(11), Nov.: 763-774.   [*AMN*]

WOOD, R. CECIL

63.058   TR   1932 Experiences in tobacco growing. *Proc Agric Soc Trin Tob* 32(8), Aug.: 275-282.   [*AMN*]

WOOD, R. CECIL & JAMES, H. M.

63.059   TR   1936 Cauliflower cultivation in the tropics. *Trop Agric* 13(8), Aug.: 218-220.   [*AGS*]

WRIGHT, G.

51.144   SV   1928 St. Vincent arrowroot.

Chapter 64

SYLVICULTURE AND LUMBERING

AIKEN, JAMES

64.001   BG   1912 Commercial classification of colony timbers.   *Timehri* 3d ser., 2
(19A), July: 65-70.   [41]   [*AMN*]

AMOS, G. L.

64.002   BG   1951 Some siliceous timbers of British Guiana. *Car For* 12(3), July: 133-
137.   [*AGS*]

ANDERSON, C. WILGRESS

64.003   BG   1914 Report on experimental tappings of balata trees. *J Bd Agric Br Gui*
8(1-2), July, Oct.: 34-39.   [*AMN*]

ANDREWS, L. R.

64.004   BC   1937 The West Indies market for B.C. lumber. *Can-W I Mag* 26(7), July:
8-10; 26(8), Aug.: 6-8.   [51]   [*NYP*]

BANCROFT, C. K.

64.005   BG   1915 Para rubber in British Guiana: 1915. *J Bd Agric Br Gui* 8(3), July:
73-74.   [*AMN*]

BANCROFT, C. K. & BAYLEY, S. H.

64.006   BG   1914 Report on the experimental bleeding of balata trees at Onderneem-
ing. *J Bd Agric Br Gui* 8(1-2), July-Oct.: 20-33.   [*AMN*]

BARBOUR, WILLIAM R.

64.007   GC   1942 Forest types of tropical America. *Car For* 3(4), July: 137-150. [*AGS*]

BEARD, JOHN STEWART

41.031   GC   1942 Montane vegetation in the Antilles.

64.008   TR   1942 Summary of silvicultural experience with cedar, *Cedrela mexicana*
Roem. in Trinidad. *Car For* 3(3), Apr.: 91-102.   [*AGS*]

64.009   WW   [1944?] FORESTRY IN THE WINDWARD ISLANDS. Bridgetown, Advocate Co.,
183p. (Development and welfare bulletin no. 11.) [66]   [*COL*]

41.033   GC   1944 Provisional list of trees and shrubs of the Lesser Antilles.

64.010   TR   1944 A silvicultural technique in Trinidad for the rehabilitation of degraded forest. *Car For* 6(1), Oct.: 1-33.   [41]   [*AGS*]

64.011   AT   [1945?] FORESTRY IN THE LEEWARD ISLANDS. BARBUDA. Bridgetown, Advocate
                Co., 13p. (Development and welfare bulletin no. 7b.) [66]   [COL]
64.012   BV   [1945?] FORESTRY IN THE LEEWARD ISLANDS: THE BRITISH VIRGIN ISLANDS.
                Bridgetown, Advocate Co., 16p. (Development and welfare bulletin
                no. 7a.)   [66]   [COL]
64.013   TR   1946 The mora forests of Trinidad, British West Indies. *J Ecol* 33(2),
                July: 173-192.   [AGS]

BECKETT, J. EDGAR
64.014   BG   1911 Rubber. *Timehri* 3d ser., 1(18A), Jan.: 32-41. [41]   [AMN]

BEEBE, WILLIAM
41.043   TR   1958 The high world of the rain forest.

BENA, PAUL
64.015   FG   1949 L'exploitation forestière doit servir de tremplin à l'essor économi-
                que du département francais de la Guyane [Lumbering must act as a
                springboard to the economic development of the French department
                of Guiana]. *Bois For Trop* no. 11, 3d trimester: 251-268.   [COL]

BENOIST, RAYMOND
64.016   FG   1925 La forêt et les bois de la Guyane Francaise [The forests and tim-
                bers of French Guiana]. *Ann Soc Lin Lyon* new ser., 71:37-44; 72:
                21-27; 73:18-24.   [AMN]

BENSON, GEORGE C.
64.017   BG   1912 The balata industry. *Timehri* 3d ser., 2(19A), July: 81-82. [50] [AMN]

BEVAN. ARTHUR
64.018   UV   1940 Possibilities for forestry in the Virgin Islands: St. Thomas, St.
                John, St. Croix. *Car For* 2(1), Oct.: 8-12.   [41]   [AGS]

BEYERINCK, F. H.
64.019   GC   1955 The value of a centralised market information service for Caribbean
                timbers. *In* CARIBBEAN TIMBERS, THEIR UTILISATION AND TRADE WITH-
                IN THE AREA: report of the Timber Conference held at Kent House,
                Trinidad, Apr. 15-22, 1953. Port of Spain. Caribbean Commission,
                p. 72-85. [51, 66]   [RIS]

BOYE, MARC
64.020   FG   1962 Les paletuviers du littoral de la Guyane Francaise: ressources et
                problemes d'exploitation [The mangroves of coastal French Guiana:
                potential and problems of exploitation]. *Cah O-M* 15(59), July-
                Sept.: 271-290.   [57]   [RIS]

BROOKS, REGINALD LAING
64.021   TR   1938 Teak production in Trinidad. *Proc Agric Soc Trin Tob* 38(7), July:
                236-241.   [AMN]
64.022   TR   1941 The Lands Advisory Committee of Trinidad. *Emp For J* 20(1): 60-
                62.   [66]   [AGS]
64.023   TR   1941 Notes on pure teak plantations in Trinidad. *Car For* 3(1), Oct.: 25-
                28.   [AGS]

64.024	TR	1941 The regeneration of mixed rain forest in Trinidad. *Car For* 2(4), July: 164-173. [*AGS*]
64.025	TR	1942 The forest policy of Trinidad and Tobago. *Car For* 3(4), July: 151-157. [66] [*AGS*]
64.026	BC	1947 TREES OF THE WEST INDIES: THEIR CULTIVATION AND CARE. London, Nelson, 70p.

BRYAN, VICTOR

| 64.027 | TR | 1952 The forests of Trinidad. *Car Commn Mon Inf B* 5(7), Feb.: 205-206. [*COL*] |

BURNS, L. V.

| 64.028 | JM | 1942 Roofing shingles in Jamaica. *Car For* 4(1), Oct.: 9-15. [35] [*AGS*] |

BURRA, J. A. N.

| *42.005* | JM | 1961 The forest and climate. |
| *42.006* | JM | 1962 The forest and watershed control. |

CAFFERY, E.

| 64.029 | BH | 1955 Old forests and new farms in British Honduras. *New Commonw* 30 (10), Nov. 14: xvi-xvii. [*AGS*] |

CASE, GERALD O.

| 64.030 | BG | 1934 BRITISH GUIANA TIMBERS. London, Metcalfe and Cooper, 73p. [*AGS*] |

CATER, JOHN C.

64.031	TR	1941 The formation of teak plantations in Trinidad with the assistance of peasant contractors. *Car For* 2(4), July: 147-153. [*AGS*]
64.032	LW	[1944?] FORESTRY IN THE LEEWARD ISLANDS. Bridgetown, Advocate Co., 106p. (Development and welfare bulletin, no. 7.) [66] [*COL*]
64.033	TR	1948 The forest industries of Trinidad & Tobago. *Car For* 9(1), Jan.: 1-14, 44, 52. [*AGS*]

CHATELAIN, G.

| 64.034 | FG | 1935 Le balata et la gomme de balata en Guyane Francaise [Balata and balata gum in French Guiana]. *Agron Colon* 24(213-214), Sept., Nov.: 80-87, 148-151. [*AGS*] |
| 64.035 | FG | 1935 L'exploitation du bois de rose en Guyane Francaise [The exploitation of rosewood in French Guiana]. *Agron Colon* 24(209-210), May-June: 133-137, 176-182. [*AGS*] |

COLLIER, H. C.

| 64.036 | JM | 1941 The logwood industry in Jamaica. *Can-W I Mag* 30(2), Feb.: 12, 14. [*NYP*] |
| 64.037 | BG | 1942 Wallaba for cellulose. *Can-W I Mag* 31(6), June: 7-9. [*NYP*] |

CORNER, EDWARD P.

| 64.038 | DM | 1921 The distillation of wood—a possible industry for Dominica. *W I Comm Circ* 36(600), Sept. 29: 409-410. [*NYP*] |

DANKS, F. S.

| 64.039 | BG | 1945 NOTES ON BRITISH GUIANA TIMBERS. Georgetown, Daily Chronicle, 28p. [*AGS*] |

DAVIS, T. A. W.

64.040   BG   1934   The balata industry in British Guiana. *Can-W I Mag* 23(5), Apr.: 140-141, 154.   [*NYP*]

DEMOUGEOT, M.

64.041   FG   1928   Les bois de la Guyane Francaise dans l'industrie de la tonnellerie [The timbers of French Guiana in the cooperage industry]. *B Ag Gen Colon* 21(239), Dec.: 1221-1231.   [66]   [*AGS*]

DEVEZ, G.

41.079   FG   1932   Les plantes utiles et les bois industriels de la Guyane [The useful plants and industrial timbers of Guiana].

DUBOIS-CHABERT, A.

64.042   FG   1959   Research begins to bear fruit. *Caribbean* 13(1), Jan.: 12-13.   [54]   [*COL*]

ENGLEDOW, Sir FRANK L.

46.064   GC   1945   REPORT ON AGRICULTURE, FISHERIES, FORESTRY AND VETERINARY MATTERS [OF THE] WEST INDIA ROYAL COMMISSION.

FAHEY, HAROLD NEAL

64.043   TR   1942   History of Trinidad rubber industry. *Proc Agric Soc Trin Tob* 42(4), Dec.: 271-275.   [*AMN*]

FANSHAWE, D. B.

41.086   BG   1954   Forest types of British Guiana.

FAWCETT, WILLIAM

64.044   JM   1909   Woods and forests in Jamaica. *Proc Agric Soc Trin Tob* 9(5), May: 229-232.   [*AMN*]

FORBES, G. P. A.

64.045   BG   1959   The forests of British Guiana and their future development. *Timehri* 4th ser., 38, Sept.: 57-61.   [*AMN*]

FRASER, H.

64.046   WW   1956   Forest preservation in the Windward Islands. *Car For* 17(1-2), Jan.-June: 25-28.   [66]   [*AGS*]

64.047   WW   1957   THE PRINCIPAL TIMBER TREES OF THE WINDWARD ISLANDS. [Bridgetown, Advocate Co.?] 32p. (Development and welfare in the West Indies, Bulletin no. 35.)

GILL, TOM

64.048   GC   1931   TROPICAL FORESTS OF THE CARIBBEAN. Baltimore, Pub. by the Tropical Plant Research Foundation in cooperation with the Charles Lathrop Pack Forestry Trust, 317p.   [*AGS*]

GILMOUR, JOHN D.

64.049   BG   1949   Exploitation of the forests of British Guiana. *Emp For Rev* 28(2), June: 131-136.   [66]   [*AGS*]

GIMON, P.

64.050   FG   1951 Une expérience d'exploitation forestière en Guyane Francaise [A lumbering experiment in French Guiana]. *Bois For Trop* 17(1st trimester): 26-32.   [66]   [*COL*]

GONGGRIJP, J. W.

54.020   SR   1948 Biddrage tot de kennis van 's lands domein in Suriname betreffende bauxiet en hout [Contribution to the knowledge of the value of Surinam's crownland in relationship to bauxite and lumber].

GOODMAN, EILEEN

64.051   BH   1937 British Honduras—The forest colony. *Can-W I Mag* 26(11), Nov.: 12-14.   [51]   [*NYP*]

GORDON, W. A.

64.052   BC   1961 Forest management in the Caribbean. *Car For* 22(1-2), Jan.-June: 21-25.   [66]   [*AGS*]

GRAHAM, CYNTHIA

64.053   BG   1954 A colonial problem for the protectionist. *Timehri* 4th ser., 1(33), Oct.: 28-29.   [66]

GREBERT, RENE

41.108   GD   1934 Les forêts de la Guadeloupe [The forests of Guadeloupe].

GUNTHER, A.E.

41.112   TR   1942 The distribution and status of Mora Forest *(Mora excelsa)* in the Ortoire Basin, Trinidad, B.W.I.

HAGLEY, W. H.

64.054   GR   1940 Forestry in Grenada. *Car For* 1(2), Jan.: 5-6.   [*AGS*]

HAMAN, MILES & WOOD, B. R.

64.055   BG   1928 Forests of British Guiana. *Trop Wd* 15, Sept. 1: 1-13.   [*COL*]

HARDY, F.; DUTHIE, D. W. & RODRIGUEZ, G.

57.035   TR   1936 STUDIES IN WEST INDIAN SOILS. (X)-THE CACAO AND FOREST SOILS OF TRINIDAD. (B)-SOUTH-CENTRAL DISTRICT.

HARDY, F. & RODRIGUES, G.

57.040   SL   1947 STUDIES IN WEST INDIAN SOILS. (XII)-THE AGRICULTURAL AND FOREST SOILS OF ST. LUCIA.

HARRIS, W.

64.056   JM   1909 The timbers of Jamaica. *W I B* 9(4): 297-328.   [*AMN*]

HARRISON, Sir JOHN B.

64.057   BG   1908 Rubber experiments in British Guiana. *W I B* 9(3): 254-257.   [*AMN*]

HART, J. H.

64.058   BC   1901 Rubber planting in the West Indies. *W I B* 2(2): 100-113.   [*AMN*]

64.059   TR   1907 Progress of the rubber industry in Trinidad. *W I B* 8(2): 195-199.
                                                                                      [*AMN*]

HEESTERMAN, J. E.

51.064   GC   1955 Marketing of Caribbean timbers.

64.060   GC   1956 Forestry. *Caribbean* 10(4), Nov.: 95-97.   [66]   [*COL*]

HEIM de BALSAC, F.; DEFORGE, A.; HEIM de BALSAC, H. & LEFEVRE, L.

41.121   FG   1929 Contribution à l'étude des écorces tannifères de la Guyane Fran-
                       caise [Contribution to the study of the tanniferous barks of French
                       Guiana].

HEINSDIJK, D.

64.061   SR   1953 Bosbouwkundige foto-interpretatie [Interpretation of sylvicul-
                       ture photographs]. Paramaribo, Centraal Bureau Luchtkaartering
                       te Paramaribo, 19p. (Publ. no. 13.)

HENRIQUEZ, P. C.

66.061   CU   1962 Problems relating to hydrology, water conservation, erosion control,
                       reforestation and agriculture in Curacao.

HINGSTON, R. W. G.

41.125   BG   1930 In the canopy of the rain-forest.

HODGE, L. P.

41.129   BG   1918 Some of the constructional woods.

HODGE, W. H.

41.130   DM   1942 A synopsis of the palms of Dominica.

HOHENKERK, L. S.

64.062   BG   1917 A list of British Guiana woods. *Timehri* 3d ser., 4(21), June: 244-
                       293.   [*AMN*]

41.133   BG   1918/ Botanical identifications of British Guiana trees and plants.
                       22

64.063   BG   1918 The Kokerit palm. *J. Bd Agric Br Gui* 11(2), Apr.: 43-52.   [*AMN*]

64.064   BG   1923 A review of the timber industry of British Guiana. *J Bd Agric Br
                       Gui* 16(1), Jan.: 1-22.   [*AMN*]

HOMULLE, H. J.

64.065   SR   1919/ Houtdistillatie in Suriname [Wood distillation in Surinam]. *W I G*
                       20 1(2): 151-156.   [*COL*]

HUGHES, J. HENRY

41.146   BG   1946 Forest resources.

HUGUET, LOUIS & MARIE, ERNEST

64.066   FA   1951 Les plantations d'acajou d'Amérique et des Antilles Francaises
                       [Mahogany plantations in the Americas and in the French Antilles].
                       Bois For Trop 17, 1st trimester: 12-25.   [*COL*]

JONES, B. HOWELL

64.067   BG   1907 Rubber in British Guiana. *WIB* 8(2): 200-208.   [*AMN*]

JUNKER, L.

64.068   SR   1946 De toekomst van de houtexploitatie in Suriname [The future of the lumber exploitation in Surinam]. *WIG* 27:69-88.   [*COL*]

KLUGE, H. C.

14.018   SR   1923 Curious loggers of the world, the Boschneger of Surinam: descendants of escaped slaves fill important place in South American logging.

LALOR, G. C.

64.069   JM   1961 The logwood dye industry. *Inf B Scient Res Coun* 2(1), June: 16-18.   [*COL*]

[LAMB, A. F. A.?]

64.070   BH   1946 NOTES ON FORTY-TWO SECONDARY HARDWOOD TIMBERS OF BRITISH HONDURAS.   [Belize?] British Honduras, Government Printer, 116p. (Forest department bulletin no. 1.)

LAMB, A. F. A.

64.071   TR   1951 Forestry in Trinidad and Tobago. *J Agric Soc Trin Tob* 51(4), Dec.: 405-413.   [*AMN*]

64.072   TR   1953 Wood preservation on estates. *J Agric Soc Trin Tob* 53(4), Dec.: 423-425.   [*AMN*]

64.073   TR   1955 Forestry on private estates. *J Agric Soc Trin Tob* 55(2), June: 169-183.   [*AMN*]

64.074   TR   1955 Trinidad's teak forests. *J Agric Soc Trin Tob* 55(1), Mar.: 27-34.   [*AMN*]

64.075   BH/   1960 Policy and economic problems in the conversion of old growth for-
         TR   ests to managed stands in tropical South America. *Car For* 21(3-4), July-Dec.: 61-67.   [66]   [*AGS*]

LAMONT, Sir NORMAN

64.076   BC   1932 Timber prospects in the tropics: West Indian woods that count; boundless possibilities. *Proc Agric Soc Trin Tob* 32(7), July: 236-239.   [*AMN*]

LANG, W. G.

64.077   SL   1954 Forest utilization in Saint Lucia, British West Indies. *Car For* 15 (3-4), July-Oct.: 120-123.   [*AGS*]

LEWIS, C. D. & SWABEY, C.

64.078   JM   1944 Notes on furniture cracking in Jamaica. *Car For* 5(2), Jan.: 94-97.   [*AGS*]

MARIE, ERNEST

41.167   MT   1949 Notes sur les reboisements en *Swietenia macrophylla King* [Notes on reforestation with *Swietenia macrophylla King*] *Car For* 10(3), July: 205-222.   [64]   [*AGS*]

MARSHALL, R. C.

64.079   TR   1925 Forestry in Trinidad and Tobago. *Proc Agric Soc Trin Tob* 25(8), Aug.: 291-294.   [*AMN*]

64.080   TR   1926 Preliminary notes on the seasoning of local timber. *Proc Agric Soc Trin Tob* 26(4), Apr.: 197-212.   [*AMN*]
64.081   TR   1932 Which are our most useful timber trees? *Proc Agric Soc Trin Tob* 32(7), July: 229-235.   [*AMN*]

MATTHEWS, D. M.
64.082   TR   1930 Forestry in Trinidad. *J For* 28(1), Jan.: 72-77.   [*AGS*]

MILLER, W. A.
64.083   BH   1941 Mahogany logging in British Honduras. *Car For* 2(2), Jan.: 67-72.   [*AGS*]

MOORE, DAVID
59.032 TR   1956 A forester's thoughts on cocoa plantations.
64.084   TR   1958 The effects of an expanding economy on the tropical shelterwood system in Trinidad. *J Agric Soc Trin Tob* 58(1), Mar.: 27-37. [*AMN*]
64.085   TR   1962 The utilisation of teak thinnings in Trinidad and Tobago. *Car For* 23(2): 82-86.   [*AGS*]

MOORE, J. C.
64.086   DM/   1907 Summary of results of tapping rubber trees at Dominica and St. Lucia.
         SL   *W I B* 8(2): 204-208.   [*AMN*]

MORAIS, ALLAN I.
64.087   GC   1954 Caribbean timber: a survey of production and overseas trade. *Car Commn Mon Inf B* 7(2), Feb.: 158-159.   [*COL*]

MURRAY, C. H.
64.088   TR   1961 Teak and fire in Trinidad. *Car For* 22(3-4), July-Dec.: 57-61. [*AGS*]

PALMER, M. B.
64.089   BH   1951 Mahogany is important factor in economy of British Honduras. *Can-W I Mag* 41(8), Aug.: 36-37.   [*NYP*]

PEARSON, HENRY C.
64.090   SR   1911 India-rubber in Dutch Guiana. *India Rubb Wld* 43(4), Jan. 1: 115-118; 43(5), Feb. 1: 149-152; 43(6), Mar. 1: 189-191; 44(1), Apr. 1: 221-226; 44(2), May 1: 257-261.   [*NYP*]

PERTCHIK, BERNARD & HARRIET
41.186 GC   1951 FLOWERING TREES OF THE CARIBBEAN.

POWELL, DULCIE A.
64.091   JM   1962 The mahogany and Jamaica. *Inf B Scient Res Coun* 3(2), Sept.: 26-29.   [*RIS*]

QUESTEL, ADRIEN
41.191 GD   1946 Les palmiers de la Guadeloupe et dépendances [The palm trees of Guadeloupe and her dependencies].

ROSS, PHILIP
64.092   TR   1958 The utilisation of teak in Trinidad. *Car For* 19(3-4), July-Dec.: 80-84.   [*AGS*]

SHARP, T. H.

64.093   JM   1907   Rubber cultivation in Jamaica. *W I B* 8(2): 191-194.   [*AMN*]

SINGH, JAY R.

64.094   BG   1951   Large modern saw-milling plant for British Guiana. *New Commonw* 22(6), Dec.: 447-449.   [*AGS*]

SMEATHERS, R.

64.095   TR   1943   The manufacture of shingles from local woods in Trinidad and To-bago. *Car For* 4(3), Apr.: 107-111.   [35]   [*AGS*]

SMITH, J. H. NELSON

52.086   BH   1941   Use of British Honduras woods for railway sleepers or cross ties.

64.096   BH   1942   The formation and management of mahogany plantations at Silk Grass Forest Reserve. *Car For* 3(2), Jan.: 75-78.   [*AGS*]

41.216   BH   1945   Forest associations of British Honduras, parts II-III.

SNELLEMAN, J. F.

64.097   SR   1922/ Hout en planken [Wood and lumber]. *W I G* 4:437-443.   [*COL*]
               23

STANDLEY, PAUL C. & RECORD, SAMUEL J.

41.220   BH   1936   THE FORESTS AND FLORA OF BRITISH HONDURAS.

STEHLE, HENRI

64.098   MT   1941   Classification des essences forestières de la Martinique d'après leur utilisation [Classification of timbers in Martinique according to their use] *Car For* 3(1), Oct.: 29-31.   [*AGS*]

41.223   FA   1941   Conditions éco-sociologiques et évolution des forêts des Antilles Francaises [Socio-ecological conditions and development of forests in the French Antilles].

64.099   MT   1941   Plan d'aménagement et d'exploitation rationnelle de la forêt martini-quaise [Plan for the parceling out and rational exploitation of Martinique's forests]. *Car For* 3(1), Oct.: 32-38.   [66]   [*AGS*]

41.226   FA   1943   Classification des arbres à latex et à secretions de gommes, res-ines et matières colorantes aux Antilles Francaises [Classifica-tion of latex- and gum-yielding trees, resins and dyes in the French Antilles].

41.227   FA   1943   La vegetation muscinale des Antilles Francaises et son intérêt dans la valorisation sylvicole [Mosses in the French Antilles, and their importance to sylviculture].

41.229   GC   1945   Forest types of the Caribbean Islands.

41.230   GC   1947   Notes taxonomiques, xylologiques et géographiques sur les châttaig-niers du genre *Sloanea* des Petites Antilles [Taxonomic, xylologic, and geographic notes on *Sloanea* genus chestnut trees in the Lesser Antilles].

STEHLE, HENRI & Mme.

41.231   GC   1947   Liste complementaire des arbres et arbustes des Petites Antilles [Complementary list of trees and shrubs in the Lesser Antilles].

STEHLE, HENRI & MARIE, E.

41.234   GC   1947 Le magnolia, *Talauma dodecapetala*, des Petites Antilles: monographie sylvo-botanique [The magnolia *Talauma dodecapetala*, of the Lesser Antilles: sylvo-botanical monograph].

STEVENSON, N. S.

64.100   BH   1938 The evolution of vegetation survey and rural planning in British Honduras. *Emp For J* 17(1): 9-26.   [41,46,67]   [*AGS*]

64.101   BH   1940 Balsa in British Honduras. *Car For* 1(3), Apr.: 1-3.   [*AGS*]

41.236   BH   1942 Forest associations of British Honduras.

STOCKDALE, Sir FRANK A.

41.237   BG   1911 The indigenous "rubber" trees of British Guiana.

STORER, DOROTHY P.

41.239   JM   1958 FAMILIAR TREES AND CULTIVATED PLANTS OF JAMAICA.

SWABEY, CHRISTOPHER

64.102   JM   1939 Forestry in Jamaica. *Emp For J* 18(1): 19-29.   [*AGS*]

64.103   JM   1940 Reservation policy in Jamaica. *Car For* 1(2), Jan.: 10-12. [66] [*AGS*]

64.104   BH   1941 An islander looks at the mainland. *Car For* 3(1), Oct.: 39-41. [*AGS*]

64.105   JM   1941 Supply of tanning materials in Jamaica. *Car For* 2(3), Apr.: 145-146.   [*AGS*]

64.106   JM   1942 The development of forest policy in Jamaica. *Emp For J* 21(2): 89-100.   [66]   [*AGS*]

64.107   JM   1945 FORESTRY IN JAMAICA. Kingston, 44p. (Forest Dept. Forestry bulletin no. 1.)   [41]   [*AGS*]

64.108   SR   1950 Forestry in Dutch Guiana. *Emp For Rev* 29(2), June: 125-131.   [*AGS*]

64.109   BG   1950 Note on the development of forest policy in British Guiana. *Timehri* 4th ser., 1(29), Aug.: 27-35.   [5, 66]

64.110   BG   1951 Note on the development of forest policy in British Guiana. *Car For* 12(4), Oct.: 159-170.   [5,66]   [*AGS*]

SWABEY, CHRISTOPHER & LEWIS, C. BERNARD

64.111   CM   1946 FORESTRY IN THE CAYMAN ISLANDS. [Bridgetown?] Barbados, Advocate Co., 31p. (Development and welfare in the West Indies, bulletin no. 23.)   [66]   [*AGS*]

VIEIRA, V. & RICHARDSON, H.

64.112   BG   1957 Forest conditions, problems and programmes in British Guiana. *Car For* 18(1-2), Jan.-June: 44-48.   [66]   [*AGS*]

WADSWORTH, FRANK H., et al.

41.253   GC   1960 Records of forest plantation growth in Mexico, the West Indies and Central and South America.

WARDLAW, C. W.

57.068   SL   1929 Soils and flora; notes on a botanical and soil inspection of the St. Lucia banana and forest lands.

WESTERMANN, J. H.

64.113   GC   1952 CONSERVATION IN THE CARIBBEAN. Utrecht, publications of the Foundation for Scientific Research in Surinam and the Netherlands Antilles, 121p. [66]   [*NYP*]

WHITTON, B. A.

41.264   BG   1962 Forests and dominant legumes of the Amatuk region, British Guiana.

WILLEMS, V. J.

64.114   BG   1957 Haulin' greenheart. *Timehri* 4th ser., 1(36), Oct.: 36-39.

WISHART, H. A.

64.115   BG   1915 The conservation and characteristics of colony timber. *Timehri* 3d ser., 3(20B), May: 293-303.   [66]   [*AMN*]

WOODHOUSE, W. M.

64.116   BC   1955 Problems of the consumer in the British West Indies. *In* CARIBBEAN TIMBERS, THEIR UTILISATION AND TRADE WITHIN THE AREA: REPORT OF THE TIMBER CONFERENCE HELD AT KENT HOUSE, TRINIDAD, APR. 15-22, 1953. Port of Spain, Caribbean Commission, p.41-55.   [*RIS*]

Chapter 65

LIVESTOCK AND PASTURAGE

ABRAHAM, A. A.

65.001   BG   1918 Notes on caponizing. *J Bd Agric Br Gui* 11(4), Oct.: 164-166.   [*AMN*]

ADENIYI, S. A. & WILSON, P. N.

65.002   TR   1960 Studies on pangola grass at I.C.T.A., Trinidad: I. Effects of fertilizer application at time of establishment, and cutting interval, on the yield of ungrazed pangola grass. *Trop Agric* 37(4), Oct.: 271-282.   [*AGS*]

ALLAN, J. A.

41.012   BB   1957 The grasses of Barbados.

ANDERSON, C. B. W.

65.003   BG   1921 Our milk supply. *J Bd Agr Br Gui* 14(3), July: 177-187.   [*AMN*]

ARNOLD, R. M.

65.004   JM   1955 Growth of the dairy industry in Jamaica (1940-1953). *Trop Agric* 32(1), Jan.: 38-44.   [*AGS*]

65.005   JM   1955 30 million quarts of milk. *Caribbean* 9(4), Nov.: 84-88. [66] [*COL*]

BAYLEY, S. H.

65.006   BG   1913 Poultry keeping for profit in British Guiana. *J Bd Agric Br Gui* 7(1), July: 46-49.   [*AMN*]

BLAICH, O. P. & DETTERING, T. P.

65.007   BG   1956 Management of the dairy-beef enterprise: Fairfield-Abary District 1952-1953. Georgetown, Dept. of Agriculture, 24p.

BRATT, A. E.

65.008   BG   1918 The dairy farm in British Guiana. *J Bd Agric Br Gui* 11(4), Oct.: 158-163.   [*AMN*]

BROCK, STANLEY E.

65.009   BG   1964 Longhorns of British Guiana. *Geogr Mag* 36(10), Feb.: 583-593. [*AGS*]

BRUCE, S. N.

63.004   BG   1926 A local industry.

BURKE, S. C.

65.010   JM   1907 Horses and horse breeding in Jamaica. *W I B* 8(3): 241-244.   [*AMN*]

BUTTENSHAW, W. R.

65.011   BB   1905 Barbados woolless sheep. *W I B* 6(2): 187-197.   [*AMN*]

CATHCART, J. W.

65.012   TR   1925 Stock-raising in the West Indies. *W I Comm Circ* 40(701), Aug. 13:
                   327.   [*NYP*]

CORK, P. C.

65.013   JM   1902 Stock rearing in Jamaica. *W I B* 3(3): 203-206.   [*AMN*]

DUTHIE, D. W.

65.014   BG   1939 Mineral deficiency and cattle raising in British Guiana. *Agric J Br
                   Gui* 10(4): 194-204.   [57]   [*AGS*]

ENGLEDOW, Sir FRANK L.

46.064   GC   1945 REPORT ON AGRICULTURE, FISHERIES, FORESTRY AND VETERINARY MAT-
                   TERS [OF THE] WEST INDIA ROYAL COMMISSION.

FLOCH, HERVE ALEXANDRE

65.015   FG   1955 A propos d'alimentation en Guyane Francaise. Elevage de porcs
                   et arbre à pain [On nutrition in French Guiana. Pig-raising and the
                   breadfruit tree]. *Archs Inst Past Guy L'In* 383, Nov. 10 (6p.) [30, 60]

GONGGRIJP, J. W.

65.016   SR   1923/ Surinaamsche savanna's en veeteelt [Surinam's savannahs and cat-
           24   tle breeding]. *W I G* 5:337-352.   [66]   [*COL*]

GOOD, W. A.

65.017   BG   1946 Dairy farming along the coastlands of British Guiana. *Timehri* 4th
                   ser., 1(27), July: 53-57.

GOSSET, B. S.

65.018   JM   1907 Indian cattle in Jamaica. *W I B* 8(3): 229-240.   [*AMN*]

GRANSAULL, EDWARD

65.019   TR   1921 Our livestock. *Proc Agric Soc Trin Tob* 21(7), July: 212-218. [*AMN*]

GUILBRIDE, P. D. L.

28.259   GC   1952/ Veterinary public health: the importance of animal disease to public
           53   health in the Caribbean, with special reference to Jamaica.

GUILBRIDE, P. D. L.; YOUNG, VIOLA MAE & NORSEN, JEANETTE

65.020   JM   1955 A bacteriological survey of milk and milk products in Jamaica. *W I
                   Med J* 4(1), Mar.: 43-48.   [*COL*]

HALY, JOHN H.

65.021   BG   1918 Notes on cattle raising on the coastland savannahs. *J Bd Agric Br
                   Gui* 11(4). Oct.: 144-146.   [*AMN*]

HARRISON, E.

65.022 TR 1944 The breeding and artificial insemination of dairy cows in Trinidad, B.W.I. *Trop Agric* 21(1), Jan.: 3-7. [*AGS*]

HEESTERMAN, J. E.

65.023 GC 1955 USE OF INDUSTRIAL BY-PRODUCTS AS STOCK FEED. Port of Spain, Caribbean Commission, 25p. [49,66] [*RIS*]

HITCHCOCK, A. S.

41.127 BG 1922 Grasses of British Guiana.
41.128 BG 1923 Grasses of British Guiana.

HOGG, PETER G.

65.024 BG 1953 RESEARCH PROGRAM FOR LIVESTOCK IMPROVEMENTS AND GRASSLAND MANAGEMENT AT THE EBINI LIVESTOCK STATION, BRITISH GUIANA. Georgetown, [Dept. of Agriculture; printed by] "Daily Chronicle," 21p.

HOUGHTON, T. R.

65.025 TR 1960 Management of pigs for pork production in Trinidad. *J Agric Soc Trin Tob* 60(2), June: 182-202. [*AMN*]
41.136 TR 1960 The water buffalo in Trinidad.

HOWE, J. W.

65.026 GC 1937 Livestock in the West Indies. *Proc Agric Soc Trin Tob* 37(12), Dec.: 479-485. [*AMN*]
65.027 JM 1940 Livestock improvement in Jamaica in war time. *Trop Agric* 17(9), Sept.: 175-176. [66] [*AGS*]

HOWES, J. R.

65.028 TR 1952 Food for thought. *J Agric Soc Trin Tob* 52(3), Sept.: 283-293. [*AMN*]
65.029 BC 1954 The adaptability of livestock to their environment with special reference to the West Indies. *J Agric Soc Trin Tob* 54(4), Dec.: 411-421. [*AMN*]
65.030 SR 1955 Grass and livestock production in Suriname. *J Agric Soc Trin Tob* 55(2), June: 185-200. [*AMN*]
65.031 TR 1956 Livestock buildings at the college New Farm. *J Agric Soc Trin Tob* 56(2), June: 169-181. [35] [*AMN*]
65.032 TR 1956 Poultry husbandry in the tropics. *J Agric Soc Trin Tob* 56(3), Sept.: 383-397. [*AMN*]

HOWES, J. R. & CAMPBELL, J. S.

65.033 TR 1953 Grass and its utilisation in Trinidad. *Trop Agric* 30(1), Jan.-Mar.: 3-14. [*AGS*]

HOWES, J. R. & WEBB, G. W. HUMPHREY

65.034 TR 1953 Poultry husbandry in the wet tropics. *J Agric Soc Trin Tob* 53(4), Dec.: 427-440. [*AMN*]

HUGGINS, H. D.

65.035 BG 1943 AN ECONOMIC SURVEY OF DAIRY-FARMING IN EAST DEMERARA. [Georgetown?] B.G., Argosy Co., 40p. (Dept. of Agriculture, British Guiana. Economic intelligence series.) [*NYP*]

HUTSON, L. R.

65.036   TR   1953 Progress in dairying at St. Joseph Stock Farm, 1948-52. *J Agric Soc Trin Tob* 53(3), Sept.: 279-284.   [*AMN*]

HYNAM, C. A. S. & HUTSON, L. R.

65.037   AT/   1944 Hay-making under conditions obtaining in the drier West Indian is-
          SM   lands. *Trop Agric* 21(7), July: 133-135.   [*AGS*]

KEMPF, M.

65.038   GD   1963 L'élevage de vaches laitières de Beauport [The raising of milk
                     cows in Beauport]. *B Pedag* 1(6-8), Apr.-June: 32-36.   [*RIS*]

LENS, TH.

65.039   CU   1919/ Struisvogelteelt op Curacao [Ostrich-breeding on Curacao]. *W I G*
          20   1(2): 3-12.   [*COL*]

LEYDEN, T. P.

65.040   JM   1907 Dairying in Jamaica. *W I B* 8(3): 245-249.   [*AMN*]

LEYS, J. J.

65.041   SR   1924/ De veeteelt in Suriname [Cattle breeding in Surinam]. *W I G* 6:405-
          25   418, 441-460.   [*COL*]

MAULE, J. P.

65.042   JM/   1952 Experimental breeding of dairy cattle for hot climates. *J Agric Soc
          TR   Trin Tob* 52(1), Mar.: 43-52.   [*AMN*]

MEADEN, C. W.

65.043   TR   1905 Butter making in Trinidad. *W I B* 6(2): 181-187.   [*AMN*]

MEADEN, C. W. & HART, J. H.

65.044   TR   1901 Zebu cattle in Trinidad. *W I B* 2(2): 166-169.   [*AMN*]

METIVIER, H. V. M.

65.045   TR   1923 Pig rearing. *J Bd Agric Br Gui* 16(3), July: 166-175.   [*AMN*]
65.046   TR   1928 Lecture.   Subject:—The work carried out at the Government Farm
                     with special reference to the grading up of dairy cattle. *Proc Agric
                     Soc Trin Tob* 28(10), Oct.: 401-412.   [*AMN*]
65.047   TR   1946 Address . . . on Prof. Miller's report on veterinary and animal hus-
                     bandry matters in Trinidad and Tobago. *Proc Agric Soc Trin Tob*
                     46(1), Mar.: 49-64.   [66]   [*AMN*]
65.048   TR   1950 The improvement of cattle and horsekind in the colony of Trinidad
                     and Tobago. *Proc Agric Soc Trin Tob* 50(2), June: 133-143.   [*AMN*]
65.049   TR   1951 The livestock work of the Department of Agriculture. *J Agric Soc
                     Trin Tob* 51(2), June: 367-372.   [*AMN*]

METIVIER, H. V. M. et al.

65.050   TR   1951 Report on the dairy farming industry. *J Agric Soc Trin Tob* 51(4),
                     Dec.: 425-441.   [*AMN*]

MILLER, WILLIAM C.

65.051 BG [n.d.] SURVEY OF ANIMAL HUSBANDRY, FEEDING, MANAGEMENT AND VETERINARY SERVICES IN THE WEST INDIES. BRITISH GUIANA REPORT. [Bridgetown?] Barbados, Advocate Co., 44p. (Development and welfare in the West Indies, bulletin no. 19A.) [66] [*RIS*]

65.052 TR [n.d.] SURVEY OF ANIMAL HUSBANDRY, FEEDING, MANAGEMENT AND VETERINARY SERVICES IN THE WEST INDIES. TRINIDAD AND TOBAGO REPORT. Bridgetown, Advocate Co., 40p. (Development and welfare bulletin no. 19.) [66] [*COL*]

MULLIN, JOHN

65.053 BG 1918 Cattle raising on crown lands in British Guiana. *J Bd Agric Br Gui* 11(3), July: 78-85. [*AMN*]

OAKES, A. J.; BOND, R. M. & SKOV, O.

65.054 UV 1959 Pangola grass *(Digitaria decumbens Stent)* in the United States Virgin Islands *Trop Agric* 36(2), Apr.: 130-137. [*AGS*]

PACILLY,

65.055 TR/ 1938 Notes sur l'élevage à Trinidad et en Guyane Angiaise [Notes on the BG livestock production in Trinidad and British Guiana]. *Agron Colon* 27(246), June: 177-183. [*AGS*]

PATERSON, D. D.

65.056 TR 1936 The growth and utilisation of fodder grasses in Trinidad. *Trop Agric* 13(4), Apr.: 98-103. [*AGS*]

65.057 TR 1937 Forage production in Trinidad. *Trop Agric* 14(12), Dec.: 337-341. [*AGS*]

PEACOCKE, NORA E.

65.058 BG 1953 Livestock research in relation to agricultural policy in the Caribbean. *Car Commn Mon Inf B* 6(11), June: 251-252. [66] [*AGS*]

RHOAD, A. O.

65.059 GC 1951 New developments and special problems in livestock management. *Car Commn Mon Inf B* 4(9), Apr.: 747-752. [66] [*AGS*]

ROMNEY, D. H.

65.060 BH 1960 Productivity of pasture in British Honduras—I. *Trop Agric* 37(2), Apr.: 135-142. [*AGS*]

ROSE-ROSETTE, ROBERT

65.061 MT 1958 Some veterinary aspects of the Martinique livestock industry. *Caribbean* 12(3), Oct.: 58-59. [*COL*]

SAUNDERS, P. T.

65.062 LW/ 1914 A veterinary survey of the Windward and Leeward Islands. *W I B* WW 14(3): 153-167. [*AMN*]

SCOTT, Mrs. F. E.

65.063 TR 1923 Notes on poultry raising. *J Bd Agric Br Gui* 16(4), Oct.: 223-232. [*AMN*]

SHANNON, J. LIONEL

65.064   TR   1940 Cattle raising as an adjunct to citrus growing in Trinidad. *Proc Agric Soc Trin Tob* 40(3), Sept.: 215-222.   [*AMN*]

65.065   TR   1947 Care and management of dairy goats in Trinidad and Tobago. *Proc Agric Soc Trin Tob* 47(3), Sept.: 215-228.   [*AMN*]

65.066   TR   1948 A few practical suggestions on poultry-keeping in Trinidad and Tobago. *Proc Agric Soc Trin Tob* 48(1), Mar.: 46-57.   [*AMN*]

65.067   JM/
        TR   1950 Housing and management of livestock. *Proc Agric Soc Trin Tob* 50(1), Mar.: 95-99.   [*AMN*]

65.068   TR   1952 Some possibilities of tropical kudzu in Trinidad and Tobago. *J Agric Soc Trin Tob* 52(3), Sept.: 331-335.   [*AMN*]

65.069   TR   1956 Care and management of dairy goats in Trinidad and Tobago. *J Agric Soc Trin Tob* 56(1), Mar.: 118-134.   [*AMN*]

65.070   BC   1956 History of dairy goats in the West Indies. *J Agric Soc Trin Tob* 56(1), Mar.: 19-33.   [66]   [*AMN*]

65.071   TR   1956 Possibilities of a pig industry in Trinidad. *J Agric Soc Trin Tob* 56(3), Sept.: 375-381.   [*AMN*]

STEHLE, HENRI

65.072   GC   1956 SURVEY OF FORAGE CROPS IN THE CARIBBEAN. Port of Spain, Central Secretariat, Caribbean Commission, 389p.

STEVENSON, G. C.

65.073   BG   1949 Notes on the grazing lands of British Guiana. *Trop Agric* 26(7-12), July-Dec.: 103-106.   [*AGS*]

STONE, E. F.

65.074   TR   1935 Poultry raising in citrus orchards. *Proc Agric Soc Trin Tob* 35(6), June: 205-210.   [60]   [*AMN*]

TURNER, H. E.

65.075   BG   1938 A short history of the Rupununi savannahs with special reference to the livestock industry. *Agric J Br Gui* 9(4): 230-236. [5]   [*AGS*]

TYWANG, C. B.

65.076   TR   1951 The institution and work of the Trinidad Goat Society. *J Agric Soc Trin Tob* 51(1), Mar.: 33-36.   [*AMN*]

UNSWORTH, P.; CAMPBELL, L. & BUTTERWORTH, M. H.

65.077   TR   1959 The problem of fluctuating fodder supply in Trinidad. *J Agric Soc Trin Tob* 59(3), Sept.: 355-369.   [*AMN*]

WARNER, HENRY

65.078   TR   1921 Our milk supply. *Proc Agric Soc Trin Tob* 21(6), June: 175-179.   [*AMN*]

WATTS, Sir FRANCIS

65.079   BC   1914 The production of pork and bacon. *W I B* 14(4): 221-227. [66] [*AMN*]

WEBB, G. W. HUMPHREY

65.080   TR   1950 Animal and plant breeding and genetics: a survey and history of dairy cattle of Trinidad and suggested policies for their improvement. *Trop Agric* 27(1-3), Jan.-Mar.: 18-23.   [66]   [*AGS*]

WILSON, P. N.

65.081   TR   1958   Animal husbandry—the problem child of Trinidad agriculture. *J Agric Soc Trin Tob* 58(4), Dec.: 425-467.   [*AMN*]

65.082   TR   1959   Animal husbandry investigations at I.C.T.A. with special reference to the management of cattle on pangola pastures. *J Agric Soc Trin Tob* 59(4), Dec.: 455-468.   [*AMN*]

65.083   TR   1960   Grass—the world's most important crop. *J Agric Soc Trin Tob* 60 (4), Dec.: 483-521.   [*AMN*]

WILSON, P. N. & HERRERA, E.

1.050   TR   1961   List of completed research work carried out at the Imperial College of Tropical Agriculture on animal and grassland husbandry.

WISE, K. S.

65.084   BG   1907   Observations on the milk supply of Georgetown. *Br Gui Med Annual 1906* 15:51-58.   [28]   [*ACM*]

WISE, K. S. & MINETT, E. P.

28.601   BG   1913   Review of the milk question in British Guiana.

ECONOMIC
AND
SOCIAL
PROSPECTS

Chapter 66

DEVELOPMENT AND CHANGE

ABRAHAM, A. A.

46.001   BG   1918 The agricultural development of the North Western District, during the years 1907-1918.

ACHARD, CH.

28.001   FG   1939 Mission en Guyane [Guiana expedition].

ADAMS, INEZ & MASUOKA, J.

8.001   TR   1961 Emerging elites and culture change.

AHRENS, H.

50.002   SR   1922/ Kolonisatie op particulier land in Suriname met Javanen onder
                23   contract onder de thans geldende immigratie wetten [Colonization with Javenese contract laborers on privately owned land in Surinam under the current immigration laws].

AIKEN, JAMES

66.001   BG   1915 "Timehri" and development. *Timehri* 3d ser., 3(20B), May: 169-210.
                [52]   [*AMN*]

ALCALA, V. O.

66.002   GC   1957 About community development...a review.   *Caribbean* 10(8), Mar.:
                192-195.   [*COL*]
66.003   GC   1959 Highlights of the conference on social development in the West
                Indies. *Caribbean* 13(6), June: 114-116.   [33]   [*COL*]

ALEXANDER, JOHN J. G.

66.004   JM   1946 Growing pains in Jamaica. *America* 75(21), Aug. 24: 494-495. [*COL*]

ALLEN, DEVERE

66.005   GC   1943 THE CARIBBEAN: LABORATORY OF WORLD COOPERATION. New York,
                League for Industrial Democracy, 40p. (Pamphlet series.)   [*COL*]

ARMSTRONG, ELIZABETH H.

66.006   GC   1946 Report on the West Indian Conference. *Dep St B* 14(359), May 19:
                840-845.   [*AGS*]

66.007   GC   1949 West Indian Conference: third session. *Dep St B* 20(503), Feb. 20:
                          221-226.   [*AGS*]

            ARNOLD, R. M.
65.005   JM   1955 30 million quarts of milk.

            ARNTZ, W.
66.008   SR   1925/ Het Suriname vraagstuk [The Surinam problem]. *WIG* 7:252-264. [37]
                    26   [*COL*]

            ASBECK, W. D. H. van
23.003   SR   1919 De Evangelische of Moravische Broeder-Gemeente in Suriname [The
                          Evangelical or Moravian Brethren in Surinam].

            ASQUITH, JUSTICE, et al.
32.015   BC   1945 REPORT OF THE COMMISSION ON HIGHER EDUCATION IN THE COLONIES.

            AUCHINLECK, GILBERT; SMITH, G. WHITFIELD &
            BERTRAND, WALTER
47.001   GN/   1914 Government schemes of land settlement in Grenada and the Grena-
            GR   dines.

            BADCOCK, W. J.
46.005   BB   1960 The problems relative to soil conservation in the Scotland District.

            BAILEY, BERYL LOFTMAN
25.005   GC   [1962] Language studies in the independent university.

            BALDWIN, RICHARD
66.009   BG   1948 Rupununi and its neighbor—Rio Branco. *Timehri* 4th ser., 1(28),
                          Dec.: 47-53.

            BANCROFT, C. K.
49.001   BG/   1917 The making of panama hats: a suitable industry for British Guiana.
            SR
41.024   BG   1918 Botanical aspect of the sea defence problem.

            BARI, VALESKA
66.010   UV   1925/ What to do with the Virgin Islands? *Nth Am Rev* 222, Dec., Jan.,
                    26 Feb.: 266-273.   [*COL*]

            BARKER, AUBREY
36.001   GC   1958 Progress, planning and people.

            BARON van LYNDEN, W. E. K.
46.007   SR   1932/ Landbouwvoorlichting en landbouwonderwijs in Suriname [Agri-
                    33 cultural guidance and agricultural education in Surinam].

            BARRY, JOHN
49.002   JM/   1946 Mulberry planting.
            TR

BARTELS, E.
55.001   AR   1956   Aruba moves ahead.
55.002   GC   1956   Government can help.

BARTLETT, KENNETH A.
37.019   UV   1957   The U.S. Virgin Islands Corporation.

BASCOM, F. C. S.
50.008   BG   1912   The labour question: the problem stated.

BATAILLE, EMILE C.
49.003   BG   1939   Report on industrial possibilities in British Guiana and on the establishment of an industrial center.
49.004   BG   1942   Possibilities for industrial enterprise in British Guiana.

BEARD, JOHN STEWART
64.009   WW   [1944?]   Forestry in the Windward Islands.
64.011   AT   [1945?]   Forestry in the Leeward Islands: Barbuda.
64.012   BV   [1945?]   Forestry in the Leeward Islands: the British Virgin Islands.

BEASLEY, CYRIL GEORGE
44.007   BC   1956   Prospects and obstacles to economic development.

BEAUREGARD, C. F.
66.011   GC   1963   The Caribbean organization and development in the Caribbean. *Chron W I Comm* 78(1391), Dec.: 644-646.   [*NYP*]

BECKETT, J. EDGAR
46.009   BG   1905   HINTS ON AGRICULTURE IN BRITISH GUIANA.
11.003   BG   1917   The black peasant proprietor.
66.012   BG   1918   Some stray thoughts on our people. *Timehri* 3d ser., 5(22), Aug.: 91-97.   [*AMN*]
66.013   BG   1919   Some home truths. *Timehri* 3d ser., 6(23), Sept.: 186-195.   [*AMN*]
66.014   BG   1921   Progress? *Timehri* 3d ser., 7(24), Aug.: 131-147.   [*AMN*]

BECKFORD, G. L. F.
46.010   TR   1965   Agriculture in the development of Trinidad and Tobago: a comment.

BECKLES, LYNNE
16.003   JM   1961   Race and colour in Jamaica.

BERGH, V. H. van den
54.006   CU   1935/   Petroleum, het levens-elixer voor Curacao [Petroleum, the elixer of 36   life for Curacao].

BERRILL, KENNETH
44.013   BG   1961   A comment [on "The economic future of British Guiana" by Peter Newman, in *Social Econ Stud* 9(3)].

BEST, ETHEL
50.010   UV   1936   Economic problems of the women of the Virgin Islands of the United States.

BEUKERING, J. A. van
46.012   SR   1952 Types of farming.

BEYERINCK, F. H.
64.019   GC   1955 The value of a centralised market information service for Caribbean
                        timbers.

BEYLERS, H. de
17.002   FG   1951 Immigration en Guyane [Immigration into Guiana].

BIRAC, ANTHONY
66.015   JM   1942 Jamaica. *New Stsm Natn* 24(605), Sept. 26: 203.

BIRD, V. C.
50.011   AT   1950 Labour in the Leewards.

BISHOP, G. D.
32.021   JM   1962 The shortage of science teachers in underdeveloped territories.

BLANCAN, ANDRE
66.016   GD   1904 La crise de la Guadeloupe: ses causes, ses remèdes [The crisis
                        in Guadeloupe: its causes and remedies]. Paris, Librairie nouvelle
                        de droit et de jurisprudence, 206p. (Ph.D. dissertation.)   [*COL*]

BLOOD, Sir HILARY
37.030   BH   1960 British Honduras: land of opportunity.

BLUME, HELMUT
47.007   JM   1961 Die gegenwärtigen Wandlungen in der Verbreitung von Gross- und
                        Kleinbetreiben auf den Grossen Antillen [Contemporary changes in
                        the distribution of large- and small-holdings in the Greater Antilles].

BOEKE, J.
56.009   NA   1948 Eenige opmerkingen over de visscherij naar aanleiding van het
                        Rapport Welvaartsplan Nederlandsche Antillen 1946 [Some remarks
                        about fishing, inspired by the Welfare Plan Report of the Dutch
                        Antilles 1946].

BOHEEMEN, H. van
32.025   SR   1947 Onderwijshervorming in Suriname [School reform in Surinam].

BOND, RICHARD M.
46.018   UV   1957 The federal experiment station in U.S. Virgin Islands.

BONE, LOUIS W.
32.027   GG   1962 Secondary education in the Guianas.

BOONACKER, J.
46.020   SR   1932/ Hoe kan Suriname's landbouw tot ontwikkeling komen [How can
                   33   Surinam's agriculture be developed]?

BORNN, D. VICTOR
66.017   UV   1954 On the road to stability. *Car Commn Mon Inf B* 8(4-5), Nov.-Dec.:
                        82-85.   [*COL*]

BORNN, ROY W.
33.003   UV   1949 Further extension of social security to Virgin Islands.

BOUGH, JAMES A.
66.018   GC   1949 The Caribbean Commission. *Int Org* 3(4), Nov.: 643-655.

BOULDING, K. E.
66.019   BG   1961 Social dynamics in West Indian society [cf. Newman's article in *Social Econ Stud* 9(3)]. *Social Econ Stud* 10(1), Mar.: 25-34.   [44]
                                                [*RIS*]

BOUMAN, L. F.
55.004   NA   1949 Tourism in the Netherlands West Indies.
55.005   NW   1959 Islands to windward.

BOWEN, CALVIN
66.020   JM   1953 Ten-year plan for Jamaica. *New Commonw* 25(4), Feb. 16: 170. [*AGS*]

BRACEWELL, SMITH
54.009   BG   1950 The search for minerals in British Guiana.

BRAINE, BERNARD
62.004   BG/   1953 Caribbean contribution to relief of world rice shortage.
          TR

BRAITHWAITE, LLOYD E.
38.023   BC   1957 'Federal' associations and institutions in the West Indies.
31.013   GC   1961 Social and economic changes in the Caribbean.
31.014   GC   1963 The changing social scene.

BRANDON, H. G.
62.005   SR   1932/ Proefneming voor machinale hoeverijstcultuur op de plantage Guade-
                33 loup in Suriname in 1925-26 [Experiments with mechanical field-rice cultivation on the Guadeloup plantation in Surinam in 1925-26].

BRANDS, C. F. J.
66.021   SR   1933/ De toekomst van Suriname [The future of Surinam]. *W I G* 15:309-
                34 312.   [*COL*]

BREEVELD, F.
44.023   SR   1958 Electriciteit in het oerwoud [Electricity in the primeval forest].

BRETON, B. O.
49.007   AT   1956 Antigua—industrial development.

BROAD, D. & FERGUSON, W.
51.017   BC   1956 Trade opportunities for the U. K.

BROOKS, REGINALD LAING
64.022   TR   1941 The Lands Advisory Committee of Trinidad.
64.025   TR   1942 The forest policy of Trinidad and Tobago.

BROWN, G. ARTHUR
44.025   JM   1958 Economic development and the private sector.

BROWN, HEADLEY & ANDERSON, ERROL
47.008   BC   1963/ Economic development in the West Indies and the peasantry.
                    64

BROWN, HERBERT H.
56.011   LW/   1945 The fisheries of the Windward and Leeward Islands.
            WW

BROWN, JOHN
32.033   SL   1962 Education and development of St. Lucia.
32.034   SL   1962 Lines of approach to adult education.

BROWN, JOHN, ed.
32.035   SL   1962 An approach to adult education.

BROWN, W. J.
37.045   JM   1948 Jamaica boss.

BRUCE, GEORGE
44.029   JM   1961 Jamaica's 10-year miracle.

BRYAN, VICTOR
46.024   TR   1951 Agricultural policy.

BUCK, EDWARD CLARK
52.016   BG   1919 Proposed railway development of the hinterland of British Guiana.

BUENEMAN, E. R.
35.003   TB   1958 The Tobago story—example of cooperation at all levels.

BUIE, T. S.
57.007   BB   1955 Report of study of the Scotland District, Barbados, B.W.I., with
                    recommendations for a soil conservation program.

BURGESS, CHARLES J.
35.004   GC   1951 Issues in Caribbean housing improvement.
49.008   GC   1952 Prewar industrial development.
46.027   GC   1952 Some sociological factors in agricultural development in the Carib-
                    bean.
49.009   GC   1952 World War II and industrialisation.
49.010   GC   1953 The achievements of industrialisation policy in the Caribbean.
49.011   GC   1953 The future of industrialisation in the Caribbean.
49.012   GC   1953 Post war industrialisation policy.

BURNS, Sir ALAN CUTHBERT
66.022   BC   1949 Weaknesses of British West Indian administration. *Crown Colon* 19
                    (208), Mar.: 147-149.   [37]   [*NYP*]

BURRA, J. A. N.
42.006   JM   1962 The forest and watershed control.

BUTLER, HUGH A., et al.
66.023   UV   1954 Virgin Islands report. Washington, U.S. Govt. Print. Off., 143p.
                                                                          [*NYP*]

CAIRES, P. F. de
28.081   GC   1951 The international yellow fever problem in the Caribbean Islands.

CALVER, W. A.
33.005   BB   [1945?] REPORTS ON THE BARBADOS POLICE FORCE AND THE BARBADOS (BRIDGE-
                TOWN) FIRE BRIGADE.

CAMPBELL, BETTY
30.005   TR   1948 Malnutrition and allied problems in Trinidad and Tobago.

CAMPBELL, LEWIS
46.030   GC   1962 Production methods in West Indies agriculture.

CAMPBELL, THELMA P.
31.016   GC   1963 The role of youth clubs in preparing for maturity.

CAMPO, E. J. à
62.006   SR   1955 Het Wageningen-project [The Wageningen project].

CANADAY, WARD M.
66.024   GC   1949 U. S. economic policy in the Caribbean. *Dep St B* 20(521), June 26:
                813-819.   [*COL*]

CARASCO, F. J. & SCHOUTEN, S. A.
17.004   SR/   1947 Emigration to Surinam.
          BC

CAREY-JONES, N. S.
44.031   BH   1953 THE PATTERN OF A DEPENDENT ECONOMY: A STUDY OF THE NATIONAL
                INCOME OF BRITISH HONDURAS.

CARLE, R. BENITEZ
55.007   GC   1959 The tourist potential of the Caribbean.

CARLEY, MARY MANNING
28.083   JM   1943 MEDICAL SERVICES IN JAMAICA.

CARLEY, VERNA A. & STARCH, ELMER A.
66.025   JM   1955 REPORT ON COMMUNITY DEVELOPMENT PROGRAMS IN JAMAICA, PUERTO
                RICO, BOLIVIA, AND PERU, BY TEAM NUMBER II. Washington, D. C., In-
                ternational Cooperation Administration, 76p.   [*UNL*]

CASE, GERALD O.
44.032   BG   1946 Power resources of British Guiana.
49.014   BG   1946 Problems affecting industrialisation of the interior of British Guiana.

CATER, JOHN C.
64.032   LW   [1944?] FORESTRY IN THE LEEWARD ISLANDS.

CHAMPION, HAROLD
49.016   JM   1955 Industrial era for Jamaica.

CHAPMAN, DONALD

66.026   JM   1962 Jamaica cuts loose. *Venture* 14(1), Jan.: 4, 8.   [*COL*]

CHAPMAN, ESTHER

66.027   JM   1954 DEVELOPMENT IN JAMAICA: YEAR OF PROGRESS, 1954. Kingston, Ara-
                wak Press, 209p.   [*AGS*]

CHAPMAN, JOHN L.

35.006   SV   1951 Aided self-help housing in St. Vincent.

CHARLES, HENRI

44.034   GD   1947 La Guadeloupe: un cas d'émancipation coloniale et de rétablisse-
                ment économique après la guerre [Guadeloupe: a case history of
                political emancipation and economic revival after the war].

CHARLES, L. J.

28.093   BG   1953 Re-infestation problems in an *Aedes Aegypti*—free area in British
                Guiana.

CHARPENTIER, S. & G.

66.028   FG   1954 An Indianist experiment in French Guiana. *Boln Indig* 14(2), June:
                133-141.   [13, 14, 33]   [*COL*]

CHOUBERT, BORIS

66.029   FG   1960 L'Institut francais d'Amerique tropicale (I. F.A.T.): pilot agency
                in French Guiana. *Caribbean* 14(4), Apr.: 73-79, 100.   [40, 41, 57]
                                                                                         [*COL*]

CLEGG, J. B.

49.018   JM   1952 Commercial and industrial prospects in Jamaica.

COMBER, STAFFORD X.

52.020   BG   1919 Interior communications for British Guiana.

COMITAS, LAMBROS

56.017   JM   1962 Fishermen and cooperation in rural Jamaica.

CONSEIL, L. B.

56.018   MT   1926 LA QUESTION DE LA PÊCHE INDUSTRIELLE À LA MARTINIQUE [THE QUES-
                TION OF INDUSTRIAL FISHING IN MARTINIQUE].

COOL, P.

28.110   SR   1924/ De nieuwe afdeling van het militaire hospitaal te Paramaribo voor
                25 besmettelijke ziekten [The new section for contagious diseases in
                the military hospital in Paramaribo].

COORE, DAVID

37.068   JM   [1961?] Government and the community.

COSTELLO, M.

35.009   BG   1951 The possibilities of prefabrication.
35.010   BG   1952 Rural housing problems: with notes on self-help housing and the
                possibilities of prefabrication.

COYAUD, YVES

62.008   FG   1952 Les possibilités rizicoles de la Guyane Francaise [The rice-grow-
                ing possibilities in French Guiana].

COZIER, EDWARD L.

46.038   SL   1956 Agricultural progress in St. Lucia.

66.030   BB   1958 Lesson from Barbados; how to triumph over adversity. *Can-W l Mag*
                      48(4), Apr.: 12-13, 18.   [*NYP*]

CROFT, W. D.; SPRINGER. H. W. & CHRISTOPHERSON, H. S.

51.039   BC   1958 Report of the Trade and Tariffs Commission.

CROUCHER, H. H. & SWABEY, C.

46.041   JM   1938 SOIL EROSION AND CONSERVATION IN JAMAICA, 1937.

CROWLEY, DANIEL JOHN

66.031   SL   [1959?] CONSERVATISM AND CHANGE IN SAINT LUCIA: ACTAS DEL XXXIII CON-
                      GRESO INTERNACIONAL DE AMERICANISTAS, San José, Costa Rica,
                      July 20-27, 1958. [n.p.] Editorial Lehmann, p.704-715. [5]   [*RIS*]

CRUICKSHANK, J. GRAHAM

36.005   BG   1918 "King William's people."

CUMPER, GEORGE E.

66.032   BG/   [1950?] This is the Evans Report. *Car Q* 1(3): 39-44.
          BH

50.022   BB   1959 REPORT ON EMPLOYMENT IN BARBADOS.

8.018   JM   [1961?] Notes on social structure in Jamaica.

66.033   JM   [1961?] The success of the Conference: a personal evaluation. *In* CUMPER,
                      GEORGE, ed. REPORT OF THE CONFERENCE ON SOCIAL DEVELOPMENT
                      IN JAMAICA. Kingston, Standing Committee on Social Services,
                      p.114-121.   [*RIS*]

44.045   JM/   1961 Investment criteria: a comment [on Newman's article in *Social Econ*
          BG   *Stud* 9(3)].

CUMPER, GEORGE E., ed.

66.034   JM   [1961?] REPORT OF THE CONFERENCE ON SOCIAL DEVELOPMENT IN JAMAICA.
                      Kingston, Standing Committee on Social Services, 181p.   [*RIS*]

CURTIN, PHILIP D.

37.085   GC   1955 The United States in the Caribbean.

CUSH, J. M.

46.045   BG   1920 Possibilities of farming on the banks of the Berbice River.

DANKLEFSEN, MILDRED MARIE

58.029   JM   1952 RECENT TRENDS IN THE SUGAR INDUSTRY OF JAMAICA.

DASH, J. SYDNEY

46.049   BC   1955 Making the most of agriculture.

DAVENPORT, WILLIAM HUNT

8.019   JM   1956 A COMPARATIVE STUDY OF TWO JAMAICAN FISHING COMMUNITIES.

DAVIDSON, H. K. & MINKES, A. L.

66.035   JM   1954 Social factors in the economic problems of Jamaica. *J Agric Econ*
                      11(1), June: 69-80.   [8,9,44]   [*NYP*]

DAVIDSON, LEWIS

23.032 JM   1945 First things first: a study of the Presbyterian Church in Jamaica.

66.036 JM   [1961?] Acceptance of social change. *In* CUMPER, GEORGE, ed. Report of the Conference on Social Development in Jamaica. Kingston, Standing Committee on Social Services, p.111-113. [20]   [*RIS*]

DAVIS, J. MERLE

23.033 JM   1942 The church in the new Jamaica: a study of the economic and social basis of the Evangelical Church in Jamaica.

DAVSON, Sir EDWARD R.

66.037 BG   1908 British Guiana and its development. *J Roy Colon Inst* 39(5), Apr.: 313-337.   [*NYP*]

37.091 BC   1919 Problems of the West Indies.

DEMOUGEOT, M.

64.041 FG   1928 Les bois de la Guyane Francaise dans l'industrie de la tonnellerie [The timbers of French Guiana in the cooperage industry].

DENHAM, Sir EDWARD

66.038 BG   1934 The present state of British Guiana. *W I Comm Circ* 49(931), June 7: 229-230.   [*NYP*]

DENNY, J. F.

46.052 BG   1921 The farmer's progress.

DeSYLLAS, L. M.

35.012 BB   [1944?] Report on preliminary housing survey of two blocks of Chapman's Lane Tenantry, Bridgetown (June-July, 1944); and comments on the Report by the Town Planning Adviser and the Housing Board.

DICKINSON, THOMAS H.

44.051 UV   1927 Economic crisis in the Virgin Islands.

DICKINSON, THOMAS H., et al.

32.056 UV   1929 Report of the educational survey of the Virgin Islands.

DIJK, M. van

5.046 SE   1929/ Nog eens: verzuimd Sint Eustatius [Once again: neglected St.
        30 Eustatius].

DILLARD, J. L.

25.022 GC   1962 Purism and prescriptivism as applied to the Caribbean Creoles— tentative classification.

DOWNIE, JACK

44.052 BH   1959 An economic policy for British Honduras.

DRESDEN, D. & GOUDRIAAN, J.

66.039 CU   1947 Rapport Welvaartsplan Nederlandse Antillen 1946 [Report about the Welfare Plan, Netherlands Antilles 1946]. Willemstad, 67p.
        [46]   [*NYP*]

DRIMMLEN, C. van

45.009   SR   1923/ Een uitweg voor verzinkend Suriname [A way out of sinking
                 24 Surinam].

DUCLOS, B. HAVARD

46.057   GC   1957 REPORT ON AGRICULTURAL DEVELOPMENT IN THE CARIBBEAN.

DUFOUGERE, W.

37.101   FG   1921 De l'utilisation rationnelle de la main-d'ouevre pénale en Guyane
                 [On the rational use of forced labor in Guiana].

DUMPLETON, C. W.

66.040   BC   1956 The colonial development corporation in the Caribbean. *Statist*
                 Sept.: 65.

DUNLOP, W. R.

56.021   BC   1915 A method of sponge cultivation and its prospects in the Lesser
                 Antilles: with notes on other possible shallow water fisheries.

44.053   BG   1925 Economic research in tropical development, with special reference
                 to British Guiana and British Malaya.

EARLE, A. F.

44.054   JM   1953 Incentives to private investment as an aspect of development
                 programmes.

EBERLEIN, HAROLD DONALDSON

35.015   UV   1935 Housing in the Virgin Islands.

EDWARDS, DAVID T.

46.058   JM   1954 An economic study of agriculture in the Yallahs Valley area of Ja-
46.059   JM   1954 Remedies proposed by the International Bank Mission.

EDWARDS, W. H.

46.062   CM   1938 REPORT ON AN AGRICULTURAL SURVEY IN THE CAYMAN ISLANDS.

EEKHOUT, J. J. W.

66.041   SR   1926 Heeft Suriname een toekomst [Does Surinam have a future]? *In* IN-
                 DISCH GENOOTSCHAP. VERGADERING VAN 10 DECEMBER, 1926. The
                 Hague, Nijhoff, bls. 101-135. [17]   [*AGS*]

EGERTON, Sir WALTER

52.026   BG   1915 A railway and hinterland development.
2.072   BG   1918 British Guiana and the problem of its development.

EMMART, A. D.

66.042   GC   [n.d.] CARIBBEAN COOPERATION. Washington, D. C., Anglo-American Carib-
                 bean Commission.   [*AGS*]

ERICKSEN, E. GORDON

7.019   BC   1962 THE WEST INDIES POPULATION PROBLEM: DIMENSIONS FOR ACTION.

ESDRAS, MARCEL
28.146   FA   1960 Les congrès des médecins de langue francaise de l'hémisphere
                         Américain [Congresses of French-speaking physicians in the West-
                         ern Hemisphere].

ETIENNE, FLORY
66.043   GC   1952 LA COMMISSION DES CARAÏBES [THE CARIBBEAN COMMISSION]. Paris,
                         Maurice Lavergne, 192p. (Ph.D. dissertation, University of Paris.)
                                                                                  [COL]

ETTINGER, J. van
53.015   CU   1930/ Bankwezen in Curacao 1906-1928 [Banking institutions in Curacao,
                     31 1906-1928].
53.016   CU   1938 Wijziging van de regeling nopens het circulatiebankwezen van
                         Curacao [Modification of the rule about the circulation banking
                         institutions of Curacao].

EVANS, Sir GEOFFREY
66.044   GC   1939 Note on the possibilities for the agricultural settlement of involun-
                         tary refugees from Central Europe in the hinterland of British
                         Guiana. In REPORT OF THE BRITISH GUIANA COMMISSION TO THE PRES-
                         DENT'S ADVISORY COMMITTEE ON POLITICAL REFUGEES. Washington,
                         D. C. [no. 5] (29p., 5 l.)   [46]   [AGS]
46.065   BC   1942 West Indian agriculture.
66.045   BG/   1949 Resettlement problems in the British Caribbean colonies. United
           BH   Emp 40(3), May-June: 105-110.   [AGS]

EVANS, Sir GEOFFREY, et al.
66.046   BG/   1948 REPORT OF THE BRITISH GUIANA AND BRITISH HONDURAS SETTLEMENT
           BH   COMMISSION. London, H.M.S.O., 359p. (Cmd. 7533)   [37]

EVANS, LUTHER HARRIS
66.047   UV   1935 Unrest in the Virgin Islands. For Policy Rep 11(2), Mar. 27:14-24.
                                                                                  [NYP]

FAHEY, HAROLD NEAL
46.066   TR   1940 Re-adjustment of Trinidad's agriculture, its necessity, and policy
                         required for same.
46.067   TR   1944 The necessity of resuscitating Trinidad's agriculture.

FARLEY, RAWLE
16.010   BG   1955 The substance and the shadow—a study of the relations between
                         white planters and free coloured in a slave society in British
                         Guiana.
50.047   BC   1958 Caribbean labour comes of age.
46.070   BG   1958 Economic and social change on a Caribbean frontier.
49.022   BC   1958 Nationalism and industrial development in the British Caribbean.
44.059   BG   1962 Kaldor's budget in retrospect: reason and unreason in a developing
                         area: reflections on the 1962 budget in British Guiana.

FARLEY, RAWLE; FLANDERS, ALLAN & ROPER, JOE
50.050   BC   1961 Industrial relations and the British Caribbean..

FAULKNER, O. T. & SHEPHARD, C. Y.
46.071   BC   1943 Mixed farming: the basis of a system for West Indian peasants.

FAUVEL, LUC
37.112   FA   1955 Les conséquences économiques et sociales de l'assimilation administrative des Antilles Francaises [The economic and social consequences of the political assimilation of the French Antilles].

FENTEM, ARLIN D.
43.053   SV   1961 COMMERCIAL GEOGRAPHY OF ST. VINCENT.

FINCH, KENNETH W.
49.023   TR   1962 A commercial approach to rural electrification.

FINCH, T. F.
57.017   JM   1959 Soil and land-use surveys. No. 7: Jamaica—Parish of Clarendon.
             1961 Soil and land-use surveys. No. 11: Jamaica—Parish of Portland.

FINDLAY, G. G. & HOLDSWORTH, W. W.
23.045   BC   1921 The history of the Wesleyan Methodist Missionary Society, v. 2.

FISHER, NORMAN
43.054   GC   1953 Caribbean problem: education, food, and human resources.

FOLLETT-SMITH, R. R.
58.039   BG   1958 British Guiana's sugar industry: thirty years of progress.

FOREMAN, R. A.
47.013   SL   1958 LAND SETTLEMENT SCHEME FOR SAINT LUCIA: BASED ON A SURVEY OF THE AGRICULTURAL AND SOCIAL CONDITIONS OF THE ISLAND ... ON A VISIT FROM 24.3.58-26.4.58.

FOSTER, BEN R.
47.014   UV   1947 Homesteading in the Virgin Islands.

FOX, ANNETTE BAKER
33.008   GC   1949 FREEDOM AND WELFARE IN THE CARIBBEAN: A COLONIAL DILEMMA.

FRAMPTON, A. de K.
47.015   BC   1952 Land tenure in relation to the British West Indies.

FRAMPTON, A. de K., et al.
66.048   TB   1957 DEVELOPMENT PLAN FOR TOBAGO: REPORT OF THE TEAM WHICH VISITED TOBAGO IN MARCH/APRIL, 1957. Bridgetown, Advocate Co., 172p. (Development and Welfare Bulletin no. 34.)
66.049   SV   1959 Report and recommendations for the development of Saint Vincent by team of experts following its visit in November, 1957. Bridgetown, Advocate Co., 125p.

FRANCIS, SYBIL E.
35.017   JM   1953 A land settlement project in Jamaica.

FRASER, H.
64.046   WW   1956 Forest preservation in the Windward Islands.

FREDHOLM, A.
32.067   TR   1912 Agricultural education in Trinidad—past, present and future.

FREILICH, MORRIS
67.005   TR   1960 Cultural models and land holdings.

FREITAS, G. V. de
37.117   BG   1961 British Guiana clears the decks.

FREITAS, Q. B. de
28.200   BG   1942 Some observations on the proposed scheme for British Guiana for the improvement of public health and sanitary measures.

FREITAS, Q. B. de, et al.
28.203   BG   1940 Report of the Sub-committee of the Infant Welfare and Maternity League of British Guiana.

GAAY FORTMAN, B. de
44.064   CU   1921/ Curacao: De voorstellen van den Gouverneur in het belang van de
            22   economische opheffing der kolonie [The suggestions of the Governor toward the economic development of the colony].
66.050   NA   1921/ De vooruitgang der Nederlandsche West-Indische eilanden [The
            22   progress of the Dutch West Indian islands]. *W I G* 3:113-144. [*COL*]
5.061   CU   1938 Curacao onder de regeering van Koningin Wilhelmina 1898-1938 [Curacao under the Government of Queen Wilhelmina 1898-1938].
44.084   CU   1938 Economische en sociale vraagstukken in Curacao [Economic and social problems in Curacao].
46.074   NL   1948 De landbouwplannen van den Gezaghebber van Rades [The agricultural plans of the District Commissioner van Rades].

GAMMANS, L. D.
37.136   JM   1947 Self-governing Jamaica.

GARDNER-MEDWIN, R. J.
36.006   BC   1948 Major problems of town planning in the West Indies.

GATES, RALPH CHARLES
66.051   GC   1961 A MONOGRAPH ON COOPERATIVE DEVELOPMENT IN THE CARIBBEAN. San Juan, Pto. Rico, Caribbean Commission, 13p. [33, 46, 48]   [*RIS*]

GEORGE, Mc.
46.075   AT   1956 Antigua peasant agriculture.

GIBBS, BERNARD, ed.
66.052   SV   [1947?] A PLAN OF DEVELOPMENT FOR THE COLONY OF ST. VINCENT, WINDWARD ISLANDS, BRITISH WEST INDIES. Port of Spain, Guardian Commercial Printery, 821p.   [*RIS*]

GIGLIOLI, E. G.
62.013   BG   1959 Mechanized rice production at the Mahaicony-Abary Scheme, British Guiana.

GIGLIOLI, GEORGE
28.216   BG   1939 Notes on health conditions on the southern Rupununi savannahs.
28.218   BG   1946 Malaria and agriculture in British Guiana.
28.219   BG   1948 Immediate and long-term economic effects accruing from the control of mosquito-transmitted diseases in British Guiana.

GILLETTE, H. P. S.
28.228 BC 1960 Comments on Dr. Thomas's report of the chest service for the Federation of the West Indies.

GILMOUR, JOHN D.
64.049 BG 1949 Exploitation of the forests of British Guiana.

GILMOUR, W. SANTON
28.229 BB [n.d.] TUBERCULOSIS SURVEY AND RECOMMENDATIONS.

GIMON, P.
64.050 FG 1951 Une expérience d'exploitation forestière en Guyane Francaise [A lumbering experiment in French Guiana].

GONGGRIJP, J. W.
65.016 SR 1923/ Surinaamsche savanna's en veeteelt [Surinam's savannahs and 24 cattle breeding].
66.053 SR 1955 Some remarks on the Brokopondo Project. *Vox Guy* 1(6): 145-148. [*RIS*]

GOODE, RICHARD
44.090 JM 1956 Taxation and economic development in Jamaica.

GORDON, DAVID L.
66.054 BH 1954 THE ECONOMIC DEVELOPMENT PROGRAM OF BRITISH HONDURAS. Washington, D. C. International Bank for Reconstruction and Development, 34p. [*NYP*]
66.055 BH [1955?] THE ECONOMIC DEVELOPMENT PROGRAM OF BRITISH HONDURAS. Washington, D. C., International Bank for Reconstruction and Development, 34p.

GORDON, HOPETON
56.025 JM 1964 Commentary: a note on Jamaica's marine fisheries.

GORDON, SHIRLEY C.
32.070 TR 1962 The Keenan report, 1869. Part I: The elementary school system in Trinidad.
32.074 TR [1963?] Documents which have guided educational policy in the West Indies —3: Patrick Joseph Keenan's report 1869—Pt. II: Secondary and higher education.
32.078 BC 1964 Documents which have guided educational policy in the West Indies, No. 8: Report of the Commissioners Mayhew and Marriott on secondary and primary education in Trinidad, Barbados, Leeward Islands and Windward Islands, 1931-32.

GORDON, W. A.
64.052 BC 1961 Forest management in the Caribbean.

GORE-ORMSBY, W.
46.077 BC 1922 The progress of the West Indies.

GOVEIA, ELSA V.
66.056 BC 1965 Small societies in transition: past history and present planning in the West Indies. *New Wld Q* 2(1), Dead Season: 71-79. [5] [*RIS*]

GRAHAM, CYNTHIA
64.053 BG 1954 A colonial problem for the protectionist.

GRANSAULL, EDWARD
17.011 TR 1916 Causes of emigration from the colony.

GRANT, ANDREW
52.031   BG   1930 Railways necessary to progress.
52.032   BG   1931 Railroad construction advocated.

GRANT, C. H.
66.057   BG   1965 The politics of community development in British Guiana 1954-57.
                      Social Econ Stud 14(2), June: 170-182.   [37]   [*RIS*]

GRANT, LOUIS STRATHMORE
28.245   JM   1956 Modern trends in preventive medicine in the Caribbean: a review.

GRATTAN, C. HARTLEY
66.058   GC   1948 Caribbean: detritus of empire. *Jew Fron* 15(7), July: 20-24.   [*COL*]

GREENIDGE, C. W. W.
66.059   BH   1942 British Honduras. *Contemp Rev* 162, Aug.: 93-98.   [*COL*]
2.086   BC   1949 The present outlook in the British West Indies.

GROOTE, J. F.
52.033   AR/   1950 The new harbours of Aruba and Curacao.
           CU

GUPPY, JOHN LECHMERE
60.031   TR   1932 Cashew nuts: as a possible local agricultural industry.

GUYADEEN, K. D.
57.019   SV   1957 A note on soil conservation work in St. Vincent, B.W.I.

HAAN, J. H. de
46.080   SR   1953 The Lelydorp project.
46.081   SR   1955 De landstreekontwikkeling in Suriname [Development of rural regions in Surinam].

HAAN, J. H. de & HENDRIKS, J. A. H.
46.082   SR   1954 Lelydorp project—a pilot scheme for land-development in Surinam.

HAGERTY, T. F.
31.033   AR   1963 The Junior Achievement Programme in Aruba.

HAGLUND, ELSA
35.019   GC   1958 HOUSING AND HOME IMPROVEMENT IN THE CARIBBEAN.

HAJARY, H. N.
9.012   SR   1937 De verwacht wordende groote gebeurtenis onder de Britsch-Indiërs in Suriname [The expected big event among British Indians in Surinam].

HALL, C. J. J. van
59.015   SR   1933/ De proeven van Dr. Fernandes in de koffie-proeffabriek in Suriname
                  34 [The experiments of Dr. Fernandes in the experimental coffee-factory in Surinam].

HAMMOND, S. A.
32.086   BC   1945 COST OF EDUCATION.

HANRATH, JOHANNES J.

52.034	SR	1952	"Planning" met betrekking tot het binnenlandse verkeer van Suriname [Planning of inland traffic of Surinam].
52.035	SR	1952	DE ZEESCHEEPVAART VAN SURINAME: VOORSTELLEN VOER DE TEEKOMSTIGE VERKEERSONTWIKKELING VAN SURINAME [THE SEA TRAFFIC OF SURINAM: PROPOSALS FOR THE FUTURE DEVELOPMENT OF TRANSPORTATION AND TRAFFIC OF SURINAM].
43.063	SR	1956	The economic-geographical structure of Surinam.

HANSON, DONALD R.

35.020	GC	1955	Caribbean housing.

HARDY, F.; McDONALD, J. A. & RODRIGUEZ, G.

57.038	AT	1933	STUDIES IN WEST INDIAN SOILS. (V)—THE SUGAR-CANE SOILS OF ANTIGUA.

HARDY, F.; ROBINSON, C. K. & RODRIGUEZ, G.

57.039	SV	1934	STUDIES IN WEST INDIAN SOILS. (VIII)—THE AGRICULTURAL SOILS OF ST. VINCENT.

HARDY, F.; RODRIGUES, G. & NANTON, W. R. E.

57.042	MS	[1949?]	STUDIES IN WEST INDIAN SOILS. (XI)—THE AGRICULTURAL SOILS OF MONTSERRAT.

HARDY, F.; SMART, H. P. & RODRIGUEZ, G.

57.043	BH	1935	STUDIES IN WEST INDIAN SOILS. (IX)—SOME SOIL-TYPES OF BRITISH HONDURAS, CENTRAL AMERICA.

HAREWOOD, JACK

50.058	BC	1956	A system of labour force statistics.

HARKNESS, J. W. P.

28.267	BC	1949	Montego Bay Conference Report. E: Report of the Fourth Conference of Heads of British West Indian Medical Departments.
28.268	BC	1950	Some aspects of public health progress in the British Caribbean territories during the period 1947-50.

HARLOW, VINCENT TODD

37.158	BG	1951	British Guiana and British colonial policy.

HARRIS, BRITTON

49.034	GC	1953	The role of government in industrial development in the Caribbean.

HARRISON, Sir JOHN B.

44.099	BG	1918	Now and then; or, Notes on the Society and its work in 1897 and in 1918.

HARTOG, JOHAN

36.007	CU/ AR	1947	De voorgenomen uitbreiding van Willemstad op Curacao, Oranjestad en St. Nicolaas op Aruba [The contemplated expansion of Willemstad in Curacao, of Oranjestad and St. Nicolaas in Aruba].
23.062	AR	1952	Aruba's oudste kerk 1750-1816-1952 [Aruba's oldest church 1750-1816-1952].

HAVORD, G.

57.045   TR   1961 Soil and land-use surveys. No. 13: A detailed soil and land capability survey of a cacao area in Trinidad.

HAYDEN, HOWARD

32.094   BB   [1945?] A policy for education.

HAZLEWOOD, ARTHUR

44.100   JM   1956 The Hicks Report on finance and taxation in Jamaica: a comment.

HEESTERMAN, J.E.

35.021   GC   1951 New materials and methods of construction.
30.033   GC   1953 Standardising milk fat content.
65.023   GC   1955 Use of industrial by-products as stock feed.
64.060   GC   1956 Forestry.
49.037   GC   1956 Industry.
55.015   BN   1957 A development plan for Bonaire.

HENDRICKSEN, H. E.

32.096   TR   1912 •Agricultural education.

HENDRICKS, J. A. H.

46.089   SR   1956 Het Lelydorpplan in Suriname: inleiding tot het vraagstuk van de landontwikkeling op arme gronden in een tropisch gebeid [The Lelydorp plan in Surinam: introduction to the problem of land development on inferior soils in a tropical area].

HENFREY, COLIN

66.060   BG   1961 S.O.S. from Guiana. *Commonw J* 4(3), May-June: 122-127. [13] [*AGS*]

HENRIQUEZ, P. C.

66.061   CU   1962 Problems relating to hydrology, water conservation, erosion control, reforestation and agriculture in Curacao. [Willemstad, Curacao, Sold by Boekhandel Salas; The Hague, Sold by M. Nijhoff], 54p. (Uitgaven van de Natuurwetenschappelijke Werkgroep Nederlandse Antillen, no. 14.) [40, 46, 57, 64]   [*RIS*]

HENRIQUEZ, P. COHEN

66.062   NC   1934/ Is grooter bloei van West Indië mogelijk? [Is greater prosperity of 35 the West Indies possible]? *W I G* 16:337-366.   [*COL*]

HESS, ERNEST

56.029   BB   1962 Fisheries development programme, 1961-1965.

HICKLING, C. F.

56.030   BC   [1950?] The fisheries of the British West Indies: report on a visit in 1949.

HICKS, JOHN R. & URSULA K.

44.101   JM   1955 Report on finance and taxation in Jamaica.

HILL, L. C.

37.178   JM   1943 Report on the reform of local government in Jamaica.

HILL, L. C.
37.179   JM   1945 Jamaica gets reform program.

HILL, LUKE M.
52.039   BG   1912 Railway discussion 1902: the possibilities of railway development
                      in British Guiana.
36.009   BG   1915 The municipality of Georgetown.

HILL, ROLLA B.
28.282   GC   1947 The International Health Division of the Rockefeller Foundation in
                      the Caribbean.

HOARE, SAMUEL
37.181   BH   1921 The problem of crown colony government in the Caribbean.

HOLDRIDGE, DESMOND
2.100   BG   1939 An investigation of the prospect for white settlement in British
                      Guiana.

HOLMES, OLIVE
66.063   BC/   1944 Anglo-American Caribbean Commission-pattern for colonial coopera-
          VI   tion. *For Policy Rep* 20(19), Dec. 15: 238-247.   [*AGS*]

HOLSTEIN, CASPER
66.064   UV   1925 The Virgin Islands. *Opportunity* 3(34), Oct.: 304-306. [37]   [*COL*]
66.065   UV   1926 The Virgin Islands: past and present. *Opportunity* 4(47), Nov.:
                      344-345. [37]   [*COL*]

HORN, EDWIN
35.023   BC   [n.d.] The West Indies: report of a survey on housing, November 1956-
                      May 1957.

HOTCHKISS, J. C. & MRS. J. C.
46.092   BC   1954 The education of the small scale farmer and his family for better
                      farm and home living in the British Caribbean.

HOWE, J. W.
65.027   JM   1940 Livestock improvement in Jamaica in war time.

HOWES, H. W.
32.100   GC   1955 Fundamental, adult, literacy and community education in the
                      West Indies.

HOYOS, F. A.
32.102   BB   1948 Barbados aims at high level education.

HOYT, ELIZABETH E.
44.107   JM   1959 Changing standards of living in Jamaica.
50.066   JM   1960 Voluntary unemployment and unemployability in Jamaica with special
                      reference to the standard of living.

HUCK, SUSAN L. M.
66.066   BH   1962 British Honduras: an evaluation. Ph.D. dissertation, Clark Univers-
                      ity, 277p. [37]

HUGGINS, H. D.

32.103   BC   1949 Institute of Social and Economic Research at U.C.W.I.
66.067   BC   1949 Social science research, *Car Q* 1(1), Apr.-June: 21-25. [67]
44.109   JM   1953 Employment, economic development and incentive financing in
                      Jamaica.
54.026   GC   1965 Aluminum in changing communities.

HUGGINS, H. D., ed.

44.110   BC   1958 [PROCEEDINGS OF THE] STUDY CONFERENCE ON ECONOMIC DEVELOPMENT
                      IN UNDERDEVELOPED COUNTRIES [held at the University College of
                      the West Indies, Aug. 5-15, 1957].

HUGGINS, H. D. & CUMPER, G. E.

44.111   JM/   1958 Economic development in a context of low population pressure.
          BG

HUGGINS, Sir JOHN

33.013   BC   1944 West Indies development and welfare organiation.

HUNTE, GEORGE HUTCHINSON

58.059   BB   1955 Barbados ... sugar and tourism.
55.016   BC   1957 Tourism: a federal approach.
55.017   BB   1959 Barbados in the federal tourist picture.

HURAULT, JEAN

13.039   FG   1963 Les Indiens de Guyane Francaise: problèmes pratiques d'adminis-
                      tration et de contacts de civilisation [The Indians of French Guiana:
                      practical problems of administration and culture contact].

HUSSEIN, AHMED & TAYLOR, CARL C.

66.068   JM/   1953 Report of the Mission on Rural Community Organization and De-
          TR   velopment in the Caribbean area and Mexico. [New York?] United
                      Nations, March, 45p. [8]

HUTTON, J. E.

23.073   GC   [1922?] A HISTORY OF MORAVIAN MISSIONS.

IDYLL, CLARENCE P.; WHITELEATHER, R. T.; & HOWARD, GERALD V.

56.031   GC   1950 Potentialities of the Caribbean fisheries and recommendations for
                      their realization.

IMRIE, Sir JOHN

44.117   TR   1958 REPORT ON THE FINANCE OF THE THREE MUNICIPALITIES AND THE WORK-
                      ING OF THE COUNTY COUNCILS IN TRINIDAD AND TOBAGO.

INTERNATIONAL BANK FOR RECONSTRUCTION AND DEVELOPMENT

66.069   JM   1952 THE ECONOMIC DEVELOPMENT OF JAMAICA. Baltimore, Johns Hopkins
                      Press, 288p. [44, 46, 52]   [*RIS*]
66.070   SR   1952 SURINAM; RECOMMENDATIONS FOR A TEN YEAR DEVELOPMENT PROGRAM.
                      Baltimore, Johns Hopkins Press, 101p. [44, 46, 52]   [*RIS*]
66.071   BG   1953 THE ECONOMIC DEVELOPMENT OF BRITISH GUIANA. Baltimore, Johns
                      Hopkins Press, 366p. [44, 46, 52]   [*RIS*]

IRVINE, JAMES, et al.
32.105   BC   [1945?] REPORT OF THE WEST INDIES COMMITTEE OF THE COMMISSION ON HIGHER EDUCATION IN THE COLONIES.

ISSA, ABE
55.018   BC   [1959?] A SURVEY OF THE TOURIST POTENTIAL OF THE EASTERN CARIBBEAN: WITH PARTICULAR REFERENCE TO THE DEVELOPMENT OF BEACHES, THE BUILDING OF HOTELS, AND THE PROVISION OF ANCILLARY FACILITIES AND AMENITIES FOR THE TOURIST INDUSTRY.
55.019   BC   1959 Tourism will be the biggest industry within ten years.

JACOBS, H. P.
42.016   JM   1951 Jamaica after the hurricane.
44.120   JM   1955 Production pattern.

JAMEAU, JEAN
66.072   FG   1935 LA GUYANE FRANCAISE [FRENCH GUIANA]. Paris, Impr. Heldé, 47p. [*AGS*]

JAMES, ERIC GEORGE
37.208   JM   1956 ADMINISTRATIVE INSTITUTIONS AND SOCIAL CHANGE IN JAMAICA, BRITISH WEST INDIES—A STUDY IN CULTURAL ADAPTATION.

JAMES, PRESTON E.
43.079   GC   1960 Man-land relations in the Caribbean area.

JAMES, S. A.
32.106   SL   1962 Adult education and community development.

JEAN, SALLY LUCAS
28.290   UV   1933 Virgin Islands: school health program—utilization of existing facilities.

JENNY WEYERMAN, J. W.
28.292   SR   1923/ Eene waterleiding voor Paramaribo [Water works for Paramaribo].
             24
28.293   SR   1927/ Van waar moet het water komen voor eene waterleiding te Para-
             28 maribo [From where do we get the water for waterworks in Para-maribo]?

JERVIS, T. S.
66.073   BC   [n.d.] ROBUSTA COFFEE PRODUCTION IN THE EASTERN CARIBBEAN: REPORT ON A VISIT FROM SEPTEMBER 1956 TO JANUARY 1957. Bridgetown, Advocate Co., 39p. (Development and Welfare bulletin.) [46]

JOHNSON, J. T. C.
28.294   BB   1926 A REPORT TO THE PUBLIC HEALTH COMMISSIONERS ON THE ORGANIZA-TION OF THE MEDICAL AND SANITARY SERVICES OF THE COLONY OF BAR-BADOS, WITH RECOMMENDATIONS.

JOLLY, A. L.
59.018   TR   1942 Address delivered to Agricultural Society of Trinidad and Tobago, setting forth results of work with respect to cocoa investigations.
59.021   GR   1942 Uniformity trials on estate cacao fields in Grenada, B.W.I.
46.102   TR   1952 Unit farms.

46.105   BC   1954 Research into the problems of small scale farming in British Carib-
                        bean countries.
46.107   GC   1954 Small scale farming management problems.
46.108   TR   1955 Peasant experimental farms.
46.110   GC   1956 Agriculture.
46.114   TR   1957 The future of Trinidad's agriculture.

JONES, CHESTER LLOYD
66.074   GC   1931 CARIBBEAN BACKGROUNDS AND PROSPECTS. New York, D. Appleton,
                        354p. [37]   [AGS]

JONES, CLEMENT W., et al.
52.040   BC   1948 REPORT ON WEST INDIAN SHIPPING SERVICES.

JONES, T. A.
46.118   BC   1960 Some aspects of improved land utilisation.

JONKERS, A.
66.075   NC   1953 Hoofdtrekken van de ontwikkeling van Suriname en de Nederlandse
                        Antillen [Main features of the development of Surinam and the
                        Dutch Antilles]. *W I G* 34:113-159. [5]   [COL]

JORDAN, HENRY P.
66.076   GC   1944 Regional experiment in the Caribbean. *Curr Hist* 6(33), May: 398-
                        404.   [COL]

JOSEF, W.
46.119   SR   1958 Tienjarenplan en Plan-Wageningen [The Ten Year Plan and the
                        Wageningen Plan].

JUNKER, L.
46.121   SR   1932/ De cultuurwaarde van Suriname [The value of Surinam's cultivations].
                  33

KADLEIGH, SERGEI
35.025   JM   [1961?] Our housing needs.

KANDEL, I. L., et al.
32.109   JM   [1943?] REPORT OF THE COMMITTEE APPOINTED TO ENQUIRE INTO THE SYSTEM
                        OF SECONDARY EDUCATION IN JAMAICA.

KARAMAT ALI, M. A.
66.077   SR   1963 De evolutie van de Hindostanse volksgroep in het kader van de
                        Surinaamse samenleving [The evolution of the Hindustani group
                        within the framework of Surinam society]. *In* LUTCHMAN, W. I., ed.
                        VAN BRITS-INDISCH EMIGRANT TOT BURGER VAN SURINAME. The Hague,
                        Drukkerij Wieringa, p.105-122. [12]

KARWICK, LEE
55.020   GC   1956 A growing industry.
55.021   GC   1959 Boosting Caribbean tourism.

KESLER, C. K.

53.025   CU   1929/ De ontwikkeling van een modern bankbedrijf [The development of a
               30   modern banking system].

28.308   SR   1931/ Een paar opmerkingen [A few remarks].
               32

60.044   SR   1932/ Bacoven in Suriname [Bacoven in Surinam].
               33

KING, JOSEPH A.

66.078   BG   1913   Colonisation and settlement on coast, river, and savannah. *Timehri*
               3d ser., 3(20A), Sept.: 97-104.   [*AMN*]

KINGSBURY, ROBERT C.

43.083   GR   1960   Commercial geography of Grenada.
43.084   BV   1960   Commercial geography of the British Virgin Islands.
43.085   GN   1960   Commercial geography of the Grenadines.
43.086   TR   1960   Commercial geography of Trinidad and Tobago.

KING-WEBSTER, W. A.

56.033   TR   1956   Caronage fishing centre—a "combined operation."

KITTERMASTER, Sir HAROLD

44.126   BH   1933   British Honduras faces forward.

KLAASESZ, J.

44.127   SR   1952   The Surinam Development Fund and the small man.

KLEIN, W. C.

44.128   GG   1940   Economische binnenland-penitratie in de vier Guyana's [Penetra-
               tion into the interior regions of the four Guianas for economic
               reasons].

KLERK, CORNELIS JOHANNES MARIA de

50.074   SR   1953   De immigratie der Hindoestanen in Suriname [The immigration
               of Hindus to Surinam].

KLUVERS, B. J.

52.046   SR   1921/ Een wegracé door het moeras naar Coronie [A road plan for travers-
               22   ing the swamps to Coronie].

66.079   SR   1922/ Beschouwingen over het Rapport Pyttersen [Observations about the
               23   Pyttersen Report]. *W I G* 4:481-504.   [*COL*]

66.080   SR   1922/ Nog eens het Rapport Pyttersen [The Pyttersen Report once more].
               23   *W I G* 4:653-658.   [*COL*]

KNAPPERT, L.

23.090   CU   1939   Wigboldt Rasvelt en zijne gemeente op Curacao, 1730-1757 [Wigboldt
               Rasvelt and his congregation on Curacao].

KNIGHT, RUDOLPH H.

37.216   BC   1960   La planificación y la política en el Caribe Británico [Economic
               planning and politics in the British West Indies].

KNOWLES, WILLIAM H.

66.081   JM   1956 Social consequences of economic change in Jamaica. *Ann Am Acad Polit Social Sci* 305, May: 134-144. [44]

KNOX, A. D.

49.046   JM   1956 Note on pioneer industry legislation.

KONTAK, W. J. F.

66.082   GC   1963 SOME IMPORTANT CARIBBEAN QUESTIONS. Antigonish, N.S., St. Francis Xavier University, 65p.   [*RIS*]

KOOL, R.

66.083   SR   1956/ Kolonisatie van blanken in het Surinaamse Wageningen-project
                   57   [Colonization of white settlers in the Wageningen project of Suri-nam]. *W I G* 37:25-40.   [*COL*]

44.131   SR   1956 Paramaribo; het economische leven van een stad in een tropisch land [Paramaribo; economic life of a town in a tropical land].

KRUIJER, GERARDUS JOHANNES

36.010   SR   1951 Urbanisme in Suriname [Urbanism in Surinam].
33.018   SR   1952 "Social welfare work" in Brits West-Indie en het maatschappelijk werk in Suriname's Tienjarenplan [Social welfare work in the British West Indies and social work in Surinam's Ten Year Plan].
32.113   JM   1952 De 4-H Clubs van Jamaica.
8.036   JM   1956 SOCIOLOGICAL REPORT ON THE CHRISTIANA AREA.
46.130   JM   1958 Het Christianagebied; een landhervormings-project in Jamaica [The Christiana area—a land reform project in Jamaica].
34.009   JM   1958 Family size and family planning: a pilot survey among Jamaican mothers.
66.084   SR   1958 Sociale consequenties van het Tienjarenplan [Social consequences of the Ten Year Plan]. *Vox Guy* 3(2), July: 49-53. [10]   [*RIS*]
66.085   JM   1961 Evaluatieonderzoek in Jamaica [Evaluation research in Jamaica]. *Tijdschr Econ Social Geogr* 52(6), June: 147-157.   [*AGS*]

KRUIJER, GERARDUS JOHANNES & NUIS, A.

46.131   JM   1960 REPORT ON AN EVALUATION OF THE FARM DEVELOPMENT SCHEME: FIRST PLAN: 1955-1960.

**KRUIJER, GERARDUS JOHANNES; VEENENBOS, J. S. &
WESTERMANN, J. H.**

66.086   NW   1953 Richtlijnen voor de economische en sociale ontwikkeling der Boven-windse Eilanden [Directives for the economic and social develop-ment of the Windward Islands]. *In* KRUIJER, G. J.; VEENENBOS, J. S. & WESTERMANN, J. H., comps. BOVENWINDENRAPPORT. Am-sterdam, Voorlichtingsinstituut voor het Welvaartsplan Nederlandse Antillen, December, 67p. [33]

LADEL, ROBERT

52.049   FG   1956 French Guiana—telecommunications.

LAMB, A. F. A.

64.075   BH/   1960 Policy and economic problems in the conversion of old growth
           TR   forests to managed stands in tropical South America.

LASHLEY, T.O.
35.028   BB   [1945?] Report on a housing survey of eight slum tenantries in Bridgetown, June 1944-April 1945.
35.029   BB   1953 Barbados attacks the housing problem.

LASSALLE, C.F.
41.157   TR   1921 A mosquito survey of Trinidad.

LAW, LOUIS S.
55.024   GC   1950 Survey of tourism in the Caribbean.
55.025   GC   1953 Promoting the Caribbean as a summer tourist resort.

LAWTON, OLWEN
66.087   LW/   1956 Report on the Leewards and the Windwards. *New Commonw* 32(8),
WW   Oct. 15: 375-378.   [*AGS*]

LEE, ULRIC
33.021   TR   1959 Report to the honourable the Premier by the Honourable Ulric
Lee on the reorganisation of the public service.

LEIGHTON, FRED
49.047   BC   1951 Report on handicrafts and cottage industries in the British West
Indies.
49.048   BC   1952 Handicrafts and cottage industries in the British West Indies.

LENS, TH.
17.015   SR   1927/ Emigratie naar Suriname [Emigration to Surinam].
28

LE PAGE, R.B.
25.063   BC   1952 A survey of dialects in the British Caribbean.
25.064   BC   1955 The language problem of the British Caribbean.

LEPPER, G.W.
54.035   BB   1949 Report on oil development policy in Barbados.

LEPRETTE, JACQUES
66.088   GC   1960 De la Commission des Caraïbes à l'Organisation des Caraïbes
[From the Caribbean Commission to the Caribbean Organization].
Annuar Fr Dr Int 6:685-706.   [*COL*]

LEWIS, A.B.
46.133   GC   1951 A land improvement programme for the Caribbean.

LEWIS, GORDON K.
32.120   BC   1959 Technical and human resources in the Caribbean.

LEWIS, W. ARTHUR
50.083   BC   1939 Labour in the West Indies: the birth of a workers' movement.
44.138   JM   1944 An economic plan for Jamaica.
49.050   BC   1950 The industrialization of the British West Indies.
46.134   GC   1951 Issues in land settlement policy.
32.121   JM   1961 Education and economic development.

LICHTVELD, LOU

66.089   SR   1953 SURINAME'S NATIONALE ASPIRATIES (EEN AANLEIDING TOT DISCUSSIES
                    OVER DE GRONDSLAGEN VAN EEN AL-OMVATTEND ONTWIKKELINGSPLAN)
                    [SURINAM'S NATIONAL ASPIRATIONS (LEADING TO DISCUSSION OF THE
                    PRINCIPLES OF A GENERAL PLAN OF DEVELOPMENT)]. Amsterdam,
                    Arbeiderspers. [37]

LIDEN, CONRAD H.

66.090   BG   1956 Technical assistance in British Guiana. *Caribbean* 9(12), July:
                    261-263. [46]   [*RIS*]

LIEMS, J. A.

60.049   SR   1922/ Het klein-landbouw bedrijf en de vruchten cultuur in Suriname
                 23 [Small scale agriculture and fruit cultures in Surinam].

LIER, RUDOLF A. J. van

66.091   SR   1954/ Cultuur en wetenschap in Koninkrijksverband [Culture and science
                 55 within the framework of the Kingdom]. *Vox Guy* 1(4-5), Nov.-Jan.:
                     6-11.

66.092   SR   1954 Le plan de développement de Surinam [The development plan for
                    Surinam] [by] R.A.L. [sic] van Lier. *In* PROCEEDINGS OF THE SYM-
                    POSIUM INTERCOLONIAL, June 27-July 3, 1952. Bordeaux, Impr. Del-
                    mas, (p.167-177.)   [44, 46]   [*RIS*]

LIMBURG STIRUM, O. E. G., Graaf van

37.228   SK/   1924/ De opheffing der strafkolonie: Fransch Guyana en haar mogelijke
         FG   25 gevolgen voor Suriname [The abolition of the penal colony in French
                     Guiana and its possible results for Surinam].

66.093   SR   1927/ Het Surinamaamsche vraagstuk [The problem of Surinam]. *W I G*
                 28 9:203-229.   [*COL*]

LOCHHEAD, A. V. S.

33.022   TR   [1956?] REPORT ON ADMINISTRATION OF THE SOCIAL SERVICES IN TRINIDAD AND
                        TOBAGO: WITH PARTICULAR REFERENCE TO CO-ORDINATION.

66.094   TR   1956 Social change in Trinidad. *Venture* 7(10), Mar.: 4-5.   [*COL*]

LOGAN, HANCE

51.088   GC   1925 Hance Logan, M. P., gives Parliament account of his mission to
                    West Indies.

LONG, ANTON V.

66.095   JM   1956 JAMAICA AND THE NEW ORDER 1827-1847. Kingston, Institute of Social
                    and Economic Research, University College of the West Indies,
                    166p. (Special series, no. 1.) [5, 8]

LOXTON, R. F.; RUTHERFORD, G. K. & SPECTOR, J.

57.048   BG   1958 SOIL AND LAND-USE SURVEYS. No. 2: BRITISH GUIANA—THE RUPUNUNI
                    SAVANNAS.

LUKE, Sir STEPHEN

33.023   BC   [1954?] DEVELOPMENT AND WELFARE IN THE WEST INDIES 1953.
33.024   BC   [1955?] DEVELOPMENT AND WELFARE IN THE WEST INDIES 1954.
33.025   BC   1955 Organising development and welfare on the spot.

33.026	BC	1956 The work of the Development and Welfare Organisation.
33.027	BC	1957 DEVELOPMENT AND WELFARE IN THE WEST INDIES, 1955-1956.
33.028	BC	1958 Development and welfare in the West Indies, 1957.

MacINNES, C. M.
33.029   BC   1955 Development and welfare in the British West Indies.

MacKNIGHT, JESSE M.
44.141   SR   1957 Economic developments in Surinam, 1956.

McNAMARA, ROSALIND
54.042   BG   1959 British Guiana's Mackenzie story.

McNEILL, GEORGE
23.099   JM   1911 THE STORY OF OUR MISSIONS: THE WEST INDIES.

MacPHERSON, Sir JOHN
33.031   BC   1947 DEVELOPMENT AND WELFARE IN THE WEST INDIES, 1945-46.

McREYNOLDS, FRANCES R. P.
55.029   GC   1946 The Caribbean plans for tourists.

MADDEN, F.
66.096   BC   1954 Social and economic conditions of the British West Indies. *In* PRO-
CEEDINGS OF THE SYMPOSIUM INTERCOLONIAL, June 27-July 3, 1952.
Bordeaux, Impr. Delmas, p.125-135. [33, 44, 46]   [*RIS*]

MADDOX, JAMES G.
46.137   GC   1952 The major land utilization problems of the Caribbean areas.

MARCANO, RODERICK G.
28.349   TR   1963 Twenty-five years of public health in the city of Port-of-Spain.

MARCKWARDT, ALBERT H.
25.073   JM   1962 Applied linguistics.

MARIE-JOSEPH, E.
44.144   FC   1962 Réalités économiques [Economic facts].

MARIER, ROGER
33.032   JM   1953 SOCIAL WELFARE WORK IN JAMAICA.

MARKLE, GOWER
32.131   BC   [n.d.] Report of Labour Education Survey.

MARRIOTT, F. C. & MAYHEW, ARTHUR
32.132   BC   1933 REPORT OF A COMMISSION TO CONSIDER PROBLEMS OF SECONDARY AND
PRIMARY EDUCATION IN TRINIDAD, BARBADOS, LEEWARD ISLANDS AND
THE WINDWARD ISLANDS, 1931-32.

MARRYSHOW, JULIAN A.
44.145   BC   1954 The Regional Economic Committee of the British West Indies,
British Guiana and British Honduras.

MARSHALL, DOUGLAS
66.097   BC   1953 Possibilities worth investigation in the British Caribbean. *New Commonw* 25(8), Apr.: 375-376.   [*AGS*]

MARTIN, LAWRENCE & SYLVIA
37.254   GC   1941 Outpost no. 2: the West Indies.

MARTIN-KAYE, P. H. A. & BADCOCK, J.
40.121   BB   1962 Geological background to soil conservation and land rehabilitation measures in Barbados, W. I.

MASON, G. B.
28.351   BC   1922 The British West Indies medical services.

MASSON, GEORGE H.
28.352   TR   1910 Indentured labour and preventable diseases.

MATTHEWS, CEDRIC O. J.
46.139   GC   1951 Agricultural labour and mechanisation.

MAURICE, JOSEPH
46.140   MT   1963 L'expansion de l'économie agricole de la Martinique [The expansion of Martinique's agricultural economy].

MEEHAN, M. J.
44.147   GG   1927 Economic development of the Guianas.

MENKMAN, W. R.
7.043   SR   1927/ Dokteren over de West [Attempt to improve the West].
                28
60.057   SR   1930/ Heeft in Suriname een vruchtenbedrijf kans van slagen [Has fruit
                31   cultivation in Surinam a chance of success]?
44.151   CU   1931/ Enkele voorloopige opmerkingen aangaande de voorloopige Curaca-
                32   osche begrooting voor 1936 [Some preliminary remarks about the tentative budget of Curacao for the year 1936].
66.098   SE   1932/ Sint Eustatius' gouden tijd [The golden age of St. Eustatius]. *W I G*
                33   14:369-396.   [5, 44]   [*COL*]
60.058   SR   1934/ De hervatting van de Surinaamsche bacovencultuur [The resumption
                35   of the cultivation of bacoven of Surinam].
66.099   SR   1934/ Kan Nederland worden opgewekt on het Surinaamsche binnenland te
                35   laten exploreeren [Can the Netherlands be stimulated to explore the interior of Surinam]? *W I G* 16:145-150.   [*COL*]
46.143   SR   1940 Landbouw-economische politiek in Suriname [Agricultural-economic policy in Surinam].
44.155   NA   1948 De economische ontwikkeling der Boven- en Benedenwindse Eilanden [The economic development of the Windward and Leeward Islands].
66.100   NC   1948 Westindische samenwerking [West Indian cooperation]. *W I G* 29: 368-372.   [*COL*]
49.053   SR   1949 Industrie en industrialisatie in Suriname [Industry and industrialization in Surinam].
23.104   SM/   1958 St. Maarten en St. Barthélemy, 1911-1951.
          SB

MERRILL, GORDON CLARK
19.031   BC   1961 The survival of the past in the West Indies.

METIVIER, H. V. M.

65.047   TR   1946 Address ... on Prof. Miller's report on veterinary and animal hus-
                      bandry matters in Trinidad and Tobago.

METRAUX, RHODA

66.101   MS   1957 Montserrat, B.W.I.: some implications of suspended culture change.
                      Trans N Y Acad Sci 2d ser., 20(2), Dec.: 205-211. [20]   [*RIS*]

MIDAS, ANDRE

66.102   GC   1957 A brief historical sketch of the West Indian Conference. *Caribbean*
                      11(4), Nov.: 74-77.   [*COL*]

MILLARD, I. S.

66.103   JM   1950 The village schoolmaster as community development leader. *Mass
                      Educ B* 1(3), June: 42-45. [63]   [*NYP*]

MILLER, H.

46.145   JM   1958 The role of surveys in planning agricultural development in Jamaica.

MILLER, WILLIAM C.

65.051   BG   [n.d.] SURVEY OF ANIMAL HUSBANDRY, FEEDING, MANAGEMENT AND VETERINARY
                        SERVICES IN THE WEST INDIES. BRITISH GUIANA REPORT.

65.052   TR   [n.d.] SURVEY OF ANIMAL HUSBANDRY, FEEDING, MANAGEMENT AND VETERINARY
                        SERVICES IN THE WEST INDIES. TRINIDAD AND TOBAGO REPORT.

MORAIS, ALLAN I.

32.140   GC   1953 Statistical education in the Caribbean.

MORGAN, D. J.

44.157   JM   1957 Finance and taxation in Jamaica.

MOSER, C. A.

44.158   JM   1957 THE MEASUREMENT OF LEVELS OF LIVING WITH SPECIAL REFERENCE TO
                      JAMAICA.

MOSS, GUIDO,

52.064   TR   1961 BUS TRANSPORTATION IN TRINIDAD AND TOBAGO [BY THE] NATIONAL
                      CITY MANAGEMENT CO., CHICAGO, ILL. [Guido Moss, engineer].

MOTTA, STANLEY

51.106   JM   1961 The role of commerce in independent Jamaica.

MULLER van VOORST, S.

66.104   SR   1920/ De middelen tot opheffing van Suriname uit zijn verval [The ways
          21   to raise Surinam from its decline]. *W I G* 2:370-384, 433-444. [*COL*]

MULLINGS, LLEWELLYN MAXIMILLIAN

54.049   JM   1961 DEVELOPMENT OF JAMAICAN BAUXITE RESOURCES.

MURRAY, D. B.

46.148   TR   1962 The agricultural needs of Trinidad and Tobago with independence.

NARAINE, S. S.

66.105   BG   1961 The Public Works Department and sea defences in British Guiana. *Timehri* 4th ser., no. 40, Oct.: 47-56.   [40]   [*AMN*]

NEHAUL, B. B. G., et al.

28.398   BG   1962 Conference of the Council of Caribbean Branches of the British Medical Association.

NETTLEFORD, REX

32.145   JM   [1961?] New goals in education.

37.279   JM/   1962 Political education in the developing Caribbean.
            BG/
            BH

NEUMARK, S. DANIEL

46.150   GC   1951 The importance of agriculture in Caribbean economy.

NEWBOLD, C. E. & GILLETTE, H. P. S.

28.399   TR   1949 Self-clearing sea heads for low drainage through surf and consequent effects on the incidence of malaria.

NEWMAN, PETER KENNETH

44.162   BG   1960 The economic future of British Guiana.

44.163   BG   1961 Epilogue on British Guiana [reply to comments on his article in *Social Econ Stud* 9(3)].

NICHOLAS, RICHARD U.

52.065   BG   1939 The development of transportation routes under the projected colonization of refugees in British Guiana.

NICHOLLS, H. A. ALFORD

46.151   BC   1901 Legislation to control bush fires.

46.152   BC   1902 The harmfulness of bush fires.

NICOL, J. L.

32.146   BC   1956 Education.

NIEHOFF, ARTHUR

12.023   TR   1959 The survival of Hindu institutions in an alien environment.

NORMAN, FRANK A.

50.092   BC   1952 Whitehall to West Indies.

NUNAN, JOSEPH J.

52.066   BG   1915 Railways, twelve years after.

OBERG, KALERVO

10.031   SR   1955 INTERACTION AND DEVELOPMENT OF ETHNIC GROUPS IN SURINAM.

OBERG, KALERVO & HINDORI, GEORGE

46.154   SR   1963 GROOT HENAR POLDER: POLDER SETTLEMENT STUDY NO. II.

OBERG, KALERVO & MAY, EDWARD

46.155   SR   1961 POLDER SETTLEMENT STUDY NO. I: LA POULE.

OGILVIE, J. A.

28.402 BC 1930 A peep into West Indian medical history.

OLIVIER, SYDNEY, 1st Baron RAMSDEN

46.156 JM 1915 Recent developments in Jamaica: internal and external, by Sir Sydney Olivier.

46.157 JM 1929 The improvement of Negro agriculture, by Lord Olivier.

11.021 JM 1929 Progress of a Negro peasantry, by Lord Olivier.

16.027 JM 1935 A key to the colour question, by Lord Olivier.

OLIVIER, SYDNEY, 1st Baron RAMSDEN & SEMPLE, D. M.

58.073 BC 1930 Report of the West Indian Sugar Commission [pref. signed: Olivier and D.M. Semple].

ORMSBY-GORE, W.

66.106 BC 1922 British West Indies. *United Emp* new ser., 13(7), July: 454-466. [*AGS*]

OSBORNE, CHRISTOPHER

49.056 TR 1956 Handicraft in Trinidad.

OUDSCHANS DENTZ, FRED

54.051 SR 1920/ De bauxietnijverheid en de stichting van een nieuwe stad in Suri-
21 name [The bauxite industry and the founding of a new city in Surinam].

66.107 SR 1921 Progress of Surinam. *Timehri* 3d ser., 7(24), Aug.: 77-82. [67] [*AMN*]

66.108 CU 1926/ De opkomst van Curacao [The development of Curacao]. *W I G* 8:
27 357-369. [*COL*]

32.147 CU/ 1933/ Stichtingen en fondsen in de West [Institutions and foundations in
SR/ 35 the West].
BG

33.035 SR 1954 Een welvaartsplan voor Suriname in 1770 voorgesteld door Gouverneur Jan Nepveu [A welfare plan for Surinam proposed by Governor Jan Nepveu in 1770].

OWEN, G. H.

31.059 JM 1963 Vocational guidance and education for adolescents.

PAGE, H. J.

46.160 TR 1949 Agricultural research at the Imperial College of Tropical Agriculture, Trinidad, B.W.I.

46.161 GC 1951 Agricultural research in relation to Caribbean economy.

PANDAY, R. M. N.

12.025 SR 1963 De sociaal-economische betekenis van de Hindustaanse bevolkingsgroep in Suriname [The socio-economic importance of the Hindustani community in Surinam].

PANHUYS, L. C. van

52.069 SR 1922/ Denkbeelden en plannen nopens een kustspoorweg in Suriname
23 [Plans and ideas about a coastal railroad in Surinam].

66.109 SR 1933/ Ir. A. A. Meyers over het kolonisatievraagstuk [Ir. A. A. Meyers about
34 the problem of colonization]. *W I G* 15:102-104. [*COL*]

PARKER, C. SANDBACH
66.110   BG   1913 The development of British Guiana. *United Emp* new ser., 4(5),
                        May: 422-429. [5]   [*AGS*]

PATTERSON, BRUCE
2.178   BC   1954 Britain's Caribbean colonies: tragic, doomed lands?

PAYNE, ERNEST A.
23.118   JM   1946 FREEDOM IN JAMAICA; SOME CHAPTERS IN THE STORY OF THE BAPTIST
                        MISSIONARY SOCIETY, 2d ed.

PEACOCKE, NORA E.
35.034   GC   1953 Building research in the Caribbean.
65.058   BG   1953 Livestock research in relation to agricultural policy in the
                        Caribbean.
46.167   GC   1953 Research in relation to extension services in the Caribbean.

PEAN, CHARLES
37.310   FG   1953 THE CONQUEST OF DEVIL'S ISLAND.

PEARSE, ANDREW C.
32.154   TR   [1952?] Outside the walls.
32.155   GC   1955 Vocational and community education in the Caribbean.

PECK, H. AUSTIN
44.183   JM   1958 Economic planning in Jamaica: a critique.

PERRONETTE, H.
28.420   MT   1948 Public health services in Martinique have been reorganised.

PETTER, G. S. V.; HARLOW, F. J. & MATHESON, J. A. L.
32.156   BC   1957 REPORT OF THE MISSION ON HIGHER TECHNICAL EDUCATION IN THE
                        BRITISH CARIBBEAN.

PHILLIPS, ROSALIND
66.111   GC   1957 Technical assistance with special reference to its role in the
                        Caribbean. *Caribbean* 10(8), Mar.: 205-208.   [*COL*]

PITT, D. T.
28.425   BC   1943 Comment on medical section of Sir F. Stockdale's report.

PLAATS, G. van der
46.169   NW   1923/ Eenige beschouwingen over de toekomst van den landbouw op de
                   24   Bovenwindsche Eilanden [Some observations about the future of
                        agriculture on the Windward Islands].

PLATT, B. S.
30.045   BC   1946 NUTRITION IN THE BRITISH WEST INDIES.

PLENEL, ALAIN
37.317   FA   1963 Libération nationale et assimilation à la Martinique et à la Guade-
                        loupe [National liberation and (political) assimilation in Martinique
                        and Guadeloupe].

PLUMMER, HARRY CHAPIN

52.070   CU   1913 Improving a harbor of Curacao: one effect of the Panama Canal's completion.

POOLE, BERNARD L.

66.112   GC   1951 THE CARIBBEAN COMMISSION: BACKGROUND OF COOPERATION IN THE WEST INDIES. Columbia, S. C., University of South Carolina Press, 303p.   [COL]

POUND, F. J.

59.035   TR   1944 Government's scheme for cacao rehabilitation.

PREIJ, L. C.

52.071   SR   1934/ De waarde van bliegtuigen voor Suriname [The value of airplanes
                35 for Surinam], [by] L. C. Prey.

52.072   SR   1938 Suriname en het luchtverkeer [Surinam and air traffic].

PRICE, R. W.

57.052   JM   1959 SOIL AND LAND-USE SURVEYS. No. 8: JAMAICA—PARISH OF ST. JAMES.

57.053   JM   1960 SOIL AND LAND-USE SURVEYS. No. 12: JAMAICA—PARISH OF HANOVER.

PROUDFOOT, MALCOLM J.

17.021   GC   1950 POPULATION MOVEMENTS IN THE CARIBBEAN.

PYTTERSEN, T.J.

66.113   SR   1922/ Beschouwingen over het Rapport Pyttersen [Observations about the
                23 Pyttersen Report]. W I G 4:553-556.   [COL]

66.114   SR   1922/ Opbouw [Development]. W I G 4:421-436 (1922/23); 5:35-44, 110-
                24 124, 353-370 (1923/24).   [COL]

RAGATZ, LOWELL JOSEPH

45.028   GC   1928 FALL OF THE PLANTER CLASS IN THE BRITISH CARIBBEAN, 1763-1833.

RANCE, Sir HUBERT ELVIN

33.037   BC   [1950?] DEVELOPMENT AND WELFARE IN THE WEST INDIES, 1947-49.

35.036   TR   1951 Government expenditures in Trinidad and Tobago.

44.195   TR   1953 Trinidad report.

RANKIN, JESSIE

66.115   BG   1954 A plea for national parks. *Timehri* 4th ser., 1(33), Oct.: 12-13. [41]

RANKINE, J. D.

66.116   BB   [n.d.] A TEN YEAR DEVELOPMENT PLAN FOR BARBADOS: SKETCH PLAN OF DE-
                VELOPMENT, 1946-56. [Bridgetown?] Barbados, Advocate Co.   [33]

READ, MARGARET

32.161   BC   1955 EDUCATION AND SOCIAL CHANGE IN TROPICAL AREAS.

REID, CHARLES FREDERICK

32.163   UV   1938 Federal support and control of education in the territories and outlying possessions.

32.164   UV   1941 EDUCATION IN THE TERRITORIES AND OUTLYING POSSESSIONS OF THE
                        UNITED STATES.

            RENNER, AGNES CECELIA
51.120   JM   1940 TRENDS IN THE TRADE OF JAMAICA.

            REVERT, EUGENE
66.117   GC   1954 La Commission Caraïbe [The Caribbean Commission]. *In* PROCEED-
                        INGS OF THE SYMPOSIUM INTERCOLONIAL, June 27-July 3, 1952.
                        Bordeaux, Impr. Delmas, p.144-146.   [*RIS*]

            RHOAD, A. O.
65.059   GC   1951 New developments and special problems in livestock management.

            RICHARDSON, J. HENRY
33.038   BG   1955 REPORT ON SOCIAL SECURITY IN BRITISH GUIANA, APRIL, 1954.

            RICHARDSON, LEIGH
37.334   BH   1955 P. U. P. plan for British Honduras.

            RICHARDSON, W. A.
52.077   BC   1961 The place of radio in the West Indies, by Willy Richardson.

            RICKARDS, COLIN
66.118   BH   1962 British Honduras after "Hurricane Hattie." *New Commonw* 40(6),
                        June: 359-362.   [*AGS*]

            RIESGO, RAYMOND R.
44.198   JM   1958 Economic developments in Jamaica.1957.

            RIJNDERS, B. J. C.
23.129   SR   1947 Het werk van de Evangelische Broedergemeente in Suriname [The
                        work of the United Brethren in Surinam].

            ROBERTS, GEORGE WOODROW
7.067   BC   1958 Note on population and growth.
7.070   BC   1962 Prospects for population growth in the West Indies.
7.071   GC   1963 The demographic position of the Caribbean.

            ROBERTS, LYDIA J.
33.041   GC   1952 First Caribbean Conference on Home Economics and Education
                        in Nutrition.

            ROBERTS, WALTER
62.022   BG   1959 Rice in British Guiana: a preliminary review.

            ROBERTS, WALTER ADOLPHE, et al.
66.119   JM   1937 ONWARD JAMAICA. New York, Jamaica Progressive League of New
                        York, 8p.   [*NYP*]
66.120   JM   1938 WE ADVOCATE A SOCIAL AND ECONOMIC PROGRAM FOR JAMAICA. New
                        York, Jamaica Progressive League of New York, 7 p.   [33]   [*NYP*]

ROBINSON, C. K.

46.185   GC   1952 Food crops for local consumption.

46.186   TR   1953 The food production programme of Trinidad and Tobago.

RODDAM, GEORGE

40.144   BB   1948 Reports on the ground water resources of Barbados, B.W.I. and their utilization.

RODWAY, JAMES

66.121   BG   1917 Tropical development. *Timehri* 3d ser., 4(21), June: 117-123.   [10] [AMN]

66.122   BG   1921 Stages of progress. *Timehri* 3d ser., 7(24), Aug.: 1-23.   [AMN]

ROMER, HANS

66.123   UV   1936 Die Virgin-Islands: ein unerfreuliches Kapitel der amerikanischen Kolonialpolitik [The Virgin Islands; a displeasing chapter of American colonial policy]. *Z Polit* 26(10), Oct.: 578-586.   [COL]

ROMNEY, D. H., ed.

46.188   BH   1959 Land in British Honduras: report of the British Honduras Land Use Survey Team.

ROSE, F. G.

28.447   BG   1921 The progress of sanitation in British Guiana.

ROSE, H.

44.201   BC   1961 Economic prospects for the West Indies.

ROSE, JOHN C. & LEWIS, ANTHONY C.

36.016   SL   1949 Report on the new town planning proposals; redevelopment of central area, Castries, St. Lucia 1948.

ROSE, W. V.

56.047   BB   1955 Memorandum on the Barbados fishing industry for consideration by the Marketing Committee.

ROSEN, JOSEPH A.

66.124   BG   1939 Problem of large scale settlement of refugees from middle European countries in British Guiana. *In* Report of the British Guiana Commission to the President's Advisory Committee on Political Refugees. Washington, D. C. [no. 8] (27p.) [17]   [AGS]

ROSKILL, O. W.

49.062   WW   1951 Scope for industrial development in the Windward Islands.

ROTH, VINCENT

55.033   BG   1944 Development of a tourist industry in the interior.

66.125   BC   1919 Some lesser known potentialities of the northwestern district. *Timehri* 3d ser., 6(23), Sept.: 133-135.   [AMN]

37.350   BG   1952 Amerindians and the state: a brief history of the Guiana Amerindians vis-a-vis the government.

ROWAAN, P. A.
63.047   SR   1941 Surinaamsche honing als exportproduct [Surinam honey as an export product].

RUBIN, VERA
31.064   TR   1963 The adolescent: his expectations and his society.

RUHOMAN, JOSEPH
12.027   BG   1921 The Creole East Indian.

RUSCOE, GORDON C.
32.170   JM   1963 DYSFUNCTIONALITY IN JAMAICAN EDUCATION.

RUTGERS, A. A. L.
66.126   SR   1934/ De ombouw van Suriname [The reconstruction of Surinam]. *W I G*
                      35   16:241-249.   [*COL*]
5.192   SR   1938 Suriname onder de regering van Koningin Wilhelmina 1898-1938
                      [Surinam under the government of Queen Wilhelmina 1898-1938].

RYLE-DAVIES, W.
50.105   JM   [1961?] Employment in a developing economy.

ST. JOHNSTON, Sir REGINALD
44.205   LW   1935 The situation in the Leeward Islands.

SAMLALSINGH, RUBY S.
33.043   BG   1959 Application of social welfare principles to the rural development
                      programme on sugar estates in British Guiana.

SANDS, W. N.
46.193   SV   1914 Method of working small holdings under the land settlement scheme,
                      St. Vincent.

SAUTET, JACQUES
28.467   GC   1953 Health of the worker and industrial medicine.

SCHAFFNER, BERTRAM
31.067   GC   1963 Special problems in setting up a mental health programme in an
                      international region: the Caribbean.

SCHALKWIJK, F. G.
66.127   SR   1937 De herovering van Suriname [The recapture of Surinam]. *W I G* 19:
                      44-54.   [*COL*]

SCHOCH, C. F.
66.128   SR   1923/ Onze twaalfde provincie in nood [Our twelfth province in distress].
                      24   *W I G* 5:498-518.   [*COL*]
66.129   SR   1924/ Wat kan Suriname zelf doen [What can Surinam itself do]? *W I G* 6:
                      25   97-106.   [*COL*]
46.194   SR   1926/ De ondernemersraad voor Suriname en zijne voorstellen betreffende
                      27   den grooten landbouw [The Council of employers for Surinam and its
                      suggestions for large-scale agriculture].

SCHULZE, ADOLF
23.136	GC	1931/ 200 Jahre Brüdermission [200 years of the Brothers' missions].
		32

SCHUTZ, H.
23.137	SR	1934/ Herrnhutter nederzetting leiding 7B [The Moravian settlement
		35	line 7B].
23.138	SR	1935/ Sporen van tweehonderd jaar Herrnhutterzending [Traces of two
		36	hundred years of Moravian missionary work].

SCHWARZ, ERNST
66.130	JM	1955 Progressive government in Jamaica: the Manley Plan. *Facts Fig*
		4(3-4), Mar.-Apr.: 1-4. [37]	[*NYP*]

SCOTT, JOHN P.
31.068	UV	1963 Recreation programs for adolescents in the Virgin Islands.

SEAFORTH, COMPTON E.
28.477	GC	1962 Drugs from the West Indies.

SEALY, THEODORE
66.131	BC	1952 Why the West Indies need help. *Listener* 47(1199), Feb. 21: 289-
		290.	[*NYP*]

SEARL, D. M.
55.034	TR	1956 Tourism in Trinidad.

SEDNEY, JULES
50.108	SR	1955 Het werkgelegenheidsaspect van het Surinaamse Tienjarenplan
		[The aspect of employment opportunities under the Surinam Ten
		Year Plan].

SEEL, Sir GEORGE
33.044	BC	[1952?] DEVELOPMENT AND WELFARE IN THE WEST INDIES, 1951.
46.195	BG	1952 Some of the problems facing British Guiana agriculture.
33.045	BC	[1953?] Development and welfare in the West Indies, 1952.

SEERS, DUDLEY
38.110	BC	1957 Federation of the British West Indies: the economic and financial
		aspects.
44.211	BC	1962 Economic programming in a country newly independent.

SEGGAR, W. H.
13.073	BG	1952 The Mazaruni Amerindian district.
66.132	BG	1954 Some aspects of development of a remote interior district. *Timehri*
		4th ser., 1(33), Oct.: 30-40. [13]
66.133	BG	1959 Community development amongst Amerindians. *Timehri* 4th ser.,
		38, Sept.: 21-24. [8, 13]	[*AMN*]

SENIOR, CLARENCE
66.134	BC	1958 Demography and economic development. *In* HUGGINS, H. D., ed.
		[PROCEEDINGS OF THE] STUDY CONFERENCE ON ECONOMIC DEVELOPMENT

IN UNDERDEVELOPED COUNTRIES [held at the University College of the West Indies, Aug. 5-15, 1957]. *Social Econ Stud* 7(3), Sept.: 9-23. [7]   [*RIS*]

SERTIMA, J. van

| 36.017 | BG | 1915 The municipality of New Amsterdam. |
| 66.135 | BG | 1921 Progress in New Amsterdam. *Timehri* 3d ser., 7(24), Aug.: 24-28. [36] |

[*AMN*]

SHAFFER, ALICE

| 28.485 | GC | 1952 UNICEF in the Caribbean. |

SHANNON, J. LIONEL

| 65.070 | BC | 1956 History of dairy goats in the West Indies. |

SHAW, EARL BENNETT

| 56.048 | UV | 1933 The fishing industry of the Virgin Islands of the United States. |
| 43.135 | BG | 1940 The Rupununi savannahs of British Guiana. |

SHENFIELD, A. A.

| 49.064 | BC | 1956 Industrialisation—and opportunities for British capital in the British West Indies. |
| 66.136 | BC | 1958 Economic advance in the West Indies. *New Commonw* 35(8), Apr. 14: 356-359. [37, 38] [*AGS*] |

SHEPHARD, C. Y.

46.203	GC	1954 Background to agricultural extension in the Caribbean.
46.205	JM	1955 Agricultural extension.
46.206	JM	1955 Jamaica: report on agriculture.
48.012	TR	1957 Postscript.

SHERLOCK, PHILIP M.

32.179	BC	[1952?] The extra-mural programme.
32.181	BC	1957 Aims and priorities in education.
48.013	BC	1958 The co-operative movement in the British Caribbean.
2.218	GC	1963 CARIBBEAN CITIZEN.

SICCAMA, H.

| 66.137 | BG | 1915 The sea defences of British Guiana. *Timehri* 3d ser., 3(20B), May: 223-225. [40] [*AMN*] |

SIMEY, THOMAS S.

37.373	BC	[1944?] PRINCIPLES OF PRISON REFORM.
33.048	BC	1946 WELFARE AND PLANNING IN THE WEST INDIES.
33.049	JM	1962 Sociology, social administration, and social work.

SIMMS, Rev. Canon WILLIAM

| 32.184 | JM | 1900 Agricultural education. |
| 32.185 | JM | 1900 The proposed agricultural department and agricultural teaching in Jamaica. |

SIMONS, R. D.

| 66.138 | SR | 1947 Suriname's ontvoogding en het welvaartsplan [Surinam's emancipation and the welfare plan]. *W I G* 28:222-235. [33] [*COL*] |

SIMPSON, GEORGE EATON

| 50.114 | GC | 1962 | Employment policy problems in a multiracial society. |
| 8.054 | GC | 1962 | Social stratification in the Caribbean. |

SKEETE, C. C.

42.031   BB   1944 NOTES ON WEST INDIAN HURRICANES WITH SPECIAL REFERENCE TO BARBADOS.

SKINNARD, FREDERICK W.

66.139   BC   1949 Development in the West Indies: some doubts and disappointments. *Venture* 1(8), Sept.: 3-4.   [COL]

SLOTHOUWER, L.

3.281   NW   1929/ De Nederlandsche Bovenwindsche Eilanden [The Dutch Windward
            30 Islands].

SMITH, E. P.

44.220   TR   1955 Trinidad ... oil-agriculture-industry.

SMITH, FRANCES McREYNOLDS

66.140   GC   1958 The Caribbean Commission: prototype of regional cooperation. *In* WILGUS, A. CURTIS, ed. THE CARIBBEAN: BRITISH, DUTCH, FRENCH, UNITED STATES [papers delivered at the Eighth Conference on the Caribbean held at the University of Florida, Dec. 5-7, 1957]. Gainesville, University of Florida Press, p.276-299. (Publications of the School of Inter-American Studies, ser. 1, v. 8.)   [RIS]

SMITH, Rev. G. W.

23.156   GC   [1939?] Conquests of Christ in the West Indies: a short history of Evangelical missions.

SMITH, M. G.

50.117	JM	1956	A REPORT ON LABOUR SUPPLY IN RURAL JAMAICA.
37.385	BC	1962	Short-range prospects in the British Caribbean.
8.060	GR	1965	Structure and crisis in Grenada, 1950-1954.

SMITH, M. G.; AUGIER, ROY & NETTLEFORD, REX

23.158   JM   1960 THE RAS TAFARI MOVEMENT IN KINGSTON, JAMAICA.

SOULBURY, HERWALD RAMSBOTHAM 1st Viscount, et al.

58.094   SK   1949 Report of the commission appointed to enquire into the organisation of the sugar industry of St. Christopher; the Right Honorable Lord Soulbury, chairman.

SOUTHWELL, N.

66.141   AT   1963/ Social and economic revolution in Antigua. *Social Scient* 1:9.
            64

SPECKMANN, JOHAN DIRK

32.188   SR   1962/ Enkele uitkomsten van een sociologisch onderzoek onder de Hindo-
            63 staanse leerlingen van de mulo-school in Nieuw Nickerie [Results of a sociological investigation among the Hindustani pupils of a high school in New Nickerie].

12.034   SR   1963 Het proces van sociale verandering bij de Hindostaanse bevolkingsgroep in Suriname [The process of social change among the Hindustanis in Surinam].

SPENCE, R. O. H.
66.142   BG   1912 Surveying and mapping in British Guiana. *Timehri* 3d ser., 2(19A),
                        July: 56-63.   [40]   [*AMN*]
66.143   BG   1918 The development of British Guiana. *United Emp* new ser., 9(2),
                        Feb.: 61-65.   [*AGS*]

SPOON, W.
51.131   SR   1932/ Enkele Surinaamsche producten in Nederland in 1932 [Some Surinam
          33   products in the Netherlands in 1932].

SPRINGER, HUGH W.
38.115   BC   1961 The West Indies emergent: problems and prospects.

STAAL, G. J.
10.051   SR   1927/ Stroomingen in Suriname [Currents in Surinam].
          28
6.068   SR   1928/ Nettelbecks plannen [The plans of Nettelbeck].
          29

STAEHELIN, F.
23.160   SR/   [1912?] Die Mission der Brüdergemeine in Suriname und Berbice im acht-
          BG   zehnten Jahrhundert [The Moravian Brethren mission in Surinam and
                        Berbice in the 18th century].

STAGE, H. H. & GIGLIOLI, G.
28.496   BG   1947 Observations on mosquito and malaria control in the Caribbean area.
                        Part II: British Guiana.

STAHEL, GEROLD
46.210   SR   1933/ De cultuurwaarde van Suriname [The value of Surinam's cultivations].
          34

STAHEL, GEROLD & REYNE, A.
66.144   SR   1920/ Een vreemdelingen laboratorium voor biologisch onderzoek in Suri-
          21   name [A laboratory of foreigners for biological research in Surinam].
                W I G 2:65-76.   [*COL*]

STANFORD, OLLY N.
32.192   TR   1945 The 4-H clubs movement.

STARK, J., et al.
57.057   BG   1959 Soil and land-use surveys. No. 5: British Guiana.

STARK, J.; RUTHERFORD, G. K.; SPECTOR, J. & JONES, T. A.
57.058   BG   1959 Soil and land-use surveys. No. 6: British Guiana.

STARKEY, OTIS P.
43.139   MS   1960 Commercial geography of Montserrat.
43.140   BB   1961 Commercial geography of Barbados.
43.141   SK/   1961 Commercial geography of St. Kitts-Nevis.
          NV
43.142   SL   1961 Commercial geography of St. Lucia.
43.143   BC   1961 Commercial geography of the Eastern British Caribbean.

STEHLE, HENRI

64.099 MT 1941 Plan d'aménagement et d'exploitation rationnelle de la fôret martiniquaise [Plan for the parceling out and rational exploitation of Martinique's forests].

46.211 FC 1950 New agricultural research centre set up for French Caribbean Departments.

46.212 FA 1954 Research into the problems of small scale farming in the French West Indies.

STEMBRIDGE, E. C.

66.145 BG 1931 The centenary of British Guiana—the colony then and now. *W I Comm Circ* 46(861), Oct. 1: 387-389. [*NYP*]

STERN, PETER M.

7.078 GC 1958 Population factors.

STEVENS, PETER H. M.

36.020 BC 1957 Planning in the West Indies.

STOCKDALE, Sir FRANK A.

33.050 BC [1943?] DEVELOPMENT AND WELFARE IN THE WEST INDIES: PROGRESS REPORT FOR 1942-1943.

66.146 BC 1943 DEVELOPMENT AND WELFARE IN THE WEST INDIES 1940-42. London, H.M. S.O., 93p. ([Gt. Brit. Colonial Office]. Development and welfare in the West Indies. Colonial no. 184.) [*COL*]

28.504 BC 1943 Development and welfare in the West Indies 1940-1942.
33.051 BC 1945 The British West Indies.
33.052 BC 1945 Development and welfare in the West Indies 1943-1944.
66.147 GC 1947 The work of the Caribbean Commission. *Int Aff* 23(2), Apr.: 213-220. [*AGS*]

STOCKDALE, Sir FRANK A., ed.

46.213 BB 1941 AGRICULTURAL DEVELOPMENT IN BARBADOS: DESPATCHES FROM THE COMPTROLLER FOR DEVELOPMENT AND WELFARE IN THE WEST INDIES TO HIS EXCELLENCY THE GOVERNOR OF BARBADOS.

STOCKDALE, Sir FRANK A.; GARDNER-MEDWIN, R. & SYLLAS, S. M. de

35.043 BC 1948 Recent planning developments in the colonies.

STOLNITZ, GEORGE J.

28.506 GC 1958 The revolution in death control in nonindustrial countries.

STRONG, M. S.

30.052 JM 1959 Jamaicans change their eating habits.

STUART, G. MOODY

32.196 TR 1919 Agricultural college and re-organization of the Imperial Department of Agriculture.

32.197 BC 1920 Agricultural college for the West Indies.

SUCHTELEN, N. van

59.051 SR 1964 Vijftien jaar nieuwe cacaocultuur in Suriname, 1945-1960 [Fifteen years of the cacao-growing revival in Surinam, 1945-1960].

SWABEY, CHRISTOPHER

64.103   JM   1940 Reservation policy in Jamaica.
64.106   JM   1942 The development of forest policy in Jamaica.
64.109   BG   1950 Note on the development of forest policy in British Guiana.
64.110   BG   1951 Note on the development of forest policy in British Guiana.

SWABEY, CHRISTOPHER, & LEWIS, C. BERNARD

64.111   CM   1946 FORESTRY IN THE CAYMAN ISLANDS.

TAUSSIG, CHARLES W.

66.148   GC   1946 A four-power program in the Caribbean. *For Aff* 84(4), July: 699-710.
                                                                                    [*AGS*]

TAYLOR, CARL C.

46.214   JM   1953 Some land situations and problems in Caribbean countries.

TAYLOR, G. T.

56.049   SL   1960 Fisheries training school in St. Lucia.

TAYLOR, S. A. G.

46.215   JM   1955 An account of the development of the water resources of the Claren-
                      don Plains.

TAYLOR, S. A. G. & CHUBB, L. J.

40.184   JM   1957 The hydrogeology of the Clarendon Plains, Jamaica.

TERVOOREN, E. P. M.

66.149   SR   1954/ De financiering van het Tienjarenplan en de Nederlandse bijstand
                55   [The financing of the Ten Year Plan of Development and the contri-
                      bution of the Netherlands]. *Vox Guy* 1(4-5), Nov.-Jan.: 61-72.   [10,
                      44]

TEUNISSEN, H.

49.070   SR   1957 The Brokopondo Plan.

THAYSEN, A. C.

46.217   GC   1950 Can politics feed our millions?

THOMAS, C. Y.

44.229   BC   1964 Short-term improvements in Caribbean economic planning.

THOMAS, CLIVE Y.

59.054   GR/   1964 Projections of cocoa output in Grenada, Trinidad and Jamaica, 1960-
          TR/   1975.
          JM

THOMPSON, ERNEST F.

56.051   JM   1945 The fisheries of Jamaica.
56.052   CM   [1946?] THE FISHERIES OF CAYMAN ISLANDS.

THOMPSON, RALPH

44.231   VI   1935 The promise of the Virgin Islands.

TIGGELMAN, G. P.

46.221 SR 1954 Research into the problems of small scale farming in Surinam.

THORNE, A. A.

66.150 BG 1912 British Guianese progress and limitations. *Timehri* 3d ser., 2(19B), Dec.: 377-382.

THORNE, ALFRED P.

44.233 JM 1956 Some general comments on the Hicks Report.

44.235 BG 1961 British Guiana's development programme: analysis of the Berrill report and Newman article [in *Social Econ Stud* 9(3)].

TIETZE, CHRISTOPHER

34.020 BB 1957 THE FAMILY PLANNING SERVICE IN BARBADOS.

34.021 BB 1958 THE EFFECTIVENESS OF THE FAMILY PLANNING SERVICE IN BARBADOS.

TIETZE, CHRISTOPHER & ALLEYNE, CHARLES

34.022 BB 1959 A family planning service in the West Indies.

TUCKER, LEONARD, comp.

23.164 JM 1914 "GLORIOUS LIBERTY": THE STORY OF A HUNDRED YEARS' WORK OF THE JAMAICA BAPTIST MISSION.

TURNER, P. E.

58.106 BB 1945 REPORT ON DEVELOPMENTS IN SUGAR-CANE AGRICULTURE IN BARBADOS WITH SPECIAL REFERENCE TO METHODS OF TILLAGE, DRAINAGE AND CONTOUR CULTIVATION.

UMBGROVE, F. H.

66.151 SR 1923/ Een middel om Suriname uit het moeras te helpen [Ways to help 24 Surinam out of its difficulties]. *W I G* 5:601-612. [*COL*]

66.152 SR 1927/ Het verval van Suriname pogingen tot herstel [The deterioration of 28 Surinam. Attempts to recover it]. *W I G* 9:379-384. [*COL*]

VANDERCOOK, JOHN WOMACK

66.153 SR 1926 A Klondike in the tropics: an article on legendary El Dorado, now Surinam. *Wld Today* 48(3), Aug.: 259-271. [*NYP*]

VERNON, K. C.

57.063 JM 1958 SOIL AND LAND-USE SURVEYS. No. 1: JAMAICA—PARISH OF ST. CATHERINE.

57.064 JM 1959 SOIL AND LAND-USE SURVEYS. No. 4: JAMAICA—PARISH OF ST. ANDREW.

57.065 JM 1960 SOIL AND LAND-USE SURVEYS. No. 10: JAMAICA—PARISH OF ST. MARY.

VERNON, K. C.; PAYNE, HUGH & SPECTOR, J.

57.066 GR/ 1959 SOIL AND LAND-USE SURVEYS. No. 9: GRENADA.
CR

VERRILL, ALPHEUS HYATT

51.140 GC 1918 Some lands of opportunity.

VERTEUIL, ERIC de

28.541 TR 1943 The urgent need for a medical and health policy for Trinidad.

VERWEY, R. A.

66.154   CU   1938 De sociale ontwikkelingsgang van Curacao [The tempo of social development of Curacao]. *W I G* 20:161-174.   [*COL*]

VIEIRA, V. & RICHARDSON, H.

64.112   BG   1957 Forest conditions, problems and programmes in British Guiana.

VIGNON, ROBERT

44.240   FG   1954 French Guiana: looking ahead.

VOULLAIRE, W. R.

23.168   SR   1926 SURINAM: LE PAYS, LES HABITANTS ET LA MISSION MORAVE [SURINAM: THE LAND, THE INHABITANTS, AND THE MORAVIAN MISSION].

WAKEFIELD, A. J., et al.

46.225   TR   1951 REPORT OF THE AGRICULTURAL POLICY COMMITTEE OF TRINIDAD AND TOBAGO.

WALKER, DORSEY E.

66.155   JM   1951 Some realistic aspects of the progress of Jamaica, 1895-1947. *J Negro Educ* 20(2), Spring: 148-159.

WALLE, J. van de

66.156   BB   1947 Barbados aan den vooravond van veranderingen [Barbados on the eve of changing conditions]. *W I G* 28:239-248, 257-268.   [*COL*]
49.073   CU   1948 De industriële voorsprong van Curacao [The industrial headstart of Curacao].

WATERMAN, JAMES A.

28.556   BC   1942 A suggested maternity scheme for the West Indies.
28.559   TR   1944 A national health service with special reference to Trinidad.

WATSON, J. P.; SPECTOR, J. & JONES, T. A.

57.069   SV   1958 SOIL AND LAND-USE SURVEYS. No. 3: ST. VINCENT.

WATTS, Sir FRANCIS

65.079   BC   1914 The production of pork and bacon.
46.227   MS   1915 Agricultural industries of Montserrat.
46.228   DM   1915 The development of Dominica.
58.123   AT   1915 Review of ten years' work of the Antigua Sugar Factory (Gunthorpes).
46.230   BC   [1921?] Tropical departments of agriculture with special reference to the West Indies.

WEBB, G. W. HUMPHREY

65.080   TR   1950 Animal and plant breeding and genetics: a survey and history of dairy cattle of Trinidad and suggested policies for their improvement.

WEEVER, GUY E. L. de

66.157   BG   1934 The development of British Guiana. *Contemp Rev* 146(826), Oct.: 457-465.   [*AGS*]

WEEVER, P. M. de

46.233   BG   1921 Our future peasantry.

WEISS, H.

23.169   SR   1919 Het zendingswerk der Herrnhutters in de Oerwouden van de Boven-
                     Suriname [Missionary work of the Moravian Brethren in the jungles
                     of the Upper Surinam River].

23.170   SR   1920/ De zending der Hernhutters onder de Indianen in Berbice en Suri-
               21   name, 1738-1816 [The mission of the Moravians among the Indians
                    in Berbice and Surinam, 1738-1816].

WELLER, THOMAS H.

28.578   GC   1961 Research in the health services in the Caribbean.

WELLS, A. F. & D.

53.042   BC   1953 FRIENDLY SOCIETIES IN THE WEST INDIES.

WELLS, A. V.

28.581   SL   1961 Malaria eradication in St. Lucia, West Indies.

WENGER, O. C.

28.583   TR   1946 CARIBBEAN MEDICAL CENTER.

WESTERMANN, J. H.

46.235   NA   1947 Natuurbescherming op de Nederlandsche Antillen, haar etische,
                     aesthetische, wetenschappelijke en economische perspectieven
                     [The protection of nature on the Dutch Antilles, its ethical, es-
                     thetical, scientific and economic perspectives].

64.113   GC   1952 CONSERVATION IN THE CARIBBEAN.
41.263   GC   1953 NATURE PRESERVATION IN THE CARIBBEAN.

WESTON, S. BURNS

66.158   GC   1944 The Anglo-American Caribbean Commission. In FRAZIER, E. F. &
                     WILLIAMS, E., eds. THE ECONOMIC FUTURE OF THE CARIBBEAN.
                     Washington, D. C., Howard University Press, p.73-74.

66.159   GC   1944 The Caribbean: laboratory for colonial policy. Antioch Rev 4(3),
                     Fall: 370-382.   [COL]

WHITE, EIRENE

66.160   BG   1954 Prospects in British Guiana. Venture 5(12), Mar.: 3-4.   [COL]

WHITE, JOHN W.

66.161   BC/ 1957 United States technical assistance in the Caribbean. In WILGUS,
         SR   A. CURTIS, ed. THE CARIBBEAN: CONTEMPORARY INTERNATIONAL RE-
                    LATIONS [papers delivered at the Seventh Conference on the Carib-
                    bean held at the University of Florida, Dec. 6-8, 1956]. Gaines-
                    ville, University of Florida Press, p.129-134. (Publications of the
                    School of Inter-American Studies, ser. 1, v. 7.)   [RIS]

WHITE, SENIOR

28.586   TR   1947 Malaria work in Trinidad.

WHITELEATHER, RICHARD T. & BROWN, HERBERT H.

56.055   TR/ 1945 An experimental fishery survey in Trinidad, Tobago and British
         BG   Guiana.

WIDENLOCHER, WILLIAM

66.162   FA   1962 Les Antilles Francaises—une révolution à faire [The French West Indies—a revolution in the making]. *Rev Guad* 46, Jan.-Mar.: 31-34.
                                                                                                                             [*RIS*]

WIGHT, Sir GERALD

35.045   TR   1951 A proposal for the future financing of public housing in Trinidad and Tobago.

WILLIAMS, ERIC EUSTACE

33.055   BC   1947 The new British colonial policy of development and welfare.
32.218   BC   1950 EDUCATION IN THE BRITISH WEST INDIES.
46.237   GC   1952 Agricultural development.
49.074   BC   1952 Industrial development.
66.163   GC   1954 Survey of some major Caribbean developments in 1953. *Car Commn Mon Inf B* 7(6), Jan.: 121-124.   [*COL*]
37.428   TR   1955 THE CASE FOR PARTY POLITICS IN TRINIDAD AND TOBAGO.
37.429   TR   1955 CONSTITUTION REFORM IN TRINIDAD AND TOBAGO.
44.250   TR   1955 ECONOMIC PROBLEMS OF TRINIDAD AND TOBAGO.
66.164   GC   1955 MY RELATIONS WITH THE CARIBBEAN COMMISSION, 1953-1955. Port of Spain, Ben Durham Print. Works, 51p.
66.165   TR   1960 PERSPECTIVES FOR THE WEST INDIES. Port of Spain, PNM Pub. Co., 11p. [2, 37, 38]   [*RIS*]
66.166   GC   1961 MASSA DAY DONE. Port of Spain, PNM Pub. Co., 19p. [20, 45]   [*RIS*]

WILLIAMS, ERIC EUSTACE, ed.

32.220   GC   1953 Evaluation of existing facilities for vocational training in the Caribbean and proposals for their improvement. Prepared jointly by Lucien Dulau [et al.] and coordinated by Eric Williams.

WILLIAMSON, C.

37.430   BC   1952 Britain's new colonial policy: 1940-1951.

WILLOCK, G. W.

44.252   BG   1955 British Guiana ... economic recovery after political misadventure.

WILSON, ROY & SNELL, H.

66.167   BG   1927 The future of British Guiana. *W I Comm Circ* 42(751), July 14: 273-282.   [*NYP*]

WISHART, H. A.

64.115   BG   1915 The conservation and characteristics of colony timber.

WIT, THEODORUS PETRUS MARIA de

62.027   SR   1957 The Wageningen rice scheme in Suriname.

WONG, PAUL G.

35.046   SR   1953 The aided self-help housing programme in Surinam.

WOOD, E. F. L.

66.168   BC   1922 Report on his visit to the West Indies and British Guiana, December 1921-February 1922. London, H.M.S.O., 101p. (Cmd. 1679.)   [*AGS*]

WOOD, SYDNEY MAKEPEACE

57.073   JM   1961 Coastal erosion and its control.

WOODHAM, WARREN

50.128   JM   1962 ELEMENTS OF A MANPOWER PROGRAMME FOR A DEVELOPING COUNTRY: A
                           JAMAICAN CASE STUDY.

WOODHOUSE, W. M.

35.048   BC   1955 Housing in the West Indies.

WORSWICK, G. D. N.

44.253   JM   1956 Financing development.

WORTS, G. F.

40.225   BG   1958 A BRIEF APPRAISAL OF GROUND-WATER CONDITIONS AND PROPOSED
                           PROGRAM FOR WATER-RESOURCES INVESTIGATIONS IN THE COASTAL
                           ARTESIAN BASIN OF BRITISH GUIANA.

WRIGHT, JAMES

33.056   JM   1947 Lucky Hill Community Project.

YOUNG, BRUCE S.

66.169   JM   1964 Jamaica's long term development programme: a comment. *Social
                           Econ Stud* 13(3), Sept.: 370-376.   [*RIS*]

ZAAL, G. PH.

28.609   SR   1937 Het drinkwatervraagstuk in Suriname en het stadium zijner oploss-
                           ing [The problem of drinking water in Surinam and the stage of its
                           solution].

ZEIDLER, GERHARD

37.438   FG   1940 CAYENNE—HELL LET LOOSE!

Chapter 67

THEORY AND METHODOLOGY

ADAMS, RICHARD N.
45.001 GC 1959 On the relations between plantation and "Creole cultures."

ARONOFF, JOEL
31.004 SK 1965 The inter-relationship of psychological and cultural systems: a case study of a rural West Indian village.

AUGELLI, JOHN P.
43.004 GC 1962 The rimland-mainland concept of culture areas in Middle America.

BACK, KURT W. & STYCOS, J. MAYONE
34.002 JM 1959 THE SURVEY UNDER UNUSUAL CONDITIONS: THE JAMAICA HUMAN FERTILITY INVESTIGATION.

BAILEY, BERYL LOFTMAN
25.005 GC 1962 Language studies in the independent university.

BEEBE, WILLIAM
41.041 BG 1921 The Neotropical Research Station of the New York Zoological Society.

BENJAMIN, ELSIE
7.007 JM 1944 Jamaica takes a census.

BETHEL, JEANETTE
44.015 JM 1961 Some national income aggregates for Jamaica at constant prices.

BLAKE, JUDITH
34.005 JM 1958 A reply to Mr. [Lloyd E.] Braithwaite [*Social Econ Stud* 6(4), Dec. 1957: 523-571].

BRAITHWAITE, LLOYD E.
34.007 BC 1957 Sociology and demographic research in the British Caribbean.
67.001 BC 1960 The present status of the social sciences in the British Caribbean. *In* RUBIN, VERA, ed. CARIBBEAN STUDIES: A SYMPOSIUM. Seattle, University of Washington Press, p.99-109.   [*RIS*]

BUCHLER, IRA R.
29.007 CM 1964 Caymanian folk medicine: a problem in applied anthropology.

831

BULLBROOK, JOHN ALBERT

4.019   TR   1953 ON THE EXCAVATION OF A SHELL MOUND AT PALO SECO, TRINIDAD, B.W.I.

BURROWES, W. D.

46.028   JM   1952 SAMPLE SURVEY OF PRODUCTION OF SELECTED AGRICULTURAL PRODUCTS, 1950.

CASSIDY, FREDERIC G.

25.013   GC   1959 English language studies in the Caribbean.

DAVENPORT, WILLIAM HUNT

67.002   JM   1960 Jamaican fishing: a game theory analysis. *In* MINTZ, SIDNEY W., comp. PAPERS IN CARIBBEAN ANTHROPOLOGY. New Haven, Dept. of Anthropology, Yale University, no. 59 (11p.) (Yale University publications in anthropology, no. 57-64.) [56]   [*RIS*]

DAVIDSON, LEWIS

31.023   JM   1963 The adolescent's struggle for emancipation.

DESPRES, LEO A.

67.003   BG   1964 The implications of nationalist politics in British Guiana for the development of cultural theory. *Am Anthrop* 66(5), Oct.: 1051-1075. [8, 10, 19, 37]   [*RIS*]

Du RY, C.J.

4.034   NL   1960 Notes on the pottery of Aruba, Curacao and Bonaire.

ELLIS, ROBERT ARTHUR

8.021   JM   1955 SOCIAL STRATIFICATION IN A JAMAICAN MARKET TOWN.

FERRER, V. O.

67.004   BG   1951 Eye estimation of paddy yields in British Guiana. *Trop Agric* 28 (1-6), Jan.-June: 63-67. [62]   [*AGS*]

FREILICH, MORRIS

67.005   TR   1960 Cultural models and land holdings. *Anthrop Q* 33(4), Oct.: 188-197. [47, 57, 66]   [*RIS*]
67.006   TR   1963 The natural experiment, ecology and culture. *Sw J Anthrop* 19(1), Spring: 21-37. [10]   [*RIS*]

GILLIN, JOHN P.

10.014   GC   1951 Is there a modern Caribbean culture?

GREENFIELD, SIDNEY M.

9.011   GC   1962 Households, families and kinship systems in the West Indies.

GRINDER, ROBERT E.

27.025   JM   1964 Negro-white differences in intellectual performance: a receding controversy.

HAREWOOD, JACK

50.058   BC   1956 A system of labour force statistics.

HEEKEREN, H. R. van
4.059   NL   1930 Studies on the archeology of the Netherlands Antilles, II: A survey of the non-ceramic artifacts of Aruba, Curacao and Bonaire.

HERSKOVITS, MELVILLE JEAN
11.011   GC   1930 The Negro in the New World: the statement of a problem.
67.007   GC   1931 The New World Negro as an anthropological problem. *Man* 31, Apr.: 68-69. [11, 14]   [*COL*]
67.008   GC   1938 African ethnology and the New World Negro. *Man* 38(5), Jan.: 9-10. [11, 14]
19.019   GC   1938 Les noirs du Nouveau Monde: sujet de recherches africanistes [The New World Negroes: a subject for Africanist research].
67.009   GC   1946 Problem, method and theory in Afroamerican studies. *Phylon* 7(4): 337-354. [11, 14, 19]   [*COL*]
67.010   GC   1948 The contribution of Afroamerican studies to Africanist research. *Am Anthrop* new ser., 50(1, pt. 1), Jan.-Mar.: 1-10. [19]   [*COL*]
67.011   GC   1951 The present status and needs of Afroamerican research. *J Negro Hist* 36(2), Apr.: 123-147. [11, 19]   [*COL*]
31.034   GC   1952 Some psychological implications of Afroamerican studies.
67.012   GC   1960 The ahistorical approach to Afroamerican studies: a critique. *Am Anthrop* 62(4), Aug.: 559-568. [11, 19]   [*RIS*]

HODNETT, G. E. & NANTON, W. R. E.
47.021   BC   1959 Definitions of a farm and a farmer in agricultural statistics in the West Indies.

HOROWITZ, MICHAEL M.
67.013   GC   1960 A typology of rural community forms in the Caribbean. *Anthrop Q* 33(4), Oct.: 177-187. [8]   [*RIS*]

HUGGINS, H. D.
66.067   BC   1949 Social science research.

KINLOCH, J. B.
41.152   BH   1940 Mapping vegetational types in British Honduras from aerial photographs.

LICHTVELD, LOU
25.070   GC   1954 Enerlei Creools [One kind of Creole].

LONGABAUGH, RICHARD HAROLD
18.044   BB   1962 THE DESCRIPTION OF MOTHER-CHILD INTERACTION.

MANNERS, ROBERT A.
67.014   GC   1960 Methods of community-analysis in the Caribbean. *In* RUBIN, VERA, CARIBBEAN STUDIES: A SYMPOSIUM, 2D ED. Seattle, University of Washington Press, p.80-98.   [*RIS*]
44.143   BC   1965 Remittances and the unit of analysis in anthropological research.

MAU, JAMES A.; HILL, RICHARD J. & BELL, WENDELL
20.012   JM   1961 Scale analyses of status perception and status attitude in Jamaica and the United States.

MAUNDER, W. F.

50.089   JM   1960 Employment in an underdeveloped area: a sample survey of Kingston, Jamaica.

METRAUX, RHODA & ABEL, THEODORA M.

31.052   MS   1957 Normal and deviant behavior in a peasant community: Montserrat, B. W. I.

MINTZ, SIDNEY W.

67.015   GC   1964 Melville J. Herskovits and Caribbean studies: a retrospective tribute. *Car Stud* 4(2), July: 42-51.   [11, 19]   [*RIS*]

MORAIS, ALLAN I.

2.160   GC   1952 Statistical organisation in the Caribbean. *Car Commn Mon Inf B* 6(4), Nov.: 84-86.   [67]   [*AGS*]
32.139   GC   1953 Practical training for the Caribbean.
67.016   GC   1953 Rudimentary practices in statistical presentation. *W I B* 7(2), Sept.: 25-28.   [*AMN*]
32.140   GC   1953 Statistical education in the Caribbean.

MOSER, C. A.

44.158   JM   1957 THE MEASUREMENT OF LEVELS OF LIVING WITH SPECIAL REFERENCE TO JAMAICA.

MURRA, JOHN V.

9.027   FA   1957 Studies in family organization in the French Caribbean.

O'LOUGHLIN, CARLEEN

46.158   GC   1957 The measurement and significance of agricultural sector statistics in national accounting.

OUDSCHANS DENTZ, FRED

66.107   SR   1921 Progress of Surinam.

PADILLA, ELENA

67.017   GC   1960 Contemporary social-rural types in the Caribbean region. *In* RUBIN, VERA, ed. CARIBBEAN STUDIES: A SYMPOSIUM, 2D ED. Seattle, University of Washington Press, p.22-23.   [47]   [*RIS*]
10.033   GC   1960 Peasants, plantations, and pluralism.

PAGET, E.

46.162   BC   1961 Value, valuation and use of land in the West Indies.

PANHUYS, L. C. van

67.018   NC   1922/ De jongste botanische en zoologische onderzoekingen van het ei-
          23   land Krakatau als een aansporing tot wetenschappelijke waarnemingen ook in Suriname en Curacao [The latest botanical and zoological research of the island Krakatoa as encouragment to scientific research in Surinam and Curacao]. *W IG* 4:373-386. [41] [*COL*]

PEARSE, ANDREW C.

67.019   BC   1956 Ethnography and the lay scholar in the Caribbean. *W I G* 36(2-4), May: 133-146.   [19, 22, 24]   [*RIS*]

RODMAN, HYMAN
8.049   GC   1959 On understanding lower-class behavior.

RODNEY, WALTER
67.020   BC   1963/ The role of the historian in a developing West Indies. *Social Scient*
64 1: 13-14, 16.   [5]   [*RIS*]

RODWAY, JAMES
67.021   BG   1918 The "good old times" in Guiana. *Timehri* 3d ser., 5(22), Aug.: 120-
139.   [5]   [*AMN*]

ROWE, RICHARD R. & THORNDIKE, ROBERT L.
31.062   UV   1963 Virgin Islands intelligence testing survey.

RUBIN, VERA
67.022   GC   1960 Cultural perspectives in Caribbean research. *In* RUBIN, VERA, ed.
Caribbean studies: a symposium, 2d ed. Seattle, University of
Washington Press, p.110-122.   [*RIS*]
20.016   BC   1962 Culture, politics and race relations.

SCHWARTZ, BARTON M.
67.023   TR   1963 Induced competition: a technique to increase field data and rapport.
Am Anthrop 65(5), Oct.: 1112-1113.   [*RIS*]

SIMPSON, GEORGE EATON
10.041   GC   1962 The peoples and cultures of the Caribbean area.

SKINNER, G. C.
58.092   TR   1928 Sugar cost accounts.

SMITH, M. G.
67.024   GC   [1955?] A framework for Caribbean studies. Mona, Extra-mural Dept.,
University College of the West Indies, 70p. (Caribbean affairs.)
[8]   [*RIS*]
19.037   GC   1960 The African heritage in the Caribbean.
10.045   GC   1960 Social and cultural pluralism.
8.058   JM   1963 Aimless, wandering adolescent groups.

SMITH, M. G. & KRUIJER, G. J.
67.025   JM   1957 A sociological manual for extension workers in the Caribbean.
Kingston, University College of the West Indies, 255p. (Caribbean
affairs series.)   [2, 8]   [*RIS*]

SMITH, RAYMOND THOMAS
9.045   GC   1963 Culture and social structure in the Caribbean: some recent work on
family and kinship studies.

STEVENSON, N. S.
64.100   BH   1938 The evolution of vegetation surevy and rural planning in British
Honduras.

STYCOS, J. MAYONE
67.026   JM   1954 Unusual applications of research: studies of fertility in underdeveloped areas. *Hum Org* 13(1), Spring: 9-12. [34]   [*COL*]

STYCOS, J. MAYONE & BLAKE, JUDITH
9.053   JM   1954 The Jamaican Family Life Project: some objectives and methods.

TAYLOR, DOUGLAS, C. & ROUSE. IRVING
4.144   GC   1955 Linguistic and archeological time depth in the West Indies.

VOORHOEVE, JAN
25.113   SR   1961 A project for the study of Creole language history in Surinam.

WAGENAAR HUMMELINCK, P.
41.257   NA   1951 Natuurwetenschappelijke belangstelling voor de Nederlandse Antillen [Scientific interest in the Netherlands Antilles].
4.153   NL   1953/ Rotstekeningen van Curacao, Aruba en Bonaire [Linear rock designs of Curacao, Aruba and Bonaire].
                  61

WEATHERLY, U. G.
67.027   GC   1923 The West Indies as a sociological laboratory. *Am J Sociol* 29(3), Nov.: 290-304. [2]   [*COL*]

WILLCOX, HORACE
4.154   BH   1954 Removal and restoration of the monuments of Caracol.

WILLIAMS, ERIC EUSTACE
5.219   BC   1964 BRITISH HISTORIANS AND THE WEST INDIES.

YDE, JENS
13.095   BG   1962 Britisch-Guiana und Nord-Pará [British Guiana and Northern Pará (Brazil)].

ZONNEVELD, J. I. S.
67.028   GC   1953 Notes on the use of aerial photography in the Caribbean countries. *Car Commn Mon Inf B* 6(12), July: 267-272. [40]   [*AGS*]

AUTHOR
INDEX

AUTHOR INDEX

Capra, Giuseppe. 22.031
Caracciolo, Harry A. 51.020
Carasco, F.J. 17.004
Carew, Jan 21.003
Carey, A.T. 18.008
Carey, Ellen 28.082
Carey-Jones, N.S. 44.031
Cargill, Morris 2.032
Carle, R. Benitez 55.007
Carlee, J.J.A. 50.016
Carley, Mary Manning 2.033 28.083 32.044
Carley, Verna A. 66.025
Carlin, Clair 46.031
Carlson, C.G. 40.208
Carmichael, Gertrude. 5.028 41.058
Carmody, P. 58.017 58.018
Carnegie, A.L. 28.084
Carpenter, Reginald 28.085
Carr, A.B. 63.008
Carr, Andrew T. 19.004 22.017
                              22.018 23.060
Carr, David 3.047
Carrel, Frank. 3.048
Carstairs, C.Y. 38.028
Carter, E.H. 5.029
Carter, J.E.L. 4.027
Carter, Samuel E. 31.017
Carteret, P.E.V. de. . . see
    De Carteret, P.E.V.
Cartier van Dissel, E.F. Verkade-. . . see
    Verkade-Cartier van Dissel, E.F.
Carto, W.L. 55.008
Cary-Elwes, C.I. 26.002
Case, Gerald O. 40.031 44.032
                    46.032 49.014 64.030
Case, Henry W. 3.049
Caselitz, F.H. . . . 28.252 28.253 28.291
Casserley, C.J. 49.015
Casserly, F.L. 51.021
Cassidy, Frederic G. 25.011 25.012
            25.013 25.014 25.015 25.066
Casta-Lumio, Lucien. 50.017
Castagne, Patrick. 22.019
Castelli, Enrico 60.013 60.014
Castor, Ursula S. 28.503
Cater, John C. 46.033 64.031
                            64.032 64.033
Cathcart, J.W. 65.012
Cavassori, Ermes 37.056
Cave, Hugh B. 3.050
Cave, J.M. 46.084
Cazalet. 37.057

Cazanove, Dr. 28.086
Cecil, C.H. . 2.034   3.051 18.009 22.020
            28.087 41.059 51.022 54.013
Cederstrom, D.J. 40.032 40.033
Celarié, Henriette. . 2.035   3.052   3.053
Cesaire, Aimé 37.058
Cespedes, Francisco S. 32.045
Chabert, A. Dubois- . . . see
    Dubois-Chabert, A.
Chambers, H.D. . . 28.088 28.089 28.090
Chambertrand, Gilbert de 22.021
                            24.013 24.014
Champion, Harold 49.016
Chandler, Alfred D. 17.005
Chandos, Dane. 3.054
Chang, Carlisle 22.022
Channer, D.M. 30.064
Channon, J.A. 42.007
Chapin, Howard M. 52.018
Chapman, Donald 66.026
Chapman, Esther. . . 3.055 21.004 37.059
                    37.060 50.018 66.027
Chapman, John L. 35.006
Chapman, T. 1.006 63.009
Chapman, V.J. . . . 40.034 40.175 41.060
Chardon, Carlos E. 44.033
Charles, E.D.B. 28.091
Charles, Henri 44.034
Charles, L.J. 28.092 28.093
Charley, A. 58.019
Charpentier, G. 66.028
Charpentier, Geneviève 51.023
Charpentier, [Guy?] Suzy 10.008
Charpentier, S. 66.028
Charter, C.F. 58.108 58.111
Chartol, Ed. 55.009
Chase, Philip P. 56.012
Chateau, E.D. 8.006
Chatelain, G. 64.034 64.035
Chatelain, Jean 37.061
Cheesman, E.E. 41.061
Cheesman, W.J.W. 48.004
Chemin Dupontès, P. 2.036 43.025
Chen, W.N. 28.250 28.254
Chenery, E.M. 57.008 57.009
Chevalier, Louis 17.006
Chiles, Kenly. 49.017
Chilstone, E.M. 37.062
Chinloy, T. 58.020
Chisholm, Hester Dorothy 37.063
Chot, Robert 3.056
Choubert, Boris . . 40.035 40.036 [contd]

Heilly, G. d' 2.016
Heilprin, Angelo . . . . 3.138　3.139
Heim, Roger 2.096
Heim de Balsac, F. 41.121
Heim de Balsac, H. 41.121
Heinsdijk, D. . . . . 41.122　64.061
Hellinga, W. Gs. . . . . .25.040　25.041
　　　　　　　25.085　25.086　32.095
Hellmer-Wullen, Hilda von. 6.028
Helsdingen, W.H. van. . . . 37.164　37.165
　　　　　　37.166　37.167　37.168　37.169
Helwig, G.V. 10.017
Henderson, Doug 51.065
Henderson, Gilroy. 3.140
Henderson, John. 3.141
Henderson, Judith. 18.026
Hendrick, S. Purcell 23.063
Hendricksen, H.E. 32.096
Hendriks, J.A.H. . . . . . . 46.082　46.089
　　　　　　　　　　　57.013　57.014
Henfrey, Colin . . . 13.035　37.170　66.060
Hengel, J.W.A. van 53.023
Henin, S. 57.046
Henle, Fritz 3.142
Hennessy, James Pope- . . . *see*
　　Pope-Hennessy, James
Henri, Edmond 37.171
Henric, S. 9.013
Henriques, Fernando . . . . . 2.097　9.014
　　　　　9.015　9.016　16.014　16.015
Henriquez, O.S. 49.040
Henriquez, P.C. 66.061
Henriquez, P. Cohen . . . . 24.029　24.030
　　　　　　　　　　　49.041　66.062
Henry, Arthur. 5.083
Henry, Bessie M. 49.042
Henry, C.C. . . . . 58.056　63.030
Henry, Frances 8.028
Henry, M.U. . . . . .28.275　28.276
Henshall, Janet Daphne 43.064
Henzell, L.I. 58.057
Hepburn, Andrew. 3.143
Herbert, Charles W. 3.144
Herderschee, A. Franssen. . . *see*
　　Franssen Herderschee, A.
Herklots, G.A.C. . . . . . . 32.096　41.123
Herlinger, R. 28.591
Hermans, Hans G. . . . . . . 37.172　37.173
Hermes Aguilar, Luis A. 39.030
Hermes, João Severiano da Fonseco 39.029
Herrera, E. . . . . 1.006　1.050
Herrick, Robert. 16.016

Herron, C.R. 52.059
Herskovits, Frances S. . . .11.012　14.006
　　　　　　　　　　22.076　24.032
Herskovits, Melville Jean. . 5.164　8.029
　　　　　　　　　11.011　11.012
　　14.005　14.006　19.017　19.018
　　19.019　22.072　22.073　22.074
　　22.075　22.076　24.031　24.032
　　25.042　31.034　67.007　67.008
　　67.009　67.010　67.011　67.012
Hervé, P. 46.090
Heshuysen, F. van 4.061
Hess, Ernest 56.029
Hesselberg, Engelbret 6.029
Hesseling, D.C. . . 24.029　24.030　25.043
Hessling, H.A. 7.031
Hewick, J.E. 10.018
Hewitt, C.W. 60.063
Hewitt, J.M. 37.174
Hewitt, W. 31.035
Hewitt-Myring, Philip . . . 38.053　38.054
Heyligers, J.C. Th. G.J. 5.084
Heyrel, Jean 43.066
Heyward, DuBose 3.145
Hickerson, Harold. 8.030
Hickerton, J.P. 3.146
Hickling, C.F. 56.030
Hicks, John R. 44.101
Hicks, Ursula K. 44.101
Higdon, E.K. 37.175
Higham, C.S.S. . . . . 5.085　6.030
　　　　　　　　　37.176　37.188
Hildebrand, Ingegerd 5.086
Hilfman, P.A. 15.019
Hill, A. Edward 28.277
Hill, Mrs. A. St. 7.032
Hill, Arthur H. 50.063
Hill, Claire McDowell 41.124
Hill, Clifford S. . . . . 18.027　18.028
Hill, Errol . . . . . . 22.077　22.078　22.079
Hill, Frank 50.065
Hill, Kenneth R. . . . . 27.036　28.021
　　　　　　　　　28.278　28.279
　　28.280　28.281　28.378　28.495
Hill, L.C. . . . . 37.178　37.179
Hill, Luke M. . . . . 36.008　36.009　52.039
Hill, O. Mary . . . . 3.147　51.066
Hill, Richard J. 20.012
Hill, Rolla B. . . . . 28.282　41.124
Hill, Vincent G. . . 28.283　40.085　54.024
Hilliard, Hugh Scott- . . . *see*
　　Scott-Hilliard, Hugh

Lavigne, Pierre 50.081

Law, Louis S. 55.024 55.025
  55.026 55.027

Lawley, David Baxter 32.118

Lawrence, George E. 23.094

Lawrie, I.D. 58.112

Laws, Geoffrey. 3.178

Lawton, Olwen 66.087

Layne, Frederick 33.020

Leach, MacEdward 24.043

Leaf, Earl 22.086

Leake, H. Martin 47.024 47.025

Lebedeff, V. 40.106 40.107

Le Bihan. 51.083

Le Blant, Robert. . . *see*
  Blant, Robert le

Leblond, Marius-Ary 2.016 2.127

Leborgne, Yvon 21.011

Le Boucher, Léon 3.179

Lecuiller, A. 30.020 30.021 30.022

Ledlie, J.C. 37.224

Lee, C.U. 28.327

Lee, Frank F. 18.034 18.035
  18.036 18.037

Lee, Guy 56.034

Lee, James W. 4.085

Lee, Kendrick 2.128

Lee, Rosemary. 18.038

Lee, Ulric. 33.021

Leechman, Alleyne 2.129 32.119

Leefmans, J. 18.039

Lees, Ronald E.M. 28.328 28.329 30.034

Leeuw, Hendrik de 2.130 3.180

Leeuwin, R.S. 18.040

Lefèvre, L. 41.121

Le Gallo, C. 41.158

Leger, Marcel . . . 28.330 28.331 28.332
  28.333 28.334 28.335

Légier, Emile 58.064

Legray, Jacques. 2.131 2.132

Leighton, Fred. 49.047 49.048

Leims, J.A. 50.082

Leiris, Michel 2.133 19.027

Leitch, Adelaide 3.181 49.049

Lekis, Lisa 22.087

Lelyveld, Th. van 19.028

LeMaire, G.W. 54.034

Lemaire, M. Neveu-. . . *see*
  Neveu-Lemaire, M.

Lemery, Henry 5.124

Lenox-Coningham, G.P. 40.108

Lens, Th. 17.015 45.014 65.039

Lenz, Rudolfo 25.062

Leonard, E.R.. . . . . 51.084

Le Page, Adrien 2.134

Le Page, R.B. 25.063 25.064
  25.065 25.066 25.067

Lepper, G.W. 54.035

Leprette, Jacques 66.088

Leroi-Gourhan, André 2.135 2.136

Lescene, G.T. 28.336

Leschaloupe, Constance Marie. . . . 22.088

Letang, Casimir 25.068

Lethem, Sir Gordon J. 3.182

Le Toumelin, Jacques-Yves 3.183

Levitt, Kari. 52.043

Levo, Edith Miriam 38.065

Levo, John E. 2.137

Levy, Babette M. 23.095

Levy, Claude. 6.041 38.066

Levy, Roy. 31.045

Levy, W.J. Inc. 54.036

Lewes, M.D. 54.037

Lewis, A.B. 46.133

Lewis, Anthony C. 36.016

Lewis, C. Bernard 5.125 41.159 64.111

Lewis, C.D. 64.078

Lewis, E.P. 9.024

Lewis, E.R. 18.041

Lewis, Gordon K. . 32.120 37.225 37.226
  38.068 38.069 38.070

Lewis, John B. 41.160

Lewis, L.F.E. 28.337 31.046
  31.047 31.048

Lewis, W. Arthur. . 32.121 32.122 38.067
  38.071 44.138 44.139
  46.134 49.050 50.083

Lewthwaite, R. 28.338

Leyden, T.P. 65.040

Leys, J.J. 32.123 65.041

Liachowitz, Claire 28.339

Lichtveld, Lou . . . 14.020 21.012 24.044
  25.069 25.070 29.015 29.016
  32.124 32.125 35.030 66.089

Lichtveld, U.M. 51.085

Lickert, Rev. 13.047

Lickfold, E.R. 51.086

Liden, Conrad H. 66.090

Liems, J.A. 46.135 60.049 60.050

Lier, Rudolf A.J. van . . . 6.042 7.039
  8.038 8.039 8.040
  10.026 66.091 66.092

Lier, Willem F. van 14.021 23.096

Lighton, G. 36.011 40.109

GEOGRAPHICAL
INDEX

BRITISH HONDURAS   [BH]   [*contd*]
CHAP.
4 [*contd*]   .145 .146 .147 .148 .154 .155
5 .047 .223
9 .048 .049 .050
13 .011 .074 .083 .084 .086 .087
15 .016
22 .134
23 .022 .041
26 .030
27 .021 .026 .035
28 .340 .350
30 .035
37 .030 .056 .084 .181 .190 .191 .198 .279
   .280 .334 .372 .407 .408 .409 .410
39 .001 .002 .003 .017 .018 .020 .021 .022
   .023 .024 .026 .029 .030 .032 .034 .035
   .037 .042 .045
40 .047 .063 .135 .136 .154
41 .078 .152 .164 .206 .216 .219 .220 .236
42 .034
43 .043 .050 .056 .070
44 .020 .031 .052 .112 .126 .146 .186 .227
46 .188 .202
50 .090 .121
51 .142
52 .086
56 .038 .050
57 .043
60 .010
62 .011
64 .029 .051 .070 .075 .083 .089 .096 .100
   .101 .104
65 .060
66 .032 .045 .046 .054 .055 .059 .066 .118

BRITISH VIRGIN ISLANDS   [BV]
See also Tortola, Virgin Islands-General &
British Caribbean
CHAP.
2 .137 .169
3 .134 .305
28 .096
32 .089
40 .101 .115 .120
43 .084
44 .173
49 .042
50 .056
64 .012

CAICOS ISLANDS   [CC]
See also Turks & Caicos Islands, Jamaica
& British Caribbean
CHAP.
4 .009
51 .048
52 .024

CARRIACOU   [CR]
See also Grenadines, Windward Islands &
British Caribbean
CHAP.
9 .038 .039 .040
22 .114
32 .151
40 .117 .191
43 .082
47 .029 .032
57 .066

CAYMAN ISLANDS   [CM]
See also Jamaica & British Caribbean
CHAP.
2 .062 .063
3 .211
5 .087 .093
8 .005
25 .026
27 .017 .018
29 .007
31 .022
37 .237
40 .051 .122
41 .107
43 .016 .044
46 .025 .062
56 .052
64 .111

CURACAO   [CU]
See also Netherlands Leward Islands,
Netherlands Antilles & Netherlands Carib-
bean
CHAP.
1 .043
2 .012 .013 .038 .069 .081 .095 .099 .172
3 .038 .068 .085 .091 .094 .180 .208 .213
   .247 .271 .304 .329

[*contd*]

GENERAL CARIBBEAN   [GC]   [*contd*]

CHAP.

41 [*contd*]   .192 .208 .209 .210 .229 .230
 .231 .234 .244 .245 .252 .253 .259 .263
42 .001 .007 .025 .029 .033 .035 .036
43 .001 .004 .006 .017 .018 .025 .033 .049
 .054 .069 .079 .104 .120 .121 .123 .129
 .133
44 .033 .095 .116 .142 .216 .248 .249
45 .001 .016 .018 .020 .028 .031 .036 .038
46 .023 .027 .030 .036 .057 .064 .103 .106
 .107 .109 .110 .111 .112 .113 .115 .133
 .134 .137 .139 .144 .150 .158 .161 .167
 .185 .192 .203 .216 .217 .237 .238
47 .020 .031
48 .002 .003 .004 .009 .015
49 .008 .009 .010 .011 .012 .034 .037 .045
 .055 .058
50 .003 .004 .036 .046 .099 .107 .114
51 .012 .053 .064 .088 .092 .097 .103 .113
 .123 .124 .140 .143
52 .010 .014 .017 .047 .059 .091 .096
53 .037 .038
54 .023 .026 .059 .061 .064
55 .002 .003 .007 .020 .021 .022 .024 .025
 .029 .039 .040
56 .023 .031 .035
57 .028
58 .060 .082 .085 .130
60 .018 .051 .078 .086
61 .005 .012
63 .005 .051
64 .007 .019 .048 .060 .087 .113
65 .023 .026 .059 .072
66 .002 .003 .005 .006 .007 .011 .018 .024
 .042 .043 .044 .051 .058 .074 .076 .082
 .088 .102 .111 .112 .117 .140 .147 .148
 .158 .159 .163 .164 .166
67 .007 .008 .009 .010 .011 .012 .013 .014
 .015 .016 .017 .022 .024 .027 .028

GRENADA   [GR]

*See also Windward Islands & British Carib-
bean*

CHAP.

 2 .084 .161 .221
 4 .024 .025 .069 .114
 5 .150 .172
 8 .059 .060
22 .114

[*contd*]

GRENADA   [GR]   [*contd*]

CHAP.

23 .035 .036 .157
28 .029 .097 .098 .128
29 .017
32 .088 .129 .151
35 .018
37 .176 .375
40 .055
41 .076 .098
43 .083 .110
44 .010
47 .001 .032
50 .103
55 .028 .032
56 .037
57 .037 .066
59 .020 .021 .029 .034 .054 .056
61 .025
63 .056
64 .054

GRENADINES   [GN]

*See also individual islands, Windward Is-
lands & British Caribbean*

CHAP.

40 .055 .056
41 .076 .138
43 .085
47 .001
61 .025

GUADELOUPE   [GD]

*See also French Antilles & French Carib-
bean*

CHAP.

 2 .020 .035 .134 .180 .208
 3 .179 .253 .306
 4 .043 .106
 5 .009 .018 .122 .152
 6 .002 .061
 7 .020 .040 .056
 9 .013
19 .003
22 .004
24 .069
25 .068 .120
28 .159 .355 .356 .419 .423 .466

[*contd*]

GUADELOUPE [GD] *[contd]*

CHAP.
31 .009 .010 .027
32 .166
33 .040
34 .012
37 .196
40 .168
41 .093 .108 .191 .221 .222 .232 .233
43 .003 .061 .094 .096 .109 .132
44 .034
46 .093 .094 .126 .184
51 .013 .014 .056 .083
52 .011
55 .009 .038
56 .019
58 .063
60 .036
65 .038
66 .016

GUIANAS – GENERAL [GG]

See also British Guiana, French Guiana &
Surinam

CHAP.
1 .042 .049
2 .120 .200
3 .137
4 .125
5 .157 .196
6 .018
9 .007
10 .037 .043
13 .001 .025 .029 .030 .052 .055
15 .033
19 .026
26 .003 .009 .012 .014 .018
28 .124
32 .027
39 .031
40 .036 .196 .220
43 .045 .047 .101
44 .128 .147 .209
54 .065
62 .021

GUYANA

See British Guiana

JAMAICA [JM]

See also British Caribbean

CHAP.
1 .009 .025
2 .001 .025 .031 .032 .033 .047 .048 .052
.059 .097 .107 .138 .140 .149 .151 .167
.168 .198 .221 .226 .267
3 .026 .032 .044 .050 .055 .067 .069 .073
.074 .086 .141 .154 .160 .168 .172 .173
.187 .209 .216 .217 .220 .223 .229 .234
.250 .266 .277 .293 .307 .309 .322
4 .010 .030 .031 .033 .042 .065 .066 .067
.085 .086 .087 .088 .090 .099 .137 .149
5 .016 .017 .031 .033 .037 .039 .040 .042
.044 .052 .068 .082 .125 .148 .149 .170
.179 .182 .183 .184 .185 .186 .187 .197
.202 .204 .205 .206 .207 .208 .209
6 .009 .013 .021 .026 .038 .064 .065 .066
.083
7 .007 .011 .012 .061 .065 .069 .073
8 .004 .007 .008 .009 .011 .012 .016 .018
.019 .021 .022 .023 .036 .037 .041 .043
.046 .057 .058 .063 .066
9 .003 .005 .014 .015 .016 .028 .037 .053
.059
10 .012 .017 .032 .035 .046 .052
11 .004 .007 .010 .019 .021 .022 .025 .028
.037
13 .074
15 .002 .009 .015 .020 .022 .024 .027
16 .003 .013 .014 .015 .020 .023 .024 .025
.027 .028 .029 .031 .033
17 .003 .007 .010 .017 .025
18 .009 .015 .056 .064 .065
19 .002 .010 .012 .016 .022 .030 .033
20 .001 .004 .012 .017 .018 .020
21 .007 .013 .018 .019
22 .006 .007 .008 .009 .013 .025 .027 .047
.048 .081 .094 .101 .120 .121 .122 .135
.148
23 .004 .005 .027 .030 .031 .032 .033 .034
.041 .063 .064 .065 .066 .067 .072 .097
.099 .101 .107 .108 .118 .124 .146 .147
.148 .149 .150 .151 .152 .158 .164 .172
.173 .174
24 .002 .005 .006 .007 .008 .009 .017 .027
.036 .037 .038 .043 .080 .071 .076
25 .004 .011 .012 .014 .015 .019 .066 .067
.073
27 .016 .017 .023 .024 .025 .027 .028 .029
.038

[contd]

JAMAICA [JM] [contd]

CHAP.
64 .028 .036 .044 .056 .069 .078 .091 .093
   .102 .103 .105 .106 .107
65 .004 .005 .010 .013 .018 .020 .027 .040
   .042 .067
66 .004 .015 .020 .025 .026 .027 .033 .034
   .035 .036 .068 .069 .081 .085 .095 .103
   .119 .120 .130 .155 .169
67 .002 .025 .026

LEEWARD ISLANDS [LW]

*See also individual islands & British Carib-
bean*

CHAP.
 2 .023 .045 .249
 3 .024
 5 .085
28 .023 .092
32 .032 .133
37 .063 .064 .176 .214 .360 .389
40 .120
41 .073
44 .172 .174 .204 .205
46 .116 .190 .200 .201
47 .009 .012 .022
50 .056
51 .126
54 .043
56 .011
58 .016 .119 .120
60 .002
61 .035 .036 .037 .038
64 .032
65 .062
66 .087

Les SAINTES [LS]

*See Guadeloupe, French Antilles & French
Caribbean*

MARIE GALANTE [MG]

*See also Guadeloupe, French Antilles &
French Caribbean*

CHAP.
43 .093

MARTINIQUE [MT]

*See also French Antilles & French Carib-
bean*

CHAP.
 2 .015 .076 .183 .203
 3 .007 .070 .105 .202 .214 .246 .262 .286
   .291 .325
 4 .032 .055 .108 .109 .110 .111
 5 .008 .070 .110 .111 .134 .178
 6 .003 .011 .034
 7 .058
 8 .032 .065
 9 .019 .022 .023
21 .015
22 .128
23 .040 .068 .069 .122 .128
24 .034 .041 .067
25 .020 .028 .053 .101 .105
27 .002 .003 .004 .005 .006 .011 .030 .031
   .032
28 .379 .420
31 .061
32 .168 .169
36 .014
37 .098 .150 .221 .282 .332 .388 .401
40 .002 .069 .081 .096 .128 .147 .171
41 .167 .224
43 .013 .037 .038 .039 .040 .062 .066 .073
   .091 .106 .127
44 .049 .123
46 .125 .140 .180 .181
50 .035
51 .015 .093
55 .030
56 .005 .018 .036 .045
58 .061
59 .026
64 .098 .099
65 .061

MONTSERRAT [MS]

*See also Leeward Islands & British Carib-
bean*

CHAP.
23 .094
28 .258
31 .001 .002 .003 .052
32 .171
35 .035
40 .108 .138

[contd]

SAINT EUSTATIUS [SE] [*contd*]

CHAP.
5 .046 .053 .095 .096 .107 .120 .135 .136
6 .027
23 .050
31 .044
40 .088 .215
46 .079
51 .069 .072
57 .041
66 .098

SAINT JOHN [SJ]

See also United States Virgin Islands & Virgin Islands-General

CHAP.
4 .022
25 .048
28 .421
40 .049 .050
44 .213
63 .049

SAINT KITTS [SK]

See also St. Kitts-Nevis-Anguilla, Leeward Islands & British Caribbean

CHAP.
2 .004
3 .063
4 .015
5 .021 .084 .115 .116 .117 .215 .222
20 .006
28 .243
31 .004
35 .039
40 .061 .088 .187 .217 .221
41 .010 .071
43 .030 .107 .141
57 .041
58 .094 .105 .109 .110 .118 .122 .124
61 .018 .022
63 .010

SAINT KITTS-NEVIS-ANGUILLA [KNA]

See also St. Kitts, Nevis, Anguilla, Leeward Islands & British Caribbean

CHAP.
3 .040
28 .486

[*contd*]

SAINT KITTS-NEVIS-ANGUILLA [KNA]
[*contd*]

CHAP.
30 .032
31 .071
40 .053
44 .170

SAINT LUCIA [SL]

See also Windward Islands & British Caribbean

CHAP.
2 .051
3 .079 .090
4 .071 .073 .150
5 .023 .024 .103
13 .042 .089
19 .006
22 .042 .136
23 .028 .029 .037
24 .018 .020 .077 .078
25 .001
28 .025 .056 .095 .134 .328 .329 .337 .580 .581
30 .034
32 .013 .033 .034 .035 .106 .134
36 .016
37 .289
40 .054 .199
43 .142 .147
44 .177
46 .038
47 .013
50 .067
56 .012 .049
57 .040 .067 .068
60 .048 .088
64 .077 .086
66 .031

SAINT MARTIN/SAINT MAARTEN [SM]

See also Guadeloupe, French Antilles, French Caribbean
and/or
Netherlands Windward Islands, Netherlands Antilles, Netherlands Caribbean

CHAP.
3 .088
5 .109 .121 .159 .160
23 .089 .104
25 .078 .079

[*contd*]

[*contd*]

[*contd*]

CHAP.
17 .004 .007 .015 .018 .027 .028 .029
18 .039 .040
19 .011 .017 .018 .023 .024 .025 .028 .032
   .034 .035 .038
22 .031 .032 .033 .034 .050 .051 .075 .076
   .084 .085 .089 .090 .104 .105 .106 .107
   .108 .109 .110 .111 .112 .116 .129 .130
   .141
23 .003 .008 .038 .052 .053 .054 .055 .077
   .078 .079 .081 .084 .085 .088 .096 .098
   .100 .103 .114 .115 .116 .117 .119 .120
   .129 .133 .134 .135 .137 .138 .160 .165
   .166 .167 .168 .169 .170
24 .001 .011 .012 .028 .029 .032 .040 .044
   .050 .056 .057 .058 .059 .062 .063 .064
   .065 .066
25 .007 .009 .024 .025 .027 .032 .033 .034
   .037 .041 .042 .044 .069 .075 .077 .080
   .083 .084 .085 .086 .088 .089 .091 .092
   .094 .101 .106 .107 .108 .109 .110 .111
   .112 .113 .114 .115 .116 .117
26 .004 .005 .006 .007 .008 .015 .016 .017
   .019 .020 .021 .022 .023 .026 .060
27 .009 .012 .013 .014 .015 .019 .020
28 .017 .037 .038 .039 .041 .042 .043 .044
   .045 .046 .054 .071 .072 .073 .102 .103
   .104 .105 .106 .107 .109 .110 .147 .156
   .204 .205 .292 .293 .298 .299 .308 .312
   .313 .314 .315 .316 .317 .319 .320 .321
   .322 .339 .357 .363 .406 .413 .414 .433
   .439 .440 .470 .487 .507 .509 .511 .518
   .576 .588 .589 .593 .594 .605 .606 .609
29 .005 .006 .014 .015 .016 .018 .019 .020
   .021 .026
30 .037 .039
32 .014 .025 .026 .057 .064 .095 .108 .117
   .123 .134 .137 .143 .147 .149 .172 .175
   .188 .201 .210
33 .018 .034 .035 .054
35 .030 .046
36 .010 .018
37 .018 .025 .027 .034 .048 .073 .097 .103
   .115 .138 .151 .154 .215 .218 .223 .227
   .228 .229 .230 .231 .264 .265 .266 .268
   .271 .293 .295 .296 .298 .299 .300 .301
   .302 .303 .323 .324 .326 .348 .354 .355
   .356 .357 .390 .391 .392 .402 .415 .420
   .431 .434
39 .006 .007 .008 .009 .010 .011 .012 .013
   .014 .015 .040 .   [*contd*]

CHAP.
40 .005 .006 .007 .013 .014 .027 .028 .029
   .030 .041 .052 .058 .059 .065 .067 .068
   .070 .075 .093 .094 .098 .153 .156 .159
   .172 .173 .177 .233 .234 .235 .236 .237
   .238 .240
41 .099 .100 .102 .103 .115 .119 .122 .134
   .153 .156 .161 .177 .179 .180 .183 .184
   .205 .218 .254 .262
43 .015 .034 .063 .087 .115 .117 .118 .148
44 .002 .017 .022 .023 .037 .038 .060 .094
   .105 .124 .125 .127 .129 .131 .136 .141
   .148 .149 .159 .178 .179 .180 .181 .189
   .192 .193 .197 .219 .221 .237 .241 .242
   .243 .245 .247
45 .004 .005 .009 .017 .032 .035
46 .007 .012 .016 .017 .019 .020 .022 .055
   .056 .072 .080 .081 .082 .089 .119 .121
   .122 .123 .127 .135 .142 .143 .153 .154
   .155 .163 .174 .175 .176 .177 .178 .179
   .191 .194 .210 .221 .223 .224 .226 .242
47 .004 .005 .023 .026 .027 .028 .034
49 .001 .028 .033 .053 .057 .066 .070
50 .001 .002 .038 .052 .070 .071 .073 .074
   .075 .082 .106 .108 .119 .125
51 .002 .008 .010 .078 .082 .085 .111 .131
   .132 .133 .135 .136 .138
52 .015 .025 .034 .035 .041 .046 .068 .069
   .071 .072 .073 .074 .075 .078 .079 .080
   .081
53 .013 .018 .026 .027 .029 .032 .041 .043
54 .001 .007 .017 .020 .021 .025 .029 .030
   .038 .039 .041 .050 .051 .054 .070 .074
   .078 .086
56 .042 .043 .044 .054
57 .013 .014
58 .010 .032 .078
59 .014 .015 .036 .037 .049 .050 .051 .060
60 .007 .020 .022 .041 .044 .049 .050 .057
   .058 .064 .072 .087
61 .023
62 .005 .006 .020 .025 .026 .027 .028
63 .033 .045 .047
64 .061 .065 .068 .090 .097 .108
65 .016 .030 .041
66 .008 .021 .041 .053 .070 .077 .079 .080
   .083 .084 .089 .091 .092 .093 .099 .104
   .107 .109 .113 .114 .126 .127 .128 .129
   .138 .144 .149 .151 .153 .161

[contd]

[contd]

UNITED STATES VIRGIN ISLANDS   [UV]
[*contd*]
CHAP.
43 .011 .020 .131 .134 .136
44 .024 .051 .236
46 .018 .218
47 .014
50 .010
56 .022 .048
61 .022 .029
63 .052
64 .018
65 .054
66 .010 .017 .023 .047 .064 .065 .123

VIRGIN ISLANDS – GENERAL   [VI]
See also individual British & United States Virgin Islands
CHAP.
2 .118 .187 .239
3 .089 .165
7 .075
40 .126
43 .002
44 .231
66 .063

WINDWARD ISLANDS   [WW]
See also individual islands & British Caribbean
CHAP.
2 .046
3 .024 .059 .183 .246
13 .082 .083
22 .044
26 .001
28 .092
37 .160
40 .171
41 .021 .047 .073
44 .172 .174
46 .037 .116 .190 .200 .201
47 .009 .012
49 .062
51 .126
56 .011
60 .005 .006
64 .009 .046 .047
65 .062
66 .087